W9-AXX-756

What's New in *The Internet Unleashed*, Second Edition

Expanded Coverage of the World Wide Web

In the last year, the use of the Web has exploded. With popular browsers such as Mosaic and Netscape, Web access has become as important as Internet access. Web information is integrated throughout the book, but for a primer, turn to Chapter 28, "Navigating the World Wide Web."

New Chapters

- **Chapter 1, "The Idea of the Internet."** Author Jill Ellsworth discusses how the Internet has affected society.
- **Chapter 19, "Internet Teleconferencing: MBone, CU-SeeMe, and Maven."** Kevin Mullet examines one of the hottest topics on the Internet: teleconferencing.
- **Chapter 30, "New Tools: FSP, Harvest, and Hyper-G."** Billy Barron presents three new tools available on the Internet and gives odds on whether they'll flourish in the coming years.
- **Chapter 33, "Providing Information with E-Mail Robots."** Dave Taylor considers two different e-mail auto-responders that offer simple ways to automate the way you respond to electronic mail.
- **Chapter 36, "Creating Web Pages with HTML."** Brandon Plewe provides an up-and-running tutorial on how to use HTML to create your own Web pages.
- **Chapter 37, "Setting Up a World Wide Web Server."** Kevin Mullet shows readers how to create their own Web sites.
- **Chapter 42, "Digital Cash."** Rosalind Resnick presents methods online merchants are using to handle the issue of legal tender and payments for goods and services.
- **Chapter 62, "How the Web Is Changing the Internet."** John December examines how the popularity of the World Wide Web and graphical browsers have changed—and are still changing—the way information is presented on the Internet.
- **Chapter 63, "Spamming and Cancelbots."** Kevin Savetz discusses the mass posting of a message to too many newsgroups (spamming) and programs written by annoyed Internetters to remove the offending message (cancelbots).
- **Chapter 66, "Games Online."** Kevin Savetz shows readers how to relax and have fun with the Internet by seeking out the best games.
- **Chapter 67, "Cool Web Worlds."** Angela Gunn takes readers on two tours of the best of the Web.
- **Chapter 68, "Online Art Galleries."** Angela Gunn presents the intersection of art and the Internet.

As a final note, everyone knows that the Internet is in a constant state of flux. As a result, in addition to these new chapters, many of the old chapters have new and updated information.

The Internet

UNLEASHED
SECOND EDITION

201 West 103rd Street
Indianapolis, IN 46290

Copyright©, 1995 by Sams.net Publishing

SECOND EDITION

All rights reserved. No part of this book shall be reproduced, stored in a retrieval system, or transmitted by any means, electronic, mechanical, photocopying, recording, or otherwise, without written permission from the publisher. No patent liability is assumed with respect to the use of the information contained herein. Although every precaution has been taken in the preparation of this book, the publisher and author assume no responsibility for errors or omissions. Neither is any liability assumed for damages resulting from the use of the information contained herein. For information, address Sams.net Publishing, a division of Macmillan Computer Publishing, 201 W. 103rd Street, Indianapolis, IN 46290.

International Standard Book Number: 0-672-30714-6

Library of Congress Catalog Number: 95-67642

98 97 96 95   5 4 3 2 1

Interpretation of the printing code: the rightmost double-digit number is the year of the book's printing; the rightmost single-digit number, the number of the book's printing. For example, a printing code of 95-1 shows that the first printing of the book occurred in 1995.

Composed in AGaramond and MCPdigital by Macmillan Computer Publishing.

Printed in the United States of America

Trademarks

All terms mentioned in this book that are known to be trademarks or service marks have been appropriately capitalized. Sams.net Publishing cannot attest to the accuracy of this information. Use of a term in this book should not be regarded as affecting the validity of any trademark or service mark.

Publisher
Richard K. Swadley

Acquisitions Manager
Greg Wiegand

Development Manager
Dean Miller

Managing Editor
Cindy Morrow

Marketing Manager
Gregg Bushyeager

Assistant Marketing Manager
Michelle Milner

Acquisitions Editor
Mark Taber

Development Editors
Dean Miller
Mark Taber

Production Editor
Alice Martina Smith

Copy Editor
Anne Owen

Editorial/Graphics Coordinator
Bill Whitmer

Formatter
Frank Sinclair

Editorial Assistants
Carol Ackerman
Sharon Cox
Lynette Quinn

Technical Reviewers
Billy Barron
Kevin Savetz

Cover Designer
Tim Amrhein

Book Designer
Alyssa Yesh

Imprint Manager
Kelly Dobbs

Imprint Supervisor
Katy Bodenmiller

Manufacturing Coordinator
Paul Gilchrist

Graphic Image Specialists
Becky Beheler
Brad Dixon
Teresa Forrester
Jason Hand
Cheryl Laugner
Clint Lahen
Laura Robbins
Michael Reynolds
Craig Small

Page Layout
Carol Bowers
Mary Ann Cosby
Terrie Deemer
Louisa Klucznik
Ayanna Lacey
Casey Price
Jill Tompkins
Susan Van Ness
Dennis Wesner
Michelle Worthington

Proofreading
Mona Brown
Michael Brumitt
Mike Dietsch
Mike Henry
Donna Harbin
Kevin Laseau
Paula Lowell
Suzanne Tully
Donna Martin
Kim Mitchell
Brian-Kent Proffitt
Erich J. Richter
SA Springer
Elaine Voci-Reed

Indexers
Chris Cleveland
Bront Davis

Contents

Part II How the Internet Works

Part III Plugging Into the Internet

Part IV Communicating with Others

Part VII Using the Internet: Business

Part IX   Using the Internet: Education

Part X   Using the Internet: Community and Government

Part XI Internet Issues and Controversies

Acknowledgments

Over one hundred people contributed directly in some way to the production of *The Internet Unleashed*, Second Edition. It was an enormous undertaking—one that truly couldn't have been done without each and every person in our extraordinary team of authors, editors, technical reviewers, editorial assistants and coordinators, design and production specialists, proofreaders, indexers, and others. Their expertise, talent, and dedication are evident on every page of this book.

Although most of those who had a direct hand in *The Internet Unleashed* are listed somewhere on the pages in the front of this book, those not named on any page are the many, many others—friends, coworkers, spouses, children, parents, and online acquaintances—who contributed indirectly to the book with their words of support and encouragement, with their willingness to look over a rough draft or explain some arcane technical detail one more time, and with their patience and endurance through all the long evenings and weekends spent without their loved ones. We all thank them all.

Foreword

What we have unleashed is not about computers. Just as sex, drugs, and rock 'n' roll were the defining common ground of the previous generation, the emerging culture in this era has all those sharp edges plus one: the Internet. Like sex, drugs, and rock 'n' roll, the Internet is a consciousness-raising event. It is a state of mind more than anything else.

A person on the Internet sees the world in a different light. He or she views the world as global, sees power as decidedly decentralized, sees every far-flung member both as a producer as well as a consumer (a *prosumer*, says Alvin Toffler), sees all parts of the world as equidistant—no matter how large the globe gets—and every participant as responsible for manufacturing truth out of a noisy cacophony of ideas, opinions, and facts. There is no central meaning, no official canon, no manufactured consent rippling through the wires from which one can borrow a viewpoint. Instead, every idea has a backer, and every backer has an idea, while contradiction, paradox, irony, and multifaceted truth rise up in a flood. More than any other experience in modern times, the Internet revives Thomas Jefferson's 200-year-old dream of thinking individuals self-actualizing a democracy.

This almost spiritual vision that people have while on the Internet is all the more remarkable for how unexpected it has been. The Internet, after all, is nothing more than a bunch of highly engineered pieces of rock braided together with strands of metal or glass. It is routine technology. Computers, which have been in our lives for 20 years, have made our life faster, but not that much different. Nobody expected a new culture, a new thrill, or even a new politics to be born when we married calculating circuits with the ordinary telephone; but that's exactly what happened.

Other machines, such as the automobile and the air conditioner, have radically reshaped our lives and the landscape of our civilization. The Internet (and its future progeny) is another of those disrupting machines and may yet surpass the scope of all the others together in altering how we live.

To grasp the full importance and utility of the Internet, it is best to approach it as a new platform. The Internet is a computing machine whose exact size and boundaries are unknown. All we do know is that new portions and new uses are being added to it at such an accelerating rate that it may be more of an explosion than a thing. It is an explosion that increases in value the more that it booms. It is a distributed computer consisting of maybe 20 million individually maintained CPUs in perpetual upgrade, with no one in charge and no one in customer service, and with a most nerdy interface. And this *ad hoc* mega-machine has no manual.

It is the last point that this book addresses. So vast is this embryonic machine, and so fast is it developing into something else, that no single human can fathom it deeply enough to claim expertise on the whole, as one might a microcomputer. Instead, we have the impression that the Internet is almost ecological in scale. All we can hope for are local experts to guide us where we need to go and to let us peek at their notes.

The Internet shall ever be this way. As fast as we build it—and tire of its insight—it will out-run the leash of what we know.

Kevin Kelly
Wired
San Francisco
March 1994

About the Authors

Section Editors

Billy Barron (billy@metronet.com) is the network services manager for the University of Texas at Dallas. He has an M.S. degree in Computer Science from the University of North Texas and has contributed to such books as *Tricks of the Internet Gurus* and *Accessing Online Bibliographic Databases*, as well as writing for periodicals. **(Section Editor: Part V, "Finding Information," and Part VI, "Sharing Information." Author: Chapter 20, "Finding Information: Introduction and Tips"; Chapter 21, "Finding People on the Internet"; Chapter 30, "New Tools: FSP, Harvest, and Hyper-G"; Chapter 31, "Sharing Information: An Introduction"; Chapter 50, "Colleges and Universities on the Internet"; and Chapter 58, "Crackers and Viruses.")**

Jill H. Ellsworth, Ph.D. (je@world.std.com, http://www.oak-ridge.com/orr.html) is a university professor, an Internet consultant for Fortune 500 companies, and a frequent speaker about business, marketing, and education on the Internet. She is the author of *Education on the Internet* (Sams Publishing, 1994) and *The Internet Business Book* (Wiley, 1994), and co-author of *Marketing on the Internet: Multimedia Strategies for the World Wide Web* (Wiley, 1995). **(Section Editor: Part I, "The Internet Explosion"; Part II, "How the Internet Works"; Part VIII, "Using the Internet: Libraries"; and Part IX: "Using the Internet: Education." Author: Chapter 1, "The Idea of the Internet"; Chapter 38, "Business Growth on the Internet"; Chapter 39, "Why Do Business on the Internet?"; Chapter 40, "Marketing Your Products and Services"; and Chapter 53, "Distance Education.")**

Kevin M. Savetz (savetz@northcoast.com, http://homepage) is a computer journalist who writes for a variety of magazines, including *Internet World, Byte, Internet Business Journal, CD-ROM World, Online Access,* and *Wired.* He publishes the Internet Services FAQ list and is the author of *Your Internet Consultant: The FAQs of Life* (Sams Publishing, 1994). **(Section Editor: Part III, "Plugging Into the Internet"; Part XI, "Internet Issues and Controversies"; and Part XII, "Internet Diversion and Fun." Author: Chapter 7, "Finding Access as a User"; Chapter 8; "Finding Access as an Organization"; Chapter 63, "Spamming and Cancelbots"; Chapter 66, "Games Online"; and Appendix E, "Favorite Internet Books.")**

Contributing Authors

Philip Baczewski (baczewski@unt.edu) is the assistant director of academic computing at the University of North Texas in Denton, Texas. He holds a doctoral degree in music composition; in addition to his activities in computing support and instruction, he is active as a composer of classical music and as a researcher in the field of music cognition. (**Chapter 24, "Archie: An Archive of Archives."**)

Steve Bang (bang@rain.org) gives workshops on e-mail and trains University of California, Santa Barbara, faculty, staff, and students in the use of the Internet. Steve has written articles on the Internet and contributed to Sams Publishing's *Navigating the Internet*. (**Chapter 51, "ERIC and Educational Resources," and Appendix C, "UNIX Basics and Tips."**)

James Barnett (spingo@echonyc.com) is a New York City-based interactive and online media consultant whose *Spingo World Media* has provided services for Elektra Records, Marvel Comics, and *American Photo* magazine. He's also a graphic designer, cartoonist, and master of the one-note guitar solo. (**Chapter 54, "Virtual Communities: ECHO and the WELL."**)

Fred Barrie (barrie@unr.edu) is a graduate student in Computer Science at the University of Nevada, Reno. He is also a co-developer of Veronica and is always experimenting on the network. (**Chapter 26, "Searching Gopherspace with Veronica."**)

Kevin D. Barron (kdb@itp.ucsb.edu) is the system manager for the Institute of Theoretical Physics at the University of California, Santa Barbara. He has been roaming the Net for more than 11 years; for the past several years, he has taught "Beyond E-Mail," a seminar on navigating the Internet. (**Chapter 22, "FTP: Fetching Files from Everywhere"; Chapter 34, "Setting Up an FTP Server"; and Chapter 35, "Creating Your Own Gopher."**)

Robert J. Berger (rberger@internex.net) is the founder and CEO of InterNex Information Services, Inc., an Internet service company headquartered in Silicon Valley. InterNex specializes in cost-effective high-bandwidth Internet connectivity such as ISDN. In addition, the InterNex Server Bureau offers services that facilitate using the Internet for commerce. (**Chapter 10, "High-Speed Internet Connections."**)

Tom Caldwell (tcaldwell@rns.com) is manager of information systems for Rockwell Network Systems, located in Santa Barbara, CA. He holds a Master of Science degree in Engineering and Computer Science from Cal Poly, San Luis Obispo, and has over 7 years' experience supporting the Internet and computer networking. (**Chapter 11, "Managing Internet Security."**)

Andy Carvin (acarvin@k12.cnidr.org) is a technology consultant at the Corporation for Public Broadcasting in Washington, D.C. He is the coordinator of the EdWeb Project (http://k12.cnidr.org:90) and the Listserv WWWEDU. His articles have appeared in *GNN*, *On the Horizon*, and other education and technology journals. (**Chapter 49, "K through 12 Teachers on the Internet."**)

John December (decemj@rpi.edu, http://www.rpi.edu/~decemj) publishes several World Wide Web-based documents and publications about the Internet and the Web. Co-author of *The World Wide Web Unleashed* (Sams Publishing) and a Ph.D. candidate in Communication and Rhetoric at Rensselaer Polytechnic Institute, he is an experienced Web navigator and researcher. **(Chapter 62, "How the Web Is Changing the Internet.")**

Ron Dippold (rdippold@qualcomm.com) is an engineer in the high-tech communications field. He is an author of much information related to computers and handles most new group voting for Usenet. He also possesses one pair of flameproof underwear for safe Usenet posting. **(Chapter 12, "Internet E-Mail: An Overview"; Chapter 13, "Internet E-Mail: UNIX"; Chapter 14, "Internet E-Mail: DOS, Windows, and Macintosh"; Chapter 15, "Internet E-Mail: Gateways"; and Appendix B, "Tools Every Internetter Should Have.")**

William Dutcher (dutcherb@nic.ddn.mil) teaches the Defense Data Network (DDN) course for Network Solutions, which manages the Internet Network Information Center (InterNIC) and the DDN NIC. Based in the Washington D.C. area, Dutcher also runs TeraByte Data Systems, a systems training and consulting company. **(Chapter 9, "Connecting a LAN to the Internet.")**

Matthew V. Ellsworth (oakridge@world.std.com) researches and writes books and articles about the Internet. His company, Oak Ridge Reasearch (http://www.oak-ridge.com/orr.html) provides Web-page consulting and authoring services. He holds degrees from Michigan State and Syracuse Universities, and now lives in a Texas Hill Country house he designed. **(Chapter 3, "Forces Shaping the Internet"; Chapter 4, "The Future of the Internet"; and Chapter 6, "Domain Names and Internet Addresses.")**

Cliff Figallo (fig@well.sf.ca.us) was director of the Whole Earth 'Lectronic Link (the WELL) from 1986 to 1992. He then spent a year as the online liaison for the Electronic Frontier Foundation. Today, he writes and consults in the areas of online community-building and commercial Internet applications. **(Chapter 54, "Virtual Communities: ECHO and the WELL.")**

Mark Gibbs (mgibbs@rain.org) has consulted, lectured, and written articles and books about the network market. He is the author of Sams Publishing's *Do-It-Yourself Networking with LANtastic* and *The Absolute Beginner's Guide to Networking*; he is co-author of *Navigating the Internet*. **(Chapter 27, "WAIS: The Database of Databases.")**

Angela Gunn (agunn@pipeline.com) is a journalist specializing in the Internet and online communications. She is a contributor to *Home Office Computing, PC Magazine, Computer Shopper*, and *Internet World*, and is the author of *Plug-n-Play Mosaic for Windows* (Sams Publishing, 1994). **(Chapter 67, "Cool Web Worlds," and Chapter 68, "Online Art Galleries.")**

Judy Hallman (judy_hallman@unc.edu) is Campus-Wide Information Systems Manager, Office of Information Technology (OIT), University of North Carolina at Chapel Hill (UNC-CH). She is also WebMaster of the UNC-CH home page. She has worked for the university since 1967 and is Executive Director and Vice President of Triangle Free-Net. **(Chapter 52, "Campus-Wide Information Systems.")**

John Iliff (pp001654@interramp.com) is the Head Reference and Systems Librarian at Pinellas Park Public Library (FL). He's been using the Internet since 1991, and is co-moderator of the PUBLIB and PUBLIB-NET Listservs. He has been widely featured as a speaker on the Internet. **(Chapter 44, "Net-Surfing Public Librarians," and Chapter 45, "Library of Congress: The Power of Information.")**

Andrew Kantor (ak@panix.com) is senior editor at *Internet World* magazine. He gives seminars at trade shows and for local organizations; his weekly radio show, "The Internet Minute," debuts on certain National Public Radio stations in the Summer of 1995. **(Chapter 59, "Information Overload.")**

Susan Kinnell (susan.c@bkstr.ucsb.edu) works for the University of California, Santa Barbara, Bookstore as Custom Publishing Manager and for Santa Barbara City College in Continuing Education as a computer instructor. She has authored several technical manuals, edited bibliographies for a local publishing company, and recently published *CD-ROM for Schools* (Eight Bit Books, 1995). **(Chapter 46, "Discussion List for School Libraries: A Case Study.")**

Diane K. Kovacs (dkovacs@kentvm.kent.edu) is an instructor and reference librarian at Kent State University libraries. She is the editor-in-chief of the *Directory of Scholarly Electronic Conferences*, which is published by the Association of Research Libraries. She has written and spoken frequently on the topic of scholarly resources on the academic networks and also has taught workshops on using the Internet resources for scholarly research. **(Chapter 32, "Creating and Administering Mailing Lists.")**

Elizabeth Lane Lawley (liz@itcs.com) is the founder and director of Internet Training & Consulting Services (ITCS), based in Tuscaloosa, Alabama, and the co-author of *Internet Primer for Information Professionals* (Meckler, 1992). She received her M.L.S. degree from the University of Michigan in 1987, and worked for the Library of Congress and Congressional Information Service, Inc. **(Chapter 41, "Selecting an Internet Consultant or Trainer.")**

Terrence J. Miller (terrynaples@delphi.com), a writer transplanted to Florida from Washington, D.C., is active with computer groups, was a founding member of the Free-Net organizing committee in Washington, and now is organizing a committee in Naples, FL. He likes to join and form groups. **(Chapter 55, "Community Computing and Free-Nets.")**

David H. Mitchell (diaspar@bix.com) is the founder of the Diaspar Virtual Reality Network, writer about tele-things, space activist, and reader of science fiction. **(Chapter 65, "Virtual Reality on the Internet.")**

Martin Moore has been wandering the Internet for nearly 10 years. The founder of MDP, Inc., Moore has written three books, numerous magazine articles, and is currently fascinated with the multimedia aspects of the Internet. **(Chapter 2, "Introducing the Internet"; Chapter 5, "The Network of Networks"; and Chapter 6, "Domain Names and Internet Addresses.")**

Kevin Mullet (kevinm@rice.edu) is a network specialist for Texas Rice University and Sesquinet regional network. When he's not indulging his interests in Internet service provision, system security, community computing, and personal teleconferencing, he proselytizes about the global culture of the Internet while trying to brew a perfect cup of coffee. **(Chapter 19, "Internet Teleconferencing: MBone, CU-SeeMe, and Maven," and Chapter 37, "Setting Up a World Wide Web Server.")**

Janet Murray (jmurray@psg.com) is the librarian at a comprehensive public high school in Portland, Oregon, and a co-founder of K12Net. Her FidoNet bulletin board system, HI TECH TOOLS for Librarians, feeds K12Net conferences to more than 30 systems from Hawaii to New Brunswick as well as to the international and Usenet gateway systems. **(Chapter 48, "Schoolkids and the Net.")**

Lay Wah Ooi (ooi@metronet.com) is a UNIX system administrator at Titan Client/Server Technologies. She graduated from the University of North Texas with a Computer Science degree and has worked at Sprint, one of the principle Internet backbone providers, as a software engineer/UNIX system administrator. **(Chapter 18, "Live Conversations: Internet Relay Chat and Other Methods," and Chapter 23, "Logging in to Other Computers with Telnet and Rlogin.")**

Maggie Parhamovich (magoo@nevada.edu) is head of the Government Documents department at James R. Dickinson Library, University of Nevada, Las Vegas. She conducted training and developed resources for the Internet while on an ALA/USIA Library Fellowship at Dalhousie University, Nova Scotia, and the University of New Brunswick in Canada. **(Chapter 57, "Federal Information on the Internet.")**

Tim Parker (tparker@tpci.com) is a consultant and writer based in Ottawa, Ontario. He is a columnist and writer for several magazines, including *UNIX World, Computer Language*, and *UNIX Review*. He has published six books, the last two on UNIX. When not writing, Tim spends his time white-water kayaking, flying, and scuba diving. **(Chapter 17, "Reading and Posting the News: Using Usenet.")**

Phillip W. Paxton is a development editor at Sams Publishing, specializing in the Internet, programming languages, databases, operating systems, and emerging technologies. A former systems programmer and DBA, his spare time is spent juggling seven balls and playing cribbage. **(Chapter 16, "Joining Discussions: Using Listservs and Mailing Lists.")**

Brandon Plewe (plewe@acsu.buffalo.edu, http://wings.buffalo.edu/~plewe/) is Assistant Coordinator of Network Information Services at the State University of New York at Buffalo. He has an M.A. degree in Geography from SUNY/Buffalo. Besides managing the University's CWIS, he has built several geography-related services on the WWW, including the Virtual Tourist. **(Chapter 36, "Creating Web Pages with HTML.")**

Joseph Poirier (snag@acca.nmsu.edu) is a software engineer for Network Design Technologies, Inc., where he designs and implements object-oriented telecommunications network optimization software. He graduated from Purdue University in 1990 with a B.S. degree in computer science. Known as *Snag* on several muds, he can frequently be found playing cards in the virtual poker halls. He is the one wearing the bunny slippers. **(Chapter 64, "Interactive Multiuser Realities: MUDs, MOOs, MUCKs, and MUSHes.")**

Rosalind Resnick (rosalind@harrison.win.net) is a freelance writer, author, and consultant specializing in business and technology. She is the co-author of *The Internet Business Guide* (Sams Publishing, 1994) and the author of *Exploring the World of Online Services* (Sybex, 1993). Her twice-monthly newsletter, *Interactive Publishing Alert,* tracks trends and developments in electronic newspaper and magazine publishing. **(Chapter 42, "Digital Cash.")**

Lance Rose (elrose@path.net) is an attorney and writer who works with high-tech and information companies. He is the author of *NetLaw,* the online legal guide, and writes for *Boardwatch Magazine* and *Wired.* He has spoken at Internet World; ONE BBS CON; Comdex; New Media Expo; Computers, Freedom and Privacy; and other network events. **(Chapter 60, "Copyright on the Networks," and Chapter 61, "Freedom of Online Speech.")**

Lou Rosenfeld (lou@argus-inc.com) is President of Argus Associates, Inc. (http://argus-inc.com), an Internet publishing and marketing company that specializes in information organization and evaluation. While working as a librarian at the University of Michigan, Lou founded and now manages the Clearinghouse for Subject-Oriented Internet Resource Guides (http://www.lib.umich.edu/chhome.html), a popular Internet reference resource. **(Chapter 43, "The Internet in Academic Libraries.")**

David H. Rothman (rothman@clark.net) is author of *The Electronic Citizen,* which Sams will publish in the Fall of 1995. An electronic activist as far back as the mid-1980s, Rothman's work has appeared in publications ranging from *The Washington Post* to *Computerworld.* His current cause is TeleRead, a proposal for an online national library affordable to all. **(Chapter 56, "Net Activism.")**

Peter Scott (scottp@herald.usask.ca) is the manager of small systems at the University of Saskatchewan Libraries. He is the author of Hytelnet and other hypertext software programs, a frequent speaker at Internet conferences, and a past president of the Saskatoon Free-Net Association. **(Chapter 29, "Opening Doors with Hytelnet.")**

Richard J. Smith (rjs@lis.pitt.edu) has taught the use of the Internet in graduate courses and workshops since 1991. He is the co-author of Sams Publishing's *Navigating the Internet;* tens of thousands have participated in his online Internet tutorials. **(Chapter 27, "WAIS: The Database of Databases.")**

Dave Taylor (`taylor@netcom.com`) is a long-time Internet expert, having sent his first Internet e-mail message in 1980. Author of both the Elm mail system and Embot, he's a prolific UNIX programmer, interface designer, and writer. He is the author of *Teach Yourself UNIX in a* Week (Sams Publishing, 1994) and co-author of *The Internet Business Guide* (Sams Publishing, 1994). **(Chapter 33, "Providing Information with E-Mail Robots.")**

Glenn Vanderburg (`glv@metronet.com`) is a UNIX and network software developer at the University of Texas at Dallas. He's been active on the Internet since 1986, and has worked on e-mail systems, special-purpose languages, and network management. Currently, he's interested in practical applications of the World Wide Web, MIME-based e-mail, and autonomous network agents. **(Chapter 28, "Navigating the World Wide Web.")**

Laura Windsor (`windsor@ouvaxa.cats.ohiou.edu`) is an instructional librarian at Ohio University in Athens, Ohio. She has a B.A. degree from Texas Christian University in Ft. Worth and an A.M.L.S. degree from the University of Michigan. She has fun surfing the Net, as well as teaching the Internet to people of all ages and expertise. **(Chapter 47, "The Virtual Library.")**

Introduction

The book you're now holding in your hands is a very real, very weighty demonstration of the power of the Internet.

Without the Internet, it would have been impossible to gather together such a diverse and experienced collection of authors—even if we had somehow managed to track down all these people, staying in touch with them all and passing ideas and files back and forth would have been far more difficult without the Internet. To be sure, in producing this book, we all relied on the traditional tools of the business—paper and the telephone and the U.S. Mail—but not nearly as heavily as we relied on such Internet tools as e-mail, file transfer, newsgroups, FAQ lists, and some powerful search tools.

The Internet Unleashed, Second Edition, will help you discover the potential that awaits you on the Internet. Other books are available that tell you how to get online and use the basic tools of the Internet, but *The Internet Unleashed*, Second Edition, is unlike any of them.

We dig deeper into the Internet. We don't just tell you how to use the World Wide Web, for example, we tell you how to set up and develop content for your own Web server—or to start a mailing list, or to establish an FTP or Gopher site. And we also tell you how to put these Internet tools and resources to work—whether you're in business, education, libraries, government, or community networking.

Even more importantly, *The Internet Unleashed*, Second Edition, is not the product of a single author, or even two or three authors. No single individual has the depth of knowledge or experience to do justice to the incredible richness and power of the Internet. We sought knowledgeable authors, all experts in their own fields, to contribute to this work. The names you see in this book are the names you'll inevitably come across in your explorations on the Net. Many of them are actively and prominently involved in contributing their work to the Internet: maintaining FAQ lists, publishing electronic books and journals, moderating newsgroups and mailing lists, building community networks and Free-Nets, teaching workshops and training seminars (online and otherwise), maintaining FTP, Gopher, and Web sites, and developing the new Internet tools we'll be using tomorrow.

Audience

The Internet Unleashed, Second Edition, is designed to have something for everyone, whether you're an individual user, a user on a network, or a technical professional. And it shouldn't matter what profession you're in—this book has sections for business professionals, librarians and information professionals, teachers and students, and government or community workers.

Organization of this Book

We start out in Parts I and II, as so many Internet books do, with a history of the Internet. It's important to understand how the Internet developed, how it's structured, how things change and develop, and what kind of behavior is expected—for new users and even for those who are more experienced. The Internet did not appear overnight all full-grown, with structure and rules all predetermined. The Internet grew organically over time. And as a result, taking the time to read through these introductory chapters will help you better understand some of the Internet's peculiarities—and dangers.

In Part III, "Plugging Into the Internet," we take up the question would-be Internet users the world over ask: how do I get connected? Kevin Savetz discusses the various general options, both for individual dial-up users and for businesses or other organizations that may want to hook up an entire office or company. Bill Dutcher explains how to connect an existing local area network (LAN) to the Internet. Bob Berger discusses the options for high-speed Internet connections. Tom Caldwell tells you how to secure your site against Internet intruders.

In Part IV, "Communicating with Others," Ron Dippold, with some help from Billy Barron in this edition, has written four big chapters on the mother of all Internet functions: e-mail. And then Phil Paxton, Tim Parker, Lay Wah Ooi, and Kevin Mullet go on to tell you how to join and use mailing lists, how to read and post messages using Usenet newsgroups, how to join live conversations with Internet Relay Chat, and how to set up live teleconferencing over the Internet with MBone, CU-SeeMe, and Maven.

In Part V, "Finding Information," we show you the other major Internet function—finding and exploiting resources. Billy Barron kicks the section off with an overview of the tools we'll use, along with some general pointers and tips, and then we go into every major Internet tool or resource out there: Kevin Barron on FTP, Lay Wah Ooi on Telnet, Philip Baczewski on Archie, Paul Lindner and Danny Iacovou on Gopher, Fred Barrie on Veronica, Rich Smith and Mark Gibbs on WAIS, Glenn Vanderburg on the World Wide Web, Peter Scott on Hytelnet, and Billy Barron on new tools like FSP, Harvest, and Hyper-G.

In Part VI, "Sharing Information," Billy Barron opens with an overview chapter; then Diane Kovacs tells how to create and administer a mailing list, Dave Taylor describes how to provide information with e-mail robots, Kevin Barron details the procedures involved in setting up FTP and Gopher servers, Brandon Plewe tells how to create World Wide Web pages with HTML, and Kevin Mullet gives an overview of setting up a Web server.

In Part VII, "Using the Internet: Business," Jill Ellsworth debunks the myth that the Internet is hostile to business. She tells you what you can—and cannot—do, and provides you with numerous ideas and examples for putting the Internet and its resources to work. Rosalind Resnick contributes a chapter on digital cash, and Elizabeth Lane Lawley outlines what to look for when you're choosing an Internet trainer or consultant for your business.

In Part VIII, "Using the Internet: Libraries," Susan Kinnell, Lou Rosenfeld, John Iliff, and Laura Windsor demonstrate the immense utility that academic, K–12, and public libraries have found on the Internet.

In Part IX, "Using the Internet: Education," Jill Ellsworth, Andy Carvin, Janet Murray, Billy Barron, and Steve Bang show teachers, students, and parents how the Internet can break down the restrictions of classroom walls and open up an exciting world of possibilities to students of all ages.

In Part X, "Using the Internet: Community and Government," several authors approach the idea of building an online community with the tools that the Internet has to offer. James Barnett and Cliff Figallo combine their efforts in a chapter on virtual communities, with special emphasis on ECHO and the WELL. Terrence Miller profiles the community networking efforts of Tom Grundner. David Rothman gives us a look at activism on the Internet. And Maggie Parhamovich summarizes federal information that's available online.

In Part XI, "Internet Issues and Controversies," we bring you up to date on some current hot Internet topics for discussion: Billy Barron on crackers and viruses, Andrew Kantor on information overload, attorney Lance Rose on copyright on the networks and freedom of online speech, John December on how the Web is changing the Internet, and Kevin Savetz on spamming and cancelbots.

In Part XII, "Internet Diversion and Fun," we wrap up the chapters in the book with a quick look at some of the more interesting sides of the Internet: Joseph Poirier on MUDs, MOOs, MUCKs, and MUSHes; David Mitchell on virtual reality on the Internet; Kevin Savetz on online games, and Angela Gunn on cool Web worlds and online art galleries.

Finally, the appendixes provide you with lists for future reference of access providers, tools every Internetter should have, UNIX basics and tips, Internet domain names, and reviews of some of the best printed books about the Internet. (Other than this one, of course!)

PART

The Internet Explosion

The Idea of the Internet

1

by Jill H. Ellsworth

... in a net I seek to hold the wind.

—*Wyatt*

The Internet is the network that is changing the way people communicate, interact, and define community.

The Internet has a spirit of invention within the human community it encompasses as expressed in the tools, software, and hardware that are used. It crosses time and space in a way we could only dream of before, creating a virtual place and community.

The Internet represents a changing paradigm for human interaction. It is a collaborative medium, in which you can access information and data; it is a place for learning, for commerce, for entertainment, and a place to intensively interact with people. This book explores the conceptual structure and nature of the Internet and explains the tools and protocols of the Internet.

The Internet creates points of contact for widely dispersed people across time and distance. There are daily person-to-person exchanges that can have an enormous impact on how we as individuals think and how we come to understand global issues. Time on the Internet tends to be accelerated and compressed, creating what I call "Internet Time." Things happen and change fast. It is a little like what people call dog years: they say that one year for a dog is like seven for a person; on the Internet, one day is like a month or longer.

The Internet—Global Expansion

As a network of networks, the Internet connects computers around the world using a standardized set of procedures called TCP/IP. The number of networks linked to the Internet now is in excess of 45,000, with approximately 5 million host computers connected to these networks. And the Internet is growing by roughly 10 percent a *month*. It is the largest intentional association of people and machines yet invented and it is growing every day.

The Internet is not owned by any one person or group. No one is in charge; it is a cooperative venture. The Internet has moved from being primarily an educational and scientific network to a primarily commercial network. Currently, the commercial domains account for almost 60 percent of address registrations.

Joining Up

Not all that long ago, the only way to get on the Internet was through an educational, governmental, or related business entity. By and large, the only people using the Internet were researchers and scientists.

But how times have changed. The majority of Internet users used to be VT-100 terminals attached to DEC VAX machines; that has shifted to dial-up connections to UNIX boxes using Internet services providers (ISPs). Now access can be obtained through a variety of means, including ISDN, dial-up SLIP/PPP, and permanent high-speed connections up to T3. In addition, the commercial services such as CompuServe, America Online, and Prodigy are providing some Internet-related services, with more expected.

The average user now has powerful access to the Internet, with the ability to use all the Internet tools including e-mail, File Transfer Protocol (FTP), Gopher, the World Wide Web (WWW), Internet Relay Chat (IRC), and more.

We have seen the Internet move from the realm of professors, researchers, and scientists to the domain of children, educators, and business owners—individuals of all ages and walks of life.

Communication—People and Computers

On the Internet, communication can be person to person, computer to computer, or person to computer:

- From rather basic beginnings, e-mail now can have binary attachments such as images, sound, and formatted files.
- The number of Usenet newsgroups now numbers somewhere above 10,000 and the newsgroups continue to grow in variety and type.
- Internet Relay Chat provides real-time conversations and is used by some software as a vehicle for other types of real-time human communication as well.

The trend is towards more and better real-time interaction including video and sound using teleconferencing, virtual reality techniques, and improved speed and throughput.

The Internet Makes a Difference

Regularly, the Internet has impact on the lives of millions of people. A few examples are given in the following sections.

The Power of the Internet: Being Inteled

Professor Thomas Nicely noticed that he had been running into a calculation problem on his computer and suspected that it was caused by the CPU: the Pentium chip. He spent several months figuring out the problem, and he was right: the chip could not divide correctly under certain circumstances. He was not alone in that finding, but the chip manufacturer, Intel, downplayed the situation. And then the Internet came into play.

Dr. Nicely posted a message on the Internet, reporting his findings, and the problem he was having with Intel. *Boom!* The word was out and spread like wildfire: there was a calculation problem with the Pentium. In the ensuing weeks, Intel dodged and ducked, but then IBM decided to stop selling the chip in its computers.

People talk, and when they talk on the Internet, the world tunes in. People share information very rapidly; they compare notes and make the facts easy to verify. A critical mass is much easier to create.

And in this case, a company's credibility and reputation went on the line very quickly and very publicly. Now, when this kind of thing happens to a company, the Net calls it "being inteled."

Letting in the Light

In Canada, Karla Homolka was put on trial for murder. She was accused of killing two people, but defended herself saying that her husband made her do it. The government sought to ensure a fair trial by prohibiting the news media from covering it after the trial began. The government had not counted on the Internet, though. Many Canadians were disturbed by the news blackout. Others outside the blackout area began to report the story on the global Internet. Although the government attempted to stop the postings, it was unsuccessful. The upshot was that the information was made available.

Crossing Culture and Distance

The following was written in English and sent on the Internet from an 11-year-old Bosnian girl to a boy in Los Angeles who had lost a friend in a drive-by, gang-related shooting:

> I live in what you call it Bosnia and know that it is like with your gangs in Angles [Los Angeles]. Many lost friends I count and know that I may die soon before growing up and this seems the same for you I think. I am sorry for you but glad also to know that it is the same for you.

Their exchange went on for several months, but stopped abruptly one day. No one knows what happened to the Bosnian girl, only that she stopped writing.

Of course, she started a conversation that continues on.

Information—The Wealth of the Internet

What the Internet does best, in addition to connecting people with people, is to make available, through a variety of means, rich storehouses of information of all kinds: science, research, commercial, education, community, government, diversions, and on and on. The range and depth of this information can support serious research in thousands of areas, or provide a fascinating trip for the casual Net surfer.

A Few Caution Lights on the Information Highway

Not surprisingly, the Internet is not a perfect place—it reflects the people and communities that comprise it.

The Internet has concerns about security in commercial transactions, authentication of messages, and the integrity of computers and data. For example, there have been cases of "crackers" stealing credit card numbers from a Web site and of bogus messages being sent from a CEO to employees.

In addition, the quality, validity, and type of information, files, and images are of concern.

In each case, however, there are ways of working around the issues; many groups and individuals are working on new solutions and improvements in firewalls, secure transaction methodologies, personal search agents, and selective message filtering and sorting systems.

Diversions and Entertainment

The Internet has shifted from a place where serious scientists conducted research. Now, there are a lot of entertaining and interesting things to be found on the Internet: Using appropriate software (a GUI) for example, you can see video clips of the *Tonight Show*. Take a quick trip out to `http://www.nbctonightshow.com/` and browse the video and sound clips.

If you are headed for a vacation in Moscow, you can get information about flying in a MiG-29 Fulcrum B supersonic fighter. Yes, you can actually fly in the fighter. And how did I find about this once-in-a-lifetime opportunity to suit-up in a high-performance g-suit and hurl myself aloft? I found full information, pictures, sound, and video on the Internet at `http://www.intnet.net/mig29`.

Where Is It All Headed?

The single constant about the Internet is change. We know with certitude that the Internet will keep evolving. The Internet has already fundamentally changed the way people communicate—it has a long reach, it is fast, it has a leveling effect: people talk to people regardless of station in life. New tools and protocols will continue to enhance human communication.

Introducing the Internet

by Martin Moore

This chapter provides a brief history of the Internet. And yet, no exact history can be written about the Internet because the Internet is not an easily definable thing. It is a consensus of ideas, an agreement among friends and colleagues, a reflection of technological trends. It is evidence of the notion that communication among peoples is a good thing; it is a quiet affirmation of individual initiative. In short, the Internet is a very large concept.

Therefore, what you will read in the following pages is the history of a number of discrete events that, when combined in history, resulted in the Internet.

From the Cold War—A Hot Network

The 1960s were a peculiar time in the United States. The start of the decade saw the arrival of nuclear missiles in Cuba. The simmering Cold War with Russia rose to a near boil; the threat of nuclear annihilation was a constant in nearly everyone's daily life.

Concurrent with the blockade of Cuba, the beginning of the Vietnam conflict, and political intrigue in many Third World countries, the Cold War was being fought in research labs, fueled by federal spending and public fear. It was thought that the ability to create and keep a technological edge would determine the winner of the war. Technological advances were coming in a rush, and nowhere were they coming more quickly than in the field of computers.

By the late 1960s, every major federally funded research center, including for-profit businesses and universities, had a computer facility equipped with the latest technology that America's burgeoning computer industry could offer.

The idea developed quickly that these various computer centers could be connected to share data. But the actual means by which they would be connected was colored by the ever-present Russian threat. Any network linking these defense-related centers had to be capable of withstanding disruption by a nuclear attack.

The Advanced Research Projects Agency (ARPA) within the Department of Defense was charged with finding the best way to interconnect these various computer sites.

The government's research did not start in a vacuum. Both the National Physics Lab in the United Kingdom and France's Societé Internationale de Télécommunications Aeronautiques were experimenting with a means of intercomputer communications called *packet switching*, which provides tremendous flexibility and reliability in moving commands and data from one computer to another.

PACKET SWITCHING VERSUS CIRCUIT SWITCHING

Packet switching solved the difficult problem of creating a network that could survive attack while providing the greatest communications flexibility. To understand the advantages of packet switching, consider the following analogy. Suppose that you work

Introducing the Internet

2

by Martin Moore

for a company that has three buildings (as shown in Figure 2.1); you want to link the computers in each building. You can string a telephone line from A to B, another from A to C, and another from B to C. When the computer in building A has a message for the computer in building C, it switches to Circuit AC and sends the message. A similar process occurs if the computer in building C has a message for the computer in building B. It turns on Circuit BC and sends the message. This is called *circuit switching,* a method that works just fine as long as all the circuits are in place and functioning.

But what happens if a large object falls from the sky, smashing one of the telephone poles between buildings A and B, thus destroying Circuit AB? The computer in building A can no longer communicate with the computer in building B.

There is another way: Instead of depending on a circuit to send a message between buildings A and B, you can stuff your message into an electronic envelope (called a *packet*), put building B's address on the outside of the packet, and, if B can't receive it, send it to any computer on the network that can receive it. In this case, building C would receive the packet, read the address on it, and send it out over its working lines to building B.

Packet switching does not rely on fixed connections between two computers. Rather, messages are contained in packets, which can be routed among computers until they reach their final destination. Very large messages are divided into several packets, each of which is addressed and contains a sequence number so that the message can be reassembled at its destination. In the early days of the Internet, every computer contained a list of all the other computers it knew about on the network. The list had to be updated on a regular basis and was difficult to maintain. Today, a number of computers throughout the world are responsible for keeping track of and registering new computer names on the Internet. (See Chapter 6, "Domain Names and Internet Addresses," for more on domain names.)

Packets can be nearly any size, but they rarely exceed 1,500 bytes in length. The packet "envelope" usually contains a "to" address, a "from" address, information about the size of the particular packet, and information on where the packet fits in the series of packets that make up a large message. The computer that receives the packet checks particular predefined locations within each packet to get this information.

Packets offer the following benefits:

- Information is divided into discrete chunks that can be routed independently, along various routes, to the destination and then reassembled.

- If a packet disappears or is corrupted during transmission, only the damaged packet must be re-sent, not the whole message.

- Packets can be encoded for security.

- Packets can be compressed to save transmission time.

- A packet can contain information about itself (a checksum) that the receiver can use to validate the accuracy of the contents.

- By use of a standard packet *protocol* (an agreement on exactly how the packets are to be handled and routed), computers and networks using different kinds of hardware and software can be linked together.

- The best use of communications links can be made because packets from various locations on the network can be intermixed. Instead of getting a "busy signal" until another site is totally finished sending packets, new packets can be slipped into small breaks in the traffic—sort of like carrying on a conversation between the words of someone else's conversation.

FIGURE 2.1.

Circuit switching depends on functioning circuits between any two computers that are communicating.

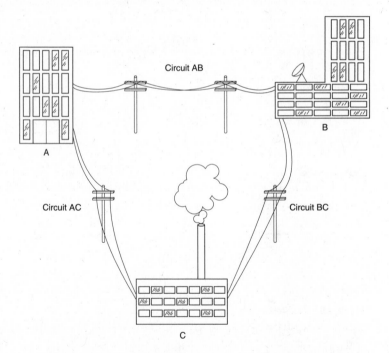

ARPA funded a study by the firm Bolt Beranek and Newman (BBN) to find out how communications between these research centers and military installations could be maintained in spite of a nuclear attack. By 1969, BBN had come up with a packet-switching network protocol called the Network Control Protocol and had designed a network controlling computer called an Information Message Processor (IMP), which could manage the network tasks for mainframe computers. The very first IMP was installed at UCLA that same year. By 1970, the first packet-switched computer network in the United States had been created. As shown in Figure 2.2, ARPAnet connected the University of California at Los Angeles, the University of California at Santa Barbara, Stanford University, and the University of Utah in Salt Lake City.

FIGURE 2.2.

The original ARPAnet connected four university campuses.

This was the start of the Internet—four universities connected by a packet-switching network funded by ARPA. If any one link of the network failed, information could still be routed along the remaining links. This satisfied the original criteria for developing a computer network that could withstand hostile attack.

By using packets for communications, each computer was at a peer level with every other computer on the network. This arrangement decentralized network control. No one computer was the master and all had equal standing on the network. This fundamental design element was key in encouraging the growth of networks throughout the world and the eventual linking of many of these networks into one world-wide Internet.

By 1972, there were 40 different sites attached to ARPAnet. The electronic traffic between these sites included small text files sent between individual users—a transfer called *electronic mail* or *e-mail*. The University of Utah was the first to control a remote computer over the network—a process called *remote login* or *rlogin*. Large text and data files were transferred between computers on ARPAnet using *File Transfer Protocol* (*FTP*). Thus, by 1972, the core technology was in place.

Outcome of the First ICCC

In 1972, the first International Conference on Computer Communications was held in Washington, D.C. Attended by representatives from around the world, the conference sought an agreement about communication protocols between different computers and networks. Vinton Cerf, who was involved in the establishment of the ARPAnet at UCLA, was named the first chairman of the InterNetwork Working Group, a group that was charged with creating a protocol that could be used by nearly any computer network in the world to communicate with any other network.

The year following the ICCC, ARPA, newly renamed Defense Advanced Research Projects Agency (DARPA), began a program called the Internetting Project to study how to link packet-switching networks together.

These two projects resulted in the development and introduction of the two basic Internet protocols. In 1974, Vinton Cerf and Robert Kahn released the Internet Protocol (IP) and the Transmission Control Protocol (TCP). These two protocols defined the way in which messages (files or commands) are passed among computer networks on the Internet.

TCP/IP—AN OVERVIEW

Fundamentally, *communications protocols* are rules that govern the way one machine communicates with another. We can use the English language to demonstrate. When you are reading text written in English, you have some idea of what rules—protocols—govern the language. For example, you know that most sentences start with a capitalized word, and that a sentence ends with some sort of punctuation mark. In between, sentence fragments are separated by commas, semicolons, or colons. Large thoughts are divided into paragraphs (unless you are Norman Mailer), and so on. Thus, there are commonly understood rules governing written communication.

The Internet Protocol (IP) is a similar body of rules that forms the foundation for all communications over the Internet. Among the rules the IP establishes are these:

1. Every *node* (computer) on the Internet has an Internet address made up of four numbers, and each number is less than 256. (For example, my Internet provider's address is 192.108.254.10.) The address numbers are separated by periods when written out.

2. All messages are divided into packets of information.

3. Each message packet is assembled (electronically speaking) into an IP envelope.

4. The IP envelope contains the address to which the envelope is being sent and the address of the computer sending the message.

Some of the computers that make up the Internet are called *routers*. These computers are responsible for directing packets sent out on the Internet to the correct destination. Not every computer on the Internet is a router, nor is it necessary that every computer on the Internet know the location and path to the computer that the packet is being sent to. It is analogous to your mail carrier picking up an envelope you have addressed to Aunt Flo who lives on 220 E. West St. in Walla Walla, Washington. The person who picked up your mail may not even know where Walla Walla is. But your mail carrier carries the envelope to a post office that routes the envelope to a central post office near Walla Walla, which, in turn, routes the envelope to Aunt Flo's local post office, where a postal carrier picks it up and delivers it to 220 E. West St.

The IP address contains finer and finer location information as you read from left to right. The first IP number indicates which major part of Internet the destination network is on; the right-most number indicates the specific machine being addressed. Again using my Internet provider as an example, the right-most number (10) in the IP address 192.108.254.10 is a Sun workstation named Kelly.

Most protocols have layers, and the Internet protocols are no exception. The Internet Protocol (IP) is the foundation; laying on top of the IP is yet another protocol called the Transmission Control Protocol (TCP). Most often, you see these two protocols referred to together as TCP/IP.

TCP is used to handle large amounts of data and to handle situations in which the transmitted data is corrupted. TCP divides large messages into multiple packets. Each packet is then assembled into a TCP envelope, which is in turn assembled into an IP envelope. At the receiving end, the TCP envelopes are separated from the IP envelopes and the original message or data is reassembled. If one or more packets are corrupted (as indicated by bad checksums), the originating computer is sent a request to issue a replacement for the bad packet.

The work done by Kahn and Cerf continues to serve the Internet community. TCP/IP is the protocol of choice in most new networks established today. The approach used in TCP/IP is so straightforward that the original goal of creating a communications pathway among many different kinds of networks using their own internal protocols continues to be met.

It was, however, a curious, counter-intuitive event (given the times and the Cold War fears) that truly made the Internet broadly available: DARPA decided to release TCP/IP to the world, free of charge, with no restrictions. In other words, a core technology that solved the problem of computer-network reliability in times of war was suddenly released to the world.

UNIX and Digital Equipment Corporation

The next part of the Internet story involves the development of a new concept in computer operating systems and a low-cost minicomputer.

Digital Equipment Corporation (DEC) was one of the early developers of the minicomputer, a breakthrough in relatively low-cost computers for the masses (as opposed to the large mainframes from IBM and Control Data that cost hundreds of thousands or even millions of dollars). DEC developed the PDP series of computers, followed in the early 1970s by the VAX family of computers. These moderately powerful computers could be afforded by many colleges, universities, and high-tech businesses. Originally, the VAX computers were only shipped with operating system software called VMS, but that was soon to change.

About the same time, researchers at AT&T Bell Labs were experimenting with a home-grown, multitasking, operating system that ran on DEC minicomputers: a system called UNIX.

UNIX was, from the beginning, an operating system that understood networking. In 1976, Mike Lesk at AT&T Bell Labs created a software package called the UNIX-to-UNIX Copy Program, or UUCP. With UUCP, any UNIX computer with a modem could call any other UNIX computer with a modem and transfer files. AT&T Bell Labs starting shipping UUCP with UNIX version 7 in 1977.

Here was a widely available and affordable computer that could run an operating system that actually had built-in support for networking. The UNIX/DEC combination spread like wildfire throughout industry and academia. Networking was no longer an esoteric act performed on expensive, government-sponsored computer facilities. All those slightly renegade UNIX users quickly understood and adopted the idea of networking.

UNIX was the original "open" system, and it promoted an anarchistic attitude toward computing. Clashes between traditional data processing organizations (with their rightful focus on limited access and security) were the antithesis of the UNIX approach. As much as anything else, UNIX was a game, and its users were global players.

AN UNDERGROUND NETWORK

The   community was held in some disrepute by the data-processing community in many companies. While working at Tektronix, Inc. in the late 1970s and early 1980s, I had the privilege of watching a bit of anarchistic behavior unfold.

During that time, a new business unit inside Tektronix was started for developing products to serve the emerging microcomputer marketplace. During the course of creating the business unit, the company purchased several DEC VAX computers and the decision was made to use the UNIX operating system. In addition, the computers were networked to one another internally, and a few modems were purchased to provide dial-up capability. Of course, if users could dial in, they could usually dial out, too.

There was a certain amount of fear at the corporate level about having a computer network—used to develop new products—communicating with other computer sites. Because UNIX was a fairly open operating system, it was difficult to guarantee that outsiders could not break into the development computers and steal designs. Therefore, Tektronix had a list of approved external sites. Any site not on the list could not be dialed up, nor could any site that was not on the list dial in to Tektronix's computers.

Within 20 miles or so of the Tektronix site was a private institution of higher learning called Reed College. Because of the rambunctious nature of college students, it was determined that there would be no computer-to-computer communications between Reed College and Tektronix.

Not everyone at the lower levels believed in this policy. In fact, there were those determined to demonstrate the folly of placing artificial limitations on a computer network. Work was immediately undertaken to establish an alternative, "underground," connection to Reed College. This connection is shown in Figure 2.3.

Tektronix could not communicate directly with Reed College. However, the University of California at Berkeley was on the approved list. UC Berkeley could, in turn, establish a link between its UNIX computers and Duke University in North Carolina. Duke had a link to Reed. Therefore, a long-distance link was established between the VAX computers in Beaverton, Oregon, and Reed College's computers in Portland, Oregon.

This UUCP network was carried over the public telephone system, which was drafted to serve as the information superhighway of the moment.

The wide distribution of DEC minicomputers running the UNIX operating system created a very large, casual network of computers running over the public telephone systems. This was the epitome of a decentralized, ungoverned network.

FIGURE 2.3.
Using UUCP to make a local call.

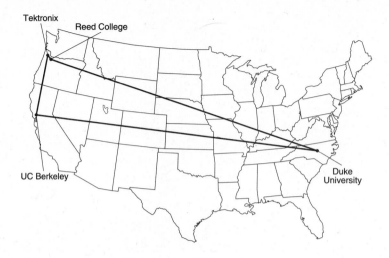

Independent Network Evolution

Toward the end of the 1970s, networks were starting to pop up everywhere, and they ran on all kinds of computers.

In 1977, the University of Wisconsin decided to create a network for science researchers. More than 100 researchers used Theorynet to trade e-mail messages with one another.

At this time, ARPAnet was serving a select number of research centers, but not all. Many centers, including the University of Wisconsin, were justifiably concerned that sites connected to the ARPAnet over its high-speed dedicated network were receiving an unfair advantage when compared to non-ARPAnet sites depending on slower telephone lines and UUCP. Wisconsin felt that there might be a real need for another network: one like ARPAnet but focused specifically on computer science. In 1979, a meeting was held between a number of researchers from various universities (including Wisconsin), DARPA, and the National Science Foundation.

That meeting in 1979 turned out to be the launch meeting for the creation of the Computer Science Research Network (CSnet), funded in large part by the National Science Foundation.

The story swings back now to Vinton Cerf. In 1980, Cerf suggested connecting ARPAnet and CSnet with a gateway, using the TCP/IP protocols he and Robert Kahn had developed. Cerf also suggested that CSnet could exist as a collection of several independent networks that shared a gateway to ARPAnet (see Figure 2.4).

It can be argued that this was the real birth of the Internet. Keep in mind that the Internet does not exist as a physical entity. You cannot reach your finger out and touch anything that can be called the Internet. The Internet is a collection of independent, free-standing networks that have come to an agreement about how to talk to one another. That is what Vinton Cerf envisioned when he suggested coupling CSnet to ARPAnet.

FIGURE 2.4.

The new CSnet linked to ARPAnet with a gateway.

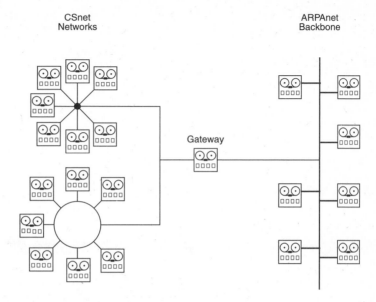

By 1982, researchers could dial in to CSnet to read and send e-mail both to sites within CSnet and to sites within ARPAnet. Thus was born the physical implementation of Internet.

Start Spreading the News

While CSnet was being created and joined to ARPAnet, Steve Bellovin was busy at the University of North Carolina. Steve had the idea for a software application to create an electronic newspaper.

Actually, the newspaper paradigm doesn't quite fit unless your local newspaper has an editorial section as large as all the rest of the newspaper to which you can respond instantly. News on the Internet is definitely interactive, promoting letters to the editor, letters to authors, and even letters to innocent bystanders.

Steve's concept was turned into Release A of Usenet, developed by Steve Daniel and Tom Truscutt. This first release firmed up the concept of newsgroups and newsgroup hierarchies. The newsgroup hierarchies have since been expanded (and, in one notable case, sidestepped), but the fundamental operation remains the same.

Usenet's function was to provide a network that would enable any user to submit an article that would be routed to all computers on the network. It allowed any user to send a message that all other users on the network could have access to, or to all users that subscribed to one or more specific newsgroups. UUCP was called into action; very soon, a series of computers were calling one another, copying files back and forth. If a user posted an article, it was distributed to the host computer and sent out over the network, moving from host to host.

USENET IS ORGANIZED

In the beginning of Usenet, there were only two hierarchies: The mod hierarchy was intended to discuss product modifications and bug fixes; the net hierarchy was used to discuss network-related issues. Starting in 1986, the Usenet hierarchies underwent a major change, and seven new main hierarchies were created in the Great Renaming:

comp	computer-related discussions
news	news about Usenet
rec	recreation discussions
sci	science discussions
soc	sociological discussion
talk	chit-chat
misc	miscellaneous discussions

The creation of the new hierarchies allowed for a more logical grouping of messages. Groups were organized by category, subcategory, sub-subcategory, and so on. For example, under sci, there are now a number of subcategories such as chem, physics, and med (medicine). Under these subcategories are further subcategories. These groups are listed in a standard way such as this:

```
sci.med.pharmacy
sci.med.psychobiology
sci.med.nutrition
```

Of equal importance, however, was that a number of controversial discussions began, which also created subgroups. These were all lumped into the talk hierarchy, and they fostered a certain amount of sponsor censorship.

In the early days of Usenet, news feeds were being leaked on to the DARPA-sponsored ARPAnet. By the time the official ARPAnet overseers noticed that there may have been news traffic unsuitable for forwarding over a government network, it was too late. This prompted the creation of a new protocol called Network News Transfer Protocol (NNTP), which is used to carry Usenet news over TCP/IP connections only to sites that want it.

More top-level categories have been added. One of the most popular of these is alt The alt groups have a simpler procedure for adding new groups (see Chapter 17, "Reading and Posting the News: Using Usenet," for information about group creation).The alt category has grown rapidly and now includes some of the most esoteric, often interesting, and borderline (un)acceptable groups.

Usenet now has over 10,000 different groups. If you can think of a topic, there's probably already a group discussing it!

1983—The Year of the Network

By 1983, it seemed that networks were cropping up everywhere. Within the halls of the City University of New York, Bitnet emerged. (Bitnet is an acronym for the Because It's Time Network.) Bitnet is another source of news and opinion. Bitnet uses a mechanism called the *Listserv*. Under Bitnet operation, if you want to read the postings to a specific group, you subscribe to that discussion group by sending an e-mail subscription request to the appropriate Listserv. Newly posted articles are routed directly to all of the group's subscribers using e-mail.

Bitnet is waning in popularity and use, but there are now lists supported by programs such as listproc, majordomo, and L-Soft. Many former Bitnet sites are porting their lists to the Internet directly.

The use of Listserver software to support discussion groups migrated to other parts of the Internet, and the number of discussion groups is continuing to grow. As of this writing, there are more than 7,500 discussion lists available on the Internet.

In San Francisco, another important network was born: FidoNet. In 1983, Tom Jennings wrote a personal computer bulletin-board system called FidoBBS. The software rapidly grew in popularity, and soon there were Fido bulletin boards across the nation. The following year, Jennings released FidoNet, a networking package that could link all the different Fido bulletin boards using a modem and telephone line; FidoNet allows users to send e-mail to one another to create discussion groups just like Usenet and Bitnet.

By 1987, the UNIX-to-UNIX Copy (UUCP) software originally developed for the UNIX operating system was ported to the IBM PC and its clones; thus, FidoNet could share traffic with Usenet.

Because it is based on the PC, FidoNet is used world wide, linking all kinds of users to the larger Internet family.

Supercomputing and the National Science Foundation

In the latter half of the 1980s, a new concern worried the U.S. government, a fear that America's lead in the high-end computing platform business would be eroded by foreign competition. One of the outcomes of that fear was the creation of the National Science Foundation Network (NSFnet), which linked a handful of supercomputer centers across the United States. The purpose of NSFnet was to provide the highest quality computing services to researchers nationwide.

The NSFnet sites were linked by state-of-the-art transmission lines. Each of the sites in turn served as the central point for a local network or networks. The number of key sites grew over the years to more than 14, divided into two different regions: East and West.

Network Evolution and Growth

While NSFnet was being formed, the existing networks were undergoing transformations, and new networks were being developed.

In 1983, the military portion of ARPAnet was spun off into its own network, Milnet (which soon disappeared from view). ARPAnet, the grandfather of networks, was slowly being supplanted by NSFnet; in 1990, ARPAnet was removed from service.

In 1989, Bitnet merged with CSnet, the Computer Science Research Network established a decade earlier. However, in two short years, CSnet closed down, shunted aside by NSFnet.

Although at this point it may seem that all existing networks were being consumed by NSFnet, nothing could be further from the truth. New, independent networks emerged, including services such as CompuServe, Prodigy, and America Online. Businesses, particularly those involved in research and product development, created huge networks, most of which are linked to the Internet.

At the other end of the scale, alternative, independent networks continue to come and go (there are no rules that say you cannot start your own network any time you like and link it into the vast Internet). Indeed, these small, local, or international networks benefit greatly from the larger, federally supported networks because their packets can "go along for the ride," using the NSFnet high-speed transmission lines to move data from one end of the continent to the other.

It's a Wonder It Survived

As you've seen, the Internet is an amalgam of over 45,000 different, independent networks with a system largely open to all.

Looking back, we see that it could have been far different. Computer networking was started with federal funding. The government could have stepped in at any time during the past 20 years and seriously restricted its development. Fortunately, that didn't happen. Industry as well could have prevented communications with the outside world. That too, for the most part, has not happened.

The result is an Internet that spans the globe. You can send e-mail to the South Pole, Fiji, Germany, and even to the land that had such a large and inadvertent role in the development of networks in the first place—Russia.

Forces Shaping the Internet

3

by Matthew V. Ellsworth and Martin Moore

Chapter 2, "Introducing the Internet," covered some of the key developments since 1968 that have lead to the current state of the Internet, including the following:

- The federal government's decision to create an attack-proof computer network using packet switching.
- The decision to allow universal access to the TCP/IP protocol.
- The federal government's continued funding for leading-edge, high-speed electronic communications pathways.
- The creation and wide disbursement of the UNIX operating system and its UUCP file-copying protocol.
- The creation of Usenet as a network dedicated to communications among network users.

With this kind of foundation in place, and with the obvious benefit to both industry and academia of widely available computer networking, the Internet could do nothing but grow.

This chapter looks at the current state of the Internet and the forces that shaped it. In addition, it touches lightly on the primary features of the network, all of which are covered in greater depth in the chapters that follow.

A Growth Market

In 1990, the Federal Networking Council (one of the governing bodies of the Internet) made a radical policy change. Previously, if an organization wanted to become a member of the Internet, it had to seek sponsorship by a U.S. government agency. The Federal Networking Council dropped that requirement, allowing any organization to apply for membership without justifying the connection. This launched what is commonly referred to as the "commercialization" of the Internet. It also launched a period of extraordinary growth.

The Amazing Statistics

Each of the original four sites linked together by the original ARPAnet had its own local network. From that four-network system, the Internet has grown to include over 45,000 networks worldwide (see Figure 3.1).

In the United States, these networks are found in all states. Figure 3.2 shows their current distribution.

FIGURE 3.1.

Growth in the number of networks connected to the Internet.

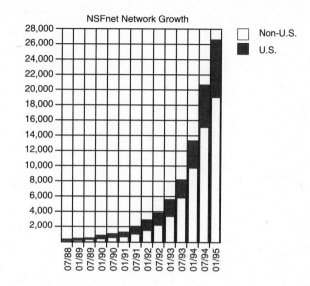

FIGURE 3.2.

The number of networks linked to the Internet in each state.

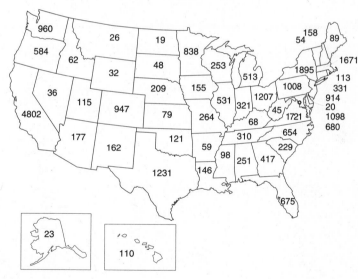

Although the U.S. and Europe are the most intensively networked areas of the world, many countries have networks linked to the Internet (see Table 3.1).

Table 3.1. The number of networks linked to the Internet in each country.

Country	Number of Networks	Country	Number of Networks
Algeria	3	Hong Kong	80
Argentina	23	Hungary	163
Armenia	3	Iceland	31
Australia	1,825	India	12
Austria	377	Indonesia	50
Belgium	123	Ireland	167
Bermuda	14	Israel	195
Brazil	162	Italy	478
Bulgaria	9	Jamaica	13
Burkina Faso	2	Japan	1,669
Cameroon	1	Kazakhstan	1
Canada	3,295	Kenya	1
Chile	86	Korea, South	449
China	24	Kuwait	8
Colombia	5	Latvia	6
Costa Rica	6	Lebanon	1
Croatia	31	Liechtenstein	3
Cyprus	25	Lituania	1
Czech Republic	369	Luxembourg	44
Denmark	45	Macao	1
Ecuador	85	Malaysia	6
Egypt	7	Mexico	114
Estonia	49	Morocco	1
Fiji	1	Netherlands	350
Finland	605	New Caledonia	1
France	1,843	New Zealand	354
French Polynesia	1	Nicaragua	1
Germany	1,620	Niger	1
Ghana	1	Norway	211
Greece	95	Panama	1
Guam	5	Peru	116

Country	Number of Networks	Country	Number of Networks
Philippines	45	Sweden	356
Poland	131	Switzerland	313
Portugal	92	Taiwan	632
Puerto Rico	7	Thailand	77
Romania	26	Tunisia	19
Russian Federate	369	Turkey	90
Senegal	11	Ukraine	52
Singapore	101	United Arab Emirates	3
Slovakia	69	United Kingdom	1,394
Slovenia	46	United States	26,681
South Africa	363	Uruguay	1
Spain	252	Uzbekistan	1
Sri Lanka	1	Venezuela	13
Swaziland	1	Virgin Islands	4

In addition to growth in the number of networks connected to the Internet, many of these networks have grown themselves—adding many new sites to the Internet. Figure 3.3 shows the growth in the number of host computers connected by these networks.

FIGURE 3.3.

Increase in the number of Internet host computers.

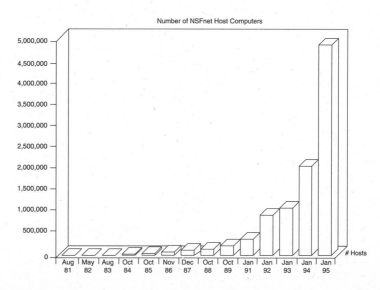

Computers and networks on the Internet are quite easy to count; people are not. Although some computers on the Internet provide access for only one person, most provide access for many people. Universities, businesses, and organizations may have one computer used for Internet access that is used by dozens or even thousands of people. Current estimates for the number of people on the Internet are as high as 30 million with access to the full scope of Internet tools and protocols, and up to 50 million with at least e-mail access to the Internet.

The Internet's phenomenal growth has made it a virtual household word, whether people know anything specific about it or not. The growth has also involved a good deal of activity among businesses that have found a new world-wide marketplace and a new way of doing business. Communications companies, telephone companies, and cable television firms are doing whatever they can to make sure they're not left behind because they view the next five years as the "early days" in the rush to connect everyone's PC to everyone else's PC.

The Superhighway

Backbones are primary networks that serve as the framework for the global Internet. In the early days, the ARPAnet was the backbone network for Internet. Today, several networks serve as Internet backbones. In addition to several commercial networks such as CIX, Sprint, and MCI, one of the most important backbones is NSFnet. The NSFnet is sponsored by the National Science Foundation, but it is managed and operated by an organization called Advanced Network & Services, Inc. (ANS). NSFnet is in the process of being phased out in the coming months.

Backbone networks provide the speed of communication, the ability to transfer large amounts of data (high bandwidth), and the reliability necessary to the Internet. The NSFnet backbone, for example, is comparable to a high-speed transport running from coast to coast. Imagine that you walk from your house to your car at 3.5 miles per hour (MPH), which is roughly analogous to your PC's modem communicating with an Internet server at 9,600 bps. Then you drive to the transport station at an average of 50 MPH—comparable to your Internet server communicating with an NSFnet node at 56,000 bps. Once you are on the hypothetical high-speed transport, you're whisked from San Francisco to Boston in about three seconds, analogous to the NSFnet T3 connection, which runs at 45,000,000 bps.

This high-speed data flow across the United States and to other countries is accomplished by fiber-optic cabling as well as by using satellites to relay data over radio channels. With these high-speed links, interactions with computers half way around the globe take place within a few seconds, and e-mail during the quieter times of day is often delivered in less than a minute.

As the commercial sector improves its ability to transfer the massive data flow, the NSF is being phased out as the central, pivotal network. The evolution continues.

Figure 3.4 shows a map of the core NSFnet backbone network as it currently looks as it travels across the contiguous 48 states. In addition to the primary network and switching systems shown in Figure 3.4, there is a second tier of switching systems connected to each primary node shown on the map.

FIGURE 3.4.

The NSFnet core backbone network service.

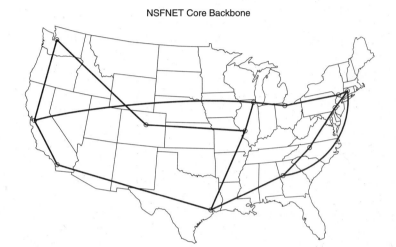

NSFNET Core Backbone

History suggests that the structure of Internet networks will continue to change. Much of this change will go unnoticed by most individual Internet users except in the improvements in the range and flexibility of the system.

Who's in Charge Here?

How can such an amorphous collection of networks be managed? As mentioned in Chapter 2, the Internet is more nearly an agreement among friends than a structured, organized, establishment. However, there are two entities that have exerted a significant amount of influence over the Internet: NSFnet and the Internet Society.

NSF

Because the National Science Foundation funded most of NSFnet, and because NSFnet became probably the most important American backbone of the Internet, the NSF had a significant voice in how the Internet was operated in the United States—but only in terms of how the Internet uses NSFnet.

In 1990, the NSF created Advanced Network and Services Inc. (ANS), a corporation formed by Merit (Michigan Education and Research Infrastructure Triad), the IBM computer company, and the MCI telecommunications company. ANS was chartered with the operation of the NSFnet backbone.

The NSF and ANS have been very generous in sharing the network backbone. Before 1992, as long as users of the NSFnet backbone followed the NSF's acceptable use policy (see sidebar), the NSFnet was available to Internet users. This acceptable use policy and its precursors shaped the Internet forcefully, and the effects of this AUP are still much in evidence. The AUP is critical to understanding the commercial revolution currently underway.

NSFNET BACKBONE SERVICES' ACCEPTABLE USE POLICY (JUNE 1992)

GENERAL PRINCIPLE:

1. NSFnet backbone services are provided to support open research and education in and among U.S. research and instructional institutions, plus research arms of for-profit firms when engaged in open scholarly communication and research. Use for other purposes is not acceptable.

SPECIFICALLY ACCEPTABLE USES:

2. Communication with foreign researchers and educators in connection with research or instruction, as long as any network that the foreign user employs for such communication provides reciprocal access to U.S. researchers and educators.

3. Communication and exchange for professional development, to maintain currency, or to debate issues in a field or subfield of knowledge.

4. Use for disciplinary society, university association, government advisory, or standards activities related to the user's research and instructional activities.

5. Use in applying for or administering grants or contracts for research or instruction, but not for other fundraising or public relations activities.

6. Any other administrative communications or activities in direct support of research and instruction.

7. Announcements of new products or services for use in research or instruction, but not advertising of any kind.

8. Any traffic originating from a network of another member agency of the Federal Networking Council if the traffic meets the acceptable-use policy of that agency.

9. Communication incidental to otherwise acceptable use, except for illegal or specifically unacceptable use.

UNACCEPTABLE USES:

10. Use for for-profit activities, unless covered by the General Principle or as a specifically acceptable use.

11. Extensive use for private or personal business.

This statement applies to use of the NSFnet backbone only. NSF expects that connecting networks will formulate their own use policies. The NSF Division of Networking and Communications Research and Infrastructure will resolve any questions about this policy or its interpretation.

The most current version of the acceptable-use policy is still available from Merit by anonymous FTP to `nic.merit.edu` in the file `/nsfnet/acceptable/use.policies/nsfnet.txt`, but the current value of this document is largely as an historical document that shaped the Internet.

The acceptable-use policy left issues of personal and business use of the Internet unclear to many. It generally tended to stifle large-scale access for businesses and individuals other than certain organizations such as universities. That has all, of course, changed in recent years.

In 1992, the NSF extended ANS's contract to run NSFnet. The National Science Foundation made it clear then that NSF is a customer of ANS, and the limitations outlined by the acceptable-use policy applied *only* to traffic from the NSF. This changed the commonly held interpretations of how the Internet could be used.

Suddenly, the door opened. The burden is now on ANS to set policy concerning the Internet's use of the network backbone, but it is very clear that commercial use of the backbone is no longer prohibited by the NSF.

Internet access providers and some networks are increasingly by-passing the backbone altogether by using a variety of alternative direct links. For these networks, using other links removes much of whatever still remains of the NSF influence on their networking policies.

The next chapter looks at what the opening of Internet to commercial use may mean.

The Internet Society

The other, more direct source of control over the Internet comes from the Internet Society. Yet even this control is subject to voluntary cooperation among members—and it isn't really very direct.

The Internet Society is an international body made up of volunteers. In its own words:

The Society will provide assistance and support to groups and organizations involved in the use, operation, and evolution of the Internet. It will provide support for forums in which technical and operational questions can be discussed and provide mechanisms through which the interested parties can be informed and educated about the Internet, its function, use, operation, and the interests of its constituents.

What you do not see in that statement is any suggestion that the Internet Society runs the Internet. It does not. However, it is the most influential body involved with the Internet, and its members do a significant amount of work to keep us all up and running on the network. (To join the Internet Society, request an information package by sending e-mail to `isoc@isoc.org`. Dues are $70 a year for individuals, $25 a year for individuals who happen to be students.)

The Internet Society acts as a benevolent advisor, with its members belonging to several subgroups, or forums, within the Society. One of those is the Internet Architecture Board (IAB). The IAB was formed in 1983 to encourage research about the Internet. Today, the IAB produces standards for interconnecting networks by creating task forces such as the Internet Engineering Task Force (IETF) and the Internet Research Task Force (IRTF).

The Internet Research Task Force is made up, like its parent organization, of a group of volunteers who keep an eye on long-term technological developments that may (or should) impact the Internet. The Engineering Task Force develops protocol standards for the Internet. For example, one of the Engineering Task Force teams revised a document called "Issues in Designing a Transport Protocol for Audio and Video Conferences and other Multiparticipant Real-Time Applications."

Multimedia conferencing is a very logical next step for the Internet. Because many businesses are installing multimedia conferencing systems, it should not be surprising that the Internet Society is examining the question of how to use the network to transmit and receive video and audio as well as text.

As a final indicator of the kind of work being done to improve the Internet, research has begun on a communications system that can move data at the incredible speed of 300 million bps—nearly an order of magnitude faster than the current T3 technology, which moves data at 45 million bps.

Keeping Up with the Latest

The Internet is a dynamic, constantly changing environment. One of the ways to stay current and up to date on what's going on with the Internet is to read the *Internet Monthly* report, available from a number of sources, including Merit. (FTP to `nic.merit.edu` and look in the `newsletters` directory.)

Another good source of Internet information is the *NSF Network News*, which is transmitted to the entire United States and 44 different countries around the world. (Send e-mail to `newsletter-request@is.internic.net`.)

You can get more information about all kinds of networking information and statistics from InterNic at `http://www.internic.net`. This site offers access to a variety of guides and services.

The next chapter focuses on where these forces are likely to take the Internet in the near future.

The Future of the Internet

4

by Matthew V. Ellsworth

Predicting the future is hardly an exact art—there are often unexpected twists and turns in history that produce unexpected paths. There are, however, some well established trends, and internal and external forces on the Internet that make near-term predictions reasonably safe (even without a call to the Psychic Friends Hotline).

Growth

The incredible growth of the Internet is likely to continue. The Internet is not yet running up against any major physical or technical constraints, although the time may come when this will be true. The ease of using alternative routes for data packets allows for expansion of the system in increments—a totally new system does not have to be built every time there is increased need for bandwidth. Also, the Internet tolerates interaction of systems of dramatically different capabilities. On a daily basis, people with high-speed T1 connections to the Internet interact successfully with those using 2,400 baud dial-in accounts. The expansion of high bandwidth communications technologies such as fiber optics and direct satellite communications should easily coexist with the existing Internet.

Another influence on growth is the recent development of easy-to-use, graphically oriented, "point-and-click" software for the Internet. This is encouraging a large group of people to use the Internet who found the Internet interface too daunting before.

Secure Communications

With the current vigorous efforts to develop secure transaction procedures for business uses including sales transactions online, there seems little doubt that secure transactions, authentication, and other secure communications will be commonplace—probably within a year. Dozens of secure transaction methods exist now, with encryption methods holding the greatest promise. The challenge at this point is to make these encryption methods convenient and user friendly. With the capabilities and current expansion of the World Wide Web, these features will certainly have to be incorporated in Web browsers and Web servers. The winners in that realm are likely to become the *de facto* standards for secure transactions.

The World Wide Web Takes Over

With the exception of e-mail, the WWW (World Wide Web) has become the most used user interface for the Internet—way ahead of Gopher, the former leader. With the ability of most Web browsers to provide an interface for the other Internet protocols, the WWW will become the primary face of the Internet: many new Internauts will not know, or need to know, how to use FTP, Gopher, or any of the other applications.

Most of the early growth of the WWW came through use of freeware or shareware Web browsers. Now, however, many companies are developing more fully featured browsers that will soon be plentifully available at retail outlets.

The integration of a variety of text, file, and image viewers (such as Adobe Acrobat and PostScript) into current browsers allows information to be distributed in a variety of fully formatted ways. This allows publications to be distributed with full control over layout, text, fonts, image positions, and size.

Pictures and other graphics are now common on the World Wide Web. Sound and movie files are available but not widely used. With the increasing sale of multimedia-capable computers, and the spread of World Wide Web graphical browser use, full multimedia Internet sites should be commonplace within a couple years.

Commercialization

Tens of thousands of businesses are already actively using the Internet for various business functions, including marketing and sales. As secure transactions and multimedia become commonplace on the Internet, expect an even faster rush by businesses to the Internet.

The secure transactions not only protect the customer and business, but will create a comfortable environment for doing business. The multimedia capabilities of color, movement, and sound will allow for effective advertising and interaction between customer and business.

The place for businesses to be on the Internet now, and in the foreseeable future, is on the World Wide Web. Web access providers are making access to the Web much easier with turnkey virtual storefronts and cybermall services. These virtual storefronts and cybermalls can be expected to grow dramatically as businesses that are now only marginally aware of how to do business on the Internet purchase these ready-to-use services.

Publishing Will Never Be the Same Again

Publishers of magazines, newspapers, and books are increasingly going online. Some are offering excerpts and promotional materials and providing online order forms for their traditional paper-based publications. Others, however, are experimenting with online electronic publication. This has brought the issue of intellectual property rights to the forefront. How can an author or publisher protect against duplication and distribution of a copyrighted digital version of a work? Various technical options involving the imbedding of identity codes within a file are being considered, as are new laws to protect these documents. This issue is a tough one. Intensive discussion and research on this issue is a certainty for the next few years—the nature of the solutions is not yet clear.

Access

Local calling area dial-up phone access to the Internet is continuing to be provided to smaller and smaller communities (without some governmental action, however, rural areas will continue to be a toll call away from the Internet). One possible bypass for this problem involves the frequencies allocated recently by the Federal Communications Commission for personal communications devices. These, and satellite links, may make the Internet av ailable almost anywhere.

Government Influence: The National Information Infrastructure

Government actions in the past sometimes affected the Internet in random or unplanned ways. Now, however, the U.S. government has directly and positively addressed the development of networks through the concept of a "National Information Infrastructure."

The United States Advisory Council of the National Information Infrastructure was created in September 1993. The following sidebar shows their "Agenda for Action."

THE NATIONAL INFORMATION INFRASTRUCTURE

Agenda for Action—Executive Summary

All Americans have a stake in the construction of an advanced National Information Infrastructure (NII), a seamless web of communications networks, computers, databases, and consumer electronics that will put vast amounts of information at users' fingertips. Development of the NII can help unleash an information revolution that will change forever the way people live, work, and interact with each other:

■ People could live almost anywhere they wanted, without foregoing opportunities for useful and fulfilling employment, by "telecommuting" to their offices through an electronic highway.

■ The best schools, teachers, and courses would be available to all students, without regard to geography, distance, resources, or disability.

■ Services that improve America's health care system and respond to other important social needs could be available online, without waiting in line, when and where you needed them.

Private sector firms are already developing and deploying that infrastructure today. Nevertheless, there remain essential roles for government in this process. Carefully crafted government action will complement and enhance the efforts of the private sector and ensure the growth of an information infrastructure available to all Americans at reasonable cost. In developing our policy initiatives in this area, the Administration will work in close partnership with business, labor, academia, the public, Congress, and state and local governments. Our efforts will be guided by the following principles and objectives:

- Promote private sector investment, through appropriate tax and regulatory policies.

- Extend the "universal service" concept to ensure that information resources are available to all at affordable prices. Because information means empowerment—and employment—the government has a duty to ensure that all Americans have access to the resources and job-creation potential of the Information Age.

- Act as a catalyst to promote technological innovation and new applications. Commit important government research programs and grants to help the private sector develop and demonstrate technologies needed for the NII, and develop the applications and services that will maximize its value to users.

- Promote seamless, interactive, user-driven operation of the NII. As the NII evolves into a "network of networks," the government will ensure that users can transfer information across networks easily and efficiently. To increase the likelihood that the NII will be both interactive and, to a large extent, user driven, the government must reform regulations and policies that may inadvertently hamper the development of interactive applications.

- Ensure information security and network reliability. The NII must be trustworthy and secure, protecting the privacy of its users. Government action will also ensure that the overall system remains reliable, quickly repairable in the event of a failure, and—perhaps most importantly—easy to use.

- Improve management of the radio frequency spectrum, an increasingly critical resource.

- Protect intellectual property rights. The Administration will investigate how to strengthen domestic copyright laws and international intellectual property treaties to prevent piracy and to protect the integrity of intellectual property.

- Coordinate with other levels of government and with other nations. Because information crosses state, regional, and national boundaries, coordination is critical to avoid needless obstacles and prevent unfair policies that handicap U.S. industry.

- Provide access to government information and improve government procurement. The Administration will seek to ensure that Federal agencies, in concert with state and local governments, use the NII to expand the information

> available to the public, ensuring that the immense reservoir of government information is available to the public easily and equitably. Additionally, Federal procurement policies for telecommunications and information services and equipment will be designed to promote important technical developments for the NII and to provide attractive incentives for the private sector to contribute to NII development.
>
> The time for action is now. Every day brings news of change: new technologies such as hand-held computerized assistants; new ventures and mergers combining businesses that not long ago seemed discrete and insular; new legal decisions that challenge the separation of computer, cable, and telephone companies. These changes promise substantial benefits for the American people, but only if government understands fully its implications and begins working with the private sector and other interested parties to shape the evolution of the communications infrastructure.
>
> The benefits of the NII for the nation are immense. An advanced information infrastructure will enable U.S. firms to compete and win in the global economy, generating good jobs for the American people and economic growth for the nation. As importantly, the NII can transform the lives of the American people—ameliorating the constraints of geography, disability, and economic status—giving all Americans a fair opportunity to go as far as their talents and ambitions will take them.

This is certainly a bold, broad, fascinating vision. Only time will tell how much of this is implemented and how it will be integrated with the Internet. It does, however, dovetail well with current trends on the Internet, and the hopes of many currently on the Internet.

Out on a Limb

Moving a little farther out on the limb, we come to the ever illusive "video conferencing." Various companies, businesses, and groups have been predicting widely available video conferencing for almost 50 years, but despite project after project backed by major communications companies, it just hasn't become an everyday means of communicating.

A combination of hardware, software, and communications trends now makes large scale, worldwide, inexpensive video conferencing on the Internet likely within the next year and a half. Some audio and video experiments are already taking place: MBone Radio, Internet Multicasting, CU-SeeMe, I-Phone, and so on; these should lead to interactive video conferencing.

NOTE

For more information on Internet-based video conferencing, see Chapter 19, "Internet Teleconferencing: MBone, CU-SeeMe, and Maven."

Video conferencing software is now available from several sources that provide motion-video, sound, and simultaneous file transfers between computers connected to an ISDN line (56 Kbps). Phone companies are increasingly offering ISDN to their customers; in some areas of the United States, regulators are requiring that ISDN be available to all customers within the next few years.

Not that we'll necessarily have to wait for ISDN at our local telephone pole—the latest crop of modems currently selling in retail stores provides 28.8 Kbaud rates (approximately half the bandwidth of an ISDN line). With some compromises in features and video quality, some current video conferencing software can be adapted for Internet use.

Hardware development is also heading in the right direction for video conferencing: an increasing number of computers are being sold "multimedia ready," or are being upgraded with multimedia hardware and software. Thus, the base of computers that have sound and color video capabilities is rapidly increasing.

Video input to computers is also becoming easier and less expensive. Macintosh users have available easy-to-install video cameras, a number of which are currently offering on the Internet real-time snapshots of various locations around the world. To see some of these remote cameras and machines connected to the Internet, go to `http://www.eskimo.com/~irving/web-voyeur.html`.

The particular ways these hardware and software elements are brought together will influence the branches Internet video takes, but innovative applications will too, and the possibilities are intriguing:

- Video mail
- Online education:
    - Real-time and archived lectures and demonstrations
    - Counseling, student questions, and feedback
- Virtual classrooms
- Remote sensing and monitoring:
    - Security cameras at environmentally dangerous or sensitive sites
    - Scientific instrument readings at remote or dangerous sites
    - Flood and dangerous weather monitoring
    - Construction or other project monitoring
    - Monitoring important world events

- Virtual reunions of families and friends
- Business:
    - Advertising
    - Product demonstrations or instruction videos
    - Troubleshooting assistance
- Meetings
    - Business
    - Membership organizations
- Virtual attendance at remote events, conferences, and performances

And many, many more possibilities....

A Final Thought

Although this chapter samples some of the near-term future features of the Internet, remember that the Internet is a participatory sport—where it develops from here could be influenced by you.

PART

II

How the Internet Works

The Network of Networks

5

by Martin Moore

This chapter is a brief dip into the network pool. There are literally hundreds of books available that detail how networks work. This chapter, however, gives you an overview of how networks function, and how the Internet moves millions of bits of information around the world every hour of every day. Previous chapters explained how the networks that make up the Internet networked together with the aid of TCP/IP protocols. The networks that make up the Internet, themselves, use a variety of techniques and protocols to make links within their own networks. This chapter is about how these networks work.

Keep in mind that the Internet is actually a constantly metamorphosing collection of many different kinds of networks. Internet traffic races down telephone lines, flashes from a mountaintop to a high tower on the plains using microwave relays, bounces off geosynchronous communications satellites orbiting the Earth 22,000 miles away, enters a laser beam stuck in one end of a fiber-optic cable, comes out the other end, zips around an Ethernet cable strung from one point to another in your office, and speeds through a converter straight to your computer. *Bang!*

A Network Is...

Of course, nothing with computer networks is quite as simple and straightforward as you might hope. The first concept to adopt is that of *layering*. Every network has several layers of functionality. Accepting the risk of insulting your intelligence, I'll describe how these layers work by using a very primitive two-node network.

You have two tin cans and a length of string. Poke a hole in the bottom of each can, feed one end of the string through each hole, and tie a knot in each end. If you and a friend (each holding a can) move apart until the string is taut between the cans, you create the first layer in the network: the physical layer. When either of you speaks into a can, the sound waves are transformed into mechanical vibrations in the bottom of the can (the diaphragm) and then are transmitted down the length of string to the other can where they are converted back into sound waves by the bottom of the second can (now a speaker).

If you pull the string tight and both begin to talk at once, you create what's known in the network trade as a *data collision*. In other words, if everybody talks and nobody listens, people don't communicate. Therefore, you have to build your first communications protocol layer: an agreement between you and your friend that before you speak, you will listen.

Having agreed how to start, you listen, hear nothing, and then begin speaking into your node (can). Your friend listens and then hears you start to speak. But, taking great exception to something you say, he begins to respond without waiting for you to stop speaking. Another data collision occurs. How do you solve this? You create another protocol layer that says, "When I am done talking, I will say 'over,' just like in the movies."

These are the two aspects of any network: physical and metaphysical. The physical aspect concerns the actual transmission medium. If it's a wire, how quickly can you change voltages on the wire, and what are the minimum and maximum voltage levels? The metaphysical aspect is represented by various protocol layers in which network software running on machine A understands what machine B is trying to say.

Networks vary widely in the physical aspect. A network can be as simple as two PCs connected by their serial ports and an RS-232 cable, or multiple PCs sharing a printer by way of an infrared beam bounced off the ceiling. Some networks rely on a pair of wires twisted around each other, and others use coaxial shielded cable or fiber-optic cable.

Network Mediums

Using wire to transmit signals has been the norm since the days of the telegraph. A single pair of wires strung between poles can carry a low-quality telephone conversation for some distance. Wires such as these, however, have a couple problems: electro-mechanical interference (EMI) and crosstalk. A magnetic field can create an electrical current—noise (EMI)—in the line, generated, for example, by a lightning storm or an electric motor. If a network uses two lines—one to carry one conversation and another to carry a different conversation—and the wires are in close physical proximity, crosstalk occurs. The magnetic field created by one wire causes noise in the other wire.

Several methods have been tried to overcome these two deficiencies. The first is to twist the wires together in pairs, called, obviously enough, *twisted pairs*. Twisted pairs have been used for years by the telephone company and have the bandwidth (see the "Bandwidth Determines Quantity of Data" sidebar) to handle several simultaneous telephone conversations.

BANDWIDTH DETERMINES QUANTITY OF DATA

Any communications medium can be discussed in terms of *bandwidth*: the range of frequencies that can be passed from one end of the medium to the other.

For example, in the early days of public telephone systems, bandwidth was very limited. Each conversation required a pair of telephone wires, and only one conversation could occur at a time. People who lived in rural America most likely shared a party line with their neighbors. When someone called, people listened to the number of rings to determine who was being called.

However, as twisted pairs came into use, available bandwidth went well beyond the 3,500 Hz needed for one conversation. This enabled the creation of *multiplexed* telephone lines. A fairly narrow range of frequencies (300 to 3,500 Hz) is required to carry voice signals. Several of these relatively low-frequency voice signals can be used to modulate one higher, carrier frequency. (In other words, the voice signals are added to, or incorporated within, the higher "carrier" frequency in a manner similar to what radio stations do with a radio frequency carrier and voice frequencies.) The process of combining several voice signals into one is called *multiplexing*. Suppose that a twisted-pair cable has a bandwidth of 1,000 Hz to 18,000 Hz, as shown in Figure 5.1.

You could then broadcast four carrier frequencies at 3, 7, 11, and 15 KHz, and modulate them with the audio frequencies. This creates four voice channels over a single pair of wires. Filters at the receiving end separate the signals.

Twisted pairs can actually handle upwards of 100 voice channels.

FIGURE 5.1.

Multiplexing signals on a single line.

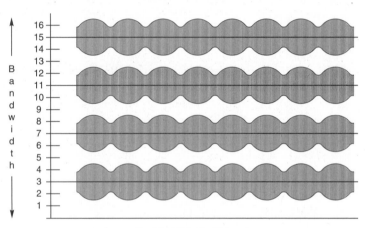

Modulated Carrier Channels

Another method (better than twisted pairs) of overcoming EMI and crosstalk is to place one wire inside the other, separated by an insulator—the coaxial cable. Coaxial cable can handle a bandwidth several orders of magnitude greater than twisted-pair wires: nearly 10,000 analog voice channels and superior rejection of EMI and crosstalk.

The bandwidth champion, however, is fiber-optic cabling. Because of its nearly complete immunity to outside interference, and a bandwidth of several gigahertz, fiber-optic cabling can carry a tremendous amount of data. Fiber-optic cables contain one or more very thin glass rods (the thickness of a human hair) with the useful characteristic of being able to conduct a light shown into one end to the other end of the cable, with very little loss. Laser light is modulated to carry the signals at rates above 140 million bits per second (bps). Compare this to the upper limit of 28,800 bps transmission speeds available from currently popular modems used over normal phone lines (the fiber optics are about a thousand times faster).

Network Topologies

Connecting one computer with another computer is a straightforward task; when several computers are linked, however, there are a number of different ways they can be connected—and each method has advantages and disadvantages. Figure 5.2 shows several network topologies in use throughout the Internet.

FIGURE 5.2.

Computers are connected to networks in a variety of ways.

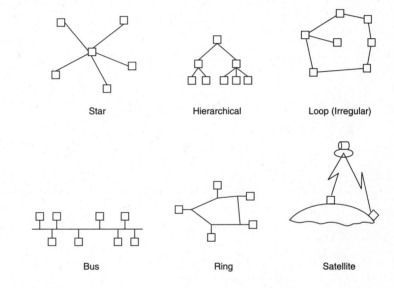

Star

Hierarchical

Loop (Irregular)

Bus

Ring

Satellite

The star, hierarchical, and loop arrangements are all *point-to-point topologies*. In this kind of topology, each computer can communicate with its nearest neighbors, but depends on those neighbors to relay data or commands to other computers on the network. The star topology is an extreme example of this configuration because every computer on the network must communicate with the central computer. The other extreme in point-to-point topologies is when all computers are connected to all other computers in a fully connected network.

The bus, ring, and satellite configurations are *broadcast topologies*. The fundamental concept behind this topology is that a message is placed on the bus, in the ring, or broadcast from a satellite. The message contains the name of the intended receiving computer node. All computers listen constantly; when a message addressed to a specific computer arrives, the message is captured and stored. Only one node can broadcast a message at a time. There are two very popular broadcast topologies in use today: the bus-based Ethernet, and the ring-based Token Ring network.

Ethernet

Ethernet is a popular bus-based broadcast topology that gained wide acceptance in the 1980s. Ethernet can transfer data at up to 10 million bps. A four-node Ethernet network is shown in Figure 5.3.

FIGURE 5.3.

The Ethernet is a popular bus-based topology.

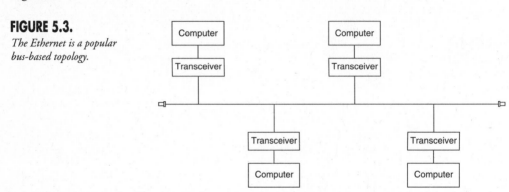

The network starts with a single cable (which may be coaxial, twisted pairs, or fiber optic). Each computer that taps into the cable must use a transceiver; the computer connects to the transceiver. Transceivers may be circuit boards that plug into a computer's motherboard; other types of transceivers may be connected to the computer's serial or parallel port.

When the message is composed, the sending computer must "listen" to the network (through the transceiver) to see whether any other computer is sending a message at the moment. If not, the sending computer can begin transmitting the message onto the bus. If other traffic is on the bus, the computer must wait before trying again. Finally, while transmitting the message, the computer also simultaneously listens to the bus to see whether the message the bus is carrying is the same as the one it is broadcasting. If not, another computer has begun transmission at almost the same time, and a collision is occurring. When that happens, both computers stop transmitting and wait a random amount of time before trying again. This procedure of listening, and then sending while listening, is called *carrier sense multiple access with collision detection* (CSMA/CD). When a transceiver loads a message onto the bus, it creates a carrier signal, which all the other transceivers listen for.

Token Ring

Another broadcast topology in wide use is the Token Ring network. Unlike the loop, which requires each computer in the loop to load every message into itself before passing the message on or keeping it, the ring requires that each computer be attached to a repeater, as shown in Figure 5.4. Although Token Ring networks appear to be self contained and isolated from the rest of the Internet world, one computer in the ring is usually assigned the task of serving as the gateway computer. The gateway is responsible for converting incoming, external traffic into a form acceptable to the Token Ring. Likewise, outbound traffic is converted to the appropriate communications protocol.

FIGURE 5.4.

A Token Ring network uses repeaters to continue sending messages around the ring until they are read by the receiving computer.

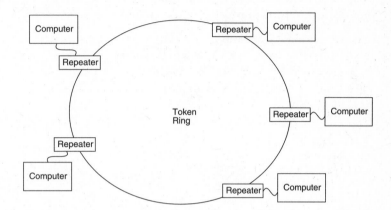

The Token Ring, developed by IBM, has an interesting way of letting each node on the ring tell when the ring is available to broadcast a message. An electronic *token* is created and placed on the ring by one of the computers (usually, a single computer node has the responsibility of creating and issuing the token). This token (which is really a packet containing a fixed data word) loops around the ring, passing through each repeater. If no node issues a message, the token continues its circuitous route. However, when a computer node does transmit a message, the token is captured by that computer's repeater, modified, and sent back out onto the ring. This newly modified token passes around the ring, but is not recognized by any of the other repeaters; therefore, it indicates to them that the ring is busy and cannot be used.

The sending computer prepares a message with a destination address and places the message on the ring. As the packet passes through all the other repeaters in the ring, each repeater reads the packet header to see whether the message is addressed to its node. If the message is not addressed to its node, the repeater passes the message to the next repeater in the ring. If the message is addressed to its node, that repeater sends a copy of the message to its node and passes the message on around the ring. When the message makes a complete circuit around the ring to the originator, the originator reinstates the token, indicating that it is done with the ring. The ring then becomes available to any other node.

As with Ethernet, there is no built-in way for the sender of a message to verify that it was received, beyond the fact that the packet made a complete circuit around the ring; if the receiver was listening, the receiver should have captured the message. Passing an acknowledgment message around the ring is the responsibility of the next higher protocol level.

Network Protocols

Mentioned in the preceding sections were different protocol "layers" used in network communications. The specifics of each layer, and the number of layers, varies from type to type. The protocol architecture provided in the following example is typical of many networks.

The International Standards Organization (ISO) has developed an architecture that defines seven layers of network protocol (used by many network developers) as a base definition. These seven layers are shown in Figure 5.5. Keep in mind that protocol layers are, fundamentally, agreements between computers about how to communicate with one another. They are the "rules of the road."

FIGURE 5.5.

The ISO's seven layers of protocol.

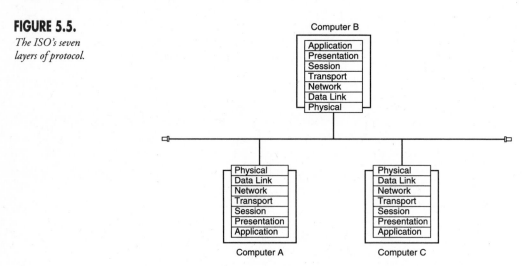

The advantage of layering communication protocols is two-fold:

1. New versions or updates can be written for each layer without affecting the layer before or after. For example, improvements to the Network layer should not require any changes to the Data Link layer, and any improvements made at this level ripple upward so that higher levels benefit without having to be modified.

2. Two computers on the network need to use only the layers appropriate for the task they are doing.

Each layer in a protocol system such as this uses the previous layer or layers to take action.

The first layer is the Physical layer. This is the definition of how 1s and 0s are passed over the network medium, what control signals are used, and the mechanical properties of the network itself (cable size, connector, and so on). In fact, this is the only layer in which actual communications occur. All the other layers exist as software within the computer that directs and modifies the behavior of the Physical layer.

The following chart briefly describes each of the remaining layers.

Layer	Description
Data Link	This layer provides the low-level error detection and correction functions of the network. For example, if a packet is corrupted during transmission, the Data Link layer is responsible for retransmitting the packet.
Network	This layer is responsible for routing packets across the network. If you want to e-mail a large file to another site, for example, the Network protocol layer divides your file into packets, addresses the packets, and sends them out over the network.
Transport	This is an intermediate layer that higher layers use to communicate with the network. This layer hides all the gruesome details necessary to actually make a connection between two computers.
Session	This layer manages the current connection, or session, between two computers. Keep in mind that in packet-switched networks, your computer does not have a full-time connection to a remote computer (even though it may seem so). Your commands to the remote computer are broken into packets and transmitted to the remote machine where they are reassembled and responded to. The Session layer keeps communications flowing until you're done. This layer also validates users that log on your computer through the Internet.
Presentation	The Presentation layer does all the necessary conversion to make sure that both computers are speaking the same language. For example, you may be logged on a Digital Equipment Corporation workstation that uses the ASCII representation for text. If you want to send text to a friend who works with an older IBM mainframe, you have two choices: you can convert the file to an EBCDIC representation and then send the file, or you can let your friend's computer's Presentation layer take care of the conversion for you. Presentation layers also can be used to automatically encode and decode data for transport over the Net.
Application	This is the highest layer in the ISO standard and is represented by the programs you use directly.

Network protocols are critical to intermachine communication. Fortunately, most of us don't have to worry about these various layers. Systems developers have done all the worrying for us.

The original Internet protocol, which is still used today, is the set developed by Vinton Cerf and Robert Kahn in 1974: Internet Protocol (IP) and Transmission Control Protocol (TCP), known collectively as TCP/IP.

The TCP/IP protocols have layering similar to the ISO protocols and are, in fact, used more widely throughout the Internet than the ISO protocols. A simplistic view is that the Internet Protocol (IP) takes care of addressing packets, and the Transmission Control Protocol (TCP) takes care of dividing your message into packets—and then relies on IP to mail them. When a message is received, the reverse happens. The IP captures the various packets and feeds them to TCP—which makes sure that they are all there—and then reassembles the packets into a single message.

Routing

Now that you understand how messages are sent from one computer node to another within a network, the next question is, "How can an e-mail message get from your network to a single user on a network across the country?"

You may recall from earlier chapters that the success of the Internet depends a lot on the fact that it is a packet-switched network. Messages between computers are converted to small packets that are rapidly routed to their destinations. Each packet contains destination and source addresses, as well as other information that makes routing possible.

In a simple ring topology, a packet is routed around the ring until it gets back to the sender. The assumption is that the receiver saw the packet with its address on it and copied the packet as it went by. However, not every network is a ring. In fact, the Internet is made up of all the possible types of topologies. There must be a more rational way of getting packets from point A to point B. Consider the mixed network shown in Figure 5.6.

FIGURE 5.6.

Mixed network types complicate the delivery of packets.

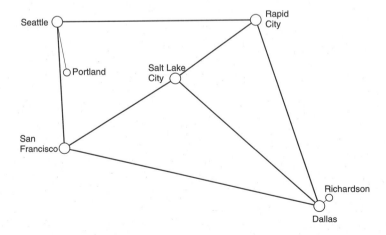

Suppose that you want to send a message from your computer on a small network in Portland, Oregon, to a friend in Richardson, Texas. What are the options?

- You could sit in Portland with a network map and lay out a specific route to Richardson. But what happens if one of the links is broken?

- You could keep a list of all possible routes (a routing table) to Richardson in your computer. Your computer could keep trying different routes until it succeeds. However, keeping the list up to date is a bother; it requires that every computer on every network keep a routing table up to date.

- All network nodes could declare one centralized point (Salt Lake City, for example) in the entire network; this point would be responsible for rerouting packets to their appropriate destinations. But what happens if that centralized point goes down?

- One node in each local network could be responsible for keeping track of all the other remote networks.

The fact is that all these approaches (and even more) have been used in the past. Today, the Internet is so large—consisting of thousands of networks—that keeping track of routing information is difficult. Some years ago, every computer on the Internet was responsible for keeping routing information. Now, computers called *routers* are used to forward packets in the appropriate direction.

For example, a router in Portland may know that all packets destined for anywhere near Dallas have to go first to Seattle. In Seattle, another router may know that it has two options to route packets to Dallas: by way of San Francisco or by way of Rapid City. The router in Seattle may pick the route with the least traffic at the moment—for example, to Rapid City. In Rapid City, another router knows there are a couple of paths available. Once the packet arrives in the Dallas router, the packet is sent over a local line to your friend's computer in Richardson (or to his or her Internet access provider's computer). This way, no one computer must keep track of all possible destinations. The routers are responsible for making the major moves; the local machines manage to get the packet to its final destination.

Keep in mind that a large message is broken into a number of packets. Not all packets are necessarily sent out over the same route. The route selected depends on traffic loads and what backbones are working at the moment.

Another method of routing is the "nearest neighbor" method, or *centralized adaptive routing*. A central node within each network knows only about its direct connections to the outside world. For example, in Figure 5.6, Seattle knows about Portland, San Francisco, and Rapid City; Rapid City knows about Seattle, Salt Lake City, and Dallas, but doesn't know about San Francisco.

These are some of the many routing strategies that remain in use today.

Yes, But...

Given that everything you send out on the Internet is divided into chunks called packets and then reassembled at the other end, you may be saying to yourself, "Yes, I can see how that would work for e-mail or sending somebody a file, but that can't be how it works all the time. What about when I'm actually logged on to another computer using Telnet?"

The fact is, all communications over the Internet (and any other packet-switched network) are done in just this way. If you have used Telnet and are logged on to a computer 1,200 miles away, all your commands and all the responses to your commands are being packetized and routed over the Internet. As an Internet user, you may have noticed that the responses from the remote computer slow down occasionally, or there seem to be long, inexplicable pauses. Sometimes that's because some of the packets were routed a different way and took a while to catch up to the rest.

It doesn't matter whether you're a Gopher guru, an FTP fanatic, or love to wax profound on Usenet; all your communications are divided into packets and routed over the Internet.

The Internet Protocols are in an active period of change and development. There are groups considering changes and new protocols such at VRTP (Virtual Reality Transport Protocol), SHTTP (Secure HyperText Transport Protocol), and others. In addition, many new algorithms for compression and for making better use of existing bandwidth are on the horizon.

Domain Names and Internet Addresses

6

*by Martin Moore
and Matthew V.
Ellsworth*

In 1963, the United States Postal Service divided the country into small geographical zones and assigned each zone a ZIP code, which is a five-digit number that enables the postal service to very quickly determine how to route mail.

Your local post office sends all its nonlocal outgoing mail to its nearby main office, where the mail is sorted by ZIP code. The sorted mail is then sent to a distribution center, where it is gathered together and shipped out to the appropriate receiving distribution center (see Figure 6.1).

FIGURE 6.1.

Internet addresses are used in much the same way as your ZIP code.

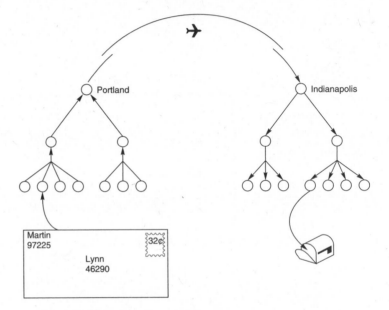

If I address an envelope to my pal Lynn at ZIP code 46290, my mail carrier takes the envelope to the local post office (where they check to see whether the envelope is addressed to a local ZIP code); if it doesn't have a local ZIP, they pass it on to a collection center in Portland. There, envelopes are sorted: any with *46* as the first two digits of the ZIP code are destined for Indianapolis in central Indiana. My envelope is dropped into the Indianapolis bag, and off it goes. Once in Indianapolis, the reverse happens, and the envelope lands in Lynn's local post office. Only then does someone look at the street address. A valid five-digit ZIP code removes the necessity of including a city and state on your envelope (although you should include them in case the post office can't read the ZIP code numbers). The final sorting by postal carrier area is done at the local post office, and then Lynn receives the envelope.

More recently, in 1983, the postal service added another four digits to the ZIP code, enabling the post office to determine your street with the nine-digit number.

Internet Addresses

The ZIP code is decoded left to right, with the first number identifying the largest geographical area. Each next number (moving right) signifies smaller areas, and the last four digits of the nine-digit number represent the actual street.

A similar thing happens over the Internet. Every computer on the Internet has a specific address called the *Internet Protocol (IP) address*. Each person that uses a computer on the Internet also has a user name that is combined with the IP address to make their full Internet address.

The IP address is made up of four numbers; each number is less than 256. (For example, my Internet provider's address is 192.108.254.10.) The address numbers are separated by periods when written out. As with ZIP codes, IP addresses are decoded from left to right. The first three digits identify the largest divisions of the network.(The numeric IP addresses are not based on geographic location.) The next numbers (moving right) signify smaller virtual locations; the final numbers represent the computer you use to access the Internet.

A computer with an IP address is part of the Internet; but if you use your personal computer to dial in to an Internet access provider, your PC does not need an IP address (unless you are making a SLIP or PPP connection). Your PC serves as an intelligent terminal connected to your Internet provider's computer with a phone line and modem. Your PC is, in effect, just one of several terminals using the common address.

For example, if you want to send me mail, you can do so on some systems by e-mailing to this address:

```
martinm@192.108.254.10
```

The martinm is my user name, given to me by the system operator that runs the computer I use to access the Internet. It could just as well have been mmoore, or even just a number, as long as it uniquely identifies me as a user on the system.

The at (@) symbol is used to separate the user name from the IP address. The IP address is the four-part number, described previously. Much more commonly, however, addresses are made up of your user name attached to the front of a domain name: foo@bar.com.

Domain Names

As mentioned in the preceding section, on some systems, you use the IP address to send me mail. More commonly, you use the domain name of the Internet provider's computer. Most people have a hard time remembering a long string of numbers containing periods. For those of us who are challenged by long numbers, the Internet provides domain names.

Domain names represent the IP address and are intended to be simpler to understand and easier to remember. If you want to use a domain name to send me e-mail (instead of the IP address used in the preceding section), you address the e-mail as follows:

```
martinm@teleport.com
```

The `teleport` part of the domain name is the unique name of the computer attached to the Internet. The `.com` portion of the domain name identifies what kind of operation this computer serves—in this case, a commercial (`com`) service.

Domain names can have many parts, each separated by a period (usually referred to on the Internet as a *dot*). However, instead of providing the largest group on the left (as with IP addresses), domain names provide the largest grouping on the right. In other words, in an IP address, the number to the left of the first period is the largest grouping possible within Internet. It defines the network being used. The rightmost number in an IP address identifies one actual computer. Domain names are just the opposite. The largest grouping within the name is the rightmost part of the name, and the specific computer's name is the leftmost part.

Here are some examples:

Domain Name	What It Means
`cs.wisc.edu`	This is a computer in the computer science (`cs`) department at the University of Wisconsin (`wisc`), which is an educational (`edu`) institution.
`xcf.berkeley.edu`	The University of California at Berkeley (`berkeley`) has a computer named `xcf` somewhere in its hallowed halls. Again, UC Berkeley is an educational (`edu`) institution.
`spacelink.msfc.nasa.gov`	The federal government has its own domain name (`gov`). This is a computer named `spacelink` at Marshall Space Flight Center (`msfc`), which is part of NASA (`nasa`).
`prep.ai.mit.edu`	A computer named `prep` is probably in the Artificial Intelligence (`ai`) lab at the Massachusetts Institute of Technology (`mit`), an educational (`edu`) institution.

These domain names are certainly more readily remembered than the IP addresses they represent. Here are several well-recognized, high-level domains in use within the Internet:

Domain Name	Meaning
`com`	Commercial domains used by corporations or companies that have Internet access. The commercial domain also is used by Internet providers such as `teleport.com`.

Domain Name	Meaning
edu	This domain name is used primarily in the United States to identify educational sites.
gov	The U.S. government.
mil	U.S. military sites use the mil domain name.
net	Some networks choose to use this domain name in identifying themselves. For example, some state-run networks use the net domain name because, although educational sites may be tied into the network, the network serves state and local offices as well.
org	This name is used by organizations. The Internet Society, for example, uses the domain name isoc.org.

You will discover other high-level domain names in use around the world. For example, Internet traffic from Australia usually uses .au as the final element of the domain name; .nz means the computer is located in New Zealand; and .de is used by Germany.

All these domain names are part of what is called the *Domain Name System*. The Domain Name System uses a number of computers scattered throughout the Internet to keep track of which computers are located within its geographical area. When you send e-mail to teleport.com, for example, your host computer sends a request to the nameserver to check its database for the IP number for teleport.com. When the IP number is received back by your host computer, it matches that IP number with your message and sends it out on the Internet.

Since the inception of the Domain Name System in 1983 at the University of Wisconsin, the Internet has been easier to use.

The Internet Network Information Center (NIC) manages the naming of Internet nodes. Anyone who wants a domain name must apply for the name.

UUCP Addresses

When you read a Usenet message, you see a line in the message header named *Path*. Following Path is usually a long list of domain names separated by exclamation points (referred to on the Internet as *bangs*). This list shows the route that particular message followed to arrive on your computer. The path for one message, for example, was listed as follows:

```
teleport.com!news.world.net!news.sprintlink.net!demon!uknet!piex!howland.
reston.ans.net!math.ohiostate.edu!cyber2.cyberstor.ca!nntp.cs.ubc.ca!unixg.ubc.ca
```

This pathname lists the most recent transaction first and the first transaction last. In this example the `teleport.com` computer got the message from a computer on `world.net`. The message passed through part of the Sprint network, through the United Kingdom's Internet network (`uknet`), through Ohio State, and so on. The last domain name on the list is the computer from which the message originated. In this case, the University of British Columbia in Canada (`ubc.ca`). *Whew!*

The use of the bang (!) was started in the UNIX community with the advent of UUCP. Recall that UUCP (UNIX-to-UNIX Copy) was one of the original network packages that enabled UNIX-based computers to call one another and transmit files and commands back and forth. When UUCP was created, the developers needed a way to identify other UNIX sites by name. They developed a domain name system very similar to the one used today on the Internet. The primary difference between the Internet domain name system and the UUCP system is that an exclamation mark is used to separate the elements of the UUCP address instead of a dot.

Nearly all UNIX sites use the Internet Domain Name System conventions today. At some sites, however, a local network may still use UUCP addressing for internal routing and the Domain Name System for external communications. If you do see a UUCP address, it may look something like this:

```
zeus!charlieb@teleport.com
```

Here, the computer that communicates with Internet is named `teleport.com`. However, `teleport.com` is connected to a UUCP local area network. One of the computers on the local area network is named `zeus`, and the user named `charlieb` has an account on `zeus`. Therefore, mail comes from the Internet into `teleport.com`, which sends the file on to a computer called `zeus`, and to the user named `charlieb`.

As time goes by, UUCP addresses may disappear entirely.

One other naming system you may run across uses a percent sign (%) as a secondary naming mechanism. In a UUCP address, a percent sign may be used as follows:

```
charlieb%zeus@teleport.com
```

Here, the `teleport.com` computer is responsible for communicating with `zeus` to make sure that `charlieb` gets the message.

The Bitnet

Another early, major player in the networking world was Bitnet (the Because It's Time Network), formed by City University of New York. Like every other network in the world, Bitnet needed to create a naming system to help users get around their system. Although it is no longer used much in North America, Bitnet is still used in various countries around the globe.

The Bitnet creators limited both user and address names to eight uppercase characters. A Bitnet address looks like this:

```
NAMEMIKE@BITNIC
```

Notice that the at (@) symbol is used to separate the user name from the machine name, just as it does with Internet domain names.

If you need to send mail to someone on Bitnet, and you are an Internet user, append the characters `.bitnet` to the end of the Bitnet address, as follows:

```
NAMEMIKE@BITNIC.bitnet
```

The mail will get through.

Uniform Resource Locators: Finally, Some Simplicity

As the World Wide Web developed on the Internet, it adopted a standardized way of specifying a particular site, or file, on the Web. Currently, the addressing system uses URLs (Uniform Resource Locators). These URLs combine information about the type of protocol being used, the address of the site where the resource is located, the subdirectory location, and (where used) the name of the file.

Here is a typical World Wide Web URL:

```
HTTP://www.ncsa.uiuc.edu/SDG/Software/Mosaic/MetaIndex.html
```

This URL is composed of these components:

- ■ **HTTP**—Type of Internet protocol used for storage and transmission of information.
- ■ **://**—Standard URL punctuation.
- ■ **www.ncsa.uiuc.edu**—Domain name of the site where the resource is stored.
- ■ **/SDG/Software/Mosaic/**—The directory path to the resource stored on the remote computer (in this case, a file).
- ■ **MetaIndex.html**—The name of the file to be retrieved.

Occasionally, a URL contains a "port number." When this happens, the port number is placed directly after the site address in this manner:

```
HTTP://www.ncsa.uiuc.edu:80/SDG/Software/Mosaic/MetaIndex.html
```

URLs provide a consistent, easily understood method of listing many different kinds of Internet sites—in addition to World Wide Web sites.

Gopher

The popular menu-oriented Gopher system usually has addresses such as this:

```
gopher.std.com/pub
```

In the URL format, Gopher addresses look like this:

```
gopher://gopher.std.com/pub
```

Telnet

The remote computer login system (Telnet) can use a URL such as the following:

```
telnet://std.com
```

FTP

The location, directory path, and name of a specific file at an FTP file storage site can be specified in a URL such as the following:

```
ftp://ftp.std.com/pub/oakridge/unleashed.txt
```

Usenet News

Usenet newsgroups are listed in a different format from other URLs. The newsgroup `alt.business` is listed in a URL like the following:

```
news:alt.business
```

Not Just Good To Look At

The value of the URL goes far beyond its use as a standardized way of telling humans where to find things on the Internet. The real power of URLs comes when they are used with Web browsers and other programs that provide interfaces between you and the Internet. URLs provide the full set of information to the program—not only about where the resource is located and what its name is, but also what protocol should be used to retrieve it. The URL, therefore, provides a method to shield the Internet user from much of the complexity of the Internet.

PART

Plugging Into the Internet

Finding Access as a User

7

by Kevin M. Savetz

One of the most challenging aspects of using the Internet might surprise you. It's not learning to use a dozen new programs to navigate the network, or even finding out about all the interesting places to explore. The biggest challenge for most of us—finding Internet access—comes before these other tasks.

Before you can explore the Internet, you have to "plug in." That is, you must have access to a computer that is connected to the network. When you buy a telephone, it doesn't work right out of the box. Before you make that first call, you must plug your phone into a telephone line and hear a dial tone. Similarly, you can't dial up the Internet's services until your modem or local area network can connect with a computer that is part of the Internet. Once you have an "Internet dial tone," you can access the Internet's resources.

Because the Internet is a cooperative effort, there is no Internet, Inc. to sign up with and send a check to. Instead, you must find a service that is plugged into the Internet. Not every online service is part of the Internet, and as you will see, the tools available at various services differ considerably. The Internet "dial tone" can take many forms, so there are many choices and features to consider.

The computer your computer connects with to gain access to the Internet is called a *host*. The company or institution that operates the host is called a *service provider* (or *ISP*—Internet service provider). Because of the array of computers and people that compose the Internet, service providers range from billion-dollar commercial, online services to tiny bulletin board systems running out of someone's basement. Regardless of where you're connected, your service provider is the person or company on the other side of your Internet link; *host* refers to the computer to which you connect.

Getting telephone service is simple and decision free; you ask the local phone company for a line and you get it. Getting an Internet "dial tone" isn't so straightforward. You have to choose your access method, think about what services you'll use, compare prices, and finally sign up with a service provider. At the risk of taking this analogy too far (or is it too late?), imagine having to choose your phone company before you could even make a phone call. It wouldn't be as simple, but you would have the benefit of choosing exactly what services you could use and the price you would pay. That's the way it is with Internet access.

Because you connect to the Internet with a phone call, you probably want an Internet service provider that has a phone number in your area, lest you be forced to pay the phone company steep long-distance charges. In the past year or two, Internet service providers have been popping up like weeds; it has become a *lot* easier to find a local "on ramp" to the Internet, even if you don't live in a metropolis.

Types of Internet Connections

Individuals and small businesses can best access the Internet using a dial-up connection, which is what this chapter focuses on. A *dial-up connection* means your modem dials a host computer to access the Internet—and you go about your business. Your phone line is tied up only while you're using the Internet. When you're done, hang up the modem and free up the phone line. Dial-up access means that you won't need a lot of expensive hardware or a high-speed leased phone line—you just need a computer, a modem, a plain old phone line, an account with a service provider, and the appropriate software.

If you are trying to connect a large group of people who require simultaneous, extremely fast connections to the Internet, dial-up access may not be the best choice. If you're connecting more than 20 people who require simultaneous and permanent Internet connections, you may very well need that leased line, plus that expensive equipment. (For more information on finding leased-line access, see Chapter 8, "Finding Access as a Organization.")

Tools of the Trade

There are a multitude of services you can use to access the Internet, including a public-access service provider, a commercial online service, or a community bulletin board system. Some connections give you access to a wide variety of Internet services and tools; others limit you to only electronic mail, Usenet, or other services. Before investing in a connection, consider the features and drawbacks of each.

Not all Internet connections are created equal. Many Internet service providers do not offer "full" access to the Internet's functions. (For that matter, what one provider calls "full" access may differ from another's concept of full access.) The most basic level of Internet access is electronic mail, which enables you to exchange e-mail with users on the Internet and other networks. Electronic mail is to the Internet what salt and pepper are to a chef: pretty useful, always available, but not all that exciting by itself.

A more complete Internet connection includes access to Usenet (also known as *newsgroups* or *netnews*)—the "bulletin board" of the Internet, where you can read and post messages on any of 9,000-plus topics.

An even better Internet connection features still more tools—programs that enable you to connect with other people and computers in "real time." These include Telnet, FTP (File Transfer Protocol), and Gopher.

The brass ring of Internet tools is the World Wide Web—this is the tool that provides a snazzy hypertext, (possibly) graphical interface. Again, not all providers offer all services, so you have to decide what you need before signing up.

Besides the tools available to you, the service provider you choose determines the type of interface you see once you are online. The interface determines how the Internet appears to you (as simple text on the screen, as a menu interface, or with graphics and sounds). The service provider also determines whether you receive access to the "raw, uncensored Internet" (which, although complete, can be trickier to navigate) or a customized front-end (which can be easier to use, but might limit what you can do online.)

Command-Line Access

Command-line access through a local Internet service provider is cost effective, simple to learn, and similar across different computing platforms. The term *command-line access* can be a misnomer because access through a local Internet service provider can be through a command-line (*a la* the UNIX operating system, for example) or a simple menu-driven interface.

Command-line access is easy to set up; it is generally a little less expensive than other types of Internet connections. Command-line access works reliably from any kind of personal computer because specialized software isn't needed. This is beneficial if you use, for example, a Macintosh at home and a 486 running Windows at the office. Although these computers are very different, Internet access using a command line is similar in both machines.

Finding a public access site for a command-line account or dial-up IP link is usually more difficult than joining a commercial online service. Although there are only a few commercial online services, there are hundreds of service providers offering command-line accounts. Each one seems to offer different features, pricing structures, and local access locations.

A command-line account is a popular way to use the network. This kind of access is simple to use and, unlike an IP link, doesn't require complicated software configuration on your own computer.

NOTE

If you are a college student or faculty member, check with your campus computer center to learn about available online facilities. Many schools offer free accounts to students and staff. Similarly, your business may offer Internet access to employees—if you know the right person to ask. Finding access at your institution is a great way to get a free Internet account. However, beware of special restrictions imposed by your institution. Most schools frown darkly on use of these accounts for business or other nonacademic activities. Such policies may be as simple as posted rules or as elaborate as firewalls preventing you from using multiuser dungeons, Internet Relay Chat, and other interesting stuff.

If you already know someone who is part of the Internet community, ask that person how he or she gets access. If that person lives near you and is happy with the service, chances are that service will be right for you, too.

Dial-Up IP Links

Dial-up IP links such as Serial Line Internet Protocol (SLIP) and Point to Point Protocol (PPP) connect your computer directly to the Internet while you're dialed in. You can run networking applications for electronic mail, FTP, Gopher, Telnet, and other tools locally from your own computer instead of relying on another host (as you do with a command-line account). IP links are more robust than other types of accounts—for example, they enable you to connect to multiple sites simultaneously. You can have an FTP session in one window, Telnet in another, and Gopher in yet another. And if you don't like the software you're using for e-mail (or for reading Usenet news, or whatever), you can switch to something else. With an IP link, you're generally not married to any particular software.

Dial-up IP links are usually a bit more expensive than command-line accounts. And although you can use a slow modem, you should use a 9,600 bps or faster modem for IP access.

Because the software for a dial-up IP link resides in your computer, you have to find it and install it yourself. You have to configure many pieces of software on your computer, and take complex steps that command-line users need not worry about. The software you need includes several programs: one each for e-mail, FTP, Telnet, Gopher, World Wide Web, and so on. If you're new to the Internet, setting up this software can be a frustrating welcome to the "information highway." Once everything's set up the first time, however, IP links are easier to use than command-line accounts. (If you're new to computers or frustrate easily, consider hiring a consultant for a couple hours to help get the show on the road.)

If you are using an IP link, you have to choose between two types of access: SLIP or PPP. What you use depends on which software is available for your computer and what your service provider offers. Find out whether your provider supports SLIP or PPP and if you can access either using your computer system. (If you have the choice, choose PPP over SLIP. PPP is better implemented and a little faster than SLIP.)

Commercial Online Services

Commercial online services are large computer systems available around the world. Unlike providers that offer only a link to the Internet, commercial online services offer a variety of services other than Internet access, such as databases, online shopping, games, and file libraries. You've probably heard of some of them: CompuServe, Prodigy, America Online, and Delphi, among others.

When I wrote this chapter for the first edition of this book in late 1993, only two commercial online services offered any Internet service worth talking about. Today, every major online service offers Internet access. Some of them don't offer every tool (the "whole enchilada") but they all offer a strong collection of tools. Online services (which typically charge per minute) are almost always more expensive than IP links and they may offer features you don't need—especially if all you want is a pipeline to the Net.

An important advantage of commercial online services is that, unlike most public access providers, commercial online services can be accessed with a local phone call from hundreds of cities. Commercial services are linked to packet-switching networks such as SprintNet and Tymnet, which may provide a local phone number for access—even though the service's computers are actually in Virginia, Cleveland, or somewhere else. Packet-switching networks are nice, but they can drive up the price of using a commercial service and they aren't always available in rural areas.

Delphi was the first nationwide service to provide full Internet access. Its text-only command-line interface won't win any beauty contests, but Delphi makes it easy enough to find your way around. The price is minimal: $20 a month for 20 hours of service. Delphi's voice information line is 1-800-695-4005.

America Online and Prodigy both offer graphical Internet interfaces. As of this writing, AOL provides e-mail, Gopher, FTP, and WAIS access; a World Wide Web browser should be ready any day now, hopefully by the time you read this. Prodigy was the first commercial service to offer a graphical Web interface. Prodigy also offers e-mail and a Web browser for Windows users, but (as I write this) no other Internet tools. CompuServe offers a variety of Internet tools, too. You can use its command-line interface or (if you have a Macintosh or a Windows computer) you can use a snazzier graphical interface. AOL's voice information line is 1-800-827-6364. Prodigy's information line is 1-800-PRODIGY. CompuServe's information line is 1-800-609-1674. All three of these services offer a nearly identical pricing structure: under $10 a month for a few hours online plus about $3.50 for each extra hour. Call for current prices. Like the stock market, this stuff changes fast.

There are other online services, too, each offering various levels of Internet service. All commercial online services are clamoring to provide the "whole enchilada" of Internet tools, and I suspect that they all will—very soon.

Bulletin Board Systems

You also can access the Internet using a local bulletin board system (BBS). Getting to the Internet through a BBS can be a dubious proposition for many reasons. Although there are tens of thousands of fine bulletin board systems around the world, few offer complete and reliable Internet access.

Finding a reliable BBS for accessing the Internet can be a crapshoot. Anyone can run a bulletin board: the system operator behind the BBS may be a seasoned professional or a 12-year-old kid hacking away in his bedroom. Some BBSes are professional operations that charge for access; others are more fleeting. Some have dozens of telephone lines; many have only one or two. Most BBSes are not dedicated to providing Internet access. Most of the time, they have their own conferences for chatting, as well as files for downloading. Internet access, if available, usually comes second to the board's own community.

Some BBSes are part of networks other than the Internet (such as FidoNet or OneNet.) Don't be fooled by imitations! Demand Internet by name. Not all types of bulletin boards can offer Internet access, and those that do usually can't offer the full gamut of Internet services. (Several types of bulletin board software can provide Internet e-mail and Usenet newsgroups but lack programs such as Telnet, FTP, and the World Wide Web.)

For these reasons, accessing the Internet through a bulletin board system is probably not a reliable choice.

Choosing a Service Provider

Finding the right access may mean one quick phone call to a local user who's "in the know," or it can mean hours of phone calls and research. Is it worth it? Absolutely. Getting on the Internet is like buying a house or planning a vacation—there are options to consider, choices to make, and in the end, a worthwhile prize.

No matter which method of access you want, you should know certain specific things about service providers before making your decision. Arm yourself with the information in this section and begin contacting promising service providers and asking questions.

Hopefully, you will be able to stick with one service for a long time. Staying with one service means you won't have to keep learning new interfaces and commands (which is handy) because no two services are exactly alike. You will also have a stable e-mail address so that your corespondents can find you. Internet service providers vary wildly in services and prices; be sure to check out all your options.

Don't worry too much about finding the perfect Internet service provider the first time around. Just getting online the first time is usually one of the most difficult tasks. Once you're online, you'll find a wealth of information about other—possibly better—ways to connect to the Internet. You can change your service provider any time. Although it's cumbersome to set up a new account, don't feel locked into a particular service provider or type of service.

Once you decide on an IP connection or command-line account, begin with a recent listing of service providers. Start by turning to Appendix A, "Internet Access Providers." Service providers come and go daily, so the list in the back of the book is probably fading with age, but it should get you on the right track.

If you have associates with Internet access, see whether you can enlist their aid in finding a service provider near you. There are a several lists of Internet service providers on the Internet itself. The catch-22 is, of course, that you have to be on the Internet to get them. If you're itching to get on the Net pronto, without all this tomfoolery, call Delphi or America Online and you can be online tonight. Once you're exploring the Net, you can find the perfect service provider for your needs. Or you may decide that Delphi or America Online is perfect for you.

NIXPUB

NIXPUB is a large listing of public access and free UNIX providers. Not all the providers in the NIXPUB list offer full Internet service; some offer only e-mail or Usenet newsgroups. NIXPUB is available by using anonymous FTP to the following address:

```
ftp://vfl.paramax.com:/pub/pubnet/nixpub.long
```

Alternatively, you can receive NIXPUB through e-mail. Send mail to this address (the subject/message body is unimportant):

```
nixpub@access.digex.com
```

PDIAL

If you already have an Internet e-mail account (or you know someone who does), you can receive PDIAL, another large listing of service providers, by sending electronic mail with a subject line of Send PDIAL to this address:

```
info-deli-server@netcom.com
```

> **NOTE**
>
> Once upon a time, PDIAL was the finest list of Internet providers available. However, as of this writing, it hasn't been updated in months and is hopelessly out of date. There are rumors that the person who publishes the PDIAL list will be updating it again soon.

ISP Lists on the World Wide Web

If your begged, borrowed, or stolen Internet account has access to the World Wide Web, check out the following sites. Each of these Web pages offers a list of Internet service providers. It's worth checking them all out—there are a lot of service providers and it's hard to keep up-to-date information; the information at each of these sites is likely to differ.

InterNIC: http://www.internic.net/

Celestin Company Directories: http://www.teleport.com/~cci/directories/dir

Network-USA's ISP Catalog: `http://www.netusa.net/ISP/`

Best.com's ISP list: `http://www.best.com/~ophelia/isp.html`

Internet Tools Offered

Find out what Internet tools are available from the hosts you are considering. Some services that claim to offer Internet access offer only a limited selection of tools. Be sure to plan ahead. For example, although you may think you need only Internet electronic mail, you will be gravely disappointed if later you want to try out FTP or Gopher and discover you can't access those services from your host. Tools to ask for are these:

- **E-mail:** See the rest of the list for some things to know.

- **Delivery:** Is e-mail delivered the instant you send it, or is it *batched* (delivered only a few times a day)? Batching of e-mail probably saves your service provider money, but it considerably slows down the delivery of your electronic mail.

- **Low charges:** Does the service charge you to send and receive e-mail? A small number of services charge, based on the number of messages delivered or the size of your e-mail. Try to avoid using services that charge this way. Charges based on e-mail usage limits the range of nifty things you will do with electronic mail and can bring unwelcome surprises when the bill comes.

- **Telnet:** Does the service allow you to connect in real-time to other Internet hosts? For example, can you access databases and library catalogs?

- **FTP:** Is there a limit to the amount of information you can transfer with FTP?

- **Usenet news:** Does your host offer a full Usenet feed? How about value-added news like ClariNet (which features newswire feeds and syndicated feature writers)?

- **Gopher client:** Does the service provider give you a front end to the Internet's menu-oriented Gopher tool?

- **World Wide Web client:** Does the service include access to the World Wide Web? If so, do you get a graphical browser or a text-based one?

- **Internet Relay Chat (IRC) client:** Does the service offer access to Internet Relay Chat (a sort of Internet coffee house and pick-up bar)?

- **Online help:** Are "manual pages" or other online help systems installed on the host?

Cost

For most of us, price is a primary motivating factor in choosing a service provider. Some public access command-line services charge a flat monthly fee for unlimited online time (some as little as $15 a month). Others charge an hourly fee or a combination of the two. A few others charge by the amount of data you transfer. (This archaic method of billing is becoming decreasingly common because it's hard to judge just how many kilobytes have flowed across your screen in an online session. Avoid services that charge this way, if you can.)

High prices don't necessarily mean good service. Low prices don't always mean you're getting a good deal. An extremely high price may indicate that the service provider is inexperienced or is offering a level of service you don't need. A very low price may show inexperience on the part of the provider or indicate a lack of willingness to support you later.

Local Access

The service provider's charge may not be your only cost. If your host is not a local phone call from your location (and if it isn't accessible through a packet-switching network or an 800 number), you will have to pay long-distance or toll telephone charges. Some services that do offer packet-switch access (Tymnet, SprintNet, and so on) charge extra for that service. All services that offer toll-free access using 800 numbers charge extra for it. 800 surcharges are generally much steeper than packet-switching charges. If a service provider with the tools you want isn't a local phone call away (which is very likely, unless you live in a large, technologically adept city), a host that is accessible through a packet-switching network or an 800 line can save you from nasty surprises on your phone bill.

Speed

Your fancy 28.8 Kbps modem will slow to a snail's pace if it can't connect to a system that's as fast as it is. Find out the fastest speed your host can support. Transferring a large file at 2,400 bps can be agony, so get the fastest connection you can. (If you'll be connecting to a packet-switching network, find out what modem speed the local hub of the network supports. Big cities typically have 9,600 bps or faster access; rural communities typically make do with 2,400 bps.) Some services charge extra for connecting with faster modems, so know what you'll be expected to pay based on your modem speed. This practice has decreased in recent years. Look twice at any service provider that discriminates against those with quick modems.

Interface

What does your interface look like once you're online? What you find varies from service to service. There are hundreds of types of computers on the Internet—from tiny personal computers to medium-sized workstations to behemoth mainframes—and each one looks different online. The service you choose may feature an elegant graphical interface, a slightly elegant menu-driven interface, or a decidedly inelegant UNIX prompt.

Although I've already set myself up to receive tons of hate mail from lovers of UNIX, I will say this: the interface you choose (and ultimately the service provider you use) depends on your expertise and patience. Although a command-line UNIX interface is harder at first to use, with practice and patience, it is definitely more powerful than any menu-driven program can be.

Storage Space

If you won't be using an IP connection, you'll sometimes need to store some information on your local host computer. Find out how much information you can store there. Some service providers have a strict limit (for example, 2M); others may let you purchase extra disk space when you need it. The hard disk on your host computer can hold only a limited amount of information, and the system administrators want to be sure there is enough space to go around.

Software

Don't forget that you need communication software that enables your computer to talk to the modem. Most modems come with software, and there are dozens of software packages available for every computer system. Some are free, some are shareware, and others are commercial software. The software you need depends on your computer system and what service you will connect to. Users of dial-up command-line services and text-based commercial services can use freeware or shareware terminal programs (such as Zterm for the Mac and Procomm for PCs.)

You need special software to access some commercial online services and bulletin board systems (such as Prodigy and America Online) that use graphics instead of text. You must get this software from the online service before signing on the first time—it's usually free. You also need special software on your computer if you're connecting with an IP link (such as Chameleon for Windows, Internet in a Box, or MacTCP and MacPPP for Mac users). Most of this software is commercial, although some of it is freeware.

Access Restrictions

Find out what the service's appropriate-use policies are before you sign up. Certain systems may be inappropriate for certain activities. Some networks that are part of the Internet are dedicated to education and research; therefore, they don't allow commercial activity. If you're thinking of putting your business online, find out what the network's acceptable-use policies are.

Games and multiuser dungeons are another sticky issue with certain systems, especially at educational and business institutions.

If you'll be reading news on the Usenet, find out whether a site you are considering has a full Usenet feed. A full Usenet feed approaches 90M of information a day, so many sites cut back on less popular newsgroups to save disk space. (It's likely that you won't miss them unless you want to know about water sports in Finland or the goings-on in a particular literature class at an obscure East Coast university.) Other sites don't feed newsgroups with explicit sexual content.

Reliability and Performance

Nothing in the world is more frustrating than trying to log in to check your electronic mail only to find that your host is down, the phone lines are busy, or network connectivity has been lost. The problem is twice as bad when you need to send an important piece of e-mail immediately but your host is in the Land of Oz.

Although loss of connectivity just when you need the Internet most can happen with any service provider, make an effort to learn how reliable a potential host is. Call the service's modem number at peak usage times (during the business day and from 6 to 11 P.M.) If you hear a busy signal, the service provider probably doesn't have enough phone lines to handle their current customers. If there is no answer at all, you should wonder aloud why the system is unavailable.

Many systems have scheduled downtime (usually in the wee hours of the night) for system maintenance and backups.

Even when the system is running, performance is an issue. An overworked computer runs much more slowly than an underworked one. Some systems can theoretically handle hundreds of users simultaneously but get bogged down with more than a few dozen. (Performance also depends on what the users are doing online. Telnet, for example, uses far less computing power than do database searches or compiling programs.) There isn't much you can do to test performance before you try the service for yourself. However, you can ask the administrator how many users the system can handle reliably at once, how many users are typically online at peak usage times, and whether your service provider plans to put a cap on new accounts when a performance limit is reached.

Find out whether there is a service guarantee. If so, what is it, and what does it include?

Security

Find out what measures the system administrators take to ensure that your information will remain private. Security isn't an enormous issue for casual Internet users, although most of us want to have some assurance that our files, electronic mail, and other information will be free from prying eyes.

Find out the system's policy on system administrators reading private e-mail. This should be of special concern to you if you gain access to the Internet using a bulletin board system. System administrators can peruse anything and everything on their computers, so you must rely on their honesty and integrity to keep their noses out of your files. Some systems try to promise privacy, and others clearly state that nothing is private.

Technical Support

Computers aren't the only component of a successful network; the people who use them make all the difference. While you are asking questions about a host's service, think about the service's support. Are the people you are talking to helpful and knowledgeable? Are they responsive to your questions and concerns? Are they willing to explain the simple stuff to you, or are you treated like a bother? After you sign on the service, it is likely that you will be asking many more questions. Be sure that the technical support team is willing and able to assist you.

What methods are provided for you to reach the technical support team? Every online service provides technical support through electronic mail, but e-mail won't do you any good if you can't sign on the system or you need immediate assistance. Find out whether there is a technical-support hotline or a voice mail system where you can leave a message.

Finally, don't just take the service provider's word for anything; check references. Get a list of three to five references and call or e-mail those folks. Ask about the service, technical support, system problems (such as unexplained downtime), and so on.

With a little preparation, your first Internet interaction can be a wonderful experience instead of a frustrating, expensive disaster.

Finding Access as an Organization

8

by Kevin M. Savetz

Large organizations and businesses that want to plug into the Internet must consider issues, problems, and technologies that don't affect those who want just individual access. Connecting a large group of people to the Internet takes time, thought, and money. With research, planning, and experimentation, you can find the right kind of access—at the right price—for your organization.

Dial-Up or Dedicated?

Dedicated Internet access isn't right for everyone: it's perfect for some applications and a decidedly bad choice for others. This section looks at the pros and cons of dedicated Internet access and what kind of users can benefit most from it.

A *dedicated* Internet connection links your organization's local area network (LAN), mainframe, or minicomputer to the Internet. After this connection is made, the connected computer or computers have a fast, full-time Internet connection. The local area network at your site can include IBM PC compatibles, Macintoshes, UNIX boxes—in fact, any computers with the hardware necessary to be part of a network.

Dedicated access is expensive. The costs include a high-speed leased telephone line, a CSU/DSU (a kind of high-speed digital modem), a router to connect your LAN to the CSU/DSU, and installation charges. In addition, if the computers at your site aren't already networked, they must be before they can access the Internet. A dedicated connection is also expensive in terms of time to set up and maintain.

A dedicated Internet line provides very fast, round-the-clock access for a large group of people. How many people? Many people suggest 20 users, but it will become clear that this number is not a hard-and-fast rule. What access method you can best use depends on the needs and resources of your group.

Could your organization use many *dial-up* accounts rather than dedicated access? Absolutely. Dial-up service doesn't require a hefty investment in equipment or dedicated phone lines. However, dial-up access is usually much slower than a dedicated connection, ties up your traditional phone lines, and usually isn't cost effective with more than a few users.

Dial-up users must wait for their modems to dial and connect; computers at an organization with dedicated access have Internet connectivity all the time. The speedy connection makes the perfect stomping ground for those who need (or want) to receive flashy graphics and use point-and-click interfaces.

Who Needs Dedicated Internet Access?

Any organization can get Internet access—businesses, nonprofit organizations, computer clubs, schools and colleges, whoever. You don't even have to be an organization to set yourself up with dedicated Internet access. If you've got several thousand dollars burning a hole in your pocket, you're welcome to plug into the Net. This scenario isn't very likely, however, so this chapter assumes that you're thinking of connecting your medium or large business, school, or other group.

In addition to dedicated-connection equipment costs, you need a person with the expertise to set up and maintain the Internet connection, hardware, LAN, and so on. Don't underestimate the effort it can take to set up these things. Consultation and system setup can be a full-time job. After things are running smoothly, maintenance can take a part-time or a full-time position (depending on your equipment and the scope of your network link). You also need technical support personnel to answer questions and troubleshoot problems with the network.

How Dedicated Access Works

Although dedicated access can seem much more complicated than dial-up access, it is in fact very similar: a computer at your site is hooked, with a telephone line and a communications device, to a service provider, from which you get Internet access.

At least one computer on your local area network must be configured with TCP/IP software, the programs that instruct the computer how to communicate with the Internet. Your LAN is attached to a router, which connects the LAN to a telephone link. Between the router and the telephone line is a CSU/DSU, a digital conversion device similar to a modem (see Figure 8.1). (A CSU/DSU works over digital lines and is much faster than a standard modem.)

At the other end of the telephone line, your service provider has similar equipment: a CSU/DSU to exchange information with your equipment, a router (shared by many users—you rent one "port" for your use), and a computer linked to the Internet.

FIGURE 8.1.

Elements of a dedicated Internet connection.

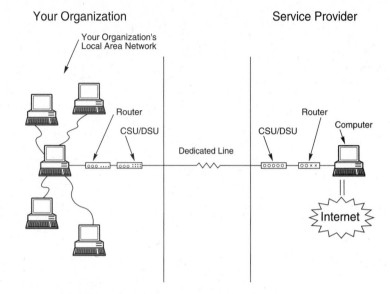

Types of Leased Lines

Because dedicated Internet access is available 24 hours a day, 7 days a week, you must lease a phone line. Area phone companies (such as Pacific Bell), long-distance companies (*à la* Sprint and AT&T), and specialized telephone companies can provide your leased line. Most Internet service providers use circuits from one specific company.

Phone lines can be likened to pipes: as the diameter of a pipe increases, the amount of water that can flow through in a given time also increases. The amount of information that can flow through a connection in a certain time is referred to as "bandwidth." A bigger pipe means greater bandwidth.

Dedicated connections can run from moderate to very fast speeds. Depending on the type of connection, you can transfer data from 56 Kbps (a connection of this speed can transmit the text of the Bible in about 11 minutes) to 45 Mbps (which can transfer the Bible nearly 50 times per minute).

How much bandwidth you use depends on how much information you need to send and receive and how quickly you want to exchange it. The price of your leased line is most likely a fixed monthly charge based on what connection speed you choose. Some types of connections cost more the farther you are from your remote host; other connections, such as frame relay and switched multimegabit digital service (SMDS), are usually charged at one rate no matter where you're connected.

What type of connections are available? The most cost-effective connections are digital, frame relay, and SMDS. A digital connection can carry your data at speeds from 56 Kbps (over a switched-56 line) to 45 Mbps (over a T1 line). The speed at which your data moves depends on the type of CSU/DSU you and your service provider use. It will come as no surprise that faster equipment costs more.

Frame relay and SMDS are new technologies emerging as cost-effective alternatives to digital telephone service. Frame relay moves data from 56 Kbps up to 512 Kbps. SMDS connections work at speeds from 56 Kbps to 10 Mbps. SMDS and frame relay connections are "distance independent"—you pay the same for a connection across the street as for a connection across the nation, a welcome plus for organizations with a distant Internet service provider.

Why a Digital Connection?

Now, a little confession. Although all the types of lines explained in the preceding section are digital connections, it is possible to connect your local area network to an Internet service provider using a dedicated analog line. This type of connection uses standard modems rather than CSU/DSUs but has serious drawbacks.

First, analog connections are much slower than digital ones (28.8 Kbps is the maximum analog speed). Even if that speed seems fast enough now, a connection at that speed can effectively handle only a few simultaneous users, with little room for growth. The number of simultaneous users isn't easily determined. In fact, the limiting factor isn't the number of users, but the type of activity they're engaged in. Bandwidth-intensive activities, like use of File Transfer Protocol, quickly sap the resources of a low-volume connection. Certain other applications need relatively little information to pass through, allowing hundreds of simultaneous users without an adverse affect on speed.

Choosing a Service Provider

An important distinction between a dedicated (leased) line and a traditional phone line is that dedicated lines are—barring unfortunate backhoe accidents—always connected. Unlike with dial-up access, it is important to pick a service provider you can remain happy with for a long time. With a dedicated line, you can't just hang up and dial someone better.

Some service providers that offer dial-up user access (as discussed in the preceding chapter) also provide dedicated access; others do not. Still other services, called *mid-level networks*, provide dedicated access service only to organizations and other networks.

A list of Internet service providers who offer dedicated service is at the end of this chapter in Table 8.1. The list isn't complete, but it can get you started on the road to finding the perfect service provider.

As you compare your choices of dedicated service providers, you will find that prices vary wildly depending on the provider, the speed and type of service you want, and your geographic location. You must consider many of the elements discussed in the preceding chapter (such as technical support, security, and reliability), plus others. Ask the questions posed in the following sections—and thoroughly understand the answers you receive—before signing up with any service provider.

Equipment Required

What hardware do you need at your site to connect to the service provider? Who supplies the hardware for the connection? Some service providers own and maintain all the equipment on both sides of the connection. Other providers insist that you purchase and maintain the routers, CSU/DSUs, and other equipment for both sides of the connection. Other service providers prefer other scenarios.

The more equipment your service provider owns and maintains, the higher your monthly fee. The trade-off is fewer worries for you; if a piece of equipment should fail, your provider's service guarantee (the provider *does* offer a guarantee, right?) will quickly replace or repair the hardware to minimize downtime.

If you choose to buy all the necessary equipment at the start, your initial costs are much higher, but you will most likely save money in the long run with lower service fees. Get hardware recommendations from your service provider to be sure that the equipment you buy is compatible with the provider's system. Remember that owning the equipment means replacing or repairing hardware that breaks—and being off the Net until it is fixed.

Software Needed

Will your service provider help you find and set up the software necessary on your side of the connection to talk to the Internet? Usually, many pieces of software are needed, including TCP/IP, mail routing, and domain name system software. You'll probably also want a selection of Internet tools, such as an electronic mail reader, Telnet, FTP, Gopher, World Wide Web, and so on. Some service providers visit your site to help set up the myriad pieces of software. Others offer technical support by telephone.

Cost

The price you pay for a dedicated Internet link can vary considerably. Your service provider may charge a flat monthly fee or may charge based on how much data flows through your link. Your rate also varies depending on the speed of your service, whether you rent or own the CSU/DSUs and router, and so on.

When you begin your service, you can expect certain one-time charges: an installation fee at your service provider, an installation fee for your leased line, two CSU/DSUs (if you're buying both), and the local router.

Your monthly charges include a service provider fee, port connection (for use of one of the ports on your service provider's router), and telephone line charges.

Optional Services

Your service provider may offer additional services for your dedicated connection. These can personalize your connection and inform your users. Among these options are the following:

- **Usenet:** Your service provider may be able to feed your site Usenet newsgroups. Many service providers offer this service for an extra fee. Even if you get a full feed without charge, remember that the Usenet is a disk space glutton, using about 90M a day. (This amount will surely rise as the Internet's population continues its phenomenal expansion.)

- **Domain name:** You can choose to set up a unique Internet "domain name" for your organization. This means that your organization's own network of computers has its own Internet name for incoming and outgoing electronic mail. For example, BMUG (a huge computer users' group based in Berkeley, California) has a domain name of `bmug.org`. To send mail to that system, you can send to *JoeUser*@`bmug.org`. Farallon Computer Products' domain name is, aptly, `farallon.com`. Your service provider may charge you a small amount (no more than $50) to set up your own domain name, but the name can add prestige to your Net connection—and it looks mighty cool on a business card!

Selecting an Internet Consultant or Trainer

Feeling overwhelmed? The more people find out about the Internet, the more they want to know. A peek at the Internet's treasures can pique the interest of even the most skeptical would-be Luddite. But anyone who has experienced the steep learning curve associated with surfing the Net knows that a good teacher can make all the difference. So, consider investing time and money in a consultant or trainer. An expert tour guide can determine whether Internet access becomes a cost-effective productivity booster or an expensive time waster.

When you begin searching for a trainer or consultant to guide you and your organization through the sometimes stormy Internet waters, you must establish certain criteria. You want to select a provider who can truly meet the needs of your organization, someone who can show you how the Internet can help you be more productive. Remember that your needs are unique; every profession, every organization, and every individual has a different set of needs and expectations of what technology can do for them. You shouldn't settle for a one-size-fits-all solution—no such creature exists, and a good Internet training or consulting company knows that.

Evaluate potential providers to make sure that they understand your specific needs and are prepared to make presentations or offer advice based on those needs. How do you make sure that your trainer or consultant can meet your needs? Create a detailed needs assessment. After all, if you don't know what your requirements are, communicating those needs to your prospective provider may be difficult.

To begin, identify the expected recipients of the services you require. Do you need training or consulting services for your technical staff? For managers? For customers? For yourself? What a network system administrator needs to know about the Internet may be quite different from the needs of a marketing staff member or the concerns of a manager focusing on bottom-line issues. Before you can complete any other questions in your assessment, you must know who in your organization is the consumer of these services.

The next question seems simple on its face, but it provides the framework for the rest of the assessment. In its most general form, the question is "what skills do you expect participants to gain from the training?"

The next question to consider is "What do we already know?" If you're new to the Internet, you may be tempted to say "nothing," but that answer often is an exaggeration. The fact that you're reading this book means that you already know more about the Internet than most people. By informing the prospective provider of what you already know, you ensure that you do not pay him or her to teach that material to you again. The best use of your funds is to get information not easily available in your organization.

The obvious follow-up question to "What do we know?" is "What don't we know?" Don't answer in the broadest sense of the question but in relation to what your goals for the training or consulting project are. If you want consulting on how to connect to the Internet, and you already know what the primary options are, what you don't know may be how to implement those options or what the associated costs may be. If you're looking for a trainer to show your already Internet-competent staff how to train others on use of the Internet, what you don't know is what training techniques and methods are most useful in the training process. Knowing what you *don't* need is as important as knowing what you *do* need.

List of Dedicated Access Service Providers

Table 8.1 lists service providers that offer dedicated Internet access. This list is not complete, but it can get you started on the search for the perfect service provider for your needs. The list is from InterNIC Information services; for the most recent edition, send electronic mail to `info@is.internic.net`, or call 619-455-4600.

Table 8.1. InterNIC Internet service providers list.

ACM Network Services Nationwide	
Angela Abbott	1-817-776-6876 (phone)
`account-info@acm.org`	1-817-751-7785 (fax)
AlterNet Nationwide	
A service of UUNET Technologies, Inc.	
`alternet-info@uunet.uu.net`	1-800-4UUNET3 (phone)
American Information Systems Illinois	
Josh Schneider	1-708-413-8400 (phone)
`schneid@ais.net`	1-708-413-8401 (fax)
ANS Nationwide	
Sales and Information	1-800-456-8267 (phone)
`info@ans.net`	1-703-758-7717 (fax)
APK Public Access Ohio	
Zbigniew Tyrlik	1-216-481-9428 (phone)
`support@wariat.org`	
BARRNet California, Nevada	
Sales	1-415-725-1790 (phone)
`info@barrnet.net`	1-415-725-3119 (fax)

continues

Table 8.1. continued

Beckemeyer Development California	
Sales	1-510-530-9637 (phone)
info@bdt.com	1-510-530-0451 (fax)
California Online! California	
Christopher Ward	1-707-586-3060 (phone)
cward@calon.com	1-707-588-8642 (fax)
CCnet Communications California	
Information	1-510-988-0680 (phone)
info@ccnet.com	1-510-998-0689 (fax)
Centurion Technology, Inc. Florida	
Jeffery Jablow	1-813-572-5556 (phone)
jablow@cent.com	1-813-572-1452 (fax)
CERFnet Western United States	
CERFnet Hotline	1-800-876-2373,
sales@cerf.net	1-619-455-3900 (phone)
	1-619-455-3990 (fax)
CICnet Midwestern United States	
Marketing and Sales Dept.	1-800-947-4754,
info@cic.net	1-313-998-6703 (phone)
	1-313-998-6105 (fax)
Clark Internet Services Northeastern United States	
ClarkNet Office	1-800-735-2258,
info@clark.net	1-410-730-9764 (phone)
	1-410-730-9765 (fax)
Cloud 9 Internet New York	
Scott Drassinower	1-914-682-0626 (phone)
scottd@cloud9.net	1-914-682-0506 (fax)
CO Supernet Colorado	
Guy Cook	1-303-296-8202 (phone)
gcook@csn.org	1-303-273-3475 (fax)
CONCERT North Carolina	
Naomi Courter	1-919-248-1999 (phone)
info@concert.net	1-919-248-1405 (fax)

Connix   Connecticut

Jim Hogue   1-203-349-7059 (phone)

office@connix.com

CRL Network Services   California

Sales   1-415-837-5300 (phone)

sales@crl.com

CSUnet   California

Gary Jones   1-310-985-9661 (phone)

nethelp@csu.net

CTS Network Services   California

Sales   1-619-637-3637 (phone)

support@cts.com   1-619-637-3630 (fax)

CyberGate, Inc.   Florida

Dan Sullivan   1-305-428-4283 (phone)

sales@gate.net   1-305-428-7977 (fax)

DFW Internet Services, Inc.   Texas

Jack Beech   1-817-332-5116 (phone)

sales@dfw.net   1-817-870-1501 (fax)

DHM Information Management   California

Dirk Harms-Merbitz   1-310-214-3349 (phone)

dharms@dhm.com   1-310-214-3090 (fax)

Digital Express Group, Inc.   Nationwide

John Todd   1-800-969-9090 (phone)

sales@access.digex.net   1-301-220-0477 (fax)

EarthLink Network, Inc.   California

Sky Dayton   1-213-644-9500 (phone)

info@earthlink.net   1-213-644-9510 (fax)

The Eden Matrix   Texas

John Herzer   1-512-478-9900 (phone)

jch@eden.com   1-512-478-9936 (fax)

The Edge   Tennessee

Tim Choate   1-615-455-9915 (phone)

info@edge.net   1-615-454-2042 (fax)

continues

Table 8.1. continued

Escape (Kazan Corp)   New York

Sales   1-212-888-8780 (phone)

info@escape.com   1-212-832-0344 (fax)

Evergreen Internet   Arizona

Phil Broadbent   1-602-230-9330 (phone)

sales@libre.com   1-602-230-9773 (fax)

Florida Online   Florida

Jerry Russell   1-407-635-8888 (phone)

jerry@ditigal.net   1-407-635-9050 (fax)

FullFeed Communications   Wisconsin

Katie Stachoviak   1-608-246-4239 (phone)

info@fullfeed.com

Fxnet   North and South Carolina

Sales   1-704-338-4670 (phone)

info@fx.net   1-704-338-4679 (fax)

Global Enterprise Services   Nationwide

Sergio Heker, President   1-800-35-TIGER (phone)

market@jvnc.net   1-609-897-7310 (fax)

HoloNet   Nationwide

HoloNet Staff   1-510-704-0160 (phone)

support@holonet.net   1-510-704-8019 (fax)

IACNet   Ohio

Devon Sean McCullough   1-513-887-8877 (phone)

info@iac.net

ICNet   Michigan, Ohio

Ivars Upatnieks   1-313-998-0090 (phone)

info@ic.net

IDS World Network   Northeastern United States

Information   1-800-IDS-1680 (phone)

info@ids.net

Innovative Data Services   Michigan

Sales   1-810-478-3554 (phone)

info@id.net   1-810-478-2950 (fax)

INS Info Services   Iowa

Customer Service   1-800-546-6587 (phone)

`service@ins.infonet.net`   1-515-830-0345 (fax)

INTAC Access Corporation   New Jersey

Sales   1-201-944-1417 (phone)

`info@intac.com`   1-201-944-1434 (fax)

InterAccess   Illinois

Lev Kaye   1-800-967-1580 (phone)

`info@interaccess.com`   1-708-498-3289 (fax)

The Internet Access Company   Massachusetts

Sales   1-617-276-7200 (phone)

`info@tiac.net`   1-617-275-2224 (fax)

Internet Access Online   Ohio

Sales   1-514-887-8877 (phone)

`sales@iac.com`

Internet Atlanta   Georgia

Dorn Hetzel   1-404-410-9000 (phone)

`info@atlanta.com`   1-404-410-9005 (fax)

Internet Express   Colorado

Customer Service   1-800-592-1240 (phone)

`service@usa.net`   1-719-592-1201 (fax)

Internet On-Ramp, Inc.   Washington

Sales   1-509-927-7267 (phone)

`info@on-ramp.ior.com`   1-509-927-0273 (fax)

Internetworks   Nationwide

Internetworks, Inc.   1-503-233-4774 (phone)

`info@i.net`   1-503-233-4773 (fax)

Interport Communications Corp   New York

Sales and Information   1-212-989-1128 (phone)

`info@interport.net`

IQuest Network Services   Indiana

Robert Hoquim   1-800-844-UNIX,

`info@iquest.net`   1-317-259-5050 (phone)

                                               1-317-259-7289 (fax)

continues

Table 8.1. continued

Kaiwan Corp.   California

Rachel Hwang   1-714-638-2139 (phone)

sales@kaiwan.com   1-714-638-0455 (fax)

Li Net, Inc.   New York

Michael Reilly   1-516-476-1168 (phone)

questions@li.net

Lightside, Inc.   California

Fred Condo   1-818-858-9261 (phone)

lightside@lightside.com   1-818-858-8982 (fax)

Los Nettos   Los Angeles Area

Joe Kemp   1-310-822-1511 (phone)

los-nettos-info@isi.edu   1-310-823-6714 (fax)

maine.net, Inc.   Maine

Andy Robinson   1-207-780-6381 (phone)

atr@maine.net   1-207-780-6301 (fax)

MCSNet   Illinois

Karl Denninger   1-312-248-8649 (phone)

info@mcs.net   1-312-248-8649 (fax)

MichNet/Merit   Michigan

Recruiting Staff   1-313-764-9430 (phone)

info@merit.edu   1-313-747-3185 (fax)

MIDnet   Midwestern United States

Network Inf Ctr   1-402-472-7600 (phone)

nic@westie.mid.net   1-402-472-5640 (fax)

MRNet   Minnesota

Dennis Fazio   1-612-342-2570 (phone)

info@MR.Net   1-612-342-2873 (fax)

MSEN   Michigan

Owen Medd   1-313-998-4562 (phone)

info@msen.com   1-313-998-4563 (fax)

MV Communications   New Hampshire

Sales   1-603-429-2223 (phone)

info@mv.mv.com

NEARNET   Northeastern United States

NEARNET Information Hotline   1-617-873-8730 (phone)

nearnet-join@near.net   1-617-873-5620 (fax)

NeoSoft, Inc.   Texas

Jay Williams   1-713-684-5969 (phone)

jmw3@neosoft.com   1-713-684-5922 (fax)

NET99   Nationwide

Joseph Stroup   1-800-638-9947 (phone)

joe@ns.net99.net   1-602-249-1161 (fax)

NetAxis   Connecticut

Luis Hernandez   1-203-969-0618 (phone)

luis@netaxis.com   1-203-921-1544 (fax)

NETCOM   United States

Business or Personal Sales   1-800-501-8649,

info@netcom.com   1-408-554-8649 (phone)

                                                           1-408-241-9145 (fax)

netILLINOIS   Illinois

Peter Roll   1-708-866-1825 (phone)

proll@illinois.net   1-708-866-1857 (fax)

Network Intensive   California

Sales and Information   1-800-273-5600 (phone)

info@ni.net   1-714-450-8410 (fax)

The Network Link, Inc.   California

Steve Froeschke   1-619-278-5943 (phone)

stevef@tnl1.tnwl.com

NevadaNet   Nevada

Brad D. Lee   1-702-784-4827 (phone)

braddlee@nevada.edu   1-702-784-1108 (fax)

continues

Table 8.1. continued

New Mexico Technet, Inc.   New Mexico

Marianne Granoff   1-505-345-6555 (phone)

granoff@technet.nm.org   1-505-435-6559 (fax)

New York Net   New York

Bob Tinkelman   1-718-776-6811 (phone)

sales@new-york.net   1-718-217-9407 (fax)

Northcoast Internet   California

Kevin Savetz   1-707-443-8696 (phone)

support@northcoast.com

NorthWest CommLink   Washington

Garlend Tyacke   1-206-336-0103 (phone)

gtyacke@nwcl.net

Northwest Nexus, Inc.   Washington

Information   1-206-455-3505 (phone)

info@nwnexus.wa.com   1-206-455-4672 (fax)

NorthwestNet   Northwestern United States

Member Relations   1-206-562-3000 (phone)

info@nwnet.net   1-206-562-4822 (fax)

NYSERNet   New York

Sales   1-315-453-2912 (phone)

info@nysernet.org   1-315-453-3052 (fax)

OARnet   Ohio

Alison Brown   1-614-292-8100 (phone)

alison@oar.net   1-614-292-7168 (fax)

Old Colorado City Comm   Colorado

Sales   1-719-528-5849 (phone)

thefox@oldcolo.com   1-719-528-5869 (fax)

PACCOM   Hawaii

Torben Nielsen   1-808-956-3499 (phone)

torben@hawaii.edu

Panix   Eastern United States

New User Staff   1-212-741-4400 (phone)

info-person@panix.com   1-212-741-5311 (fax)

Ping   Georgia

Brett Koller   1-800-746-4635,

bdk@ping.com   1-404-399-1670 (phone)

Pioneer Global   Massachusetts

Craig Komins   1-617-375-0200 (phone)

sales@pn.com   1-617-375-0201 (fax)

Planet Access Networks   New Jersey

Fred Laparo   1-201-691-4704 (phone)

fred@planet.net   1-201-691-7588 (fax)

PREPnet   Pennsylvania

Thomas Bajzek   1-412-268-7870 (phone)

twb+@andrew.cmu.edu   1-412-268-7875 (fax)

Primenet   Arizona

Clay Johnston   1-602-870-1010 x109 (phone)

info@primenet.com   1-602-870-1010 (fax)

PSCNET   Eastern United States (PA, OH, WV)

Eugene Hastings   1-412-268-4960 (phone)

pscnet-admin@psc.edu   1-412-268-5832 (fax)

PSINet   Nationwide

PSI, Inc.   1-800-82PSI82,

info@psi.com   1-703-620-6651 (phone)

                                                     1-703-620-2430 (fax)
                                                     1-800-79FAX79 (faxback)

QuakeNet   California

Sales   1-415-655-6607 (phone)

info@quake.net

The Rabbit Network, Inc.   Michigan

Customer Liaison Services   1-800-456-0094 (phone)

info@rabbit.net   1-810-790-0156 (fax)

continues

Table 8.1. continued

RAINet   Oregon, SW Washington

| Robert Chew | 1-503-227-5665 (phone) |
| `info@rain.net` | 1-503-297-9078 (fax) |

Red River Net   Minnesota, North and South Dakota

| Craig Lien | 1-701-232-2227 (phone) |
| `lien@rrnet.com` | |

Rocky Mountain Internet, Inc.   Colorado

| Rich Mount | 1-800-900-RMII (phone) |
| `mountr@rmii.com` | 1-719-576-0301 (fax) |

Schunix   Massachusetts

| Robert Schultz | 1-508-853-0258 (phone) |
| `info@schunix.com` | 1-508-757-1645 (fax) |

Scruz-Net   California

Matthew Kaufman	1-800-319-5555,
`info@scruz.net`	1-408-457-5050 (phone)
	1-408-457-1020 (fax)

SeaNet   Seattle

| Igor Klimenko | 1-206-343-7828 (phone) |
| `igor@seanet.com` | 1-206-628-0722 (fax) |

Sibylline, Inc.   Arkansas

| Dan Faules | 1-501-521-4660 (phone) |
| `info@sibylline.com` | 1-501-521-4659 (fax) |

Sesquinet   Texas

| Farrell Gerbode | 1-713-527-4988 (phone) |
| `farrell@rice.edu` | 1-713-527-6099 (fax) |

Sims, Inc.   South Carolina

| Jim Sims | 1-803-762-4956 (phone) |
| `info@sims.net` | 1-803-762-4956 (fax) |

South Coast Computing Services   Texas

| Sales | 1-800-221-6478 (phone) |
| `sales@sccsi.com` | 1-713-917-5005 (fax) |

SprintLink   Nationwide

SprintLink   1-800-817-7755 (phone)

info@sprintlink.net   1-703-904-2680 (fax)

SURAnet   Southeastern United States

Kimberly Donaldson   1-301-982-4600 (phone)

kdonalds@sura.net   1-301-982-4605 (fax)

Synergy Communications   Nationwide

Jamie Saker   1-402-346-4638 (phone)

jsaker@synergy.net   1-402-346-0208 (fax)

Telerama Public Access   Pennsylvania

Peter Berger   1-412-481-3505 (phone)

sysop@telerama.lm.com   1-412-481-8568 (fax)

THEnet   Texas

Frank Sayre   1-512-471-2444 (phone)

f.sayre@utexas.edu   1-512-471-2449 (fax)

ThoughtPort Inc.   Nationwide

David Bartlett   1-314-474-6870 (phone)

info@thoughtport.com   1-314-474-4122 (fax)

UltraNet Communications, Inc.   Massachusetts

Sales   1-508-229-8400,

info@ultranet.com   1-800-763-8111 (phone)

                                                  1-508-229-2375 (fax)

US Net, Inc.   Eastern United States

Services   1-301-572-5926 (phone)

info@us.net   1-301-572-5201 (fax)

VERnet   Virginia

James Jokl   1-804-924-0616 (phone)

net-info@ver.net   1-804-982-4715 (fax)

ViaNet Communications   California

Joe McGuckin   1-415-903-2242 (phone)

info@via.net   1-415-903-2241 (fax)

continues

Table 8.1. continued

Vnet Internet Access, Inc. North Carolina	
Sales	1-800-377-3282 (phone)
info@vnet.net	1-704-334-6880
WestNet Western United States	
Lillian or Chris	1-914-967-7816 (phone)
staff@westnet.net	
WiscNet Wisconsin	
Tad Pinkerton	1-608-262-8874 (phone)
tad@cs.wisc.edu	1-608-262-4679 (fax)
WLN Washington	
Rushton Brandis	1-800-DIAL-WLN,
info@wln.com	1-206-923-4000 (phone)
	1-206-923-4009 (fax)
WorldWide Access Illinois	
Kathleen Vrona	1-708-367-1870 (phone)
support@wwa.com	1-708-367-1872 (fax)
WVNET West Virginia	
Harper Grimm	1-304-293-5192 (phone)
cc011041@wvnvms.wvnet.edu	1-304-293-5540 (fax)
Xmission Utah	
Support	1-801-539-0852 (phone)
support@xmission.com	1-801-539-0853 (fax)

Connecting a LAN to the Internet

9

*by William Dutcher
and updated by
Kevin M. Savetz*

Connecting a local area network to the Internet isn't necessarily hard; it's just a lot of work. What makes it problematic is that it's one of those computer networking problems for which nobody's yet developed a complete, shrink-wrapped solution. Buy this box, load this software, and cyberspace—here we come.

Unfortunately, connecting a LAN to the Internet seems to be one of those tasks that ranks in difficulty with VTAM sysgens for IBM mainframes and determining exactly what all those files called AUTOEXEC.BAT really do. Establishing an Internet connection isn't quite as formidable a task as programming a VCR to record one program while you watch another, but it's close. At least it seems that way to anyone who has tried it. There aren't very many cookbook Internet connection recipes, because everyone seems to start out with a different set of ingredients.

One of the problems is that there isn't just one single way to connect your LAN or your host to the Internet. There are several ways to do it, and each depends on the services your users expect to use, how much system configuration you can do, and the type of connection for which you're willing to pay.

So it isn't, unfortunately, a plug-and-play operation. You must do some up-front work to analyze how you're going to configure your connection from your LAN or local host to the Internet, and what to expect once you get there.

First, you must address some basic issues to determine what you're going to get out of your Internet connection. Here are some questions that systems and network administrators must answer before proceeding with an Internet connection:

- What Internet services do users expect to use? Electronic mail? File transfer? Bulletin boards?

- Who will absorb the costs of the Internet connection? If the end users will pay, how will cost accounting be done?

- Do users want to send and receive electronic mail with other users on the Internet? (Most do.) If so, where will users' mailboxes be, and who will administer the mailboxes?

- Should your LAN electronic mail system be connected to the Internet? LAN users can send and receive electronic mail through the LAN electronic mail system, rather than by making a specific connection to an Internet electronic mail system.

- Can or will the PCs on your LAN run another protocol (TCP/IP) in addition to the native LAN protocol?

- Do you have a host that already runs TCP/IP, or do you plan to install a host that can?

- Is a router available to route packets from your LAN to the Internet?

These questions indicate that there are several alternatives to connecting your network environment to the Internet. Your answers help indicate which type of connection is most appropriate for your situation.

Start with the Basics

Let's start with an understanding of the basics of connecting to the Internet. The Internet is a group of computer networks connected by data communications circuits, which are phone lines. There are hundreds of separate networks in the group of interconnected networks called the Internet. All you want to do is to connect somewhere to one of them. That one connection is all you need to get users on your LAN into the Internet. It's much like the one connection from your telephone at home that interconnects you to any other telephone in the world. As long as you're connected to one local phone system, you're connected to all of them. An Internet connection works the same way.

So, you need that connection to the Internet. If you're part of a university or a research organization, you may already be part of a network that is one of the Internet's member networks. If you're not, that connection will probably be provided by an Internet access provider. These companies give organizations outside the member network community a port through which they can connect to the Internet. They charge a fee for this service and offer different types of services and capabilities (see Chapter 8, "Finding Access as an Organization").

Things are simpler for military installations that want to connect to the Department of Defense's Defense Information Systems Network (DISN), formerly called the Defense Data Network (DDN). Hosts running TCP/IP, or devices on LANs that run TCP/IP, connect directly to an X.25 packet-switching node (PSN) or to a router that connects to the DISN backbone. The part of the DISN that carries unclassified traffic connects through gateways to the Internet.

It would be convenient if establishing that phone line connection to the Internet were enough, but remember, this isn't an average shrink-wrapped application. One end of the phone line goes to the Internet access provider, but the other end is yours. Your end of the line plugs into a modem or a CSU/DSU. Providing the RS-232 port on your network for the connection to the back end of the modem is another one of those Internet connection problems.

IP Routers

On most networks, you have to configure a router, either in a separate router box or in a host or server configured to act as a router. The router redirects, or routes, traffic from your network out onto the Internet, for delivery to its destination.

The second problem is communicating over that connection to the other hosts on the Internet. An Internet *host* is a computer system to or from which you transfer files. It can accept logins from remote terminals and run programs. It also can originate, receive, store, or forward electronic mail.

So that all hosts can communicate on the Internet, the use of a standard set of communications protocols has been agreed on so that everyone speaks the same language. That language, or *protocol*, is the Transmission Control Protocol (TCP) and the Internet Protocol (IP), usually referred to by a single acronym, TCP/IP. The hosts on your network must speak TCP/IP because, by common agreement, all other hosts on the Internet speak TCP/IP.

On the Internet, as on other systems that use this standard set of protocols, TCP/IP implies the use of application-level protocols, such as the File Transfer Protocol (FTP) and a virtual terminal protocol, Telnet. These are two of the most commonly used Internet application protocols, but there are several others.

Your hosts have to run TCP/IP and higher-level applications, or something has to run them for them. If your LAN workstations don't run TCP/IP, a local host can do it for them. Alternatively, your Internet access provider may have a host that can do it for you. Another option is to subscribe to an information service or electronic mail system that gives you Internet access as part of the information or electronic mail access package. This option limits the availability of Internet services, but it allows you to sidestep most of the thorny issues of Internet connection.

If you want to connect your LAN-based electronic mail system to the Internet, you have the task of establishing an electronic mail gateway. The *gateway* translates your local electronic mail address to Internet addresses and then forwards messages to the Internet. A response to your message from a user on the Internet traverses the Internet and is forwarded back to the electronic mail gateway on your LAN. The gateway translates your Internet address back into a local electronic mail system address and delivers the mail. The translation by the gateway is necessary, because your Internet mail address and your LAN electronic mail address are usually different.

Administrative Details

The first decision point is to determine how you want to connect your LAN to the Internet. You may be directly or indirectly connected to the Internet. A host or network that is *directly connected* has full access to all the other networks that make up the Internet. Traditionally, full connectivity to the Internet has been limited to organizations that have some sort of government sponsorship. However, as interest in and use of the Internet has grown, commercial service providers—designed to provide Internet connection for commercial and individual customers—have been permitted to offer direct Internet connections.

An *indirectly connected* network is a LAN or a separate network that connects to the Internet through another computer system. The intermediary system provides Internet access, but it may allow only limited services, such as only electronic mail.

An IP Address of Your Own

Directly connected networks need an officially designated Internet Protocol (IP) network address. Hosts on directly connected networks have IP addresses that identify them differently from any other host.

Because you will be connecting your LAN, host, or gateway to a world-wide collection of systems that use the TCP/IP protocols, you need a unique set of IP addresses that identify your systems. You also need an IP address for each host that runs the IP protocol. For example, the IP address 150.48.236.5 uniquely identifies a host running the IP protocol anywhere in the world.

IP addresses are similar to Ethernet network adapter card addresses. Every Ethernet adapter has a unique, 48-bit Ethernet address that identifies it. Similarly, every IP host has a unique IP address that identifies it. The implication of this is that a host or a workstation attached both to a LAN and the Internet has two mutually exclusive addresses. One is for LAN access; the other is for Internet access.

To ensure uniqueness, Ethernet addresses are assigned by the Institute of Electrical and Electronics Engineers (IEEE), which assigns blocks of Ethernet (and Token Ring) numbers to adapter manufacturers. The uniqueness of your IP addresses is established by the InterNIC.

An *IP address* is a 48-bit binary number expressed as a series of four decimal digits. It is composed of two parts: a network number and a host number. The first part of the number is the network number, and the last part is the number of the host on that network. A host with the IP address 150.48.236.5 is located on network 150.48.0.0, and it is host 0.0.236.5 on that network. In this case, the first two numbers indicate the network number and the last two specify the host on that network. Other types of IP addresses use either the first octet for a network number and the last three octets for a host number, or they use the first three octets as a network number and the last octet for a host number.

Your LAN gateway to the Internet will "advertise" to other hosts on the Internet that it knows how to get to any host on a network for which it acts as an Internet gateway. The other hosts and gateways on the Internet don't know and don't care where a specific host is located. All they need to know is how to route IP datagrams to the host or gateway that "fronts" for a specific network. The gateway then forwards the traffic to the appropriate host.

To connect your LAN and its hosts to the Internet, you must apply to the Internetwork Network Information Center for a network number. Contact the InterNIC for the application and for information about the application process. Its address, phone number, and Internet address are given here:

> InterNIC Registration Services
> c/o Network Solutions Inc.
> 505 Huntmar Park Drive
> Herndon, VA 22070
> 1-800-444-4345
> `hostmaster@internic.net`

If you are connecting your own network of hosts to the Internet, you also need a domain name. A *domain* is an organizational entity that helps identify the hosts in your network by giving them common text names that can be mapped back to IP addresses. The InterNIC also approves requests for domain names after determining that a new domain name is unique.

Connecting to the Internet

Establishing a connection to the Internet usually means providing these four primary connectivity elements:

- A host that can run the TCP/IP protocols
- End-user applications to access Internet hosts for electronic mail exchange, file transfer, and host login access
- A router, or a host or server that acts as a router, to direct traffic from a LAN or another network to the Internet
- A communications line to carry traffic to and from the router

Often, the simplest way to connect to the Internet is to let somebody else do it for you. You can subscribe to an Internet access service that handles all the gory details of Internet access for you. For a monthly use or connection fee, an Internet access provider can give you Internet connectivity across a standard dial-up line. The Internet access provider gives you dial-up access to its host. The Internet access provider's host runs TCP/IP, connects to the Internet, runs the TCP/IP protocols, and routes traffic to and from the Internet. In addition, the access provider usually maintains users' Internet mailboxes and administers mailbox usage.

Reaching the Internet through an access provider carries the extra benefit of little extra expense for hardware, software, or support. Users on a LAN can use standard communications software, such as Crosstalk or Procomm Plus, to dial out of the network through a directly attached modem, or one on a communications server or a modem pool. The most common requirement is that the user's PC emulate a VT-100 terminal (to get full-screen service) but that capability is built into any communications software sold today.

For a relatively low use or connection fee, the Internet access provider lets you have access to all the Internet's electronic mail, file transfer, and host login services. For example, Digital Express (DigEx), of Greenbelt, MD (1-301-220-2020), charges about $20 per month plus a one-time $25 setup charge for dial-up access to its host. The DigEx host gives its users a full Internet connection, a mailbox, and up to 5M of storage space.

Performance Systems International (PSI) of Herndon, VA (1-800-827-7482), offers a similar setup. PSI subscribers use their own PSILink Software to connect to the Internet through local dial-up ports in more than 100 U.S. cities. Users get an Internet mailbox only (PSILink Lite) or a mailbox and FTP (PSILink Basic). Costs range from $9 per month for DOS access to PSI Lite at 9,600 bps, to $39 per month for Windows access to PSI Basic at 14,400 bps, plus a one-time $19 setup fee.

Another Internet access provider, Delphi, of Cambridge, MA (1-800-544-4005), charges $10 to $20 per month for Internet access, depending on how much you intend to use the service and how long you will be connected. Delphi also provides an Internet mailbox and access to the full set of Internet applications, such as FTP and Telnet.

For users who need only electronic mail access, there's an even simpler solution. Commercial online data services and electronic mail systems, such as MCI Mail, Prodigy, and CompuServe, can access the Internet's electronic mail systems through their own electronic mail gateways.

For example, MCI Mail users can dial up the local MCI Mail node on an 800 number (1-800-234-6245), access their MCI Mail mailboxes, and send and receive electronic mail with users on several other electronic mail systems—including the Internet. Normal MCI Mail message charges apply (45 cents for a message of less than 500 characters and $1 for up to 10,000 characters) for any message, even one destined for an Internet address. An MCI Mail user can send an electronic mail message to an Internet user by embedding the recipient's Internet address in the address of the MCI Mail message.

Internet Access Directly from Your LAN

Dial-up access through an Internet access provider can be an expensive solution for an organization with many users who want Internet access, particularly if they are already connected to a LAN. Usage charges can mount quickly, and each user needs a separate account for his or her mailbox.

One solution is to establish a dedicated connection from the LAN to the Internet. The dedicated connection is a communications line to the Internet access provider that gives you access to the Internet. You provide the rest of the connection, including the hosts, router, and TCP/IP applications.

Another solution is to run TCP/IP on PCs and workstations on the LAN and to install an IP router, which is connected to an Internet access provider over a leased line. This is practical for

LANs with PCs as workstations and network servers but no host computer, such as a network of PCs and servers on a LAN running Novell NetWare or Banyan Vines.

Let's use a NetWare LAN as an example. The basic configuration is to run a TCP/IP client on each PC on the LAN, giving each PC the capability to direct IP datagrams to the Internet through a router on the LAN. On the Internet, TCP/IP hosts provide the server-side processes to honor client-side FTP, TFTP, and Telnet requests.

Back on the LAN, a NetWare server or a dedicated device acts as a router, forwarding IP datagrams to and from the Internet service provider's access point. In a typical network configuration that has interconnected LANs, you may already have a router (such as a cisco or Wellfleet router) to forward IPX traffic to other NetWare LANs. That same router can route IP traffic to the Internet.

To gain access to the Internet, make arrangements with an Internet access provider to provide a port for your use and acquire the leased line to the access provider's Internet access point. Then configure the router port to route IP traffic (assuming that you have already requested and been assigned an official IP network address by the InterNIC).

Your router acts as a gateway for the devices on the LAN behind it. You have to assign the router port the IP network number of the network for which it will act as a gateway. For example, if you have been assigned a network address of `200.100.50.0`, your router acts as the gateway for the PCs on your LAN, which have IP addresses of `200.100.50.1`, `200.100.50.2`, and so forth.

To run client-side processes, networked PCs can run Novell's LAN Workplace for DOS software or another client-side software program, such as the Clarkson utilities, FTP Software's PC/TCP, or NetManage's Chameleon. This software gives users' PCs access to the standard suite of client-side applications, such as FTP and Telnet. It also links those application-level protocols to the lower-level TCP and IP network protocols.

A workstation using LAN Workplace for DOS uses the TCP/IP protocols instead of NetWare's native SPX/IPX protocols for communications with TCP/IP servers on the Internet. Users' PCs create IP datagrams addressed to the router. The router forwards the IP datagrams to the Internet for delivery to the correct host.

At the same time, the PCs also use the Novell IPX/SPX protocols to communicate with NetWare servers—unless the NetWare servers are configured to run only the TCP/IP protocols. IPX and SPX are efficient protocols for NetWare servers, but if your LAN has both PCs and UNIX systems (such as Sun workstations), you may want to standardize on TCP/IP.

If you are running LAN Workplace for DOS, the key configuration file for Internet access is NET.CFG. This file contains the PC's IP address, as well as other configuration parameters. In most cases, NET.CFG can be run without modification, except for adding the IP address and the address of the default router on the LAN. You may specify only one default router in

NET.CFG (it is specified by its IP address). All other routers (if any others exist) are determined dynamically by the Routing Information Protocol (RIP).

PCs running Microsoft's Windows NT Advanced Server are easier to configure for TCP/IP use because TCP/IP is Microsoft's preferred protocol for communications between workstations and Windows NT servers on different LANs. In the Windows NT world, a PC that can communicate with a Windows NT server runs Windows NT, the Microsoft LAN Manager client for DOS, or Microsoft's upscale Windows for Workgroups (WFW) client. Of course, Windows NT and WFW are fully integrated with Windows. The DOS client loads before Windows and accesses the NT server through the Windows File Manager. This book refers to all three Windows NT clients.

Windows NT clients use Microsoft's NetBIOS extension, NetBEUI, to reach a Windows NT server on its local LAN segment, and TCP/IP to reach Windows NT servers on other LAN segments. Routers running IP connect the LAN segments together. However, because Windows NT clients already run TCP/IP, they are already set up to create IP datagrams that can be routed to the Internet. Network workstations only need application software, such as an FTP or Telnet program, to achieve full Internet access. TCP/IP applications are not part of the Windows NT client software.

Both the Windows NT and the WFW software include Windows utilities to configure a workstation's IP address and to bind them to the adapter through NDIS drivers. In the DOS client, the workstation's IP address and the pointer to the default gateway are parameters in `\lanman.dos\protocol.ini`. In both the WFW and DOS clients, the NetBIOS names and IP address of Windows NT workstations and Windows NT servers on other networks must be in the LMHOSTS file. If they are not in LMHOSTS, the client has no way of determining the IP address of a host or domain controller on another LAN.

NDIS and ODI

PCs on a LAN can run both TCP/IP and the network operating system's native protocols. Most PCs on a LAN use a network operating system for communications between networked workstations and network servers. Most networked PCs don't use TCP/IP as their native protocol.

For example, Novell's NetWare uses its own proprietary protocols for LAN communications: the Internet Packet Exchange (IPX) and Sequenced Packet Exchange (SPX) protocols. If your networked PCs are to be Internet hosts and have their own IP addresses, they also have to run the TCP/IP protocol stack.

In the days before extended memory managers, running different protocol stacks meant rebooting each time a different protocol was run. Rebooting gave the PC a different network identity because the protocols were bound separately to the PC's network interface card.

However, NIC and NOS vendors, led by 3Com, Microsoft, and Novell, have developed both standard and NOS-specific interfaces between their protocols and NICs. The benefit of these interfaces is that more than one protocol stack can run at the same time, eliminating the need to reboot every time.

For example, 3Com and Microsoft developed the Network Driver Interchange Standard (NDIS), a software specification for a NIC equivalent to an API for network protocols. Instead of writing a driver for a specific NIC, the network software—even TCP/IP—can interface to the standard NDIS NIC driver, which can be bound to several sets of LAN transport and network protocols.

Novell's Open Data Link Exchange Interface (ODI) provides an equivalent capability for the NetWare shell. ODI is the NetWare 3.11 enabler for running both SPX/IPX and TCP/IP at the same time, binding both to the same NIC.

In NetWare 4.*x*, Novell has added a more sophisticated capability: Virtual Loadable Modules (VLMs). The NetWare 4.*x* client loads other network protocols on demand. Each protocol is a separate "loadable module" that loads into memory and runs only on demand, instead of remaining in (and using up) memory all the time. A VLM is the client-side version of the NetWare server's NetWare Loadable Modules (NLMs).

Microsoft's Windows NT simplifies PC configuration matters for TCP/IP protocol use. It uses TCP/IP as its native protocol between LANs, relying on NetBEUI for LAN communications on a device's local LAN segment. To round out the top NOS players, Banyan Vines, like NetWare, uses its own proprietary protocols (Vines VIPX and VIP), but offers TCP/IP as a separately configured optional protocol.

Matters are much simpler if a minicomputer or mainframe host (rather than individual PCs) is the TCP/IP host and terminals or PCs on the network connect to the host as terminals. A UNIX host, for example, already runs TCP/IP for most LAN and WAN communications anyway. Users who access the host through terminals or PC terminal sessions have eliminated much of the need for configuring TCP/IP on individual workstations.

Minicomputer Access

Many LANs are composed completely of PCs, workstations, and servers. Traditionally, devices connected to the Internet were host computers, such as DEC VAXes or IBM hosts. Today, many Internet hosts are host computers, and the population has expanded to include DEC Alphas, Sun systems, HP minis, IBM AS/400s, and many others.

The LAN-connected minicomputer or mainframe that acts as both a router and a host is another alternative for Internet access. Unlike a LAN server, the minicomputer can run the UNIX operating system as its native device operating system. In this case, it's not UNIX *per se* that is important, but what comes with UNIX. Most UNIX operating systems include the TCP/IP protocols, electronic mail process handlers, and FTP and Telnet client and server processes. The system administrator can configure these services for Internet access.

UNIX systems are the most common Internet hosts. They include all the tools to be well-appointed Internet hosts, IP routers, or both. They use TCP/IP as their native protocols. Also, they can create and manage users' mailboxes, act as routers, and run the communications protocols necessary to connect to the Internet.

The system administrator must configure the UNIX system kernel to support TCP/IP processes. Each UNIX system is configured differently, so we'll describe general principles rather than system specifics. The basic UNIX kernel configuration supports networking on a LAN interface (usually Ethernet), an X.25 serial interface, or both. By default, the system is set up as a router to forward IP datagrams to another network interface.

The kernel configuration binds the TCP and IP protocols to the UNIX kernel, but other processes (called *daemons* in UNIX terminology) must be started to service the other routing and service protocols needed to route traffic and deliver datagrams. For example, the routed and named processes start the Routing Information Protocol (RIP) and the Domain Name Service (DNS) processes, respectively. Another superserver process, inetd, calls processes dynamically as they are needed, such as FTP, Telnet, and rlogin.

Then the IP address and subnetwork mask (if applicable) of each serial or LAN interface are configured. Each network interface has its own IP address, but the IP process also has to know how to interface to a specific network-level process below it, such as X.25 or the IEEE 802.2 Logical Link Control (LLC) layer. The UNIX ifconfig command and its associated parameters are used to configure each network interface.

The ifconfig command also creates a routing table for the network interfaces that have been assigned IP addresses. For a directly connected Internet host, one of the interfaces can be configured to support an Internet data link protocol, such as the Serial Line Interface Protocol (SLIP) or the Point-to-Point Protocol (PPP).

A host with a direct connection to the Internet uses either SLIP or PPP as the protocol on its interface to the Internet. A DISN host, by contrast, uses the DDN standard X.25 protocol. Both SLIP and PPP are wide area network protocols for encapsulating IP datagrams for transmission to the next router or gateway on the Internet. Ethernet, by contrast, is a protocol that can encapsulate IP datagrams for transmission and delivery on a local area network. A router or a gateway forwards the IP datagrams to their destination, encapsulating and de-encapsulating the datagrams in different protocols.

Both SLIP and PPP were created to enable hosts on the Internet to communicate over serial lines. Both SLIP and PPP support asynchronous dial-up and synchronous, private-line transmission. Either can be used for a connection to an Internet access provider, but the one your system uses depends on what your system and the Internet access provider's system support.

SLIP frames datagrams with special characters that specify the beginning and the end of a datagram. It's a simple technique, not unlike that used by Xmodem, to send blocks of characters asynchronously. Developed in the interest of simplicity, SLIP does not do error detection, nor can it support data compression. Its main purpose is to transmit IP datagrams.

PPP is a standard Internet serial line protocol. It was developed to address SLIP's weaknesses. Like other protocols, such as IBM's SDLC, PPP is similar to the High-Level Data Link Control (HDLC) protocol. PPP includes facilities to negotiate connection establishment and termination, and to negotiate connection options. It also can do error detection, so it can guarantee reliable data delivery, regardless of line quality.

Gateway Protocols

If the host and the router are separate devices, the host must know where the gateway is so that it can send IP datagrams to it for transmission to the Internet. So, the host configuration must specify a default gateway to which it directs Internet traffic. On a LAN, the default gateway is the port of the router that is the gateway from the LAN to the Internet. The gateway's IP address is listed as the default gateway. In other words, it's the gateway to which is sent traffic not bound for any IP network address that the host knows about.

If the host connects directly to the Internet, it has to advertise its existence to the rest of the Internet through a standard Internet gateway protocol. Many hosts, even ones directly connected to the Internet, have to advertise only the existence of networks reachable through them.

The most commonly used routing protocol is the Routing Information Protocol (RIP). Systems that connect other networks to the Internet use the Exterior Gateway Protocol, or EGP. This protocol is being replaced by the newer Border Gateway Protocol (BGP). In any case, one of these routing protocols (usually RIP) must be configured so that devices on the network can make routing decisions. In UNIX systems, the gated process runs RIP, BGP, and EGP, and the routing is configured through it.

If terminals on the LAN access the host through a terminal server, configuring the host for Internet access hasn't changed how they use the host. They're still terminals running applications on the host, but now they can FTP through their local host to other hosts on the Internet. PC users can either run client-side FTP and Telnet applications for communications with other Internet hosts or they can connect to their local host by emulating a terminal.

Electronic Mail Gateways

Not all users need or want to transfer files and log on to remote systems across the Internet. For many users, electronic mail is all the Internet access they ever need.

One of the more common requirements for Internet access is to integrate a LAN's electronic mail system and the Internet's extensive electronic mail network. For example, LAN users may send and receive electronic mail using a LAN mail package, such as cc:mail or Microsoft Mail. Despite the problems this may create for system administrators, users want any electronic mail to be accessible through their own local electronic mail system, even users on the Internet. It's done with a LAN electronic mail system's native gateway, or a more general X.400 electronic mail gateway.

An *electronic mail gateway* translates the address of a LAN electronic mail message into an address that is comprehensible by another electronic mail system, then forwards it for delivery to the foreign mail system. Forwarding it to the other electronic mail system can involve transmitting electronic mail messages across a wide area network (WAN) using a protocol such as X.25. In addition, forwarding electronic mail to the Internet may also require that the gateway use a TCP/IP electronic mail delivery application protocol, such as the Simple Mail Transport Protocol (SMTP).

Many electronic mail system vendors provide optional gateways from their mail systems into other vendors' mail systems. These native gateways are designed to take electronic mail from a specific electronic mail system and convert it into a format comprehensible by another vendor's mail system. For example, cc:mail makes a gateway from cc:mail to Lotus Notes Mail. It helps that both products are from the same company (Lotus), but the electronic mail formats and addressing conventions of cc:mail and Notes Mail are different, and addresses must be translated between the two.

Most electronic mail systems can configure an electronic mail gateway to forward mail to the Internet. The key to making this work is a translation table that translates native electronic mail system addresses into Internet addresses and vice-versa, and a process that executes SMTP. Users embed an Internet address into a native mail address. The gateway identifies the message as one bound to an external mail system, strips off the native mail system address, and forwards it to the external foreign mail system.

For example, cc:mail allows the system administrator (the Postmaster) to set up foreign domains. The cc:mail system knows that anything addressed to a foreign domain belongs elsewhere, such as the Internet. For example, a user may address a cc:mail message to John Smith at {jsmith@falcon.bigco.com}@internet. The Postmaster has configured the cc:mail post office to know that internet is a foreign domain. The cc:mail post office strips off the cc:mail user name (John Smith), and forwards the mail to the Internet for delivery.

Coming the other way, an Internet electronic mail message addressed to the Internet addressee jsmith@falcon.bigco.com may come into the LAN electronic mail system gateway from an Internet access provider. The LAN gateway has to map the user name jsmith to the LAN mail addressee John Smith@BigCo, and deliver it to the appropriate server.

To transmit the electronic mail to the Internet, the gateway or server running a message handler (the Connectivity Manager of Novell's Message Handling Service, or MHS, is an example of one) picks up mail and forwards it to the Internet access provider, or directly to the Internet.

If the gateway connects directly to the Internet, the gateway has to act like a standard Internet host. That is, it has to run the TCP/IP protocols, as well as the Simple Mail Transport Protocol (SMTP) to deliver mail to another Internet host.

X.400 Gateways to the Internet

Another variation of a native mail gateway to the Internet is the X.400 gateway to the Internet. Many commercial electronic mail systems, such as MCI Mail, Sprint Telemail, and CompuServe, transfer electronic mail messages to and from the Internet through X.400 gateways. The X.400 gateway is a convenient way to get electronic mail into and out of a LAN electronic mail system. In addition, it can transfer electronic mail to any other system that has an X.400 gateway.

At the risk of oversimplifying a seriously complicated subject, X.400 is a CCITT standard for addressing and exchanging electronic mail between different electronic mail systems. The address of a mail message is converted to a standard X.400 format and transferred from an electronic mail system gateway to an X.400 Message Transfer Agent (MTA). The MTA transfers the message to another MTA at the destination mail system.

Many WAN carriers operate X.400 MTAs that accept electronic mail messages from a variety of systems with X.400 gateways and then forward X.400 messages to destination systems with their own X.400 gateways. The Internet can be one of the X.400 systems, as can your LAN electronic mail system.

For example, Sprint's Telemail system acts as an X.400 MTA for mail from the Internet destined for other electronic mail systems. If a router on your LAN has an X.25 link to the Sprint Telemail system, mail messages in X.400 format can be directed from the Internet to Sprint, then transferred across the X.25 link to your router. The router transfers the messages to the local X.400 MTA, and the MTA forwards them to the electronic mail system's X.400 gateway for conversion back into the native mail system format.

The Domain Name Service

The TCP and IP protocols provide common communications mechanisms for all users of the Internet. Given the IP address of a destination, the Internet's hosts, gateways, and routers deliver the message.

However, getting the exact IP address can be a problem. Just like dialing a phone number, being close rarely counts. You have to be exact. An IP address is all numbers and can be up to 12 digits long. The correct digits can be hard to remember. Besides, Internet hosts are rarely referred to by number, but by name. We can easily remember that the files we want are on `moosehead.bottle.com`, or that a correspondent's electronic mail address is `cjones@engine.railroad.com`.

In each case, the name of an Internet host is specified as part of the mnemonic by which we refer to Internet hosts. For example, Casey Jones' mailbox is on the Internet host `engine.railroad.com`, and `moosehead.bottle.com` is the name of a host. However, neither text name is an IP address. If we don't specify the IP address of the host, something has to do it for us.

Fortunately, part of the infrastructure of the Internet is a service that translates text host names into numeric IP addresses. It's the Domain Name Service (DNS), which lives on a host on your local LAN, somewhere on your network, or out on the Internet. DNS provides name-to-IP address translation as a convenience for Internet users. It's the Internet's version of the telephone system's Directory Assistance, or a name service or clearinghouse in a LAN network operating system.

The DNS maintains a set of tables that map host names to IP addresses. For example, an instance of the DNS that knows about the hosts in the `railroad.com` domain might have an address table that looks like this:

Host	IP Address
`engine.railroad.com`	155.155.10.79
`caboose.railroad.com`	191.207.221.3
`freightcar.railroad.com`	172.157.12.165

If a user of an electronic mail application specified that the message was to be delivered to `cjones@engine.railroad.com`, the electronic mail service has to translate `engine.railroad.com` to an IP address before it can hand it over to SMTP, TCP, and IP for delivery. If the local host doesn't know the IP address of `engine.railroad.com`, it can ask the nearest DNS to translate it.

Because it's inefficient to keep asking the DNS to resolve every IP address, most hosts have access to a local table, the *hosts table*, usually in a file called HOSTS.TXT. The table can be stored on a host on the LAN, or each host or PC can keep its own local hosts table.

So, a request for IP address resolution goes first to the hosts table. If the host name isn't in the hosts table, a request goes out to the host specified as the DNS server for resolution.

DNS servers themselves are arranged in a hierarchy, passing DNS queries to other DNS servers for resolution. At the highest level of the hierarchy are top-level domains. Hosts are arranged into major top-level domains. There may be (and usually are) other levels of domains below each level of the hierarchy.

The host `engine.railroad.com` is really the host named `engine` in the `railroad` domain, which is part of the top-level `com` domain. There is a DNS server for each level in the hierarchy, and DNS queries are passed to the DNS server at the appropriate level in the hierarchy for resolution.

The last part of the name of most Internet hosts is one of the six top levels of the Internet naming hierarchy for the United States. The top-level domains, and the operators of hosts usually in each, are as follows

Domain Name	Meaning
.com	Commercial organizations
.edu	Universities
.mil	Department of Defense and other military agencies
.gov	Government agencies
.net	Network resources
.org	Other organizations

To resolve the IP address of an Internet host from its symbolic name, users' PCs need a pointer to the nearest Domain Name Service (DNS) server or a local copy of the hosts file. With Novell's LAN Workplace for DOS, the RESOLV.CFG file points to the root name server. If the DNS server is not available or can't resolve a name, the inquiry goes to the hosts file in \NET\TCP.

In Microsoft's client software for Windows NT, the name of the host is specified in the initial configuration screens. If you use the standard (and free) DOS client instead of Windows NT as your workstation operating system or Windows for Workgroups, the DNS server address is in \LANMAN.DOS\PROTOCOL.INI. In a standard Windows configuration, the name is in the \WINDOWS\PROTOCOL.INI file.

In each of these implementations, the name of the nearest DNS server is specified as an IP address, rather than a host name. This arrangement avoids the trap of trying to find a DNS host if you only have the name of the DNS server and not its IP address. Therefore, the IP address of the nearest DNS host (as well as a host that has the HOSTS.TXT file) is usually part of the initial system configuration.

High-Speed Internet Connections

10

by Robert J. Berger

Plain old telephone service (or POTS, as it's affectionately called in the telephony business) is the conventional analog phone service we all use on a daily basis. POTS has a very long history. It is ubiquitously deployed and enjoys the status of universal service, which means that POTS is available everywhere and is incredibly inexpensive.

The major down side of POTS for Internauts is that the *bandwidth* (how fast bits flow) is severely constrained. A somewhat lesser issue is that the time to set up a call (from when you dial to when you connect to the other party) is slow, particularly when you add in the time for a modem to negotiate speeds and encoding protocols.

Bandwidth plays an important part in how responsive a connection feels and can become an obvious limitation when you start downloading large files, such as weather pictures or a software distribution. With POTS bandwidths, you start a transfer and have time to go out for lunch.

This chapter describes high-speed connection services available today that may give you a chance only to get up for a cup of coffee rather than have lunch. The chapter also describes upcoming services that will erase the distinction between local area networks (LANs) and wide area networks (WANs), meaning you won't even get a sip of that coffee.

Limitations of Plain Old Telephone Service (POTS)

POTS has fundamental limitations that have been stretched just about as much as possible. These limitations make POTS unusable for Internet connections of the future.

Tuned for Voice (Low) Bandwidth

The fundamental problem with POTS is that it is an analog technology tuned for the distribution of voice information. Digital data was not even an idea when the POTS technology was being deployed. Therefore, POTS is a less than optimal solution for connecting you and your computer to the inherently digital Internet.

The bandwidth required to transmit analog voice is around 3,000 cycles per second, which is the raw bandwidth of a POTS line. For the last several years, modem manufacturers have done a remarkable job of squeezing every last bit out of that 3,000 hertz of bandwidth. Manufacturers accomplish this with various analog encoding tricks, such as frequency shift keying (300 to 2,400 bits per second), quadrature amplitude modulation (4,800 to 9,600 bps), and phase quadrature modulation (9,600 bps and above). With the introduction of V.FAST (28,000 bps), modems are reaching theoretical limits of what they can do with these limited analog lines.

So-called *high-speed modems* can reach their top performance only if they are used on lines and connections in top shape. If the line has any noise or other problem, the modems are forced to fall back to lower speeds. Thus you have no guarantee of the performance of these modems, which can vary on a call-by-call basis.

Slow Modem Connection

How fast a connection your computer can make with the Internet is important when you want true IP connectivity. For example, if you are using SLIP or PPP to connect your computer to an Internet service provider, the SLIP/PPP driver may automatically bring up the connection when packets are waiting to be sent. (See "Packet Services," later in this chapter.) You don't have to explicitly make a connection; instead, you just have your mail tool retrieve your mail or click a Mosaic hyperlink and the driver automatically brings up the link. As you read your mail, the driver automatically brings down the phone connection because no packets have gone by for a specified period of time.

This automatic making and breaking of the connection creates a virtual permanent connection. The user does not notice that the SLIP/PPP driver is saving him or her connect charges unless the delay caused by call setup is too long.

The techniques used by today's modems tend to add overhead to the startup of the call. When added to the 4-second to 10-second delay of an analog call setup, establishing a complete connection between your computer and a remote site can take 20 seconds to a minute. This time is not bad for a remote login session that may last ten minutes or longer. When you want to create a virtual permanent connection, however, this procedure becomes frustrating.

New Possibilities with Higher Bandwidth

Today, most Internauts experience the Internet by firing up a terminal emulator communications program on their PC or Mac and dialing in to a remote UNIX system connected to the Internet. The PC acts like a dumb terminal from the 1970s: it can display only ASCII text. To see graphics or try out some software, users first have to FTP the file to their UNIX account and then transfer the file from the UNIX machine to their PC. Then the user can display the graphics or run the program.

Direct IP Connections for GUI Applications

A much more satisfying way to surf the Net is to have a direct IP connection between your computer and the Internet. This way, you can use Internet clients with graphical user interfaces (GUIs) that take full advantage of the capabilities of your native machine and the Internet.

A 14.4 kilobits per second (Kbps) modem can support a direct IP connection using SLIP or PPP as the link protocol sent over the phone line between your computer and the Internet provider. The use of SLIP or PPP means that your computer has true Internet connectivity, allowing full client-server GUI applications and native access to all Internet services. Unfortunately, these modem speeds give you only a taste of being fully connected to the Internet. Having a connection of 56 Kbps or faster is when you really feel the Internet surf is up!

Higher-speed access offers enough bandwidth to use tools such as Mosaic as an everyday tool. No longer do you have to try your patience every time you fire up, waiting for each graphic to download. Instead, you can zip around the Net through all the various hyperlinks. Listening to some of the audio links or viewing graphics and MPEG movies becomes feasible.

Realistic Access to Large Databases and File Transfers

Generally, all the browsing/searching/retrieval tools such as Gopher, WAIS, and FTP become more pleasurable to use with higher bandwidth. Much of the added pleasure is that you can comfortably use the graphical versions of these tools. More importantly, you now can explore much more, because each access or retrieval is at least 10 times faster.

Trailblazing new Gopher spaces is even more fun when you can open several documents or directories simultaneously. Finally, you can feasibly view those satellite weather pictures on a daily basis.

WAIS searches are more practical because you can view more of the retrieved documents and iterate the next search much faster.

Transferring large software distributions or image databases with FTP is something you now can do regularly. You also have less of a need to archive Internet material on your computer because you can easily FTP the material again at a later date.

Simultaneous Activities

Having a   direct, high-speed Internet link also supports the ability to do multiple activities simultaneously over the same link. For example, you can transfer several large files with FTP and at the same time read news or carry on an IRC (Internet Relay Chat) conversation.

Sophisticated Remote Access

A high-speed direct Internet link allows some activities that are too painful to do over a modem-speed IP link. For example, using the X Window system to access remote X clients is feasible with performance similar to local clients. High-speed links enable you to mount remote file systems across the Internet using the Network File System (NFS) or the Andrew File System (AFS). Some of the major software archive sites, such as the University of Michigan, offer their archives as remotely mountable. If you have the right software, you can make the archive site's disks seem as though they are part of your computer system, eliminating the need to use FTP to copy files from the remote site.

Farallon has started shipping Timbuktu Pro, which enables Macintosh users to remotely access other Macintosh (and eventually Windows) systems over TCP/IP. At ISDN (integrated services digital network) speeds (128 Kbps) or greater, the interaction is very smooth.

Multimedia

The Internet is a hotbed of multimedia activity, and multimedia requires substantial bandwidth. Today, the Internet offers services usable at ISDN and T1 speeds (even with as little as 14.4 Kbps if you have a little patience). Carl Malamud's Internet Multicasting Service is generating gigabytes of audio (as well as publishing gigabytes of federal databases). The program Internet Talk Radio covers science and technology, and the Internet Town Hall is devoted to public affairs. For more information, point your Web browser to `http://town.hall.org`.

Each hour program of 8-bit, 8K samples/second pulse code modulated audio (AM radio quality) takes up 30M of storage, and the Internet Multicasting Service produces anywhere from 30 to 90 minutes of programming per day! You can download the programs from a variety of FTP archive sites around the Internet that replicate the files originating at the site, `ftp.uu.net`. Downloading an hour program takes about 6 hours with a 14.4 Kbps modem, 42 minutes with ISDN, or about 3.5 minutes with a T1.

Other people are publishing audio and video clips as well. Adam Curry of `curryco.com` has record cuts and QuickTime video clips available. Some publishers provide entire albums online, bypassing the record companies. Many research centers offer a variety of scientific visualizations as QuickTime or MPEG videos.

Video Conferencing

To better understand the impact of real-time audio/video network services, the Internet Society's Internet Engineering Task Force (IETF) has been running an experimental multicasting backbone (MBone) testbed. MBone enables multiple channels of real-time 8-bit audio and slow-scan video to transmit across the Internet. Each channel takes up between 100 and 300 Kbps of bandwidth and is implemented using special routing software on workstations.

At this time, the MBone is a hand-crafted virtual network superimposed on top of the Internet backbone. MBone primarily is used to transmit IETF meetings, but during off hours, people rotate being disk jockeys and playing music. MBone also transmits special events such as the Hubble satellite repair space walk. If you are a network wizard and have a UNIX workstation, you can access the MBone using publicly available software.

More conventional video conferencing is available using any commercial or freeware video conferencing package that works with TCP/IP. Many UNIX workstations now offer hardware and software to support video conferences over ISDN and TCP/IP. Sun offers ShowMe as well as several configurations of SparcStations that have built-in video capabilities. SGI offers the Indy, which has built-in video conferencing.

Quite a bit of research and development is going on in the arena of network video conferencing. Much of the research includes free software implementations. Most of the software is for UNIX workstations, but a few Mac and PC implementations also are available.

Alternatives to POTS

The preceding sections emphasized the wide variety of demands for bandwidth greater than the measly 14.4 Kbps of POTS. The main questions are how fast do you want to go, how much money do you have to spend, and when do you want the service?

Currently, technological and regulatory environments are going through nonlinear transformations. The preceding decade was somewhat staid in terms of wide area network improvements. The 1990s will see bandwidth into our homes and businesses jump from the minuscule 14.4 Kbps to hundreds of Mbps and eventually to gigabit speeds. Just like the doubling of MIPS (millions of instructions per second) and quadrupling of M/SIMM every two years, this huge expansion of bandwidth will usher in new markets, products, and possibilities. The following sections describe the digital offerings of today and the expectations for the next few years.

Physical Links

The *physical links* are the actual wires and low-level encoding protocols that transport the data. These links range from POTS, switched/dedicated 56 (56 Kbps), ISDN (56 Kbps to 128 Kbps), T1 (1.54 Mbps), cable TV (4 to 10 Mbps), to the very high-end fiber optics of T3 and SONET (45 Mbps to gigabits). Physical links can be divided into the categories of switched and dedicated services. POTS, switched 56, and ISDN have the familiar characteristic of allowing you to dial each call and thus select who you connect with on a call-by-call basis.

The *dedicated services* of dedicated 56, T1, and T3 are point-to-point, meaning that you contract with a phone company to connect a wire from your site to the remote site. A dedicated service can connect only two fixed points; you are charged each month for the mileage between your site and the remote site. Although you get dedicated, full-time connections that support constant two-way services, the cost of setting up the connection and the monthly cost are very high.

Packet services (described later in this chapter in "Packet Services") on top of dedicated physical links can remove the cost of long distance point-to-point connections because you pay only for the mileage to the nearest point of presence (POP). Each Internet provider or phone company sets up POPs all around the territories they serve. This minimizes the distance charges for their customers.

Switched 56

Switched 56 was one of the first digital offerings that had somewhat reasonable pricing. This technology uses many of the same infrastructure facilities (wires and central office switches) as POTS. Like POTS, you can dial the connection on a call-by-call basis. The difference is that switched 56 delivers a digital connection at a reliable 56 Kbps. The problem is that the technology requires dedicated trunk lines and is an old analog/digital hybrid, which is expensive to support and maintain. Most phone companies plan to phase out switched 56 as ISDN and other more advanced technologies are more widely deployed. Switched 56 is compatible with ISDN, so a switched 56 call can connect to an ISDN phone.

Switched 56 service costs $40 to $90 a month, with installation in the $500 price range. Calls carry per-minute charges similar to standard business POTS calls. You need a specialized piece of hardware to connect your computer to the switched 56 line. For Internet access, this hardware usually is a bridge or router with an Ethernet interface that connects to your LAN on one side and a switched 56 interface that connects to the telephone network on the other side. This equipment is in the price range of $2,000 to $6,000, depending on what features you require.

Dedicated 56

Dedicated 56 is effectively the same as switched 56 except for the obvious fact that it's dedicated. Instead of enabling you to dial your connection, dedicated 56 is a fixed, point-to-point service. This technology currently is the most common way to connect a computer or LAN to the Internet. The early Internet backbone was based on dedicated 56.

Most Internet providers that support dedicated 56 service offer POPs within a short distance to most metropolitan areas. Some providers cover the cost of the line setup and monthly service charge if you are within 100 miles of their POP. Other providers charge the line setup and monthly fees separate from the Internet service. Dedicated 56 line setup is a couple thousand dollars, and the monthly fees are about $100 plus about $8 per mile. Startup fees for the Internet service over dedicated 56 range from $1,000 to $5,000, and the monthly fees range from $400 to $1,000. A router and a CSU/DSU (a unit that converts the telephone signal into a standard computer interface such as V.35) is required to connect your computer or LAN to the dedicated 56 line. These items run in the $2,500 to $7,000 range.

Dedicated 56 is considered the most cost-effective way to have a full-time connection to the Internet and have enough bandwidth to use many of the services available on the Net. In the next few years, however, other services should replace dedicated 56, offering significantly higher bandwidth at similar costs.

ISDN

Although ISDN has a reputation of standing for I Still Don't Know, many local exchange carriers (LECs, otherwise known as the local phone company) finally are rolling out ISDN services at reasonable prices. ISDN is one of the more promising telephone technologies for supporting cost-effective, higher-bandwidth Internet access. ISDN is expected to act as a transitional bridge for the next several years until the significantly higher bandwidths of fiber optics are more widely deployed. Because of ISDN's promise as the best price/performance solution for connecting people to the Internet, this section goes into more depth than other sections.

Work on ISDN started in 1968. At that time, developers envisioned ISDN to merge supervisory call setup, voice, fax, teletext, videotext, and data on a digital network (hence Integrated Services Digital Network). The world was very different then. AT&T still owned and controlled almost all the U.S. phone systems. Researchers were just beginning to work with LANs in advanced technology laboratories. PCs were not yet invented and mainframes were king. 64 Kbps seemed like a great deal of bandwidth (just as 64K of RAM seemed like an incredible amount for a computer). At that time, many experts thought digital PBXs (corporate ISDN telephone switches) would be the way to connect corporate computers and terminals to each other.

With this mind-set, large international committees of telephone engineers conceived and developed ISDN. ISDN is better than conventional POTS, but ISDN is a real compromise in terms of supporting data communications.

An ISDN basic rate interface (BRI) is the line used to connect an individual device to a PBX or central office switch. The BRI line uses the same twisted-pair wiring of POTS, so the telephone company does not need to change the millions of miles of copper wire already in place throughout the country. However, each central office in every community must upgrade telephone switches to modern digital switches such as the AT&T 5ESS or the Northern Telecom DMS-100.

Fortunately, most telephone companies have made these investments in many territories over the last decade or so. Most metropolitan areas around the U.S. are ready for ISDN. All that is needed to have widespread ISDN deployment in the U.S. is to file the proper tariffs, add some software/hardware upgrades to the installed switches, and train the telephone installers. Most U.S. LECs expect 85 to 95 percent deployment by mid-1995. Europe is even better off in terms of ISDN deployment, which has been tariffed and deployed for several years already.

ISDN Technology

ISDN BRI has three full duplex channels: two B channels each carrying 64 Kbps and one D channel at 16 Kbps. You can think of the two B channels as two phone lines that coexist on one wire (see Figure 10.1). For data communications, the two 64 Kbps B channels can be combined to produce 128 Kbps throughput.

FIGURE 10.1.

ISDN BRI channels.

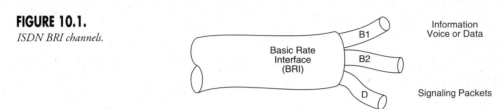

The D channel does all the signaling to set up a call out-of-band from the B channels. This technique is quite different from the normal analog phone lines (where all signaling is inband). The tones you hear when you punch the numbers on a touch-tone phone are the signals that tell the switches how to set up the call. These DTMF (dual-tone multifrequency) tones are transmitted on the same channel as your voice; thus they are in the same band as the primary signal (your voice).

D channel signaling is implemented using X.25 packets (described later in this chapter in "Packet Services"). Instead of sending out touch-tone signals to tell the switch how to make the connection, the D channel sends data packets from your phone/computer to the switch. This method enables ISDN to set up the call in tenths of a second versus the 8 to 10 seconds of conventional dial or touch-tone calling. Therefore, ISDN is ideal for supporting virtual permanent connections.

Because of the separate out-of-band D channel signaling, ISDN can handle call setup, features, and special functions in parallel with one or two voice or data connections on the two B channels. For example, instead of issuing the obnoxious *beep* or *click* of call waiting, ISDN sends a data packet from the central office to your phone or computer. The data packet can include the phone number of the second calling party. Your phone or computer then can decide how to handle the second call, based on the phone number. It can signal busy, display a message to you, or send a message to the calling phone, asking the caller to hold.

ISDN hardware devices used to connect a computer to the ISDN network are called *terminal adapters*. These devices range from boards that plug into your computer to external devices that connect to your computer with serial, parallel, SCSI, or Ethernet interfaces. Some adapters connect just a single computer; other adapters can connect an entire LAN.

To support an Internet connection, the Internet service provider you dial must support the protocols used by the ISDN terminal adapter. Many current terminal adapters use proprietary protocols, making interoperability difficult to support. Experts predict that in the next year, PPP will emerge as the standard for ISDN, although most providers will support other official standards, such as frame relay (RFC 1294) and X.25, as well as *de facto* standards (Combinet).

Many Internet providers are waiting for hardware manufacturers to implement these standards before they offer ISDN service.

The providers who support ISDN have standardized specific hardware implementations to ensure interoperability. Figure 10.2 shows how ISDN customers connect to an Internet provider.

FIGURE 10.2.

ISDN customer/provider connectivity.

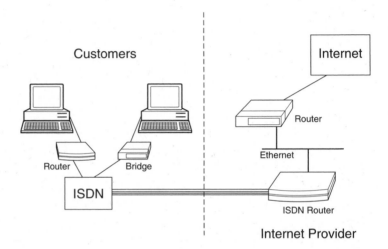

The combination of low cost, true digital connectivity, higher bandwidth, and fast call setup makes ISDN the best cost/performance solution for connecting computers or small LANs to the Internet (see Figure 10.3). In most areas, ISDN is best suited for situations in which you require client access to the Internet (for example, you want to use FTP, Mosaic, Gopher, or Telnet to access services on the Internet). Because of tariff restrictions (described later in this section), ISDN is not cost effective if you want to run a server on your host or LAN that remote Internet clients will access at random times.

Although the pricing for ISDN lines is not much more than that of conventional POTS lines ($25 to $275 to install, $20 to $30 per month), most local phone companies do not offer flat-rate tariffs for ISDN; you incur a usage charge for each minute you are connected. Pacific Bell charges the same rate for an ISDN B channel call as for a conventional POTS business call: four cents for the first minute, one cent for each minute thereafter. Two B channel calls that give you the full 128 Kbps of the BRI cost twice as much per minute. Users, Internet providers, and equipment manufacturers are applying pressure to the LECs through the public utility commissions, so a good chance exists that flat-rate tariffs for ISDN will become more widespread.

A few local phone companies do offer flat rates in the $60 to $90 per month range. In these cases, ISDN can be a cost-effective replacement for dedicated services such as dedicated 56 and fractional T1s, and you can use ISDN for both client and server applications.

The bottom line is that, for many applications, ISDN is the current price/performance leader. Costs for terminal adapters are rapidly dropping and becoming competitive with analog modem solutions, but with performance that is 10 times greater. Equipment costs for connecting an individual computer to an ISDN Internet provider run in the $500 to $1,500 range, and connecting a LAN with a router starts at $2,500.

FIGURE 10.3.

POTS versus ISDN performance.

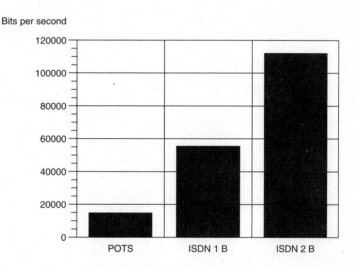

T1

T1 service offers 1.54 Mbps over two twisted-pair copper wires. This service is a telephone technology offered by LECs and Inter Exchange Carriers (IECs, otherwise known as the long-distance phone companies). Until a few years ago, a mesh of T1s made up the Internet backbone. T1 service is today's primary choice for connecting academic and corporate networks to the Internet because of its bandwidth capacity and price point.

Before 1984, customers outside the Bell System generally could not receive T1 service. Today, T1s are used for a wide range of high-bandwidth services in addition to Internet links. T1s can deliver a single channel of 1.54 Mbps of synchronous data, or you can carve T1s into 24 different 64 Kbps channels that can mix digital voice and data. Current T1 technology requires repeaters every 6,000 feet.

As with other dedicated point-to-point connections, users of T1-based Internet services must pay to have a T1 run from their site to the nearest POP of their Internet provider. The physical T1 costs about $2,000 to $5,000 for setup and $300 to $500 per month, plus $20 to $50 per mile. T1 Internet service costs another $2,000 to $10,000 for setup and $1,000 to $3,000 per month.

Hardware to support an Internet T1 link includes a router ($5,000 and up) and a CSU/DSU (if it's not built into the router). The cost of T1 service and hardware is expected to drop as it transforms into ADSL/HDSL technology, described in the next section.

ADSL/HDSL

Asymmetrical digital subscriber line (ADSL) and high-speed digital subscriber line (HDSL) were developed at Bellcore Labs as a way to use existing telephone copper twisted-pair and switching capacity to deliver low-cost video-on-demand services in competition with cable TV. ADSL and HDSL use much of the same telephone infrastructure as T1. By drawing on many of the same technology developments that were driving FDDI (fiber distribution data interface) over copper and Fast Ethernet, Bellcore was able to upgrade the capacity of the T1 four-wire link from 1.54 Mbps to more than 6 Mbps.

The *A* in ADSL stands for *asymmetrical*, which, in this case, means that the line has more bandwidth going into the home than out. Developers envisioned that an ADSL line would contain multiple channels of information at different bandwidths. The lower bandwidth channels would be full duplex (that is, they can support bidirectional data at the same time). HDSL uses the same techniques to squeeze more bandwidth into a T1 line, but HDSL is fully symmetrical.

For example, a single ADSL line (four wires) can include a POTS channel that terminates in the traditional RJ11 connector and works even if the other services go down. Another portion of the ADSL line can carry full ISDN, two B+D channels on an RJ45 connector. An optional full-duplex H0 (384 Kbps) channel can also be available.

The bulk of the bandwidth of the ADSL line is unidirectional and comes only from the information provider and into your home or office. You can carve the bandwidth to contain a mix of MPEG1 (1.54 Mbps), MPEG2 (3 Mbps), real-time video (6 Mbps), or compressed HDTV (6 Mbps). This way, you can have four MPEG1 signals coming in simultaneously (in case your family cannot decide to watch the same program).

ADSL is excellent for delivering Internet service. Depending on your needs and pocketbook, you can use the ISDN channels for 64 Kbps to 128 Kbps links, the H0 channel for 384 Kbps, or a combination of the H0 and 1.54 Mbps for an asymmetrical link in which you have 384 Kbps upstream bandwidth and 1.54 Mbps downstream bandwidth (for data that comes to you). This scenario generally is ideal for Internet clients, because you have very high bandwidth for the data that comes to you (like transferring a file with FTP from a remote site).

Unfortunately, no one has yet deployed ADSL on a commercial basis. Some regional Bell operating companies (or the *baby Bells*) have decided to forego ADSL deployment and jump directly to fiber optics. Some carriers plan to offer ADSL in stages. The first stage became available in 1994 and offers POTS, ISDN, and a single MPEG1 channel. Starting in 1995, the full ADSL technology should begin to appear.

No pricing is yet available, but because ADSL is expected to compete with cable TV, the costs should be quite low. Internet feeds using the H0 or MPEG channels probably will have a premium price caused by the floors that traditional T1 service has set.

Cable TV

Like ISDN, cable TV (CATV) delivery of the Internet promises to lower the cost of high bandwidth Internet connectivity. At this time, only a few Internet providers are promising CATV services.

Two major classes of Internet exist over CATV. One class is *symmetrical*, in which channels on the CATV plant simulate an Ethernet. In this case, special interface adapters connect the CATV cable to the LAN of the user. These symmetrical services can deliver Ethernet speeds, but they carry a large price tag in terms of the equipment ($4,000 to $10,000) and can support only a limited number of simultaneous users on a single channel. The symmetrical service is ideal for corporate users who need to connect large LANs in a metropolitan area, but this service doesn't look cost-effective for individuals and smaller LANs for a few years.

Under a Defense Advanced Research Projects Agency grant, Hybrid Networks, Inc. has developed a more cost-effective solution available in a few cities. Like ADSL, Hybrid uses an asymmetrical delivery mechanism; you get Ethernet speeds in one direction. Fortunately, the speed is in the good direction: traffic from the Internet cloud comes to the user at around 10 Mbps. Traffic from the user back to the Internet travels at the rate supplied by a telephone connection (14.4 Kbps V.32, 28 Kbps V.FAST, 128 Kbps ISDN).

Because many IP services use some form of handshaking, the speed (actually, the latency) of the backchannel has a big impact on the downstream bandwidth. By using 2 B ISDN rather than POTS for the backchannel, the overall speed doubles for operations such as FTP.

Security is built into the Hybrid Networks system by using DES encryption on packets sent to each user; a listener on the cable cannot eavesdrop easily on other people's packets. The user does not need to worry about keys because the system manages them transparently.

Hybrid Networks, Inc. and other entities can run a hybrid access system (HAS) point of presence (POP) in any region that offers this service. The HAS POP connects to the Internet, private networks, and information providers using traditional IP networking technology (WAN links such as T1 or T3 and routers).

The HAS POP uses both conventional routers and a custom Hybrid router to handle the IP traffic (see Figure 10.4). The Hybrid router does all the work of encrypting the packets and modulating the carrier with the aggregate data to be sent to the cable TV head end. This signal (the IN channel) resembles a conventional broadcast TV signal and can be transmitted using any conventional over-the-air or cable TV distribution technology.

FIGURE 10.4.

Hybrid networks architecture.

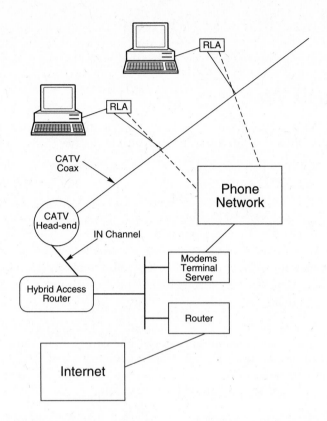

Traditional routers can drive multiple Hybrid routers and IN channels to send packets destined for a particular cable system to the appropriate cable head end. Therefore, all of a region's cable systems do not have to carry duplicate traffic. Regional systems can scale nicely because each cable channel carries traffic only for that particular system. You can add cable channels if traffic on any one cable system channel becomes overloaded.

The receiver at the user's site is a product of Hybrid Networks that acts as an RF (radio frequency) modem and network interface. The receiver connects to the cable TV system using the same cable connected to your TV or VCR. Hybrid Networks calls this device the *remote link adapter* (RLA) and plans to offer a few variations on the theme.

An RLA has an Ethernet interface that connects to your LAN, a CATV interface that connects to your CATV coax cable, and an RS-232 port that can connect to a modem or ISDN terminal adapter. When you start up an IP client, the RLA automatically calls the service provider for the backchannel connection. The downstream connection comes over the CATV link.

Current RLAs cost in the $1,000 to $1,500 price range, plus the cost of the modem or ISDN terminal adapter. The good news is that the service ranges from $60 to $100 per month (plus your basic cable and phone bills). This service is an outstanding buy for the amount of bandwidth you can get. Asymmetrical services such as Hybrid Networks are suitable only for client-style access and cannot easily offer services to the Internet.

Wireless Technology

Today, wireless is used mostly to deliver low-speed e-mail connections by companies such as Radiomail of San Mateo, California. But wireless promises to deliver speeds at least as fast as an ISDN B channel (64 Kbps) for metropolitan area networks (MANs). Companies such as Tetherless Access, Ltd. of Fremont, California, are developing technologies based on spread spectrum radio, using radio spectrum that does not require licensing from the FCC.

Originally, the military created spread spectrum technology to overcome jamming by hostile forces. This technology is created by modulating the radio frequency signal with a spreading sequence or by causing the carrier signal to hop between frequencies. By spreading the utilization of the radio frequency bandwidth over a wide frequency range rather than using a narrow bandwidth like traditional AM and FM radios, spread spectrum radios can better share the available radio bandwidth.

By combining spread spectrum techniques with variable-power, cellular deployment of nodes, developers can create MANs that enable deployment of hundreds of thousands of units in a small area like a city. When TCP/IP serves as the protocol, each unit can transmit and receive data at 64 Kbps, supporting both mobile and stationary wireless Internet connections. Of course, some of the nodes must connect to an Internet backbone to tie the wireless network to the greater Internet.

Spread spectrum radios with interfaces and software to support TCP/IP start in the $1,500 to $2,500 price range. Like most electronics that move from the laboratory to the mass market, these prices should fall dramatically in the next few years. You can expect to roam and still be connected to the Internet in the near future!

Fiber Optics and Gigabit Networks

A big jump in performance occurs when you leave the limitations of electrons being pushed through copper wire and move to photons pumping through fiber-optics cable. Light travels at much higher frequencies and enables much higher signal bandwidths than electrical or microwave signals. Optical transmission is more reliable and less error-prone because it is not susceptible to interference from electromagnetic radiation. Fiber optics also offer much lower attenuation rates and can run in longer lengths before a repeater is required.

T3 was the first commercial service that used fiber optics for WANs. T3 supports 45 Mbps, which is very low performance for fiber. The main advantage of T3 is its availability—the existing classes of routers can support T3. Internet connections based on T3 run in the $26,000 per month price range and require router hardware in the $50,000 to $150,000 range. But T3 is really a stopgap until the phone companies deploy SONET.

Synchronous optical network (SONET) is the international standard for a synchronous digital hierarchy (SDH) where speeds are denoted as multiples of 51.84 Mbps.

Data Rate (Mbps)	Synchronous Optical Carrier Level Designation	Transport Signal Designation	CCIT Designation
51.84	OC-1	STS-1	—
155.52	OC-3	STS-3	STM-1
622.08	OC-12	STS-12	STM-4
1,244.16	OC-24	STS-24	STM-8
2,488.32	OC-48	STS-48	STM-16

Now this is high bandwidth! The phone companies plan to use this technology to merge voice, data, and variable resolution video onto one network. SONET is designed to encapsulate all this traffic into a common package called *cells*. The standard expected to be used throughout the world is called *asynchronous transfer mode* (ATM), as described in the following section, "Packet Services."

Commercial OC-3 ATM services have been announced by some of the Inter Exchange Carriers such as Sprint, AT&T, MCI, and Willtel. Gigabit networks are available only in some experimental testbeds that are cooperative undertakings between government and private industry groups. The U.S. government is coordinating many of these testbeds under the High Performance Computing and Communications (HPCC) Program. Most of the $1 billion annual funding is going into supercomputer research, but about 15 percent is going into gigabit network research.

Many experts believe that the NSFnet (National Science Foundation network) backbone will be replaced by a gigabit network (or at least an OC-12 network) in the next year or so as part of the National Research and Education Network (NREN) project sponsored by the NSF. The network is supposed to connect only supercomputers, but the contract has a loophole that enables the contractor to sell excess capacity to the open market.

In the meantime, the phone and cable companies plan to spend over $100 billion on laying a fiber-optic infrastructure over the next decade or so, replacing the copper twisted-pair and coaxial cables that go into our homes and businesses. An incredible amount of fiber is already deployed, much of it still *dark* (that is, not connected to any light sources).

> **NOTE**
>
> When companies lay cable or fiber, they put down many more strands than they plan to use for quite a while because the cost of digging is much higher than the cable itself. Currently, court battles are occurring to force the phone companies to rent out this *dark* fiber at cost plus profit, which is much lower than what a phone company can sell *light* fiber bundled with a service. You can expect some areas to have a glut of fiber bandwidth in the near future.

Packet Services

So far, this chapter has primarily discussed the physical link needed to connect computers and LANs to the Internet. IP, the protocol used by the Internet, requires a lower-level protocol that enables it to ride on the physical link. On Ethernet, the protocol is called the media access control (MAC) layer. Physical links such as POTS, dedicated 56, ISDN, and T1 usually use the Serial Line Internet Protocol (SLIP) or the more modern Point to Point Protocol (PPP). SLIP and PPP were developed by the Internet community through the Internet Engineering Task Force (IETF), which uses a consensus-based, experimental model for setting standards that produces very practical and effective standards with rapid evolution.

The telecom industry creates standards using a very large and formal international committee mechanism. This process, which tends to take a very long time to create and deploy standards, is starting to change as the two worlds collide and intermix, as you can see in the rapidity of ATM deployment.

The first packet-style service offered by phone companies was X.25, which charged on an expensive per-kilobyte basis and had a protocol only an international committee could like. X.25 is not a very good carrier of IP because IP is a very lightweight protocol. IP has just enough information to say where it's coming from, where it's going, what type packet it is, and how big it is. The IP layer doesn't worry about error detection, correction, or recovery. IP has no built-in handshaking, link negotiation, or packet ordering. Upper layers such as TCP handle all these issues, but only if required. Thus, only those applications that require extra overhead for such services carry that burden.

X.25 embeds a very complicated error-handling and handshaking mechanism into the protocol. This mechanism makes the protocol unwieldy for many applications because the overhead takes up so much of the communications channel instead of just moving bits. Transporting IP over X.25 is possible, but is generally avoided because the utilization of a communications channel such as dedicated 56 or T1 is very poor compared to other transport protocols.

In many cases, you gain an advantage using an underlying packet mechanism to transport IP from your computer or LAN to an Internet provider rather than having a direct point-to-point connection. Packet services enable you to establish a point-to-point link between yourself and the nearest POP for the packet service (such as an Internet provider, a local phone company, or a long-distance phone company). Many new packet services enable you to pay a flat fee that is not distance or usage sensitive, making your connection to your Internet provider less expensive.

Over the last few years, we have seen an onslaught of new WAN services that are much better tuned to support IP than X.25. These services include frame relay, switched multi-megabyte digital services (SMDS), asynchronous transfer mode (ATM), and even wide area Ethernet. Most of these WANs ride on top of fiber-optic physical links.

Both frame relay and SMDS now are offered by most LECs and some IECs. Physical links that carry frame relay and SMDS include dedicated 56, ISDN, and T1. SMDS also runs on T3. These services are priced so that you pay a flat fee—in some cases, you can pay for a committed rate. *Committed rate* means that you pay only for a portion of the bandwidth of the link. The provider guarantees that you get only what you pay for. However, if the network is not congested, you can use the extra headroom of the link and not pay any extra. For example, if you can use a T1 for the physical link, you may choose to sign up for a committed rate of 56 Kbps. But because the network is frequently not congested, you can use the full 1.54 Mbps of the link!

ATM is a cell relay protocol and is different from frame relay and SMDS in that ATM has small, fixed-size cells. The cell size of 53 bytes (5 bytes for control and 48 bytes for data) was a compromise between the United States and European communities. Europe wanted a very small 16-byte data cell to optimize for voice. The United States realized that data requires a larger cell size and asked for 128-byte cells. The international committee compromised in what may turn out to be an unfortunate 53-byte cell. The small size means that the cell has about a 10 percent overhead at minimum, which is the concern of the folks making the routers, switches, and networks.

ATM is coming on like a locomotive compared to most telco standards. Just a few years ago, ATM was a proposal; today most of the required standards are in place, hardware and services are commercially available, and customers are starting to use ATM. For the next couple of years, only large corporate and government networks will use ATM. But we can expect ATM to come down in price rapidly and eventually become the underlying fabric for the Internet as well as telephone and mass market video distribution.

NOTE

Today, the choices for connecting to the Internet are somewhat limited. ISDN is the most affordable higher-speed service, delivering up to 128 Kbps without compression at costs not much greater than POTS. But just around the corner are lots of new technologies bringing bandwidths that are literally orders of magnitude faster than today's Internet backbone.

Like the incredible increases in CPU power and memory capacity of computers over the last decade, the rapid growth in low-cost, high-bandwidth connectivity will usher in new possibilities you can barely imagine now. Whole new markets, products, and technologies will arise. Now is the time to start paddling and get ready to catch the wave!

Available Services

The only vendors known to offer ISDN at the time of publication are these:

Internex Information Services, Inc.
Voice:	415-473-3060
Fax:	415-473-3062
E-mail:	info@internex.net
FTP:	ftp://ftp.internex.net:/pub/internex
Gopher:	gopher.internex.net
Mosaic/WWW:	http://www.internex.net

Colorado SuperNet
Voice:	303-273-3471
Fax:	303-273-3475
E-mail:	info@csn.org
FTP:	ftp://csn.org/CSN/reports/DialinInfo.txt

OARnet
Voice:	614-292-8100
E-mail:	nic@oar.net
FTP:	ftp://ftp.oar.net
Gopher:	gopher://gopher.oar.net

Santa Cruz Community Internet
Voice:	408-457-5050
E-mail:	info@scruz.net
FTP:	ftp://ftp.scruz.net:/pub/datasheet

Performance System International, Inc.
Voice: 703-904-4100
Fax: 703-904-4200
E-mail: `info@psi.com`
FTP: `ftp://ftp.psi.com:/info/uupsi-man.ascii`

Nuance Network Services
Voice: 205-533-4296
E-mail: `staff@nuance.com`

Internet Sources

The following are some of my favorite sources of information on the subjects touched on in this chapter. Use them as starting points to find out more. They can lead you to rich veins of information within the Internet.

Electronic Frontier Foundation

The Electronic Frontier Foundation has led the way to ensure that the national information highway can be built for all to access. EFF's founder, Mitch Kapor (also a founder of Lotus), was one of the early advocates of using ISDN to get Internet into our homes and businesses. EFF has produced several papers on ISDN and Open Networks in general. You can FTP the EFF at `ftp://ftp.eff.org:/pub/EFF/Policy/Open_Platform`, or access it by WWW at `http://www.eff.org`.

FAQs (Frequently Asked Questions)

ISDN: `rtfm.mit.edu`
                   `pub/usenet-by-group/comp.dcom.isdn/`
                   `comp.dcom.isdn_Frequently_Asked_Questions`
ATM/SMDS: `rtfm.mit.edu`
                   `pub/usenet-by-group/comp.dcom.cell-relay/comp.dcom.cell-relay` (FAQ: ATM, SMDS, and related technologies)
Telecom Acronyms: `lcs.mit.edu`
                   `telecom-archives/glossaries/*`
Telecom FAQ: `lcs.mit.edu`
                   `telecom-archives/new-readers/frequently.asked.question`
MBone: `venera.isi.edu`
                   `mbone/faq.txt`

Usenet Newsgroups

This list contains some of the key newsgroups:

```
comp.dcom.isdn
comp.org.eff.news (ATM/SMDS)
comp.org.eff.talk (Electronic Frontier Foundation)
```

Mailing Lists

You can access mailing lists by sending an e-mail message to the address specified in each of the following sections. Your e-mail inbox will be filled with messages on the subjects described.

Telecom Digest

This service contains technical discussions of telephones, modems, and data communications. It is maintained by Patrick Townson.

```
telecom@eecs.nwu.edu          (items for publication)
telecom@bu-cs.bu.edu          (alternate for preceding address)
telecom-request@eecs.nwu.edu  (address changes, maintenance)
ptownson@eecs.nwu.edu         (personal mail to maintainer)
```

ISDN Discussion List 1

This list contains primarily technical discussions of ISDN in the U.S. Send submissions to the list to the following address:

```
ISDN@List.Prime.COM
```

If you want to cancel your subscription, send e-mail to this address:

```
ISDN-Cancel@List.Prime.COM
```

To start a subscription, send e-mail to this address:

```
ISDN-Subscribe@List.Prime.COM
```

Send all other administrative correspondence to the following site:

```
ISDN-Request@List.Prime.COM
```

The Acting List Coordinator can be contacted at this address:

```
NetAdmin@Relay.Prime.COM
```

ISDN Discussion List 2

This list covers all aspects specific to ISDN (protocols, services, applications, experiences, status, coverage, and implementations). The discussion includes both data and voice, and is open for broadband-ISDN and other related issues. This list is more international than the first ISDN list and is a pure mail exploder. Its Internet address is as follows:

```
isdn@teknologi.agderforskning.no
```

An archive of the list is available by anonymous FTP to the following address:

```
ugle.unit.no, file archives/isdn
```

List coordinator, Per Sigmond, is available at this address:

```
Per.Sigmond@teknologi.agderforskning.no
```

Current Cites

Current Cites is a monthly publication of Information Systems Instruction and Support—*The Library*, The University of California, Berkeley. Contributors include Teri Rinne, David Rez, Vivienne Roumani, Mark Takaro, and Roy Tennant.

Over 30 journals in library and information technology are scanned for selected articles on these subjects: optical disk technologies, computer networks and networking, information transfer, expert systems and artificial intelligence, electronic publishing, and hypermedia and multimedia. Brief annotations accompany the citations.

Direct subscriptions also are available free of charge by sending a request with the message sub cites <*your name*> to the following address:

```
listserv@library.berkeley.edu
```

An archive is available from FTP at this address:

```
ftp://ftp.lib.berkeley.edu/pub/Current.Cites
```

National Research and Education Network Discussion

Participate in freewheeling unmoderated discussions on the NREN/NII. To subscribe, send e-mail to this address:

```
nren-discuss-request@psi.com
```

To post, send e-mail to this address:

```
nren-discuss@psi.com
```

Commercialization/Privatization of the Internet Discussion

This discussion is mostly about who will fund, pay for, and own the Internet, and other economic/political issues. Sometimes, the discussion gets into architectural issues.

To subscribe, send e-mail to this address:

```
com-priv-request@psi.com
```

To post, send e-mail to this address:

```
com-priv@psi.com
```

Other Sources

National ISDN Users Forum
National Institute of Standards and Technology
Building 223, Room B364
Gaithersburg, MD 20899
Voice: 301-975-2937
Fax: 301-926-9675
BBS: 301-869-7281

Bellcore
Karen E. FitzGerald, Director ISDN Product Management
445 South Street MRE 2G-141
PO Box 1910
Morristown, NJ 07962-1910
Voice: 201-829-4947
Fax: 201-829-2632

REFERENCE WORKS

AT&T Bell Laboratories, *Engineering and Operations in the Bell System*, ISBN 0-932764-04-5.

Heldan, Robert K., *Future Telecommunications*, ISBN 0-07-028039-8, McGraw-Hill, Inc.

Lynch, Daniel C. and Rose, Marshall T. (editors), *Internet System Handbook*, ISBN 0-201-56741-5, Addison-Wesley Publishing Co.

Partridge, Craig, *Gigabit Networking*, ISBN 0-201-56333-9, Addison-Wesley Publishing Co.

Powers, Jr., John T. and Stair II, Henry H., *Megabit Data Communications: A Guide for Professionals*, ISBN 0-13-573569-6, Prentice-Hall, Inc.

Stallings, William, *ISDN: An Introduction*, ISBN 0-02-415471-7, Macmillan Publishing Company.

U.S. Office of Technology Assessment, *Advanced Network Technology—Background Paper*, S/N 052-003-01326-6, U.S. Superintendent of Documents.

Managing Internet Security

11

by Tom Caldwell

With additional Internet connections being added every day, the management of any Internet site should be concerned with security issues. No site that is connected has absolutely foolproof security, but with the proper knowledge and education, an adequate security level can be maintained to suit the requirements of any organization.

This chapter explains many of the primary issues surrounding Internet security. It is designed to prepare the beginning site administrator or help managers understand system security issues that should be included in the Internet site installation.

Connection to the Internet provides a vast collection of information tools to the corporate or educational user. But for every positive use of the Internet's tools, there is a dark side where people plot to maliciously misuse services. Maintaining the proper level of security at your site can help ensure that people will gain the most from this vast resource of information technology. The following pages explain some basic concepts, tools, and organizational skills needed to maintain various levels of security on the Internet computer resource. These skills can be the "ounce of prevention" needed to guard against a security-related catastrophe in your organization.

Too Much Paranoia

Most popular Usenet newsgroups post a document called a *FAQ* (short for Frequently Asked Questions). Recently, there was such a posting in the newsgroup comp.security.misc. The article mentions that implementing computer security can turn ordinary people into rampaging paranoids.

Often, after a system break-in, everybody wants to jump on the bandwagon of system security. People who may be bored with their own job want to play the exciting game of securing the castle from the bad guys. This becomes even worse when the system administrator goes overboard and loses focus of the primary reason why the computer is connected to the Internet.

Unfortunately, such extreme paranoia often ends up rendering the computer overly restrictive and difficult to use. The FAQ article stated that one university system administrator banned the head of a department from the college mainframe for using a restricted network utility. In the end, the system administrator had a difficult task justifying his implementation of computer security to an unsympathetic department committee.

People can take computer security too far and get caught up in the excitement or knowledge that they may be doing battle with a movie-like computer monster. They forget that the computer is attached to the Internet to provide a positive support service and a competitive advantage to the organization. There must be a balance between responsibly managing the security of an Internet system and providing a system that is easy to use from the network user's standpoint.

I enjoy living in a city where the presence of security is almost hidden from view. When I walk the streets, I don't see barbed wire and bars on every window. I use city services—such as the buses, pay phones, outdoor cafes, and highways—free of hassle. Only once in a while do I see a firearm or interact with the police to ensure that my activities and possessions remain "safe."

My attitude about computer security is the same. When a group of people use the Internet, they want to freely enjoy accessing the resources of the great network. As they access and move information around the globe, they do not want to be hampered by productive services that have been turned off, or have to perform easy tasks in a way that needs pages of notes to accomplish, or endure daily badgering from the system administrators about security.

Remember that beginning computer users usually are afraid their ignorance will lead to trouble. If your Internet environment maintains an attitude of paranoia, you may be hampering productivity and restricting the education the network can provide. An effective environment should encourage people to take advantage of network technology but still ensure a responsibility to maintain the security of the organization's environment and the protection of user files.

Should Your Computer Be on the Internet?

Some sites contain classified or highly confidential information. Computers that contain this level of information should not be on the Internet at all. For those sites, highly advanced security mechanisms should be in place and a great effort should be made to secure the data. You should consider your site sensitive if any of the following conditions apply:

- You process data that the government considers sensitive.
- You process financial transactions in which a single transaction can exceed $25,000 or the total transactions exceed $2.5 million.
- You process data whose release time is tightly controlled and whose early release could provide significant financial advantage—or disadvantage.
- The computer supports a life-critical processing task.
- Your organization has enemies with a history of terrorism or violent protests.
- The data on your computer contains trade secret information that would be of direct value to a competitor. This is important in a corporate environment. Make sure that the computer that contains the "family jewels" does not have connectivity with the Internet. Make sure that the site security policy distributed to new account users explicitly states that they must not keep competitive information on the Internet firewall or on any computer connected to the Internet.

Level of Security

One of the tasks of securing a system is to define a security philosophy or plan. This is commonly referred to as a *site security policy*.

A smart businessperson always creates a business plan before venturing into an investment. When attaching a computer to the Internet, it is prudent to know how you will handle network security. This action is part of being responsible and well organized.

The security policy should include how you plan to prevent break-ins, detect break-ins, and educate users not to blindly contribute to break-ins by opening security holes on your computer.

When creating a policy, you should understand the following:

- The system you are protecting
- Why it needs protection
- The value of what is protected
- Who is responsible

The site manager should understand what the "appropriate" use of the Internet is and understand what level of performance will be maintained on the system. Before creating your site security policy, be sure to get a copy of RFC 1244 (Request for Comments 1244, available at `ftp://is.internic.net:rfc/rfc1244.txt`). This document is entitled *Site Security Handbook* and outlines exactly what your security policy should cover. The IETF Security Policy Working Group (SPWG) also is working on a set of recommended security policy guidelines for the Internet network.

Cost, Time, and Money

When creating a security policy, the level of security should be planned by estimating the cost of installation and maintenance versus return on investment.

Unless you are part of a very large organization, computer security is probably only one of many responsibilities you have. Generally, security must be implemented so that a single person can be responsible for protecting the organization's assets but can also remain free to perform many other services at the same time.

Time is money and this realization must be figured into the security equation. Checking daily logs, monitoring security programs, and viewing user activity takes a lot of effort and a large amount of time. One of the most expensive parts of maintaining an organization is the payroll expense. Time is expensive and should be used effectively. Some of the tools and concepts mentioned in this chapter can be used to effectively manage the security of a system in a cost-effective manner.

Your security policy also should reflect the computer and network equipment used to maintain the security at your site. Will you create a firewall? How much does a firewall cost to implement? Can your budget afford it? How much time will different types of equipment save you? Is what you are protecting worth the investment? Figure 11.1 compares the cost of various security configurations in terms of cost and value.

FIGURE 11.1.

Security investment strategies (Cost = man-hours + capital expense).

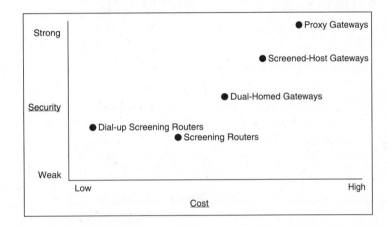

If you are not a network guru or a computer wizard, I recommend setting up a simple firewall and dedicating one computer to providing Internet connectivity.

Most computers that provide Internet networking services run the UNIX operating system. There are many security tools on the Internet to help minimize the time spent managing UNIX security while providing a healthy degree of system security.

Recently, I have been experimenting with the Windows NT Advanced Server. I expect that future implementations of Internet connectivity will include other popular operating systems. Vendors such as Microsoft have built into their software many security mechanisms that greatly enhance site protection from a possible Internet attack. For example, the Windows NT Advanced Server has been designed to conform to government C2 security standards.

Fun versus Secure

When planning a policy design for Internet connectivity, a system manager should have a clear idea of how restrictive the environment will be to users.

Why are you connecting to the Internet in the first place? Probably to provide your user community with a range of services that provide information. The key is to define that range so that users can freely access information without being discouraged by security restraints.

Remember that typical users are unsure of themselves. In light of this, the Internet connection should not be a bad experience. On the other hand, you don't want to leave security doors wide open for an amateur cracker. The whole purpose of this chapter is to help provide the average system manager who is connecting to the Internet some sensible security guidelines.

Who Is There To Be Afraid Of?

One of the first lessons to learn is terminology. For a long time, people have misused the term *hacker* to mean *cracker*. In the Internet community, a *cracker* is a person who maliciously attempts to break into other people's computer systems.

Once a person breaks into a computer, they spend valuable resource dollars (especially if the authorized user pays a monthly bill for the service). Even worse, a cracker typically rearranges the operating system's functionality with back doors, Trojan horses, games, or open security holes for others. The ultimate disaster is when a cracker erases files or disks, cancels programs, or crashes a system. In the PC world, the term *cracker* is used to describe someone who tampers with copy protection software to illegally distribute the program.

The more accepted meaning of the term *hacker* is a person who has expertise in the area of computing and networking. A hacker enjoys digging into how an operating system interoperates with a network and invents methods of expanding the capabilities of a system. Hackers on my systems usually help me find security holes and help keep the operating system tuned so that users benefit. A hacker can become a cracker when the individual crosses an ethical line and uses his or her talents in an illegal or unprofessional manner.

Why People Break In

Rarely do crackers attack systems for monetary gain. Typically, crackers attack as a test of their skills, to gain status with their peers, as a game, or (more commonly), to use your computer as a stepping-stone to break into another computer. Most crackers cover their tracks to make apprehension difficult.

Another possibility is that your competitors may want to break into your system to secure information that would help them succeed against you in the marketplace. This happens very infrequently compared to other reasons.

A possible source of computer break-ins is from employees or ex-employees. With the recent recession and large number of layoffs in the corporate world, a cracker of this type usually carries a grudge. I have heard about ex-employees changing a computer firm's source code enough to ensure that new product releases fail. Because many of these people are amateur crackers who do not spend a great deal of time breaking into computer systems, they typically use an entry point left exposed when they left the company. (This is another important reason to stay organized.) A small degree of prevention and the implementation of some standard security tools can protect your system from harm.

Eugene Spafford, in a paper entitled "Are Computer Hacker Break-Ins Ethical?," presents five false justifications of why people break into computers or create vandalware:

- Information should be free and belong to everyone. The intruder believes there are no boundaries or restraints to prevent people from examining information; thus, there is no need for security.

- To point out computer security problems to a community that may not otherwise notice the security holes.

- To make use of idle machines. Most machines are not used to their full capacity, so an intruder is using extra resources that would otherwise have been wasted.

- The student hacker argument states that system crackers are simply learning how computers operate. By writing worms and viruses, the person is getting an education in a cost-effective manner.

- Crackers are protectors of society (this one seems most popular with European intruders). The crackers are keeping an eye out for "Big Brother" and protecting us from data abuse. Do we really want these malicious individuals "protecting" us from computer monitoring and abusive record keeping?

What People Do When They Break In

Crackers will break in to multiple computers (I have seen more than 10 break-ins during a single episode) to make it difficult to find their point of origin. This activity is known as *connection laundering* in the Internet world.

An example of this is when the cracker logs in to five computers one at a time to perform a malicious stunt on a sixth computer. To track this cracker, the management of all six computers must log the person's activity and turn the logs into a central coordinator like CERT (defined later). This coordinator compares the logs and traces the movements of the cracker through each system.

You can see why it is usually difficult to prove the guilt of a cracker. That doesn't mean it is impossible, because the authorities do catch people and (usually) confiscate their equipment. Most crackers like to boast about their conquests and leave activity trace logs on their local systems as proof of their deeds. It is very important to maintain a system that makes break-ins difficult. If a cracker can't break into your system with a few simple tools, they will likely move to another system.

As discussed later in this chapter, it is very important to maintain user activity logs. You cannot track or detect possible break-ins without adequate activity logs.

If you want to read about an administrator who lured and studied an active cracker at AT&T Bell Laboratories, read an article by Bill Cheswick entitled "An Evening with Berferd, in Which a Cracker Is Lured, Endured, and Studied." Bill and his staff created a "chroot" jail where the cracker unknowingly logged in to a restrictive environment. The staff then watched as the cracker attempted to use an arsenal of cracking tools to gain control of the system. The administrators were able to gain useful information to improve the security of their systems. At the end of their observation, the cracker attempted to erase all the disks on the computer system. Most occurrences of an Internet related break-in are not catastrophic and are usually done as a challenge or a game.

How People Break In

Now that you've learned about who breaks into a computer, why people break into computers, and what they do once they are in, it is time to discuss how people break into computers.

To understand how people break in, you must understand the following aspects of your system:

- The network connection
- The network environment
- The types of services you offer
- How to protect yourself from disaster
- Computer passwords
- The design of your defense system
- Types of attacks to expect
- Security tools available
- How educated users are when it comes to security

This sounds like a large amount of information to cover. Yet a very basic understanding of these topics can help you protect computers from an outside threat on the Internet.

Types of Connections to the Internet

One of the key elements of computer security is understanding the connection to the Internet. The more you understand this link, the greater success you will have with security tools. Internet links typically range from low-cost dial-up solutions to higher-cost leased lines. Their functionality ranges from user-to-LAN connectivity to LAN-to-LAN connectivity. As you know, part of your investment cost is the associated cost of the Internet link. Each of the links described in the following sections affects the amount of time you spend monitoring security.

> **NOTE**
>
> For more detail on the different types of Internet connections, see Chapter 7, "Finding Access as a User," and Chapter 8, "Finding Access as an Organization."

Low-Cost Connectivity

The lowest cost Internet connection is when you have PC accounts on an Internet computer and leave the security to someone else. Most Internet service providers sell you an account on their Internet computer you can use for Internet connectivity.

Typically, the user dials in using a PC modem and a communications software package. This is one of the best ways to find out whether the Internet is useful to your organization without making a large initial investment. The only security you need to implement here is to teach users about maintaining secure passwords and to make sure that they don't abandon the account. A cracker typically looks for an account that is seldom or never logged on to. In that way, there is less chance the authorized account user will detect and report a break-in.

An even lower-cost method of using Internet electronic mail is to get a CompuServe or America Online account for your computer users. Again, sensible password security should be demonstrated by the person who uses the account.

A low-cost purchased account should never be shared by multiple users. This is a security gap that is taken advantage of by many crackers. When a group of people want joint access to the Internet network, they should have separate accounts. If an intruder breaks in and runs your bill up into the thousands of dollars, you want to go to one responsible person to trace account activity. When multiple people share an account, the password is rarely changed and is typically shared publicly. There have been cases in which people allow children or friends to use their accounts—thus creating more opportunity for security to be breached and operators to open up security holes on the system.

Modem and Terminal Server Security

If you are setting up Internet access using a bank of modems or terminal servers, you should take some precautions. Misconfigured hardware easily creates an open security door for an intruder. Make sure that the following items are checked before allowing people to use the modem equipment:

- If a user who has dialed up to a modem hangs up, the system should log them out.
- If a user logs off, the modem should disconnect the phone call and hang up the modem.

- If the connection from the terminal server to the system is disconnected, the system should log off.

- If the terminal server is connected to a modem and the user hangs up, the terminal server should signal the system so that the account is logged off.

You should check the terminal server manuals, system manuals, and modem manuals for the proper configuration of each device.

A example of a security enhancement to dial-up modems is a security box. SecureID from Security Dynamics in Cambridge, MA, sells such a box. The system gives each user a credit card-sized device that electronically displays a generated personal identification number (PIN). The remote user must use this PIN number, along with a password, to log in to the security box and then in to the computer system. The security box changes the PIN numbers at regular intervals so that the device must be present at login time.

Dial-Up IP

When the organization has enough people who desire access to the Internet, or when the information obtained from the Internet is very large in size, a faster and more efficient link can be used.

The latest addition to many Internet service provider connections has been the dial-up router connection. This provides a link between your network and the Internet network (an arrangement commonly referred to as *LAN-to-LAN connectivity*) using the public phone lines. In this case, your local network is now part of the ever-expanding Internet network. Your users have direct access to the Internet from local computers and, conversely, the Internet community has access to your local computers.

Very cheap security solutions include the installation of a SLIP connection. SLIP is an implementation of TCP/IP, which operates over a serial line. The SLIP connection can provide a network link between two computers using modems and ordinary phone lines. One modem dials another, and the network connection takes place.

After the birth of SLIP came a more advanced solution called Point-to-Point Protocol (PPP). A PPP connection is more efficient and provides security through the enhancement of CHAP (Challenge Handshake Authentication Protocol). The use of CHAP requires a three-way handshake between the dial-up network devices using encrypted passwords. These passwords are changed using a hashing function each time the devices connect. This makes it virtually impossible for an intruder to gain access through a dial-up-IP connection into your network.

Typically, in a dial-up-IP solution, a dial-up router is used to provide the connectivity. The router is a device that passes information packets between the segment of the Internet network to which you are connected and your local network. The Internet information could be a file transfer, remote login, Gopher information, or many of the other information tools available. The router can be programmed to support your security philosophy and discourage break-ins. The best routers for Internet connectivity provide a high degree of filtering and logging and enable you to control when the connection can be made.

Packet filtering is the ability of the router to selectively pass only the packets you specify into or out of your local network. The selection process can be based on host computers, network segments, or service types. In other words, you can limit the hosts who talk to the Internet, what internal networks communicate with the Internet, and what tools can be used on the Internet connection.

A dial-up router provides a high degree of filtering. The filtering can be by host, network, or protocol. If your security philosophy wants to allow only FTP (file transfer), Gopher, and the WWW and wants to disallow remote logins from the Internet, appropriate filters can provide this protection.

The modem on the dial-up router can be set to allow Internet connectivity only during certain hours or specific days. Most crackers conduct break-ins during evenings or weekends to lessen the chances of someone detecting their activity.

If your router is set to allow Internet connectivity only during normal business hours, most Internet crackers will not be interested in your system. Employees or ex-employees usually work during business hours and may not be able to become "midnight crackers" if you block access during the evenings or weekends. Again, such filtering should match your security philosophy *and* your target of service functionality (and availability) to best suit your organizational needs.

Connections that Cost More: Leased Lines

When your Internet traffic needs grow, you can justify the cost of a leased line. Leased lines can range from a 56 Kbps line up to higher speeds. What you choose depends purely on your pocketbook. This type of connection uses a router much like the dial-up connection does. However, instead of there being "bandwidth on demand," as is so in the dial-up solution, the leased line provides a constant connection to the Internet by using a direct permanent line between you and the Internet service provider.

A popular router used for a leased-line Internet solution is the cisco router. It has the same filtering capabilities as the dial-up router, although you cannot maintain the hours of operation as you can with the dial-up line. The cracker usually has access to your computers at a more acceptable speed than the dial-up solution. It is common for a site directly connected to the Internet to extend security beyond the filtering on the router by designing some sort of advanced firewall system.

Levels of Security

An adequate level of security can be maintained by combining knowledge of computer security issues, the security features a vendor can provide on networking equipment, public domain security software, and adequate user education. What level of security is needed? That should be outlined in your security policy.

Campus Environment

In many universities, all networks have open access to the Internet. In an atmosphere of open learning, any user can directly use the resources of the Internet without the hindrances of security mechanisms that may inhibit network services.

Many corporations may want to provide Internet tools, such as FTP, Gopher, WAIS, and the WWW on the desktop workstation. This means that every network in the corporate environment may be left open to the risk of attack. The corporation's Internet security policy must include a mechanism to protect certain sensitive hosts from being open to attack.

The benefit of such an arrangement is increased productivity by letting users conveniently access Internet resources from a highly productive Macintosh or PC. Many users may not use the Internet if you require them to log in to a single Internet-connected host to access Internet information, especially if the procedure makes them learn about the complicated UNIX environment.

Router Filtering

Blindly attaching your local area network to the Internet without some way of protecting hosts that store competitive or sensitive information is an open invitation for security problems.

One of the simplest protection methods is to ensure that your router to the Internet supports filtering. Such routers are called *screening routers*. Many popular routers support packet filtering at the host level, network level, and service (protocol) level. Information is carried on the Internet network in various size packets. Each information packet carries with it a description of the source, destination, and service type (login, mail, and so forth), which enables routers to selectively filter unwanted data.

Routers can be configured to prohibit traffic from going from the Internet to an internal host or internal network subnet (an internal network can be divided into management pieces called *subnets*). Routers also can be configured to prohibit traffic that participates in dangerous services such as tFTP (trivial file transfer without passwords) and lpd (remote printing).

An example of the intelligent use of filters is to set up a filter to allow only electronic mail to reach one host on your local network. From there, the specified host can distribute the mail internally, thus reducing the number of hosts that have e-mail contact with the Internet. The famous Internet worm exploited a bug in the `sendmail` e-mail program and used it to gain access to many hosts throughout the Internet. Router filtering is one method of reducing the security risk at your facility.

Firewalls

Firewalls tend to be a compromise between ease of use and security. The local network that is available to the Internet network can be considered the "zone of risk." Without a firewall, your entire local network becomes a zone of risk.

A *firewall* reduces your zone of risk by defining a smaller area that is accessible to the Internet. By defining a smaller zone of risk, you reduce the area you need to cover to detect an Internet intruder. There are many configurations of firewalls using various components and configurations. By using only a screening router (as mentioned in the preceding section), you set up a simple firewall that reduces the area you have to worry about for security purposes.

Two basic approaches exist. The first is to design a firewall to prohibit any service that is not explicitly permitted through the Internet connection. If you don't tell your users that a service is available, turn it off.

The second approach is just the opposite. It involves designing a firewall where all services not explicitly prohibited are permitted. The difference is that, in the first case, the firewall is designed to block everything and services are enabled one by one after careful risk assessment. In the second case, the administrator must plot out the weak points in security and then disable those services that are too risky to leave available. The users often perceive the first approach as constricting and view the firewall as a hindrance to productivity. The second approach allows the users more freedom to use the Internet resources—and gives them more freedom to create security holes in your firewall configuration.

Privacy-Enhanced Electronic Mail

Recent efforts have been made to increase the security of Internet electronic mail. The enhancements center around the transparent encryption of the mail message. Using this method, electronic mail would be able to move around the Internet; servers en route to the message's destination could not read their contents.

In the present form of electronic mail (using the SMTP protocol), most mail messages are text and can be read by anyone who captures them. A growing issue concerning Internet privacy is the ethical concern of system administrators reading electronic mail to detect security infractions.

What Is the Internet to You?

Most Internet services use well-known ports to communicate. A system administrator can se-lect which services to leave on and which to turn off through various mechanisms that limit port access.

When an organization asks for a connection to the Internet, it usually has a basic idea what it wants the connection for. It may be to provide file transfer (FTP) service to a specific user base, enable members to communicate with professional peers (e-mail), or enable the organization to participate in technical discussions (Usenet news, mailing lists).

A wealth of information is also provided by Gopher, the WWW, and WAIS. Many online database systems are available through the Internet using the remote login program, Telnet. Your Internet security policy should state which services and functionality the connection will provide. I recommend turning off any other service you do not want to offer. These "other" services can open the door of opportunity for an intruder.

Turn Off Dangerous Services

Many well-known security organizations recommend that some of your services be filtered on your Internet router. These services are considered dangerous and do not have to be operated on the Internet. It is recommended that the following list of services be filtered:

- DNS zone transfers—socket 53. Only your secondary name server needs to receive these.
- tFTPd—socket 69. Trivial file transfer program. Although your organization may want to use this program locally, it should not be used on the Internet. This is a great mechanism for a cracker to use to obtain your password file. It does not require a password and, in some broken versions, allows access to the entire system.
- link—socket 87. Commonly used by intruders to break into systems.
- SunRPC & NFS—sockets 111 and 2049. The Internet should not be used to remote mount file systems.
- BSD UNIX r commands—sockets 512, 513, and 514. The programs rsh, rcp, and rlogin are dangerous—especially if an .rhosts file is present.
- lpd—socket 515. Remote printing is not very common over an Internet connection.
- uucpd—socket 540. This is UUCP (UNIX to UNIX Copy Program), which was typically used as a network before the Internet. This version operates over the Internet rather than using an earlier serial link. Be very careful when setting up UUCP. It is common to make a mistake and open up security holes. If you are not using UUCP, turn it off.

- openwindows—socket 2000. The Internet should not be used to run a remote windowing program.
- X Window—socket 6000+. Users should not be significantly increasing traffic on the Internet by running remote windows. Many major Internet routers do not let X Window packets through. There are many security holes surrounding the X Window system that can affect the security of the entire system.

System administrators should know what services they want to offer through the Internet. Any other service should be filtered through the router. You can obtain a list of the services you want by looking in the assigned numbers FAQ: `is.internic.net:rfc/rfc1700.txt`.

Don't Allow .rhost Files

Many users may keep a file named `.rhosts` in their home directories. This file lists "trusted" users from other systems that are allowed to log in to the account without a password. It also allows remote commands like `rsh` and `rcp` to be operated without a password.

The `rsh` command enables a remote person to issue a command without logging in. The `rcp` command enables a person to copy a file without ever logging in to the system. My recommendation is that `.rhosts` files are dangerous and should not be allowed on your Internet system. Run a nightly program that erases these files from your user accounts. You can send the users an automated message stating that the system security policy does not allow the `.rhost` file. Removing these files can anger your users, but every system administrator has to make that choice.

The exception may be the root account (remote execution may be required for network backups). But many vendor-supplied backup mechanisms have security workarounds so that you do not even need a root-owned `.rhost` file.

Don't Allow NFS Mounts

You can use the `showmount` command to show remote mounted file systems on a file server. Generally, on a UNIX system, the `/etc/exports` file lists the systems allowed to remote mount your file system.

It is dangerous to let a computer on the Internet be a file server for other systems. You should at least filter out NFS packets on your Internet router, but a better move is to turn off NFS completely on your Internet computer system. Many dangerous security holes surround access to your file systems.

Trusted Hosts

Trusted hosts are usually other computer systems that are thought of as secure and need a smaller degree of security when accessing your system. The list is commonly found in a file named /etc/hosts.equiv on a UNIX system. Trusted hosts can access services such as remote printing and file sharing without requiring passwords or security constraints. Be very careful about which hosts are trusted on the system connected to the Internet network.

NIS and Yellow Pages

The NIS (Network Information System, formerly called Yellow Pages) is a network database shared by multiple computers.

Typically, there is an NIS server and NIS clients. The NIS server contains information about accounts, passwords, remote file sharing, trusted hosts, and other important security information. In the past, many security bugs were found in the NIS system (these bugs are fixed in more recent versions of the database system).

Before using NIS on a network connected to the Internet, make sure that you study how each client and server file should be set up. It is very easy to accidentally create a large security hole just by leaving the default NIS configuration active or by mistyping a line in an operating system configuration file.

OS Bugs/Software Bugs

Software security holes provide a common entry point for Internet intruders. The problem resides in poorly written programs distributed with the operating system. These programs allow a user to operate them for reasons other than their original purpose.

One of the most publicized examples of a software bug has been the sendmail debug security hole. The Internet worm used it to exploit systems throughout the entire Internet network. The Internet worm also took advantage of a bug in the fingerd (finger daemon) program.

With every new release of an operating system, new security holes are created. The best way to close up these holes is to subscribe to an active security mailing list so that you will be notified immediately each time a new hole is found. If you maintain an older system, check the FTP archives at cert.org to get a list of discovered security holes in various operating systems.

Be Smart

Backups should be part of every well-run operation. If you are connected to the Internet, make sure that you run backups on a regular basis.

If an intruder breaks into a system, he or she may remove or change files. Once the break-in is detected, a good backup can help you clean up the system and put things back in order. Once, I watched someone break into a computer and change a user's account during the evening. After I locked the intruder out, I was able to quickly restore the account using backups. The next morning, the regular account user was not affected and resumed work not knowing that his account had been changed the night before (although I did have a talk with him later about creating a more secure password and keeping an eye out for peculiar things in his account).

Protect Thy Password File

One of the most vulnerable places on a computer system is the password file—typically named /etc/passwd on a UNIX operating system. The password file is the first point of attack. It has been found that more than 80 percent of all computer attacks from outside of networked systems are based on exploitation of weak passwords. A cracker can use a variety of techniques to access your password file. For a number of years, there was a security bug in the sendmail program (a program used to manage the e-mail system on a computer). A cracker could attach to the e-mail port of a computer, turn on debug mode, and then issue a command like this one:

```
mail user@anywhere.com < /etc/passwd
```

The e-mail system would then mail your password file to the cracker. Other security holes like this one presented similar access to the password file. Most well-known bugs have been fixed, and it is important that you have these fixes installed. Many of them have been fixed in newer releases of operating systems provided by vendors.

Once the cracker has your password file, he or she uses a program like CRACK and a dictionary of common passwords to try and guess your password. To write his paper "Foiling the Cracker: A Survey of, and Improvements to, Password Security," Daniel Kline collected nearly 15,000 account entries to test for "easy-to-guess passwords." He found that 21 percent of all passwords had been broken by the first week of testing. In the end, he could crack about 25 percent of the passwords. The scariest thing is that it took him only 15 minutes to crack 386 passwords (2.7 percent). I have never managed a system for which the password file was foolproof. On a regular basis, I run my own version of CRACK against my system password files and can usually break into at least one account on every system. One password is all a cracker needs to access your computer system.

Another area in which a smart system administrator must be organized is accounts. An account should always have a password. I have seen some engineers using accounts without passwords to make it easier to share group data between users. Having such a password system on the Internet (or any network) is an open invitation for an intruder to gain access to information.

An account should have an expiration date. Accounts that are no longer in use are the best targets for system intruders. Once crackers break into an unused account, they can work with a smaller chance of being detected. Placing expiration dates on accounts ensures that the accounts are removed in a timely manner when they are no longer needed.

Guest accounts are a good way to lower the level of security on a system. Having accounts for which you cannot link account responsibility to a single person is dangerous. You will never know whether there is a cracker on your system or a guest is exploring. Any guest account should have a unique name and password solely restricted to that person. Each guest should be assigned their own account with an expiration date. When the account expires, the account should be closed unless it is specifically requested to be reopened. Group accounts should be avoided on the Internet system. Again, not having a link of responsibility to a single person makes it difficult to monitor the account activity of a potential intruder.

Password Protection

One way of protecting your password file is by using a shadow password file. If you turn on the C2 security option offered under SunOS, you can see how a shadow password file is used. The encrypted password is stored in a separate secure location from the other password information. The /etc/passwd file simply stores a place holder entry. The examples below show the difference between a regular password file and one using a shadow password mechanism.

Here is a sample password file /etc/passwd (readable by all users):

```
mike:CNjlEZIADBdP6:145:17817:Mike Allison:/home2/mike:/bin/csh
jason:NZErd3xZxPkpLE:5001:20:Jason Hendrix:/home/jason:/bin/csh
caldwell:XDghFYD:350:20:Tom Caldwell:/home2/caldwell:/bin/csh
```

A sample password file with shadowing for /etc/passwd (readable by all users):

```
mike::145:17817:Mike Allison:/home2/mike:/bin/csh
jason::5001:20:Jason Hendrix:/home/jason:/bin/csh
caldwell::350:20:Tom Caldwell:/home2/caldwell:/bin/csh
```

A sample shadow password file (not readable by any user except the root):

```
mike:CNjlEZIADBdP6:6445
jason:NZErd3xZxPkpLE:6445
caldwell:XDghFYD:6445
```

By using the shadow password file, crackers have a much harder time getting to the information needed to guess passwords. They must find another way to break into your system and must spend more time and effort doing it.

User Education

People who use easy-to-guess passwords provide an open door to the cracker. Passwords should not be written down on paper or kept in desk drawers. Proper password education should be included in a site security policy that all users are issued when they receive accounts. The following password information should be included in such a site security policy.

Password Dos and Don'ts:

- **Joes.** A *Joe* is an account in which the user name is identical to the password. In the mid-1980s, it was found that almost every machine had at least one Joe account on it. Joe accounts are great for crackers because the password is easy to guess and easy to remember. Do not use a password that is your user name in reverse, capitalized, doubled, and so on.

- **Don't use the same password on every machine.** This practice may be hassle free for users because they have to remember only one password. But it is also hassle free for crackers. Once crackers break into one account (possibly on the firewall), they can freely enter many other systems by using the same password.

- **Don't write passwords down.** Having written passwords in your wallet may provide access to the computer systems if your wallet is stolen. Keeping copies of passwords in file cabinets or desk drawers is another way to jeopardize security. Select a password that is easy to remember so that you do not have to write it down.

- **Don't use your first or last name (or any combination) as a password.**

- **Don't use your spouse's or child's name as a password.** Crackers carry dictionaries full of names like these—including popular pet names.

- **Don't use a password of all digits or all the same letter (such as eeeeeeee).** Doing so reduces the time a cracker needs to crack your password.

- **Don't use personal information that is easily obtainable.** Crackers can obtain phone numbers, license numbers, social security numbers, the make of your car, and your address. It is better to stay away from personal information in your password.

- **Don't use a word that can be found in the dictionary.** Crackers use both domestic and foreign dictionaries to crack your password. A typical workstation can be used to crack a password with a 250,000-word dictionary in under five minutes. Most computer systems include online dictionaries that the cracker can use. The Internet worm also used an online dictionary to break passwords.

- **Don't use a password shorter than six characters.**

- **Don't feel secure with a very long password (such as a sentence).** Most operating systems only check the first eight characters of your password; the rest does not matter.

- **Use a password with mixed-case alphabetics.** An example is `AeBbit!`.

- **Use a password with nonalphabetic characters.** An example is `Ae,,it!`.

- **Use a password you can type quickly, without having to look at the keyboard.** If you type it in too slowly, someone can watch your keyboard strokes.

Some security experts suggest that you select a line from a favorite poem or song, then use the first letter of each word in your password. For example, "when the lights go down in the city" provides the password `Wtlgditc`. Another recommendation is to join two words with a punctuation character. An example is `toy+boat` or `little;bighorn`.

Use CRACK

Many system administrators run a password cracking program much like the ones crackers use. Do so at regular intervals to help catch an easy-to-guess password before an intruder does. You can tailor these cracking programs the same way a cracker does. One of the most popular cracking programs is CRACK. It can be obtained from many public domain archives on the Internet network.

Run NPASSWD or Passwd+

A more advanced method of preventing the use of passwords that can be easily guessed is to run a password creation program that has built-in password intelligence. These programs can enforce your password policies by keeping a user from creating an unsecured password. Two such programs are NPASSWD and Passwd+.

Who Can Read Your Password?

Many people don't understand how their passwords travel over the network when they log in to a computer. When a remote user logs in to an account on the Internet, the information flows over the network medium organized into packets.

Think of these packets as envelopes. Each one on the outside contains an address of where the information should go, a return address, and some other information that is needed for the network to process the packet. Finally, there is the content of the envelope, or the data area. When you use the U.S. Postal Service, you seal the envelope so that it is difficult for mail carriers to read the contents of your envelopes. On an Ethernet network, the information inside the packet is just as accessible as the address information. If you log in to a computer in New York from California, every piece of equipment that transfers your typed-in password can easily read and store this information. You basically have to trust that the management of each segment between California and New York provides a secure environment through which your packet travels.

Ethernet and the Broadcast Packet

The Ethernet network is a broadcast network. When you type your password on the remote computer, the Ethernet broadcasts the information to every computer on the network. This is akin to a person yelling in a crowded room.

If a college student sets up his or her computer in promiscuous mode, he or she can watch every packet on the network. It would not take much effort to create a packet-filtering program to watch for login packets and capture your login information (including your password). The password information is not encrypted and is readily available in the data portion of the packet.

How Your Packet Travels

It is a smart idea to know where your packet travels and who can see it. Does your organization share a network with the company next door? Does your computer exist on the same segment as the computer science lab at the local university?

The administrator should have an understanding of the network topology surrounding the Internet connection. (Another reason why people shouldn't use the same password for different computers.) If one of your users logs in to an account at a remote university and someone is monitoring packets, he or she can use the password information to break into your local systems.

Use Kerberos

An add-on authentication system that maintains a higher degree of security on the network is called Kerberos. Named after the three-headed watchdog that guards the gates of Hades in Greek mythology, Kerberos effectively authenticates every user for every application.

To implement this system, a server is installed to maintain three components: a database, an authentication server, and a ticket-granting server. The database contains all network user names, their passwords, the network services the users can access, and a service encryption key. To use a service, the person needs a ticket and an authenticator. This provides the security needed to ensure that the entity accessing the service remotely is actually the authorized user. The information transferred over the network is encrypted to keep crackers from viewing the access information in the packet.

More on Setting Up a Firewall

Firewalls use a variety of components and configurations to reduce the risk of security problems. As mentioned earlier in this chapter, a simple screening router can be used to create an Internet firewall (Figure 11.2 shows a screening router example). Rockwell International uses a screening router as a "Telnet diode." The Telnet diode allows outgoing Telnet connections to the Internet but prohibits incoming Telnet connections to internal hosts. This arrangement enables employees to freely log in to remote Internet servers but keeps malicious users from attacking internal computers.

FIGURE 11.2.

Screening router example.

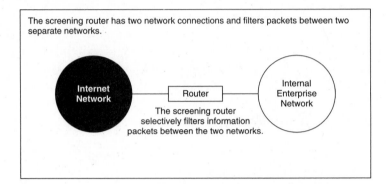

The screening router has two network connections and filters packets between two separate networks.

Internet Network — Router — Internal Enterprise Network

The screening router selectively filters information packets between the two networks.

Another component of a firewall is to use a "bastion host." *Bastions* are highly fortified parts of medieval castles that often focus on critical areas of defense. A bastion host is usually slated to provide many Internet services—such as electronic mail distribution, FTP file service, and Gopher services.

The bastion host usually receives extra security attention and is monitored more frequently than other network hosts. Some configurations of these type of hosts are called *proxy gateways* or *application level gateways*. Software programs are run on the host and act as forwarders for services such as electronic mail or Usenet news.

The services offered on a bastion host can be interactive, such as FTP or Telnet. Digital Equipment Corporation operates bastion hosts that act as proxy gateways for FTP and Telnet. These hosts filter the FTP and Telnet packets between the Internet and the internal DEC network—transparently to the user. A bastion host can be on the Internet but be accessible only to the local internal network by using a protocol other than TCP/IP (the Internet is based on this communication protocol). See Figure 11.3.

These types of bastion hosts often are called *hybrid gateways* because they use a combination of protocols to limit Internet access to the internal network. Access to the hybrid gateway can be made through serial lines or IP tunneling. A terminal server can be used to gain serial access to the hybrid gateway and then on to the Internet.

IP tunneling means taking the Internet IP information packet and enclosing it in another protocol such as X.25. You can think of it as taking an Internet envelope of information that arrives at your corporate mail room, stuffing it in a larger envelope after verifying it is not malicious in content, and then using a different carrier service to deliver it to your office. One example of a corporate firewall that uses a hybrid design is AT&T's connection to the

Internet. This design prevented the famous Internet worm from infecting any of the AT&T computers during the 1988 Internet worm crisis.

FIGURE 11.3.

One example of a bastion host with a terminal server.

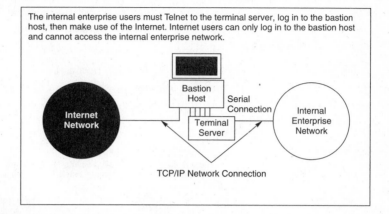

The internal enterprise users must Telnet to the terminal server, log in to the bastion host, then make use of the Internet. Internet users can only log in to the bastion host and cannot access the internal enterprise network.

Internal/External Networks (Dual-Homed Gateway)

One implementation of a bastion host is to install two network boards in the computer. One network board is connected to the Internet and the other network interface is connected to your local internal network. This is known as a *dual-homed gateway* (see Figure 11.4).

Traffic is not allowed to pass from one network interface board to the other. The most secure version is one in which logins are not allowed on the dual-homed gateway. If an intruder login occurs, it can be detected immediately and dealt with quickly. However, this adaptation does not provide very many Internet services to your local organization and may be overly restrictive. By forcing your users to first log in to the dual-homed gateway to use Internet connectivity, you can focus your attention on a single point of connectivity and also provide some Internet flexibility to the user.

FIGURE 11.4.

A dual-homed gateway.

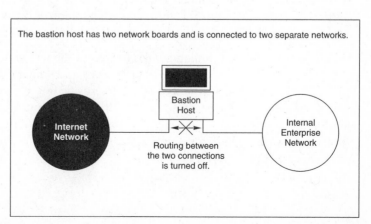

The bastion host has two network boards and is connected to two separate networks.

The drawback of this configuration is that once the intruder gains access to an account on the gateway, he or she has access to every host in your internal network. The attacker also can turn on routing between the two network interfaces and open up your entire network to attack. One advantage is that you can restrict the gateway's use during certain hours of the day or shut it down if there are security problems. It is a convenient way to manage your organization's access to the Internet.

A combination of a screening router and a bastion host can be set up to provide a *screened host gateway* (see Figure 11.5). In this configuration, the bastion host is the only host that can be seen from the Internet network. The screening router permits only a small number of services to communicate with the bastion host.

FIGURE 11.5.

Screened host gateway.

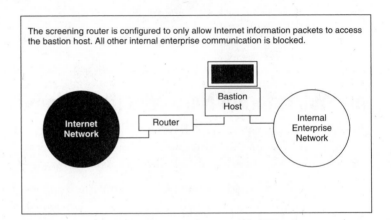

In this configuration, the screening router is sometimes referred to as the *choke* to funnel the packets through a narrow gap. The users must first log in to the bastion host to access any Internet resources. This focuses the administrator's attention on only two components: the router and the bastion host. The bastion host is also referred to as the *gate* in this configuration of a firewall. This firewall focuses any potential intruder's attention on only two components. Such an arrangement limits the battlefield and reduces the complexity of your security risk.

Another common firewall configuration is to create a subnet that is connected to the Internet but is isolated from the rest of your local network by a screening router. You can put a bastion host or any other hosts on the isolated subnet to provide Internet services. Traffic between the Internet and the screened subnet is allowed. Traffic between your local network and the screened subnet is allowed. However, traffic between the Internet, across the screened subnet, and into your local network is blocked by the screening router. Some experts refer to this subnet as a *secure subnetwork* (see Figure 11.6).

FIGURE 11.6.
A screened subnet example.

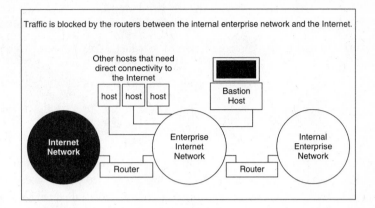

Do You Know If Someone Was in Your House?

How do you know when your system has been compromised? It can take some effort to un-cover a break-in if your system has not been significantly altered. By looking at logs, obscure events, high-resource utilization, and other out-of-the ordinary events, an administrator can detect a possible break-in.

Detecting an Attempted Break-In

Detecting a break-in can be done by using many of the public domain tools available on the Internet network. COPS is a good tool for detecting break-ins (it is described later in this chapter). When working on the system, you can run the w command to see what your users are doing and how much of the computer resources they are using.

Familiarity with the typical habits of your users not only helps you keep an eye out for peculiar events, but also helps you manage system resources. The command (on a BSD UNIX system) ps -ax lists all running programs (known as *processes*) on the computer. Typically, a program named crack or scsh might appear suspicious to your security-conscious eyes. Another tool commonly used for detecting break-ins is TCP Wrappers, discussed later in this chapter and freely available on the Internet.

Watching Logs

Another method of detecting intruders is looking in the logs. A command such as last lists all the recent logins and where they originated. The following example shows the output from the last command when run on a Sun 3/60 computer with the name server.xxx.com:

```
lars       ttyp9    Eskimo.CPH.XXX.C  Tue Nov 16 14:21 - 15:06  (00:44)
paul       FTP      Oak-Street.XXX.C  Tue Nov 16 14:13 - 14:16  (00:02)
FTP        FTP      netcom4.netcom.c  Tue Nov 16 13:42 - 13:55  (00:13)
price      ttypd    JACKSON.XXX.COM   Tue Nov 16 13:38 - 15:08  (01:29)
prasad     ttyp6    Drakes.XXX.COM    Tue Nov 16 13:29 - 14:33  (01:03)
FTP        FTP      staff.cc.purdue.  Tue Nov 16 13:09 - 13:11  (00:02)
FTP        FTP      netcom4.netc.com  Tue Nov 16 12:43 - 12:50  (00:07)
james      ttyp7    netcom4.netc.com  Tue Nov 16 13:03 - 13:05  (00:01)
rao        ttyp9    131.143.66.12     Tue Nov 16 12:40 - 14:17  (01:36)
```

As you can see, there are a number of local logins to the computer named server.xxx.com. Also notice that the anonymous FTP login was used to gain access to public files on the server (the user FTP). The user james logged in from a host called netcom4.netc.com right after someone used an anonymous FTP login from the same origin. This looks suspicious and may be worth investigating. Realizing that the user james was on vacation all last week can raise even more doubts about the credibility of the login.

The syslog file is another place to watch for attempts at break-ins. All attempts and successes at accessing system-level privileges are recorded in this log. Following is a sample syslog file:

```
Nov 28 16:15:58 spectrum login: REPEATED LOGIN FAILURES ON ttyp3 FROM
  mcl.xxx.edu, user1
Nov 28 19:58:11 spectrum login: ROOT LOGIN ttyp0 FROM cmcserver.XXX.COM
Nov 28 20:15:29 spectrum su: 'su root' failed for caldwell on /dev/ttyp0
```

The first entry shows that someone at the host mcl.xxx.edu repeatedly tried to log in and was unsuccessful. The second entry shows that the root system user logged in from the host cmcserver.xxx.com. The last entry shows that user caldwell tried to gain full-system privileges by becoming the root user. All these entries could be security-related events and should be investigated.

If you think an account may be used maliciously by someone, use the lastcomm command to display a list of commands they recently have run. Here's a sample lastcomm command output:

```
csh        S    rao      __        2.00 secs Tue Nov 23 12:42
sendmail   F    rao      ttyp7     0.44 secs Tue Nov 23 12:49
who             rao      ttyp7     0.16 secs Tue Nov 23 12:49
rm              rao      ttyp7     0.12 secs Tue Nov 23 12:49
elm             rao      ttyp7     2.11 secs Tue Nov 23 12:42
```

The first command, csh, may be suspicious. It ran as something that had the set-uid bit turned on (the s flag shows processes that ran with another user's permission).

Looking for Evidence of a Break-In

There are a number of techniques involved in searching for attempted break-ins or figuring out what a cracker has already done (if you suspect malicious activity). The five basic techniques are as follows:

1. **Differencing.** Every system administrator should run a tool that provides a checksum of critical operating system programs and files. This should be done before you connect to the Internet network. I recommend that you store the information offline on a tape or removable disk. When you suspect a break-in, you can run the utility again and compare the checksums with the original checksums. If they are different, someone may have tampered with some part of the operating system. Even though this is the safest method of detecting system tampering, simpler methods include comparing protection modes on files or looking for file size differences. The recommendation is to get a good security tool that alerts you to changes made to your system.

2. **Finding.** This is a simple method of looking for operating system files with recent modification dates. Most crackers know how to manipulate the modification dates to make a file look like it is an original. If you look at the ASCII portion of an executable file with the `strings` command, you sometimes see peculiar alerting strings. This is one of the easiest ways to find a poorly written Trojan horse program.

3. **Snooping.** A computer administrator can install monitors on a system to report future actions of a suspected cracker. This is called *snooping*.

4. **Tracking.** *Tracking* is when a person uses system logs and other audit trails to determine what an attacker has done. A good method for uncovering accounts that have been broken into is by examining the top CPU users. Many crackers run utilities that hog CPU time on a system.

5. **Psychology.** This nontechnical approach is simply to try and communicate with the cracker by leaving notes, sending the account e-mail, starting talk sessions, and so forth. This can lead to disaster or be informative—depending on the situation.

Keeping an Eye Out for Back Doors

Another important thing to look for are filenames that start with a period (.) (sometimes referred to as a *dot file*). These files are called *hidden files* because they are not seen in the normal listing of a user's directories. They are used by the system to configure a user's account. Many crackers store files in a user's account with names like . .. (dot space dot dot) or .. (dot dot space space). Normal dot files found in user directories include the optional `.mailrc` and `.exrc` files. Many crackers store their files and disguise them with the name `.mailrc` or `.exrc`. (These back doors may be difficult to detect.) Because these files are typically small, check for large file sizes in the user's home directories.

Another type of special file to look for is a set-uid file. This file has the permission set so that when it runs, it has the permissions of the file *owner*, not the typical permissions of the user that ran the program. Many system administrators create shell scripts with the set-uid bit set so that users can have extra capabilities beyond their normal account authorizations. Crackers create root-owned set-uid scripts as a way to gain system privileges without a password. You can use the find command on a UNIX system to help locate these files. The following find command displays all set-uid files owned by the user root everywhere on the system:

```
find / -user root -perm -4000 -print
```

> **NOTE**
>
> A set-uid root-owned program can be used by a normal account holder, but it gives him or her superuser access to various parts of the operating system.

A favorite in the cracking community is known as the *supershell*. A cracker takes a shell such as the Bourne shell or the C shell and changes the permission to be set-uid and the owner to be root. Then the cracker disguises it with a name like .mailrc.old and leaves it in a compromised account's home directory. To the administrator, it looks like an old copy of an electronic mail setup script. But the cracker can run it whenever he or she enters the account to instantly have a shell that effectively has all the security access of the root account (known sometimes as the *superuser*).

Another cracker trick is to log in to an account accessed through password cracking, copy a supershell into the account, and run the supershell. The cracker then erases the supershell from the directory. This effectively keeps the shell running in memory but removes evidence of it from the directory.

Yet another cracker trick is to look for program shell scripts that are run nightly by the root user as a batch file. Crackers typically modify small portions of these files so that each night a security hole is created to enable them to enter the system. Even though the administrator may find the security hole and repair it, during the evening the script reopens the security hole.

Many crackers install Trojan horses. These are most commonly replacement programs for login, Telnet, rlogin, and any other program that makes users type their passwords. The Trojan horse normally looks and appears much like the original program, but it collects the passwords and account names in a hidden file. It may possibly mail these passwords to another compromised account somewhere else. For this reason alone, an administrator should not log in to the system as the user root (administrators should log in as a normal user and then use the su program to gain root privileges; in this way, administrators may detect something funny before they compromise the root password). It is wise to use a nightly security program, such as COPS, to detect Trojan horse programs and alert you of their presence.

Reporting Break-Ins

CERT is the Computer Emergency Response Team formed by the Defense Advanced Research Projects Agency (DARPA) in November 1988, in response to the Internet worm incident. The charter of CERT is to facilitate its response to computer security events involving Internet hosts, to raise the community's awareness of computer security issues, and to conduct research in the area of improving system security. CERT provides 24-hour technical assistance in response to computer security incidents, product vulnerability assistance, technical security documents, and security seminars.

If you encounter a security problem such as a break-in, a virus, a worm, or a software bug that creates a security hole, contact an Emergency Response Center. CERT is a common group to contact. For more information about CERT, read the newsgroups `comp.security.announce` and `comp.security.misc`.

Does Your Computer Have Worms?

The first mention of a computer worm was in the classic 1975 science fiction novel, *The Shockwave Rider*, by John Brunner. In the book, the tapeworm was a program that lived inside computers and spread to other machines. Xerox went on to experiment with worms and reported them in the communications of the ACM.

The definition of a *computer worm* is a program that can run by itself and propagate a fully working version of itself to other machines. The famous Internet worm that spread in November 1988 brought the Internet to a state of inoperability. It spread from machine to machine by exploiting a bug in the `sendmail` and `fingerd` programs. The worm attacked computers by trying to use easy-to-guess passwords such as Joes and attacked accounts using the owner's first or last name (available from the `finger` command to outside Internet users). The worm also used the standard online dictionary and a small dictionary of its own of commonly used passwords. A full description of the Internet worm can be found on the FTP server at Purdue University.

Fred Cohen of USC describes a *computer virus* as a section of programming code that adds itself to other computer programs. In other words, it modifies operating systems or running programs to include an evolved copy of itself. This section of code cannot run by itself and requires a host program before it can replicate. Virus programs are common in the PC computer world, and many off-the-shelf vendor solutions are offered to keep your personal computer free from viral infections. If you are interested in looking into these bizarre creatures of computer vandalism, start with the FAQ for the Usenet newsgroup `comp.virus` or the mail list `VIRUS-L` (both groups are identical except that one is a newsgroup and the other is a mail list).

Another form of vandalware is the Trojan horse. A program that does something a programmer wants to do but that is prohibited by a user is often called a *Trojan horse*. A few months ago, a Trojan horse showed up on a computer system. The beast was a modified version of the

Telnet daemon that did everything the normal Telnet daemon should do—including ask users for their passwords when they logged in to the system. This special version not only asked users for their passwords, it also collected these passwords in a hidden file on the system. The intruder expected to come back and collect these passwords to break into other accounts and systems on our network.

Other vandalware terms you may see referenced on the Internet are *rabbits* (which spread wildly within or among computer systems, disrupting network traffic) and *bacterium* (whose main goal is to replicate in a system and consume CPU time until the computer is halted).

Programs that Enhance Security

There are programs freely available on the Internet to enhance the security of your computer system. Most of the packages are designed for the UNIX operating system because it is the most commonly attached computer on the Internet. UNIX hosts are typically used as bastion hosts and gateways.

COPS

The COPS package contains a variety of scripts to form a security testing system. It addresses common security holes and can be run at regular intervals to ensure that your system is secure. The package includes the Kuang expert system, which takes a set of rules and tries to break into your system like a malicious user would. It then reports on your security weaknesses.

One version is written in perl, another is written in shell scripts and C. Both versions are continually modified to include recent UNIX security holes. The configuration of the package is fairly easy and can be installed without having a degree in computer science. The package, currently maintained by Dan Farmer, is available at `archive.cis.ohio-state.edu: /pub/cops`. It was originally developed under the direction of Gene Spafford at Purdue University.

CRACK and UFC

CRACK was written by Alec Muffett to break insecure passwords. It can be used both by the cracker to break into systems and by the administrator to check the integrity of the password file. It has a friendly front-end interface and a networking option to spread the load over various computers on the network.

UFC, written by Michael Glad, is a fast version of the crypt algorithm. It can be combined with CRACK to enhance the ability to check easy-to-guess passwords.

CRACK and UFC are available from `FTP.uu.net:/usenet/comp.sources.misc/volume28`.

> **NOTE**
>
> It has been debated for some time whether to make these tools readily available on the Internet to irresponsible and malicious people. Logic dictates that it is more important for system administrators to readily have these tools than the bad guys. Most crackers have had these tools for years, anyway.

NPASSWD and Passwd+

The NPASSWD and Passwd+ programs provide a replacement for the UNIX `passwd` command that is used to change a user's password. The programs try to prevent a user from choosing a poor password that a program like CRACK could break. NPASSWD was written by Clyde Hoover; Passwd+ was written by Matt Bishop. Use the Internet service Archie to find the most recent versions of these programs.

SecureLib

William LeFebvre enhanced the security of three UNIX kernel calls to check for "allowed" hosts before permitting network connections to your Internet host. The latest version of these library routines is stored at `eecs.nwu.edu: /pub/securelib.tar`.

Shadow

Shadow is a set of program replacements for your UNIX system. It keeps the password entry in a separately guarded file rather than in the normal password file. Shadow also provides for terminal access control and includes user and group administration. Written by John F. Haugh II, it is available from `FTP.uu.net: /usenet/comp.sources.misc/volume38/shadow`.

TCP Wrappers

TCP Wrappers provides a front-end filtering capability to many of the network services in the UNIX operating system. The extra logging information it provides can help detect an intruder who is trying to break into your Internet system. The package can also be set up to prevent illegitimate connections from being made to your computer. TCP Wrappers was designed by Wietse Venema of the Eindhoven University of Technology, the Netherlands. You can obtain TCP Wrappers from `ftp://ftp.cert.org: /pub/network_tools/tcp_wrappers_7.2.tar`.

User Education

Make sure that you prepare a handout for all your Internet account users. Users should know what the acceptable use of the Internet is and the conduct that is ethically accepted. They should be aware of the security problems weak passwords represent and should be educated on keeping their account secure. You should provide a list of contacts just in case someone detects a security problem on the system or sees some peculiar activity. A copy of your site security policy should be available at all times.

Where To Go from Here

By using many of the information tools found in this chapter, you should be able to locate quite a bit of information about security. If you get stuck and need information, try to find a Gopher server with Veronica and run the query `security`.

Internet FTP Sites for Security

One of the first places to look for security information is from CERT. You can use the FTP (File Transfer Protocol) network tool to retrieve information from the site `cert.org`. The first file to download should be `CERT.FAQ` (CERT Frequently Asked Questions). This file includes information about how the information is organized on the CERT file server `cert.org`.

Usenet Newsgroups

The following is a list of Usenet newsgroups that discuss security-related issues:

Newsgroup	Description
`alt.security`	This forum discusses computer security but also includes other issues such as car locks and alarm systems.
`comp.security.announce`	This list is used to distribute CERT security advisories.
`comp.security.misc`	A forum for the discussion of computer security (tends to be related to UNIX security issues).
`comp.virus`	This newsgroup discusses computer virus issues.
`comp.risks`	This forum discusses the risks to the public from computers and related systems.

Mail Lists

A few Internet mailing lists can provide you with updated information about computer security. The Computer Emergency Response Team Coordination Center (CERT/CC) has established a list for the purpose of exchanging information and security tools and techniques. Membership is restricted to system programmers, system administrators, and others with legitimate interest in computer security tools. An administrator can subscribe by sending e-mail to `cert-tools-request@cert.org`. Other CERT mailing lists include an security advisory list called `cert-advisory`. You can join this list by sending e-mail to `cert-advisory-request@cert.org`.

Another security-related mail list is `VIRUS-L`, which focuses on computer virus issues. You can subscribe by sending the string `SUB VIRUS-L` and your name in the body of an e-mail message to `listserv@lehigh.edu`. A similar list named `VALERT-L` exists at the same location and is used for sending urgent virus-related warnings to computer users. To join, send the string `SUB VALERT-L` and your name in the body of an e-mail message to `listserv@lehigh.edu`.

Organizations and Groups

New organizations are being formed every day to deal with the security-related threats on the Internet. CERT has been mentioned a number of times in this chapter. Other organizations include COAST, FIRST, ASIS, CSI, NIST, and the CIAC. All these organizations are designed to help the system administrator manage a usable system that is secure.

COAST (Computer Operations, Audit, and Security Tools) is a project coordinated by Gene Spafford at the Department of Computer Sciences at Purdue University. The goal of this project is to create a research program that explores new approaches to computer security and computer system management. Further information can be obtained from `ftp://coast.cs.purdue.edu/pub/Purdue/papers/spafford`.

REFERENCE WORKS

Bishop, Matt, "Privacy Enhanced Electronic Mail," Department of Mathematics and Computer Science, Dartmouth College, Hanover, NH. Available from `FTP.dartmouth.edu:/pub/security`.

Brand, Russel L., "Coping with the Threat of Computer Security Incidents: A Primer from Prevention through Recovery," June 8, 1990.

Brunner, John, *The Shockwave Rider*, Harper and Row, 1975.

Carl-Mitchel, Smoot and Quarterman, John S., "Building Internet Firewalls," *UNIXWORLD*, February 1992.

Carl-Mitchel, Smoot and Quarterman, John S., "Tutorial: tcp_wrappers," *UNIXWORLD*, July 1993.

CERT Coordination Center, "Packet Filtering for Firewall Systems." Available from `cert.org`.

CERT Coordination Center, "DARPA Establishes Computer Emergency Response Team," December 13, 1988. Available from `cert.org`.

CERT Coordination Center, "The CERT Coordination Center FAQ," Revision 7, JPO#93-025 and ESC#93-0115, January 1993. Available from `cert.org`.

CERT Coordination Center, "CERT Coordination Center Generic Security Information," November 5, 1993. Available from `cert.org`.

Cheswick, Bill, "The Design of a Secure Internet Gateway," USENIX proceedings. Available from `research.att.com`: `/dist/secure_internet_gateway.ps`.

Cheswick, Bill, "An Evening with Berferd, in Which a Cracker Is Lured, Endured, and Studied," USENIX proceedings, January 20, 1990. Available from `research.att.com`:`/dist/internet_security/berford.ps`.

Cohen, Fred, "Computer Viruses: Theory and Experiments," Proceedings of the 7th National Computer Security Conference, pp. 240-63, 1984.

Curry, David A., "Improving the Security of your UNIX System," (Technical Report ITSTD-721-FR-90-21), Menlo Park, CA: SRI International, April 1990.

Dichter, Carl, "Easy UNIX Security," *UNIX Review*, Volume 11 No. 4, April 1993.

Farmer, Daniel, "The COPS Security Checker System," Purdue Technical Report CSD-TR-993, Department of Computer Sciences, Purdue University, West Lafayette, IN, September 19, 1991. Available from `FTP.cs.purdue.edu`:`/pub/spaf/security`.

Klien, Daniel V., "Foiling the Cracker: A Survey of, and Improvements to, Password Security," Carnegie Mellon University, Software Engineering Institute, Pittsburgh, PA.

Muffet, Alec and many other contributors, "Almost Everything You Ever Wanted To Know About Security (But Were Afraid To Ask)," Usenet news list `comp.security.misc` FAQ, June 6, 1992. Posted at regular intervals on the Usenet news list `comp.security.misc`.

Network Working Group, "Site Security Handbook," July 1991. Available from any repository of RFCs on the Internet or from `cert.org`: `/pub/security`.

Pethia, Richard D. and Van Wyk, Kenneth R., "Computer Emergency Response—An International Problem," CERT/Coordination Center, Software Engineering Institute, Carnegie Mellon University, Pittsburgh, PA. Available from `cert.org`.

Ranum, Marcus J., "Thinking about Firewalls," Trusted Information Systems, Glenwood, MD.

Salmone, Salvatore, "Internetwork Security: Unsafe at Any Node?" *DATA COMMU-NICATIONS*, September 1993.

Spafford, Eugene H., "The Internet Worm Program: An Analysis," Purdue Technical Report CSD-TR-823, Department of Computer Sciences, Purdue University, West Lafayette, IN, December 8, 1988. Available from `FTP.cs.purdue.edu:/pub/spaf/security`.

Spafford, Eugene H., "Are Computer Hacker Break-ins Ethical?" Purdue Technical Report CSD-TR-994, Department of Computer Sciences, Purdue University, West Lafayette, IN, July 1990. Available from `FTP.cs.purdue.edu:/pub/spaf/security`.

Spafford, Eugene H., "The Internet Worm Incident," Purdue Technical Report CSD-TR-933, Department of Computer Sciences, Purdue University, West Lafayette, IN, September 19, 1991. Available from `FTP.cs.purdue.edu:/pub/spaf/security`.

Spafford, Eugene H., "Policies and Planning Can Prevent Security Incidents," Workshop Handouts, Department of Computer Sciences, Purdue University, West Lafayette, IN, August 1992. Available from `FTP.cs.purdue.edu:/pub/spaf/security`.

Spafford, Eugene H., "Research on Techniques and Tools for Computer Security: The COAST Project and Laboratory," Department of Computer Sciences, Purdue University, West Lafayette, IN, October 25, 1993. Available from `FTP.cs.purdue.edu:/pub/spaf/COAST`.

Venema, Wietse., "TCP Wrapper," Mathematics and Computer Science, Eidhoven University of Technology, The Netherlands. Available from `cert.org:/pub/tools/tcp_wrappers`.

Wack, John P. and Carnahan, Lisa J., "Computer Viruses and Related Threats: A Management Guide," NIST Special Publication, Computer Systems Technology. Available from `cert.org:/pub/security`.

PART

IV

Communicating with Others

Internet E-Mail: An Overview

12

*by Ron Dippold
revised for this edit-
ion by Billy Barron*

As is explored further in Chapter 15, "Internet E-Mail: Gateways," one of the prime advantages of the Internet is almost universal electronic mail (e-mail) access. Any computer network, BBS, service, or e-mail company that wants to can hook into the Internet and allow e-mail to and from anyone else who is connected to the Internet directly or indirectly.

This chapter covers the basic concepts of Internet mail. After this chapter, read Chapter 13, "Internet E-Mail: UNIX," if you are using a UNIX machine to read and send your e-mail (skip the UNIX chapter if your mail is on a microcomputer). If you are using a PC or Mac to read and send your e-mail, read Chapter 14, "Internet E-Mail: DOS, Windows, and Macintosh." One exception, however, is if you are using PINE on a PC; if that is true, read the PINE section in Chapter 13 because PC PINE is almost identical to UNIX PINE.

E-Mail Basics

Before getting into specifics, you should read about a few fundamental concepts.

E-Mail Parts

E-mail consists of two basic parts: the control information and the content. The *control information* contains information about the message: who it came from, where it's going, when it was sent, what it's about, and whether it's regular or extra crispy. The *content* is the actual message being sent (which is usually considered the important part).

On the Internet, the control information is referred to as the *header*; the content is referred to as the *body* or *text* of the message.

E-Mail Addressing

When you send snail mail (through the postal service), you place both your address and the recipient's address in the "control" part of the letter—the outside of the envelope. Both you and the post office are using an agreed-on address standard: name, street address, city, state, and ZIP code. There are some variations to this standard, but that's basically it.

But what if you want to send e-mail to Joe Blow on his computer at Cyberdine Systems? If you think about it, you'll realize that you need something similar. First, your mail has to get to Joe's computer system; then it has to get to Joe.

The form of addressing you see most often on the Internet is known simply as Internet addressing; it looks like this:

```
localname@domain
```

Both sides are extendable. The *domain* portion should get you to a machine, and the *localname* portion should get you to the user you want. The *domain*, which is read from right to left, specifies a series of encapsulated logical domains. Here's an example:

```
tadpole@booboo.marketing.gigantico.com
```

The far-right domain, com, indicates that this is a commercial site; the gigantico specifies the name of the company or entity; marketing further specifies a department in gigantico; booboo is a specific computer in the marketing department; and the user on that machine is tadpole.

This is what is known as a *fully qualified domain name*—you have given complete instructions on how to reach tadpole, down to the very machine he reads mail on. In many cases, this much detail is not necessary. For example, the gigantico mail computer should know where tadpole's mail is located—unless it's a very primitive computer—and should get his mail to him correctly after it's inside the company. In this case, tadpole@gigantico.com would be sufficient. Generally, the domain contains two to four parts.

By Internet convention, the domain is case insensitive. That is, any machine routing mail from one place to another should realize that gigantico.com, GigantiCo.Com, and GIGANTICO.COM are all the same site.

The right part of the domain name is known as the *top-level domain*. The most common top-level domains are com (commercial site), edu (educational site), gov (government site), net (networking organizations) and mil (military site). Actually, these are usually U.S. sites. Other countries' top-level domains usually start with the two-letter ISO code for that country—for example, ca for Canada or de for Germany. However, that rule of thumb is not foolproof because there are sites in Canada with edu or com top-level domains and the us domain also exists for the United States.

The *localname*, on the other side of that @, is usually just the user's mail ID. It can be the user's name, the user's initials, random numbers, or anything else the site decides on. Although the *localname* should be case insensitive, this is not required, so mail to Tadpole@gigantico.com may not reach tadpole@gigantico.com. Most sites assume case insensitive addresses, but a few don't.

When mail travels from the Internet to another network (or vice versa), it's common to see very strange Internet addresses, with all sorts of odd characters involved. In this case, you may see some addressing for the other network tacked on to the Internet address. For example, you may see billy%untvaxb.bitnet@cunyvm.cuny.edu (we won't cover the explanation of this because it gets complex and confusing).

E-Mail Layers

Sending e-mail involves several layers of protocols. Starting from the bottom in a crude layering are the following layers:

- **Hardware.** Our machines must physically be able to talk to each other on some sort of low-level communications link. This hardware could be a modem, a dedicated line, or a satellite system. This layer takes care of everything needed to make sure that you can send a stream of bits from one site to another.

- **Link.** This layer manages all the complexities of maintaining logical channels from one site to another. You will probably have multiple data streams running over the same hardware link, and this layer has to manage that situation. This layer also usually ensures that the data received has no errors. TCP/IP, SLIP, UUCP, and PPP are examples of this layer.

- **Mail Transport Agent (MTA).** MTAs are responsible for handling all the complexities of moving a piece of mail from one site to another, including managing the routing. MTAs can be complex beasts.

- **User Agent (UA).** Known more specifically as Mail User Agent (MUA). This is the layer that most concerns us. The User Agent attempts to make access to the Mail Transport Agent as painless as possible. User Agents are what you, the user, run to access your e-mail and send your own messages. You read about several of these User Agents in the next two chapters.

Some Basic E-Mail Concepts

Using e-mail involves a few concepts, but if you look carefully, you will realize that almost all of them originally came from the Postal System or memos. It is not hard to grasp them.

First, you can Carbon Copy (cc) e-mail messages just like you can with a letter. In addition, there is a Blind Carbon Copy (bcc) feature in most e-mail systems that allows you to secretly send a copy of the letter to a person just as you can with paper letters.

When you have a lot of paper mail, you end up filing it into file folders in your filing cabinet. The same applies to e-mail. You can file your messages into folders. With some e-mail packages, this feature is called the *mailbox*.

Instead of a Rolodex or a little black book, you may have an address book. Some e-mail packages allow you to have multiple address books so that you can put your friends in one address book and your work associates in another. Finally, you may have an e-mail system that has workgroup or global address books. These are usually maintained by the system administrator and contain a large number of commonly used addresses. At a company, this address book may contain the e-mail addresses of all employees who work there.

Mail Standards

It would be nice to ignore Mail Transport Agents altogether, but they are an important factor in the design of User Agents. Obviously, standards for sending e-mail from one place to another are necessary. But what standards?

RFCs—Internet Standards

Standards on the Internet are created in a wonderfully anarchic manner. Any person (or group) who thinks he or she has a good idea prepares an RFC (Request For Comment) detailing the proposal. If other people think the idea is good, it is implemented. If not, it will languish, unused.

RFCs are actually a little more general than this—in addition to standards, there are *commentary RFCs*. This type of RFC can be a specific commentary on another RFC, a commentary on the general direction of the Internet, meeting minutes, or whatever the person felt was important enough to turn into an RFC. For example, RFC 146 (each RFC is given a unique number) is "Views on issues relevant to data sharing on computer networks."

For those interested in e-mail, the two most important RFCs are RFC 821, "Simple Mail Transfer Protocol," and RFC 822, "Standard for the format of ARPA Internet text messages." There are also other fascinating documents in the list.

If you have a WAIS (Wide Area Information Server) client or Telnet available, you can use the WAIS servers to find RFCs. You can find them at `telnet://ds.internic.net/wais/`; you want the `rfcs` database.

FTP is what most users probably end up using; it's superior to WAIS in some ways and definitely more convenient than using one of the mail servers. The RFCs are stored at `ftp://ds.internic.net/rfc/`. For an index, retrieve `rfc-index.txt`. For help with FTP, see Chapter 22, "FTP: Fetching Files from Everywhere."

If you don't have FTP access, you can send mail to the Internet address `mailserv@ds.internic.net` and include one or more of the following commands in the body of the message:

```
document-by-name rfcnnnn
file /ftp/rfc/rfc-index.txt
help
```

Replace the *nnnn* in the first command with the number of the RFC you want to retrieve. The second command retrieves an index. Keep in mind that some of these documents are very large—hundreds of thousands of bytes. The index itself is 200,000 bytes. Don't accidentally swamp your mailbox.

RFC 821—Simple Mail Transfer Protocol

Simple Mail Transfer Protocol (SMTP) is the underlying transmission mechanism for almost all the mail on the Internet. The standard was published in August 1982 by J.B. Postel. Although some extensions have been added, it's still used pretty much as it was proposed.

SMTP is a simple peer-to-peer model. Each host that wants to receive mail sets up an SMTP server. When the host wants to send mail to another host, it contacts that host's SMTP server as an SMTP sender. When another host wants to send mail to your host, that host contacts your SMTP server, which then acts as an SMTP receiver.

RFC 822—Internet Text Message Format

RFC 822 is actually "Standard for the format of ARPA Internet text messages," but few people have referred to the Internet as ARPAnet for a long time. This standard has been updated a few times, but everyone still refers to the RFC 822 format.

Anyway, RFC 822 describes the format that the Internet uses to transfer messages. It is useful to understand the format because you need it when you are trying to figure out why e-mail bounced, why you cannot reply to a message, or when you have some other problem. If you think this will never happen to you, you are in for a surprise.

Mail Addresses

RFC 821 and RFC 822 specified (although they didn't invent) a mail addressing format discussed earlier in this chapter. All addresses are of this form:

```
localname@domain
```

Message Header

The basic format for a message is simple: multiple header lines, a blank line, and then the message text (body). Each *header line* contains information about the message and uses the form `keyword: value`. The `keyword` should be only a single word, but the `value` can be multiple words (it depends on what the keyword accepts). A header can stretch over several lines; every continuation line should start with a space or tab. The term *header* can refer to either the entire header or a single item of the header.

Here are some examples:

```
From: dr_zachary@lost.inspace.com
Subject: This is a subject line. Note how it breaks over
  two lines whereas the start of headers are flush left.
To: crow@mst3k.com
```

Tabs and spaces are both treated as generic, word-separation characters. If a keyword requires a one-word value, and the value you want to use includes spaces, surround everything with quotation marks. As an example, the address rdippold@bozos.edu is perfectly valid and can be given as follows:

```
From: rdippold@bozos.edu
```

However, the address Bob Smith@wubba.com includes a space, which can confuse mailers, so it must be given as follows:

```
From: "Bob Smith"@wubba.com
```

For this reason, it is rare that such an address is given. Generally, this address would be assigned as Bob_Smith@wubba.com (or wubba.com would automatically translate between the two) because it is simpler.

Basic Headers

The only header absolutely required for a message you want to send is the To header:

```
To: address
```

However, the mailer usually adds other headers. Generally, you'll also want to add a Subject header so that the receiver can see what the message is about:

```
Subject: message subject
```

You may also want to add a From header so that the receiver can reply to your mail:

```
From: your_address
```

Here's a simple message:

```
From: mickj
To: keithr
Subject: Where's the sugar?

Me bag of cane sugar is missing, Keef. I don't suppose you might
know something about it, eh?
```

The mailer at your site adds some other headers (such as the date); any machines along the way add their own information.

Common Headers

The easiest way to learn about the other headers is to look at a real message header. Only the names and addresses have been changed to protect the guilty:

```
From jeff@mathcs.amour.edu Thu  Mar 30 07:49:44 1995
Received: from tofu.com by happy.tofu.com; id HAA04319
sendmail 8.6.4/QC-client-2.0 via ESMTP
Thu, 30 Mar 1995 07:49:42 -0800 for <rdippold@happy.tofu.com>
Received: from amour.mathcs.amour.edu by tofu.com; id HAA28169
sendmail 8.6.4/QC-main-2.2 via SMTP
Thu, 30 Mar 1995 07:49:40 -0800 for <rdippold@tofu.com>
Received: from cssun.mathcs.amour.edu by
amour.mathcs.amour.edu (5.65/Amour_mathcs.3.4.15) via SMTP
id AA28633 ; Thu, 30 Mar 95 10:49:38 -0500
From: jeff@mathcs.amour.edu (Jeff Budd {guest - asst uucpMC})
Sender: jeff@ee.amour.edu
Message-Id: <9503301549.AA28633@amour.mathcs.amour.edu>
Subject: sci.physics results
To: rdippold@tofu.com (Ron Dippold)
Date: Thu, 30 Mar 1995 10:49:37 -0500 (EST)
Reply-To: jeff@mathcs.amour.edu, jeff@hobbit.moth.com
X-Mailer: <PC Eudora Version 2.0>
Cc: group-advice@uunet.UU.NET
Cc: aleff@ux1.cso.uiuc.edu (Hans-Jorg Aleff)
In-Reply-To: <CMM.0.90.0.755815603.rdippold@happy.tofu.com>
Mime-Version: 1.0
Content-Type: text/plain; charset=US-ASCII
Content-Transfer-Encoding: 7bit
Content-Length: 20432
```

This is a message from Jeff to me regarding the Usenet group `sci.physics`. From the top:

```
From jeff@mathcs.amour.edu Thu Mar 30 07:49:44 1995
```

This is the line my mail program uses to separate one message in the mail file from another.

```
Received: from tofu.com by happy.tofu.com; id HAA04319
sendmail 8.6.4/QC-client-2.0 via ESMTP
Thu, 30 Mar 1995 07:49:42 -0800 for <rdippold@happy.tofu.com>
```

This section is interesting; it's the last machine-to-machine mail transfer (each transfer adds a `Received` line at the top of the message, so the first listed is the last that occurred). In this case, the machine `happy.tofu.com` received the message from the machine `tofu.com` (the central e-mail machine for `tofu.com`). The transfer was done with sendmail 8.6.4, and the protocol used was ESMTP, which is an extended version of SMTP. The date and time of the transfer are given, as is the address of the intended recipient.

```
Received: from amour.mathcs.amour.edu by tofu.com; id HAA28169
sendmail 8.6.4/QC-main-2.2 via SMTP
Thu, 30 Mar 1995 07:49:40 -0800 for <rdippold@tofu.com>
```

This portion of the header is the mail transfer that actually got the e-mail to `tofu.com`. In this case, the machine `amour.matchs.amour.edu` sent the message with SMTP using sendmail to `tofu.com` at the time given.

```
Received: from cssun.mathcs.amour.edu by
amour.mathcs.amour.edu (5.65/Amour_mathcs.3.4.15) via SMTP
id AA28633 ; Thu, 30 Mar 95 10:49:38 -0500
```

This portion is the first mail transfer. The machine `cssun.mathcs.amour.edu` (where the message presumably originated) sent it to `amour.mathcs.amour.edu`, which is presumably the central e-mail gateway for `amour.edu`. The message was sent with SMTP at the time given.

```
From: jeff@mathcs.amour.edu (Jeff Budd {guest - asst uucpMC})
```

The person who sent the message is Jeff Budd. His address, in case I want to reply, is `jeff@mathcs.amour.edu`

```
Sender: jeff@ee.amour.edu
```

The `Sender` header is the identity of the person sending the message. In most cases, it should be the same as the `From` field and can be left out. However, it is used when secretaries send mail in the names of the people they work for, or if a single member of the group specified in `From` sends the message. In this case, Jeff used the `ee` machine to send the mail rather than the `mathcs` machine he gave in his `From` address. Therefore, the mail program added the `Sender` field so that I would know where the message "really" came from. Not a big deal here, but if the `From` and `Sender` fields are radically different, the message might be a forgery.

```
Message-Id: <9503301549.AA28633@amour.mathcs.amour.edu>
```

The `Message-Id` header is used for tracking down errors; every message has a unique `Message-Id` header. There should never be another message with this `Message-Id`.

The following line is the subject of the message:

```
Subject: Re: sci.physics results
```

When my mail program shows me the overview of the message, it shows me who the message is from, the date, and the subject. The `Re` indicates that it's a reply to a previous message.

```
To: rdippold@tofu.com (Ron Dippold)
```

This is who the message is for (me, in this case).

```
Date: Thu, 30 Mar1995 10:49:37 -0500 (EST)
```

This line gives the date the message was sent. You'll read more about date formats later.

```
Reply-To: jeff@mathcs.amour.edu, jeff@hobbit.moth.com
```

If the sender does not want a reply to be sent to the address given in the `From` line, he or she inserts a `Reply-To` line; any replies should be sent to this address. In this case, my answer to this message will go to two separate addresses: `jeff@mathcs.amour.edu` and `jeff@hobbit.moth.com`. The `amour` address is faster, but it's unreliable, so Jeff likes to have replies go to both addresses. Normally, `Reply-To` is used only on special occasions, but it can also be used if the address given in your `From` line is incorrect and you can't fix it for some reason (because of a lazy administrator, for example).

```
X-Mailer: <PC Eudora Version 2.0>
```

Keywords starting with x- are special. You can create any such x- keyword with whatever you think is important and use it as a header. In this case, the mailing software that was used to send the message (PC Eudora) inserted its own ID in a little bit of self-promotion.

```
Cc: group-stuff@xxnet.XX.NET
Cc: jones@ux1.cso.krill.edu (Josef Jones)
```

The message was also sent (carbon copied) to the addresses group-stuff@xxnet.XX.NET and jones@ux1.cso.krill.edu. This information could also have been specified in a single Cc line by separating the addresses with a comma.

```
In-Reply-To: <CMM.0.90.0.755815603.rdippold@happy.tofu.com>
```

The message is in reply to a message I sent with this Message-Id.

```
Mime-Version: 1.0
```

This line deals with something to be discussed later: MIME message format.

```
Content-Type: text/plain; charset=US-ASCII
Content-Transfer-Encoding: 7bit
```

These MIME headers indicate that the contents of the mail are simple text with no high ASCII characters, such as PC graphics characters. If any machine along the way cares to send only 7 bits of each character, the message should still transfer okay.

```
Content-Length: 20432
```

The length of the body of the message is 20,432 bytes.

Some Other Headers

```
Bcc: recipient
```

The Bcc (blind carbon copy) field is like the Cc field, except that those whose addresses appear in the Cc or From fields don't see the Bcc header.

```
Keywords: keyword, keyword
```

This header specifies keywords that relate to the message. These keywords are sometimes used by the e-mail program to do searches, but this is totally dependent on the program.

```
Comments: comments
```

This header allows comments on the message to be sent without disturbing the body of the message.

```
Encrypted: software keyhelp
```

This header indicates that the message body is encrypted with the encryption software *software*, and the optional *keyhelp* helps select the key to decode with. Note that the header itself cannot be encrypted, because it contains vital routing information.

Date Fields

Dates used in RFC 822 headers are of the following form:

```
Mon, 27 Mar 95 15:34 -800
```

The day of week is optional. The time is given as 24-hour format (00:00 through 23:59) local time. The last field is the time zone in one of several formats:

Format	Meaning
UT or GMT	Universal/Greenwich mean time
EST or EDT	Eastern time zone
CST or CDT	Central time zone
MST or MDT	Mountain time zone
PST or PDT	Pacific time zone
–HHMM	HH hours and MM minutes earlier than UT
+HHMM	HH hours and MM minutes later than UT

Z	Universal time
A	UT minus 1 hour
M	UT minus 12 hours
N	UT plus 1 hour
Y	UT plus 12 hours

The `-HHMM` format is probably the least confusing. In my opinion, `-0800` makes it much easier to translate the time to local time than PST does. The Z through Y zones are military codes.

X.400 to RFC 822 Mapping

Another common form of addressing used by many of the big commercial e-mail providers such as AT&T, Sprint, and MCI is X.400. There exist gateways between these systems and the Internet, but X.400 is much more restrictive than RFC 822 about which characters are allowed in addresses. Because X.400 addressing is complex and cumbersome, it is not covered here. See Chapter 15, "Internet E-Mail: Gateways," for more information (alternatively, read RFC 1327).

RFC 1521—MIME

MIME (Multipurpose Internet Mail Extensions) addresses a giant limitation in Internet message standards. Generally, messages are assumed to be all low-bit ASCII text (ASCII values 0 through 127). This situation makes it tough to send information such as sounds, videos, programs, or even some non-English character sets in an Internet message. Much of this type of information is probably altered, assuming that it doesn't break the mailers first. There are ways around this problem, such as preprocessing all the information to 7 bits and then reconstructing it on the receiving end (see the discussion of uuencode, later in this chapter). Both the sender and receiver must agree on a format and have programs to deal with it. It's also inconvenient when X.400 messages (which allow encapsulated data) must be passed through a section of the Internet—it would be extremely helpful if the message that reentered the X.400 network contained the same encapsulated data.

A MIME message allows this sort of data to be passed through in a consistent manner. The header fields you need to look for are `MIME-Version` and `Content-Type`. These are the Content-Types defined in RFC 1521:

Content-Type	Description
text	Plain text information. A subtype, `richtext`, is defined in RFC 1341.
multipart	For messages consisting of multiple independent data parts.

continues

Content-Type	Description
message	An encapsulated message, which can be all or part of a full RFC 822 message. There is a partial option to the message Content-Type for partial messages, which allows one message to be divided into several smaller parts. There also is an external-body option that allows a reference to an external source, such as a file on an FTP site.
image	Still-image data that can be sent to a graphical display, fax machine, printer, and so on. The two initial subtypes are the common JPEG and GIF image formats.
audio	Audio data, which requires a speaker of some sort to listen to the contents.
video	Moving picture data. The initial subtype for this is the MPEG standard.
application	Some other data to be processed by the mail application. The primary subtype, octet-stream, is used for a stream of simple binary data. In most cases, the recommended action is to write the data to a file for the user. This file is what is used to send a program by mail. Another subtype, PostScript, is defined for sending PostScript documents.

The Content-Type you see on most messages for now is this one:

```
text/plain; charset=us-ascii
```

This Content-Type just means plain text with a U.S. ASCII character set. In fact, MIME-aware mailers that don't find the Content-Type field assume this value.

The other important header is the Content-Transfer-Encoding field, which tells how the data is encoded. If you want to send binary (8-bit) data over channels that assume 7 bits (most Internet mail servers), you still must encode that data down to 7 bits.

Those interested in further information should read the RFC or FTP to ftp.netcom.com and get the document pub/mdg/mime.txt, a MIME overview by Mark Grand. If you want to see some sample MIME messages, FTP to thumper.bellcore.com and look in the directory pub/nsb/samples. For those with Usenet access, the group comp.mail.mime discusses this subject.

MIME hasn't completely arrived by most practical standards. Although a lot of people are interested and programs are starting to support MIME, it's not yet universal. Carnegie Mellon's huge Andrew system handles MIME. The Gopher client for NextStep 3.0 has MIME support. The WWW (World Wide Web) uses MIME messages for transferring information. Metamail is a useful program that other mail programs can call to display MIME messages. The PINE mail program (discussed in the next chapter) and the Eudora mail program (discussed in Chapter 14, "Internet E-Mail: DOS, Windows, and Macintosh"), among others, offer some support for MIME. New Content-Types and subtypes are being registered all the time.

POP2 (RFC 937) and POP3 (RFC 1725)

The POP (Post Office Protocol) protocol comes in multiple versions, such as POP2 and POP3. Following is a general discussion because both protocols are in widespread use. Suppose that you want to use a PC or Mac to read your e-mail, but you only dial up the Internet every once in a while. POP or IMAP (Interactive Mail Access Protocol, discussed in the following section) is the solution to your problems.

With POP, your incoming e-mail spools onto a server machine, usually UNIX based, somewhere. When your computer connects to that server, it downloads the e-mail to your computer. You do all your e-mail processing on your computer.

POP is supported by numerous e-mail packages including Eudora, Pegasus Mail, and Z-Mail.

IMAP (RFC 1730)

One situation POP does not resolve is if you have a computer at home and one at work; you want to read your e-mail with a package on your home microcomputer but you also want to read it when you are at work. You also want to be able to access all your folders. IMAP is the solution to your problems.

IMAP's proponents see no reason that POP should continue to exist since IMAP has arrived. IMAP is supported by several e-mail packages including PINE, ECSMail, and Mailstrom.

Other Standards

You can find other standards by reading the RFCs. In fact, any two sites that want to talk to each other can use any protocol they agree on, such as L'il Joe's Own Protocol. The trick is to make sure that other sites can still handle the mail after they've processed it.

Standards Summary

Wow, all that to send a simple message. Don't let it get you down. In most cases, all you have to remember is this:

```
From: me
To: them
Subject: description

Message body here.
```

You've seen how SMTP can be used to send mail (you can even SMTP yourself), but you don't really want to do that every time you send mail. And how do you read mail? Read on, MacDuff.

Mail Transfer Agents

Earlier, you read that a Mail Transfer Agent (MTA) routes e-mail. Normally, only the system administrators worry about the details of the MTA and how it works. I mention MTAs here only so that you will be familiar with the terminology when you run across it.

The most famous MTA is sendmail, which comes with almost all UNIX machines. Although it is a very mature, robust product, it is most well known because of the periodic security holes people find. Other well-known MTAs you may run across include MMDF, PMDF, and smail.

Mail Filters

When you start getting a lot of e-mail, you begin to wonder whether you can filter and sort that e-mail before you begin to read it. Others have had the same idea.

Some mail packages, such as Pegasus Mail, include a filtering and sorting function as an integral part of the mail program itself. On other systems, especially UNIX-based systems, there are separate mail-filtering programs. The UNIX filtering programs are discussed briefly in the next chapter.

The major functions of mail filtering generally are filing, trashing, and marking. In *filing*, the incoming message is placed in a folder you have specified. A good use of this is when you want to read a mailing list but you do not want it mixed up with your other e-mail. *Trashing* is what it sounds like: getting rid of messages you don't want to see. This is useful when you do not want to read messages from a certain person. Finally, *marking* is the ability to mark important messages as being such.

I should point out that filtering has its limitations. With many filtering systems, you can only filter based on who the message is from and the subject. Even more advanced filtering packages that search the entire message cannot understand the actual meaning of the message and can only look for particular words in the text.

Uuencode and Split

There's one last introductory subject to cover. In the absence of MIME, how do you send programs and data through e-mail? Because there are so many people who don't have FTP access, yet do have e-mail access, it's guaranteed that this problem would be addressed. Indeed, there are several solutions, but the most widespread is the use of uuencode and uudecode.

Uuencode and BinHex

Uuencode takes an 8-bit (that is, a *binary*) file and encodes it as 6-bit printable characters. Because all Internet mail sites pass normal ASCII printable characters unmodified, the data should make it through to the other side. Some Mac users use a similar program (called BinHex) which serves the same purpose but is not compatible with uuencode.

> **NOTE**
>
> The uuencoded file is about 35 percent larger than the original file; 33 percent of that comes from converting 8-bit bytes to 6-bit bytes, and the rest comes from control information in the encoding, like the end-of-line markers.

Versions of uuencode exist for almost every platform there is. The next chapter discusses uuencode on UNIX (the original version of the program).

Split

What if you want to send a 200,000-byte file? If you use uuencode, you add 35 percent for a 270,000-byte file after encoding. That's a hefty message by any estimation. Although you usually don't run into any problem with normal messages, some sites have a limit on message size—usually around 64,000 bytes. If you send your file as one big chunk, only a fourth of it might get there. And unlike a hologram, the entire thing is needed to reconstruct the file. You must split the file into smaller chunks. A UNIX split program is described in the next chapter; similar programs exist for other platforms.

E-Mail Security

New Internet users tend to think that e-mail is secure and private. This is a mistake. There is no postal service that protects your e-mail.

The first problem is that it is relatively easy to forge a mail message to make it look like it came from a certain person. E-mail experts can almost always detect forged e-mail messages by looking at the headers. A good defense you can use is to look at the style of the message. Does it sound like something the sender would say? If not, then be suspicious.

Another problem is that—although there are some laws against it—people can intercept e-mail messages during transit without you knowing it. Your own system administrator most likely can look at your e-mail and may even be able to do it legally, especially if he or she is investigating a security leak.

Digital Signatures

The solution to the forgery problem is known as a *digital signature*. It is possible to include a digital signature on e-mail messages so that you can validate whether the sender is who he or she says it is. However, if the sender has his or her password stolen, someone may be able to still forge a message in his or her name.

Encryption

You can also encrypt e-mail messages. Remember how, as a kid, you encoded messages with your secret decoder ring? Encoding e-mail messages is like that, but it's an automatic process and is much, much more secure.

Using the latest algorithms, it is virtually impossible for someone besides the recipient to decrypt your messages.

Packages

Two major software systems for e-mail encryption and digital signatures control most of the market. They are PEM (Privacy Enhanced Mail) and PGP (Pretty Good Privacy). PEM is a purely commercial effort that depends on heavily centralized control mechanisms. In other words, PEM-based solutions tend to be expensive and require a complex infrastructure to be put in place.

The alternative PGP is based on the efforts of one person, Phil Zimmerman. PGP is free to individuals and educational institutions (others must pay for the software). PGP is based on the concept of a web of trust. You validate that you know your friends. Your friends validate that they know their friends. You assign a value to how much you trust your friends to validate their friends; this value tells PGP how much you trust their friends. The good thing about PGP is that it is easy for friends to start exchanging encrypted e-mail. The bad news is that it still requires an infrastructure to make it a good global solution.

Unfortunately, the support in e-mail packages for PGP and PEM are minimal at this point. Also, the standards for using these encryption systems with MIME are still being developed. We are at least a couple of years away from widespread deployment of e-mail encryption.

> **NOTE**
>
> Chapter 13, "Internet E-Mail: UNIX," discusses UNIX e-mail packages; continue your reading with this chapter if you are using a UNIX-based Internet service provider. Chapter 14, "Internet E-Mail: DOS, Windows, and Macintosh," is about PC and Mac e-mail packages; read this one if your e-mail package runs directly on your microcomputer.

Internet E-Mail: UNIX

13

*by Ron Dippold
revised for this
edition by
Billy Barron*

The Internet is, at heart, a UNIX network. It and its many services were closely tied to UNIX at the start, and that relationship continues to this day. Most UNIX implementations come with, or allow easy addition of, a whole suite of utilities for Internet connectivity. UNIX machines tend to be networked, and there is a good chance that your Internet access comes either directly or indirectly through some box running UNIX.

Many UNIX e-mail packages have primitive user interfaces, but that is changing. On the other hand, UNIX e-mail packages tend to be extremely powerful and flexible. Microcomputer-based e-mail, discussed in the next chapter, tends to be strong on user interfaces and less powerful.

Mail Programs

In the last chapter, we looked at the lower levels of e-mail. This chapter is concerned with User Agents for UNIX—the e-mail programs themselves. These programs are supposed to take care of all the hassles involved with retrieving and sending mail. You'll find that they vary widely in capability.

Incoming Mail

To access e-mail on UNIX, you don't actually have to run any sort of e-mail program. When your mail host receives a message for you, it places the message in your incoming mail spool file, usually `/var/spool/mail/yourid`, `/usr/mail/yourid`, or `/usr/spool/mail/yourid`.

All new messages are lumped together in the same file, divided by some separator your e-mail program should recognize. The most common separator is the characters From at the start of a line. Another separator, used in the MMDF format, is four Ctrl+A (ASCII 001) characters.

Mail

Most UNIX systems come with a basic program named, simply, *mail.* The Sun manual pages for mail claim that it is "a comfortable, flexible, interactive program for composing, sending, and receiving electronic messages." Flexible and interactive, yes; comfortable, no. But mail or a variation of it is on most systems. The mail version reviewed here is the common Sun mail program, but there are clones all over the place.

Simple Sending

In its simplest use, mail can be an easy mail-sending device. Just use the following line:

```
mail -s "subject" recipient < message
```

On some systems, you may have to use the `mailx` command instead of `mail`. You can't place headers in the message text. Or rather, you can, but the headers are treated as part of the message body—mail wants to control all the headers.

The `< message` part isn't required. If you don't give it, mail prompts you for the message text. If you do give it, it is a pre-prepared file that contains the message.

The `-s "subject"` part is optional, but if you don't include it, your e-mail won't have a subject when it is received. If you didn't include the `< message` part and are entering the message by hand, mail prompts you for the subject.

You can specify multiple recipients, separated by spaces.

Sending Mail

You can enter e-mail by hand as opposed to sending a prepared message. Just type **mail** **recipient**.

You are prompted to enter a subject. After entering the subject, you can type your message in a line mode (that provides very limited editing capability using tilde escape commands). If you enter the message in line mode, press Ctrl+D to send the mail when you are finished typing the message.

You can use a number of tilde escape commands to control various mail functions. These commands are indicated by a tilde (~) as the first character of a line, followed by the escape command. If you really want to have a tilde as the first character of a line of your message, enter it twice (~~).

NOTE

In normal use, I recommend the use of only one tilde escape command: ~v. The ~v command puts you in the editor defined by the UNIX environment variable VISUAL. By default, this is usually the vi editor, which is not the best editor for entering e-mail but does work. (Other editors such as emacs are also available.) If you ever need other tilde commands, type ~?.

You are placed in your editor; type your message. When you finish your message, save and exit the editor to return to the manual entry mode. Press Ctrl+D to send the message. You are then prompted for Carbon Copy addresses. Enter any that you want to use.

If you do not use ~v, you can manually enter your message and press Enter or Return at the end of every line. Remember that in this mode, you can not back up lines to correct mistakes. When you get to the end of the message, press Ctrl+D.

Reading Your Mail

If you start mail without any arguments (that is, if you just type **mail**), the program looks in your incoming mailbox for new e-mail. If it finds any, it places you into command mode. The first thing mail does is show you the e-mail waiting for you:

```
Mail version SMI 4.0 Wed Mar22 10:38:28 PDT 1995 Type ? for help.
"/var/spool/mail/rdippold": 2 messages 2 new
>N 1 jeff@goo.goo.com  Sat Mar 4 23:18  20/1045 Voting
N 2 rdippold           Sun Mar 5 01:19  13/347  This is a test
&
```

This message shows that I have two new e-mail messages waiting. One is from jeff@goo.goo.com, sent Saturday, March 4, at 11:18 P.M. It is 20 lines long and 1,045 characters (including the header). The subject of the message is Voting. The second message is one I sent to myself.

The > in the left column of the first message indicates that it is the *current message*—if I don't specify a message number, any command I give acts on this message. The Ns next to messages 1 and 2 indicate that they are new messages. The & is mail's prompt.

Note that there are many *mailboxes*, in the sense of files containing mail messages. There are two defaults, plus any you create yourself. The first standard mailbox is the incoming mailbox referred to earlier, usually stored at /usr/spool/mail/*yourid*, /usr/mail/*yourid*, or /var/spool/mail/*yourid*. This is your "system" mailbox. The second standard mailbox contains all your old, previously read messages (unless you've deleted them). This is a file called mbox in your home directory. You can also define as many mailboxes, or folders, as you want. Any file with saved messages is technically a mailbox, so simply executing a save or copy command on a message to another file creates another mailbox, which you can switch to later.

The general procedure for reading new e-mail is to press **n** to view each message; press **r** to reply to a message; press **d** to delete it (if you don't want it saved in mbox). You can follow any of these commands by a number (for example, you can read the fifth message by typing **n 5** or delete the tenth message by typing **d 10**.

As with most UNIX e-mail programs, messages are not deleted until you exit the mail program. Until then, you can type **undelete #** where the pound sign is the message number you want to undelete (the message you previously marked to be deleted).

Folders

Mail supports folders. You can see your available folders by using the folders command. You can switch to a particular folder by using the file *folder* command (replace *folder* with the folder name).

You can move messages into folders with the command copy *message folder*. The *message* parameter is the message number to be moved. The *folder* parameter is the name of the folder to which you want to move the message.

Common Mail Variables

Mail has several variables that affect its behavior. These variables act as a way to customize mail to your preferences. These variables are lost when you exit mail, so you should place any variable settings you want to use all the time in your .mailrc file (see "The .mailrc File," below).

You use the set command to change the value of these variables. For example, type **set VISUAL=emacs** to set the full-screen editor to the emacs editor. Type **set** by itself to see all the current variables.

To change the location of where mail thinks your folders are, use the set *folder=directory* command. By default, when replying, mail puts a tab in front of the other person's text. You can change this default with set indentprefix=*prefix* where *prefix* is the prefix character you want to use. The most common use of this command is set indentprefix=>.

The set replyall command configures mail so that whenever you reply, the message goes to all the people on the Cc line as well as those on the From line.

The *.mailrc* File

It would be a real pain in the neck to have to configure mail each time for the way you like to work. Instead, you can use the source command to read in a file as a series of mail commands. By using the source command, you can have a file that sets up your mail configuration the way you like it. But you still have to type **source myconfig** every time you run mail, and this method doesn't work if you type **mail henry** and never see a command line.

The solution is the .mailrc file. This file lives in your home directory and is automatically executed every time you start mail, just as if you had typed **source .mailrc**. Usually, the .mailrc file contains mail variables, but you can include other mail commands as well. The following sample .mailrc file uses many variables and commands not discussed in this chapter, but it will give you an idea of some of the other options available in mail:

```
# Example .mailrc file for Ron Dippold
echo Running Ron's .mailrc file
#
# The next lines set up aliases for sending mail
alias bill williamf@wubba.com
alias me rdippold@tofu.com
alias mit mail-server@rtfm.mit.edu
#
```

```
# These are some alternate addresses which I go by
alternates rdippold voting ronnied
#
# Discard "Received:" headers, which we don't care about
discard received
#
# Now set some variables
set alwaysignored
set autoprint

set crt=20
set editheaders
set folder=/usr/rdippold/mailboxes
set indentprefix=" > "
set keep
set metoo
set prompt="mail> "
set quiet
set screen=20
set sign="                            - Ron Dippold"
set Sign="Ron Dippold  - rdippold@tofu.com - (619) 555-1212"
set VISUAL=emacs
#
# This next bit is kind of neat - if I'm using a terminal, even my regular editor
# should be emacs. Why would I want to use a line editor? If for some reason
# I'm not using a terminal, then I'll grudgingly use ex, a line editor.
if t
set EDITOR=emacs
else
set EDITOR=ex
endif
echo Done processing Ron's .mailrc file. You may cheer.
```

TIP

To leave mail, just type **quit**. There are many mail commands not described in this chapter. You can discover them by looking at the mail manual page (type **man mail**) or by typing **help** within mail.

Mail Summary

The basic mail program is fairly flexible and powerful. The user interface is enough to send most people crying home to their parent or legal guardian, so there have been no shortage of replacement mail programs. In fact, you probably won't use mail. I spent the time explaining it because the same basic principles apply to the rest of the mail programs out there.

Elm

Elm is...impressive. It's written to be an easy-to-use, full-screen UNIX e-mail system, but it actually comes with an impressive amount of configurability and power. Elm comes with more than 100 pages of PostScript-formatted documentation.

Elm includes support for AT&T Mail forms, which makes it easy to fill out a standardized form and mail it off. Elm has some MIME support, but for real MIME support, you need the metamail package (available by anonymous FTP from `thumper.bellcore.com`).

Getting Elm

As of the time of this writing, Elm was at version 2.4.

> **NOTE**
>
> You can use anonymous FTP to get Elm from `ftp://ftp.uu.net/networking/mail/elm` or from `ftp://wuarchive.wustl.edu/mirrors/elm`.

The packed source-code file (which you need to build Elm) is about 1M, and the packed documentation is about 250K. Elm is not for those whose disk space is scarce. However, if you're looking for a friendly and fairly powerful mail program, it may be worth getting some guru with disk space to burn to get Elm running for you—Elm doesn't require a huge amount of space when it's running.

You start Elm by typing **elm**.

Elm Files

Elm places an `.elm` directory in your home directory to contain configuration items (such as the `elmrc` configuration file). It also makes a `Mail` directory for your mail folders (unless you change that setting).

Elm Interface

Elm itself is actually fairly simple. The messages are presented as header summaries (see Figure 13.1). You scroll a selection bar up and down the list of messages and press a key to perform an action on the message. The basic list of keys you need to know is reasonably small and usually appears at the bottom of the screen, but there are many esoteric functions assigned to esoteric keys. Almost every key has a function.

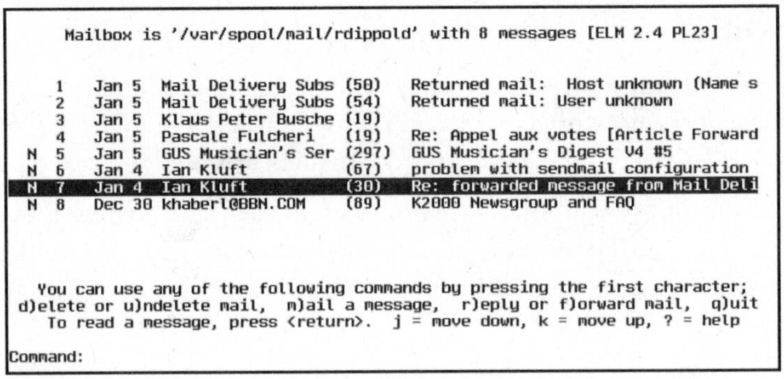

FIGURE 13.1.

The main Elm screen. I have eight messages in my mailbox; four are new. Message 7 is selected.

```
        Mailbox is '/var/spool/mail/rdippold' with 8 messages [ELM 2.4 PL23]

       1   Jan 5  Mail Delivery Subs (50)   Returned mail:  Host unknown (Name s
       2   Jan 5  Mail Delivery Subs (54)   Returned mail: User unknown
       3   Jan 5  Klaus Peter Busche  (19)
       4   Jan 5  Pascale Fulcheri    (19)  Re: Appel aux votes [Article Forward
  N    5   Jan 5  GUS Musician's Ser (297)  GUS Musician's Digest V4 #5
  N    6   Jan 4  Ian Kluft           (67)  problem with sendmail configuration
  N    7   Jan 4  Ian Kluft           (30)  Re: forwarded message from Mail Deli
  N    8   Dec 30 khaberl@BBN.COM     (89)  K2000 Newsgroup and FAQ



      You can use any of the following commands by pressing the first character;
    d)elete or u)ndelete mail,  m)ail a message,  r)eply or f)orward mail,  q)uit
        To read a message, press <return>.  j = move down, k = move up, ? = help

 Command:
```

Elm has respectable online help. Type **?** to get help; type **??** to get a list of all valid keys.

After you select a message, press Enter or the spacebar to view it. You will be in a simple full-screen e-mail lister. Most of the keys that affect e-mail also work from this screen.

Elm Sending

To send a message in Elm, use the m command. Entering messages in Elm is easy. Just enter the name of the recipient and the subject, and Elm sends you into the editor. When you exit the editor, you have several options:

Option	Description
e	Edit the message again.
!	Exit to a command shell. Type exit to get back to Elm.
h	Edit the message headers (see Figure 13.2).
c	Save a copy of the message.
i	Spell-check the message.
s	Send the message.
f	Forget about it—don't send the message.

Pick the appropriate command. If you pick s, your message goes to the recipient.

Elm Options

If you press o from the main menu, you see the Elm options screen. The options shown in Figure 13.3 are explained in Table 13.1.

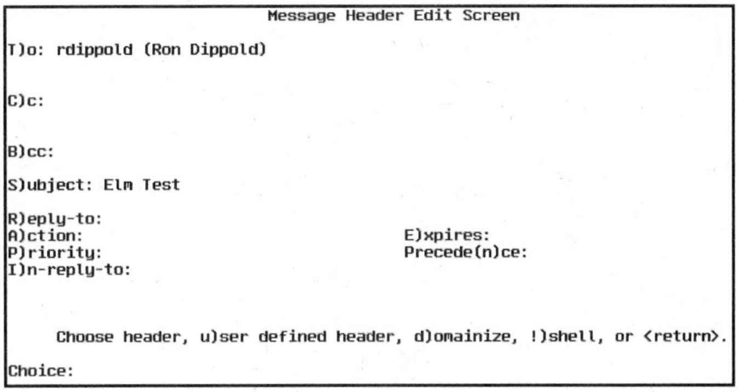

#### Chapter 13

FIGURE 13.2.

Editing the message headers is easier than it sounds—Elm comes with an option screen for this task.

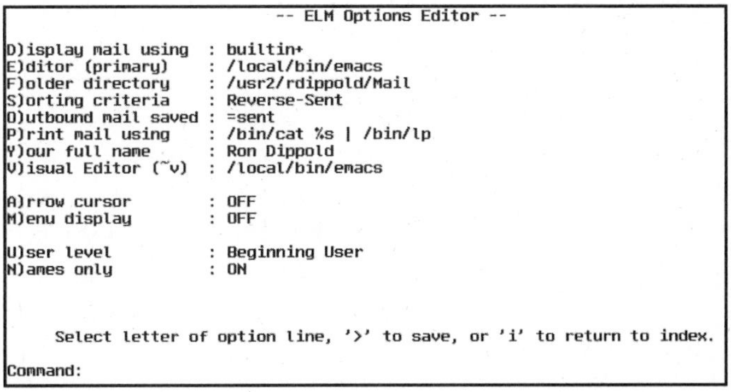

```
                    Message Header Edit Screen
T)o: rdippold (Ron Dippold)

C)c:

B)cc:

S)ubject: Elm Test

R)eply-to:
A)ction:                              E)xpires:
P)riority:                            Precede(n)ce:
I)n-reply-to:


     Choose header, u)ser defined header, d)omainize, !)shell, or <return>.
Choice:
```

FIGURE 13.3.

An example option screen.

```
                    -- ELM Options Editor --
D)isplay mail using   : builtin+
E)ditor (primary)     : /local/bin/emacs
F)older directory     : /usr2/rdippold/Mail
S)orting criteria     : Reverse-Sent
O)utbound mail saved  : =sent
P)rint mail using     : /bin/cat %s | /bin/lp
Y)our full name       : Ron Dippold
V)isual Editor (~v)   : /local/bin/emacs

A)rrow cursor         : OFF
M)enu display         : OFF

U)ser level           : Beginning User
N)ames only           : ON


     Select letter of option line, '>' to save, or 'i' to return to index.
Command:
```

Table 13.1. Elm options available from the option screen.

Option	Description
D	Your message display program. By default, Elm uses its own built-in message displayer (builtin+). Change this value to more if you like the UNIX pager.
E	The editor used for outbound messages. Elm comes with a built-in editor, which is rather puny. If you regularly use a good full-screen editor, the outbound editor should be the same as your visual editor (see the entry for the V option).
F	The directory in which your e-mail folders are kept. By default, Elm uses the Mail directory under your root directory.
S	Specification of how folders are sorted. Most options you would want to use (and some you wouldn't) are allowed for. I normally use Mailbox Order, which is effectively unsorted. When you select this option, it goes through the list of valid options.

continues

Table 13.1. continued

Option	Description
O	You can specify a folder in which all the e-mail you send is kept. By default, this is =sent, which means the folder sent stored in the file sent in your Elm Mail directory.
P	This is the command used to print your e-mail. Place the characters %s in the command to specify where Elm can put the name of the file to print to the programs you invoke. For example, you can use /bin/lp %s to invoke the printer on some System V systems.
Y	Your full name is the equivalent of the personal name in other e-mail programs. The text you specify here is sent in the From field as a comment: ab3443@bravenew.world.com *(Your Full Name)*.
V	*Visual editor* is a strange way of saying *full-screen editor*. This is usually emacs, vi, or pico; specify your favorite.
A	If the Arrow Cursor setting is off, an inverse highlight bar is used to choose messages. If you're on a very slow link, that method may be too slow; it may also be that you cannot see inverse highlights on your old clunker terminal. In both cases, you can set this option on to get a -> to the left of the screen to select messages.
M	Normally, Elm gives a short menu of the most important keys at the bottom of the screen. Although this menu is nice, it takes up room where you could show message headers (after a while, you learn what the keys are). Turn off this option to free that screen space.
U	The User Level option isn't well defined, but there are three levels: beginner, intermediate, and advanced. Beginners won't have some commands available (there's no need to scare them).
N	Normally, Elm shows only the name of the sender when you reply to a message. If you turn off the Names Only option, both the name and the address are shown.

Don't forget to press > to save your options when you're done!

More Elm Options

Even if you don't want to change any of the options shown in the Elm options screen, you should press > from the options screen. Doing so creates the file .elm/elmrc in your home directory. You can edit this file to set all sorts of nifty options, most of which can't be configured from inside Elm.

> **TIP**
>
> The .elm/elmrc file can be somewhat deceiving if you forget that all lines starting with # are comments. You can change values until you're blue in the face, but unless you get rid of those #s, Elm uses its default values.

You can find help for all the settings in the Ref.guide, which comes with Elm. Therefore, this chapter does not detail all the Elm settings.

Reading Messages in Elm

Reading messages in Elm is simple. Use the arrow keys to highlight the message you want to read and then press Enter or Return. Elm displays the selected message.

Continue pressing Enter to see the various pages of the message. When you want to go back to the message list, press **i** (Index).

To reply to a message, highlight the message and press **r**. The rest of the reply function works like the send function.

Highlight a message and press **d** to delete the message. If you change your mind, notice that once a message is deleted, the cursor skips over that message when you press the arrow keys. However, you can type the message number by itself to go directly to the deleted message. Once the message is highlighted, you can press **u** to undelete.

Folders

Folders are one of Elm's strengths. If you want to see what folders you currently have, the command depends on your version of Elm. With version 2.4 (and probably future versions), press **c** (for change folder) and then press **=***. For earlier versions, press **c** and then press **?**.

To switch to a folder, use the c command. Then Elm prompts you for the folder name. Enter the name of the folder preceded by an equal sign. For example, to switch to the fun folder, type **=fun**.

To save a message into a particular folder, highlight the message and use the s command. The default folder name that appears is the *userid* of the person who sent you the mail. If you do not want the default, type = and the name of the folder to which you want to save the message.

Elm Replaces Mail

Elm handles the same command-line arguments as mail (and more), so you can use Elm instead of mail to send an automatic command-line message. The following line works just fine:

```
elm -s "subject" recipient < messagefile
```

If you don't give the < *messagefile* information, Elm prompts you, just like mail does.

And More Elm

Elm is actually much more powerful than it appears at first glance. In addition to Elm itself, a host of associated programs are available. Read the documentation for a full description of how to use each program. These associated programs serve a variety of purposes such as telling people you are on vacation, telling you immediately when new mail arrives, and so on.

There are also several programs (chkalias, elmalias, and so on) that help manage Elm's aliases feature, which is fairly robust. Aliases enable you to define user nicknames and group of names so that you can specify just joeb rather than his full address of joe_buttafucco@incredibly_long_name.fisher.edu.

Elm Documentation

Elm comes with much documentation and includes specific guides for aliases, the filter program, and mail forms. Be sure to browse Users.guide and Ref.guide for hints.

> **NOTE**
>
> If you think you are going to be a serious Elm user, the Usenet group comp.mail.elm carries a discussion on it. The Elm Frequently Asked Questions list (FAQ) is available at ftp://ghost.dsi.unimi.it/pub/Elm/Elm-FAQ.Z. It's also posted to the Usenet group news.answers once a month.

Elm Summary

In its simplest configuration, Elm is easier to use than mail. Elm also comes with quite a few useful additional programs, if you don't mind the complexity of the add-ins. But what if Elm is still too complex for you?

PINE

PINE, in a vein similar to Elm, is a product from the University of Washington that's designed to act on simple one-key menu operations. PINE originally stood for "PINE Is Not Elm," but recently has been changed to mean "Program for Internet News and E-mail." PINE supports MIME. MS-DOS and UNIX versions of PINE are available. PINE uses a message editor, pico, which can also be used as a stand-alone program. PINE handles multiple folders or incoming mailboxes quite well. PINE can read Usenet news, although it currently does not offer all the features of a full-featured news reader.

Getting PINE

> **NOTE**
>
> To get PINE, anonymously FTP to `ftp://ftp.cac.washington.edu/mail`.

At the time of this writing, the latest version of PINE was version 3.91. The compressed distribution code, `pine.tar.z`, was 2M in size. As a nice touch, precompiled versions for AIX3.2, HP/UX 9.01, Linux, NeXTstep, Solaris 2.X (SPARC), and SunOS 4.1.3 (SPARC) systems are available in the `UNIX-BINARIES` subdirectory. Most of these files are around 2M in size (the AIX executable file weighs in at 4M).

If you already have a version of PINE, you should know that some versions of PINE let you fetch the latest version of itself from the PINE Update Server.

PINE Configuration

You can totally configure PINE 3.9x from within the program itself. If you have an older version of PINE, you must edit a file called `.pinerc` (not covered here). The PINE configuration screen can be reached by pressing **s** and then **c** from the main menu.

If you installed PINE yourself, make sure that you set *personal-name* (your own name, for example, John Smith), *smtp-server* (if you're using SMTP—you probably should ask your system administrator for this value if PINE cannot send a message successfully), and *inbox-path* (very important, usually `/var/spool/mail/yourid`). The rest is gravy. The `sort-key` setting is nice if you like to be organized. The `image-viewer` setting is a necessity if you want to view GIF or JPEG files that arrive in MIME messages. However, if you are a PINE user and not the system administrator, you will probably find PINE preconfigured for your system and do not need to make any changes unless you want to.

PINE Interface

PINE is designed to be easy to use (see Figure 13.4). Most functions are keyed off of "hotkeys." These hotkeys change from screen to screen, but an effort was made to keep them consistent where possible. The bottom of the screen lists some of the currently acceptable commands.

Press **?** on most screens to get help; on screens where text entry is called for, press Ctrl+G to get help. The Ctrl+G combination isn't very intuitive, but PINE always reminds you of it. (Any "normal" key may be something you want to enter as part of the text, so something strange has to be used to access help.) The help is fairly detailed (see Figure 13.5).

FIGURE 13.4.

PINE's main menu. Note the simplicity. Here I have just entered PINE and have one new message waiting.

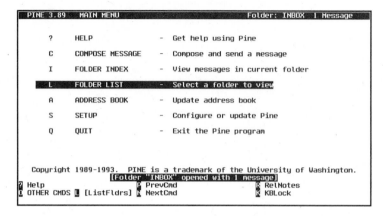

FIGURE 13.5.

This is a PINE help screen for the Address Book.

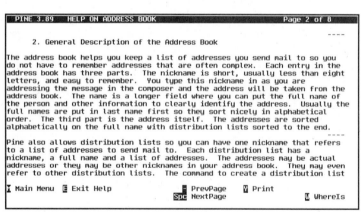

When hotkeys aren't practical (such as when you're selecting one mail message out of dozens), a selection bar is used. You can move it with the arrow keys and press a hotkey to take appropriate action against the selected message.

Finally, there are a few places where you just must actually type something, such as when you enter message text. If this bugs you, be cheered by the fact that voice recognition systems are improving rapidly.

PINE Folders

PINE makes good use of the concept of multiple folders. By default, PINE creates three folders: INBOX (your incoming e-mail), sent-mail (e-mail you've sent), and saved-messages (a generic place for you to save messages). You can define folders of your own for storing e-mail that should be grouped with other mail. Switching to another folder is as simple as pressing **L** (for List Folders) from almost any menu. By default, all folders except INBOX are created in a mail directory under your home directory; INBOX is wherever your system places your new e-mail. To create a new folder, press **L** to get the folder list, press **A** (for Add), and type the name of the new folder.

When you open a folder, you see an overview of all the messages in the folder (see Figure 13.6). Use your cursor to select a message to read, press Return, and you are in a full-screen message viewer.

FIGURE 13.6.

This screen shows my incoming e-mail; there are four messages, three I haven't seen. The third message is selected (from the look of it, I botched an address).

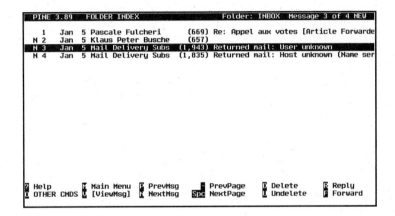

PINE Address Book

The PINE Address Book is useful (access the Address Book screen by pressing **A** from the main menu). The basic concept is the same as the nicknames, or aliases, of mail and Elm: you want to create fast names you can use to refer to nasty long addresses or lists of addresses (see Figure 13.7).

FIGURE 13.7.

A sample address book that shows some nicknames for the bizarre people I e-mail. Note the mailing list mylist *at the bottom.*

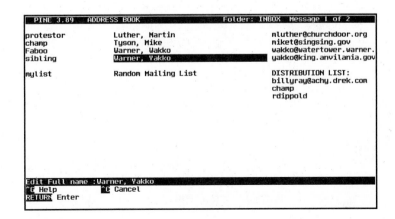

Instead of sending e-mail to wakko@watertower.warner.com, I can define that address to be associated with a nickname wakko. When I compose a message and enter **wakko** as the recipient, PINE replaces that alias with the full address. You can also create list aliases, which send e-mail to several addresses. For example, I can define the alias warners to send mail to wakko, yakko, and dot. PINE takes care of expanding the alias name into addresses for me.

You can create an alias when you are reading a message or looking at an index of messages. The Takeaddr command searches the current message for the From field, shows it to you, and asks you for a nickname for this address. Using this feature, you can define nicknames on the fly.

PINE *Compose Message*

Compose is PINE's equivalent of other programs' send command. Compose enables you to specify who you want to send the message to and then enter your message text. You can start a composition by pressing **c** from most menus. The editor is easy to use, and even includes a primitive spell checker (see Figure 13.8).

FIGURE 13.8.

The editor screen, used to send a "help" message to the mail server at MIT. Because I spelled it wrong (it should be mail-server*), the User Unknown error was generated.*

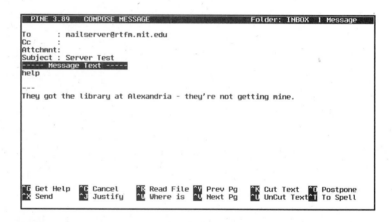

There's one item in the editor screen that may be puzzling: Attchmnt (it stands for *Attachment* and refers to an attached file). Use this field to specify the name of a file you want to send with the message using MIME format. If the receiver has a MIME-capable e-mail reader, the receiver should be able to "detach" the file and use it for whatever nefarious purpose you intended. When you're viewing a message, PINE enables you to view or save an attached MIME file by pressing the **v** key.

One of the advanced features of PINE is its capability to stop a composition in the middle and continue it at a later date. The function is known as Postpone and can be accessed by pressing Ctrl+O. Thereafter, every time you enter Compose mode (in a few minutes, hours, days, or years), you are prompted whether you want to continue the postponed composition.

Reading Messages

Reading messages in PINE is almost identical to reading them in Elm. You highlight what you want with the arrow keys and press Enter or Return. After reading the message, press **I** (for Index) to go back to the messages screen.

Press **D** to delete a message; press **U** to undelete a message (PINE does not skip undeleted messages like Elm does). Finally, you can reply to a message by pressing **R**.

PINE Summary

PINE is easy to use, is fairly powerful, does MIME, and has good help. If you can live with a large mail program and if menu-driven programs don't drive you crazy, it's certainly worth looking at.

User Mail Agents Summary

This chapter has described several e-mail programs, from the most primitive to the most user friendly. Is this all of them? Not by any means! I'll list a few more here.

NOTE

For a complete list of e-mail programs, find the "UNIX E-Mail Software Survey FAQ," which is posted once a month to the Usenet group `news.answers`. By reading the `comp.mail.misc` group, you should learn about any exciting new products.

Program	Description
mailx	This is AT&T's version of mail. You wouldn't want to use this any more than you would want to use mail, but it's fairly common and should be mentioned.
metamail	The metamail program isn't really a normal User Mail Agent. Rather, regular e-mail programs can take MIME messages they don't know how to handle and pass them on to metamail, which may be able to do something with them. You can anonymously FTP to `thumper.bellcore.com` and look in `pub/nsb` for the source code.
MH	Mail Handler (MH). MH is different in that each command is a different program. Why use a separate user interface when you can do everything from the UNIX shell? This program is obviously not for novices, but it may be your cup of tea. MH has MIME support and is

continues

Program	Description
	standard with some UNIX systems. You can find it at `ftp://ftp.uci.edu/pub/mh/mh-6.8.tar.Z` if you are interested (this is the latest version as of this writing). The Usenet group `comp.mail.mh` is for discussions of MH. There's also an `emacs` interface for MH called MH-E.
mush	Mail User's Shell (mush). This program stands out because it enables you to configure everything, even its internal workings, with a UNIX shell-type scripting language. You can build a totally custom mail environment for yourself. The mush program has evolved into a commercial product, Z-Mail, which is very advanced. For information on either product, mail `info@z-code.com`. The Usenet group `comp.mail.mush` is for mush discussion.
ECSMail	ECSMail is a relatively new, but nice graphical interface to UNIX e-mail. See `ftp://isagate.isac.ca/ecsmail/`.

There are other programs (including several for other platforms as discussed in the next chapter), but if none of those listed or discussed fits your needs, read the `comp.mail.misc` Usenet group to see what else may be out there.

Mail Filters

Chapter 12 introduced the concept of a mail filter. Now let's take a look at the packages available on UNIX for filtering messages.

Procmail

Procmail is designed to "do" things to your e-mail before you see it. It can sort your e-mail into separate folders (useful if you subscribe to different mailing lists) or get a substantial amount of e-mail that can be split off separately so that you can forward the messages to another address. Procmail lets you preprocess your e-mail; for example, you can pass it through a formatter. You can have Procmail generate automatic replies, or have it execute programs when certain types of mail are received. You can even run mail servers and mailing lists with it (more on these entities in later chapters). Procmail has been extensively tested, is fast, and has scads of error checking built in. You can pick up the latest version at `ftp://ftp.informatik.rwth-aachen.de/pub/unix/Procmail.tar.Z`.

Deliver

Although Procmail is the king-of-the-hill for mail filter programs, I personally like Deliver. With Deliver, you write shell scripts to handle all incoming messages. Although this usually requires more work on your part than filtering with Procmail, Deliver is very clean, is almost infinitely flexible, and set limits on what you can do with your e-mail based only on how well you can program scripts. The speed shouldn't be too much of a concern on that fast machine of yours. Deliver can be found at `ftp://oak.oakland.edu/pub2/unix-c/mail/deliver.tar.Z`.

Mailagent

I can't personally recommend or say bad things about the Mailagent program because I'm not very familiar with it, but it's another well-known e-mail filter. This one is written in the perl language, which means you can do almost anything with your e-mail. Mailagent comes with many built-in features. I suggest you look at this one if you know perl; it can be found at `ftp://isfs.kuis.kyoto-u.ac.jp/utils/perl-archive/perl-mailagent.tar.Z`.

Elm Filter

The simple Elm Filter filtering program comes with Elm. It is a nice program to use if your filtering needs are minimal or you are just getting started and want something simple to use. If you want something really powerful, use one of the other programs described here.

Uuencode and Split

The following sections describe how to use uuencode and split. Uuencode converts a binary file to text; split splits a large file into multiple pieces. For general information on these topics, refer to Chapter 12, "Internet E-Mail: An Overview."

Uuencode

Here's a simple example of how uuencode works. The file `test1` contains the text `This is a test`. To run the file through uuencode and place the result in `test1.uue`, you use the following command:

```
uuencode test1 test1 > test1.uue
```

This is the standard uuencode command format: first the name of the file you want to encode, then the name you want the file to have when it is unpacked on the other end, then the > symbol and the name of the encoded file. Normally, you want the file to have the same name when it is unpacked as it does now, so both names (`test1` and `test1` in this example) usually are the same in any uuencode you do. When you `cat test1.uue`, you get the following result:

```
begin 660 test1
.5&AI<R!I<R!A('1E<W1!

end
```

The first line contains uuencode's `begin` signal, the UNIX file permissions for the file, and the name to which the file should be unpacked. The second line contains the encoded data, which can consist of only printable characters. Then there's a blank line, followed by `end` to end the file. You can freely send the uuencoded file through almost any mail system.

You can even send the uuencoded data directly to someone else without an intermediate file:

```
uuencode ttt.exe ttt.exe ¦ mail -s "Tic Tac Toe" mybuddy
```

Uudecode

When you receive an e-mail message that has been uuencoded, you have to decode it. For that you use uudecode. First, save the uuencoded e-mail message to a file. Then decode it with the following command:

```
uudecode test1.uue
```

Simple as that. Well, not quite. A lot of other crud such as message headers winds up in the `test1.uue` file. Sometimes, the sender adds some commentary before the data. Uudecode is supposed to find the beginning of the actual uuencoded data in the file, but sometimes it gets confused. You may have to use your editor to trim off everything before the `begin` line and after the `end` line.

Now look at the resulting file with **cat test1**:

```
This is a test
```

It worked! Of course, you could have just sent this sentence through the mail without encoding and decoding it. If you want to send programs through the mail, you should encode and decode them—and the process should work the same way as described here. It's tough to show the contents of program files in print—except as a hex dump, which would probably send weaker readers screaming. Therefore, I used just the simple sentence in this example.

Split

But wait! All is not paradise. The test1 file was short; had it been a long file (generally, greater than 100K), we may have had problems sending it to certain networks with UUCP. In Chapter 12, we talked about splitting a mail message. Now we will cover the commands you use to do it.

Although you can split a file manually, there's a UNIX program that does the job for you: split. Just tell split the number of lines you want in each piece of the split file, and split goes *snicker-snack*, sending that big file galumphing back. The number of lines you specify doesn't tell you the size, exactly, but you can experiment. I find that using 800 lines per piece gives you nice safe 50,000-byte chunks. Here's how it works:

```
uuencode bigfile bigfile > bigfile.uue
split -800 bigfile.uue splits
mail -s "Bigfile.uue 1/3" mybuddy < splitsaa
mail -s "Bigfile.uue 2/3" mybuddy < splitsab
mail -s "Bigfile.uue 3/3" mybuddy < splitsac
rm bigfile.uue splits??
```

The hidden piece of the puzzle is that the split command needs the number of lines, the name of the file to be split, and a base name for the output files. In this case, the base name for the output files is splits. The split program then names the resulting files splitsaa, splitsab, splitsac, and if necessary, all the way up to splitszz. Split can divide a large file into as many as 676 pieces. If that's not enough, seriously consider using other methods to send data.

In the example, the subject lines (-s) use the convention 1/3, 2/3, and 3/3 to let the receiver know how many total pieces there are and which piece of the whole each message is.

The receiver has to save all the messages into a big file, edit out everything except the uuencoded stuff, and then run uudecode on the resulting file. Although it's a cumbersome process, it works. If you do this a lot, look into programs that automate the uuencode splitting and mailing and the recombining plus uudecoding. There's a program for everything.

Internet E-Mail: DOS, Windows, and Macintosh

14

by Ron Dippold
revised for this
edition by
Philip
Baczewski

What if you don't have UNIX and you want to send Internet mail, or you have a UNIX system but want to use your personal computer to handle mail?

The first alternative is to let someone else do the work for you—subscribe to a BBS or an online service that offers Internet mail connectivity. See the next chapter, "Internet E-Mail: Gateways," for more information. The alternative explored in this chapter involves hooking your personal computer into an existing mail system.

Background

What? You skipped all of Chapter 12, "Internet E-Mail: An Overview"? Shame, shame! Seriously, please go back and read it; an understanding of Internet mail on other systems still relies on concepts of SMTP, Internet addressing, and more. If you want to learn more about how Internet e-mail software works (including the programs discussed in this chapter), review the "Sendmail" section of Chapter 12.

Methods of Access

A microcomputer can be used to receive Internet electronic mail in a number of ways. It can be as simple as using the computer as a terminal to read Internet mail on a UNIX machine on the host system, or it can be as complex as using your microcomputer as a full-fledged Internet mail gateway that not only lets you read your mail, but also transmits and receives it using Internet protocols. The middle ground may be the most flexible use of a microcomputer for electronic mail: use the micro to read and compose mail messages while using a Internet-connected host to manage a mailbox and actually transmit and receive the messages.

Not a Full Node

First of all, you can always get Internet mail on another platform by setting up a complete mail system yourself. Many bulletin board systems (BBSes) that support Internet mail or Usenet groups use this method. They receive what is known as a *feed* from a real Internet site that agrees to support these smaller sites. Once or twice a day, the site calls the Internet site and grabs any new mail or Usenet news, then sends any mail or postings from its side. These smaller sites have their own domain names and act as independent sites.

That option is always available to you for mail, but it's not the topic here. In this chapter, I am looking for the solution to the following problem: I have mail waiting for me at a central mail site and want to access it remotely. I also want to be able to compose mail offline and send it to that site for mailing.

Mail Clients

Mail clients are a simple concept. Sometimes you don't want to implement a "real" Internet node on your computer for reasons of space, speed, and complexity of setup. You can let an existing system handle all the real mail problems and just connect to it to get your mail.

Here's a real-life example: I normally do all my mail on my UNIX system, where all my new mail arrives. I use Elm—no problem. Sometimes, however, such as when I'm on the road, I don't want to (or can't) spend much time online reading my mail. In this case, I use a mail reader; it connects to the UNIX system, downloads all my new mail, and then disconnects. Then I can browse the mail at my convenience and enter responses. When I've read all my mail, I reconnect just long enough to have my mail reader upload my responses and then I disconnect.

Some people like to use this method all the time with their personal computers at work because many of the mail clients have a user interface greatly superior to what they can get on their UNIX systems. Or the computer department may have given them a mail-only account, reasoning that this route is less of a hassle for them than trying to help Windows users learn UNIX.

E-mail and Local Area Networks

In an office setting, electronic mail is often provided by software running on a local area network (LAN). Novell NetWare is most common for PC networks; AppleShare is the standard for Macintosh networks. Apple Computer has also introduced Powershare, a part of its Apple Open Collaboration Environment (AOCE).

The one thing the LAN systems have in common when supporting e-mail is that they must support some type of gateway to send mail the Internet. Some gateways still require an Internet-connected host to handle the actual transfer of e-mail to its final destination. It can take a bit of time on the part of a LAN administrator to set up and configure an Internet mail gateway, but the result allows office and Internet mail to be read from the same e-mail program.

TCP/IP and Microcomputer E-mail

In computer lingo, the UNIX system is known as the *server* and my PC is known as a *client*. Now I've got a new problem: how do the client and server exchange mail?

First, the client and server must connect. The standard protocol with which two machines on the Internet talk to each other is known as TCP/IP (Transmission Control Protocol/Internet Protocol). TCP (RFC 793) provides error-free logical channels between connected machines (or even separate processes on the same machine). It doesn't specify the underlying physical connections. TCP runs on top of IP (RFC 791), which allows two processes to exchange *datagrams* (blocks of data). IP runs on top of whatever hardware you want to use to connect the machines. Within a site, that hardware is usually Ethernet, but it could be X.25, AppleTalk, serial connections, or even two cans and a string or a series of semaphore posts (although I wouldn't want to write the drivers for either of those last two).

For most mail solutions, you need some form of the TCP/IP protocol stack and driver (like the ones that come with TCP/IP packages: FTP Software's PC/TCP and NetManage's Chameleon software). Here, I'll touch on some important points related to microcomputer e-mail.

Packet Drivers

Packet drivers solve several problems for DOS PCs that use various networking protocols. Back in the old days, applications that wanted to talk over Ethernet boards would access the boards directly. It was too bad if you wanted to access the board from multiple applications. And it was doubly too bad if you wanted to bring out a new board—you had to get all the applications to know about your board. Finally, multiple protocol support was almost impossible (you couldn't do TCP/IP and Novell file systems and PC-NFS at the same time).

To fix these problems, FTP Software came up with the packet driver specification and made it public. *Packet drivers* are small pieces of software that talk to the Ethernet card and to any software that wants to use the card. They even handle multiple incoming types of messages and can notify the appropriate software when data intended for it has arrived. With packet drivers, an application no longer has to use special code to talk to each card: it just talks to the packet driver and forgets about the card being used. The maker of a new card can make it instantly compatible with much of the software out there just by providing a packet driver.

And because the packet drivers can handle multiple types of incoming and outgoing data, multiple network applications are possible. Therefore (in the most popular example), you can use TCP/IP and still use your Novell file servers simultaneously.

Actually, because this specification does such a good job of hiding the Ethernet card, you can have packet drivers for something that really isn't an Ethernet card. There are packet drivers for serial lines, packet drivers for other hardware, and even packet drivers to interface to other network software drivers, such as IPX or NDIS. This is technically known as a *shim*.

Finally, the packet driver specification is in the public domain, and so are the packet drivers themselves (it's in the best interests of the network card manufacturers that this is so). The drivers used to be collected as the Clarkson packet drivers and are now maintained as the Crynwr (no, that's not a typo) drivers. You can anonymously FTP them (and other packet driver utilities) from, among other places, `ftp://ftp.cc.utexas.edu/microlib/dos/network/packet`.

People using Novell networks often use Novell's Open Data-Link Interface (ODI) drivers. This and other protocol stacks, like 3Com and Microsoft's Network Driver Interchange Standard (NDIS), attempt to make using multiple protocols easier on a LAN. If programs written to the packet driver specification are to work with these other kinds of drivers, an additional driver is needed to translate back and forth. These shims are available for both ODI and NDIS at the same FTP site just mentioned, as well as at other FTP sites on the Internet. For more information about ODI and NDIS, see Chapter 9, "Connecting a LAN to the Internet."

Note that packet drivers are not the end-all of networking; they're just a start. To talk to something else, you have to run some sort of protocol on top of the packet drivers—usually a TCP/IP stack that interfaces with the packet driver.

Real TCP/IP for PCs

Several companies manufacture full TCP/IP suites for PCs. FTP Software offers them for DOS, for example, and IBM offers them for OS/2. Novell's LAN Workplace is another popular suite available for both DOS and Windows. These usually come with a full range of utilities that operate over TCP/IP, such as FTP, Telnet, and `finger`.

There is a problem, however; the TCP standard specifies just the protocol, not really the procedure calls made to set up a connection. Each TCP/IP vendor uses its own standard for programming a socket (one end of a connection). Your TCP/IP software may not work with a utility that uses TCP/IP because it's looking for another TCP/IP library. Be careful when you are matching utilities with network packages.

Waterloo TCP/IP Library

Waterloo is one of the most popular of several free TCP/IP libraries available. Having this library solves the programmers' dilemmas about which TCP/IP stack they should support—they can just include Waterloo in their program. Because the Waterloo TCP/IP talks to the generic packet drivers described earlier, almost no compatibility problems are involved. This concern doesn't really apply much to you, the user. But it does mean that several programs out there require only the addition of a packet driver to run, so you don't need a separate TCP/IP stack.

On the other hand, including the TCP/IP library in the program adds two problems. First, it increases the size of the programs (they have to have the TCP/IP logic that normally resides outside of the program). Second, you can't really run the program simultaneously with something that wants to use another TCP/IP stack. These are just some of the tradeoffs involved.

WinSock

If you're running under Windows, you're in luck. There is a socket interface specification standard that has been gathering increasing support: Windows Sockets, otherwise known as WinSock, or WinSocketAPI. This interface specifies a set of calls applications can make to interface with TCP/IP software. If your TCP/IP package supports the WinSock interface, any program written to use the WinSock interface should function. No fuss, no muss, no hassle. Lately, most TCP/IP software shipping has included WinSock capabilities.

> **NOTE**
>
> There is even a set of free WinSock programs you can get with FTP at
> `ftp://ftp.cica.indiana.edu/pub/pc/win3/winsock`.

The big problem with WinSock is what the name implies: it works only for Windows. DOS users are still on their own.

MacTCP

MacTCP is a TCP/IP protocol stack for the Macintosh. As of System 7.5, it is supplied by Apple Computer as part of the Macintosh operating system and as an add-on to earlier versions of the Macintosh OS. Many commercial as well as shareware programs are written to use MacTCP to accomplish Internet operations.

MacTCP must be configured with appropriate Internet network information, like IP address, gateway, and other parameters. Once that information is set, you can select a variety of transports, such as Ethernet, SLIP, or PPP. Having MacTCP in place makes using e-mail clients and other Internet programs not only possible, but fairly transparent as well.

SLIP and PPP

For those who want to run TCP/IP over serial lines (a modem, in other words), SLIP (Serial Line IP—RFC 1055) is a simple "nonstandard for transmission of IP datagrams over serial lines." Most annex servers for computer systems offer SLIP capability.

There are some extensions to this concept. TCP/IP headers are quite large when compared to the speed of most modems, so RFC 1144 details a method of compressing them that many servers implement (this is sometimes known as CSLIP). You can find SLIP implemented for a packet driver as part of the Crynwr packet driver set.

Point-to-Point Protocol (PPP), detailed in RFC 1171, is another popular connection method. PPP is a bit more efficient and flexible than SLIP and supports more than just Internet protocols.

SLIP and PPP are available to Macintosh users in freely distributed versions. InterCon Systems Corporation has written InterSLIP, which you can use on as many computers as you want—as long as use is limited to private, noncommercial purposes. MacPPP was developed by the Merit Network, Inc. and the University of Michigan. It consists of a network extension and a control panel installed in your Macintosh system folder. Both can be found on any of the Info-Mac archive sites, such as `ftp://ftp.uu.net/archive/systems/mac/info-mac/Communication/MacTCP/` (don't forget that there are many other Info-Mac archive mirror sites as well).

Apple's AOCE

The Apple Open Collaboration Environment (AOCE) seeks to integrate communication and collaboration more closely with the desktop. It does this by integrating messaging services with the operating system by providing a desktop mailbox, supporting catalogs and information card files, supporting digital signing, providing a password keychain for transparent access to multiple network systems, providing a built-in mail program (AppleMail), and supporting mail-enabled applications.

There are two parts to AOCE. Powershare is a server component that can provide a central mail gateway and global catalog support. Powertalk is the desktop component that can act as a client to the Powershare server but also maintain local messaging resources. Powertalk is included in System 7.5 and was also part of an OS version called System 7 Pro. AOCE can serve as a basis for sending Internet mail either using the Powershare server or using the capabilities of Powertalk installed on an individual Macintosh in combination with an SMTP gateway installed on either the server or on the Macintosh.

Mail Protocols

Okay, you have established a link of some sort between your system and the host system. They can exchange data. How, specifically, do they exchange mail?

UUCP and FIDO

The UUCP and FIDO protocols are commonly used by sites exchanging information with each other. UUCP originated with UNIX machines that communicated by directly dialing one another over modems and exchanging information. For microcomputers, this same scheme is the foundation of the FidoNet BBS mail exchange (many people's first entry to the Internet). However, these protocols are usually in the realm of system administration and are not usually applicable for single-person mail—unless you're a real sucker for punishment. There are now easier and more standard ways for micros to exchange Internet mail. If you're interested in UUCP, however, read the Usenet group `comp.mail.uucp`.

SMTP

SMTP, as covered in Chapter 12, is a simple way for your client to send mail. All your mail program has to do is connect to the host and use the simple `sendmail` commands. However, unless your machine is set up as a full-mail node that the mail host knows about, it can't easily return the favor. But your machine can connect to the mail host and use the SMTP TURN command to turn around the link and let the host machine transfer mail to you (some programs use this method).

POP3 (RFC 1460)

Post Office Protocol 3 (POP3) is a protocol designed to handle the problem of having a mail client fetch mail from the mail server without too much complexity. You can see some resemblance here to SMTP.

First, the host must have a POP3 server running (by convention, on TCP socket 110). The host sends a greeting, the client sends commands, and the host responds. Finally, the client disconnects.

All commands are a single keyword followed, in some cases, by an argument.

Unlike UNIX, which likes to end lines with a simple line feed, POP3 requires command and response lines to be terminated with a carriage return and line feed (CRLF). Responses consist of a return code and a keyword, and possibly some extra information. The two return codes are +OK and -ERR.

If there is a multiple-line response (such as the text of a mail message), the end is indicated by a period (.) on a line by itself. To prevent confusion, if the actual text of the reply includes a period as the first character of the line, the server inserts another period. It's up to the client to undo this. POP3 should be sounding very similar to SMTP.

Because everything is done in a somewhat human-readable format, you can run a test yourself by Telnetting to port 110 on your mail host.

You may see references to POP2 (RFC 937). POP2 is an ancestor of POP3 and should not be used if possible.

POP3 Authorization State

When the client connects to the server, the server sends a one-line response, such as the following and enters Authorization state, waiting for user authorization:

```
+OK POP3 - Foobar, Inc. POP3 server ready
```

The client then sends the following message to identify the user to the host:

```
USER userid
```

The server should respond with something like this:

```
+OK Userid recognized, please send password
-ERR Never heard of you
```

If the response is positive, the client should send the following message:

```
PASS password
```

In this syntax, password is the account password for the user ID. There are three possible response types:

```
+OK Welcome, your account has 3 new messages (15234 octets)
-ERR Invalid password. Try again.
-ERR Couldn't lock your incoming mailbox.
```

The third response type requires some explanation. The POP3 client must have exclusive access to your incoming mailbox so that no other program changes it while it is trying to do its stuff, and vice versa, because this interference would cause confusion or even loss of data. If some other program has exclusive access to your mailbox (that is, it has the mailbox "locked"), the POP3 client can't get it, and you must try again later.

In addition, the word octets in the first line should be explained. An *octet* is simply 8 bits, or what is commonly known as a byte. The word *octet* is used rather than byte to prevent possible confusion with nonstandard byte sizes. A successful authorization dialog looks like the following:

```
USER rdippold
+OK Please send password
PASS doohickey
+OK maildrop has 3 messages (1432 octets)
```

APOP is an optional way to log on. Although it's given as part of the POP3 standards, the server doesn't have to implement it. APOP is a way of dealing with the problem of password transmission. Because many people like to have their client log on every five minutes or so to look for mail, and because this action involves sending the user name and password each time, there is increased risk that someone using a network snooper can grab both and, thus, have access to someone's mail account. APOP requires that the server send a unique message in its greeting every time someone logs on. This usually can be done by combining the process ID of the server with the system clock value, or some similar method. The client grabs this message, manipulates it with the text of a "shared secret" value that both the server and the client know using the MD5 algorithm (explained in RFC 1321) to get a "digest" value, and then logs on to the server by sending the user ID and the digest. Think of the shared secret as a password, but it should be longer than a password, because the longer it is, the harder it is for someone else to break it. Here's an example (the digest value follows APOP rdippold):

```
+OK POP3 server ready <1432.699723421@foo.bar.com>
APOP rdippold c4c9334bac560ecc979e58001b3e22fb
+OK maildrop has 3 messages (1432 octets)
```

The server then manipulates the text with the shared secret using the same algorithm and compares the digest against the one sent. If they're the same, the user is logged on. Because of the nature of the MD5 algorithm, it should be almost impossible for someone to calculate the password working backward from the greeting message, user ID, and digest, if someone should happen to intercept them. Because that person gets a different greeting if he or she connects, the digest intercepted is worthless.

Assuming an eventual positive response, the POP3 host is now in the transaction state.

POP3 Transaction State

The transaction state is where all the real work is done. The client can issue any of the commands discussed in the following paragraphs.

The STAT command should cause the host to reply with two numbers: a count of waiting messages and a count of the number of bytes in the waiting messages. For example, the following response indicates 9 messages for a total of 13,453 octets (bytes):

```
+OK 9 13453
```

The LIST command is used to get information about specific waiting messages. If used by itself, it should return information about each message, one message per line. If a specific message number is given after LIST, only information for that message is given. Here's an example showing LIST by itself, LIST with a valid message number, and LIST with an invalid message number:

```
LIST
+OK 3 messages (3045 octets)
1 570
2 658
3 1817
.
```

```
LIST 2
+OK 2 658
LIST 9
-ERR No such message
```

The RETR command actually retrieves a specific message. The only argument is the number of the message. Here's an example of RETR with a valid message number and RETR with an invalid message number:

```
RETR 1
+OK 570 octets

This is the text of the message. It should be 570 bytes long.
I'm not going to type the whole thing, actually; just pretend
there are 570 bytes here, okay?

This should have an RFC 822 header too. Note how this message ends with a "." by
itself:
.
RETR 9
-ERR No such message
```

The DELE command is used to delete a message on the server. Some users like to keep all their messages on the client machine, in which case every message retrieval (RETR) should be followed by a DELE command. Others prefer to keep their messages on the host machine, for space reasons or so that they can be accessed with multiple pieces of software. The only parameter to use with the DELE command is the message number. Here are several examples:

```
DELE 2
+OK Message 2 deleted
DELE 9
-ERR No such message
DELE 2
-ERR Message 2 already deleted
```

The NOOP command does nothing except force the server to respond:

```
NOOP
+OK Nothing done
```

The server keeps track of the highest accessed message number that has been retrieved in that session. The client can use the LAST command to find the number of the highest accessed message, and can then presume that any following messages have not been seen by the user. Here's an example that uses LAST:

```
STAT
+OK 6 12341
LAST
+OK 2
RETR 4
+OK 3021 octets
Text of message 4 goes here.
.
LAST
+OK 4
```

RSET is used to reset parameters if things go wrong. All messages marked to be deleted are unmarked and the LAST counter is reset to zero. Here's an example:

```
LAST
+OK 4
LIST 2
-ERR Message 2 has been deleted
RSET
LAST
+OK 0
LIST 2
+OK 2 570
```

A smart client can selectively undelete a message by doing a STAT, LAST, and LIST to get the current state (if it didn't have them saved already), doing a RSET to reset the server, and then redeleting all the messages except the one to undelete.

TOP is an optional command (the other commands shown must be supported by a POP3 server). The parameters passed are a message number and (optionally) the number of lines of message body to show. The server then sends the entire RFC 822 header of the message plus the specified number of lines of text in the message. It's extremely useful to be able to get just the header like this so that the client can show the user a message summary (sender, subject, date, and size) without taking the time to retrieve the entire message body. Retrieving just part of the body is useful for showing the user the first part of the message so that the user can decide whether to read the entire thing. Here's an example of TOP:

```
TOP 2 1
+OK
From: joeblow@mondrain.com
To: me@my.site.com
Subject: How's it going?
```

```
Date: 12 Oct 94 13:12:32 -800
This is the first line of the message.
TOP 9
-ERR No such message
```

An optional XTND command allows further extension of the protocol. The client sends XTND *keyword options*, and the server should respond with a +OK if it supports those extensions and an -ERR if it doesn't. The XTND XMIT command supported by the Berkeley POP3 server allows you to send messages with POP3 as well as receive them.

When you're done, use QUIT to delete all the messages marked for deletion and unlock the incoming mail file:

```
QUIT
+OK POP3 mail server closing connection (2 messages remain)
```

POP3 Limitations

POP3 includes no way for you to send mail back to the host (without the XTND XMIT extension). That's because SMTP already takes care of that process. You can use POP3 for retrieval and SMTP for sending. A disadvantage of POP3 is that once the mail is retrieved from the host post office, it resides only on the local machine. Reading mail from several locations can be difficult to manage. IMAP, described in the following section, was developed partially as an alternative to address management of a host post office from multiple locations on the Internet.

IMAP (RFC 1176 or RFC 1203)

IMAP (Interactive Mail Access Protocol) tries to solve the same basic problem as POP3, but it specifies a bit more complex set of functions. IMAP puts more of the burden on the server, which should allow less data to be transferred from server to client, and should ease the work of the client. The server also has a much larger role in managing the mailbox of the user. Ironically, however, this added complexity seems to have resulted in its not being nearly as well supported as POP3.

The standard is complex enough that I won't cover it here in detail (if you're interested, read the RFCs). IMAP certainly does have a nice set of options for retrieving data from the host and making the host do the work for you. It allows for multiple simultaneous accesses to a mailbox (if the implementation allows it), as well as unsolicited server information sent to the client.

Here's a quick command summary:

Command	Function
NOOP	Do nothing but force the server to return a response.
LOGIN *userid password*	Log on to the server.
LOGOUT	Exit the server.
SELECT *mailbox*	Switch to another mailbox on the server (the default is INBOX). The server returns the number of messages and how many are new.
CHECK	Check for new mail and changes.
EXPUNGE	Force the immediate physical deletion of mail marked for deletion.
COPY *sequence mailbox*	Copy the specified *sequence* of messages from the current mailbox to the one specified by *mailbox*.
FETCH *sequence selection*	Retrieve the *selection* text for the specified message *sequence*. Flags include ALL, ENVELOPE, FAST, FLAGS, INTERNALDATE, RFC822, RFC822.HEADER, RFC822.SIZE, and RFC822.TEXT. For example, you can retrieve the headers and flags for messages 2 through 5 with FETCH 2:5 (FLAGS RFC822.HEADER). The parentheses are used to group multiple items.
STORE *sequence selection value*	The opposite of FETCH. Change the value of the *selection* to *value*. Using this command, you can change the header, text, or (most importantly) flags of a message on the server.
SEARCH *criteria*	Reply with the numbers of the messages that match your search *criteria* (which can be quite complex). You can search based on flags, dates, header text, body text, sender, subject, and so on, and you can combine criteria.
BBOARD *bboard*	Select a BBOARD, which is something akin to a shared mailbox.
FIND *type pattern*	Return the names of all files of *type* (MAILBOXES or BBOARDS) that match the given *pattern*, which can include wildcards. The command FIND BBOARDS PC* finds *PCTEST, PCMAIL,* and *PCHELP.*

Command	Function
READONLY	Change the current mailbox to read only.
READWRITE	Change the current mailbox to read and write.
SUPPORTED.VERSIONS	Ask the server to return a list of supported IMAP versions.
SELECT.VERSION (*major minor*)	Set the server to behave like IMAP version *major minor*. For example, to select version 3, level 0, specify **SELECT.VERSION (3 0)**. This must be a version reported by SUPPORTED.VERSIONS.
SELECT.FEATURES *features*	Set server options as reported in SUPPORTED.VERSIONS.
FLAGS	Return a list of flags supported by the server.
SET.FLAGS *flags_list*	Set the user-definable flags (keywords) for this mailbox.

You may have noticed that IMAP is basically a remote implementation of the mail program. If your mail client and host both support IMAP, you should use it rather than POP3 because it is more efficient and can provide you more flexibility in managing your mail.

Other Mail Protocols

Another mail protocol specified by RFC is PCMAIL (RFC 1056). Again, there are many different proprietary methods. You just need one that works with whatever you're using, which in most cases is SMTP or POP3. However, it won't hurt to see what's available.

Desirable Features

Before discussing actual mail clients, look at some desirable features of these products so that you have a basis for comparison.

- **TCP/IP or SLIP:** Ideally, your client should be able to access whatever network your mail host is on. Otherwise, why bother? TCP/IP and TCP/SLIP are the most common network protocols.

- **SMTP:** The most common way for a mail client to send mail is to use the SMTP server on the mail host. If your software doesn't have this, it had better support some other method that your host understands. Some mail clients also support SMTP connections from the host as a way to get incoming messages.

- **POP3:** POP3 is the most widely supported way for a mail client to retrieve mail from the mail host. Again, if your mail client doesn't support POP3, it had better have some method that your host understands.

■ **Mail (POP3) Server:** Your software must be able to specify a host to connect to in order to get mail. It is helpful if you can specify multiple hosts in case one is down. Generally, however, if the mail host is down, no mail is going anywhere.

■ **Mail (Send) Server:** By default, the client should use the same host for sending mail that it uses for retrieving messages. However, in some cases, it is desirable to use a different host to send mail; some client software enables you to specify a separate host for sending.

■ **Retrieve on Startup:** Ideally, the client should enable you to specify whether it should immediately try to retrieve mail from the host when you start it. Normally, you want to take this action, but it may take a while to do this. You may just want to look at old mail, in which case you want this feature off.

■ **Timed Retrieval:** The client should enable you to specify an interval at which mail should be checked. After this period has passed, the client should connect to the host, check for new mail, retrieve it (or retrieve information about it), and, optionally, beep or show a message indicating that new mail has been found. For a machine connected directly to a host on the same network with Ethernet, this interval can be every five minutes. If you're dialing in with a modem, you may want to set this option to occur once a day, every few hours, or never.

■ **Delete on Retrieve:** If you see your mail client as your primary mail program (that is, if you always use it to access mail), you probably want it to retrieve any new mail found to the client and automatically delete it from the host. On the other hand, if you are using several programs to access your mail, or if you are using this client temporarily while on vacation, you may want to think of the retrieved mail as a temporary copy and leave a copy on the host so that other programs can read it.

■ **Header Only or Full Text:** A server that supports sending just the header of a message (such as the APOP command in POP3) can save some initial time. The client needs to download only information about the message, not the actual message. If you choose to look at a message, it asks the host for the text of that message. This capability is useful if you have a fast permanent connection to the host (such as Ethernet) and you view the host as your primary mail file. On the other hand, if you're using an intermittent connection, or your mail client is your primary mail file, you may as well retrieve the whole text of the message. Then when the user wants to see it, you can retrieve it from disk.

■ **Name Server Support:** A machine domain name, like mail.foobar.com, is actually just a logical name for a machine uniquely identified by an IP number that looks like this: 129.042.11.12. The advantage to domain names is that they are easier to remember. Also, if the IP number of the machine changes (if it's replaced by a new machine, for example), the domain name can remain the same (the existing name is mapped to the new IP number—the number is absolute and the domain name is variable).

However, turning a name into the number requires that your client support DNS (Domain Name Service). Otherwise, it may require you to enter the machine's addresses as IP addresses rather than the domain addresses, which can be a pain.

■ **Other Mail Items:** A full-featured mail client has the same features available to a good user agent operating under UNIX. You shouldn't have to give up your options to use a mail client. These options include mail aliases, a decent editor, a signature file, specification of different header fields (especially `Reply-To` fields), support for MIME, and an address book.

Mail Clients

What about actual mail clients? What's out there? Clients come from a number of sources, some commercial and some free. Following are some ideas about where to find clients and some specific clients you may want to investigate.

There are far too many mail clients for me to describe. Luckily, most mail packages offer some sort of demo (or even a fully functioning program) over Internet FTP, so if one mail client doesn't meet your needs, find some others. Use Archie (described in Chapter 24, "Archie: An Archive of Archives") to find them.

Remote Login

This isn't really a remote client, but if all else fails, your host should have some way for you to log on remotely with a terminal emulator and use whatever mail program you normally use on your host. Although it's expensive in phone charges if done long distance, and you won't get a nifty user interface, it does work, and all your mail will be in one place.

Your TCP/IP Package

Your TCP/IP package is one place to look for a primitive mail client. Look for programs with names such as `mailer`, `mail`, `pop2`, or `pop3`. If you're masochistic enough, you can even use these programs for something other than experimentation.

Chameleon

Chameleon, from NetManage, is actually a full TCP/IP implementation for Windows. It has WinSock support and many standard TCP/IP utilities. It includes FTP, Telnet, TN3270, `mail`, `ping`, TFTP, NSLookup, `finger`, `whois`, Gopher, news, MIME support for Mail, an SNMP agent, and NFS support.

You can try a Chameleon Sampler, which runs only over serial lines (supporting SLIP, CSLIP, and PPP) and includes FTP, Telnet, TN3270, `mail`, and `ping` applications. There's also a monitoring tool named Newt, although you have to look for it.

> **NOTE**
>
> The Chameleon Sampler is available from `ftp://ftp.netmanage.com/pub/demos/` `chameleon`. See `Readme.txt` for installation instructions. For information about other NetManage products, see `http:/www.netmanage.com`.

The utilities are nicely done and take advantage of the Windows environment. For example, the FTP client allows you to select remote files with the mouse; you perform actions on those files with buttons or menu commands. The ability to scroll through and select remote files is a huge improvement over the command-line FTP clients. The interface also hides much of what's going on so as not to confuse the user. Because Chameleon is a full TCP/IP setup, you can even get it and add another superior mailer to it later, such as Eudora or Pegasus Mail.

Not to say that the Chameleon mail program is a slouch—it's nicely designed to work with Windows. It supports multiple mail accounts per PC, and multiple mailboxes per account. It has an address book, a simple rules editor to route incoming mail, a mail log, a built-in editor, and a complete font and color configuration. You can specify separate SMTP and POP gateways. You can set timers for how often to retrieve mail, how often to try to deliver pending mail, and how long to wait for a piece of outgoing mail before giving up on it as undeliverable.

The CommSet

The CommSet, from Cybernetic Control Inc., is a commercial TCP/IP package for DOS. It is exceptional in that it combines all its utilities in one package and allows multiple simultaneous windowed sessions. This wouldn't be a big deal under UNIX, but it is under DOS. It means you don't need a multitasker, even if that would work (many TCP/IP packages for DOS don't allow you to do multitasking—they get confused). In addition, the utilities are designed to be user friendly. Everything is mouse and menu driven, although expert users can get around fast with keystrokes and user-defined macros. CommSet is a full suite of utilities, and it does its own TCP. But it does include a POP3/SMTP mailer, which is why it's included here. CommSet runs on top of standard packet drivers and also provides its own SLIP drivers.

Although CommSet is constantly being upgraded, it currently offers the following modules: NewsReader, POP3 Mailer, Telnet, Editor, Gopher, FTP, `finger`, Monitor, `ping`, NSLookup, `whois`, ISO-3166 table, and ASCII table. For DOS access and control, there are Help, Command, File Browser, Fake DOS, Serial Terminal, and Full Screen Editor modules.

You can FTP a demo version of CommSet from `ftp://ftp.cybercon.nb.ca/commset`, call 1-506-364-8192 (Canada), or send e-mail to `info@cybercon.nb.ca` to request information. The FTP server tells you as you log in which files you need.

Because this discussion is about mailers specifically, let's look more closely at CommSet's POP3 mailer.

First, because all sessions are active at once, the POP3 mailer can operate in the background, checking your mail every so often. Configuration is fairly comprehensive. The most basic information you enter (in the Network Settings box) is the POP3 server name, your user ID, and your password. Because CommSet is a full set of TCP utilities, it enables you to use real domain names rather than IP addresses.

In the Download Settings box, you have several options, including what to make the mail directory on your client machine, whether the client should automatically fetch messages whenever it is started, how often to check for messages, and whether it should delete messages on the host after retrieving them to your machine.

Finally, for uploading messages, you can specify an alternative machine for sending messages (in case you don't want to use the POP3 server for this) and whether to batch messages so that you can upload them all at once. For composing replies, you can set options such as your time zone, whether or not you want to include reply text, a signature file to include, and a separate address for the `Reply-to:` line (if needed).

Messages are shown in the one-line-per-message summary form you've come to expect from mail programs (see Figure 14.1), although the contents of the summary are changeable, as is the sort order. When you highlight a message and press Enter, CommSet's full-screen browser shows the message; if you decide to reply, CommSet's full-screen editor is used.

FIGURE 14.1.

CommSet's POP3 mail client is shown in the foreground CommSet window. I'm about to empty my box of deleted messages.

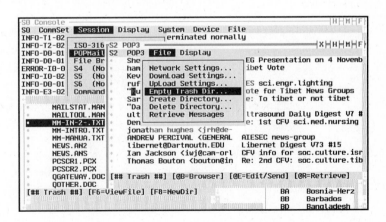

All in all, although CommSet is not the most full-featured mail program ever, it works well and its integration with the rest of the CommSet package makes it attractive. Dale Edgar, lead programmer, is also quite open to suggestions for future versions, which is a plus.

Eudora

Eudora was written specifically as an easy-to-use windowed mail client. Eudora versions are available for both Windows and the Macintosh, meaning that if your office has both PCs and Macs (as ours does), you can use similar clients for both platforms. Extended POP3 is supported, so you can send messages with POP3 if the server supports it.

Eudora was written as a Mac mail program by Steve Dorner at the University of Illinois. Dorner was eventually hired by QUALCOMM Incorporated, which has continued to update the program and has produced a Windows version as well.

Besides the Windows/Mac division, there are two main branches of the Eudora family tree. Version 1.x of Eudora is free; version 2.x is commercial. Version 1.x will continue to be made freely available and maintained as far as bug fixes go, but all real development (meaning nifty new features) is done in version 2.x and later.

The system requirements for Eudora on the host side are SMTP capability (to send mail) and POP3 capability (to receive mail). For the Macintosh, System 6 is supported by version 1.3, and System 7 is required for versions 1.4 and 2.x. You need an Ethernet card, a DDP/IP gateway, or a modem for a physical connection, and MacTCP for networking. A version of MacTCP with limited site licenses is provided for Eudora use only. Finally, Eudora for Mac takes about 340K of RAM. For PCs, you need to run Windows 3.1 or later with WinSock 1.1-compliant networking software, an Ethernet card or a modem, 640K of RAM, and a mouse (not required, but you would be insane not to use one with Windows).

> **NOTE**
>
> To test the free versions of Eudora, access `ftp://ftp.qualcomm.com`. The PC version is kept under `/quest/windows/eudora` (get all the files). The Mac version is under `/quest/mac/eudora`. For the Mac, you must decide which version you want to try: if you have System 6, you need the version in the 1.3 directory. Otherwise, grab the one in the 1.5 (or higher) directory. Be sure to get the `README.first` file, which tells you what all those files and utilities are. At a minimum, grab Eudora, the manual, and the release notes. The `E_BY_QC` packed file tells you the differences between the free version you're getting and the latest commercial version.

Windows Eudora 2.0.1 and higher supports what Qualcomm calls "direct serial dialup." If you have a dial-in account that enables you to use Telnet, you can dispense with running TCP/IP on your machine. Just have Eudora dial the modem, log in under your account, do all the connections necessary for SMTP and POP3 directly, and then hang up.

Pricing is around $65 in single-unit quantities. A Macintosh version with the Spellswell spelling checker sells for $99. Eudora has a 30-day money-back guarantee. Call 1-800-2-EUDORA or send e-mail to eudora-sales@qualcomm.com.

Eudora is a fairly mature product, so a lot of "wish list" stuff has already been included. In fact, it's one of the most complete mail programs I've seen yet. I won't even try to describe all the features, although if you can think of it, Eudora probably has it.

Eudora normally runs in the background, periodically polling the host for your mail (as specified) and popping up a message when new mail is found (at your discretion). Each mailbox (by default, just your In box) gets its own window, showing the now-standard one line of status information per message, with a large array of flags on the left side. After you select a message for viewing, the message appears in its own window with its own set of options. Multiple mailboxes can be open simultaneously. In fact, Eudora's philosophy seems to be "more windows is good"—you can have almost all windows open at once, including your mailboxes, nicknames (see Figure 14.2), filters, several mail messages, configuration, and more. If you minimize the windows, they go to the bottom of the Eudora window as icons. Click them to restore them. And (this is particularly impressive) when you exit Eudora and start it up again, it is exactly as you left it, windows and all!

FIGURE 14.2.

Creating a new nickname in Eudora. Note the message and mailbox windows in the background.

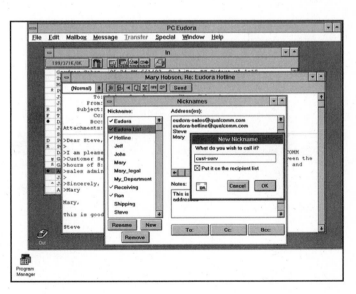

Everything is pretty easy to use. As much as some UNIX types despise them, the windows and menu systems first commercialized by the Mac make it easy to get around. The Windows version offers icon toolbars so that you can click the appropriate icon to take whatever action you want.

Eudora has many mailbox management features, including comprehensive find and sort functionality, the capability to sort incoming and outgoing mail into different user-defined mailboxes based on content, automatic prioritization of mail based on content, and hierarchical mailboxes (mailboxes within mailboxes). It allows multiple nickname files so that in addition to user nicknames, different groups and departments can maintain their own mailing lists. You can create mail templates from outgoing mail for use in the future. Mail can be individually tagged to go out at the next connection, at a specific time, right now, or to be put on indefinite hold. You can even add your own sound for incoming mail notification.

Eudora supports MIME functionality—you can attach and decode multiple files and binary data to messages, and translate between different international character sets. You also can specify the programs to call to display other types of MIME data, such as spreadsheets, pictures, video, or audio.

If you're running a Mac, Eudora has System 7 support, including aliases, drag and drop, and AppleEvents. It also supports RFC 1342 for nonASCII text in headers.

If you're looking for a mail client with a good user interface that runs over TCP/IP or over a modem, that runs under Windows or the Macintosh, and that you don't mind having to pay for (some people are funny about that), I'd say Eudora is a worthy choice.

PINE

PC-PINE, from the University of Washington, is a DOS/Windows version of the UNIX PINE User Mail Agent discussed in Chapter 13, "Internet E-Mail: UNIX." If you run PINE on your UNIX and DOS systems, you can have a consistent user interface between platforms. It's also fairly user friendly and utterly free. Note that PINE requires that your host support IMAP2 for message retrieval. If it just does POP3, you can't use PINE as it currently exists. It uses standard SMTP to send mail.

> **NOTE**
>
> To get PC-PINE, access `ftp://ftp.cac.washington.edu/pine/pcpine`. PINE is available for the following network software: FTP's PC/TCP (`pcpine_f.zip`), generic packet driver using built-in Waterloo TCP/IP (`pcpine_p.zip`), Novell's LAN WorkPlace (`pcpine_n.zip`), and Sun's PC/NFS (`pcpine_s.zip`). A version of PINE that runs under Windows and uses WinSock is available as `pcpine_w.zip`. The Windows version, however, is not written as a graphical interface and uses the same interface as the DOS version. Each is around 1.2M unpacked.

See Chapter 12, "Internet E-Mail: An Overview," for more information on PINE. The DOS version is essentially the same as the UNIX version (it's easier that way). Highlights include an address book, an easy-to-use menu interface, easy multiple mailboxes, and MIME file support.

In addition to mail, PINE allows primitive reading of Usenet newsgroups using NNTP. PINE also includes a full-screen editor, `pico`, as a stand-alone program (in case you want to use it for other things). For more information, you can also see the PINE World Wide Web page at `http://www.cac.washington.edu/pine`.

ECSMail

ECSMail isn't so much an electronic mail client as it is an electronic mail system. It is described by its developers as a product for developing enterprise mail systems. It includes mail clients, yes, but it also handles message transport and message services so that you can build an entire mail system. All the pieces support RFC 822 and MIME, as well as X.400. All pieces run under UNIX, OS/2, OpenVMS, and Windows NT; the mail clients also run under MS-DOS, Windows, and Mac System 7.

The ECSMail clients can provide a solution for those seeking to support IMAP from multiple platforms. The complete ECSMail package may be more than you need, but if you want to build a large mail system from the ground up, it's worth asking about. Contact ECS (in Canada) by calling 1-403-420-8081 or send e-mail to ECS Sales at `ecs-sales@edm.isac.ca`. A demonstration copy of the Microsoft Windows version of ECSMail is available at `ftp://ftp.srv.ualberta.ca/pub/windows/utilities/ecs.tar.Z`.

This Windows version of ECSMail supports IMAP2 and SMTP and can deliver MIME format messages. Although it is available for demonstration purposes, it is not in the public domain and should be treated accordingly.

Mailstrom

Mailstrom is a Macintosh IMAP mail client originally developed at the Stanford University Medical School. The University of Michigan has adapted a version to supply their campus with Macintosh access to their IMAP mail server. The University of Michigan implementation is version 1.055. Versions 1.05 and 1.04 can also be found by doing an Archie search on `mailstrom`.

Mail-It

Mail-It 2.0, from Unipalm Ltd, is a mail client for Windows 3.1. It's tightly integrated with Windows and Windows MAPI (Mail API). It supports SMTP, POP2, POP3, and UUCP for mail transport.

Mail-It's features include MIME support, drag and drop, hierarchical folders (folders within folders, for better organization), interaction with mail-enabled applications and MAPI directory services, and an address book. If you want a client written specifically for Windows, this is something to look at.

As of this writing, Mail-It 2.0.2 is the current version. Send e-mail to `mail-it@unipalm.co.uk`, or call 1-800-368-0312 (in the United Kingdom, call +44-(0)223-250100) for more information.

PC Mail Manager

PC-MM, from ICL ProSystems AB, is a Windows mail client that uses the WinSock API. It handles mail using SMTP and IMAP2 (but does not support POP3).

PC-MM does MIME, features drag and drop, handles local-based and server-based folders, has an integrated address book, and does some message sorting and tagging.

You can contact Lars Haberg at ICL by sending e-mail to `Lars_Hagberg@li.icl.se`, or call (Sweden) ICL at +46 (0)13 11 70 00.

Iride

Iride is a MIME user agent for the Macintosh, developed by the GNBTS (Gruppo Nazionale Bioingegneria sezione di Trieste). It supports POP3 and SMTP for message receive and send, and runs on MacTCP 1.1 or higher.

Iride supports many types of MIME messages, but you must install 32-bit QuickDraw if you want to use images.

You can retrieve it from `ftp://gnbts.univ.trieste.it/mime/Iride.sea.hqx`.

ProLine

ProLine is one of those pieces of software that makes people say, "Hey! How did they do that?" ProLine is a bulletin board system that runs on an Apple II system (usually with a hard drive, but it's not required) and emulates a UNIX system to a scary degree. It contains built-in networking for Usenet news and Internet mail (you can set up your own little BBS just to do mail if you don't want to set up the full-fledged thing). And once you've got the basic mail service, it's not that much harder to set up ProLine so that you can get Usenet news. This isn't some penny-ante UNIX rip-off, either; it has a UNIX shell built in, a configurable user shell, a file system, most standard UNIX utilities, and, of course, games. And if you don't have an Apple II now, used Apple IIs are dirt cheap.

For more information about ProLine, contact the Morgan Davis Group (U.S.) at 1-619-670-0563 or the BBS at 1-619-670-5379 or fax at 1-619-670-9643. Alternatively, send e-mail to `mdavis@pro-sol.cts.com`.

LAN Server-Related Mail Products

In the past, mail systems written for local area networks were, for the most part, not developed to communicate beyond a small group of file servers. The one exception is cc:Mail (currently from Lotus), which has had an SMTP gateway for a number of years. Other products, like WordPerfect Office Mail, were written to an MHS mail transport standard and had to rely on third-party products for SMTP mail transfer before vendors supplied their own solutions (which may or may not have been reliable).

Fortunately, this set of mail developers no longer ignores Internet mail. Products such as Groupwise (Novell/WordPerfect's follow-up to WordPerfect Office Mail), cc:Mail, QuickMail, Microsoft Mail, and Da Vinci now have SMTP mail gateway support of one kind or another.

In addition to these commercial offerings, there are several other programs you may find useful if you are trying to support Internet mail from a file server system.

Pegasus Mail

Pegasus Mail, by David Harris, is for Novell v2.15 or higher. It supports MHS and SMTP and includes DOS, Windows, and Macintosh versions (for wide platform support with a single program). Pegasus Mail does MIME, and many utilities (including an SMTP gateway and mailing list manager for Novell named Mercury) are available if you don't mind digging in. Pegasus enables you to be quite flexible about setting up user-defined mail gateways. The included Guide program is quite useful for helping you install it and answering configuration questions.

Pegasus Mail itself is very complete and has many useful features (see Figure 14.3), not the least of which is its support for MIME file attachments. New mail filtering, in the PC version only, allows many actions to take place based on incoming mail headers, including copy, move, delete, forward, extract files, append, print, send file, add or remove user from list, and run a separate program.

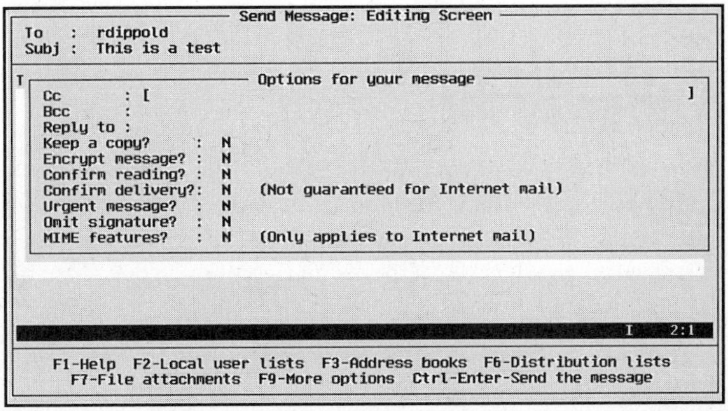

FIGURE 14.3.

An example of some of the outgoing mail options of Pegasus Mail, including encryption and delivery confirmation.

```
                            Send Message: Editing Screen
  To   :  rdippold
  Subj :  This is a test

  T ┌────────────────── Options for your message ──────────────────┐
    │ Cc        : [                                                ] │
    │ Bcc       :                                                    │
    │ Reply to  :                                                    │
    │ Keep a copy?      :  N                                         │
    │ Encrypt message?  :  N                                         │
    │ Confirm reading?  :  N                                         │
    │ Confirm delivery? :  N    (Not guaranteed for Internet mail)   │
    │ Urgent message?   :  N                                         │
    │ Omit signature?   :  N                                         │
    │ MIME features?    :  N    (Only applies to Internet mail)      │
    └───────────────────────────────────────────────────────────────┘


                                                          I    2:1

       F1-Help  F2-Local user lists  F3-Address books  F6-Distribution lists
            F7-File attachments  F9-More options  Ctrl-Enter-Send the message
```

Pegasus Mail comes with its own internal editor, which is tightly integrated with the rest of the program, although you can define an external editor to use.

> **NOTE**
>
> All the versions and add-on utilities for Pegasus Mail can be found at `ftp://risc.ua.edu/pub/network/pegasus`. Read the `0index` file to find out what's what. The software is free, but manuals cost money: pricing is $150 U.S. for a five-copy license. You can contact David Harris by fax in New Zealand at +64 34 53 66 12, or send inquiries to `david@pmail.gen.nz`.

iGate

iGate is one of those specialized need programs. iGate, from Smart Systems, is an SMTP system for WordPerfect Office Mail version 3. It runs under the Office Connection server and doesn't require existing TCP/IP stacks or MHS support.

If this sounds like what you need, you can send mail to `smart@actrix.gen.nz`, or fax to (New Zealand) +64 63 56 14 84.

StarNine

StarNine, a developer and manufacturer of Macintosh e-mail gateways, has two products that may be of interest to Macintosh Internet users. One is a Powershare (server) SMTP gateway; the other is a Powertalk (individual) gateway. The Powershare gateway decodes mail enclosures and attachments (including MIME) and places them in the AppleMail attachments box. StarNine also provides gateways for QuickMail and Microsoft Mail.

You can reach StarNine by phone at 1-510-649-4949, by fax at 1-510-548-0393, and with postal mail at 2550 Ninth Street, Suite 112, Berkeley, CA 94710. You can also contact `info@starnine.com` for sales and product information.

Other Tactics

If you have Usenet capability, read the group `comp.mail.misc` (and possibly `alt.internet.services`) for more information. Use Archie to look around for mail clients or mail agents. New programs are appearing all the time. If all else fails, ask someone who knows more, or resign yourself to a special mail account on one of the many Internet service providers or Internet mail providers.

Internet E-Mail: Gateways

15

by Ron Dippold

The Internet extends beyond its physical presence of computers linked together by direct connections. Internet mail now reaches almost all major computer services and networks, including many bulletin board system (BBS) networks. This connectivity solves the obvious problem of how someone on one computer service or network can send information to someone on a different service or network. Because most services charge monthly fees, maintaining a separate account on each service could be ruinous to your finances. And snail mail (the plain old post office) is just too slow and inefficient to someone who has experienced the world of electronic mail. How do you keep just a single account and still send mail to people on other networks? This chapter answers this question in detail.

Internet Mail

The simple solution to internetwork communication is to hook two services together using a *gateway*—a device that passes messages from one network to another and handles all formatting and addressing problems that may come up. But gateways take time to set up. You have to program the interface to the gateway on both services. Both services must work together to decide the best way to handle any problems that are sure to arise (such as what to do with messages from one service that are too long for the other to handle). Someone has to set up the gateway hardware, operate it, and handle billing. Now consider that as the number of services grows, the number of gateways you need to set up also grows. GEnie has to be able to send messages to CompuServe, America Online, MCI Mail, Prodigy, and more. And any new service must set up gateways to all the existing services. This confusion is obviously fodder for a good number of mental breakdowns.

What is needed is a *central service* that can handle messages from and to each of the existing services—GEnie doesn't send messages to SprintMail; it sends them to the central service and the central service sends the mail to SprintMail. In this way, each service maintains only a single gateway to the central service. New services can use the already established format of the central service, obviating the need to reinvent the wheel each time. This central service should be widespread, shouldn't be owned by a direct competitor of any of the existing services, and should have reasonable rates. Of course, this central service is the Internet.

Strictly speaking, the Internet actually is a competitor to the existing services because it offers the same attractions the services offer. People who don't have Internet access through school or business usually acquire access through an information service—and many of the big services realize users could choose them. Delphi has taken this concept to heart and has become just an Internet service provider.

Address Formatting

One remaining problem still exists: how to address mail to someone at another site. Many services use their own unique user naming scheme. The most obvious example is CompuServe's octal addressing scheme, where accounts are represented as 12345,678. Not only do you have to worry about getting the mail to CompuServe, you have to know that Internet doesn't like commas in addresses, nor does it like spaces—which is a problem for other networks.

The easiest way to find someone's address is to ask them. If they don't know, their service can give address information on request. As with snail mail, after you have an address that works, you can settle down to worrying about the content of your messages.

However, sometimes you have an account at another site and you need to send something now, or sometimes you cannot easily ask a person's address. Suppose that you are having a problem with a game, and instead of trying to get through telephone lines that are chronically busy, you want to contact the manufacturer electronically. (Many companies and organizations have service representatives on CompuServe. You can send a detailed description of a problem and, surprisingly often, you receive an informative and helpful response in return.) But contacting the representative to ask his or her Internet address can be troublesome. In another example from Usenet, Rush Limbaugh has a CompuServe account and apparently gives out only the CompuServe address. Because many people want to send fan mail and hate mail his way, a frequent request in several newsgroups is "How do I send mail to him from Internet?" This chapter covers these addressing issues.

Basic Addressing Issues

The basic Internet mail address format is *userid@site.domain*. The *userid* is the person's account identification at that site. A user ID can be rdippold, RonDippold, ron_dippold, or abc1138—whatever format the site chooses to use. The *site* is the name the receiving site has given itself and is usually fairly obvious. CompuServe's site name is compuserve; America Online's site name is aol. The *domain* is one of several larger groupings of sites. The two most common domains are edu and com, which are usually U.S. educational and commercial sites, although exceptions do exist. In many countries outside the United States, the domain name is a two-character country abbreviation, such as au for Australia.

This basic format is extensible—jsmith@foo.bar.bozo.edu is a perfectly valid address. Likewise, you sometimes see extensions *before* the user ID, separated from the rest of the address with % or !. These extensions give additional routing information for sites that need it.

Regardless of the extensions used, all modern services that offer Internet mail use some version of this basic format to do addressing.

Planned Obsolescence

If anything is faster than the speed at which information moves, it's the speed at which information goes obsolete. All the information in this chapter should be accurate at the time it is written (early 1995). But the material will go out of date quickly. Luckily, aging usually occurs because a new service arrives and the information is simply less complete rather than inaccurate. In that case, if you want to get mail to a new service not described in this book, you can use the information in this book as an example (or you can just ask the service). Rarely will information in this book actually change, but it may happen. Luckily, the bigger the service, the less likely the change; the information here on how to send mail to CompuServe should be valid for a long, long time. Just keep in mind that anything in the computer world is mercurial.

If you have access to Usenet, the groups `comp.mail.misc`, `alt.internet.services`, and `alt.online-service` should keep you up to date with the latest information. Alternatively, a fairly complete and periodically updated list of services and how to reach them is available by sending Internet mail to `mail-server@rtfm.mit.edu`. Include the following line in the body of the message: `send usenet/news.answers/mail/inter-network-guide`.

The account `mail-server@rtfm.mit.edu` is a standard Internet mail account; you may have to see one of the following entries to determine how to send mail to this account from your site. For example, from CompuServe, you send the mail to `>INTERNET:mail-server@rtfm.mit.edu`. The `send` command in the body of the message you are mailing stays the same for any site.

If you need more help, you can find several useful tips in "Services that Provide Gateways," later in this chapter.

Financial Concerns

Mail sent or received usually ends up costing someone money. Often, the recipient pays if you send mail from the Internet; because the recipient's commercial service has no way to charge you for the message, the service charges the recipient instead, like postage due. You really shouldn't send mail to someone unless you know the recipient is willing to accept the mail or it will not cost them anything; perhaps the recipient told you to send the mail or they advertised their account number. Most technical support accounts fall into the latter category.

The pricing (and the pricing scheme) changes even faster than the information—about once a year on average. Therefore, this chapter does not give rates; check with your service provider for information.

Services that Provide Gateways

This section explains how to send mail to and from the major services. As an example, Chris Smith is exchanging mail on the various services with Pat Jones, who is on the Internet as `pjones@foo.bar.edu`. Notice that addresses such as `pjones@foo.bar.edu` are in monospaced type to set them off from the surrounding text. Parts of addresses you should replace with specific information are in *monospaced italic*. The address *userid*`@aol.com` is an address at America Online where you replace *userid* with the actual account name of the recipient. The other replacement word you see in this chapter is *domain*. Although *domain* sometimes refers to just com or edu, it also refers to everything after the @ in an Internet address. Hence you can replace *userid*@*domain* with pjones@foo.bar.edu.

Except where necessary, this chapter gives only the Internet address of the service and how to send mail to the Internet from the service. To send from one nonInternet service to another, you must determine from this information how to send mail from your service to the Internet and then how to send mail from the Internet to the destination service. Combining the two steps should give you the full address, as the following example shows:

> You are on CompuServe and want to send mail to Jeff Brown on GEnie. Looking up the information in the following sections, you find that GEnie's Internet mail format is *userid*@genie.geis.com. To send mail from CompuServe to Internet, the format is >INTERNET:*userid*@*domain*. Thus, you should address the mail to >INTERNET:jbrown@genie.geis.com, assuming that you know Jeff's user ID on GEnie is jbrown.

America Online

America Online (AOL) is a major U.S. commercial information service. The standard Internet address for a user at America Online is *userid*@aol.com. To send Internet mail from AOL, you don't need to use any special formatting; just use the address directly—*userid*@*domain*.

AOL lets you use abbreviated domains for AppleLink, CompuServe, or GEnie. Address your mail to *userid*@applelink, *userid*@cis, or *userid*@genie, respectively.

Example Internet to AOL:	csmith@aol.com
Example AOL to Internet:	pjones@foo.bar.edu
Example AOL to CompuServe:	11111,222@cis

AppleLink

AppleLink is Apple Computer, Inc.'s network. Addressing mail to AppleLink is easy; the format is *userid*@applelink.apple.com. Sending mail to Internet is a bit trickier—you must address it to *userid*@*site*@internet#. The entire sending address must be 35 characters or less, so sending mail to some sites may be impossible.

> Example AppleLink to America Online: csmith@aol.com@internet#

AT&T Mail

AT&T Mail is a commercial e-mail service provided by AT&T. Sending mail from Internet to AT&T Mail is easy; the format is *userid*@attmail.com. You send mail to Internet in this format: internet!*domain*!*userid*.

> Example AT&T Mail to Internet: internet!foo.bar.edu!pjones

Bitnet

Bitnet is an academic network that is becoming less important as more educational sites hook into the Internet. However, the network still exists for now. To send mail from the Internet to Bitnet, address it to *userid%bitnetsitename*.bitnet@*gateway*. The *gateway* must be a host site on both the Internet and Bitnet. A commonly used gateway is mitvma.mit.edu, but your Bitnet site may have a closer gateway you can use—ask the administrators.

Sending mail from Bitnet to the Internet should be fairly easy. To use one of the Bitnet-Internet gateways, systems must be running a mailer capable of certain addressing standards. Also, almost all Bitnet sites are on the Internet as well.

Example Bitnet to Internet: pjones@foo.bar.edu

Example Internet to Bitnet: csmith%uxavax.bitnet@mitvma.mit.edu

BIX

BIX is the Byte Information eXchange, a commercial service oriented toward technical users. Delphi bought the service, but it still operates separately. Sending mail from the Internet to BIX is easy; the format is *userid*@bix.com. To send mail to the Internet, choose Internet Services from the main menu.

CompuServe

CompuServe is a large commercial service operated by CompuServe, Inc. The format from the Internet to CompuServe is *userid*@compuserve.com. The format has one quirk: CompuServe IDs are of the form 77777,777—because commas are not allowed in Internet addresses, you must replace the comma with a period. To get to the Internet from CompuServe use: >INTERNET:*userid*@*domain*.

Example Internet to CompuServe: 12345.677@compuserve.com

Example CompuServe to Internet: >INTERNET:pjones@foo.bar.edu

Connect PIN

Connect PIN is the commercial Connect Professional Information Network. To send mail from the Internet to Connect, use *userid*@connectinc.com. Getting from Connect to the Internet is a bit more difficult. You must send the message to DASN and make the first line of the message "*userid*@*domain*"@DASN. Notice the use of the required double quotation marks (") here.

Delphi

Delphi is a commercial service now devoted to offering Internet access. Delphi is a real Internet site, so standard Internet addressing works. To send mail from the Internet to Delphi, use *userid*@delphi.com. To send mail from Delphi to the Internet, use *userid*@*domain*.

FidoNet

FidoNet is a large international BBS network run over the phone lines. This network is not as fast as the Internet, but access is usually cheaper, and chances are your area has a FidoNet BBS. Because FidoNet is run over phone lines, BBS operators incur charges for any mail transferred, so please don't send large messages to FidoNet sites. In fact, many sites limit messages to 8K or 16K; parts of your larger message will not get through.

To send mail from the Internet to FidoNet, you must know the network address of the specific FidoNet BBS the recipient is on. The address is of the form Z:N/F.P. To send mail to that site, use *userid*@pP.fF.nN.zZ.fidonet.org. If the address is like 1:2/3, leave out the pP. part. In the *userid*, replace any spaces or other nonalphanumeric characters with periods (.). To send mail from FidoNet to the Internet, use *userid*@*domain* ON *gateway*. The *gateway* is a special FidoNet site that acts as an Internet gateway. You can use 1:1/31.

Example FidoNet to Internet:	pjones@foo.bar.edu ON 1:1/31
Example Internet to FidoNet:	chris.smith@p4.f3.n2.z1.fidonet.org

GEnie

GEnie is General Electric Information Services, another commercial service. To send mail from the Internet to GEnie, use *userid*@genie.geis.com. From GEnie to the Internet is *userid*@*domain*@INET#.

Example GEnie to Internet:	pjones@foo.bar.edu@INET#
Example Internet to GEnie:	csmith@genie.geis.com

Gold 400

GNS Gold 400 is British Telecom's commercial X.400 system. From the Internet to Gold 400, use *userid*@*org_unit*.*org*.*prmd*.gold-400.gb. The recipient must give you the *userid*, *org_unit* (organization unit), *org* (organization), and *prmd* (private mail domain).

To send mail from Gold 400 to the Internet, use `/DD.RFC-822=`*`userid@domain`*`/O=uknet/PRMD=uk.ac/ADMD=gold 400/C=GB/`. If you have any special characters in the *userid*, see the "X.400 Addressing" section, later in this chapter, to learn how to encode those characters.

Example Gold 400 to Internet: `DD.RFC-822=pjones(a)foo.bar.edu/O=uknet/`
                                          `PRMD=uk.ac/ADMD=gold 400/C=GB`

Example Internet to Gold 400:   `csmith@foo.bar.baz.gold-400.gb`

IBMMAIL

IBMMAIL is IBM's commercial mail system. Internet addressing through this system suffers from horrible mainframeitis. Sending a message can give old IBM programmers flashbacks to JCL (Job Control Language). Don't panic.

To send mail from the Internet to IBMMAIL, use *`userid`*`@ibmmail.com`. The *userid* consists of a country code, company code, and user code, so you must ask for the recipient's address.

To send mail from IBMMAIL to the Internet, send the message to `IBMMAIL(INTERNET)`. Then place the following lines at the top of the message (with no initial spaces):

```
/INTERNET
/TO userid@domain
/REPORT
/END
```

MCI Mail

MCI Mail is MCI's commercial e-mail service. To mail from the Internet to MCI Mail, you have several options. All users have a name (Pat Jones) and a phone number (555-9999) associated with their account. The phone number is unique, so you can always send mail to *`number`*`@mcimail.com`. If you know that only one P Jones has an MCI Mail account, you can send mail to *`FLast`*`@mcimail.com`, where *F* is the first initial and *Last* is the last name. If you know that the system has only one Pat Jones, you can send mail to *`First_Last`*`@mcimail.com`, where *First* is the first name and *Last* is the last name. Note the underscore (_) between the names.

To send mail from MCI Mail to the Internet, enter this line at MCI Mail's `To` prompt: *`name`* `(EMS)`. You don't actually need the *name* for addressing, but you can insert the recipient's real name. MCI Mail then prompts you with `EMS:`, and you respond with `INTERNET`. Finally, the service asks for `Mbx:`, and you respond with *`userid@domain`*.

Example Internet to MCI Mail: `Pat_Jones@mcimail.com1234567@mcimail.com`

Prodigy

Prodigy is the Prodigy Information Services (Sears and IBM) large commercial service. To send mail from the Internet to Prodigy, use `userid@prodigy.com`.

At the time of this writing, Prodigy is undergoing many changes; the information presented here may be out of date when you read this. Check with Prodigy for the latest information. Sending mail from Prodigy to the Internet is a little difficult. Support for sending to the Internet isn't integrated into the main Prodigy software, so you have to use some offline Mail Manager software. The software works only on IBM PCs, and you must pay $4.95 to download the Mail Manager. To download when you're online, jump to `ABOUT MAIL MANAGER`. The Mail Manager leads you through the download procedure.

> Example Internet to Prodigy: `foob09z@prodigy.com`

SprintMail

If AT&T and MCI have commercial mail services, obviously Sprint isn't going to be left out. SprintMail is Sprint's commercial X.400 mail service. To send mail from the Internet to SprintMail, use `/G=first/S=last/O=organization/ADMD=TELE-MAIL/C=US/@sprint.com`. The `first` and `last` placeholders are the recipient's first and last name, respectively; `organization` is an organization name you need to get from the recipient.

To send mail from SprintMail to the Internet, use `C:USA,A:TELEMAIL,P:INTERNET,` `"RFC-822":<userid(a)domain>) DEL`. As with other X.400 services, if `userid` has any special characters, you should refer to the "X.400 Addressing" section, later in this chapter, for information on how to encode these characters.

> Example SprintMail to Internet: `C:USA,A:TELEMAIL,P:INTERNET,`
> `"RFC-822":<pjones(a)foo.bar.edu>) DEL`
>
> Example Internet to SprintMail: `G=Chris/S=Smith/O=Foo Inc/ADMD=TELEMAIL/C=US/`
> `@sprint.com`

WWIVNet

WWIVNet is the largest of several networks for BBSes running WWIV software. Traffic from node to node is long distance in several places, and the gateway site uses long distance as well, so please be courteous and don't send or receive anything large (over 8K or so).

To send mail from Internet to WWIVNet, you must get the recipient's node number and user ID number. Use the format `userid-node@wwiv.tfsquad.mn.org`. To send mail from WWIVNet to Internet, use `userid#domain@506`.

> Example WWIVNet to Internet: `pjones#foo.bar.edu@506`
> Example Internet to WWIVNet: `12-3456@wwiv.tfsquad.mn.org`

Fussy Address Concerns

When dealing with computers, the devil is in the details (along with a host of minor demons). The following sections present a few details that can rise up to snap at you in certain situations.

Case Sensitivity

Internet addresses are, for the most part, case insensitive; that is, addresses ignore capitalization. For a given address, *userid@domain*, any address router should ignore the capitalization of the *domain*—pjones@Foo.BAR.CoM, pjones@foo.bar.com, and pjones@FOO.BAR.COM all should get to the correct address. The *userid* also is usually case insensitive, but the individual site or service can change to enforce case sensitivity if they don't have decent programmers.

By UNIX custom, you should give addresses in all lowercase letters when possible. However, if you receive the address of someone on another service or network, be careful to preserve all the capitalization when you send a message. Uppercase and lowercase discrepancies usually are not a problem, but why take chances?

X.400 Addressing

The Internet uses what is known as RFC 822 addressing. Many of the large commercial services that specialize in electronic mail use what is known as X.400 addressing, which looks like */X=value/Y=value/Z=value*. You can use this addressing from the Internet (refer to some of the X.400 services in the preceding pages). However, one major problem exists: RFC 822 addressing allows many characters that choke X.400 addressing. X.400 dislikes punctuation characters in its values, including the @ sign, which causes difficulty in sending mail to someone on the Internet.

Whenever an Internet address has a special character, use the following substitutions:

For	Use
@	(a)
%	(p)
!	(b)
"	(q)
_	(u)
(	(l)
)	®

For any other special character, like #, substitute (*xxx*) where *xxx* is the three-digit decimal ASCII code for the character. For #, the code is (035).

After converting the Internet address *uunet.uu.net!bob#test@foo.bar.com* into an address for MCI Mail, Gold 400, or any other X.400 service, you have the following address:

```
uunet.uu.net(b)bob(035)test(a)foo.bar.com.
```

The format is not convenient, but at least it works.

NOTE

Useless trivia: (b) replaces ! because in ancient computer times ! often was called *bang*; addresses containing *bangs* were known as *bangpaths*.

THE HUNT FOR THE ELUSIVE ADDRESS

At times, it is difficult to find people's e-mail addresses. Chapter 21, "Finding People on the Internet," offers much advice. Much of the information in Chapter 21 applies to people who are not directly on the Internet, but who can access it only through a gateway.

Joining Discussions: Using Listservs and Mailing Lists

16

by Phillip Paxton

Although e-mail is convenient for sending messages to someone else, sending a message to more than one user at the same time requires saving a copy of the message and sending it to the additional parties. Alternatively, you must create a distribution list of users who will receive the message and designate this list at the time the message is sent. If a list is used regularly and each user on the list keeps an individual version, each user is required to maintain that list. This means anyone wanting to join such a group is at the mercy of every user already on the list.

Duplication of effort coupled with the lack of control makes this a tenuous solution. Much better is a single, central list that requires a user to be added or deleted only once. All mail sent to such a list is forwarded to everyone on the list. This type of list is common on the Internet and is discussed later in this chapter. If we extend the features of such a list, we can allow each user to control the ability to receive mail, receive copies of the mail they post, and search previous messages for specific information. This is what Listservs do. Rather than burden someone with a full-time job of maintaining a list, Listservs allow those who want to subscribe to a list take care of themselves.

Listservs are one of the most accessible Internet resources available to those who don't have full Internet access; you need only an e-mail gateway. Many Internet-related books ignore or diminish the role of Listservs. Because of the Listserv system's role in the Internet's history and its continued growth and popularity, it is silly to overlook such a flexible, powerful, and useful Internet facility.

The Listserv system provides a mechanism for self-sufficiency, but this doesn't mean you are on your own. Each site running Listserv software has at least one person designated as the Postmaster. The Postmaster is responsible for the upkeep of the Listserv software (although this is usually done automatically using the Listserv system) and serves as a contact point to help resolve technical and list-oriented problems. If you need to contact the site Postmaster, send e-mail to POSTMAST@*siteaddress* (notice that POSTMASTER is truncated to POSTMAST to conform to an eight-letter user ID restriction).

The person you are most likely to contact is the list owner. The list owner is one or more individuals responsible for maintaining the list, helping users who have difficulties, and settling disputes. It's not unusual for someone to post a request publicly for the list owner to contact them. The preferred method of contact is to review the list and use the information there to send mail directly to the list owners.

NOTE

Before diving deeper into this subject, a few notes should be made regarding conventions. References in this chapter to lists refer to VM operating system Listserv-based lists, unless otherwise stated. Every effort has been made to use real information and real messages as examples. The origin of the messages has been altered to protect privacy, and some users' e-mail addresses have been altered for the same reason.

An Introduction to Listservs

Listserv-based lists provide users with the ability to govern themselves. You can subscribe and unsubscribe to the lists of your choice, control your subscription options, search through the archives of previous messages, and so on. Most lists are open to the public, although some are moderated and require the list owner to approve of messages before they are distributed.

Using the Listserv system requires little knowledge beyond that used to operate your e-mail system. Special methods required to tap into an Internet gateway (usually through an online service) are exceptions to the system requirements. Interacting with Listserv is as simple as sending someone e-mail. The commands are simple. The Listserv system even has the ability to *peer itself*—that is, you can split the list across several, even distant, sites to spread the load imposed by a heavily trafficked list.

> **NOTE**
>
> Many texts that provide cursory information about Listserv tell you to leave blank the subject line of an e-mail header. If you have used different e-mail software—even on the same computer—you have probably discovered that many e-mail software packages do not allow a blank subject line. In actuality, the Listserv software ignores the subject line when processing commands.

A Brief History

The Listserv system originally started as a standard e-mail distribution list common to many users of the Internet today—all messages sent to a list were automatically redistributed to everyone listed as a subscriber. This was software written by EDUCOM and installed at BITNIC. As the desire and needs of the subscribers grew and additional features were needed to accommodate the volume of e-mail, Listserv became the Revised Listserv.

Dr. Eric Thomas developed this new list processor at the Ecole Centrale de Paris in France. This new generation of list processing provided for a broader understanding of users' needs and self-sufficiency. The new software included the ability to automatically subscribe and unsubscribe, get online help, communicate between multiple sites to improve efficiency, and specify different types of subscription settings to provide flexibility. As the Listserv system grows, Dr. Thomas has worked to ensure that each version is backward compatible with the previous version, allowing the system to continue to progress without requiring everyone to relearn how to use it.

Versions of the Listserv software are now underway for other operating systems. A Listserv-like system for UNIX is now available and running at many sites but is not as robust as Dr. Thomas' Listserv system. The subscription process has been automated, and a rudimentary help facility is available, but the various sites are not interconnected and self-organizing; that is, they are stand-alone sites. This means you have to examine each site for the lists it has to offer; you cannot retrieve a global list of lists.

How Listservs Work

As you become familiar with the Listserv environment, you notice one interesting characteristic about the names of the lists: they have a maximum of eight letters. This is no coincidence. As noted earlier in this chapter, the Listserv software was written for the VM/CMS operating system. VM (and many other IBM operating systems) allows no more than eight letters in a user ID.

A Listserv list is created as a user ID (usually by the technical support or systems staff) under VM. A control file is then created (again, usually by the support staff) that designates the *list owners* (those who can control the list and act on behalf of users when problems occur) and various options selected for the list (including default options). The control file is sent to the Listserv user ID. This step identifies the list to Listserv and can be used to activate the list.

A user ID with the name LISTSERV is the "brain" for each of the sites that supports the Listserv system. All commands related to list subscriptions and options should be sent to this user ID: all commands should be sent to LISTSERV@*where_ever* and all messages for others to read should be sent to *listname@where_ever*.

Because all messages sent to a list are redistributed to all active subscribers, stray commands are often sent to everyone. Also, it is not unusual for someone to post this message to a list: "would someone please add me to this list?" A follow-up message from a subscriber is almost always posted, explaining the subscription process. The original requester does not see the message (because he or she is not yet a subscriber) so these efforts are in vain.

Advantages and Disadvantages of Listserv

No system is perfect; even Listserv has flaws. Some users feel these flaws are severe enough to prevent them from using the lists. Although the flaws *are* annoying, you'll find that the shortcomings are not insurmountable. Listserv software continues to develop and improve. Subscribers can now specify topics of interest and receive only messages addressing those interests. Another feature has been added that allows a subscriber to receive one large block of messages in a digest format instead of many individual messages. This is convenient for those gaining access to the Internet through a paid service provider where charges may be based on the number of messages received and are almost always based on connect time. The digest form allows you to log on, download your e-mail in one file, and disconnect to read the mail offline at your leisure.

One inconvenience is the e-mail orientation of Listserv; everything arrives through your mailbox. If you are using a paid provider service that monitors or charges for e-mail use, this may be inconvenient. This drawback is offset by a positive attribute: because you are probably familiar with your e-mail software, you won't have to learn a new command structure for handling list traffic.

Another inconvenience of Listserv is that it cannot automatically address mail to the list owners. Other software packages allow you to direct mail to the owner or maintainer of a list or forum without knowing their name or e-mail address. To send mail to the Listserv list owner directly, you must know the address. For information on this process, read "Reviewing the List," later in this chapter. Do not do as some inconsiderate users do and post a request to the list asking the list owners to contact them.

Finally, no easy mechanism exists for determining where you have subscriptions. The only organized method of knowing about your subscriptions is to keep a list, perhaps a list of mail aliases, or an online address book that contains a list. You don't have to know which lists you have to remove your subscription from because you can unsubscribe from all lists. See "Unsubscribing from All Lists," later in this chapter, for information about this procedure.

Despite some of these inconveniences, the Listserv system has several redeeming features. The self-organizing structure allows you to quickly and easily find information about available lists and topics. Many other discussion lists tend to appear and disappear like mushrooms and have no formal mechanism that allows users to locate them.

The Listserv system also permits a high degree of independence. Other discussion lists require owner intervention just to add or remove users from a subscription list. Allowing users to control their own fate provides more free time (in theory) for list owners to improve their lists.

Finally, using the Listserv system doesn't require full Internet access. You can access these lists if the online system you use has an e-mail gateway to the Internet. Because most paid providers have (or will have soon) e-mail gateways, Listserv makes it easy to tap into the information exchanged.

General Use and Etiquette

The Listserv software system is structured to make Internet users self-sufficient. It's generally expected that you will provide for yourself. This includes subscribing and unsubscribing (except for moderated lists), searching the archives for previously discussed topics, and determining whether or not the list is "alive."

At times, you must rely on the list owner to intervene on your behalf, but doing so publicly is not the preferred method. All the commands you need to avoid inflicting yourself on fellow subscribers and eliminate embarrassment can be found in this chapter. Anyone who learns how to subscribe to a list is expected to know how to unsubscribe as well.

> **TIP**
>
> Because messages sent to a list are redistributed to all active subscribers, never send Listserv commands to the list; always send them to the Listserv user ID.

After subscribing to a list, it is a wise practice to lurk. *Lurking* is the practice of watching but not posting; you're an electronic Peeping Tom. Doing so allows you time to acclimate yourself with the posters and participants, gauge the volume (number of messages) of the list, and determine whether this is where you want to spend your time. Newbie users are exposed when they subscribe to the *Star Trek* Listserv (STREK-L@PCCVM.BITNET) and post a message such as "I like the pointy-eared guy. What's his name?" or subscribe to the chess Listserv (CHESS-L@GREARN.BITNET) and post "I just learned to play last year. Please send me your favorite opening."

Before posting, consider your audience. Eventually, you'll find others with whom you have something in common. You'll be tempted to exchange messages, which are extensions of list conversations. It's polite to take these message threads offline; not everyone is interested in hearing the various tidbits of information you and your cohorts exchange. They're irrelevant to the list's purpose.

The world is not going to end because you do not provide for yourself. But you reduce or eliminate the aggravation caused to fellow users by familiarizing yourself with the commands and the actions they perform. Generally, the Internet community is open minded and tolerant of diversity. Jumping in without consideration for current policies and practices, however, is similar to doing a cannonball off the diving board, splashing your hosts, and realizing you never learned to swim.

Finding Lists

The Listserv system's self-organizing ability provides an advantage over other e-mail-based discussion lists. Finding lists of interest is simple; messages like "Does anyone know of a Listserv about such-and-such topic?" are unnecessary and annoying.

There are three primary methods for finding lists: online references, directories, and texts (including Gopher and Veronica); subscribing to NEW-LIST and receiving an announcement; and using the built-in LIST command.

Online References

The online references and dictionaries are regularly updated materials. They are provided by individuals who collect information about either general topics representing a cross-section of the Internet's offerings or resources of interest to specific special-interest groups.

NEW-LIST is for users who create new lists (both Listserv and non-Listserv) to notify others. This list is also used by persons posting inquiries while looking for specific lists, Listservs, and news. The address of NEW-LIST is vm1.nodak.edu (for those who don't trust Listserv to forward your subscription request). See "Subscribing and Unsubscribing," later in this chapter, for information about subscribing to Listservs.

The *LIST* Command

The LIST command is the Listserv equivalent to a library's card catalog; it allows users to exploit Listserv's self-organizing capability. The scope (or range) of the LIST command depends on the options you specify. If you are interested in becoming a charter member of a Listserv, you may find yourself checking for new lists more often than is practical. Using the LIST command daily or weekly is probably too often. If early exposure to a new list is important, you should probably subscribe to NEW-LIST.

Local Use of the *LIST* Command

If the LIST command is used without options, it provides a list of lists for the site receiving the command. Here's the abbreviated output from sending the LIST command to listserv@indycms.iupui.edu:

```
> LIST
AATG       American Association of Teachers of German
ACCESS-L   Microsoft Access Database Discussion List
APOSEC52   Alpha Phi Omega Region 6 (Sections 48/52/54)
ARNBOARD   ARNOVA Board of Directors
BIBSOFT    Discussion of software for citations and bibliographies
BKGAMMON   Backgammon strategy
BRTHPRNT   List for Birthparents of Adoptees
C-L        Discussion of C Programming
CENTINFO   Center Availability Information
COMPACT    IUPUI Campus Compact
CSCI207    Learning List for CSCI207
DISTLABS   Teaching Science Labs Via Distance
EXCEL-L    Microsoft Excel Developers List
FACOUNCL   IUPUI Faculty Council Mail List
FITNESS    Fitness and the IUPUI campus
FREE-L     Fathers' Rights and Equality Exchange
```

The *LIST GLOBAL* Command

The LIST GLOBAL command is self-descriptive. It returns a list of all known public lists. If you do not send the command to a backbone site, it is forwarded to a backbone for you. A *backbone site* is a primary or large site. Because Listserv forwards LIST GLOBAL requests on your behalf, it is not necessary to know the addresses of your backbone sites.

> **TIP**
>
> If you are using an online service that charges for either large numbers of messages or large messages, check to see whether it has an online library that contains files, such as the LISTSERV LISTS file. Another possibility is to try using a Gopher (see Chapter 25, "Using and Finding Gophers") or Veronica (see Chapter 26, "Searching Gopherspace with Veronica"), both of which frequently provide access to the global list.

Before sending the LIST GLOBAL command, you should be prepared for the results. At the time of this writing, more than 4,000 lists existed. This means a rather lengthy list of lists when you to try to determine what's changed since the last time you submitted the command.

> **NOTE**
>
> The emphasis on Bitnet addresses in the LIST GLOBAL result does not mean you have to become a full-time Bitnet-to-Internet translator. Listserv is usually smart enough to forward commands to the correct site.

Following is a portion of the output received from the LIST GLOBAL command (do you really want to read through 100 pages now?). The *Network-Wide ID* column gives the name of the list, the *Full Address* column is the Bitnet address, and the *List Title* column gives the description of the list designated by the list owner.

```
List of all Listserv lists known to Listserv@YALEVM on 28 Feb 1994 22:55

Network-wide ID  Full address     List title
-------          ------           ------
AUSTEN-L         AUSTEN-L@MCGILL1 Jane Austen discussion list
AUSTLIT          AUSTLIT@NDSUVM1  Austrian Literature
AUTISM           AUTISM@SJUVM     SJU Autism and Developmental
                                  Disabilities List
AUTOCAD          AUTOCAD@JHUVM    AUTOCAD Discussion List
AUTOCAT          AUTOCAT@UBVM     AUTOCAT: Library cataloging and
                                  authorities +
```

```
AUTORACE        AUTORACE@VTVM1        AUTORACE - A Discussion of Auto
                                      Racing
AUTOS-L         AUTOS-L@TRITU         The List For Classic And Sports Cars
AVHIMA-L        AVHIMA-L@UIUCVMD      American Veterinary Health
                                      Information Manag+
AVIATION        AVIATION@BRUFPB       General Aviation List
AWARDS-B        AWARDS-B@OSUVM1       Commerce Business Daily - Awards
AWARE-L         AWARE-L@UKANVM        Discussion of the dual platform
                                      authoring pr+
AWR-L           AWR-L@TTUVM1          A WRITER'S REPERTOIRE
AXE-LIST        AXE-LIST@MCGILL1      Quebec Literature Studies
```

Reducing the Volume of *LIST GLOBAL*

Faced with the prospect of browsing more than 4,000 lines of text to find interesting lists, most users resort to reading the text file into an editor or word processor and using a search command. Listserv has a mechanism to reduce the list automatically. An extension of the LIST GLOBAL command enables you to specify text to be found in the name or description of the list. The form of the command extension is LIST GLOBAL/*text* where *text* is text string for which you want to look in the list name or description.

The next output example shows a list of information supplied by Listserv when the LIST GLOBAL/GAME command is submitted. The /*text* extension is not a cure-all. Some lists may have cryptic names resulting from the eight-letter restriction, or may not be described in the way you expect. However, it often reduces the search time.

```
Excerpt from the Listserv lists known to Listserv@YALEVM on 31 Jan 1994 01:07
Search string: GAME

Network-wide ID  Full address        List title
-------          ------              ------
CONSIM-L         CONSIM-L@UALTAVM    Conflict simulation Games
DIPL-L           DIPL-L@MITVMA       Discussion Group for the Game of
                                     Diplomacy
D20A-L           D20A-L@MITVMA       10 Player Diplomacy Game List (Sam
                                     Huntsman +
GAMES-L          GAMES-L@BROWNVM     (Peered) Computer Games List
GAMES-L@GREARN   (Peered) Computer Games List
GAMES-L@KRSNUCC1 (Peered) Computer Games List
GAMES-L@UTARLVM1 (Peered) Computer Games List
GMAST-L          GMAST-L@UTCVM       Gamemasters Interest Group
MYTHUS-L         MYTHUS-L@BROWNVM    Mythus Fantasy Roleplaying Game List
SHADOWRN         SHADOWRN@HEARN      Discussion of the Fantasy game
                                     ShadowRun
STARGAME         STARGAME@PCCVM      STARTREK Role Playing game list
```

Subscribing and Unsubscribing

The following sections describe the all-important activities of subscribing and unsubscribing to Listserv.

Subscribing to a List

The SUBSCRIBE command requires little documentation, aside from the need to identify yourself to Listserv. SUBSCRIBE can be abbreviated SUB, producing the following command syntax:

```
SUB listname firstname lastname
```

Remember to insert the correct name of the list for `listname`, and your first and last names in place of `firstname` and `lastname`. Listserv is designed to allow you to send this command to any Listserv user ID; your request is forwarded to the proper host site (you are notified should forwarding occur). Here is a copy of the notice received from a subscription request to the FOLKLORE list:

```
Your subscription to the FOLKLORE list (Folklore Discussion List) has been
accepted.

Please save this message for future reference, especially if you are not familiar
with Listserv. This might look like a waste of disk space now, but in 6 months
you will be glad you saved this information when you realize that you cannot
remember what are the lists you are subscribed to, or what is the command to
leave the list to avoid filling up your mailbox while you are on vacation. In
fact, you should create a new mail folder for subscription confirmation messages
like this one, and for the "welcome messages" from the list owners that you will
occasionally receive after subscribing to a new list.

To send a message to all the people currently subscribed to the list, just send
mail to FOLKLORE@TAMVM1.TAMU.EDU. This is called "sending mail to the list",
because you send mail to a single address and Listserv makes copies for all the
people who have subscribed. This address (FOLKLORE@TAMVM1.TAMU.EDU) is also
called the "list address". You must never try to send any command to that
address, because it is distributed to  all the people who have subscribed. All
commands must be sent to the "Listserv address", Listserv@TAMVM1.BITNET (or
Listserv@TAMVM1.TAMU.EDU). It is very important to understand the difference
between the two, but fortunately it is not complicated. The Listserv address is
like a FAX number, and the list address is like a normal phone line. If you make
your FAX call someone's regular phone number by mistake, it is an unpleasant
experience for him but you will probably be excused the first time. If you do it
regularly, however, he will probably get upset and send you a nasty complaint. It
is the same with mailing lists, with the difference that you are calling hundreds
or thousands of people at the same time, so a lot more people get annoyed if you
use the wrong number.
```

```
You may leave the list at any time by sending a "SIGNOFF FOLKLORE" command to
Listserv@TAMVM1.BITNET (or Listserv@TAMVM1.TAMU.EDU). You can also tell Listserv
how you want it to confirm the receipt of messages you send to the list. If you
do not trust the system, send a "SET  FOLKLORE REPRO" command and Listserv will
send you a copy of your own messages so that you can see that the message was
distributed and did not get damaged on the way. After a while, you may find that
this is getting annoying, especially if your mail program does not tell you that
the message is from you when it informs you that new mail has arrived from
FOLKLORE. If you send a "SET FOLKLORE ACK NOREPRO" command, Listserv will mail
you a short acknowledgment instead, which will look different in your mailbox
directory. With most mail programs, you will know immediately that this is an
acknowledgment you can read later. Finally, you can turn off acknowledgments
completely with "SET FOLKLORE NOACK NOREPRO".

Contributions sent to this list are automatically archived. You can get a list of
the available archive files by sending an "INDEX FOLKLORE" command to
Listserv@TAMVM1.BITNET (or Listserv@TAMVM1.TAMU.EDU). You can then order these
files with a "GET FOLKLORE LOGxxxx" command, or using Listserv's database search
facilities. Send an "INFO DATABASE" command for more information on the latter.

Please note that it is presently possible for anybody to determine that you are
signed up to the list through the use of the "REVIEW" command, which returns the
e-mail address and name of all the subscribers. If you do not want your name to
be visible, just issue a "SET FOLKLORE CONCEAL" command.

More information on Listserv commands can be found in the Listserv reference
card, which you can retrieve by sending an "INFO  REFCARD" command to
Listserv@TAMVM1.BITNET (or Listserv@TAMVM1.TAMU.EDU).
```

This message is a *template*—it is nearly the same for every subscription confirmation, except for the list name and addressing information. If you read this listing carefully, you will see much of the information users need to avoid posting queries like "How do I sign off this list?" or "How do I receive copies of the mail I send?"—the message even fills in the addresses specific to this list.

NOTE

If you misspell your name or want to change it, the SUB command allows you to do so. If you submit the SUB command to a list that understands you to be a subscriber, it makes the name change for you.

Providing Confirmation and Renewal

Some lists require confirmation after an initial subscription request. The following example shows a portion of the message returned by Listserv when a subscription request is submitted to a list requiring confirmation. You may wonder why confirmation is be needed. Consider what would happen if you leave your user ID logged on and unattended. Someone can easily send a subscription request to a list with a high volume of mail, perhaps even on the order of several hundred messages per day. Requiring confirmation can help avoid this problem.

```
Your command:

SUBSCRIBE ACCESS-L firstname lastname

has been received. You must now reply to this message (as explained below) to
complete your subscription. The purpose of this confirmation procedure is to
check that the address Listserv is about to add to the list for you is working
properly. This is a typical procedure for high-volume lists and all new
subscribers are subjected to it - no offense meant. We have tried to make this
confirmation as simple and painless as possible, and apologize for the
inconvenience.
```

Historically, most Internet users come from academic institutions (hence the reference in many Internet circles to the "September" cycle of new users). This means a fairly high rate of turnover because of student users who are away several months of the year. Even in the world of the Internet today, where businesses are connecting at dizzying rates, turnover exists. Listserv permits the list owner to require renewal of your subscription, usually once a year, to alleviate the burden of weeding out expired user IDs or the user IDs of persons who may still be subscribed but have no interest in the list. This list is also used by persons looking for specific groups who post inquiries.

Unsubscribing from a List

The UNSUBSCRIBE command (which can be abbreviated UNSUB) or the SIGNOFF command removes you from the specified list. The command syntax is as follows:

```
UNSUB listname
```

This is the output from a successful UNSUB request:

```
You have been removed from the FOLKLORE list.
```

If you try to remove yourself from a list that doesn't consider you to be a subscriber, you receive two messages. The following example shows the first message that resulted from an unsuccessful attempt to unsubscribe from WIN3-L:

```
> UNSUB WIN3-L
You do not appear to have subscribed to list WIN3-L. You are being mailed some
additional information, with a few hints on getting your subscription cancelled.
Please read this mail message before trying anything else.
```

The next output extract provides the first few lines from the follow-up message. If you cannot resolve the problem using the information provided in this response, you should attempt to contact one of the list owners. Instructions for determining the list owners' e-mail addresses are found in "Reviewing the List," later in this chapter.

```
No entry for your me@here address could be found in the WIN3-L list at
UICVM. Here are a number of possible reasons why you might still be getting mail
from the list.
```

TIP

If you cannot reach any of the list owners for assistance and you are subscribed to a high-volume list, consider using the SET *listname* NOMAIL command (details provided later in this chapter). This command stems the tide of e-mail until you can unsubscribe. Using this command is preferred to a public message, which will only irritate your fellow subscribers.

Unsubscribing from All Lists

If it becomes necessary for you to unsubscribe from all the lists to which you are subscribed, Listserv has just the tool: an extension of the UNSUB or SIGNOFF command. This extension tells Listserv to distribute the request to all known Listserv sites and attempt to remove you from any of the lists under their control. No special information is provided for this command. The syntax is as follows:

```
SIGNOFF * ( NETWIDE
```

Processing your request takes place in two steps. The following example shows the output from the first step, which indicates that UNSUB requests will be passed along to other servers. If you know your user ID will be deleted or out of service, it is only courteous to remove yourself from lists in advance. Many users do not realize that their inaction causes extra work for others when the mail begins bouncing. Many support personnel ignore this command when removing a user ID from their system and address individual messages to each of the lists found in the mailbox to ask for removal.

```
> UNSUB * ( NETWIDE
Your request will be forwarded to 259 servers.
```

Making Inquiries About Your Subscription

Although Listserv doesn't enable you to determine which lists you are subscribed to in a global fashion, you can determine the subscription parameters for a particular list. You also can list information about a particular list. Some lists allow you to retrieve information about the list only if you are listed as a subscriber. This option is turned on or off by the list owners.

Find Your Subscription Settings with *QUERY*

The QUERY command returns the subscription values for a particular list. In addition to providing information about your subscription, the QUERY command can quickly tell you whether you are subscribed to a list. If you believe you are a subscriber and receive information from the Listserv system to the contrary, use the REVIEW command (explained in the next section) to determine whether Listserv has you subscribed with a different e-mail address.

```
> QUERY ACCESS-L
Distribution options for firstname lastname <me@here>,
list ACCESS-L: Ack= Yes, Mail= Yes, Files= Yes,
Repro= No, Header= Short(BSMTP), Renewal= Yes, Conceal= No
```

Reviewing the List

You should use the REVIEW command to obtain specific information about the list—default subscription values for new subscribers, a list of the users and their e-mail addresses, and a list of users who have not concealed their subscription. Here is some of the information returned when reviewing the WORDS-L list:

```
*     English Language Discussion Group
*
*     Review=          Public
*     Subscription=    Open,Confirm
*     Send=            Public
*     Daily-Threshold= 300
*     Notify=          Yes
*     Reply-to=        List,Respect
*     Files=           No
*     Default-options= Repro
*     Confidential=    No
*     Validate=        Store Only
*     Renewal=         6-Monthly,Delay(14)
*     X-Tags=          Comment
*     Stats=           Normal
*     Ack=             No
*     Notebook=        No
*     Digest=          Yes,Same,Daily
*     Owner=           maynor@ra.msstate.edu (Natalie Maynor)
*     Owner=           alileste@idbsu.idbsu.edu (Dan Lester)
*     Owner=           lncjb@cc.newcastle.edu.au (Carolyn Baird)
*     Owner=           fna104@uriacc.uri.edu (Jim Bradley)
*     Owner=           hide:,quiet:
*     Owner=           maynor@cs.msstate.edu (Bernard Chien Perro)
*     Owner=           hide:,quiet:
*     Owner=           harold@uga
*     Errors-to=       maynor@ra.msstate.edu
*     Errors-to=       alileste@idbsu.idbsu.edu
*     Errors-to=       lncjb@cc.newcastle.edu.au
*     Errors-to=       fna104@uriacc.uri.edu
*     Editor=          maynor@ra.msstate.edu
*     Editor=          alileste@idbsu.idbsu.edu
*     Editor=          lncjb@cc.newcastle.edu.au
*     Editor=          fna104@uriacc.uri.edu
*     Mail-Via=        DIST2
```

Setting Subscription Options

Other discussion list methods can be implemented using e-mail, but you are usually limited to the options of receiving mail or not receiving mail: If you are a subscriber, you receive mail; when you are removed from the list, you do not receive mail. The Listserv software, however, has several options you can set.

Several of these options are described in the subscription message you receive (see the output listing, earlier in this chapter, for a successful subscription request) in a format customized for that particular list. The following sections list options you'll find helpful, as well as information about why and when you may want to use them. This is not an exhaustive list, but the commonly used options are described. You can retrieve additional Listserv commands using the information in "Using the INFO Command for More Information," later in this chapter.

Controlling Your Ability To Receive Mail

The MAIL/NOMAIL option instructs Listserv about your desire to receive or halt posted messages. Using this command enables you to control the e-mail flow but still retain your subscription. The syntax of the command indicating a desire to stop receiving messages is as follows:

```
SET listname NOMAIL
```

The counter command that restores your ability to receive mail is this:

```
SET listname MAIL
```

You'll find this handy in several situations. If you return from vacation, or your system was brought down for an extended period of time, you can find yourself digging out from underneath an avalanche of messages when you return. Imagine how much mail you can have waiting for you if a high-volume list sends several hundred messages daily and you're gone for a week. If you feel you have missed something, you can retrieve relevant archives (if that option is established for the list) at your convenience. Look at the sections later in this chapter that explain the archive structure and how to list, search, and retrieve list archives.

> **TIP**
>
> Another reason to keep a list subscription and not receive messages is for the purpose of research. Many older lists have extensive archives that are nice to search. If you are interested in material previously posted (perhaps on a computer-related forum for solutions to a particular problem) but don't care to receive e-mail, the NOMAIL option is exactly what you need.

Receiving Copies of the Messages You Post

Many unknowing or inexperienced users post messages to a list asking, "Why don't I receive copies of my own messages? Are my messages being posted? Please let me know." The Listserv system has an option called REPRO, which indicates your desire to receive copies of the messages you post to the list.

A good rule of thumb is to expect lists to default to Repro=No. If you want to receive copies of your own messages (a sign the list is at least functional when traffic is light), use this syntax:

```
SET listname REPRO
```

Turn the option off with this syntax:

```
SET listname NOREPRO
```

Concealing Your Subscription

You may find it necessary to conceal your subscription to a particular list; perhaps the list focuses on issues of a personal nature and you'd rather others—for example, your employer—not know you are a subscriber. The CONCEAL command prevents others from seeing your name and e-mail address when they retrieve list information with the REVIEW command. You should know, however, that this command does not prevent others from seeing your presence if you post messages to the list. You can only hope a list that is this important allows only subscribed users to search the archives. This means that someone wanting to check up on you has to join the list and take the chance of exposing themselves.

The syntax of the command to conceal yourself is as follows:

```
SET listname CONCEAL
```

Here is the reverse command:

```
SET listname NOCONCEAL
```

Shortening the Headers Body with *SHORT*

Because Listserv is efficient enough to send copies of messages once to each site (whenever possible), it lists each of the recipients at that site in the To header field. If the number of users at your site is more than a handful, this list can get cumbersome. The list of recipients also compromises your privacy because your name and user ID are on each message received by your associates. The list of To recipients can be abbreviated to a nondescript Multiple users by using the following command syntax:

```
SET listname SHORT
```

The full list of headers can be turned on using the following command syntax:

```
SET listname FULL
```

Files and Archives

Although many other Internet-related discussion groups and Usenet newsgroups keep archives available with anonymous FTP, Listserv makes archives available directly. Most lists archive all messages automatically. They also have the ability to store files for retrieval, as well as storing groups of files known as *packages*. A package permits making one retrieval request instead of requesting many files individually.

The Listserv system possesses a powerful searching mechanism. Without it, you are required to retrieve entire archive files and search them manually. The following sections are not a comprehensive tutorial to the searching mechanisms; after reading them, however, you will be able to perform simple searches and have enough information to survive as you learn.

Listing Available Files

The INDEX command provides a list of files available at the site hosting the Listserv. Following is a summarized output from an INDEX request submitted to listserv@uicvm.uic.edu, host of WIN3-L. The most important columns are the filename, file type, and file description. Remember that Listserv is structured for the VM operating system. VM organizes files by filename and file type (there's also a filemode, but that is not relevant here).

```
*   Master Listserv filelist
*                               rec            last-change
```

```
*filename filetype  GET  PUT -fm lrecl nrecs  date     time     File description
*  ----      ----    -    -   --  ---   ---    --       --       --------

Listserv FILELIST   ALL  CTL  V   107   105 95/01/31 22:19:33 Lists all available
  ➡Listserv files
NOTEBOOK FILELIST   NAD  N/A  V    95   N/A 95/01/26 11:23:51 List of available
  ➡notebooks
INFO     FILELIST   ALL  LMC  V   102   100 94/09/16 22:02:58 List of information
  ➡files about Listserv
TOOLS    FILELIST   ALL  LMC  V    97   223 94/09/16 22:03:04 Software tools for
  ➡use with Listserv
CONTROL  FILELIST   ALL  LMC  V    96   139 95/01/25 13:49:14 Control datafiles
  ➡used by Listserv
```

The master list has been obtained, but it contains only high-level material and doesn't include information about the intended target: WIN3-L. Submitting a new INDEX request in the form INDEX WIN3-L produces output similar to the following. This is a list of files associated with WIN3-L.

```
*   WIN3-L FILELIST for Listserv@UICVM.
*   WIN3-L files
*                            rec            last - change
*filename filetype  GET  PUT -fm lrecl nrecs date     time     File description
*  ----      ----    -    -   --  ---   ---   --       --       --------
WINDOWS  FAQ         ALL OWN  .    .     0    ........ ........

*   NOTEBOOK archives for the list
*   (Monthly notebook)
*                            rec            last - change
*filename filetype  GET  PUT -fm lrecl nrecs date     time     File description
*  ----      ----    -    -   --  ---   ---   --       --       --------
*
*   NOTEBOOK archives for the list
*   (Weekly notebook)
*                            rec            last - change
*filename filetype  GET  PUT -fm lrecl nrecs date     time     File description
*  ----      ----    -    -   --  ---   ---   --       --       --------
WIN3-L   LOG9201A   PRV OWN  V    80  2920 95/01/07 23:04:35 Started on Sun,
  ➡1 Jan 1995 10:15:44 EST
WIN3-L   LOG9201B   PRV OWN  V    80  4359 95/01/14 22:58:49 Started on Fri,
  ➡8 Jan 1995 08:32:00 CET
WIN3-L   LOG9201C   PRV OWN  V    80  3674 95/01/21 22:43:27 Started on Sun,
  ➡15 Jan 1995 00:29:10 -0600
WIN3-L   LOG9201D   PRV OWN  V    80  2656 95/01/28 09:02:49 Started on Sat,
  ➡21 Jan 1995 23:17:00 PST
WIN3-L   LOG9201E   PRV OWN  V    80  1335 95/01/29 09:54:12 Started on Sun,
  ➡29 Jan 1995 10:11:25 EST
WIN3-L   LOG9401D   PRV OWN  V    82 11507 94/01/28 23:48:41 Started on Sat,
  ➡22 Jan 1994 00:50:00 EDT
WIN3-L   LOG9401E   PRV OWN  V    80  5651 94/01/31 23:31:36 Started on Fri,
  ➡28 Jan 1994 21:43:00 EST
WIN3-L   LOG9402A   PRV OWN  V    79   240 94/02/01 02:04:32 Started on Mon,
  ➡31 Jan 1994 22:21:57 -0800
```

The files with a file type prefix of LOG are archives. The files have a timestamp: LOG*yynn* tells the year (*yy*) and number (*nn*) of the archive. The ninth line of the listing indicates that notebooks are reset monthly (now we know that each number indicates the month the archive log was created). Some lists have enough activity to warrant weekly logs. The final letter at the end of the filename (for example, A, B, or C) indicates smaller archives within the month. Whenever a log archive becomes large, the letter is incremented to keep the same datestamp but provide a unique file type.

Retrieving

The filename and file type become important when you want to retrieve a file. The proper command syntax to indicate which file you want sent to you is as follows:

```
GET filename filetype
```

If you retrieve too much material during a 24-hour period, you are notified by Listserv and told how much time must expire before you can retrieve more files. If a specific file is desired, you shouldn't have any problems, but if you are retrieving log archives and searching them, you may want to investigate the Listserv searching mechanism.

Archives

A demonstration of the LIST command has provided you with a list of files associated with the WIN3-L list. As a quick review, each message posted to the list is archived in a log file if the list owner has specified this option. Sites working with little or no spare disk space may not permit list archives.

Indexing

The INDEX command is local; that is, it is relevant only for the site you send it to. If you send the command INDEX *listname* to a Listserv user ID, it returns a list of files associated with the list. This list includes the archived files (if this feature has been designated by the list owner). If you want to retrieve a file, use the GET command. The command structure is GET *filename filetype* (to conform to the VM operating system's structure of a filename and file type). After the request is processed, the desired file is returned to you.

Searching and Retrieving

The Listserv system supports a powerful searching mechanism. The minute details of this function are beyond the scope of this book. The INFO command provides you with the information you need to retrieve the necessary documents. The Listserv system lets you search for more than just specific words. Archived messages can be searched based on the date they were written, words they contain, words they don't contain, who posted the message, similarities of words, and combinations of all of these.

Here is a simple search request:

```
//
Database Search DD=MyJob
//MyJob DD  *
Search Easter Egg in Win3-L
Index
/*
```

If this is submitted as an e-mail message and sent to listserv@uicvm.uic.edu by an active subscriber, an index of messages that contain the words *easter* and *egg* is returned. (*Easter eggs* are the hidden screens software designers sometimes add to programs as an artistic touch.) If you use this sample command file as an example and build on it using the online references, it's possible to find just about anything you are looking for. The searching mechanism is one of the most understated features of the Listserv system and is probably more powerful than those available in commercial systems that permit user searches against unstructured text.

Using the *INFO* Command for More Information

The INFO command is the method for requesting help. You can send this command to any of the Listserv user IDs, and a file will be sent to you in response to your request. Use the INFO ? command to retrieve a current list of relevant help topics. Most topics listed are available to all users. Some are available only to those who own or maintain lists, others only to Postmasters, and still others only to those who help coordinate the Listserv software system.

REFERENCE WORKS

Heim, Michael. "Humanistic Discussion and the Online Conference." *Philosophy Today.* 30 (Winter 1986): pp. 278-88.

Hiltz, S.R., & Turroff, M. (1993). *The Network Nation: Human Communication via Computer*, Boston: Massachusetts Institute of Technology.

Katzen, May. "The Impact of New Technologies on Scholarly Communication." In *Multi-Media Communications*, ed. May. Katzen, pp. 16-50. Westport, CT: Greenwood Press, 1982.

Kerr, Elaine B. "Electronic Leadership: A Guide To Moderating Online Conferences." *IEEE Transactions on Professional Communication* PC 29, no. 1 (1986): pp. 12-18.

Kovacs, M.J., Kovacs, D.K. (1991). "The state of scholarly electronic conferencing." Electronic Networking: Research Applications and Policy, 1, pp. 29-36.

Kovacs, Diane K. "GovDoc-L: An Online Intellectual Community of Documents, Librarians, and Other Individuals Concerned with Access to Government Information." *Government Publications Review* 17 (September/October 1990): pp. 411-20.

Pfaffenberger, Bryan. "Research Networks, Scientific Communication, and the Personal Computer." IEEE Transactions on Professional Communication PC 29, no. 1 (1986): pp. 30-33.

Quarterman, John S. "The Matrix: Computer Networks and Conferencing Systems Worldwide." Bedford, MA: Digital Press, 1990.

Rafaeli, Sheizaf. "The Electronic Bulletin Board: A Computer-Driven Mass Medium." *Computers and the Social Sciences* 2, no. 3 (1986): pp. 123-36.

Rice, Ronald E., and Donald Case. "Electronic Message Systems in the University: A Description of Use and Utility." *Journal of Communication* 33, no. 1 (1983): pp. 131-52.

Richardson, John. "The Limitations to Electronic Communication in the Research Community." Paper delivered at the Information Technology and the Research Process Conference, Cranfield, UK, July 1989.

Spitzer, Michael. "Writing Style in Computer Conferences." IEEE Transactions on Professional Communication PC 29, no. 1 (1986): pp. 19-22.

Sproull, Lee, and Sara Kiesler. "Reducing Social Context Cues: Electronic Mail in Organizational Communication." *Management Science* 32 (November 1986): 1 pp. 492-512.

Steinfield, Charles W. "Computer-Mediated Communication Systems." Annual Review of Information Science and Technology 21 (1986): pp. 167-202.

Reading and Posting the News: Using Usenet

by Tim Parker

```
Article 123 (534 more) in alt.newbies
From: fflintstone@bedrock.com
Newsgroups: alt.newbies alt.newusers
Subject: IS ANYONE OUT THERE?
Date: 20 Jan 1994 13:45:12
Lines: 6

HELLO.  IS ANYONE OUT THERE READING THIS MESSAGE?

IM REALLY INTO MOUNTAIN BIKING.  ITS SO COOL!!!!

FRED


Article 145 (345 more) in alt.newbies
From: rmaclean@bnr.ca.edu
Newsgroups: alt.newbies
Subject: Re: IS ANYONE OUT THERE?
Date: 20 Jan 1994 20:12:34
Lines: 12

> HELLO.  IS ANYONE OUT THERE READING THIS MESSAGE?
Only a few million of us! (Well, those of us who subscribe to
this newsgroup, at any rate.)

> IM REALLY INTO MOUNTAIN BIKING.  ITS SO COOL!!!!
Since you are obviously a newbie, you won't get flamed too much.
Try checking out newsgroups under rec.bicycles, such as
rec.bicycles.tech, rec.bicycles.misc, or rec.bicycles.soc (there
are others).

> FRED
Nice to meet you Fred.  By the way, there's no need to shout.
Check out the posting guidelines in new.announce.newusers.

  ¦ \
 / ¦  \   I'd rather             Roy MacLean
 / ¦ ___\  be sailing            rmaclean@bnr.ca.edu
 - - - - -
-------------------------------------------------------------
```

Welcome to Usenet! These are only two of the thousands of articles that are posted to Usenet every day.

Usenet is one of the most misunderstood aspects of the Internet; at the same time, it is one of the most popular and frequently used. To many users, especially those who don't use the Internet's mail facilities, Usenet *is* the Internet.

Usenet was developed to facilitate discussion groups (called *newsgroups*) in which any user can participate in a public dialog with everyone else on the network. By the end of 1994, Usenet carried more than 9,000 different newsgroups totaling 100M of information every day, covering every imaginable topic (as well as some unimaginable ones!). Usenet is supported in hundreds of countries and reaches millions of users.

Understanding what Usenet is, how newsgroups are managed, and how to best interact with the newsreader utilities is the focus of this chapter. This information can help you better use this popular Internet feature.

What Is Usenet?

Despite many people's preconceived notions, Usenet is not a formal network. Instead, it is a number of machines that exchange electronic mail tagged with predetermined subject headers. The mail is referred to as an *article*; the subjects are *newsgroups*.

Any computer that can attach itself to the Internet can become part of Usenet by implementing the software that downloads and uploads newsgroup mail. This software implements the Network News Transfer Protocol (NNTP), which lets your machine interact with others that handle the news. NNTP software is an integral part of most UNIX versions and most DOS and Macintosh Internet access software packages, so typically there is no additional software to purchase.

Usenet is not a company or organization. No single person or entity controls Usenet, and there is no authority that manages it (other than the local machine system administrator who can decide what news is downloaded). This implies that Usenet is not funded by any public or governmental body. Usenet's nodes are maintained by corporations, educational institutions, or individuals who choose to implement the newsgroup system at their own expense.

Controlling what happens on Usenet is left up to the users. They tend to decide what newsgroups will be of interest and thus should be supported; users also monitor other users. Badly behaved users are subjected to attacks through articles and private e-mail in the hope that public pressure will force them to conform to the general guidelines developed for using Usenet (often called *netiquette*). In extreme cases, a system administrator receives enough complaints about a user that the user's access privileges may be revoked.

Usenet is not a UNIX-exclusive system. Any operating system can access Usenet newsgroups by implementing the software that manages the transfer of Usenet mail. There is no single Usenet software program; a suite of programs work together to manage different aspects. Versions of the required utilities are available for most popular platforms, including the Macintosh, DOS-based PCs, VAX VMS, and many others.

Newsgroup Naming Conventions

Usenet newsgroups are named using a set of conventions. Because newsgroups are usually created only by general consensus, these naming conventions are enforced by the community as a whole.

Newsgroups lead off with an identifier that tells the type of newsgroup it is, followed by a more specific name. The major groups are as follows:

Group Name	Meaning
biz	Business related groups
comp	Dealing with computers, computer science, and software
sci	Scientific subjects such as astronomy and biology
misc	Newsgroups that don't readily fall under any other category
soc	Groups addressing social issues and socializing
talk	Debate-oriented groups that encourage lengthy discussions
news	General news and topical subjects
rec	Groups aimed toward arts, hobbies, and recreational activities
alt	Groups that have a more limited distribution than the standard Usenet newsgroups but that are usually much freer as far as content than formal groups

All the group subjects, except for alt, are usually circulated world wide. The alt groups are usually selectively circulated, depending on the system. They are not usually carried world wide. Many users think of the alt newsgroups as an underground set of newsgroups, where anarchy reigns.

The second part of the newsgroup name identifies the major subject area. For example, rec.bicycles involves the subject of (surprise!) bicycles. However, most subjects have further subgroups dedicated to more specific aspects of the general topic. So, for example, if you have a question about bicycle maintenance, you could post to rec.bicycles.tech. To read about other people's rides or ask about bicycle routes in your area, check out rec.bicycles.rides. Follow up with the social aspects of biking by reading rec.bicycles.soc.

Even more specification can be encountered, especially in the comp and sci groups. For example, comp.ibm.software.microsoft.word and comp.ibm.software.microsoft.excel both deal with specific software packages for the IBM PC. Newsgroups with five or six layers are rare, but three levels is common.

The alt (alternate) newsgroups can mirror the normal Usenet newsgroups (for example, there are rec.autos.antique and alt.autos.antique newsgroups), but sometimes there is no corresponding non-alt group name. The alt groups serve a couple of purposes. They can be used for local-interest groups that may not be distributed beyond a small area in the country. They also can be considered a less rigidly behaved version of the usual newsgroup.

It is not uncommon to find more flaming (explained in "Flames, Shouting, and Smileys," later in this chapter) and nasty posts in alt newsgroups. Most Usenet users recognize that there are fewer restrictions on expected behavior in alt groups. Although this can sometimes get out of hand, the alt groups are often very interesting. Not all sites accept alt groups.

Sometimes, a new newsgroup is created that has a title representing a joke or insult to someone, such as alt.ed.is.a.dope. These are not real newsgroups; they are created for the sole purpose of showing how clever the creator is in his or her high level of witticism. Usually, they fail. These "bogus newsgroups" show up with annoying regularity—usually a few a week—and can slow down a news session while the reader handles the new newsgroup names.

Although you can create new newsgroups, this is usually a decision made by the user group after a "call for votes." If enough people express interest in a new group, it is created and joins the list of supported newsgroups. Most users have no need to know the mechanism for creating a new newsgroups, but you can find information about the process in the newsgroups news.announce.newuser and news.groups.

Moderated Newsgroups

Some newsgroups do not allow postings without the article being vetted by someone. Such groups are called *moderated newsgroups*, of which there are quite a few. In a moderated newsgroup, one individual receives a post before it is freely released to the network. That person has the power to refuse admission to the posting if the subject is irrelevant to the group, doesn't contribute anything useful, or is considered in poor taste.

Because moderated newsgroups rely on an individual to screen all posts, an article takes longer to appear in a moderated newsgroup. A full list of moderated newsgroups is usually available in the newsgroup new.announce.newuser; in addition, many newsgroup headers clearly indicate whether the newsgroup is moderated.

Moderated newsgroups are usually better behaved than ones that aren't moderated because the moderator eliminates useless postings. There is definitely much less "flaming," which brings us to the next subject.

Flames, Shouting, and Smileys

Usenet has its own behavior patterns and jargon. Most of the important terms are introduced in the next few pages, but a couple concepts are worth noting now.

One of the first terms you encounter (which applies directly to you) is *newbie*. A newbie is a newcomer to Usenet. There are typical newbie questions that everyone expects, most of which are easily answered by reading newsgroup traffic. Many common questions a newbie has are answered on the newsgroups' Frequently Asked Questions (FAQ) postings, which are typically related to the newsgroups' topic. FAQs cover all the basic information a newcomer to the newsgroup may want, as well as providing lots of background material on the subject. FAQs are often posted to the newsgroup at regular intervals, as well as to the news.answers newsgroup. Most FAQs are available from FTP sites, too. If, after watching the messages for a couple weeks, you can't find the FAQ for a newsgroup, post a short, simple question asking for directions.

A *lurker* reads Usenet newsgroups but doesn't post. Estimates from large corporations that download newsgroups indicate that less than 10 percent of all newsreaders actually post messages. As a newbie, you should be a lurker for a while, until you understand the network operation and general rules. There's nothing wrong with being a lurker!

Another term you hear a lot is *surfing*. To *surf the Usenet* is to move through many newsgroups, visiting quite a few each time. When you surf, you can cover a lot of different subjects, touching on each briefly.

One of the most commonly encountered Usenet terms is *flame*. A flame happens when one user gets mad at another and sends sarcastic, insulting, or downright nasty comments. A flame is usually triggered by a silly comment or a major breach of the network's rules. There are even dedicated newsgroups whose sole purpose is to post flames or flame someone else!

Most newbies don't get flamed as readily as Usenet veterans (who should know better). Tolerance is higher when the other users know you are a beginner, but that's not a license to act irresponsibly. Persisting in obnoxious behavior or repeatedly asking stupid questions will most certainly get you singed!

In some cases, flaming become rampant with many users participating. Such sessions can go on for months, and insults mount with each new posting. Sometimes, these sessions are entertaining; usually they are just boring for others. These types of affairs are called *flame wars*.

You often see the comment Don't flame me! in a posting. This usually means the poster knows he or she is posting something contentious or silly, and is begging indulgence for some reason.

Usenet even allows people to shout at each other. Most posts are properly typed using uppercase and lowercase letters—as one would expect (although some users seem to ignore the use of the Shift key entirely). When a user wants to emphasize something, he or she usually writes in CAPTIAL LETTERS. This is the Usenet equivalent of shouting.

It is considered bad practice to shout excessively. Shouting works much better when you emphasize the important word or phrase; typing in uppercase letters for more than a sentence is not advisable. It may result in you getting yelled at!

Smileys have become popular over the last few years. A smiley is a combination of characters that represents a pictorial expression, usually facial. There are even entire books dedicated to different smileys.

A smiley is used to emphasize that you are saying something in jest, or tongue in cheek. A typical smiley looks like this : -) which, when viewed from the side, looks like two eyes, a nose, and a smiling mouth. You will see many variations on smileys in postings, some obvious (such as : - } for a wry smile) to long complex character strings that take a while to figure out. Use smileys sparingly.

Abbreviations are rampant in newsgroup postings because they simplify the typing process and cut down on article lengths. Common abbreviations are IMHO (in my humble option), TTYL (talk to you later), OTOH (on the other hand), BTW (by the way), and ROTFL (rolling on the floor, laughing). You may occasionally encounter the sign <G>—the short form for a grin!

Another common convention is to lightly emphasize a word or phrase by placing it between asterisks. Asterisks indicate a level of emphasis between normal text and shouting, such as I *think* that....

NOTE

Some users post abbreviations that are not obvious, resulting in a guessing game to figure out their meaning. Again, the rule is to stick with common abbreviations and use them only occasionally.

WHAT IS A NEWSREADER?

You'll hear the term *newsreader* used a lot. A newsreader, as its name implies, is a piece of software designed to let you read news easily. There isn't a single newsreader—the name applies to a whole family of software packages, some of which are discussed later in this chapter.

Newsreaders obtain the news for you from the news server (the computer that holds all the news articles on your network), sorts it into threads (if the newsreader supports them), displays the articles one at a time, and lets you either reply to it or move to the next article. Some newsreaders are quite complicated and can take a while to learn; others are very simple.

You don't have to have a newsreader to read news. Some other software packages, such as the World Wide Web's Mosaic and Netscape, can display news for you. Having a dedicated newsreader is your decision, but remember that they tend to be better at their purpose than other tools. Now all you have to decide is which newsreader is best for you!

Browsing Newsgroups

The fun of Usenet is in reading the daily postings to all the newsgroups. When you become familiar with Usenet, you will be able to select only those newsgroups and articles that interest you; but most newbies want to see many different newsgroups.

Check These Newsgroups First!

New Usenet users can take advantage of a wealth of information about Usenet, the newsgroups, and netiquette; this information is maintained in several special areas. Most of these groups are tagged with the name newuser somewhere in the newsgroup name.

The basic source of information for new users is the newsgroup news.announce.newusers. This newsgroup holds a continuously evolving set of articles that explain all aspects of Usenet and the newsgroups themselves. A good way to start using Usenet is to check this newsgroup for documents of interest—perhaps saving them to a file for printing and future reference.

Within the news.announce.newusers newsgroup are several standard postings that make up a guidebook to Usenet, including these:

- A Primer on How To Work with the Usenet Community
- Answers to Frequently Asked Questions about Usenet
- Emily Postnews Answers Your Questions on Netiquette
- Hints for Writing Style for Usenet
- Rules for Posting to Usenet

Also within the group are several long lists of active newsgroups and what they cover, a guide to various sources of information about the different newsgroups, and access information for different networks.

The articles on news.announce.newusers are renewed on a regular basis so that they will be available, in spite of news software retention dates.

Another useful newsgroup for new users is news.answers, which has two purposes. One is to hold periodic informational postings from the different newsgroups, such as their FAQ (Frequently Asked Questions) lists. Another purpose is to answer basic questions about Usenet and newsreaders. This area is monitored by a surprisingly large number of users who are all willing to help a newcomer with advice or suggestions. You should read the articles in the news.announce.newuser newsgroup before posting a question to news.newusers.questions, the newsgroup for new users' queries and responses.

Getting Help on Usenet Basics

The news.newusers.questions newsgroup is a good place to post questions about Usenet, but try to find the answers first yourself. Some problems you will encounter have nothing to do with Usenet but with your local site's access to it. For this reason, you should ask your local user group for help before posting questions to the Net; others may have no idea how to fix a problem specific to your site.

Try to avoid questions that are answered in local man pages, such as about a command used within readnews. If you are having problems with a newsreader, examine the man pages or online command summary before asking the network for help.

If you do post a question, the more information you can supply to other newsgroup readers, the better. If the question is related to hardware, specify the machine model, operating system and version, and the newsreader you are using. You also should provide a detailed explanation of the problem. Simply stating "My readnews doesn't work!" won't get you many helpful answers.

Threads

A single article usually generates responses along the same line. The sequence of articles following a subject is called a *thread*. Threads are easy to spot by the persistent use of quotes, or inclusion of parts of previous posts. Another obvious way to spot threads is the use of Re: in the subject header.

Straying off a subject is common, which means that the thread eventually discusses something totally unrelated to the original subject. Threads sometimes change so much that they should be redirected to another newsgroup. Gun control and abortion are two that show up in an amazing number of threads, and in groups quite unrelated to the topic.

Threads can be useful if your newsreader supports following them. When you follow a thread, you can continue through the subject without lots of other postings getting in the way; following threads is a more logical browsing option for those who want it.

Sometimes, someone asks a question through e-mail instead of posting it to the newsgroups. This usually happens when there is not enough interest in the newsgroup to sustain a group discussion. For example, you may want to know about the benefits of Y Brand Spinnaker Retaining Wire, but doubt that the subject will interest everyone in rec.sailing. In your message, you may say "Please reply to rmaclean@bnr.ca.edu."

Another common reason to request a reply through e-mail is to avoid a flood of responses cluttering the newsgroup with the same information. When the subject has been exhausted, the requester sometimes assembles the replies into a single collection and posts the results for the rest of the network to read.

Posting to Usenet

Although reading articles is fun, many Usenet users believe that getting involved adds to the experience. Posting articles and replying to other postings make Usenet a more participatory process.

Test Newsgroups

When you are ready to start posting articles, you should ensure that your postings will go out to the network correctly. If you have an environment variable incorrectly set or your system has no posting capabilities, you could be wasting time looking for your posts.

Also, users new to posting frequently have a case of the jitters and want to make sure that their posts are clean and readable. To help verify that everything is working correctly, Usenet has a few newsgroups dedicated to test postings.

The most common test newsgroups are `misc.test` and `alt.test`. These newsgroups contain nothing more than postings from other users looking for their first network-wide article or trying out new signature blocks (discussed in "Creating a `.signature` File"). To post to these groups, use a newsreader to scan an article or two; then select the command to post to the current newsgroup.

Most test newsgroups send you an automatic reply when your posting is received. Other test newsgroups don't send a reply, so you have to scan the articles for your posting (which can be awkward when there are hundreds of new articles a day).

Using the test newsgroups is preferable to posting to an active newsgroup. As you read news, you will see the occasional post labeled `test`, with some silly content. The user couldn't be bothered learning to post to `misc.test` or `alt.test`. Such conduct frequently leads to flames. Whatever you do, try not to test with a post to a regular newsgroup.

Creating a *.signature* File

To the bottom of almost every posting are attached a few lines that give you contact information for the sender, sometimes coupled with a graphic or quotation that the sender thinks is appropriate (or worse, cute). These lines are called the *signature*.

Instead of writing these lines at the end of every post, you can create one file that can be copied to the end of your text. Doing so saves you time and also provides some consistency to your posts that others will begin to recognize.

Typically, the file that contains these lines is called `.signature`, and it resides in your home directory. Many news posting routines automatically look for this file in your home directory and include it for you. The `.signature` file makes it very easy to tag your posts with information that can steer a reader back to you. If your posting system doesn't automatically include your `.signature` file, check its configuration file (such as `elmrc` in the `.elm` directory for the Elm mailer).

One key to a good signature file is brevity. Although some posters have enormous signatures running 10 lines or more, this length is a waste of space and time. It is also usually annoying to others who must page through it all. A good guideline is to limit the signature to four lines or less. Indeed, many newsreaders truncate any signature longer than four lines, so you are wasting your time producing long ones.

A signature should minimally contain your full name, user name, company name, and Internet address. This information enables someone reading your posts to reply to you directly instead of to the newsgroup. Some users also specify a telephone and fax number.

Additional material can add a personal touch to a `.signature` file. Typically, this can be a little ASCII-character generated figure or pithy saying. Many users like to rotate quotations in their signature file to lend a bit of originality and share particularly interesting quotes. You can see lots of examples of both graphics and quotations when you read articles.

Try not to cram too much into a signature block. You want it to clearly communicate who you are and perhaps add a personal touch, but you don't want it to be so busy that posters are distracted or don't bother looking at it. Be careful when using graphics, because special character sets do not show up on all terminals.

Test your signature by e-mailing a message to yourself or a friend, or by posting a sample message to one of the test newsgroups (such as `alt.test` or `misc.test`). If you want to see some complex signature files (and ones that have incurred the wrath of others by being too long or objectionable), see the newsgroup, `alt.fan.warlord`.

Cross-Posting

Sometimes, postings can apply to more than one newsgroup. Usenet lets you post to more than one group by specifying all the groups on a header line in your article. This process is called *cross-posting*.

Some users cross-post on a regular basis, but this can be annoying to those who read the groups and encounter the same message several times. As a general rule, don't cross-post unless your message really should be in several locations. When replying to an article that was cross-posted, you may want to remove many of the newsgroups so that the chain doesn't get out of hand.

Netiquette

A user's behavior on the network is governed by a set of guidelines called *netiquette*. A complete document is devoted to the subject, *Emily Postnews Answers Your Questions on Netiquette* in `news.announce.newusers`. It is well worth your time to capture this article and read it.

As a general rule, insulting or degrading any other network user is a cardinal sin and should be avoided. Insults are sure to reduce everyone else's opinion of you, which may affect you in the future. Some users have a reputation for being obnoxious, and their postings are frequently filtered out and unread.

Keep posts clear, short, and succinct. Long, wordy articles that are train-of-thought may be fine when you write them, but edit them before you post. Otherwise, readers will skip the article altogether—even though you may have something important to say.

Obviously, correct spelling and grammar are appreciated. The odd spelling mistake is bound to creep in, but an attempt at proper language is appreciated by all those who read the article.

Personal messages are a no-no. Anything that is meant to be shared by only two or three people should be handled through e-mail, not Usenet. Following this rule saves millions of others from wasting time reading your personal comments—not to mention the hours of transmission time saved as the article works its way around the globe.

When excerpting (or quoting) other articles in a reply, keep it short. You should never quote more than the necessary lines in a follow-up. Quote just enough to provide context or to show why you are posting a reply.

Posting business items, especially advertisements for a company or service, should be done with extreme care. Most newsgroups frown on commercial items; a few newsgroups tolerate them only in exceptional circumstances. You will probably be flamed if you offer your spouse's cat-sitting service over the Net. Get-rich-quick schemes are always on the network, with plenty of testimonials and guarantees. The posters of these deserve more than flames; in many cases, they are barred from accessing Usenet by irate system administrators.

At least once a year, there is a posting about some poor person who is trying to enter the Guinness Book for collecting postcards, e-mail addresses, business cards, or credit card numbers. These posts are usually bogus and should be treated as garbage.

A common problem occurs when a user asks a simple question and receives dozens of replies. If you read an article that asks for something most people should know, you may want to delay posting a reply until you see whether anyone else does. This can prevent cluttering a newsgroup and reduces the number of redundant articles you must wade through. In a similar vein, if you are asking a question that could generate lots of replies, you should ask for e-mail.

Distribution

Most news systems enable you to specify how widely your posting is distributed. For example, you can keep your post within your company's network, within a geographical region, or to the entire network (called the "world").

Most users post to the world without giving it a second thought. However, if you post the message "There's a hole in Hwy 7 outside of Carp" to the entire network, you can be assured of a few nasty comments about your distribution habits from those in Japan and Australia who think Carp is a fish, not a place.

When you are posting, make sure that you carefully consider distribution. Only post to the world if the subject fits into a nongeographical discussion and may be of interest to everyone else.

DOS AND DO NOTS OF POSTING

A few guidelines can help you get the most out of your time on Usenet (and cut down on the amount of flames you receive):

- Keep your posting direct and to the point
- Try to use proper grammar and spelling
- Use sarcasm and similar forms of speech carefully
- Define your subject clearly
- Use the correct newsgroup
- Limit the distribution if necessary
- Use a short signature file
- If you flame, expect to get it back in greater intensity

Usenet is a fun, informative, and interesting network. Many use it daily for entertainment. Don't be one of the few malcontents on the network, because it will definitely catch up with you one day.

Usenet History

Usenet grew out of a release of UNIX called UNIX V7, which implemented the UUCP (UNIX to UNIX Copy) program. In 1979, two graduate students at Duke University, Jim Ellis and Tom Truscott, began to use UUCP to exchange information between their UNIX machines.

Other users began using UUCP and found it could be expanded to provide better intermachine communications. At the University of North Carolina, Steve Bellovin used shell scripts to write the first version of the news software for use between Duke and UNC, allowing messages and general commentary to be passed between the two universities.

This system was described at a Usenix conference in 1980, spreading interest in the software even wider. Steve Daniel was the first to implement the news software in the C programming language. This version eventually became the first general release of the news software, which was called Release A.

To cope with the increasing volume as new news sites began to communicate by adding themselves to the expanding informal network, two University of California students, Mark Horton and Matt Glickman, rewrote the software and added new functionality. After a further revision of their Release B, news was finally generally released in 1982 as version 2.1.

The Center for Seismic Studies' Rick Adams took over maintenance of the software in 1984, at which point it was up to release 2.10.2. One of Rick's first additions was the capability for moderated newsgroups, resulting in release 3.11 in 1986.

Since then, several contributors have added features to the software, the most important of which was a complete rewrite of the basic software, undertaken in 1987 by the University of Toronto's Geoff Collyer and Henry Spencer. Their rewrite greatly increased the speed with which mail could be processed. Over the next few years, the basic news package went through some minor revisions but has remained true to Collyer and Spencer's version.

Newsreader software lets you read articles in newsgroups as they arrive. The original reader was called readnews, and it remains one of the most widely used newsreader packages, primarily because is it easy to use and is available on practically every UNIX system.

Several alternative newsreaders were developed, typically expanding on the features offered by readnews. Software such as rn (a more flexible version of readnews), trn (threaded readnews), and vnews (visual newsreader) became freely distributed. With the popularity of graphical user interfaces, newsreaders were ported to these environments; resulting software includes xrn (X Window-based readnews). Most of the readnews variants share a basic command set, although each adds features that may appeal to some users.

Some other Internet tools let you read newsgroups, too; some of the better known are the World Wide Web's Mosaic and Netscape. Gopher can also be used to lead to news sites. The problem with most of these tools is that they only allow you to read news, not to reply or post your own articles.

The User and News: Choosing Software

Several application programs are in general distribution for reading and sending news. Most programs are public domain, so there is little or no cost associated with obtaining them. Some commercial applications have appeared, but few offer anything not available in a freely distributed alternative.

The newsreaders available at a particular site are chosen by the system administrator and staff. The programs readnews, postnews, and vnews are basic packages for reading and replying. The most commonly available newsreaders are rn and trn, which add considerable power and flexibility. Screen-oriented software includes xrn, an X implementation that is one of the most sophisticated packages currently available.

All these newsreaders rely on low-level programs for the actual mechanics of receiving and sending news articles, but the user is isolated from them by the reader itself.

Three kinds of programs are involved in the underlying layer of news: pagers, editors, and mailers. A *pager* is a program that displays messages on-screen, usually one screen at a time. Typical UNIX pagers are more and pg. *Editors* are used to write articles and e-mail posts and can be of any type as long as they have the capability to save ASCII text. Most UNIX systems have the vi editor; others use public domain editors such as emacs. *Mailers* are responsible for directing articles and e-mail notes to the network and subsequently to the intended recipients.

Lately, several graphical interfaces to newsgroups have become popular, presenting a friendly icon-driven approach to the newsgroups. These software packages are available for all GUI-based systems, including Windows, Macintosh, and both X and Motif for the UNIX platform. Graphical packages don't usually offer more features than character-based systems, but they are better to look at and easier for newbies to work with.

The following sections discuss the more common character-based interfaces; near the end of the chapter, a few graphical interfaces are described. If you can run a graphical interface (especially on a DOS, Windows, or Macintosh machine), you will probably find a graphical interface a better choice than the character-based systems.

The *.newsrc* File

Most newsreaders use a file called .newsrc to list the newsgroups in which the user is interested. Usually, the file is created by the newsreader and kept in the user's home directory, although some systems keep it in a news directory within the home directory.

When you first use a reader, you won't have a .newsrc file, so the reader creates one for you. Sometimes, the system default newsgroups are used; other systems require that you manually select the newsgroups in which you are interested from the complete list (this process can be very time consuming). If you have started a reader (such as readnews) for the first time, you may think the machine has locked up because nothing happens for several minutes. Actually, the reader has discovered that no .newsrc file exists and is busily creating one for you.

TIP

One of the easiest ways to begin using news quickly is to copy someone else's .newsrc file. Of course, you then start with that person's selected newsgroups, and you can't see articles they have already read unless you reset the numbering.

The .newsrc file contains a list of all newsgroups currently handled by the host system, even those not wanted by the user. At regular intervals (usually daily), the reader scans the incoming news and compares its newsgroups with those in .newsrc to indicate which newsgroups are new and which have been dropped.

A portion of a typical .newsrc file is shown here. Each line shows a newsgroup name in full, followed by the numbers of the articles that have been read.

```
news.newusers.questions: 1-1406
news.software.anu-news: 1-745
news.software.notes!
rec.arts.misc!
rec.arts.movies: 1-363,456,463
comp.os.os2.programmer: 1-23
comp.sys.amiga!
comp.sys.amiga.multimedia!
comp.sys.amiga.programmer!
rec.audio: 1-56242
rec.audio.high-end: 1-8963
rec.autos: 1-83746,84635,85647,86756
rec.autos.antique: 1-3998
alt.test!
comp.ai!
rec.arts.startrek: 1-12837
```

Although the numbers are usually contiguous (such as 1-8376), you may have skipped some articles, so the numbering is disjointed (such as 1-243,354-345,423). Hyphens are used to show contiguous blocks, with the numbers used inclusively (1-34 indicates that you have read article numbers 1 through 34). Commas separate individual pieces of several ranges. The .newsrc file can be edited with any ASCII text editor.

An exclamation mark (!) after the newsgroup name (as in the newsgroup comp.ai in the example) indicates that the newsgroup is *unsubscribed*. This means that you do not want to read any articles posted to the newsgroup.

The order of newsgroups in the .newsrc file can be important because most readers show incoming news in the order of the newsgroups in this file—unless a specific instruction to do otherwise is given.

Downloading and Aging Articles

Most Usenet recipients download on a daily basis, usually in the early morning. Larger systems can download on a more regular basis, so it is common to find large companies and educational facilities that download newsgroups four times a day.

The system administrator has control over the newsgroups that are downloaded. Many sites do not allow full access to all newsgroups—not because of the cost of such downloads, but because of the content of some newsgroups. For example, many corporations don't download any newsgroup with the words *sex* or *erotica* as part of the newsgroup name. Others may not accept any `alt` newsgroups if they tend more to the unruly side.

Articles are not kept on a system indefinitely. A typical daily download of all newsgroups exceeds 100M, so keeping a few weeks' worth of material can easily chew up disk space. Most systems "age" articles and remove them after they are a predetermined number of days old. Many systems keep articles for a week, but some cut that number down to three or four days.

If the site downloads only a few selected newsgroups, the aging may be set to very long intervals. For example, if you are an OS/2 developer and download all the OS/2 newsgroups, keeping the hints and programming examples around for several months may be useful. Each system establishes its own download and aging guidelines.

Getting Help on Readers

Most Usenet newsgroup readers are not commercial applications. Instead, they have been developed and are distributed and supported by dedicated programmers who want to share their applications. The more popular newsreaders have developed the support of large communities, with suggestions and refinements implemented as they arise.

Because there is no single, standard newsreader, users sometimes have difficulty getting started and learning about the readers available at their site. Getting help can vary from being impossible to very easy.

The first place to start learning about a newsreader and getting help on its commands is on your system. Most newsreaders have man (manual) pages, which are available when you type the `man` command and the name of the reader (for example, `man rn`). If there is a help file (called a *man page*) for that reader, it is formatted and displayed.

Command summaries are available in most newsreaders when you enter `?` at any command prompt. Some use the command `help`, which displays brief summaries (a few recently developed newsreaders have online tutorials that make learning the system easy).

Failing all these options (or getting stuck with a man page that is difficult to understand), it's time to turn to other users on your system or on the Usenet network for help. Don't feel badly about posting a request for more information on a newsgroup. Just be careful where you post it. Most Net users are happy to assist newcomers.

readnews

The readnews program was the original newsreader and is still in use on many systems. It was used as the basis for more sophisticated readers such as rn, although readnews retains a simplistic approach that many find better than the command-heavy rn, vnews, and xrn. Practically any system that downloads news has readnews available, so it is a good place to start.

The readnews reader has a small command set that is displayed at any prompt when you enter **?**. Although the command summary is brief, often it is all you need to figure out an action. Several useful command-line options are supported by readnews, as described later in this chapter.

Reading News

The easiest way to use readnews is to type the command alone, with no arguments. The readnews reader presents newsgroups in the order they occur in the .newsrc file. For each article readnews encounters, it displays header information, including the newsgroup title, an article count, the subject of the posting, the user name, and machine pathname of the poster. The article count shows the current location within the articles on the system. The header Article 3 of 56 means that there are 56 articles currently available, with the third one shown for you. Despite the total shown in the header, some articles may not be available on your system because they have been dropped or lost. Generally, however, these numbers are a good guideline.

Following the header information, readnews prompts you with the number of lines left in the posting and the question More? [ynq]. You can use any of several commands with this prompt, even though the prompt lists only three: y, n, and q.

If you want to read the rest of the article, enter **y**. Entering **n** (for *no* or *next*, depending on the way you look at it) skips to the next article. The **q** (for *quit*) option quits readnews and updates your .newsrc file to include the article numbers that have been offered. Another option you may want to use is **x** (exit), which quits readnews but doesn't update the .newsrc file (meaning that you are shown the same articles the next time you use readnews).

Most implementations of readnews let you back up to the previous article with the p command; the command displays the article immediately before the currently displayed one. Not all readers support the p command, so nothing may happen when you use it.

A command similar to the p command is b (for *back*). This command moves you to the article immediately preceding the one currently shown. In most cases, b and p perform the same task unless you have bounced to articles out of sequence.

You can read a specific article by entering its number. This is sometimes useful when a posting refers to a specific article (which is not reliable because the numbering can differ from system to system), or when you are following a series of articles on a particular topic (called a *thread*).

To display the current article's number and position in the newsgroup, as well as the newsgroup you are currently reading, use the # command. It gives a one-line summary and repeats the More? prompt.

When following a thread, it is handy to be able to switch between two articles. The hyphen (-) command lets you do this. The hyphen command toggles between the currently displayed article and the previously displayed one.

You can save a copy of an article in a file with either the s (save) or w (write) command. You normally provide a filename (which can include a full path) such as s /usr/tparker/saved_news. If no path is specified, the user's home directory is used (unless the reader has been configured to save files in a news directory under the user's home directory). Both s and w perform the same function. The s command was used originally, but the w version was added later to retain compatibility with popular UNIX editors.

If a filename is not specified when an s or w command is issued, readnews assumes the default filename, Articles, in your home directory. If the file Articles does not exist, it is created. If it does exist, the article to be saved is appended to the file. Obviously, this file can become quite large if you indiscriminately save to it. Experienced users use the Articles file for articles they want to retain for only a few days. These articles are purged at regular intervals. Articles you want to keep for a while should be saved under a specific filename, preferably indicating the subject matter.

An article can be marked as unread with the e command (which, according to readnews lore, stands for *erase* any reference to the article in the .newsrc file). When e is used, the article is not marked as read and it reappears at the next session. You may want to use this command when reading an article you want to think about, do some research on before replying to, or want to reread to better understand.

When an article is tagged with an e command, it is considered to be held. After you issue the command, readnews responds with a prompt that tells you how many articles have been held during the current session. Holding an article is not a guaranteed method for recalling it at a future session. Because most systems age articles in all newsgroups, you can recall the held article only as long as it is physically on the system. If you want to be sure that it is available in the future, save the article to a file.

Another method of tagging an article as unread is with the + command. This command tags the next article as unread and skips over it. This command is seldom used because few users want to mark mail as unread when they haven't seen the subject. The + and e commands differ because e marks the *current* article as unread; + marks the *next* one and then skips it.

There are two ways to display more details about the header information, which includes all the routing instructions. The h command displays how the article was routed over the networks. The H option offers maximum verbosity, showing everything from the routing to the news software used. This information is seldom of interest except when trying to backtrack to the originator's location or when debugging the reader's software.

Occasionally, you may want to mark many articles as read even though you haven't really seen them. You may want to do this when you haven't read news for a while and don't want to wade through the backlog. The K command (uppercase is important) marks all the articles in the newsgroup as read, so that the next update can begin with only the latest news. After you issue a K command, readnews updates the .newsrc file and moves on to the next newsgroup.

When readnews has finished with the last message of the current newsgroup, it moves to the next newsgroup listed in .newsrc. You can force the move to the next newsgroup with the N command; the next article you see is the first article in the subsequent newsgroup listed in the .newsrc file.

If you want to specify the newsgroup to jump to, specify its name after the N command; the command N alt.autos.antique moves you to the specified group, skipping everything in between. The P command moves you to the previous newsgroup (just as the n and p commands move to the next and previous articles within a newsgroup).

If you change your mind about subscribing to a newsgroup, you can always unsubscribe with the U command. This command marks your .newsrc file so that you don't see the contents of that newsgroup again. (If you want to resubscribe, the easiest method is to edit the .newsrc file and remove the exclamation mark from the end of the newsgroup's name.)

Every so often, you'll see an article (or part of one) that looks like gibberish. The sender may have encrypted part or all of the posting. If the encryption is private, only someone else with the encryption key can decipher it. (Sending encrypted articles through newsgroups is considered very bad practice. Something that private should be sent by e-mail.)

Most encryptions are performed with a simple offset encryption technique called a *Caesar cipher*, in which each letter of the alphabet is replaced by the one 13 characters away (with the letters wrapping around at both ends), so the letter *a* appears as *n*, and so on. This process is sometimes called *rot13* (rotation by 13 characters).

Encryptions are used in newsgroups when the poster wants to hide part of the post from the casual reader's glance. Typical uses are to encrypt the punch line for a joke, an answer to a puzzle, or a plot line for a movie. Less frequently, off-color or risqué jokes are encrypted. Most newsreaders have an option to decode an encrypted message automatically, or on user command. The D command (again, uppercase is important—the lowercase d command is used with article digests) decrypts the message for you.

Finally, readnews lets you execute any shell command with the usual escape character, the exclamation mark (!). For example, entering ! lp Articles at the More? prompt instructs the shell to print a copy of the file, Articles, and return you to the newsreader.

One useful feature of the shell command is that you can specify the current article you are reading with the environment variable $A. You can use this variable on any shell command, such as ! cat $A >> news_stuff, which appends the current article to the specified file.

Posting Articles

When you want to send a reply to an article, there are two ways to do it. The first is to send private mail to the originator (as you do with a mail program). The second is to post your reply to the newsgroup for the rest of the world to see. Newsgroup readers handle the posting process somewhat differently, but the usual manner is described here.

General posting to newsgroups has caused traffic to increase enormously, even though the posting may be of interest to only one or two people. It is considered good netiquette to post to the Net only if more than the original poster is interested in your comments. Unfortunately, some users ignore this guideline completely, with the result that many articles that have little to do with the newsgroup or to the groups' participants in general are posted.

Sending Mail to the Poster

Sending mail to the poster is easy, because the reader software can extract the addressing information and pass it to the mail program. To reply by e-mail directly to the poster, use the r (reply) command.

When readnews receives the r command, it places you in the system default editor (usually vi). The header details, including the subject line, are included at the top of your reply (you can edit it as you want). When you save the text, your reply is sent through the mail program.

In most cases, readnews uses the Path line of the article header (which indicates who posted the article) as the To line for the mail program. Occasionally, this can cause problems if the poster doesn't use a proper UUCP format in his or her name, or when messages are posted from a nonuser site. Lately, anonymous access sites have become popular, wherein the poster's name is not provided. It is difficult to reply to these people directly because most anonymous sites don't properly route mail to the originator.

The rd command is similar to the r command, except that it ignores all the header information and lets you specify it directly. The rd option is frequently used when a message is short and the recipient's address is known.

Posting a Reply to the Newsgroup

To post a reply to the newsgroup (and the rest of the world), use the f (for *forward* or *follow-up*) command. The original article's header is included in your reply, so the subject is kept the same as the original article unless you specifically overwrite it. When you enter f, you see a message prompting you to enter a short comment or summary, which is used to tag your contribution, ending with a blank line. Many posters skip this step completely.

After you type your brief summary and leave a blank line (follow the blank line by pressing Return) to indicate the end of your text, readnews asks whether you want to include a copy of the original post. Some users like to keep part of the original in their reply so that the context is clearly understood, but superfluous text should be deleted. (It is considered bad netiquette to include more than 10 lines of the original article because of the wasted space. Others prefer what has become known as the "fifty-percent rule," which says that no more than half your posting should comprise quoted material.)

If you tell readnews you want to include a copy of the original article, the original article is placed into your reply with each line of the original prefaced with the > symbol (indicating that the line was extracted from another posting). If more than one previous post is included, the > symbols are cumulative, so the second direct quoting shows >>.

Then readnews enters the default editor, in which you can type your reply to the article, as well as edit any included original text. After saving your text, readnews asks what you want to do with the reply. You are given five options: send (post it to the newsgroup), edit the reply, list (display) the reply, write (save) the reply to a file, or quit without posting the reply.

If you elect to post, readnews responds with a confirmation and returns you to the current article's More? prompt. A slight variation on the f command is fd, which acts exactly the same as the f command except that the original article's header material is not included in your reply.

At times, you may regret sending a post to the network; although it is impossible to prevent everyone from seeing the post, you can perform some damage control. The c (cancel) command deletes an article you have posted. Because of the nature of the network, the c command takes some time and may not be effective at all sites. Usually, however, a cancel command can remove an article that hasn't been read by others within a day or so.

Only the poster and the system superuser can cancel a post. When canceled, the news system actually sends another message to all sites that instructs those sites to delete the message. The distribution of the cancel message and its processing can take some time.

In most cases, postings to newsgroups are done from the news server at specified intervals, not when each posting is received. If the posting hasn't left your site, it is much easier to prevent it from entering the Usenet newsgroups. In general, however, once a message has been sent, it's too late to prevent it from being seen by others. So think twice before posting.

Digests

A *digest* is a collection of articles that have been strung together into a larger file by someone. This collection is distributed as a single file to make transmittal easier and to keep all the articles grouped together.

Digests often are assembled for a particular subject. One user may have posted a question on the network, collected all the answers into a digest, and reposted them for others to examine.

A digest retains all the header information of the originals, so the file looks like a series of newsgroup articles one after another. The readnews reader displays the entire file as one large article, ignoring separations between the embedded articles.

The d command instructs readnews to treat each article within a digest as a separate article, shown in the same manner as all other articles. The d command scans through the digest, looking for header information, and uses that to break up the file. Using the d command lets you read a digest in exactly the same manner you read individual newsgroup articles.

Table 17.1 lists the commands you can use with readnews.

Table 17.1. The readnews commands.

Command	Description
y	Read current mail
n	Read next article
q	Quit and update .newsrc
x	Quit without updating .newsrc
-	Display last article read
b	Back up one article
num	Go to the specified article number
s	Save the article to a file
w	Save the article to a file
e	Mark current article as unread
+	Mark next article as unread and then skip it
K	Mark all articles in the newsgroup as read
D	Decrypt the article
d	Read digest articles individually
f	Post a reply to the newsgroup
fd	Post without the header information
r	Send mail to the poster
rd	Send mail without the header information
c	Cancel a message you posted
?	Display command summary

continues

Table 17.1. continued

Command	Description
h	Show header information
H	Show complete header information
#	Display current article and newsgroup name
N	Move to next newsgroup
P	Move to previous newsgroup
U	Unsubscribe to this newsgroup
!	Execute a shell command

Command-Line Options

There are several useful command-line options you can use to control the way the system behaves when starting readnews. The most commonly used option is -n, which specifies the newsgroup to be read. When expanding the argument, readnews matches all newsgroups that start with the specified string.

The command readnews -n rec.video instructs readnews to display articles only in newsgroups that start with rec.video, such as rec.video itself, rec.video.laserdisk, and rec.video.vcrs. After they have all been shown, readnews exits.

The -t option is similar to -n, except that it provides string matching across the entire name instead of just from the start of the name. For example, readnews -t video displays all newsgroups with the letters *video* in their names. Sometimes, this causes matches you don't particularly want (such as matching comp.automata when you specified "auto" on a quest for articles about cars). Practice teaches you to specify enough letters to see only those newsgroups in which you are interested.

You can specify more than one string at a time with either the -n or -t option; the command readnews -t video, audio shows all newsgroups with either *video* or *audio* in the titles. You can even use both options at once, as in readnews -n alt.video -t audio, but the two options are combined so that only one newsgroup starting with alt.video and having the text *audio* in the title is shown (quite unlikely to have any matches in this example).

The -x option lets you read all articles whether you have read them before or not. Essentially, this option ignores the article numbers in the .newsrc file. This option is useful when you remember seeing an article in a newsgroup but don't remember where it was or when you saw it. Unfortunately, all postings on the system are displayed, which can provide quite a few to sort through.

You can specify dates in the readnews command to limit the articles matched. This is accomplished with the -a option. The command readnews -a last sunday shows all the articles received since last Sunday. Dates can be specified in absolute terms or by relative days of the week, as in this example, which readnews converts for you.

Of course, all these options can be combined in strange and wonderful combinations. The command readnews -t autos -a yesterday -x displays all articles received since yesterday that are in newsgroups with the string *autos* in their titles, whether you have seen them or not.

The -l and -e options are handy when you don't want to look at each article in a newsgroup. They differ only in whether .newsrc is updated. These options display the article number and subjects so that you can select the ones that interest you. The command readnews -l -t autos shows all subject titles for newsgroups with *autos* in their titles. (It is often useful to redirect the output to a file or the printer, such as readnews -l -t laserdisks > new_articles.)

You must restart readnews after generating output with either the -l or -e options because either option exits the reader once the title list has been displayed. With the -l option, no changes are made to the .newsrc file (the -l option is usually used if you haven't actually read any articles yet).

The -e option does update .newsrc to reflect that all the articles have been read. This is a fast method of marking all new articles as read and then reading specifically only those whose titles interest you—saving you the time of scanning lots of articles you may not want to see. Of course, if the subject titles don't match the contents, you may miss something interesting!

A great deal of news follows a subject thread, with replies from one original posting. Some users like to use the -f option, which shows only the original articles and none of the replies. The -f option works particularly well with the -e and -l options, although it doesn't show you which subjects are the "hot" topics of the week.

To start with the latest articles and work backward, use the -r option. It shows the articles in reverse order, based on their article numbers. This option can be useful if you haven't looked at a newsgroup in a while and don't want to scan dozens or hundreds of articles. Coupled with the K command (mark all articles as read), the -r option is a fast method for bringing the .newsrc file up to date in a particular newsgroup.

The -h option uses short headers for articles. This option is mostly used when communicating at a slow baud rate (such as over a modem), when you want to spend the least amount of time writing excess and unwanted information. You can still use the readnews h and H options to show more header information about an article if necessary.

Another option that is useful over modems is -u, which instructs readnews to update the .newsrc file every five minutes. Normally .newsrc is updated only when you exit the reader, but if a modem drops the line in the middle of a session, all the articles you have read since the start must be reread the next time.

The -s option shows you all the available articles, compared to the ones you currently receive. It lets you note new additions to the newsgroup downloads that may have passed you by when they were first received.

The -p option instructs readnews to suppress all questions, such as the More? prompt. This option is usually used when all output is sent to the printer or a file.

You can change the readnews interface to resemble other applications. The -M option switches to an interface similar to mailx. The -c option uses an interface such as mail or Mail. Commands such as header and p (for displaying an article) are active. For more information on the commands used by the mail programs, check the local documentation for the mailer used at your site.

These optional interfaces are often used by beginners who may know the mail commands but are unfamiliar with readnews. Although the mail interfaces are adequate, they are not as powerful or friendly as the readnews system. You cannot, for example, move backward and forward through the articles in a mail interface. Users are encouraged to learn the proper newsreader interface rather than relying on either of these alternatives.

Table 17.2 lists the command-line options for readnews.

Table 17.2. The readnews command-line options.

Command-Line Option	Description
-n *string*	Display newsgroups starting with *string*
-t *string*	Display all newsgroups with *string* in their names
-a *date*	Display articles received since *date*
-x	Display all articles, even if they have been read
-l	Show article subject titles; don't update .newsrc
-e	Show article subject titles and update .newsrc
-r	Show articles in reverse order
-f	Show original articles only, suppressing replies
-h	Show short headers only
-s	Display the site and user subscription lists
-p	Suppress questions
-u	Update .newsrc every five minutes
-M	Use mailx-like interface
-c	Use a mail-like or Mail-like interface

readnews Environment Variables

The readnews program relies on several environment variables to define aspects of the reader's behavior. These should all be defined in your shell's startup file (.profile, .cshrc, .kshrc, or .login). A simple .profile (Bourne shell) readnews configuration is shown here:

```
# configuration info for readnews
EDITOR="/bin/emacs"          # use emacs as the editor
MAILER="/bin/mail"           # use mail as the mailer
PAGER="/usr/bin/less"        # use "less" as the pager
SHELL="/bin/sh"              # Bourne shell for shell commands
NEWSBOX="~/News"             # store saved articles in News dir
NAME="Tim Parker"            # my user name
ORGANIZATION="TPCI"          # my organization name
NEWSOPTS="-h -r"             # use these startup options
```

The EDITOR, MAILER, and PAGER variables can be set to any available program, as long as the full path is specified or the program is in the search path. The SHELL used for executing shell commands is usually the one you default to, for simplicity's sake. If you don't specify values for these variables, they default to the vi editor, the mail program, and the more pager. The default shell is usually the login shell.

The NEWSBOX variable specifies where files are to be saved. In the sample .profile file, all save commands are written to a directory called News within the home directory (written as ~ for the shell to expand). The default value is your home directory.

The NAME and ORGANIZATION variables should reflect your real name and company name. If you don't specify these variables, NAME defaults to your user name from /etc/passwd, and ORGANIZATION defaults to the system site name.

Some Usenet users think it is funny to invent other names when posting contentious articles, but this is a childish practice. The use of "cute" pseudonyms (such as *The Masked Avenger* and *The Flame Artist*) is similarly considered in bad taste.

The NEWSOPTS are specified just as they are on the command line. The specified options are added to the readnews command-line expansion when it starts. The default value is no options. (See Table 17.3 for a list of readnews environment variables and their descriptions.)

Table 17.3. The readnews environment variables.

Variable	Description
EDITOR	Editor to use for writing replies
MAILER	Mail program to use to send replies

continues

Table 17.3. continued

Variable	*Description*
PAGER	Program used for paging articles
SHELL	Shell to run when an ! is issued
NEWSBOX	File or directory to which to save articles
NAME	Your user name (used in headers)
ORGANIZATION	Your company name (used in headers)
NEWSOPTS	Default options to use when starting readnews

vnews

Another popular newsreader is vnews (visual news). This program uses a screen-oriented approach instead of readnews' line-oriented interface. The vnews reader has a number of advantages over line-oriented displays because it can always show you information that might be useful. The vnews reader works only on screen-addressable terminals, but practically every terminal manufactured in the last 20 years meets that requirement.

You start vnews with the command vnews; you see the full-screen display. At the top of the vnews screen is the header information, much as it would appear with readnews. At the bottom of the screen is a line of information that shows the prompt, the current newsgroup name, the number of the current article, the total number of articles in the newsgroup, and the current date and time.

The middle of the screen is blank until you instruct vnews to display the article whose header is displayed. This is where a trade-off in newsreaders becomes an issue. Some users like to see as much as they can on-screen; others prefer not to see the body of the article until they have decided to read it, based on the subject line. The vnews reader follows the latter philosophy. The approach you prefer will help you decide whether vnews is appropriate for your use.

Many of the vnews commands are the same as those used by readnews, so trying vnews for a while doesn't require you to learn new commands. There are several new commands added, but these are explained in the vnews help file, obtained by entering ? at any prompt.

Not all systems support vnews, but it does have a loyal following on the network. Its screen-oriented approach is different from that of readnews, and many find it preferable. If it is available on your system, try it out.

rn

The readnews newsreader provides all the basic functions a user needs. You can use it to scan mail, move around newsgroups, and subscribe or unsubscribe to newsgroups. However, readnews has limitations. It cannot manage a set of articles at once (such as deleting all articles dealing with snow), it cannot search through articles for text (where was that comment about the bug you just found in Windows?), and it cannot follow a subject thread (because it is limited to displaying one article after another in numeric sequence).

One of the most frequently desired features is the capability to follow a thread. Following threads lets you read articles in the same subject series, similar to a readnews digest, but without waiting for someone to assemble the digest posting. Having to interrupt a sequence of articles dealing with solving a compiler bug to read someone's comments about her poodle can be frustrating and derail a train of thought. Following threads is also a means of feeling more involved in the debate.

All these features and many new commands are packed into rn (short for *readnews*), written by Larry Wall and available free of charge from the network archives. The new features result in a larger and slower program than readnews, but the extra capabilities compensate for the slightly slower response.

This chapter doesn't look at all rn's commands. (That would require several chapters.) Instead, it examines the most useful ones. For a full list of rn's features, find a man page or help guide on the network. The help guide tends to move around, with no single newsgroup as home, so you may want to ask in news.answers.

Starting rn

The rn reader uses the .newsrc file, just as readnews does. One nice feature about rn is that when it is started, it creates a backup copy of the .newsrc file (called .oldnewsrc) so that if anything goes wrong, you can always step back to the previous version. When starting with the previous version, the only thing missing is changes from the crashed session.

When you start rn after each newsgroup download, rn checks the .newsrc file for consistency with the downloaded list of newsgroups. The first time you run rn, it may take a couple of minutes, but after that it requires only a few seconds.

If any new newsgroups have been added or some have been dropped, you receive messages about them. You get to decide whether you want to subscribe to the new groups after each name is displayed:

```
Newsgroup alt.carrots not in .newsrc - add? [yn]
```

Your .newsrc file is updated to reflect your decisions.

If a newsgroup is dropped, rn sends a message to you that a bogus newsgroup has been found and changes the .newsrc file to remove any subscription.

Most rn commands are single letters, with many of them performing the same function as they do in readnews. Users who are moving from readnews to rn don't have to relearn a basic command set, which adds to rn's popularity.

You start rn by typing the name, with the option to specify a set of newsgroups to display immediately. For example, the command rn autos displays all newsgroups with the word *autos* in the name. The rn program responds with a list of the newsgroups that match and the number of articles in each:

```
Unread news in rec.autos           123 articles
Unread news in rec.autos.antique    34 articles
Unread news in rec.autos.tech       56 articles
Unread news in alt.autos.antique    12 articles
```

After presenting the list, rn autos displays the newsgroups one at a time and lets you decide whether to read them or not:

```
******** 123 unread articles in rec.autos-read now? [ynq]
```

rn now waits for you to issue a command. Despite the fact that it only shows three options in its prompt, there are many commands available. The same is true with most prompts, so you must assume that rn displays only the most common options. To get a list of all commands, you can enter **h** at any prompt.

You can use rn without a newsgroup specifier, but part of the power of rn is its capability to match strings. This lets you selectively move through the newsgroups in any order you want. rn's matching is over the entire newsgroup name, so if you specify **rn ibm**, you get every newsgroup with the letters *ibm* in the name.

If you answer yes to the read now? prompt, the articles in that newsgroup are displayed. If you answer no, you are prompted for the next newsgroup that matches your pattern. (Actually, the lowercase n and p commands go to newsgroups with unread articles only. The uppercase N and P commands go to the newsgroup whether there are unread articles or not.) After all the newsgroups have been cycled through, rn starts again at the top.

You can use the p (for *previous*) command to move back up the list of newsgroups. As with readnews, the - command toggles between the current and previous newsgroups. Some rn newsgroup movement commands are borrowed from the UNIX operating system. The

^ command moves to the first newsgroup in the list that has unread articles; the $ command moves to the last newsgroup. You also can use the command 1 to go to the first newsgroup—regardless of whether it has unread articles.

You can change the newsgroups you are reading using a couple of different commands. If you know the entire name of the newsgroup, use the g (*go*) command. If you are currently reading a bicycle newsgroup and decide that four wheels are better, type the command **g rec.autos** at the read now prompt to switch to the articles in that newsgroup.

To search for a new newsgroup with unread articles using a string, use the / command. Following up on the last example, suppose that after reading rec.autos, you conclude that four wheels aren't better than two, so maybe one wheel is the solution. At the read now. prompt, you enter **/unicycle** to scan through all the newsgroups to find the first one whose name matches the string *unicycle*. If there are none, you return to where you were when you issued the command. Assuming that there are a few unicycle newsgroups, you would be positioned at the first one on the list, and you would start again from the read now. prompt within the single-wheeled world.

The / command searches forward from the current newsgroup's position in .newsrc. The ? command specified with a string searches backward through the file, so **?unicycle** scans in the opposite direction to **/unicycle**.

Both / and ? have their origins in UNIX search patterns, and rn even supports the ^ (start) and $ (end) formats. Therefore, specifying **/^alt** causes rn to look for the first newsgroup that starts with *alt*. Similarly, **?vintage$** would search backward through the .newsrc list for the first newsgroup ending with *vintage*. If you haven't used these UNIX formats before, don't worry. They are seldom used in rn except by those who like to push the software to its maximum capabilities.

The c (for *catchup*) command lets you mark all articles as read within a newsgroup. This is useful when you've been away from the newsgroup for a while and don't want to read backlogged articles. The rn reader displays the following message to confirm that you really intended to issue the c command:

```
Do you really want to mark everything as read? [yn]
```

Exiting from rn is simple. The q (quit) command exits and updates the .newsrc file. The x (exit) command exits without changing the .newsrc file.

By using the u command at the read now prompt, you can specify that you want to unsubscribe to a newsgroup. There is no single subscribe command because you can subscribe to a newsgroup by different methods. The easiest way is to specify the newsgroup to go to, with either the g alt.jokes or rn alt.jokes format. The rn program displays a message telling you that you don't currently subscribe to the newsgroup and asking whether you want to. An alternative method is to edit the .newsrc file with an editor.

You can use rn to order your favorite newsgroups within .newsrc, but this process is best left for a more detailed discussion of rn. If you really want to know, check the documentation for rn, or ask a Usenet rn user.

One useful feature of rn is its capability to show a list of the subject headers of unread mail. When you use the = command, rn displays a list of the article numbers and subjects:

```
345 Star Wars Trilogy Special Edition
346 Problems with laserdisk player
347 Re: Star Wars Trilogy Special Edition
348 Cleaning the laser assembly in a Sony
349 Lousy quality pressing in Highlander
350 Side Timing (was: How many mins per side?)
351 Re: Abyss SE problems
352 Re: Star Wars Trilogy Special Edition
353 Where do I buy disks in Chicago
354 Reissue of Highlander letterbox
...
364 chapter titles for bambi
365 Warped disk problem
366 Re: Star Wars Trilogy Special Edition
 [Type space to continue]
```

If there is more than one screenful of subjects, press the spacebar to move to the next screen. The subject display is useful when you want to scan a large amount of news for articles that may be of interest to you. Because rn lets you move through the mail in many different ways, the subject display can save you a considerable amount of time. Table 17.4 lists the rn newsgroup commands.

Table 17.4. The rn newsgroup commands.

Command	Description
n	Go to the next newsgroup with unread articles
N	Go to the next newsgroup, regardless of article status
p	Go to the previous newsgroup with unread articles
P	Go to the previous newsgroup, regardless of article status
-	Go to the previous newsgroup
1	Go to the first newsgroup
^	Go to the first newsgroup with unread articles
$	Go to the last newsgroup

Command	Description
q	Quit rn and update .newsrc
x	Quit rn but don't update .newsrc
g	Go to the specified newsgroup
/ *string*	Search forward for a newsgroup that matches *string*
? *string*	Search backward for a newsgroup that matches *string*
u	Unsubscribe to a newsgroup
c	Mark all articles as read
=	Display subject headers for all unread mail
Ctrl+N	Find the next article with the same subject
Ctrl+P	Find the previous article with the same subject

Reading Articles

For simple article reading, rn behaves much as readnews does. The article-movement commands are the same as rn's for moving between newsgroups, albeit with many new features added.

After you have indicated that you want to read a newsgroup, the first unread article is shown. If there is more than one screenful of articles, only the first screen is shown. The -MORE- prompt at the last line waits for you to press the spacebar to display the next screen. If you want to page up only half the screen so that text on the lower half remains visible (sometimes useful when examining code, a list, or to keep the context clear), use the d command to display only half of the new page, scrolling the lower half of the current screen to the top.

A q or n command at the -MORE- prompt skips the rest of the article and moves to the next one. To back up a screen, use the b command. To start reading the article from the top, press Ctrl+R (hold down the Ctrl key and press R).

At the end of each article you read, you'll see the standard rn command prompt:

```
End of article 345 (of 254)-what next? [npq]
```

To move to the next article, use the n (next) command or press the spacebar. The q option also moves to the next article, but with a slight twist.

There are differences in how rn handles marking an article as read. If you use the n command, the article is marked as read. Using q moves to the next article, but doesn't mark the article as read. With both commands, the next unread article is displayed. The p command moves to the previous unread article—if there is one—not to the article previously displayed.

A slight variation occurs with the N and P commands, which move to the next and previous articles respectively, whether they have already been read or not. The P command is frequently used when you skip through an article too quickly and want to return and reread it.

Most users use the n command for most movement purposes, because it is easiest to stay with one key when paging quickly through news. The n command updates the .newsrc file properly. It can sometimes be frustrating to see the same articles popping up from a previous session because you used q instead of n. The q command is used when an article looks interesting and you think you may want to return to it later, but don't have the incentive to save it to a file.

While inside an article, the pager is used. (It is similar to the System V more pager.) If you want to perform a text search while inside an article (for example, to search for a string in a long article), type the text followed by a g at the -MORE- prompt. If you type **g firebird**, the pager does a case-insensitive search for the string *firebird* in the current article. To repeat the search in the article, use the G command.

Consistent with readnews and the rn newsgroup commands, the - command toggles between the current article and the last one displayed. The ^ command moves to the first unread article; $ moves to the end of the newsgroup (past the last article). You can move directly to any article by specifying its article number (easily obtained using the = command).

To decrypt an encrypted article that uses the Caesar cipher (13-character displacement), use the Ctrl+X command. As mentioned in the readnews section, this cipher is often used to hide endings to jokes, movie plot lines, or particularly obnoxious comments.

You can mark an article as unread (so that you can return to it later) in two ways. The m command marks it as unread, but it could reappear later in the session if you move through the newsgroup completely. The M command marks the article as unread, but you won't see it again in the current session. Using either command, the article is displayed again in the next session. When you use the m command, rn responds with this message:

```
Article 534 marked as still unread
```

If you use the M alternative, the message is this (just like a movie sequel):

```
Article 534 will return
```

Table 17.5 lists the rn article commands.

Table 15.5. The `rn` article commands.

Command	Description
q	Go to the end of the current article
n	Move to the next unread article
N	Move to the next article, even if read
p	Move to the previous unread article
P	Move to the previous article, even if read
b	Move back one screen
spacebar	Display the next screen
Enter	Display the next line
d	Display the next half screen
-	Toggle to the previously displayed article
^	Move to the first unread article in the newsgroup
$	Move to the end of the newsgroup
number	Move to the specified article *number*
Ctrl+R	Start at the top of current article again
v	Restart display with complete header details
Ctrl+X	Decrypt article using the 13-character offset
g string	Search for *string* within an article
G	Repeat the previous search
m	Mark as unread
M	Mark as unread after the session is completed
j	Mark the current article as read and go to its end
c	Mark all articles in the newsgroup as read
s	Save to a file
w	Save to a file without the header
S	Save to a file using an optional shell
W	Save to a file without the header using an optional shell
r	Reply by e-mail
R	Reply by e-mail including the original article
f	Post a reply to the newsgroup
F	Post a reply to the newsgroup including the original

continues

Table 15.5. continued

Command	Description
&&	Define or display macros
k	Mark all articles with the same subject as read
K	Same as k and update the kill file
Ctrl+K	Edit the kill file

> **NOTE**
>
> In a *kill file*, you can enter names of users, sending sites, subjects, and keywords that filter out articles automatically. For example, you can specify that any articles from etreijs@tpci.com are to be ignored because this person is always long winded and boring. The exact format of the kill file differs with the newsreader, but the principle is the same.

Searching for Articles Within a Newsgroup

You sometimes want to search for an article you remember reading, such as the one yesterday that mentioned the new microwave-controlled mouse. A set of useful search commands lets rn find the articles for you. You even can specify whether to search just the subject lines, the entire header (for a name or e-mail address, for example), or the entire article.

This chapter has discussed how to search through newsgroup names. The same syntax is applicable within a newsgroup. For example, to search subject lines in the current newsgroup for the mouse article, use /microwave/r or /mouse/r. The option /r searches all articles, including those already read. If /r isn't used, only unread articles are searched.

If rn can't find a match, it replies with the message Not found. If it is successful, rn displays the first article that matches. Case is not significant in the search, so you don't have to worry about how the string was capitalized. If you want case-sensitive searches, use the option /c (the command /UniForum/c searches all unread subject lines for the exact string *UniForum*).

The command just used searches only the subject line. Options after the command can expand the search. Appending the string /h performs the search over the entire header body. If your search for the microwave-controlled mouse doesn't succeed, but you know it was posted by someone at micromouse.com, you can search the headers for articles from them with /micromouse/h.

If you want to search already read articles too, append the /r option as well; the command becomes /micromouse/hr. Note that you don't need two slashes at the end of the name to separate options.

To scan entire articles (which takes a while), use the /a option. To scan for the first unread article mentioning 12-bolt PosiTraction axles for 1969 Firebirds within the rec.autos group, you issue a command such as /posi/a from within that newsgroup.

The / search commands operate from the current article forward through the newsgroup. To move backward (which is usually the case when you want to search previously read mail), use the ? instead. To search for a previously read article on the Toronto Bluejays, for example, use the command ?Toronto?/rac.

As you can see, the options in the search strings can be combined freely, as long as they follow the string surrounded by the forward or backward search characters. A quick word of warning: searching large newsgroups for strings in the entire article body can sometimes take quite a while.

If rn displays a match that isn't the one you want, you can invoke the previous search again using the short form of the search character (either / or ?). This repeats the same search string from the current article. See the following list for search characters and their purposes:

Search Character	Meaning
/string	Scan forward for unread articles with *string* in the subject line
?string	Scan backward for unread articles with *string* in the subject line
/h	Search the headers
/a	Search the entire article
/r	Search read articles as well
/c	Make the search case sensitive
/	Repeat previous forward search
?	Repeat previous backward search

Following Threads

One of the most popular features of rn is its capability to follow a subject. The sequence of articles that makes up the subject can be scattered throughout the newsgroup, but rn pulls the articles into order to make reading the series (thread) easier.

To follow a thread, you enter what rn calls the *subject mode*. When you have an article displayed for which you want to follow the replies, press the key combination Ctrl+N. This tells rn to find the next article with the same subject as the current one; rn switches itself into subject mode.

You can now move through the articles in the subject thread. You can tell when you are in subject mode because the subject line changes to display the word (SAME) before the subject. Also, the prompt at the end of each article changes to look like this:

```
End of article 345 (of 365)- what next? [^Nnpq]
```

In this line, ^N is the display form for Ctrl+N. To move to the next article in the thread, press the spacebar.

The Ctrl+P command moves you to the previous article with the same subject (similar to the way Ctrl+N moves to the next article). Using these two commands, you can follow a thread back and forth from the current position. Both sequences leave you in subject mode.

To leave subject mode, use any of the normal movement commands such as n or p; you return to the regular mode.

Aside from being useful in following a subject through the newsgroup, subject mode also lets you remove a thread you don't want to read. Suppose that a flame fest has broken out in the current newsgroup, and you don't particularly want to read dozens of posts of name calling and insults. Get into subject mode by pressing Ctrl+N and then use the k (for *kill*) command to mark all the articles on that subject as read. Then you won't see any with that subject title during your rn session.

Saving Articles to a File

You can save an article to a file anywhere in your directory structure. There are two basic commands to accomplish this: s (save) and w (write).

Both commands accept full pathnames, or they prompt for the location in which the file is to be saved. If no pathname is specified, a directory called News under the user's home directory is used. When you try to save an article, rn responds with this message:

```
File /tpci/u1/tparker/News/newstuff doesn't exist-
use mailbox format [ynq]
```

The filename you specified is shown with the complete pathname. The offer to use the mailbox format means that the file is saved that so it can be read with the UNIX mail utilities using the -f option (for example, you can type **mail -f newstuff**). If you don't use the mailbox format, the file is saved in a normal format. For most users, it doesn't matter which format you save the file in because both formats can be examined with a pager such as more or pg; the file can also be directed to a printer.

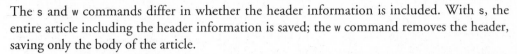
The s and w commands differ in whether the header information is included. With s, the entire article including the header information is saved; the w command removes the header, saving only the body of the article.

There are uppercase versions of the s and w commands that employ a shell specified by an environment variable within the rn system. For most users, the two versions are the same. Some advanced users may employ different shells for their normal work within rn.

Replying to Articles

Getting involved in the discussions is the fun part of Usenet. As with readnews, you can reply to articles with rn either by posting a reply to the newsgroup or through private e-mail to the original poster.

To use rn to reply to an article through e-mail, use the r or R (reply) commands. The R version includes the original posting as a quoted portion of the new message (which you should edit). Apart from a few more descriptive messages from rn, the process is the same as that of readnews. The R command gives you the option to cancel the reply at the last moment. The last question you see from rn asks you whether to include your .signature file.

To post to a newsgroup, use the f or F (follow-up) commands. The F format includes the previous article. Most systems respond with a message about how millions of people are reading your post and ask if you're sure you want to waste their time and system resources. These messages tend to discourage a lot of new users from posting, but you soon learn to ignore them.

When you use the follow-up commands, rn asks whether you have a prepared file to include. You may have written a response offline or have part of another document you want to include. At this prompt, provide the filename for rn to read into the editor's buffer. After you type the text of a follow-up, rn verifies whether you really want to send the posting to the newsgroup.

Filtering Articles

When you want to avoid reading mail from a particularly abusive person, eliminate a thread that has become boring, or simply don't want to read any articles about Mustangs in the rec.autos newsgroup, you can use rn's kill file capabilities.

A *kill file* instructs rn to immediately mark all the mail that matches some pattern as read, so that you never see it. The kill file is a file containing commands in the following form:

```
/string/j
```

The j instructs rn to mark the articles as read.

There is actually more than one kind of kill file. One that applies to all newsgroups is called a *global kill file*. Each newsgroup can have its own kill file, too (called a *local kill file*).

You can kill a subject from the newsgroup reader using the k command. All unread articles with the same subject title are marked as read; rn responds with a message such as this one:

```
Marking subject "John's a twit" as read.
```

The K command marks the subject as read, too, but also adds the subject to the rn kill file for the newsgroup. The prompt from rn is after you use the K command looks like this:

```
Marking subject "John's a twit" as read.
Depositing command in /tpci/u1/tparker/newsgroup/KILL...
```

The reader then scans the rest of the newsgroup, which echoes a message to you whenever it marks an article as read:

```
Searching...
53      junked
56      junked
67      junked
89      junked
done
```

After the search, the prompt reappears.

To edit a kill file, use the command Ctrl+K. If you issue this command from a newsgroup-level prompt, you edit the global kill file. If you issue the command from inside a newsgroup at an article-level prompt, you edit the local kill file. Until you become proficient with rn, you may want to defer from editing this file too much. Luckily, you always can delete the file and start over.

Macros

The capability to abbreviate long commands is a popular feature in UNIX. (The C shell and Korn shell are favorites because of their aliasing capabilities.) The rn newsreader can do this too; it calls aliases *macros*.

A macro is a command string abbreviated to a few letters. For example, you may have the command g `rec.autos.tech` abbreviated to car. Typing **car** at the newsgroup prompt issues the longer command for you. In many cases, macros don't really save a lot of time or typing, but they are useful when you perform the same commands day after day.

To create a macro, enter two ampersands (**&&**) in a row followed by the abbreviation and the full command string. To create the macro mentioned in the last paragraph, type this command at the newsgroup prompt:

```
&& car g rec.autos.tech
```

When a macro is called, it isn't executed until you press Enter or Return; this allows you to edit the string if you want.

If you enter **&&** by itself, rn displays all the currently defined macros:

```
*********** End of newsgroups-what next? [npq] &&
Macros:
car     g rec.autos.tech
m1      g rec.audio.high-end
m2      g rec.autos.vintage
m3      g rec.video.laserdisk
su      s unix_stuff
sv      s video_stuff
```

Unfortunately, a macro defined at a command prompt is lost when you leave the current session. Luckily, macros can be defined in the .rnmac file. This file contains the desired macros, one per line. For the preceding macros, the .rnmac file would look like this:

```
car     g rec.autos.tech
m1      g rec.audio.high-end
m2      g rec.autos.vintage
m3      g rec.video.laserdisk
su      s unix_stuff
sv      s video_stuff
...
```

When you start rn, the .rnmac file is read and all the defined macros become active throughout the session.

Batch Processing

A powerful feature of rn is *batch processing*. With this feature, you can provide all complex command sequences for finding and marking news articles. However, the use of this feature requires a good knowledge of UNIX and is beyond the scope of this book. For more information on batch processing, read the rn documentation.

Environment Variables

The behavior of rn is controlled by a set of environment variables defined in the startup shell files. Valid environment variables for rn are listed in Table 17.6.

Table 17.6. The rn environment variables.

Variable	Meaning
NAME	Your full name
ORGANIZATION	The name of your company
ATTRIBUTION	Used to describe quoted material in follow-ups
YOUSAID	Used to describe quoted material in e-mail
DOTDIR	Where to find .newsrc
HOME	Home directory name
KILLGLOBAL	Where to find the global kill file
KILLLOCAL	Where to find the local kill files
MAILFILE	Where to check for mail
RNINIT	Optional filename containing settings
RNMACRO	Location of macro definition file
SAVEDIR	Default directory to save files
SAVENAME	Default name to save files
EDITOR	Default editor
MAILPOSTER	Mail program command
SHELL	Shell for use in addressing UNIX
VISUAL	Alternative editor name

Most variable functions are clear from their short explanations. The ATTRIBUTION and YOUSAID strings are used when quoting articles, such as "*username* said" and "In your posting you said...." These strings are automatically used in front of the body of the text being quoted. The default values supplied by the newsreader are usually good enough for most users.

trn

The program trn is a threaded version of rn and was developed by Wayne Davison of Borland International. *Threaded* means that the articles are connected by the reader in reply order. It is possible to follow threads with rn, but trn does a better job of it.

It is easy to think that an original posting can branch out into a tree-like structure. With trn, a representation of this tree structure is displayed in the header so that you know where you are in the sequence.

The display is shown in the upper-right corner of the header and looks like this:

```
+-(1)--(3)--[2]
¦-(1)+-<4>
¦     \-[2]--[1]
\-(2)+-[3]
     \-[2]
```

The numbers represent the number of articles in the thread, with different branches from the original subject shown as branches on the diagram. The shapes of the brackets surrounding the numbers indicate whether the thread is selected for reading (marked with angle brackets < >), articles that are read (marked by parentheses ( )), or unread (marked by square brackets [ ]).

A branch in the tree, of which there are several in the previous example, occurs whenever the subject title is changed. Because of the evolving nature of newsgroups, some branches have no relationship to the original posted subject—which is why some branches may not be read. There's no use reading posts in which you are not interested when there are hundreds of other articles to read.

To help solve this problem, a subject selector has been added to trn. The difference between a *selector* and a *thread* is that the selector displays all subjects that match a string—even those that are cross-referenced. Using the selector takes practice but it does enable you to eliminate subject titles in a thread that are not of interest.

A major advantage of trn is that it enables you to know when there are replies to an article later in the newsgroup. This may save you from posting duplicate information, or worse, embarrassing yourself by stepping in at the wrong time.

Once you start it, trn behaves like rn, except that you are in thread mode. Each posting is followed through the reply sequence before the next subject is displayed; trn keeps track of which threads and messages you have read.

The commands for moving through trn are the same as those you use with rn, although with a few new ones added. Especially useful are the J command (that kills an entire thread) and , (that kills the current article and all its replies). Kill files have been expanded considerably over those used with rn.

The command set for managing threads and other aspects of trn is very complex. A man page is available for trn that is quite lengthy (44 pages at last count) and covers all aspects of the newsreader. Unfortunately, it is written as a command reference instead of as a tutorial, so new Usenet users may want to start with readnews or rn until they feel confident with the commands.

Use trn if you have it, even if you stay with the basic rn commands (all of which work with trn). The tree display and slightly different presentation of the header information is useful. As you gain confidence and want to start experimenting, the help screens and man pages let you begin to tap trn's full power.

xrn

With the popularity of the X and Motif graphical user interfaces, it was inevitable that newsreaders would be ported to take advantage of the features windowed interfaces offer. The most popular X-based newsreader is xrn, which is unfortunately found on only a few systems.

xrn maintains compatibility with readnews and rn commands, but enables the user much more control over the reader. The help file and man page for xrn is even larger than trn's; configuring it properly can be a chore. When xrn is working properly, however, it is graphically pleasing and easy to use.

If you work on an X-based workstation, you have an interesting choice. Although xrn is graphically more pleasing, it's slower than rn or readnews. Although rn runs fine in a shell window, xrn shows complete newsgroup listings that let you be more selective about what you read. Ultimately, the choice is yours.

Graphical Newsreaders

With the explosive growth in Usenet use among Windows and Macintosh users, graphical newsreaders for those environments have become popular and easily available. Commercial vendors of Internet software products often include a newsreader as part of their package; in addition, a healthy shareware market has developed. There are over a dozen graphically based newsreaders currently available for Windows and Macintosh users, so the choice of which to use is usually based on availability, cost, and features.

Unfortunately, many Windows-based and Macintosh-based newsreaders require a TCP/IP connection to allow them to connect to the news host and transfer postings. This can cause some problems when setting up and configuring the package if you are not familiar with TCP/IP or don't have it available on your system or network. Check the software package before you install it to ensure that it will work with your system.

Typically, a graphical newsreader presents you with a list of available newsgroups and unread mail in that newsgroup. Figure 17.1 shows the newsreader window from MKS Internet Anywhere, a popular commercial package for accessing the Internet. The icons across the top of the window let you access commands with the mouse instead of using the sometimes awkward commands used by character-based newsreaders. Pull-down menus offer many other features.

FIGURE 17.1.

The MKS Internet Anywhere newsreader displays all newsgroups with unread postings. Icons allow rapid movement between postings and newsgroups.

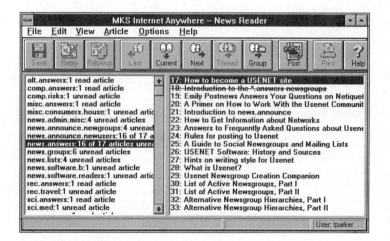

The left part of the Internet Anywhere window shows newsgroups with unread mail; the right part lists the subjects of the postings. Clicking a posting displays the mail (see Figure 17.2). When working within a newsgroup, more icons become active to allow you to reply to mail, follow the thread, or change newsgroups.

The behavior of newsreaders differs depending on whether you are downloading mail from a news server or simply reading mail from a connected machine (either over a network or through a modem). Most graphical newsreaders use a configuration file that allows you to select the newsgroups of interest to you. Figure 17.3 shows the MKS Internet Anywhere newsgroup subscription window. From this window, you can select the newsgroups you want to download each day.

Even if you don't download newsgroups to your own machine, many newsreaders allow you to customize the behavior of the system. Figure 17.4 shows the configuration screen from WinVN, a popular Windows-based shareware newsreader.

FIGURE 17.2.

The Internet Anywhere newsreader displays unread postings. Following threads is simply a matter of clicking an icon.

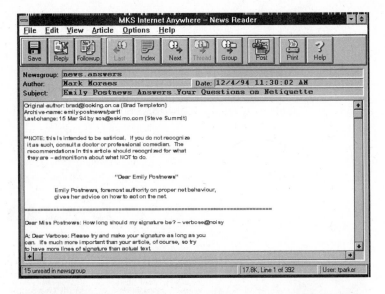

FIGURE 17.3.

Internet Anywhere's newsgroup subscription window allows you to select the newsgroups to download (not necessary if you read news from a local server).

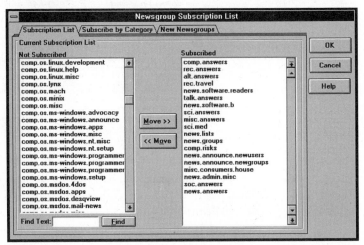

Reading, replying, following threads, and searching for postings are all quite easy with graphical interfaces because of icons and pull-down menus. These systems eliminate the need to memorize command sequences.

Most graphically based newsreaders look the same, presenting news and newsgroups in windows that differ only marginally in layout, icons, and menus. Figures 17.1 through 17.3 showed some representatives of these systems; the following sections describe some of the most popular newsreaders in more detail.

FIGURE 17.4.

WinVN's configuration screen lets you control the behavior of the newsreader.

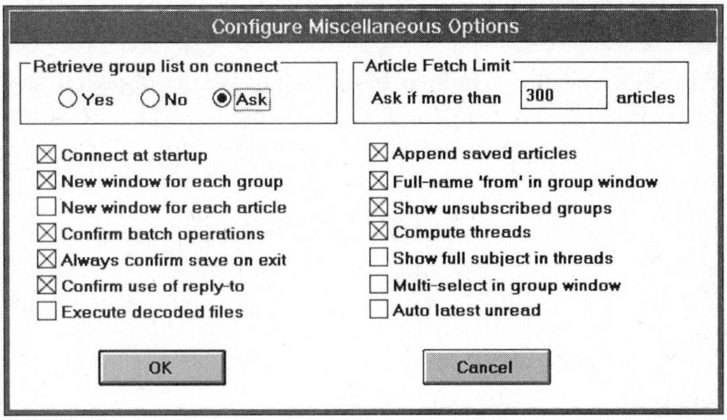

Configure Miscellaneous Options

Retrieve group list on connect
○ Yes ○ No ◉ Ask

Article Fetch Limit
Ask if more than [300] articles

☒ Connect at startup
☒ New window for each group
☐ New window for each article
☒ Confirm batch operations
☒ Always confirm save on exit
☒ Confirm use of reply-to
☐ Execute decoded files

☒ Append saved articles
☒ Full-name 'from' in group window
☒ Show unsubscribed groups
☒ Compute threads
☐ Show full subject in threads
☐ Multi-select in group window
☐ Auto latest unread

OK   Cancel

Trumpet

Trumpet is one of the most popular Windows-based newsreaders, written as shareware by Peter Tattam. Trumpet installs easily on a Windows machine (although you have to know the details about your news server to configure it). Trumpet requires a direct connection of a supported type to the news server, otherwise it can't be used to read news. Figure 17.5 shows one of the two primary Trumpet configuration screens.

FIGURE 17.5.

Trumpet requires information about your system, you, and how to contact your news server before it can be used to read news.

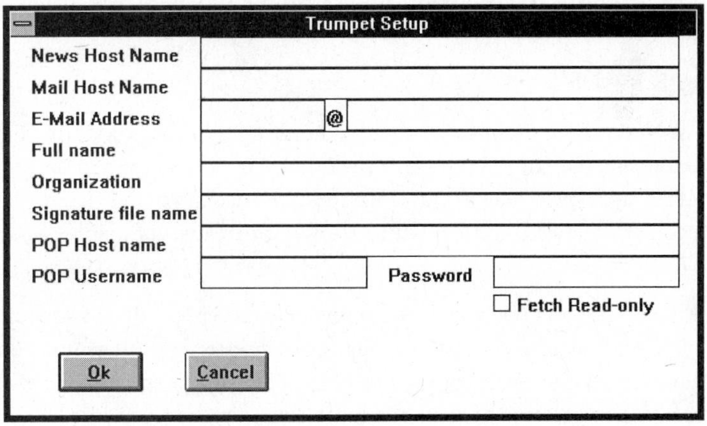

Trumpet Setup

News Host Name
Mail Host Name
E-Mail Address   [@   ]
Full name
Organization
Signature file name
POP Host name
POP Username   Password
☐ Fetch Read-only

Ok   Cancel

Once installed, Trumpet displays a split screen that allows you to subscribe to newsgroups. From there, a window with a list of all newsgroups with unread mail is displayed; you can select any newsgroup or posting title to display the contents. Threads can be followed easily with a menu choice, although the default is not to follow threads.

WinVN

WinVN is a flexible Windows-based newsreader developed by several programmers. It requires Windows Sockets to be installed if it is to work properly. (A shareware product called WinSock—developed by the author of Trumpet—implements sockets.) WinVN's configuration screen was shown in Figure 17.4.

WinVN uses a large, clutter-free screen for most purposes such as listing newsgroups and articles. The lack of icons means you need pull-down menus or keyboard keystrokes to accomplish most tasks. WinVN is very good at handling file attachments with several encoding types for binaries.

PINE

PINE (which originally stood for PINE is Not Elm) is a combination e-mail and newsreader available for many platforms, including UNIX, DOS, and Macintosh. The cross-platform capabilities can be an advantage to users who work on different machines and don't want to change e-mail and newsreader packages on each platform. PINE is freeware.

PINE has a set of single-character keys that control most of the functions within a window. On the other hand, PINE's interface is somewhat confusing because it does not always follow GUI standards. For example, the Windows version doesn't behave like most other Windows applications. PINE also offers no capability to handle threads.

Air News

Air News is the newsreader included in Spry Corporations Internet in a Box software package, a commercial (not shareware) product. Air News is a sophisticated newsreader with several advantages over WinVN and Trumpet, especially when more than one news server is accessible. Air News is very good at showing threads; its display is similar to the Windows File Manager.

Air News allows you to maintain several personal groups of subscribed newsgroups so that you can have a separate personal group for computer-related groups, another for your hobbies, and another for the talk groups. Air News also supports multiple windows so that you can have several newsgroups open at the same time.

The Air News interface is a little cleaner and easier to use than Trumpet's; moving through several newsgroups or articles quickly is easy. The primary disadvantage of Air News (other than having to pay for it) is its lack of integrated encoding and decoding. Instead, a separate utility must be executed.

MKS Newsreader

The newsreader included with MKS Internet Anywhere was shown in Figures 17.1, 17.2, and 17.3. It is integrated with the rest of the Internet Anywhere package, which includes FTP and Telnet utilities and e-mail and connectivity packages. The MKS newsreader is simple to set up and use once the connections to a server have been established.

A control panel is available that lets you tell the MKS system how often to poll the news server and which newsgroups to allow access to. The control panel allows system administrators to remove access to some newsgroups that may be deemed offensive or a waste of time. The list of active and available newsgroups is set in a dialog box, as shown in Figure 17.6.

FIGURE 17.6.

MKS Internet Anywhere allows control of which newsgroups are received, which can be posted to, and how to contact the moderator of moderated newsgroups.

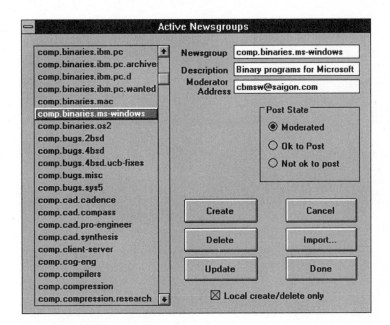

NewsWatcher for the Macintosh

One of the best Macintosh-based newsreaders is NewsWatcher, written by John Norstad. It is well designed, has excellent documentation, and is absolutely free! NewsWatcher requires TCP (either MacTCP or a third-party implementation).

NewsWatcher is easy to install and configure for your own favorite newsgroups. It lets you perform all the functions any Windows or UNIX-based newsreader offers. Curiously, NewsWatcher is still labeled as a beta software release, even though it has been available for quite a while.

USING MOSAIC AND OTHER INTERNET TOOLS

If you only occasionally read newsgroups, you may not want to use a dedicated newsreader. Many other Internet tools, such as the Mosaic and Netscape products for browsing through the World Wide Web, allow you to specify a news server and newsgroups as part of their interfaces.

Using this method is usually a little more cumbersome than a dedicated newsreader, and most such tools do not allow you to post, so you should use them only when you can't use a dedicated newsreader for some reason.

Live Conversations: Internet Relay Chat and Other Methods

18

*by Lay Wah Ooi
revised for this
edition by Billy
Barron*

Most Internet communication facilities work asynchronously. You rarely read your e-mail within moments of its being sent. People put information into Web, Gopher, and FTP servers; others access that information at different times. However, as has been proven by the telephone, real-time synchronous communications between two geographically distant people is valuable.

Over the years, the Internet and other wide area networks (such as Bitnet, Span, and Hepnet) have offered synchronous communication facilities that people have used for live conversations. Span and Hepnet were based on DEC's DECnet protocol, which includes a program called Phone. Phone is similar to the Talk program described in this chapter, but Phone is more powerful than Talk. In fact, some of the functionality of Phone should be added to Talk. Bitnet offers a facility generally called Tell, but VAX users know it as Send. These protocols were extremely useful on Bitnet and were the predecessors to the largely unused, but useful, Internet Message Send Protocol.

Most importantly, a Bitnet facility known as Bitnet Relay was created by leveraging off of Tell. In many ways, it is the direct predecessor to Internet Relay Chat (IRC). Although Bitnet Relay still lives, it is dying (as is Bitnet itself). In fact, the author of Bitnet Relay can regularly be found on IRC these days.

Real-time communication facilities are extremely popular on the Internet. They are also extremely useful.

Talk

Talk is a facility for holding one-on-one conversations but has no native facility for holding conference calls. The command is very simple to use. Normally, you can just type **talk** *user@hostname*. For example, type **talk goodguy@tetris.utdallas.edu**. Then goodguy is told he or she is being called and is given the command to respond on the screen.

It is up to goodguy to decide whether he or she wants to respond. If goodguy does respond, you and he or she are each given half a screen in which you can type. Your text is always on the top half of the screen; the other person's text is at the bottom. You see all keystrokes as you press them and both you and your correspondent can type at the same time. To see what it really looks like, see Figure 18.1.

When you finish your conversation, either of you can press Ctrl+C to end the call. Afterwards, both you and your correspondent are placed back at the command prompt.

FIGURE 18.1.

A sample Talk session.

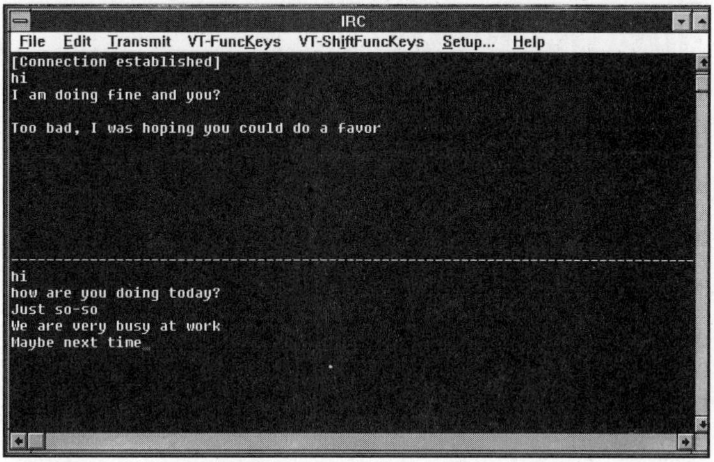

Incompatibilities

Unfortunately, the original Talk protocol had a bug that prevented all systems in the world from talking to each other. The protocol was later fixed and called *new talk* (*ntalk* for short). Unfortunately, some vendors, notably Sun, refused to adopt the new protocol. Therefore, the old protocol has lived on and is called *old talk* by many people.

What this means is that if you are on a machine that supports one protocol and the machine of the person you want to talk to supports the other protocol, you are out of luck. Because source code for both versions of Talk can be found on the Internet, it is possible that your system administrator can install the other version of the protocol (leaving the original in place). Normally, you must issue a different command for each of the two protocols, but at least you can talk to everybody you want to.

Software

Talk software comes with almost all versions of UNIX (although you must verify which version of the protocol it is). Source code for Talk can be found using Archie. Another version of Talk for UNIX, called YTalk, allows conference calls and overcomes the protocol differences.

Versions of Talk are also available for other platforms such as VAX/VMS and Windows. For these machines, Talk is most often a part of the TCP/IP package for the machine, which must be purchased.

Internet Relay Chat

Internet Relay Chat (IRC) is comparable to multiuser chat facilities on BBSes or an online service. However, IRC is larger and more global than any of these systems. At any given moment, thousands of people—and quite possibly, tens of thousands at times—simultaneously use IRC. In contrast, Talk is almost always just one-on-one conversations.

IRC was created during the late 1980s by Jarkko Oikarinen (who is sometimes on IRC as *Wiz*). He was writing a chat facility for a BBS in Finland. However, at some point, he gave the software to others who set it up. They connected their various servers together to form the IRC network.

During the Gulf War and the coup against Mikhail Gorbachev, IRC made big news. IRC was used for real-time communications regarding these events by eyewitnesses.

Uses

IRC has a reputation of being for frivolous communications. In truth, the bulk of IRC conversations *are* frivolous. In addition, IRC has many games you can play. So is the use of IRC at public universities just a waste of our tax dollars?

The answer is no. Valuable conversations are also going on. As already mentioned, live news reports can be found on IRC. On occasion, some people use IRC to get the answers to UNIX system administration questions. Actually, you can get the answer to any question. People hold real meetings on IRC, too.

Architecture

IRC is a client-server protocol. The user runs a client and specifies an IRC server to be used. Various IRC servers can be connected to form an IRC network.

The main IRC network is known as EFnet (Eris Free network) but few people call it that. Many people think that EFnet is all of IRC, but it is not. The primary alternative to EFnet is known as Undernet.

EFnet is chaos: there are an enormous number of users, occasional rogue operators, and painful robots. Although it is not well managed, EFnet does remain useful. However, its naysayers think its death is on the way. Some of them formed Undernet, which has strict controls in place. You can still talk about anything on Undernet, but the operators are carefully selected and abuse is not tolerated.

In addition to the main IRC network, many smaller ones exist. Lamenet and Dalnet are a few examples. Additionally, some stand-alone servers are running here and there.

Acquiring IRC Software

IRC software is available for numerous operating systems, including UNIX, Mac, MS-DOS, Windows, OS/2, VM/CMS, VMS, and even Amiga. They all can be found at `ftp://ftp.undernet.org/pub/irc/clients`.

The UNIX client, known as `ircII`, is probably the most popular and has the most active development support. This chapter uses `ircII` to explain how to use IRC.

The installation of IRC is not covered here. If you have a UNIX-based Internet service provider, IRC is probably already installed. If not, ask your system supervisor to install it. Companies and universities may discourage its use because it tends to be used for frivolous activities and takes up resources (especially dial-up modems); be understanding if your system administrator refuses your request.

IRC clients can also be accessed by Telnet. However, this is not recommended for several reasons. First, it increases the load on the Internet. The Telnet clients also tend to be slow and limit the number of people using them. Finally, you have no way to customize your IRC setup and must do it manually every time you use IRC. However, accessing IRC through Telnet is a nice way to try IRC before you invest the time installing a client. A partial list of sites that let you use IRC through Telnet is available in the FAQs described later in this chapter.

Starting IRC

Normally, you start IRC by typing **irc** at the prompt. The `irc` command connects you to the server specified at the time the client was compiled. By default, your *IRC nickname* is your user ID (more on this later).

You can change all of this by using a configuration script called `.ircrc`, which must be in your home directory. The `.ircrc` file can contain any of the IRC commands discussed in this chapter. The commands in the `.ircrc` file are run each time IRC is started.

If you do not want to use the server specified at the time the `irc` command was compiled, change it with the `/server` command. (By the way, all IRC commands start with a slash.) The syntax is as follows:

```
/server hostname
```

For example, use `/server dewey.cc.utexas.edu` to connect to the IRC server called Dewey at the University of Texas at Austin.

Nicknames

Nicknames are what they sound like. Those of you who were CBers in the 1970s know them by the term *handles*. When in IRC, you do not talk to people by their Internet address; you always use their nicknames.

You must be careful however. A person can have multiple nicknames and switch between them; you may have to look under several nicknames to find the person. The other problem—which has happened to a lot of people— is that you may log in to IRC and find that someone else is using your nickname. In that case, you have to use another one. The worst part is that people on IRC can start confusing the two of you.

Nicknames are set with the /nick command followed by the nickname desired. For example, if you want your nickname to be *DarthVader*, type /**nick DarthVader**.

If you want more information about someone who is currently on IRC, use the /whois *nickname* command. For example, if you use *DarthVader* as your nickname, other users can find out about you by typing /**whois DarthVader**. The /whois command gives you the person's user ID, host name, real name, the channel they are on, the server they are connected to, and finally the amount of time that they have been idle (see Figure 18.2) . Please note that it is possible for people to forge some of this information, so do not trust it as always being valid.

FIGURE 18.2.

A sample /whois *command.*

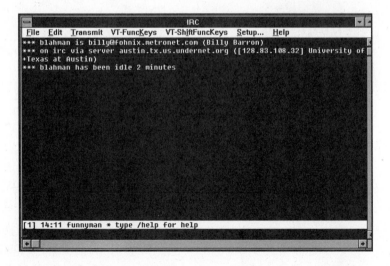

If someone has recently disconnected from IRC, you can still get information about him or her. Instead of using /whois, use /whowas. Otherwise, the command works the same. However, after a period of time, the information is purged from the system and you cannot find out who somebody was.

Sometimes, you want to be notified when a certain nickname signs on IRC. Use the /notify command to do that. Type /**notify** *nickname* to activate the notification facility. For example, if you want to know when goodguy logs in, type /**notify goodguy**.

Channels

IRC is divided into *channels*. Each channel is similar to a channel on a CB system. All the people on that channel hear (or see) all the messages sent to that channel. Under normal circumstances, anybody can send messages on a channel. In IRC syntax, all channel names must start with a pound sign (#).

There are numerous channels on IRC. Some are transient and others are permanent (for all practical purposes). Table 18.1 lists some "permanent" IRC channels on EFnet.

Table 18.1. Some "permanent" IRC channels.

Channel Name	Purpose
#hottub	Simulates a conversation around a hot tub
#sex	Discussions of sex (not for sensitive people)
#talk	General discussions
#unix	Discussions about UNIX (very useful for getting questions answered)

There are two commands for seeing the available channels: /list and /names. The /list command lists all the visible channels, the number of users, and the topic of the channel. The /names command lists all the visible channels and the names of the people on that channel (see Figure 18.3).

> **CAUTION**
>
> On a large IRC network, the /names and /list commands can generate more output than you want. This caution definitely applies to EFnet and may also be true for Undernet.

In Figure 18.3, you may notice that some people have an at symbol (@) in front of their nicknames. This symbol identifies the people known as *channel operators* (*channel ops* for short). The person who creates a channel is automatically a channel operator. This person (or anyone who has channel-op privileges) can *op you* (that is, make you a channel operator).

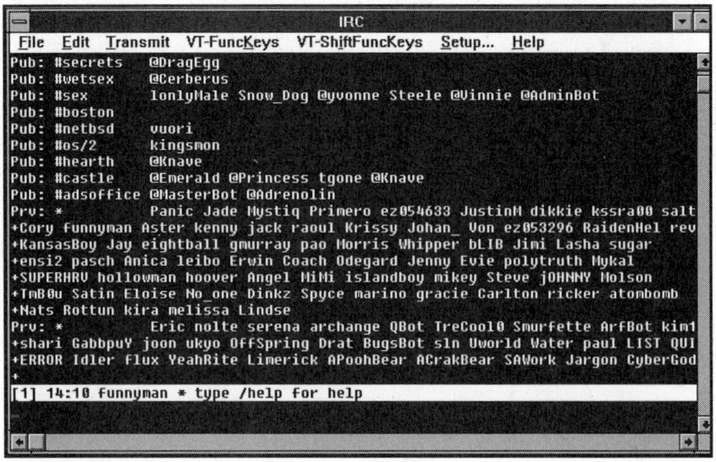

FIGURE 18.3.

A sample output from the IRC /names command.

```
┌─────────────────────────────  IRC  ─────────────────────────────┐
│ File   Edit   Transmit   VT-FuncKeys   VT-ShiftFuncKeys   Setup...   Help │
│ Pub: #secrets    @DragEgg                                        │
│ Pub: #wetsex     @Cerberus                                       │
│ Pub: #sex        lonlyMale Snow_Dog @yvonne Steele @Vinnie @AdminBot │
│ Pub: #boston                                                     │
│ Pub: #netbsd     vuori                                           │
│ Pub: #os/2       kingsmon                                        │
│ Pub: #hearth     @Knave                                          │
│ Pub: #castle     @Emerald @Princess tgone @Knave                 │
│ Pub: #adsoffice  @MasterBot @Adrenolin                           │
│ Prv: *           Panic Jade Mystiq Primero ez054633 JustinM dikkie kssra00 salt │
│ +Cory Funnyman Aster kenny jack raoul Krissy Johan_ Von ez053296 RaidenHel rev │
│ +KansasBoy Jay eightball gmurray pao Morris Whipper bLIB Jimi Lasha sugar │
│ +ensi2 pasch Anica leibo Erwin Coach Odegard Jenny Evie polytruth Mykal │
│ +SUPERHRV hollowman hoover Angel MiMi islandboy mikey Steve jOHNNY Molson │
│ +TmB0u Satin Eloise No_one Dinkz Spyce marino gracie Carlton ricker atombomb │
│ +Nats Rottun kira melissa Lindse                                 │
│ Prv: *           Eric nolte serena archange QBot TreCool0 Smurfette ArfBot kim1 │
│ +shari GabbpuY joon ukyo OffSpring Drat BugsBot sln Uworld Water paul LIST QUI │
│ +ERROR Idler Flux YeahRite Limerick APoohBear ACrakBear SAWork Jargon CyberGod │
│ +                                                                │
│ [1] 14:10 funnyman * type /help for help                         │
└─────────────────────────────────────────────────────────────────┘
```

The channel operator controls the channel. He or she can kick people off the channel or change channel settings using the /mode command. You can get the full list of modes by using the help feature (described later in this chapter); here, we are concerned with only a few of the most important ones. The basic syntaxes of the command are as follows:

```
/mode #channel [+-]<modes> [parameters]
/mode nickname [+-]<modes>
```

The plus sign (+) turns on the mode; the minus sign (–) turns it off.

For example, the command /mode #channel +i makes the channel *invite only*: only people invited to a channel can join (more about inviting in a minute). The /mode your_nickname +i command makes you *invisible* so that people cannot find you with a /list or /names command. The /mode #channel +s command makes the channel *secret*, which basically means invisible. The /mode #channel +o nickname command gives channel-op privilege to nickname.

Although we said earlier that anybody can send a message to a channel, that is not true if a channel has been made *moderated* by the /mode #channel +m command. In this case, only channel operators and people who have been given voice mode by a channel operator can speak. Channel operators can give voice mode to particular users with the /mode #channel +v nickname command. Others can only hear what is being said but cannot add their own comments.

To see the users on a particular channel, use the /who #channel command. This command lists users' nicknames, Internet addresses, and real names (which are usually just comments).

If a channel already exists, you type **/join #channel** to join it. If you use the /join command with a channel name that does not already exist, the command creates a channel with that name and makes you the channel operator on it.

At times, you may want to invite a person to join you on a channel. Do this with the /invite *nickname #channel* command. The person is then asked to join you with a message like *** DarthVader invites you to channel #sillyness.

To leave a channel, use the /part or /leave command (both are same). You can type /**part** #**channel** to leave a specific channel or /**part** * to leave your current channel.

Sending Messages

Until now, all the IRC commands you have seen started with a slash. If you type something that does not start with a slash, that "message" is sent to IRC. By default, the message is sent to the channel you are currently on. Other people see your messages starting with your nickname in angle brackets. In Figure 18.4, look at the first line for an example.

However, sometimes you want to send a private message. The facility for doing so is the /msg command. Type /**msg** *nickname message*. The *message* goes to the specified person; no other IRC users can see it. The intended user sees your nickname followed by the message between two asterisks (*).

> **NOTE**
>
> Although the /msg command is supposed to deliver private messages, it is possible that someone has installed an IRC server that uses a code modification to let him or her intercept private messages.

If you want to deliver a really private message, the next level of security is DCC (Direct Client-to-Client). With DCC, instead of your messages being passed through the IRC servers, your client and the other person's client make a direct connection that bypasses the IRC servers. To set up a DCC session, type /**dcc chat** *nickname*. When you want to send a private message to that person, type /**msg** =*nickname message* or /**dmsg** *nickname message*. The other user sees the message; your nickname between two equal signs precedes the message. For examples of the types of messages discussed so far, see Figure 18.4.

A final level of security actually encrypts your messages. You set up the encrypted session by typing /**encrypt** *nickname key*. The other person must also type this command (each of you uses the other's *nickname* and both of you specify the same *key*). Exchanging keys in a secure manner is an interesting challenge. The documentation for IRC says the default encryption system is not very secure. You can select your own external encryption program if you want.

In addition to sending messages, your nickname can perform actions. For example, if your romantic interest is online and in the same channel as you, you can type /**me kisses my love**. The message * DarthVader kisses my love * appears on the channel.

FIGURE 18.4.

A sample conversation using various types of messages.

```
┌─────────────────────────────── IRC ──────────────────────────────┐
│ File  Edit  Transmit  VT-FuncKeys  VT-ShiftFuncKeys  Setup...  Help│
│<blahman> hi all                                                   │
│> hi blahman                                                       │
│-> *blahman* long time no see                                      │
│*blahman* no joke                                                  │
│=blahman= hey, let's be more private                               │
│=> =blahman= sure no problem                                       │
│                                                                   │
│                                                                   │
│                                                                   │
│                                                                   │
│                                                                   │
│[1] 14:22 Funnyman on #bookdemo * type /help for help              │
└───────────────────────────────────────────────────────────────────┘
```

Earlier, we said that if you do not precede what you type with a slash, the text you type is sent as a message to the channel. This is true with one exception: If you are talking to a certain person quite a bit and want to have these messages sent to that person instead of to the general channel, you can use the /query command to redirect the messages. The syntax is /query *nickname* (/query =*nickname* in the case of a DCC conversation).

At times, you may run across someone who annoys or harasses you. Fortunately, you can tune that person out using the /ignore command. The /ignore command is very configurable. Only the most basic uses are covered here. To prevent the messages from a particular nickname from appearing on your screen (although other people still see it), type /**ignore** *nickname* **all**. Unfortunately, that person can change his or her nickname and start talking to you again. To prevent this, you can also type /**ignore** *user@host* **all**, where *user* is the user ID and *host* is the user's host name.

File Transfer

You can transfer files over IRC using another variation of the /dcc command. You type /**dcc send** *nickname* *filename*. When the file gets there, the recipient is notified. At that point, the file can be received by the command /dcc get *nickname* *filename*. You can also cancel a file sent to you by using /dcc close send *nickname* *filename*.

Help

With ircII, it is fairly easy to get help: type **/help**. However, the help screens are numerous. If you cannot find what you are looking for and need a quick answer, the best approach is often to ask someone on IRC what the command is called and then look at the help page for that command.

If you are not in a rush, you can ask your question of a Usenet newsgroup such as alt.irc.questions. Alternatively, you can take a look at the IRC FAQs found in the IRC newsgroups or at ftp://rtfm.mit.edu/pub/usenet/alt.irc/.

Quitting

The normal way to quit IRC is to type **/quit**, **/signoff**, **/bye**, or **/exit**. These commands log you out of the IRC server and put you back at the prompt. All these commands support an optional *message* parameter (for example, /quit going home). The *message* is sent to all your active channels.

Others prefer to use the /away command: If you type **/away *message*** and someone sends you a message, the *message* is sent back to that person. If you use /away, you must keep your IRC client running—which your system administrator may not appreciate.

Security

Be warned that there are many crackers on IRC who like to prey on novice Internet users. Here are some guidelines you can follow to avoid being taken advantage of:

- If someone asks you to type a strange command, do not do it. The unknown command may give crackers information about your system that your system administrator does not want known; alternatively, the unknown command may damage your account.

- Never give your password to anyone on IRC even if you know that person in real life. The password may spread and give dozens of people access to your account. We have seen this happen on more than one occasion.

- Never give out any private information such as credit card numbers. You could be the victim of a scam.

- Never use an executable program sent to you by a stranger on IRC. There is the possibility that it is a Trojan horse or can do other damage to your account.

If you ever run across any problems of this nature, contact your IRC server administrator or your local system administrator. You can find out who the IRC server administrator is by using the /admin command. Every IRC server administrator has special powers on the IRC network to kick people off if they are breaking the rules. However, do not involve the IRC server administrators over personal disagreements.

Bots

A *bot* is an abbreviation for *robot*. A bot is a program that interacts with IRC and looks like another IRC user. Bots usually have the word *bot* in their nicknames. The good bots run games, provide files, or provide some other useful IRC services. Unfortunately, there are numerous harmful bots that can have negative effects on IRC.

Most IRC novices think bots are cool. Most IRC experts think they are annoying. One of the most annoying kind is those that pretend to be real people.

Before running a bot, we strongly suggest that you spend a lot of time on IRC interacting with numerous bots. You should run bot code only for those bots you completely understand. Sometimes, crackers give novices bots that leave the novice's account open for attack. Make sure that you have a positive and useful purpose to which you want to put the bot. Finally, make sure that your system administrator and the IRC server you are using both allow bots.

Etiquette

Just like e-mail, IRC has some etiquette that all IRC users should follow. Most of the rules are fairly obvious.

First of all, you should not send messages to people when they have asked you to stop talking to them. Related to this, never send a massive amount of text to other IRC users or channels. This rule definitely includes any kind of ASCII graphic pictures. Massive text or graphics files can overflow some people's modems, making IRC unusable for them.

Most importantly, do not do anything destructive to harm IRC. Trying to break IRC security is an obvious no-no. You should also never run annoying bots that flood IRC with messages or kick people off.

Internet Teleconferencing: MBone, CU-SeeMe, and Maven

19

by Kevin Mullet

Multimedia Teleconferencing on the Internet: Is It for You?

Most readers of this book probably already know that numerous vendors offer high-bandwidth, near-broadcast quality, schedule-invasive teleconferencing that requires specially equipped conference rooms, video and audio technicians who ride shotgun during the conference, a separate dedicated network between all teleconference sites, and a convenient place to pour all the excess cash in your budget.

What you may not know is that if you're willing to suffer the slings and arrows of outrageous fortune on the bleeding edge of the Internet, you can engage in teleconferencing over your existing Internet infrastructure with moderately little investment in time and equipment.

Shoulder Surfing a Typical Internet Teleconference

Not everything used for teleconferencing can talk to everything else. The tools and the dynamics of a "typical" Internet teleconference can vary not only from site to site, but from conference to conference as people switch software depending on what the people on the other end are using.

A typical Internet teleconference can be between two or more people using a freely available package called CU-SeeMe. CU-SeeMe provides audio/video teleconferencing on a Mac and video-only teleconferencing on a PC. In the example shown in Figure 19.1, the participants are conferencing over their desktop computers at frame rates that vary between .5 and 1/2 to 15 frames per second (depending on the available bandwidth).

FIGURE 19.1.

Internet teleconferencing can be a highly valuable tool in bringing together diverse locations. This keepsolid session lets anyone on the Internet with keepsolid software participate.

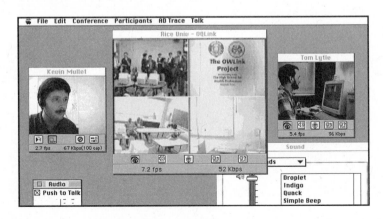

Look at the Participants window menu (shown in Figure 19.2) to see the chosen session nicknames of the video participants and several "lurkers" as well (these folks may be people without the ability to send video, who have chosen not to actively participate in the conference, or who have been blocked from participating because the conference is using a private conference ID number).

FIGURE 19.2.

Ubiquitous teleconferencing is another reason to become a mouse potato. Freely available software like keepsolid permits teleconferencing on-the-fly.

Each of the active participants can send audio to the group; alternatively, he or she can click the microphone symbol at the bottom of another participant's video window to speak privately with that individual.

What's important about the conference is that it takes place over the same Internet infrastructure that the participants' e-mail, file server, Usenet news, WWW, and other traffic also occupies. This is both good and bad.

The benefit of teleconferencing on the same Internet you use for everything else is that you no longer need an entirely separate network and set of conference rooms to do teleconferencing. In addition, the number of people you can reach just exploded. Now, virtually anyone with 56 Kilobits (Kb) or better bandwidth access to the Internet can engage in teleconferencing by adding some freely available software and minimal hardware to their Macintosh, PC, UNIX, or VMS workstation.

The down side is that because your teleconference shares the same bandwidth as your other applications, it can also negatively impact the performance of those applications, slowing down the workplace for the benefit of a teleconference that may or may not be as important as the other traffic it displaces.

What Is and Isn't Realistic

Internet-based teleconferencing doesn't lend itself well to every teleconferencing application. If, for example, the purpose of a teleconference is to review video of industrial time/motion studies, critically analyze sports performance at normal speed playback, or play a string quartet with each player in a different location, you are far better off looking at one of the proprietary solutions, at least for the time being.

If, however, you want to have off-the-cuff conferences with numerous associates who may be anywhere from a couple hundred feet to several thousand miles apart and do so with little or no advance setup, without leaving the desk in your office or home, the present state of technology in Internet teleconferencing holds promise.

What kind of performance can you realistically expect? The technology discussed in this chapter can usually be relied on to deliver 10 to 15 frames per second of video on the same LAN, 5 to 15 frames per second between different LANs at the same site, and 0 to 15 frames per second of video between any two arbitrary Internet sites with no intervening circuits of less than 56 Kilobit bandwidth. Your mileage, of course, will vary depending on numerous factors. These factors include things such as how many other applications are relying on your network and the demands those applications make on the available bandwidth. More subtle issues also come into play, such as how often the scene changes in any given video window. (This is important because the video applications discussed here use something called *velocity compression*, which gives priority to updating fast-changing parts of a scene before updating more static portions. Because of this, you may see a partial image for a minute or so when you bring up a new video conferencing window.)

Audio performance is the other factor that depends greatly on immediate bandwidth availability. The dynamics of human communication are such that most teleconferences (those between people who can both see and hear) communicate more information through audio than through video. If the video portion of the connection begins to drop frames, the result is usually just annoying. If audio drops off, it often means more than just the loss of a few seconds of audio: you often lose additional time asking for something to be repeated and repeating it. Many types of conferences, however, don't lend themselves well to interjections from the audience; the bit of audio information that dropped out may just be lost; the listener has to imagine what may have been said, with the result that he or she understands that much less of the subject material.

Other teleconferencing components (such as slides) are almost equally well suited to spotty communications and good, wide-bandwidth networks. These kinds of elements take longer to communicate and the user can request retransmission within the application without impacting the people involved. Displays of slides or scheduling information don't have the real-time demands of audio and video and therefore can be considered to have comparatively negligible impact on network resources.

When To Fish and When To Cut Bait

Once you start Internet teleconferencing, you should be aware of some signs that indicate you could be better off using another type of teleconferencing until Internet tools are available that do what you need or until the present tools improve to do what you want. Such signs include the security demands of the teleconference, the reliability of product support, and a requirement for consistent, broadcast-quality teleconferencing.

Two audio clients described here, Visual Audio Tool and Network Voice Terminal, each offer DES encryption to provide greater security and privacy for conferencing. Other types of Internet teleconferencing clients, such as video and whiteboard applications, don't offer encryption. This means that although most of the information in a teleconference can be concealed from all but the most skilled intruders, the video, whiteboard, and other data streams are not encrypted, leaving potentially vital portions of your conference open to the public. (Because the conference is transmitted over numerous local and wide area networks, any curious people can watch the packets race by on their local Ethernet and snoop on your conference without your knowledge.) Doing so is beyond the expertise of the vast majority of Internet users, but then again, the vast majority of Internet users aren't predisposed to intentionally violate other people's security.

Frequently, the "you get what you pay for" principle of economics fosters a belief that software acquired from the Internet is necessarily bug ridden and functionally unsupported. An unfortunate fact is that many commercial and academic sites don't embrace Internet teleconferencing because they mistrust anything that doesn't cost an arm and a leg. This, no doubt, stems from a desire for ultimate accountability—to have someone take responsibility for the failure of a product. Experience indicates that paying more for support doesn't necessarily result in a better product. No computing product, be it software or hardware, is used in an environment in which all equipment and software come from a single vendor. Finding such genetically pure computing environments is about as likely as finding an entirely American-made automobile.

In real-word, composite environments, vendors have traditionally dismissed errant product behavior as caused by some other vendor's product. Clearly, a commercial commitment to support doesn't always mean that the vendor will even acknowledge the problem. The argument in favor of using only commercially supported packages can degrade to this: even if actual support is unavailable, identifying a specific vendor with a given system results in a target for litigation. Management by lawsuit, however, isn't management at all but the failure thereof.

Using applications developed and informally supported through the Internet doesn't necessarily mean that the support is substandard or below the level available through commercial channels. The most substantial difference between informal Internet-based support and commercial support is that the burden for evaluating the reliability of multiple, often contradictory, sources of support rests with you, the customer. Unlike bandwidth and restrictive legislation, ego is never in short supply on the Internet. The more obscure your problem or request, the more likely you are to get detailed descriptions of what you need to do or where you need to go. Relying on the Internet for support of major resources, therefore, is less of a journey to the Oracle and more of a trial by jury. The *a posteriori* nature of Net-based support means that if you are doing anything non-unique, chances are that many people on the Net have already worked out a way to do it. It may even be valid to argue that the Internet can better support some applications because it is more of a melting pot than any single vendor's support facility; such an environment yields more valuable experience than a vendor-pure lab.

> **NOTE**
>
> *A priori* can be found at `http://www.nr.no/ordbok/engelsk?a+priori`; *a posteriori* can be found at `http://www.nr.no/ordbok/engelsk?a+posteriori`.
>
> All that being said, however, the very best support is frequently from commercial vendors with whom you have a proactive, committed relationship. The decision about where the best support can be found for teleconferencing isn't cut and dry and the conclusion you come to may very well lead you to a high-end commercial solution and away from use of the Internet.

The Holy Grail of teleconferencing is so-called *broadcast-quality video* with video frame rates of at least 24 frames per second and audio sampling on par with compact discs. Developing standards such as H.261 coding hold great promise for high-quality teleconferencing, but the current state of Internet teleconferencing is a level of magnitude less than the glitchless broadcast-quality product available with commercial products. Without a doubt, many applications require that level of quality—even at the cost of a parallel network to carry it and a parallel staff to run and maintain it. Even in such situations, it may be possible to reserve the "fine china" of a dedicated teleconferencing infrastructure for occasions that require it and to use the "paper plate" applications from the Internet when the type of conferencing needed doesn't justify the economics of the larger system.

If none of the issues just discussed have torpedoed your enthusiasm for Internet-based teleconferencing, let's move on to some even grayer issues such as bandwidth use, interoperability, and site security.

Internet Teleconferencing Rides Again

The best and worst thing about Internet teleconferencing is that is uses the same network you use for everything else—from frivolous perusals of packetized flights of fancy to the most mission-critical NFS mounts, Netware file services, and SQL databases. Some LAN and WAN protocols offer traffic prioritization, but not all hardware supports it, nor do most networks use such protocols. The bursty nature of teleconferencing can drag the available bandwidth of your network down and can cause noticeable or significant decreases in the availability of services from other relatively high-bandwidth applications like file servers, X Window, large-scale network management, and so forth.

These are not insurmountable problems. Some applications can assist your efforts to make the teleconferencing as nonintrusive to the other tasks on your network as possible. The INRIA Video-Conferencing System (described in "The Applications," later in this chapter) can automatically control the bandwidth it uses by monitoring feedback information it receives over the network. Most broadcast applications can be adjusted to have an upper threshold for transmission bandwidth. The CU-SeeMe reflector that enables many-to-many communication with the CU-SeeMe software for microcomputers can place a hard limit on the bandwidth any particular client can use, disconnecting them for a preset amount of time if that limit is exceeded.

In addition to the available technical constraints, social constraints are also a good idea. A little peer pressure applied at appropriate points can go a long way toward taming the human and software bandwidth hogs. After a little initial testing, you should be able to determine whether your network can bear the load of one or two teleconferences, each with three of four video participants and three or four "lurkers" (non-transmitting participants who just watch and listen). Before long, you should have a feel for whether you can be indiscriminate about when you teleconference or whether you should wait for periods of nonpeak usage.

No new application is born into a vacuum, and teleconferencing is no exception. You may already have existing teleconferencing, telemetry, or other remote-sensing systems that must tie into your teleconferencing system. Niche requirements can make demands on your teleconferencing system that off-the-Net software cannot address.

The level of security required for the information transmitted in a teleconference can easily rule out the feasibility of Internet teleconferencing. A more subtle issue is the degree to which your internal network must be opened to teleconference with external sites. Most security firewall arrangements, whether protocol or host based, can accommodate teleconferencing without sacrificing anything but bandwidth, privacy of teleconference content and methods, and the minimal information about your network architecture that can be gleaned from teleconference traffic.

These are some of the larger issues you should think about as you consider making the move to Internet-based teleconferencing. Certainly, teleconferencing is so useful—and just plain fun—that it's probably a one-way street. Any organization introduced to Internet teleconferencing is no more likely to go back to not using it than they are to stop using the World Wide Web once they start that.

The MBone: A Multimedia Backbone for the Internet

The Internet has a few different teleconferencing infrastructures, each with a limited amount of interoperability. One, CU-SeeMe, is a development project funded by the National Science Foundation and has taken the approach of loading all the functionality into a single piece of software. The other, the Internet Multicast Backbone, or MBone, carries its multimedia conferences to and from a wide variety of software. Although the software for both these networks can facilitate conferences between just two people without any kind of special network accommodations, the following discussion covers the wider possibilities of many-to-many conferencing.

A Brief History

The summer of 1968 may have been the summer of love, but 1988 was the summer of the MBone, and there was a "whole lotta hackin' goin' on." During that summer, the first Internet multicast took place, appropriately enough, between two of the original four ARPAnet sites: Bolt, Beranek, and Newman (BBN) and Stanford University (both of which have been important contributors to the Internet since 1969—before it was called the Internet).

The MBone (see Figure 19.3) relies on a type of networking called *IP multicasting*. Multicasting is a kind of middle ground between unicasts (in which one computer communicates with one other computer) and broadcasts (in which one computer talks to all the computers on a particular network). When one computer multicasts, it sends information to a group of computers, *not all of which may be on the same network.*

FIGURE 19.3.

A monument to creativity and ingenuity, the MBone is one of the most successful experiments undertaken on the global Internet.

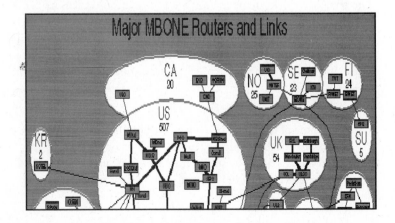

Since the early conferences in the late 1980s, the MBone has grown steadily; by the end of 1994, it included over 1,200 individual networks. The content of the MBone has grown from simple documentation of the Internet Engineering Task Force meetings to a variety of programming from underwater research to speeches at the National Press Club.

The Applications

Following are brief summaries of several applications that run on the MBone. All these applications run on UNIX (or something similar, depending on your talent at porting source code). With the exception of Shared Mosaic, each of these applications can be found through URL `http://www.eit.com/techinfo/mbone/mc-soft.html`. Shared Mosaic can be found through URL `http://www.eit.com/software/mosaic/sh-mosaic.html`.

Lawrence Berkeley Lab's Visual Audio Tool (VAT)

Lawrence Berkeley Lab's Visual Audio Tool (VAT) (shown in Figure 19.4) is the software used for most audio conferencing on the Internet. VAT's features include automatic input and output gain control, a conference/lecture mode toggle, and a VU meter and volume slider for both input and output. The user interface is also modifiable using the popular Tool Control Language.

FIGURE 19.4.

LBL's Visual Audio Tool.

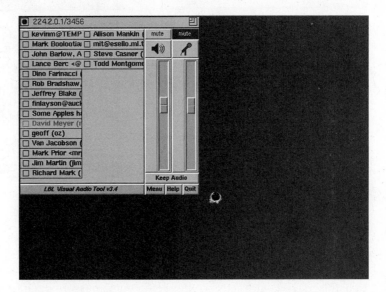

VAT can encode and decode in a variety of audio formats with a range of bandwidth requirements from 9 Kbps to 78 Kbps. At press time, work was being done on a 4,800 bps format; a 2,400 bps format was being considered. VAT can also serve as a mixer to adapt bandwidth and mix numerous audio streams into a single stream, or as a converter from one audio format into another.

VAT can send and receive DES-encrypted audio streams. Because most teleconferences over the Internet don't yet have the frame rate to make lip-reading practical, encrypted audio serves to conceal a great deal of the information conveyed in any given conference.

Network Voice Terminal (NeVoT)

Network Voice Terminal (NeVoT) is an audio client from Henning Schulzrinne of GMD Fokus in Berlin (see Figure 19.5). Like VAT, NeVoT includes an interface controlled by the increasingly popular Tool Control Language, the ability to operate in either gateway or client mode, the ability to run several conferences at once, and the ability to use DES-based voice encryption. Unlike VAT, NeVoT can run in either mono or stereo mode.

FIGURE 19.5.

The Network Voice Terminal MBone audio client.

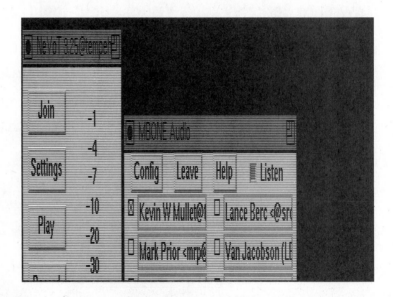

NetVideo

NetVideo, also referred to as *nv*, is the most widely-used MBone video client. As seen in Figure 19.6, NetVideo permits transmitting stations to control the bandwidth they use. Given appropriate hardware, NetVideo also permits the user to switch between sending black-and-white or color images. NetVideo can encode video in numerous formats, including Cornell University's CU-SeeMe (refer to "Teleconferencing on a Beer Budget: CU-SeeMe and Maven," later in this chapter).

In addition to conventional NTSC or PAL video input, NetVideo has also incorporated a number of "grabbers" that grab video from workstation displays and feed the contents or partial contents of a display window into a conference video stream. Different display types use different grabbers. Some displays show stills of the grabbed area; others show the grabbed area dynamically in real time.

FIGURE 19.6.

Netvideo can transmit video from a video camera, but it can also use an X Window as a display source (such as the rebroadcast FrameMaker window shown here).

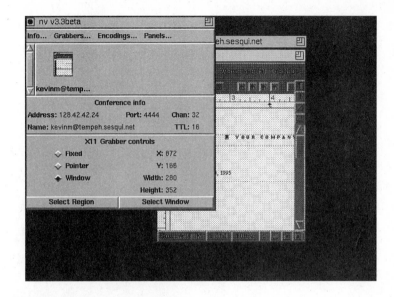

INRIA Video-Conferencing System (IVS)

INRIA Video-Conferencing System (IVS) is a one-stop shopping application for audio/video teleconferencing. The software in the IVS system, IVS (see Figure 19.7), ivs_replay, ivs_playback, and ivsd combine to give the user a single application cluster that receives and sends both audio and video in numerous encoding formats. The combination also records and replays previously recorded conferences and can notify you when another IVS user wants to conference with you.

FIGURE 19.7.

The INRIA Video-Conferencing System has the useful feature of being able to "page" people to engage them in a teleconference.

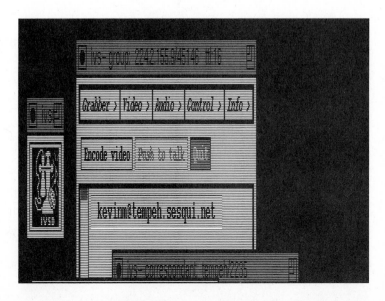

Lawrence Berkeley Laboratory Network Research Group's VIC

VIC, the Internet video conferencing tool in the Lawrence Berkeley Laboratory Network Research Group suite of multimedia teleconferencing tools (see Figure 19.8), was still in beta test at press time, but was nonetheless available to the general Net public. VIC's strong points include voice-activated video switching and the ability to use H.261 video encoding.

FIGURE 19.8.

The flexible VIC is Lawrence Berkeley Lab's contribution to the video part of Internet teleconferenceing.

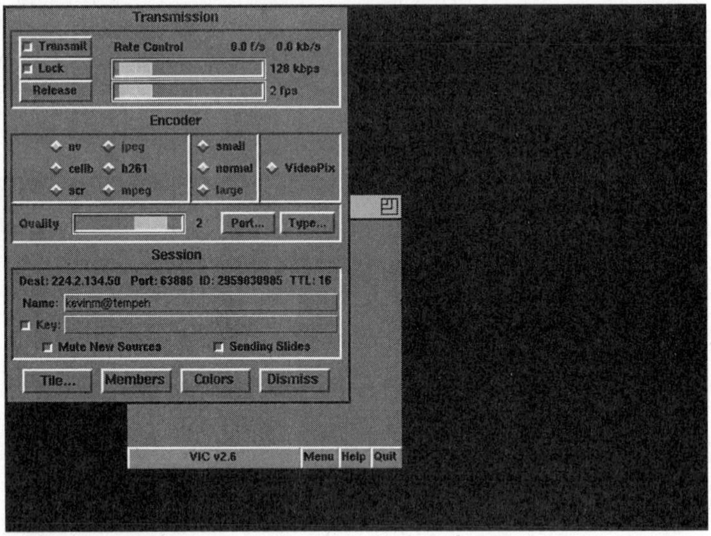

The Shared Whiteboard Tool

The Shared Whiteboard Tool (wb) is LBL's version of a combination whiteboard and slide projector. Participants can import plain text or PostScript source files; they can also use built-in drawing tools to enhance or create new images on the multipage whiteboard display (see Figure 19.9).

Image Multicaster Client

The IMage Multicaster (IMM) client pictured in Figure 19.10 is an MBone client designed for low-bandwidth background downloads of images such as satellite imagery and art gallery images. An advantage of using IMM over other applications to download a series of files is that through the use of IP multicasting, IMM can download the same files to all the participants in a given session simultaneously, making corrections for individual errors afterward when necessary.

FIGURE 19.9.

This electronic whiteboard lets numerous users around the world display pages of text and graphics and mark them up simultaneously.

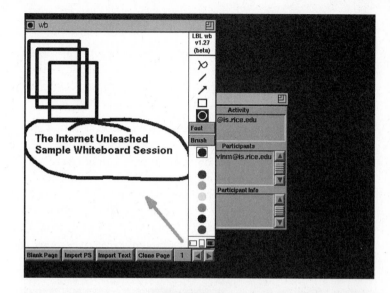

FIGURE 19.10.

IMM has a creative answer to the load problem of many people downloading the same graphics from the same place.

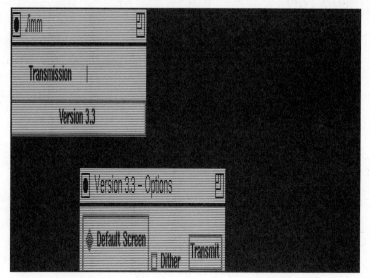

Shared Mosaic

Enterprise Integration Technologies' Shared Mosaic is an extension of NCSA's Mosaic for X. Any two normal IP unicast machines can use Shared Mosaic to cooperatively browse the Web in a one-to-one conference. Any reasonable number of workstations equipped to handle IP multicasting can cooperatively browse the Web as well. The synchronization model is described as "loosely controlled"—a nice way of saying it's a free-for-all. Anyone can control the browsing.

How To Coordinate a Teleconference

Once you have all these nifty MBone clients (or as many as you could fit on your available storage), you're ready to teleconference. Calling someone on the phone to tell them you want to teleconference seems a bit out of the spirit of things. If you're not running IVS and IVSD, how are you supposed to go about coordinating things?

The most popular way of coordinating conferences is with a *session directory*, or SD (see Figure 19.11). SD is a kind of automated television schedule. Persons who want to advertise a conference can set it up in SD, plug in whatever parameters they need, specify whether they're doing video, audio, and/or whiteboard, give the time, date, description, and a few other things, and their entry shows up in a list of upcoming and current conference events in the application's main window. All anyone has to do at that point is double-click the listing to start up all the required clients with the appropriate parameters to participate in the conference. Not surprisingly, the particular clients used for different types of sessions (video, audio, and so on) are controlled by a TCL script.

FIGURE 19.11.

A kind of television schedule for the MBone, Session Directory lets you schedule and advertise your own conferences as well as launch you into others' conferences.

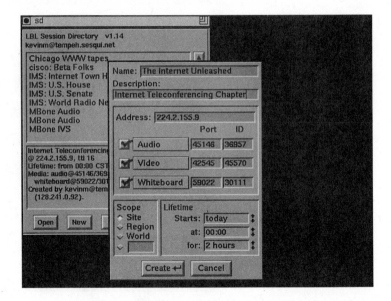

If Session Directory is a kind of television guide, the Multimedia Conference Control (MMCC) program delivers video on demand. Users of MMCC (shown in Figure 19.12) can page one or more other users of MMCC and engage them in a teleconference. With MMCC, you don't have to schedule a meeting ahead of time and you can restrict your guest list to a subset of folks running MMCC.

FIGURE 19.12.

Naturally, all teleconferences aren't for public consumption. The MultiMedia Conference Control program helps coordinate and initiate multiparty Internet teleconferences.

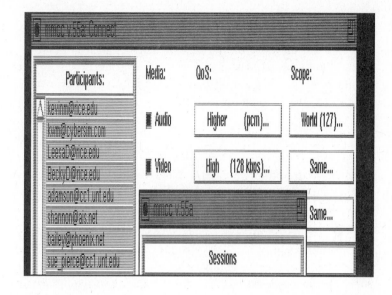

The MultiMedia Phone Service, MMPhone (shown in Figure 19.13), is specifically designed for unicast (one-to-one) teleconferencing. Users indicate the parameters of their conference on a World Wide Web form that they submit; their correspondent receives a MIME-format mail message with all the necessary information to begin the session.

FIGURE 19.13.

The MultiMedia Phone Service uses existing Web tools to coordinate one-to-one teleconferencing. Fill out the form; your local software runs automatically and an e-mail invitation goes out to the other party.

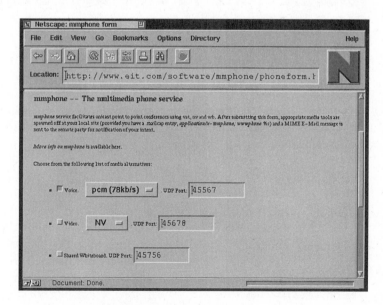

Doing It

The checklist for being on the MBone includes an IP route to an MBone provider that can route IP multicast packets to you over your existing 56 Kb or better Internet connection, and presumes routers that can do IP multicasting or a UNIX machine running mrouted, the IP multicast router daemon.

It is necessary to acquire an MBone "feed" and UNIX machines acting as multicast routers (also called *mrouters*) because IP multicasting is not a feature built into to all, or even a majority, of Internet Protocol routers today. Because the call for this feature has thus far outstripped the ability of the industry to meet demand, the freely available mrouted software is used on UNIX machines to "tunnel" IP multicast traffic inside conventionally routed IP traffic to build a network within a network: the MBone.

The industry is beginning to recognize the value of this technology; some UNIX-style operating systems such as SGI Irix 5.x, DEC OSF 2.x, BSDI, NetBSD, FreeBSD, and Sun Solaris 2.x, now have the ability to do IP multicasting without third-party patches to the kernel of the operating system. For those systems that require patches to be full players on the MBone, the patches, along with the mrouted software can be acquired through URL http://www.eit.com/techinfo/mbone/mc-soft.html for the client software.

Teleconferencing on a Beer Budget: CU-SeeMe and Maven

Some microcomputer-based software with a limited amount of interoperability can interact with the MBone. The following discussions are limited to software that has at least a limited amount of interoperability with the MBone. Although other software (such as Internet VoiceChat) shows a great deal of promise, discussion of software that doesn't interoperate with the MBone is beyond the scope of this chapter because it doesn't contribute to the availability of a single teleconferencing infrastructure.

CU-SeeMe

Cornell University's CU-SeeMe (see Figure 19.14), developed at the Cornell Information Technology organization (CIT), is a teleconferencing application that comes in two flavors: a Mac-based client and a PC-based client. At press time, the Macintosh client supports audio, video, and a "talk" interface in which participants can type to each other; the PC client was video-only, but an audio version was in alpha-testing. At press time, both versions only supported black-and-white video.

FIGURE 19.14.

Now every office can have a window with a view—here, CU-SeeMe tunes in to the NASA Select network while there's a mission.

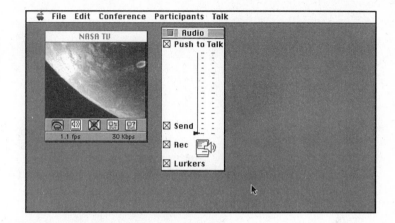

Like its MBone cousins described earlier in this chapter, CU-SeeMe can be used with no additional software for point-to-point, one-on-one teleconferencing—just like an ordinary telephone call. The addition of UNIX-based "reflector" software, however, permits a CU-SeeMe client to send its video (and audio and talk, if from a Mac) transmission to the reflector machine, to which any number of additional CU-SeeMe clients can attach and participate or simply lurk.

CU-SeeMe has become the Model-T of Internet-based teleconferencing. It's the first teleconferencing application that doesn't require a comparatively high-end workstation or operating system but has captured the enthusiasm of a global audience. A recent indicator that CU-SeeMe had gained acceptance into hitherto unpenetrated markets was the CU-SeeMe-based pay-per-view broadcast of the Houston livestock show and rodeo. Whether it's a live broadcast from a Space Shuttle mission or a view of someone's empty office in Norway, CU-SeeMe is quickly becoming the most ubiquitous teleconferencing application on the Net.

Maven

Maven, named after a Yiddish word for *knowledgeable person*, is an audio conferencing application for Macintoshes. Maven can use four encoding formats: u-law, which is a good lowest common denominator when interacting with other teleconferencing applications; Intel DVI, which is used by VAT; Linear, which is the native Mac audio format; and u-mod, which uses comparatively little bandwidth at the expense of some audio quality.

Maven (shown in Figure 19.15) requires no reflector to work, although the CU-SeeMe reflector has made accommodations for Maven/VAT audio format (refer to "Tab A and Slot B," later in this chapter).

FIGURE 19.15.

Maven is the audio software used in the Mac version of CU-See Me. Here, a Maven user talks to two VAT users, neither of whom can hear each other, but both of whom can hear the Maven user (who can hear them all).

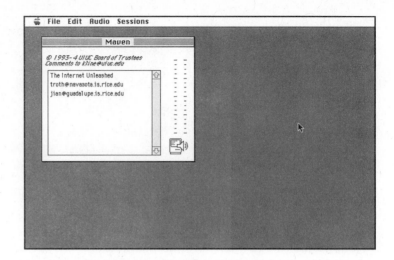

Once you start Maven, you can add participants one at a time; such participants can be copies of VAT or the CU-SeeMe reflector or other Mavens running on the Net. Participants can be removed from your list only if they shut down—there's no facility short of quitting Maven for removing participants from a conference yourself.

Many folks are using Maven without realizing it. The code for Maven was included in the Mac CU-SeeMe for the sound functionality (which makes it a little easier to understand why the Mac CU-SeeMe client is the only one so far that has been in general release with audio support).

The Bottom Line: What Time and Equipment Do You Need?

Setting up an MBone site is considerably more labor and time intensive than bringing yourself up with CU-SeeMe. Both MBone and CU-SeeMe require an IP route between each of the participants and either the mrouter or the CU-SeeMe reflector for many-to-many communications. The requirements in addition to the IP level are, in both cases, narrow enough to afford what would be adequate firewall reliability in most circumstances. Both MBone and CU-SeeMe software can be used for point-to-point communications.

One difference between CU-SeeMe and IP multicast clients is that you can be up and running on CU-SeeMe inside of five minutes by downloading a list of public or semi-public reflectors and the appropriate client for your machine and then running it. As long as you have a working WinSock or Mac TCP installation (whichever is appropriate), no installation is necessary for CU-SeeMe besides putting the software where you want it. Configuration is possible with both clients, but not required. With a stripped-down Mac, you can be watching and listening to conferences all over the world as soon as you bring up the software. The Cornell University reflector is usually a good place to find a conference that includes people from all over the country or the world.

If you have a Mac AV, you can plug in your mike and a camcorder and be a full player right now. If you have a nonAV Mac, you can use a digitizer board or a Connectix Quick-Cam (a serial-attached camera, digitizer, and microphone that costs around $100).

Although going from zero to CU-SeeMe can take about 5 minutes, bringing up each MBone client takes a bit longer, depending on how you go about it. Many FTP sites have precompiled binaries for the most common machines and operating systems. If you decide to use a precompiled binary, at least for initial evaluation, each installation of an IP multicast client should take about 5 to 10 minutes to complete. If, however, you prefer to start with source code and compile your clients to optimize them for your individual system, allow at least a half hour to an hour to take each client from download to startup.

Once you have your clients set up and have tested them against public CU-SeeMe reflectors or with point-to-point conferencing, what's next? If you decide to go for many-to-many conferencing using your own infrastructure, you must bring up a CU-SeeMe reflector or an IP multicast backbone. The former can be done in about 10 to 15 minutes (including the time it takes to read the documentation). The latter route involves several strategic decisions with regard to who you want to get your IP multicast feed from, where you want to run your mrouted daemons, which organizational subnets can handle the load of teleconferencing, and most important of all, what you're going to do to maintain this beast and ensure that present and future employees know how to make appropriate use of it.

Tab A and Slot B

Without common standards to link these teleconferencing tools, all you would have is a virtual tower of Babel. The key pieces in interoperability between microcomputer-based teleconferencing and IP multicasting are NetVideo, the CU-SeeMe reflector, and VAT. Naturally, any audio clients that use Intel DVI encoding can serve the same role as VAT in this equation; any video clients that use CU-SeeMe encoding (currently, only NetVideo fits this bill) can serve the same role as NetVideo.

To understand how things work together, it's necessary to understand the reason for the fundamental difference between the MBone and the CU-SeeMe architectures. Typically, clients that participate in the MBone are capable of IP multicasting (meaning that they can share the burden of distributing their traffic to an arbitrary group of computers that may or may not be on the same local area network). Typical clients that participate in CU-SeeMe (PCs and Macintoshes) cannot support IP multicasting. This means that their audio and video transmissions must go to an intermediary piece—a reflector—to be made available to other

CU-SeeMe clients. Those other CU-SeeMe clients, however, are equally unable to support IP multicasting, so they must connect to the reflector to participate in a conference.

A notable side effect of this is that although both CU-SeeMe and MBone-based conferences can have numerous video and audio streams in a single conference, CU-SeeMe is currently limited to participating in only one conference at a time. A workstation on the MBone, however, can participate in as many conferences as practical hardware limits permit.

- Two or more CU-SeeMe reflectors can be linked to load-share across geographical or organizational distances. The reflector can be configured to enforce an arbitrary upper limit on the amount of bandwidth that may be consumed by any single transmitting participant. The combination of these two factors can be used to provide high and low bandwidth reflectors for the same conference.

- The reflector can be configured to participate in one VAT and one NetVideo multicast session. Multiple concurrent VAT and NetVideo sessions are not currently supported.

- The reflector can make its conferences available to both VAT and NetVideo clients in unicast mode, which means that the CU-SeeMe reflector can also be used to make the MBone available to non-IP multicast-capable workstations capable of running VAT or NetVideo.

- Any of the clients listed earlier in this chapter can talk to another of the same client for one-to-one teleconferencing.

- NetVideo must use CU-SeeMe encoding to interoperate with the CU-SeeMe reflector.

Where To Go from Here

Getting on board with Internet teleconferencing is not unlike being one of the Mercury seven. As you learn about the MBone and CU-SeeMe, a lot of your satisfaction will come from seeing it get off the ground. The quality and strength of the tools involved is increasing just fast enough to keep you from resting on your laurels for any comfortable period of time.

It's impossible to guarantee that things will work well all the time, that you will always have at least 10 (or even 5) frames a second of video, or even that every teleconference will be worth the effort it takes to set up. What is likely, however, is that, as with any new communications medium, you will begin to use Internet teleconferencing to replace some of the media you already use (such as the telephone and e-mail). You will also find new ways to exploit this technology to do things that were so impractical before that they never occurred to you.

Following are a few URLs that can help you move on in your own research to discover whether Internet-based teleconferencing is for you. It's probable that your first successful teleconference on the Internet will inspire the same enthusiasm and amazement as your first time at bat with NCSA Mosaic. One thing is certain: Internet teleconferencing will have no less of an impact on the world than Mosaic did on the World Wide Web.

MBone Starting Points

- MBone Information Web:

```
http://www.eit.com/techinfo/mbone/mbone.html
```

- Frequently Asked Questions (FAQs) on the Multicast Backbone (MBone):

```
http://www.research.att.com/mbone-faq.html
```

- NPS World Wide Web home page: Multicast Backbone (MBone):

```
ftp://taurus.cs.nps.navy.mil/pub/mosaic/mbone.html
```

- Dan's Quick and Dirty Guide to Getting Connected to the MBone:

```
ftp://genome-ftp.stanford.edu/pub/mbone/mbone-connect
```

CU-SeeMe and Maven Starting Points

- The CU-SeeMe Clients, Reflector, and FAQ:

```
ftp://gated.cornell.edu/pub/video/
```

- Cornell Video: "CU-SeeMe":

```
http://pipkin.lut.ac.uk/~ben/video/cuseeme.html
```

- Maven:

  ```
  http://pipkin.lut.ac.uk/~ben/video/maven.html
  ```

- CU-SeeMe Desktop Video-Conferencing:

  ```
  http://www.indstate.edu/msattler/sci-tech/comp/CU-SeeMe/index.html
  ```

V

PART

Finding Information

Finding Information: Introduction and Tips

20

by Billy Barron

A primary purpose, if not *the* primary purpose, of the Internet is the sharing of information between universities, companies, governments, nonprofit organizations, and individuals. At present, millions of pieces of information are available on the Internet in a variety of formats. Many people call this an *information overload* or an *information wasteland*. This need not be the case, however. In this chapter, you receive the knowledge and tools needed to navigate the Internet and find the information you are looking for. We hope that the tips in this chapter help you avoid much of the information you have no interest in.

History

In the early days of the Internet, the information situation was vastly different, but it is important to understand the past to understand the present. The original part of the Internet, the ARPAnet, was funded as a research project in computer networking. Needless to say, people quickly started using the network for exchanging information. Because the number of sites on the Internet was relatively few, however, users could find just about any information they were looking for—or find out that it was not available on the network at all. Advanced information-searching tools were not needed. The traditional method of providing information on the Internet in those early days was the anonymous File Transfer Protocol (FTP) site, which is discussed in more detail later.

In the mid-1980s, the Internet started experiencing exponential growth, which continues to this day. Universities and other users began placing information services—such as library catalogs known as Online Public Access Catalogs (OPACs) and systems known as Campus Wide Information Systems (CWIS)—online. These services, which contain information about specific universities, were accessible with the Telnet and rlogin protocols. Quickly, people discovered that they could no longer easily find the information they sought on the Internet. For the remainder of the 1980s and even through 1991, the situation was still not too bad. A handful of electronic guides appeared during the end of this period to help users find what they were looking for on the Internet.

These guides were just an electronic equivalent of a paper list. In fact, it was common that these electronic lists were printed and used as a paper reference book. Later, several of the guides even had official print editions. However, by the early 1990s, many of the guide authors became overwhelmed with just the sheer number of additions and changes to the guides.

In 1990 and 1991, new ways to provide information on the Internet—such as Wide Area Information Servers (WAIS), Gopher, and the World Wide Web (WWW)—hit the scene. These systems enable many Internet users to make information easily accessible on the Net. Previously, only professional computer professionals had easy methods of providing information. The result was that the number of pieces of information on the Internet soared from thousands of items to millions of items in a short period.

Meanwhile, tools such as Archie, Veronica, and Jughead came out to help people search for information. Although these tools are heavily used on the Internet, they are still going through an evolution and are becoming more sophisticated over time.

The first major electronic hypertext guide to Internet resources—Hytelnet—became available at the end of 1990. Since then, several of the earlier guides have been discontinued (because of author burnout). At least one major guide is now generated electronically. Also, instead of general guides, it is more common today to find specialized guides on topics such as agriculture and law all over the Internet.

In 1993, the United States government funded the Internet Network Information Center (InterNIC) to help users find Internet access and information on the Internet.

Consequences of Internet History

What effect has this history had on the current state of information on Internet? The effects can be seen just about everywhere in the current state of the Internet. Let's look at the effects:

- The tools for searching the Internet are useful, but still in an early state of development. Some tools do not cover everything in their domain. Others attempt to cover everything but do not provide fine-grain searching. Debates on the best searching methods are still common.

- The network is growing so fast that methods of finding information quickly become obsolete.

- High rates of Internet growth mean that popular sites that make information available to the Internet community often go from being lightly loaded to having a crippling load in a matter of months.

- The quick change rate of the network means that guides and tools must deal with out-of-date information. Ed Vielmetti, a well-known Internet access provider and researcher, once said that "the half-life of an Internet resource is six months."

- Because many tools are available, an information provider must decide how best to get the information to the target audience. This includes the decision to spend or not spend the extra time making the information available in multiple formats.

- It is important for all sites to make some information freely available—even if they offer for-pay information, too. A real benefit of the Internet is being able to search for information without worrying about being charged. However, this system works only as long as people share information freely. If a large number of sites start using free information without providing any in return, the system of free exchange will gradually fall apart. This could turn the Internet into a system such as CompuServe or Prodigy. This is not to say that there is anything wrong with having for-pay information on the Internet, but making all the information on the Internet available on a for-pay basis is not a good thing.

■ Contacts are an important way to find information. Internet users should feel free to pass along valuable Internet information sources to friends and contacts.

■ Sometimes, a piece of information will exist on the Internet but you will not find it. You have to accept this when it happens.

Information Location Methods

At different times on the Internet, different information location methods have been used. Today, all information location methods exist in parallel. Each method has its strengths and weaknesses, but all are useful in their own way. The different information locations are these:

■ **Serendipity.** This is the original method of finding information on the Internet because no better tools existed. *Serendipity* means discovery by accident—and that is exactly what the method is. You can never predict what you are going to find or when you are going to find it using serendipity. Often, you do not find what you are looking for at all. However, serendipity does have a few strengths.

One strength is that some information on the network can only be found this way. Serendipity also can be fun because of its unpredictable nature. Finally, serendipity often turns up that piece of information you never thought existed, but which is useful once you know about it.

■ **Resource Guides.** The user looks in a document, finds a resource, and then uses it. In the past, you had to use serendipity to find resource guides. Now resource guides of resource guides are available.

■ **Browsing.** Browsing is the same as walking into the library or bookstore and directly perusing the shelves. You may start in Science Fiction but eventually end up scanning the shelves in Philosophy. Gopher is the electronic equivalent of browsing.

■ **Searching.** Searching is the same as looking at an index or a card catalog. On the Internet, searching usually works by picking a searching tool and then entering some keywords to search for. WAIS, Veronica, Jughead, Lycos, WebCrawler, and Archie are all searching tools—each with its own purpose.

■ **Hypertext.** Hypertext can be thought of as a special form of browsing. However, the differences between the two methods are important. Browse is usually a menu-driven system; in a hypertext document, words, phrases, or even pictures contain links to another document. If you select a link, you enter a new document. The closest nonelectronic comparison I can make are the *SEE ALSO* lines in the encyclopedia. Hypertext is just a more advanced electronic form of this.

The proponents of hypertext argue that it leaves traditional browsing methods in the dust. The arguments against hypertext can be summed up in one commonly stated sentence: "You see a lot of little hypertext links all the same." This sentence is a quote from the Infocom text adventure game Zork, and it's true. The basic problem with hypertext is that most people start looking at the links and may even traverse a few. But after a few jumps, the user is reading materials on an entirely different subject. Also, people tend to get lost in the hypertext links.

Good hypertext can be really good. Unfortunately, the majority of hypertext seems to fall somewhere in the poor-to-bad category. Hopefully, over time, people's skills at writing hypertext material will improve. Over the last few years, there has been only a small improvement in hypertext authoring skills. In addition, HTML (HyperText Markup Language) is getting more advanced (which may help to some degree).

This book covers three different hypertext systems. The first is Hytelnet, which is a good piece of hypertext. The second is the fast growing World Wide Web, which is made up of millions of hypertext documents. The quality of these documents goes all the way from excellent to terrible—with the majority of them somewhere in between. The third hypertext system is relatively small and unknown but shows some signs that it could be the next World Wide Web in size. It is called Hyper-G.

When using the Internet, it is important to be able to take advantage of all five information location methods. Some pieces of information on the Internet can be found with only one method.

Information Location Tools

Many of the chapters in this part of the book describe individual tools for finding information on the Internet. It is important to know when to use one tool over another one.

You often select a tool based on where the information is stored. At other times, an information resource on the Internet is in multiple formats.

Here's a brief list of specific Internet tools:

■ **FTP.** File Transfer Protocol is the oldest commonly used method of transferring files on the Internet. It works in two different modes. The first is that it can be used to transfer files between any two accounts on the Internet (however, this requires knowing the passwords of both accounts). The other mode is known as *anonymous FTP.* An anonymous FTP site enables anyone to connect into the system and download files.

FTP by itself has no facility to let the user know in advance where a particular file is available. FTP as a facility of sharing documents is somewhat on the decline because of the newer tools, but it is still the primary way to acquire computer software over the Internet. See Chapter 22, "FTP: Fetching Files from Everywhere."

- **Telnet/rlogin.** Telnet and rlogin enable an Internet user to log in to a remote computer. The user can use a private account on the remote computer or a public one. Public accounts are set up around the network for services such as CWISes, OPACs, and BBSes. Hytelnet documents all the known public Telnet sites; look in the current version of Hytelnet to find what sites are available. See Chapter 23, "Logging in to Other Computers with Telnet and Rlogin."

- **Archie.** Archie enables users to use a search method to find where files are available for anonymous FTP on the Internet. However, Archie's database does not contain all the anonymous FTP sites on the Internet (you may have to fall back on serendipity). In the near future, Archie will also allow searches of other kinds of Internet information. See Chapter 24, "Archie: An Archive of Archives."

- **Gopher.** Gopher is sometimes called "Internet duct tape" because it glues together a variety of systems on the Internet. In reality, Gopher was designed as a CWIS and document delivery system, but it has been expanded greatly over time. It is menu driven; menu items can be documents, menus, FTP sites, Archie searches, Telnets, WAIS, or other kinds of information on the Internet. Gopher uses the browsing method. See Chapter 25, "Using and Finding Gophers."

- **Veronica and Jughead.** Veronica and Jughead add searching capabilities to Gopher. Veronica regularly finds all the Gopher items in the world that are connected to the master Gopher server at the University of Minnesota. Jughead allows searches of just a single Gopher server. See Chapter 26, "Searching Gopherspace with Veronica."

- **WAIS.** WAIS creates databases of documents that can be searched. There is even a WAIS database that contains the location of other WAIS databases. See Chapter 27, "WAIS: The Database of Databases."

- **WWW.** The World Wide Web is similar to Gopher, but instead of being menu driven, it is hypertext based. The WWW appears to be a much better platform for multimedia documents than Gopher. Like Gopher, however, the WWW can act as a front-end for just about any piece of information on the Internet. Mosaic and Netscape are two of the major clients to the World Wide Web. See Chapter 28, "Navigating the World Wide Web."

- **Hytelnet.** Hytelnet documents all the public access Telnet sites in the world. In addition, it includes some tips on using the custom user interfaces of some Telnet sites. See Chapter 29, "Opening Doors with Hytelnet."

- **FSP.** File Service Protocol is an alternative to anonymous FTP that eliminates some of the server performance problems of FTP. See Chapter 30, "New Tools: FSP, Harvest, and Hyper-G."

- **Harvest.** Harvest attempts to make indexing Internet information easy. Harvest is described in Chapter 30.

■ **WWW spiders.** Lycos, WebCrawler, and JumpStation are just a few of the indexing systems available for the Web. They are each slightly different and are described in Chapter 28.

■ **Hyper-G.** Hyper-G is a second-generation hypertext system with the potential to solve most of the problems of the World Wide Web largely by replacing the Web. Hyper-G is also described in Chapter 30.

Finding People and Computers

In addition to the information-finding tools described in this part of the book, Chapter 21, "Finding People on the Internet," explains how to find people—and their computers—on the Internet. It may be necessary for you to refer to some of the other chapters in this section because Telnet, WAIS, the WWW, and Gopher are all useful tools for finding people. In addition, Chapter 21 describes several tools that are unique to the problems of finding people on the Internet.

Some Final Tips

When you first start looking for information on the Internet, do yourself a favor and look for something that interests you instead of a boring topic. If you are interested in rock music, don't waste your time looking for *Moby Dick* (although information on the novel is available). You can search for lyrics to the Blue Oyster Cult song "Don't Fear the Reaper"—if you hunt around, you can find them (try using Archie or Veronica to find the lyrics). Remember that the Internet can be fun and fascinating if you let it be. Don't think it is boring!

If you want to hone your searching skills, you can join the Internet Hunt contest held monthly. Every month, the context moderator asks a few questions that have answers on the Internet. People around the world try to find the answer and send in the answers. The winners receive prizes!

Remember that if you cannot find a piece of information you are looking for, you can always find a mailing list or newsgroup on the topic. Look for tips in the FAQ (Frequently Asked Questions) file for the newsgroup. If you do not see a tip, feel free to post a question. Someone will usually provide an answer.

Now review the following chapters on finding information. You do not necessarily have to read them in order; start with the one that interests you most.

Finding People on the Internet

by Billy Barron

One of the most frustrating and frequently asked questions Internet users have is how to find other people on the network. This chapter explains various methods you can use to locate people on the Internet.

Why Finding Internet Users Is Difficult

New Internet users often expect to find tools similar to the telephone system when they want to find other people on the network. The telephone companies have a vast advantage over the Internet because the telephone system has relatively few telephone companies. Each company controls a geographic region, and the company knows about every telephone in that region. The telephone system has three major tools that people use to locate other people and businesses: the white pages, the yellow pages, and directory assistance.

Although many white-pages systems are available on the Internet, the systems are not well coordinated and often are incompatible. Some of the directory-service software tools are not designed to deal with multiple sites. The white-pages services you can access typically cover a single company or university. A company or university has only a few thousand names at most. Most telephone white pages cover tens or hundreds of thousands of people. In addition, some Internet sites do not give out information about their sites for security reasons, much like an unlisted phone number. In relative terms, an individual white-pages phone book is more useful than the white-pages system of a single Internet site. However, more global Internet white-pages services are being developed.

Yellow-pages systems on the Internet have been discussed only over the last couple years. (In discussing yellow pages, note that this chapter is not talking about Sun's NIS system, which previously was called Yellow Pages.) Yellow pages serve a commercial purpose. In the earlier days of the Internet, most sites were government or academic, not commercial. Very few people were selling anything on the network, so users didn't need yellow pages. These days, however, many businesses are connecting to the Internet and offering services. Therefore, yellow-pages services are starting to develop.

Telephone directory assistance has always worked because the telephone company knows everybody's telephone number. But as you learned from the discussion of white pages, nobody on the Internet has all this information. Also, the telephone company has an easy way to bill you for this service. Such a billing system has not been worked out for the Internet—even if the information were available. Primitive forms of directory service do exist on the Internet and are discussed at the end of the chapter as methods of last resort.

Nonelectronic Directory Methods

With Internet's high technology, many users overlook the simplest and often the quickest methods of finding someone on the Internet. Many effective methods of finding an Internet address do not use a computer or the Internet at all.

Looking at a person's business card is a good place to start. Listing e-mail addresses on business cards is becoming increasingly common. Often you find an Internet address on the card, but at other times you may find Bitnet, CompuServe, or some other type of e-mail address. By the time this book is printed, Bitnet probably will be just about obsolete. Therefore, any Bitnet address you find will likely be invalid. Even so, the address may give you a clue about the person's user ID. If you have a CompuServe address such as `53470,3243`, you can turn it into an Internet address by replacing the comma with a period and adding `@compuserve.com` to the end of the address. Therefore, the person's Internet address is `53470.3243@compuserve.com`.

Business cards are not the only place to look. If the person in question writes magazine articles or books, for example, you may find an Internet address in one of these publications. However, the older the publication, the higher the chance that the address is obsolete.

Unfortunately, literally dozens, if not hundreds, of other networks have addressing schemes different from the Internet. If you are dealing with another network, you should read the *Inter-Network Mail Guide,* by Scott Yanoff. The guide is frequently posted to newsgroups like `alt.internet.services`, `news.answers`, or `comp.mail.misc`. If this guide does not help, you may want to ask your Internet support person or organization for some assistance. In most cases, you can turn this address into one you can use from the Internet.

If you are looking for someone in a foreign country who may not be on the Internet or even have e-mail at all, start by looking in the *International E-Mail Accessibility FAQ* (Frequently Asked Questions) posted frequently to `news.answers`. This guide lets you know the current state of e-mail in various countries. If you find that the country has no external e-mail, this FAQ stops you from wasting time trying to dig up an e-mail address.

Many professional organizations print membership lists with postal addresses, phone numbers, and the like. Conferences often do the same with a list of people who attended. Over the last few years, many of these organizations have begun adding Internet addresses to their lists.

A few paper-based Internet directories are now published. The white-pages books are largely generated from lists of Usenet posters. This information is also available online as files (`http://rtfm.mit.edu/pub/usenet-address/lists`) as well as a WAIS database (as described later in this chapter). The paper version is much more convenient, although it often has out-of-date entries. Paper-based Internet yellow pages exist also and can be useful, although they also go out of date quickly.

The final nonelectronic method of finding someone's Internet address is just to call him or her on the telephone and ask. For years, many users have preferred this method. Fortunately, the Internet has reached a point in its maturity where using the network itself is a reasonable way to find someone, as the next section explains.

Types of Directory Servers

A *directory server* is a place on the network that stores phone numbers, addresses, e-mail addresses, and the like. A *directory service client* is a program the searcher uses when looking for people. The client sends the server a request for information and the server returns the requested information. A thorough explanation on how to use servers comes later in this chapter.

Many types of directory servers are available on the Internet. The oldest type of server probably is the WHOIS directory server. This server originally was designed so that the Network Information Center could keep a list of contacts for all networks connected to the Internet. Since then, many sites have brought up WHOIS as their local directory server.

The successor to WHOIS appears to be a system called WHOIS++, still quite new and under development. No one knows how important WHOIS++ will be in the future, but do not be surprised to see WHOIS++ in use.

CSO (Computing Services Office) NameService is a phone-directory system written by the University of Illinois at Urbana-Champaign. This system enables you to search on multiple fields and is quite fast. CSO also has the advantage of being relatively easy to install—often an important criteria for overworked computing staffs.

Some users also look at the WAIS (wide area information services) software and decide it is an effective method of bringing up a directory server. The down side is that WAIS searches the whole file of directory entries and cannot search individual fields like CSO NameService can. This means you cannot search for *Mitch* as only a last name. WAIS shows you all occurrences of the name *Mitch*, whether it is a last name or something else (such as a first name or a street name).

X.500 originally was part of the Open Systems Interconnect (OSI) protocol stack. However, X.500 was useful enough that people ported it over to run on Transmission Control Protocol/Internet Protocol (TCP/IP). X.500 has a hierarchical scheme in which the world is broken into countries, states, cities, organizations, departments, and so on. X.500 is not easy to install and is a major resource hog. Even so, the system appears to be picking up steam. Many commercial vendors are promising support for X.500 in their products. In addition, as of the end of 1994, the current OSI Consortium version of the server is now freely available for educational and nonprofit organizations.

Types of Directory Service Clients

As you go through this chapter, you may notice some overlap among the different directory services. The primary reason is that the writers of many directory service clients try to allow access to as many directory servers as possible. To accommodate this overlap, the rest of this chapter is organized by client software. Note that different clients can access the same directory server.

Things You Need To Know in Advance

The term JANET (Joint Academic Network) is mentioned several times in this chapter. JANET has been a major network in the United Kingdom for a number of years, and many resources in the United Kingdom are available only through JANET. Fortunately, the Internet and JANET are well linked. Whenever this chapter mentions a JANET site, you can access the site using Telnet to `sun.nsf.ac.uk`, logging in as `janet`, and pressing Enter for the password prompt. When the `Hostname` prompt comes up, enter the JANET address. Please be aware that JANET and Internet addresses are inverts of each other. The JANET address `uk.ac.aston.quipu` is known as `quipu.aston.ac.uk` on the Internet.

When you attempt to use some of the directory clients and servers, be prepared for a few problems. When I was writing this chapter for the first edition of this book, I found that several of the directory servers and clients that had previously worked were broken when I tested them. Some organizations consider their directory servers to be very important. Other organizations do not, and they may leave a broken directory server down for days, weeks, or even permanently. Additionally, some sites do not load all their people into their directory server. For example, many universities do not load their students into the directory server. Finally, beware of obsolete information. Many sites do not update the information in the directory server regularly. If you locate an e-mail address or phone number that does not work, suspect that it is out of date.

Gopher

Through Gopher, you can find your way to most of the directory server information in the world. Joel Cooper at the University of Notre Dame has compiled a Gopher menu containing a large number of sites accessible by a variety of methods including CSO, WAIS, WHOIS, and X.500. You can find this menu on the University of Notre Dame Gopher (`gopher.nd.edu`) under Non-Notre Dame Information Sources/Phone Books—Other Institutions. The URL is `gopher://gopher.nd.edu:70/11/Non-Notre%20Dame%20Information%20Sources/Phone%20Books--Other%20Institutions`.

On the Gopher menu, the directory servers are broken down by geographic region. Select the geographic region you want. You end up with a menu that has WAIS indexes and CSO NameServer entries. If you select a WAIS index, you just enter the person's name. Gopher returns the results to you. If you select one of the CSO entries, Gopher gives you a list of fields you can search. Enter only the fields you want to search. You don't need to fill in every blank (in fact, doing so may prevent you from finding the person). Press Enter, and Gopher lists the entries that match.

The X.500 menu is a separate menu. Move through the menus until you get to the menu of the organization you want to search. Select the search item for the organization and enter the name of the person you want to find. The process may take a while, but eventually Gopher should return a list of people who match your search string. Select the appropriate person and you get detailed information.

Gopher also has a gateway to WHOIS servers, which is available at `gopher://sipb.mit.edu:70/1B%3aInternet%20whois%20servers`. All the WHOIS databases show up as WAIS search items.

X.500

There are many X.500 clients including FRED, dish, and SD.

FRED is one of the most popular X.500 clients, yet is the easiest to use. Although you can install FRED directly on your computer system, most likely it has not been installed there. If not, many publicly accessible FRED clients are available through the Internet, as well as other X.500 clients (see Table 21.1). Some can be found on JANET (see Table 21.2).

Table 21.1. X.500 clients available through Telnet.

Site	Address	User ID
Aston University (UK)	quipu.aston.ac.uk	de
Computer Tech Inst (GR)	wp.csi.forth.gr	wp
Denmark	login.dkuug.dk	ds
FUNET, Finland	nic.funet.fi	dua
Italy	jolly.nis.garr.it	de
King's College	dir.kcl.ac.uk	de
Monash University (AU)	nice.cc.monash.edu.au	fred
Poland	ipx1.mat.torun.edu.pl	de
PSINET, USA	wp1.psi.net	fred
Spain	ocelote.cica.es	directorio
Sweden	wp.umu.se	de
Switzerland	nic.switch.ch	dua
Trinity College, Ireland	ashe.cs.tcd.ie	de
University of Adelaide (AU)	whitepages.adelaide.edu.au	fred
University of London CC	paradise.ulcc.ac.uk	dua
University of Sydney (AU)	jethro.ucc.su.oz.au	fred

> **NOTE**
>
> If a user ID is specified in Table 21.1 or 21.2, use it as the user ID to log in to that system. If no user ID is given, you are automatically logged in when you connect to that service. In neither case must you apply for a personal account.

Table 21.2. X.500 clients available through JANET.

Site	Address
Brunel University	uk.ac.brunel.dir
Manchester Computing Centre	uk.ac.mcc.dir
Manchester Institute of Science & Technology	uk.ac.umist.dir
Manchester University	uk.ac.mbs.dir
Sussex University	uk.ac.susx.dir
University of Leeds	uk.ac.leeds.dir
University of Manchester	uk.ac.man.dir

In the following example, the user connects to the University of Adelaide's FRED client with Telnet. Suppose that the user has heard vaguely of a Dr. Stanton there. The user uses the whois *name* command.

```
fred> whois stanton
David William STANTON (1)                          +61 8 303 7130
Adelaide, SA 5005
AUSTRALIA
FAX:     +61 8 332 7381
Telex:   number: 89031, country: AA, answerback: UNIVAD
Title:   Mr
Name:    David William STANTON, Applied Mathematics, Faculty of Mathemat
ical and Computer Sciences, The University of Adelaide, AU (1)
Modified: Mon Nov  1 20:30:31 1993
by: Manager, DMD, The University of Adelaide, AU (2)
```

Unfortunately, this search revealed no e-mail address, but at least it turned up phone and fax numbers.

WHOIS

The WHOIS database also has a client program called WHOIS. This program is available on most UNIX machines. The basic syntax is whois -h *server name*. The following example shows how to search for a friend, Roy Tennant, at the University of California at Berkeley:

```
%whois -h whois.berkeley.edu tennant
UNIVERSITY OF CALIFORNIA AT BERKELEY WHOIS SERVER     (v 4.0 - 13 Oct 93)

Searching in campus faculty and staff directory for TENNANT

TENNANT, Elaine C.                                    Last update 06/23/93
Associate Professor
Ger            1414 Dwinelle       674-3111           674-7121

ETENNANT@GARNET.Berkeley.EDU
TENNANT, Roy                                          Last update 07/08/93
Head Information Systems Instruction&Support
Lib            2990 Lib            674-5201           (FAX) 674-6200
Info Sys Instr  &Support
RTENNANT@LIBRARY.Berkeley.EDU

End of directory search.
```

You can acquire a list of available WHOIS servers at ftp://sipb.mit.edu/pub/whois/whois-servers.list.

Knowbot Information Service

The Knowbot Information Service (KIS) attempts to be a front-end for a variety of directory servers. The servers include WHOIS, X.500, and MCI Mail. KIS defaults to using some of the servers (but not all of them). You often may have to tell KIS something about the location of the person you want to find. KIS is available at telnet://info.cnri.reston.va.us:185/ or telnet://sol.bucknell.edu:185/ (see Chapter 23, "Logging in to Other Computers with Telnet and Rlogin," for more information on how to use Telnet). Suppose that you are looking for William Green of the University of Texas at Austin. The KIS client uses the query *name* command to search:

```
> query Green, William

The ds.internic.net whois server is being queried:
----------
Green, William C. (WCG11)               w.green@UTEXAS.EDU
University of Texas
Computation Center (12700)
```

```
Austin, TX 78712
(512) 432-9873

Record last updated on 25-Feb-93.

The rs.internic.net whois server is being queried:

No match for name "GREEN,WILLIAM".

The nic.ddn.mil whois server is being queried:

Green, William A. [CAPT] (WAG9) 46AREFS@ACFP1.ACFP.AF.MIL
(907) 356-1475/0154/5793 (DSN) 472-1475/0154
Green, William C. (WCG11)        w.green@UTEXAS.EDU                    (512) 432-9873
```

PH

Although most of the world uses Gopher to interface with CSO NameService directory servers these days, CSO has its own client called PH. PH has a few useful features, such as the capability to update your own information in the CSO database (if your site allows). If you have a PH client installed, the basic syntax you use is ph -s *server name*. The following example shows how to use the PH client:

```
%ph -s x500.tc.umn.edu paul lindner
-------------------
name: Paul M Lindner
: Paul M Lindner-1
campus: Minneapolis
delivery_method: mhs
department: Distributed Computing Services
home_address: 222 W Delaware Ave
: Minneapolis, MN 55406
home_phone: +1 612-873-7382
host: maroon.tc.umn.edu
last_name: Lindner
mailbox_assigned: lindner@maroon.tc.umn.edu
mailbox_preferred: lindner@boombox.micro.umn.edu
office_address: 152 SHEP LAB
: Minneapolis, MN 55455
office_phone: +1 612-606-8123
title: Tu Jr Applic Prog
userid: lindner
x400_address: /I=M/G=Paul/S=Lindner-1/OU=mail/O=tc/PRMD=umn.edu/ADMD= /C=us/
-------------------
```

A list of known CSO servers is available at ftp://casbah.acns.nwu.edu/pub/ph/admin/helptext.

The World Wide Web

Many directory servers are available through the World Wide Web (WWW), including gateways to WHOIS and X.500. In addition, WWW can access any directory service available on Gopher. Individual sites such as CERN also have their directory servers in WWW. Unfortunately, finding items in WWW is difficult, and no central listing of directory servers in WWW seems to be available.

To see the CERN directory server in WWW, point your WWW client, such as Mosaic or Lynx, to http://info.cern.ch/. Select the item called *phone numbers, offices and e-mail addresses.* Then find the search command in your client—in Lynx, the command is s or /—and enter the person's name. WWW returns a list of matching entries.

The Internet has several public access WWW clients available (see Table 21.3). These clients support different user interfaces, so if you do not like one interface, try another. The login ID for all clients is www except for Arizona, where it is uainfo with password uainfo.

Table 21.3. WWW clients available through Telnet.

Site	Address
Budapest, Hungary	fserv.kfki.hu
FUNET, Finland	info.funet.fi
Hebrew University of Jerusalem	vms.huji.ac.il
Indiana University	www.law.indiana.edu
Slovakia Academy of Science	sun.uakom.sk
University of Arizona	lanka.ccit.arizona.edu
University of Kansas	ukanaix.cc.ukans.edu

The AT&T 800 directory can be found on the Web at http://att.net/dir800 for browsing. In addition, there is a search index at http://harvest.cs.colorado.edu/brokers/800/query.html.

Finally, there is a service called Four11 (named after the directory service phone number). Four11 contains over a half million e-mail addresses and can find people anywhere in the world. Four11 offers some commercial databases; searching the e-mail directory is free. To set up an account, connect to http://www.four11.com/.

WAIS

Some directories are in WAIS format (see Table 21.4). In these directories, you can use a WAIS client, such as swais, xwais, or waissearch. In particular, the WAIS database's Usenet addresses contain the e-mail address of anyone who has posted to Usenet recently. This resource is useful if you know someone who regularly posts to Usenet, but you cannot remember his or her address. You also can find WAIS in some Gopher servers.

Table 21.4. Addresses in WAIS databases.

Site	WAIS Database
FidoNet (BBS) SysOps	fidonet-nodelist
Internet Managers as of 1990	internet-phonebook
Monash University, Australia	monashuni-phonedir
San Diego State University	SDSU_PhoneBook
San Francisco State University	sfsu-phones
University of Economics and Business Administration, Vienna	wu-wein-phonebk
University of North Carolina	UNC_Student_phone UNC_Staff_phone
U.S. Army Corps of Engineers	usace-spk-phonebook
U.S. Congress	US-Congress-Phone-FAX
Usenet posters	usenet-addresses

College E-Mail Addresses

If you are looking for someone at a college, you can consult a document called *College E-Mail Addresses* about the e-mail address formats at universities. This document lists the formats of e-mail addresses for dozens of universities and also offers tips on site-specific ways to find an e-mail address. This document is posted regularly on the newsgroup soc.college and also can be found at one of the following sites:

```
ftp://ftp.qucis.queensu.ca/pub/dalamb/college-email/faq*.text
ftp://rtfm.mit.edu/pub/usenet/soc.college/College_Email_Addresses.
```

Custom Clients

Many sites have their own custom directory service clients, as shown in Table 21.5. Each client has its own user interface and capabilities. Some clients are quite good and other clients are not. The major differences are in ease of use and reliability.

Table 21.5. Custom clients available through Telnet.

Site	Address	User ID/Port Number
DDN Info. Center	nic.ddn.mil	whois
InterNIC	rs.internic.net	whois
OCEAN Info. Center	delocn.udel.edu	INFO
Ohio State University	osu.edu	
University of Colorado	directory.colorado.edu	853
University of Maryland	info.umd.edu	954
University of Pennsylvania	nisc.upenn.edu	whois

Serverless Clients

As mentioned earlier, many sites have a server with outdated information or no server at all. This section describes a few methods for finding people that may work on these sites.

If you know the Internet address of a major machine at the site of the person you want to find, you can try the crude but sometimes effective `finger` method. You can try the command `finger` *lastname@address* or `finger` *firstname@address*. Suppose that you are looking for me and you know that the University of Texas at Dallas has a machine with the address `utdallas.edu`. You could try the command `finger billy@utdallas.edu` or `finger barron@utdallas.edu`.

Mike Schwartz of the University of Colorado knew about the `finger` method and a few other ways to find people using crude tools. He created a program called NetFind that combines these tools with data he gathered on Internet address and site names. NetFind is a helpful tool for finding someone on the Internet; try this program if other methods fail.

Some systems have NetFind directly installed. On these systems, use the NetFind command: `netfind` *name key key*. The *name* is the first name, last name, or user ID of the person you want to find. Any number of *keys* can follow the name. Each *key* describes where the person works (the name of the organization, city, state, country, or department). In the following example, you search for Billy Barron, assuming that he works at a university in Denton for an academic computing department:

```
%netfind barron denton university academic

[lots of detailed information skipped]

SUMMARY:
- "barron" is currently logged in. Among the machines searched,
the machine from which this user has been logged in the longest is
```

```
sol.acs.unt.edu, since Nov 21 18:05:41.
- The most promising email address for "barron"
based on the above search is
billy@sol.acs.unt.edu.
```

Sometimes, NetFind's summary is wrong, but the correct address turns up in the detailed information (not shown in the preceding listing). If the suggested address does not work, pay attention to the details and see if you can find the answer there. The developer is updating NetFind regularly. Every version is smarter and better than the preceding version at finding addresses.

In the preceding example, you started with an invalid assumption that used to be true. I haven't worked for UNT in Denton, Texas, for quite a while. However, the e-mail address still works in this case. As a favor, the University of North Texas (UNT) forwards my e-mail to my correct address at UTD. As a general rule, do not count on someone's e-mail being forwarded to their new location (even though forwarding does occasionally work).

A gateway between Gopher and NetFind exists on a variety of gopher servers. One is University of Minnesota (`gopher://mudhoney.micro.umn.edu:4320/1netfind%20`) and another is in Czechoslovakia (`gopher://gopher.vslib.cz:4320/1netfind%20`). You can find NetFind on the server in the Worldwide Connections/Searchable Internet Resources/NetFind menu. The format for doing the search in Gopher is the same as with the native NetFind client, except that you leave out the word *netfind*.

If you do not have access to NetFind through Gopher and do not have a local client, many sites around the Internet provide a public NetFind client (see Table 21.6). Because all the NetFind public clients work from the same data and give the same results, connect to the client closest to you regardless of where you are searching.

Table 21.6. NetFind clients available through Telnet (use `netfind` as the user ID).

Site	*Address*
AARNET, Australia	`archie.au`
California State University	`eis.calstate.edu`
Chile	`malloco.irg.puc.cl`
France	`netfind.fnet.fr`
Imperial College, UK	`monolith.cc.ic.ac.uk`
InterNIC, USA	`ds.internic.net`
Korea NIC	`nic.nm.kr`
McGill University, Canada	`netfind.ee.mcgill.ca`

continues

Table 21.6. continued

Site	Address
Poland	netfind.icm.edu.pl
San Jose State University, USA	netfind.sjsu.edu
TECHNET, Singapore	lincoln.technet.sg
Slovak Academy of Science	nic.uakom.sk
University of Alabama, Birmingham, USA	redmont.cis.uab.edu
University of Colorado, USA	bruno.cs.colorado.edu
University of Minnesota, USA	mudhoney.micro.umn.edu
Venezuela	dino.conicit.ve

Merit Network NetMail Database

If you know the user ID of the person you want to find but have no idea of the nodename, you can try the Merit Network NetMail Database. To use the database, Telnet to hermes.merit.edu and enter **netmailsites** at the Which Host? prompt.

```
****  Merit Net Mail Sites Database  ****

At the prompt, enter the name or partial name of an institution,
place, or computer. Type HELP for assistance.

You may issue up to three queries.

Press <Return> to stop, 3 remaining queries.
Enter the name of the site -> utdallas

There are 3 sites found for UTDALLAS

Internet Sites:
HALFWAY.UTDALLAS.EDU
UTDALLAS.EDU


Bitnet Sites:
UTDALLAS                    University of Texas Dallas Academic
Computer Ctr

Type HELP ADDRESS for information on how to use a mail site name.
```

Hytelnet

Hytelnet is a hypertext program that contains Telnet sites. Among other things, Hytelnet contains the Telnet addresses of all known directory service clients available publicly through Telnet. Although this chapter lists the currently available public clients, new clients will have appeared by the time you read this book. You can find these clients in the Hytelnet program. You can acquire Hytelnet at `ftp://ftp.usask.ca/pub/hytelnet`. Look at the README file to see what files you need to download for your computer. You also can access Hytelnet by using the Washington & Lee University Gopher server (`gopher://liberty.uc.wlu.edu:70/11/internet/hytelnet`). Hytelnet is described in more detail in Chapter 29, "Opening Doors with Hytelnet."

Methods of Last Resort

This section discusses the few methods left for trying to find a person on the Internet. Use these methods only if other methods have failed, including trying to call the person directly on the telephone. With the following methods, you usually have to get a third party involved— and this person may not get paid to provide such a service.

First, ask your own local Internet support person for help. These people often know about finding Internet users in new ways that may have come along since this book was published.

A Usenet newsgroup called `soc.net-people` exists for trying to find other people. You can try posting to this newsgroup (a long shot but it may pay off).

On Internet Relay Chat (IRC), people commonly ask questions looking for someone else on the Internet. If you try this method, you probably should ask only on public channels or ask someone with a high probability of knowing, such as a coworker at the same site.

If you know the nodename of a computer at the same location, try sending mail to the postmaster account on that node. For example, suppose that you are trying to reach someone at the computer science department of the University of Texas at Austin. You know the nodename `cs.utexas.edu` is at that location. Therefore, you try the address `postmaster@cs.utexas.edu`. A related trick: if you happen to know the e-mail address of a computer support person at the site, try asking him or her. In either case, you should phrase the letter as politely as possible. A friendly tone increases the likelihood of a response and the probability that the person did a thorough search before responding.

If you have friends at the same site as the person you are trying to reach, try them also. Avoid asking people randomly at the remote site. To understand, imagine that someone you did not know called you at home and asked you for the phone number of someone else you did not know.

If you have the postal mail address of the person, try sending an old-fashioned letter asking for his or her e-mail address. You may want to ask for a phone number too, so that you can reach the person quicker.

If none of the preceding methods work, you unfortunately may have to give up your search.

FTP: Fetching Files from Everywhere

22

by Kevin D. Barron

File Transfer Protocol (FTP) is one of the most venerable methods of transferring files from one computer to another. The earliest specification for FTP dates from April 1971. It is still the workhorse of the Internet and will remain so for many years. Two crucial aspects of FTP make it particularly useful: its capability to transfer files between computers of completely dissimilar types and its provision for public file sharing.

This chapter elaborates on the procedures for using FTP, beginning with some simple examples. The chapter also deals with finding sources: How do you find that super-slick software you heard was available through FTP? You also learn about Mac and PC use of FTP, including some tools for those platforms. Also described are additional tools, ranging from X Window interfaces to FTP using e-mail. The "Advanced Use" section, later in this chapter, explores the uses of automated login and wildcards.

Basic Operation

In essence, there are two ways of using FTP. You can use it to transfer files from machine to machine or to access public files that exist on anonymous FTP servers. This latter use is the most common, because there are innumerable anonymous servers providing everything from aardvark fonts to computer operating systems to ZOO files.

Publicly accessible FTP servers are called *anonymous servers* because of the procedure used to connect to them. Traditionally, the account logged on to a server was anonymous; currently, it is common to use the FTP account. Similarly, the traditional password was *guest*, but most current systems request the use of your e-mail address as the password. For example, if you want to connect to a machine called amber.fubar.com, you enter the following:

```
ftp amber.fubar.com
```

If your system can connect to that machine, you see something similar to the following:

```
Connected to amber.fubar.com.
220 amber ftp server (SunOS 4.1) ready.
Name (amber:kdb): ftp
331 Guest login ok, send ident as password.
Password:
230 Guest login ok, access restrictions apply.
ftp>
```

The first line confirms the connection to the desired machine. The line beginning with 220 indicates that the FTP server process is ready (in this case, running under SunOS 4.1). Next, the system prompts for a Name matching your current username on the FTP machine. If you had an account with that name, you could press Return. In this example, ftp is entered as the username, which is followed by the request to send ident (e-mail address) as password. The password is not echoed back, so you cannot see any typing mistakes you make. However, in most cases, you enter only your username followed by @ (most FTP servers can determine your e-mail address anyway).

The final response (the line beginning with 230) indicates that you are logged in and can execute all available commands. To get a list of those commands, enter a ?. To get information on a given command, enter ? followed by the command, as in this example:

```
ftp> ? dir
dir            list contents of remote directory
```

The dir command is the equivalent of the UNIX ls -l (or the DOS DIR command). Note that the directory being listed is referred to as the *remote directory*. The server's side is always considered the remote; the machine on which you originate the FTP process is known as *local*. The concept of local versus remote is important because it underlies many of the FTP commands and procedures. For example, when you want to change directories on the remote machine, use the cd command. However, to change directories on the local machine, use the lcd (local cd) command.

Another concept important in FTP is the client-server model. When you engage FTP, you are actually running the FTP client on your machine. The client intercepts commands and interprets them, passing on the appropriate requests to the server. One of the reasons it is important to keep this in mind is that not all servers have the same commands available. Thus, the remotehelp command is useful for listing the commands supported by the remote server.

Continuing with the example session, the next step is to obtain a directory listing to see what files and directories are available. As noted, you obtain this listing with the dir command:

```
ftp> dir
200 PORT command successful.
150 ASCII data connection for /bin/ls (193.131.225.1,3247) (0 bytes). total 5
drwxr-xr-x  2 root  system         512 Nov 29  1994 bin
drwxr-xr-x  2 root  system         512 Sep  8  1994 dev
drwxr-xr-x  2 root  system         512 Nov 29  1994 etc
drwxrwxr-x 24 ftp   system        1024 Dec 19 00:18 pub
drwxr-xr-x  3 root  system         512 Nov 29  1994 usr
226 ASCII Transfer complete.
436 bytes received in  0.047 seconds (9.1 Kbytes/s)
```

The dir command produced a listing typical of many servers. The bin, dev, etc, and usr directories are of little interest because they contain only system files to enable FTP to operate normally.

As is usually the case, the pub directory is the one you want. If you don't see a pub directory, chances are the server has put you there automatically. To change to the pub directory, use the cd command:

```
ftp> cd pub
250 CWD command successful.
ftp> dir
200 PORT command successful.
150 ASCII data connection for /bin/ls (193.131.225.1,3248) (0 bytes).
total 18
-rw-rw-r--   1 ftp    daemon        15248 Jan 14 19:23 LS-lR.Z
-rw-rw-r--   1 ftp    daemon         5323 Dec  9  9:18 README
drwxrwxr-x   2 ftp    staff           512 Feb 17  1995 axel
-rw-rw-rw-   1 ftp    daemon        71258 Jan  6  1995 donen.ps
drwxr-xr-x   9 ftp    daemon          512 Sep  1  1994 mailers
-rw-rw-rw-   1 ftp    daemon         3443 Dec 19 00:18 netrc
-rw-rw-r--   1 ftp    daemon       319616 Oct 27 18:21 superbridge.sea
-rwxr-xr-x   1 ftp    daemon        19272 Oct 21  1994 quest.hqx
-rw-r-r--    1 ftp    daemon        28425 Nov  9  1994 vxw
226 ASCII Transfer complete.
3092 bytes received in 0.55 seconds (5.5 Kbytes/s)
```

The format you receive back from the dir command depends on the system to which you're connected. In this example, the system is a UNIX machine running SunOS, so you see the equivalent of an ls -lga command (see the discussion of file listings in Appendix C of this book).

Assume that you want the README file: download it by typing **get README**. A file named README is placed in the directory you were in when you started the FTP program. If you want to use another name for the file to avoid overwriting an existing README file, specify the name as follows:

```
get README amber.readme
```

This get command results in the README file being copied to your local host with the name amber.readme.

Transfer Mode

The default transfer mode is ASCII, meaning that the transfer is treated as text (IBM mainframers take heart—ASCII should really be called *text* because it gets translated to EBCDIC automatically in the mainframe world). This means that the file is readable on the local host because it is translated according to the local requirement. However, the translation is beneficial only with text files; it can make other files unusable.

Binary files, such as executable programs, require the binary transfer mode. This mode is also referred to as *image* because it copies an exact image of the original. Of course, even though the copied program is an exact duplicate, it does not change the fact that a binary program can run only on the machine for which it is compiled. In other words, a PC binary runs only on a PC, regardless of where it is transferred by FTP. However, you can transfer that PC binary using a machine of a completely different type, transfer the file to a PC, and the file will run.

The question, then, is how to determine which transfer mode to use for a given file? One method uses file extensions, or suffixes, to discern the file type. (Table 22.1 lists some common file types and their transfer modes.) Unfortunately, only some files are flagged by a telling extension. Mostly, using file extensions is a question of educated guesswork. If a file is not marked by one of the extensions listed in Table 22.1 and is not executable (that is, a dir listing of the file shows no x—see Appendix C), chances are it can be transferred in ASCII mode. On the other hand, if you know that the remote and local hosts are identical, you can use binary mode for both text and data files. Because you have a 50/50 chance of being right, transfer the file in binary mode and then check it on the local machine. NonASCII machines are becoming less common, so the translation of ASCII mode often is not required.

Table 22.1. File types, extensions, and transfer mode.

File Type	Extension	Transfer Mode
Text	N/A	ASCII
Shell archive	.SHAR	ASCII
uuencoded	.UUE	ASCII
Binhex	.HQX	ASCII
PostScript	.PS	ASCII
Tar file	.TAR	Binary
Compressed	.Z .ZIP .SIT .ZOO	Binary
Executable	.EXE .COM	Binary

To switch to binary mode, type **binary**. Following is an example of downloading the ls-1R.Z file from the server:

```
ftp> binary
200 Type set to I.
ftp> get LS-1R.Z
200 PORT command successful.
150 Binary data connection for LS-1R.Z (193.131.225.1,3924) (15248 bytes).
226 Binary Transfer complete.
```

```
local: LS-1R.Z remote: LS-1R.Z
15248 bytes received in 0.0044 seconds (3.4e+03 Kbytes/s)
ftp>
```

The message, Type set to I, shows the server's response: the transfer type has been set to Image (a synonym for binary mode). To return to ASCII mode, type **ascii**. The server responds with Type set to A (or something similar).

When you finish your session, type **bye** or **quit** to close your connection to the server. The server politely responds with Goodbye, and you are returned to your system prompt.

Netiquette

Anonymous FTP servers are usually running as "public services" on machines that have other work to do. Common courtesy—*netiquette*, as it is referred to on the Net—requires that you respect those servers that request usage to be restricted to off-hours (usually outside of 8 A.M. to 6 P.M. local time). Many larger servers announce that service is available 24 hours a day. However, massive downloads that *can* be done during off-hours *should* be done at those hours if possible. Even machines that are dedicated servers can simultaneously serve only a finite number of FTP sessions; file transfers that take a long time preclude others from making use of the system.

Another aspect of netiquette involves the login process. Although many implementations of the FTP server do not enforce the use of your e-mail address as the password, you should get in the habit of supplying the address nonetheless (as mentioned earlier in this chapter, your username followed by an @ will suffice). Because logging your user ID and site is becoming standard procedure, it is not a question of losing anonymity. Rather, the question concerns courtesy. As Jon Granrose repeatedly pointed out in his anonymous FTP listings, FTP is a privilege, not a right.

Essential Commands

The supported FTP commands vary somewhat from one type of server to another, but a core group of essential commands exists and is supported by almost all FTP programs. The best way to determine whether a command is supported is to try it. If it fails, obtain a listing of commands by issuing the help command. This command (which usually has ? as a synonym) lists the commands the local client supports. Once connected to a server, you can type **remotehelp** to obtain a listing of the supported commands on the server.

For most purposes, however, the list in Table 22.2 (in which curly braces { } indicate optional arguments) should be all you require.

Table 22.2. A list of essential FTP commands.

FTP Command	*Description*
account {*info*}	Supplies additional accounting information where required on certain hosts. If you do not include *info* with the account command, the system prompts for it.
ascii	Changes the transfer mode to ASCII. This is the default mode. *See also* binary.
bell	Sounds a bell after completion of file transfer in either direction.
binary	Changes transfer mode to binary. This is required for transferring an executable, image, or any other nonASCII file (unless the file has been converted to ASCII using uuencode, binhex, or some similar program). *See also* ascii.
bye	Terminates the FTP session. The bye command logs you off the remote host and closes the connection, returning you to your local host prompt. The synonym is quit.
cd *remote-directory*{/*remote-directory*}	Changes the (current) working directory on the remote host to *remote-directory*. Most FTP servers support changes of more than one level (for example, cd pub/docs/goodstuff). *See* the lcd command to change directories on your local host.
cdup or cd ..	Changes the working directory to the directory above the current directory. Note that cd .. is not supported by all servers.
close	Closes out the remote host connection but stays within the FTP client.
delete *remote-file*	Deletes the named file on the remote host (if you have write permission on it). *See also* mdelete.
dir {*remote-directory*} {*local-file*}	Provides a detailed listing of the current working directory on the remote host. If *remote-directory* is specified, the listing is of

continues

Table 22.2. continued

FTP Command	Description
	that directory. In addition, if `local-file` is specified, the directory listing is downloaded to that file. To save the contents of the current working directory in a file, specify the `remote-directory` as . (does not work on all servers). *See also* `ls` and `mdir`.
get `remote-file` {`local-file`}	Transfers the file `remote-file` from the remote host. The file is stored on the local host with the same name, unless you specify `local-file`. *See also* `mget` and `put`.
hash	Turns on the hash mark (#) indicator to provide visual verification of data transfer. A hash mark (or pound sign) is printed for each block of data transferred. The hash mark is off by default because it is only useful for debugging. To turn it back off, enter the `hash` command again.
help {`command`}	Provides a summary list of available commands on your client. To get brief information on a specific command, type **help command**. *See also* `remotehelp`.
lcd {`directory`}	Changes directories on the local host. Without specifying a directory, you are placed in your home directory; otherwise you are placed in the specified directory (for the duration of your FTP session). This is particularly useful when you don't want to download into the directory in which you started the FTP session.
ls {`remote-directory`} {`local-file`}	Provides a short listing of the current working directory on the remote host. If `remote-directory` is specified, the listing is of that directory. In addition, if `local-file` is specified, the directory listing is downloaded to that file. To save the contents of the current working directory in a file, specify the `remote-directory` as . (does not work on all servers). *See also* `dir` and `mdir`.

FTP Command	Description
`mdelete {remote-files ...}`	Deletes multiple files on the remote host (if you have the appropriate permissions). You can follow the `mdelete` command with each individual filename, or you can use wildcard characters (* or ?) *See also* `delete` and `prompt`.
`mdir remote-directory {local-file}`	Provides a detailed listing of the specified directories on the remote host. If *remote-directory* is specified with wildcard characters (* or ?), directory name expansion takes place on the server. In addition, if *local-file* is specified, the directory listings are saved to that file. *See also* `ls` and `dir`.
`mget remote-files ...`	Downloads multiple files from the remote host to your local host. The remote filenames can be listed individually, separated by a space, or with wildcard characters (* and ?). *See also* `get`, `mput`, and `prompt`.
`mkdir directory-name`	Creates a directory named *directory-name* on the remote host (if you have write permission). *See also* `rmdir`.
`mput remote-files ...`	Uploads multiple files from the remote host to your local host. The remote filenames can be listed individually, separated by a space, or with wildcard characters (* and ?). *See also* `get`, `mget`, and `prompt`.
`open host-name {port}`	Attempts to open an FTP connection to the named host. An optional *port* number can be specified.
`prompt`	Asks for confirmation before transferring using `mget` or `mput`. Toggles off/on; on by default. Prompting is particularly useful when using `mget` with wildcards to transfer a single file.
`put local-file {remote-file}`	Transfers the file *local-file* to the remote host. The file is stored on the remote host with the same name—unless you specify *remote-file*. *See also* `get` and `mput`.

continues

Table 22.2. continued

FTP Command	Description
pwd	Prints the current working directory of the remote host.
quit	Closes any open connection and exits from FTP. The synonym is bye.
remotehelp {command}	Provides a summary of supported commands on the server. To get brief information on a specific server command, type **remotehelp command**. *See also* help.
rmdir directory-name	Removes a directory named directory-name from the remote host (if you have write permission). *See also* mkdir.
user {username}	Enables you to specify the user to log in as. This command is mostly used when you make a mistake entering the username. You can simply retype it—rather than closing the connection and starting over.

Common Problems

The following error message captures what is probably the most common problem when trying to FTP to a site:

```
unknown host
```

Often enough, the reason for this error is the mistyping of the host address. Check the spelling of the hostname and try again. If you still get an error message and you have access to the ping command, you can verify the existence and accessibility of a host by typing this command:

```
ping -s {hostname} 1 1
```

This command sends the named host one byte in one packet. The purpose here is twofold: the command determines whether your host is a valid hostname, and the procedure demonstrates whether the site is reachable from your host. If so, you will have a numeric address to try:

```
amber ~ > ping -s cerf.net 1 1
PING cerf.net: 1 data bytes
9 bytes from nic.cerf.net (192.102.249.3): icmp_seq=0.
----nic.cerf.net PING Statistics----
1 packets transmitted, 1 packets received, 0% packet loss
```

The important thing to note is that the numeric address is given (in this example, the numeric address is 192.102.249.3), which can be used in place of the full site name (in this example, nic.cerf.net). If your FTP client does not have access to a nameserver, using the numeric address is often necessary.

Another problem arises because not all sites accept anonymous FTP connections. Just because a site has an FTP server does not mean that anonymous FTP service is enabled. In fact, most UNIX machines are shipped with a functional FTP server. However, as shipped, the server only enables users listed in the system password file to access their own accounts.

Finally, not all anonymous FTP sites accept *ftp* as the username. Although ftp is becoming as common as anonymous for the login, some servers do not accept it. Make sure that you try the anonymous login before flaming the administrator of a site.

Finding Sites

If you know where to find what you are looking for, you can connect to that site. But how do you find the name of an appropriate site—or worse, the name of a program or file? The complete answer is beyond the scope of this chapter. However, several approaches fall within the realm of FTP.

The usual method to locate files in the FTP domain is the Archie program (discussed in Chapter 24, "Archie: An Archive of Archives"). You should use Archie, but if you find it is impractical for your site, don't despair. Before Archie existed, there were lists of FTP sites that briefly described what collections those sites maintained.

Probably the most comprehensive list was maintained by Jon Granrose at pilot.njin.net. Although very dated, this file is still somewhat useful because it can provide a starting point for searching for general archive sites (for example, mac, X11, and TeX). The file is called ftp-list and can be obtained from any of the following sites:

```
ftp.gsfc.nasa.gov:/pub/ftp-list
funet.fi:/netinfo/ftp-list
nic.cerf.net:/pub/doc/ftp.list.Z
```

Jon Granrose apparently last updated the list in December 1991.

> **NOTE**
>
> Because IP numbers tend to change more frequently than host names, it is prudent to
> try the names rather than the numbers listed. Given the date on this list, however, even
> the host names are likely to be out of date.

More recently, the list was updated by Tom Czarnik. Using a slightly different format, Czarnik
compiled a substantial list. However, the last version he edited seems to be from April 1993.
The list is currently maintained by Perry Rovers. It can be found at the following sites:

```
oak.oakland.edu:/pub/msdos/info/ftp-list.zip
garbo.uwasa.fi:/pc/doc-net/ftp-list.zip
```

The list also can be obtained from the mail-server at MIT. Send mail to `mail-server@rtfm.mit.edu` with no subject line; for the body of the message, enter this text:

```
send usenet/news.answers/ftp-list/faq
```

When using these listings, remember that they are dated. You can obtain more current information by using the Archie services. If Archie is not available, however, the `ftp-list` can provide a useful starting point for your search.

Mac/PC Usage

If you use a microcomputer (a Mac or a PC) directly connected to the Internet, you can use
FTP to transfer files directly to and from your desktop. A good example is Fetch, a program for
the Mac that not only downloads programs with a few clicks of a mouse button, it also automatically unbinhexes binaries on the fly! The end result is usually a program that is ready to
run or a self-extracting archive (with an `.SEA` extension) that you can double-click to start. As
with all the programs mentioned in this chapter, consult Archie to find the latest version and
nearest source.

Although no single program is available for the PC that is the exact equivalent of Fetch, there
are some very good packages. One of these is the NCSA Telnet package, which includes an
FTP utility. Several suites of TCP/IP software, such as Chameleon or Internet in a Box, contain useful FTP programs.

When transferring files to and from a microcomputer, it is important to remember which is the client and which is the server. With an application such as Fetch, the Mac acts as a client connecting to an FTP server. When you get a file in this case, you are transferring it *from* the server *to* your Mac.

On the other hand, when using the FTP function of NCSA Telnet, you are actually running the FTP client on the host to which you connected, and your Mac (or PC) becomes the server. When you get a file in this case, you are getting it *from* your Mac, not the host to which you connected. The logic seems to be reversed, unless you keep in mind that your microcomputer is the server.

CAUTION

By default, the FTP server is enabled while you are running NCSA Telnet. This potentially allows anyone on the Internet to access and download the files on your microcomputer! To avoid this problem, ensure that you have set up an NCSA Telnet password file.

If your microcomputer is not directly connected to the Internet, you can still download software from FTP servers using a two-step process. First, FTP the file from the remote server to a local host. Then use traditional file transfer such as ZModem or Kermit to download from the local host to your PC.

Some of the main sites for Mac or PC archives are listed in Table 22.3. Because of the popularity of these sites, they are commonly not accessible at peak hours. Fortunately, popular sites are mirrored at other sites, so it is often more convenient to use a mirror site.

Table 22.3. Primary FTP sites for Mac and DOS archives.

Site	Specialty	Mirrored By
archive.umich.edu	Mac, DOS	nic.switch.edu, archie.au
ftp.apple.com	Mac	ftp.lu.se
ftp.funet.fi	DOS	ftp.lth.se
ftp.microsoft.com	DOS	ftp.uni-kl.de
microlib.cc.utexas.edu	Mac, DOS	bongo.cc.utexas.edu
oak.oakland.edu	DOS	archie.au
omnigate.clarkson.edu	DOS	utsun.s.u-tokyo.ac.jp
plains.nodak.edu	DOS	archive.umich.edu
sumex-aim.stanford.edu	Mac	wuarchive.wustl.edu

Tools

As mentioned earlier in this chapter, Fetch is an extremely useful Mac interface to FTP. Similarly, other programs facilitate FTP usage on other platforms. For example, users of OpenWindows can obtain the ftptool distribution. Table 22.4 shows some other FTP tools.

Table 22.4. Examples of various FTP resources.

Tool	OS	Type
minuet	DOS	Client
soss	DOS	Server
trumpet	DOS	Client
wftpd	DOS/Windows	Server
NCSA_Telnet	DOS, Mac	Client/server
fetch	Mac	Client
xferit	Mac	Client
anarchie	Mac	Client
ftptool	UNIX	Client
moxftp	UNIX	Client
ncftp	UNIX	Client
wuarchive-ftpd	UNIX	Server
xgetftp	UNIX	Client

The ftptool utility was written as shareware by Mike Sullivan at Sun Microsystems. It has features that provide a significant advantage over the standard UNIX FTP client. Batch mode, for example, provides the capability to select items in various directories and transfer them all at once. The advantage is that you don't have to wait for one file to transfer before moving to another directory. And because ftptool is a windowed application, you can iconify it or move to another window while the batch transfer takes place.

In addition to enabling you to make better use of your time, ftptool also makes intelligent use of computer resources. Specifically, you can use a cache file to store remote directories rather than retrieve them repeatedly; users of the .netrc file will be glad to know that ftptool can read the .netrc (for more details on .netrc, see "Advanced Use," later in this chapter).

For those who prefer (or require) a more generic X-client, there is the moxftp distribution. This name comes from the three versions of the client: mftp (Motif), oftp (OpenWin), and xftp (Athena). Most versions of UNIX can run at least one of these versions.

For the command-line diehard, `ncftp` provides a much nicer interface than the standard FTP client. The `ncftp` client features the following :

- No more typing **anonymous** plus your e-mail address every time you want to FTP anonymously. You don't have to have the site in your `.netrc` file.
- No more typing complete site names. Sites in your `.netrc` can be abbreviated. Type **o wuar** to call wuarchive.wustl.edu.
- Use your pager (such as `more`) to read remote files (and also compressed files).
- Use your pager to view remote directory listings.
- Transfers feature a progress meter.
- You can keep a log of your actions. See what the path was of that file you downloaded yesterday so that you don't have to look for it today.
- Comes with a built-in mini-`nslookup`.
- The `ls` command is `ls -CF`. Some FTP `ls` commands were identical to the `dir` command, but `ls` is more flexible, so that you can do things like this:

```
ls -flags directory
```

- You can use the `redial` command for a remote host until you connect.
- Don't feel like typing a long filename? Use a wildcard in single-file commands such as `get` and `page`.
- Supports colon mode so that you can type **ncftp cse.unl.edu:/pub/foo**, to copy `foo` into your current directory.
- You can redisplay the last directory listing without getting it across the network.
- Detects when new mail arrives.
- `ncftp` is quieter by default; who cares if the `PORT` command was successful—if you do, turn verbose on. :-)

FTP by Mail

If you do not have direct access to the Internet but can send e-mail, you can still make use of FTP. Several services are available that provide an e-mail interface to FTP. One such service, BITftp, is for users of Bitnet only (other users are rejected). To obtain a help file, send mail to `bitftp@pucc.bitnet` with `help` as the one-line message.

Another useful example is FTPmail, which is located at Digital Equipment Corp (DEC) in Palo Alto, California. FTPmail was written by Paul Vixie at DEC, and is in use at the following sites:

```
ftpmail@decwrl.dec.com
ftpmail@src.doc.ic.ac.uk
ftpmail@cs.uow.edu.au
ftpmail@grasp1.univ-lyon1.fr
ftpmail@ftp.uni-stuttgart.de
```

As with BITftp, you can get information from these servers by sending the help message to `ftpmail@gatekeeper.dec.com`. (Table 22.5 contains examples from that help file.)

Table 22.5. Examples of FTPmail requests.

Desired Function	*Body of Mail Message*

Connect to default server (normally `gatekeeper.dec.com`) and obtain a root directory listing	`connect`
	`ls`
	`quit`

Connect to default server and obtain the README.FTP file	`connect`
	`get README.ftp`
	`quit`

Connect to default server and get the gnuemacs sources	`connect`
	`binary`
	`uuencode`
	`chdir /pu/GNU`
	`get emacs-18.58.tar.Z`
	`quit`

Connect to `ftp.uu.net` and obtain a root directory listing	`connect ftp.uu.net`
	`binary`
	`chdir /index/master`
	`get by-name.Z`
	`quit`

To send an FTP request to the mailserver, you use one `connect` command and no more than one `cd` command. The commands are sent in the body of your mail message; the subject line can be blank or used for something like *job requests* (the mailserver returns the same subject line you send).

Unless you specify otherwise, the results of your request are sent back in chunks of 64,000 characters. Note that binary transfers must be preceded by the `binary` command, otherwise an ASCII transfer is attempted. When the binary mode is selected, automatic btoa (binary-to-ASCII) encoding takes place (uuencode can be specified).

Advanced Use

Even though many sophisticated tools simplify the use of FTP, knowledge of some advanced FTP features can make the normal interface preferable in some ways. For example, mget and mput provide a means to transfer multiple files; their nominal syntax is as follows:

```
mget {list of files}
mput {list of files}
```

However, they also can be used in conjunction with wildcards to ease the difficulties associated with long filenames:

```
ftp> mget alt*
mget alt.sex.bestiality.barney.Z?
```

The use of wildcards varies, so remember that the server may have a different syntax than the client. Although the mput command is expanding wildcards on the client side, mget wildcard functionality is based on the server's syntax.

Another useful trick is to use - as the name of the file to be downloaded. For example, if you want to look at a README file, you could type this:

```
get README -
```

This command tells the FTP client to output the received file to standard output (your screen). The only problem with this method is that the entire file is dumped to the screen without pause. On a short file, this may be acceptable if you can scroll back your window buffer, but on longer files it can be cumbersome.

Alternatively, if you are on a UNIX system, you can use the pipe (¦) operator to read a file directly into a pager. That is, when you use get to retrieve a readable file, you can use ¦more as the name of the file you want to "save." For example:

```
get README ¦more
```

This syntax downloads the README file, but rather than saving another README file in your current directory, the command pipes the file to screen using the more program. Of course, if you prefer the less pager, feel free to use that program instead: it's more or less the same. :-)

Lastly, note that although the file is not stored on the local system using these techniques, the entire file nonetheless travels across the network. If you have to look at a long file several times, it is probably best to download it and then view it as you normally would. You can view the file without terminating your FTP session by using the shell escape character(!). An example of this technique follows:

```
get README readme.new
150 ASCII data connection...
1634 bytes received in 0.052 seconds (30 Kbytes/s)
ftp> !more readme.new
```

Once you are finished reading the file, or if you quit out of the more program, you return to the FTP prompt. If you don't take too long reading the file (generally, you have 15 minutes), you can continue your FTP session. If you do take a long time between sending commands to the remote host, the session is terminated.

To simplify the process of logging in to an FTP site, the UNIX client reads a startup file called .netrc in your home directory. The client scans the file for an entry matching the site to which you are currently connected; if one is found, the information is passed to the server. Note that if the .netrc file contains the password token and the file is readable by anyone other than you, the process aborts.

The format of .netrc is as follows:

```
machine    {ftphost}
login      {username}
password   {password}
{optional macro}
```

Here is an alternative format for .netrc:

```
machine {ftphost} login {username} password {password}
{optional macro}
```

The FTP client parses the machine tokens for an entry matching the site to which you are trying to connect. Once it finds an entry, it continues to process the entry until another machine token is reached (or an EOF is encountered). The login and password strings are passed to the server, saving you the trouble of entering them each time. However, you should use the password token only on anonymous sites.

Another convenience offered by the `.netrc` file is its ability to use macros. A practical use of the macro feature is to change the directory; you can also use a macro to `get` a file. For example, the following `.netrc` entry logs the user into the site, changes the directory, and gets a file:

```
machine ftp.cadence.com login anonymous password joe@
macdef init
cd jobs
get joblist
quit
```

The `macdef` command functions the same as in interactive use: it defines a macro. The `init` macro is a special case, however, because it is invoked automatically at login. Therefore, this entry is essentially an automated procedure for downloading the `joblist` file.

Note that the `macdef` function requires a null line to mark the end of the macro. This also applies to the last entry in the `.netrc`—where it is often forgotten.

Another "automagic" function is the built-in compression in the wuarchive server. Compressed files can be automatically uncompressed before downloading. To activate this feature, omit the extension from the compressed file when specifying the `get` command. For example, if the file is called `foo.bar.Z` and you specify **get foo.bar**, the file is uncompressed automatically. This function is not available on the standard servers and is one good argument for installing your own server.

REFERENCE WORKS

CERT, "FTP security notes," FTP at `cert.org:/pub/tech_tips/anonymous_ftp`, June 1993.

_____, "Wuarchive Ftpd Vulnerability," FTP at `cert.org:/pub/cert_advisories/CA-93:06.wuarchive.ftpd.vulnerability`, June 1993.

_____, "AIX FTP Vulnerability," FTP at `cert.org:/pub/cert_advisories/CA-92:09.AIX.anonymous.ftp.vulnerability`, October 1992.

_____, "Ftpd Hole," FTP at `cert.org:/pub/cert_advisories/CA-88:01.ftpd.hole`, January 1988.

Czarnik, Tom, "ftp.list" FTP at `askhp.ask.uni-karlsruhe.de:/pub/info/ftp.list.sites.Z`, April 1993.

December, John, "Internet Tools," FTP at `ftp.rpi.edu:/pub/communications/internet-tools.txt`, December 1993.

Gleason, Mike, "Ncftp Blurb," FTP at `world.std.com:/src/network/ncftp/Blurb`, September 1993.

Granrose, Jon, "ftp-list" FTP at `ftp.gsfc.nasa.gov:/pub/ftp-list`, December 1991.

Lemson, David, "Compression Notes," FTP at `ftp.cso.uiuc.edu:/doc/pcnet/compression`, July 1993.

Postel, J., and J. Reynolds "File Transfer Protocol," RFC 959 FTP at `nic.merit.edu:/documents/rfc/rfc0959.txt`, October 1985.

Rovers, Perry, aftp-list.FAQ, FTP at `oak.oakland.edu:/pub/msdos/info/ftp-list.zip`, January 1994.

Logging in to Other Computers with Telnet and Rlogin

23

by Lay Wah Ooi

Remote login is the ability to use another computer on the Internet or a TCP/IP network as if you were sitting at it. Researchers use remote login to access supercomputers. Libraries use it to check remote online library catalogs. Individuals can even use it to order CDs — compact discs, not Certificates of Deposit. : -)

This chapter talks about Telnet, TN3270, and rlogin. All three of these programs are used to remotely log in to other computers. Each serves a slightly different purpose, although Telnet is the most widely used. Telnet is available on almost any platform in existence. TN3270 is also very common, although it is not always available. The rlogin program is primarily available on UNIX and VMS machines, although it does exist on some other platforms.

Telnet

Telnet is a program that lets you communicate with another machine using the Telnet protocol. Suppose that you are in Texas and you want to run a program on a computer several hundred miles away in Virginia; if your local machine and the remote machine in Virginia are connected to the same network running TCP/IP or on the Internet, and you have an account on the remote machine in Virginia, you can remotely log in to that machine to run your program instead of traveling all the way to Virginia to complete your tasks.

Telnet allows you to log in to a remote machine and execute commands on the remote machine as if you were using the remote machine locally. The syntax of the UNIX version of Telnet is as follows:

```
telnet [host [port]]
```

In this syntax, *host* is the name or IP address of the machine you want to connect to; *port* is the port number of the remote machine. The default port is 23.

If you issue the following command at the UNIX prompt, you can connect to the machine jaring at port 23 in Malaysia:

```
% telnet jaring.my
Trying...
Connected to jaring.my.
Escape character is '^]'.


SunOS UNIX (jaring)

login:
```

If you have a valid user ID on that machine, you can enter your account name at the login prompt now.

Command Mode

If you type only **telnet** and press Enter at the UNIX prompt, you are in the command mode of Telnet:

```
% telnet
telnet>
```

Telnet waits for you to enter a command. All commands can be found in the Telnet help (enter either **help** or **?**). Commands may be abbreviated. The result of the help command is shown in the following listing:

```
close      Close current connection
display    Display operating parameters
mode       Try to enter line-by-line or character-at-a-time mode
open       Connect to a site
quit       Exit Telnet
send       Transmit special characters
set        Set operating parameters
status     Print status information
toggle     Toggle operating parameters
z          Suspend Telnet
!          Shell escape
?          Print help information
```

To get more information on each command, use the following command in command mode:

```
command ?
```

In this syntax, *command* is the actual command name (for example, send, status, and so on).

In addition to getting help from within Telnet in command mode, you can display the UNIX man page for Telnet by issuing the command **man telnet** at the UNIX prompt.

Typing **telnet cs.unt.edu** at the UNIX prompt (normally a % or $) is the same as typing **open cs.unt.edu** in the Telnet command mode:

```
telnet> open cs.unt.edu
Trying...
Connected to ponder.csci.unt.edu.
Escape character is '^]'.


DYNIX(R) V3.1.4   (ponder)

login:
```

The open command opens a connection to the specified machine (in this case, to cs.unt.edu). For some machines, you can abbreviate open as o.

The line Connected to ponder.csci.unt.edu. indicates that you are connected to the machine ponder in the Computer Science department at the University of North Texas. You have probably noticed that the original address cs.unt.edu is different from the "connected to" address ponder.csci.unt.edu. In this case, both addresses refer to the same machine. You can find out more about it by typing **nslookup cs.unt.edu** on most UNIX machines (you will discover that cs.unt.edu is an alias of ponder.csci.unt.edu). Some Telnet clients show you the same address you entered instead of the original name of the alias.

At the login: prompt, type your user ID (the ID for your account on the remote machine). For example, to log in on cs.unt.edu as ooi, I type **ooi**. Then you see the Password: prompt. After entering the password, you are connected to ponder and you see the remote prompt:

```
@Ponder>>
```

You can now use the machine ponder as if you were logged in there locally. After you finish using that machine, enter **logout** or **exit** to log out from the remote machine.

Telnet Ports

As mentioned earlier, the default Telnet port is port 23. If you Telnet to a remote machine without specifying a port, you are connected to port 23, which is the standard port for an interactive login (that is, a login: prompt). However, you can also Telnet to other available ports on the machine if they are set up for something. For example, you can Telnet to port 2034 of camms2.caos.kun.nl to get the periodic table of elements:

```
% telnet camms2.caos.kun.nl 2034
Trying...
Connected to camms2.caos.kun.nl.
Escape character is '^]'.
```

```
(camms2) Ultrix 4.3:
          The Electronic Periodic Table of the Elements
          CAOS/CAMM Center, KUN, Nijmegen, NL. May 1993
                    Commands:  {key} - {action}
a - Abbreviations Table              n - Numbered Table
b - Basic Metric Units               o - (future implement.)
c - Properties of Metals as Conductors  p - Redraw Symbols Table
d - Documentation/ Reference Text    q - (future implement.)
e - Periodic Table (Newlands, 1865)  r - Radii,Ionic w states
f - Periodic Table (Medeleev, 1872)  s - Show element groups
g - Draw Group Labels                t - (future implement.)
h - Move left                        u - Show e-config. on PT
i - Information on specific element  v - Visual Enhancement
j - Move down                        w - (future implement.)
k - Move up                          x - Exit/Quit
l - Move right                       y - (future implement.)
m - Metrix Prefixes                  z - (future implement.)
```

You can get a list of Telnet-accessible Internet sites compiled by Scott Yanoff from `ftp://ftp.csd.uwm.edu/pub/inet.services.txt`. This list has a lot of Internet sites to which you can Telnet for different purposes. In addition, refer to Chapter 29 of this book, "Opening Doors with Hytelnet," which covers Hytelnet, a software package that lists Telnet sites.

Escape Character

What do you do if your screen locks up when you are in a Telnet session? "Turn off the computer!" "No, kick it!" "No, reboot it!"

Sadly, none of these is the correct answer. You can always *escape out* instead of turning off your computer. Escape lets you get to command mode from the Telnet session. When you are in command mode, you can issue a `quit` or `close` command to terminate the Telnet session.

How do you get to command mode by escaping from the Telnet session? The escape character is usually Ctrl+] (sometimes represented as ^]); press and hold the Ctrl key and press the right bracket). When you first start your Telnet session, Telnet reminds you of the escape sequence:

```
% telnet cs.unt.edu
Trying...
Connected to ponder.csci.unt.edu.
Escape character is '^]'.


DYNIX(R) V3.1.4  (ponder)

login:
```

The line `Escape character is '^]'` lists the escape character you want to remember when you are stuck in a Telnet session. Simply press Ctrl+] to return to the command mode with the Telnet prompt:

```
telnet>
```

To quit the session, type **quit** or **close** at the `telnet>` prompt. Likewise, to return to the Telnet session, press Enter or Return (you go back to where you were before you pressed the escape sequence).

Miscellaneous Commands

Telnet has some other useful commands in addition to `quit`, `close`, and `open` that you can use from command mode. The following sections describe a few of these commands.

The *set* Command

Occasionally, you may want to Telnet from one machine to another, and then Telnet from the second machine to another machine. Before you Telnet to the second machine, issue the following command at the `telnet>` prompt:

```
set escape character
```

This command sets the escape character of the second Telnet session to something other than the original ^] escape character. If you don't set the escape character to something else for the second Telnet session, when you press Ctrl+], you return to the command mode of the first Telnet session.

The *status* Command

The status command shows the current status of the Telnet session you are in:

```
telnet> status
Connected to ponder.csci.unt.edu.
Operating in character-at-a-time mode.
Escape character is '^]'.
```

In this example, the Telnet session is currently connected to `ponder.csci.unt.edu`, input mode is character-at-a-time mode (that is, Telnet sends a character at a time to the remote machine as you type), and the escape character is `^]` (Ctrl+]).

The z Command

If your shell supports *job control* (that is, if you can suspend and resume processes), you can use the z command. Typing **z** at the `telnet>` prompt lets you temporarily get out of the Telnet session and back to your local machine. When you "get back to your local machine," you see the prompt you normally do before you start Telnet. Type **fg** to bring the Telnet session back to the foreground.

Of course, these are not the only commands you can use in command mode. I will let you explore the rest. :-)

TN3270

You cannot use Telnet to access an IBM mainframe or compatible machine unless the mainframe has a protocol converter. However, TN3270 is a full-screen, full-duplex 3270 emulation program that lets you access these types of machines. TN3270 is actually a version of Telnet that has been modified to emulate a 3270 terminal. In fact, some TN3270 programs act just like normal Telnet if you do not connect to an IBM mainframe.

If you try to connect to the IBM mainframe `vm.acs.unt.edu` (the University of North Texas VM machine) with Telnet, you get the following response:

```
%telnet vm.acs.unt.edu
Trying...
Connected to vm.acs.unt.edu.
Escape character is '^]'.
Connection closed by foreign host.
%
```

The mainframe refused to bring you to a 3270 mode with Telnet. However, if you use TN3270 to access that same machine, it negotiates nicely into 3270 emulation mode; it's just as if you were using a 3270 terminal connected to the mainframe:

```
%tn3270 vm.acs.unt.edu

VM/XA SP ONLINE
```

```
THE   COMPUTING   CENTER

                    UU      UU    NNN    NN    TTTTTTTTTT
                    UU      UU    NNNN   NN    TTTTTTTTTT
                    UU      UU    NN NN  NN        TT
                    UU      UU    NN  NN NN        TT
                    UUUUUUUUUUU   NN   NNNN        TT
                     UUUUUUUUU    NN    NNN        TT

R E L E A S E   2 . 1



  Fill in your USERID and PASSWORD and press ENTER
  (Your password will not appear when you type it)
  USERID   ===>
  PASSWORD ===>

  COMMAND  ===>
                                              RUNNING   UNTVM1
```

TN3270 uses /etc/map3270 and your terminal type to determine what kind of key mapping it should use when connected to the mainframe. You can edit /etc/map3270 to make the keys work the way you want them to; if you do not have the root password to modify /etc/map3270, you can use mset to modify the key map. For more information, type **man mset** at the UNIX prompt.

By default, you quit a TN3270 session by pressing Ctrl+C and typing **quit** or **close.** Sometimes, however, system administrators want to make TN3270 work as much like Telnet as possible, and change the escape key from Ctrl+C to Telnet's Ctrl+] escape key.

Rlogin

The rlogin program is like Telnet in that it lets you log in to a remote machine from your local machine. Other than that basic similarity, there are many differences between rlogin and Telnet. Rlogin stands for *remote login.*

Rlogin allows you to remotely log in to an equivalent host without entering a user ID or password — if the remote host has the right information in either the /etc/hosts.equiv or .rhosts file. The .rhosts file must be in your account on the remote host; it can be owned by root or by you. The format of .rhosts is as follows:

```
hostname username
```

In this syntax, *hostname* can be your local hostname or the name of the machine you want to remotely log in from. The *username* is the same as your login name on the machine you remotely log in from. A + in either field means anything; for example, the following line in .rhosts means that user abc can remotely log in from any host to the machine without a password:

```
+ abc
```

The following .rhosts line means that anybody from thishost can log in to your account without a password:

```
thishost +
```

You can omit the *username* if it is the same on both hosts. However, both of these examples are very dangerous security holes. In the first example, anybody on the Internet with the user ID abc can log into your account. In the second example, any user on thishost can log in to your account. Therefore, these two examples are not recommended for real-life use.

The /etc/hosts.equiv file is used by the system administrator. Hosts that have the same set of user IDs are included in this file so that rlogin users can switch between hosts without ever specifying their passwords. However, if a host that uses a different set of user IDs is included in that file, a security problem arises: the wrong people may be able to access your account without a password.

> **CAUTION**
>
> If you are a system administrator, please note that some UNIX vendors put a + in the /etc/hosts.equiv file by default. This must be removed immediately.

Examples

This section presents some sample rlogin sessions.

In this first example, I have a .rhosts file in my home directory on ponder.csci.unt.edu. The file contains my local host and login ID, as shown here:

```
metronet.com ooi
```

To rlogin from metronet.com from my account ooi to ponder.csci.unt.edu, I issue the following command:

```
%rlogin ponder.csci.unt.edu
Last login: Mon Jan  2 20:35:55 from feenix.metronet.

                            Welcome to
                  The University of North Texas
                  Department of Computer Science
                            Denton
                         T e x a s

                  -* Sequent Symmetry - S81 *-

        #*******************************************#
        #    For assistance send mail to 'sysadm'   #
        #                   or                       #
        #            call 817-555-2642,3076          #
        #*******************************************#

            Type 'news' for local ponder news items.

        To view these messages again type 'more /etc/motd'

**********************************************************************


My information shows that you are logged in on a vt100.

@Ponder>>
```

If I delete my .rhosts file and try the same rlogin sequence, here is what I get:

```
% rlogin ponder.csci.unt.edu
Password:
```

Because I no longer have a .rhosts file in my account on ponder.csci.unt.edu, I was prompted for a password. If I don't enter the correct password, it throws me back to the login prompt so that I must enter a login ID *and* password. If your login name on the remote host is different than the one on your local host, you can use the rlogin command with the -l option, provided that you have a .rhosts file or an entry in /etc/hosts.equiv on the remote host:

```
rlogin remote-host -l remote-login-id
```

Terminal Settings

Your terminal settings are usually propagated to the remote host when you use `rlogin` to connect to it. These settings include the terminal type, the number of rows, and the number of columns. In fact, if you resize your rlogin window in a GUI environment, the remote host automatically picks that up.

When you use Telnet and TN3270, the terminal settings are fixed by default. If you want to change the terminal settings, you must do it manually when you resize the window or make any other changes.

Escape Character

Can you use Ctrl+] with rlogin like you do in Telnet to escape out of a session? No! Instead, you use ~! to shell out from the remote host back to the local host. The tilde (~) is the escape character and the exclamation point (!) is used to shell out.

```
@Ponder>> ~!
%
```

To get back to the remote host from the shell, type **exit**:

```
% exit
exit
[Returning to remote]

@Ponder>>
```

If you ever get stuck on the remote host during a rlogin session, type ~. (tilde period) to exit from the rlogin session totally:

```
@Ponder>> ~.
Closed connection.
%
```

You can also suspend your rlogin process by typing ~ (tilde) and then pressing Ctrl+Z:

```
@Ponder>> ~^Z

Stopped.
%
```

This sequence brings you back to your local host. Simply type **fg** to return to the foreground rlogin session:

```
% fg
rlogin ponder.csci.unt.edu

@Ponder>>
```

To exit from the remote host, use your usual logout procedure.

Other Platforms for Telnet, TN3270, and Rlogin

Although this chapter focuses on the UNIX versions of the Telnet, TN3270, and rlogin programs (UNIX versions are the most common; many other versions are based on the UNIX source code), Telnet, TN3270, and rlogin programs exist for many other platforms. Some graphical versions that support color exist for GUI-based systems such as Windows and X.

Figure 23.1 shows a Telnet session from Novell's LAN Workplace under Windows. Figure 23.2 is an example of a TN3270 session from the same package. In both cases, notice the pull-down menus at the top. The TN3270 session also has some buttons at the top of the screen; click them to send special TN3270 keys such as PA1 and Clear to the remote host.

FIGURE 23.1.

A sample Telnet session under Windows.

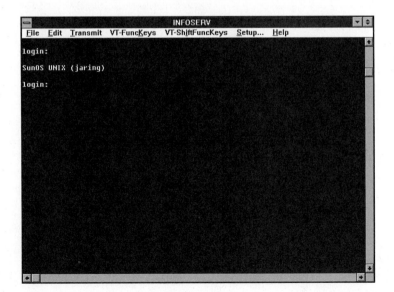

#### Chapter 23

FIGURE 23.2.

A sample TN3270 session under Windows.

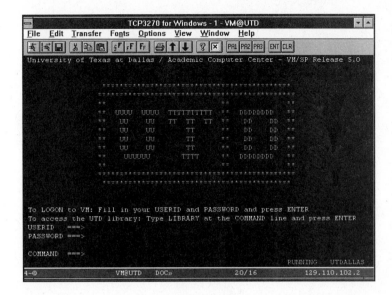

The Telnet, TN3270, and rlogin programs will always remain important to people who own multiple computer accounts. However, we are seeing that there is an increasing trend to make information databases client-server based instead of having users use a remote login program to access the databases. This trend will continue as the Web continues its growth. Even library systems, which have traditionally been accessible with Telnet, are gradually switching to a client-server protocol known as Z39.50.

Archie: An Archive of Archives

24

by Philip Baczewski

Anonymous FTP can be one of the most exciting Internet discoveries you can make. Once you become aware of the enormous amount of information and software available on the Internet, the challenge becomes finding the particular item you need when you need it. This is where Archie comes to the rescue. Says Peter Deutsch, one of the creators of Archie:

> *The Archie service is a collection of resource discovery tools that together provide an electronic directory service for locating information in an Internet environment. Originally created to track the contents of anonymous FTP archive sites, the Archie service is now being expanded to include a variety of other online directories and resource listings.*

Archie's primary use is to locate specific files available with anonymous FTP somewhere on the Internet. However, the latest versions of the Archie software can be applied to information gathering and distributed database tasks beyond anonymous FTP. Archie's anonymous FTP database is not absolutely comprehensive. There is a limit to the number of FTP sites that can be included in Archie's database; however, the database is extensive and indexes many of the most popular anonymous FTP locations.

Archie started as a project of the McGill University School of Computer Science to meet their internal needs for locating anonymous FTP sites. As with many other Internet resources, a good idea, once made public, spreads quickly. This is true of Archie. From its original site at McGill University in Canada, the Archie service has spread throughout the world and is accessible from anywhere on the Internet.

In 1992, Peter Deutsch and Alan Emtage (two of Archie's original creators) created a company named Bunyip Information Systems to develop a commercially supported version of the software. Version 3.0 of Archie was the initial result of this effort.

Why Use Archie?

Archie is not the only way to find files available for anonymous FTP. Often, electronic mailing lists and newsgroups can be good sources of FTP information related to a particular topic or computing system. These forums, however, require that you do one of the following:

- Happen to see a message about a particular piece of software or document that is available through anonymous FTP
- Post an inquiry, hope that someone will reply, and then wait for an answer

Depending on the activity level of a particular mailing list or newsgroup, either of these occurrences is possible. It is obvious, however, that either scenario requires patience and perhaps a little bit of luck.

Archie has the advantage of being automated and immediately or almost immediately accessible; it also enables you to conduct multiple attempts to search for a particular item of interest. As you will see, you can access Archie in a number of ways, and Archie offers several methods of searching for a program or file.

How Is Archie Used?

There are three primary ways to access the Archie service. If you use a computer directly connected to the Internet, it may be possible to run an Archie client program. The client performs the communication tasks with an Archie server to accomplish your search. The client program must be installed on your computer. (Client programs are available for many popular computer systems. Clients are most numerous for UNIX operating systems; however, DOS, Windows, and Macintosh clients are also available.) Using an Archie client enables you to enter one command (usually `archie`) to specify your search parameters. You can use various command options to control how the search is accomplished (more about Archie clients later).

With a direct connection to the Internet and access to a Telnet client program, you can establish a remote terminal session with an Archie server and enter commands interactively. You simply Telnet to the closest Archie server and log in as `archie`. (For a list of Archie servers, see the sidebar entitled, "Archie Servers Throughout the World," later in this chapter.) You can then enter commands at the prompt; the results return to your terminal session screen. Most Archie servers support a limited number of direct connections, so the Telnet method is often the most difficult to accomplish when the servers are busy. Because client programs and electronic mail both demand fewer resources of the Archie server, it may actually be quicker in the long run to use either of those methods for performing your Archie search.

If you do not have direct access to the Internet, you can still use Archie if you can send electronic mail to the Internet. You can send e-mail to an Archie server with your search commands in the mail message body; the Archie server e-mails the results back to you. This is the least interactive method of using Archie, but it is often useful when you want to do an unattended search of the Archie database. You can just fire off a mail message and later, when you next read your mail, the results will be awaiting you.

The Different Parts of Archie

The heart of the Archie service is a database of the file systems of anonymous FTP sites (which number in the thousands). Each server maintains its own database. Special resource discovery software runs each night to update about one thirtieth of the database so that each file system image is updated approximately once a month. This procedure ensures a reasonably accurate representation of contents at the FTP sites without creating an overly large amount of traffic on the Internet. Servers are set up to share information as well, so that starting a new server does not necessarily require a comprehensive resource discovery operation.

A second database maintained at Archie servers is the `whatis` database. The `whatis` database cross-references numerous terms with associated file or directory names. Not surprisingly, you can search the `whatis` database using the `whatis` command. Because the Archie database indexes filenames within directory structures, your search for a name that seems intuitive may not find the exact software you want. If you search for a term in the whatis database, the server returns the names of associated files that you can then locate with a normal Archie command. Note that you can only search the whatis database using the Telnet or e-mail methods of using Archie. The Archie client programs are only capable of searching the file system database.

The various Archie servers are obviously a very important part of the Archie service. They are, in fact, the very foundation of the information management process. As you have seen so far, the servers collect and maintain the anonymous FTP site information, maintain the whatis database, and accept and process queries to either database using one of the three methods described earlier. The Archie servers are generally computers running the UNIX operating system and are connected to the Internet. These computers are maintained for the most part by universities and network service organizations and are offered as a public resource to Internet users.

ARCHIE SERVERS THROUGHOUT THE WORLD

As you can see from the following list, Archie is a world-wide service. You can specify any of the addresses below as the primary server for an Archie client. You can Telnet to these addresses to use Archie interactively, or you can send e-mail to archie@<*server address*> with appropriate search commands. This list was adapted from a list found on the Bunyip anonymous FTP site. The file can be found at: ftp://ftp.bunyip.com/pub/bunyip-docs/serverlist.

Server Address	Numeric Address	Location
archie.au	139.130.23.2	Australia
archie.univie.ac.at	131.130.1.23	Austria
archie.bunyip.com	192.77.55.2	Canada
archie.cs.mcgill.ca	132.206.51.250	Canada
archie.uqam.ca	132.208.250.10	Canada
archie.funet.fi	128.214.6.102	Finland
archie.univ-rennes1.fr	129.20.254.2	France
archie.th-darmstadt.de	130.83.22.1	Germany
archie.ac.il	132.65.16.8	Israel
archie.unipi.it	131.114.21.10	Italy
archie.wide.ad.jp	133.4.3.6	Japan
archie.hana.nm.kr	128.134.1.1	Korea
archie.sogang.ac.kr	163.239.1.11	Korea
archie.uninett.no	128.39.2.20	Norway
archie.rediris.es	130.206.1.2	Spain
archie.luth.se	130.240.12.23	Sweden
archie.switch.ch	130.59.1.40	Switzerland

archie.switch.ch	130.59.10.40	Switzerland
archie.ncu.edu.tw	192.83.166.12	Taiwan
archie.doc.ic.ac.uk	146.169.16.11	UK
archie.doc.ic.ac.uk	146.169.17.5	UK
archie.doc.ic.ac.uk	146.169.2.10	UK
archie.doc.ic.ac.uk	146.169.32.5	UK
archie.doc.ic.ac.uk	146.169.33.5	UK
archie.doc.ic.ac.uk	146.169.43.1	UK
archie.doc.ic.ac.uk	155.198.1.40	UK
archie.doc.ic.ac.uk	155.198.191.4	UK
archie.hensa.ac.uk	129.12.43.17	UK
archie.sura.net	128.167.254.195	USA(MD)
archie.unl.edu	129.93.1.14	USA(NE)
archie.internic.net	192.20.225.200	USA(NJ)
archie.internic.net	192.20.239.132	USA(NJ)
archie.internic.net	198.49.45.10	USA(NJ)
archie.rutgers.edu	128.6.18.15	USA(NJ)
archie.ans.net	147.225.1.10	USA(NY)

As you can see from the preceding sidebar, there is probably an Archie server near you. When selecting a server, it is best to use one that is closest to you through the Internet. If you attempt to use Archie with Telnet and that server is busy, you can select an alternative location. You should take care, however, in selecting an alternative site. If you are in the western United States, and the University of Nebraska server is busy, it probably does not make sense to try the one in Korea. You can, but you will be adding to the bandwidth of a transoceanic network link and probably will not be receiving the best network performance, either. The New York or Maryland server may be a better choice.

The Archie client programs provide you with the most direct access to the Archie FTP file system database. Because the clients are based on the Prospero file system, they do not have access to the whatis database. The Prospero file system is software used to organize and search file references (and is partially the basis for the Archie service itself).

ARCHIE CLIENT PROGRAMS

Listed below are the most commonly used Archie client programs. There may be client programs available for other systems; however, these are the ones most widely available on anonymous FTP sites.

Filename	Author Name and Address	Description
`c-archie-1.[1-3].tar.Z`	Brendan Kehoe (brendan@cs.widener.edu)	Command-line program written in C
`c-archie-1.[2,3] -for-vms.com`	Brendan Kehoe (brendan@cs.widener.edu)	Command-line program written for DECVAX/VMS
`archie.el`	Brendan Kehoe (brendan@cs.widener.edu)	Command-line interface written for emacs
`perl-archie-3.8.tar.Z`	Khun Yee Fung (clipper@csd.uwo.ca)	Command-line program written in perl
`xarchie-1.[1-3].tar.Z`	George Ferguson (ferguson@cs.rochester.edu)	X11(R4) client program using the Athena widget set
`archie-one-liner.sh`	Mark Moraes University of Toronto	UNIX shell program
`NeXTArchie.tar.Z`	Scott Stark (me@superc.che.udel.edu)	NeXTStep client program
`mac-archie-client-09.hqx`	Chris J McNeil (cmcneil@macc2.mta.ca)	Macintosh client
`Anarchie-140.sit`	Peter Lewis (peter@kagi.com)	Macintosh FTP and Archie client
`archie.zip`	Brad Clemens (bkc@omnigate.clarkson.edu)	PC DOS client program
`wsarch06.zip`	David Woakes (david@maxwell.demon.co.uk)	Windows WinSock client

The Archie client programs commonly available usually run on computers with UNIX operating systems. The reason for this may be that UNIX computers have traditionally been the foundation for many Internet networks and protocols; the Archie service itself is greatly dependent on UNIX systems. Clients are available, however, for NeXTStep (admittedly a flavor of UNIX), VAX VMS, DOS, and even IBM's VM/CMS (see the sidebar entitled "A Note for IBM Mainframe Users").

ARCHIE CLIENT PROGRAM ANONYMOUS FTP SITES

These sites on the Internet are good places to look for the most common Archie client programs. Most of them maintain copies of the various client programs listed in the preceding sidebar and can be accessed with anonymous FTP.

```
ftp://ftp.bunyip.com/pub/archie-clients
ftp://gatekeeper.dec.com/.3/net/infosys/archie/clients
ftp://cs.columbia.edu/archives/mirror2/uunet/networking/info-service/archie/
   clients
ftp://sunsite.unc.edu/pub/packages/infosystems/archie
ftp://ftp.mr.net/pub/Info/archie/clients
ftp://ftp.sura.net/pub/archie/clients
ftp://ftp.uu.net/networking/info-service/archie/clients
ftp://ftp.luth.se/pub/infosystems/archie/clients
```

Anarchie Sites:

```
ftp://redback.cs.uwa.edu.au//Others/PeterLewis/
ftp://amug.org/peterlewis/
ftp://nic.switch.ch/software/mac/peterlewis/
```

A NOTE FOR IBM MAINFRAME USERS

Even if you use an IBM mainframe, Archie may still be accessible to you. An MVS Archie client was written by Alasdair Grant at the University of Cambridge Computer Laboratory. This served as the basis for a VM/CMS client written by Arthur J. Ecock (ECKCU@CUNYVM.CUNY.EDU) at the City University of New York. The VM/CMS client requires IBM's VM/TCP version 2 or greater and the freely available RXSOCKET software package. The Archie client is distributed with version 2 of the RXSOCKET software. The package is available on the Bitnet Listserv installation at CUNYVM. You can retrieve the package by sending a mail message to listserv@cunyvm.cuny.edu with SENDME RXSOCKET PACKAGE as the first line of the message.

Using Archie

A client program may be the simplest way to use Archie, and the simplest way to use a client program may be as follows:

```
archie string
```

In this syntax, *string* is any search string you want to specify. By default, the search tries to exactly match the string you specify. For example (using the popular Kermit public domain file transfer protocol as our guinea pig), if you know that there is a file out there named c-kermit, the following command should return one or more sites where a file with that name is available:

```
archie c-kermit
```

Not all files are that easy, however, and often the names are longer than your search string or they have the string embedded somewhere within them. Fortunately, the Archie clients have some options you can use to be more or less specific when doing your search. For example, this command returns all occurrences of files that contain the exact substring *c-kermit* (capitalization is respected):

```
archie -c c-kermit
```

NOTE

For the sake of this discussion, the examples reflect the use of the Archie C client, written by Brendan Kehoe. Other clients, however, support the same or similar command options. The DOS client options, for example, are quite similar to the C client options. The Windows and Macintosh clients provide fields to enter a search string and provide an interface for specifying a search type and a target Archie server. If you retrieve a particular client with anonymous FTP, be sure to retrieve any documentation or manual files that accompany that client. These files provide the exact command syntax and options.

A SAMPLE ARCHIE CLIENT QUERY

The following is an example of using an Archie command-line client program to perform a substring search of the Archie database in which case is ignored. For the sake of space, the output listing has been edited. A normal search returns a default maximum of 95 "hits" of the search string.

```
archie -s c-kermit

Host gatekeeper.dec.com
Location: /.2/usenet/comp.sources.unix/volume1
      FILE -r-r-r- 6994 Jun 1 1989 c-kermit.ann.Z
      FILE -r-r-r- 3208 Dec 1 1986 c-kermit.old.Z

Host uhunix2.uhcc.hawaii.edu
Location: /pub/amiga/fish/f0/ff026
      FILE -rw-r-r- 238032 Jul 9 1992 C-kermit.lha


Host osl.csc.ncsu.edu
Location: /pub/communications
      FILE -rw-r-r- 617243 Aug 31 1992 C-Kermit_5a.tar.Z

Host ftp.shsu.edu
Location: /KERMIT.DIR;1
      FILE -rw-r-x-w- 2   Dec 1 1992 C-KERMIT-V5A-DOC.ZIP-LST;1
      FILE -rw-r-x-w- 3   Dec 1 1992 C-KERMIT-V5A-EXE.ZIP-LST;1
      FILE -rw-r-x-w- 11  Dec 1 1992 C-KERMIT-V5A-SRC.ZIP-LST;1

Host ftp.utoledo.edu
Location: /KERMIT_ROOT.DIR;1/KERMIT_BINARY.DIR;1
      FILE -r--x-w- 1084  Apr 4 1993 VMS-C-KERMIT-MULTINET.EXE;1
      FILE -r--x-w- 1133  Apr 4 1993 VMS-C-KERMIT-WOLLONGONG.EXE;1

Host wuarchive.wustl.edu
Location: /systems/amiga/aminet/comm/misc
      FILE -rw-rw-r- 697822 Dec 11 1992 C-Kermit-5A-188.lha

Location: /systems/mac/info-mac/Old/comm
      FILE -rw-r-r- 198461 Sep 29 1991 mac-kermit-098-63.hqx

Host ugle.unit.no
Location: /pub/kermit/os2
      DIRECTORY drwxrwxr-x 1024 Jan 11 1993 c-kermit
Location: /pub/kermit/vms
      DIRECTORY drwxrwxr-x 1024 Aug 16 09:46 c-kermit
```

The preceding sidebar shows yet another variation on this search example. The -s option specifies a search in which the string is matched anywhere within a target file and the case of the letters is ignored. You can see by the example that the results vary quite a bit. Note the variations: c-kermit, C-kermit, C-KERMIT, VMS-C-KERMIT, and mac-kermit (yes, mac-kermit contains the substring c-kermit).

Perhaps it is appropriate for a note about the output Archie returns to you. The word Host indicates each Internet anonymous FTP host (so far, pretty simple). Under each host, you see one or more designations of Location: which shows you the file path to the location of the file. In other words, when doing an anonymous FTP file transfer, once connected, you can use this command to move to the directory where the file is stored: cd *path*, where *path* is the complete string that follows Location:. After the location is the designation FILE or DIRECTORY, depending on which is found, followed by a UNIX-style permissions listing, a file date, and the filename itself. This information is usually enough to do a successful anonymous FTP download to retrieve the file you want.

Following are more of the options available with the C Archie client program. They not only tell you how to control your Archie search, but also reveal a bit about the operation of the client itself. (If you use the client on a UNIX operating system, you can usually enter the command **man archie** to see these options as well as other information.)

Option	Description
-	A - by itself enables you to search for that character in a substring. For example, the command archie -c - -v5, looks for the occurrences of -v5 in a filename.
-c	Searches substrings while respecting the case of the letters.
-e	Performs an exact string match (the default).
-h *hostname*	Tells the client to query the Archie server specified by *hostname*.
-L	Shows a list of the Archie servers known to the client program when it was compiled, as well as the name of the client's default Archie server. For a current server list, send e-mail to archie@archie.mcgill.ca (or to Archie at any Archie server) with the text servers as the body of the message.
-m *hits*	Specifies the maximum number of search string matches (database *hits*) to return (the default is 95).
-o *filename*	Specifies the name of a file in which to store the results of a query.
-r	Specifies that the next argument is a regular expression for specifying the search string.
-s	Searches substrings without respecting the case of the letters.
-t	Sorts the results by descending date.
-V	Prompts the server to print some status comments while performing long searches.

The options -c, -r, and -s are mutually exclusive; if more than one of these is specified, only the last one is used. Using -e with any of these three options causes the server to first check for an exact match and then perform a substring or regular expression search.

Accessing an Archie Server with Telnet

If your computer supports remote terminal sessions over the Internet with a Telnet client program, you can connect to an Archie server directly. As mentioned previously, this is not always the most efficient way to perform a search, and the use of client programs is encouraged to save both network and server resources. One thing you can easily do through a direct connection, which clients do not support, is a search of the `whatis` database.

To connect to an Archie server, enter this command:

```
telnet server
```

In this syntax, *server* is one of the servers listed in the sidebar, "Archie Servers Throughout the World," earlier in this chapter. You are prompted for a username, to which you should reply **Archie**. At this point, you receive one of two messages. The server may tell you that there are too many people using it and to try a different site. The server follows such a message by immediately closing the Telnet session. The alternative to this rejection message is a greeting by the server followed by an Archie prompt.

A SAMPLE ARCHIE TELNET SESSION

The following shows a sample Archie query done in a Telnet session to an Archie server. The server used is kept anonymous to prevent it from bearing the brunt of too many test sessions. This example shows a typical session using a `whatis` command, setting some search parameters, and finding a file.

```
telnet archie.xxx.xxx
Trying xxx.xx.x.xx ...
Connected to xxxxxxx.xxx.xxx.
Escape character is '^]'.
SunOS UNIX
login: archie
password: archie
Last login: Sun Jan 2 21:46:06
SunOS Release 4.1.2 #1: Wed Dec 16 12:10:12 EST 1992
########################################################################

Welcome to the ARCHIE server.

Please report problems to archie-admin@foo.edu. We encourage
people to use client software to connect rather than actually logging in.
Client software is available on ftp.xxx.xxx in the /pub/archie/clients directory

If you need further instructions, type help at the archie> prompt.
########################################################################
```

```
archie> whatis kermit

c-kermit.ann          C-Kermit & USENET
ckermit               The 'C' implementation of Kermit
cu-shar               Allows kermit, cu, and UUCP to all share the same lines
dialout               Kill getty and kermit programs
kermit                Communications software package
kermit.hdb            Kermit patches to enable dial to use HDB database
okstate               UUCP Access to Kermit Distribution
unboo.bas             Decode Kermit boo format

archie> set search sub
archie> set maxhits 5
archie> set sortby hostname
archie> prog c-kermit

# matches / % database searched:    5 / 7%
Sorting by hostname


Host ftp.cs.uni-sb.de   (134.96.7.254)
Last updated 00:05  6 Jul 1993

Location: /pub/comm
     FILE      rw-r-r-    412196  Jul  2  1990   C-kermit.tar.Z

Host ftp.uu.net   (192.48.96.9)
Last updated 05:27 31 Jul 1993

Location: /usenet/comp.sources.unix/volume1
     FILE      rw-rw-r-     3208  Nov 30  1986   c-kermit.old.Z
     FILE      rw-rw-r-     6994  May 31  1989   c-kermit.ann.Z

Host imag.imag.fr   (129.88.32.1)
Last updated 00:37 19 Sep 1993

Location: /a/durga/Ftp/archive/macintosh/serial-com
     FILE      rw-r-r-    198461  May 20  1992   mac-kermit-098-63.hqx
Location: /ftp.old/archive/macintosh/serial-com
     FILE      rw-r-r-    198461  May 20  1992   mac-kermit-098-63.hqx

archie> quit
Connection closed by foreign host.
```

You can enter a number of commands at the Archie prompt. The command prog *string* executes a database search for the particular *string*. The set command allows you to control how the search is accomplished. The search in the preceding sidebar used the following commands:

Command	Meaning
set search sub	Specifies a substring search without respect for case
set maxhits 5	Sets the maximum number of matches to five
set sortby hostname	Specifies that the results are sorted alphabetically by host name
prog c-kermit	Begins the actual search on the string c-kermit

The maxhits number of 5 is chosen to keep the example output brief. While doing the search, some servers keep you apprised of how many hits are found as well as the percentage of the database that is searched. In the preceding example, notice that the server had to search only about 7 percent of the database before finding 5 matches. It is also obvious that this is not a complete search, so by controlling the maxhits variable (by default 100), you can control how much of the database is searched. If you find what you are looking for early in the search, you may not need to change the maxhits value. Depending on the frequency of the string, you may have to increase the maxhits value or be more restrictive in the string for which you search (see "About Archie Regular Expressions," later in this chapter, for information).

Some of the commands and their parameters you can enter at the Archie prompt are listed in Table 24.1 (these apply to version 3.0 of the Archie server).

Table 24.1. Archie commands available in version 3.0 of the Archie server.

Command	Meaning
bye	Closes your session with the Archie server.
exit	Acts the same as bye.
help *topic*	You can type **help** by itself to receive a general message and to enter the help system, or you can enter it followed by a supported topic name, for example, help set.
list *string*	You can enter list by itself to obtain a list of all known sites in the Archie database. Enter list with a search string to match a string or regular expression to the site names.
prog *string*	Specifies a search string or regular expression depending on the value of the search variable (refer to Table 24.2).
set *variable value*	Enables you to control your search by setting various variables to arbitrary or specific values (refer to Table 24.2).

continues

Table 24.1. continued

Command	Meaning
quit	Acts the same as exit.
site *string*	Lists the files found at a particular archive site.
unset *variable*	Clears the value of the specified variable and resets it to the default value (if any).
whatis *string*	Searches the whatis database for the term matching *string*.

The commands set and prog may be the most used when you access an Archie server directly. The variables that can be set are listed in Table 24.2.

Table 24.2. Variables for use with the set and prog commands.

Variable	Meaning
autologout *number*	Sets the number of minutes before an automatic log out occurs.
mailto *string*	Sets an address to which output is to be mailed (rather than printed on the screen).
maxhits *number*	Specifies the maximum number of matches before the server stops searching.
pager	The command set pager specifies that the output pauses between pages; unset pager turns off this feature.
search *value*	Specifies how the database search is to occur—the possible values are sub (a case-insensitive substring match), subcase (a case-sensitive substring match), exact (an exact match), and regex (a regular expression search). Compound searches can be done by combining values using the format *value1_value2*—if *value1* is not successful, the server attempts a search with *value2*; for example, exact_sub.
sortby *value*	Controls how the search results are sorted—the possible values are none (an unsorted listing), filename (sorted by filename), hostname (sorted by host name), size (sorted by file size), and time (sorted by modification time). Note that any of these options can be specified with an r immediately preceding the value to receive a listing in reverse order (you can even specify rnone, although this option has no effect).

Variable	Meaning
status	The command set status causes the server to report search progress; unset status turns off this feature.
term *string*	Enables you to describe your terminal; for example, if you use a VT-100, you can type **term vt100**.

Accessing Archie with E-Mail

You can reach Archie with electronic mail by sending a message to the address archie@*server*, where *server* is any of the servers listed in the sidebar, "Archie Servers Throughout the World," earlier in this chapter. The server commands should be placed in the subject and body of the e-mail message. Although most servers respond to an e-mail request, a response is not guaranteed. If you have a question about a specific server, send e-mail to the address archie-admin@*server*.

Archie servers have one feature that can be both helpful and annoying. If the server receives a message with an unknown command, an incorrect command, or no command, it treats the message as a help request and returns the complete help file. This is helpful if you want the help file but annoying if you just happened to misspell your command. A help request also supersedes all other commands. So if you make a mistake, all you get is help.

The server parses your subject line for a command. This means that if you need to do only one command, you can send a mail message with a subject line and no message body. Alternatively, you can either include a valid command as the subject of your message or leave the subject blank.

The commands supported in an e-mail message search are identical to the ones valid for a direct Telnet connection. You can even send the command help *topic* to find information about a particular feature without receiving the entire help file. The following sidebar shows an example of output returned from an e-mail query.

A SAMPLE ARCHIE E-MAIL SEARCH

The following listing shows what to expect to see if you send an e-mail message to an Archie server. The first of the output shows the result of a whatis command. The search itself is limited to five hits, a case-insensitive search is used, and the output is sorted by last modification time.

```
>> whatis kermit
c-kermit.ann              C-Kermit & USENET
ckermit                   The 'C' implementation of Kermit
cu-shar                   Allows kermit, cu, and UUCP to all share the same
lines
dialout                   Kill getty and kermit programs
kermit                    Communications software package
kermit.hdb                Kermit patches to enable dial to use HDB database
okstate                   UUCP Access to Kermit Distribution
unboo.bas                 Decode Kermit boo format

>> set search sub
>> set maxhits 5
>> set sortby time
>> prog c-kermit

# Search type: sub.

Host freebsd.cdrom.com       (192.153.46.2)
Last updated 03:49 11 Nov 1993
Location: /pub/aminet/comm/misc
     FILE -rw-r-r-   697822 bytes 00:00 12 Dec 1992 C-Kermit-5A-188.lha

Host ftp.wustl.edu    (128.252.135.4)
Last updated 09:12 22 Dec 1993
Location: /systems/amiga/aminet/comm/misc
     FILE -rw-rw-r-    47 bytes 00:00 12 Dec 1992 C-Kermit-5A-188.readme

Host freebsd.cdrom.com       (192.153.46.2)
Last updated 03:49 11 Nov 1993
Location: /pub/aminet/comm/misc
     FILE -rw-r-r-    47 bytes 00:00 12 Dec 1992 C-Kermit-5A-188.readme

Host ftp.wustl.edu    (128.252.135.4)

Last updated 09:12 22 Dec 1993
Location: /systems/amiga/aminet/comm/misc
     FILE -rw-rw-r-   697822 bytes 00:00 11 Dec 1992 C-Kermit-5A-188.lha
Location: /systems/mac/info-mac/Old/comm
     FILE -rw-r-r-    198461 bytes 23:00 29 Sep 1991 mac-kermit-098-63.hqx
```

The output from a successful e-mail query echoes the commands you specify, prefixed by two greater-than signs (>>). The rest of the output should look rather familiar by now.

Accessing Archie with Gopher

Archie searches can be performed with a Gopher client courtesy of a Gopher gateway to the Archie service. Unfortunately, success in using the Gopher gateway still depends on getting access to the very busy Archie servers. In addition, popular Gopher sites that support the Archie gateway may themselves be so busy that access is impossible. The Gopher interface does provide a sometimes useful alternative to client, e-mail, or Telnet access to Archie, especially if you can access it at low-use times.

Choosing an FTP Site and Files from an Archie Listing

By definition, Archie returns listings of files available for anonymous FTP. However, because any search may return numerous site listings for the same file, you are often faced with a decision about which site to use. Following are some guidelines for selecting a site.

- Consider Internet site distance. If faced with multiple possibilities, select the one you know is nearest to your site. There is no need to cross an ocean if the file is available "next door."

- Select sites that, by their names, appear to be established anonymous FTP services. Such sites often have more resources to handle FTP requests (the chances of your FTP connection being rejected is slimmer). The string FTP in the address is a giveaway in this regard, as is the inclusion of the string archive. Network service organizations often have a domain name of .net and can be good archive sources for network information and software in particular.

- Choose a site that has the most items you need. You probably won't save any network bandwidth with this method, but you will save time if you do not have to establish multiple FTP connections.

- If you are unsure whether a particular file is the one you need, the names in the directory path often provide a clue. A file named C-Kermit in the path /systems/amiga is probably not a Mac version of that program. Also, because the complete file systems are indexed by Archie, be selective about which directory paths you use. Most files publicly offered for anonymous FTP are in a /pub directory. Finally, software distributions are usually offered in some archive or compressed format. Although there may be times you want to retrieve just an executable file, most of the time you want the complete distribution, including documentation and possibly source code.

About Archie Regular Expressions

If you are a UNIX guru, you probably know lots about regular expressions. The rest of us mere mortals must pick up as much useful information about this topic as we can maintain in our brains—just enough to be useful. What are *regular expressions*? They are simply symbolic ways to specify patterns of strings by using wildcards and other substitution characters. Archie regular expressions are a combination of UNIX regular expressions and Archie's own syntax.

You can use a regular expression as a search string in an Archie query by using the `-r` option with an Archie client or using the command `set search regex` when doing a Telnet or e-mail search. When using regular expressions with a client program (especially on a UNIX system), the string should be enclosed in double or single quotation marks.

The possible elements of an Archie regular expression are given in the following chart:

Element	Meaning
^	When used at the start of an expression, anchors the characters following to the beginning of the string. In other words, `^c-kermit` finds all file occurrences beginning with the exact string `c-kermit`.
$	When used at the end of an expression, anchors the preceding characters to the end of the string. For example, `txt$` finds all file occurrences ending with the exact string `txt`.
.	Represents an arbitrary character.
*	Represents multiple repetitions of the character immediately preceding it.
\	Causes the character immediately following it to be treated as a literal part of the string. For example, `\.txt` searches for the actual string `.txt` rather than an arbitrary character followed by `txt`.
[]	Encloses lists or ranges of characters that can be substituted in that position. For example, `a[b-d]e` returns `abe`, `ace`, or `ade`. Single characters, lists, and ranges of character can be included within one pair of brackets. Prefixing the contents of the brackets with ^ returns any match that is *not* one of the listed characters.

With these elements in hand, you can be quite detailed in your search specification. Note that regular expression searches are acted on as if they are case-sensitive substring searches, once the expression has been interpreted.

Here are some examples:

Search String	What It Does
`^c.*\.txt$`	Matches any string that begins with `c` (`^c`), is followed by any number of arbitrary characters (`.*`), is then followed by the occurrence of a period (`\.`), and ends in the string `txt` (`txt$`)
`^kermit\.[Vv]5$`	Returns `kermit.v5` or `kermit.V5`

The sidebar entitled "A Sample Regular Expression Search" shows what you can specify if you are looking for occurrences of the string c-kermit associated with the word *sun*. The *C*, the *K*, and the *S* may or may not be capitalized. The output of the search is successful in returning some matches. (These are not program files; they but appear to be archived news messages that may have the information you desire.)

A SAMPLE REGULAR EXPRESSION SEARCH

Following is a search done with an Archie client program and using the regular expression feature of the server. The search looks for the occurrence of any number of arbitrary characters (.*), followed by either case of the letter *c* ([cC]), followed by the character –, followed by either case of the letter *k*, followed by the string ermit, followed by any number of arbitrary characters, followed by either case of the letter *s*, followed by the string un, followed by any number of arbitrary characters. (Phew!)

```
archie -m 500 -r '.*[cC]-[kK]ermit.*[sS]un.*'
Host lth.se
Location: /pub/netnews/sys.sun/volume90/nov
     FILE -r-r-r-      1213  Nov 26 1990  C-Kermit.Sun.and.vi
Location: /pub/netnews/sys.sun/volume91/jun
     FILE -r-r-r-       336  Jun  5 1991  C-Kermit.needed.for.Sun
```

The Future of Archie

Bunyip is not content to rest on its laurels. Future applications of Archie may include other databases collected directly from the Internet, using the model that has proved to be so successful for organizing the anonymous FTP archives. These additions may include databases of information about Internet services, people on the Internet, and other databases and information resources.

For More Information About Archie

To contact Bunyip, use the following postal address:

Bunyip Information Systems
310 St. Catherine St. West
Suite 202
Montreal, Quebec, Canada H2X 2A1
Phone: 1-514-875-8611
Fax: 1-514-875-8134

You can send e-mail to the following addresses:

`info@bunyip.com`	For information about Bunyip Information Systems
`archie-group@bunyip.com`	For inquiries about Archie
`archie-admin@server`	For information about the administration of an individual server

Using and Finding Gophers

25

by Paul Lindner and Danny Iacovou

The Internet Gopher is one of the most useful Internet tools used today. Gopher's ease of use and simplicity are perfect for the beginner, and its well-ordered structure makes it useful for even the most veteran Internet user.

The Gopher concept is simple. You start an application called a *Gopher client* on your computer. This software retrieves information from machines called *Gopher servers*. The information can be in any number of formats. Text, movies, sounds, images: Gopher can store and retrieve them all. To date (February 1995) there are more than 9 million items stored on 6,000+ servers world wide. This giant amount of information is commonly called *Gopherspace*.

Navigating this massive amount of information is easy. Gopher organizes information in a series of browsable *menus* and lets you search for information that matches specific keywords. You can either browse the menus, delving deeper and deeper to find specific information, or you can search select menu items that find specific items for you.

Getting on Gopher

Your first step in accessing the wealth of information contained in Gopher is to acquire a Gopher client. A Gopher client consists of software you install on your machine. Clients are available for most platforms that have TCP/IP installed.

You will most likely get the client software from your Internet provider. Alternatively, you can get free Gopher software over the Internet on the FTP site `boombox.micro.umn.edu`, in the directory `/pub/gopher`. Other options for accessing Gopher include using it through a commercial online service such as America Online or Delphi, or buying Internet software packages from your local software store.

If you cannot run any of these clients, you can connect to what's known as a *public Gopher client*. These machines let you anonymously log in to run the UNIX Gopher client. This isn't the best way to do things, however: the terminal client doesn't take advantage of your personal computer's graphics, mouse, memory or disk.

The following Gopher clients allow public Gopher access connections using Telnet as of this writing:

Hostname	IP#	Login	Area
consultant.micro.umn.edu	134.84.132.4	gopher	North America
ux1.cso.uiuc.edu	128.174.5.59	gopher	North America
sailor.lib.md.us	192.188.199.5	gopher	North America
panda.uiowa.edu	128.255.40.201	panda	North America
gopher.msu.edu	35.8.2.61	gopher	North America
gopher.sunet.se	192.36.125.10	gopher	Sweden

Hostname	IP#	Login	Area
hugin.ub2.lu.se	130.235.162.12	gopher	Sweden
info.anu.edu.au	150.203.84.20	info	Australia
tolten.puc.cl	146.155.1.16	gopher	South America
ecnet.ec	157.100.45.2	gopher	Ecuador
gan.ncc.go.jp	160.190.10.1	gopher	Japan
gopher.th-darmstadt.de	130.83.55.75	gopher	Germany
gopher.uv.es	147.156.1.12	gopher	Spain
info.brad.ac.uk	143.53.2.5	gopher	United Kingdom

One of these machines should be close to you. To use these public clients, start the Telnet software on your machine and use it to connect to the hostname listed in the preceding chart. When you connect, you are prompted to log in. Type the specific login name from the chart (for example, **gopher**) and press Enter.

Navigating Gopher

Your Gopher client retrieves a menu at startup. This menu is commonly called your *root*, or *home*, Gopher server. It is your entry point into the Gopher system. From this entry point, you can select items that take you seamlessly to machines throughout the world.

Figure 25.1 shows the home Gopher server menu at the University of Minnesota. It contains a number of broad categories and two search options.

FIGURE 25.1.

The home Gopher server menu at the University of Minnesota.

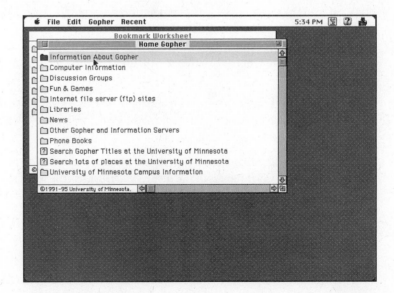

Assume that you're looking for a manicotti recipe for a dinner party. You may guess that recipes are in the Fun & Games category (cooking is such enjoyment!). Choosing that menu reveals a number of choices: Games, Humor, Movies, and, yes, Recipes.

Once you select the Recipes menu item with your mouse or keyboard, you find the information organized into different categories. There are menus (no pun intended) for Breads, Beverages, Italian, and so on. By continuing to choose from these menus, you can find that manicotti recipe you're looking for (refer to Figure 25.2).

FIGURE 25.2.

You can use Gopher menus to find just about anything—including a recipe for manicotti.

Gopher searches offer a more direct way of finding the same information. Instead of browsing from menu to menu, Gopher searches let you directly find documents that match specific words and phrases.

You could also find the manicotti recipe using a search. Select the Search Recipes menu item and type the word **manicotti**. The resulting menu contains only those items that contain the word *manicotti* (see Figure 25.3).

In this case, the search turns up two items: the recipe you viewed previously and a recipe for Pizza Rustica. This document is in the menu because it has the word *manicotti* in the text. These Gopher search items are commonly called *full-text indices* because you can search for an occurrence of a word in the complete text of the document.

FIGURE 25.3.

You can search for specific text, too. Here are all the recipe files that have the word manicotti *in them.*

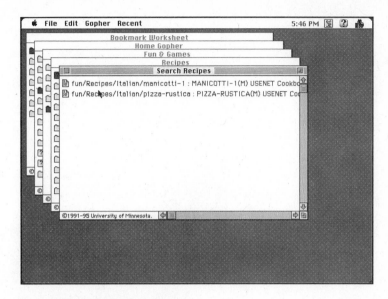

Information in Gopherspace

So far, this chapter has just scratched the surface of the millions of documents contained in the Gopher system. A wealth of text, graphics, sound, and movies awaits you.

You can use the simple browsing and searching methods described in the preceding section to find any document. However, you may need special software called *helper applications* to view nontext documents. Helper applications take care of the mundane job of displaying the multitude of file formats available in Gopher.

Helper applications are implemented in one of two ways. The first is to write them as part of the Gopher client. The second is to allow the user to specify the external helper application to be called by the Gopher client to display a particular document type. Most Gopher clients take the second approach to solving the problem (except for very simple file types, like text).

You can specify which external applications should be called to display documents (refer to Figure 25.4). This arrangement gives you the freedom and flexibility to select an application that can display the document in the most efficient manner. You can later change your mind if a better document viewer comes along.

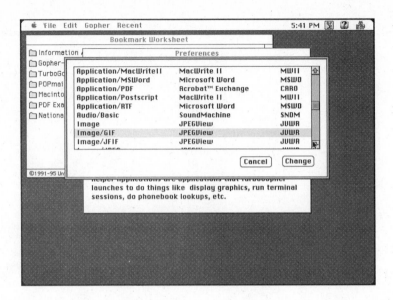

FIGURE 25.4.

Selecting the application you want to use to display a document.

Check the documentation for your helper application for specific information about setting up the application. Then you, too, can display movies, sounds, and images from all over the world.

Telnet Sessions with Gopher

In your travels through Gopherspace, you may chance across Telnet and TN3270 sites. These special Gopher menu items connect you to large mainframe computers using terminal emulation. Many popular services still run in this fashion: library card catalogs and MUDs are the most popular of these types of services.

Access these terminal-based information services by selecting the session from the Gopher menu. The Gopher client then initiates a terminal session to the correct host. Like image viewers or audio players, Gopher clients generally require an external helper application to make the terminal connection. One type of helper application emulates a VT-100 terminal session. These are known as *Telnet clients*. Other software emulates the popular IBM mainframe terminal, the 3270.

When you run across a terminal session in Gopherspace, your client informs you that you will be making a terminal connection to different machine. Your Gopher client then launches the correct terminal emulator helper application, and you are connected to the mainframe service. In the example shown in Figure 25.5, TurboGopher has launched the Telnet application.

FIGURE 25.5.

Using TurboGopher to launch the Telnet application.

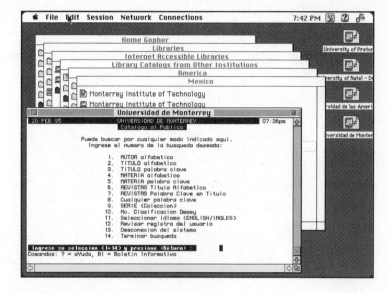

Advanced Search Mechanisms

As you use Gopher, you will find many items that allow you to search for documents. The preceding examples used just a single word to search for items. You can do much more sophisticated searches, however. Many search items support *Boolean searches*. To see how to enter Boolean queries, let's run through an example session.

Suppose that you want to find information about serial cables on a NeXT computer. Although you could have used *Next* as the search string, that results in a menu of 36 items—far too many.

You can reduce the number of items returned by the search by using the Boolean AND operation. To do this, construct a query using the search string Next AND serial. This syntax asks for only the documents that contain *Next* **and** *serial* in their titles. This search string produces a manageable list of items: just one.

```
Home Gopher server: gopher.tc.umn.edu
   1.   Information About Gopher/
   2.   Computer Information/
   3.   Discussion Groups/
   4.   Fun & Games/
+----------Search Gopher Titles at the University of Minnesota-------------+
¦                                                                          ¦
¦ Words to search for                                                      ¦
¦                                                                          ¦
¦ Next and serial-------------------------------------------------------   ¦
¦                                                                          ¦
¦ [Help: ^-]  [Cancel: ^G]                                                 ¦
+--------------------------------------------------------------------------+
```

Now suppose that as you look for serial cables for your NeXT computer, you decide to search for serial cables for your Macintosh computers as well. So what you are looking for is the list of items containing *Next* **or** *Macintosh* **and** *serial* in their titles. To formulate this query, specify it as follows:

```
Home Gopher server: gopher.tc.umn.edu

    1.   Information About Gopher/
    2.   Computer Information/
    3.   Discussion Groups/
    4.   Fun & Games/
+----------Search Gopher Titles at the University of Minnesota-----------+
|                                                                        |
| Words to search for                                                    |
|                                                                        |
| (Next or Macintosh) and serial-------------------------------------    |
|                                                                        |
| [Help: ^-]  [Cancel: ^G]                                               |
+------------------------------------------------------------------------+
```

The parentheses ( ) allow you to group terms together. Be careful when you use parentheses. You want a list of items about serial cables specifically. If you specified the search as `Next or (Macintosh and serial)`, you get a combined list of documents about Next machines and a list of documents about Macintosh serial cables.

Suppose that as you conducted this search, you saw that some of the items referred to MIDI cables. Because you aren't interested in MIDI cables, you can exclude the items referring to MIDI cables by using the Boolean `NOT` operator. The new search asks for items containing *Next* **or** *Macintosh* **and** *serial* **and not** *midi* in their titles. To formulate this query, specify it as follows:

```
Home Gopher server: gopher.tc.umn.edu

    1.   Information About Gopher/
    2.   Computer Information/
    3.   Discussion Groups/
    4.   Fun & Games/
+----------Search Gopher Titles at the University of Minnesota-----------+
|                                                                        |
| Words to search for                                                    |
|                                                                        |
| (Next or Macintosh) and serial and (not midi)------------------------  |
|                                                                        |
| [Help: ^-]  [Cancel: ^G]                                               |
+------------------------------------------------------------------------+
```

As you can see, formulating search queries is fairly easy—even complicated searches such as the last one. If you are having trouble formulating the search, try writing it in plain English, as we did in the previous examples. Doing so can help you specify searches that quickly find the information you want.

Searching for People Using Gopher

You can search for people on the Internet using Gopher. Use your Gopher client to connect to the server gopher.tc.umn.edu. Once there, select the item Phone Books. You can then select Phone Books at Other Institutions or Internet Wide Email Address Searches.

> **NOTE**
>
> One thing to keep in mind is that although many institutions around the world make the e-mail addresses of their associates publicly available, many do not.

If you use the Phone Books at other Institutions section, you must first browse for the institution with which the person you are looking for is associated. The institutions are organized in a hierarchy based on geography—much in the same way the registered Gopher servers are organized. Once you search for and find the institution you want, you can search for the person in question.

Institutions generally use one of two searching methods. The first is a *CSO nameserver*, the other is a *WHOIS server*. Your Gopher client has some way of indicating whether the search method is a CSO nameserver or not.

If the institution is using a CSO nameserver, you are presented with a form to fill out. The more information you can specify, the narrower the results of your search will be. You can search for people by specifying only their name or by searching on a number of other fields. Keep in mind that you can search for people using their first name and last name and by using * as a wildcard. For example, if you are looking for all the people named *Scott* at the U.S. Department of Education, complete the form as shown in Figure 25.6.

If the institution uses a WHOIS server, you are presented with the standard Gopher search interface when you try to search for a person. If this happens, try entering the person's first and last names—or just the last name, depending on how things are implemented on the remote server. If you've never consulted that particular WHOIS server before, you have no way of knowing what format is expected, so be heuristic. The results of your search may be displayed in a document named Raw Search Results, or you may receive multiple documents back from your search. To view your search results, be sure to select the documents returned.

In the Phone Books at Other Institutions menu (in addition to the listing of institutions by geographical location), is a directory called X.500 Gateway (experimental). As you can with the CSO and WHOIS servers, you can search for people using the ISO standard protocol X.500. Again, you must first locate the institution with which the person you are looking for is associated. Once you find the institution, type the name of the person, organization, country, locality, and so on. Currently, only exact matching is supported (that is, you have to get the name right). A future version may do approximate searches (for example, SOUNDEX).

FIGURE 25.6.

Using a Gopher CSO nameserver to search the U.S. Department of Education for all people named Scott.

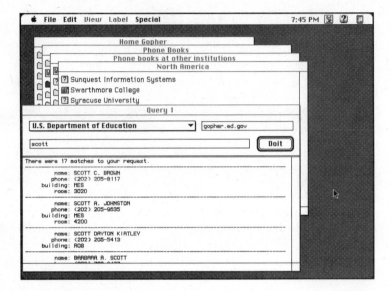

If you enter the Internet-Wide E-mail Address Searches section, you use a program called Netfind. Netfind is the easier of the search engines to use. When you connect to a Netfind server, you are greeted with a menu resembling this one:

```
Top level choices:
    1. Help
    2. Search
    3. Seed database lookup
    4. Options
    5. Quit (exit server)
```

By selecting the second option, you are expected to specify your search in the following format:

```
username locationkey1 locationkey2 locationkey3 ....
```

For example, to search for John Doe at the University of Minnesota, you can specify the search using the following four keys:

```
doe university minnesota minneapolis
```

You can also generate keys by taking a site's domain (if you know it) and replacing the periods with spaces. The domain `micro.umn.edu` results in the keys `micro`, `umn`, and `edu`. You can then reformulate your search using these keys:

```
doe micro umn edu
```

Keys are not case sensitive and may be specified in any order. Multiple keys are related by the logical AND operation across all keys. It is possible to specify too many keys, causing your search to fail; if this happens, try specifying your search using fewer keys. On a similar note, you can specify too few keys; if this happens, Netfind lists some of the matching institutions and asks you to formulate a more specific search. You can use the keys presented in the list in future search strings.

By selecting the `Seed Database Lookup` option, you can search the Netfind seed database without actually performing any searches. You may want to search this database to resolve any acronyms you run across. You can vary the information displayed by choosing the option `Toggle Seed Database Search Output Format`. Results from seed lookups can be used as keys in future searches.

Bookmarks

As you delve deeper and deeper into Gopherspace, you'll likely find areas you frequent quite often. Perhaps you search an index very often, or find yourself selecting many menus to get back to the recipe database you love. There is an easier way to keep track of your favorite Gopher resources: *bookmarks*.

Bookmarks in Gopherspace work in much the same way they do in real life. In the traditional sense, bookmarks provide a place holder for a particular page in a book. In Gopherspace, bookmarks provide a place holder for a particular Gopher item. This item can be a document, a directory, a search engine, a movie, a sound—just about anything. A bookmark can be placed on any item residing in Gopherspace.

If you want to save your place in Gopherspace, use your client's `set bookmark` command. The current item is added to your bookmark list. Some clients (like WSGopher) even allow you to store and sort your bookmarks in specific categories (see Figure 25.7).

When you want to return to the section of Gopherspace at which you dropped a bookmark, all you have to do is look at your list of bookmarks, select the saved item from the list, and you are transported back to the saved location. Most Gopher clients let you use only a single list for your bookmarks, but WSGopher allows a wide selection of bookmarks (refer to Figure 25.8).

FIGURE 25.7.

Save your place in Gopherspace with a bookmark—and keep your bookmarks organized by category.

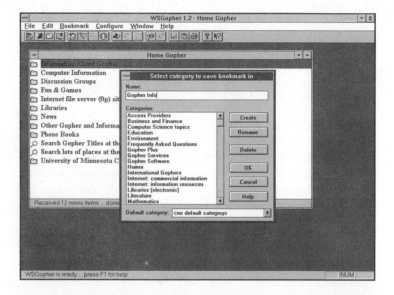

FIGURE 25.8.

WSGopher has a large selection of bookmark categories you can use to organize your own bookmarks.

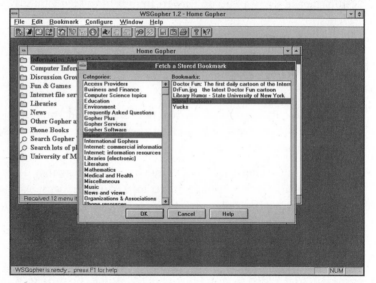

Bookmarks free you from memorizing names and locations and are an efficient way of navigating Gopherspace. In addition to saving time, you also save network resources by connecting directly with the server you want to use.

When Good Gophers Go Bad

As you navigate Gopherspace, you will come across items you don't think are working quite right. There may be items you want to see improved, or documents that may have some grievous errors in them. Or even worse, a site may be impossible to connect to. Like any real-world system, Gopherspace isn't perfect.

What can you do about such matters? The best thing to do is to tell someone about your grievances. You can make Gopherspace a better place by voicing your opinion. Let Gopher server administrators know of ways they can improve their servers. Most system administrators welcome such comments and are thankful to receive them. The question now is, how do you contact the system administrator?

If you are running a Gopher+ client, your client supports a way of looking at an item's Attribute information. One Attribute that may be available is the ADMIN attribute. The ADMIN attribute may look something like this:

```
Admin=The Ringmaster <gopher@circus.sams.com>
```

Using this attribute, you see that the administrator for this item is the Ringmaster and can be reached at the following e-mail address: gopher@circus.sams.com.

If the ADMIN attribute isn't available for a particular item, you can still reach the system administrator. Another attribute that is sure to be available is the HOST attribute. It looks something like this:

```
Host=boombox.micro.umn.edu
```

Although this information doesn't give you the exact address of the system administrator, it does give you a very good clue about where you can voice your comments. Send e-mail to the postmaster at the address of the HOST machine. In the preceding example, you send e-mail to postmaster@boombox.micro.umn.edu.

This person can either respond to your comments directly or know where to forward your e-mail so that is it handled accordingly.

Bolts, Nuts, and Gopher Guts...Under the Fur

Now that you've been using Gopher to do more sophisticated tasks, you're probably wondering, how does it all work?

The Gopher system has been called *brutally simple.* That's one reason why Gopher software exists for almost every platform that can possibly attach to the Internet.

You've already seen features of the Gopher client (the software that allows you to navigate the Gopher system quickly and easily). The client runs on your own computer, using the computer's resources to its best advantage. It may cache documents in memory, store files on your local hard disk, or use graphics and user interface elements familiar to you. You can get specialized Gopher clients for most platforms including Macintosh, Microsoft Windows, OS/2, DOS, UNIX, VMS, Amiga, and others.

The Gopher client retrieves documents from a Gopher server. A Gopher server is a machine that stores documents and "serves" them on demand. Servers typically run 24 hours a day and are usually fast machines that can handle many requests per minute. The server software generally allows you to create a hierarchical tree of items to browse, provides utilities to generate full-text indexes, and offers provisions for running external scripts.

The Gopher server and client communicate with each other through what's called the *Gopher protocol.* The Gopher protocol is simple: a Gopher client opens a connection with a Gopher server. The client then sends the name of an item to retrieve along with any search terms. The server sends back the desired information (or an error response if the request is invalid). Figure 25.9 graphically shows the workings of the Gopher protocol.

FIGURE 25.9.

The Gopher protocol.

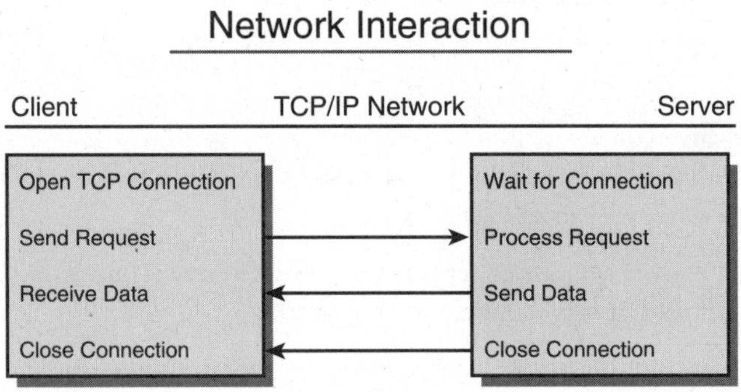

Network Interaction

Client	TCP/IP Network	Server

Open TCP Connection		Wait for Connection
Send Request	→	Process Request
Receive Data	←	Send Data
Close Connection	←	Close Connection

The main type of document that Gopher servers store is a *Gopher menu file.* This document is formatted in a specific way to represent items in a menu. Its format is shown in Figure 25.10.

FIGURE 25.10.

The format of a Gopher menu file.

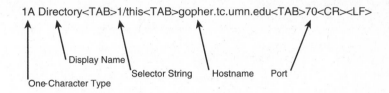

1A Directory<TAB>1/this<TAB>gopher.tc.umn.edu<TAB>70<CR><LF>

Each line of the Gopher menu document represents one item. The first character of each line denotes the type of the document. The menu or display name follows this single character. A TAB character separates the name from the selector string. The *selector string* is a unique iden-tifier for a document on each server. Usually, the selector string is a variation of the filename. TAB characters also separate the Internet hostname and port from the selector string. The line ends with a carriage return character and a linefeed character.

In most cases, you can retrieve the document referred to by the menu by connecting to the server's Internet hostname at the specified port and sending the selector string of the item. Some exceptions: the Telnet, CSO, and TN3270 types interpret the fields differently.

The type character can denote many different document types. Table 25.1 lists the more com-mon Gopher types.

Table 25.1. Common Gopher types.

Type	Description
0	Item is a plain text file.
1	Item is a Gopher directory.
2	Item is a CSO (qi) phone-book server. The hostname is the name of the machine to connect to. The selector string is unused.
3	Error.
4	Item is a BinHexed Macintosh file.
5	Item is DOS binary archive of some sort.
6	Item is a UNIX uuencoded file.
7	Item is an Index-Search server.
8	Item points to a text-based Telnet session. The selector string is the name to log in as, the hostname is the host to connect to using Telnet protocol.
9	Item is a binary file.
g	Item is a GIF image.
h	Item is a HTML document.
I	Item is a graphic image.

continues

Table 25.1. continued

Type	Description
i	Displays unselectable "inline" text.
M	Item contains a MIME encapsulated mail message.
P	Item is an Adobe Portable Document Format (PDF).
s	Item is a sound.
T	Item points to an IBM TN3270-based Telnet session. The selector string is the name to log in as, the hostname is the host to connect to using Telnet/TN3270 protocol.

The guiding philosophy of Gopher has been (and always will be) to keep things simple. The clients are simple and easy to use. Servers simply construct Gopher menus from their directory lists. The Gopher protocol is as bare-bones as it gets.

Gopher+

Once people started using Gopher, they quickly bumped up against its limits. These limits are caused by the method of transferring data between the server and client (the Gopher protocol). The simplicity of Gopher was also its limitation: there just wasn't much room to efficiently accommodate the various enhancements many people wanted.

At the very first Gopher Conference in 1992, the University of Minnesota Gopher Team proposed a suite of extensions to Gopher called Gopher+. These enhancements include the following:

- The ability to have multiple formats of a document associated with a single menu item (for example, a single menu item can be available in plain text, PostScript, and rich text format)
- A method of attaching a short description to a Gopher item (called an *abstract*)
- The ability to request that a client fill out a form before retrieving an item
- A simple method of determining whether a document was transferred correctly

To use these Gopher+ features, you need a Gopher+ server and a Gopher+ client. Gopher+ servers currently exist for Macintosh and UNIX platforms. The Macintosh version, GopherSurfer, can be obtained through anonymous FTP on boombox.micro.umn.edu in the /pub/gopher/Mac_server directory. The Gopher+ server more commonly used is the University of Minnesota's UNIX server. Releases higher than 2.0 support the Gopher+ extensions. The server and client can be retrieved with anonymous FTP from boombox.micro.umn.edu in the /pub/gopher/Unix directory. The latest production version as of this writing was gopher2_1_2.tar.Z.

The new Gopher+ server works with the older non-Gopher+ clients. However, the older clients cannot access the new features of Gopher+. Additionally, all Gopher+ clients support the old Gopher servers; you can upgrade either client or server at your convenience.

Unless you look closely, it's difficult to see the difference between Gopher and Gopher+. Both offer the same quick, easy user interface. In fact, you may not notice anything different in the following menu other than the version number and the double question mark on item 3:

```
              Internet Gopher Information Client v2.0.16

                    Home Gopher server: circus.sams.com

  -->   1. Introduction.
        2. Weather Forecasts/
        3. Cotton Candy Order Form <??>
        4. Clowns in a Balloon <Image>

  Press ? for Help, q to Quit                          Page: 1/1
```

There's a lot more here than first appears. If you use your client's item information command, you quickly notice some differences:

```
Link Info (0k)                                            100%
+-------------------------------------------------------------+
#
Type=1+
Name=Introduction
Path=0/cover
Host=circus.sams.com
Port=70
Admin=Ringmaster <gopher@circus.sams.com>
ModDate=Wed Aug 10 20:51:13 1994 <19940810205113>
URL: gopher://circus.sams.com:70/00/cover

ABSTRACT
--------
The Introduction file is meant as a quick guide to this server.
Please read this file first because it contains very useful information.


Size        Language       Document Type
----------  ------------   ----------------------------
3k          English (USA)  text/plain
18k         English (USA)  application/rtf
14k         German         application/x-wordmasher


+-------------------------------------------------------------+
[Help: ?]  [Exit: u]
```

Aren't things starting to look different? You can now find the name and e-mail address of the administrator of the document (`Ringmaster`, at `gopher@circus.sams.com`), the time the document was last modified (August 10, 1994), and the Universal Resource Locator (URL: `gopher://circus.sams.com:70/00/cover`). You can get an idea of what's in the document by reading the abstract. The bottom of the display shows the different versions of this document. There are three total: two in the English language and one in German. The first item is an ASCII text version that's 3K in size. The next is in Rich Text Format, and the third is in a fictitious word processor called WordMasher. If you select this document, your client tries to figure out which version you want. Different clients do this in different ways. The UNIX client asks you which you want, as shown in the following example:

```
+-------------------Introduction-----------------------+
|                                                      |
|  -->   1. Text/plain English (USA) [3k] (default)    |
|        2. application/rtf English (USA) [18k]        |
|        3. application/x-wordmasher English (USA) [12k] |
|                                                      |
| Choose a document type (1-3):                        |
| [Help: ?]  [Cancel: ^G]                              |
+------------------------------------------------------+
```

If you choose item 2, the Gopher client transfers the Rich Text version of the document to your computer; the appropriate helper application handles the file. The different formats of a document are called *alternative views*.

Now go back to the main menu and select the `Cotton Candy Order Form`. When you select this item, your client fetches a set of questions from the server and asks for your input:

```
+--------------------Cotton Candy Order Form---------------+
|                                                         |
| Name:                    _____  |
| Phone No:                _____  |
| E-mail Address:          _____  |
|                                                         |
| Color:                   Red                            |
| On a stick?:             Yes                            |
|                                                         |
| [Help: ^-]  [Cancel: ^G]                                |
+---------------------------------------------------------+
```

You must fill out the form before you can retrieve the document. The data you fill in is transferred to a specific program on the server that interprets your input and acts on it in some way. In the case of this form, you can order a case of cotton candy.

Gopher+ adds many features to the simple base of Gopher. From its forms to multiple document support, Gopher+ improves Gopher in all areas. Additionally, the open-ended design of

Gopher+ means that Gopher software of the future will not have to change too much to meet new needs.

Choice of Gopher Tools

You can find a veritable cornucopia when choosing software to browse Gopher servers. There are tools for most major platforms out there.

The main collection point for these tools is at the University of Minnesota on the machine `boombox.micro.umn.edu`. This machine has most known Gopher software in the `/pub/gopher` directory. You can access `boombox.micro.umn.edu` through FTP or using Gopher itself.

Determining what client to use may at first seem like a huge task to tackle; in reality, it isn't very hard.

Does the client understand the Gopher+ protocol? Older, non-Gopher+ clients do not have many features that make Gopher great. Without Gopher+, you cannot use forms, look at alternate views, or check an item's Attribute information.

Since the introduction of the Gopher+ protocol, the Gopher community has integrated Gopher+ features into their servers. Today, most people assume that you navigate Gopherspace using a Gopher+ client. Although you can still obtain older clients that haven't been upgraded to the Gopher+ protocol, it is not recommended that you use these clients.

> **NOTE**
>
> There are also some programs, called *orphans*, available. PC Gopher III, Hgopher, and others haven't been upgraded in some time. Think twice before using these older Gopher clients. There is likely a newer, better program out there that will meet your needs.

To keep on track with the current development of the various Gopher clients, you may want to read the Usenet newsgroup `comp.infosystems.gopher`. Most authors of the various clients frequent this newsgroup. You can ask questions about specific clients, suggest features, and report bugs. Also found in this newsgroup is a FAQ (Frequently Asked Question) file, which is updated monthly. The FAQ has a section in it about the different clients, what platforms they run under, and where to go to get the software. The FAQ is also available on one of the University of Minnesota's Gopher servers. The URL to this FAQ is as follows:

```
<URL:gopher://mudhoney.micro.umn.edu:70/00/Gopher.FAQ>
```

Following are some mini-reviews that give you a grasp of the features each Gopher client package offers. Commercial packages are available for many of these platforms, too.

TurboGopher

Arguably the fastest client out there, TurboGopher is *the* Gopher client to have on your Macintosh. It gets its speed by displaying information as soon as it comes in and only parsing what's exactly necessary (see Figure 25.11).

TurboGopher supports all Gopher+ features, including forms and alternate views. Many of the screen graphics used as figures in this chapter are from TurboGopher.

Development of TurboGopher takes place at the University of Minnesota.

FIGURE 25.11.

TurboGopher is the only Gopher client you'll need on your Mac.

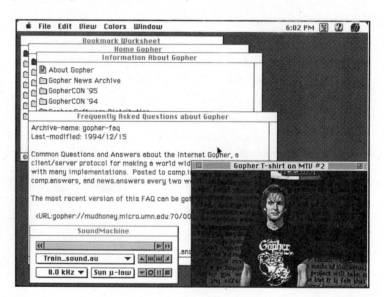

WSGopher

WSGopher is the leading Gopher client for Windows. There have been many Gopher clients for Windows; the first, GopherBook, was written in Asymmetrics ToolBook Language. After GopherBook, the floodgates opened; Hgopher arrived, followed shortly by BCgopher and WinGopher from NOTIS systems.

WSGopher stands above them all (see Figure 25.12). It borrows many of the ideas used in TurboGopher, including allowing multiple downloads and displaying information as it arrives from the network. WSGopher also has excellent capabilities for maintaining and organizing bookmarks.

Using and Finding Gophers

WSGopher supports all the Gopher+ features including forms, alternative views, and more. It was developed by Dave Brooks at the Idaho National Engineering Laboratory.

FIGURE 25.12.

WSGopher is all you need to hit Gopherspace from Windows.

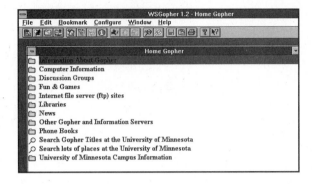

UNIX/VMS Gopher

The UNIX/VMS terminal client is part of the UNIX/VMS distribution put out by the University of Minnesota. The client works on any number of standard terminals, including the common VT-100.

You'll find many pleasing features with this client. It supports bookmarks, localized messages in French, German, Spanish, and more (refer to Figure 25.13).

FIGURE 25.13.

The UNIX Gopher client of choice.

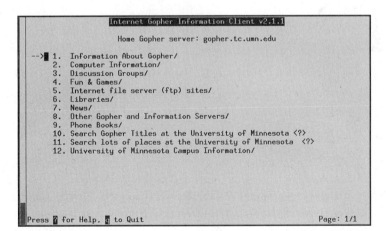

Mosaic/Netscape

Currently, Mosaic and Netscape are the best clients available for browsing Gopher sites using X Window. Even though the main focus for these clients is the World Wide Web, you'll find they do a good job of browsing Gopher sites (see Figure 25.14).

The only down side is that they do not support the Gopher+ features.

FIGURE 25.14.

*Browse Gopher sites
using a WWW client
such as Netscape.*

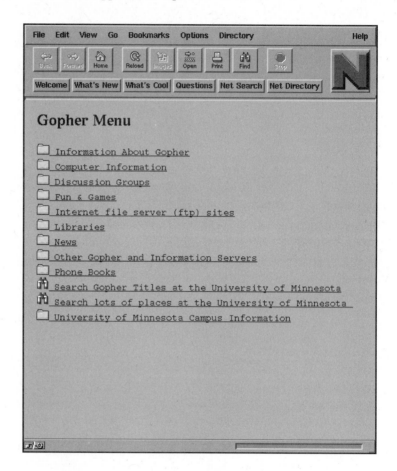

Minuet

Minuet (Minnesota Internet Users Essential Tool) is a DOS application that combines the following functions into one integrated package: POP mail client, Gopher+ client, Telnet, FTP, NetNews reader, and World Wide Web browser. In addition, it comes with a suite of handy desk accessories: `finger`, IP finder, an address book, a Webster client, two calculators, a calendar, and an ASCII table. Figure 25.15 shows one of the Minuet screens.

You can find Minuet at `boombox.micro.umn.edu` in the `/pub/pc/minuet` directory. Look for the file `minuarc.exe`. It is a self-extracting archive that contains the Minuet application and associated files.

FIGURE 25.15.

A DOS Gopher client like Minuet can fill many needs.

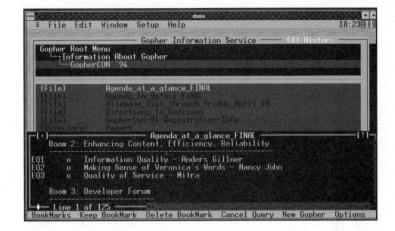

Where To Go from Here

Now that you've got some cool Gopher software, you can use it to go to some cool Gopher sites. Each site name is followed by a URL (Uniform Resource Locator). Many newer Gopher clients support this feature.

The following sections describe only a smattering of the interesting Gopher sites out there. In the process of exploring these sites, you'll no doubt find ones that cater to your own interests.

C-SPAN (Cable-Satellite Public Affairs Network)

```
<URL:gopher://c-span.org:70/1>
```

A server devoted to the C-Span television network. Look here for recent C-SPAN press releases, historic documents and speeches, transcripts and publications, congressional election results, reports, articles, and much more.

ACLU Free Reading Room

```
<URL:gopher://aclu.org:6601/1>
```

The ACLU Free Reading Room makes available to users of the Internet a growing collection of ACLU publications and information resources. Currently, the collection includes a basic line of publications on issues of high public interest; the current issue of its membership newsletter, *Civil Liberties*; a growing collection of recent public policy reports and action guides;

Congressional voting records for the 103rd Congress; letters to elected officials and congressional testimony; selected ACLU legal briefs submitted in Supreme Court cases; and an archive of news releases from the National Office.

Children, Youth, and Family Consortium Clearinghouse

```
<URL:gopher://tinman.mes.umn.edu:80/1>
```

A server focusing on families, adoption information, parenthood, and infants and children. It provides great articles and lists available resources, programs, and services.

ECHO

```
<URL:gopher://echonyc.com:70/1>
```

NYC's favorite BBS is on the Internet. The ECHO Gopher originates on ECHO, the electronic salon/Internet gateway based in New York City. The ECHO Gopher is intended to serve as the definitive cultural Gopher for New York City and elsewhere.

Comics Archive at Texas A&M

```
<URL:gopher://gopher.tamu.edu:70/11/.dir/comics.dir>
```

Comic books, comic strips, animation, and *more*! The one-stop source to get you through your comic frenzy habit. With this server, anytime you are in Gopherspace it can be Saturday morning cartoon time—without the commercials.

Adam Curry's Music Server

```
<URL:gopher://metaverse.com:70/1>
```

A Gopher server brought to you by MTV's renegade VJ, Adam Curry. Look here to find what's hot in today's music scene. This server is full of audio files, images, and movies. Adam Curry also keeps you up to date on some of the hot TV shows.

KIDLINK

```
<URL:gopher://kids.ccit.duq.edu:70/11/>
```

KIDLINK offers a Gopher server focusing on youth ages 10 through 15. It is full of projects to get them involved in a global dialog through e-mail and other telecommunications exchanges. While you are here, be sure to check out the art gallery!

187resist: Immigrant Rights in California

```
<URL:gopher://garnet.berkeley.edu:1870/1>
```

This Gopher server is an information provider for those studying and working in the area of immigrant rights and California's Proposition 187. It is a project of the Center for Community Economic Research, which is dedicated to creating connections between universities and communities. This Gopher is part of a larger project known as the Economic Democracy Information Network (EDIN), which promotes the use of information technology to create virtual conferences and research connections for the needs of communities.

Hearts of Space

```
<URL:gopher://hos.com:70/1>
```

National Public Radio's *Hearts of Space* program has its own Gopher server. Use it to get playlists, lists of stations carrying *Hearts of Space* radio, and information on records and where to get them. The server also has record release sheets and digitized images of their covers.

The Future of Gopher

Gopher is still chugging along, simple as ever. However, a number of changes on the horizon will alter the face of Gopher.

The first of these changes is a virtual reality representation of Gopher. You will soon be able to view a Gopher directory in three dimensions. You will be able to "drive" through a scene to find information. Sophisticated new search tools will cluster information into different areas so that you can easily grasp the results of a search. You may be able to follow "footprints" to the most popular items on a particular server.

After these aspects of 3D Gopher are completed, there are plans to add people to the scene. You will be able to see and talk to other people browsing the same information—you will be able to explore Gopher areas with your friends.

The possibilities for learning, entertainment, and interaction with Gopher are enormous!

On a more mundane, but perhaps more important, level is URN support. An URN is a Universal Resource Name. The way most information systems work is with a location reference. That's like me telling you about this really neat book I saw at the library, on the fifth shelf, ten books over. When you get to your library, the book may have moved—plus, you may not be at the bookstore or library closest to you. URNs solve these problems by having a naming scheme for items on the Internet, making Gopherspace faster and more simple.

Searching Gopherspace with Veronica

26

by Fred Barrie

How can you find a copy of the General Accounting Office's 1993 transition report on health care reform, get a great recipe for a chicken dish, and find a summer job at Cornell University—all without leaving your home? It's simple if you use the networking tool created by Fred Barrie and Steve Foster at the University of Nevada. This tool, called Veronica, is an indexer that simplifies the search for resources found in the Internet.

The development of the Internet gave all computer users, even those in remote areas, access to computer resources formerly available only in big cities or on university campuses. However, one of the problems new users (and even some old timers) have is that they need to know what resources exist, and where those resources are located, before they can effectively use the Internet to gain information. Gopher, a tool developed at the University of Minnesota, helped Internet users by enabling them to more easily browse menus that contained the many Internet resources. Now, users no longer have to know exactly where resources are located to effectively use the Internet. Instead, they can browse Gopher to find them.

As more and more information became available on the Internet, Gopher became extremely popular, but the increase in information created problems of its own. As the number of Gopher servers increased, it took users longer to find the information they wanted. On the Gopher newsgroup, there were daily postings requesting information about whether a piece of information existed in Gopher and how to retrieve it. It became almost impossible to wade through the Gopher menus and make any sense out of them. To effectively use Gopher, Gopher gurus had to "burrow" through Gopher servers, adding interesting Gopher items to their bookmark lists almost daily so that when the need arose, they would be ready. That's where Veronica comes in. It helps simplify searching for information and making connections to information in Gopherspace.

With Veronica, Gopher users simply have to type keywords to initiate a search of the titles of menu items in Gopher. For example, if you type the word `chicken`, you receive a list of approximately 577 titles that contain the word *chicken*. There are chicken jokes and recipes ranging from chicken curry to chicken casserole. Then you can select the menu item that contains the information you want. If it's in Gopher, Veronica can help you find it quickly.

How To Use Veronica

One of the great features of Veronica is that if you have mastered Gopher, you know how to use Veronica. Veronica was built specifically for Gopher. Veronica works with Gopher by creating Gopher menus that contain direct links to the information requested. Previous indexing methods of the network only had hints on how to get the information, such as "FTP to this host and retrieve that file." A novice can use Veronica for the first time and get exactly what he or she wants. However, Veronica has many, many options for the advanced user. It allows a user to restrict or expand the search of Gopher menu titles. It also allows logical-query operators for the construction of complicated searches. However, keep in mind that Veronica is not a full text index. It can index only *titles* of Gopher menu items.

To access Veronica, first start up Gopher and connect to the main Gopher server for Veronica (gopher.unr.edu). If the default Gopher server you connect to does not have a link to Veronica, you can access it directly by connecting to gopher.unr.edu. If you have a UNIX Gopher client, you can access Veronica by typing **gopher gopher.unr.edu** and selecting the Veronica directory. The listing of Veronica searches provided by this server contains a list of currently running Veronica searches.

You should be aware of some restrictions in Veronica. First, searches are not case-sensitive: the queries veronica and VERONICA are identical. In addition, all Veronica searches have a default number of 200 menu items, which means that only the first 200 items found are returned when you submit a query. This prevents users who accidentally type the keyword **Gopher** from getting the 10,000 plus menu items that are in Veronica. If you want to see more than the default 200 Gopher items, add the option -m followed by an integer number. To get the first 400 results, for example, add -m400 to your query. To see fewer items than the default of 200, use the -m option with an integer less than the default. If you want to see all records in the Veronica database that match your criteria, add the -m option without any number to your query.

One of the simplest searches in Veronica is on a single keyword. The following example shows a search on the keyword internet:

```
Internet Gopher Information Client 2.0 pl10
Search ALL of Gopherspace ( 3300 servers ) using veronica
     1.   Search gopherspace at NYSERNet <?>
     2.   Search gopherspace at PSINet <?>
 --> 3.   Search gopherspace at University of Pisa <?>
     4.   Search gopherspace at University of Cologne <?>
     5.   Search Gopher Directory Titles at NYSERNet <?>
     6.   Search Gopher Directory Titles at PSINet <?>
lqqqqqqqqqqqqqqqqqqqSearch gopherspace at University of Pisaqqqqqqqqqqqqqqqqqqqqk
x                                                                              x
x Words to search for                                                          x
x                                                                              x
x  internet                                                                    x
x                                                                              x
x                   [Cancel: ^G] [Erase: ^U] [Accept: Enter]                   x
mqqqqqqqqqqqqqqqqqqqqqqqqqqqqqqqqqqqqqqqqqqqqqqqqqqqqqqqqqqqqqqqqqqqqqqqqqqqqqqqqj
Press ? for Help, q to Quit, u to go up a menu                     Searching..\
```

This search returns a menu list of records that have the word *internet* in the title field:

```
Internet Gopher Information Client 2.0 pl10
Search gopherspace at University of Pisa: internet
 -->  1.   CA-91:17.DECnet-Internet.Gateway.vulnerability.
      2.   CA-91:18.Active.Internet.tftp.Attacks.
      3.   CA-92:03.Internet.Intruder.Activity.
      4.   CA-93:14.Internet.Security.Scanner.
```

```
 5. b-43.ciac-decnet-internet-gateway.
 6. c-16.ciac-net-internet-intrusions.
 7. CA-91:17.DECnet-Internet.Gateway.vulnerability.
 8. CA-91:18.Active.Internet.tftp.Attacks.
 9. CA-92:03.Internet.Intruder.Activity.
10. CA-93:14.Internet.Security.Scanner.
11. b-43.ciac-decnet-internet-gateway.
12. c-16.ciac-net-internet-intrusions.
13. Internet Resource Guide/
14. Internet FYI Series/
15. Internet Resource Guide (ds.internic.net)/
16. Internet Resources/
17. Internet RFC documents'/
18. The Hitchhikers Guide to the Internet.
```

You can further restrict the results of a query to a certain set of Gopher types. This restriction is done by adding the -t (for *type*) option to your query. The -t flag is followed by a list of Gopher types you want to see. You can specify more than one type in the query. Simply put all the types together with no spaces after the -t. A partial list of common Gopher types can be found in Table 26.1 (refer to Chapter 25, "Using and Finding Gophers," for more information on Gopher types). To restrict the search to just Gopher directories, for example, add -t1 to your search. If you want to restrict your search to directories and text files, add -t01 to your search. The items Search Gopher Directory Titles... on the Veronica menu are Veronica searches with the -t1 option already supplied.

Table 26.1 Common Gopher types.

Type	Description
0	Item is a file
1	Item is a directory
2	Item is a CSO (qi) phone-book server
3	Error
4	Item is a BinHexed Macintosh file (discouraged)
5	Item is a DOS binary archive of some kind (discouraged)
6	Item is a UNIX uuencoded file (discouraged)
7	Item is an Index-Search server (like Veronica)
8	Item is a pointer to a Telnet session
9	Item is a binary file of some sort
I	Item is an image
s	Item is a sound

You can expand the search Veronica performs by adding the metacharacter * to the end of a string of characters. Veronica finds all words that start with that string of letters. For example, a search for chick* matches chick, chicken, chickens, and so on. This form of word stemming allows you to find all forms of a certain word—useful when you want to find the singular and plural forms of a keyword (such as star and stars).

Veronica understands the logical operators AND, OR, NOT, and parentheses. The AND operator matches Gopher titles that have both words in the title. The OR operator matches Gopher menu items that have one word or the other in the title. Another form of restriction is the NOT operator, which matches queries for which the first word is in the title and the second word is not. The parentheses operator modifies the order of interpretation of the previous operators.

The last option Veronica recognizes is -l, which creates a link file suitable for use in a Gopher server or a user's bookmark file. This option is used mostly by Gopher server administrators who want to add Gopher menu items returned by Veronica to their Gopher servers. If a Gopher server is dedicated to environmental information, for example, the server's administrator can do a search on environ* -m -l to receive a list of all titles that have words starting with *environ* and immediately put this list in the Gopher server.

> **TIP**
>
> When using the -l option, the trick is to save the file first before viewing it. When you view a file returned by a Gopher search item (of which Veronica is one), the client normally adds highlighting to the words that meet your search criteria. This highlighting causes the Gopher server to not recognize the links properly.

When you initiate Veronica with a query, Veronica reads the query from right to left and interprets operators as they are encountered. The query chicken and wine is processed in the following order: wine and chicken. If two words are next to each other, Veronica inserts an implied AND between the two adjacent keywords. If in doubt about the order of keyword interpretation, use parentheses. Also note that Veronica options cannot be concatenated together; all options must have at least one space between them.

Sometimes, it is beneficial to know where a Gopher menu item is located. The Gopher server that contains the menu item Veronica returns usually has related information you may find useful. Currently, Veronica does not maintain this information. However, your Gopher client can help you in this department. By using the Get Info about this Item option in Gopher, you can find out which host and port the items are located at and view other pertinent information. On the UNIX Gopher client, for example, you do this by pressing the = key.

Example Searches

Following are some simple searches you can do with Veronica:

`internet`	Search on the keyword `internet`. This search returns a menu list of at most 200 records that have the word *internet* in the title field.
`internet -m1000`	Search on the keyword `internet`, but show 1,000 items instead of the default of 200.
`women -t1`	Search on the keyword `women` and have only Gopher directories in the menu list.
`chicken and wine`	Search on the keywords `chicken` and `wine`. This search returns a menu list of at most 200 records that have *both chicken* and *wine* in the title field.
`chicken or wine -t1`	Search on the keywords `chicken` or `wine`, requesting directories only. This menu contains directories with the words *chicken* or *wine* or both in the title.

Following are some advanced searches you can do with Veronica:

`Chinese food not MSG`	Search for all the titles with the words *Chinese **and** food **but not** MSG*. Remember that there is an implied AND between the two words.
`chicken (wine or curry) -m`	List all titles in the Veronica database that have the words *chicken **and** either *wine **or** curry*: `chicken wine` and `chicken curry` match but not `chicken pot pie`.
`(chicken or wine) NOT (MSG or growing)`	List titles with the words *chicken **or** wine **but not** msg or growing*.
`chicken* or wine*`	Search for all titles with word *chicken, chickens,* and so on **or** *wine, wines, wineries,* and so on.

The following chart summarizes options and operators used by Veronica:

Option	Description
`-t`	Select matching Gopher types.
`-m`	Specify how many Gopher menu items to return (default is 200).
`-l`	Create a link file suitable for a Gopher server.

Option	Description
AND	Both words must be in the title.
OR	Either word must be in the title.
NOT	The first word must be in the title but not the second word.
*	Matches word stems.

How Veronica Works

Veronica has three distinct phases: a search and harvest phase, an index phase, and a user query phase. In the harvest phase, Veronica builds a database of Gopher menu items from Gopher servers. After the database is collected by Veronica, it is indexed for quick retrieval by keyword searches. The last phase, the user query, is the phase most people associate with Veronica: the searching of keywords that meet the user's criteria.

The Harvest Phase

Veronica and Gopher are both built on top of the Gopher protocol. This protocol enables individual users to communicate with servers. Without the protocol, it would be nearly impossible for a Macintosh Gopher to communicate with a VMS server. Veronica also takes advantage of this protocol when communicating between Gopher server and harvester. Because of this protocol, Gopher menu items have a common structure. The following line is a representation of a Gopher menu item's structure:

```
[Gopher Type][Title][tab][Selector String][tab][Hostname][tab][Port Number]
```

The Gopher Type is a one-character representation of the item (for example, a 0 for a text file and a 1 for a directory). The Title is the actual string of characters displayed by the Gopher client. The proper method of retrieving this item is to connect to the Hostname at the specified Port Number and send the Selector String to the server. If the item is a 0 (that is, a text file), the server sends back a text file; if the item is a 1 (that is, a directory), the server sends back a listing similar to this:

```
1About Gopher      1/AboutGopher      gopher.unr.edu      70
1Computer Services Help Desk Gopher Server      fremont.scs.unr.edu      70
1UNR Campus Information 1/UNR-Campus      gopher.unr.edu      70
1Internet Services and Other Gophers      1/OtherServices gopher.unr.edu      70
1Libraries and Reference Services      1/Libraries      gopher.unr.edu      70
1Documentation about the Internet      1/Network-Docs      gopher.unr.edu      70
1Discipline-Specific Topics      1/Selected      gopher.unr.edu      70
```

```
1Search ALL of Gopherspace     ( 3300 servers ) using veronica
    1/veronica      gopher.unr.edu     70
7Search Nevada Gopher menus by title keyword(s)     (2 servers)
    futique. scs.unr.edu      8013
.
```

In the preceding example, the first line represents a directory (Type=1) whose title string is About Gopher. The proper way to retrieve this subdirectory is to send the selector string 1/AboutGopher to the host gopher.unr.edu at port 70. The last line in this example represents a search item (Type=7) whose title string is Search Nevada Gopher.... Again, the proper way to retrieve this search item is to send an empty selector string (because no selector string was given) to the host futique.scs.unr.edu at port 70.

The search and harvest phase begins by creating a connection to a Gopher server. The harvester sends the proper selector string to the server so that the server sends back a listing of its top level menu items. For example, the following menu incorporates the list shown in the preceding example.

```
Internet Gopher Information Client v1.1
Root gopher server: gopher.unr.edu
    1.   About Gopher/
    2.   Computer Services Help Desk Gopher Server/
    3.   UNR Campus Information/
    4.   Internet Services and Other Gophers /
    5.   Libraries and Reference Services/
    6.   Documentation about the Internet/
    7.   Discipline-Specific Topics/
 -> 8.   Search ALL of Gopherspace ( 3300 servers ) using veronica/
    9.   Search Nevada Gopher menus by title keyword(s)  (2 servers) <?>
Press ? for Help, q to Quit, u to go up a menu              Page: 1/1
```

For each item in the list of the top level menu, the harvester checks to see whether the item is local to the Gopher server being harvested or if it is a link to another Gopher server. The Veronica harvester does this check to eliminate redundant Gopher links and to record new Gopher servers so that it can harvest them later. Veronica then builds a database by adding local Gopher menu items to the database.

If the item is local to the current Gopher server, the harvester must decide whether the item is a directory. A Gopher server can be thought of as a tree structure (similar to a file system structure). By traversing the subdirectories, it is possible to search the entire Gopher server. Veronica adds the directory's selector string to a list of directories for the current Gopher server. After the harvester is finished with the current directory, a new connection is made to the next subdirectory. The selector string for that directory is sent to the server and the whole process starts again for the new subdirectory.

If, on the other hand, the item is a link to another server, the harvester must decide whether the item is a new Gopher server or some other network provider like an anonymous FTP server. A text file/directory is, in the opinion of the creators of Veronica, the only true test to see whether a host-and-port combination is a real Gopher server. Other links like Telnet sessions and index searches are often not Gopher servers. If the item is a text file/directory, the hostname and port number of the server is recorded so that a harvest of that new server can be made later.

After sending the selector string to the Gopher server for the top menu items, the harvester records seven subdirectories that are local to gopher.unr.edu, one link to a Gopher server (fremont.scs.unr.edu, port 70), and the index search for use in the Veronica database (Search Nevada Gopher Menus). For each of the seven subdirectories, a separate connection is made to the Gopher server. In this manner, a Gopher server can be harvested completely. After the current server is finished, the harvester starts to search the next server in the list of Gopher servers. In this manner, all of Gopherspace can be harvested.

The harvesting of Gopherspace is done approximately every two weeks. It takes approximately two to three days to index the world's Gopher servers. The computational time, along with the strain placed on Gopher servers during the harvest, prohibits more frequent harvests.

Index Phase

In the index phase, Veronica creates indexes of the words in the titles of Gopher menu items. The Veronica indexer uses a *stop word list*, which contains some of the most common words in the English language (for example, *a*, *the*, *an*, and *for*). The stop list has a two-fold purpose: First it makes the size of the indexes smaller. Second, user queries that request these common words do not waste computation time by returning results that may not be very useful. A search on the letter *A*, for example, is usually not very beneficial.

User Query Phase

The user query phase starts when the user selects the search menu item. The Gopher client sends a message to the Veronica server with the text of the keyword (for example, chicken). The Veronica server receives the query and splits the text into atomic words. For each word, a record list is created with the information on how to retrieve the Gopher menu items from the Veronica database. After each word's record list is created, any query logic is applied. A search for Alpha and Beta creates a list that has both the words *Alpha* and *Beta* in the titles. The resulting list of Gopher menu items that meet all the user's criteria is sent back to the client, where it is presented as a menu of Gopher items that the user can immediately access.

In the example of the keyword chicken, the Gopher client presents the following screen:

```
Internet Gopher Information Client v1.1
Search gopherspace at NYSERNet: chicken
—>    1.   why.did.the.chicken.cross.the.road.
      2.   LIVER ACETONE POWDER CHICKEN.
      3.   Chicken_Little,tomato_sauce,and_agriculture-who_will_produce_tomor.
      4.   Chicken And Egg Problem With Uuencode....
      5.   Last Night'S Chicken&Egg Revisited.
      6.   Re: philosphic chicken fryers.
      7.   Re: philosphic chicken fryers.
      8.   Re: philosphic chicken fryers.
      9.   chicken-adobo.
     10.   chicken-aprict.
     11.   chicken-asian.
     12.   chicken-basil.
     13.   chicken-bourbn.
     14.   chicken-broth.
     15.   chicken-cacc-1.
     16.   chicken-cinn-1.
     17.   chicken-curry.
     18.   chicken-curry2.
Press ? for Help, q to Quit, u to go up a menu              Page: 1/12
```

The final step in the user query phase is when the user selects a menu item from the dynamically created menu Veronica presented. If you want to see the first item in this menu (why.did.the.chicken.cross.the.road?), a connection is made to a Gopher server; the user's Gopher client views the following text file:

```
Why did the chicken cross the road?
Aristotle: To actualize its potential.
Roseanne Barr: Urrrrrp. What chicken?
George Bush: To face a kinder, gentler thousand points of headlights.
Julius Caesar: To come, to see, to conquer.
Candide: To cultivate its garden.
Bill the Cat: Oop Ack.
Buddha: If you ask this question, you deny your own chicken-nature.
Moses: Know ye that it is unclean to eat the chicken that
has crossed the road, and that the chicken that crosseth the
road doth so for its own preservation.
```

Future for Veronica

Veronica is not a mature service. It is constantly under scrutiny by the developers for improvements. Veronica was and still is an experiment in network information discovery and retrieval. As the developers learn more about the network, Veronica changes. Some of the ideas the Veronica development team have in mind are listed here:

■ The ability to restrict the returned menu to items not in the set. For example, the ability to search for all items that are not text files. This is the opposite of the -t option.

■ The ability to restrict the search to a certain domain that a Gopher server is in. If you live in Australia, it would be helpful to see only Gopher menu items in Australia that meet your criteria. Conversely, the ability to see all items *not* in Australia.

■ The use of regular expressions used in UNIX programs (for example, ex and egrep).

■ The ability to search for literal matches, so that users can differentiate between gopher, GOPHER, and GoPhEr.

■ More searchable fields. With the advent of Gopher+, Gopher administrators have the ability to easily associate more information with an item in a uniform way. Some of the new fields Veronica could index are Abstracts (a short description of the item) and modification dates. Veronica will be able to index this expanded information to allow more context when searching Gopherspace.

Veronica truly lives up to the name of Very Easy Rodent Oriented Netwide Index to Computerized Archives. The developers of Veronica are constantly trying to put even more meaning to the first two words *Very Easy*.

WAIS: The Database of Databases

27

*by Richard J. Smith
and Mark Gibbs*

On the Internet, people have a remarkable desire to share knowledge. Why altruism should be a feature of cyberspace is anyone's guess, but the pioneer spirit may have something to do with it. Just as the Wild West campfire always had room for a stranger (in contrast to today's urban scene), the database always has room for another terminal. One of the great tools for finding useful stuff in many databases is WAIS.

The Wide Area Information Server (WAIS, pronounced *ways*) attempts to harness the vast data resources of the Internet by making it easy to search for and retrieve information from remote databases, called *sources* in WAIS terminology.

Sources are collections of files that consist mostly of textual material. For example, if chemistry is your forte, you can find several journals on the subject through WAIS. WAIS servers not only help you find the right source, they also handle your access to it.

Like Gopher, WAIS systems use the client-server model to make navigating around data resources easy. Unlike Gopher, WAIS does the searching for you. Currently, more than 520 sources are available through WAIS servers. A WAIS *client* (run either on your own computer or on a remote system through Telnet) talks to a WAIS *server* and asks it to perform a search for data containing a specific word or words.

Most WAIS servers are free, which means that the data is occasionally eccentric and erratic. The data can also have great gaps in coverage on some subjects and more coverage than you can believe on others. For example, you can find tons of material in WAIS about chemistry and computer science, but sources on, say, art history or the theory of juggling, are nonexistent at the moment. New WAIS servers and sources are created from time to time, so a library of Van Gogh's writings may yet be established.

WAIS is simple to use, although its text-based interface is a little user hostile. The X Window client is much easier to use, but requires that you run X Window (of course). WAIS clients are available for Macintoshes, PCs, and even supercomputers.

What Is WAIS?

WAIS was one of the first programs to be based on the Z39.50 standard. The American National Standard Z39.50—Information Retrieval Service Definition and Protocol Specification for Library Applications standard, revised by the National Information Standards Organization (NISO)—attempts to provide interconnection of computer systems despite differences in hardware and software.

WAIS was the first database system to use this standard (which may well become a universal data-search format). Unfortunately, WAIS was based on an old version of the Z39.50 standard. The newer standard is somewhat incompatible with the older one. There have been discussions about making WAIS clients and servers that can use both protocols, however.

> **NOTE**
>
> Z39.50 is similar in some respects to Structured Query Language (SQL), but it is simplified. Although this makes Z39.50 less powerful, it consequently makes it more general, so Z39.50 is likely to gain wide acceptance.

Z39.50 is an important step in making information sources on the Internet more accessible. Today, most Internet databases are accessed in ways completely different from each other. They use different standards for storing data and different tools to access that data. Although Z39.50 may change that, it is not yet clear when or how.

For example, one library catalog system may use find as its search command for a subject heading; another may use subject. Still another may use topic. If they all conformed to a standard, life would be much simpler. Z39.50-compliant systems all use the same format to construct queries. You don't have to know anything special to search a WAIS database. You just use whatever word you think may be used in relevant documents because WAIS indexes all the text in a source.

Document Rankings

After you run a search that identifies any documents, you receive a list of *hits*, or ranked document titles. The WAIS server ranks the hits from the most-relevant to the least-relevant document. Each document is scored, with the best-fitting document awarded 1,000 points. All other scores are relative to the top score.

WAIS ranks documents by the number of search words that occur in the document and the number of times those words appear.

WAIS servers also take into consideration the length of the document. WAIS servers are smart enough to exclude common words, called *stop words*, to make the search manageable. Words such as *a, about, above, across, after, the,* and so on should be excluded from your search because the frequency of their appearance in most documents makes them irrelevant in most searches. For example, if you search for *Who is Richard Simmons?*, *who* and *is* are excluded from the search because they are stop words.

> **NOTE**
>
> Stop words are controlled by the administrator of each WAIS server. In addition to generally common words, many words common to a database may become stop words. For example, the word *WAIS* may be a stop word in the database of a WAIS newsgroup; the word *Internet* may be a stop word in a database of Internet protocols.

In a WAIS server, a *word* is a series of alphanumeric characters, possibly with some embedded punctuation. A word must start with an alphabetic character: you can't search for numbers. A word can have embedded periods, ampersands, or apostrophes, but only the first kind of punctuation that you use is treated as punctuation. Any other punctuation is interpreted as a space and ends the word. `I.M.Pei` is a valid word and so is `AT&T`, but `A.T.&T.` is two words: `A.T.` and `T`.

Hyphens are not accepted as embedded punctuation because they're used so freely that they inflate the database dictionary.

Two classes of words are ignored in queries. First are *stop words* chosen by the database administrator for their complete lack of value in searching. There are 368 stop words for the public CM WAIS server. Some common stop words are *a, about, aren't, further, he, will,* and *won't*—you get the idea.

Some words are far too common to be helpful in searches. These are weeded out by the database software as the database is built. There are currently *777 buzz words* for the public CM WAIS server, each of which occurs at least 8,000 times in the database. They include words such as *able, access, account, act, action, add, added, addition, additional, address, addresses, administration,* all the way through to *winkel* (I have absolutely no idea why that one's in there).

Limitations

You cannot use Boolean logic in most WAIS searches. That is, you can't do anything other than find a single word or several words. A search for `cow and farm` searches for documents that contain *cow* and/or *and* and/or *farm*. The and should be excluded from the search. Notice that the search is "and/or" not just "and." The search for `cow farm` gives you all documents that contain any of the following:

- ■ cow and farm
- ■ just cow
- ■ just farm

You can guarantee that this limitation won't always be the way of things; already there's a new version of WAIS called FREEWAIS (get it? freeways?) which does support Boolean searches.

Also, no wildcard searching is available in WAIS. This means that you can't specify that you would accept `cows` as well as `cow`.

Unlike many regular database searches, WAIS searches can't be expanded to include articles that may talk about similar topics or to retrieve all articles that have those words (for example, `cars or automobiles or trucks or motorcycles`). Neither can you exclude words in a search (for example, `cars but not trucks`).

You can, however, increase the number of relevant documents by using more specific terms in a search. A search for `car automobile crash statistics` may retrieve more pertinent documents on the subject you want.

What Is Available?

The sources available through WAIS are as varied as the groups that communicate over the Internet: Renaissance music, beer brewing, Aesop's fables, software reviews, recipes, ZIP code information, a thesaurus, environmental reports, and many other databases are available.

The WAIS system for Thinking Machines alone gives access to more than 60,000 documents, including weather maps and forecasts, the *CIA World Factbook*, a collection of molecular biology abstracts, Usenet's *Info Mac* digests, and the Connection Machine's FORTRAN manual (a must for pipe-stress freaks and crystallography addicts). The Massachusetts Institute of Technology makes a compendium of classical and modern poetry available through WAIS.

Where To Get WAIS

WAIS was developed by Thinking Machines Corporation, Apple Computer, and Dow Jones; access to the system is available free from Thinking Machines by connecting to `telnet://quake.think.com/WAIS`.

As an alternative, WAIS client software (both executable and source) is available through anonymous FTP at Thinking Machines (use the same Internet address) in the `pub/wais/` directory. WAIS clients are available for a number of operating systems (X Window, DOS, Macintosh, and others), but they do require that your computer have some kind of TCP/IP connection to the Internet.

Searching WAIS

You can access WAIS in three ways. You can Telnet to `quake.think.com` and log in as `wais`, or you can run a local WAIS client. Your system administrator may have set up your system so that typing **wais** automatically connects you to whatever WAIS service is available. Another way to get to WAIS is through Gopher. You'll find an entry on Gopher menus such as `Other Gopher and Information Servers` that will lead you eventually to WAIS.

The first screen you see on WAIS is a list of the WAIS servers and sources available. At the time of this writing, 529 WAIS sources are available through the WAIS client at Thinking Machines, starting with `aarnet-resource-guide` and ending with `zipcodes`.

The following example screen gives you a reference number for each source, the location of the WAIS server in brackets, the name of the server, and the cost of searching that library. At this time, all WAIS servers available through Thinking Machines are free.

```
#       Server                        Source                    Cost
001:    [           archie.au]  aarnet-resource-guide           Free
002:    [      munin.ub2.lu.se]  academic_email_conf            Free
003:    [wraith.cs.uow.edu.au]  acronyms                        Free
004:    [     archive.orst.edu]  aeronautics                    Free
005:    [ bloat.media.mit.edu]  Aesop-Fables                    Free
006:    [ ftp.cs.colorado.edu]  aftp-cs-colorado-edu            Free
007:    [nostromo.oes.orst.ed]  agricultural-market-news        Free
008:    [     archive.orst.edu]  alt.drugs                      Free
009:    [     wais.oit.unc.edu]  alt.gopher                     Free
010:    [sun-wais.oit.unc.edu]  alt.sys.sun                     Free
011:    [     wais.oit.unc.edu]  alt.wais                       Free
012:    [alfred.ccs.carleton.]  amiga-slip                      Free
013:    [      munin.ub2.lu.se]  amiga_fish_contents            Free
014:    [    coombs.anu.edu.au]  ANU-Aboriginal-Studies   $0.00/minute
015:    [    coombs.anu.edu.au]  ANU-Asian-Computing      $0.00/minute
016:    [    coombs.anu.edu.au]  ANU-Asian-Religions      $0.00/minute
017:    [    coombs.anu.edu.au]  ANU-CAUT-Projects        $0.00/minute
018:    [    coombs.anu.edu.au]  ANU-French-Databanks     $0.00/minute

Keywords:
<space> selects, w for keywords, arrows move, <return> searches, q quits, or ?
```

You are now ready to conduct a search. As is true with Gopher, the problem with using WAIS is deciding which of the 529 libraries to search. An added problem is that the names of the servers don't necessarily describe what they contain. Fortunately, a directory of servers is available that contains short abstracts of the contents of each server and other information about the source of the server. Until you know exactly which server you want to search, you should start with the directory of servers.

How do you get there? The preceding screen looks like an alphabetical list of WAIS servers, so using the down-arrow key can do the trick but may take a while. Issuing the ? (help) command to reveal the online help that comes with this client displays the following information:

```
SWAIS                      Source Selection Help          Page:  1
j, down arrow, ^N      Move Down one source
k, up arrow, ^P        Move Up one source
J, ^V, ^D              Move Down one screen
K, <esc> v, ^U         Move Up one screen
###                    Position to source number ##
/sss                   Search for source sss
<space>, <period>      Select current source
=                      Deselect all sources
v, <comma>             View current source info
```

```
<ret>                   Perform search
s                       Select new sources (refresh sources list)
w                       Select new keywords
X, -                    Remove current source permanently
o                       Set and show swais options
h, ?                    Show this help display
H                       Display program history
q                       Leave this program
Press any key to continue
```

This help screen tells you how to move through the screens of the source directory. WAIS uses UNIX editor commands for moving around (the j and J, for example, are UNIX editor commands for moving down by line or by screen). Try your Page Down and arrow keys; they may work if you're using VT-100 terminal emulation. The /sss is an important command because it quickly moves the pointer to a source on a specific line. Also note that the space or period selects a source; the equal sign deselects all sources.

> **NOTE**
>
> Unless your terminal emulator does a good VT-100 emulation, don't bother with swais; you'll go crazy trying to figure out what's going on.

> **TIP**
>
> Here's a feature not covered in the swais help screen: use the spacebar or period on a selected source to deselect it.

It's too bad that the directory of servers isn't the first item on the list of sources. You know the name, so use a forward slash with the name of the server to get there. Type /**dir** to get close; after the screen is refreshed with names of new sources, use the down arrow key or type **j** once to highlight the directory of servers.

```
SWAIS                         Source Selection      Sources: 429
#               Server              Source               Cost
145:  [       ds.internic.net] ddbs-info               Free
146:  [            irit.irit.fr] directory-irit-fr       Free
147:  [        quake.think.com] directory-of-servers    Free
148:  [        zenon.inria.fr] directory-zenon-inria-fr  Free
149:  [        zenon.inria.fr] disco-mm-zenon-inria-fr   Free
150:  [           wais.cic.net] disi-catalog            Free
151:  [        munin.ub2.lu.se] dit-library             Free
152:  [ ridgisd.er.usgs.gov] DOE_Climate_Data           Free
153:  [           wais.cic.net] domain-contacts          Free
```

```
154:   [        wais.cic.net]  domain-organizations          Free
155:   [ ftp.cs.colorado.edu]  dynamic-archie                Free
156:   [  wais.wu-wien.ac.at]  earlym-l                      Free
157:   [           bio.vu.nl]  EC-enzyme                     Free
158:   [        kumr.lns.com]  edis                          Free
159:   [    ivory.educom.edu]  educom                        Free
160:   [        wais.eff.org]  eff-documents                 Free
161:   [        wais.eff.org]  eff-talk                      Free
162:   [     quake.think.com]  EIA-Petroleum-Supply-Monthly  Free
```

Remember that you are not searching a huge database containing source materials but a database of descriptions of source databases. The terms you choose should reflect what the author or owner of the database would probably use to describe it.

The following example search uses the words wais and Z39.50 to find information on the NISO standard and how WAIS uses it. WAIS uses the words wais and Z39.50 to retrieve search results that contain those words (see the following example). The information is returned in *ranked order*—the order WAIS thinks is most likely to contain your information. The first item, scored 1,000, is the one WAIS thinks is most likely to contain what you're looking for.

```
SWAIS                           Search Results              Items: 40
#     Score    Source                         Title         Lines
001:  [1000]  (directory-of-se)  cool-cfl                      76
002:  [ 953]  (directory-of-se)  dynamic-archie                59
003:  [ 858]  (directory-of-se)  wais-docs                     24
004:  [ 834]  (directory-of-se)  wais-talk-archives            18
005:  [ 810]  (directory-of-se)  alt.wais                      18
006:  [ 810]  (directory-of-se)  wais-discussion-archives      18
007:  [ 691]  (directory-of-se)  cool-net                      50
008:  [ 572]  (directory-of-se)  aftp-cs-colorado-edu         144
009:  [ 476]  (directory-of-se)  bionic-directory-of-servers   31
010:  [ 452]  (directory-of-se)  cicnet-wais-servers           55
011:  [ 381]  (directory-of-se)  cool-lex                      59
012:  [ 333]  (directory-of-se)  IUBio-INFO                    71
013:  [ 333]  (directory-of-se)  directory-of-servers          32
014:  [ 333]  (directory-of-se)  sample-pictures               23
015:  [ 333]  (directory-of-se)  utsun.s.u-tokyo.ac.jp         32
016:  [ 309]  (directory-of-se)  journalism.periodicals        58
017:  [ 309]  (directory-of-se)  x.500.working-group           38
018:  [ 286]  (directory-of-se)  ANU-Theses-Abstracts          89
```

This search resulted in some irrelevant sources. For example, cool-cfl is a database of files from a group concerned with conservation in libraries, archives, and museums. This might be a bug in WAIS—not improbable; Internet software is being developed and improved continuously.

The second source, dynamic-archie, discusses a Dynamic WAIS prototype at the University of Colorado that performs Archie searches with WAIS. This could be useful...and so could the next four sources. The rest don't seem to be relevant.

The information that describes the sources in WAIS is determined by the owners of the source. Some sources, such as ERIC databases, give detailed information that makes the directory of sources a valuable tool in finding out which sources are relevant. Other sources have minimal descriptions that aren't very useful or won't be found through the directory of services. Such source descriptions are probably of use only to people who know they are available in the WAIS database.

From here, press the letter s to return to the sources, using the /wais command to select the three sources with *wais* in the name.

```
SWAIS                      Source Selection              Sources: 429
#             Server                      Source        Cost
415: * [    quake.think.com]  wais-discussion-archives   Free
416: * [    quake.think.com]  wais-docs                  Free
417: * [    quake.think.com]  wais-talk-archives         Free
418: [hermes.ecn.purdue.ed]  water-quality              Free
419: [    quake.think.com]  weather                    Free
420: [    sunsite.unc.edu]  White-House-Papers         Free
421: [    wais.nic.ddn.mil]  whois                      Free
422: [    sunsite.unc.edu]  winsock                    Free
423: [ cmns-moon.think.com]  world-factbook             Free
424: [    quake.think.com]  world91a                   Free
425: [        wais.cic.net]  wuarchive                  Free
426: [        wais.cic.net]  x.500.working-group        Free
427: [wais.unidata.ucar.ed]  xgks                       Free
428: [        cs.widener.edu]  zen-internet               Free
429: [    quake.think.com]  zipcodes                   Free
```

You could also select the alt.wais group (the one ranked fifth in your initial search), but these three will work. Using Z39.50 as a search criterion simplifies the search; the word *wais* is probably scattered throughout most of the documents, lessening its relevance to the search. To enter the search text, select the sources you want to search; you are then prompted for keywords. After typing the keywords, press Enter; WAIS searches each selected source and ranks the results according to their relevance.

```
SWAIS                          Search Results              Items: 39
#   Score    Source                    Title               Lines
001: [1000] (      wais-docs)  z3950-spec                 2674
002: [1000] (wais-talk-archi)  Edward Vie Re: [wald@mhuxd.att.com: more  383
003: [1000] (wais-discussion)  Clifford L Re: The Z39.50 Protocol: Ques  325
004: [ 939] (wais-discussion)  Brewster K Re: online version of the z39  2659
005: [ 893] (wais-discussion)  akel@seq1. Re: Net resource list model(s  347
006: [ 823] (      wais-docs)  waisprot                   1004
007: [ 800] (wais-discussion)  Michael Sc Re: Dynamic WAIS prototype an   27
008: [ 338] (wais-discussion)  harvard!ap Re: Z39.50 Product Announceme   51
009: [ 333] (      wais-docs)  protspec                    915
010: [ 331] (wais-discussion)  Unknown Subject              6
```

```
011:   [ 331] (wais-discussion)   uriel wile Re: poetry server is up [most    31
012:   [ 313] (wais-talk-archi)   brewster@q Re: Re: Information about z39     69
013:   [ 313] (wais-talk-archi)   ses@cmns.t Re:  Z39.50 1992                 171
014:   [ 313] (wais-talk-archi)   ses@cmns.t Re:   Z39.50 1992                 90
015:   [ 308] (wais-discussion)   Brewster K Re:Hooking up WAIS with othe      66
016:   [ 292] (wais-discussion)   Brewster K Re: [morris@Think.COM: it's s     25
017:   [ 286] (wais-talk-archi)   mitra@pand Re:Z39.50 1992                    71
018:   [ 284] (wais-discussion)   Brewster K Re: WAIS-discussion digest #6     18
```

The results look promising. The first Z39.50 is ranked 1,000. In fact, the first three seem to be relevant. The name of the information source is given, along with the title of the information. In this case, the title appears to come from e-mail message subject headings. Finally, the screen gives the number of lines contained in the information.

From here, you can read each result and have pertinent results e-mailed to you or even to another person. At the search result screen, type the letter m to receive a prompt asking for an e-mail address. If none of the documents are relevant, you can go back to the sources and redefine the search strategies or add additional appropriate sources to search. The sample documents contain the desired information, so this search has worked.

Because WAIS uses natural language query in its search mode and searches the full-text index of the source, changing any of the search words produces different results. Using a natural language search such as how does wais use Z39.50 protocol produces the following results:

```
SWAIS                           Search Results                Items: 39
#     Score    Source            Title                              Lines
001:  [1000]  (     wais-docs)  z3950-spec                          2674
002:  [1000]  (wais-talk-archi)  Edward Vie Re: [wald@mhuxd.att.com: more  383
003:  [1000]  (wais-discussion)  Michael Sc Re: Dynamic WAIS prototype an   27
004:  [ 998]  (wais-discussion)  Brewster K Re: online version of the z39  2659
005:  [ 777]  (wais-talk-archi)  news-mail- Re: WAIS-discussion digest #4  554
006:  [ 675]  (wais-talk-archi)  news-mail- Re: WAIS-discussion digest #3  535
007:  [ 640]  (wais-talk-archi)  news-mail- Re: WAIS-discussion digest #3  636
008:  [ 629]  (wais-talk-archi)  brewster@t Re: WAIS-discussion digest #5  749
009:  [ 608]  (wais-talk-archi)  news-mail- Re: WAIS-discussion digest #4  601
010:  [ 607]  (wais-talk-archi)  fad@think. Re: WAIS Corporate Paper - "   424
011:  [ 607]  (wais-talk-archi)  composer@b Re: WAIS, A Sketch of an Over   449
012:  [ 589]  (wais-talk-archi)  news-mail- Re: WAIS-discussion digest #4  621
013:  [ 549]  (wais-talk-archi)  news-mail- Re: WAIS-discussion digest #3  575
014:  [ 524]  (wais-talk-archi)  brewster@t Re: WAIS-discussion digest #4  682
015:  [ 515]  (wais-talk-archi)  news-mail- Re: WAIS-discussion digest #3  521
016:  [ 510]  (wais-talk-archi)  news-mail- Re: WAIS-discussion digest #4  480
017:  [ 507]  (wais-discussion)  akel@seq1. Re: Net resource list model(s  347
018:  [ 495]  (wais-discussion)  Unknown Subject                           6
```

Although many of the results are duplicates of the search using just the text Z39.50, some new documents are listed. An extensive search for all relevant documents may mean using different search strategies and a variety of WAIS source servers.

WAIS Indexing

In addition to its search features, WAIS also functions as a data-indexing tool. WAIS can take large amounts of information, index it, and make the resultant Z39.50-compliant database searchable. You can build an indexed database for your own use as a stand-alone database or, if you have a TCP/IP connection, you can make your WAIS database public by registering it with wais.com and listing it in the Directory of Sources.

To obtain the WAIS software, go to ftp://think.com/wais. This is the main distribution site for WAIS software and WAIS documentation. Both the WAIS server code and client code are available from think.com. You can find more WAIS software at ftp://ftp.cnidr.org/pub/NIDR.tools/wais, ftp://ftp.wais.com/pub, and ftp://sunsite.unc.edu/pub/wais.

Getting WAIS up and running is no trivial matter. Because it's very complicated, we'll leave that as an exercise for more daring users with time on their hands and a good supply of Valium.

The Ways of WAIS

The use of WAIS is growing slowly on the Internet. WAIS provides a convenient and efficient way to index and search large amounts of information using standards that are starting to be generally accepted on the Internet.

However, WAIS faces some tough competition. The WWW, Harvest, and Hyper-G tools offer facilities that may replace WAIS. However, it is likely that WAIS will survive and be used in niche database applications.

Navigating the World Wide Web

28

by
Glenn Vanderburg

If you've read about the Internet lately, you've probably seen some mention of the World Wide Web. It has been featured in the daily newspapers, network television, major news magazines, and, of course, in the computer industry press. The *World Wide Web* (often called *WWW*, *W3*, or just *the Web*) is drawing people and organizations to the Internet faster than ever before; this time, reality comes close to living up to the hype. The Web is visually appealing, easy to use, rich with resources both useful and useless (but nearly always fun), and truly world wide.

The World Wide Web is a *distributed hypertext* system. This means that documents contain links to other documents (*hypertext links*) and that documents on different machines, widely separated on the network, can link to each other. The Web is also a *hypermedia* system in that documents can contain sound clips and images; other media such as video clips are also common. Figure 28.1 shows a typical Web page with hypertext links highlighted and underlined.

FIGURE 28.1.

A typical World Wide Web page.

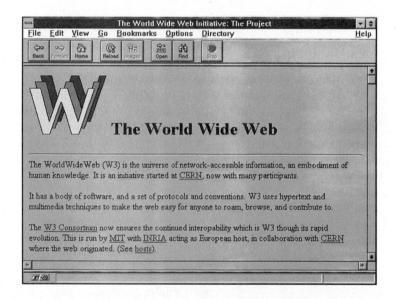

Navigating the Web is easy. While looking at one document, you can follow a link to another document by a mouse click or key press. Your *browser* (the program you use to explore the Web) will load the new document and present it to you for viewing. You can continue to follow links from there, whether you are doing serious research or just exploring for fun. Usually, the only difficult part of the process is finding your starting point for a topic, but there are Web indexes, catalogs, and search facilities that help with that process, too.

The Web has quickly become a crucial part of the Internet and its culture. If Usenet and mailing lists can be compared to the town square and restaurants where people gather and converse, then the World Wide Web fills the roles of libraries, shopping centers, and museums.

That's really just the start of it. As you will see, the Web is being used for such a wide variety of things that the only way to really get a complete feel for it is just to *use* it—to browse around, hang out, and grow familiar with the World Wide Web.

A Brief History

The Web itself is relatively new (the project was officially begun in 1990), but it has its roots in ideas that go back to 1945. This is when Vannevar Bush, then Director of the U.S. Office of Scientific Research and Development, published an article in *The Atlantic Monthly* called "As We May Think." In the article, Bush proposed the development of a mechanical filing and knowledge-retrieval system that he called the *memex*. Physically, Bush's dream bears little resemblance to the Web of today in that the memex was a personal knowledge system rather than a world-wide knowledge sharing system, and it was mechanical, making use of mirrors and microfilm. But if one ignores the physical design, the memex is the first rough design for a *hypertext* system: a system that permits documents to contain live, active links to other documents or sections of other documents so that relationships and cross-references can be examined instantly. The basic ideas of Bush's device can be seen today in the Web and similar systems, such as HyperCard on the Macintosh. Bush's paper was so influential that most consider him the "father of hypertext." (For those who are interested, "As We May Think" is available on the Web as `http://www.csi.uottawa.ca/~dduchier/misc/vbush/as-we-may-think.html`.)

In the late 1950s and 1960s, several people began attempting to realize Bush's ideas. The most famous of these people are Douglas Englebart and Ted Nelson. Englebart, working at the Stanford Research Institute, developed some experimental hypertext systems that are still amazing to people today. In the process, he invented window systems, the mouse, and several other important innovations. Nelson is known more for his writings about hypertext and his predictions about the eventual uses and forms of hypertext systems. Nelson coined the word "hypertext." At the time (and for many years after), many considered his ideas to be wildly improbable, but the World Wide Web comes quite close to his predictions.

Since Englebart and Nelson did their first experiments in the 1960s, they and others have continued to work on the concept, and some simple hypertext systems have seen wide use (Microsoft Windows' help system is an example). However, the World Wide Web, partly because it has a simple architecture and partly because it makes use of the Internet, is the first system that has demonstrated the rapid growth in information and connectedness that was envisioned by Bush, Englebart, and Nelson.

The World Wide Web project was started at CERN, the European Laboratory for Particle Physics (the initials come from its older French name, *Conseil Europeen pour la Recherche Nucleaire*) in Geneva, Switzerland, by a group led by Tim Berners-Lee. It was intended as a vehicle for real-time collaboration among physicists. Partly because of this need and because physicists at CERN wanted to collaborate with each other and also with other physicists around the world, the Web was not designed as an internal CERN system; it was designed to be world wide. Berners-Lee and others on the WWW team made several decisions that helped the Web succeed where other hypertext systems did not. They made all of the specifications open and publicly available; they designed a linking system that operated over the network and that was *inclusive* (that is, it could be adapted to use existing and future protocols, not just the ones designed to be a part of the Web). They also created sample implementations of Web servers and browsers and made them freely available.

The Web project started at CERN in 1990 and was showing slow but steady growth in 1992. This is when Marc Andreesen began working on similar collaboration and information sharing at NCSA (National Center for Supercomputing Applications). NCSA is a federally funded organization located at the University of Illinois at Urbana-Champaign (UIUC). Marc was a student who had a part-time job at NCSA developing tools for researchers. He learned about the World Wide Web and realized that he didn't have to start from scratch—the Web was designed to solve the same sorts of problems that Marc was working on. At the time, however, Web browsers were primarily text based, so Marc began writing a new browser that could mix text and graphics, taking full advantage of modern window systems such as X Window, the Macintosh, and Microsoft Windows. His new browser, combined with a few extensions to existing WWW specifications, became *NCSA Mosaic*. Compared to what had gone before, Mosaic was flashy and dazzling, combining text and graphics in the same documents. Many people began to see the potential of the Web. Mosaic, more than any other development, sparked the current interest in the Web and its explosive growth. (In fact, Mosaic made such an impression that many people think that it *is* the Web, and speak of "Mosaic pages." But the Web is independent of any one browser.)

Although CERN and NCSA were the primary forces behind the beginnings of the Web, neither controls it any longer. Because the specifications are open and inclusive, the current development of the Web is being driven by numerous forces. These forces include research groups, the Internet Society, information providers, and several new companies that have been started in order to capitalize on the Web's growth and popularity (one of which was co-founded by Mosaic's creator, Marc Andreesen). CERN and the Massachusetts Institute of Technology have started the World Wide Web Organization (W3O), a consortium intended to help coordinate future developments. However, the W3O, as it's called, is also open; its purpose is not to control but to provide a forum for cooperation—to help keep the Web from splintering into incompatible enclaves. The Web has a life of its own.

Using and Exploring the Web

To explore the Web, you use a program called a *Web browser* (or sometimes, a *Web client*). The browser makes connections over the Internet to network services, requesting network resources and displaying them to you. Most commonly, the network services are specialized Web servers, and the resources that are displayed are hypertext documents (often called *Web pages*).

However, one of the things that has made the Web such a success is that it can also connect you to some of the more traditional network services, such as FTP, Telnet, and Gopher, all using the same interface and using the hypertext documents to link them together and provide explanations.

While reading hypertext with a Web browser, certain parts of the text are highlighted or marked in some special way; those marks or highlights are *links* (refer back to Figure 28.1). A link is a pointer to some other network resource or document. By clicking a link with your mouse (or selecting it in some other way with a terminal-based browser), you direct the browser to *follow* the link. It will connect to the appropriate machine on the network, request the resource, and display it to you.

Documents on the Web that deal with similar topics are often linked together, and there are indexes that provide searchable catalogs of the available resources. By following links from one document to another, you can explore and research a topic quickly and thoroughly, and often you'll learn about related topics you hadn't even considered. If you've ever spent an hour following "see also" references in an encyclopedia just learning about new things, you'll have an idea of what the Web is like. The Web can be more fun, though, because following a link is easier and faster than looking up a new entry in an encyclopedia; the Web usually has more personality and it's often more thorough. Anyone can publish on the Web, and a great many people are publishing the things that interest them. Whether it's a serious topic or just a fun diversion, chances are that there's information about it on the World Wide Web.

The hypertext documents on the Web are written in *Hypertext Markup Language (HTML)*, version 2.0. HTML allows documents to contain other things besides text and links; for example, pictures, sound and video clips, and forms with fields that you can fill out and send back to the document's author. However, not all browsers support all the features of HTML 2.0. Today, it's hard to get the most out of the Web if your browser doesn't support forms and inline images. HTML 3.0 is currently being designed and will support features such as tables and mathematics.

Getting the Software You Need

Before you can start exploring the Web, you'll need to get a Web browser. It also helps to have a few "helper applications" your browser can use to display special document types.

Browsers

Whether your computer is a PC running Windows, a Macintosh, or a UNIX machine, you have several browsers to choose from. There are browsers available for nearly every computer environment; some are free and some are licensed for a fee. There are two primary types of browsers: *text-based*, for use on ordinary terminals or terminal emulators, and *graphical*, for use on systems with a graphical user interface.

The following sections list some of the most popular browsers and explain how to acquire them. (A list of WWW browsers is maintained by the World Wide Web Organization and can be found at `http://www.w3.org/hypertext/WWW/Clients.html`.)

Multiplatform Browsers

The Web offers several browsers that come in versions for different platforms. This section describes those browsers. One of the following may be a good choice for you if you occasionally must access the Web from different types of machines:

- **Netscape Navigator:** This is a browser from Netscape Communications Corporation. Version 1 was released in late 1994. It is supported by Windows, Macintosh, and UNIX/X. It is a fast, full-featured browser with several useful features not found in other browsers. Netscape's most useful feature is the capability to begin displaying the initial portion of a document while it is still downloading the text and images. Not only can you begin to see the document before it is fully loaded, you can begin to interact with it, scrolling or traversing links without having to wait for the full load. Netscape Navigator is a commercial product, but it's free for noncommercial use by individuals and educational institutions. If your use fits one of those categories, you can get Netscape Navigator from the locations shown in Tables 28.1, 28.2, or 28.3. Otherwise, contact `info@netscape.com` for more information.

- **NCSA Mosaic:** This is the browser that first garnered a lot of attention for the Web because of its easy user interface and its support for embedded images and other groundbreaking features. Most of those features are found in other browsers now, but Mosaic is still a good full-featured browser. Like Netscape's browser, it runs on Windows, Mac, and UNIX machines (although the UNIX versions have historically been better than the others). As of this writing, new versions of Mosaic are being tested that will support the new features of HTML 3.0, including tables and mathematics and Netscape's capability to interact with the user while a document is being retrieved. Mosaic is available free of charge.

- **AIR Mosaic:** This is a commercial adaptation of NCSA Mosaic, produced and supported by Spry, Incorporated. Spry has enhanced NCSA Mosaic and offers support services. See `http://www.spry.com/` for more information.

- **Quadralay WebWorks Mosaic:** This is another adaptation of NCSA Mosaic that has been enhanced as a commercial product and is sold with support. Currently, it is not available in a Macintosh version. Contact Quadralay at `http://www.quadralay.com/`.

Windows Browsers

In addition to the multiplatform browsers mentioned in the preceding section, there are two full-featured browsers, *Cello* and *WinWeb*, designed specifically for Windows (see Table 28.1).

Table 28.1. Windows browsers and their locations.

Browser	Location
Netscape Navigator	`ftp://ftp.netscape.com/netscape/windows`
NCSA Mosaic	`ftp://ftp.ncsa.uiuc.edu/Mosaic/Windows`
AIR Mosaic (demo version)	`ftp://ftp.spry.com/AirMosaicDemo`
Quadralay WebWorks Mosaic	`http://www.quadralay.com/products/WebWorks/Mosaic/`
Cello	`ftp://ftp.law.cornell.edu/pub/LII/Cello`
WinWeb	`ftp://ftp.einet.net/einet/pc/winweb`

Macintosh Browsers

In addition to the multiplatform browsers, there are two other browsers that run only on the Macintosh: *MacWeb*, a full-featured browser similar to WinWeb for Windows, and *Samba*, a basic browser from CERN that does not support some of the newer features, such as forms (see Table 28.2).

Table 28.2. Macintosh browsers and their locations.

Browser	Location
Netscape Navigator	`ftp://ftp.netscape.com/netscape/mac`
NCSA Mosaic	`ftp://ftp.ncsa.uiuc.edu/Mosaic/mac`
AIR Mosaic	`http://www.spry.com/`
Samba	`ftp://ftp.w3.org/pub/www/bin/mac`
MacWeb	`ftp://ftp.einet.net/einet/mac/macweb`

UNIX/X Browsers

All multiplatform browsers run on UNIX under the X Window system, in addition to the following:

- **Arena:** Arena is an experimental browser designed primarily as a testbed for new features planned for HTML 3.0. It's slow and not a particularly good browser in terms of usability, but it is interesting to see what kinds of features will be coming soon in other browsers.

■ **tkWWW:** This browser is based on the Tk window toolkit. That means it's programmable and can be controlled from other applications. It's unusual in that it assists in editing and building Web documents, but the current version is not very stable.

See Table 28.3 for a list of UNIX browsers and their locations.

Table 28.3. UNIX browsers and their locations.

Browser	Location
Netscape Navigator	`ftp://ftp.netscape.com/netscape/unix`
NCSA Mosaic	`ftp://ftp.ncsa.uiuc.edu/mosaic/unix`
AIR Mosaic	`http://www.spry.com/`
Quadralay WebWorks Mosaic	`http://www.quadralay.com/products/WebWorks/Mosaic/`
tkWWW	`ftp://ftp.aud.alcatel.com/tcl/extensions/` `tkWWW-0.12.tar.gz`
Arena	`ftp://ftp.w3.org/pub/www/arena`

Text-Mode Browsers

Finally, for UNIX users without access to X, there are several text-mode browsers:

■ **Lynx:** This is a convenient full-screen browser that supports most current features of the Web, including forms.

■ **Emacs w3-mode:** A browser mode for `emacs`. This is actually a good alternative if you're an `emacs` user because w3-mode is well-known for being quick to support new experimental features (for example, it currently supports all of HTML 3.0 except for mathematics), and it can take advantage of multiple fonts for nice formatting when you do have access to a window system. This is convenient if you have to switch back and forth between simple terminal access and your window system.

■ **CERN line-mode browser:** This is a simple prototype browser written at CERN. It is primarily a testbed and not widely used for casual browsing.

See Table 28.4 for a list of text-mode browsers and their locations.

Table 28.4. Text-mode browsers and their locations.

Browser	*Location*
Lynx	`ftp://ftp2.cc.ukans.edu/pub/lynx`
Emacs w3-mode	`ftp://ftp.cs.indiana.edu/pub/elisp/w3`
CERN line-mode browser	`ftp://ftp.w3.org/pub/www/src/WWWLineMode.tar.Z`

Helper Applications

In addition to browsers, it also helps to have some *external viewers* or *helper applications* that the browser can use to show you documents that it doesn't understand. For example, most browsers understand one or two graphics formats, but if they find an unusual format that they can't display directly, they can call a helper application to show the file.

You probably already have some programs that can be used as helper applications on your system: image viewers, PostScript previewers, and audio and video players. However, if you need others, it helps to know where to find them. Netscape has a page that describes the helper applications available for various systems; it's located at `http://home.mcom.com/assist/helper_apps/index.html`.

The way to configure browsers so that they know which helper applications to call for particular document types depends on what kind of computer you use and on the browser itself. Most UNIX browsers consult a system configuration file called *mailcap* (because it's also used for electronic mail configuration). Some Windows browsers also use a mailcap file, but others store this information in their INI files and have dialog-based configuration procedures. Macintosh browsers also have a different mechanism. Check your browser's documentation for information on this.

Staying Current

The Web is still a relatively new technology and is changing rather rapidly. It's worthwhile to try to keep your browser current so that you can use new features of the Web as they become available. Check in at your browser's home page every month or two to see what the current version status is.

There is a "Browser Checkup page" on the Web: just go to the page and it will figure out what browser and what version you're using. The page lets you know whether the browser you're using is the most up-to-date version available or not. The Browser Checkup page can be found at `http://www.city.net/checkup.cgi`.

Using WWW Browsers

Although many different browsers are available, they are remarkably similar in their interfaces. After having learned to use one browser, you should be able to learn to use a different one very easily.

In the following sections, you'll learn most of the things that browsers can do. I'll cover both graphical and textual browsers. In general, I won't get *too* specific about how particular browsers do things, but I will occasionally provide specific examples. For graphical browsers, I'll refer to *Netscape Navigator for Windows* (which is the browser used for most of the screen shots in this chapter), and I'll also give some specific examples of the textual browsers because their interfaces differ more than the graphical browsers.

Starting Up

When you start your browser, it will first load an initial page, usually called a *home page*. ("Home page" is sort of a confusing term because you'll see later that it's used to mean several different things. But in this section, I always use it to refer to the initial page that your browser loads on startup.) Most browsers let you configure the *Uniform Resource Locator* (URL), which is used to load the home page; each browser has a default. Many of the early browsers use the CERN World Wide Web Project page, but most of the newer generation of browsers have their own home pages that introduce you to the browser and its features. All default browser home pages, however, have links to important Web pages that lead to the rest of the Web. Figure 28.2 shows Netscape Navigator's home page.

FIGURE 28.2.

Netscape Navigator's home page.

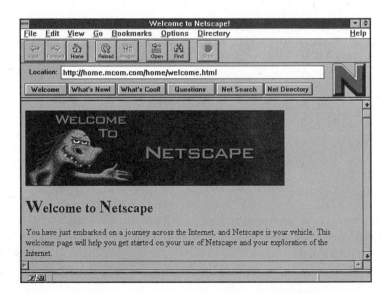

Unless your browser comes with its own home page loaded on to your local disk, you'll probably notice that loading the default home page is a little slow. This might be because it is far away from you on the network or because your link to the network is relatively slow. However, part of the reason is that the machines that hold those home pages are *busy*; thousands or millions of people all over the network are using that same browser and whenever they start up, they all connect to the same machine and load the same document. This is one reason that after you've gained some familiarity with the Web, you may want to find another page that is closer to use as a home page or one that is on a machine that's less busy. You may even want to create your own home page (see Chapter 36, "Creating Web Pages with HTML," for information on how to build your own Web pages).

Proxies

If you are in an organization that accesses the Internet from behind a firewall, you may have to use a proxy for your Web access. A Web *proxy* is a special program running on the firewall machine that forwards your Web requests to the Internet and returns the requested documents to your browser. *Firewalls* are special machines designed to shield an organization's internal network from the Internet, only permitting certain kinds of trusted traffic through. If you try to use the Web and always have trouble connecting to network hosts, you may be behind a firewall. Your browser will have to ask the proxy machine for each document, and the proxy will actually fetch the document from the Internet, passing it to the browser. Different browsers have different ways of handling this; you'll have to find out the name of your proxy; ask someone knowledgeable about your organization's Internet connection.

Following Links

World Wide Web documents, or pages, usually consist of text and pictures, just like a typical page from a book or magazine. The biggest difference is that some parts of the text (or even some of the images) are *active*; they represent links to other documents. Usually, the links are highlighted in some way so that you can tell they are there. In most graphical browsers, links are represented in a different color than the rest of the text (and image links have a colored border). By clicking the link with the mouse, you can load the other document in place of the one you're currently reading. This is called *traversing* or *selecting* a link (see Figure 28.3).

You may notice that a message in a status area of your browser's window changes as you move the mouse or cursor from link to link. If this happens, the browser is showing you the URLs of the documents associated with the links. Most browsers have an option to do this, but in some it is turned off by default. URLs are the "addresses" used on the Web to represent documents (see Chapter 6, "Domain Names and Internet Addresses," for more information about URLs).

FIGURE 28.3.

Traversing a link.

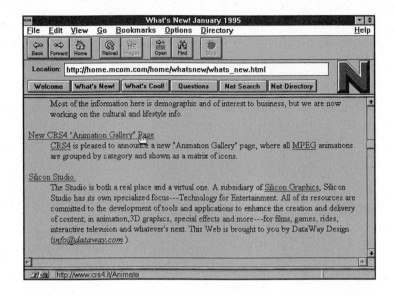

If you are using a textual browser, links can't be highlighted by a different color, so they are handled a bit differently. Lynx highlights links in bold and uses the cursor to mark the link that's ready to be selected. You use the up-arrow and down-arrow keys to move from link to link; finally, you traverse one by using the right-arrow key (Return and Enter also work). The CERN line-mode browser marks each link currently visible on-screen with a number in square brackets, like this: [1]. At the bottom of the screen, the browser prompts you for the number of a link to traverse.

Images, of course, are a problem for textual browsers. Well-designed Web pages specify text to be displayed in place of an image if the browser can't display the image. However, not all Web authors bother to specify alternate text for images; if this is the case, a textual browser usually won't display anything at all unless the image is also defined as a link, in which case Lynx displays the link as [IMAGE].

Imagemaps

Sometimes, an image represents a special type of link called an *imagemap*. With imagemaps, clicking on different parts of the image links you to different places. This is usually used to present a fancy, graphical menu of choices. Usually, the sections of the image are labeled with text in some way to tell you where to click for particular types of information. Figure 28.4 shows an imagemap with clearly labeled regions; Figure 28.5 shows an imagemap that is a literal map; for example, clicking a city name produces a weather forecast for that city.

FIGURE 28.4.

An imagemap with clearly marked regions.

FIGURE 28.5.

Another imagemap.

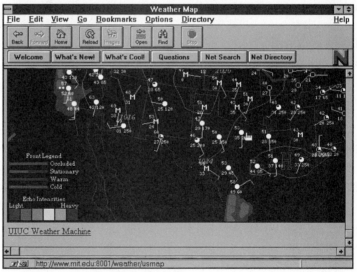

If you're using a textual browser, you can't use imagemaps. Some graphical browsers don't support them, either. However, most pages with imagemaps contain a textual link that says something like "go here to see the textual version of these pages" for the benefit of those who can't use the images.

The Different Types of Links

Each link specifies a URL, which is the address of the document to be loaded when the link is traversed. There are several different types of URLs, and each type works a little differently; therefore, it's sometimes helpful to know a little bit about them. Chapter 6, "Domain Names and Internet Addresses," describes URLs in detail, but this section gives a brief overview with an emphasis on how your browser handles each different type.

The most common type of link is HTTP. HTTP is the HyperText Transfer Protocol, designed especially for the World Wide Web at CERN. HTTP is very lightweight and fast and is used to serve most documents found on the Web today. When you traverse an HTTP link, your browser will connect to the appropriate machine, retrieve the document, and close the connection. The HTTP server will tell your browser what type of document it is so that your browser can display it correctly.

The FTP URL type is almost as common. When you traverse an FTP link, your browser connects to a machine using the File Transfer Protocol, retrieves the appropriate document, and closes the connection (see Chapter 22, "FTP: Fetching Files from Everywhere"). The FTP server does not tell the browser about the type of document, so the browser has to guess based on the file's name. Sometimes your browser's best guess may be incorrect.

If an FTP URL specifies a directory instead of an actual file, the browser will get a listing of that directory and construct a special document for display. The document is the directory listing with each file or directory name being an FTP link to that file or directory and with a special link at the top to the parent directory (see Figure 28.6). By using this facility, your Web browser can be used to explore anonymous FTP sites on the Internet.

FIGURE 28.6.

Browsing an FTP site using a Web browser.

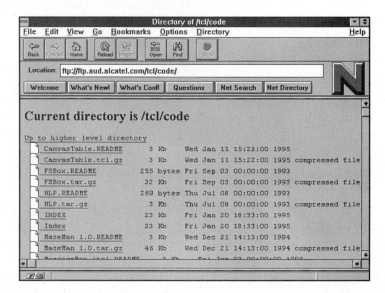

The file URL type is much like FTP except that it specifies a file on a local disk accessible to the browser. As you may guess, file URLs aren't very common on the Web at large, although you may find them useful in your own Web documents.

The Gopher URL type is used to refer to information available on Gopher servers (see Chapter 25, "Using and Finding Gophers"). Gopher is also a typed protocol, like HTTP, so your browser can do different things with documents based on their types. Typically, Gopher URLs refer to Gopher menus or text files. Your browser displays a Gopher menu as a menu of links, again with a special link at the top to take you to the parent menu.

The news URL type consists of two kinds, both of which are used to access Usenet news (see Chapter 17, "Reading and Posting the News: Using Usenet"). One type links to an individual news article that will be retrieved from your news server and displayed for you. The other type links to an entire newsgroup, and your browser will show you a list of the messages in that newsgroup with each line linked to the corresponding article. Unlike most other URL types, news URLs don't contain the name of a machine; your standard news server is used; if you don't have access to Usenet already, you can't access it through the Web. Also, news articles eventually expire and are removed from news servers, so news URLs that refer to articles are not as long-lived as most other URLs. For this reason, you don't often see news URLs in Web documents.

A Telnet URL is unusual in that it doesn't retrieve a document for you; it connects you to a service. The URL contains the name of a machine to connect to using the Internet's Telnet protocol (see Chapter 23, "Logging in to Other Computers with Telnet and Rlogin"). When you traverse a Telnet link, usually your browser will start a Telnet session (possibly in another window) with which you can log in to the other machine. Often, a Telnet URL is used to connect you to a library catalog system or some other information server that is accessed by using Telnet. Another URL type, TN3270, is similar, but it uses a version of Telnet that works with mainframe applications designed for IBM's 3270-style terminals.

A relatively new URL type, mailto, is another type that doesn't actually retrieve a document. When you traverse a mailto URL, if your browser supports this type, you are prompted to compose a mail message that will be sent to the electronic mail address contained in the URL.

Unusual Document Types

Most documents you find on the Web are in HTML (HyperText Markup Language) format, described in Chapter 36, "Creating Web Pages with HTML"; however, other types of documents exist. In some cases, you see plain text documents, images, video clips, sound recordings, Gopher menus, PostScript documents, and others. Some of these special formats are understood directly by your browser, but most of them must be displayed by helper applications. If you don't have the appropriate viewer for a document type, or if your browser doesn't know about it, you may not be able to display some documents.

Moving Forward and Back

As you traverse links from one document to another, most browsers keep track of your *path* through the Web: the list of documents you have gone through to get to your current document. By using a button, menu entry, or command (usually named "Back"), you can back up through those documents, eventually returning to your home page. After backing up through a few documents, some browsers allow you to move forward again, retracing your steps to the point at which you started backing up, without having to find and reselect the same links you traversed to get there.

This capability is a great aid to exploring. If you find a page that looks interesting, you can explore any of the links that lead from that page without worrying about losing it. If you branch off in one direction and eventually exhaust that lead, or if it turns out to be a blind alley, you can just back up and start again on another trail.

Bookmarks and Hotlists

Another aid to exploration is the *bookmark* (some browsers use *hotlists* instead, but the ideas are very similar). Like bookmarks for paper books, Web bookmarks are markers that permit you to quickly return to places of interest. You can save bookmarks to pages that are particularly interesting or that you may want to return to later. After you've saved the bookmark, it's a simple matter to return to that page later by choosing the bookmark from your list. Some browsers let you choose a bookmark from a dialog box, others have a menu of bookmarks, but the principle is the same.

Some browsers also support hierarchical bookmarks so that you can organize a long list of bookmarks into categories, making them easier to manage. Figure 28.7 shows the process of selecting a bookmark from one of the categories I've established in my copy of Netscape Navigator.

Forms

Many Web pages contain *forms*, which you can fill out with different kinds of information. In some cases, these forms just collect information for a survey; but in other cases, the forms permit you to enter information for a database query, request information on a topic, draw a picture, or play a game. Figure 28.8 shows a form used for searching the Web for pages devoted to a particular topic.

Not all browsers support forms, but most do; even the textual browser Lynx has good support for forms.

FIGURE 28.7.

Selecting a bookmark.

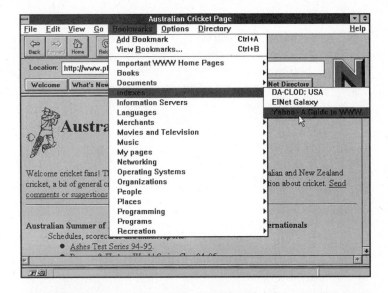

FIGURE 28.8.

A simple Web form.

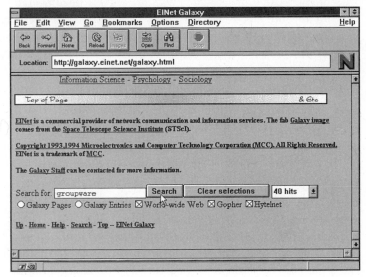

Forms can contain several different types of elements that will be familiar to users of window-based applications. *Entries* are blanks in which you can enter text. *Check boxes* are boxes with labels, and you can check as many as apply. *Radio buttons* are like check boxes, but they come in groups, and you can check only one at a time. *Menus* present a list of choices from which you can select one (and sometimes more). Finally, forms contain a *Submit* button, used to submit the form, and sometimes a *Reset* button, to clear the form and start over.

Different browsers handle forms in different ways, and textual browsers have to be especially creative. It can take some experimenting to figure out how to work all the different gadgets, but it's all right to experiment—remember that you usually can't actually submit the form until you select the Submit button. (The exception is some forms that contain only one entry: pressing Return in the entry box can submit the form.) Furthermore, if you decide not to submit the form after you've started, just back up out of the page that contains the form, choose another link, and your browser will forget all about it.

Getting Help

If you run into trouble or need to know how to do something new, it helps to be able to read your browser's documentation. All graphical browsers have a *Help* menu, and the textual browsers also have help commands that let you view help files.

Some browsers come with documentation that you install on your disk, but others simply access their current documentation from the Web. This is usually a benefit because you always see the most up-to-date documents. If you're having trouble getting anything to work, though, it's a problem. All browsers come with preliminary documentation that you'll need to get up and running; but if you can't get things to work, and you have a browser that fetches the rest of its help files over the Net, you'll have to get a friend with a connection to help you.

Speeding Things Up

If your access to the Web is over a slow link (or even if it's not), sometimes pages load slowly and you want to speed things up a bit.

Delay Image Loading

One easy way to make things seem faster is to delay the loading of images. Most graphical browsers have this facility; once enabled, your browser will load all the text for each page but not the images. Small icons are usually shown in place of the images, and you can click an icon to request that a particular image be loaded; if a page looks interesting enough, you can request that all the images be loaded. Inline images can use up a *lot* of bandwidth, so cutting them out can save a lot of time—at the expense of less exciting Web pages. The good part of the tradeoff is that you don't have to choose all or nothing. You get to decide when you want to take the time for the images and when you don't.

Browser Cache

Another strategy for speeding up your access is to make use of your browser's *cache*. Most browsers cache the documents they retrieve. When you move on to a new page, the browser saves the old page for a while, rather than throwing it away, in case you choose to revisit the page soon. In some cases, even if you don't revisit the same page, the cache will help because often pages at the same Web site share images used for markers, bullets, or dividers. If your browser loads those images into its cache for the first page at that site, subsequent pages load more quickly.

Some browsers cache old documents in memory, others use disk space; most often, it's a combination of both. Enabling the cache (if it's not enabled by default) or increasing the size of the cache can lead to increased performance.

Be careful with the cache, however, because the cache takes memory and disk storage that could be used by other applications, and you could end up slowing things down further if you make the cache too large. Be reasonable. If you have a PC with 8M of memory, using 4M for the Web cache will probably cause more problems than it will solve. Likewise, a disk cache uses disk space you might wish you had for other things. If you are running your Web browser on a multiuser machine, such as a UNIX system, you should go easy on the cache (and it might be a good idea not to use the disk cache at all) so that you don't cause too much trouble for other users.

Shared Caches

If you're using the Web from within an organization with many Web users, such as a company or university, ask one of the network administrators if the organization has a *shared* Web cache. Shared caches look and act like proxies (refer to "Proxies," earlier in this chapter), and they cache Web documents locally for a group of users. If your slow link is between you and the cache, it won't really help very much; but often the slow link is outside the organization, and a shared cache could help a lot. Because it's shared, it's less wasteful to allocate a lot of disk space to the cache because it will only cache a single copy of a document retrieved by multiple users. The cache might decrease congestion on that slow link to the outside world, which would be a win for everyone in the organization, Web surfers or not.

One Web cache your organization might want to install is a part of the Harvest system, a system for building topical indexes of Web sites (`http://harvest.cs.colorado.edu/harvest/`). Harvest is discussed in detail in Chapter 30, "New Tools: FSP, Harvest, and Hyper-G."

Problems with Caches

Caches, whether local to your browser or shared with others, sometimes cause problems. Some documents on the Web change frequently; for example, pages that contain live images of some event. Such pages are supposed to identify themselves as short-lived so that they won't be cached. However, not all such pages are set up properly, and some caches have bugs; therefore, you might find that each time you reload the page, you get the same picture. If you're using a browser cache, you can usually clear the cache; but if you're using a shared cache, you'll need to reconfigure your browser to bypass the cache if you want to see the updates regularly. (You may need to shut down your browser to do that.)

Miscellaneous Browser Functions

Most browsers also provide a host of other functions. All browsers provide the capability to type the URL you want to open (this is usually done by using a button or menu entry marked *Go* or *Open*). You can also save documents to disk, print them, or mail them to a friend. After you've grown comfortable with the basics, it's worth spending an hour or so investigating the other possibilities offered by your browser.

Setting Your Home Page

After you are familiar with your browser, you may not want to see the browser's home page each time you start up. You may have another home page that you prefer (such as your organization's home page), or you may want to build one of your own, filled with links to sites you like to visit often. To do this, you need to configure your browser to use a different startup page.

Depending on your system and browser, the way to do this may be different. Many browsers now have menu options or dialogs for setting the home page. If you can't find such an option or if you're using Windows or UNIX, try setting the environment variable WWW_HOME to the URL of the desired page. In either case, your browser's documentation should explain what to do.

Dealing with Errors

Because computers and people are involved, errors do occur on the Web. Sometimes machines are down, or there's a network problem that keeps you from reaching the machine you're interested in. At other times, a Web link points to a document that has moved, or possibly one that never existed in the first place; these are called *broken links*. Also, links occasionally point to documents you're not allowed to read—some documents on the Web are restricted to people within certain organizations.

The best way to handle such situations is to be prepared for them and not panic. If the problem looks like it might go away after a while, save a bookmark to the document and try again later (most browsers let you save a bookmark to a page even if you didn't load it successfully). In the case of a broken link, see whether the page that contained the link (or some other page at that site) contains the e-mail address of the author or maintainer of that page. Web authors usually appreciate hearing about problems with their documents, and they might reply with the correct URL. But you should also be prepared for the occasional disappointment. Sometimes, documents are withdrawn from the Web because the people or organizations responsible for them don't have time to keep them updated anymore or for other reasons. The Web is shifting and changing some, not just growing.

The Structure of Webspace

To begin navigating the World Wide Web, it's important to have some understanding of the way it all fits together and where to start.

There Is no "Top"

Many people, when they start exploring the Web for the first time, expect a unified structure, much like a directory structure, with a top-level entry point that "contains" the rest of the Web. However, like most of the Internet, the Web is not that well organized. There are "catalog" pages that attempt to categorize and index the entire Web, and there are introductory pages that attempt to provide good starting points for further exploration (as most of the browser home pages do), but none of them are complete. There is no official entry point to the World Wide Web.

You may find it helpful to think of the Web as a collection of islands in a vast ocean. Each island has some organization of its own. There are large islands and small islands, and there are connections between the islands—but there is no overall authority; there is no "official" organization to the Web.

Newcomers to the Web find this confusing at times, but it is also one of the Web's (and the Internet's) strengths: A global organizing authority would slow things down and be a barrier to the growth of the Web. Instead of a global organizing authority, several groups are attempting to survey and categorize the entire Web on a regular basis. None of the indexes produced by these groups is complete, but at some point in the future, one may emerge as *the* catalog of the Web.

Think of it this way: In the conventional publishing world, there is no real catalog of *everything* that is published. *Books in Print* covers only the United States, and there is a British equivalent that covers the U.K. and some of the former British colonies. There is a system of International Standard Book Numbers (ISBNs) and International Standard Serial Numbers (ISSNs), but there are still books and periodicals published all over the world that are not registered according to either system. The closest thing to a global catalog that we have is the United States Library of Congress, and even that has no official international status; all it has is prestige. Because of that prestige, most publishers desire to have their publications cataloged by the Library of Congress, so they register a copy there.

Perhaps soon, one or another of the unofficial World Wide Web indexes or catalogs will achieve a similar level of prestige so that nearly all the people and organizations who publish information on the Web will register their pages with that organization. Until then, though, things are much less formal.

You Can Build Your Own Structure

Although there are no "official" catalogs to the World Wide Web, there are several unofficial ones, and you can also build your own catalog of the pages that are interesting to you. If your browser has a "hotlist" or "bookmarks" so that you can save pointers to pages, use that tool. When you encounter a page that is particularly interesting, save a pointer to it. I find this particularly useful when I'm looking for one kind of information but stumble on another interesting page in the process. Rather than getting sidetracked on the new topic, I can just save a bookmark for later reference.

Other users maintain their own Web pages with links to their favorite pages on the Web. With the full structuring power of HTML at their disposal, such users have more freedom to organize their collection of links in a useful way. You may want to investigate this option if you find your collection of bookmarks getting unwieldy or if your browser doesn't allow you to organize your bookmarks hierarchically.

Ways Some Sites Structure Their Own Spaces

You usually don't have to store a reference to every page that is interesting to you. Most of the islands, or *sites*, in the Web have their own organization; from the site's home page, it is usually quite easy to find your way back to any other page at that site. In fact, most sites are organized in a loose hierarchy and provide links on each page to help you move up, down, backward, or forward in the tree of pages at that site.

Each site has slightly different ways of doing this, however, so you should learn to recognize the signs. Usually, there are links using the words *Next* or *Forward*, *Previous* or *Backward*, *Back* or *Up*, and *Home*. Following the *Next* links walks you through the pages at the site in a planned order, like reading the pages of a book in sequence. The links marked *Previous* let you go backward through that order. *Up* lets you move up a level in the hierarchy (usually this is equivalent to going back to the start of a major section). Links marked *Home* take you to the welcome page for the site. If you follow a link from somewhere else and land in the middle of a site that's organized in this way, it's easy to get to the main page for the site.

Of course, in addition to these special navigation links, there are still embedded links within the text of the pages. These might be cross-references to other pages at the same site, but remember that they can also take you away from the site completely, to related information at another site.

Avoiding Disorientation

As you browse through the Web, you travel from place to place through pages scattered all over the Internet, building a trail as you go. Some people feel disoriented if the trail gets too long. It's easy to lose track of where you are, where you've been, and how to get back to where you started.

There are several ways to avoid disorientation. For newcomers to the Web, it's best to try to keep your trail from getting too long. When you find a place that's very interesting, with leads to a lot of other interesting places, save a bookmark to that place, back up to your starting point, and jump straight to your new treasure trove to begin further exploration.

If it's important to you to know *where* you are, turn on the option in your browser that displays the URL of the current document. Because most URLs contain the name of the machine where the document is located, you can usually tell something about "where you are" (`akebono.stanford.edu` is at Stanford University, for example). However, be prepared to go to companies, universities, and countries you've never heard of.

As you gain experience with the Web, you'll learn an easier way to avoid becoming disoriented; you'll realize that concepts like "where you are" and "how to get back" don't really matter. You're always at your keyboard, looking at a document from out in the Web someplace. Save references to places you might want to visit again, and just keep exploring. Occasionally, when I've reached the end of a long exploration and feel that I've exhausted all my leads, I start clicking Back just for fun, to see where I've been. Sometimes there are 30 or 40 links between my starting point and the eventual endpoint, and that's not counting the pages that turned out to be blind alleys. When I first started exploring the Web, I wanted to always know how far I was from my home page, but now I rarely know, and I don't feel lost. It just takes a while to get used to the vastness of the Web.

Finding Things on the Web

After you find a Web page on a particular topic, it's usually easy to find other related information because pages tend to have links to other pages on the same topic—but how do you find that first page?

Earlier, I mentioned *indexes* or *catalogs* of pages on the Web. There are several of these, and they can be used to search the Web for the information you need. I'm going to give you an example using the catalog I find most useful, called *Yahoo* (`http://www.yahoo.com/`). Other indexes use different ways of gathering and organizing information and different styles of searching, and one of the others might be a better match for the way you think. Two good alternatives are *Lycos* (`http://lycos.cs.cmu.edu/`) and *WebCrawler* (`http://webcrawler.cs.washington.edu/WebCrawler/`). One of the nice things about Yahoo is that it keeps a list of other Web catalogs, and there's a link to that list on almost every page in Yahoo. Therefore, if you want to try one of the alternatives, just go to Yahoo and follow the links to the other catalogs from the Yahoo welcome page.

Figure 28.9 is a picture of the Yahoo welcome page. You can see that it is organized into categories, and you can choose the category that seems most likely to contain the information you're looking for. Often, you can find information quickly this way, and it's a good way to explore when you don't know exactly what you're looking for.

FIGURE 28.9.

Some of Yahoo's subject categories.

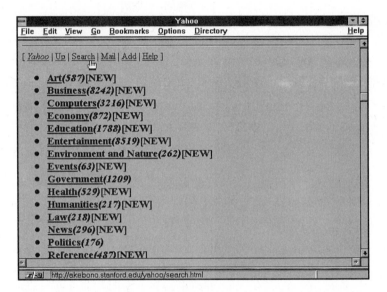

If you are uncertain about what category might be appropriate for your topic, or if it's something that could reasonably fall under more than one category, it might be better to use Yahoo's search facility. The next few figures illustrate the search process, starting with Figure 28.10, the Yahoo search form. I'm interested in learning about the comet that hit Jupiter a while back, but I can't remember the name of it, so I just enter a couple keywords that seem likely to get me what I want.

FIGURE 28.10.

Starting a Yahoo search.

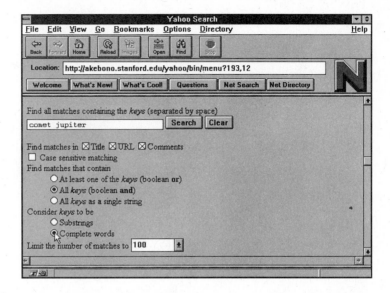

When I submit the form, Yahoo searches its entire catalog for pages that match the keywords I entered. Figure 28.11 shows the results of the search, and there are several pages about the comet impact to choose from. The result page has useful information about each of the matching pages, including a summary and a direct link to the page, so it's easy to take a look at the real thing after you've done the search. The search result also tells you how the page is classified in Yahoo's category system and includes a link to that category page so that you can investigate other pages listed in the same category. For the example, I'll follow a link to one of the comet pages that looks particularly interesting (see Figure 28.12).

FIGURE 28.11.

The result page of a Yahoo search.

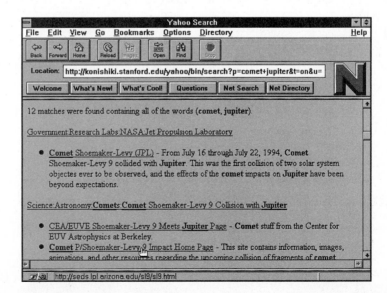

FIGURE 28.12.

One of the pages found in the Yahoo search.

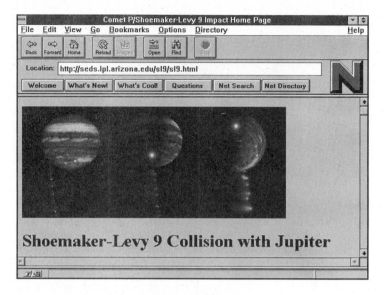

Fun, Interesting, or Useful Places

As you explore the Web, you'll build your own list of interesting places, and those places will lead to others. A little exploration tends to lead to more. To get started, though, here are a few pointers to places you may want to investigate. Some of them are just for fun, others have a wealth of serious and useful information, and still others fall somewhere in between.

Table 28.5. Fun, interesting, or useful places.

Place	Address
Web Catalogs	
Lycos	http://lycos.cs.cmu.edu/
WebCrawler	http://webcrawler.cs.washington.edu/WebCrawler/
Yahoo	http://www.yahoo.com/
Arts and Entertainment	
Hollyweb	http://www.ingress.com/users/spease/hw/hollyweb.html
Internet Underground MusicArchive	http://www.iuma.com/
JazzWeb	http://www.nwu.edu/WNUR/jazz/

Place	Address
Movie Database Browser	`http://www.msstate.edu/Movies/`
OTIS	`http://sunsite.unc.edu/otis/otis.html`

Computers and the Internet

Best of the Web	`http://wings.buffalo.edu/contest/`
Cool Site of the Day	`http://www.infi.net/cool.html`
Economics and the Internet	`http://gopher.econ.lsa.umich.edu/EconInternet.html`
MPEG Movie Archive	`http://w3.eeb.ele.tue.nl/mpeg/`
SGI Silicon Studio	`http://www.studio.sgi.com/`
Xearth	`http://www-bprc.mps.ohio-state.edu/xearth/xearth.html`

Fun

Cybersight	`http://cybersight.com/cgi-bin/cs/s?main.gmml`
Dr. Fun	`http://sunsite.unc.edu/Dave/`
World Birthday Web	`http://sunsite.unc.edu/btbin/birthday/`

Hobbies, Crafts, and Sports

America's Cup '95	`http://www.ac95.org/`
Juggling Information Service	`http://www.hal.com/services/juggle/`
LEGO Information	`http://legowww.itek.norut.no/`
Origami Page	`http://www.cs.ubc.ca/spider/jwu/origami.html`
The Sports Server	`http://www.nando.net/sptsserv.html`
Wine.com	`http://www.wine.com/wine/`

Libraries, Museums, and Information Sources

French National Center for Art and Culture Georges Pompidou	`http://www.cnac-gp.fr/index-e.html`
Library of Congress	`http://lcweb.loc.gov/homepage/lchp.html`
Raleigh News and Observer (NandO)	`http://www.nando.net/welcome.html`
The United States Holocaust Memorial Museum	`http://www.ushmm.org/`
Usenet FAQs (Frequently Asked Questions lists)	`http://www.cis.ohio-state.edu/hypertext/faq/usenet/`

continues

Table 28.5. continued

Place	Address
The WebMuseum	http://www.oir.ucf.edu/louvre/
Science	
Entomology at Colorado State University	http://www.colostate.edu/Depts/Entomology/ent.html
Face of Venus	http://stoner.eps.mcgill.ca/bud/first.html
The Nine Planets	http://seds.lpl.arizona.edu/nineplanets/nineplanets/nineplanets.html
Physics e-Print archive	http://xxx.lanl.gov/
Purdue Weather Processor	http://thunder.atms.purdue.edu/
Travel	
Guide to Australia	http://www.csu.edu.au/education/australia.html
Paris	http://meteora.ucsd.edu/~norman/paris/
Yukon Visitor's Guide	http://www.yknet.yk.ca/
Miscellaneous	
CIA	http://www.ic.gov/
PAWWS Portfolio Management Challenge	http://pawws.secapl.com/pmc.html
The White House	http://www.whitehouse.gov/

The Future of the Web

In spite of all of the current excitement, and in spite of the fact that the Web is more dazzling and comes closer to fulfilling the promise of the Internet than anything that has gone before, it is clear that the World Wide Web is in its infancy. There are pressures to provide new functionality on the Web, to improve its performance and ease of use, and to use the Web for new purposes. There is a huge amount of research and development in progress with regard to the Web. It's impossible to predict what might happen, but in this section, I'll try to give you a snapshot of some of the directions people are talking about and some of the things that may come.

Some of these new technologies and ideas are actually in production, although they are not widespread and are still being refined. Others are currently being developed; still others are no more than gleams in someone's eye. Each of them, however, stands a good chance of someday becoming an important part of the World Wide Web.

New Types of Documents

Most documents on the Web are written in HTML, the HyperText Markup Language. HTML is quite simple, and its simplicity has made it easy for the Web to get started. However, people are starting to want more from HTML than it currently offers, and alternatives are being developed.

It's unlikely, though, that any one alternative will be chosen as *the* next generation HTML; that's because people disagree with what a document markup language should look like. Those who are using the Web for publishing technical information wish that HTML provided more versatile ways of describing the *structure* of their documents; those who are doing marketing and public relations work on the Web wish that HTML gave them more control over *appearance*. People disagree on how to accomplish these goals, and there are many who consider them incompatible; therefore, there are several different groups working on possible solutions. The alternatives mentioned in the following sections are prominent examples, but there are others.

HTML 3.0

Work is proceeding on a new version of HTML, called HTML 3.0 (the version most widely supported as of this writing is HTML 2.0). HTML 3.0 attempts to correct some of the most glaring flaws in the current HTML, without going too far (most people agree that HTML should remain relatively simple and easy to implement). The most important new features of version 3.0 are tables and mathematics. The new version also cleans up some of the messy or inconsistent details of the current version.

HTML 3.0 is currently supported by two browsers that run on UNIX: Arena (which was designed specifically as a testbed for new HTML ideas) and Emacs-w3, which implements all of HTML 3.0 except for mathematics. New versions of Netscape Navigator also support many HTML 3.0 features, including tables.

General SGML

Many of those who are doing actual publishing on the Web want more versatile and flexible ways of describing the logical structure of their documents. This is particularly true for people publishing technical information that must be indexed and searched, in addition to being casually browsed by Web explorers. Many such people are hoping that the Web soon will support the Standard Generalized Markup Language (SGML).

SGML is actually a way of describing the structure of a whole class of documents. After that is done, you can mark up a particular document to show how it matches that structure. HTML is actually one simple application of SGML designed for typical textual documents; but those with more specialized documents (such as phone books and bibliographies) want to have other SGML document types to choose from when they publish on the Web.

Some information providers have chosen to store master copies of their documents in other SGML formats for searching and maintenance purposes, translating those formats to HTML for Web browsing. Other groups, however, are hoping to add SGML knowledge directly to Web browsers. Mosaic version 2.5 is supposed to come with a free version of a product called *Panorama* from SoftQuad Corporation. Panorama is capable of understanding any SGML document type and will work with Mosaic as a helper application.

Style Sheets

Users who are more concerned with the appearance of their documents than the logical structure are hoping for better ways to control that appearance. Currently, HTML gives an author very little control over how the document will be displayed.

Most of the work in this direction centers on *style sheets*. Rather than turning HTML into a full-function formatting language, the goal is to come up with a second style language that can be used to specify how various parts of an HTML document should be formatted. Some of the proposals concentrate solely on HTML, other style sheet proposals are meant to be useful with arbitrary SGML documents. One such proposal is DSSSL-Lite, which is based on the SGML-related DSSSL (Document Style Semantics and Specification Language) standard.

New Browsers

If the new document types are to become useful, there will have to be new browsers that understand them. Additionally, people are working on browsers that support different modes of use and more interactive documents.

Browsers As Tools

Earlier, I mentioned that many Web browsers ship with only minimal documentation, with the rest being available on the Web. Other applications are starting to do the same thing. Several large software systems are now shipping without extensive user documentation. When you ask the documentation for help, it fires up a Web browser to access the documentation from the network. This can be wonderful if you're connected to the Net because the documentation is always up to date, and you don't have to waste shelf or disk space for documentation you might not use very often. Soon, we'll see browsers designed to make it easy for other applications to use the browsers this way. Mosaic for UNIX already has this capability.

Currently, most applications that find their documentation on the Web are designed for UNIX systems because it's very common for UNIX systems to be connected to the network. However, as network connectivity becomes more common in the PC and Macintosh worlds, you can expect to see many more programs use Web browsers as help systems. (Of course, there will always be systems that don't have network connections. Software developers should make sure that you can get a copy of the documentation for your local disk if you need to.)

Componentware Browsers

It's already clear that browsers are going to have a hard time keeping up with all the things people want to do with the Web, and all the different kinds of documents out there. The browser you get tomorrow, which supports all the best new features, might be slow to pick up the next big advance; but not many people want to change browsers every six months.

One possible solution is to design browsers as *componentware*—instead of one big application that has a built-in understanding of many different types of documents, these browsers will be loose confederations of cooperating components, each of which understands one type of document. When the main part of the browser encounters something it doesn't understand, it looks for a component that does understand it, gives it an area of the screen to draw on (if required), and hands the document over. To support a new type of document, you won't have to upgrade your whole browser; you'll just install a new component. You may already be familiar with non-Web applications that work this way—applications that cooperate by using Microsoft's OLE (Object Linking and Embedding) system or the Apple-IBM OpenDoc system are examples of this idea.

Sun Microsystems Laboratories is developing a new Web browser based partially on this philosophy, with a working title of *HotJava*. It can readily load new components to handle document types it doesn't understand. Interestingly, HotJava's components are written in a special language designed to be *safe* so that the components cannot do unpleasant things to your system, like erasing your files or installing viruses. As a result, HotJava users can trust new components they get from the network. HotJava has the capability to automatically locate new components on the network, download them, and install them, with no requirement for the user to even know what's happening. When using HotJava, upgrades happen transparently.

Figure 28.13 shows HotJava (running on a UNIX system) displaying a page with *active content*: When I clicked the three graphs, each began an animation of a sort algorithm, moving the bars around as I watched. The image in the figure was taken just after QSort finished, with the other two still running. HotJava doesn't have built-in knowledge of how to display that page—it searches for the extension and loads it from the network when it finds something it doesn't understand.

FIGURE 28.13.

WebRunner (the original name of HotJava) displaying a page with active content.

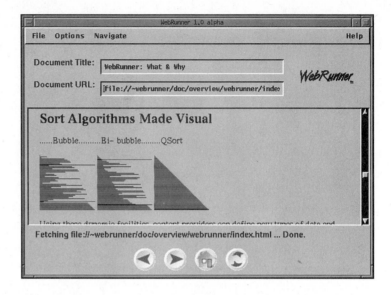

The HotJava authors have written several other interesting Web applications that demonstrate a level of interactivity not found elsewhere on the Web. It's an interesting browser that's worth watching for. The home page for more information is http://java.sun.com/.

Common Client Interface

Another strategy, similar to the componentware approach, is to give helper applications a way to interact with the browser. Currently, documents viewed by helper applications are rather static (they can't contain links to other documents, for example). The Mosaic team is developing a system called the *Common Client Interface (CCI)*, which allows helper applications to control the browser itself. This system will permit much more interactive documents and may be another way to achieve the same kinds of interesting applications the componentware browsers hope to achieve.

New Structures

The current, loose organization of the Web has its advantages, but it has its problems, too. We're certain to see many different attempts to give the Web a little more structure.

URNs

Currently, links on the Web are done in terms of URLs, or Uniform Resource Locators. As the name implies, URLs contain information about the *location* of a document. If a document moves, URLs that used to be valid suddenly become invalid. (These are called *broken links*.)

One solution currently being worked on is to use Uniform Resource Names (URNs), which would not contain information about the document's location at all. URN servers on the network would help applications translate from URNs to URLs. After this system is in place, an information provider will be able to move a document without breaking all the links to it, as long as the information provider informs the URN servers of the change.

Another application for URNs is to provide "mirrored" resources. Consider the WWW server at CERN, the home of the Web. That server has a lot of useful information and is very popular. Partly as a result of that popularity, it's also overloaded a lot of the time, so retrievals from there are slow. Additionally, it's in Europe, which slows it down even more if you are trying to get to it from the United States. It would be great if there were a copy of all of the CERN Web pages (a *mirror*) in the U.S. as well, to be closer to a large group of users and to spread the load around. However, by using URLs, it wouldn't do a lot of good because links have to point to one site or the other, and most links would probably continue to point to CERN because it seems more "authoritative."

URNs may solve this problem. URN servers will translate an URN into multiple URLs, each of them pointing to a mirror site at a different location. Then the browser can decide which site is closer and retrieve the document from there.

Hierarchical Cache Structures

In "Shared Caches," earlier in this chapter, I mentioned the use of *caches* to help speed access to commonly accessed documents. The Harvest cache system supports a hierarchy of caches with local caches first trying larger regional caches to see whether they have a copy of the document. Then the caches try a huge statewide cache before finally attempting to retrieve the document from its source. It will be interesting to see whether states or organizations begin setting up such groups of caches for Web access.

Special-Interest Catalogs

In addition to the indexes that attempt to catalog the entire Web, servers are starting to appear that have a more limited goal: They provide a clearinghouse for WWW information on a particular topic. These sites are already quite useful. One service they do not yet provide (but may in the future) is a notification service. It would be very nice if the clearinghouse site on, say, anthropology were able to notify you (through electronic mail, for example) when it learned of a new anthropological resource available on the Web.

Rating Servers

Almost certainly, many of you will have read about the availability of pornographic material on the Internet. This is of great concern to many parents, and also to many schools that are trying to introduce their students to the Internet. Some researchers have proposed the creation of "rating servers" that could provide information on the "suitability" of information at a particular site. Browsers could be configured to check with a rating server first and to allow retrieval of a document only if it were approved by the rating server (or, more likely, if it were not *disapproved*).

Some people have been concerned that this proposal would engender censorship, but the nature of the Web means that adherence to the recommendations of such servers will almost certainly be voluntary. Furthermore, such rating servers will probably be useful for other things. One example is the question of scientific peer review. Currently, scientific papers published in journals are reviewed by other scientists to ensure that the research is valid and that it follows accepted scientific practices. On the Web, where anyone can publish whatever information they like, some similar system is needed so that readers can tell whether they are reading serious science or quackery. It may be that scientific organizations (such as the American Medical Association) will set up rating servers to inform readers of those papers that have been reviewed and found to be acceptable.

Backlink Servers

One of the ways in which the Web differs from Ted Nelson's early vision of hypertext is that links are not bidirectional; that is, when you're reading one document, you can't find out what other documents have linked to it. Sometimes it would be nice to know. Suppose that you were reading a document on the Web about a revolutionary new medical technique. Wouldn't it be nice to know what other people had to say about it? If others have read the paper, certainly they would link to it if they found it useful, or write a critique (also with a link to the original) if they found the research to be flawed. It would be nice to be able to follow those links back from the current document to all the other documents that refer to it.

The current Web design has links stored inside the source document so that you can't find a link from the destination document at all. However, it is possible that future developments may have link information stored separately in *link servers* so that you can learn about links based on either the source or the destination document. Obviously, backward links would work a little differently, but this capability will be useful, nonetheless.

New Uses

Finally, people will certainly start to use the Web in new ways. Consider the following examples.

Closer Integration with E-Mail

Already, URLs are the most common way for people on the Internet to tell each other the location of interesting resources. People send URLs around in mail and Usenet posts all the time. It's inevitable that the Web and e-mail will be tied together a little more tightly. One example is the X-URI header tag people are already adding to their e-mail and Usenet posts. Usually, it contains the URL of the sender's home page. Also, at least one e-mail program can automatically recognize URLs in the text of a message and highlight them so that the reader can click on them; the URL is then automatically passed to a Web browser to be displayed.

In the future, it may be common to send HTML in the body of e-mail messages, with mail programs that understand how to display it properly.

The Web as a Gateway to Other New Services

Almost from the beginning of the Web, people have found ways to interface existing programs and applications to it. These interfaces are called *gateways*, and there are gateways to interesting systems all over the Web (two examples are the Xerox map viewer, `http://pubweb.parc.xerox.com/map/` and the Stock Quote server, `http://www.secapl.com/cgi-bin/qs`). Such gateways will continue to be an important part of the Web, and they will probably become even more common.

As completely new services come to the Internet, such as video conferencing or video on demand, we may see the Web serve as another kind of "gateway." We may use the Web as a directory of available services and the interface for accessing those services. It's easy to imagine a video catalog on the Web that you can browse and search, finally selecting a movie and arranging a time for it to be sent over the network to your home.

The Disappearance of the Web

Perhaps the most important change we may see on the Web is not so much a change in function, but a change in perception. In reality, the Web is just a gigantic, shared network file system, similar in many ways to the file system on your hard disk. Currently, it's difficult for most people to actually use it that way because fast, full-time connections to the Internet are still somewhat uncommon—but that may not be the case for long.

After you have easy access to the Internet whenever you're using your computer, it becomes easy to use the Web as an extension of your hard disk. You don't have to download a personal copy of every document that interests you. Instead, you can just store a pointer to it and retrieve it whenever necessary. There are already people who are doing this on a regular basis. It's very useful to have many applications (not just specialized "browsers") that know how to retrieve files from the Web.

For now, when you are using the World Wide Web, you're aware of it: You're using a Web browser, flying around and exploring, and traversing new links. However, when other applications use the Web in the course of helping you do your work, it won't be so obvious. You may use the Web so often that you don't even think about it—the Web will become an extension of your computer.

Opening Doors with Hytelnet

29

by Peter Scott

The amount of information available on the Internet is staggering and continues to grow. The Internet's size, as well as the lack of a centralized, governing body to issue standards for information retrieval, may cause even the bravest "navigator" frustration and confusion when attempting resource location. The compilation and maintenance of traditional paper directories is now obsolete because currency of information is all important. Any serious attempt to compile resource directories must now take place on the medium being indexed.

Today, an Internet user has access to a number of resource-discovery tools, including Gopher, the World Wide Web, Veronica, Jughead, and WAIS. But this was not the case when Hytelnet was developed. In fact, Hytelnet was the first such tool to be made freely available to the Internet community. Its original purpose, which still holds true today, was to make access to resources on the Internet as painless as possible for both the beginner and the experienced user.

This chapter explains how and why the program was developed, how to use it, and how it has been adapted by various Internet users.

Early Days

Hytelnet was developed in late 1990. It is an acronym for *HYpertext browser for TELnet-accessible sites on the InterNET*. These sites include hundreds of online public-access library catalogs, bulletin boards, campus-wide information systems, Free-Nets, network information centers, and full-text databases. Also included are an Internet glossary, a help file, and a directory of cataloging software. The initial design was aimed at the IBM-PC user, and that design still forms the basis for other versions running on different platforms.

When I first learned how to use Telnet to connect to remote sites, the only available information regarding login procedures was in paper directories. These directories were written by Art St. George (1990) and Billy Barron (1991). At that time, there was no mention of an *electronic* directory of such resources. This struck me as odd, because the lists were carrying information about an electronic procedure. I downloaded the directories, tested the information, and made connections to most of the sites listed. Immediately, a number of questions arose. Paper lists lose currency very quickly. So how often would they be updated to retain their usefulness? Obviously, more sites would be added on a continual basis; so would a user have to keep downloading new paper copies each time a change was made to the information?

I had already created a hypertext utility, called HYPERVAX, for helping people understand all the commands associated with VAX/VMS mail. This utility was renamed HYMAIL; it was designed to be driven by HyperRez (1989), written by Neil Larson from MaxThink.

Barron's list, *UNTs Accessing On-Line Bibliographic Databases*, contained entries listing full Telnet addresses, login and logout procedures, and (when available) an indication of the software running the catalog.

Program Development

The list was loaded into a very fast and powerful text editor called QEdit (1991), which is ideal for marking chunks of text and saving the text to discrete files. Each location, therefore, was housed in a discrete file. The naming of the files corresponded with the domain of the country in which the site is located (for example, FI for Finland and BR for Brazil).

The next step was to determine the arrangement of the information so that files with sensible hypertext links could be created. The HyperRez driver enables the linking of pure ASCII files with hypertext jumps. (A *jump* is text surrounded by angle brackets.) This was accomplished by creating files that listed the names of the sites belonging to a particular country. These files then had to be linked to a file naming all the countries, which is eventually linked back to the START.TXT file.

If hypertext links lead somewhere, they can be inserted into any file. It seemed like a logical step to create files for the various cataloging systems listed in the descriptions of the files. These are simply small help files that enable a user to understand how a given catalog is to be searched.

Depending on the document being formatted, hypertext creation can be frustrating and time consuming. Fortunately, Barron had created an ideal document as the basis for this purpose. My job was to design a system that users would find intuitive and not distracting. I also felt that I should create other files (such as a file explaining the functions of the arrow keys, a READ.ME file explaining what the program does, and a CUSTOM file that explains how a user can update files to keep current on all new information).

The PC version of Hytelnet is designed to run as a terminate-and-stay-resident (TSR) program. That is, the program is loaded into the computer's memory and invoked when needed. It runs as a perfect complement to communications software. While connected to a mainframe with a PC, a user can invoke the Hytelnet program by pressing Ctrl+Backspace to browse and return the program to memory when the information has been found. The arrow keys enable quick maneuverability, and the program can be reinvoked at will.

First Version Released January 1991

The first version of Hytelnet was released in January 1991. Many Internet users responded favorably to the program. The comments received were positive and encouraging, and many felt that such a directory was long overdue. One user, Richard Duggan of the University of Delaware, immediately adapted the files to run under Windows as a stand-alone program called CATALIST (1991).

As my interest in the Internet grew, I began to discover other types of Telnet-accessible resources, including bulletin boards, Free-Nets, and campus-wide information systems. What began essentially as a guide to library catalogs quickly became a complete index of Internet resources. It wasn't long before a second version of the program was released, containing hundreds of other sites.

Certain Usenet newsgroups also became a mine of information about new sites (such as `alt.bbs.internet` and `alt.internet.services`) that were becoming available for Telnet login. I decided to create my own mailing list for informing users of new sites. Now, thanks to Diane Kovacs at Kent State University, a Listserv list called `HYTEL-L` is now in operation. It keeps users up to date on new versions of Hytelnet and all new, updated, and deleted files.

NOTE

The Hytelnet updates distribution list, `HYTEL-L`, is a mailing list that sends information about new versions of the popular Hytelnet program, which gives users access to all known Telnet-accessible sites on the Internet. List members also receive announcements of new, changed, and defunct sites—announced between full versions of the program. The list is *moderated*, which means that only the list owner posts messages. Any messages you send to `HYTEL-L` are forwarded to the list owner. Feel free to contribute any of the following:

- New information about any of the sites mentioned in Hytelnet (such as changes in Telnet addresses, login procedures, or resources available).
- Any information on Telnet-accessible sites not found in Hytelnet.

Many Telnet-accessible sites contain login and logout instructions in languages other than English. If you want to volunteer to check such sites before they are posted to the list, please let me know by e-mail. State which language(s) you can handle. Messages sent to `HYTEL-L` are being gatewayed to the Usenet group, `bit.listserv.hytel-l`. All the work associated with the maintenance of the Hytelnet files is performed on the author's own time and equipment. The time is limited and the equipment is in dire need of replacement. Therefore, the author is asking for a $20 shareware fee to cover the costs of maintaining the program. Shareware is based on the principal of "try before you buy." If you or your site are regular users of the program, the author would appreciate your support. Thanks to those of you who have already contributed.

Running Hytelnet on a Personal Computer

To better show how Hytelnet operates, this section presents a sample session. Suppose that you are interested in discovering the Internet address and login procedures for the Medical College of Wisconsin library in the United States. On the PC, the command to invoke Hytelnet is entered at the DOS prompt:

```
C:\> cd hytelnet
C:\Hytelnet> HR
```

To load Hytelnet into memory, press the Ctrl+Backspace combination; the START.TXT file starts and displays the following information:

```
              Welcome to HYTELNET version 6.8
                    November 27 1994
              What is HYTELNET?        <WHATIS>
              Library catalogs         <SITES1>
              Other resources          <SITES2>
              Help files for catalogs  <OP000>
              Catalog interfaces       <SYS000>
              Internet Glossary        <GLOSSARY>
              Telnet tips              <TELNET>
              Telnet/TN3270 escape keys <ESCAPE.KEY>
              Key-stroke commands       <HELP.TXT>
    Up/Down arrows MOVE     Left/Right arrows SELECT     F1 for HELP anytime
              CONTROL/HOME returns here     ALT-T quits
    ...............................................................
HYTELNET 6.8 was written by Peter Scott
      Northern Lights Internet Solutions, Saskatoon, Sask, Canada
                  (aa375@freenet.carleton.ca)
```

In this example session, the <SITES1> link is selected to access library catalogs:

```
 On-Line Library Catalogs
<SITES1A> The Americas
<SITES1B> Europe/Scandinavia
<SITES1C> Asia/Pacific/South Africa
```

Then, <SITES1A> is selected to access information about the Americas:

```
The Americas
<BR000> Brazil
<CA000> Canada
<CL000> Chile
<MX000> Mexico
<US000> United States
<VE000> Venezuela
```

Then the <US000> link, the top-level United States directory, is selected. Because there are so many catalogs accessible in the United States, a submenu of catalogs was created, dividing the catalogs into types; from this submenu, <US000MED> is selected:

```
United States Medical Libraries
<US376> Albert Einstein College of Medicine
<US482> Arizona Health Sciences Center
<US011> Association of Operating Room Nurses
<US098> Audie L. Murphy Memorial Veterans' Administration Hospital
<US520> Bowman Gray School of Medicine, Wake Forest University
<US381> Cornell University Medical College
<US293> Creighton University Health Sciences Library
<US011> Denver Medical Library
<US145> Georgetown University Medical Center
<US214> HSLC HealthNET (Health Sciences Information Network)
<US408> Massachusetts College of Pharmacy
<US362> Medical College of Ohio
<US242> Medical College of Wisconsin
```

(Only a portion of the file is being shown for this sample session.) From this list, select the <US242> link to see information about the Medical College of Wisconsin:

```
--------------------------------------------------------
                     Medical College of Wisconsin

    TELNET ILS.LIB.MCW.EDU or 141.106.32.19
    login: library

    OPAC = INNOPAC <OP009>

    To exit, type Q
--------------------------------------------------------
```

This screen shows the Telnet address you need to access the site along with the login and exit requirements. Notice also that there is another link embedded in the file; if you select that link, you see the help for searching an INNOPAC catalog:

```
--------------------------------------------------------------
                       Using INNOPAC

     INNOPAC is very easy to use. Just press the letter
     or number next to the item that you want. There is no need
     to press the ENTER or RETURN key when choosing one of the
     menu options. For example:

   Title searches:      To search for a particular title, select
                        T on the main menu.

   Author searches:     To search for a particular author,
                        select A on the main menu.
```

```
  Subject searches:      To search for a particular subject,
                         select S on the main menu.

  Keyword searches:      Either "k" or "w" (varies from system to
                         system) as listed on the menu.

  Other search options: Different INNOPAC libraries have added
      additional search options, such as Medical Subject Headings,
      Call Number, SuDocs numbers, Reserve Lists, etc.

  Popular options available when looking at any one record
  include:

    S > Show items with the SAME SUBJECT
    Z > Show items nearby on the shelf
```

The PC version of the program doesn't make automatic connections to the remote sites. However, other versions do; they are discussed in the following section.

Other Versions of Hytelnet

In the early days of Hytelnet, many Internet users had machines other than IBM-compatible PCs and were unable to gain access to the Hytelnet files. That situation was first rectified in 1992 by Earl Fogel of the University of Saskatchewan. He designed versions of the program that run on VAX/VMS and UNIX machines. One attractive new feature of these versions is that they connect automatically to remote sites. If we had used the Fogel versions of Hytelnet in the example session shown in the preceding section, Hytelnet would have asked whether we wanted to connect. If so, the program would automatically run a Telnet session. Of course, we would still have to log in. Because there are now so many accessible sites throughout the Internet listed in Hytelnet, browsing through the program can easily become a chore. Fogel has created a search feature that enables a user to type a term and be presented with a new index; in effect, you can create customized indexes.

NOTE

The UNIX/VMS version of Hytelnet is also available for browsing through the Web at `http://access.usask.ca/cgi-bin/hytelnet`. For more information on this version, contact Earl Fogel at

`fogel@herald.usask.ca`

The UNIX, VMS, and Macintosh versions of Hytelnet are available in their own subdirectories at the FTP archive. Just change to the appropriate one for more information on downloading.

Macintosh users can thank Charles Burchill of the University of Manitoba for creating a HyperCard reader for the original Hytelnet database. It reads the specially formatted Macintosh or IBM files over a mixed network, such as Novell or AppleShare. It also can automatically launch the NCSA Telnet or TN3270 software and connect a user to a chosen site. There is also limited support for serial and dial-up connections. Burchill has designed the HyperCard reader to read letters from HYTEL-L Listserv messages or saved files from the bit.listserv.hytel-l newsgroup and automatically update the database. This version of Hytelnet runs only with HyperCard 2.1 and higher. The preferred operating system is System 7.x, but it also runs with System 6.0.5 or later.

The Hytelnet Gopher

John Doyle of Washington and Lee University has linked the information contained in the original Hytelnet database with the power of Gopher. To see this action, point your Gopher client to liberty.uc.wlu.edu 70 and move to Explore Internet Resources->Hytelnet. The URL is gopher://liberty.uc.wlu.edu:70/11/internet/hytelnet.

Doyle's design maps Hytelnet's hypertext structure into a Gopher structure by creating a directory for each of Hytelnet's hypertext menu links and each Telnet or TN3270 link. The directories also contain copies of the original Hytelnet file that created the directory. For example, follow this menu hierarchy:

```
Library Catalogs
Asia/Pacific/South
Australia
Macquarie University
```

You will find this Gopher screen:

```
1.  Macquarie University <TEL>
2.  OPAC = DYNIX.
3.  Macquarie University.
```

Item 1 is the Telnet link to the library at Macquarie University. Item 2 lists the catalog software in effect (other embedded links would also appear as menu choices). Item 3 is the original Hytelnet file that contains full login instructions and information about the site.

One particularly useful feature of the Gopher version of Hytelnet is a directory of new or revised entries. These are automatically sorted in reverse chronological order and cover postings to the Hytelnet mailing list made in the previous month. Another feature is the searchable database of the names of all the remote destinations. If you enter a term, the program retrieves a Gopher menu of links, as well as the original Hytelnet file containing the term. The URL is `gopher://liberty.uc.wlu.edu:3004/77/`.

Selected Listserv Commands

To join the HYTEL-L mailing list, send the following e-mail message to LISTSERV@KENTVM:

```
SUBSCRIBE HYTEL-L First Name Last Name
```

The list server also has an Internet address:

```
LISTSERV@KENTVM.KENT.EDU
```

To remove your name from the HYTEL-L mailing list, send the following e-mail message to LISTSERV@KENTVM:

```
UNSUBSCRIBE HYTEL-L
```

To stop HYTEL-L mail when you go on vacation, send the following e-mail message to LISTSERV@KENTVM:

```
SET HYTEL-L NOMAIL
```

To resume HYTEL-L mail delivery, send the following e-mail message to LISTSERV@KENTVM:

```
SET HYTEL-L MAIL
```

To determine what your HYTEL-L distribution settings are, send the following message to LISTSERV@KENTVM:

```
QUERY HYTEL-L
```

The QUERY command is useful to try if you stop receiving HYTEL-L mail. The moderators may have had to set you to NOMAIL because of problems with your e-mail account. To send a message to HYTEL-L, send your e-mail message to HYTEL-L@KENTVM.

To obtain a list of HYTEL-L users, send the following e-mail message to LISTSERV@KENTVM:

```
REVIEW HYTEL-L F=MAIL
```

To receive full documentation about searching the message database, send the following e-mail message to LISTSERV@KENTVM:

```
INFO DATABASE
```

A brief tutorial for Hytelnet is also available. Send the following e-mail message to LISTSERV@KENTVM:

```
GET SEARCH DOC F=MAIL
```

To see what files are available, send the following e-mail message to LISTSERV@KENTVM:

```
INDEX HYTEL-L F=MAIL
```

To retrieve a file, send the following e-mail message to LISTSERV@KENTVM:

```
GET File Name File Type
```

All messages to the conference are automatically archived for one month only. Users can search the message database for specific information using complex Boolean queries. The most reliable method of searching the database is to submit batch-search jobs to the list server in e-mail messages. Search features include nested Boolean expressions, search limitation by date and time, and SOUNDEX searches.

For more information about HYTEL-L, contact Peter Scott at

aa375@freenet.carleton.ca

His postal address is also given:

324 8th Street East
Saskatoon
Saskatchewan
Canada S7H0P5

How To Retrieve Hytelnet with FTP

This section gives the procedure for retrieving Version 6.6 of the PC version of Hytelnet with File Transfer Protocol (FTP).

To retrieve Hytelnet, follow these steps:

1. Enter one of the following commands at your system prompt:

   ```
   FTP FTP.usask.ca
   FTP 128.233.3.11
   ```

2. At the name prompt, enter **anonymous**.
3. When you see the password prompt, enter your Internet address.
4. When you see the FTP> prompt, enter **binary**.
5. At the next FTP> prompt, enter **cd pub/hytelnet/pc**.
6. Enter **get hyteln68.zip**.
7. After the transfer is finished, enter **quit**.

The Hytelnet program is archived using PKZIP.EXE. To unarchive the program, you must be able to unzip the file. If you have the file PKUNZIP.EXE, use it to unarchive the hyteln68.zip file you just downloaded. If you do not have PKUNZIP.EXE, you can retrieve it by following these instructions:

1. At the system prompt, type **ftp oak.oakland.edu**.
2. At the name prompt, enter **anonymous**.
3. When you see the password prompt, enter your Internet address.
4. At the first FTP> prompt, enter **binary**.

5. At the next FTP> prompt, enter **cd pub/msdos/zip.**

6. Enter **get pkz204g.exe.**

7. After the transfer is finished, enter **quit**.

You also can unarchive the hyteln68.zip file with UNZIP.EXE. To retrieve it, follow these instructions:

1. At your system prompt, enter **FTP oak.oakland.edu.**

2. At the Name prompt, enter **anonymous**.

3. When you see the password prompt, enter your Internet address.

4. At the first FTP> prompt, enter **binary**.

5. At the next FTP> prompt, enter **cd pub/msdos/zip**. Then enter **get unz50p1.exe.**

> **NOTE**
>
> Because of the plethora of PC communications programs, I can't give more specific instructions here. Check your software instructions for help about downloading a binary file from your Internet account to your PC.

Make a new directory on your hard disk (for example, type **mkdir hytelnet**). Copy PKUNZIP.EXE or UNZIP.EXE and HYTELN68.ZIP into the new directory. Make sure that you are in that directory and then enter **pkunzip hyteln68.zip**. PKUNZIP unarchives HYTELN68.ZIP, which contains the following files:

```
HYTELNET.ZIP

READNOW
```

The READNOW file gives full instructions for unarchiving the HYTELNET.ZIP file. (Simply put, if you are using PKUNZIP.EXE, you must unzip the HYTELNET.ZIP file with the -d parameter so that all the subdirectories are recursed. If you are using UNZIP.EXE, no parameters are required.)

To use Hytelnet, refer to the README file included with the package.

REFERENCE NAMES

Barron, Billy <billy@utdallas.edu> and Marie-Christine Mahe <mahe@yale.edu>. (1991-5). Accessing online bibliographic databases. Available from anonymous FTP: ftp.utdallas.edu: /pub/staff/billy/libguide.

Burchill, Charles <burchil@ccu.umanitoba.ca>. Write for details about the Mac version of Hytelnet.

Doyle, John <doylej@liberty.uc.wlu.edu>. Write for details about Hytelnet Gopher.

Duggan, Richard <duggan@brahms.udel.edu>. (1990). CATALIST. Newark, DE: University of Delaware. Write for more information.

Fogel, Earl (1992) <fogel@herald.usask.ca>. Write for details about UNIX and VMS versions of Hytelnet.

Larson, Neil (1989). HyperRez. California: MaxThink. Available via FTP from wuarchive.wustl.edu in the mirrors/msdos/hypertext, subdirectory hyperrez.arc.

Montulli, Lou <montulli@kuhub.cc.ukans.edu>. Write for information about Lynx.

QEdit advanced v2.15 (1991). Marietta, GA: SemWare. Available via FTP from wuarchive.wustl.edu in the mirrors/msdos/qedit subdirectory as qedit215.zip.

St. George, Art <stgeorge@unmb.bitnet>. (1990). Internet-accessible library catalogs and databases. Albuquerque, NM: University of New Mexico. Write for details.

New Tools: FSP, Harvest, and Hyper-G

30

by Billy Barron

New tools for finding information on the Internet are developed on a regular basis. Some, such as Gopher, take off immediately. Others, such as the Web, take a few years to catch on. Others still, such as Versatile Message Transfer Protocol (VMTP), never catch on.

This chapter looks at a few of the newest tools. Some of these may be important over the next several years. Others may die off, although lessons may be learned from them that may affect more mainstream protocols. The Internet is definitely a survival-of-the-fittest environment dictated by usage and not standards dictated by organizations. Although a standards-creation process exists, an official standard is only accepted if multiple working implementations exist.

The first tool to be discussed is FSP. FSP stands for File Service Protocol (although it has also been called File Slurping Protocol, Flaky Stream Protocol, and FTP's Sexier Partner). In particular, FSP is designed to solve some of the server performance problems of FTP.

The second tool is Harvest. Harvest is a generalized caching/indexing system for the Web, Gopher, and FTP. It has the potential to make the Internet more efficient and easier to use.

The final tool discussed here is Hyper-G. Hyper-G is another system like Gopher or the World Wide Web, but offers much greater functionality. Its proponents say it is going to overtake the Web the way the Web overtook Gopher. Its critics say it has some good points but that the Web has too much momentum behind it for Hyper-G to replace the Web.

FSP

FSP is designed as an alternative to anonymous FTP and is in no way geared to transfer a file between two accounts. The problem with anonymous FTP has historically been that it is extremely resource intensive on the server side. Each person connected to the server is usually an extra server process that eats up resources—especially memory. Another problem is that high-volume FTP sites can at times cause a link to be saturated.

These problems are partially fixed by the wuarchive FTP server. It limits the number of simultaneous connections and controls how much bandwidth is allocated to each user. However, FSP is even better protected against these problems than wuarchive.

FSP is slower than FTP at transferring files. It is important to note that this is a design feature and not a bug; it helps prevent FSP sites from getting flooded. FSP also conserves resources because all connections are handled by a single process on the server.

Reliability

If an FTP transfer is aborted, there is no way to continue the transfer. You must restart it from the beginning. FSP is designed to be able to continue a transfer at any point where it left off. In fact, if you really want to, you can transfer just parts of a file using FSP.

User Community

It is important to note that FSP has the reputation of being a hacker and pornography protocol. Many hackers use FSP to set up FSP servers in their accounts (which is easier to do than with FTP) and let just a few people know about it. FSP's use with pornography comes from the fact that any time an anonymous FTP site carrying pornography becomes publicly known, it is instantly brought to its knees by hundreds if not thousands of people trying to grab pictures from it. Therefore, people wanting to make pornographic pictures publicly available use FSP because it has protection against being saturated in this way. Also, there are fewer FSP users so the potential flood is much smaller.

Although these uses for FSP do exist, it is important to remember that it is a generic protocol. It is used for many other purposes and should not be thought of in just these terms.

FSP Software

FSP software exists for a variety of platforms, although UNIX has the most software. The base FSP package includes the server and the original client software, which is a set of various commands. Although these commands are useful for scripting and doing other work at the same time, they are somewhat awkward to learn. Therefore, a set of other client's programs (`fspclient`, `fspcli`, and `fspsh`) were created to be very similar to the FTP user interface. Table 30.1 lists all known versions of FSP software.

Table 30.1. Available FSP software.

Software	URL
FSP (UNIX/VMS)	`ftp://ftp.germany.eu.net/pub/networking/inet/fsp/fsp.271.tar.gz`
fspclient (UNIX)	`ftp://ftp.germany.eu.net/pub/networking/inet/fsp/fspclient.0.0-h+.tar.z`
fspcli (UNIX)	`ftp://ftp.germany.eu.net/pub/networking/inet/fsp/fspcli-1.2.1.tar.gz`
fspsh (UNIX)	`ftp://ftp.germany.eu.net/pub/networking/inet/fsp/fspsh113.zip`
FSPtool (X)	`ftp://ftp.germany.eu.net/pub/networking/inet/fsp/fsptool-1.6.1.tar.gz`
MS-Windows client	`ftp://wuarchive.wustl.edu/systems/ibmpc/win3/winsock/winfsp12.zip`
FSP for OS/2	`ftp://ftp.cdrom.com:/pub/os2/new/fsp2.10a.zip`

continues

Table 30.1. continued

Software	URL
MS-DOS client	ftp://ftp.germany.eu.net/pub/networking/inet/ fsp/pcfsp105.zip
MacFSP	ftp://ftp.pht.com/pub/mac/umich/util/comm/ macfsp1.0b13.cpt.hqx

Example Session with *fspcli*

This section looks at an example FSP session with the `fspcli` software. However, the only FSP command that really must be discussed is the `server` command. If you look closely, you will notice that all the other commands used in this sample session are the same as FTP commands. If you do not know how to use FTP, please read Chapter 22 "FTP: Fetching Files from Everywhere" (the other commands used in this sample session are explained there). Other FSP user packages that have an FTP-like interface are very similar to this sample session.

The `server` command is similar to the FTP `open` command. The only difference is that the `server` command requires you to use a port number.

```
/u/u/billy 1> fspcli
Can't open /u/billy/.fsphosts.
Do "help fspcli" for help on how to make it
****If you're new to fspcli just "help" will list commands
Could not open /u/billy/.fsprc
No server set, use "server" command to set.
0:0>server terra.stack.urc.tue.nl 21
Rdirectory mode: (owner: other)(del: N)(create: N)(mkdir: N)(private: N)
terra.stack.urc.tue.nl:/>dir
Rtotal 453
-rw-rw-rw-    1 nobody        2232 Jun  2  1993 00-README.ftp
-rw-rw-rw-    1 nobody         889 Apr 28  1994 00-dirs.txt
-rw-rw-rw-    1 nobody      219508 Dec 28 18:47 00-ls-lR.gz
-rw-rw-rw-    1 nobody      221426 Dec 28 18:47 00-ls-lR.zip
drwxrwxrwx    2 nobody         512 Feb 10  1994 esperanto
drwxrwxrwx    2 nobody        1024 Sep 21 05:58 fsp
drwxrwxrwx    2 nobody         512 Dec 22 07:32 humor
drwxrwxrwx    2 nobody         512 Dec 27 21:01 linux
drwxrwxrwx    2 nobody         512 Sep 21 05:44 msdos
drwxrwxrwx    2 nobody         512 Dec  2 05:50 scrumpel
drwxrwxrwx    2 nobody        4608 Dec 28 18:48 simtel
drwxrwxrwx    2 nobody        1536 Dec  9 04:16 win3
drwxrwxrwx    2 nobody         512 Sep 21 05:53 zyxel
terra.stack.urc.tue.nl:/>cd humor
Rdirectory mode: (owner: other)(del: N)(create: N)(mkdir: N)(private: N)
```

```
terra.stack.urc.tue.nl:/humor>dir
total 10
drwxrwxrwx    2 nobody         512 Dec 22 07:37 ascii
drwxrwxrwx    2 nobody         512 Nov 14 11:24 chainletter
drwxrwxrwx    2 nobody        1024 Dec 22 07:32 computer
drwxrwxrwx    2 nobody         512 Nov  1 09:15 internet
drwxrwxrwx    2 nobody        1536 Dec 22 07:35 lists
drwxrwxrwx    2 nobody         512 Nov 14 10:42 misc
drwxrwxrwx    2 nobody         512 Nov 14 10:47 startrek
terra.stack.urc.tue.nl:/humor>cd internet
directory mode: (owner: other)(del: N)(create: N)(mkdir: N)(private: N)
terra.stack.urc.tue.nl:/humor/internet>dir
total 28
-rw-rw-rw-    1 nobody        2630 Sep 15 09:14 Advocacy.Rules.gz
-rw-rw-rw-    1 nobody        4415 Nov  1 08:51 Smiles.Dictionary.gz
-rw-rw-rw-    1 nobody       13617 Nov  1 08:51 Smiles.List.gz
-rw-rw-rw-    1 nobody        2971 Nov  1 08:51 Smiley.Faces.gz
-rw-rw-rw-    1 nobody        1734 Jun 30 10:23 Standard.Bonehead.Reply.Form.gz
-rw-rw-rw-    1 nobody         827 Sep 15 09:14 Youngest.Poster.gz
terra.stack.urc.tue.nl:/humor/internet>get Youngest.Poster.gz
R1k  1k : Youngest.Poster.gz [827b/s]
terra.stack.urc.tue.nl:/humor/internet>quit
*poof*
```

Finding FSP Sites

Only a handful of people know about many FSP sites. However, some sites are widely known. A list of FSP sites is maintained at `ftp://ftp.germany.eu.net/pub/networking/inet/fsp/lists/fsp-charro.txt`. The list contains only about 30 FSP sites.

In that list, however, you will find some sites that limit the number of FTP connections; one of these is `wuarchive.wustl.edu`. The `wuarchive` site is well known for not allowing people in through FTP because there are too many connections. However, even at those times, you can probably still get in through FSP.

Harvest

Veronica is the principal global search system for Gopher; Jughead focuses on single-site indexes. For FTP, there is Archie. With the Web, there are a variety of search engines such as Lycos, WebCrawler, and Jumpstation. Wouldn't it be nice to have one global search engine for all protocols or to have more subject-specific indexes?

Also, wouldn't it be nice to be able to have site-wide caching for the Web, Gopher, and FTP sites to improve performance? Even better, wouldn't it be nice for your site to be indexed only once and then be included in all the indexes?

Harvest is a system that aims to address these needs and several others. It is a recent addition to the Internet (it was released in November 1994) but has the most potential for efficient solutions to resource discovery problems in today's environment. The software was developed by the Internet Research Task Force-Resource Discovery group (IRTF-RD), which includes Dr. Michael Schwartz, the man who developed NetFind.

Harvest can be broken into two major and relatively independent parts. The first one is the indexing part; the other is the caching part.

Indexing with Harvest

The Harvest indexing software looks at information on the Internet, indexes it, and then allows users to search it. The software is broken into three major divisions: the Gatherer, the Broker, and the Replicator. The Gatherer takes a list of URLs and summarizes the information at these URLs. The Broker takes information from the Gatherer to build indexes that users search. The Replicator is used to make mirror copies of a Broker index.

Harvest's indexing system is very powerful and flexible. In fact, you can implement Veronica, Archie, Jughead, or any of the Web indexers in it. Harvest's indexing offers much more than just the reimplemention of other indexers.

The Gatherer

The Gatherer looks at URLs and summarizes their contents. The results are then placed on a TCP port so that Brokers can later pick up the results of a Gatherer session.

The Gatherer uses a configuration file like the following one. Various directories are specified first. The port the Gatherer runs on is specified in this file as 8011. The LeafNodes entries tell the Gatherer to look at a single URL. The RootNodes entries tell the Gatherer to look at all URLs on the same server that are reachable from that URL. In a future version, the Gatherer will have more options, such as looking at all URLs in a specific domain.

```
Data-Directory:          /info/harvest/gatherers/utdinfo/data
Working-Directory:       /info/harvest/gatherers/utdinfo/tmp
Errorlog-File:           /info/harvest/gatherers/utdinfo/log.errors Log-File:
                         /info/harvest/gatherers/utdinfo/log.gatherer
Gatherer-Name:             UTD Information Gatherer
Gatherer-Port:             8011

<RootNodes>
http://www.utdallas.edu/
ftp://ftp.utdallas.edu/pub/
</RootNodes>
```

```
<LeafNodes>
gopher://gopher.utdallas.edu/00/UT-Dallas_Calendar_of_Events
gopher://gopher.utdallas.edu/00/UT-Dallas_Profile
</LeafNodes>
```

While the Gatherer is looking at a URL, it calls Essence to summarize the URL. Essence figures out the data type of a file based on its extension. Then Essence summarizes the file based on rules in the summarization script. For some items, the summary is just the filename and a few other pieces of information about the file. For other items, the summary is the major headings in the file. For others, it is a full text summary. Custom scripts can be written to handle any type of file imaginable. The results are then bundled together and placed on the TCP port specified.

The Broker

The Broker pulls information from one or more Gatherers and possibly other Brokers. Then it indexes all the information. In the end, it gives the user a Web interface to search through the indexed information.

Harvest is flexible about the indexing system it uses. The default is called Glimpse (an extremely space-efficient and flexible querying interface). Another choice is Nebula (very fast but less space efficient). Harvest also supports WAIS. In the future, Harvest will support commercial databases such as Ingres.

Figures 30.1 and 30.2 show the first two screens of the AT&T 800 Directory Service Broker. The AT&T 800 Directory Service Broker is a searchable phone book of 800 numbers provided by AT&T to the Internet community. The Query field specifies what you are searching for. In this case, the name of the company is the most likely entry. When ready to start the search, click the Submit button.

Lower on the page, you may find options on some Brokers and not on others. The search engine is case insensitive, meaning that it matches both uppercase and lowercase names. If you want to match parts of a name, deselect the Whole Keyword Must... box. It is possible to allow a Broker to find misspelled words by using the Misspelling Errors field. You can also control how many results you get back (the example in Figure 30.2 defaults to 50).

FIGURE 30.1.

The first screen of the AT&T 800 Broker.

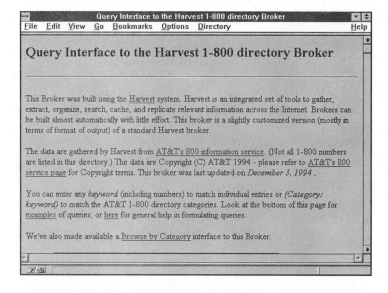

FIGURE 30.2.

The second screen of the AT&T 800 Broker.

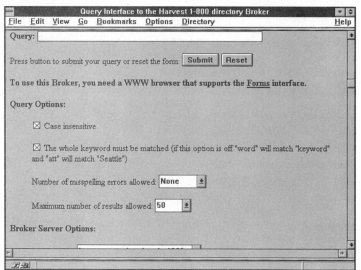

Replicators

A popular Broker can overload a server or a network link. When this happens, it would be nice if you could make a copy of the Broker on another system. (It is also a good idea to have more than one copy of a Broker to increase reliability.) The Harvest Replicator copies a Broker from one system to another with a minimal amount of trouble.

Veronica, Archie, and Lycos all suffer from overload. None of them are easy to replicate to additional sites on the Internet. If they were, there might be more servers on the Internet to distribute the load.

Caching

Caching is another important part of Harvest, although it is mostly independent of the indexing software. If you just want caching, you can install this module without installing the rest of Harvest. Here is how caching works: When an end user accesses a URL, the browser talks to the cache server. If the cache has the URL, it sends the document immediately to the browser. Because the cache should be at the same site, this transfer occurs very quickly without accessing the Internet at large.

If the cache does not have the document, the cache fetches it from the remote server. Then the cache saves a copy on disk and sends it to the browser. The next time a user needs that document, the cache has it ready for them. This arrangement greatly speeds up browsers and reduces Internet traffic.

It is important to note that the cache does not keep documents forever. After a period of time, it expires its copy of the document because documents on the Internet change over time.

Although other Web caching systems exist (see Table 30.2), one thing that makes the Harvest cache unique is that it supports hierarchical caching. In this model, local caches talk to larger, faster, regional caches to see whether they have a copy of the requested document.

Table 30.2. Alternative caching software.

Software	URL
Lagoon	`http://www.win.tue.nl/lagoon/`
CERN HTTPD	`http://info.cern.ch/hypertext/WWW/Daemon/Status.html`
DEC	`http://www.research.digital.com/SRC/personal/Steve_Glassman/CachingTheWeb.html`
HENSA	`http://nutmeg.ukc.ac.uk/new.cache.html`

Harvest Software and Server Registry

The home page for Harvest is at `http://harvest.cs.colorado.edu/`. From this page, you can find software, technical reports, and other information. These is also a mailing list for Harvest users. The subscription information can be found from the home page.

All public Harvest servers are listed in the Harvest Server Registry which can be found at `http://harvest/cs.colorado.edu/hsr/query.html`. If you bring up a Gatherer or Broker you want to be accessible to the Internet community, please list it in the Harvest Server Registry.

Hyper-G

Development on Hyper-G started in 1990 by the University of Technology, Graz, Austria. Although it was started only as a research project, the system was used for several real-world purposes. In 1993, the second phase of the project was started, which increased the emphasis on dealing with distributed information systems—especially in the Internet environment.

In the following sections, think of Hyper-G as the Web. I will point out the differences between the two.

Objects

Each item (called an *object*) in Hyper-G is stored in a document server. Each object is assigned a unique object ID by a link server. Whenever the object is moved, the object ID remains the same. Whenever the object is deleted, the object ID goes away. You can even use Hyper-G to remove any links to that object when it is deleted. All links are based on the object ID and not the physical location of the object.

Consider what happens when items are moved or deleted in Gopher or the Web. There are broken links that no one automatically knows about and which stay broken until the server administrator finds out about it. Once the administrator does, there is no guarantee that he or she can find the same item again if it has been moved to another location.

Finding Information

Hyper-G supports browsing just like Gopher and the Web do. However, in both Gopher and the Web, you have to go to extra effort to set up an index. Even then, the index is only what is designed and is not very flexible.

In Hyper-G, information about the object (such as author, date of last revision, keywords, access rights, and accounting information) is stored in the link server. Any Hyper-G user can form queries such as "give me all the objects authored by `billy@utdallas.edu` during January 1995." The negative is that Gopher+ also supports this extra information but few people enter it.

In fact, a very powerful feature of Hyper-G is its ability to find all documents that link to a particular object. This is very useful if the information provider wants to find out how information is being used. It is also useful for the end user to find related resources.

Multilingual Support

Documents that exist in multiple languages have always been a problem for Internet information services (they generally do not have a clean solution for the problem). Gopher+ implements good support for it, but experience shows that it is rarely used. It is possible that it did not catch on because of restrictive Gopher+ licensing policies and because the Web came along shortly after Gopher+. The Web's way of doing it is to have a menu with items for every language (a kludgy approach).

However, it's not hard to see the use for this facility because many companies maintain manuals in a variety of different languages. It would be advantageous to have one information system no matter what the user's language.

Hyper-G remembers what languages the user prefers in a profile and then gives that user all menus, help, and documents in that language. If the language is not available, the user may also have a second preference. Hyper-G's multilingual support is slightly more advanced than that of Gopher+ because Gopher+ did not address the help and other associated problems.

Another use of Hyper-G's multilingual support is to access user levels. A user may want to see only the novice versions of documents instead of the advanced versions. With Hyper-G, you can make a document accessible in multiple levels and have the user access the current version.

Annotations

Some Web clients, such as NCSA Mosaic, allow annotations—but only the author of the annotations can see them. Some Web programmers have kludged together some public annotation systems but none of them seem very clean.

Hyper-G supports private, public, and group annotations. In a *group annotation*, only a limited group of people can see the annotation. The annotation feature is natively supported instead of being wedged in like it is with the Web.

Although annotations offer a powerful collaborative tool, it is a tool that is misused more often than not. Most public annotations I've seen in the Web have been noisy and unimportant. However, the same can be said about Usenet, and we still find value amid the noise somehow.

Caching

In the discussion about Harvest, you learned about a cache that can be used by Web clients. The Harvest cache, however, must be separately installed and maintained. Caching in Hyper-G is automatic and a native part of the system. The big advantage of this arrangement is that it is unlikely that all Web clients on the Internet will ever have caches because the caches must be installed and maintained; it is to be hoped, however, that a significant portion of Web clients will install caches.

HTF

HTF (HyperText Format) is the language Hyper-G documents are written in. HTF for Hyper-G is similar to HTML for the Web. Both HTF and HTML are SGML-based markup languages. It is also possible to automatically translate between the two formats with minimal loss of information. To find out more about HTF, see `ftp://iicm.tu-graz.ac.at/pub/Hyper-G/doc/HTF.ps`.

Although HTF exists, Hyper-G is designed to handle any SGML-based format for which the client has a DTD (Data Table Definition) and a style sheet. Hyper-G can handle HTML as well as anything else that can be marked up with SGML. Rumors are that the Web may also head this direction one day soon. The HTML support is not finished as of yet, but it is important and may be completed by the time you read this. If it is available, it will be much easier to convert Web sites to Hyper-G.

Compatibility with Gopher and the Web

The Hyper-G server is designed to respond not only to Hyper-G requests; it can talk to Gopher and Web browsers as well. However, with Gopher and Web browsers, Hyper-G provides only limited functionality. To gain full advantage of Hyper-G, you need a Hyper-G client. Hyper-G clients can use information available in Gopher and Web servers.

Transition tools are in the works to read a Web or Gopher server and include it in a Hyper-G server automatically. However, these tools are not ready; how well they work remains to be seen.

Software Availability

Three clients exist for Hyper-G (refer to Table 30.3): a VT-100-based ASCII client that runs on UNIX; an X Window-based UNIX client known as Harmony; and the MS-Windows client known as Amadeus. The design of the system is such that clients for any operating system can exist (they just haven't been written yet). Currently, there is only one choice in Hyper-G server software.

Table 30.3. Available Hyper-G software.

Software	*URL*
Amadeus	`ftp://ftp.tu-graz.ac.at/pub/Hyper-G/Amadeus`
Harmony	`ftp://ftp.tu-graz.ac.at/pub/Hyper-G/Harmony`
Hyper-G Server	`ftp://ftp.tu-graz.ac.at/pub/Hyper-G/Server`
VT-100 Client	`ftp://ftp.tu-graz.ac.at/pub/Hyper-G/UnixClient`

technology-wise, than the Web. And because so much investment is going into Web technology right now, it may be hard for people to switch. In its current state, however, the Web does not solve all problems; Hyper-G, an upgraded Web, or something else must come along to replace the current Web.

The key to the success of any of these services will be the addition of servers and information. Also important is providing good user interfaces.

Figure 30.3 shows the Hyper-G server at the University of Auckland in New Zealand using Amadeus. The top half of the screen displays the item `Introduction`; the bottom half is the menu of items at the root of the University of Auckland server.

FIGURE 30.3.

A sample screen from Amadeus.

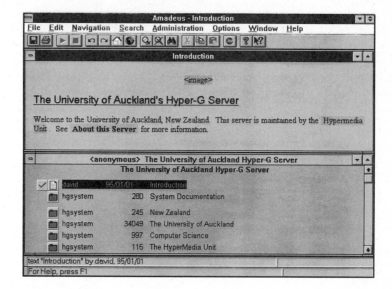

Predictions

Writing predictions for new tools is always dangerous, but I am going to do it anyway. I think it is safe to say that a protocol I have not discussed in this chapter will come out of nowhere and become very popular sometime during the next few years.

Although FSP has its good points, it will probably always be a niche application for those sites very worried about bandwidth (primarily, sites that carry GIF files). I do not see FSP replacing anonymous FTP.

Harvest is an excellent facility that is badly needed. It only has two major problems. One is that it is primarily a back-end facility that does not excite end users, even though it has the potential to benefit them greatly. The other is that the installation of the indexing software takes a little longer than many people are willing to spend. However, the benefits are enormous. I think a moderate number of sites will end up running Harvest.

Hyper-G offers much promise and solves many of the current problems with Gopher and the Web. However, Hyper-G does not address other known problems with the Internet, such as how to determine whether multiple copies of the same item exist around the Internet. From the novice user's point of view, it is not immediately obvious that Hyper-G offers much more,

VI

PART

Sharing Information

Sharing Information: An Introduction

31

by Billy Barron

In addition to getting information off the Internet, you may want to put out some information for others to look at. Although this used to be a task outside the means of the average Internet user, times have changed.

Nowadays, many Internet access providers allow you to make information available through FTP, Gopher, and the WWW for a reasonable fee. If you do not want to go through the trouble yourself to make the information available, it is relatively easy to find a consultant who can do the work for you. This chapter is geared to those who want to do the work themselves.

Making Information Available

People publishing information are faced with many choices. How do they pick the best services in which to publish their information?

In Part VI of this book, "Sharing Information," there are chapters on creating a Gopher, WWW, and FTP or Telnet server. This is not to say you do not have other choices. The following list briefly explains all the options and when you want to use each one.

- **Anonymous FTP.** If your Internet access site has an anonymous FTP server already installed and is willing to allow you to put your information on it, this is an easy way to make your information available. However, installing a new anonymous FTP server in a secure fashion is not easy. Also, your information may not be found as easily on an anonymous FTP site as it may be if it were stored in Gopher or the WWW.

- **Telnet sites.** You can also put your information on an existing Telnet site or create your own site. A major down side to this is that your information may not be easily found. The strength of newer systems such as Gopher and the WWW is that users have to know only one program to search thousands of sites; each Telnet site tends to have its own interface, which the user has to spend time learning to use.

- **WAIS.** WAIS is an excellent way to make databases of information and documents available. Installing the public domain software server can be tricky and the commercial version is relatively expensive. Once you have a server, however, adding another database is easy. With WAIS, however, end users cannot browse the information.

- **Gopher.** With Gopher, it is easy to add information; users find it just as easy to find information. Veronica and Jughead are well-established search engines. The down side is that Gopher is primarily a text-only system.

- **WWW.** The WWW is good for multimedia documents or documents that are interlinked with other documents. Documents to be put on the WWW must be converted into HyperText Markup Language (HTML), which at the present time is difficult to learn. Word processors and other software packages will start to support

HTML in the near future. Another drawback is if the target audience has slow-speed connections to the Internet or older computers, WWW is too resource intensive for them to use. Over time, this will become less of a problem.

- **Posting.** Information can always be posted to Usenet news or on a mailing list. Posting is good for timely information; however, neither posting nor e-mail is acceptable for information of long-term value.

Always remember that sharing information is what makes the Internet the Internet. If you have something valuable to share, please do so.

Generally, any type of information can be published on the network. However, a few types of information should not be published. In the U.S., for example, child pornography is against the law and should not be made available on the Internet.

It is interesting to note that other types of pornography are tolerated. However, you can find them only on Usenet and not on any of the information servers. The reason for this is not purely moral: whenever a site tries to bring up pornographic pictures for anonymous FTP or Gopher, the computer or network becomes so overloaded with users attempting to download files that something eventually crashes.

Information Formats

Information providers must select a format in which to put their information. Information users must deal with the format and convert it into something they can use.

For documents without formatting, the format of choice on the Internet is a straight text file. If a document has special formatting, but will not be edited by the user, PostScript is an excellent choice. Most users can print or view PostScript. Unfortunately, documents with special formatting that must be edited by the user are tricky. The only thing to do is to pick a popular word processing format such as Microsoft Word or WordPerfect.

For picture graphics, the most popular formats on the Internet are GIF and JPEG. Some formats popular on microcomputers (such as PCX) are almost never on the Internet. For movies, MPEG is the most common Internet format, although QuickTime is seen quite a bit, too.

It is highly recommended that you use data compression programs common to the platform used by the target audience. For PCs, use ZIP, ZOO, or ARC. For Macintosh, use StuffIt or BinHex. For UNIX, use compress or gzip. When information is to be used by multiple platforms, it is probably best to use one of the PC formats or the UNIX gzip program.

Good and Bad Sharing Practices

Not only is providing information important, providing it in a useful format is of concern, too. A poorly organized site is one that people remember and dread using. The good practices to follow are listed here:

■ **Think about the organization.** The worst thing you can do is to throw information into your server without giving it any thought. Over time, your site will grow; if you haven't planned for that, you will have a mess on your hands. Remember that users do not like to waste time searching for information and may decide that your site is not useful if it is poorly organized.

■ **Make the information pretty.** If your information is in Gopher, make sure that there are definitely less than 80 characters per line, but preferably less than 70. For the Web, refer to Chapter 36, "Creating Web Pages with HTML."

■ **Keep information as small as possible.** Although there are times when information should be kept at a maximum for archival or research reasons, most of the time, users want only the minimum information to answer their questions. For users with slow modems, this rule is doubly important because large files take sufficiently longer to download.

■ **Always keep your audience in mind.** If you are trying to sell cars over the Internet, the average buyer could care less about the mechanics involved in making the car run. So don't highlight it on your site (although it would be fine to have that information off in a corner for those who *do* care).

■ **Avoid moving information frequently.** If you have good information available, people will build links and bookmarks to it. If you move it frequently, people will have trouble finding the information. However, there comes a time on most sites when reorganization and moving items must happen. In those cases, try to announce the changes—especially to people whom you know point to your site. Some Web servers even have ways to make the change invisible.

■ **Never use the actual host name.** For your information services, always use a DNS alias instead of the real host name of the computer. You may want to move the information service to another computer; if you have an alias, people can automatically follow the change. For example, at the University of Texas at Dallas, the following aliases are in place:

FTP site:	`ftp.utdallas.edu`
Gopher server:	`gopher.utdallas.edu`
Web server	`www.utdallas.edu`

The aliases `ftp`, `gopher`, and `www` are the standard addresses used for those information services across the Internet.

■ **Always have a contact address.** Always make sure that, somewhere on your information server, you leave a note with a contact e-mail address for the server administrator. Users often notice problems with your server or with dead links long before you do.

■ **Make mirror sites.** If your service is really popular and overloaded, find a mirror site somewhere else on the Internet. Often, it is a good idea to place mirrors on other continents to reduce the traffic load on busy intercontinental Internet links.

■ **Update obsolete information.** Always remember that information must be updated. Because very few pieces of information remain the same until the end of time, plan to spend time updating old information periodically.

Creating and Administering Mailing Lists

32

*by Diane Kovacs
and Michael Kovacs*

A profound transformation of human culture is in progress, and one important aspect of it is the emergence of the virtual culture. Virtual culture is the total shared experience of reality by human beings through computers. Virtual culture includes computer-mediated communication; electronic conferences; journals; information distribution and retrieval; the construction and visualization of images, representations, and models of worlds; and personal, intellectual, institutional, and societal-related issues.

——Ermel Stepp, Director, Institute
for the Study of Virtual Culture

Discussion lists and electronic journals are created for discussion—recreational, scholarly, or otherwise. What you want your discussion list to be depends on your interests and ideas. This chapter outlines the major steps in establishing a Listserv-based discussion list. It also addresses some issues for managing discussion lists and electronic journals once they are technically set up.

There are many reasons for using the Listserv software. It provides robust electronic mail connectivity. E-mail is the most common Internet service. Listserv makes e-mail-distributed discussion lists or electronic journals practical for international distributions.

Listserv performs automated distribution to a subscriber list of discussion messages, journal issues, tables of contents, and so on. It also provides for automatic subscription, automatic distribution of user instructions, and automatic digesting and archiving. The archiving function allows keyword searching with commands delivered by e-mail.

The Listserv software was developed by Eric Thomas, from software originally developed by EDUCOM/BITNIC (the Bitnet Information Center). Listserv runs on IBM mainframe computers with VM/CMS operating systems, and uses LMAIL to distribute discussion list messages or electronic journals. Dr. Thomas has announced that UNIX, VAX/VMS, and NT versions will be available soon.

There are three basic qualifications an individual must meet before establishing a discussion list or electronic journal:

1. Knowledge of how to send standard e-mail to Internet or Bitnet addresses from a computer account connected to the Internet or Bitnet.

2. Basic understanding of the text editor on the computer account regularly used.

3. The time and motivation required to prepare and maintain the discussion list or electronic journal.

This chapter assumes only the three necessary qualifications. Many problems will arise that require more in-depth assistance than this chapter provides. It is ideal if the moderator can find a local expert. The discussion list LSTOWN-L@SEARN.SUNET.SE is designed to provide moderators with access to Listserv experts and experienced moderators. Here is a general resource list for persons interested in supporting Listserv-based lists:

- ERIC@SEARN.SUNET.SE: Eric Thomas, the author of the Listserv software.
- HELP-NET@VM.TEMPLE.EDU: A discussion list for new users of the network who need answers to simple questions.
- LSTOWN-L@SEARN.SUNET.SE: A discussion list for sharing information between Listserv-based discussion lists and electronic journal owners.
- NEWJOUR-L@E-MATH.AMS.ORG: A UNIX Listserv distribution list for the announcement of new electronic journals.
- NEW-LIST@VM1.NODAK.EDU: A Listserv distribution list for the announcement of new discussion lists.
- VPIEJ-L@VTVM1.CC.VT.EDU: An e-conference for electronic publishing issues, especially those related to scholarly electronic journals. Discussion topics include SGML, PostScript, and other e-journal formats, as well as software and hardware considerations for creating, storing, and accessing e-journals.
- TASOS@CS.BU.EDU: Anastasios Kotsikonas, the author of the UNIX Listserv software.

The role of the discussion list moderator, coordinator, list owner, or editor varies from discussion list to discussion list. For consistency, the term *discussion list moderator* is used to describe any person responsible for daily maintenance of a discussion list, regardless of how much they actually review or edit. The term *electronic journal editor* is used to describe anyone responsible for the management and organization of an electronic journal.

Listserv discussion lists require someone who is attentive (if not devoted) to these operations. The discussion list moderator or electronic journal editor should be willing and able to undertake both the technical and intellectual functions. In moderating a discussion list, a light hand and a firm commitment to the basic tenets of the discussion are best. If you don't plan to actively moderate (edit), you still have to monitor and guide the discussion. Electronic journal editing requires the same intellectual and clerical commitment as editing a paper journal. The technology replaces traditional distribution and makes interactions much simpler and faster than they are with paper journals.

Steps To Set Up a Discussion List

The steps to start a discussion list or electronic journal are given here and are detailed in the following sections:

1. Determine that there is a need for a discussion list in a given area.
2. Determine whether you are willing to make the time commitment.
3. Learn about e-mail and local editor software.
4. Find a Listserv site willing to host the discussion list or electronic journal.
5. Read the documentation.

6. Subscribe to `LSTOWN-L` (`LISTSERV@SEARN.SUNET.SE`). `LSTOWN-L` provides technical and editorial help for moderators of Listserv-based discussion lists and electronic journals.

7. Design the setup for the discussion list or electronic journal.

    a. Edit or not. Electronic journal or discussion.

    b. Name the discussion list or electronic journal.

    c. Determine the purpose of the discussion list or electronic journal.

    d. Identify potential participants or subscribers.

    e. Choose the subscription method.

    f. Set the scope of discussion.

    g. Regulate the source of the messages and how they are accessed.

8. Establish services.

9. Get editorial help.

10. Write an introductory document.

11. Establish error-handling procedures.

12. Get the Listserv owner to set up the list.

13. Announce the discussion list or electronic journal.

Determine the Need for the Discussion List

Before anything else, determine whether or not there is a need for a discussion list in an area in which you are interested. There are already thousands of established discussion lists. One of them may already be operating in the area in which you are interested.

There are several ways of determining which discussion lists already exist. The easiest way is to do a keyword subject search of the `NEW-LIST` archives, the `LISTS` (`LISTS GLOBAL`), or the `INTGRP` database (the Internet interest groups database compiled by Marty Hoag).

The following example search is useful, especially if you want to know whether any discussions for recipes or cooking exist. Address e-mail to `LISTSERV@VM1.NODAK.EDU`. The e-mail message must look like this:

```
//
Database Search DD=Rules
//Rules DD *
s recipes or cooking in NEW-LIST
Index
Print All
/*
```

To search LISTS or INTGRP, simply substitute LISTS or INTGRP for the NEW-LIST archive name and use keywords appropriate to your topic area.

The Directory of Scholarly Electronic Conferences provides subject access to electronic conferences (discussion lists, newsgroups, interest groups, and electronic forums) that are of scholarly interest. It is available by addressing e-mail to LISTSERV@KENTVM.KENT.EDU. The message must read GET ACADLIST README.

The ACADLIST README file provides further directions for retrieving any or all of the eight files that make up the directory. The file is also available through Gopher to access.usask.ca 70.

You can also send a request to NEW-LIST@VM1.NODAK.EDU, specifying SEARCH:*topic* in the subject line. The subscribers to NEW-LIST may respond to your post.

Determine Your Time Commitment

Decide whether or not you can commit 20 to 30 hours per week for the first week or two for planning and setup. Determine whether you can commit 5 to 15 hours per week for discussion list maintenance. The moderator of ACM-L spends under five hours per week because ACM-L is not edited and has only 70 subscribers. The list owner does not screen individual messages before they are sent to the discussion list. You can expect to spend as many as 15 hours per week maintaining an actively edited list. The moderators of LIBREF-L spend between 5 and 15 hours per week editing, depending on how active the discussion is.

Electronic journals require as much time as print journals in terms of the intellectual activities required for editing, reviewing, and formatting texts. This can be minimal (as with newsletters) or very time intensive (as with peer-reviewed electronic journals). The editor-in-chief of the *Electronic Journal on Virtual Culture* commits at least 8 hours per week to the journal. The week before the bimonthly issue is distributed often requires much more time. The co-editor spends an equal amount of time on the journal. The *EJVC* editors have some graduate-student clerical assistance, which eases their burden somewhat. Other activities are distributed throughout an editorial board, which also reviews the articles.

Learn about E-Mail and Local Editor Software

You must also be familiar with the mailer and editing software of your own e-mail account. You must commit a sufficient amount of time to learn how your e-mail system works. Ask your local computer support people for assistance and make sure that you have manuals for everything.

You can run a discussion list from almost any kind of mainframe or operating system, or networked microcomputer with e-mail access (including VAX/VMS, UNIX, IBM VM/CMS, Macintosh/Eudora, DOS PC/Pegasus Mail, and others). However, there are problems unique to each system. The Listserv software runs only on IBM mainframes running VM/CMS. You run your discussion list from your own e-mail account in interaction with the Listserv software running on an IBM machine. All should go smoothly if your e-mail account is on an IBM VM/CMS machine. Other systems may present problems—especially if they are only Internet connected. For assistance with other systems, consult your Listserv owner or your LSTOWN-L colleagues.

Find a Listserv Site

Locate a computer site running Listserv software. Your own site or one geographically close to you is preferable. During startup, you will have many conversations over e-mail, telephone, or in person with your Listserv owner (the person responsible for maintaining the Listserv software you will be using).

A database of all Listserv sites, called PEERS, is available for keyword subject searching. An Arkansas resident who wants to identify the closest Listserv site can search PEERS using the keyword *Arkansas*. Address e-mail to LISTSERV@VM1.NODAK.EDU (or another Listserv site with the PEERS database). Leave the subject line blank. The message must look like this:

```
//
Database Search DD=Rules
//Rules DD *
s arkansas in PEERS
Index
Print All
/*
```

Contact the Listserv owner at an identified site and ask permission to use the software and disk space for archives and files. Names and e-mail addresses of administrative and technical contacts at Listserv sites are provided in the PEERS database. Most sites give you the processing time and disk space free of charge. However, some sites do charge a fee, even for employees.

If your site does not have the Listserv software, you may want to ask your computer center to acquire it. The software is available from Eric Thomas (ERIC@SEARN.SUNET.SE). Although the software is free to most educational institutions, your computer services must commit a small amount of time and personnel for set up and maintenance.

If your site has an Internet-connected computer running the UNIX operating system, contact Anastasios Kotsikonas (TASOS@CS.BU.EDU) to obtain his UNIX Listserver software. It is not the same as the original Listserv, but it is functional.

Read the Documentation

Read the documentation. Several files are available from most Listserv sites. The most important ones are LISTOWNR MEMO, LISTKEYW MEMO, LISTSERV REFCARD, and LISTSERV MEMO. To retrieve these files, address e-mail to LISTSERV@VM1.NODAK.EDU (or another Listserv site). The message must read as follows:

```
GET LISTOWNR MEMO
GET LISTKEYW MEMO
GET LISTSERV REFCARD
GET LISTSERV MEMO
```

LISTOWNR MEMO describes commands available to discussion list moderators. These commands include those that add or delete subscribers and query whether an address is subscribed. The syntax for commands sent by the moderator on behalf of subscribers is different than that used by subscribers. For example, to add a subscriber, address mail to the Listserv address. The message must read like this:

```
ADD listname subscriber@address Firstname Lastname
```

To query for an address, the message looks like this:

```
QUERY listname FOR subscriber@address
```

To set DIGEST, NOMAIL, or MAIL, and so on, use this command:

```
SET listname NOMAIL FOR subscriber@address
```

LISTKEYW MEMO describes all the keywords you can use to set up the discussion list in the listheader. A sample follows. The characteristics of a Listserv discussion list or electronic journal are set in the header file (for example, the file for DOROTHYL is DOROTHYL LIST). Some options mentioned in this article are described following the example.

```
*  Discussion of Government Document Issues
*
*  Subscription= Open Send= editor          Confidential= no
*  Notify= Yes        Reply-to= List,Respect  Files= No
*  Validate= Store only  X-tags= Comment  Ack= yes
*  Mail-via= Dist2  Stats= normal,private  Review= Public
*
*  DEFAULT-OPTIONS= REPRO  NOTEBOOK= YES,X1/305,WEEKLY,PUBLIC
*
*  TOPICS= N&O,
*  DEFAULT-TOPICS=ALL, -N&O
*
*  Peers=  UALTAVM,PSUVM
*
*  EDITOR= raed@vmd.cso.uiuc.edu
```

```
*
*  OWNER=
*  ERRORS-TO= librk329@kentvms (Diane Kovacs)
*
*  Owner=   Quiet:
*  OWNER=   APISCITELLI@EWU.EDU  (Aimee Piscitelli)
*  OWNER=   LBARTOLO@KENTVM  (LAURA BARTOLO)
*  Owner=   DKOVACS@KENTVM  (Diane Kovacs)
*  OWNER=
*  OWNER=   C60TMS1@NIU  (TIM SKEERS)
*  OWNER=   SHAYES@VMA.CC.ND.EDU  (STEPHEN HAYES)
*  Owner=   RAED@uiucvmd  (Raeann Dossett)
*  Owner=   raed@vmd.cso.uiuc.edu  (Raeann Dossett)
*  OWNER=   MTHOMAS@TAMVM1 (MARK THOMAS)
*  OWNER=
*  OWNER=
*  Owner=   librk329@kentvms (Diane Kovacs)
*  OWNER=
*  OWNER=   MTHOMAS@TAMVENUS  (MARK THOMAS)
```

Here is a breakdown of some of the important options in this listing:

Option	Description
Owner=	This is the place to put the address of the moderator. It is useful to have more than one moderator address because these are the addresses of users authorized to make changes in the listheader (it is good to have a backup person). It is also useful for your subscribers if you include your name in parentheses following your address.
Sender=[Public,Editor]	If Sender=Editor, all mail sent to the list address is forwarded to the person addressed in the Editor field, who can then forward the mail back to the list if the posting meets approval.
Editor=[e-mail address of editor]	If Sender=Editor, the Editor field is required. Only mail sent from this address is posted to the list. All other mail sent to the list address is forwarded to this address.

`Subscription=[By_owner,Open,Closed]`	If `Sub=By_owner`, all subscription requests are forwarded to the first address in the `Owner` field (and the attempted subscriber is notified). If `Sub=Public`, anyone can subscribe to the list. If `Sub=Closed`, no one can subscribe to the list, although any of the list owners can add new subscribers.
`Notebook= [Yes,No,Frequency,Disk]`	This keyword defines whether an archive is kept and the frequency of the archiving. *Frequency* is denoted by words like `daily`, `weekly`, and `monthly`. Your Listserv owner determines the *Disk* on which the archives are stored.
`Digest= [Yes,No,Frequency]`	`Digest` defines whether the discussion list is available as an automatic digest. It also indicates the *Frequency* at which the digest is compiled and distributed (a *Frequency* of `daily` is useful for very active discussions).
`Topics= [keyterms] default-Topics=ALL`	The *keyterms* can be any words that must appear in the subject headings of messages. The `default-Topics` defines what subscribers receive unless they reset their `Topics`. The moderator can define as many as 11 topic keyterms. Listserv keeps track of what topics users define by noting the order of the keywords. It is very important that the moderator establish the order of topic keyterms and *not change that order.*
`Ack=[Yes,No,Msg]`	Defines the default value of the `Ack/NoAck` distribution option for new subscribers. Subscribers can still change the option with the `SET` command. If `Ack=Yes`, messages are sent when the user's mail file is processed. Additionally, a short acknowledgment with statistical

continues

Option	Description
	information about the mailing is sent. This is the default. If Ack=Msg, messages are sent when the user's mail file is processed. Statistical information is also sent with messages, but no acknowledgment mail is sent. If Ack=No, a single message, but no acknowledgment mail or statistics, is sent when the user's mail file is processed.
Errors-To=[Postmaster,Owner, e-mail address]	This option defines the person or list of persons to receive mail rejected from the list. The default value is Postmaster; it is recommended that the owners change it to Owner or an individual's e-mail address.
Quiet:	This option prevents the automatic notification of the list owner every time someone subscribes, unsubscribes, or changes options. If you need to know all this information, do not use the Quiet: option.
Default-options=Repro	You should almost always include this option in your listheader. Subscribers generally want to receive reassurance that their message was distributed. Putting this field in the listheader makes Repro the default value of the Repro/NoRepro distribution option for your list. Anyone posting a note to your list receives a copy of their note. The normal default (NoRepro) means that a poster receives only a message acknowledging receipt of the posting.

The LISTSERV REFCARD and LISTSERV MEMO files contain subscriber information you may want to use in your instructional documentation.

Subscribe to *LSTOWN-L@SEARN.SUNET.SE*

LSTOWN-L@SEARN.SUNET.SE provides technical and editorial help for moderators of Listserv-based discussion lists and electronic journals.

You can join before your list or journal is actually in operation. You may also want to join an active, well-run discussion list, such as HUMANIST@BROWNVM.BROWN.EDU or PACS-L@UHUPVM1.UH.EDU. You can also monitor established electronic journals, such as *PostModern Culture* (at PMC-L@NCSUVM.NCSU.EDU) or the *Electronic Journal on Virtual Culture* (at EJVC-L@KENTVM.KENT.EDU).

Design the Setup for the Discussion List

Some of the factors listed in the following sections are set up with keywords in the listheader. Others are explained in your subscriber documentation.

You must make decisions about each of the topics described in the following sections before you can set up the discussion list or electronic journal.

Edit or Not: E-journal or Discussion

Editing requires the moderator to review all messages before they are forwarded to the discussion list. Editing duties can range from merely screening erroneous postings and personal messages to the full-review process required by a peer-reviewed journal. The answer to whether you want to host an edited list depends on the amount of time you are willing to commit to the list or journal. It also depends on whether you intend to establish a discussion list or electronic journal.

Even after electing not to edit and to leave the discussion unmoderated, the moderator can still moderate. The role of the moderator combines the duties of editing a newsletter or journal with leading a seminar. The main advantages of a moderated discussion list are focus and coherence. These benefits can be very important in an active discussion list, but moderation takes care and time. An unmoderated discussion list is completely defined by its subscribers. If your discussion list has a very specific focus (such as a particular piece of software) you may not feel the need to moderate as closely.

Name the Discussion List or Electronic Journal

It is conventional to have all discussion-list names end in -L (for example, Ethics-L). A suffix of -D designates a digest (normally, one created before the DIGEST feature was developed). However, as many discussion lists break with this convention as hold to it. Time spent choosing a good name is time well spent. Any name up to eight characters can be used. Be sure to check with your Listserv owner to see whether the name is already in use by your local system.

Determine the Purpose of the Discussion List

Why are you establishing the discussion list or electronic journal? What purpose does it serve? This is important to clarify as early as possible because your answers determine how you present the discussion list or electronic journal to subscribers, colleagues, or your administration.

Identify Potential Participants or Subscribers

This is an important point to consider when you are deciding where to advertise your discussion list or electronic journal. Will you take flyers to your professional conferences or put up a poster at your local bookstore?

Choose the Subscription Method

Will members be able to subscribe by themselves or will you monitor things? Open subscription allows people to come and go as they want—without bothering you. Closed or "reviewed" subscription lets you decide who to admit. Perhaps more significantly, a reviewed subscription method gives you the opportunity to ask potential members for information—and have a reasonable chance of getting that information. You may, for example, ask for a statement of interests or a professional biography, which can be circulated to the membership to help forge a community.

Set the Scope of the Discussion

What kinds of topics do you want to discuss? In general, it's far better to have a widely defined scope so that you don't put too many restrictions in place from the beginning. Will your electronic journal be a newsletter and publish everything submitted? Will you review submissions or will they be peer reviewed? What will the scope of the articles be? These are important considerations to keep in mind.

The TOPICS keyword allows you to set up topics that subscribers can select to receive or not receive. For example GOVDOC-L@PSUVM.PSU.EDU has set TOPICS=N&O. All N&O lists are government documents that people need or want to offer to others. Not all subscribers want to see them.

Regulate the Sources of Messages

Do you want the discussion list to be open to messages from nonsubscribers? Do you want nonsubscribers to be able to read the contributions from participants on your discussion list? As moderator, you must consider these options.

Establish Services

Will your Listserv owner provide you with the computer space required to store files associated with your discussion list or electronic journal? To what extent? If your discussion list is to be primarily conversational, you may not need disk space for anything other than the archives, which can be kept by Listserv. If your discussion list is primarily concerned with distributing stable information, you need a sufficient allotment of storage space.

Get Editorial Help

Do you want to set up an editorial board or its equivalent? Can you get others to help you (for example, to assist in long-range editing tasks)? For larger discussion lists, sharing the moderation tasks is essential.

Write an Introductory Document

It's important to write a brief instructional document to introduce new subscribers to your discussion list. This document should contain a concise description of the list or journal based on the decisions you have made. The document should also provide elementary instructions on how to use Listserv so that new users can order files from the server. You may want to explain your editorial policies in the document: Even if the discussion list is unmoderated, you may have to intervene occasionally to guide discussion around an offensive or otherwise difficult topic. On such occasions, it is useful to have a statement of policy to refer to. Following is a sample discussion list welcome message. A sample electronic journal guide follows that.

Distribution of the instructional document can be done automatically by Listserv. Ask your Listserv owner to create a WELCOME file on the fileserver associated with your discussion list or electronic journal. The Listserv owner can set things up so that you can put the file and future updates directly on the fileserver without going through the Listserv owner. This is something you can negotiate. The Listserv software distributes your WELCOME instructional document to each new subscriber as he or she signs up.

```
DOROTHYL New Subscriber Instructions
Dear Networker,
Your subscription to DOROTHYL has been accepted. Please read
this memo carefully and SAVE it.
This is a posting sent to all new subscribers to
DOROTHYL:
The text below is a basic description of what the DOROTHYL
discussion list is, how it works, and how to participate.
```

```
                    TABLE OF CONTENTS
****************************************************************
1. What is DOROTHYL?
   The Mission Statement of the Conference
   Guiding Tenets of DOROTHYL
   The Technology Involved
2. How to Send Messages to DOROTHYL
   Subject Headings and Humor
   Cross-Postings from other E-conferences (lists)
3. Guidelines for Replying to Messages on DOROTHYL
4. Basic DOROTHYL Etiquette
5. Subscriber Option Commands:  NOMAIL, MAIL, DIGEST, REVIEW,
   UNSUB, etc.
6. How to retrieve Files and Archives from the fileserver.
7. Who to contact for assistance or information.
****************************************************************
```

```
(Electronic Journal on Virtual Culture)
Dear Networker,
Your subscription to the Electronic Journal on Virtual
Culture has been accepted. Please read and save this memo
because it contains useful information about submitting articles
to and receiving EJVC.
For assistance, please contact Diane Kovacs - Co-Editor
dkovacs@kentvm.kent.edu or dkovacs@kentvm
The following topics are covered in this memo.

1. EJVC:  Basic Facts and Philosophy
2. Submission Procedures and Author Guidelines
3. Archiving/Retrieval/Subscription (FTP Access, Gopher
   Access, Listserv Subscription Options)
4. Copyright Statement
5. The Editorial Board
```

Establish Error Handling Procedures

Who will handle errors? Will your Listserv owner have time? With the help of LSTOWN-L, you may be able to cope with errors yourself. Error handling is discussed every day on LSTOWN-L. The only way to learn is to start doing it yourself.

Here are some basic guidelines for setting up your error handling procedures:

- ■ Any error message that says addressee unknown, unknown userid, or user unknown indicates that the address should be deleted.

- ■ Error messages that mention "temporary" unavailability of mailing services indicate that the address should be maintained unless the problem is repeated excessively.

It is debatable whether `mailbox full` or `directory overlimit` errors indicate that the address should be deleted. Some moderators delete them and others wait to see whether the problem is cleared up.

Ask the Listserv Owner To Set Up the List

Ask the Listserv owner to set up your discussion list or electronic journal. Don't forget to test it.

Announce Your Discussion List

Send an e-mail announcement of your new discussion list to `NEW-LIST@VM1.NODAK.EDU`. Send an e-mail announcement of your new electronic journal to `NEWJOUR-L@E-MATH.AMS.ORG`.

If your discussion list or electronic journal is of interest to people in a particular academic subject area, you may want to announce it on a discussion list related to that subject. For example, an electronic journal on recent world history might be announced on `9NOV89-L@UTDALLAS`, a discussion list for issues surrounding the fall of the Berlin Wall.

Other Issues

The following sections describe some additional issues you should consider when setting up mailing lists.

Discussion List Maintenance

Table 32.1 briefly outlines the tasks you can expect to perform. Of course, different moderation styles lead to different kinds of work. This work is much easier if you have a computer and modem at home because, by nature, it is easily done in bits and pieces during odd moments.

Table 32.1. Time commitments for discussion list maintenance.

Task	Time Commitment
No editing	1 to 5 hours per week
Screening	5 to 15 hours per week
E-journal	Up to 20 hours per week
Dealing with errors	1 to 3 hours per week

Monitoring or Reviewing Submissions

Even unmoderated discussion lists must be monitored for inappropriate postings and network problems every day. You must monitor some discussion lists several times per day. You can and should respond directly to anyone who makes an inappropriate posting. Posting directly to the discussion list about such problems is considered bad etiquette, unless it is a general problem. A light touch is better than a heavy hand, but unmoderated discussion list moderators must occasionally take decisive action.

The edited discussion list needs daily attention, depending on the amount of activity. Contributions may simply be passed on to your Listserv software without modification, or you can clean up extra headers and text extracting (many mail editors enable users to include text from other messages; this is called *extracting* and can take up lots of space if not done judiciously). Digesting is now an automatic function of the Listserv software and is no longer done manually by editors.

Depending on how your discussion list is set up, you may have to monitor and respond to requests for subscription. These tasks should be done every day.

Dealing with Errors

You must monitor for and respond to errors arising from addressing problems and misbehaving software. There are three kinds of errors:

1. "Reviewed" subscriptions: errors you make when you give Listserv the addresses of new members.
2. Subscriptions made by members themselves: illegal node IDs sent by software at the user's site.
3. Other miscellaneous errors.

Errors of the first two types usually cause the Listserv software to automatically delete the bad address. There are several kinds of errors that occur when delivery of e-mail is attempted to a downed computer. There are hundreds of variations on this type of error. It is usually not acceptable to delete addresses with this type of error unless they are persistent. Another error is `user unknown` or `mailbox full`. These errors do require deletion of the bad address.

In the beginning, you will need help from a network expert. The worst consequence of bad address errors is when a "network loop" develops on an unedited discussion list. When a network loop develops, messages are sent back and forth between Listserv and mail software elsewhere on the network. As a result, members can be quickly deluged by junk mail. Note that loops and other causes of junk mail are much less likely in moderated discussion lists because the editor is always there to act as a filter. Loops can still occur in a moderated discussion list because of local mailer problems, in which case your subscribers should talk with their local computer services people.

The last (but not least) recommendation is that you password protect your discussion list. You do this by putting the following command in the header:

```
password=XXX
```

The password must be typed in the header each time a change is made before the change can be implemented. Passwords protect against unauthorized (and sometimes malicious) changes.

Problems and Solutions in Moderating the Discussion List

Often, problems result from people who do not follow rules of etiquette. Some problems that occur include these:

1. Incorrectly addressed subscription, unsubscription, or file requests.
2. Off-topic postings.
3. Flaming (*ad hominem* attacks on other subscribers).

In an electronic journal, these kinds of problems are usually dealt with by sending short messages rejecting the problem posting on the basis that the electronic journal has a specific publication mission. The law permits publications to define a topic area and to publish only in that topic.

With discussion lists, however, the lines are less distinctly drawn. Incorrectly addressed requests are best dealt with by sending the offender a guide that describes appropriate behavior. With an edited discussion, the requests need not be posted. In an unedited discussion, requests can inspire both off-topic postings discussing the problems and flaming of the poster of the misaddressed request.

Off-topic postings are the most difficult to deal with. The law covering publications *may* protect discussion lists. It is somewhat easier to control off-topic postings when the discussion list is edited. The university counsel at Kent University advised moderators of discussion lists distributed by Kent University's Listserv to define the topic area clearly and to state that the moderators reserve the right to reject any posting they deem inappropriate and to distribute a copy of that statement to all new and existing subscribers.

In unedited discussions, off-topic postings can inspire flaming and general complaints from other subscribers. In general, subscribers use peer pressure to keep the discussion on topic. This peer pressure can be as extreme as e-mail bombing (the e-mailing of multimegabyte files to the offender). E-mail bombing is done only in extreme cases to the worst offenders and can cause problems for the offender's entire site. E-mail bombing is generally frowned on by system administrators and can backfire—causing the e-mail bombers to lose their accounts.

The moderator must intervene if things get out of hand. In some cases, individuals may be asked to unsubscribe or actually be forcibly deleted from the discussion list before the problem can be solved. In such cases, lawyer waving (threatening to sue or otherwise inflict punitive damage on the moderator) frequently occurs. At this writing, no one has successfully taken a moderator to court. Moderators can find support and encouragement from other moderators in the LSTOWN-L discussion.

Very few large discussion lists are unedited. As subscription numbers increase, problems also increase. The workload for the moderator can become greater than editing. A liberal editing policy—no censorship and a specific set of guidelines for a team of moderators and editors—works very well. *Censorship* means excluding a posting because it expresses an opinion opposed to that of the moderators. It is not censorship to exclude a posting because it is off-topic. These are the same rules that govern public speech. For example, the local Democratic party can hold an open forum to discuss health care. They cannot exclude Republicans, Libertarians, Socialists, or anyone else from expressing their opinion on health care. But they are perfectly within their rights to remove anyone who insists on talking about the Democratic party's finances.

Flaming is a difficult issue. Many edited discussion lists define personal attacks as unacceptable. Almost any discussion can become emotionally charged. Some discussions are a continuous flame war; others are very polite. In general, flaming should be reserved for very specific offenses and restricted to personal e-mail. New subscribers who have been attacked privately should complain to the moderator; the moderator can then contact the flamer and request that he or she be more gentle with the new people. Attacks on the basis of ethnic background, religion, physical condition, gender, or sexual orientation occur on networks just as often as they occur in the real world. These attacks are just as reprehensible and difficult to eradicate. We can only hope to do our best to maintain a civil environment for discussion.

Moderating Styles

Each moderator moderates or edits differently, depending on his or her own tastes, subscribers, and the topic area. Political discussions tend to be very open and freewheeling. Discussions of medical interest tend to be conservative and well managed. A heavy-handed editorial style or scolding tone causes many subscribers to unsubscribe and go elsewhere. Most subscribers, however, support their moderator in efforts to keep the discussion on topic and free of misaddressed requests. If you have to stop some posting behaviors, doing so with a sense of humor is advisable and is often more effective.

Non-Listserv Software for Discussion Lists

This section describes other software that can be used to establish and manage discussion lists and electronic journals. Some common alternatives to the Listserv software are given here (in alphabetic order):

- Almanac
- MAILBASE
- PMDF Mailserv
- majordomo
- UNIX Listserver
- Usenet newsgroups (various software)
- Various homegrown list servers
- Various manually maintained lists

The first five of these (Almanac, MAILBASE, PMDF Mailserv, majordomo, and UNIX Listserver) respond to the one-word command `help` when it is sent in the main body of an e-mail message.

Almanac

Almanac is an information server designed to process file requests received through electronic mail and to provide subscription services for e-mail discussion lists. It does not automatically archive discussion lists and has no facility for searching files. Almanac can be set up for one-way distribution only—for electronic journals and newsletters, for example. Or it can be set up for two-way discussion so that subscribers can reply to any postings. Almanac was originally developed at the Oregon Extension Service at Oregon State University from a grant by the W. K. Kellogg Foundation. Almanac requires the UNIX operating system.

Almanac uses a central e-mail address (usually `almanac`) at each site where it is installed. Requests sent to that e-mail address retrieve files and provide automatic subscription and unsubscription to discussion lists. For example, at the University of Missouri, the Almanac address is `almanac@ext.missouri.edu`; a guide for Almanac users can be retrieved by addressing e-mail to that address with this message: `send guide`. A directory of the discussions available from a specific Almanac site can be retrieved by addressing e-mail to that address with this message: `send mail-catalog`.

You can subscribe to an Almanac discussion list by addressing e-mail to the Almanac address with this message:

```
subscribe <discussion name> <affiliation> <personal description>
```

In this message, `discussion name` is the name of the discussion list you want to subscribe to; `affiliation` is your institutional or organizational connection; and `personal description` is anything you want the moderators to know about you. Do not include your e-mail address;

the Almanac software identifies your correct address from the headers of the e-mail message you send to it. Unsubscribe by sending e-mail to the Almanac address with this message:

```
unsubscribe <discussion name>
```

Address mail to the discussion-name address or reply to e-mail from a discussion if you want to post messages to the discussion.

If you are the moderator (called the *supervisor* on an Almanac system), you can add or delete subscribers by addressing e-mail to the Almanac address with these messages:

```
Add <discussion name> e-mail address
Delete <discussion name> e-mail address
```

MAILBASE

MAILBASE is an excellent discussion list or electronic journal distribution software. It is currently available only in the United Kingdom. The central MAILBASE address is mailbase@uk.ac.mailbase and is run by the Networked Information Services Project, The Computing Service, University of Newcastle upon Tyne. Essentially, MAILBASE can do anything that Listserv can do except for searching file archives. In addition, the sponsors are willing to review proposals for new discussion lists or electronic journals being developed. Send e-mail to mailbase-helpline@uk.ac.mailbase.

Detailed information about MAILBASE discussion list moderation can be obtained by sending e-mail to the MAILBASE address with this message:

```
send mailbase owner-guide
```

A list of the existing discussion lists and electronic journals can be obtained by sending e-mail to the MAILBASE address with this message:

```
index
```

Subscribing and unsubscribing is done in the usual manner, by addressing e-mail to the central MAILBASE address with the following commands:

```
subscribe <discussion name> <your name>
unsubscribe <discussion name> <your name>
```

Posting to a MAILBASE distributed discussion list or electronic journal is done by addressing mail directly to `<discussion name>@mailbase.ac.uk`.

PMDF Mailserv

Mailserv is similar in capabilities and commands to the Listserv software, with the addition of discussion list reflection, electronic journal distribution, and file archiving services. However, Mailserv does not have automated discussion list archiving or file archive searching capabilities. It can be set up to send an automatic welcome message to all new subscribers. It runs on VAX/VMS systems. Mailserv is included with the widely used PMDF mail agent software package, available from Innosoft International, Inc., of Caremont, California.

Single-word commands addressed to a Mailserv site (for example, `Mailserv@oregon.uoregon.edu`) can be used to request further information:

Command	Description
HELP	Sends a help file
INDEX	Sends an index of all files currently available on that mailserver
LISTS	Sends a file containing a list of the mailing lists maintained by that mailserver

Subscribing and unsubscribing is accomplished by addressing e-mail to a Mailserv site address with the following messages:

```
subscribe <discussion name> <your name>
unsubscribe <discussion name> <your name>
```

To post messages to a Mailserv discussion list or electronic journal, address mail to the `<discussion name>@Mailserv` site address.

Majordomo

Majordomo is a UNIX-based e-mail distribution software package for discussion lists and electronic journals. Its development came out of discussions of the Internet Engineering Task Force Listserv Working Group. It functions similarly to other Listserv-like software because commands sent as the text of e-mail messages are received by the majordomo software and processed. Majordomo was written by Brent Chapman (`brent@GreatCircle.COM`). The latest version of the code is available by anonymous FTP from `FTP.GreatCircle.COM` in the directory `pub/majordomo`.

If you have any questions or require additional information about majordomo, send e-mail to `listmanager-owner@lanl.gov`.

ListProcessor (Formerly UNIX Listserver)

The UNIX Listserver (as of version 6.0a, known as ListProcessor), created by Anastasios Kotsikonas, has similar functionality to the Listserv software but runs only on UNIX computers. Support is provided for public and private hierarchical archives, moderated and unmoderated lists, peer lists, peer servers, private lists, address aliasing, news connections and gateways, mail queueing, digests, list ownership, owner preferences, crash recovery, batch processing, configurable headers, regular expressions, archive searching, and live user connections with TCP/IP. The latest version of ListProcessor is available by anonymous FTP to cs.bu.edu in the directory pub/listserv.

Homegrown and Manually Maintained List Servers

The phrase *homegrown and manually maintained list servers* covers a lot of different software and manual methods for managing discussion lists and electronic journals.

Homegrown list servers are essentially programs developed to suit the needs of local users to distribute discussion lists and electronic journals. COMSERVE is one of the most prominent of these. Hundreds of discussion lists and electronic journals are available from COMSERVE@Vm.Ecs.Rpi.Edu, which is the only site at which the COMSERVE software is used for publicly available discussion lists and electronic journals.

COMSERVE works almost exactly like the Listserv software and shares very similar commands. Information about the service can be obtained by sending e-mail to Support@Vm.Ecs.Rpi.Edu. Much locally developed list server software is available on anonymous FTP sites. Use Archie or Veronica to search for listserv or group communications; many of these sites will be identified for you. A FAQ with the subject *Mail Archive Server software list* is distributed to comp.mail.misc, comp.sources.wanted, comp.answers, and news.answers; the FAQ is maintained by Jonathan I. Kamens (jik@security.ov.com).

It is also possible, given enough account space, to manually distribute discussion lists and electronic journals. You can use nickname files or other distribution mechanisms from your own account space, depending on your computer system.

Providing Information with E-Mail Robots

33

by Dave Taylor

If you've been involved with the Internet for more than a few days, you've already realized that e-mail is the common currency, the most popular, most personal, and simultaneously most invasive of network communications. It's the only medium on the Net where everything you receive is directed to you, not to a group you're reading or a site you're maintaining. That's a great thing, but there's a price to pay. That price becomes more visible as you receive more and more electronic mail: it takes a lot of time to manage your electronic correspondence!

This isn't really news; your mailbox at home is also an open market, a free-for-all target for hundreds of bulk-mail companies, catalog salesfolk, credit card vendors, and goodness knows what else. Wouldn't it be great if you could hire someone to help you with your correspondence? A lackey who sent notes to all junk correspondents asking that you be removed from their mailing lists, who automatically responded to all requests for information without your having to get involved?

That's difficult to accomplish in the real world (I suppose that if you have sufficient funds, you can always hire someone to do this for you). With computer-based correspondence, the good news is that you can choose from a variety of programs that can do just this—and they're all free. Even better, if you're a burgeoning commercial vendor who wants to distribute information to your customers or clients without having to directly check your mail each day, these programs are just the trick. They easily answer requests for technical notes, pricing sheets, information files, and even source code and bug fixes—day or night, weekday or weekend.

This chapter considers two different e-mail *auto-responders*, as they're called. Embot offers a new, simple way to automate responding to electronic mail; Filter offers a smart programming environment for specifying any of a wide number of possible actions based on simple rules. Both of these programs require that your e-mail be received on a UNIX-based system, but don't despair: almost all low-cost Internet access accounts available are on just that type of system, whether a PC running UNIX or Linux, a Sun Microsystems machine running Solaris, or some other variant.

For less than $20 a month (and a bit of work), you can set up an automatic document-distribution system that can be accessed by over twenty million people, including everyone on CompuServe, GEnie, Prodigy, America Online, and eWorld. A definite bargain, I think.

Embot

The first of the robots described in this chapter is also the simplest: Embot. Embot scans through all your electronic mail as it arrives and automatically answers any messages that appear to be addressed to it rather than to you. It places any other mail in your usual incoming mailbox. You don't even know it's running unless you ask it for a status check. Although this is basically how all the programs described in this chapter work, the more complex programs require you to define a set of rules that define user requests, actions, and results. A typical rule might be "any message that has the subject *send catalog* should be answered with a copy of the file CATALOG."

The goal of Embot was to create a mail robot that didn't require any type of rule set to work intelligently and transparently. As a result, Embot simply looks for messages (or message subjects) that contain a specific one-word or two-word request and answers it. The one-word requests are *help* or *info* (which are synonymous with *send help* and *send info*); any file at all can be requested with the first word *send* or *get*. Rather than force the user to build an index of available files and information (which is one of the purposes of rule sets), Embot creates its own subdirectory and assumes it's okay to send copies of any file or files in that directory.

This means that once you set up Embot, it's simplicity itself to add new information to your database of available documents: simply save a copy of the file in the Embot directory. That's it. No updated rule sets, no index modifications, nothing. Immediately, Embot knows about the new file; requests that come in as quickly as two seconds after your addition can result in that file being sent in response. Updating files is similarly easy: simply replace the old version of the file with the newer one; anyone requesting the file automatically receives the most recent copy. This suggests how easy it is to offer daily price quotes, for example, or even hourly stock results through electronic mail.

Obtaining a Copy Of Embot

You can most easily get a copy of Embot by asking the master copy of the program to send you a copy of itself. Simply send an e-mail message to embot@northcoast.com. You can specify help in the subject line or in the message body, but Embot is smart enough to send you back a friendly greeting and an explanation of how to work with it— even if your message is completely blank. Here's what you most likely receive in response to your query (probably within five minutes or less):

```
Subject: Some tips on using the Embot program
Hi! I'm Embot, and I've been set up to look through e-mail messages
as they arrive here and try to extract and respond to requests for
files and other such miscellaneous tasks. I'm really quite easy to
work with - or so my Dad says - and all you have to remember is that
if you send any requests that I don't understand, I'll drop them in
the mailbox of my owner so he or she can respond by hand. That's a
lot slower, however, since humans don't think as quickly as us computers
do, but that's another subject entirely. Anyway, to get files, handouts,
and other information directly, all you need to do is know the name of
the file and send a request to me like:
        send thefilename
This can appear in the subject of the message or in the body of the
message. If you want a bunch of files, send me a single message with all
your requests in the body of the message, and I'll send them back as a
number of different e-mail messages. My owner won't even know!
```

```
To start out, send me a request to list all the available files. The easiest
way to do this is to have 'list' as either the subject of the message or
within the message body itself. I'll jump into action, build a list of
all files and information I'm authorized to send, and mail that back to
you, probably within five minutes of your request.
Once you have that, you can even reply to that message, prefacing the files
you'd like with the word 'send'.
That's about it. Any messages I don't understand, like I said, will be dropped
in the mailbox of my owner, and if you request 'help,' you'll get a copy of this
message.
If you'd like a copy of the Embot program to help you filter your own electronic
mail, I'd be delighted to help you out. You can get a copy by sending mail to me
at embot@northcoast.com. Specify 'send embot' and you'll get a copy of my
source code and installation instructions as fast as I can spell mitosis!
Thanks for working with me, and I look forward to hearing from you again
in the near future.
Bye for now.
Embot
```

Installation is relatively simple, at least for those somewhat versed in UNIX commands, but if you're a complete neophyte, you may opt to have someone help you out. Rather than provide the nuts and bolts of installation here, we note that you should read the README file closely (indeed, we recommend that you upload it to your home computer, print it out, and read through it before you actually begin typing any commands).

Once you install the program and configure it, you should ask Embot to check its own configuration by using the embot check command. Here's a typical output listing:

```
% embot check
Checking your Embot configuration...
     Account = embot, fullname = Embot
     Home directory = /home/embot
Embot home directory (/home/embot/Embot) is okay.
You don't have an Embot generic reply file (/home/embot/Embot/.default-msg)
so you won't be able to use the '-a' answer-all-mail option.
You don't have an Embot default help file (/home/embot/Embot/help) which
is definitely ungood. Please check into it ASAP!
I can't find a .forward file for you: I can't filter your e-mail without
my being added to this file or some equivalent.
Done checking your configuration.
```

Embot can detect and fix some common configuration problems, and once it is done, you have a directory called Embot that serves as your repository for any files or directories you want to make available.

The help file is automatically copied into your directory; before you go further, if you've turned on Embot by adding it to your .forward file, you can begin testing it and learning how it works.

A .forward file, in case you aren't sure, is a short file you place in your UNIX system home directory that instructs the mail delivery program to forward your messages to a specified address or program (rather than just delivering them to your mailbox). For all mail filter programs, you must create a simple .forward file that lets the system know you want to have the program check your mail.

As a first step, send yourself an e-mail message with the subject *help*. You should get back the same message you received when you sent mail to the Embot master copy on northcoast.com. Next, ask Embot for a file that isn't available: send a message with the subject send unknown-file. The response looks like this:

```
You requested file 'unknown-file' but it isn't available. The list of possible
files is as follows:
        help
        README
        embot.shar
Please send your request again, specifying one or more of these files.
Thanks!
Embot
```

You should save any files you want to have Embot distribute in the Embot directory.

Daily Life with Embot

After a while, you may find that many people send requests that can't be understood by Embot. In particular, some people send messages like "please send catalog" or "send catalog, thank you," neither of which is understood by Embot and both of which, therefore, end up in your own mailbox, requiring you to answer them by hand. This can be quite tedious if you send out dozens or hundreds of files each day. Fortunately, Embot can take over all the e-mail sent to an account, responding with a helpful message when it receives messages it doesn't understand. The Embot master copy does exactly that: try sending a message with the subject *hello* to embot@northcoast.com. Here's its response:

```
Subject: I couldn't understand your e-mail
Hi! You've mailed a message to me, but I'm Embot, not a human, so I only
understand certain specific requests and comments in my e-mail. To get
files, handouts, catalogs, and other information directly, all you need
to do is know the name of the file and send a request to me like:
        send thefilename
This can appear in the subject of the message or in the body of the message.
If you want a bunch of files, send me a single message with all your requests
in the body of the message, and I'll send them back as a number of different
e-mail messages.
To start out, send me a request to list all the available files. The easiest
way to do this is to have 'list' as either the subject of the message or
```

```
within the message body itself. I'll jump into action, build a list of all
files and information I'm authorized to send, and mail that back to you,
probably within five minutes of your request.
Once you have that, you can just reply to that message, prefacing the
files you'd like with the word 'send'.
Thanks for working with me, and I look forward to hearing from you again
in the near future.
Bye for now.
Embot
```

To turn this feature on—and don't use it for your personal account or you'll never get any personal mail delivered to your mailbox!—simply change the information in the .forward file to ¦embot -a. I highly recommend that you use a separate account and test it extensively before you publish its address for customer, client, or even use by your friends.

Embot keeps track of who requests which files from you, too. It's simple to learn what's been requested and by whom. To find out what files have been sent, for example, type **embot stats**; following is a sample list of the files accessed by Embot:

```
11 /home/embot/Embot/embot.shar
 7 /home/embot/Embot/help
 6 listing-of-files
 7 /home/embot/Embot/info
```

If you're curious about who requested a specific file (for example, your product info file), type **embot wanted info** to learn more (info, in this case, is the name of the file you've been sending). Following is a sample list of the people who have accessed the info file:

```
carlson@odin.net
marv@netcom.com
root@ns1.two.com
taylor@netcom.com
untangl@the-wire.com
untangle@io.org
zcopley@cats.ucsc.edu
```

Note that you can easily build a simple mailing list based on these addresses as a way of offering further information to those people interested in your product line. (Beware of flooding their mailbox with advertisements, however; such conduct is poorly received in the Internet community, as Rosalind Resnick and I explain in *The Internet Business Guide*, published by Sams Publishing, 1994.)

Unsure about what commands and options Embot understands? Simply type **embot help** to have the program remind you what you can do:

```
% embot help

Welcome to Embot! I understand a variety of interactive commands,
all of which should be specified on the command line:

stats           obtain statistics about embot usage, by requested file
users           produce a list of people who have accessed your embot
wanted file     see who has requested the specified file
check           Quick checks to see if things are configured OK
clear           clear your log files (your log file is 1645 bytes)

I also have a couple of different starting flags:

   -a        Respond to ALL mail sent:
             Only use this if I have my own account
   -v        For testing, this produces a log of my actions.
             Only for when I'm being used interactively!
```

Embot has a long memory: it can remember all requests from the very first day you install it, regardless of how many that represents. If you want to empty out its log file, type **embot clean** and Embot cleans up its database. If you want to retain a list of people who requested a file, however, make sure that you save a copy of the log file (once you clean the log file, the information is gone forever).

SUPPORTING FURTHER EMBOT DEVELOPMENT

Unlike the other programs described in this chapter, Embot is a shareware program; you can get a copy of the program for free, but the author requests a donation of $25 for individuals and $100 for companies that use it on a daily basis. Of course, you don't have to pay this fee and can still use the program without penalty, but with an aggressive set of changes and improvements in the works, your payment will help the author continue to grow and expand the capabilities of the program. Details of the shareware registration fee are in the file LICENSE.

Filter

Although Embot is a great solution for people seeking to simplify the distribution of files, technical reports, catalogs, source code, and other information through electronic mail, if you need more capabilities to tame your wild e-mailbox, you'll want to move up to Filter. Filter can send out not only files, catalogs, and other information, it can also delete mail from certain people, file mail from specific mailing lists into user-designated folders, and even forward specific messages to other people—all without any intervention on your part.

The trick, however, is to get things set up correctly.

Filter is based on an artificial intelligence-inspired rule set of conditions that the program checks on receipt of each and every electronic mail message. The overall form for a rule is "if a certain condition is evaluated as true, then do the specified action." If no rules are matched, Filter delivers the message to your mailbox.

The Filter Rules File

Filter is a piece of the Elm mail system, a popular screen-based electronic mail program. As a result, it is distributed (for free) as part of the Elm system and is most likely already installed on your Internet access provider's computer system (or even included with your UNIX system). The rules file for Filter lives in a file called `filter-rules` in a directory called `.elm` in your home directory. That is, if your home directory is `/home/taylor`, the Filter rules file is in `/home/taylor/.elm/filter-rules`.

There's a lot you can do with your Filter rule set. At its most fundamental, the language is simple to learn and work with; Filter helps by explaining what it doesn't understand if you make any mistakes while writing your rules.

Following is the `filter-rules` file I have in place to filter through the mail I receive at the account taylor@netcom.com:

```
#
# Filter rules so that people can request files without my
# having to mail them back one-by-one.

if (subject = "send mall" ) then
 exec "send mall %r"

if (subject = "send tyu" ) then
 exec "send tyu %r"

if (subject = "send gs" ) then
 exec "send gs %r"

if (subject = "send addme" ) then
 exec "send addme %r"

if (subject = "send toc" ) then
 exec "send tyu-toc %r"

if (subject = "send inbiz" ) then
 exec "send intbiz %r"

if (subject = "SUBSCRIBE imall-l" ) then
 delete
```

Each rule is specified in the format *if condition then action.* Each rule is considered in order, from first to last, until one matches the message that has been received. If you send me a message from your account `reader@mcp.com` with *send addme* as the subject, for example, Filter compares that subject to *send mall, send tyu,* and so on until it gets to the comparison for *send addme.* The two subjects match, so Filter invokes the associated action: `exec "send addme %r".`

The `exec` command is shorthand for *execute UNIX command;* Filter automatically replaces the cryptic `%r` with the return address of the message. Therefore, the actual `send` program is invoked with the command `send addme reader@mcp.com.`

Given that information, it's a simple and succinct C shell script that actually sends the specified file to the specified e-mail address. Here's an example of the `send` script you can use in cooperation with Filter to automatically send back information to users who request specific files or data.

```
#!/bin/csh -f
# a simple SEND shell script

cd /home/taylor/Filter-Files              # move into the file archive dir

if ( ! -f $1 ) then
  echo "I'm sorry, but file $1 is not available. Here's what is:"
  ls -CF | expand | sed 's/^/  /'
else
  mail -s "File $1, as requested" $2 < $1
endif

exit 0
```

Without delving too far into shell script programming (a task that *Teach Yourself C Shell Programming in 21 Days,* published by Sams Publishing, 1994, fulfills admirably), I will quickly note that `$1` is expanded to the first word of the command (the name of the requested file) and `$2` is expanded to the return address to which the file should be sent. As occurs within the `filter-rules` file, the C shell script tests the items between brackets and executes the action if appropriate. For the first test, `-f` tests to see whether the specified file (`$1`) exists; the prefix (`!`) reverses the logic of the test—in other words, the first test is really, "If the specified file does not exist, state that the file isn't available and list the alternatives." If the file is available, it's mailed to the user using the UNIX `mail` command.

The Filter Rules Language

Filter rules aren't as difficult to write as you may think. The language is succinct and should help you easily specify actions to help manage the tsunami of electronic mail you receive on a daily basis.

Recall that all rules are in the format *if condition then action*. There are four conditions that can be checked:

Condition	Meaning or Interpretation
from	Checks the return address of the message
subject	Lists the subject of the message, if any
to	Identifies the person to whom the message is addressed
lines	Lists the number of lines in the message

Expressions can test for equality (=), inequality (!=), or logical values. If you want to delete all messages from anyone at netcom, for example, you could use this rule:

```
if (from "@netcom.com") then delete
```

To reverse the logic of the rule, preface the rule with not:

```
if not subject = "test message"
```

To construct multiple conditions, add and between subconditions:

```
if (from="jane@edu" and lines > 30) then delete
```

Filter is quite flexible with the actual syntax of rules; if you prefer to have conditions in parenthesis, that's okay. If you prefer to think that subjects *contain* patterns rather than that subjects *equal* patterns (which is a more precise way to consider the matching strategy used), you are free to write rules like these:

```
if subject contains "send embot" then
    forward "embot@northcoast.com"
```

Any condition must be followed by an action, which can be any of the following:

Action	Meaning or Interpretation
delete	Deletes the message
save *folder*	Saves the message to the specified *folder*
savecopy *folder*	Same as save *folder*, but also delivers a copy to your mailbox
execute *command*	Feeds the message to the specified UNIX *command*
forward *address*	Forwards the message to the specified e-mail *address*
leave	Leaves the message in your mailbox (normal delivery of mail)

That's the entire Filter rules language, with one addition not yet discussed. If you want to specify a default rule at the bottom of the rule set for delivery of all messages that are not otherwise matched, you can specify the special command `always`, which looks like this:

```
always
   delete
```

In this example, any message not already matched by a previous rule is summarily deleted, which, frankly, is probably not a particularly great strategy for trimming your electronic mail (although it is no doubt quite effective).

Checking the Rules

Once you have written a set of rules that you think properly match your needs, you can ask the Filter program to double-check the syntax and notation. Simply type **filter -r** at the command line. The program scans and checks each rule, printing each to the screen as it goes. Here's an example:

```
% filter -r
Rule 1: if (subject = "send mall") then
        Execute /u1/taylor/bin/send mall <return-address>
Rule 2: if (subject = "send tyu") then
        Execute /u1/taylor/bin/send tyu <return-address>
Rule 3: if (subject = "send gs") then
        Execute /u1/taylor/bin/send gs <return-address>
Rule 4: if (subject = "send addme") then
        Execute /u1/taylor/bin/send addme <return-address>
Rule 5: if (subject = "send toc") then
        Execute /u1/taylor/bin/send tyu-toc <return-address>
Rule 6: if (subject = "send inbiz") then
        Execute /u1/taylor/bin/send intbiz <return-address>
```

If any problems are encountered, they are flagged, Here's how an error is flagged when I add a deliberate mistake to my rules file:

```
filter (04/03/95 12:26:32 taylor): Error on line 18 of rules - action "trash"
unknown
```

Daily Life with Filter

Just as with the other mail processing programs, you must tell the UNIX system that you want Filter to check your electronic mail as it's delivered. You do this by creating a .forward file in your home directory that contains the following line: ¦filter. It's a good idea, however, to use the which command to identify the full name of the Filter program on your system (the which command returns something like /usr/bin/filter). Use that name in the .forward file. The resulting line in the .forward file is something that looks like this:

```
¦/usr/bin/filter
```

Once the .forward file is in place, you're ready to roll. Filter starts checking and answering your mail without any fuss. One strategy for sending files with Embot, of course, is to tell everyone to use a specific subject line for their requests (in the section on Embot, earlier in this chapter, you can see how people send mail with subjects like *send mall* or *send intbiz* to get information without intervention).

Filter keeps track of its actions, whether they result in a message being sent to someone, a message being deleted, or even just dropped into your mailbox. You can learn what Filter has been doing by typing **filter -s** (which results in a succinct summary of actions) or **filter -S** (which offers the same summary followed by a detailed analysis of each action—that can go on for hundreds of pages!). Here's an example of the latter, greatly abbreviated:

```
% filter -S
A Summary of Filter Activity
A total of 699 messages were filtered:
The default rule of putting mail into your mailbox
     applied 441 times (63%)
Rule #1: (given to command "/u1/taylor/bin/send mall %r")
     applied 113 times (16%)
Rule #2: (given to command "/u1/taylor/bin/send tyu %r")
     applied 2 times (0%)
Rule #4: (given to command "/u1/taylor/bin/send mall %r")
     applied 15 times (2%)
Rule #5: (given to command "/u1/taylor/bin/send addme %r")
     applied 19 times (3%)
Rule #7: (given to command "/u1/taylor/bin/send promo %r")
     applied 3 times (0%)
Rule #9: (given to command "/u1/taylor/bin/send tyu-toc %r")
     applied 2 times (0%)
Rule #13: (given to command "/u1/taylor/bin/send intbiz %r")
     applied 11 times (2%)
Explicit log of each action:
Mail from JWGuirl@aol.com about send mall
     EXECUTED "/u1/taylor/bin/send mall JWGuirl@aol.com" by rule #1
Mail from HBeZee@aol.com about Description for inclusion in Mall
     PUT in mailbox: the default action
Mail from HBeZee@aol.com about send intbiz
     EXECUTED "/u1/taylor/bin/send intbiz HBeZee@aol.com" by rule #13
Mail from HBeZee@aol.com about send mall
     EXECUTED "/u1/taylor/bin/send mall HBeZee@aol.com" by rule #1
```

```
Mail from P.Ket@topos.ruu.nl about Internet Mall
    PUT in mailbox: the default action
Mail from kawabe@unisys.co.jp about send mall
    EXECUTED "/u1/taylor/bin/send mall kawabe@unisys.co.jp" by rule #1
Mail from Mailer-Daemon about Returned mail: User unknown
    PUT in mailbox: the default action
Mail from gwl1@gte.com
    PUT in mailbox: the default action
Mail from lghecht@netcom.com about Advertising in the Internet Mall
    PUT in mailbox: the default action
Mail from lhatzakis@hol.forthnet.gr about send mall
    EXECUTED "/u1/taylor/bin/send mall lhatzakis@hol.forthnet.gr" by rule #1
Mail from taylor about New mail archive server for your FAQ
    PUT in mailbox: the default action
```

Because Filter remembers every transaction, it's imperative that you occasionally clean out the log file it uses to track actions. You can do this easily when you request a summary: type **filter -sc** to produce a summary of actions and also clear the log file. If you issue the command a second time, Filter tells you it can't find a log file. No worries, though: the file is automatically re-created when the next message arrives for you.

Other Strategies for Managing Electronic Mail

Other programs can help you manage your electronic mail, including the baffling, but incredibly powerful, Procmail system for UNIX, and the many PC and Macintosh-based electronic mail front-end programs (most notably, the slick filtering system included with the full release of Eudora). For people who want to set up a simple and efficient e-mail robot that can help them promote their personal interests or business on the Internet, however, Embot and Filter can't be beat.

Nonetheless, the best way to manage the flood of electronic mail is to ask yourself the question "is this necessary?" for each message you receive. If you get unsolicited e-mail from someone selling something, for example, respond to them (and the postmaster at their site) with a brief note saying that you didn't seek the information and you don't want to receive any more messages from that party. If you're on a mailing list and it seems to be migrating from topics of interest to those that aren't of interest, sign off the list. If your customers send you mail with requests for catalogs or other automatically distributed files but are formatting the requests incorrectly, create a new account and set up Embot or some other program to answer all mail sent to that account so that you don't have to spend time with the inevitable "oops" messages you are otherwise forced to send on a daily basis.

The underlying goal is to ensure that each message you actually receive in your mailbox (after being checked and filtered by Embot, Filter, or some other program), is worth reading and considering. If you find that lots of your mail just wastes your time, you're a prime candidate for much of what I have discussed in this chapter.

Best of luck! Feel free to send me an electronic mail message with your experiences using either Embot or Filter, or with your own helpful tips for managing the flow of electronic mail. Just be careful of the subject, or my robot will respond instead!

Setting Up an FTP Server

34

by Kevin D. Barron
updated by
Billy Barron

There are many reasons for setting up an FTP server—ranging from sheer necessity to noble intentions. Whatever your reasons, you should plan carefully and consider the notes in this chapter.

The first thing to consider is how you plan to use the server. Who are the intended users? Will they best be served by a public or a private server?

The next major consideration is the software you plan to use. Does your vendor-supplied server meet your needs? Check the system manuals to determine whether you want to use that server or one of the other servers available on the Net. Three solid UNIX packages are available from the following sites:

```
ftp://uarchive.wustl.edu:/packages/wuarchive-ftpd
ftp://ftp.uu.net:/systems/unix/bsd-sources/libexec/ftpd
ftp://gatekeeper.dec.com:/pub/DEC/gwtools/ftpd.tar.gz
```

Next, sketch out an overview of how your server will be set up. This not only helps your own efforts, it makes the server easier for others to use. For example, you may want to diagram the layout in some detail. That is, create a tree structure on paper and draw in the branches you'll supply. Consider the following example:

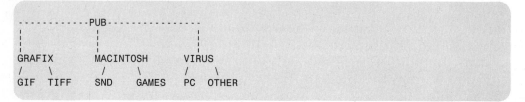

```
------------PUB----------------
    |              |            |
    |              |            |
GRAFIX        MACINTOSH      VIRUS
 /    \         /    \       /    \
GIF  TIFF     SND   GAMES   PC  OTHER
```

Add all the directories you think you might use, even if there is nothing in them yet; that way, people know what you are going to put there and will come back to look again. Adding all the directories may be a good idea, but stay reasonable. If the directories don't contain files after a few months, you should remove them.

The next step involves making decisions about access. Some sites provide an incoming directory that enables files to be put on the server anonymously. If you plan to use such a directory, remember that you have very little control over what is put there. Some sites become depositories for pirated software; others are flooded with GIFs.

The best way to deal with such security issues is to make your incoming directory execute-only; make sure that the directory has write and execute subdirectories (see the CERT "Security Notes" posted to the comp.security newsgroups or on ftp://ftp.cert.org/ for specifics). Of course, this practice may require more administration time than is available. As many FTP administrators can attest, the down side to having an incoming directory is that someone has to continuously check the directory.

Ultimately, you have to decide how much time you have to devote. An alternative to having an incoming directory is to use mail aliases (although this requires the extra work of encoding and decoding binaries). A separate alias can be set up for each topic (for example, UNIX, Windows, and network); if that does not provide sufficient granularity, you can use Procmail to filter the mail based on a subject line (use Archie to locate Procmail).

In addition to dealing with incoming files, you should set up an alias of ftp@your_ftp_server to deal with incoming mail. Using this alias is one way to keep mail related to your FTP site separate from other system mail. If this e-mail address is presented prominently—for example, in a top-level README file—people can inform you of problems with the server.

Another conventional alias is to set up an alternative name for your host in the form ftp.site.domain (for example, ftp.widgets.com). To set up such an alias (actually a cname record in a nameserver database), add the name to the nameserver that serves your site.

The procedure for installing software varies depending on the package, but the following steps provide an overview. As always, first consult the documentation distributed with your package.

1. Ensure that the FTP user account is set up properly. The user ID (number) should not conflict with that of another user; most importantly, the group ID should be unique—or as is commonly the case, should be "nobody." The shell for FTP must be left blank.

2. Create the root directory for FTP, preferably on a separate disk or partition. This is the home directory for ftpd (the FTP server) and should contain the following subdirectories: bin, dev, etc, pub, and usr. The permissions on the directories should be as follows:

```
r-xr-xr-x    root    system       ./
r-xr-xr-x    root    system       ../
--x--x--x    root    system    bin/
--x--x--x    root    system    etc/
r-xr-xr-x    root    system    pub/
--x--x--x    root    system    usr/
```

3. Copy the appropriate files into their respective directories:

```
cp /usr/bin/ls        bin/ls
cp /usr/bin/sh        bin/sh
cp /usr/lib/ld.so     usr/lib/ld.so
cp /usr/lib/libc.so.* usr/lib/
```

4. Make these three files: `etc/passwd`, `etc/group`, and `dev/zero`.

   The `passwd` file should resemble the following (see "Security," later in this chapter, for details):

   ```
   special:*:21:65534:Innat Special::
   nobody:*:65534:65534:Notta Contenda::
   ftp:*:9999:90:Anonymous Ftp account (server)::
   ```

   The `group` file should resemble the following:

   ```
   nogroup:*:65534:
   ftp:*:90:
   ```

   Use the `mknod` command to create the special `dev/zero` file:

   ```
   /usr/etc/mknod dev/zero c 3 12
   ```

5. Ensure that the files in the FTP directories are owned by root and are not writeable by FTP:

   The `bin` directory:

   ```
   --x--x--x  1 root      system     ls*
   --x--x--x  1 root      system     sh*
   ```

   The `dev` directory:

   ```
   crw--r-r--  1 root      daemon     zero
   ```

   The `etc` directory:

   ```
   -r--r--r-  1 root      system     group
   -r--r--r-  1 root      system     passwd
   ```

   The `usr` directory:

   ```
   rwxr-xr-x 2 root      system     lib/
   ```

The `usr/lib` directory:

```
-r-xr-xr-x  1 root    system    ld.so*
-rwxr-xr-x  1 root    system    libc.so.1.6*
```

6. Verify that there are FTP entries in the `/etc/services` and `/etc/inetd.conf` configuration files.

The `/etc/services` file:

```
ftp-data 20/tcp
ftp      21/tcp
```

The `/etc/inetd.conf` file:

```
ftp    stream   tcp   nowait root /usr/etc/in.ftpd in.ftpd
```

If something similar to the preceding lines does not exist in these files, you must add entries like these. In the `/etc/services` file, add the entries shown here. In the `/etc/inetd.conf` file, you may have to change the filename (that is, `/usr/etc/in.ftpd`) to the correct location of your FTP daemon; the last field must match the part of the filename after the last slash.

7. Test the account. Make sure that you can log on, use the `cd` command to access all directories under `pub`, and transfer files.

Administration

You can do several things to make your server a more hospitable place. Foremost among the things you should consider is a recursive listing of the entire contents of your server. Depending on how many files reside on your server, this listing can take up considerable space. However, you can compress the listing to conserve space.

The listing should be called `ls-1R` or `FILELIST` and should be placed in the top-level directory. On an active server, it should be updated weekly or biweekly; on less active servers, a monthly update may suffice. However, the listing should be updated at regular intervals so that users know when to check it (the frequency of the updates can be specified for users in a `README` file). If the updates are irregular, users are likely to perform their own recursive listings. Depending on the size of your server, these recursive listings can be a significant drain on resources (defeating one of the main purposes of making the file list available).

Another file you should place in the top-level directory is the README file. You can use the file to hold various information, such as the purpose of the site, the name and home phone number of the person maintaining the site, and an e-mail address to which users can send bug reports or comments. This file also can be used to point out other methods to retrieve information (Gopher, Web, mailserver, and so on), and whether your site "mirrors" other sites or archives. It also should contain information about any anomalies on your system—for example, if you have hacked the server.

Within each subdirectory, you can add another README or INDEX file to describe the contents of that directory. These files can become dated quickly, so it is a good idea to keep their descriptions fairly generic. For example, if you have a directory called amoeba that contains the current release of the mind-numbing Amoeba's Revenge game, you can point to AMOEBA.TAR.Z as the latest version (rather than listing the version number in the INDEX file). The AMEOBA.TAR.Z file could be a link to the latest version AMOEBE.5.3.TAR.Z, saving you the trouble of updating all the INDEX files—and saving users the guesswork of finding the most recent version.

> **TIP**
>
> Regarding version numbers, it is a good idea to keep at least the previous release of a given program in case there are bugs with the current one. Keep your naming convention consistent—especially when the old and new versions are in the same directory. Often, the best way to do this is to include the version number in the name of the file or directory.

Finally, if you intend for your site to be public, make sure that people can find it: register the site with the Archie folks. (See Chapter 24, "Archie: An Archive of Archives," for details.)

Compression

Disks have a nasty habit of filling up, and FTP directories seem to have a hyperactive appetite for disk space. Unfortunately, cleaning up is not as simple as moving some files to tape. On an FTP server, the files must be on the disk or they are not accessible.

The solution is to use compression, which can save between 40 and 60 percent of your disk space. Compression also saves network bandwidth because fewer bytes are transferred. Of course, not all files benefit from compression—and there is the added inconvenience of compressing and decompressing the files—but if conventions are followed, compression is certainly worthwhile.

One thing to remember is that the type of compression used should be consistent, as well as appropriate, for the files being compressed. For example, UNIX files are traditionally compressed using the `compress` command (which appends a *Z* to the filename) but the GNU `gzip` program is now also popular. DOS files are usually compressed with the ZIP format; these files can be unzipped with `PKUNZIP`.

Although there are no definitive compression rules to follow, here are a few guidelines:

- Being consistent does not mean using the same compression type for all files; in fact, different types of compression are appropriate to each file type (Mac, UNIX, and so on). The compression method should match the platform for which the file is intended—not the platform on which the FTP server is running. Admittedly, it would be convenient to use one type of compression across all platforms, but such universality seems to elude the anarchic world of computing (although the ZOO format merits consideration).

- Let your users know which compression methods you use: simply put a note in the `README` files. Rather than making users guess, a simple comment in each relevant directory can save a lot of frustration. Such pointers are particularly important if you use a new or nontraditional type of compression.

- Make the compression programs you use available on your server (when this is appropriate). This act will be greatly appreciated by your users.

Security

FTP has been around for a long time (by computer standards); most of its security issues have been thoroughly scrutinized. However, security is an ongoing concern because it is affected by OS upgrades, program changes, and file system modifications. Short of constructing a firewall, your best line of defense is vigilance.

Most FTP servers have a method of logging sessions—typically by specifying the `-l` option when `ftpd` is invoked. This option logs each session to `syslog`. The wuarchive `ftpd` has several options for logging, including user commands and file transfers (see the man page for details). Users of the FTP server who would abuse its services may be hesitant to do so if they know their activities are being logged. It is usually a good idea to put a message on the sign-on screen of your FTP server that you log all commands. The exact procedure for doing this depends on your FTP server, so check the documentation that came with it to see how to add such a message.

Of course, all the logging in the world won't help if the attackers gain root access (because they can then modify the logs). Therefore, your first line of defense must be careful scrutiny of your file permissions. Follow the file permission examples (provided earlier in this chapter) and make sure that they stay that way by running a script periodically. An example script can be found at the following address:

```
nic.sura.net:/pub/security/programs/unix/secure_ftp_script
```

In addition to ensuring that the file and directory permissions are secure, you should make sure that none of the entries from /etc/passwd appear in ~ftp/etc/passwd. Both the ~ftp/etc/passwd and ~ftp/etc/group files are used only to show ownership and group ownership for the dir or ls -l command. Neither are used for access privileges. Therefore, only the entries that must be there should be included.

Sites should make sure that the ~ftp/etc/passwd file contains no account names that are the same as those in the system's /etc/passwd file. These files should include only those entries relevant to the FTP hierarchy or necessary to show owner and group names. In addition, ensure that the password field, which follows the first colon, has been blocked. The following example of a passwd file from the anonymous FTP area on cert.org shows the use of asterisks (*) to block the password field:

```
ssphwg:*:3144:20:Site Specific Policy Handbook Working Group::
cops:*:3271:20:COPS Distribution::
cert:*:9920:20:CERT::
tools:*:9921:20:CERT Tools::
ftp:*:9922:90:Anonymous FTP::
nist:*:9923:90:NIST Files::
```

Another facet of FTP security is the ftpusers file. If this file exists, the daemon checks the names listed against the user logging in. If the name matches an entry, access is denied. If this file is not found (usually ~ftp/etc/ftpusers), any user meeting the other criteria is allowed access. You want to block access for certain user IDs for a few reasons. The first is when a user ID has special access to the system; someone using FTP into that user ID could cause great damage. The other reason is when no one will ever FTP into the account; why leave it open? The following users should be in ftpusers as a bare minimum:

```
root
bin
boot
daemon
digital
field
gateway
```

```
guest
nobody
operator
ris
sccs
sys
uucp
```

The wuarchive `ftp` server has the added feature of being able to permit access based on matching entries in a file (`~ftp/etc/ftphosts`).

FINAL RECOMMENDATION

If you want to set up an FTP site, you should read the documentation and this chapter and do it right. However, remember that managing an FTP server can be a lot of work. If you are not going to keep up the files on the FTP server and will let them become obsolete, it may be better for you not to run an FTP server at all. It is, however, your decision.

Creating Your Own Gopher

35

by Kevin D. Barron

Stories about the Internet are full of comments regarding the massive amounts of material available online. Indeed, one estimate put the figure at several terabytes (each terabyte is 1,024 gigabytes or 1,048,576 megabytes). So why should you feel the need to add to this huge volume of information? One reason is that, by providing your own server, you can readily organize the information and available resources in both an accessible and coherent manner. Perhaps another valid reason is that it makes sense for users of a shared resource to put something back in order to avoid a "tragedy of the commons" in which the resource is eventually depleted. Lastly, a Gopher server provides a flexible architecture-independent mechanism for making rich text, images, sounds, and programs available to almost any workstation or terminal on the network.

This chapter discusses things you should consider when setting up your Gopher server. Specifics relate primarily to UNIX servers (most hosts on the Internet run or are capable of running UNIX). Please note that all specific examples given or used are for heuristic purposes only and are not intended to replace the installation documentation.

Before delving into the installation process, this chapter explores some of the questions regarding the server's purpose. Then the chapter covers the process of obtaining and building the software. Subsequent sections explain the process of configuring the server, as well as designing and maintaining the Gopher data directory. Security, FTP gateways, and indexing are also covered.

Before Taking the Plunge

Before installing Gopher, you should understand the purpose of the server. Who are the targeted users, and what are their main interests? The answers may evolve over time, especially once the server is installed and users become familiar with the types of available resources. Nevertheless, establishing goals at the outset helps shape the resource to closely match user needs.

Versions of the Gopher software starting with 2.0 are not freeware. The University of Minnesota Gopher Development Team decided early in 1993 that users, other than educational and nonprofit organizations, would be charged. Therefore, if you intend to use Gopher for profit-making enterprises, make arrangements with the copyright holders of the software or use the latest 1.x version.

Related to the copyright issue is the problem of restricting data to a particular group of users. If this is one of your concerns, it may be appropriate to investigate the security features of the Gopher release you are considering using. Gopher can limit the hosts that access its resources, based on the Internet address of the host. There is also a per-user scheme in the 2.x releases (refer to "Security," later in this chapter). If the data to be served requires strict security measures, it probably shouldn't be made available to Gopher. However, even though sensitive information may not be suitable for Gopher, fear of unauthorized access or misuse should not be the deciding factor in installing a Gopher server. Security issues are constantly scrutinized by the Gopher development community, and patches are made available when necessary.

Other issues to review before installing the server concern who will maintain the data and how maintenance will be accomplished. Much of the data made available by Gopher is time dependent and requires regular updates. If the responsibilities and procedures for updating the data are not clearly defined at the beginning, chances are the updates will not be performed at appropriate intervals. Likewise, cumbersome data-support mechanisms neither facilitate nor encourage regular maintenance practices. ("Maintaining and Updating: The Care and Feeding of Gophers," later in this chapter, has suggestions regarding update mechanisms.)

A pragmatic (but more mundane) issue concerns computing resources. Certainly, one of the determining aspects of providing new services is how they will impact existing resources. Fortunately, the Gopher software features the ability to limit the load placed on the host. Of course, the host must be accessible and have sufficient cycles available for the Gopher server.

If a single host with sufficient cycles isn't available, you can spread the load over several hosts. An example of such a configuration is the "Mother" Gopher at the University of Minnesota, where six Macs serve as the front-end to more than 200,000 queries a day.

In a multihost configuration, the slower host can be used when computing power is not required, and the faster host can be used to perform database searches, downloads of large files, and so on. Note, however, that a Gopher server does not necessarily require much computational power, even for a relatively large server. A Gopher client typically incurs less overhead than does an FTP client. The Gopher daemon is also particularly frugal because it can be run as needed, rather than continuously (in high volume cases, however, you will want to run it continuously).

Another consideration to make is whether or not Gopher (or Gopher-like) resources already exist in your local area. If they do, it may be worth discussing partnerships or similar cooperative arrangements. As previously mentioned, one of the biggest concerns is (or should be) maintenance of data. Collaborative efforts can alleviate some of the maintenance requirements, enabling you to manage other aspects of Gopherspace. After all, it is far better to have one well maintained server than two poorly managed ones.

Software

Obtaining the Gopher software is a fairly straightforward task. Almost all the variants of the Gopher server can be found at `ftp://boombox.micro.umn.edu/pub/gopher`. For details, see Chapter 22, "FTP: Fetching Files from Everywhere." If Archie is available, you can use it to locate other FTP sites, perhaps one closer to your own site. Of course, if you already have a Gopher client available, you can use Gopher to download. Simply point the client at `gopher.micro.umn.edu` and select the following options in order:

```
-> 1.  Information About Gopher
    -> 5.  Gopher Software Distribution
```

Software ports are available for numerous platforms such as IBM/CMS, Mac, DOS, and VMS (see Table 35.1). In addition to the source distribution, there are many corollary programs and scripts that provide invaluable assistance to the Gopher manager (also called the *Gophermeister*).

Table 35.1. Gopher software is available from the University of Minnesota. Server packages are indicated by *.

Software	Description
*Mac_server	Gopher server for the Macintosh (now includes Gopher Surfer, the Gopher+ Mac server).
Macintosh-TurboGopher	A graphical Gopher client for the Macintosh.
NeXT	A graphical Gopher client for NeXTStep.
PC_client	A graphical Turbovision-based client for PCs running DOS and using the Clarkson/Crynwr packet drivers.
*PC_server	Two PC Gopher server implementations: one based on Phil Karn's NOS; the other uses Clarkson/Crynwr packet drivers.
*Rice_CMS	A Gopher server and client for VM/CMS systems, written at Rice University.
*UNIX	Gopher for UNIX. Includes a Gopher server, full-screen client, X Window client, and an emacs client.
*VMS	Gopher for VMS. Includes a Gopher server and full-screen client.
*VieGopher	A Gopher server and client for VM/CMS, written at Vienna.
*mvs	A Gopher server and client for MVS.
os2	A Gopher client for OS/2.

The UNIX source itself only requires between 1 and 2M (and 2M after compiling). Nevertheless, it's always a good idea to allow more space for enhancements such as new Gopher tools, upgrades, and local additions. Once the distribution is uncompressed and untarred, change to the DOC directory and carefully read the INSTALL note. Also of interest are the gopherd.8 and server.changes files, both of which document the basic server and changes from previous releases. Another must-read is the FAQ (Frequently Asked Questions) which you can find at ftp://rtfm.mit.edu/pub/usenet/news.answers/gopher-faq.

If you install indexing, read the INSTALL section appropriate to your hardware (for example, the NeXT section) closely. If indexing is to work, you must link in the index engine before building Gopher. Unless you are installing Gopher on a NeXT machine, you must download the WAIS software and build it first. You can FTP the WAIS source from `ftp://ftp.wais.com/pub/freeware/unix-src/wais8b5.1.tar.Z`.

For the NeXT machine, FTP from `ftp://boombox.micro.umn.edu/pub/gopher/Unix/NeXTtext.tar.Z`.

> **NOTE**
>
> Using the WAIS code does not imply that you also have to run the WAIS server. The Gopher daemon (`gopherd`) contains the search engine to query the indexed files generated by WAIS. (For details, see the `gopherd` man page and Chapter 27, "WAIS: The Database of Databases.")

Here is a list of other software you may want to download:

- Securegopher (secure versions of Telnet and `more`)
- TN3270 (enables Telnet sessions to mainframes)
- Kermit (provides file transfer to and from PCs)
- mm (metamail/multimedia)
- xv (X-based image viewer)

Making Gopher

If you use indexing, you must obtain and build the indexing software before building Gopher. Also be sure to link indexing into the Gopher source directory, as specified in the INSTALL note (at `gopher2.x/doc/INSTALL`).

> **NOTE**
>
> You must follow the instructions for installing the index software first—even though they follow the instructions for building Gopher.

Compiling the Gopher code is a relatively painless task, thanks to the efforts of the Gopher development community. The majority of the configuration requires assigning the directories to be used, which version of a given command to use during compiling, and so forth.

There are two files that control the compiling: `makefile.config` and `conf.h`. Most default settings in these files don't need to be changed, although you should always check. Some of the more important settings are listed in Tables 35.2 and 35.3.

Table 35.2. Configuration parameters in `makefile.config`.

Parameter	Default	What It Is
CC	cc	Your favorite C compiler.
OPT	-O	Use -O for faster code and -g for debugging.
RANLIB	ranlib	Use touch if you don't have the ranlib command.
PREFIX	/usr/local	The base directory where the software will be installed. Many other parameters use this value.
CLIENTDIR	$(PREFIX))/bin	Where the client Gopher is installed.
CLIENTLIB	$(PREFIX)/lib	Where the help files for the client are installed.
SERVERDIR	$(PREFIX)/etc	Where the server files are installed.
SERVEROPTS		Optional server features (for example, -DBIO).
DOMAIN	.micro.umn.edu	Set this to the portion of your hostname that the hostname command doesn't return.
SERVERDATA	/home/gopher	The default location of Gopher data for the Gopher server.
SERVERPORT	70	The default port for the Gopher server.

Table 35.3. Configuration parameters in `conf.h`.

Parameter	Default	What It Is
CLIENT1_HOST	gopher.tc.umn.edu	The default host to which to connect.
CLIENT2_HOST	gopher2.tc.umn.edu	The alternate host to which to connect.
CLIENT1_PORT	70	The default port for the first host.
CLIENT2_PORT	70	The default port for the alternate host. Set to 0 if there is no alternate host.
PAGER_COMMAND	more -d %s	Command used to display text.
PLAY_COMMAND	N/A	Command used to play sounds.
MAIL_COMMAND	mail	Command used to mail files.
TELNET_COMMAND	Telnet	Command used to connect to other hosts using the Telnet protocol.

Parameter	Default	What It Is
TN3270_COMMAND	tn3270	Command used to connect to IBM mainframe hosts.
IMAGE_COMMAND	xloadimage -fork %s	Command used to view image files.

Assuming that everything is configured properly, you should be able to type **make** from the top directory of the Gopher distribution to compile everything. To compile and install everything, type **make install**. The man pages, Gopher executables, help file, and Gopher daemon are installed in the locations defined in the makefile.config file.

If you have trouble, follow this foolproof checklist:

1. Reread the documentation to see whether you overlooked something.
2. Check the compatibility switches in makefile.config (see Table 35.4).
3. Check the WAIS-indexed news discussion of Gopher to see whether a similar problem has shown up there (item #2 on gopher://gopher.tc.umn.edu:70/11/ Information%20About%20Gopher).
4. Consult with your nearest systems guru.

If you are still stumped, post a succinct message to the newsgroup comp.infosystems.gopher. Queries to this group are generally answered quickly (often by members of the Gopher team at Minnesota).

Table 35.4. Compatibility definitions.

Unknown Symbol	What You Should Add to COMPAT=
strstr	-DNOSTRSTR
tempnam	-DNO_TEMPNAM
strdup	-DNO_STRDUP
bzero or bcopy	-DNO_BZERO
getwd	-DNO_GETWD
tzset	-DNO_TZSET
strcasecmp	-DNO_STRCASECMP

If everything compiled properly and is installed in the correct locations, you're ready to test the Gopher.

Test Run

Testing the Gopher server is simple; Gopher serves whichever directory to which you point it. Just make the directory, copy some sample files there, and run gopherd. For example, issue this command to make the directory /datadir/foo:

```
mkdir /datadir/foo
```

Copy some files into /datadir/foo and ensure that the files are world readable. The following command calls gopherd and runs as user nobody on the /datadir/foo directory, using port 70:

```
/usr/local/etc/gopherd -u nobody /datadir/foo 70
```

Use ps (or an equivalent command) to ensure that gopherd is running; then you can Telnet to the port specified—in this example, port 70:

```
telnet host 70
```

In this syntax, *host* is the name of the host running gopherd. The server should respond with a tab-limited string, which contains the names of the items in the top-level directory (that is, the top Gopher menu). Suppose that the data directory contains the following files:

```
.cap       Gopher_Info        World
About      Internet_Services  other_stuff
```

Typing **telnet *host* 70** displays something similar to this:

```
About This Server<tab>Gopher_Info<tab>Internet_Services<tab>Other_Stuff<tab>The
World at your Keyboard
```

To exit, escape back to Telnet (usually by pressing Ctrl+]) and type **quit**.

If you don't see something similar to the previous example, or you get an error message, check the file permissions on the datadir directory and the files in it. Also try temporarily running as root.

Configuring the Server

Once you have confirmed that the server is functional, you can proceed to the next phase of configuration.

The Gopher daemon has many options that are controlled in one of two ways. The `gopherd.conf` file contains most of the modifiable options (see Table 35.5). However, some options can be specified only in the second manner: at the command line when `gopherd` is invoked. (See Table 35.6 for a list of options and the manner of invocation. The best source for authoritative information of these parameters is almost always the man page released with the source code.)

Table 35.5. Parameters for `gopherd.conf`.

Parameter	Example	Description
hostalias	gopher.foo.bar	The host name returned by the server.
Admin:	Jack Nicholas	The name of the Gophermeister. May also contain phone number and other information.
AdminEmail:	jack@dull.boy	The e-mail address of the administrator.
Site:	Shining Hotel	The site name.
Loc:	New York, N.Y., USA	City, state, and country of the site.
Geog:	44 58 48 N 93 15 49 W	Latitude and longitude of the site.
Language:	En_US	ANSI language as used by `setlocale()`.
viewext:	.gif I 9/image gif	Map filename extensions to particular Gopher type.
ignore:	core	Filenames or extensions to ignore.

Table 35.6. Command-line options for Gopher.

Option	Description
-D	Enables copious debugging output.
-L	Loads restrict connections when the load average is above load. Your server must be compiled with the LOADRESTRICT option for this option to work.

continues

Table 35.6. continued

Option	Description
-C	Disables caching of directory retrievals. Otherwise, a directory retrieval is cached in the file .cache.
-l *logfile*	For each connection, the server logs the time, host, and transaction to the file *logfile*.
-I	Specifies that the server is running from inetd.
-o *options*	Specifies an alternative gopherd.conf file instead of the default.
-c	Do not use the system call chroot(2) before processing connections. This relies on code that attempts to ensure that files outside the Gopher data directory cannot be retrieved. Use with care and use with the -u option.
-u *user*	Run as the user named *user*. The server is run with reduced permissions (that is, with permissions other than root), which can ensure that only publicly readable files are available from the server.
gopher-data	The directory where the Gopher information resides.
gopher-port	The port number (usually 70) at which the server runs.

As with the options, there also are two methods of running gopherd. The first method is to run gopherd continuously. This method relies on a manual invocation, or more typically, an entry in the system startup files (BSD: etc/rc.local; System V: inittab and /etc/start-gopher-server). The gopherd is always running, spawning processes to deal with each "connection."

The second method is to run gopherd from inetd, which acts as a godfather process that runs gopherd only when needed. This method requires modifying both /etc/services and /etc/inetd.conf. One of the problems with this approach is that some systems, notably Sun systems running SunOS 4.1.x, support only a limited number of arguments. The workaround is to use inetd to call a script, which then invokes gopherd with all the options you choose.

Setting Up the Data Directory

Making data available for Gopher is as simple as moving files or directories into the directory specified by SERVERDATA in the makefile.config file (henceforth referred to as datadir). Of course, you must check the permissions to make sure that the files and directories are readable by the user ID that Gopher is running under. The only other caveat is that Gopher ignores core and dot files (for example, core and .hidden do not show up on the menu). Directories named bin, dev, etc, and usr are also ignored. By default, all other files and directories under the datadir are presented on the menus.

The files and directories are alphabetically listed on the menu—uppercase first. To change the order, you can use one of two schemes. The older method relies on a .cap directory that contains a file named the same as the file or directory to be reordered. Each of these .cap files must contain two lines. The first lists the name or title to be used on the menu; the second specifies the order on the menu (item number).

Suppose that the Gopher data directory contains the following files:

```
.cap        Gopher_Info        World
About       Internet_Services  other_stuff
```

And the associated .cap directory contains the following files:

```
About   other_stuff
```

If you run Gopher and look at the About menu, you see this:

```
Internet Gopher Information Client 2.0
Root gopher server: gopher.tc.umn.edu

->_ 1.   About This Server
    2.   Other Information
    3.   Gopher_Info
    4.   Internet_Services
    5.   World

Press ? for Help, q to Quit, u to go up a menu Page:1/1
```

Notice that the About filename became About This Server in the menu. To accomplish this transformation, the .cap/About file must contain the following:

```
Name=About This Server
Numb=1
```

The .cap/other_stuff file must contain the following information:

```
Name=Other Information
Numb=2
```

The Numb field supersedes the alphabetized order, so Other Information precedes all the rest. The Numb fields in your .cap files must be sequential and begin with 1.

The current scheme for renaming and renumbering menus is to use a .names file in the same directory as the file. This is the default; to use the .cap directories, you must specify -CAPFILES to SERVEROPTS in makefile.config.

There are some informally established conventions regarding the organization of the Gopher datadir. Some of these conventions are listed here:

- An About file in the top directory—and preferably in each main subdirectory
- A directory or link-pointer to other Gophers
- Indication of experimental/volatile directories
- A listing of "what's new"

These conventions are not carved in stone, and no one will flame you for not adhering to them. However, being a good Net citizen means making an effort to observe standard practices. At the very least, the top-level About file should contain some rudimentary information about the nature or purpose of the server and who to contact if you have problems.

One of the most useful conventions is to maintain a listing of what's new (with the date in the name of the file). Unfortunately, these items are often out of date and occasionally do not even mention a date! The Whatsnew program is designed to deal with the problem of new additions. It is a perl script that enables users to check new items since a specified date (or since the creation of a certain bookmark). Download it from the following address:

```
ftp://boombox.micro.umn.edu/pub/gopher/Unix/GopherTools/whatsnewd.Z
```

Another method of dealing with the maintenance of a what's new listing is an idea borrowed from FTP sites: ls-lR. This recursive listing of the data directory can (to some extent) be created automatically (using cron), which reduces the maintenance overhead. Although such listings are not yet common practice, they may become more prevalent as a result of the Veronica and Jughead programs (Veronica is described in Chapter 26, "Searching Gopherspace with Veronica"; Jughead is discussed later in this chapter).

The importance of indicating a volatile directory or menu becomes evident once you establish links to other servers. Few things are as embarrassing as being caught with repeated directory does not exist errors while showing off your server to those who pay your salary! Of course, many directories are moved over time, servers change names, and so forth (there are tools that make these discoveries for you). The point remains: "Do unto your server what you would have others do unto their servers." That is, maintain a measure of stability.

One of the double-edged swords of the Gopher world is that the ease of adding or modifying data results in the temptation to constantly improve the menu structure. Of course, this improvement comes at the cost of breaking all the bookmarks and links others have made pointing to your server. The object lesson is to plan the overall structure of your data directory carefully and avoid excessive reorganization.

However, once you establish your server, you aren't stuck with a particular configuration forever. In fact, the consensus from GopherCon seems to be that setting up a server is an iterative process, requiring several passes to get the structure honed. But common sense dictates that a server in constant flux is too confusing, eventually resulting in disuse.

On the other end of the scale, if a server's data is not updated at appropriate and regular intervals, the server will be as dysfunctional as the constantly changing one mentioned in the last paragraph. Therefore, it is paramount to ensure a balance of dynamic and static information.

Maintaining and Updating: The Care and Feeding of Gophers

Gophers may not be domesticated, but they aren't difficult to care for. Aside from periodically updating information and ensuring the validity of links to other Gophers, a Gopher server requires little system maintenance. Updating information depends on the amount of dynamic (stale-dateable) material being served. Often, this update procedure can be automated (or at least facilitated) by one of several procedures.

Gophermeisters can provide an easy mechanism for information providers to submit new material by setting up special e-mail accounts. (For example, Yale uses Procmail for providers.) Because Gopher serves up mail spools as a directory of files, information providers can send mail to the appropriate account to have it appear as a new file. In this scheme, the subject line becomes the name of the menu item. To remove dated material, the provider can delete the old mail message. This method requires access and permissions to the mail spool of the special account.

A second approach takes advantage of a distributed file system such as NFS (Network File System) or AFS (Andrew File System). (Notre Dame, for example, uses Gopher on top of AFS.) Distributed file systems enable users on remote machines to mount and modify file systems from the local host. In this way, the standard file permissions can be used to limit or grant access to any number of file systems.

NOTE

A caveat is that Gopher won't follow links outside the data directory unless Gopher is invoked with the -c option.

Updating links is an important part of maintaining a server because nothing dampens users' enthusiasm faster than repeated failed connections. Unfortunately, because of the many possible points of failure (some of which are listed here), there will always be failed connections:

- The network may be down, making the host unreachable.
- The Gopher server may have crashed or reached a load limit.
- The directory or file may have been moved, or renamed, and so forth.

Although not much can be done about the first two situations, the problem of moved files or directories can be alleviated by running the gopherhunt script. The gopherhunt script is a perl script that searches through your server for dead links. The script can be run automatically through cron, but the links must be removed or replaced manually. You can use Veronica to find the new location or source.

Another useful perl script is gee, by Bill Middleton. The README file included in the distribution states, "Gee is a tool for Gopher admins to allow quick and easy inspection of, and changes to, the Gopher archive. It uses a paged display, like the Gopher client itself, and displays files one directory at a time." Gee is compatible with most older Gopher servers and also works with the Gopher+ server's .name files. In fact, gee will convert the older .cap files into .name file format.

The gee script is available through Gopher on feenix.metronet.com in the perl scripts archive. You can also use the Gopher mailserver to obtain it by sending e-mail (with no subject) to perl-info@feenix.metronet.com with the following one-line body text:

```
send /scripts/gopher/tools/gee/gee.shar
```

The .cap files can be manipulated by a script named gmv. This simple shell script facilitates the move of links on your server by moving their .cap entries along with them.

Subject Gophers

Although most of the "other Gophers" listings are organized by location, there are a growing number of servers that have subject listings. Despite the difficulties of working without a standard classification scheme, the numbers of subject Gophers are steadily rising. *Subject Gophers* are those that either have a predominant theme (such as Geology) or contain listings of other Gophers based on subject rather than locality.

The relevance of subject Gophers to creating your own Gopher server pertains to the design issue. If the principal users of the server have a predominant area of interest, it makes sense to be able to access remote resources of a similar nature. When these resources are placed in a prominent place (that is, not buried ten layers deep), a community of interest can form.

Although many debates continue regarding the organization of subjects, you should consider how resources will be presented when designing your data directory.

A good starting point is to peruse the subject listing at Rice University, where Prentiss Riddle has gathered some of the more prominent resources and subject listings. Moreover, he has created a program to deal with the problem of merging local data with remote directories. This program, Linkmerge, is available in `ftp://boombox.micro.umm.edu/pub/gopher/Unix/GopherTools`.

Cohabiting with FTP

There is no natural law that prohibits the Gopher `datadir` from being the same as the FTP directory. Often, the data being served is similar—if not identical—so linking or duplicating massive amounts of this data becomes a senseless task. Under these circumstances, merging the Gopher and FTP directories is highly desirable. However, to maintain the functionality of both FTP and Gopher, the Gophermeister must make some adjustments.

The first issue is that of permissions and security. To provide the same access and security as an anonymous FTP site, the Gopher should be run with the `-u FTP` option (see the `gopherd` man page). A related requirement is the inclusion of the `-c` flag; otherwise you must create a `tmp` directory at the top of the `datadir` directory to enable FTP links to other sites. (Recall that the `-c` flag enables access to files and directories outside of the Gopher `datadir`, and that FTP uses the `/tmp` directory for this purpose.)

Another issue is the problem of hidden files. On the Gopher side, the `bin`, `dev`, `etc`, and `usr` directories are hidden; viewed from the FTP side, the Gopher dot files are visible. One solution is to hide the top-level Gopher directory by placing it one level above the `pub` directory and making sure that the FTP account points directly to `pub` (use this command: `make ~ftp = /datadir/pub`). Another option is to replace the FTP version of `ls` (in the `~ftp/bin` directory) with the GNU version. This option requires modifying the source to remove the `-a` option—not a task for the faint of heart.

Many sites run joint Gopher/FTP servers, and few bother to hide the Gopher dot files. As these joint servers become more commonplace, the existence of dot files will become less of an issue. Overall, the merging of Gopher and FTP directories is a viable method of reducing administrative overhead while providing greater accessibility to your data.

Security

Gopher was initially designed as a campus information service, not as the "Internet Gopher"; therefore, security was not top priority. Although Gopher has some security precautions, security problems arose once Gopher became widely distributed. As the Gopher documentation (located at `ftp://boombox.micro.umn.edu/pub/gopher/gopher_protocol/Gopher+/Gopher+.txt`) points out:

> Gopher was originally designed as an essentially anonymous document
> retrieval protocol to facilitate easy, rather than limited, access
> to information. Various kinds of restrictive mechanisms have been
> implemented at the server end (for example, access restriction by source
> IP address); however, putting sensitive information under a Gopher's nose
> is not a good idea.

The main security risk of Gopher is in using the standard Telnet and more programs. Generally, lack of security isn't a serious threat because the local users who execute these programs already have accounts on the system. Remote users use their own programs and are therefore not gaining access to the local host. However, under certain conditions, particularly when there is public access through a guest login, security problems can result in unauthorized access.

The problem of the Telnet and more programs can be redressed with the SecureGopher patch from `ftp://boombox.umn.edu/pub/gopher/Unix/GopherTools/securegopher.tar.Z`.

Another potential security problem involves the chroot() call that gopherd performs. The chroot() call is used to contain gopherd within the data directory. Unfortunately, this call must be overridden with the -c option so that links to data outside the Gopher directory can be made. If unauthorized access is attained, that user is not limited to the Gopher directory. The -u option provides a partial solution because it can be used to set the effective user ID of the gopherd to a user with minimal privileges.

Gopher release 2 (and later) contains two security schemes: per-site and per-user. The per-site scheme relies on the entries in gopherd.conf and permits or denies access based on a wide range of criteria.

The other security scheme is known as *AdmitOne* because it is ticketing based. AdmitOne is a per-user authentication that requires a password only on initial connection to the server. In any case, AdmitOne has not been widely deployed because its security is relatively weak and it requires extra effort to set up.

As with any software, it is important to keep abreast of developments in the security arena. For updates on a wide range of computer-related security issues, including Gopher, a good source to check is the CERT advisories. These advisories are available in both of the following:

- `comp.security.announce` (a moderated, CERT-only newsgroup).
- The CERT advisory mailing list. (To get on this list, send the line add *Firstname Lastname* in the body of the e-mail message to `CERT-advisory-request@cert.org`.)

CERT also maintains an FTP site (alas, no Gopher server) on `cert.org`. The site contains some useful tools and general security information, along with an archive of the advisories. The Gopher-related advisory is found under `CA-93:11_UMN_UNIX_Gopher_Vulnerability`.

The CERT advisories tend to be vague because they do not want to act as a cookbook for crackers. For details, it is best to turn to either the Gopher newsgroup or subscribe to the Listserv list at either of these sites:

- `comp.infosystems.gopher`
- `gopher-news-request@boombox.micro.umn.edu`

Indexing

Indexing is a mechanism that provides full-text searches with Gopher. Not only are all the WAIS materials available (see Chapter 27, "WAIS: The Database of Databases"), but you also can index your own data and make it searchable from within your Gopher. Any word in the indexed material is a valid keyword; for example, a search for *foo* returns a listing of all documents containing that word. Suppose that you are looking for a solution to a problem regarding Hayes modems and Sun workstations. With uncanny foresight, you made a bookmark of the `sun.managers.src` index you came across last week, so you return there and search for *Hayes*. The search returns a wealth of information, including step-by-step instructions on installing modems on Suns.

Of course, not all searches result in such favorable results. In fact, sometimes (because of network problems, excessive load, and so forth), the connection to the remote Gopher may fail. The solution is to provide local indexes by periodically FTPing them from the site of origin (the WAIS registry site `ftp.wais.com`). This registry contains a listing of all registered sites and a plethora of indexes. The most effective way to transfer these sites and indexes is to use Gene Spafford's `ftpget` script in a `cron` job (use Archie to find `ftpget`).

If the original material is available, you can index it yourself. Continuing with the previous example, the `sun.managers` mail can be saved in a file and indexed periodically. Moreover, any desired sorting can be done before indexing, so that unwanted material does not show up in the search results.

To make your own indexes, download `Wais8.b5.1.tar.Z`, `freewais`, `BIOwais`, or `NeXTtext.tar`. `Wais8.b5.1.tar.Z` is the latest release from Thinking Machines and is being distributed freely. (Read their copyright notice before using this release.) `Freewais` is a release of CNIDR and is also compatible with Gopher. `BIOwais`, by Don Gilbert, is a modified version of `wais8.b5` and supports Boolean and phrase searching. `NeXTtext.tar` is an indexing program only for the NeXT computer and does not work with other systems.

> **NOTE**
>
> You do not have to add the `-DBIO` option to the `SERVEROPTS` parameter in `makefile.config` to use Boolean and phrase searching. The `-DBIO` option is required

only for symbol searching. However, you must compile both WAIS and Gopher with the same option setting (that is, with or without `-DBIO`) or your server will core dump on searches.

Multiple Index Searches

The Gopher/WAIS combination provides the ability to incorporate multiple search files into one search. In other words, a single user-specified search can span multiple indexes. This enables the Gophermeister to be creative in combining searches to meet various needs. It also enables the spreading of the search across multiple hosts to achieve a simple but effective parallelism (that is, to speed searches and minimize load). To configure such a search, use a file ending in `.mindex` that contains something similar to the following:

```
#recipes
#
localhost 70 7/indexes/desserts
ashpool.micro.umn.edu 70 7/indexes/cakes
#
# computer info
joeboy.micro.umn.edu 70 7/indexes/cookies
```

The user sees a single search item called `desserts` but can find both cakes and cookies. Specifying `localhost`, rather than the hostname, means that the search is performed on the local machine in series. Otherwise, the Gopher daemon forks a process for each index specified.

Jughead

A slightly different type of index is known as Jughead (Jonzy's Universal Gopher Hierarchy Excavation And Display). As the acronym implies, Jughead was created in the same spirit as Archie and Veronica. ("Betty" servers also have been suggested, but so far no one has been able to come up with a good excuse for the acronym.)

With Jughead, the intent is to index the Gopher menu items (or directories). Typically, the Jughead item is placed at the top menu:

```
-> 14. Search Gopher Menu Items
```

The program is written in ANSI C by Rhett "Jonzy" Jones at the University of Utah. Jughead runs on the following architectures:

- Mac (A/UX)
- IBM RS 6000 (AIX)
- Sun (SunOS 4.1.2)
- DEC (Ultrix)

The source can be Gophered from `gopher://gopher.utah.edu:70/11/Search%20menu%20titles%20using%20jughead%20/jughead%20source`.

There is a discussion list about Jughead called `jughead-news`. To get on the list, send mail to `jughead-news-request@lists.utah.edu`.

Some of the features of Jughead are listed here:

- A threshold set at 1,024 items to prompt for a more concise search request
- The capability to override that threshold as a user
- A keyword-sensitive help command
- Delimiters on the hosts and ports when building the database

Go4gw

The `go4gw` daemon gateways Gopherspace to various Internet services. Along with the daemon, the package contains several modules, each of which interacts with `go4gw` to access a specific service. For example, the `g2archie` module provides a means of running the Archie program to locate FTP software. Other modules include `alexhack`, `areacode`, `finger`, `ftphack`, `geo` (geographic name server), `nntp` (news), `netfind`, SNMP, `webster`, and `whois`. The advantage of `go4gw`'s modularity is that it enables you to write your own gateway to practically any service on the Internet.

The `go4gw` daemon runs from `inetd`, which means that it uses less overhead by providing as-needed services to many different modules. It is written in everyone's favorite write-once-read-many language: perl. Because the modules are also written in perl, you should be conversant in perl before attempting to write your own gateway.

The source for the software is `boombox.micro.umn.edu` under the `gopher/UNIX` menu. Installation is straightforward:

1. Make sure that you have the appropriate version of perl.
2. Add the `go4gw` daemon to the `/etc/services` file by inserting the following line in the file:

```
go4gw 4320/tcp
```

3. Add go4gw to the /etc/inetd.conf file (depending on your system type) by inserting a line similar to the following in the file:

```
go4gw stream tcp nowait nobody /usr/local/etc/go4gw go4gw
```

4. In the go4gw script, configure the following variables as described:
    - The Gport variable to the port listed in /etc/services.
    - The Ghost variable to your fully qualified hostname.
    - The Gconf_file (go4gw.conf) to the location on your host.

5. Modify the go4gw.conf file for the modules present and their locations.

The go4gw.conf file has the following form:

```
gateway:user:module:gopher title
```

In this syntax, *gateway* is the name of the gateway, *user* is either a numeric user ID or name, *module* is the name of the perl script that go4gw will dynamically load, and *title* is the title that appears in the Gopher menu if go4gw is sent the string " ". The following example shows the format of the go4gw.conf file.

```
#
# gateway : user : module : gopher title
#
whois:-2:/usr/local/etc/g2whois:Whois:
nntp:-2:/usr/local/etc/g2nntp:USENET News:
webster:-2:/usr/local/etc/g2webster:Webster:
#
```

A nice feature of go4gw is that you can point a link at the daemon with the path set to " " and get a menu of all your gateways. The menu order is the same order as that in the go4gw.conf file.

Once you complete all this configuration, you should restart inetd using the following command:

```
kill HUP #inetd
```

In this syntax, *#inetd* is the process ID of inetd. Then you can test go4gw by running a Gopher client to the newly created port.

> **NOTE**
>
> When creating a Gopher server for your user community, you not only make Internet resources available to your community, you also make local resources available to others. Installing and maintaining Gopher isn't a trivial undertaking, but it isn't as difficult as it may first appear. With some forethought and the information necessary to consider the options, the process contains its own rewards.

Creating Web Pages with HTML

36

by Brandon Plewe

One of the primary foundations of the World Wide Web is the HyperText Markup Language (HTML). HTML is the primary format in which documents are distributed and viewed on the Web. Many of its features, such as platform-independent formatting, structural design, and especially hypertext, make it a very good document format for the Internet and the WWW.

This chapter gives the potential Web information provider a basic understanding of HTML and how you can create documents in this format. A brief description of the common tags and a style guide to creating good HTML documents help you on the road to getting your information onto the WWW. A few of the more advanced features, as well as a look to the future of HTML, are also covered.

Background

As one of the foundation specifications that define the Web (along with HTTP and URLs), HTML was originally developed by Tim Berners-Lee at CERN in 1989 (see Chapter 28, "Navigating the World Wide Web," for details of the Web). HTML was envisioned to be a format that would allow scientists using very different computers to share information seamlessly over the network, and several features were necessary: *Platform independence*, in which a document can be displayed similarly on computers with different capabilities (that is, fonts, graphics, and color), was vital to the varied audience. *Hypertext*, which allows for any word or phrase in one document to reference another document, would allow for easy navigation between and within the many large documents on the system. Rigorously *structured documents* would allow for advanced applications such as converting documents to and from other formats and searching text databases.

SGML and HTML

Berners-Lee chose to use the Standard Generalized Markup Language (SGML) as a pattern. As an emerging international standard, SGML had the advantages of structure and platform independence. Its status also ensured its long life, meaning that documents formatted in SGML would not need to be rebuilt a few years later.

SGML is platform independent because it focuses on encoding the *semantic structure*, or meaning, of a document, not necessarily its appearance. Thus, a chapter title would be labeled *Chapter Title,* instead of *Helvetica 18pt Centered.* Although the latter style breaks down if the document is viewed on a computer that doesn't have the Helvetica typeface or support for lettering of different sizes, the former style can be displayed (intelligently) on any system. Each reader defines the appearance of chapter titles in a way that is useful on his or her computer, and any text with that style is formatted accordingly.

Another feature of this structure is that semantically encoded text can be automatically processed more intelligently by the computer. For example, if every chapter title is marked with the label *Chapter Title*, perhaps with the chapter number as an attribute, a reader could request to see just Chapter 18; the SGML software would automatically look for the Chapter 18 title and the Chapter 19 title and extract everything between them. This could not be done with text marked with meaningless (to the computer) fonts and formatting codes.

A great advantage of SGML is its flexibility. SGML is not a format in its own right, but a specification for defining other formats. Users can create new formats to encode all the structure of certain types of documents (for example, technical manuals, phone books, and legal documents), and any SGML-capable software can understand it, simply by reading the definition first. A large number of Document Type Definitions (DTDs) have been created, both for common and very specialized documents. HTML is simply one DTD, or *application*, of SGML.

The Evolution of HTML

For several years, the use of HTML (and the WWW) grew slowly, despite these capabilities. This was primarily because it did not have enough features to do any kind of professional electronic publishing; it had some font control, but no graphics. Semantic encoding was not important to people when they couldn't make it look pretty.

Then everything changed. When NCSA first built Mosaic in early 1993, they added their own features to HTML, including inline graphics. This suddenly allowed people to attach logos, icons, photographs, and diagrams to their documents; the size and usage of the Web exploded. For the next year, the development of HTML happened on a very *ad hoc* basis. New pieces of HTML were introduced by one browser or another from time to time; some would catch on and others would disappear. Some of the additions were poorly designed and many were not even SGML compliant.

By May 1994, it was apparent that HTML was growing out of control. At the first WWW conference in Geneva, Switzerland, an HTML Working Group was organized. Its primary task was to formalize HTML, as it was being used, into an SGML DTD known as HTML Level 2 (Level 1 was defined to be HTML as it was originally designed by Tim Berners-Lee). Once standardized, it could then be safely extended to future levels, while taking advantage of the capabilities of true SGML and its formal structure. At the time of this writing, HTML Level 2 is nearing completion, having gone through several drafts, and is becoming the standard format that all WWW browsers can understand. HTML Level 2 is the format described in this chapter.

A Basic Document

Let's first take a look at a simple HTML document to see how one normally appears. The following text is a valid HTML file:

```
<HTML>
<HEAD>
        <TITLE>Bill Jones' Document</TITLE>
</HEAD>

<BODY>
        <H1>Welcome to Bill Jones' Life</H1>
        Hi, my name is Bill Jones. Here is a picture of me:<P>
        <IMG SRC="http://foobar.hsu.edu/~jones/me.gif"><P>
        <H3>A Brief Autobiography</H3>
        <UL>
                <LI>Born in <A HREF="http://www.mtsmith.vt.us/">Mount Smith,
                Vermont</A>, August 26, 1965.
                <LI>Went to college at <A HREF="http://www.wyst.edu/">Wyoming
                State College</A>, earning a degree in math.
                <LI>Now work at <A HREF="http://www.hsu.edu">Horton State
                University</A> as a professor.
        </UL>
        <HR>
        <ADDRESS>Bill Jones<BR>
                285 LaSalle Ave<BR>
                Horton, NY 12645<BR>
                (615)457-3523<BR>
                <A HREF="http://foobar.hsu.edu/~jones/mailme.html">
                jones@foobar.hsu.edu</A>
        </ADDRESS>
</BODY>
</HTML>
```

In a WWW browser, this document is rendered to look something like Figure 36.1. It is always important to remember that the HTML (as an application of SGML) only encodes the *structure* of the document. Much of the *appearance* of the document, such as type styles, color, and the window size, is under the ultimate control of the browser and the people using it. However, most browsers render things similarly; as different parts of HTML are described, their normal rendering is also given.

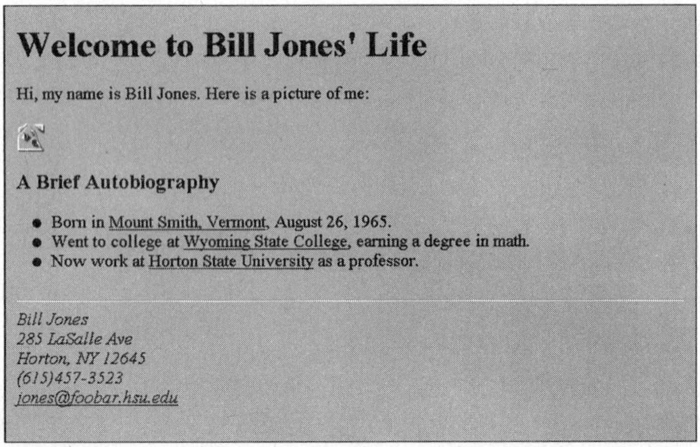

FIGURE 36.1.

A rendering of the sample HTML document.

Welcome to Bill Jones' Life

Hi, my name is Bill Jones. Here is a picture of me:

A Brief Autobiography

- Born in <u>Mount Smith, Vermont</u>, August 26, 1965.
- Went to college at <u>Wyoming State College</u>, earning a degree in math.
- Now work at <u>Horton State University</u> as a professor.

Bill Jones
285 LaSalle Ave
Horton, NY 12645
(615)457-3523
jones@foobar.hsu.edu

You can learn many things about the HyperText Markup Language from this basic document.

Basic HTML Syntax

An HTML document is a plain ASCII text file that consists of two types of contents: normal document *text* and codes, or *tags*. Tags are text strings surrounded by less-than and greater-than signs, such as <HTML> in the first line. Tags usually have the following structure:

```
<tagname attribute=value attribute=value . . . >
```

The `tagname` is the type of text being defined by the tag; the `attributes` (you can have none or several) give additional information about how the element should behave.

For example, in the <HEAD> tag in the second line of the sample HTML file, HEAD is the tagname and has no associated attributes. Farther down in the file, there is a tag with the tagname IMG and a single attribute SRC that has the value http://foobar.hsu.edu/~jones/me.gif). It is important to remember that the tagname and attribute are not case sensitive—you can use uppercase and lowercase letters as you want. The values assigned to the attributes may be case sensitive, depending on the attribute.

The tags and text combine to form *elements*. Each element represents an object in the document, such as a heading, a paragraph, or a picture. An element consists of one or two tags, and usually some associated text.

There are two types of elements: container and empty elements. *Container elements* represent a section of text and consist of body text (or other elements) delimited by a tag at the beginning and the end (the end tag is identified by a / before the tagname, and never carries any attributes). For example, in the third line of the example file, the <TITLE> and </TITLE> tags define the text between them as a title.

On the other hand, an *empty element* consists of a single tag that does not alter any text; instead, it inserts something into the document. For example, the <IMG SRC=...> tag/element places the picture in the document.

Together, container elements and empty elements completely define how a document is to be formatted and displayed. Other things normally used to format text (such as tabs, extra spaces, and carriage returns) are treated as a single space in HTML. For example, the sample HTML files could have been typed with three blank lines after every tag and ten spaces between each word but would appear exactly the same as Figure 36.1 (as it would if the entire file had been typed on a single line). Although this may make simple formatting more difficult, it allows writers to make the HTML document more readable by using programming style techniques such as extra blank spaces and tabs (as are used in the sample file) without affecting the display of the final document.

Description of Elements in Sample Document

This section looks at the elements used in the sample document. The sample file contains the common tags used in most documents (more thorough definitions of each element are given later in the chapter).

First, three container elements should appear in every HTML file:

- `<HTML>` *text* `</HTML>`: This element contains the entire file (that is, the first tag appears at the beginning of the file and the second tag appears at the end of the file) and defines the enclosed *text* as an HTML document. This, the largest, container element contains the following two container elements, in order.

- `<HEAD>` *text* `</HEAD>`: This element is the *header* and contains information about the document (usually one to three lines) that is not part of the text. It plays the same role as the running head on each page of this book: it gives context and position to the text but is not part of the narrative.

- `<BODY>` *text* `</BODY>`: This element contains other elements representing the *body text* of the document, normally almost all the file's length.

Together, these three elements create a template, which all HTML documents should follow:

```
<HTML>
<HEAD>
    Header Elements
</HEAD>
<BODY>
    Body of Document
</BODY>
</HTML>
```

The `<HEAD>` element can contain several unique elements; however, most documents contain only the one shown in the sample:

- `<TITLE>` *text* `</TITLE>`: This element is the title of the document, such as that found in the running head on each page of this book. The title is normally shown in the browser separate from the text page (for example, in the window frame or in a part of the window separate from the document).

The `<BODY>` element in the sample file contains several common elements:

- `<H1>` *text* `</H1>`: This element identifies the enclosed text as a *major heading* (for example, the title at the beginning of a document). You can have up to six levels of headings by using the tags `<H1>`, `<H2>`, on up to `<H6>` (the lower numbers signify headings of greater importance). Headings are normally rendered in a larger type (more important headings are in a larger type) with a blank space above and below.

- ■ `<P>`: This tag marks the separation between two *paragraphs* of body text (that is, text not part of some other element).

- ■ `<IMG SRC="http://foobar.hsu.edu/~jones/me.gif">`: This element places an *image* in the document, which can be found at the URL given in the SRC attribute (see Chapter 6, "Domain Names and Internet Addresses," for an explanation of URLs).

- ■ `<UL><LI>` *text* `<LI>` *text* `</UL>`: This construction provides an *unordered list* of items; the `<LI>` tag begins each item. Normally, a bullet is placed at the beginning of each entry.

- ■ `<A HREF="http://www.mtsmith.vt.us/">text</A>`: This kind of element marks a hypertext *anchor*, also known as a *hyperlink*. The *text* is highlighted in some way on-screen (in color, with an underline, or something similar); when that text is selected on-screen (that is, pointed at with the mouse), the document given by the URL in the HREF (Hypertext Reference) attribute is retrieved.

- ■ `<HR>`: This element places a *horizontal rule*, or line, across the window, normally with a space above and below.

- ■ `<ADDRESS>` *text* `</ADDRESS>`: This element marks a block of text that serves as a postal or electronic mail *address*. The address is normally rendered in a slightly different font than body text (for example, smaller, italic type) and does not use the extra space placed between body paragraphs (formatted with the `<P>` element).

- ■ `<BR>`: This element forces a *line break* in the text so that any succeeding text is placed on the next line.

Together, these elements define the document shown in Figure 36.1. They are described in more detail, along with many other valid elements, later in this chapter.

Writing Documents

Now that you have seen an HTML document in action, you're probably wondering, "How can I make one of these?" There are several options for creating HTML files, ranging from the powerful and difficult to the easy and simplistic. Most current HTML tools are not as useful as they could be, but the large demand for easy *and* powerful HTML tools ensures that they will become more robust in the near future.

Text Editors

Because HTML documents are really plain text files, the first (and currently most common) solution has been to create them using a garden-variety text editor. These can be found on almost any computer (for example, TeachText on the Macintosh, Notepad in Windows, and emacs or vi in UNIX) and are generally very easy to use. You create the HTML document by typing it exactly as it is to appear—including typing the tags by hand—and you finish with a file that looks just like the sample file shown earlier in this chapter.

The drawback of this approach is that because these editors are ignorant of the type of file you are entering, they cannot help you at all. They cannot correct poor syntax, offer any suggestions on element usage, or show how the finished product will appear in a WWW browser. You have to be careful to get the document right and often have to edit it many times to correct mistakes. If you decide to use a text editor to create an HTML document, you should also have a WWW browser available to check the document often and find any problems to be fixed.

Text Editors with HTML "Toolboxes"

Text editors that come with HTML toolboxes are similar to plain text editors in that you still see and edit the raw HTML file. However, these tools make the task of entering the HTML tags simpler by providing simple user interface tools that place correctly-formatted tags in the document automatically. The interface tools can include hotkeys, pull-down menus, toolbars, and palettes. Although these text editors can be helpful, you are still forced to look at raw HTML code without any idea of what it will look like—or even if the code on the screen is valid HTML. To help, many of these products have a special "preview" key or button that launches a WWW browser to look at the document.

Following is a list of some of the more popular editors of this type, and where to look for more information:

- BBEdit with HTML Extensions (for the Macintosh), by Charles Bellver

  ```
  http://www.uji.es/bbedit-html-extensions.html
  ```

- HTML Editor (for the Macintosh), by Rick Giles

  ```
  http://dragon.acadiau.ca:1667/~giles/HTML_Editor/Documentation.html
  ```

- HTML Assistant (for Windows), from Dalhousie University

  ```
  ftp://ftp.cs.dal.ca/htmlasst/htmlafaq.htm
  ```

- HTML Writer (for Windows), by Kris Nosack

  ```
  http://wwf.et.byu.edu/~nosackk/html-writer/
  ```

■ tkHTML (for UNIX/X), by Liem Bahneman

```
http://alfred1.u.washington.edu:8080/~roland/tkHTML/tkHTML.html
```

■ emacs with HTML-helper-mode (for UNIX), by Nelson Minar

```
http://www.reed.edu/~nelson/tools/
```

WYSIWYG HTML or SGML Editors

WYSIWYG HTML or SGML editors are much more robust and helpful than the other editors just described. WYSIWYG (what you see is what you get) editors contain most of the HTML parsing and rendering functionality of a WWW browser so that you can see what the document will probably look like as it is being created. These editors also let you easily check the document to make sure that it uses valid syntax (in fact, some editors are constantly on guard and don't allow mistakes to be made in the first place). Some of these editors are actually generic SGML editors that can read and edit documents based on DTDs other than HTML.

Although they have much potential, many of these editors have not reached the maturity level at which they are stable and easy to use. In fact, these editors often lack the handy HTML tools found in the more simple editors described in the preceding section. However, because of the heavy demand for this kind of tool, these problems are sure to be worked out in the near future. Here is a list of some popular WYSIWYG editors—most of them are commercial products, which means that they often cost money, but are better supported and maintained:

■ HoTMetaL (for Macintosh, Windows, and UNIX/X), from SoftQuad

```
http://www.sq.com/hmpro.html
```

■ Phoenix (for UNIX/X), from the University of Chicago

```
http://http.bsd.uchicago.edu/~l-newberg/phoenix-0.1.2.html
```

■ Andrew UIS with HTMLText (for UNIX/X), by Nick Williams

```
http://web.cs.city.ac.uk/homes/njw/htmltext/htmltext.html
```

Word Processor Templates

Tools in this category are not programs in their own right, but exist as macros or accessories that operate within your favorite word processor or desktop publishing program. The advantage of these templates is that they allow you to create HTML documents using the same tools and interface you use for creating normal documents; they output files in HTML instead of the program's normal format. The disadvantages are that the templates are not currently available for most word processing software and that using a large word processor to create a small, one-page document can be slow and cumbersome. However, these templates are probably very good for working on large HTML documents. Here are several currently available:

- Internet Assistant (for Microsoft Word), from Microsoft

```
http://www.microsoft.com/pages/deskapps/word/ia/default.htm
```

- GT_HTML.DOT (for Microsoft Word), from Georgia Tech University

```
http://www.gatech.edu/word_html/release.htm
```

- Internet Publisher (for WordPerfect), from Novell (to be released April 1995)

```
http://wp.novell.com/
```

HTML Converters

Many of the documents you want to contribute to the WWW likely already exist. Most people have a large number of documents previously created using a word processor or desktop publishing program; they do not want to have to recreate the documents or convert them to HTML by hand. To assist in this process, several tools can convert existing documents to HTML. They simply take the codes from the software's internal format and convert them into HTML elements.

For these converters to work cleanly, your original document should be constructed with the same philosophy as is used with HTML and SGML: using a clear, semantic structure. For example, if named styles (such as "Chapter Title," "List Item") are used in the original document, these styles can be converted directly into corresponding HTML elements ("Chapter Title" = <H1>, "List Item" = <LI>, and so on). On the other hand, nonsemantic markup, (such as "Helvetica 14pt centered") is difficult or impossible for the converter to interpret. Almost every word processor and desktop publishing program has a styles feature.

There are basically two types of HTML converter tools:

Word Processor Macros. These operate within the word processor or desktop publisher program, going through the document line by line, converting each code to an HTML equivalent. In the end, the user sees a raw HTML file that can be saved as plain text. Here are some available software packages:

- ANT_HTML.DOT (for Microsoft Word), by Jill Swift

  ```
  http://info.cern.ch/hypertext/WWW/Tools/Ant.html
  ```

- WPTOHTML (for WordPerfect/DOS 5.1 through 6.0), by Hunter Monroe

  ```
  ftp://oak.oakland.edu/SimTel/msdos/wordperf/wpt51d10.zip or wpt60d10.zip
  ftp://oak.oakland.edu/SimTel/msdos/wordperf/wpt60d10.zip
  ```

Standalone Conversion Programs. These tools are used outside the originating software. They read the original document from the disk, convert it and save the result as an HTML document. Here are a few of them; if your software is not represented, you can probably convert the file into a format that can be used by one of these tools (for example, you can convert the file into RTF format and then convert that into an HTML file):

- RTFTOHTML (for Rich Text Format files)

  ```
  ftp://ftp.cray.com/src/WWWstuff/RTF/rtftohtml_overview.html
  ```

- WebMaker (for Framemaker/UNIX), from CERN

  ```
  http://www.cern.ch/WebMaker/
  ```

- WP2X (for WordPerfect 5.1), by Michael Richardson

  ```
  http://journal.biology.carleton.ca/People/Michael_Richardson/software/
        wp2x.html
  ```

- qt2www (for Quark Xpress), by Jeremy Hylton

  ```
  http://the-tech.mit.edu/~jeremy/qt2www.html
  ```

■ Dave (for PageMaker for Mac), from Bucknell University

```
http://www.bucknell.edu/bucknellian/dave/
```

■ Internet Publisher (for WordPerfect), from Novell (to be released April 1995)

```
http://wp.novell.com/
```

Document Style and Organization

As you begin to write HTML documents, it is important that you keep in mind the following tips. Having your document obey these general style rules should make them better looking, better and more frequently used by readers, and easier for you to maintain:

■ **Thoroughly plan your information**. The only reason people put information on the WWW is because they hope others can use it (and often, the contributor expects to subsequently benefit from this use). Thus, your primary goal in organizing the documents and files you place on your server is to make your information easy for users to access.

Although this organization differs for every site, some things should be kept in mind. **Use hypertext prodigiously**; the more possible avenues people have to navigate through your information, the better the chance they find what they want. **Create navigational pages** such as directories and tables of contents to aid people in searching for information. Also, **be very clear** when describing links and menu choices; this decreases the number of wrong roads your users take.

■ **Use valid HTML.** In the early days of the World Wide Web, HTML was not well defined, and neither was the way it was to be rendered. Many tags mutated into several forms, and browsers were written to be lax in parsing documents so that they could handle the several forms in which each tag appeared. Although HTML has become more structured and stable, the browsers often still allow for variant syntaxes so that they can read the large number of old documents out there.

Although many of these "cheater" syntaxes (for example, using <UL> without <LI> to make indented paragraphs) may produce a pleasing result on your browser, their appearance varies wildly from one browser to another (some browsers ignore the lone <UL> altogether), and may produce a very poor display on somebody else's screen. Although you cannot have complete control over what appears on each user's screen, your best bet for creating fairly uniform-looking documents is to use HTML as it was designed.

■ **Use small files**. When a document is created on paper, it normally consists of one large file and is distributed as a single stack of paper. This approach is not only unnecessary in the World Wide Web, it is often undesirable. People generally don't like to read large quantities of text on a screen. If you place a 30-page document on the Web as a single piece of text, very few people will ever read the entire thing. A reader would also be very hesitant to download a 1M file when he or she is looking for a single paragraph.

The great advantage of hypertext is that it allows for nonlinear text: readers can bounce around inside and between documents, reading and understanding pieces in the order and method that best suits them individually. A good document is broken into many small files, each no more than a screen or two in length, interconnected with the <A> element to produce hyperlinks at appropriate places. Good "subdocuments" for a table of contents and index allow users to find and retrieve just those pieces of the document that they need.

■ **Don't overdo graphics**. Although the ability to display graphics as part of a document is one of the most powerful capabilities of HTML, it is often abused. Images use much more bandwidth than normal text, so a page with many large graphics takes much longer to download than one without. In fact, many users, such as those connecting over slow telephone lines and those using text-only terminals (still a large part of the Internet audience), will not even see your graphics. Graphics also increase the space your document takes on the screen, forcing people to scroll down to see the rest of the page. Here are a few good rules of thumb when dealing with graphics:

1. Concentrate your graphics where they do the most good, such as illustrations, logos, and mastheads (the large images that appear on the tops of home pages to give the service a "corporate image").

2. Cut down on the number of colors in each image. Most monitors display only 256 colors at once, so the colors of all images on the page must fit in this number. If you don't trim the images, the browser will, and it rarely does an acceptable job. If you're including photographs, they should use about 50 to 100 colors each (you can set this limit with most graphics software). Limiting colors also reduces the size of the file to be downloaded.

3. Make graphics as small (in memory size) as possible. For example, if you want to include a photograph, put a *thumbnail* (a smaller replica) of the photo in the document, which is linked to the full-size graphic that people can download if they really want to view it.

4. Most importantly, *never* rely on the graphics to communicate your message. Any important information (titles, menu choices, and so on) that appears in the graphics should also appear in the text. This may mean using the ALT attribute in the <IMG> tag, or having a duplicate page that text-only browsers can use.

■ **Test your document with multiple browsers**. Browsers vary markedly in how they render HTML. Also, some browsers (such as Netscape) use additional elements that are not part of "true" HTML and that are not supported by any other browsers. The Web has many documents that were obviously written with a single browser in mind because they look awful on all the rest.

If possible, gain access to at least two browsers (preferably a graphics one and a text-only one) that you can use to view your documents. Although the documents you create with this method may not look as good on your favorite browser as they could, they will look fairly good on all browsers.

Element Reference

The following sections provide a brief guide to almost all the elements used in HTML Level 2. For a more comprehensive reference, see the official HTML 2.0 specification at `http://www.w3.org/hypertext/WWW/MarkUp/html-spec/index.html`. Remember that the tag and attribute names are not case sensitive and can be in uppercase or lowercase letters.

<HEAD> Elements

The following tags are allowed in the header part of the HTML document.

```
<TITLE>"text"</TITLE>
```

Document title. The name of the document. The title is generally written in a larger type size than the current document to give the user a frame of reference. For example, if the document is a chapter of a book, the `<TITLE>` would probably contain the title of the book as well as the chapter title. Thus, if someone followed a hyperlink from somewhere else directly to this chapter, he or she would not be lost, but would know that this file is part of a certain book.

```
<LINK name="text" rel="text" href="URL">
```

External link. Establishes a relationship between the current document and another document. The `name` attribute gives the link a name, such as "Mail to Author." The `rel` attribute describes the type of link, such as `"made"` (the author), `"parent"` (a larger document of which this is a part), `"next"` (the succeeding section of a multifile document), and `"prev"` (the previous section). The `href` attribute points to the related document. Currently, most browsers don't make use of this tag, but future browsers will likely add a new button to the screen for each <LINK> to allow users to easily jump to the related document.

```
<META NAME="text" CONTENT="text">
```

Document meta-information. Allows for extra information about a document, such as its modification data, copyright, or abstract. This is done by setting a name and value, such as <META NAME="copyright" CONTENT="1995, Sams Publishing">. Separate <META> elements are included for each item of information. Currently, this element is seldom used in browsers.

```
<BASE HREF="URL">
```

Location of current document. Lets you specify the full URL of this document. Although it may seem redundant, this information is useful if you use relative URLs in the hyperlinks. Using this base, the hyperlinks are resolved correctly even if this document is requested with a different URL than you expect (for example, if users save it on their local disk and try to use it there).

```
<ISINDEX>
```

Searchable document. Places a search field either in the document or elsewhere on the screen, allowing people to enter keywords to search through this document. You can't just add this tag to any arbitrary document and expect it to work—your server must be set up to process this query, using a back-end search engine.

Empty Elements

As stated earlier in this chapter, *empty elements* are elements that insert objects into the document by themselves, regardless of the surrounding text. They each consist of a single tag.

```
<HR>
```

Horizontal rule. Places a horizontal line across the page, with a blank line above and below. Normally used to separate major sections of a document (for example, before an <H1> or <H2>). Some graphical browsers give the rule a 3D chiseled look.

```
<BR>
```

Line break. Forces subsequent text to the next line. Unlike the <P> tag, the text before and after the <BR> tag is still considered a single paragraph. The <BR> tag is normally used to create tight blocks of short-line information, such as mailing addresses.

```
<IMG src="URL" alt="text" align=TOP/MIDDLE/BOTTOM ISMAP>
```

Inline image. Places an image within the document, as found at the URL specified in the src attribute (which is mandatory). The most common format for these images is CompuServe's Graphics Interchange Format, or GIF. If the browser doesn't support inline images (for example, the Lynx browser does not), the text given in the optional alt attribute is displayed. If no alt attribute is given, a default placeholder such as [IMAGE] may be displayed in this situation (to ensure that nothing is displayed if the graphic cannot be shown, use the alt= attribute). The optional align attribute specifies how the image is to be aligned vertically with the current line of text (the default alignment is most often BOTTOM, but this varies by browser).

The ISMAP attribute lets you create interactive graphics, or *imagemaps*. If the syntax <A "href=http://URL1"><IMG src="URL2" ismap></A> is used and you point to a spot on the image, the x and y coordinates are passed to the hyperlink (for example, http://URL1?x,y). However, the HTTP server must be able to handle imagemap queries; see Chapter 37, "Setting Up a World Wide Web Server," for information on Web servers. For more information on imagemaps, look for the Second Edition of *The World Wide Web Unleashed*, published by Sams.

```
<!-- text -->
```

Comment. Any text inside this element is ignored. This element is used to include notes that can be read by the writer but that are not part of the text of the document (especially useful if several writers work on the same document). The useful programming technique of temporarily commenting out sections of code cannot be done here; many older browsers use a single > as the closing character of the comment, so any tags included in the comment (such as <BR>) cause the comment to end early and interpret any remaining comment text as body text.

Character Containers

Character containers allow you to format or describe words and phrases within paragraphs. Although they can be used inside nonbody blocks as well as in normal text, all but the <A> tag can produce unattractive results on some browsers.

Hypertext Links

```
<A href="URL" name="text">text</A>
```

Hypertext anchor. Used to mark the reference or the target of a hypertext link. Either the `href` or `name` attribute must be included (both are allowed, but they don't appear together very often). The `href` attribute specifies a URL to which the enclosed `text` attribute is linked (the `text` is highlighted; selecting it requests the new object); `href` can reference another HTML document, an image, or anything else that can be addressed using a URL. The hypertext anchor can also enclose an `<IMG>` tag, allowing inline graphics (such as icons) to become links.

The `name` attribute gives a unique name to the enclosed tag, allowing users and other HTML documents to point directly to this part of the document. For example, a URL such as `http://.../thisdoc.html#part1` loads `thisdoc.html` and attempts to place the text marked with `<a name="part1">` at the top of the screen.

Logical Styles

Logical styles let you give a real meaning to sections of text. Currently, they are only used for formatting, but they can be used for more intelligent types of processing, such as automatic footnoting.

```
<em>text</em>
```

Emphasis. Used to highlight sections of text for miscellaneous reasons. Normally rendered in *italics*.

```
<strong>text</strong>
```

Strong emphasis. Another form of generic highlighting. Normally rendered in **bold**.

```
<cite>text</cite>
```

Citation. Used to mark a citation to another document, such as a printed book (for example, *Great Expectations*). Normally rendered in *italics*.

```
<code>text</code>
```

Computer code. Used to mark text from a computer (for example, `hit any key`). Normally rendered in a fixed-width font such as `Courier`.

```
<var>text</var>
```

Variable. Used to mark a variable used in a mathematical formula or computer program (for example, $z = x + y$). Normally rendered in *italics*.

```
<kbd>text</kbd>
```

Keyboard input. Used to mark text that is to be typed at the keyboard by a user (for example, `hit the` **`enter`** `key`). Normally rendered in a fixed-width font such as `Courier`.

Physical Styles

Originally considered "cheater" versions of the logical styles, physical style elements have become very popular because they are similar to the way people are used to highlighting text (that is, literally instead of semantically).

```
<b>text</b>
```

Bold.

```
<i>text</i>
```

Italics.

```
<tt>text</tt>
```

Typewriter text. Rendered in a fixed-width font such as `Courier`.

Block Containers

In HTML, a *block* is defined as a piece of marked text which by itself occupies a certain amount of vertical space in a document, such as a paragraph or a heading. The following elements can be adjacent to each other, but cannot be nested (that is, you can't have a <P> inside an <H1> because they represent different types of blocks).

```
<H#>text</H#>
```

Heading (where # is 1 through 6). Acts as a title for a section of the document. The lower-number headings represent more important headings and are generally rendered in larger text. Because of a mixup in the distributed default settings, some browsers erroneously display <H5> and <H6> *smaller* than the body text. Until these two elements are displayed more consistently, they should probably be avoided when possible.

```
text<P>text
<P>text</P>
```

Paragraph. In most current browsers, this tag is used in the first form as a paragraph separator. Thus, it marks the boundary between two paragraphs of normal body text. You should not use this tag between body text and another element (for example, do not use ...<p><h1>...); because the second element implies a line break, some browsers put too much space between the elements. The second form (a container for each paragraph) represents a more valid SGML structure and will soon be the standard. However, the end tag </P> will be optional, so most documents that have been created using the first form will still work.

```
<BLOCKQUOTE>text</BLOCKQUOTE>
```

Extended quotation. Used for long quotations that exist as separate paragraphs. Normally rendered similarly to a normal paragraph, but with both margins indented.

```
<ADDRESS>text</ADDRESS>
```

Mailing address. Specifically targeted to postal addresses, this tag is commonly used to mark bylines (name of the author) and e-mail addresses. It is normally rendered in a smaller font or in italics, and usually uses the <BR> tag to separate the individual lines of the address.

```
<PRE>text</PRE>
```

Preformatted text. Because extra spaces and tabs are ignored in HTML, some kinds of text, such as poetry, tables, and computer program listings are difficult to encode. The `<PRE>` element is used with those types of text by formatting everything it contains exactly as it appears, including spaces, tabs, and line feeds.

Lists

```
<TYPE>
        <LI>text
        <LI>text
        <LI>text
        ...
</TYPE>
```

Itemized list. Creates a list containing several items, each beginning with `<LI>`. Normally indents each item one tab position. There are four types: `<UL>` is an **unordered list** (each entry is normally preceded by a bullet); `<OL>` is an **ordered list** (each entry is numbered); `<MENU>` is a **menu of choices** (similar to `<UL>` but sometimes rendered more compactly); `<DIR>` is a **directory** (designed to be a list broken into two or three columns like a disk directory; in most current browsers, the `<DIR>` element is rendered the same as `<UL>`). These lists can be nested within each other, allowing for complex list hierarchies such as outlines.

```
<DL COMPACT>
        <DT>term text
                <DD>definition text
        <DT>term text
                <DD>definition text
        ...
</DL>
```

Definition list. This syntax builds a list in which each entry has two parts, as in a glossary: a *term* (which follows the `<DT>`) and a *definition* (which follows the `<DD>`). It is normally rendered with the definition indented below the term. The optional COMPACT attribute was designed to produce a more vertically compact list in which the terms and definitions are placed in side-by-side columns, but it is ignored by most current browsers.

Forms

The forms feature of HTML is one of the things that gives the Web real power for doing live, interactive applications. The HTML form, however, is only half of this feature. Once the user fills out the form, it is submitted to a specialized program, or *script*, that takes the information and does something useful with it (for example, e-mails it to you). You must either write the script yourself (that means programming), or find a prewritten script that will suit your needs.

```
<FORM method="[GET¦POST]" action="URL">form body</FORM>
```

Form. The `<FORM>` element encloses the entire form and gives some basic definitions. The form may take up only part of the HTML document; in fact, a single document can contain several separate forms that perform different functions. The `method` attribute specified the way in which information is sent to the HTTP server; the `action` attribute gives the URL of the script that is to process the submitted information (usually `http://.../cgi-bin/scriptname`).

```
<INPUT name="text" type= size=## value="text" CHECKED>
```

Form input. This empty tag is used to place different fields in the form to allow users to enter information. The `name` attribute gives a unique name to the field; the optional `value` attribute gives a default value for this tag. When the form is submitted, the information is returned as a set of name-value pairs separated by ampersands, such as `http://.../cgi-bin/script?name=me&address=here&time=now`. The `type` attribute gives the style of object to be used and can be one of the following:

- `CHECKBOX` uses a simple on or off button. The value is ON or OFF.
- `RADIO` is similar to `CHECKBOX`, but allows you to pick one choice from many by having several radio tags with the same name but different values. Returns the `value` attribute of the checked tag (`value` is not optional with this type).
- `TEXT` places a one-line window to allow users to type in something. The returned value is the text entered.
- `IMAGE` places an image in the form, allowing users to point to it, returning the x and y pixel coordinates of the selected location. Operates similarly to `<IMG ISMAP>`, but within a form. For this type, the `SRC` and `ALIGN` attributes from the `<IMG>` element are included.
- `SUBMIT` places a button on the form that submits the form to the `action` URL in the `<FORM>` tag. The label for the button is specified by the `value` attribute.

■ RESET clears the form, returning all fields to their default values.

■ HIDDEN does not display anything on the form. It allows you to pass nonchangeable information along with the rest of the form (using the name and value attributes).

The CHECKED attribute is used with the CHECKBOX and RADIO types to signify whether the button is selected by default or not. The size attribute is used to set the window size of a text field (in characters).

```
<SELECT name="text" multiple>
        <OPTION value="text" selected>text
        <OPTION value="text">text
        ...
</SELECT>
```

Choice selection. Presents a list of possible values for the field, itemized by the <OPTION> element; normally it is displayed as a pull-down menu. The name and value fields are the same as for <INPUT>. The *text* following each <OPTION> tag is displayed in the menu; if no value attribute is given, *text* is returned if that option is selected. The multiple attribute allows more than one option to be selected; the selected attribute identifies the default choice.

```
<TEXTAREA name="text" rows=## cols=##>text</TEXTAREA>
```

Multiline text input. Similar to <INPUT TYPE="text">, but allows for many lines. The name attribute is the same as for <INPUT>, while the number values for the rows and cols attributes define the size. The *text* contained in the element is shown in the window by default.

Entities

Many characters that appear in documents can be impossible to enter in an HTML file, including characters that have special meaning to HTML (for example, the < and > characters) and international and typographic characters not found on most keyboards.

These characters can be included in documents using *entities*, pieces of text that together signify a single character. The general syntax includes an ampersand, a unique name for the character, and a semicolon. For example, Gröning produces Gröning. There are two general types, as described in the following sections.

Reserved Characters

Reserved characters are normal characters used for other purposes in HTML that can cause confusion if entered by themselves.

Entity	Displayed As
<	Less-than sign (<)
>	Greater-than sign (>)
&	Ampersand (&)
&quote;	Quotation mark (") (usually not necessary)

International Characters

International characters are characters used in most European languages other than English, referenced by names from the ISO Latin 1 character set. A few examples follow:

Entity	Displayed As
Á	Capital A with acute accent (Á)
ô	Small o with circumflex accent (ô)
Æ	Capital AE ligature (Æ)
ç	Small c with a cedilla (ç)

The Future of HTML

By the time you read this, the specification for HTML Level 2 should be complete and most browsers should be using this specification as a standard. However, Level 2 does not represent the final form of HTML. This language will continue to evolve, adding new capabilities, for years to come.

Although the current version of HTML has many powerful features, it also has its disadvantages. Suggestions are constantly being given to the HTML Working Group, which considers them for inclusion into the standard. Enhancements will likely allow a larger variety of documents to be put on the Web, make documents look better, and make them easier to manage and use.

The Presentation versus Structure Debate

The primary area currently evolving is the formatting of documents. The debate is currently raging over how much control of the appearance of the document should rest in the hands of the user and how much should be decided by the publisher. Years of research have gone into graphic design and typography and there are varied methods of using the appearance of text and graphics to communicate a particular message. To designers and publishers who have become experts in this art, it is important that the information contributor have a large degree of control over document appearance.

However, in the World Wide Web, the user can choose fonts, window sizes, colors, and many other presentation variables. Although this is a frustration to many publishers, it is an important part of the Web. Not all users have the same typefaces, colors, and screen area available and must be able to make the WWW page fit their constraints. In addition, physical differences in users place special needs on the appearance of pages; for example, sight-impaired people may want to use very large type; a blind user does not see anything at all and has the document read aloud by the computer.

A compromise must be reached. Information providers need the capability to dictate a large part of the appearance of the document when it is important. On the other hand, users need to be able to override or alter this appearance when necessary. It must always be remembered that the primary goal of the Web is the dissemination of information; the content of the documents should always be more important than their appearance. Whatever can be done to improve comprehension by users, including both dictated and alterable appearance, is important to that dissemination as well.

HTML Level 3

The next major revision of HTML was originally to be called HTML+. Because the current format is being formalized as HTML Level 2, the upcoming version has been renamed Level 3. This format, currently in development, promises to solve many of the shortcomings of Level 2. At the time of this writing, some browsers were beginning to support pieces of it; Level 3 is expected to appear in full force sometime in the middle of 1995.

The major capabilities Level 3 will add to HTML include the following:

- **Tables.** This feature, already being supported in some browsers, allows for tabular information to be displayed, similar to a spreadsheet. Many useful appearance controls, such as joined cells, optional borders, and support for other HTML elements within cells, will make this a powerful feature. It also allows for columnar text, which has been requested by designers for a long time.

- **Improved graphics**. The <FIG> element, which will replace <IMG>, has many improved capabilities such as control over horizontal alignment, HTML-encoded imagemaps, captions, and allowing text to flow beside the image.

- **Mathematics**. Many technical documents require the inclusion of complex formulae, which use many special symbols and special horizontal and vertical alignment. A whole set of new elements will be introduced to support their display.

- **Enlarged character set**. In addition to European characters, a large number of entities will be added for typographic symbols, such as ©, £, and ™. There is also discussion under way for HTML to support the Unicode character set that allows for the encoding of almost every world language.

■ **Increased presentation control**. Several additions and changes are being made to allow greater flexibility in document layouts. For example, all the block elements will allow an `align` attribute that allows text to be centered, right flush, and fully justified. New blocks for special types of paragraphs, such as abstracts and warnings, will be added as well.

■ **Stylesheets**. Another move to allow for greater provider control over presentation will be stylesheets. *Stylesheets* are separate configuration files that allow HTML writers to specify the desired characteristics of each element in a document, including font, spacing, color, justification, and such. However, if necessary, the user can still override these "suggestions."

Some of these features, such as tables, will likely be included in HTML 2.1, an interim specification; others may be pushed back to a follow-up version of Level 3, HTML 3.1 (for example, stylesheets are still in very early development). On the other hand, many features that have not even been thought of yet may find their way into Level 3 and beyond as suggestions are made by the Web community.

HTML promises to be a driving force in electronic publishing on the Internet for a long time.

Alternatives to HTML

It is doubtful that HTML will ever be able to provide all the creative design and functionality that true electronic publishing demands; it was never intended to do such. As the battle has raged over how much HTML should expand, competitors for the online format crown have begun to appear. These file types are generally geared toward more specialized applications and very little software currently exists for using them. However, some of them will likely become major (perhaps equal or superior to HTML) parts of the World Wide Web.

■ **Portable Document Format** (Adobe). PDF, the format used in Adobe Acrobat, has almost every page layout capability that can be imagined (it is based on PostScript). Acrobat readers will soon become Internet savvy and will be able to include URL hyperlinks just like HTML. The disadvantages of using PDF are these: PDF is a closed, proprietary format owned by Adobe; PDF files are much larger than the equivalent HTML file; PDF is complex, making it difficult for automatic generation by scripts and other software. Other commercial electronic document formats, such as Folio and WordPerfect Envoy, will probably also add these capabilities. For more information, address `http://www.adobe.com/Acrobat/Acrobat0.html`.

■ **Hyper-G**. This distributed hypertext system is very similar in purpose to the WWW; in fact, it is probably dumb luck that one caught on and not the other. Hyper-G has a document format called HTF that in some ways is more powerful than HTML. See Chapter 30, "New Tools: FSP, Harvest, and Hyper-G," for more information on Hyper-G.

- **Simple Vector Format/HyperCGM.** Many fields (including Engineering, Graphic Design, and Cartography) need a common format for distributing vector (object-based) graphics. Whether to create a new format from scratch or to alter an existing format such as CGM to allow for hyperlinks is still under debate. Conceivably, a strong vector graphics format could allow for completely graphics-based (rather than document-based) information systems on the Web. For more information, contact `http://www.niiip.org/svf/`.

- **Virtual Reality Modeling Language.** There is also a niche that would like to be able to distribute virtual reality over the Web. The specification is nearing completion and will allow for the design and distribution of "scenes" that give a 3D look to objects and places on the Web. For information, contact `http://vrml.wired.com/`.

- **Web-Savvy Word Processors.** When you read this, there should be at least two commercial word processors with Web support: Microsoft Word (with Internet Assistant), and WordP erfect (with Internet Publisher). These add-ons will include several new capabilities:

  - HTML creation and conversion within the word processor.

  - The word processor can act as a Web browser, reading HTML (so that you don't have to get a separate browser like Mosaic or Netscape).

  - Small standalone viewers, which can be freely distributed, so that documents can be distributed in their native format (including hypertext links and all the formatting) so that other people can view them without buying the full word processor.

For more information, contact the following sites:

```
http://www.microsoft.com/pages/deskapps/word/ia/default.htm
http://wp.novell.com/
```

Although few of these alternatives are available today, they will soon be around, increasing the flexibility (and confusion) of the WWW. They will probably become most popular in niche markets that require very specialized information types (such as maps, diagrams, and technical illustrations), and with professional publishers who need detailed presentation control that can't, or shouldn't, be part of HTML.

Setting Up a World Wide Web Server

37

by Kevin Mullet

One of the most intriguing things about the Internet is one of the facets least reported by the popular media. Not only does easily available global connectivity mean that you can get at your local library, various levels of government, and people from nearly every culture in the world easier than you can grab a soda from the corner store, it means you can make information that you are passionate about available to all those people and places as well. In a superlative expression of cutting out the middle man, most people on the Internet are able to make their social views, wants and needs, products, and other favorite things available to anyone with a "network tap." No representative government, economic distributorship, broadcast or print media, or note from your parents is needed. The first question you need ask yourself is what you want to put out there—quickly followed by "How?"

As a potential Internet information provider, you have a number of methods, limited only by your creativity. Whether you elect to use a WWW, Gopher, FTP, finger, WAIS, e-mail, or other type of server depends on what kind of information you want to publish, how much of it there is, how often it changes, how many people might want it at once, what kind of hardware and software you have available to you, and the speed of the various network connections between you and your intended audience.

If, after considering all the ancillary issues, you still want to put your information on the World Wide Web with a HyperText Transport Protocol (HTTP) server, next consider whether you should use a server to which you may already have access, or if you should bring up a server of your own. Usually, the question boils down to an issue of control. Do you have access to a server where you can store your information? Do you have enough influence to get the server configured the way you want? Does that server have access to the resources like disk space, databases, and CPU that you want to use? Is the server managed by reliable folks or by "loose cannons"? Is the fun and experience of running your own Web server worth the headaches?

If your requirements and wants and needs are unique enough in your environment to merit running your own server, the next thing to decide is which server you want to run and on which platform.

Choosing HTTP server software is not unlike choosing political candidates. Do you choose a candidate based on their personality or do you decide based on "the issues"? Do you choose a hardware platform for your server and then choose which sever software to run, or do you pick the software and let that determine the hardware platform?

Web server software, like all software, is a work in progress. Ultimately, that means many promised features are as reliable as some campaign promises. Does this mean that you should make your decision based exclusively on hardware? Probably not—many HTTP servers offer attractive, robust features that make it well worth the possible hit of using weaker hardware. A good strategy is to decide which of your hosts can potentially have access to all the really important resources you want to publish on the Web and then further limit your choice based on the features of (and your initial experience with) the HTTP servers available for those platforms.

A Deluge of Daemons

On VM, they're called *service machines*. On VMS they're *detached processes*. DOS has *TSRs*, Macintosh Systems have *INITs*, and UNIX has *daemons*. Whatever they're called in your Net-neighborhood, there is a cornucopia of choices that can serve up your HTTP.

The UNIX convention of referring to such software as a *daemon* is probably the most accurate. The term *server* usually refers to the machine on which a daemon resides, not to the software itself. The use of *daemon* (the Latin form of the middle-English *demon*) hails back to the Greek mythological *daimon* (meaning an attendant spirit or inferior divinity such as a deified hero). Depending on how well your daemon is running, however, you may be more inclined to assign it the more modern diabolical meaning.

For the purposes of this chapter, I'll follow the more popular convention of referring to the software itself as a *server*.

UNIX Servers

The current popularity and scalability of UNIX-like systems has led to the development of a variety of HTTP servers for such systems. Nowadays, UNIX is easily the most scaleable operating system in common usage, running on everything from 80286 PCs to mainframes and supercomputers and nearly everything in between. Perhaps the scope of its influence is caused because nowadays, UNIX is more of a culture from which specific operating systems arise (for example, SunOS, Linux, FreeBSD, SVR4, Dynix, and many others) than one specific product from one company. Technically, Novell may have the rights to the name *UNIX*, but that is more of a restriction on the name than on the culture and development associated with systems that are UNIX in everything but name.

The benefits of running your HTTP server on a UNIX platform include portability to more (or less) powerful hardware with a minimum of distress to your users, the probability that you'll never be at a loss for system administration talent, and the wealth of freely available software tools on the Internet to micromanage your data and coerce it into the information you want to present.

The risks of using a UNIX server include the persistent inaccessibility of a standard UNIX shell interface for neophyte users who may have learned computing on a PC or Macintosh. This limitation is important only if your information and data maintainers use the UNIX system directly. Many other options can make information available to your UNIX server and that insulate your users from UNIX; these options include e-mail robots, FTP, and remotely mounted file systems.

Another risk of using a UNIX system is that the security flaws of many UNIX systems are well known and can be overlooked by overworked, under-trained, or under-motivated system administrators. If this is likely to be true in your case, you may want to look at systems that have more obscure security flaws (and hope that anyone intent on doing harm to your system is correspondingly overworked, under trained, or under motivated). Keep in mind that the sheer popularity and widespread use of UNIX has resulted in many fine security tools and an abundance of well-thought-out research. It requires much less effort and talent to use a combination of these tools to shore up your system against attack than it does to try to repair the damage afterward. With a little persistence, any decent UNIX-style system and the network on which it resides can be made secure enough for all but the most demanding applications. Besides, if you're planning on putting ICBM launch codes on an Internet-connected HTTP server, perhaps you ought to re-think your application.

The following sections list some HTTP servers available for download from various sites on the Internet. Please note that this is a list, not a review. The issue of which server is best for you is one only you can decide. What follows is a brief overview of some of the available servers, their most prominent features, and some of the characteristics that distinguish them from other servers.

NCSA HTTPD

Server:	*NCSA HTTPD*
Platforms:	SunOS 4, Solaris 2, SGI IRIX, HP-UX, AIX, Ultrix, DEC OSF/1, NeXT, Sequent, Linux, A/UX, SCO ODT, SVR4, Amdahl UTS 2.1, HP/Apollo Domain/OS, and possibly others.
From:	The National Center for Supercomputing Applications (NCSA) at the University of Illinois at Urbana-Champaign.
URL:	`http://hoohoo.ncsa.uiuc.edu/docs/Overview.html`
Major Features:	Wildcard-based access control, CGI 1.1, server-side includes, enhanced directory listing, script hooks for PEM/PGP-based encryption, imagemaps, user authentication, user-specific HTML source directories, HTTP 1.0 and 0.9 compatibility, HTML2 forms.
Security:	Host-based filtering, user ID/password authentication, hooks for external methods of PEM and PGP encryption.
Installation:	Precompiled binaries available for some systems. C source code compiles to a single binary that can be installed to run either as a free-standing daemon or launched on demand from the `inetd` daemon.
Documentation:	Copious online documentation in the form of WWW pages at NCSA covering both installation and use in minute detail. Web-based tutorials are online for topics including CGI, HTML2

forms, access control and user authentication, graphical map creation and use, and WAIS/HTTP integration.

Age:	Version 0.5 released September 1993.
Status:	Current version is 1.3 as of January 1995.
Licensing:	Public domain.

Mention a UNIX-based HTTP server to most people in the Web community and the first one likely to come to mind is NCSA HTTPD. The National Center for Supercomputing Applications has gained notoriety on the Internet by producing freely available software for various platforms to make the Internet more accessible and enjoyable to use.

NCSA's HTTPD can be configured to run either as a stand-alone process or invoked through the UNIX inetd facility. There's a link off the main Web page for the server (see the chart at the beginning of this section) to walk you through all the steps necessary to get HTTPD up on your machine: from downloading the software through configuration and testing. Several precompiled binaries are available for several more popular machines that permit you to run the server without having to compile it first. (The variety of hardware platforms used by UNIX means that freely available software from the Internet is often distributed as source code that must be compiled to be made into a usable binary image.)

Once you've downloaded the software (and optionally compiled it), you must configure it. Configuration is accomplished by editing a handful of text files judiciously documented in the online documentation in the NCSA HTTPD Web pages. As a matter of fact, many HTTP servers and Web browsers now use Web-based documentation.

TIP

When installing an HTTP daemon, it is probably a good idea to do so where you can have at least three windows open on your screen: one for the login session in which you do the installation, one for a Web browser pointed at the online documentation, and one for a Web browser pointed at your server for testing.

You configure NCSA HTTPD in three steps: server, resource, and access configuration. Each step is typically controlled by a series of directives in a different ASCII file. Most folks can get along by changing very few of the directives. Some folks, however, can't sleep at night unless they change everything from its default value—you know who you are.

In the server configuration process, you can manipulate a variety of parameters concerning the way the HTTPD process runs, how it talks to the network, and where it should look for other configuration files. The resource configuration process dictates the specifics of how certain services are offered through your Web server, such as where the daemon should look for HTML documents, whether or not users can have private directories for their own Web publishing, and some specifics having to do with automatically generated file directories.

The access configuration process is where you can make or break the security and usability of your server. NCSA HTTPD provides two methods for controlling access to your Webspace: a global access configuration file and a per-directory access file. Global access-control files are mandatory and control such things as authentication files for users and groups, "sectioning directives" that control which access controls apply to which branches of your file system, default MIME-typing, various fine-tuning options for dynamically generated directory listings, as well as settings for the per-directory access-control files. The capabilities of the per-directory access-control file are nearly the same as for the global file with the exception of being able to limit other access-control files.

One of the greatest strengths of NCSA HTTPD lies in its near universality—it seems like everybody's doin' it. NCSA's server is the McDonald's of Web servers. It pleases most of the people most of the time and manages to come up with something fairly innovative every so often as well.

CERN HTTPD Server

Server:	CERN HTTPD
Platforms:	NeXTStep 3.2 (on NeXT and NeXT-386), SunOS 4.1.3, Solaris 2.3, HP-UX/Snake 9.0, IRIX 5.2, ULTRIX 4.3, AIX 3.2, OSF/1 2.0/3.0, VMS, Linux 1.1.29, Apple A/UX 3.1, Pyramid DC/OSx 1.1, NCR 3000 2.01.01, Amdahl UTS 2.1/4.2, SCO 3.0/3.2, DELL SVR4.0 Rev 2, Unisys SVR4, Intergraph Clipper C300/C400.
From:	Centre Europien de Recherche Nucliaire (CERN, The European Laboratory for Particle Physics).
URL:	`http://info.cern.ch/hypertext/WWW/Daemon/Status.html`
Major Features:	Features vary from platform to platform. server-side scripts, imagemaps, CGI 1.1, CGI index search interface, HTML2 forms.
Security:	Host-based filtering, user ID/password authentication, access-control lists, group-based filtering, server functions as a caching multiapplication proxy gateway to serve out services such as remote HTTP, FTP, Gopher, WAIS, and NNTP to firewalled networks.
Installation:	Source in C. Binaries available for NeXTStep 3.2 (on NeXT and NeXT-386), SunOS 4.1.3, Solaris 2.3, HP-UX/Snake 9.0,

	IRIX 5.2, ULTRIX 4.3, AIX 3.2, OSF/1 2.0/3.0, VMS, Linux 1.1.29, SCO 3.0/3.2, Intergraph Clipper C300/C400. May be called from `inetd` or run as a stand-alone server.
Documentation:	User Guide, Installation Guide, bug list, FAQ, and other documents available online at URL `http://www.w3.org/hypertext/WWW/Daemon/Status.html`.
Age:	Version 0.1 released June 1991.
Status:	Version 3.0 released September 1994. Current as of February 1995.
Licensing:	Public domain.

Not too long ago, a chapter with the scope of this one would have taken only a few pages. In the summer of 1991, just over two years after Tim Berners-Lee proposed the World Wide Web project at CERN and about seven months after he prototyped the first graphical WWW browser on the NeXT, version 0.1 of the CERN HTTPD was released (see the chart at the beginning of this section). CERN HTTPD is the old salt of the UNIX Web server set. A couple of the appeals of CERN's Web server are its staying power and the fact that it comes from CERN, the birthmother of all Web sites.

CERN's HTTPD has more to recommend it than sentimentality. A special search directive in the configuration file permits easy setup of search scripts compliant with the Common Gateway Interface (CGI) 1.1. More about CGI later. For now, keep in mind that CGI is the current platform-independent industry standard for an API that describes how back-end scripts talk to a Web server.

Another strong feature of CERN's HTTPD is its ability to sit on a firewall machine and act as a proxy server for other protocols such as HTTP, FTP, NNTP, and WAIS that wouldn't otherwise be able to leave the premises of a sensitive site. Additionally, the server can cache proxied items and act as an internal proxy to an external proxy for sites wanting or needing double-firewalled protection.

If you want to squeeze more functionality out of this server, you can use it as a Wide Area Information Server (WAIS) gateway. Understand that as you pile functions on a single daemon and a machine with limited resources, performance drops proportionately.

The CERN server isn't alone in this regard. Part of the fine art of system administration is determining when you cross the threshold of offering too many services for the resources you have available. Your site may have world-class expertise but be limited to a couple of Sun 3/60s for all your servers, or you may be at the other end of the spectrum and be resource wealthy but lack the time, inclination, or training for strategic Web service. If, like most system administrators, you have a reach that exceeds your grasp, you are well advised to back off a bit and sacrifice variety for consistency. Your users will thank you for it.

Northwestern University's GN Gopher/HTTP Server

Server:	*GN*
Platforms:	Generic UNIX-style applications with configuration accommodations made for AIX, AUX, BSD_386, Convex 0S, HPUX, Irix, Linux, NeXT, OSF1, Pyramid, SCO, Sequent, Solaris2, Sun OS4, SVR4, and Ultrix.
From:	Northwestern University.
URL:	`gopher://hopf.math.nwu.edu/`
Major Features:	Combination Gopher0 and HTTP 1.0 server. Local WAIS searches, but no WAIS gateway; global and per-directory access control based on explicit or wildcarded domain name or IP address, structured file server, automatic decompression of data files, Gopher-style scripts.
Security:	Host-based filtering.
Installation:	Source is in C. Can be run either as a stand-alone daemon or under `inetd`. No precompiled binaries available at canonical source. Well-done HTML installation documentation included with source.
Documentation:	Moderate documentation at Gopher URL.
Age:	Version 1.0 released October 1993.
Status:	Current version is 2.21 as of February 1995.
Licensing:	GNU public license: free for any use including commercial or distribution.

Pioneers who use any new technology not only have to adapt themselves to the new way of thinking but often have to adapt the previous technologies as well.

A good example is Northwestern University's GN server. GN can serve up your data using Gopher0 protocol to Gopher clients, and HTTP 1.0 to Web browsers. If you like, it can even do both out of the same TCP port! GN looks at the syntax of incoming information requests and behaves accordingly.

Like all the servers described so far, GN can either run as a stand-alone daemon or be called from the UNIX `inetd` facility. As is par for the course, GN is distributed in C source code and must be compiled to work on your intended machine.

A few global configuration settings are changed in a source code header file before compilation. The rest of GN's capabilities are controlled by menu files in each directory. These files are roughly equivalent to the `.Links` files in the University of Minnesota's Gopher server.

GN permits proprietors of existing Gopherspace to ease themselves into the WWW painlessly. Once the existing University of Minnesota Gopher tree is converted over to GN format, the resulting menu files can be left as-is or augmented to contain any desired amount of HyperText Markup Language. GN generates HTML from the existing Gopher tree when a Web client connects. The menu files can also contain any amount of HTML: from adding a few icons to an existing Gopher-style menu to a full HTML document.

GN also has the attractive feature of being able to serve structured files as a two-layer hierarchy. An e-mail folder, for example, can be split into separate records, each starting with a From header line, and listed in a menu generated on-the-fly by their respective Subject lines. A little creative symbolic linking at the UNIX shell layer can easily result in multiple presentations of the same data based on different fields.

Another nifty feature of GN is that you can keep your data files compressed and instruct GN to decompress them just before serving them out to the public. Although doing so uses up more bandwidth and time, you may want to uncompress files before serving them up if you use a compression method your target audience may not easily be able to handle.

COMPARING HTTP SERVERS

It should be apparent that each HTTP server has its own merits and detractors. It would be naive for anyone to attempt to place these servers on a linear scale and say, without qualification, that one is better than another. In fact, you may find yourself wanting to run more than one of these servers on the same machine (using different TCP ports, of course) so that you can serve up the best of their features to your audience.

There are plenty of UNIX servers around, some are commercial but most, like the ones just described, are free. A few other UNIX servers should be mentioned, however, and this is done in the following section.

Other UNIX Servers

The **Enterprise Integration Technologies Corporation** has put together a rather novel Webmaster's Starter Kit. This is a form-based installation kit for an enhanced version of NCSA HTTPD. The form asks you for a few bits of basic information about you, your site, and your host and then walks you through an Web-automated process that generates a server remotely; downloads, unpacks, and runs a shell archive; and installs and sets up your server.

The EIT HTTPD is also distinguished by a set of enhancements above and beyond the stock NCSA HTTPD. The server has been modified to give "kinder and gentler" error messages to remote users; it can also be tuned to give priority to document-specific or user-specific tasks and can redirect HTTP requests elsewhere during intentional downtime. A handful of enhancements and utilities are packaged in the kit, including a watchdog process to automatically restart the server if it hangs, a form-based home-page generator, a C library of CGI functions, a link verifier to aid in spotting lame links in hypertext documents, and a utility to convert e-mail folders into cross-linked hypertext.

EIT HTTPD can be found at URL `http://wsk.eit.com/wsk/doc/`.

Plexus is an HTTP server written in perl (which, depending on who you ask and what kind of mood they're in, stands for either Practical Extraction and Report Language or Pathologically Eclectic Rubbish Lister). The perl language has become a utilitarian staple of the UNIX community; the ease of integration with other perl programs must be numbered among Plexus' strengths. Unlike other UNIX HTTP servers, which are written in C and must be compiled, Plexus is interpreted because it's written in perl. Under normal circumstances, this is a significant performance hit, but chances are that you can run Plexus without suffering the performance ills of other interpreted languages.

Plexus was written with easy extensibility in mind; its online documentation includes a tutorial on writing your own gateways. This should make Plexus a strong contender for those sites that have unique data to be presented on the Web in a fairly standardized manner.

Plexus can be found at URL `http://bsdi.com/server/doc/plexus.html`.

Netsite is the commercial-grade Web server from Netscape Communications Corp. Netsite is a commercial product (it isn't free), but many of the folks who pay for it believe it's worth every bit of the price. The server, which is installed by using HTML2 forms, supports the standard suite of features expected from any high-end Web server and comes in two flavors. The Netsite Communications Server is a standard HTTP server designed to achieve high performance and low host resource utilization. The Netsite Commerce Server is an enhanced version of the Communications Server that purports to offer a bulletproof platform for exchange of the types of information critical to electronic commerce. Through use of RSA public-key cryptographic technology, the Commerce Server offers a combination of data encryption and server authentication that should have a fundamental impact on the amount of secure commerce taking place over the Internet.

Information about acquiring Netsite is available at `http://www.mcom.com/MCOM/products_docs/server.html`.

Servers for Microsoft Windows and IBM OS/2

Sometimes, less is more. On the Internet, everyone should be able to be both an information provider and an information consumer. Not only should you be able to keep tabs on your local, state, and federal representatives without going through the press, but they should able keep in touch with the cultures they represent without relying exclusively on pollsters. On the

World Wide Web, this idea implies the availability of *personal Web servers*—ubiquitous pieces of software that can be dropped into any or all personal workstations to serve out information from or concerning one person.

Personal Web servers aren't the only way this can be accomplished, of course. Many of the UNIX servers described in the first part of this chapter permit access to individual home directories from which users can put their own documents out on the Web. An advantage of this approach is that, although it's not strictly so by virtue of the operating system, UNIX machines often deliver more processing resources to each user than do individual PCs. An advantage of a personal Web server is that having unrestricted control over a server permits you to put items in place that require a level of privileged access and support that may not be practical in some organizations with a shared Web server. Some of these items are clickable maps and HTML2 fill-out forms. A happy medium for many people is to put the lion's share of the Web resources on larger multiuser hosts and to link to personal Web servers for resources that they can't put other places (either for reasons of practicality or resource availability).

Web servers that live on various versions of Microsoft Windows, OS/2, the Mac OS, or other traditionally single-user machines aren't necessarily under-powered relations of their larger Web cousins. Some of the Web servers you've browsed recently may actually have been PCs. So-called *personal computers* are now both client and server. On such systems, the only significant detraction may be that small personal computer operating systems don't have the rich multiuser tradition that UNIX, VM, or VMS do. Consequently, when pressing such machines into multiuser service, it's not unusual to find systemic weaknesses in drivers or software that aren't easily discovered in single-user circumstances. When you set out to use the machine on your desk as a Web server, be prepared for an interesting—although not necessarily unprofitable—life.

Alisa Systems, Inc. Windows HTTPD Server

Server:	Windows HTTPD
Platforms:	Microsoft Windows with a WinSock 1.1 compliant driver.
From:	Robert B. Denny
URL:	`http://www.city.net/win-httpd/`
Major Features:	HTTP 0.9/1.0, CGI 1.1 compliance with either DOS Virtual Machine processes or by native Windows applications, forms support, imagemaps, optional multithreading for up to 16 simultaneous users, optional Visual Basic DLL preloading for heavy CGI usage, enhanced directory listing, useful utilities.
Security:	Host-based filtering, user ID/password authentication.

continues

Server:	Windows HTTPD
Installation:	Distributed as a precompiled, ready-to-run MS Windows binary bundled with related files in a zipped archive.
Documentation:	Unzipped package includes online HTML documentation.
History:	Evolved from NCSA HTTPD for Windows, which grew out of the UNIX HTTPD.
Status:	Current version is 1.4 as of January 1995.
Licensing:	GNU public license: free for personal or non-commercial use. 30-day free trial followed by registration fee for commercial use.

To say that the Windows HTTPD is surprising is an understatement. A test machine documented in the server's home page handled well over 25,000 requests an hour, averaging around 4K each. Although there were some problems with TCP session management between some WinSock DLLs and HTTPD at press time (see `http://www.city.net/win-httpd/tcp-report.html` for more information), those problems can be worked around until the WinSock libraries in question are up to snuff.

Windows HTTPD can easily be characterized as an HTTP server for people who don't like running HTTP servers. On one level, you can download the zipped file, extract it into the default `c:\httpd` directory, double-click on the HTTPD.EXE from File Manager, and *presto-chango*, you're running a Web site (albeit one with the default demo Web pages that come with the server). On another level, the rich suite of utilities and features that come with or can be easily acquired for this server definitely make it a major player.

The utilities and added functionalities that, in some cases, have been contributed by the enthusiastic user community that Windows HTTPD has acquired are available through the URL listed in the chart at the beginning of this section. These utilities and added features include VB Server Stats, which generates periodic reports about the use of your server; a guide to using DOS perl for DOS-CGI scripts; and an imagemap editor that makes maintenance of hot regions within clickable imagemaps even easier than on UNIX.

HTTPS Server

Server:	HTTPS
Platforms:	Intel, DEC Alpha, or MIPS processor running Windows NT 3.1 final release with TCP/IP installed.
From:	European Microsoft Windows NT Academic Centre (EMWAC).
URL:	`http://emwac.ed.ac.uk/html/internet_toolchest/https/contents.htm`

Major Features:	HTTP 1.0, CGI, HTML2 forms, installed as a Windows NT service, multithreaded, integrates with WAISTOOLS for Windows NT for local WAIS searches, works with all network interfaces on multi-homed machines.
Security:	Multi-homed host support. Additional security features in commercial version.
Installation:	Configuration done through the Windows NT control panel.
Documentation:	Online at the canonical Website for the software as well as included in numerous formats in the distribution.
Age:	Still in beta, version 1.0 not released at press time.
Status:	Version 0.96 current (beta version, but is freely available) as of February 1995.
Licensing:	Free. Commercial version is also available; see Web page for details.

If you like the HTTPD for Windows but crave more horsepower, try HTTPS from the European Microsoft Windows NT Academic Centre. Not only will you run on the swifter horse of Windows NT, but you have the option of running on DEC Alpha or MIPS hardware as well.

One of the nice features of HTTPS is that you can run it on *multi-homed machines* (machines with more than one network interface) and serve the Web out of each interface. This makes HTTPS worth examining for sites with non-passable firewalls between two or more networks, although security compartmentalization of your Web tree can't really be done with the freeware version of this software (you'll have to acquire the commercial version to use WWW basic authentication and access control). The commercial version is also more of a full-blown caching firewall for HTTP, Gopher, and FTP services.

Like its Windows 3.1 cousin, HTTPS is a snap to install. Just FTP to emwac.ed.ac.uk and get the zip file containing the software appropriate for your processor from the /pub/https directory. Both DEC Alpha and Intel versions are available for download. The server installs just like any other Windows NT service and is configurable from the control panel.

At the very least, servers like HTTPS are niche software. They provide a robust platform for Web development and publication for shops that haven't yet embraced UNIX and don't have access to other Web-servable hosts systems such as VM and VMS. It's not unreasonable to look forward to the day in the not-too-distant future when Windows NT-based Web servers will inherit the mantle of VM-based and VMS-based servers, whose data will be available by back-end gateways that talk to the more user-friendly Windows NT.

As Web servers become easier to install and configure, the majority of work is put where it ought to be: providing information. The greater the percentage of time you can spend actually publishing your data, the higher the quality of your product. Certainly, the current growth in

HTML authoring tools, gateways between the Web and other information sources, and easily installed Web servers are having a tangible impact on the character of the Web and the accessibility of Web publishing to noncomputer specialists.

OS2HTTPD Server

Server:	OS2HTTPD
Platforms:	IBM OS/2 with IBM TCP/IP for OS/2 Base Kit 2.0 or later.
From:	Frankie Fan <kfan@netcom.com>
URL:	ftp://ftp.netcom.com/pub/kf/kfan/overview.html
Major Features:	HTTP 0.9/1.0, CGI 1.0/1.1/HTBIN, HTML2 forms, imagemaps, access control, server-side includes, HPFS and FAT filenames supported, REXX and OS/2 executable server scripts.
Security:	Host-based filtering.
Installation:	As with the other servers in this class, simply download the software, unzip the archive into the specified directories, and run it.
Documentation:	HTML documentation in the distribution archive as well as Web-based documentation at the canonical URL.
Age:	Ported from NCSA HTTPD 1.3
Status:	Current version is 1.04 as of February 1995.
Licensing:	Free for non-commercial use.

This section wouldn't be complete without including a reference to an HTTP server for OS/2. OS/2 has long been the also-ran of PC operating systems, but with the more recent releases, including OS/2 Warp, OS/2 has developed a sizable and devoted following.

Although many of the servers described so far in this chapter have been direct or indirect ports of the NCSA HTTPD, OS2HTTPD seems to have retained a sizable amount of the functionality of the original. Big Iron workers on the local mainframe will feel right at home developing server scripts in REXX.

One of the strong benefits of running a server in OS/2 or Windows NT is that they are true operating systems and provide stronger interprocess insulation than does MS Windows 3.x or DOS. It's much less likely that an errant process will cause your Web server to become "lost in cyberspace." When you run a Web server on Windows 3.1, however, you are subject to a range of reliability levels that are usually directly proportional to the amount of shareware experimentation or resource-envelope pushing in which you engage. For every person who has to reboot his or her Windows machine three or four times a day, there's probably some joker who's had Windows running continuously since it was originally installed. Go figure.

Serving Up the Web from a Macintosh

With all the servers available for various platforms, it should come as no surprise that there's one available for the Macintosh. With their built-in AppleTalk ports, Macintoshes have been network animals almost since their inception. For years, AppleTalk was the most pervasive network protocol in the world. Nowadays, Macs are no slouch when it comes to being both client and servers on the Internet, as demonstrated by the capabilities of the Macintosh HTTP server described in the following section.

MacHTTP Server

Server:	*MacHTTP*
Platforms:	68000-series or Power Macintoshes with System 7 and Mac TCP.
From:	BIAP Systems, Inc.
URL:	`http://www.biap.com/`
Major Features:	Optional FV-Bridge application for online commerce, CGI access to FileMaker Pro, access control by address and domain name, user ID and password authentication, remote management from other WWW browsers using AppleEvents, CGI scripts can be AppleScript or any application that returns AppleEvents (such as HyperCard), tunable performance, and usage restrictions.
Security:	Host-based filtering, user ID/password authentication, administratively defined "security realms."
Installation:	Drag-and-drop installation. Entire configuration is kept in one file, most of which can be edited indirectly through menu choices in HTTP.
Documentation:	Extensive on-Web documentation at URL listed above.
Age:	Version 1.3 released in May 1994.
Status:	Release 2.0 was current as of February 1995.
Licensing:	30-day evaluation followed by license fee. See canonical Web site listed above.

Mac HTTP has the kind of features you expect to find on a UNIX server—and a number of Mac-specific features found on no other server (see the chart at the beginning of this section). In fact, the online technical documentation states "Without MacHTTP, you'd be forced to do this on a UNIX box!"

In a roundabout way, that statement points to one of the appeals of Mac HTTP. If left-brained people are more likely to use Macintoshes, Amigas, NeXTs, or X servers running on Berkeley-extracted UNIX versions and right-brained people are more likely to use PCs, 3270 terminals attached to VM or MVS boxes, or System V UNIX at the Bourne shell prompt, Mac HTTP is likely to be more appealing to the left-brained crowd. Not that there isn't plenty here to appeal to the right-wing...uh...make that right-*brain* set.

The additional FV-Bridge application works with the server for developing credit-card charge-out applications for Internet-based commerce. The server also permits the standard set of access restrictions available on many other servers: restriction by IP address, by domain name, or based on user ID and password sets. In addition, the on-Web documentation gives examples of how to interface Mac HTTP to Filemaker Pro, Hypercard, and Mac perl.

Servers with that kind of capability and expandability can easily become indispensable once pressed into service; what was once a weird little toy in the corner of somebody's office may one day become a critical link in a new service that wasn't previously possible. The real value of Web servers like this one isn't necessarily in the tools they replace but in the entirely new applications that they make practical.

VM Servers

It's always amusing to hear someone say something along the lines of "I've been a VM system programmer for 20 years, but someone in management went to a trade show and now they want to shut down the mainframe and 'go client-server.'" Mainframes and client-server relationships aren't necessarily mutually exclusive. The fact that many of the more popular client-server applications run on PCs *and* UNIX machines is an accident of history: those systems happened to come into wide acceptance at about the same time the philosophy of client-server computing was catching on. These systems didn't have a lot of critical applications to market them, so it was natural to use PCs and UNIX for client-server applications. Mainframes happened to have been bearing an established load of centralized nonnetworked mission-critical applications, so it did not seem necessary to market mainframes as part of the client-server equation. Big Iron shops have been paying the price for that for quite a while.

Ask anyone what they don't like about mainframes; in with the arguably valid points about the cost of maintenance, cost of storage, and length of the hardware product cycle are an equal number of invalid points about 3270 interfaces, slow response, and centralization as opposed to client-server orientation. An HTTP server is an ideal application to breathe new perceptions into an allegedly tired platform.

When the mainframe is an HTTP server, there's no 3270 interface—just a Web browser. Unless users try to log in to the host or give the host an obvious "mainframy" name like webvm1, there's no way most users can discern a Web server on a mainframe from one on a UNIX box. The 3270 interface problem becomes a non-issue. Slow response time is a function of system management. If users use their PCs, Macs, X terminals, and so on as their front ends and point Web browsers at the mainframe instead of using TN3270, SNA virtual terminals, or 3270 bysynch terminals to run applications on the mainframe, a large unnecessary portion of the system load is eliminated. By making mainframe data available over a Web server instead of relying on proprietary VM-based applications, a good mainframe can be heard but not seen.

WebShare Server

Server:	WebShare
Platforms:	CMS 5 or later, with CMS pipelines and REXX/Sockets.
From:	Rick Troth `<troth@ua1vm.ua.edu>`
URL:	`http://ua1vm.ua.edu/~troth/rickvmsw/rickvmsw.html`
Major Features:	HTTP 0.9/1.0, CGI 1.0/1.1, personal Web pages, REXX CGI scripts, works on multiple-homed hosts, redirection, imagemaps, uses minidisks and shared file system.
Security:	Simple remote user identification through an RFC 1413-type ident transaction.
Installation:	REXX source code. Runs "off the shelf" and is available in either VMARC or TAR format.
Documentation:	`http://ua1vm.ua.edu/htbin/cmshelp?task+httpd` as well as additional documentation in the distribution archive.
Age:	Release 1.0 distributed in January 1994.
Status:	Release 2.2 current as of February 1995.
Licensing:	Free software; see `http://ua1vm.ua.edu/~troth/rickvmsw/cmshttpd.copyright` for restrictions.

Of the VM-based Web servers available, WebShare is the most feature rich. Through HTML2 forms with a REXX back-end engine, local mainframe data on either minidisks or the shared file system can be served in any way that can be described in REXX. Through use of a multi-homed host, appropriate REXX CGI scripts, and a related package, WebShare supports simple remote user identification by putting the result of an ident service transaction in the appropriate CGI variable

All things considered, WebShare is a pretty good chance to put your money where your mouth is when defending the life of your mainframe.

Serving Up the Web through E-Mail

The lowest common denominator is a big deal on the WWW. One of the tenets of the WWW philosophy is that users shouldn't be disenfranchised from Web access because of the machine on their desk. Although it's obvious that not all users can achieve parity of access quality, it's a perfectly realizable goal for anyone with any type of access to the Internet to have access to the great majority of information on the Web.

The same month the very first Web browser was developed at CERN (a graphical browser for the NeXT), work began on the first lowest common denominator browser: the Line Mode Browser. Development for low-end platforms has always been a common thread on the Web. Arguments that the WWW can be used only by the privileged few "information haves" (those with graphical displays) and not by the silent majority of "information have-nots" (those with text-only displays or no direct path to the Internet) just don't wash. The belief of some neophytes that the entire World Wide Web is somehow "inside Mosaic" is, naturally, invalid. Like any myth, however, that assertion has a kernel of truth. The sheer Nirvanic joy of a graphical Web browser with adequate CPU, graphics, sound, a decent Web site to browse, backbone bandwidth to get there, and other ergonomic considerations puts a lowest-common-denominator interface like e-mail to shame. Compared to the plethora of resources now available to graphical Web interfaces, many of them may as well be "inside Mosaic" (or Netscape or whatever is your personal preference for a browser).

The Internet has always had to contend with making services available to folks who have only e-mail access to the Internet. In days gone by, that contingent was made up of customers from major providers of structured network services such as CompuServe or Prodigy. As more providers join the structured-provider fray, and they all begin to offer larger amounts of direct or nearly direct Internet access to an unprecedented number of users, most e-mail orphans tend to be users on under-engineered or highly secured corporate networks.

Agora, from the W3 consortium, is a browse-by-proxy e-mail server that lets anyone with e-mail access to the Internet browse the Web from the perspective of the mail server. Hypertext documents are returned as text; links can be browsed by return mail. An informational URL can be found at `http://info.cern.ch/hypertext/WWW/Agora/Overview.html`. Agora is still being beta tested, but if you want to run it, request a copy of the software by sending e-mail to `agora-request@mail.w3.org`.

A PASSING REFERENCE TO SERVERS FOR OTHER SYSTEMS

KA9Q is a classic Internet case study of the little acorn that grew into a mighty oak. Originally written by Phil Karn (whose amateur radio call sign is *KA9Q*) to do packet radio, this piece of software has since branched out into many areas. KA9Q now exists in many flavors, and its current uses include a budget-priced IP router, network filtering firewall, SMTP/POP2/POP3 server, time server, CSO server, FTP server, Gopher server, and now, HTTP server. KA9Q is copyrighted by Phil Karn (at `karn@chicago.qualcomm.com`) and is free for use by educational institutions and Hams; other users should contact him for licensing information. The version of KA9Q available at URL `gopher://cases.pubaf.washington.edu/11c:/manual` is an ASCII-only

HTTP server. That means that binary transfers must use Gopher URLs and KA9Q's Gopher component. Everything is done with a single executable and a single configuration file and runs on a 386 or better PC under DOS. The documentation is available in several formats at the same URL.

The **Ohio State University Region 6 HTTP Server for VMS** is a DECthreads application that avoids the overhead of other non-multithreading HTTP servers for VMS. This server supports CGI, imagemaps, server-side includes, host-based access control, user ID and password authentication, and a variety of other features documented in the on-Web documentation at URL `http://kcgl1.eng.ohio-state.edu/www/doc/serverinfo.html`. Ohio State University asks in its copyright statement that the developers be acknowledged when this software is distributed.

Amiga users can go to URL `http://insti.physics.sunysb.edu/AMosaic/home.html` for information on retrieving both **Amiga Mosaic** and the Amiga port of **NCSA HTTPD for UNIX**. The Amiga version of HTTPD, which is still under development, supports CGI scripts that are AmigaDOS scripts, AmigaDOS commands, or AREXX macros.

The Creeping Feature Show

Internet applications are often replete with features, many of which were never imagined when the application was first conceived. The WWW and its associated applications aren't immune to this tendency. As is frequently the case, the more capable an application is, the more its users want "just one more thing"—until eventually these additions outnumber the original features. Such is the nature of application growth on the Internet.

The following sections briefly survey many of features important to WWW applications, especially servers.

MIME and the Web

Multimedia Internet Mail Extensions, or MIME, was developed to leverage more functionality from RFC 822/SMTP-type e-mail applications. MIME permits the attachment of single or multipart attachments such as program data, graphics, sound, video, or anything else that can be described within the context of a formal "MIME-type."

HTTP provides a framework for browsers to make either simple or full requests from the HTTP server. Simple requests are considered HTTP 0.9 requests; full requests are considered HTTP 1.0 requests.

HTTP 0.9 is provided as a stripped-down version of HTTP for more streamlined and less capable implementations. In an HTTP 0.9 request, a browser requests a document from an

HTTP server and makes certain assumptions about content based on context. The mechanics of this request can vary from client to client, but content is often presumed based on the file extension. An extension of .HTML or .HTM is usually assumed to go along with an HTML document; the .TXT extension usually goes with text, and so on. This system works much of the time, but it's far from bulletproof.

In an HTTP 1.0 request, the browser requests a document and then rattles off a list of MIME types it can accept, such as text/plain, video/QuickTime, audio/basic and so on. If the requested document contains only MIME types listed as acceptable by the browser, it is encapsulated into a MIME-format message and transmitted to the client. If not, a variety of status or error conditions and renegotiation are possible, depending on the implementations of the browser and the server.

One tangible benefit of using MIME types to define the format of data transmitted from server to client is that the user of the client can micro-manage how individual types of data are handled: the type of GIF or JPEG viewer preferred, whether they want to print PostScript as soon as they receive the file, view it on-screen, save it to a file, and so on. UNIX clients frequently use the Metamail package to define how certain MIME types are handled. PC and Macintosh clients usually have a menu set or a dedicated configuration file to perform this function.

ISMAPs, Clickable Image Maps, or Imagemaps

One of the wonderful things about the WWW is that each document can have its own unique user interface. A popular way of doing this is to create an inline graphic with clickable "hot spots" a user can point to, select, and use to control the behavior of the Web page. For example, a page may have a map of a campus; clicking on a given building may display a blueprint for that particular building. Another page may have a graphic with a photographic roster of a board of directors; clicking on a particular director may get you a roster of that director's department. Yet another page may have a fanciful company logo surrounded by custom icons representing various online services, each of which is linked to a telnet://, wais://, or another http:// URL.

Servers that support imagemaps typically have some sort table defining what coordinates define what hot spots on the map and what action should be taken. Consider this example from the NCSA HTTPD for UNIX imagemap tutorial:

```
default /X11/mosaic/public/none.html
rect http://cui_www.unige.ch/w3catalog      15,8     135,39
rect gopher://rs5.loc.gov/11/global         245,86   504,143
rect http://nearnet.gnn.com/GNN-ORA.html    117,122  175,158
```

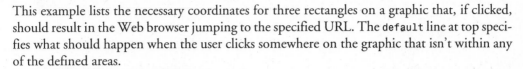

This example lists the necessary coordinates for three rectangles on a graphic that, if clicked, should result in the Web browser jumping to the specified URL. The `default` line at top specifies what should happen when the user clicks somewhere on the graphic that isn't within any of the defined areas.

A variety of utilities are available on the Net to assist in the construction of these imagemap tables; the specifics of how the server does image mapping varies between implementations.

Fancy Directories

Not surprisingly, many folks have started using Web browsers as their primary FTP clients. Information providers who know this can incorporate HTTP links to fancy directory listings in their Web pages as a kind of value-added file archive.

If you disable directory listings, users specifying an HTTP URL ending with a trailing slash will either load the designated default page, if there is one (on some systems, this is be called `index.html`), or fail. If directory listings are enabled, and the default page doesn't exist in a given directory, the user will probably see a simple listing showing the parent and child directories as well as each of the visible files in that given directory and a brief description of file type, like `text/plain`.

Extended or fancy directory listings permit the server administrator to designate an icon bitmap for specific file types, descriptive text to go at the top of the listing for individual subdirectories, as well as descriptive text for individual files like "Don't download this GIF across state lines, please."

Server-Side Include Scripts

Server-side include scripts are an easy way to solve certain challenges, but they can also give users enough rope to both hang themselves and compromise the system. Typically, the name of the script is included in the text of a document and the script is executed each time a given document is retrieved. The convention for such scripts with NCSA HTTPD, for example, is as follows:

```
<!--#command tag1="value1" tag2="value2" -->
```

Placing the script in a comment ensures that the HTML source is more portable if moved to another server.

Server-side includes are often used for applications that aren't large enough to warrant spending time putting together a full-blown HTML2 form (such as automatic counters in Web pages or pointers to dynamic events). A benefit of server-side include scripts is that no burden is placed on the Web browser to support HTML2 forms. An obvious detraction is that any time a user can give any type of unrestricted access to outside users, there's the possibility that your system can be compromised.

It is probably a good idea to use this features only on rare occasions and only for simple applications that have been gone over with a fine-tooth comb before release.

Gateways, Converters, and Filters

As anyone who's done any amount of Web publishing can tell you, the world doesn't naturally exist in HTML format. Anytime someone attempts to put some naturally existing information into HTML format, it means one of two things: they're writing HTML by hand or they're using a gateway to "HTML-ify" their information. One method isn't necessarily better than the other.

Some applications call for creative expression, such as system front ends, home pages, personal pages, and so on. Some applications call for consistent formatting, minimal distractions, and few if any hours spent in actual conversion of the data from another format. In the latter case, gateways are most useful.

Gateways abound. If you have any data in a commonly used format, the question is likely whether a gateway is available. Gateways, converters, and filters are available on the Net for getting HTML out of XFind, Hytelnet, e-mail, Usenet news, VMS Help, WAIS, Oracle, Techinfo, Lotus Notes, O2 OQL, `finger`, PostScript, Microsoft Word, WordPerfect, FrameMaker, `troff`, LaTeX/BibTeX, Texinfo, DECwrite, Interleaf, QuarkXPress, PageMaker, Scribe, Powerpoint, Linuxdoc, Rainbow, C, C++, Lisp, Fortran, SGML, Emacs Info, and AmigaGuide.

Whether some of these items are browser or server issues depends on how you implement them. If you have a directory full of MS Word documents and a CGI script that dynamically converts them to HTML just before viewing, it is a server issue. Other ways of using these gateways, converters, and filters may make them more appropriate for a browser.

The Common Gateway Interface

One of the reasons why there are so many archives of extensions and scripts for various Web servers is the Common Gateway Interface, or CGI. CGI is an Application Programming Interface specification that addresses environment variables, command lines, standard input, and standard output issues, In particular, CGI is concerned with how servers communicate with back-end scripts that dynamically produce the output of a given Web page instead of relying on the contents of a static file. CGI scripts, for example, are the most common way of handling HTML2 fill-out forms.

Most servers permit CGI scripts to be written in one of a number of languages. Depending on your server, CGI scripts can be written in perl (the most common language for CGI scripts), C, Visual Basic, DCL, and even DOS Batch (if you're a masochist).

All servers that support the CGI can process HTML2 fill-out forms. Web browsers can use two methods to send the contents of a form to the HTTP server: GET and POST. The difference between the two is how the contents are conveyed to the server. Each HTTP client has its default method, but the method may be explicitly selected within the HTML for the form. (Refer to Chapter 28, "Navigating the World Wide Web," for more information.)

Methods to the Madness: *GET, PUT,* and *POST*

One of the big differences between HTTP 0.9 and HTTP 1.0 is the pallet of methods that can be used within the context of an HTTP session to talk between the Web browser client and the HTTP server. With HTTP 0.9, only GET is used; as of the December 1994 second edition, HTTP 1.0 requires the GET and HEAD methods and defines optional methods called PUT, POST, DELETE, LINK, and UNLINK. All this really means is that HTTP1.0 servers and clients can provide a great deal more flexibility when communicating back and forth.

The GET method means that the Web browser connects to the server and tries to "get" a specific Universal Resource Locator. The HEAD method works just like the GET method but it doesn't return any actual documents (just header information). The vast majority of Web browsers use the GET method.

The POST method was specifically created for passing information that is "subordinate of the resource identified by the URL in the Request-Line" (in plain talk, this means that if you've got a Web page that requests information from you, you can use the POST method to return it to the server).

Both the GET and POST methods can be used for HTML2-type forms. If the GET method is used, the contents of your form are appended to the right side of the URL when the form is submitted to the server and passed to the CGI script as a variable called QUERY_STRING. If the POST method is used, the length of the data submitted by the form is passed to the CGI script as the variable CONTENT_LENGTH and the data is passed in standard input.

NOTE

It is recommended that you use POST instead of GET whenever possible because the method used to pass the subordinate data to the server with GET has a tendency to run into arbitrary URL length restrictions on some servers.

Hippy Guerrillas and Fascist Pyramids: Security on the Web

The WWW is the first killer application on the Internet that has attracted wide-spread interest in electronic commerce. Already, a plethora of companies are selling their goods individually and through numerous online shopping malls. There is, however, a fly in the ointment.

Communication of financial information over the Internet seems to require that such information pass from the source to the destination in privacy. That requires communication that is either physically or virtually secure. Because the Internet is built on shared communications media, virtual security seems to be the only choice available. Virtual security implies encryption of data—and that's the problem.

The NIST, NSA, and U.S. Commerce Department place restrictions on cryptography when it's used for data encryption. This can very well mean that to use encryption for electronic commerce on the Internet, steps must be taken to ensure the citizenship of any users of such services as well as the national origin of all sites ultimately receiving data from such servers. On the Internet, or even on any complex network a fraction of the size of the Internet, this is a practical impossibility.

Political quandary not withstanding, here are a few URLs that may help you sort out what your legal obligations are and help you come to a basic understanding of some of the issues involved:

Cryptography Export Control Archives:

```
http://www.cygnus.com/~gnu/export.html
```

Cryptography home page:

```
http://retriever.cs.umbc.edu/~mohan/Work/crypt.html
```

Technical progress usually outstrips social progress, and the security of the WWW is no exception. Web security has advanced on several fronts; the following sections provide a brief survey of some of the developments.

DNS and IP Address-Based Access Control

Most HTTP servers provide access control. IP address-based access control is the ability to block or permit access to a server or individual document based on all or part of the IP address of the requesting host. An example of this is to permit all of the University of North Texas to access a server by explicitly permitting their entire block of IP addresses, which all begin with `129.120`, to access the service.

DNS-based access control is the ability to afford the same type of protection based on all or some of the requesting host's Internet domain name. An example of DNS-based access control is to permit the University of North Texas site to access the server by explicitly permitting all hosts that have an Internet domain name ending in `unt.edu` (such as `vaxa.acs.unt.edu` or `mvssp.coe.unt.edu`).

Because no Internet access can take place without an IP address, IP-address restriction seems to be a good method for ensuring security. Because nearly all hosts at most sites are assigned domain names, DNS-based access control seems to be a sound idea as well.

Although these approaches great starting points, there are enough problems with them to warrant looking for additional protection. IP address-based filtering and DNS-based filtering seek to protect you from machines that violate your security. Nevertheless, machines don't violate security—people do. People can move from machine to machine and from a blocked site to a trusted site with relative ease. Because there's no shortage of unauthenticated access to the Internet, it's a little like trying to build a dam with chicken wire: nice foundation, but now we need some cement. Additionally, recent Internet history has proven that the expertise required to forge or "spoof" Internet addresses and domain names is not in short supply.

WWW Telnet-Level Access Authorization

In October 1993, the Access Authorization Basic Protection Scheme was incorporated into the CERN WWW Common Library, which is used for numerous HTTP clients and servers. The AA scheme, sometimes known as WWW Telnet-level access authorization, provides for clear text transmission of user IDs and passwords and has hooks for the use of schemes like Kerberose or RIPEM. On the surface, this approach seems to be an excellent safeguard, but the scope of its protection is narrow. If used with an encryption method, such as NCSA has done with their use of PGP/PEM encryption, the AA scheme provides an excellent way of authenticating access to resources over the Net.

A central problem the AA scheme does not address, however, is the security of the document as it passes from one relatively secure site, over umpteen broadcast networks with an unknown level of security, to another relatively secure site.

One of the proposals on the table that would address this problem is the Secure HTTP proposal by Rescorla and Schiffman of Enterprise Integration Technologies. This proposal provides for a spectrum of security measures including digital signatures, public-key encryption, privacy domains, and key exchanges.

Where Web security is concerned, it will be interesting to see how the social challenges presented by the technical capability of the Internet are addressed.

VII

PART

Using the Internet: Business

Business Growth on the Internet

38

by Jill H. Ellsworth

One of the fastest growing and hottest topics of discussion and activity on the Internet is commercial use of the network. Discussion lists far and wide are talking about "acceptable use" of the Internet, the rapid growth of business use of the Internet, what to do about it, and how to get on the bandwagon.

Questions like these are popping up everywhere:

- What can you really do on the Internet?
- Can I advertise?
- Can I actually sell services and products?
- What are others doing?
- Why would I want to do business on the Internet?

These issues are addressed in this and the following chapters on the growth of business use of the Internet.

The number of Internet users is growing at the phenomenal rate of 10 percent a month! In addition, the business and commercial component is the largest and fastest growing segment of the Internet. The details are amazing and important to anyone interested in maintaining competitiveness in this age of global communications. Part I of this book discusses this growth in some detail, but the following section, as an executive summary, briefly recaps the important points.

How the Internet Has Grown

Initially, the Internet grew slowly, but across time, it has grown to include more than 45,000 connected networks in more than 200 nations. Statistics about the Internet are almost always estimates because the numbers change so frequently.

There is a huge transition occurring with the Internet—it is in the midst of moving to a new structure, evolving from NSFnet to the National Information Infrastructure (NII). A couple years ago, the National Science Foundation sent out "NSF solicitation 93-52," calling for new components of a national backbone; contractors have been chosen to implement the NII.

The new scheme has no central coordinating authority; it depends to a large degree on the cooperation of regional and national telephone companies, academic institutions, businesses, and network providers. Officially, NSFnet ceases to exist on April 30, 1995, but several components of the "new system" are not yet online and the transition promises to be bumpy and more lengthy than planned. For businesses (and, to a lesser degree, all users), this means 12 to 18 months of some mild uncertainty about the network.

The Internet is currently made up of over 45,000 networks world wide; depending on whose data you use, there are approximately 30 million people who have some kind of Internet connectivity. Broadly, the Internet includes individuals, groups, organizations, schools, universities, commercial services, companies, governments, and Free-Nets.

Network Wizards' DNS survey (put out by the Internet Society) reports that in the last quarter of 1994, the Internet experienced its largest growth in recent history—a rate of 26 percent—to 4.851 million hosts in more than 200 countries world wide.

There are some interesting recent trends and statistics:

- Internet growth is estimated to be close to 10 percent a month
- Growth of the commercial sector has been increasing by 10 to 13 percent a month
- It is estimated that there will be 5.5 million hosts by the second quarter of 1995, and that the .com sector could reach 1,950,000 in the same time
- The World Wide Web is growing faster than any other protocol on the Internet—at a rate that could triple its size in one year

The Internet is a voluntary cooperative undertaking, in which the conjoined networks have agreed on certain communication protocols regarding e-mail addressing, how packets are sent and received, and so on. Although there are groups and committees that work on this cooperation, in the end, no one body is in charge.

Although a network that joins the Internet becomes part of the Internet, it retains control and ownership of its own network. Control is therefore shared among the 45,000 networks currently connected to the Internet. The National Science Foundation has been a very influential part of the Internet, but this has never put them fully in control because networks can communicate directly with each other using other network systems.

Businesses joining the Internet find that this cooperative venture is very different from any other organization with which they work. The Internet has an unusual history, is not governed in the way other organizations are, and has a significant community culture of cooperation, sharing data, and providing services and information for free.

How Business Use of the Internet Has Increased

The commercial sector of the Internet (both .com and .net domains) is currently growing faster than any other sector. A year ago, .com became the sector with the most domain names; now it is estimated that it will have 65 percent of the domain names by the second quarter of 1995.

The Internet access marketplace alone in the United States now exceeds $1 billion in annual revenues, according to a recent survey conducted by the Maloff Co.

The data shown in Table 38.1, extrapolated from InterNIC and other data, compares the relative size of the commercial domain with government/military, education/research, and organizational/network domain registrations. This distribution continues to change each month, swinging towards the commercial domain. Every month, the number of unique commercial registered domains represented increases by 10 to almost 14 percent from the previous month.

Table 38.1. Relative sizes of Internet domains.

Domain	Percentage of Total
Government/Military	16.7
Commercial	65.2
Education/Research	7.1
Organization/Net	11.0

Although the commercial sector of the Internet is the most rapidly growing sector, the Web has become the fastest growing protocol—and the Web is where business is spending its time these days.

In June 1993, there were close to 130 Web servers, but by November 1994, there were nearly 9,000 servers. According to Sun Microsystems (reported in *Business Week*, 2/27/95), current estimates are 27,000 to 30,000 sites, and the number is doubling every 53 days. Researchers at Carnegie Mellon estimate that there are more than five million documents stored on Web servers, doubling every six months or so. The Lycos index has indexed more than two and a half million individual Web addresses (URLs)—and remember that Lycos is an incomplete index. The majority of these sites and documents are related to commercial ventures.

You can access a humorous site to have a look at all the various Internet traffic and demographic data. The site is called the U-Do-It Internet Estimator, from GNN:

```
http://gnn.com/news/feature/inet-demo/net.measure.html
```

U-Do-It offers hotlinks to the data sources such as InterNIC, Texas Internet Consulting (John Quarterman), and others.

Who Are the Commercial Power Users of the Internet?

A group of businesses form the power users of the Internet. The commercial power users of the Internet are in a broad scope of industries, including high-technology manufacturers, computer-related industries, oil companies, pharmaceutical companies, healthcare-related industries, financial services, and banks. The growth in traffic from some of these companies exceeded 90 percent in the first quarter of 1995 compared to the preceding quarter. Based on figures from NSF and InterNIC, these are the top 10 companies using the Internet based on traffic volume and the number of externally reachable hosts:

LSI Logic Corporation
Bell Communications
Xerox Corporation
Dell Computer
Pyramid Technology
PSI
Honeywell Incorporated
Amgen Incorporated
Cray Research Incorporated
General Dynamics

Other power users of the Internet include Bristol-Meyers Pharmaceutical, Cadence Design Systems, Sterling Software, A.C. Nielson Company, Demon Systems, General Dynamics, General Motors, and Monsanto.

Who Else Is Using the Internet?

Not only industry giants use the Internet. Many small companies and individual entrepreneurs use the Internet through inexpensive access service providers such as `netcom.com`, , `pipeline.com`, `delphi.com`, `world.std.com`, and PSINet. In fact, access services have increased and expanded rapidly in the last year. They provide a full range of Internet services to individuals and small-to-medium-sized businesses. Some commercial services such as America Online, CompuServe, and Prodigy now provide a limited variety of Internet services—and all have plans to expand that access.

Major financial institutions such as J.P. Morgan & Co., Lehman Brothers, Paine Webber, and the Federal Reserve Board have started to use the Internet. According to NSF, these companies are retrieving 10 times as much data as they are sending out, suggesting that they are using the Internet to support their financial research functions. The same is true for medical institutions. Companies such as Massachusetts General, Health and Welfare Canada, and Rush Presbyterian retrieve more data than they send out by a 10:1 ratio.

Where To Go from Here

You can expect a number of influences and developments to have an impact on doing business on the Internet and the Web:

- **Virtual Reality.** Virtual Reality Transfer Protocols (VRTP) are in the works and will make virtual showrooms and product demonstrations possible.

- **HTML.** HyperText Markup Language is undergoing changes in the number and kinds of tags and operations that can be embedded in a document. The updated HTML will make Web pages even more useful to businesses with more options, more variety, and better flexibility to format text, fields, indexes, and feedback to page owners.

- **Cybermalls, Virtual Factory Outlets, and Storefronts.** Virtual stores, malls, and outlets are growing exponentially, providing opportunities for commercial activities.

- **Security and Authentication.** Security issues of many kinds are being addressed for the Internet and the Web. The Internet will support more secure transactions, secure HTTP, better authentication of messages and virtual signatures, enhanced privacy e-mail, and more sophisticated encryption. Virtual money and virtual transactions in general are going to positively affect sales and marketing on the Web.

Don't be surprised by the business activity on the Internet. A few years ago, these question were often asked on the Internet itself: "Can you do business on the Internet?" and "Are there any businesses on the Internet?" Now there are hundreds or thousands of Internet sites with their own .com (commercial) or .net Internet domain names.

Why Do Business on the Internet?

39

by Jill H. Ellsworth

Someday, digital network communication will be as common as copiers, telephones, computers, and fax machines are today. Doing business without the network will seem odd.

Businesses are joining the Internet faster than any other group of network users. Businesses of all types and sizes have found that the Internet can serve a large variety of their needs including marketing, customer and vendor support, the exchange of information, and joint ventures for research and development. With the aid of the Internet, companies also can develop new products, take orders, receive electronic publications and documents, and retrieve data from specialty databases. Businesses can find technical advice, create and maintain business relationships, obtain market intelligence, ferret out good deals, locate people with needed skills, and even provide products directly.

The look and feel of the network is usually friendly and informal and often seems more like a conversation among neighbors—indeed, the Internet is a virtual community. On the Internet, companies expect straightforward, content-rich exchanges. Conversations on the network clearly imply that companies should and do give back to the Internet or offer value-added services. These contributions are required to maintain goodwill and cooperation on the Internet. The Internet is a place where valuable information and assistance is routinely given freely.

Taking advantage of the speed and size of the Internet, commercial ventures are finding a place in cyberspace—a place where they can reach customers, promote their products, and provide information to others.

Benefiting from Business on the Internet

Why do business on the Internet? The following list describes some of the benefits:

- Global communications
- Corporate logistics
- Competitive advantage
- Information resources
- Customer feedback and support
- Marketing and sales
- Collaboration and development
- Vendor support and networking

The following sections take a more detailed look at these benefits of having a business presence on the Internet.

Global Communication

Certainly a variety of other global communications methods are available to businesses today, but the unique advantages of digital networked communications are important to consider. Because it is a truly global network, the Internet offers a business the opportunity for rapid communications with people and organizations across the globe, enlarging the visibility of a business a thousandfold. For Americans and Canadians, the fact that English has become the common language of the Internet is a great advantage in making contacts and pursuing resources and markets worldwide. Being on the Internet allows a company to truly have a world market.

Because of inexpensive access, the Internet is connecting even small, rural industries. Although the corporate giants certainly produce a great deal of traffic, the global network keeps small, out-of-the-way businesses in touch as well; mutual funds are sold from a ranch in Montana, and one-person software companies flourish in the foothills of the Rockies.

Good communications enable more global corporate management control, aiding in consistency of results. Companies can be in touch with suppliers, branches, and subsidiaries in an effort to exert more control over variables. Companies can establish, negotiate, and maintain standards online. In addition, businesses can improve employee morale by involving them in discussions about the business even outside their own unit, division, or regional office.

Corporate Logistics

Increasingly, logistical concerns can dominate production and customer service issues for businesses. Because the Internet is the anywhere-anytime network, employees, suppliers, customers, and others can keep in touch more efficiently. The use of e-mail and teleconferencing facilitates communication between markets, even in Europe and Asia.

Businesses can maintain communications by way of *asynchronous methods*, meaning that both parties do not need to be online or in the same place at one time; rather, parties can exchange mail and information across time and distance freely. This method reduces the need to be so aware of time zone differences and variations in the phone and mail systems of various countries. Using the Internet lessens logistical concerns because employees do not need to be in the same room or city for meetings. Companies can create and edit documents collaboratively in this asynchronous environment.

As a bonus, *synchronous communication* also is possible using Talk, MOOs (Multiuser Object-Oriented environments), and Internet Relay Chat (IRC). Online real-time meetings are both possible and commonplace—individuals in Ulan Bator, Singapore, and Old Dimebox, Texas can be online simultaneously. You can hold meetings with people you have never met face-to-face or create *ad hoc* groups of colleagues for working at a distance.

Listserver or group computer-conferencing software is another tool that can improve internal and external communications by helping to overcome logistical concerns. These services can help keep all members of a work unit up to date and involved no matter where or when they log in.

Although you can link telephone conversations in a conference call, this procedure is rare because it requires a great deal of preplanning, scheduling, and dealing with the politics of deciding who to include. With discussions on the Internet, you can read or post messages any time, and new people can join in, depending on their knowledge and interest.

Telecommuting is increasingly common, and some corporations have employees in far-removed places who never physically come to work. Companies can form and maintain work teams online when employees are working at a distance, either as their normal mode or when they are temporarily out of town.

In some cases, the Internet has helped to create virtual companies—the employees live and work at a distance using electronic means for keeping in touch. Employees may meet face-to-face only occasionally or may never come to a common physical place.

Competitive Advantage

The ability to have the latest information about your marketplace and an awareness of the state-of-the-art in your industry allows you to keep your competitive edge. Learning what other companies are doing, knowing the kinds of information available, and discovering new markets can assist a company in maintaining a competitive advantage. Businesses enhance these efforts by being connected to and active on the Internet.

The Internet is a two-way knowledge conduit (compared to the one-way knowledge conduit of video or paper-based publications). The exchange of public information (as opposed to proprietary information) is crucial for meeting the needs of customers, business partners, and collaborators, as well as the general public. You can join existing conversations in the form of discussion lists—experts estimate that more than 8,000 of these lists exist. Some lists focus on marketing, accounting, public relations, the use of high-technology processes and materials, and TQM (total quality management). You can form your own list by using one of the various list management software packages such as Listserver or Listprocessor. Businesses also are starting their own discussions using just the distribution capability of their e-mail accounts.

Many companies use the Internet to search for successful practices of corporate and product improvement. In some cases, this search is overtly part of a TQM plan, or it may simply be a way of finding new solutions to problems. An awareness of the current state of affairs in any industry can give a company a competitive advantage; access to information about products, new ideas, and the current status quo is invaluable.

Information Resources

The name of the game on the Internet is information. In the movie *The Graduate*, the young man was told that the secret of future success was plastics. Today the secret of success is information, and the Internet is the largest storehouse of up-to-date information in the world. Much of that information is free or available at very little cost.

Corporations need up-to-date information of all kinds, and many businesses rely on state-of-the-art scientific and governmental information for their operations. This information abounds on the Internet in sites all over the world.

Access to information through the Internet is staggering. With over 5.5 million machines connected, the system has a multitude of databases, Web sites, Gopher sites, FTP (File Transfer Protocol) sites, and Usenet and Listserv discussion lists. So much material is available that managing the information has become a task itself. Parts III and IV of this book describe the tools needed to access this information, address e-mail, use discussion groups and lists, use Usenet, and have live conversations. Part V covers WWW, FTP, Telnet, Gopher, Veronica, and Archie.

Electronic newsletters, documents, programs, searchable databases, and online experts are available in large numbers. Some users have called this abundance *information overload*; others have compared using the Internet to drinking from a firehose.

But specifically, what kinds of information are available? The following list gives you just a taste of the thousands of resources available:

- **Agricultural Market News:** Commodity reports. Access with WAIS at `agricultural-market-news.src`.

- **Asia Pacific Networking Group:** They gather, organize, and disseminate a broad range of Asia Pacific information. URL: `http://dorae.kaist.ac.kr/`.

- **Catalog of Electronic Texts (Alex):** Access to online books and other documents: `http://www.lib.ncsu.edu/stacks/alex-index.html`.

- **Census Data at the Census Bureau:** The United States Census Bureau home page: `http://www.census.gov/`.

- **Centre for Labour Studies:** Australian labor research data, labor briefings, international labor data from the University of Adelaide, Australia. Gopher to `jarrah.itd.adelaide.edu.au`.

- **CIA World Fact Book:** Demographic, geographic, social, and monetary information. Telnet to `info.rutgers.edu` and choose `library`, then choose `reference`. Or FTP to `nic.funet.fi` and look in the `/pub/doc/World_facts` subdirectory. A searchable set of the fact books is available at `http://reenic.utexas.edu/reenic/Internet/Ref/ciafbks.html`.

- **Dow Jones News Retrieval:** Investment, economic, and business related articles in abstract and full-text form. Telnet to `djnr.dowjones.com` (this service has a fee).

- **ECIX (the Environmental Exchange Archive):** FTP to `igc.org`, log in as anonymous, and look in the `/pub/ECIX` or `/pub/ECIXfiles` directories.

- **Geography Server:** Information on population, latitude, longitude, and elevation. Telnet to `martini.eecs.umich.edu 3000` and type **help** for assistance.

- **Global Land Information System:** Information on land use maps. Telnet to `glis.cr.usgs.gov` and log in as `guest`.

- **Internet Business Pages:** FTP to `ftp.msen.com` or e-mail to `ibp-info@msen.com` with the subject *send description*. Also available through Gopher: `gopher://gopher.msen.com/11/ibp`.

- **Israeli R&D Archive:** Information on R&D projects, information on high-technology incubator projects. Telnet to `vms.huji.ac.il` and log in as `mop`.

- **LEXIS:** Database of more than 1,000 legal databases and court decisions. Telnet to `lexis.meaddata.com` (this service has fee).

- **Library of Congress Information Center:** Information locator service. Telnet to `locis.loc.gov` and log in as `marvel`, or use a WWW browser to access the LOC at `http://www.loc.gov/`.

- **National Center for Biotechnology Information:** Enzyme and protein site dictionary, DNA sequence analysis, Swiss protein sequence databank. FTP to `ncbi.nlm.nih.gov` or e-mail to `repository@ncbi.nlm.nih.gov`.

- **National Online Media Association:** Trade association and lobbying information regarding online media. Subscribe to the `natbbs` mailing list by sending e-mail to `natbbs-request@echonyc.com`.

- **Patent Titles by E-mail:** Weekly mailings of all patents issued and ordering information on specific patents can be obtained using e-mail from `patents-request@world.std.com`.

- **Research Results Database:** Summaries of agricultural and economic research. Access with WAIS at `usda-rrdb.src`.

- **Science and Technology Information System:** National Science Foundation information, grant material, and databases. Telnet to `stis.nsf.gov` and log in as `public`, or use Gopher for access: `gopher://x.nsf.gov:70/11/STISINFO`.

- **Smithsonian Image Archives:** Archive of binary images. URL is `http://sunsite.unc.edu/pub/multimedia/pictures/smithsonian`.

- **Software archives:** For IBM compatible software, FTP to `oak.oakland.edu` and log in as anonymous. For Macintosh software, FTP to `sumex-aim.stanford.edu` in the `/info-mac` subdirectory.

- **U.S. Federal Budget, Singapore's IT2000 Plan for Information Technology, and general business and economic information:** All available by Gopher to `cwis.usc.edu`.

- **Washington and Lee Law Library:** Extensive access to Internet tools, law libraries, and documents. Telnet to `liberty.uc.wlu.edu`, log in as `lawlib`, and use `lawlib` as the password; or FTP to `liberty.uc.wlu.edu`, log in as anonymous, and locate the `/pub/lawlib` directory. Alternatively, you can use a WWW browser to access W&L at `http://honor.uc.wlu.edu:1020/`.

Customer Feedback and Support

Among the top Internet uses by businesses is in the domain of customer support. Customers can reach companies at any time of the day or night using e-mail and can obtain information by way of Gopher, WWW, FTP, conferences, and e-mail.

Many companies maintain World Wide Web sites, , Gophers, and FTP sites for customer use during working and nonworking hours. These services enable customers to receive assistance, get product information, and leave questions for replies during working hours. Some companies offer information files on Frequently Asked Questions (FAQs) for customers and potential customers.

Customers of some companies find that they can place orders online and even receive products online (when the product is software or information), particularly through interactive Web sites.

The value of genuine customer and public feedback cannot be overstated. In these days of a highly competitive marketplace, valid information about changing and improving your product can make the difference between success and failure. The use of the Internet facilitates a close relationship with the customer.

Many companies, especially in the computer industry, maintain help forums on commercial services such as America Online and CompuServe. Some companies also provide technical support online, as well as opportunities for customer surveys and feedback through Web sites and e-mail.

Because of the Internet protocols, the Internet provides opportunities to exchange information in both ASCII and binary form. You can quickly send and receive executable programs, e-mail, word processor files, databases, spreadsheets, graphics, even sound and animated pictures. The network can send the equivalent of a 20-volume set of encyclopedias literally in seconds. This rapid exchange benefits corporate communication and correspondence with customers and vendors alike.

Marketing and Sales

By creating a corporate presence on the Internet or the Web, businesses can participate in online marketing. Although advertising *per se* is a bit problematic on the Internet, companies can use the network for marketing services and products. Companies can establish this presence on the Internet by way of such tools as Usenet, Gopher, FTP, Telnet, and e-mail. The singlemost popular tool is a Web site, which lets users reach out and touch the company.

By observing Internet activities and participating in discussions, companies can create a sharper marketing focus for themselves. Businesses can carry out marketing research online. And, as mentioned earlier, companies can create and support actual sales distribution channels.

Collaboration and Development

The formation of partnerships among companies is increasingly common, and the Internet facilitates this collaboration for product design, vendor channels, research, and development.

Many companies are in the position of having to comply with government rules, regulations, executive orders, or laws, which can be confusing. The Internet facilitates compliance with government guidelines and policies; many companies participate in Gophers, Web sites, and FTP sites in an effort to maintain their compliance levels. These services may be maintained by companies, organizations, government units, educational institutions, or more likely, collaborative arrangements.

Businesses using the Internet can build internal and external links to create a virtual community. Using e-mail and distribution lists, individuals engage in wide-ranging discourses on business and industry even among competing organizations. Genuine exchanges focused on improving the industry as a whole are becoming more common.

In times past, companies tended to either maintain separate corporate projects or acquire a product or company to enlarge a product line or create a new division. With the advent of new managerial styles, bottom-up product development, and the creation of lateral work teams, the Internet facilitates new ways of doing business and maintaining communication.

Collaborative approaches have been greatly enhanced by the Internet with its wealth of information, its capability of supporting telecommuting and time-shifted communication, and its success in linking far-flung enterprises rather seamlessly. In addition, such collaboration adds to the creative atmosphere needed to compete in the marketplace.

Vendor Support and Networking

The Internet provides a fast method for networking with vendors and suppliers, increasing speed and variety in your procurement process. With its global tentacles, the Internet can help businesses locate new suppliers and keep in better touch with them. If you are using a software company in Moscow, milling machines from Germany, and suppliers from Spain, the Internet can help you keep in touch and maintain supply schedules. In addition, small suppliers can network with and compete with larger, more well-known suppliers.

The Internet assists companies in maintaining zero inventory systems because of the speed of communications. Telephone systems world-wide vary in quality and availability but Internet connections tend to be reliable.

Understanding Network Culture

Internet users have some expectations and ways of doing business on the system. If you understand them at the beginning, these methods can make doing business on the Internet easier and more comprehensible.

Internet Ethics

The Internet community values individualism, free access to information, mutual support, the exchange of ideas, and the idea that the network is valuable and must be protected. People usually speak for themselves, rather than from stations of rank, title, or status. This conduct makes the network a rich environment for the exchange of ideas. Because of the value of this diversity, you can find material and ideas that may stretch or challenge your own ideas.

Networkers protect the free-flow of ideas and often offer their ideas and expect genuine participation from you. A substantial portion of the information available on the Internet is compiled voluntarily and offered with no expectation of monetary reward, but with the expectation of similar contributions by others.

Implications for Corporate Culture

This virtual culture has its own values, social structure, shared history, and metaphors. The Internet is a global culture with some distinct characteristics; time, place, national origin, status, and even personality are redefined because these signs are not as obvious in a digital message as they are in face-to-face communication. In the now classic New Yorker cartoon, a dog is typing at a computer while talking to another dog next to him. He says, "On the Internet, nobody knows you're a dog."

The power of the Internet is changing some very traditional corporations: employees of all formal titles and ranks talk freely about the business, share ideas, and offer suggestions. E-mail can change the face of a corporation. In a business or industry, computer-mediated communications can change structural, social, and hierarchical barriers and norms, and affect standard operating procedures. The Internet also affects the corporate culture, or organizational norms. As lines of formal communication are modified, sometimes lines of authority are modified as well.

Employees above and below on the organizational chart may be reading Internet discussions; make sure that what you say is for public consumption—you never know who is listening. Be aware that other people from your company and industry may be participating in the same discussions. Also, because many Internet discussion systems archive the messages, other users may read your postings a year or more later.

Face-to-face meetings and decision-making situations differ in numerous ways from their online counterparts. People who often dominate meetings and conversations because of rank or personal style may be no more visible online than people who are less likely to contribute in a face-to-face meeting. The primary contributing member of a group may be quite different when he or she uses e-mail or group computer conferencing. Systems that change these organizational hierarchies may prove very productive, especially when the users are working on mutual goals and objectives.

Getting Your Business on the Internet

Creating a business presence on the Internet offers many advantages: communications, logistics, information, customer support, gaining competitive advantages, and opportunities for marketing and collaboration.

Marketing Your Products and Services

40

by Jill H. Ellsworth

The use of the Internet as an entrepreneurial tool is increasing. It is an audience-participation sport, in which two-way communication is the valued norm. The Internet is the home of lawyers, doctors, Native American chiefs, production planners, academics, corporate mail-room clerks, and CEOs.

Unlike the passive, consumer-oriented model—the model of top-down delivery to consumers—the Internet encourages interaction. It encourages consumers to be information providers as well, particularly through Web pages. This is a grassroots approach to marketing, coming proactively from the bottom up.

The Internet is breaking down some distinctions of large versus small business, rural versus urban, and local versus global, and it allows for market visibility.

Marketing using the Internet is innovative, interesting, and lively. There are no mass markets of undifferentiated people on the Internet, only communities of people and individuals brought together by common interests. You reach people one by one and group by group, which for most businesses is quite unusual. The distinction between reactive marketing and invasive advertising is critical. This virtual community is information, subject, and interactively oriented, as opposed to most advertising, which is image and sound oriented, relatively content free, and outwardly directed (even on the Web). The Web is an active medium as opposed to traditional advertising, which is targeted at a passive consumer.

For penetrating new markets, getting the data to the user's machine, and getting product information out, the Internet has valuable functions.

Marketing versus Advertising

Currently, advertising has an in-your-face attitude. Consumers are bombarded with images and sound designed to get them to buy the product. Very little (some would say no) advertising is rich in content. Indeed, it is the very content-free, intrusive nature of advertising that gets in the way on the Internet. The Internet values information—the line between information provider and consumer on the nets is blurry. Hucksterism is usually met by a barrage of *flaming*: pointed, irritated, negative messages demanding that the advertiser cease and desist.

Net culture currently prohibits, in a general way, unsolicited advertisements but permits information-rich, value-added approaches to marketing, such as the kind found on Web pages. Even in light of the multimedia nature of the Web, Net marketing is information intensive at its best. Good Internet marketing concentrates on providing valuable information and services as part of its efforts to sell products and services.

As viewed on the Internet, *advertising* is intrusive and content free; *marketing*, on the other hand, is active, runs on discourse, and provides something of value. To be successful in this medium, businesses must be seen to be contributing to the Net, or as some call it, "giving back to the Net." The customs of the Internet require this giving back to the network.

The key to living comfortably with your neighbors on the Net is to observe the rule that sending solicited information is fine, but sending unsolicited information is not. Web pages in particular are a way of providing solicited information. Businesses for the most part have to change their normal ways of doing business—they have to make a paradigm change.

The presentation of opportunities for information exchange and interaction is the key to creating a successful business presence on the Internet. Yellow pages, billboard, and virtual storefront all offer many possibilities, including those listed here:

- **Yellow Pages**

    World Wide Web
    FTP archives
    Gopher server
    BBS
    Usenet news
    WAIS
    E-mail

- **Billboard**

    `.plan`, `plan.txt`, `.profile` files
    Signature blocks
    E-mail
    Greeting cards

- **Virtual Storefront**

    Combines some of the activities from both the yellow-page approach and billboard approach but goes further: it includes the capability to deliver actual products and take orders, probably best demonstrated by World Wide Web pages.

If You Build It, They Will Come (Maybe)

Creating an Internet information service to market your products and services can take many forms. Many current business marketing activities can be adapted to Internet methods. For example, it is popular these days to include a "bingo card" in magazines for various companies to provide information and literature. The potential customer circles the numbers, mails the card, and six to eight weeks later, receives the information. By using data entry forms on a Web page or a Gopher server, that same customer can receive the information with e-mail in seconds, while their interest is still high.

Here are some of the kinds of marketing items that can successfully be translated into Internet activities:

- Product flyers or introductory information
- Product announcements
- Product specifications sheets
- Pricing information
- Catalogs
- Events and demos
- Free software
- Customer support
- Company contacts
- Promotional notices of specials and sales
- Documentation and manuals
- Multimedia descriptions
- Market or customer surveys and needs assessments
- Product performance data
- Service evaluations
- Reviews and product commentary
- Customer service information and functions
- Job placement or recruitment notices
- Dialogs with customers and others

These kinds of activities and others are easily carried out in nonintrusive ways on the Internet.

Creating an Information Service

There are numerous vehicles for offering information and services in the Internet environment, such as these:

- World Wide Web sites
- Gopher sites
- Anonymous FTP sites including banners and document archives
- `.plan/plan.txt/profile` fingerable files
- Eye-catching signatures
- Bulletin board services (BBSes)

- Usenet newsgroups
- Listservers and conferences
- Newsletters, newspapers, and 'zines
- E-mail, including fax and Telex
- Greeting cards
- WAIS

World Wide Web

The World Wide Web (WWW) is still a relatively new resource for the Internet. It is based on a technology called *hypertext* and the Internet protocol, HyperText Transfer Protocol (HTTP).

Web sites are the fastest growing place for doing business on the Internet. They provide a mulitmedia approach to information that emulates many of the features of advertising in traditional media.

Many businesses are creating their documents using the HyperText Markup Language (HTML) so that WWW searches can reach and use their documents. Others are contracting for HTML writing services, or using the services of a provider.

To provide information using WWW, you must create a link between an existing document and a resource on your system, or resources existing anywhere on the Web.

Businesses can host their own server, rent Web space on the server of a Web services provider, or lease space as a virtual storefront in a cybermall or kiosk.

GUI Web browsers like Mosaic and Netscape use this system, as does the text-based browser, Lynx. For more information, see Chapter 28, "Navigating the World Wide Web," Chapter 36, "Creating Web Pages with HTML," and Chapter 37, "Setting Up a World Wide Web Server."

The following are some excellent resources for getting a sense of marketing on the Internet and Web:

- Thomas Ho's Commerce page

```
http://www.engr.iupui.edu/~ho/interests/commmenu.html
```

- Yahoo's Business Resources

```
http://www.yahoo.com/Economy/Business/miscellaneous/
```

- EINet Galaxy Business and Commerce

  ```
  http://www.einet.net/galaxy/Business-and-Commerce.html
  ```

- Washington and Lee—Commerce, Business, and Accounting

  ```
  http://honor.uc.wlu.edu:1020/%20%20%23hf/cl
  ```

- CommerceNet

  ```
  http://www.commerce.net
  ```

- Commercial Sites Index

  ```
  http://www.directory.net/
  ```

- The BBC

  ```
  http://www.bbcnc.org.uk/index.html
  ```

- Apollo Advertising

  ```
  http://apollo.co.uk/
  ```

- BizWeb

  ```
  http://www.bizweb.com/
  ```

Using Gophers

A Gopher, in this case, is not a small, furry rodent. As described in Chapter 25, "Using and Finding Gophers," a Gopher is a menu-driven lookup tool that enables you to "burrow" through the Internet and select documents and resources for retrieval or printing. If you locate something interesting on one of the menus, you can read it, print it, or have it mailed back to your e-mail box. You can browse documents, images, and (if your Gopher client and machine permit it) sound clips.

You can access Gopher through Telnet or by using your own Gopher client. Many businesses are setting up their own Gophers on their local machines, which are accessible by all the other Gophers in the world. They set up the "pointers" for information access. This can provide access to virtually all the resources mentioned previously: product information and pricing, new product announcements, newsletters, free software, demonstrations, and so forth. Many sites provide full text of important documents, order forms, and so forth. A sample Gopher root menu is shown here:

```
Root gopher server: gopher.fonorola.net
 —>  1.  Home of The Gopher (UofMN)/
      2.  All the Gopher Servers in the Gopher Space/
      3.  A COOL Gopher to try!!!.../
      4.  Canadian Domain/
      5.  Internet Business Journal/
      6.  Internet Registration Templates/
      7.  Phone Books/
      8.  Search WAIS Databases.
      9.  Training Now - For Tomorrow/
     10.  USENET News/
     11.  Veronica and Jughead/
     12.  fONOROLA's NIC Public Directory/
     13.  fONOROLA's Software Archive/
     14.  in.coming/
     15.  martin95/
     16.  newsform.
     17.  published/
```

This example shows you the root Gopher server, with information on other Gophers, Canadian business information, the *Internet Business Journal*, Usenet access, and fONOROLA's software archive. If you see an item on a Gopher menu you don't understand, such as martin95/ in this example, just type the number and press Enter to explore that item.

The following menu shows the next menu under the root, where I investigated the *Internet Business Journal* (item number 5 on the preceding menu). You are provided options for articles, a contest, directories, and other publications.

```
 —>  1.  Adbuster Article.
      2.  Contest (win 500.00).
      3.  Directory of Internet Trainers and Consultants.
      4.  How to Advertise on the Internet/
      5.  Index to Volume One/
      6.  Internet Advertising FAQ/
      7.  Internet Advertising Review/
```

```
 8.  Internet_and_Business_Course.
 9.  Sample Issues/
10.  Strangelove's Essays/
11.  Subscription Information
```

Next, I explored the Sample Issues of the *Internet Business Journal* and discovered that I could get the full text of a back issue. I e-mailed it to myself, and in just seconds, I was browsing the newsletter.

Examine what one company has done here with the following Gopher:

```
—>1.  Full_Text_[1866-lines].
   2.  Table_of_Contents.
   3.  Advertising_on_the_Internet.
   4.  The_Newspaper_of_the_Future.
   5.  Industry_Profile.
   6.  Satellite-Delivered_Usenet_Newsfeed.
   7.  The_Essential_Internet.
   8.  The_Merger.
   9.  Resources_for_Business.
  10.  Government_Online.
  11.  How_to_Use_the_Internet.
  12.  Internet_Publishing_News.
  13.  Software_on_the_Net.
  14.  Internet_Access_News.
```

This company provides a Gopher that presents information on business journals and advertising, the full text of back issues of a related e-journal, access to all the Gophers in the world for further searching, access to Mac servers, Usenet news, access to Veronica and to WAIS, access to information on the Canadian economy, and last but by no means least, information on the company itself. This company has followed some of the guidelines for marketing on the Internet, including providing information-rich resources, and free information and services. In addition, the company has been able to nonintrusively market its products.

Gopherspace (that is, the world-wide collection of files available to Gopher servers) is searchable using a program called Veronica. Veronica can search through Gopherspace for single words or use more complex Boolean searches for combinations of words. This means that your business information can be found through Gophers world wide. Notice that the sample Gopher menu listed earlier in this section allows the use of Veronica (as option 11 on the menu). More information on Veronica can be found in Chapter 26, "Searching Gopherspace with Veronica."

Setting up Gophers is not difficult. More information on setting up your own Gopher can be found in Chapter 35, "Creating Your Own Gopher."

Using Anonymous FTP To Distribute Information

As outlined in Chapter 22, "FTP: Fetching Files from Everywhere," the Internet File Transfer Protocol (FTP) enables you to fetch documents and programs from publicly accessible sites, called *anonymous FTP sites*. Increasingly, companies are setting up archives of information such as product descriptions, news releases, price lists, and promotional events and information, as well as demos and executable programs.

Generally, to use FTP, you invoke the FTP program; at the prompt, you enter the address of the remote machine. When you reach it, remember to type **user anonymous** and use your e-mail address as the password.

You can FTP to a site, look around a bit in various directories, and then download files (text and binary) and software programs and demos (binary) to your local machine. Many companies even put up a "banner" so that when you log in, you get an advertisement along with information about the archive. This is what a directory listing might look like:

```
>dir
<Opening ASCII mode data connection for /bin/ls.
total 392
-rw-r-r-     1 root     daemon    145157 May 28  1992 .find.codes
drwx---      2 114      daemon       512 Mar 15 23:45 .obs
drwxrwsr-x   9 1862     803         1024 Dec 28 15:47 AW
drwxrwsr-x   7 2391     2391         512 Dec 21 08:04 Kluwer
drwxrwxr-x   3 src      src          512 Mar 15 02:07 OBS
drwxr-xr-x   5 1650     1650         512 Feb 25  1993 Quantum
drwxrwxr-x   2 112      daemon       512 Dec  6 22:08 RAT-archive
-rw-rw-r-    1 root     src         1739 Apr 21 16:46 README
drwxrwsr-x   2 1965     1965         512 Dec  3 14:36 Softpro
drwxrwxr-x   7 103      10           512 Aug 14 23:27 amo
drwxrwxr-x   3 108      10           512 Oct 18 23:15 archives
lrwxrwxrwx   1 root     daemon         7 May  1 20:43 bcs- >amo
dr-xr-xr-x   2 root     daemon       512 Nov 10  1992 bin
lrwxrwxrwx   1 108      10             8 May 11 04:42 bmug ->
drwxrwxr-x   4 103      10           512 Nov  1 22:30 consultants
drwxrwxr-x   2 root     10           512 Jun 24 19:48 dist
drwxr-xr-x   6 4115     daemon       512 Dec 22 20:29 epimbe
dr-xr-xr-x   3 root     daemon       512 Nov 10  1992 etc
lrwxrwxrwx   1 root     daemon         1 Mar  9  1993 ftp -> .
drwxrwxr-x   2 root     src          512 Nov 10  1992 info-future
drwxr-xr-x   2 root     0           8192 Jul 27  1992 lost+found
drwxrwxr-x 201 obi      src         4608 Jan  3 22:01 obi
drwxrwxr-x   5 root     daemon       512 Dec 22 19:00 periodicals
drwxrwx-x    2 root     10           512 Nov 16 01:24 private
drwxrwxrwt 124 root     0           4096 Jan  4 15:10 pub
lrwxrwxrwx   1 root     daemon         7 Oct  6 17:38 softpro ->
drwxrwxr-x  69 root     src         1536 Sep 29 21:55 src
drwxrwxr-x   7 ftp      ftp          512 Dec 21 19:31 vendors
drwxr-xr-x   2 root     ftp          512 Nov 16 18:18 world-info
<Transfer complete.
```

Although you can't see it in this listing, this FTP site has a banner, telling you how to sign up for a new account on `world.std.com` and showing you where to FTP information from the `world-info` subdirectory. The contents of the `world-info` subdirectory, where you can get information on corporate mailboxes, a description of services, hints for using the service, and a primer for new users, look like this:

```
-rw-rw-r-  1 ftp      daemon     5726 Aug 31 19:27 corporate-mailbox
-rw-rw-r-  1 root     daemon    12546 Nov 19 04:26 description
-rw-rw-r-  1 root     daemon    37355 Nov 16 18:17 hints
-rw-r-r-   1 root     daemon    62580 Nov 16 18:17 primer
<Transfer complete.
```

FTP sites are searchable using an Internet tool called Archie. Archie can search for file titles throughout the world. This means that your information can be discovered by individuals next door or a continent away. The individuals then can FTP to your site and pick up the information at any time. More information on FTP can be found in Chapter 24, "Archie: An Archive of Archives."

Remember that at most FTP sites, the filenames and directory names are case sensitive: for example, `Information` is different than `information`. Using FTP is a bit arcane. To set up your own anonymous FTP site, you should work with your user-support services, or perhaps a commercial company that provides services. FTP is a powerful, information-rich tool, accessible through the usual FTP methods, but also through e-mail using BITftp or FTPMail for those who only have e-mail access to the Internet.

Using .plan, plan.txt, or profile with Finger

Many machines enable you to use an Internet utility called `finger`. This command enables you to gain information about institutions and users. The general `finger` utility tells you basic information about an individual, such as his or her login name, last login, and whether he or she has mail waiting—provided that you know which machine to query. For example, `finger marybrown@toaster.world.com` hunts for a user named Mary Brown at the machine named `toaster` at the World Company.

Many individuals create what is called a `.plan` or `plan.txt` file that replies with more than the basic information directly to the screen. In some cases, the file is quite large, containing a great deal of information. Different operating systems, such as UNIX, VMS, and others, use different names for these files.

A sample `.plan` file looks like this:

```
-User          -Full Name
mbrown         Mary Jane Brown              Log in Fri 6-May
10:01 AM from netnet.com

Plan:
*****  Brown Internet Consulting Services  ***
***A Subsidiary of World Corporate Training and Development***
Are you interested in gaining greater facility with the tools
of the Internet? Our firm, BICS, can help you. We are offering
workshops for corporate Internet users on the following
schedule:

Minneapolis         May 10-11
Dallas              June 14-15
Lansing             July 1-2

Cost: $500.00, group rates available.

Call 555/555-5555 for more information or e-mail me at
mbrown@toaster.world.com, FAX 555/555-5555
```

Another `.plan` file can have a list of specials or prices such as this:

```
XX COMPUTER COMPANY
10 Maple Tree Court
Oakville, TX  12345
Voice: (555) 555-5555   (days, nights or weekends)
FAX:   (555) 555-5555
jones@xx.com

(We now have a monthly e-mailing list that you
can request to receive.)
-------------------------------
*NOTE: Some prices are negotiable and can fluctuate based on
market prices, so e-mail for a custom quote. Ask about any items
that you don't see listed*

*********************** SPECIALS ***************************
486 CPU Heat Sink Fans                         Only $ 15!
2M VESA Local Bus 24-bit SVGA Video Card       Only $105!
Sound Galaxy BXII (100% SoundBlaster Compatible)  Only $ 45!
Seagate 3390A FASTEST 850M DRIVE               Only $425!
Western Digital 340M IDE Hard Drive, 3-yr warranty Only $199!
```

Attention is usually drawn to the file brought back by `finger` by a statement in the signature block of messages, or sometimes on distributed texts and information, or even in announcements of services. Some UNIX machines even allow for animated `finger` files to be returned. Almost anything can go into a `finger` file because, by its very nature, it is a solicited communication.

You should discuss the use of these kinds of files and the use of the `finger` utility with your system user services personnel because they may have policies regarding their use.

Signatures

Signature blocks, or .sigs (pronounced *dot sigs*), are short attachments to e-mail and Usenet messages. Usually attached at the bottom of messages and postings, they should run six or fewer lines because some mailers truncate these lines at the bottom of files. The signature blocks are designed to identify the sender with a name, an e-mail address, a home page URL, and perhaps telephone numbers. Sometimes they contain witty sayings or small ASCII graphics. It is here that people put something such as "finger `marybrown@toaster.world.com` for more information about our corporate training workshops," or "retrieve the file `:training.txt` from our FTP site at `toaster.world.com`." Some .sigs now have embedded small corporate logos as well.

Here are some examples of signature files with business-related information:

```
Mark James <mjames@cow.dec.com>                    (__)
Dairy Enzyme Corporation                           (oo)
Research Circle                        / ——————\/
Midwest, MI                           /   ¦       ¦¦
http://cow.dec.com/cow.html        *    ¦¦———¦¦
Drink more milk!............             ^^       ^^
Contact me about our new milk irradiation products!
```

Or:

```
****************************************   Buck Hardy
*    LOOKING FOR A HOMEPAGE CREATOR ?  *   GBSI International
*      I've got lots of experience.    *   555/555-555
* Finger Bucky@handy.gbsi.com to see   *   Operations
* my resume, or e-mail me for a copy.  *   St. Paul, In
http://www.xxx.com/hardyhome.html
****************************************
```

Or:

```
-----------------------------------
Harrison Grandstaff  HGH Communications     HG@whippet.hgh.com
Business Phone: 555-555-5555                 http://whippet.hgh.com/hgh.html
Are you looking for Internet Business Consulting?
We can provide a wide range of services including Web Pages
Send an e-mail message for information to info@whippet.hgh.com
-----------------------------------
```

The signature blocks appear at the end of e-mail and Usenet postings as identification of the sender. Each mailer supports different methods for inserting these at the ends of messages. Some mailers allow you to set up the signature block as a file that you attach, some require that it be entered from the keyboard, and others support the use of macros with your communication software.

If you have questions about signatures, your best bet is to talk to your system support personnel or read your software documentation files for additional site-specific and mailer-specific information.

Bulletin Board Services

Many companies support computer conferencing on so-called BBSes. These allow for group conference discussion and have forums for postings. For Internet use, these BBS services are accessible by way of Telnet. Many times, these have limited guest accounts for initial browsing, but full use usually requires registration, during which you give your name, phone number, address, and e-mail address to access some kinds of information.

BBSes are very much less popular than either Gophers or Web sites, but they enable a company to have discussion forums around several of their products and services, to provide demonstrations, or to offer trial subscriptions. BBSes have largely been supplanted by Web pages.

Usenet Newsgroups

"We are able to read the Usenet news, which had resulted in several useful techniques and ideas coming to our attention that we might not otherwise have been aware of." This response from a product development specialist with a major pharmaceuticals company shows one attribute of the Usenet newsgroups—information exchange in service of product development.

> **NOTE**
>
> Usenet newsgroups are often confused with the Internet itself. The Internet is the connection, and Usenet is just one application running on the Net. It is a distributed system of message interchanges focused around topics or newsgroups.

As one person wrote recently on the Net, "I don't advertise, I post." This attitude is especially true in the Usenet newsgroups, where people exchange ideas and information rapidly. You will find numerous modest product announcements, press releases, and many signatures with business information. Also under the `.biz` category, you will find commercial groups. In Chapter 17, "Reading and Posting the News: Using Usenet," you see that Usenet is, in some ways, not owned by anyone and that each group has its own charter stating its purpose, goals, and acceptable practices. Most of the `.biz` groups explicitly allow and have commercial postings. Many businesses have their own Usenet group, devoted to their own interests. This is a sample listing of some of the `.biz` groups:

```
(unmod)   1 biz.americast
          2 biz.americast...
          3 biz.books...
( mod )   4 biz.clarinet
          5 biz.clarinet...
          6 biz.comp...
(unmod)   7 biz.config
(unmod)   8 biz.control
(unmod)   9 biz.dec
         10 biz.dec...
         11 biz.digex...
         12 biz.jobs...
(unmod)  13 biz.misc
         14 biz.next...
         15 biz.oreilly...
(unmod)  16 biz.pagesat
         17 biz.pagesat...
         18 biz.sco...
(unmod)  19 biz.stolen
         20 biz.tadpole...
(unmod)  21 biz.test
         22 biz.univel...
(unmod)  23 biz.zeos
         24 biz.zeos...
```

The `mod` and `unmod` refer to whether the group is monitored by a person. Moderated groups have a person who serves as an administrator, who in some cases screens posts for flaming and appropriateness of content. In unmoderated groups, every message is posted as it arrives, warts and all. The following two sample menu entries show two different approaches. In one case, the company is posting its announcements; in the other, it is offering samples:

```
**( mod )   1 biz.oreilly.announce
**( mod )   1 biz.americast.samples
```

Another newsgroup called `biz.books.technical` welcomes anyone to review current technical books; instructions are given for having a book reviewed. Publishers or authors who want to have their books reviewed and added to the list should have copies sent to `XXX@YYY.COM`. The notice also gives the address and procedures for publishers to have their books reviewed, and it includes a copyright notice and permission to distribute the reviews unedited.

In addition to the announcements, descriptions, price lists, and discussion found in Usenet's `.biz` groups, there are considerable opportunities to form business partnerships through the groups. Here's an example:

```
Article #1055 (1096 is last):
Newsgroups: biz.comp.hardware
From: Mikhail Rostopovich <commerce@softsoft.spb.su>
Subject: Look for business partner
Date: Thu Sept 21 01:37:23 1995

Hi BizNetters!
Really good small firm from Moscow, Russia, looks for business partners.
We want to resell in Russia good but low-cost computer parts and systems
like 486/Pentium motherboards, SIMM 4M & 8M, Sound cards, sVGA cards,
hard drives & streamers, sVGA monitors, high-speed modems, 486 and Pentium
notebooks, CDROMs, software under UNIX, OS/2 Warp, and MS Windows, MS Windows
NT, and so on. Used equipment will be good too.
At first sales volume can be $50,000 per month.
Please send us your suggestions (in terms CIF SPB).

Mikhail Rostopovich,
Softsoft Ltd. Director

rostop@softsoft.spb.su or commerce@softsoft.spb.su
Softsofts BBS 7-555-5555555 14.4 HST DS
voice 7-555-5555555 10:00-16:00 Moscow time
```

Listservs and Conferences

Listservs are very popular for distributed discussion groups, as mentioned in Chapter 16, "Joining Discussions: Using Listservs and Mailing Lists." They are a method of maintaining conversations of all kinds. Some lists are started by individuals with an interest in a subject, a product, or an industry. The number of existing lists is currently in excess of 3,000, and the lists focus on almost any topic imaginable. Many companies have begun discussions focusing on their industry as a way to invite participation regarding important issues, regulations, techniques, high technology, and so on.

Some lists are appropriate for certain products; generally, announcements are well tolerated by the natives. Use caution in posting because postings inappropriate to the subject and tone of a list cause protests. For example, the following posting may appear on a general network happenings list and on a couple of programming-oriented lists:

```
***** NEW BOOK ANNOUNCEMENT FROM FRAMUS PUBLISHERS *****

IRREVERSIBLE SYNTAX IN UNNATURAL LANGUAGE

edited by
Beamish X. Folderol, Michigan University

Table of Contents and Order Form are attached below.
```

```
More information, including Preface, can be obtained via
        anonymous ftp from universe.com in the file
              Framus/books/irreversible_syntax.ps
```

The notice included a full table of contents and—here's the hook—a handy e-mail order form. It is not unusual to offer a free chapter or section from the FTP site as well.

Participation on appropriate lists can also give a business or corporation visibility on the Net. Frequent, thoughtful postings and participation can draw attention to the activities of the business by giving information and enabling collaboration and partnerships. In addition, the use of signature files is useful on lists because each message gets distributed to all members.

Following are some interesting lists for those in business, marketing, product development, and other positions:

```
TBIRDS      TBIRDS@ARIZVM1      Discussion of International Business
            listserv.arizona.edu
BIZNET      BIZNET@ARIZVM1      NCBES Black Technical Business Net
            listserv.arizona.edu
GISBUS-L    GISBUS-L@ECUVM1     Geographic Info Systems for Business
            ecuvm.cis.ecu.edu
SIMEDU-L    SIMEDU-L@NMSUVM1    Simulation Apps in Business/Education
            nmsu.edu
AWARDS-B    AWARDS-B@OSUVM1     Commerce Business Daily - Awards
            vm1.ucc.okstate.edu
PROCUR-B    PROCUR-B@OSUVM1     Commerce Business Daily - Procure
            vm1.ucc.okstate.edu
JAPAN       JAPAN@PUCC          Japanese Business and Economics Net
            PUCC.Princeton.EDU
E-EUROPE    E-EUROPE@PUCC       Eastern Europe Business Network
            PUCC.Princeton.EDU
BUSETH-L    BUSETH-L@UBVM       Business Ethics Computer Network
            ubvm.cc.buffalo.edu
PCBR-L      PCBR-L@UHCCVM       Pacific Business Researchers Forum
            UHCCVM.UHCC.Hawaii.Edu
GLOBMKT     GLOBMKT@UKCC        Applied Global Marketing
            ukcc.uky.edu
RITIM-L     RITIM-L@URIACC      Telecommunications and Info Marketing
            URIACC.URI.EDU
IL-ADS      IL-ADS@TAUNIVM      Israel Bulletin Board for Advertising
            vm.tau.ac.il
RURALDEV    RURALDEV@KSUVM      Community and Rural Econ Development
            ksuvm.ksu.edu
ECONOMY     ECONOMY@acadvm1.uottawa.ca   Economic Probs in Less Dev Countries
CARECON     CARECON@YORKVM1     Caribbean Economy
            VM1.YorkU.CA
HEP2-L      HEP2-L@LISTSERV.AMERICAN.EDU   Marketing with Technology
MARKET-L    Market-L@nervm.nerdc.ufl.edu   For the Discussion of Marketing
Inet-Marketing  Inet-marketing@einet.net  Marketing on the Internet Discussion
            (a listproc subscription)
```

Subscriptions to these lists are generally made through the Listserv protocol, as outlined in Chapter 16. This means that, for example, you send your e-mail subscription request to listserv@uriacc.uri.edu, with no subject line and the message subscribe ritim-l *yourfirstname yourlastname*.

To effectively use these groups, choose something interesting and relevant, subscribe, and participate. After you sign up for a list, the Listserv begins e-mailing all messages posted to the list directly to you. High-traffic lists can generate 30 or more messages a day; low-traffic lists can generate fewer than one message every week or so. Subscribing to several high-volume lists could result in your finding 200 messages in your e-mailbox every time you log in! Try a couple of lists before signing up for more to be sure that the number of pieces of e-mail does not exceed the time you have available to read and process them. I have found that the best way to participate is to sign up and read the messages for a few days before jumping in. This method enables you to get a feel for the list and gradually become a contributing member. Remember, many lists prohibit advertising, so this is a good situation in which to use a small, low-key signature, or to perhaps offer information by e-mail on a product under discussion.

Some usage conventions and netiquette (Net etiquette) are observed on the lists. Knowing some of the conventions can make the newcomer less obvious and make requests for help more productive. One of the most important tips is to pause and think before sending. This facile medium can encourage quick, off-the-cuff responses you may regret both for their immediate effect and for their effect as the list archives are read and reread many months or years in the future. When posting to a list, remember that many lists have memberships of more than 1,000 people in many professions and at many levels. Think about what and how something is said and about how the posting may be interpreted when received by others who aren't aware of the context. To paraphrase Congreve, *reply in haste, repent at leisure*.

Each person develops a personal communication style, or online persona. Some individuals, as in face-to-face interaction and conversation, are more or less outgoing than others. Some users develop a different Net personality. It is important to remember that what the .sig says may or may not represent the whole truth and nothing but the truth. Frequently, the lists become levelers, offering a way for all kinds of people to engage in discussion without titles, without knowledge of gender or handicaps, and where status issues and degrees can be less obvious or important.

Some companies have started their own discussion lists, particularly focused on their own products. An example is SMS—SNUG@uncvm1.oit.unc.edu—Shared Medical Systems National User Group conference. This conference is designed to foster communication centering the business, technical, and operational uses of the SMS Inc. products.

Some short-term lists feature dialog with well-known experts, Net personalities, or high-ranking government or corporate officers. These lists provide a way for interested parties to mix with prominent people. Many companies from the traditional print media provide these opportunities with columnists, editors, and guests.

More about e-mailing and lists can be found in Part IV of this book, "Communicating with Others."

Newsletters, Newspapers, and 'zines

There are several ways in which companies use the publication of newsletters and newspapers. In some cases, businesses have started their own electronic newsletters for customers and interested others. The newsletters are overtly designed to be about their products and items of interest to their customers. Newsletters are easily distributed by e-mail, Gopher, Listservs, the World Wide Web, and FTP.

Newsletters can contain information of a general or product-oriented nature. Most newsletters are distributed on request through e-mail or Listservs designed for the purpose. Others can be fetched through Gopher, WWW, and FTP. Some come in both electronic and paper editions to meet the needs of a wider range of individuals.

In some cases, companies turn their catalogs into newsletters or 'zines. They take listings of products, descriptions, and prices and add much more content and news. They add articles, profiles, or short news clippings that are of interest. In some cases, they profile some of the people involved in the creation of the product or service.

A *'zine* is a small, creative, even experimental magazine. Some companies have created 'zines to pique interest and attract attention. The 'zines are more *avant garde* than newsletters and newspapers. These often appeal to the younger residents of the Net.

Some newsletters are underwritten by various commercial ventures and are similar to newspapers because they include ads for services and products. For example, one free electronic newsletter about the Macintosh has a blurb something like this at the top of each issue:

```
This issue of ZZZZ is sponsored in part by:
ABCD Technologies - 555/555-5555  77777.77@compuserve.com
Makers of hard drives, tape drives, memory, and
accessories. For ABCD price lists, e-mail:
abcd-prices@zzzz.com
```

The blurb is an advertisement to be sure, but subscribers are free to ignore it or to request the information mentioned.

The Library of Congress is issuing International Standard Serial Numbers (ISSN) to electronic publications that intend to be regular serial publications. You can get information on this from the Library of Congress Information System (LOCIS) by Telnet to `locis.loc.gov`; log in as `marvel`. LOCIS has information on copyrights as well.

E-mail, Fax, and Telex

In addition to being the ubiquitous communication tool of the Internet, e-mail provides a quick and easy method for working with potential customers. Also, some commercial services do not provide Telnet or FTP services, so these customers are reachable only through e-mail. In a `plan` file or signature, you can always identify yourself with your e-mail address.

Many mail programs also enable you to set up automatic replies. The replies are sent out directly by the software to any e-mail sent to a particular box. These reply mailboxes often have `-request` or `-info` somewhere in the user name, such as `global-info` as seen in the next example. These mailboxes can be used in a signature, in a `plan` file, or at the end of an announcement or flyer:

```
=+=+=+=+=+=+=+=+=+=+=+=+=+=+=+=+=+=+=+=+=+=+=+=+=+==+=+
¦  The Global Translators                            ¦
¦  We will translate among German, French,           ¦
¦  and English for your business communication needs.¦
¦  0000 Randolph,  Randoph, MI xxxxx-xxxx            ¦
=+=+=+=+=+=+=+=+=+=+=+=+=+=+=+=+=+=+=+=+=+=+=+=+=+=
¦  For information, E-Mail: global-info@reynard.com  ¦
=+=+=+=+=+=+=+=+=+=+=+=+=+=+=+=+=+=+=+=+=+=+=+=+=+=
```

This type of mailbox is normally configured to grab the e-mail address of the person asking for information and directly reply with an information sheet on the services Global Translators offers. It can also be configured to save the e-mail message in a file to develop a prospects list.

Many mailers can be configured to accept a distribution list so that they can create Listserv-like mailing systems. Of course, e-mail requests can be handled like any other e-mail by a person—one piece at a time. This is often the case with customer support functions for which there is a mailbox for customer feedback or questions handled by various individuals in the company. It is not unusual to see a customer-relations-representatives contact list like the following one in customer literature, both electronic and paper based:

```
***Our Customer Relations Staff Representatives***

REP           PRODUCT              E-MAIL

Mary Smith, all xyz products     msith@oberon.com
Fred Jones, abc and def products fjones@oberon.com
Jack Smith, all plockta products jsmith@oberon.com
Ann Blue,   xyz technical support ablue@oberon.com

Any of us can be contacted on our Web site:
http://www.oberon.com/top1.html
```

Increasingly, it is common to include Web page URLs and e-mail addresses on all business communications, including such paper-based items as letterhead, business cards, product literature, flyers, and advertisements in addition to any electronic communication.

Multipurpose Internet Mail Extensions (MIME) allows for the inclusion of multiple parts of a message, thus providing for multimedia enclosures or additions to e-mail. You must have a mailer and machine that permit sound and video to use this capability. (See Chapter 12, "Internet E-Mail: An Overview," for more information on MIME.)

E-mail can also be used to send faxes and telexes through some of the commercial services such as CompuServe and Delphi. This capability can provide quick response to information requests.

Wide Area Information Servers (WAIS)

WAIS is a distributed text-based tool for working with collections of data—enabling you to search through Internet archives for articles containing groups of words. The system is based on the Z39.50 standard. Businesses are running WAIS servers with information on their services and products. The software, usually provided with your client, enables you to create these sources. One of these, called `waisindex`, takes a set of files and builds an index of them. The index is what WAIS uses to return information to the searcher.

Most businesses find WAIS a good way of making documents and specifications regarding products and services easily available. Some even make their catalogs available on WAIS.

Because WAIS is still fairly new, look for developments in the future.

Greeting Cards

A rather new manifestation on the Internet is the *greeting card*. These small e-mail and `.plan` file-based messages, usually very light and humorous in tone, give a greeting to the recipient. Some of these messages even have animation if they can run under certain mailers and systems, such as UNIX.

Currently, greeting cards are considered to be borderline activities if sent unsolicited. The safest method is to put something in your signature file that lets people know that they can receive the greeting.

> **CAUTION**
>
> Although it almost goes without saying, you should exercise caution when dealing with online marketing. Not all signatures represent the person or business behind them. Not all `.plan` files are accurate or true. The Internet is a community that prizes genuine exchanges; news of problems with Net marketing travels almost at the speed of light.

Where from Here?

The Internet is always changing. So, too, will the methods for marketing on the Internet. The best way to keep abreast of those changes is to stay plugged in to the lists, to Usenet, and to your network of e-mailers.

New methods of secure transaction and improved authentication protocols such as Secure HTTP will make Web marketing and selling even more popular. Business-to-business Web transactions are steadily growing, and direct selling from a page will become more commonplace.

MIME and MOOs will provide enhancements to Internet services. When Virtual Reality Transfer Protocol (VRTP) matures, all kinds of virtual stores, showrooms, and businesses will emerge on the Web. MIME can provide audio and visual material to make all kinds of e-mail interactions more interesting. More on MIME can be found in Chapter 12, "Internet E-Mail: An Overview." MOOs provide opportunities for real-time interactions, enhancing almost any business function. You may even try participating in Internet Talk Radio, a digital radio audio broadcast. See Chapter 18, "Live Conversations: Internet Relay Chat and Other Methods," and Chapter 19, "Internet Teleconferencing: MBone, CU-SeeMe, and Maven," for more information on live conversations.

Creating an Internet information service and corporate presence can allow a business, large or small, urban or rural, to reap many benefits.

An example of a corporate presence is the NBC Nightly News crew, on the Internet as nightly@nbc.com. They received more than 4,500 messages in the first three days after they announced their e-mail address. Just think: your business can be on this same Internet.

Selecting an Internet Consultant or Trainer

41

by Elizabeth Lane Lawley

The more people find out about the Internet, the more they want to know. A peek at the Internet's treasures can pique the interest of even the most skeptical would-be Luddite. But anyone who has experienced the steep learning curve associated with surfing the Net knows that a good teacher can make all the difference. An expert tour guide can determine whether Internet access becomes a cost-effective productivity booster or an expensive time-waster.

When you begin searching for a trainer or consultant to guide you and your business through the sometimes stormy Internet waters, you must establish certain criteria. You want to select a provider who can truly meet the needs of your company, someone who can show you how the Internet can help you be more productive. You don't want a person who leaves you feeling that the Internet is simply an overpriced technical toy. This chapter discusses how you can ensure that the trainer or consultant you select will meet your unique needs.

From the very beginning, you must remember that your needs are unique; every profession, every organization, and every individual has a different set of needs and expectations of what technology can do for them. Just as a good word processing class for secretaries is likely to differ substantially in content from a class designed for technical writers, an Internet presentation or consultation should take into account the specific focus of your organization. You shouldn't settle for a one-size-fits-all solution—no such creature exists, and a good Internet training or consulting company knows that.

This requirement doesn't mean that every presentation must be built from ground zero; few of us have the funds available to demand that level of customization. However, you can evaluate potential providers to make sure that they understand your specific needs and are prepared to make presentations or offer advice based on those needs. What works for a public relations company may not be appropriate for a publisher, and what makes the Internet worthwhile to a financial brokerage firm may be very different from what justifies the expense to a retailer.

So how do you make sure that your trainer or consultant can meet your needs? The first step is a simple one but often overlooked. You must do a detailed needs assessment. After all, if you don't know what your requirements are, communicating those needs to your prospective provider may be difficult. Think about purchasing a car—would you be likely to go to a dealership first and ask the salesperson to pick out the best car for you? Or would you look around, think about what you really need, and then negotiate with a dealer for the vehicle you know will meet your needs? Most of us would take the latter route—and you should do the same thing when making a decision about training or consulting services.

The next section in this chapter takes an in-depth look at the needs assessment process for training and consulting services. Then you learn the process of designing an effective Request for Proposals (RFP) for those services. Finally, the chapter describes the evaluation and selection process leading to a final decision.

Conducting a Needs Assessment

To structure your needs assessment, you must anticipate the questions a prospective service provider is likely to ask—or questions they should ask if they genuinely want to serve your needs. In some ways, your needs assessment is as much about what the provider needs to know as it is about what you need to receive.

To begin, you must identify the expected recipients of the services you require. Do you need training or consulting services for your technical staff? For managers? For customers? For yourself? Without a clearly defined audience, most training and consulting services are bound for failure. What a network system administrator needs to know about the Internet may be quite different from the needs of a marketing staff member or the concerns of a manager focusing on bottom-line issues. Before you can complete any other questions in your assessment, you need to know who in your organization will be the consumer of these services.

The next question seems simple on its face, but it provides the framework for the rest of the assessment. In its most general form, the question is "What are our goals for this project?" More specifically, you need to determine what information you want the trainer or consultant to bring to your organization. For a training project, what skills do you expect participants to gain from the presentations? For a consultant, what information do you expect him or her to provide for you, and for what purpose? Although the answer to this question may shift as you continue with your needs assessment, or even in the process of receiving the services, it is important to frame the question early and use it as a point of reference for the rest of your assessment. Keeping the answer general is fine; this chapter deals more with specifics as it progresses through the needs assessment process.

The next question to consider is "What do we already know?" If you're new to the Internet, you may be tempted to say "nothing," but that answer often is an exaggeration. The fact that you're reading this book means that you already know more about the Internet than most people. By informing the prospective provider of what you already know, you ensure that you will not pay him or her to teach the material to you again. The best use of your funds is to get information not easily available in your organization. You may be surprised at how many organizations hire consultants at exorbitant rates to tell them things that the systems administrator down the hall already knows. To protect yourself from this sort of mistake, consider these specific questions:

- What do we know about uses of the Internet for our organization? Have we seen our colleagues or competitors putting Internet services to use? Have staff or customers suggested uses for the Internet in the organization?

- What do we know about our options for Internet connectivity? Have we talked to colleagues? To vendors? Have we read books or articles describing connectivity options? If we already have access, do we know what the advantages and disadvantages of our connection are, and what other types of connections would provide?

■ What do we know about communications technology? Do we understand how modems work? Do we have local or wide area networks, and do we know how they operate? Are we familiar with telecommunications terminology like *baud rate, uploading, downloading, analog, digital,* and *packet switching*?

The obvious follow-up question to "What do we know?" is "What *don't* we know?" Don't answer in the broadest sense of the question but in relation to what your goals for the training or consulting project are. If you want consulting on how to connect to the Internet, and you already know what the primary options are, what you don't know may be how to implement those options or what the associated costs may be. If you need training on how to use Internet communication features, and you already are familiar with electronic mail on your local area network, the focus of your presentation should be on the specifics of Internet communications, not on the advantages and uses of electronic mail or a comparison of e-mail software features. If you're looking for a trainer to show your already Internet-competent staff how to train others on use of the Internet, what you don't know is what training techniques and methods will be most useful in the training process. Knowing what you don't need is as important as knowing what you do need. This knowledge can prevent you from contracting unnecessary services and prevent the provider from supplying you with superfluous services rather than services that truly meet your needs.

As this chapter steps through the process of designing an RFP for Internet training or consulting services, the discussion draws on the answers you have given to these needs assessment questions.

Designing an RFP

One of the keys to successful procurement of services is the design of the RFP (Request for Proposals). Unfortunately, most people looking for an Internet trainer or consultant never bother to create or distribute an RFP. They hear about a provider from a friend (or a friend of a friend, or from an advertisement or article), negotiate with that provider, and hire him or her. Although this informal process can work out well, if you use it you may never know whether you missed an opportunity to deal with a provider who could meet your needs better (and perhaps even less expensively) than the one you chose. For this reason, it's worth the time and effort to put together an RFP that allows you to evaluate and select from a range of choices. The number of trainers and consultants providing expert assistance on Internet topics is growing, and this growth means you have more choices and more control. Don't pass up your opportunity to negotiate the best services possible for your organization!

Components of a Good RFP

Preparing a good RFP doesn't have to be a difficult or onerous task. Too many people believe a good RFP has to be 50 pages long and filled with dry and technical language. In fact, some of the best RFPs are short and to the point, giving only the key information a provider needs to prepare a proposal. A thorough RFP enables the provider to do the following:

- Determine immediately whether he or she can meet the needs of your organization
- Ensure that the proposal covers the material you need to make a good decision

Executive Summary

The first part of the RFP should be a brief summary of what type of proposal you are soliciting. The summary should include a very general statement of the project goals and scope, as well as some discussion of the budgetary constraints for the project. Writing this section last often makes sense, even though it appears first, because the summary should outline the information provided in more detail in the rest of the RFP. After you have filled in the details of the other sections, condensing the material into an accurate summary is easier.

Description of Organization

After the executive summary, the RFP should contain a detailed description of your organization. This description should include the following elements:

- The name of the organization and a brief description of its mission and goals.
- The size of the organization, including any subsidiaries.
- A brief overview of the organization's current telecommunications configuration, including any Internet connections, local or wide area networks, or use of modems for other business activities.

This description enables the consultant or trainer to begin customizing a response to suit your specific needs. An appropriate presentation for a publishing firm may be completely different from a presentation to the dean of a college or university. By starting out with a description of the environment the provider will service, you contribute to the development of a proposal that clearly addresses your requirements, instead of encouraging the submission of a one-size-fits-all (or more likely, one-size-fits-none) solution.

Specific Project Goals

The next critical component of the RFP is a clear statement of your project goals. The following list includes some issues to address for training:

- What is the proposed topic (or topics) of the required presentation?
- What skills do you expect participants to gain from the training?
- How long will the training session(s) be, and how many sessions are needed?
- How many participants are to be trained?
- What materials must be provided? Workbooks? Textbooks? Overheads?

For consulting, you should include the following issues:

- Who, specifically, will receive the consulting services? Middle managers? Company presidents? Trainers? Information specialists? Marketers? Engineers?
- What knowledge do you expect participants to gain from the consulting process?
- What specific products do you expect the consultant to provide? A written report? A properly configured computer? A working Internet connection?

You should already have the answers to these questions—from the needs assessment you did to prepare for the project. These pieces of information are the second building block in the provider's development of a proposal to meet your needs.

Budget and Other Constraints

After the description of project goals and requirements, you should specify the constraints involved. The two most important constraints are the budget and the time frame. The provider must know the limit of funds (or range of funds) available for the project, as well as when you want the services provided. If a conflict arises in either of these areas, the provider has the option of negotiating with you for a variance in the stated constraints. However, these restrictions can help eliminate providers who are unable to offer services in your price range or during your required dates.

Response Outline and Criteria for Evaluation

A helpful tip is to provide a brief outline of what material the provider should include in the RFP response, as well as an explanation of what criteria you will use to evaluate the responses. For example, do you expect a fully itemized budget as part of the cost estimate? Do you require examples of prepared materials? By specifying the format for the responses and the required supplementary materials, you accomplish two things. First, you make the response easier to prepare for the provider, which can result in a larger number of useful responses. Second, you ensure that the responses are in a standard form, making evaluation of the responses substantially easier.

In addition, providing a specific list of criteria you will use to evaluate the proposal allows the provider to focus on the aspects of the proposal most important for your needs. If the most important criteria is previous experience with similar organizations, and cost is no object, providers would be foolish to spend the bulk of their time preparing detailed cost justifications for each aspect of the proposal. On the other hand, if budget is a major factor in your decision, that item should receive more attention than other items in both the preparation and the evaluation of the proposal. In addition, carefully enumerating and weighting criteria in advance allows your organization to evaluate the proposals in an equitable manner, minimizing conflicts in the selection process.

Finding Trainers and Consultants

After you have prepared an RFP, make sure that as many potential providers as possible have access to it. What providers don't know about, they can't respond to. So where are all the Internet consultants and trainers, and how can you get your RFP into their hands? The following sections describe some of the many places you can find potential providers.

Referrals

A good starting place for information on suitable providers is referrals from your colleagues. By drawing on the knowledge of others in your field, you can immediately locate experienced providers doing work for similar organizations. A referral also makes the chance more likely that the provider can put together an appropriate response to your RFP, drawing on his or her experience in doing similar presentations or consultations. Remember, however, that a referral is only a *starting* place. The company that gave the perfect training presentation for another organization may be able to meet your needs as well, but you have no guarantee that another provider couldn't provide the same or better services, and possibly at a lower price. Make sure that you broaden the distribution of your RFP through some of the channels in the following sections.

Network Sources

If you already have access to the Internet (or to an electronic mail service with an Internet delivery option such as CompuServe, America Online, or MCI Mail), you can ensure that your RFP gets wide distribution by taking advantage of mailing lists on the network. You also can identify service providers through resources and materials they make available over the Internet.

Mailing Lists

Mailing lists targeted toward service providers are an excellent place to begin distributing an announcement of your RFP. In particular, the NETTRAIN mailing list for Internet trainers and the Net-Happenings mailing list for general Internet-related announcements are excellent distribution media for announcements of a training or consulting RFP. In fact, if providers aren't monitoring NETTRAIN or keeping an eye on Net-Happenings, they're likely to miss out not only on announcements of training or consulting contracts, but also on critical information about network resources and applications that they should be using in their presentations and materials. To subscribe to the Net-Happenings mailing list, send the message SUBSCRIBE NET-HAPPENINGS to majordomo@ds.internic.net. You can subscribe to NETTRAIN by sending an e-mail message containing only the line SUBSCRIBE NETTRAIN *Firstname Lastname* to LISTSERV@UBVM.cc.buffalo.edu.

In addition to posting to mailing lists frequented by service providers, consider posting your announcement to mailing lists on topics related to your area of business—you can find mailing lists devoted to everything from education to advertising. Using this method of distribution, you can send your RFP announcement to providers who are familiar with your topics and also get additional referrals from colleagues in your field.

Gopher and WWW Servers

Another network resource that can help you locate providers of training or consulting services is the growing network of Gopher and World Wide Web servers providing information on Internet services and activities. By using a search tool like Veronica (for Gopher) or Yahoo (for the Web) to locate information on Internet training or consulting topics, you often can find references to service providers. Some of these references are in the form of announcements the providers make themselves; other references may be posted by satisfied (or dissatisfied!) customers of certain providers. For more information on Veronica, see Chapter 26, "Searching Gopherspace with Veronica." For more information on finding information on the World Wide Web, see Chapter 28, "Navigating the World Wide Web."

Organizations and Associations

Although the industry has no official Internet Trainers Association or Organization of Internet Consultants, a number of Internet-related organizations exist that may be able to assist you in locating appropriate service providers. A glance through the membership directory of the Internet Society (http://info.isoc.org/), for example, is likely to yield information on a number of training and consulting providers. You also can check with professional organizations in your own field and solicit referrals from colleagues.

Conferences

Professional and trade conferences can be good ways to find out about consultants and trainers offering services in your field. Service organizations may have an information booth set up as part of the conference exhibits, they may have representatives attending meetings and presentations, or they may even have representatives making presentations at the conference. Even if the people you meet at the conference cannot provide the services you need, they may be able to recommend other companies that can meet your needs. And again, you have the opportunity to ask colleagues for recommendations. Information on Internet World, one of the industry's most popular conferences, is available at `http://www.mecklerweb.com/shows/internet/iwhome.htm`.

Commercial Directories

As publishers discover the popularity of the Internet, many of them are beginning to publish printed directories of Internet resources and organizations. In particular, publications focusing on the business community are likely to provide directories of vendors meeting the needs of the readership. The *Internet Business Review*, published by Strangelove Press, already has released a directory of Internet trainers and consultants and expects to update this list regularly (it's at `gopher://gopher.fonorola.net/11/Internet%20Business%20Journal`). Other publishers are likely to follow this lead, so you may want to check with the publishers of Internet-related journals.

Advertisements

The growth in Internet publishing has led to more venues for Internet trainers and consultants to advertise their services. Although you may not see too many ads for these services in newspapers and popular magazines, journals and newsletters focusing on Internet topics are likely to draw advertisements for exactly the services you need. A quick look through recent issues of Internet-related publications may yield a number of promising candidates.

Articles

If you're looking for consultants or trainers with experience in your field, you may want to look for people who have published articles or books on topics relevant to your interests. If a consultant has written a number of articles about Internet use for a trade publication in your field, he or she already has become familiar with the issues and resources of interest to you and your colleagues. If a trainer has written about a method of training you believe may be particularly useful in your organization, you may want to send an RFP to his or her organization.

Making Your Selection

After you have sent RFPs to the many candidates found in network, print, and collegial resources, you must sort through the resulting responses to your requests for proposals. If you have done a good job of writing your RFP, this job will not be nearly as difficult as if you were starting from scratch. First of all, the proposals should follow the format laid out in the RFP, which makes comparing the proposals easier.

> **TIP**
>
> You should consider proposals that don't follow your structure *only* if none of the properly prepared proposals meets your requirements; the failure to provide a proposal that meets your specifications is an indication of a provider's likely failure in giving you services that meet your specifications.

Second, you have a set of clear criteria on which to base your evaluations, making the process of reading and ranking the proposals far less ambiguous and frustrating.

Which proposal you end up selecting as the winner depends completely on how you have ranked different aspects of the RFP. If price is the most important aspect, you may be willing to accept fewer references or a sketchier outline of proposed services. If having a tailored presentation is the critical aspect, information from references and examples of materials from past presentations probably will be the deciding factors. What's important is to know *before* you get the proposals which aspects are most important to your decision-making and to communicate that message to your prospective service providers through the RFP.

Working with Your Consultant or Trainer

After you have made a selection, don't expect to sit back and play a passive role as the provider services your organization. To ensure that what you receive is really what you want and need, you must actively involve yourself in the planning and provision of services. Being involved doesn't mean you should do the consultant's or trainer's work for them, but you do need to ensure that the lines of communication stay open so that no unwelcome surprises appear. Establish a regular time for the provider to talk or meet with you, and make sure that you get copies of work in progress along the way. By providing input during the entire process, you help ensure that the product you receive—whether it's a training session or a consulting report—is what you expected.

Evaluating Services Provided

After the project is done, your job still isn't complete. A final evaluation of the services provided can help you and the trainer or consultant. If the job was well done, can you identify what aspects made it successful so that you can replicate your success in the future? If you had problems, can you identify where those problems arose so that you can prevent them from occurring in other projects?

Like your selection criteria, your final evaluation criteria is based on what aspects are most important to your organization. However, some questions to consider include the following:

- Did the provider meet the stated requirements and objectives of the project?
- Were the services provided at a cost within budget constraints?
- Did the services leave you and your organization with a better understanding of the Internet and its resources?

Some organizations require a written summary or evaluation of services at the completion of a training or consulting project. Even if you don't do an evaluation, it's well worth taking the time to structure your thoughts about the services so that you know what you have done right and wrong; you can make future decisions with that knowledge firmly in mind.

Digital Cash

42

by Rosalind Resnick
with research by
Heidi Anderson

There's no shortage of places for merchants to peddle their wares on the Internet. The trouble is getting paid.

One of the biggest stumbling blocks to commerce on the Internet is the lack of universally accepted legal tender—that is, electronic cash. Unlike the real world, where dollars, francs, lire, deutsche marks, even wampum beads are exchanged for goods and services, there are no equivalent cyberbucks that Internet shoppers can use to make their purchases. The payment systems that do exist on the Internet are fraught with problems. Despite a slew of new security technologies, credit card numbers still can't be safely sent through the network, and setting up an account with an Internet merchant is troublesome and time consuming. What's more, there's no handy way to peddle a 25-cent poem or chocolate-chip-cookie recipe.

The good news is that *digital cash*—a system in which online shoppers swap real dollars for Internet scrip to pay for goods and services—is on the way. This chapter looks at the pros and cons of the Internet payment systems in use today and examine some companies pioneering digital cash systems: DigiCash, First Virtual, NetCash, and CyberCash. You also get a glimpse of the future of Internet payment systems and find out which system is best for your business.

Internet Payment Systems Today

Closely tied to the problem of Internet payment is the issue of Internet security. Unlike commercial online services such as CompuServe and Prodigy, the Internet is not a secure network—thieves and vandals who hang out on the network routinely hack their way into Internet-connected computers and filch passwords and other confidential data. For online merchants, that means the risk that precious customer credit card data can be pilfered—a chilling prospect for companies and customers alike. That risked turned into chilling reality in February 1995 when notorious hacker Kevin Mitnick was arrested and charged with computer fraud andaccess device fraud—including stealing an estimated 20,000 credit card numbers and thousands of data files from an Internet access provider.

Currently, there are four main ways that business is transacted on the Internet:

- ■ Toll-free (800) numbers
- ■ Shopping clubs
- ■ Online credit card entry
- ■ Offline ordering

Many Internet merchants display their goods and services in cybermalls on the World Wide Web but post their toll-free 800 numbers online so that Internet shoppers can order by phone. One example, shown in Figure 42.1, is PC Gifts and Flowers the Internet version of Prodigy's popular PC Flowers shopping service. Although not as convenient as allowing shoppers to type their credit card information online, phone ordering is more secure and more comfortable for the customer.

FIGURE 42.1.

PC Gifts and Flowers takes orders on a toll-free number because of the risk of credit card theft on the Internet.

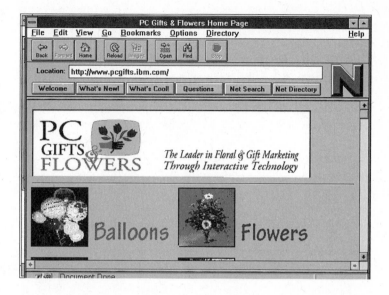

Another option is shopping clubs, which skirt the credit card security issue in a different way. For example, Internet Shopping Network, a Web-based catalog retailer of computer hardware and software, requires new customers to join the club by submitting their credit card information by fax; any purchases are charged to that card. A cybermall called Downtown Anywhere employs a Personal Payment system that lets any shopper with a credit card and a touch-tone phone acquire a Personal Payment Password that can be used for online purchases in Downtown Anywhere and at other participating sites. In seconds, information about online purchases of goods or services is transmitted by e-mail or fax to the merchants offering those products.

Many Internet merchants offer online order blanks so that shoppers can type their credit card numbers directly onto their Web sites—despite the risks involved. Even though server-based encryption programs like Enterprise Integration Technologies' Secure-HTTP protocol and Netscape Communications' Commerce Server are now available, few storefronts or cybermalls have yet to purchase or install them. In the meantime, many merchants are using on-the-fly security techniques such as PGP (Pretty Good Encryption) or simply crossing their fingers and taking their chances. Another problem with credit cards is that they're not well suited to small transactions or micro-purchases. On a 10-cent item, a bank or credit card company spends more money processing the transaction than the item costs.

Finally, some Internet merchants transact their sales offline by asking customers to send them checks. For example, I publish an electronic newsletter called *Interactive Publishing Alert* that offers potential subscribers two ways of paying for their subscriptions: check or credit card order. To activate their subscriptions, subscribers either mail a check made out to my company, Interactive Communications International, Inc., or they send me a fax containing their credit card number, expiration date, and signature. Although this system works fine for full-year $295 subscriptions, it's a pain in the neck to handle $20 single-copy issues or $9.95 special supplements this way.

The Rise of E-Money on the Net

Trouble is, all four of these payment systems (phone ordering, shopping clubs, credit card billing, and checks) have serious drawbacks when it comes to doing business on the Internet. Clearly, a better solution is electronic cash. With e-cash, or *digital cash*, as it's known, you simply transfer money from your checking account to your digital cash account, converting real-world dollars or other currency into digital coins stored on your hard drive. When you spend those coins on Internet goods or services, the transaction is credited to the merchant's account by the clearing bank and the proceeds are deposited into the merchant's bank account. Digital coins can't easily be stolen or faked, reducing the risk for both the buyer and seller.

> **NOTE**
>
> Having digital coins on your hard drive is analogous to having cash in your wallet. A thief may be able to steal the contents of your wallet, but he can't clean out your entire bank account the way he could if he got hold of your ATM card and password.

What's more, digital coins are perfect for handling micro-payments, making it possible for all kinds of booklets, pamphlets, and other low-cost bits of information to be marketed world wide.

"Famous writers and columnists might find it profitable to use this medium to write 10-cent and 20-cent articles," speculates Arnold Kling, formerly of *The Federal Reserve*, in an article about Internet banking now posted on the Global Network Navigator Internet site. "Nonfiction authors with only 20 pages of things to say could issue pithy $2 online pamphlets, rather than repetitive $20 books."

And these small sums do add up.

The following sections describe the four leading electronic cash systems vying to be top dollar.

DigiCash

In May 1994, an Amsterdam-based company called DigiCash rolled out an electronic cash system that lets Internet users pay for products and services without typing credit card numbers or mailing checks. Founded by David Chaum, a bearded, ponytailed Los Angeles native who holds a doctorate in cryptography, DigiCash previously pioneered a similar system for automatic highway toll collection using what are known as "smart cards."

Although the DigiCash system (`http://www.digicash.com`) shown in Figure 42.2 is still in the testing phase, 500 customers and approximately 25 online merchants around the world (including Encyclopedia Brittanica and the Massachusetts Institute of Technology) are already swapping play money for goods and services ranging from books to groceries. If the talks now underway between DigiCash and bankers are successful, soon real money can be exchanged through the system.

FIGURE 42.2.

DigiCash, an Amsterdam-based electronic cash company, lets Internet shoppers pay for products and services without typing credit card numbers or mailing checks.

"You can pay for access to a database, buy software or a newsletter by e-mail, play a computer game over the Net, receive $5 owed you by a friend, or just order a pizza," says Chaum, the company's managing director. "The possibilities are truly unlimited."

Some of the online merchants accepting DigiCash money include:

- Big Mac, which sells Monty Python scenes
- Bytown Electronic Marketplace, which offers electronic novelty items from Ottawa and also has a Document Rack online
- Wane's Online Grocery Store
- MIT's IESL Bookstore
- *The Weekly e-Mail,* the electronic version of South Africa's *The Weekly Mail & Guardian* newspaper

Of the four e-cash systems profiled in this chapter, DigiCash most closely resembles real money. Here's how it works:

First, you convert a certain sum of money from your bank account into electronic cash; if your bank doesn't participate in the DigiCash system, you must open an account at a bank that does. The DigiCash software then stores the digital "coins" on your computer's hard drive until you spend them (you don't earn interest on that money because you've already withdrawn it from the bank—just as with an ATM machine).

You can spend your digital money at any shop accepting electronic cash without first having to open a charge account there or typing in a credit card number—still risky business on the free-wheeling Internet. Buying goods and services is as easy as using your mouse to "drag and drop" your coins into an online store. The merchant then takes your money and deposits it at a participating bank. Unlike credit card transactions, merchants don't have to ante up a percentage of their sales, although bankers may decide to charge a fee for converting digital cash to real money.

The nice thing about electronic currency is that it enjoys the privacy of paper cash at the same time it ensures security by using *encryption* (coded messages that can't be cracked by online pickpockets) and by using digital signatures. The company's previous digital cash products ("chip cards" and "electronic wallets") have relied on a tamper-resistant chip for storing monetary value. Now, "all you have to do is download the software and you're up and running," Chaum says.

Like real-world cash, DigiCash coins also possess another important feature—anonymity. Because the merchant sees only the bank's signature and not Joe's, Joe remains anonymous throughout the entire process, enabling Joe to purchase anything he wants without fear of embarrassment.

Interestingly, the DigiCash system isn't restricted to the Internet alone. In February, DigiCash announced it was nearing completion on a technology that allows e-cash to be used on smart cards, which are popular in Europe where many currencies coexist. The technology, code-named *Blue*, uses a low-cost chip that takes advantage of DigiCash's encryption technology.

Of course, the DigiCash system isn't foolproof by any means. As with credit cards, it's possible for someone to steal your digital encryption key and use it to make purchases you may not find out about until it's too late.

DIGICASH'S FIRST CUSTOMER

Paul Robichaux had been reading papers published by David Chaum and was intrigued by his ideas on electronic money. So, when Robichaux discovered that DigiCash was putting up an experimental World Wide Web server, he decided to put Chaum's ideas to the test by enrolling his own company, Fairgate Technologies, as Chaum's first online merchant.

"[The people at DigiCash] were very cooperative and helpful in giving me the tools I needed to set up," says Robichaux, the company's principal engineer. "They have the infrastructure, the client software."

However, until DigiCash finds a bank to partner with, it won't be able to offer Fairgate what it needs to sell big-ticket items on the Internet. Until then, Robichaux says, DigiCash will remain an experiment.

"Until I can exchange DigiCash for real money, it's hard for me to convince people to let me sell [their products]," he says. "They don't have a way for me to take my e-cash and turn it into American dollars."

First Virtual Holdings

While DigiCash is experimenting with Internet money, First Virtual Holdings is pioneering Internet credit.

At First Virtual (`http://www.fv.com`), shown in Figure 42.3, Internet shoppers access the First Virtual Web server and set up an account by giving First Virtual their credit card number. But instead of getting cyberbucks as they do with DigiCash, shoppers get online accounts. Once shoppers see something they want to buy, they simply give their account number to the merchant by typing it into the First Virtual server. Unlike DigiCash, there's no software to download and install.

FIGURE 42.3.

First Virtual, a Web-based cybermall that sells electronic information products, is pioneering Internet credit.

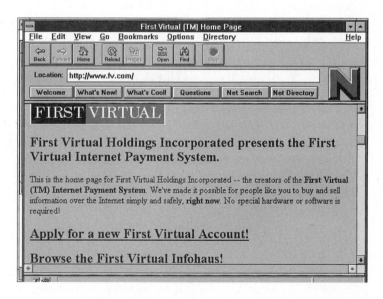

The merchant, who pays First Virtual a $10 registration fee plus a 2-percent commission on each sale, ships the product to the customer. Every week, the merchant supplies a list of sales to First Virtual, which, in turn, sends e-mail to the customer confirming the order.

If the buyer wants to keep the product, he or she notifies First Virtual, which charges it to the appropriate credit card. If the buyer decides to return it, no money changes hands.

To be sure, there are some serious drawbacks to this system for participating merchants: namely, the system requires the seller to ship a product and trust the buyer to pay for it. Although First Virtual says it will close accounts of shoppers who do nothing but return products, the burden is clearly on the merchant.

Another drawback is that, at this point, the system is available only to vendors of information, not tangible goods. Although this fits well with the Internet's current demographic profile, the less computer-savvy buyers who are now making their presence felt in cyberspace may want products they can see and feel.

"One of the big barriers is...being able to make actual deliveries of goods," says Robichaux of Fairgate Technologies, whose company is currently negotiating with First Virtual for space in its mall. "First Virtual says that if you use [their] system to sell physical items and someone rips you off, that's your problem, not ours."

Another drawback to the system is the large volume of e-mail that exchanges hands. A buyer and seller can't meet in real time and exchange cash for goods; instead, a bank must act as a go-between.

Still, for all these faults, First Virtual has something that DigiCash doesn't: a real bank as a partner. By teaming up with FirstUSA, First Virtual has been able to start handling real transactions, rather than run it with funny money as an experiment.

PEDDLING INFORMATION ON FIRST VIRTUAL

If Mike Walsh had a dollar for every time hes been mentioned in the media, he'd be a rich man.

Actually, Walsh, the owner of Internet Info, a market research firm in Falls Church, VA, isn't doing too badly—although it isn't because of the lists of commercial domain names he peddles for $10 apiece on Internet cybermalls like OpenMarket and First Virtual.

"Sales on the Internet have been insignificant," Walsh says. "Contacts made have been tremendous. Requests for consulting work have been more than I can handle."

Walsh's experience typifies that of many entrepreneurs trying to peddle information on the Internet: tons of publicity, relatively little in the way of direct sales.

"I got and continue to get sales from both the OpenMarket and First Virtual Systems. More than I expected," Walsh says. "I also got a lot of calls from people who didn't want to put up with the mechanics of the purchasing process. [But] I suspect that my sales would be 10 times higher if people felt confident and familiar with entering their credit card info into the system."

NetCash

Yet another digital cash experiment is NetCash, the Internet's answer to travelers' checks. The oldest of the payment systems profiled in this chapter, NetCash has been up and running with e-mail since May 1994; its Web site was almost complete as of this writing.

Developed by Bob Houston, president of Software Technologies in Germantown, MD, NetCash `http://www.netbank.com/~netcash/`, shown in Figure 42.4, is both easy to use and fairly secure.

FIGURE 42.4.

NetCash lets shoppers purchase goods and services using electronic coupons and is the Internet's answer to travelers' checks.

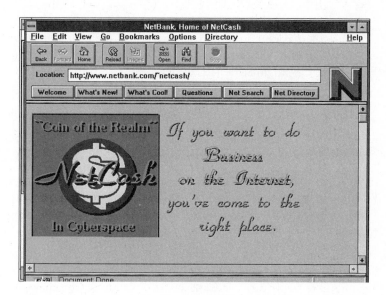

It works like this: Internet shoppers enter their checking account or credit card number into an on-screen form and e-mail it to the NetCash system. This entitles the buyers to buy electronic coupons from NetCash for their face value plus a 2-percent commission. Each coupon is marked with a serial number.

The shopper then browses NetCash's merchant list—currently, it's through e-mail, although soon it will be through the Web site as well. Once the shopper selects a product to buy, he or she makes the purchase by sending NetCash coupons to the merchant. The merchant redeems the coupons at the NetCash NetBank (a computer program and not a physical location); NetCash takes 2 percent off the top as its fee. Currently, NetCash's most active merchant is *Boardwatch* magazine, which sells subscriptions. Other NetCash merchants include software companies and music and video stores.

> **NOTE**
>
> The NetCash coupons themselves are transferred with e-mail. The consumer sends a check or money order by snail mail to NetCash, which exchanges it for the coupons and sends them by e-mail to the consumer. A coupon looks like this:
>
> `NetCash US$ 10.00 E123456H789012W`
>
> The consumer e-mails the coupon to the merchant, who e-mails it to the NetCash bank for redemption.

Because there is no minimum transaction fee, the NetCash system is ideal for micro-sales. However, because the system is not totally secure, NetCash isn't as good a way to sell bigger-ticket items. (And, in fact, NetCash has placed a $100 ceiling on vendors' offerings.)

"We prefer people to use existing systems for larger transaction items," Houston says. "We don't want them buying houses or cars online. One hundred dollars is the limit on any one item."

Along with the low ceiling and lack of total security, NetCash has some other drawbacks. Shoppers are not as anonymous as those using DigiCash; and until the Web site opens, NetCash shoppers must retrieve a list of vendors by e-mail, which isn't as easy to use as a Web browser.

On the other hand, NetCash is up and running now, handling real transactions and helping Internet merchants make money. Although Houston won't release sales figures, he says that several thousand people have registered to shop on the system.

Also, unlike First Virtual, vendors can sell tangible products, not just electronic information. NetCash users can have products shipped by postal mail, and they can also order by telephone so long as they give their NetCash serial number to the merchant. There is no minimum transaction.

CyberCash

While many companies are creating cash substitutes that can be passed across the Internet, CyberCash is working on a way to let Internet consumers use something they're already thinking of as money—their credit cards.

CyberCash (`http://www.cybercash.com`), launched in August 1994 by Bill Melton and Dan Lynch, comes close to providing a secure solution for sending credit card information across the Internet. The Reston, Virginia, company has teamed up with encryption experts Enterprise Integration Technologies, Trusted Information Systems, and RSA Data Security, Inc. to create a way to encode credit card data so that it can be sent through cyberspace safe from hackers. Rather than acting as a bank that exchanges offline money for cash that can be spent online, CyberCash acts as an Internet postal service (see Figure 42.5).

FIGURE 42.5.

CyberCash provides a relatively secure way for Internet shoppers to use credit cards on the network.

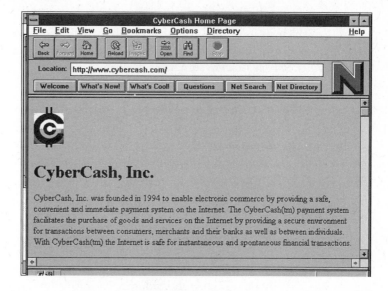

Heres how the system works: A consumer downloads the free, graphical CyberCash interface, views the merchandise online, and presses the CyberCash "pay" button. This action notifies the merchant to send an online invoice to the consumer, who fills in his or her name and credit card information in an order blank. The credit card information is then encrypted and sent to the merchant, who sends the invoice and identification information to the CyberCash server.

Once this information reaches the server, the CyberCash computer sends a standard credit card authorization to the merchant's bank and forwards the response to the merchant, who ships out the product or service. The entire process is conducted quickly and with little cost to the buyer (CyberCash likens it to the cost of a postage stamp; CyberCash's processing fees are in line with those of systems now in place).

CyberCash's advantage to Internet shoppers is that it's cheap and easy to use. Buyers do not have to set up special accounts with a bank or with CyberCash as they do with NetCash; they just type in credit card data. The main advantage to the merchant is that payment is guaranteed before any product is shipped, unlike the First Virtual system. And, in theory, merchants can use the CyberCash system to sell any product online that they can sell offline—they're not restricted to non-physical goods or services under $100.

The main drawback to the system is that it's still in the trial stage and has yet to prove its worth. CyberCash signed a deal with Wells Fargo Bank of San Francisco last December, enabling merchants with accounts at Wells Fargo to sell their products through the system. Merchants with other banks, however, cannot market items. To date, only a handful of merchants are participating in the test, and a release date not been announced, although the system is expected to be ready within the next few months. Another minor disadvantage of the CyberCash system is that buyers must have credit cards, although most Internet consumers presumably have them or they probably wouldn't have been able to open an online account.

The CyberCash system is expanding into other areas as well: CyberCash accounts for organizations (in which an individual uses the organization's "key" to conduct a transaction) and electronic cash payments (which allow merchants to sell products that are too inexpensive to process cost effectively, such as searchable databases).

The Future of Digital Cash

Because of the problems involved in getting paid, Internet commerce is still more hype than reality—that is, there are still more shops than shoppers. And each of the four payment systems profiled in this chapter have limitations; in the end, none of them may emerge as the Internet's answer to universally accepted legal tender. Of the four, however, we believe that DigiCash's system holds the greatest potential for widespread acceptability. It's easy to use, it's anonymous, and it's not restricted to the Internet. In Europe, where smart cards are more common than in the United States, DigiCash's offline capabilities could make it the system of choice.

At the same time, it's also possible that all four systems will coexist in the future—along with credit card entry, shopping clubs, and offline payment methods like toll-free phone ordering and checks sent by postal mail. The key for Internet merchants is to show online shoppers that they have a choice in how they pay: a choice that's convenient, secure, and suited to their individual needs.

PART

Using the Internet: Libraries

The Internet in Academic Libraries

43

by Lou Rosenfeld

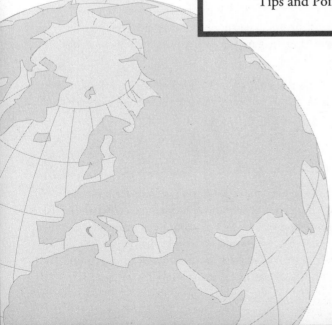

If you are reading this chapter, chances are you're a university or college librarian who is just learning about the Internet for the first time, or maybe you already have some experience with the Internet and would like to pick up some new ideas. Either way, you're probably in a perilous situation: Your patrons are marching outside your door, torches in hand, demanding increased access to the Internet. Maybe your library's director has just come from an Internet demonstration, saying "Boy, that's a neat system! Get it up and running for next semester."

The purpose of this chapter is to demonstrate how the Internet can improve your library's services. This chapter won't try to convince you that the Internet is a good thing—if the previous chapters haven't done that already, nothing will. This chapter tries to show you how the Internet is good for academic libraries, describes some simple approaches and feasible projects (based primarily on experiences at the University of Michigan library), and tries to steer you clear of some pitfalls specific to academic libraries.

Why Bother with the Internet?

Maybe you've been to Internet workshops, heard from the Internet evangelists, and seen the coverage in popular media. Maybe you've used the Internet for years. But despite all the recent hype, it's still obvious that the Internet is, to put it mildly, a mess. As an information professional, you know that it is extremely difficult to determine the existence and location of an information resource on the Internet. And should you find it, you know that probably 90 percent of the information it contains is incomplete, mislabeled, out-of-date, inaccurate, or just plain junk. The Internet is an anarchic environment in which everyone and their brother can make information available, and you can bet that the majority of them never took classes in collection development or cataloging.

An academic library's patrons are familiar with a different kind of information-seeking experience: more controlled, with some assurances of quality. Will you be able to convince your patrons that the Internet is going to be useful to them? For that matter, can you convince your colleagues on the library staff?

Of course, you knew it wouldn't be easy in the first place. You will find that many staff members are unsympathetic or unsupportive of your efforts to bring the Internet to your library. Even if they see value in the Internet, they are often too busy trying to fulfill their daily responsibilities to consider new projects. Library administrators, all too experienced with the headaches of bringing up integrated library systems, may see installing the necessary connectivity, hardware, and software as an extremely expensive proposition of questionable value.

But many of your patrons are already on the Internet—or will be soon. There are approximately 27 million Internet users today, a good number of whom are academics. What these folks find on the Internet is useful information; good or bad, it is often quite complementary to the information they find in a library. As librarians, we should remember that we are in the information business, and we should attempt to provide access to all forms of information, including those on the Internet. More importantly, if patrons don't see the library as a place that meets the majority of their information needs, academic libraries will likely see their campus-wide support (and funding) diminish.

Besides, librarians are perhaps more likely than anyone else to find ways to reduce the chaos of the Internet and make its information resources more usable. Whether through the implementation of cataloging standards, quality and authority control, pathfinding, or other approaches, librarians should strive to make more useful what the technologists have made so easy: the processes of retrieving and "publishing" information over global networks that have been made a great deal easier by the rise in popularity of HTML and the World Wide Web.

Doing What We've Always Done —Only Better

Many new technologies are first applied to improve the performance of existing systems. People often find it easier to understand new technologies in terms of what they already know and do. The following sections discuss how the Internet can make existing academic library services faster and more efficient; later in this chapter, you learn how the Internet can make libraries more effective by offering patrons creative new services.

Public/Reference Services

Of all academic librarians, reference librarians have probably benefited the most from using the Internet. The wealth of information found in FTP archives, Gopher servers, and World Wide Web servers extends the scope of information available to them. Many reference librarians find that once they've identified quality Internet resources, these resources are often more valuable than their print and commercial online counterparts.

As an example, consider the U.S. Department of Commerce's electronic Economic Bulletin Board, which provides information on leading economic indicators. Dialing in by modem, the University of Michigan library downloads new files from this resource almost every day and provides Internet access through its Gopher and WWW servers. This information is obviously much more up to date than its printed counterparts. General reference librarians, government documents librarians, and patrons can access this resource simultaneously. And of course, it is available at no charge. In this case, it's hard to argue that a print or commercial version would be more valuable.

However, it may not be fair to compare the various media for accessing information. In fact, it's often not an either/or situation; in many cases, these different media are combined in the delivery of a single service. For example, Dialog and OCLC have made their commercial databases available to educational institutions over the Internet. The resulting information is exactly the same, but the telecommunications charges are greatly reduced, if not completely eliminated.

It may be even more illuminating to hear how "real" reference librarians have used the Internet. The following quotations come from the document entitled "22 Internet Reference Success Stories," compiled by Karen G. Schneider, and posted to various Listservs. Each of these describes some of the benefits derived from the Internet by academic librarians and their patrons. Note that two relatively simple and common Internet tools, Gopher and Veronica, are used to locate information in both bibliographic and full text formats.

Rachel Cassel, Binghamton University, New York: "A patron was looking for the text of the UN declaration of human rights in 1948. We did a Veronica search and located the full text of the document at the Gopher `kragar.eff.org` path `/academic/civil-liberty/human-rights.un`. I've seen a problem instructors have given in classes on Gopher where they have students use Veronica to search for data to compare the unemployment rates of Detroit and Los Angeles."

Jane Frances Kinkus, Mississippi State University, Mississippi: "I used a Gopher server to locate ACM/SIGGRAPH's list of publications. A patron knew that so-and-so was writing a book, probably to be published by ACM/SIGGRAPH, and I verified that, according to ACM/SIGGRAPH's list, this book had not been published."

The Internet does not enhance bibliographic instruction *per se*, but does extend its scope substantially. Beginning with card catalogs and print indexes, and on through online catalogs and CD-ROM products, the trend in bibliographic instruction has been to bring the patron in increasingly direct contact with the library's holdings and resources. And as technologies become more essential to information delivery, it has been necessary to increase the technical training of patrons. The Internet is the next logical step in this progression. In terms of cost, availability, and geographic proximity, its information is perhaps even more accessible to the patron than any other kind. But understanding the Internet and its offerings requires extensive knowledge of new technologies, as well as the kinds of search strategies and navigational techniques that are generally the domain of librarians. So bibliographic instruction may face increased demand as patrons seek information from this exciting new environment and are frustrated along the way.

At the University of Michigan's graduate library, there has been a steady demand for Internet workshops, primarily those geared toward Gopher users among both library staff and the campus population. These workshops, which generally run for one hour, have been relatively easy to prepare in terms of lectures, demonstrations, and instructional materials because most patrons find that using the Gopher software is almost self explanatory. In fact, planning at least half the session for "freestyle" hands-on exploration (augmented by suggested exercises that involve searching Gopherspace and WWW exploration) makes for a very enjoyable experience for instructors and attendees alike.

Technical Services

The Internet greatly enhances both circulation and inter-library loan primarily through increased access to online catalogs. If your library has an online catalog, it makes sense to make it available to patrons over the Internet. Online catalogs allow a patron greater convenience in completing an online search; additionally, the patron can check holdings records at the office or at home to avoid coming to the library for a book that has already been checked out. Studies have demonstrated that people tend to use the information geographically closest to them, such as a personal or departmental collection, or, if they have a desktop computer, information accessible over a network. Thus, providing Internet access to your catalog places it on the patron's desktop and can actually increase the use of your library's collection.

In fact, hundreds of libraries all over the world have made their catalogs accessible over the Internet. One of the main reasons librarians use the Internet is to access the online catalogs of other libraries. Extensive guides to Internet-accessible library catalogs have been prepared by Art St. George and Ron Larsen, and by Billy Barron; the Hytelnet system, discussed in Chapter 29, "Opening Doors with Hytelnet," provides direct menu-based access to these catalogs.

If a patron comes to your desk with a potential inter-library loan request, you may find a nearby library that can help without going through the hoops of OCLC, RLIN, or another bibliographic utility. It's known that many libraries keep their own catalogs more up-to-date than the information they provide to these utilities. Finding the book in a nearby library's catalog, copying the bibliographic information from the screen, and forwarding it to the other library in an electronic mail message can greatly speed the ILL process. In fact, patrons are often more than willing to go to a nearby library themselves to use the book, avoiding ILL altogether.

Catalogers can also benefit from using remote online catalogs in much the same way they use OCLC and RLIN. Enhanced copy cataloging is an obvious benefit of this practice. Additionally, a cataloger of, say, Slavic materials may use the Internet to directly access the online system of a library with a well-respected collection of Russian and Polish works.

There is a flip side to the benefits derived from having off-campus folks access your library's catalog. Increased usage of your catalog may heighten the strain placed on your system; similarly, more external ILL requests may tax your collection. Now that your catalog's potential user base has been broadened considerably, it may be necessary to redesign certain aspects of your catalog, such as blocking unauthorized access to commercial database services offered on your catalog, or changing online help features. Many online catalogs were originally designed to be accessed only from within libraries and only from computers administered by the library staff. In this scenario, providing on-screen instructions on how to log off the catalog would be ill-advised because a naive patron may feel obligated to do so after each session. However, it may be prudent to provide this information to patrons who access the catalog remotely. Unfortunately, there are few hard-and-fast rules for deciding such issues.

Doing What We've Never Done Before

The Internet opens up countless new possibilities for academic libraries and their patrons. From gleaning information from electronic communities to joining the ranks of "publishers," academic librarians are using the Internet in creative ways, and in the process are gaining increased recognition and respect from other professions. Such positive exposure is not only an enjoyable experience for librarians, but also may solidify the often-shaky standing of academic libraries on college campuses.

People: The Internet's Greatest Information Resource

Following are two more "success stories" from Karen G. Schneider's compilation.

Susan G. Miles, Central Michigan University, Michigan: "When there was some question about the prudent practice of obtaining HIV testing for an adoptive infant born to an at-risk mother, I queried the NETNEWS group `sci.med.aids`.

"Within a week, I received replies from all over the country, several from professionals working at specialized clinics, MDs, and the Pediatric AIDS Foundation. The information was invaluable and the patrons were greatly relieved."

Mary I. Piette, Utah State University, Utah: "I worked with a young graduate student this summer who, as a doctoral candidate in natural resources and as a graduate in anthropology, was looking for information on women in pastoral systems in Morocco and Africa. [On the Internet,] I listed our findings and where we were looking, and found a network of people all over the United States and Britain....We found incredible help and a new network of colleagues."

These librarians used mailing lists or Usenet newsgroups to solicit assistance from specific electronic "communities." There are literally thousands of such communities dealing with almost every topic imaginable. A brief query to one or more of these communities is read by dozens, hundreds, or perhaps thousands of people who are interested (if not expert) in that topic. Such a query can elicit dozens of well-conceived, helpful responses (as well as some less-than-helpful ones, of course).

Librarians have always relied on expert individuals for assistance; this approach is in no way unique to the Internet environment. But the ability to contact so many individuals quickly and cheaply, and to rapidly receive so much free advice in return, is certainly a special quality unique to the Internet. The open and helpful attitude that occurs in many mailing lists and newsgroups is augmented by the equalizing effect of the medium. The pioneers and experts in a field are often as likely to respond to your query as the generalists and novices. In effect, queries such as those mentioned here create temporary "special interest groups" among those who respond. A topic such as "women in pastoral systems in Morocco" probably isn't discussed often, and the process of responding to it may be as thought provoking and gratifying for the respondents as it is for the originator of the query.

Many academic library patrons are unfamiliar with the Internet and therefore will be awed by a librarian who can harvest the human sources of knowledge available over mailing lists and newsgroups. However, some patrons in academia are old hands in these media; in fact, in many fields, especially the hard sciences, the bulk of new knowledge is exchanged in the "invisible colleges" supported by electronic discussion groups. The pioneers of a field may share their working papers and technical reports with each other electronically six months or a year before their ideas are published in print. For academic librarians involved in these fields, simply keeping up with the latest journal issues won't impress patrons; in these cases, it's a necessity for librarians to monitor the related mailing lists and newsgroups.

Academic librarians themselves can also benefit from participating in electronic discussion groups in a number of ways. Job performance can be improved, for example, by asking subscribers to the library administration Listserv (`libadmin@umab.umd.edu`) for their opinions on a specific management technique, or by contacting other Notis-savvy librarians (`notis-l@uicvm.uic.edu`) for tips on handling the new circulation module. Librarians can enhance their professional activities by participating in discussion groups centered around professional societies; an example is the ALA Social Responsibility Round Table Feminist Task Force (`feminist@mitvma.mit.edu`). Many mailing lists and newsgroups are useful for learning about new information resources, especially those available on the Internet. Gleason Sackman's net-happenings (`net-happenings@is.internic.net` with a majordomo subscription) is one of the most valuable and best-known of these notification lists.

Academic Libraries as Internet Publishers

The technologies and tools used for making information available on the Internet are relatively inexpensive and easy to implement. The ready availability of Gopher and World Wide Web software is in large part responsible for the recent information explosion on the Internet because, in addition to being popular among users, they don't demand much expertise from the server's administrators. Nor do these packages demand much of the data itself, which can often remain in plain ASCII text format. This kind of "publishing" requires a much broader definition than the traditional sense of the word; certainly, there are electronic journals (such as *Psycoloquy* and *Public Access Computing Systems Review*) that undergo processes of refereeing and peer-review equal to print journals. But the majority of information undergoes no such review, resulting in the quality problems described earlier. The information is simply made accessible by individuals or institutions, using Gophers, Listservs, the World Wide Web, and other Internet tools, to anyone who is interested. Thus, on the Internet, publishing can be defined as the act of making information available for use by communities, regardless of the level of filtering involved.

With extensive knowledge of the nature of information, of patron needs, and of specific subject domains, academic librarians possess a unique blend of skills that can go a long way in improving the Internet's "publishing" process. So it's no surprise that academic libraries have become involved more and more in enhancing this information environment. They are accomplishing this in two ways: libraries are making new, high-quality information resources available on the Internet; and libraries are adding value to existing information resources through repackaging and applying quality-control mechanisms.

A number of quality resources have been made available to the Internet community by the University of Michigan library (`http://www.lib.umich.edu/libhome/index.html`). In addition to the popular Economic Bulletin Board (mentioned earlier in this chapter), the library's Gopher and WWW server has made U.S. census data for the state of Michigan available. This resource provides statistical tables at various levels: state, county, city, and township. The library's Systems Office was already experienced in handling government data tapes and the statistical analysis software needed to create these tables, and its personnel successfully collaborated with staff reference and government-documents librarians to determine table layouts. Probably the first census resource available in Gopherspace, it has served as a model for other institutions' efforts at bringing up census data.

Similarly, once the government-documents librarian had realized the ease of adding data to the library's Gopher, she compiled a number of other useful resources, including the U.S. Congress's committee assignments. This information primarily was taken from various print sources and keyed in by student staff; the files were added to the library's Gopher and WAIS-indexed for full-text searching, and then publicized to librarians on various Listservs, such as the Government Documents list (`govdoc-1@psuvm.psu.edu`). From planning to implementation to successful publicity, the entire project took up only a small part of an already busy week.

Adding value to existing resources on the Internet is at least as important as adding new high-quality resources. Academic librarians can improve on the efforts of other information providers in ways that don't require a huge time investment and, in the process, provide direct benefits to their patrons. In fact, information providers are often grateful for the kind of assistance librarians can provide.

The "art of repackaging" information for specific audiences and uses manifests itself in two ways: through relabeling (or indexing) existing information and by combining existing information in new and more useful ways. The first case may include working with a campus computing center or other group that maintains an anonymous FTP archive to use more explicit file and directory names and to provide explanatory "readme" files to assist users. Relabeling also may involve working with a remote Gopher site to improve the terminology used in the design of a popular resource's menu labels. For example, University of Michigan librarians found a number of United Nations data files that seemed appropriate to point to from the library's Gopher. However, these files' Gopher menu labels were less than ideal; it was resolved not to include these pointers in the library's Gopher until their labels were substantially improved. Instead of waiting for these changes to happen, the University of Michigan librarians initiated a relationship with the maintainers of these files and subsequently provided them with a more concise and comprehensible naming scheme for files. These files were then added to the remote site's Gopher, thus making the information more usable. This informal collaborative effort was made possible by the open and unassuming nature of the Internet.

This kind of repackaging is being made even easier by the use of material written in HTML for the World Wide Web. The Web provides a particularly useful interface for arranging and re-arranging data and resources in nonlinear trees.

The second kind of repackaging involves assembling related resources in a single central location. We know how difficult it is to find information on a specific topic among such heterogeneous and distributed resources. By doing what is, in effect, the "legwork" of Internet searching, the academic librarian can pull together and evaluate the items useful to his or her patron community. The "sum is greater than the parts" perfectly describes the results of this repackaging process, because there is often an increased and synergistic use of a related group of resources where before there may have been little or no use of the individual resources. An extensive collection of relevant resources is an excellent carrot with which to entice patrons. Repackaging can be accomplished by compiling a directory or guide to the various topics' Internet resources, or by organizing a Gopher or World Wide Web server by subject or by audience. For example, a committee consisting of librarians expert in different subject areas runs the University of Michigan library's Gopher server. It is logical that these librarians take responsibilities for the various subject branches in the Gopher because they are in close touch with their patron communities, they understand the content of the relevant resources, and they are interested in monitoring developments in their specific subject areas. They also return to their communities and "market" the new resources they've added, thus improving patrons' impressions of the library and its staff.

Other Projects and Services

As the information explosion continues at an alarming clip, current-awareness services become increasingly necessary for any researcher, academic or otherwise, who wants to keep up with his or her field. Fortunately, combining the Internet's tools for moving data with existing information resources can make it quite simple to create a current-awareness service. At the University of Michigan library, a "quick and dirty" professional reading service was established to serve staff librarians and the faculty and students of the School of Information and Library Studies. Electronic tables of contents for over one hundred information and library-studies journals were already being produced by volunteers at BUBL (the Bulletin Board for Libraries) at `http://www.bubl.bath.ac.uk/BUBL/`, a cooperative effort of librarians primarily in the United Kingdom. It was decided that simply directing patrons and librarians to this bulletin board was insufficient; instead, automatically sending these tables of contents directly to patrons with electronic mail seemed to offer more promise. To this end, a self-service "subscription" service was established; this service requires patrons to subscribe to any of the approximately one hundred mailing lists that were created to correspond to each journal title. The X.500 directory service, a standard application that is increasingly common to academic TCP/IP networks, makes it easy to create and maintain mailing lists. Thanks to an arrangement with BUBL, the tables-of-contents files are obtained as soon as they are released. These files are then automatically "fed" to a simple script, which in turn mails each journal to its corresponding X.500 mailing list. This system is much quicker than photocopying and routing tables of contents to every interested patron, and less expensive than maintaining special subscriptions of journals solely for forwarding from patron to patron.

Academic librarians may consider building much more ambitious current-awareness services. Such services would go beyond informing patrons of new items within a particular resource; instead, as Paul Evan Peters suggests, these services would inform patrons of the actual existence of such resources. Within the context of the Internet, librarians could monitor specific subject areas and forward information on relevant high-quality resources to faculty groups and individuals. This type of service represents an activist extension of both the traditional selection process and the kind of "Internet resource discovery" already involved in maintaining subject-oriented Gopher and World Wide Web servers.

Entering the Internet environment can enable academic librarians and their libraries to play a greater and often rewarding role in uncharted territories. For example, the MLink project (`http://mlink.hh.lib.umich.edu/MLink.html`), which extended the University of Michigan library's reference services to a group of public libraries around the state, achieved improved service and greater visibility by providing a high-quality Gopher server to the community. Libraries may be more likely to get involved in collaborations with other libraries and with nonlibrary units as well. For example, staff from the University of Michigan library contributed to efforts at Yale University's computing center to maintain a Gopher and WWW branch (`http://www.library.yale.edu/`) for connections to Internet-accessible library catalogs. Because so much of the productive activity on the Internet depends on this type of collaborative work, librarians find themselves teaming with computer programmers, university administrators, faculty, and others at their own institutions and elsewhere, many of whom they have not had the opportunity to work with before. These encounters are excellent opportunities to demonstrate the value of librarianship to those who may have questioned it and to learn more about the issues dealt with in other fields.

The Internet and the Academic Library: Tips and Pointers

Although the Internet can enhance or create new library services, there are many related issues that deserve consideration. The following sections discuss a few of the issues that will crop up at one time or another for just about every academic library joining the Net.

Bringing Up the Internet: Some Considerations

Your goal simply may be to bring the Internet to your library and its patrons. But it's even more important to determine just what kind of connectivity you need before you start. Having the Internet "up and running" means different things to different people. Access to the Internet may be as minimal as having an account somewhere that can exchange electronic mail with others on the Internet. It can also mean that your library has its own server-class computers and direct TCP/IP connectivity from workstations throughout the building. Similarly, your patrons are likely to have an even greater range of levels of Internet access.

With so many factors involved, things can quickly get confusing. For this reason, your best bet is to follow these two rules:

- **Plan to implement at least the same level of connectivity that the majority of your patrons already have.** You want your patrons to consider your library as technically advanced as they are. Of course, to find this out, you must survey your users. Simple questions such as "Do you have an account that allows you to use electronic mail?", "Do you use a modem to access your account?", and "Which of the following do you use: WWW, Telnet, FTP, Gopher, ...?" can go a long way in helping determine the level of connectivity and expertise that best characterizes your patrons. You also can find out what the campus' level of connectivity is from the computing center, your library's system office, or departmental system administrators. Keep in mind that by the time your network is operational, your patron community's connectivity already may have been upgraded; if it's possible, give some consideration to a state-of-the-art configuration.

- **Determine what type of services you want to provide and make sure that your connectivity and equipment allow you to run those services.** Initially, you may want to allow patrons to use workstations solely to Telnet to a public Gopher site run by another institution. Perhaps you will be Gopher-izing your own information resources or putting together WWW home pages, and you want to allow patrons to use the friendlier, more powerful client applications from library workstations. Each case requires very different types of connectivity, hardware, and maintenance, and no single piece of advice can cover all situations, whether technical or budgetary.

Who should be responsible for bringing the Internet to an academic library? Traditionally, the Internet has come to academic libraries through the extremes of the library hierarchy, and often with significant levels of tension between the two. Administrators frequently take their libraries on great leaps forward into the realm of the Internet and are responsible for large-scale changes, such as improvements in network connectivity. The librarians "in the trenches" may have been using the Internet for years, often without realizing it, through direct contact with their patron communities; beginning with sending electronic mail and accessing other libraries' catalogs, they likely are increasing their Internet skills. Connectivity and hardware are expensive propositions for an academic library and may require the creative budgeting that can be done only by upper management. However, the connectivity hardware and the flashy new machines will go unused if there is lackadaisical interest or resistance on the part of the rank and file. The vision of library management, greatly shaped by the highly coordinated efforts needed to bring up an integrated library system, may clash with the decentralized nature of the Internet's information environment and the makeshift tools already in the hands of lower-level staff.

Somewhere in between, of course, lies an ideal solution that combines aspects of rapid top-down revolution and gradual grassroots evolution. As lower-level librarians work where the rubber meets the road, they are more likely to be in tune with what kinds of services their patrons need. These librarians, already busy with existing responsibilities, will resist new pressures on their time that are handed down from on high. The pace of change should be dictated by those in the trenches, and the role of library administrators should be one of offering encouragement and technical support as the changes begin to assert themselves.

Note that the preceding paragraph describes the ideal solution. For numerous reasons—some budgetary, some time-sensitive, and some just plain turf-oriented—this scenario is not likely to happen very often. Library administrators themselves are under increasing pressure from provosts and presidents to rapidly move their libraries ahead in the arena of information technology. For these reasons, our old friend, the library committee, is likely the best solution for bringing the Internet to the academic library. A committee drawn from all levels of a library's hierarchy and representing various aspects of public and technical services can actually be quite effective if it understands that the Internet is indeed radically different from traditional information environments.

Generating Staff Support

One of the main charges of an Internet implementation committee is to ensure that librarians will have tangible support in their efforts to become users and builders of the Internet. This can be accomplished through regularly offered training sessions and, more importantly, through encouraging Internet exploration and experimentation. Training sessions should not portray the Internet as a panacea, but instead should honestly describe the bad as well as the good because few skeptical librarians will appreciate a "sell job." Additionally, such sessions should teach the use of the Internet's many tools but should also demonstrate how the Internet can be used practically in libraries. Sessions ideally should be led by an experienced and respected librarian who can use pertinent examples and anecdotes (rather than by a member of another profession or department) to validate further the learning experience. If no such librarian exists on campus, it is well worth the investment to borrow one from elsewhere.

Encouraging staff to spend time personally exploring the Internet is a difficult decision on the manager's part because this time-consuming process can affect the already strapped workloads of various library units. However, today's unguided explorations bring tangible returns tomorrow in many ways. And because most ALA-accredited degree programs don't yet require Internet competency, "surfing" the Internet and experimenting with bringing up servers are the only ways to build the necessary in-house expertise. Librarians should be encouraged to play and, if they are bringing up a server, to make mistakes. Such mistakes are never irreparable or costly in the low-overhead environment of the Internet.

Integrating the Internet into All Aspects of Your Library's Collection

Aside from introducing aspects of the Internet into the library's job descriptions, the Internet's information resources also should be integrated fully into the library's holdings and related policies. As mentioned earlier, the resources available over the Internet augment and complement a library's holdings, and as such should be relied on like other parts of its collection. Similarly, an academic library's collection-development policy should be modified to include this environment. It is a mistake to create separate policies for the treatment of Internet resources because such policies reinforce existing walls between the Internet environment and traditional environments. However, it is still useful to design policies that recognize the different characteristics of the Internet's resources. For example, when making decisions on which remote resources to point to from a Gopher server, ease of access, not ownership, is a key difference in comparison to traditional collection development.

Think Big

Most of all, academic librarians should see the Internet as a liberating influence because its low cost and powerful tools provide many opportunities to implement new and creative services. Aside from making bibliographic and full-text files available, librarians can begin to experiment with the publishing of nontraditional formats. For example, music librarians from various institutions can now consider cooperatively mounting a great collection of audio files by using tools like Mosaic or Netscape, or making documents available in portable document formats like Acrobat. Would this have been possible a few years ago? Would these librarians have been able to create the same level of community in the days before electronic mailing lists? Although the Internet game can be expensive and difficult to play, there really is no excuse for academic libraries to sit this one out. In the next century, information will be used on college campuses in different ways than we can now imagine. It is up to academic librarians to lead this charge, instead of being run over by it.

REFERENCE WORKS

Atkinson, R. May 1993. "Networks, Hypertext, and Academic Information Services: Some Longer-Range Implications." College & Research Libraries 54 (3): 199-215.

Dell, E. Y., and N. I. Henry. March 1993. "A Resource Sharing Project Using Ariel Technology." Medical Reference Services Quarterly 12 (1).

Jordan, J., and L. Brintle. February 1993. "Coalition for Communication: Developing a Public Communication System." Computers in Libraries 13 (2): 29-32.

Kountz, J. 1992. "Tomorrow's Libraries: More than a Modular Telephone Jack, Less than a Complete Revolution—Perspectives of a Provocateur." Library Hi Tech 10 (4): 39-50.

Lynch, C. A. 1989. "Linking Library Automation Systems in the Internet: Functional Requirements, Planning, and Policy Issues." Library Hi Tech 7 (4): 7-18.

Mitchell, M., and L. M. Saunders. April 1991. "The Virtual Library: An Agenda for the 1990s." Computers in Libraries 11 (4): 8, 10-11.

Peters, P. E. April 1992. "Networked Information Resources and Services: Next Steps." Computers in Libraries 12 (4): 46-55.

Summerhill, C. A. 1992. "Internetworking: New Opportunities and Challenges in Resource Sharing." Resource Sharing and Information Networks 8 (1): 105-25.

Sutton, B. December 1992. "The Networked Future of Academic Libraries." Illinois Libraries 74 (6): 500-06.

Net-Surfing Public Librarians

44

by John Iliff

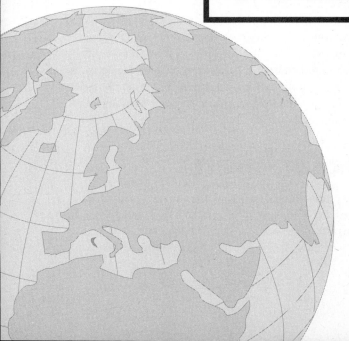

The public library is a place with long-running stereotypes. The image of Marian the Librarian comes to mind, with her index finger firmly affixed to pursed lips, hissing *Shhhhh!* The Beach Boys sang about the library as the place where kids tell their parents they are going when their real intention is to have "Fun, fun, fun until Daddy takes the T-Bird away."

If you haven't noticed, public libraries have changed. They are in the forefront of providing new information technology. Libraries were the first major markets for CD-ROM products, and computerized library catalogs are the rule not the exception. For more than 20 years, librarians have used computer networks to facilitate interlibrary loans—the borrowing of books between libraries. The primary users of commercial databases are librarians.

If Marian the Librarian was working in a public library today, she wouldn't have time to shush noisy library users; her hands would be busy at a computer keyboard. Kids are coming to libraries to have fun, fun, fun playing computer games like *Where in the World Is Carmen Sandiego.* Get rid of those stereotypes—public libraries are on the cutting edge of technology.

True to form, librarians are embracing the Internet as another method to serve their public. The number of public librarians gaining access to the Internet is growing exponentially; librarians were discussing Internet terminology and techniques well before the present burst of attention in the general press. Although some public librarians have yet to begin using the Internet, many already are.

Like others, the participation of public librarians on the Internet has grown exponentially. In early 1992, I conducted a survey of several library-oriented Listservs. The survey merely asked any public librarians with Internet access to reply; the survey garnered a mere twenty respondents. A year later, a similar survey garnered well over three hundred replies. In 1995, a review of just two Listservs revealed well over three thousand public librarians with Internet addresses.

One significant aspect of librarians' increased involvement in the Internet is that librarians provide equitable access for the public as a whole. The Internet clearly offers many valuable tools, but as the Internet now stands, many people cannot afford to access or do not understand how to maneuver in this vast resource. Public libraries comprise a ready-made network of institutions providing equal access to information, so a logical step is that public libraries continue the tradition with the Internet. Public libraries can ensure that our society has no new gulf between information-haves and information-have-nots.

E-Mail and Electronic Conferences

The most common use of the Internet by public librarians is electronic mail, or e-mail. Like the postal service, electronic mail is a way of delivering messages. Unlike postal mail, however, electronic mail is sent within seconds to anyone in the world with an Internet address. Because postal mail is relatively slow, public librarians (as well as other Net users) call it *snail mail.*

At the most fundamental level, public librarians use e-mail to communicate from one individual to another. E-mail is considerably less expensive than long-distance phone calls, and because the receiver of messages doesn't have to be in to receive the message, phone tag is eliminated. Best yet, e-mail helps eliminate the need for meetings and long-distance travel because librarians can compare notes without coming face to face.

With e-mail, librarians can communicate with no geographic limitations. Friendships and working relationships are developing on an intercontinental basis as librarians collaborate on a variety of tasks. In many instances, users of e-mail never meet—they get to know each other only by the bits and bytes they send each other. This way of meeting is ideal because visual prejudices are discarded and the merit of a person is determined purely by the worth of his or her ideas.

Listservs

Like others on the Internet, librarians have used e-mail to develop what are variably called *Listservs, e-conferences, mail reflectors,* or *lists.* With this service, relatively simple software transmits all messages sent to the conference to all the interested parties. Recipients of these messages, called *subscribers,* can send messages to the list as well as receive them.

Electronic conferences come in two forms: moderated and unmoderated. On *unmoderated lists,* the computer software sends all messages without any human intervention. *Moderated lists* involve human intervention before messages are sent (or in Net parlance, are *posted*). Moderators can ensure that discussions remain on topic, as well as provide assistance to the list subscribers. Fortunately, most librarian lists on the Internet are moderated.

STUMPERS

STUMPERS is a straightforward and useful implementation of Listserv software (refer to Chapter 32, "Creating and Administering Mailing Lists," for more information on Listserv). Here, librarians send difficult, or stumper, questions to the list subscribers. The questions range from ones as simple as locating recipes to erudite questions involving scientific formulas. With STUMPERS, librarians can draw on the collective wisdom of librarians and libraries throughout the world. Rarely does a question sent to this conference go unanswered.

PACS-L

The oldest and most popular of all librarian-related lists is PACS-L. In this conference, the focus is on computer systems and related topics. Among the types of issues under discussion are the development of electronic journals and new advances in information technology. PACS-L is the flagship of librarian electronic conferences.

LIBADMIN

Another Listserv service public librarians use is LIBADMIN. On this conference, sometimes called the *boss list*, librarians discuss administrative concerns such as long-range planning and personnel issues. Job openings are advertised on this list (and on many other librarian lists).

LIBREF-L

LIBREF-L is an electronic forum with an emphasis on library reference topics. Librarians discuss new technology in the reference process, the best reference resources, and a host of other matters. The originator of this conference, Diane Kovacs, maintains an electronic directory of electronic conferences, not only in the library field but throughout academia. Public librarians have found this resource useful in locating electronic discussions on a variety of topics.

PUBLIB and PUBLIB-NET

Beginning in December 1992, public librarians obtained their own Listserv with the appearance of PUBLIB (rhymes with *fib*). Housed on the main computer in NYSERNet, a mid-level Internet provider for the state of New York, PUBLIB's growth has been spectacular. Starting with 200 subscribers, the list grew in two years to almost 3,000 users from every continent except Antarctica (no public libraries are in Antarctica yet). One significant factor for the growth of PUBLIB is that it enjoys the leadership of Jean Armour Polly, the most experienced Net-surfing librarian around.

PUBLIB originally was designed to focus on the Internet and its applications within public libraries. Within a short period of time, the emphasis of the list broadened to include all issues of the public library world. In March 1993, PUBLIB-NET was created to dispense messages sent to PUBLIB having only an Internet emphasis. In effect, PUBLIB-NET is a list within a list, but the service has proven useful for users interested in the development of the Internet in public libraries but not interested in reading about the myriad of other issues public librarians confront.

SUBSCRIBING TO LISTSERV

The process for subscribing and unsubscribing to Listserv is easy but can be fraught with mistakes. Users must keep in mind that to subscribe or unsubscribe to a list requires sending messages to a separate Internet address than the address for posting messages. For example, if a fictional person named Joan Smith wants to subscribe to PUBLIB, she sends a message to address `listserv@nysernet.org`. The message contains this simple line: `sub publib Joan Smith`. If Joan Smith wants to post a message to the readers of PUBLIB, she sends a message to `publib@nysernet.org`. Many new users embarrass themselves by sending messages to a list's posting software with messages such as sub this list Joan Smith. The mistake is inescapable after the Listserv distributes the message, and in many instances the message is read by thousands around the world!

The following list contains the subscription addresses for the listservs mentioned in this chapter:

Listserv	*Subscription Address*
LIBADMIN:	listserv@umab.umd.edu
LIBREF-L:	listserv@kentvm.kent.edu
PACS-L:	listserv@uhupvm1.uh.edu
PUBLIB:	listserv@nysernet.org
PUBLIB-NET:	listserv@nysernet.org
PUBYAC:	listserv@nysernet.org
STUMPERS-L:	mailserv@crf.cuis.edu

Because public libraries are public institutions, the topics covered on PUBLIB are the same as those encountered by the society at large. Homelessness, latchkey children, and illiteracy all have been discussed on PUBLIB. Also, PUBLIB has covered specific public library concerns, such as whether libraries should lend hand tools, whether overdue fines are worthwhile, and what is the best software for securing CD-ROM workstations against teenage hackers.

Following is a list of subject headings for messages that appear on a typical PUBLIB day. The sample messages include a job opening announcement, a question regarding how libraries are using barcodes, and a query on methods for arranging picture files. One message (number 10) includes an announcement of the linking of Seattle Public Library's catalog to the Internet. The messages with Re: at the beginning are responses to previous messages. These ongoing discussions, called *threads*, can continue for months. Item number 11 is an announcement by LITA (Library Information and Technology Association), a division the American Library Association (ALA). In general, the ALA has been aggressive using e-mail on the Internet, conducting surveys, making announcements, and providing electronic journals and newsletters. One notable ALA newsletter is *ALAWON*, the Washington Office Newsletter. This irregularly published periodical keeps librarians informed of developments in Washington (many librarians have mobilized to respond to important legislation as a result of this publication).

```
1.    User Support and Training Positions Open at NYSERNet, Inc..
2.    Re: Ref. Question: Graduate Degree through online study.
3.    On The Lighter Side.
4.    PICTURE FILE.
5.    periodicals for gay/lesbian teens.
6.    3rd party collect calls.
7.    Re: Query: Black library users and Internet.
8.    REFORMATTING A VERTICAL FILE.
9.    BARCODE.
10.   Public Internet Access at Seattle Publib
11.   LITA NEWSLETTER NOW AVAILABLE ONLINE.
```

The following is an example of a posting on PUBLIB. This message, which was an attempt to locate humorous reference experiences, garnered 10 responses. Most responses arrived within two weeks, although this topic has continued on the list in one form or another for several months.

```
>From publll  Wed Sep 22 23:14:101994
Date: Wed, 22 May 95 23:14:10 -0400
From: publll (Publib Poster)
Received: by nysernet.ORG (5.65/3.1.090690-NYSERnet Inc.)id
       AA16304; 22 May 95  23:14:10 -0400
Message-Id: <9309230314.AA16304@nysernet.ORG>
To: publib
Subject: On The Lighter Side
I think anyone who works in a library has humorous moments, it comes with working
with the public. As a reference librarian one of my funniest moments was when a
patron asked for a "urology," and after a few questions and answers I learned she
was actually looking for a eulogy. A friend out west told me about a patron who
asked for maps to uncharted isles, and another librarian told me about a student
who was looking for an English translation of Shakespeare. PUBLIB's very own Jean
Armour Polly was once asked for a photograph of dinosaurs, and I had a similar
request for a photo of Julius Caesar.
Do you have similar stories? Of course, our intention here is not to poke fun at
our patrons, we LOVE the folks who keep us employed. Rather, it might be fun just
to hear of those crazy moments that made you laugh.
Please post any stories to me, and I'll post back to PUBLIB.
Keep smiling-

John Iliff
on Coquina Key, FL
p00710@psilink.com
```

PUBYAC

In 1993, PUBYAC was created as the first specialized, public librarian discussion list. On this conference, children and youth-service librarians trade ideas. Discussions range from comparing story-telling techniques to how to entice reluctant teenage readers into the library. Youth-service librarians around the world have found PUBYAC indispensable.

Usenet

Like Listserv conferences, Usenet (also called News or Usenet news) provides topic-oriented discussions. Usenet is a *distributed bulletin board,* meaning that Usenet conferences, called *newsgroups,* are distributed from central sites, enabling users to drop in and out of discussions. On Listserv, all users receive all messages, but on Usenet, users pick what messages they receive. This feature is a definite advantage, and some Listserv conferences are now available on Usenet—notably PACS-L and LIBREF-L as well as some solely library-oriented newsgroups such as soc.libraries.talk. E-mail overload can be a problem for subscribers of Listservs, and Usenet offers a good remedy.

Usenet is huge, covering virtually every topic people can devise. The breadth of subjects provides public librarians with the chance to contact thousands of aficionados, experts, and arm-chair philosophers on everything from rock and roll to Visual Basic programming. For example, one librarian was asked to locate information for a local Bonsai Club (Bonsai are those little Japanese trees). Not surprisingly, the librarian found two active Usenet newsgroups on the subject (alt.bonsai and rec.arts.bonsai) and was able to put the local club in contact with Bonsai growers from around the world.

Hot Internet Resources for Public Librarians

Outside of e-mail, the Internet provides a slew of resources for public librarians. By using Internet tools such as Telnet, Gopher, the World Wide Web, and File Transfer Protocol (FTP), public librarians can connect with other computers on the Internet in live sessions.

Throughout history, the worth of a library (and the ability of a librarian to provide information) has been determined by the size of the library collection. For people with access to a large library, information was easy to obtain. For people in rural areas or in equally remote inner cities, information was often hard to come by. The Internet changes this disadvantage, giving a librarian in Plentywood, Montana, the same Internet resources available to a librarian at Columbia University. The only limitation is the skill of the librarian at getting to the information.

NOTE

A few cautionary words are in order. Although the Internet offers vast resources, it does not (yet) replace a good reference collection. As the Internet now exists, some strong areas have excellent information, but the Internet cannot meet every information need. The World Book Encyclopedia is still a must, but that doesn't mean the Internet can't be extremely useful.

Catalog of Federal Domestic Assistance

One source of good information on the Internet is the U.S. Government. A good example is the *Catalog of Federal Domestic Assistance*. This large book is available in almost every public library in the United States. The *Catalog* is filled with federal program after federal program that can aid citizens. Unfortunately, in paper form, the *Catalog* is almost entirely useless: the index is unworkable. As every reference librarian knows, this potentially valuable resource usually sits unused on shelves. Many people have made a career out of taking information from the *Catalog* and making it available in expensive packages featured on infomercials.

The *Catalog*'s use has changed, however. The *Catalog* is now available on the Internet by using convenient Gopher software. As a result (thanks to computer indexing), the *Catalog* is transformed into a powerful tool. In one example, a public librarian assisted a handicapped person in finding federal programs that would help her open a business. Using the Internet version of the *Catalog*, the librarian located the information and printed it in a few minutes. As an experiment, the same search was done with the paper form of the *Catalog*—it took 40 minutes, including time for copying and reviewing text. The *Catalog of Federal Domestic Assistance* is available in Gopherspace to `gopher://solar.rtd.utk.edu:70/70/Federal/CFDA` (see the following Note box.)

> **NOTE**
>
> **About the address conventions used in this chapter:**
>
> Information about finding the resources described in this chapter can be found at the specified URL site.
>
> If you are new to the Internet, this information may seem confusing. If an item is available from Telnet, the address is indicated as well as the login information (for example, to connect to the Seattle Public Library with Telnet, the address is `spl.lib.wa.us` and the login is `library`). A listing for a resource in Gopherspace, in the World Wide Web, or with File Transfer Protocol (FTP) follows the Uniform Resource Locator convention; for example, the URL `gopher://marvel.loc.gov/70/11/copyright` indicates that the Uniform Resource Locator is for a Gopher address at `marvel.loc.gov` with a directory that contains copyright information. Merely type the information provided using your favorite Net software, and you'll find the designated resource!

LOCIS

Through its Marvel Gopher, the Library of Congress World Wide Web page, as well as direct Telnet, the Library of Congress has a very useful service for public librarians: LOCIS (the Library of Congress Information System). On LOCIS, the greater portion of the Library of

Congress card catalog is available—with more than 20 million records. LOCIS is particularly useful for librarians trying to locate obscure titles or complete bibliographic data on newly released titles. LOCIS also houses a list of copyrighted works beginning in 1978, including film, sound recordings, and software. In addition, the LOCIS database contains a tracking system for bills in Congress. Part of the tracking system contains a list of bills proposed by each legislator in the course of various congressional sessions. This system helps keep library users informed on what their representatives are really doing in Washington. LOCIS is available through Telnet to `locis.loc.gov`, on the World Wide Web at `http://lcweb.loc.gov`, and in Gopherspace to `gopher://marvel.loc.gov`.

White House Information

The Executive branch of the U.S. Government also is becoming an active player on the Internet. Both the President and Vice President have Internet e-mail addresses (`president@whitehouse.gov` and `vice.president@whitehouse.gov`). In addition, the President provides press releases and position papers on a variety of subjects. Public librarians are finding these sources useful for obtaining the president's views—unaltered by the press. In one case, current Clinton position papers were obtained for a graduate student in a remote study course. This student did not have access to her home campus library and also did not have borrowing privileges at a nearby university. With the Internet, however, quality information such as the Clinton papers were conveniently available in her neighborhood branch public library. White House documents are available on the World Wide Web at `http://www.whitehouse.gov` and in Gopherspace to `gopher://gopher.tamu.edu`.

FedWorld

The National Technical Information Service, an independent agency in the U.S. Federal Government charged with providing technical resources, has developed FedWorld. This unique gateway service provides a seamless link to over 100 federal government electronic bulletin board systems (BBS). These BBSes, most using the same type of software used by amateur BBS operators, contain a wealth of information for public libraries. Virtually every major U.S. agency is represented, including NASA, the Census Department, the Department of Energy, and the Commerce Department. Each BBS contains pronouncements from the agencies and downloadable files containing government documents as well as software.

An example of a BBS available on FedWorld is the Consumer Information Center BBS, produced by the General Services Administration. This system maintains message and bulletin areas in which citizens can query agency representatives as well as obtain hundreds of useful documents. Included on this system is the *Consumer Information Catalog* (and many of the documents advertised in the catalog). You can access information on how to purchase a car, how to get the best price for insurance, or how to avoid getting AIDS. The availability of the

Consumer Information Catalog is particularly useful for public librarians. This item is very popular, and with this resource online, no public library with Internet access need ever be without a current issue. FedWorld is available through Telnet to `fedworld.gov`.

National Institutes of Health

The National Institutes of Health (NIH) Gopher and World Wide Web servers provide excellent information on medical topics. Included is CancerNet, which contains readable and current information on cancer and cancer treatment. These NIH servers also contain the National AIDS Information Clearinghouse, which provides a variety of documents on AIDS. Among the documents are instructions on how to care for AIDS patients, a discussion on condoms and sexually transmitted diseases, and recent reports from the Center for Disease Control. As any public librarian knows, this information is in high demand; providing it can save lives. The NIH servers are available on the World Wide Web at `http://www.nih.gov` and in Gopherspace to `gopher://gopher.nih.gov`.

Weather Underground

Weather information is available on the Internet (among other places) through the Weather Underground at the University of Michigan. This service gives up-to-date forecasts and weather conditions for cities and states in the United States as provided by the National Weather Service. With this service, librarians can rapidly obtain weather information for library users, particularly travelers. The Weather Underground also displays ski forecasts, Canadian weather forecasts, U.S. Marine coastal forecasts, severe weather information, and temperatures from major cities around the world. The Weather Underground is available through Telnet to `downwind.sprl.umich.edu`, port 3000.

Geographic Name Server

Another useful service from the University of Michigan is the U.S. Geographic Name Server. This easy-to-use service gives a variety of geographic information for cities and towns around the United States. Included are population data, elevation, latitude and longitude, area codes, and ZIP codes. For example, the Geographic Server locates Hell in Michigan at latitude 42° 26' north and longitude 83° 59' 6" west. The Server locates Nirvana in Michigan also, but slightly north and west at latitude 43° 54' 9" north and longitude 85° 42' 43" west. Unfortunately, the Geographic Name Server does not indicate whether the roads to Hell are paved with good intentions! The Geographic Name Server is available through Telnet to `martini.eecs.umich.edu`, port 3000.

UnCover and Journal Graphics at CARL

The Colorado Association of Research Libraries (CARL) provides two sources of information increasingly used by public librarians: the UnCover and the Journal Graphics databases. Available through Telnet to pac.carl.org, the CARL system's UnCover service is a vast index of 14,000 magazine and journal titles with more than four million article records. The database is growing by 750,000 articles each year. The CARL staff scans the table of contents to magazines owned by member libraries and uses the scanned information as the basis for its database. Through the UnCover service, you can order articles for a nominal fee charged against a credit card. Delivery is by fax or mail.

The UnCover service is particularly useful for smaller public libraries. In these libraries, subscriptions to more specialized journals and indexes are limited or nonexistent. UnCover provides an index to a multitude of journals and magazines, and enables users to obtain the articles. In one example, a user in a small city library asked for articles by a botanist she had met. In the past, this library could do nothing but refer the patron to a larger academic library. With UnCover, however, the library located and obtained several articles written by the botanist within 48 hours.

The Journal Graphics database also is accessible on the CARL system. Journal Graphics, as most people have seen at the conclusion of national news programs on television, is a service that provides full transcripts of telecasts and radio programs. The networks covered by Journal Graphics include ABC, CNN, CBS, NBC, PBS, and National Public Radio; the CARL database consists of 75,000 records of programs ranging from recipe exchanges to debates on war and peace. Each record contains the program title, the names of key persons, and an abstract. Full text of the transcript is available by fax or mail for a reasonable charge (credit cards accepted). CARL and the UnCover and Journal Graphics databases are available through Telnet to pac.carl.org.

Public Domain Books

A nightmare for any public librarian is a sudden demand for a well-known book, of which the library owns only one or a few copies. This event typically happens when, say, all the seventh graders in a junior high are required to read *Alice's Adventures in Wonderland* or after a movie version of a classic, such as Charles Dickens' *A Christmas Carol*, is broadcast on television. The response of library users is often, "How can the library not have more copies of this book? It's a classic!"

Project Gutenberg provides a solution to this dilemma by redistributing public domain books in electronic form on the Internet. Public domain titles are not subject to copyrights; as a consequence, these books are free for replication. Included in the Project Gutenberg collection are such classics as *The Federalist Papers, Alice's Adventures in Wonderland, Moby Dick*, and the complete works of Shakespeare. The number of Gutenberg books, which are collected and made computer-ready largely through volunteer effort, is growing at a steady rate. Because of Project Gutenberg, public librarians now have a virtually infinite supply of many of the great works of literature. The Project Gutenberg books are available in a number of places on the World Wide Web, including `http://info.cern.ch/roeber/Misc/Gutenberg.html` and `gopher://spinaltap.micro.umn.edu:70/11/Gutenberg` and `ftp://mrcnext.cso.uiuc.edu/pub/etext`.

ELECTRONIC BOOKS?

Why would anyone want to use an electronic book? After all, no one wants to curl up in bed with a computer. Electronic books *do* have value, however. First, they take up no physical space other than an infinitesimal amount on a computer hard disk. The book never has to be printed until needed, providing a public librarian with an ideal example of just-in-time service. Instead of occupying shelf space, the book is used only when needed. Many electronic books also are computer searchable. With an electronic book, you can rapidly locate a keyword or phrase in context. Try to find where the Queen says, "Off with her head!" in *Alice's Adventures in Wonderland*. By computer, this search takes seconds; by paper, it can be an arduous task.

One particularly good public domain book on the Internet is the *CIA World Fact Book*. The Central Intelligence Agency, among its many activities, collects abundant information on countries throughout the world. In the *Fact Book*, virtually every country and territory on the planet has a geographic description, economic data, and sociological information. Also provided is a conversion table on weights and measures, a directory of international organizations, and a cross-reference of geographic names. With the *Fact Book*, no public library need ever be caught without easily reproduced information on a country the next time an international crisis develops. The *CIA World Fact Book* is available on the World Wide Web at `http://www.ic.gov` and in Gopherspace to `umslvma.umsl.edu:70/11/Library/GOVDOCS`.

Another effort involving the dissemination of public domain material is the Online Book Initiative (OBI). This initiative is an ambitious project in which the organizers are collecting an impressive array of public domain books and documents, including such classics as Dickens' *A Christmas Carol*, a large number of resources on computers, and position papers by political leaders. By using OBI, public librarians add a few hundred titles to their collections without taking an inch of shelf space.

Access to the OBI is available through Telnet to The World—a dial-up UNIX system. Telnet to `world.std.com` (there is a nominal fee for direct access). For information, call 617-739-0202. OBI is also available on the World Wide Web at `http://www.std.com`, in Gopherspace to `gopher://ftp.std.com:70/11/obi`, and by FTP through `ftp://ftp.std.com/obi`.

Library Policies

Public librarians are constantly struggling to have fair and comprehensive policies. As in any public institution, having a good policy in place ensures consistent and equitable service. This plan is particularly true as librarians struggle with censorship attempts; a good policy ensures that books and other materials are selected without bias.

The Electronic Frontier Foundation Gopher provides an area called the Library Policy Archive, which includes position papers from the American Library Association on such topics as intellectual freedom and censorship. With these documents, public librarians can avoid having to reinvent the wheel and can borrow statements for policies that may be challenged in court as censors step up their attempts to suppress the availability of some material. The Library Policy Archive is available in Gopherspace to `gopher://gopher.eff.org:70/11/CAF/library` and by FTP through `ftp://ftp.eff.org/CAF/library`.

Employment Information

For job seekers, the public library has always been a good resource for locating potential employers. Out-of-state newspapers, company directories, and resume books are useful tools widely available in libraries. The Internet adds to these resources with the Online Career Center. Offered by MSEN, the Online Career Center is provided free of charge by an association of employers. Included is a large database of job openings in a variety of fields, plus company profiles and a resume file of job hunters. Job openings and resumes are loaded on an almost daily basis. No job resource is as current and comprehensive as this service; public librarians are finding it invaluable in helping library users locate jobs. The Online Career Center is available on the World Wide Web at `http://www.iquest.net` and in Gopherspace to `gopher://dorite.iquest.net`.

Another good Internet source for locating job openings is ACADEME This Week. ACADEME is a resource that lists a summary of articles appearing in the *Chronicle of Higher Education*—the newspaper for academics in the United States. Included in ACADEME is a list of job ads that appear in the *Chronicle*. Because the emphasis in the *Chronicle* is academia, the job openings are almost exclusively at colleges and universities. Nonetheless, many job openings are provided, and public librarians are using ACADEME to good effect for some of their users. ACADEME is available in Gopherspace to `gopher://chronicle.merit.edu`.

U.S. Federal job openings also are listed on the Internet. Many of the FedWorld BBSes list job openings within individual agencies. Various Federal job openings are also provided on the Dartmouth College Gopher. The coverage in the Dartmouth service is uneven (not all areas of the United States are covered) but the number of jobs listed is considerable. The Federal Job listings from Dartmouth College are available in Gopherspace to `gopher://dartcms1.dartmouth.edu`.

Library Catalogs

Libraries have made a great impact on the Internet landscape by providing Telnet access to their online catalogs. Public libraries are no exception, and dozens of catalogs now are available with Telnet—from Abilene, Kansas, to Wellington, New Zealand. This service benefits public libraries considerably. First, library users can conveniently check the catalogs from their homes and offices. Additionally, Telnet access to library catalogs helps public librarians develop their library collections by seeing what books and items other libraries are buying. Also, viewing other systems gives librarians the opportunity to see how other online catalogs are arranged and how they function.

One complication in connecting to library catalogs is the large number of catalogs available. Peter Scott, at the University of Saskatchewan, has helped with this problem by developing an easy-to-use program called Hytelnet. On this freely distributed product, all libraries with Telnet connections are listed in menus that group libraries together logically . For example, public libraries are listed together, libraries are grouped geographically, and different library catalog systems are assembled collectively. Even more advantageous, when a user selects a library catalog for viewing, Hytelnet automatically makes the connection.

To sample Hytelnet and view library catalogs on the Internet, Telnet to `access.usask.ca` and log in as `hytelnet`. It is also available on the World Wide Web at `http://www.usask.ca/cgi-bin/hytelnet`, and in Gopherspace at `gopher://liberty.uc.wlu.edu:70/11/internet/hytelnet`.

Another way public librarians are providing access to their online catalogs is through local community computing systems. The idea behind community computing is simple: members of the community pool their resources, buy a computer and phone lines, and then let all members of the community dial in to share and look at available information. *Free-Nets*, which started in Cleveland and have spread to communities throughout the world, are the most common form of community computing systems. In almost all the community systems, local library catalogs are available. Additionally, public librarians have been actively involved in promoting these systems. In Peoria, Illinois, terminals are provided in the libraries for access to the local Free-Net; in Tallahassee, Florida, the public library houses the local Free-Net office. Because many community computing systems are available through Telnet, libraries providing their catalogs on these systems also are providing Internet access. To sample a community computing system with an available public library catalog, try the Heartland Free-Net in Peoria, Illinois. Telnet to `heartland.bradley.edu` and log in as `bbguest`.

Commercial Services

Public librarians have been using commercial information providers such as Dialog and BRS for almost 20 years. These vast services provide a multitude of indexes; in addition, full-text material is available from a variety of sources. Up-to-date data on virtually any company of any

size is accessible. Of course, all this information is provided for a fee, sometimes an expensive one. The Internet helps to alleviate these costs by providing Telnet access to these services. Using the Internet, public librarians have been able to reduce their telecommunications costs by as much as two-thirds—roughly about $6.00 to 7.00 per hour. There are several available through Telnet: Dialog (`dialog.com`), BRS (`brs.com`), ORBIT (`orbit.com`), and Dow Jones News Retrieval (`djnr.dowjones.com`).

One relatively inexpensive commercial resource on the Internet is the ClariNews service. Available as a Usenet news feed, as well as by Gopher on The World, ClariNews provides same-day news feeds from U.P.I. and Reuters. By accessing ClariNews from The World, public librarians can tap into news as it happens for pennies a day; unlike the local newspaper, space is never a problem. All the news is fit to print. As an example, the ClariNews service is available on The World Gopher. Access to this portion of The World Gopher is available only through Telnet to `world.std.com`. Contact The World for cost information.

The Internet Public Library

The University of Michigan School of Information and Library Studies has created the Internet Public Library, an online, 24-hour-a-day, public library designed to provide services and information. It has an online reference division, services for youth, user education division, and professional services for librarians. It can be accessed on the World Wide Web at `http://ipl.sils.umich.edu`.

The Public Library as Internet Gateway

Public librarians are providing access to the Internet not only as intermediaries but also directly for their users. One notable case is Liverpool Public Library. Located in upstate New York, Liverpool has consistently been at the forefront in using new technology in public libraries. At Liverpool, patrons merely walk in, select a designated terminal, and start to access the Internet. Reports are that the program is working well.

Some public libraries are giving access to the Internet from online catalogs. At Seattle Public Library, users have the option of connecting to a menu of Internet choices, including UnCover, Heartland Free-Net, the Geographic Name Server, the Library of Congress Marvel Gopher, and several library catalogs from the Seattle area. The designers of the Seattle catalog provide well-placed prompts to help prevent users from getting lost in the wilds of the Net. By offering user access to the Internet, Seattle is setting a good example for other public libraries. Following is a display of the Internet menu from Seattle's online catalog. Note that the menu may have changed since this book was written. The Seattle Public Library's catalog is available on Hytelnet and through Telnet to `spl.lib.wa.us` (log in as `library`).

```
              SEATTLE PUBLIC LIBRARY CATALOG 6:59pm
                  DIAL PAC     14 ITEMS
                  GATEWAY ACCESS                      PAGE 1 OF 1


      1.AAA              Seattle Public Library Gopher
      2.GGO              Green Gopher
      3.GNS              Geographic Name Finder
      4.GPO              Gov't. Prt. Off. Online Access Services
      5.HRTLD            Heartland Free-net
      6.KCLS             King County Library System
      7.KCOS             King County Online Services
      8.MARVEL           Library of Congress (via telnet)
      9.PAN              PAN (Public Access Network)
     10.SCN              Seattle Community Network
     11.UNC2             Uncover (periodical index)
     12.UWIN             UW Information Navigator
     13.UWTHR            Weather
     14.WH2              White House News (via telnet)


   Enter a Gate Code, line number, or select an option below :
   Commands:  Q = Quit, ? = Help, EL = Extd List
```

Visit Your Local Public Library

This chapter has discussed only a fraction of the Internet resources used by public librarians. Many more services are available. All the resources on the Internet are, obviously, not exclusive to public librarians. Anyone with the right equipment and connections can use the Internet. What your public librarian has to offer are the skills of an information professional—searching and providing information is what she or he does for a living. Give your local public library a visit and ask what Internet resources it is using. If the librarian is using the Internet, spend some time talking. In most cases, you will find a well-trained infonaut eager to share the boundless resources available in cyberspace.

Library of Congress: The Power of Information

45

by John Iliff

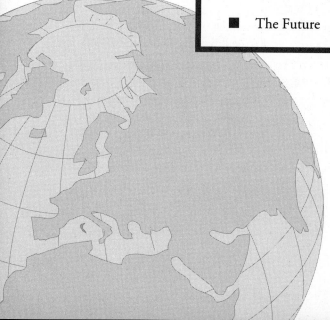

The U.S. Library of Congress (LOC) has been part of the American historical landscape for almost 200 years. As presidents, both Thomas Jefferson and John Adams encouraged the development of the library. Our nation's forebears recognized that the nation's legislators needed wide-ranging sources of knowledge to accomplish their tasks. Jefferson, in particular, acknowledged a need for the library. Following the destruction of the library in the War of 1812, the bulk of Jefferson's personal books formed the basis of the renewed collection. The idea that information is power was not lost on the founders of the United States.

The Library of Congress plays two important roles. Its official role is to live up to its name—to provide information for the United States legislative body. Its unofficial, but no less important, role is to be the repository of information for the nation as a whole. Almost from its beginning, the collection has served people outside of Congress, including the President, members of the cabinet, Supreme Court justices, and eventually average citizens. Over time, the LOC has provided many services, including copyright registration, maintenance of a comprehensive collection, provision of services for the blind and physically handicapped, and interlibrary loans of LOC materials to library users everywhere.

With the development of computers and telecommunications, namely the Internet, the Library of Congress has begun to expand access to its resources in new ways. Information previously accessible only by mail, or not at all, is available in the instant it takes data to travel over the Internet's high-speed lines. The nation's library has begun to enter every living room, office, school, and library in the country. Thomas Jefferson would be impressed.

LOCIS

One of the first forays the Library of Congress made into the Net universe is LOCIS—the Library of Congress Information Service. The LOC has been providing electronic information to members of Congress for many years, but with LOCIS, much of that information now is available for everyone; just Telnet to `locis.loc.gov` to see the following welcome screen:

```
L O C I S :  LIBRARY OF CONGRESS INFORMATION SYSTEM
To make a choice: type a number, then press ENTER

1   Library of Congress Catalog      4   Braille and Audio

2   Federal Legislation              5   Organizations

3   Copyright Information            6   Foreign Law

*    *    *    *    *    *        *    *    *    *    *
7   Searching Hours and Basics
8   Documentation and Classes
```

```
9   Library of Congress General Information

12   Comments and Logoff

Choice:
- ------------------------------
```

The Catalog

LOCIS contains several databases with a mind-boggling 27 million records, and the system is growing every day. Among the databases available is the *Library of Congress Catalog*, with records of materials in a variety of formats, including books, magazines, maps, sheet music, recordings, films, and software. If an item is published, its record is likely part of the LOC *Catalog*.

For the average person, one benefit in using the *Catalog* is identifying a book or other work for which you remember only part of the title. You can locate titles easily by using keyword searching. The LOCIS database also provides a comprehensive record of works by individual creators, so you can see, for example, all the works by Stephen King or some other favorite author.

Although LOCIS provides a good list of the LOC's contents, full-text versions of these items are not available. Additionally, just because the *Catalog* includes an item does not mean the material is available for loan. The Library of Congress collection is considered the library of last resort for obtaining books and other sources of information. LOCIS, however, does give a comprehensive view of what material has been produced, which can be significant if you are searching for information.

Federal Legislation

Another database available on LOCIS is a tracking system of federal legislation. The database has two versions: one version for Congress and another for the public. The public-accessible portion of the LOCIS Bill Digest includes the status of bills, a brief summary of bills, and which members of Congress proposed the legislation. The sessions covered include the current and preceding sessions dating to 1973. From declarations on Arbor Day to gun control legislation, the LOCIS bill-tracking system gives a clear picture of what Congress is actually doing.

National Referral Center

LOCIS also provides access to the National Referral Center Resources File (NRCRF). This database contains a listing of over 14,000 organizations that provide information, quite simply, to anyone. The organizations listed are primarily research oriented, with an emphasis on the sciences and social sciences. This database is indexed by organizational name and by subject. The information provided includes the address and phone number of the organization as well as a description of available resources. One caveat in using the NRCRF is that the database is not necessarily kept up to date. The information provided, however, is often worthwhile.

From Copyright to Foreign Law

LOCIS contains three other databases: Copyright, Braille and Audio resources for the handicapped, and Foreign Law. The Copyright section lists all materials registered for copyright since 1978. This material includes not only books, but all other works that fall under copyright protection (such as film and software). Additionally, the Copyright database contains copyright history information indicating records of copyright transfer, lapse of copyright, and so on. This information is valuable for locating the owners of works, when works were registered, and so on.

The Braille and Audio portion of LOCIS is a large database of materials that the blind and other handicapped persons can use to meet their special needs. The materials listed are widely available free of charge to eligible persons through the National Library Service for the Blind and Physically Handicapped.

The Foreign Law database contains abstracts of foreign laws and citations from legal journals. The emphasis in this database is primarily on Hispanic legal systems.

Special Services for Librarians

LOCIS gives a wide range of information for citizens in general, but the Library of Congress also provides specialized information for librarians with ALIX (Automated Library and Information eXchange). ALIX is the result of an LOC cooperative program to encourage exchange of information among federal libraries. Accessible by Telnet to fedworld.gov (choose ALIX from the federal bulletin board system area), this service gives librarians an abundance of resources. ALIX includes discussion areas on library issues, news on libraries and librarianship, and hundreds of useful computer files. ALIX is a prime example of the Library of Congress' ongoing role as the primary library in the country, and it is an invaluable service for librarians.

The LOC also provides an electronic newsletter called the *LC Cataloging Newsline* (LCCN). Available for free through Listserv software, you can obtain a subscription by sending an e-mail message to listproc@loc.gov with the message subscribe lccn followed by the subscriber's first and last names. The topics in this newsletter involve library cataloging (the classifying of material so that library users can locate the information they need). LCCN gives librarians a quick and paperless read on important topics.

Marvel

The Library of Congress entered the Internet world in a very big way with the development of Marvel—the Machine Assisted Realization of the Virtual Electronic Library. Using Gopher software, Marvel gives menu-driven access to a large number of resources inside and outside the Library of Congress. Available by Telnet to `marvel.loc.gov` or by Gopher to `gopher://marvel.loc.gov` port 70, Marvel is one of the best Gophers in Gopherspace.

The following example shows the initial Marvel menu. Each selection on this menu leads to other menus. For example, included in item 6 is LOCIS—and Marvel provides easy access to this system. Item 5, Copyright, gives a broad overview of the LOC's Copyright program. Included in this overview are full-text circulars that describe how to obtain copyrights and how to obtain ISBNs and ISSNs—those mysterious-looking numbers in the front of books and magazines.

```
Internet Gopher Information Client v2.0.14

                      Library of Congress MARVEL
  ->   1.  About LC MARVEL/
       2.  Events, Facilities, Publications, and Services/
       3.  Research and Reference (Public Services)/
       4.  Libraries and Publishers (Technical Services)/
       5.  Copyright/
       6.  Library of Congress Online Systems/
       7.  Employee Information/
       8.  U.S. Congress/
       9.  Government Information/
      10.  Global Electronic Library (by Subject)/
      11.  Internet Resources/
      12.  What's New on LC MARVEL/
      13.  Search LC MARVEL Menus/
Press ? for Help, q to Quit                            Page: 1/1
```

Federal Information

One area in which Marvel is particularly strong is in linking Internet-available U.S. federal information sources. The type of resources Marvel pulls together include other Gophers, library catalogs, and databases. All this information is available by direct access on the Internet, but with Marvel, the information is provided in one easy-to-use format. Among the agencies and departments represented are the National Institutes of Health, the National Library of Medicine (access to the entire NLM catalog is available), and NASA.

Global Electronic Library

Another strength of Marvel is the Global Electronic Library (item 10 in the Marvel menu). This portion of Marvel groups together Internet resources by commonly used subject headings, such as *economics* or *history*. The Marvel caretakers have paid attention to selecting quality services. Users can switch conveniently to a variety of free resources including electronic journals, bulletin board services, searchable databases, and so on. The Global Electronic Library is a well-organized entryway to some of the best free resources on the Internet.

Exhibits

Another way the Library of Congress uses the Internet is with FTP, or File Transfer Protocol. The LOC is famed for excellent exhibits, but before the Internet, only people in Washington could see the displays. With FTP, however, Internet users can see scanned graphics and text files from some of the current and past exhibits—all obtained in a flash over high-speed Internet lines. The collection includes the following exhibits: "Revelations from the Russian Archive"; "Rome Reborn: The Vatican Library and Renaissance Culture"; "1492: An Ongoing Voyage"; and "Scrolls from the Dead Sea." Provided free of charge in each exhibit are the graphics files, accompanying text, and the software to view the graphics. The only restriction is that you use the material for noncommercial purposes only. (To access the LOC exhibits, FTP to `ftp://ftp.loc.gov`, log in as anonymous, and use your e-mail address for the password. The exhibits are in the `/pub` directory.)

Library of Congress on the World Wide Web

The crowning glory of the LOC on the Internet is the Library of Congress on the World Wide Web. The LOC Web pages bring the Marvel Gopher and LOCIS into a single interface. Additionally, with easy-to-use Web browsers such as Netscape and Mosaic, the LOC Web pages present hundreds of the library's sound, film, and graphic files so that they can be effortlessly reproduced.

> **CAUTION**
>
> Remember that copyright laws also apply to computer files obtained from the Internet; reproduction of computer files can be illegal. Be sure to read all license and copyright restrictions before reproducing software. Respect the rights of authors!

Among the files included on the LOC Web are selections from the American Memory Project (with early films from Thomas Edison and John Porter, a massive number of photographs from the U.S. Civil War, and other fascinating historical resources). As the Marvel system does with Gopher systems, the LOC Web service links a huge number of World Wide Web services by subject, including a host of U.S. Government World Wide Web resources.

Also available is a link to the LOC-created THOMAS Web service, a collection of information on the U.S. Congress. Included on THOMAS (named for Thomas Jefferson) is the full text of legislation beginning with the 1993-1994 103rd Congress, the full text of the *Congressional Record*, and easy access to a directory of the current members of Congress. To view the Library of Congress on the World Wide Web, point your Web browser to `http://lcweb.loc.gov`. To sample the THOMAS Web service, either select it from the LOC Web server or point your browser to `http://thomas.loc.gov`.

The Future

With Marvel, LOCIS, FTP exhibits, the Library of Congress World Wide Web, and other efforts, the Library of Congress staff is demonstrating how to use the Internet to good effect. After taking successful first steps, full-text access is one possible direction for the future. As telecommunications and computer storage become even more sophisticated and less expensive, a central site will be able to provide abundant full-text, and even multimedia, material. A logical choice for that site is the Library of Congress. The LOC holds a massive amount of information; just making its public domain material available would be a significant achievement. As the central registrar of copyrights, the LOC also seems to be a logical site for the electronic distribution of copyrighted material (after working out some method of ensuring payment). Whatever happens, keep your eye on the library that John Adams and Thomas Jefferson created. Great things are sure to happen.

Discussion List for School Libraries: A Case Study

46

by Susan Kinnell

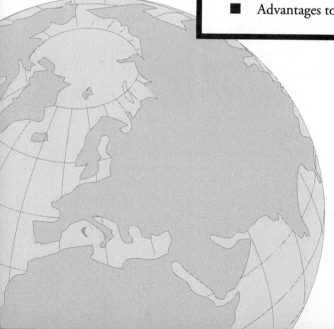

Although the largest number of Internet users are probably not from elementary, middle, and high schools, a growing number of teachers and librarians from these schools are finding that the Internet offers a variety of very useful resources. Access to current events and documents (such as White House press releases) are invaluable in teaching civics, government, and U.S. history classes. Faster access to ERIC (the Educational Resources Information Center), with its thousands of citations to educational literature, is a definite benefit of being able to use the national online networks. ERIC, the largest education database in the world, includes abstracts of documents and journal articles, in addition to papers, conference proceedings, literature reviews, and curriculum materials.

But because of the wide variety of searching tools and methods on different systems in different locations used on the Internet to access ERIC, the level of difficulty and frustration in using the system was high for K–12 educators. In 1992, the U.S. Department of Education funded the development of a pilot program called AskERIC, which was coordinated and implemented by the ERIC people at Syracuse University. AskERIC is a question-and-answer system that enables anyone with access to the Internet to ask a question about K–12 education. The question is handled by the AskERIC information specialists and, normally, an answer is sent back within 48 hours. This human intermediary is quite unique for the Internet and enables novice users to gain full access to information contained in the ERIC databases.

Another advantage to school use of the Internet is the large and diverse assortment of discussion groups, bulletin boards, and electronic mail systems available. The Kids' Network, K12Net, FrEdMail, and the National Education Association School Renewal Network are just a few of the many networks available within the big network called the Internet. Collaboration between content specialists, access to government and corporate libraries and databases, and the invaluable contact between working members of the same profession in different parts of the country are all part of the growing attraction that the Internet has for K–12 education.

One example of this kind of networking is called LM_NET:

> *The students had all left for the day, the aide had straightened the library and sorted the overdue notices, and Mrs. Burton, a 10-year veteran of her school library, sighed and leaned back in her chair. It was quiet, for the first time all day. She glanced at the clock and decided she had time for a quick check of her LM_NET account. Maybe, just maybe, someone might have answered her online request for information for an advanced class in French. She needed addresses for schools in France that the students could write to. She flipped on the modem switch and activated her telecommunications program. Moments later, she was logging on to her Internet account and requesting her electronic mailbox. "New mail," she read. "Good; maybe someone will know what I need for this class tomorrow." She frowned to herself. Tomorrow—that's what the teacher had said. Did he think she was a magician? She scrolled through her messages: more trouble in California schools, librarians being replaced by clerical staff—or not being replaced at all. Several messages about a new CD-ROM player that was working well on a library network;*

two or three new requests for help with local problems; and then, a-ha! an answer to her plea. A librarian in Montana had some advice about where to find what she needed—and the next message was from Virginia, with a different solution for her dilemma. This was great! Three more messages, one from Peter Milbury about stopping your mail when on vacation, a query about using a time clock, and one about food problems in the school library. And then another answer for her, this time from Texas. Mrs. Burton smiled to herself as she noted the information, logged off, glanced around the library to make sure that everything was shipshape, turned off the lights, and went home. Maybe she was a magician after all...thanks to LM_NET.

LM_NET is a discussion list on the Internet especially for school library media specialists. As simple as that statement is, it needs some explanation for those who are not familiar with the Internet and what it can provide. A *list* is a specific group of people who have access to the Internet and who share a common interest. A message sent to the Listserv is routed to every person in the group so that information of interest to the whole group can be shared quickly and easily. Discussion lists on the Internet include groups of people with just about every specialized interest imaginable, from specific hardware to software development to the same occupational interests. Let's have a look at LM_NET as an example of how librarians can network together.

LM_NET was started in June 1992 by Mike Eisenberg, an assistant professor at the School of Information Sciences, Syracuse University, and the director of the ERIC Clearinghouse on Information Resources. He had discussed the feasibility of putting together a list for school-library media specialists with Ann Weeks, Executive Director of the American Association of School Librarians (AASL). The initial Listserv was set up by Academic Computing Services at Syracuse and was merged several weeks later with the "Leading Edge Librarian" Internet group in California. This latter group was started by Peter Milbury, Pleasant Valley Senior High School librarian in Chico, California, who became "co-owner" of the new list with Mike Eisenberg.

LM_NET is intended for school library personnel and people with an interest in school libraries. For new subscribers, the instructions are very clear:

- Conversation on LM_NET should focus on topics of interest to the school library media community, including the latest on school library media services, operations, and activities. It is a list for practitioners helping practitioners, sharing ideas, solving problems, telling each other about new publications and upcoming conferences, asking for assistance, and linking schools through their library media centers.

- The LM_NET list is open to **all** school library media specialists world wide as well as people involved with the school library media field. It is not for general librarians or educators. The activity and discussion is focused on school library media. But the list can be used by library media people for many different things—to ask for input, share ideas and information, link programs that are geographically remote, make contacts, and so on.

Although there are members of LM_NET who are not school library media people, the vast majority are working members of that profession. They come from every state in the union and from every possible type of K–12 school—elementary, middle, junior, and senior high—large, small, private, public, urban, and rural. Library media specialists are finding that the LM_NET is a marvelous forum for airing their views, for trying to find solutions, for picking up bits of insider information, and simply for experiencing the pleasure of contact with others who share their goals, their dreams, and their problems.

Joining LM_NET

If you decide you want to join the LM_NET, what do you have to do? There are no applications to fill out, no dues to pay. Simply log on to the Internet and send a message to the address `listserv@suvm.syr.edu`. Put nothing in the subject line. The text of your message should be very simple: use the word *subscribe* followed by your Internet address and your full name written out. When I joined LM_NET, the text of my message looked like this: `subscribe susek@rain.org Susan Kinnell`.

Within 48 hours, a response to your message is sent back, and you are asked to reply. Once that exchange has been successfully completed, you are added to the Listserv and start receiving messages every day from library media people everywhere. One of the first messages is a Skills Index that lists people who are experts in particular areas and who are willing to share their expertise with beginners. Another message is a detailed list of instructions on how to handle various aspects of the LM_NET. The next day, your mailbox is full of messages from other members—messages that contain questions, hot tips on the latest books, worthwhile conferences, and much more.

Stopping Your Mail

Because the daily volume of mail is so high, you may find it a good idea to stop all mail for any period of time if you are not going to be able to access your account. Do this by sending the message `set lm_net nomail`. This message is addressed to the list of LM_NET, not to the list members.

To restart your mail, send the following message to the same address: `set lm_net mail`. Leave the subject line blank when you send a restart mail message.

LM_NET Addresses

The administrative address should be used for all mail intended for the people running the list, not for the members themselves. The address for sending a message to everyone on LM_NET is `lm_net@suvm.syr.edu`.

Ways To Use LM_NET

There are six general ways of using LM_NET. Each has a different approach and a different usefulness. Become familiar with each of them so that you can decide which method will work best for you at different times.

- **Lurking:** When you lurk on LM_NET, you log on, read the messages, and quietly slip away. No one knows you're there and no one gets any mail from you because you don't send any. There's nothing wrong with this approach, and it's a good way to learn about the topics and the people who are discussing things online. However, pretty soon you will want to take part in some of the discussions or ask a question of your own. When all members of a list contribute something to the group, the group becomes better and more valuable.

- **Target/Hit:** If you have a specific question to ask, and it's more than likely you will get multiple responses to that question, a good way to proceed is with the Target/Hit approach. When you send out your question, you ask for all responses to be directed back to you personally. You then compile the responses and put out one single message that summarizes the responses you received. That way, everyone on the list does not have to read every response individually. Because some people aren't interested in your question or the responses, it saves time and energy for them not to have to delete every response as it comes in.

  The method to use when creating a Target/Hit message is to type `TARGET-> My question is` in the subject line of your message header. In the body of the message, ask the question and ask people to respond to you directly. When you have enough responses to your question, post a message back on LM_NET as `A HIT-> Responses to my question`. It isn't appropriate to use the Target/Hit format every time a question is posed on LM_NET, but it does save time and space by condensing all responses to specific questions for the majority of LM_NETters.

- **Digest:** If you find that you are overwhelmed by the number of messages you are receiving on LM_NET, you can ask to have all your messages put into a digest. All messages are compiled into one message and posted to your mailbox once a day. You may end up with one very long message, but it saves space in your mailbox. To turn this feature on, send a message to the administrative address (`listserv@suvm.syr.edu` or `listserv@suvm.bitnet`). In the body of the message, type `set lm_net digest`. That's all. The administrators in Syracuse do the rest. If you want to turn the digest feature off, send a message to the administrative address with the following text: `set lm_net mail`.

- **Mentor:** If you find that you are completely intimidated or bewildered by the many options afforded to you through the Internet and LM_NET, you can request a mentor. This system pairs an experienced user with a novice in a kind of buddy system. You get to know your mentor, ask questions, and learn the ins and outs of a sometimes very confusing new world.

- **Monitor:** Many of the more experienced people on LM_NET are also taking part in other discussion lists or forums in other parts of the Internet or other online services. They act as a monitor of another list and report back whatever interesting information they glean to the members of LM_NET. Because there are literally hundreds of other groups with highly specialized interests on the LM_NET (or on CompuServe, America Online, Prodigy, and so on), monitors can save you a world of time and bring information to your fingertips you may never have realized was available. Watch for these reports, and don't hesitate to mention any other source of online information that you hear about to the administrators of LM_NET.

- **Archive:** Finally, there is the Archive resource at Syracuse. All the conversations on LM_NET are archived using the AskERIC Gopher and are available for searching at a later date. If you remember a discussion that you didn't download at the time, you can still retrieve it and read it.

What Can You Do with LM_NET?

The most valuable thing you can do with LM_NET is to make contact with other library people all over the country. This contact is invaluable because of the range of expertise and experience represented by the LM_NET members, and because of the range of topics and ideas discussed daily on the Listserv. Until you have experienced it for yourself, you cannot believe the depth and breadth of information that is a few keystrokes away from anyone with Internet access. The following are a few of the subjects that have been discussed:

- **The bigger issues:** Will online information replace print? When? How? What are people feeling about this change in their schools and their libraries? (This whole discussion started with a relatively simple question about the *Readers Guide* and whether or not people were keeping it in print or switching to online sources of information.)

  How will publishing initiatives on the World Wide Web affect librarians? How can librarians measure the quality of online material given the evolution and volatility of their sources?

  Will school library personnel be replaced or "made redundant" by current budget cuts and stale thinking? (A massive appeal was made by several LM_NET members in the San Diego area as the school board there prepared to make some major changes in funding staff positions.)

  What impact will technology have on our educational system as a whole? How are schools, libraries, faculty, and staff handling the transition into a multimedia world?

- **Hardware and software issues:** What are members doing about networking their libraries? How is it working? There is much concern about specific pieces of equipment, such as CD-ROM drives, mini-changers, videodisc players, and so on. The feedback from others who have used the same equipment you are contemplating buying for your library is priceless. Recommendations about new equipment and new configurations are also frequent, as are queries about what software is best for what task.

- **Timeless issues:** What do you do about food in your library? Do you use a time clock in your library? Does it work well? Discipline, reading levels, after-school hours, gender issues in school clubs, and other problems are discussed, usually with great ideas and practical solutions.

- **Collection development:** What books should I buy for a South African literature collection? Does anyone have a good source for Appalachian crafts, quilts, or Eskimo history? Where can I find a good magazine about brides from an African-American viewpoint? Does anyone know anything about a given magazine? Is it any good, or should I get rid of it?

- **Curriculum integration:** A social sciences teacher wants to make contact with students in Scotland, Ireland, and Iceland. Does anyone know of any sources or addresses?

- **The Internet:** The best resources on the Internet for high schools; an interesting new Web site, Gopher, or list; the best place to find the text of a speech; and many other tips are all part of the daily exchange on LM_NET. The administrators of the LM_NET are online at least once or twice a week with reminders about online etiquette, nifty new Internet sources, and housekeeping details for keeping the whole Listserv running smoothly.

- **Professional research:** Many student librarians are members of LM_NET and frequently ask questions of the practicing librarians on LM_NET. In exchange, the practicing librarians get to hear about the professional research going on in academic schools around the country.

Advantages to LM_NET

Call it networking, call it an isolation-buster, or call it a genuine information resource—there are real people out there with opinions, ideas, problems, and questions. You can meet with these people and take part in this bigger community of school-library media personnel from your own desk, every day of the week. No travel time, no conference fees and hotel bills, and no time off from work.

More important than this individual help is the knowledge that you are part of a larger community of similarly occupied people, a community of people whose size can be a deciding factor in helping to determine the direction of product development, community support, and professional leadership. Although there are more than 70,000 school library media people in this country, there are only about 1,200 on LM_NET. That's less than 2 percent of the total, but it's an involved, caring, and vocal 2 percent. The word is spreading, and there will be many more members in the years to come. LM_NET is easy to use, inexpensive, and a resource beyond comparison for the school librarians who want to move beyond the walls of their own schools.

The Virtual Library

by Laura Windsor

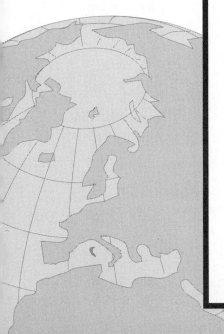

Cruising the superhighway of cyberspace, you have files to obtain, information to store, games to play, news for the day-all are part of this wonderful resource called the Internet. Users access the Internet daily to find answers to questions, see what's happening around the world, educate kids, educate adults. These examples barely scratch the surface when we speak of a dispersed "virtual" library that exists for people with access to a computer and a modem.

The number of people using a personal computer at home is growing by the day. The number of people accessing the Internet is increasing by the minute. We are in the middle of a world revolution that everyone can win. We have a tremendous potential to effectively synthesize knowledge gained from the vast array of Net resources into daily operations-in education, government, industry, medicine, the arts, science, technology, and the list goes on.

What is a virtual library? For most of us, the whole Internet is *the* Virtual Library. This library without walls can exist anywhere and enable people to access the information they need, regardless of where it is, what time of day it is, and without the use of an intermediary. Who owns the Internet? The world! The people! The masses! The Internet is a global collaboration, and the Virtual Library is everywhere on the Internet.

The idea of a virtual library is attractive. Of course, other virtual libraries besides the Internet do exist. An increasing number of companies and institutions are creating their own smaller virtual libraries by producing and obtaining data in only digital formats. Documents and reports the organization already owns are being optically scanned (a technique in which all text and graphics in paper format are scanned to translate the material into a digital format and put into a computer system).

The scanning of documents into digital form is becoming a popular choice for many users. The ability to scan text documents as well as graphics and convert them into digital form is feasible and is happening in many areas. Digital information saves space, time, and enables individuals to be more productive.

The Virtual Library Collection

The sources for our Virtual Library range from basic information on every topic under the sun to complex equations used for physics. Classical literature, children's stories, propulsion system specifications, space shuttle mission objectives in detail, available grants, and software programs are just some of the topics.

The interweaving of networks around the world has produced the definitive reference tool. More access points are made available daily as more and more people set up computer systems to tap into this major array of information.

Do you need to find the meaning of a term? You can look up the word in the Virtual Library, which has full-text dictionaries. Need to know what an acronym stands for? Look it up in an acronym dictionary on the Net. Doing a history paper and need to know more about the Alamo?

On the Net, you can get specifications of the original fort and a detailed diagram. Finding this information in print takes much longer than using the Internet. Need a copy of *Romeo and Juliet* but all the copies are checked out of your school library? Get the full text from the Internet.

> **NOTE**
>
> For a dictionary, Telnet to `chem.ucsd.edu` and log in as `webster`. For an acronym dictionary, Gopher to `veronica.scs.unr.edu` and search all of Gopherspace. Select Veronica at the University of Cologne (`koeln`) and type **acronym dictionary**. For a sketch and description of the Alamo (at the same site), type **alamo**; at the next menu, there is an ASCII sketch of the Alamo. For a copy of *Romeo and Juliet*, get it at `ftp://terminator.rs.itd.umich.edu/shakespeare/tragedies`.
>
> Many people think the Internet is hard to use. It can be; however, once you use it, read some books about it, learn a few commands, and have some good sites written down or memorized, you're more than ready. I decided to time myself to see how long it would take to actually use the resources in the previous paragraph. I dialed in to log in to my account. I first went to the dictionary at `chem.ucsd.edu`, logged in, and searched for the definition of *albatross*. I then Gophered to `veronica.scs.unr.edu` and searched Gopherspace, selecting Veronica at the University of Cologne (`koeln`). I typed `acronym dictionary` and selected one. Then I chose the option to search the dictionary by keyword and typed `SCSI`. I found that it means "Small Computer System Interface." I then typed `alamo` at the same site and found a sketch of the Alamo and a description. When I left the system, I was given the options of mailing, saving, printing, or quitting. I decided to mail the Alamo information to myself. Then it was time to get *Romeo and Juliet*. First, I had to find out where it was, so I used Archie. I Telnetted to `archie.sura.net` and logged in as `qarchie`. At the prompt, I typed `prog romeo`, and a list began to scroll across the screen with locations. I chose `terminator.rs.itd.umich.edu` and FTPed the complete play from there. When I got back to my home account, I had the complete text of the play. I also had new mail: the Alamo sketch and description. This all took nine minutes-a pretty productive nine minutes, in my opinion.

Education

The ramifications of the Virtual Library resources already are seen by students who have access to the Internet at home, school, or a public library. The magnitude of information available for study is not the only significant factor; software programs are appearing in increasing numbers.

Software programs have been used for years as an instructional medium to assist students. This teaching method is more and more the one of choice as multimedia packages get better. Many expensive software programs available on computer store shelves have comparable competition on the Net at FTP sites-and these programs are free for the taking.

The use of educational software will increase because of the tremendous technological advances in graphics and sound. More and more people have color monitors and at least some form of sound. Graphics quality is more vivid and eye-catching than ever. Good visuals and sound effects, in addition to textual material, enhance learning and comprehension for almost everyone. Interactive media in education is a hit with kids, and because this media commands active rather than passive interaction, students are more likely to pay attention and retain what they learn.

We should expect math and science scores to make great gains over the next several years as more and more students gain access to computers. Learning with a computer touch screen, keyboard, or mouse enables just about anyone to use the tool. Also, voice-activated systems are already in development and ultimately will make the Virtual Library even easier to use.

Practical Usage

Librarians who are lucky enough to have access to the Internet at a busy reference desk use it a lot to answer questions. For example, many college students in business classes have to do research on companies. A great Internet source for finding information on public companies is EDGAR, a database of annual reports, 10-K reports, and other financial publications filed electronically with the Securities and Exchange Commission (SEC). A simple Gopher search can obtain very up-to-date data.

Following is a portion of the first page of Boeing's 10-K report which is in its full text. This type of business information has become vital to students and others interested in companies.

```
windsorl@erau:  gopher town.hall.org

Root gopher server: town.hall.org

      1.  Welcome to the Internet Town Hall.
      2.  Federal Reserve Board/
      3.  Final Snapshot of the Networld+Interop
      4.  General Services Administration/
  ->  5.  SEC EDGAR/
      6.  U.S. Patent and Trademark Office/
```

```
    1.   About the Internet EDGAR Dissemination Project.
->  2.   Search EDGAR Archives <?>
    3.   SEC EDGAR Documentation/
    4.   Guide to SEC Corporate Filings/
    5.   Daily Index Files/
    6.   Full Index Files/




 -----------Search EDGAR Archives----------------
 |                                               |
 |                                               |
 |   Words to search for:   Boeing               |
 |                                               |
 |                                               |
 |                                               |
 |-------------------------|                     |
 |                                               |
 |    [Cancel ^G] [Accept - Enter]               |
 |-------------------------|
```

```
....boeing     Searching Text...

EDGAR Archives: boeing

->  1.  BOEING CO 10-K (03/17/1994).
    2.  BOEING CO 10-Q (05/13/1994).
    3.  BOEING CO DEF 14A (03/15/1994).
    4.  BOEING CO S-8 (03/22/1994).




.................................................
                  UNITED STATES
         SECURITIES AND EXCHANGE COMMISSION
                Washington, D.C. 20549

                    FORM 10-K

   ANNUAL REPORT PURSUANT TO SECTION 13 OR 15(d) OF
         THE SECURITIES EXCHANGE ACT OF 1934

      For the fiscal year ended December 31, 1993

            Commission file number 1-442

               THE BOEING COMPANY

          7755 East Marginal Way South
            Seattle, Washington 98108
            Telephone:  (206) 655-2121
        State of incorporation:   Delaware
     IRS identification number:  91-0425694
```

Another type of question the Internet can be used to answer is to find travel advisory information for people interested in visiting a foreign country. A popular Gopher site is Washington & Lee University, where they have a simple menu.

```
windsorl@erau (8)%  gopher liberty.uc.wlu.edu

   1.  W&L University Information/
   2.  Netlink Server/
   3.  Libraries and Information Access/
   4.  Explore Internet Resources/
   5.  Finding Gopher Resources/
-> 6.  W&L Gopher - All Menu Entries  <?>
   7.  W&L Gopher - Local Entries  <?>


    ----------------Search------------------------------
   |                                                     |
   | Words to search for:  travel advisories             |
   |                                                     |
   |                                                     |
   |                [Cancel ^G] [Accept-Enter]           |
    -----------------------------

 Searching  : travel advisories

->   1.  U.S. State Department Travel Advisories/
     2.  US-State Department Travel Advisories ...
     3.  US-State-Department-Travel-Advisories/
     4.  U.S. State Department Travel Advisories <?>



1.   U.S. State Department Travel Advisories

     1.  Travel-Advisories-Information.
->   2.  Search US-State-Department-Travel-Advisories <?>
     3.  Current-Advisories/
     4.  FTP-Archive/


View item number: 2


  -->  Words to search for    cuba



STATE DEPARTMENT TRAVEL INFORMATION - Cuba
============================================================
Cuba - Consular Information Sheet
October 27, 1992
```

```
U.S. Representation:  The United States does not maintain an embassy in Cuba.
U.S. citizens who travel to Cuba can contact and register with the U.S.
Interests Section of the Swiss Embassy. The  U.S. Interests Section is located
in Havana at Calzada between L & M, Vedado; telephone 33-3550 through 33-3559.

Country Description:  Cuba is a developing country under the Communist rule of
Fidel Castro.  The United States has no direct diplomatic relations with Cuba.

Entry Requirements:  U.S. citizens need a Treasury Department license in order
to engage in any transactions related to travel to and within Cuba.  Information
and the required license may be obtained by contacting the Licensing Division,
Office of Foreign Assets Control at the Department of the Treasury
(202/622-2480).

Should a license be granted, a passport and a visa are also
required for entry to Cuba.  For current information on Cuba entry and customs
requirements, travelers can contact the Cuba Interests Section, an office of the
Cuban Government located at 2630 and 2639 16th Street N.W., Washington, D.C.
20009, tel: (202) 797-8518.
```

Washington & Lee also has a Web interface at `http://honor.uc.wlu.edu:1020/`.

This is just a portion of the information available. Following the data just listed is information on medical facilities, crime information, currency regulations, and tips for travelers.

The travel advisories are at `gopher.stolaf.edu` but can be accessed easily through other avenues.

Another question many librarians get is "How do I find a job?" The Internet is a great source. One site that has become very popular is the Online Career Center, accessible by Gopher at `msen.com`.

The following listing shows the `msen.com` main menu and a search for a librarian job.

```
windsorl@erau (2)%  gopher msen.com

    1.  About The Msen Gopher (updated 1 May 1994).
    2.  About Msen - introducing Msen Internet Training!/
    3.  What's New in the Msen Gopher/
    4.  Msen News Service/
    5.  Msen _Internet Review_/
    6.  Internet Business Pages/
    7.  Msen MarketPlace/
    8.  Good Causes/
    9.  Netsurfing -- Interesting things to play with/
   10.  Selected Internet Resources/
   11.  FTP sites - search for software on the Internet/
   12.  Other Gopher and Information Servers/
   13.  Ann Arbor / Detroit Weather.
   14.  Ann Arbor Civic Information/
->15.  The Online Career Center/
```

```
-->  15. The Online Career Center/

       1.  Questions and Comments to: occ@mail.msen.com.
       2.  About Online Career Center/
       3.  Company Sponsors and Profiles/
       4.  Employment Events/
       5.  Career Assistance/
       6.  FAQ - Frequently Asked Questions about OCC/
       7.  '94 College & University Resume Books/Diskettes/
  ->   8.  * Search Jobs/
       9.  * Search Resumes/
      10.  * Other Employment Databases//
      11.  Recruitment Advertising Agencies/
      12.  "Online Career Center" On Campus/
      13.  Help Files: Keyword Search/Enter Resume/Print/
      14.  How To Enter A Resume.
      15.  Online Career Center Liability Policy.

   1.  Browse Jobs:  Jobs and Profiles By Company/
   2.  Browse Jobs:  Jobs By State/
   3.  Browse Jobs:  Jobs By City/
   4.  Keyword Search: Contract Jobs <?>
 ->5.  Keyword Search: Search All Jobs <?>
   6.  Northeast: CT/ME/MA/NH/NY/RI/VT <?>
   7.  East:DE/MD/NJ/PA/VA/WV/DC <?>
   8.  Midwest:IL/IN/KS/KY/MI/OH/WI <?>
   9.  South:AL/FL/GA/MS/NC/SC/TN <?>
  10.  North Central:IA/MN/NE/ND/SD <?>
  11.  South Central:AR/LA/MO/OK/TX <?>
  12.  West:AZ/CA/CO/HI/NV/NM/UT <?>
  13.  Northwest:AK/ID/MT/OR/WA/WY <?>
  14.  Canada:All Provinces <?>
  15.  International: International Jobs/

 -->  5.  Keyword Search:   Search All Jobs <?>


       Words to search for:    librarian



                  [Cancel ^G] [Accept - Enter]



Searching...

librarian

   1.  940603: Teacher - Elementary Librarian (MS) ..Public
   2.  940603: Project Librarian - Data Processing (CA) ..
   3.  940603: Media Specialist (MA) /
```

```
 4.  940603: Librarian - Technical College (OH)
=>5. 940603: Assistant Librarian (NY) / Corning Community College.
 6.  940531: Programmer Analyst I (TEA-4566/$33,792/Austin, Texas).
 7.  940529: Tape Librarian, Tape Clerks - IBM 3490 (GA)
 8.  940529: Secondary Librarian - Junior High (MS)
 9.  940529: Secondary Librarian - High School (MS)
10.  940529: Librarian I, Cataloger (MI) / Grand Rapids
11.  940529: Librarian I, Branch-Childrens (MI)
12.  940529: Librarian (OR) / Willamette University.
13.  940529: Librarian (FL) / City of Pensacola.
14.  940529: High School Media Librarian (MA) ..
15.  940524: Librarian/Indexer DoD Secret-Hadron, Inc.-MD.
16.  940520: Teacher - Elementary Librarian (MS) ..Public
17.  940520: School Librarian (NY R )
18.  940520: Project Librarian - Data Processing (CA)


View item number:    5


--> 5.  940603: Assistant Librarian (NY) / Corning Community College.


*****************Subject: Assistant Librarian (NY) / Corning Community College
Date: 03 Jun 1994 13:51:43 -0400
Location: New York   Eastern

Assistant Librarian (NY)
Corning Community College
One Academic Drive
Corning, New York 14830

Contact: Director of Human Resources

Description:
A 10 month standard fulltime position to start in August.
Essential functions include primary responsibility for
external services and automated systems and shared
responsibility for reference and library instruction. Please
send letter of application, resume, and the names and
telephone numbers of three professional references by June
15th.   If you need assistance in creating an inexpensive
yet  professional resume, cover letter, and laser printed
envelope to send to this or other open positions, please
contact Digital Documents at (315) 834-9252. 24-hour
turnaround in most cases.

Qualifications:
Master's degree in Library-Information Science from an ALA
accredited school. Library experience required.

Company:
A member of the SUNY System. AA. EOE.
```

```
Status: Full-time
Salary: Competitive
Location: in northeast
Starting date: August
Closing date:  June 15th
Source: NYSYRACUS

(C) 1994 Gonyea and Associates, Inc. All Rights Reserved.
Help Wanted-USA is a service of Gonyea and Associates, Inc.,
3543 Enterprise Road East, SafetyHarbor, FL34695
```

The Online Career Center is becoming more popular by the month. It is great since it is updated frequently.

Another popular Internet site is all those library catalogs. Why? Because it's nice to see what other libraries have. This can come in handy for many reasons. For example, a student once asked about sources on discrimination. He had to write a paper on racism. He said everyone else in his class was going to write on black versus white and he really wanted his paper to be different. He wanted his paper to be about discrimination in his home country of Puerto Rico.

One of the great things about the library catalogs on the Internet is that they provide bibliographic information on items you can't usually find on your own without the Net. It would be hard to know what sources the student should use for this paper because, for most libraries, there isn't an easy way to find sources of information on racism in Puerto Rico. With the Internet, however, you can go to the University of Puerto Rico and see what they have in their collection that can at least provide a title and author of a good book.

Selecting Libraries at hundreds of Gopher sites on the Internet leads you to the following Yale site:

```
            Libraries on the Internet


  ->    1.  Americas/
        2.  Asia and Pacific/
        3.  Europe and Middle-East/
        4.  South Africa/
        5.  unknown/

        1.  Brazil/
        2.  Canada/
        3.  Chile/
        4.  Mexico/
  ->    5.  Puerto Rico/
        6.  United States/
        7.  Venezuela/
```

```
                University of Puerto Rico

 ONLINE UNIVERSITY OF PUERTO RICO - LIBRARIES SYSTEM/


                UPRENET - LIBRARY SYSTEM
       LOS CAMBIOS EFECTUADOS DURANTE OCTUBRE/NOVIEMBRE 1993
 ESTARANVIGENTES HASTA NUEVO AVISO. PARA INFORMACION MAS
 DETALLADA, FAVOR DE ENTRAR A NOTIS Y VER LAS PANTALLAS
   DE "NEWS".

 THE CHANGES MADE TO THE ON-LINE LIBRARY SYSTEM DURING OCTOBER/NOVEMBER 1993 WILL
 REMAIN IN EFFECT UNTIL FURTHER NOTICE. FOR MORE INFORMATION, PLEASE CONNECT TO
 NOTIS AND SEE THE "NEWS"

           UNIVERSIDAD DE PUERTO RICOD600


    OPAC        UPR Libraries
    OPAC-MED    Medical Sciences Library


    IMED        MEDLINE: Jan 90 - Aug 93
    MEDS        MEDLINE: 9/23/93 thru 4/28/94 (See NEWS)

 Database Selection: opac

  UPR Libraries  Introduction

 WELCOME TO THE UNIVERSITY OF PUERTO RICO ON-LINE CATALOG!


    Use the following command:        To search by:
               A=               Author
               T=               Title
               S=               Subject (ALL subjects)
               C=               Call Number (Dewey Decimal System)
               CL=              Call Number (Library of Congress and
                                National Library of Medicine)
               K=               Keyword

    Begin a new search on any screen.
    For information on searching, press <ENTER>.
    Type CHO for database menu.

    For Library News, type NEWS and press <ENTER>.Type STOP to exit.

      Enter search command
 **********************************
    k=racism and puerto rico      *
 **********************************
   RACISM AND PUERTO RICO   12 Entries Found
```

```
 1 Efectos psicologicos del racismo en el ind  Amaro, Sylvia
 2 Efectos psicologicos del racismo en el ind  Amaro, Sylvia
 3 Los efectos del prejuicio racial en estudi  Santiago de
 4 El prejuicio racial en Puerto Rico          Blanco, Tomas
 5 El prejuicio racial en Puerto Rico          Blanco, Tomas
 6 El texto libre de prejuicios sexuales y ra  Pico de Hernandez
 7 El texto libre de prejuicios sexuales y ra  Pico, Isabel
 8 El texto libre de prejuicios sexuales y ra  Pico de Hernandez
 9 El texto libre de prejuicios sexuales y ra  Pico de Hernandez
10 El texto libre de prejuicios sexuales y ra  Pico de Hernandez
11 El texto libre de prejuicios sexuales y ra  Pico, Isabel
12 Ideas, creencias, actitudes Puerto Rico
*************************************************************
```

Science, Technology, and Industry

The impact the Internet has on the areas of science, technology, and industry will effect all of us. Faster transmission of information-whether the information is in the form of electronic journals, conference events, reports on research, messages posted to appropriate Listservs and newsgroups, or colleague communication-is vital to remain on the cutting edge. We can already see accomplishments resulting from some of the navigational tools that have been developed, sites with good interfaces, better computers, better access methods, and so on.

Everyone is increasingly inundated with too much to read and not enough time to read it. Scientists, researchers, and business people are demanding ways to selectively manage what they access; many of them know the Net is the logical place. The navigating tools and indexing software used now are essential for finding information, and the people in these fields will have the most impact on developing new and better ways to access information.

Manufacturing methods that have been streamlined will get even better and more efficient. Small businesses have the chance to access industry information; a few years ago, only a huge corporation could afford the commercial services that provided this information-not to mention the cost of large computer systems to store all the data. Companies as well as governments can speed up the design and production of new products and services by communicating across the country or the globe and using information from the Virtual Library.

Medicine

Undoubtedly, medicine is an area that concerns all people. Imagine the ability to send x-ray images of a patient from one doctor to a specialist across the country for a diagnosis. Collaborating on research results about AIDS at the various institutes doing experimentation could save many lives. No lag time. Using the Virtual Library means saving money, time, and eliminating many bureaucratic characteristics inherent in current health care services.

Duplication Elimination

Several individuals in different fields have addressed the duplication of efforts as a problem. In some cases, this problem is caused by competition for grant money; people don't want to share results or cooperate. This was undoubtedly a major factor in the minds of the Treatment Action Group (TAG) who critiqued AIDS research at the National Institute of Health (NIH). They made recommendations to give the Office of AIDS Research (OAR) more authority over the Institute's $1.1 billion AIDS budget.

Supposedly, OAR is responsible for coordinating research at all NIH research centers. However, the organization has no say over the budget, which many see as a problem. Congress has already incorporated some of TAG's recommendations into legislation. With 21 institutes doing AIDS research under the auspices of NIH, the last thing anyone should be doing is duplicating efforts. There should be timely information made available to not only the researchers, but also to AIDS patients. The Internet could be used for disseminating information quickly.

A duplication of efforts within the government is also being addressed by the push to reinvent government. The National Performance Review (NPR) headed by Vice President Al Gore agreed that duplication of effort was a major hurdle to government efficiency. It was also identified by outsiders in various disciplines as an inhibitor to progress. For an overview of the mission and goals of the NPR, have a look at `ftp://SunSITE.unc.edu/pub/academic/political-science/National_Performance_Review/nprintro.txt`. The Internet is a source that will be used more and more to quickly disseminate information, eliminating redundant efforts and hopefully leading to more cooperative ventures.

An important point to remember is that the Internet is a global entity; it's not like a new TV network series you watch to decide whether it will last through the end of the season. The Internet is here to stay. Imagine cutting down on the duplication of research by industry, government, research institutes, and universities. How many times has ABC University spent 1.5 million dollars on a project that duplicates what XYZ Institute did? Too many. Why? Because no one at either place was aware of what the other institution was doing.

Decreasing the duplication of research efforts will be cost effective for all. More scholarly articles are now available electronically, which speeds up the communication process. Publishing an article in a scholarly print journal can involve tremendous lag between the time the article is finished and the time it is published-over a year at times. This lengthy process is caused by the time it takes to complete peer review. It takes months to review manuscripts, edit them, add comments to the author, and wait for responses. Many times, an editorial board meets only every few months.

Get real. The Net eliminates that because everything is processed electronically. Feedback can quickly go back and forth. Some e-journal editors even post the articles for reader's comments before the final draft is ready. This sure beats waiting for letters to appear in the next issue.

Speed it up. Use the Virtual Library. Find the cure for the disease faster; find out whether a research report already exists on an experiment your company is getting ready to launch; before submitting a grant proposal for a water pollution eradication machine, find out what alternatives other organizations are using now.

The Virtual Library is full of medical and health information for the individual. More communication is taking place between professionals who are affected by the tremendous technological advances in the medical field, not to mention the advances of the Virtual Library utility. Patients also are communicating-not just with doctors but with other patients from all over the world. Many questions left unanswered by one sector of the population have been answered by another sector through the Internet.

A Powerful Presence

Not everything is available from the Virtual Library yet. But what is out there is increasing at an incredible pace-files to retrieve at FTP sites, full-text documents for the taking, tons of government information on every subject imaginable. Commercial services are popping up all around, and although many people fear that consumer costs for access to the Internet will skyrocket, some commercial services have done an excellent job of developing good Internet sites-and they don't all charge fees. This free access is likely to change, but in a capitalist society, competition is fierce. The push for better interactive software programs and access to popular database sites along the Virtual Library superhighway may fuel the commercial as well as private and government sectors.

Liberation

The Net has liberated so many individuals. People who used to be scared of computers are now discovering the worth of the machines by exploring and communicating. People who feel alone can reach out and talk to someone else-entire groups, for that matter. Kids in rural areas may be over 200 miles from a major city but can get together with other kids their age and feel a part of the world. Learn something! Play something! Use the Virtual Library-it belongs to the world.

The Internet has brought liberation and enlightenment. Celebrations are in order for the advances in communication possibilities. But liberty in its purist form eventually leads to a sense of responsibility: Who's in charge of the Virtual Library resources? Who determines whether a service has a charge or is free? Why can't I search a database that appears on a particular college library's menu for free? Who decides what should be on all the menus I see while navigating? What's important? How can we be sure this information is correct?

Who's in Charge of the Virtual Library?

Because the Virtual Library most of us use is the whole Internet, we must remind ourselves that it is not the only system. Some common standards have emerged for enabling different computer systems to get along with each other. Other than these standards, each network connected to the Internet has its own rules. For most institutions, agencies, companies, and individual service providers, a person (or persons) is in charge of that particular network, and he or she makes decisions based on the organization's users. For example, a university has a person who determines what would best suit the students and faculty at that particular Internet site.

Rules are put into effect by people who oversee the local network. After users start navigating to other sites on the network, however, they run across other systems whose rules may be entirely different-stricter, more lenient, and so on.

These rules undoubtedly lead to frustration, but many institutions are limited in what they can offer to people outside their domain. Many colleges and universities (which comprise a huge portion of the Internet sites) have licensed databases on their menus. After selecting a menu, an individual must enter a user identification code and password. These codes are necessary because the institution has paid a site license fee, which means that only so many users can use a particular database. Because of these restrictions, schools cannot allow access to anyone not associated with that school.

Online Services and Document Delivery

Online services have been around for years. They are generally considered expensive; until recently, a librarian or information specialist conducted searches for library users, researchers, scientists, teachers, and so on. With the Virtual Library, many of these services now are available to individuals who never knew the services existed. The services are for the most part commercial and still expensive (depending on the particular service provider and database) but accessibility is far greater than ever before.

In addition to searching databases and finding relevant references of interest, a service such as CARL UnCover can provide document delivery. *Document delivery* speeds up the research process by enabling users to order full-text items from their terminals. The documents are then mailed, faxed, or sent electronically. Many vendors who offer such a service can deliver within 24 hours. For people willing to pay, this service is great. People who cannot afford it must rely on other sources of information. One of the glories of the Net is that if you cannot get the information at the first site, you can keep on navigating and hopefully latch on to a free source.

The following shows a search with CARL UnCover, in which the term *bogus parts* leads to the discovery of several interesting articles.

```
windsor1@erau: telnet database.carl.org

EXIT    PAC
Enter Choice> PAC
Welcome to the CARL system
         CARL Corporation offers access to the following
                 groups of databases:

             1. Library Catalogs
                     (including Government Publications)

             2. Current Article Indexes and Access
                     (including UnCover and ERIC)

             3. Information Databases
                     (including Encyclopedia)

             4. Other Library Systems
             5. Library and System News

  Enter the NUMBER of your choice, and press the <RETURN> key >>2

                         Welcome to
                          UnCover
             The Article Access and Delivery Solution

UnCover contains records describing journals and their contents. Over 4000
current citations
are added daily.  UnCover offers you the opportunity to order fax copies of
articles from
this database.

Type  ?  for details.
For information about a new service, UnCover Complete, type ?C

         Enter   N   for   NAME search
                 W   for   WORD search
                 B   to    BROWSE by journal title
                 QS  for   QUICKSEARCH information
                 S   to    STOP or SWITCH to another database
         Type the letter for the kind of search you want,
           and end each line you type by pressing <RETURN>

                 SELECTED DATABASE:  UnCover
ENTER   COMMAND (? FOR HELP) >>  w

                 SELECTED DATABASE: UnCover

   Enter word or words (no more than one line, please)
         separated by spaces and press <RETURN>.
```

```
>bogus parts
WORKING...
BOGUS      76 ITEMS          UnCover
BOGUS + PARTS     15 ITEMS

BOGUS + PARTS     15 ITEMS  UnCover

To ADD a new word, enter it,
<D>ISPLAY to see the current list, or
<Q>UIT for a new search:


NEW WORD(S): d
  1            (Commuter air international 04/01/94)
     Could Bogus Parts get into Your Inventory?

  2            (Aviation week & space technology 04/05/93)
     U.S. indicts broker in alleged parts scam: Pratt & W...

  3            (Aviation week and space technology 03/15/93)
     Twin task forces battle bogus parts.

  4            (Aviation week & space technology 03/01/93)
     Military surplus goods fuel bogus parts market.
---------------------------------------------------------------
```

Access

A world full of information still has people who are information poor. Experts are currently discussing how to provide access to people who have no computer at home and cannot use the great Virtual Library that remains under constant construction and improvement.

On the other side of the coin are the thousands of individuals who have accounts to access the Virtual Library but never do. This lack of involvement is caused in part by the nature of large entities on the Internet. People who work at universities, companies, government agencies, and so on, may have an account (or can obtain an account easily) at no charge because Internet access is considered a benefit of the job. The institution pays a fee each year for access and therefore everyone at that site can use the Virtual Library for communicating, connecting to other sites, obtaining software, and so on. Many people don't use that privilege, however, because they feel they have no need for it, don't like computers, or just don't want to learn the basic commands to get around in the Virtual Library.

The dilemma is how to give entrance to people who need the Internet and don't have it. Public libraries are the place most people think of in terms of a community access point. Unfortunately, many public libraries cannot afford the necessary hardware. Undoubtedly, government interest, legislation, and consumers will continue to focus on this issue.

Linkage

A goal of vital importance for the Virtual Library is to continue to offer easy communication. Great inventions, discoveries, and scientific breakthroughs were not all products of research through traditional information sources. Almost all important milestones involved communication in one form or another. It's quite amazing to read a book like *Double Helix* by James Watson and realize that the discovery of the DNA structure was very much contingent on colleagues communicating-letters, articles, passing conversations, and so on. The process is so much easier now; asking questions of researchers across continents involves only an e-mail address.

With electronic linkage, you can correspond with colleagues you have never personally met. Groups of people with similar interests suddenly have a large number of individuals with whom they can share concerns and problems, seek advice, and correct misconceptions.

Communicating with people in other countries is a constant learning experience. Learning never stops. If countries are fortunate enough to have the necessary hardware and accessibility to the Internet, they experience a dramatic increase in the number of minds working to solve problems like hunger, pollution, and disease. With access to a Virtual Library, many people who have had to do without for so long can better educate themselves. Why rely on outdated books and information when access to current information is at hand? The uses of this global tool are never ending. All disciplines will be affected for the better; as problems arise, solutions will follow.

Linkage means site to site, individual to individual, terminal to terminal. If you get through to a system you need, you can contact another user through e-mail and ask for help. Often other users are glad to locate information and e-mail it back. Internet users normally are sincerely grateful when another user takes time to do a favor. Avoid the pitfall of abusing other users of the Virtual Library. The sense of responsibility that accompanies liberation and enlightenment falls on all our shoulders, not just on those of one system administrator or some entity. It's our Virtual Library, so let's take care of it.

The Force

The Virtual Library is a force electrifying millions of users. It has revolutionized communication to the point of no return. The wheels of ingenuity continue to spin at an incredible rate. As more sites connect to the Internet, more challenges present themselves. The wonder of it all is that the frustrations lead to answers, which is problem solving at its best. Waves of users are gaining confidence in using the Virtual Library, but believe it or not, not everyone welcomes this challenge.

When things begin to change drastically in any realm, many people resist because change represents a threat to tradition. People who oppose change present a force themselves. We can help alleviate the problems these people fear by educating them on the worth of the Virtual Library, the necessity for it, and its amazing capabilities.

For those who are unpersuaded: beware. The surf's up and there's no low tide in the foreseeable future. Developers forge on, and users multiply and demand more. Scientists, doctors, auto workers, pilots, and teachers continue to discover new ways to do things, new information to enable them to better their work and lives, and to restore their faith in a pioneering spirit. Nothing stops those individuals who continue to invent, to find new ways to use technology, make better hardware, to develop operating systems, and to produce better navigating tools that help maximize the Virtual Library's use. These people are the truly inspired pioneers who continue to give users reasons to revel in their accomplishments.

PART

IX

Using the Internet: Education

Schoolkids and the Net

48

by Janet Murray

The Internet is about the rise of not merely a new technology, but a new culture, a global culture where time, space, borders, and even personal identity are radically redefined.

——*Michael Strangelove, 1993*

Telecommunications technology serves the pre-university educational community in a variety of significant ways:

- Teachers can overcome their professional isolation by communicating with their colleagues.

- Students can overcome geographic and social isolation through electronic correspondence.

- Participants gain by sharing experimental data, effective teaching and learning strategies, and timely access to information.

- The use of telecommunications addresses educational reform by promoting collaborative learning.

- And perhaps, kids who share the events of their daily lives with peers from other cultures can discover a commonality that transcends politics and traditional stereotypes to create a truly global village.

This chapter discusses telecommunications initiatives in primary and secondary schools.

The Virtual Classroom

Teachers of art, music, or business education are frequently one-of-a-kinds in their buildings; telecommunications offers a daily electronic convention with others in distant locations. In August 1993, a South African teacher asked for help in designing a curriculum to teach computer skills. A teacher in Tennessee promptly shared an extensive outline as well as strategies for effective teaching with limited equipment. Informal software reviews based on classroom experience are more helpful than glossy brochures and vendors' glowing reports. As one teacher commented, "As the only computer specialist in the school and district, it is invaluable to me to have contact with other professionals using computers in new and innovative ways" (Honey, 1993).

Librarians seeking to automate their circulation system or select CD-ROM applications receive valuable advice from their peers who have already begun providing electronic access to information. Classroom teachers who have been abruptly infused with handicapped students have shared strategies for classroom management and more effective instruction. Telecommunications erases geographic boundaries for educators who are pursuing a common goal and are willing to share their expertise.

An early experiment in teleconnectivity demonstrated how electronic links can help overcome geographic isolation. The experiment connected students in a one-room Eskimo school near the Arctic Circle with students in Alberta, New York, Oregon, and Texas. Correspondents were challenged to guess what item located in the remote classroom probably would not be found in any of the other participating schools. The answer (a wood stove) delighted the puzzled urban students and their supervising teachers.

For the student who is physically handicapped, exceptionally gifted, or otherwise set apart from classmates, telecommunications offers an environment in which contributions are evaluated based on content rather than the age, appearance, race, or ethnic background of the contributor. Teachers in rural schools can expand their gifted students' horizons by giving them access to appropriate peers to stimulate their intellectual and artistic creativity. That telecommunications minimizes social isolation for students with special needs was emphasized in an electronic message posted by Queen Elizabeth II:

> *During this visit to the Whitefield Centre I have been heartened to see the emphasis placed upon helping young people towards independence by the use of technology. Through John and Adam, who are using this computer to write and send this letter for me, I send greetings to the many children worldwide who are being helped and encouraged to play a full part in the world.*

> ——k12.ed.special, *transposed from CHATBACK, July 28, 1993*

The 'Lectronic Lab

A popular project facilitated by telecommunications incorporates geographic location, history, and the gathering of scientific data. Students, located at different latitudes on approximately the same longitude, have attempted to replicate Eratosthenes' experiment to measure the circumference of the earth by measuring the length of a shadow cast by a stick at true noon on the same day. Establishing true noon requires some sophisticated calculations to adjust for longitudinal variations, and the experiment is repeated over several weeks to compensate for uncooperative weather. The students post their measurements and collaborate on the calculations. In one such exercise, their results were accurate to within 7 percent of the scientifically measured circumference.

A New Zealand student who proposed studying the effect of the earth's rotation on the way toilets flush wanted to demonstrate that water drains clockwise in the southern hemisphere and counterclockwise in the northern hemisphere. A respondent from the University of Colorado in Boulder explained that the Coriolis force cannot be documented so easily because other factors also affect the way water drains. The respondent provided detailed instructions for conducting a scientifically verifiable experiment.

Participants in the National Geographic Society's Kids Network collect local scientific data pertaining to weather, pollution, solar energy, and the water supply and share it with students at other locations. Scientists guide the students' exploration of geographic patterns through letters, maps, and graphs. Collecting, comparing, processing, and evaluating data is a significant activity among students who have access to telecommunications resources.

Improvement in the clarity and quality of students' written expression is a widely documented result of experiments in electronic correspondence. Teachers find that students who write for a real audience composed of their peers are highly motivated to make themselves understood; timely feedback from other students reinforces the value of effective communication. Correspondence with native speakers in another language similarly improves students' writing skills while expanding their understanding of other cultures.

Today's students will spend all their working and learning lives in the Information Age. Students who know how to efficiently locate and evaluate pertinent information can gain a competitive edge. K–12 educators (in schools serving kindergarten through 12th grade) who taught students to use online information retrieval sources report a significant impact on the students' acquisition of higher-level thinking skills. In her national study of telecommunications and K–12 educators, Margaret Honey concluded: "Critical thinking, data analysis, problem solving, and independent thinking develop when students use a technology that supports research, communication, and analysis."

When it is important to obtain current information, online sources are always more up to date than print sources. News retrieval services, scientific databases, educational resources, and social studies databases are examples of popular electronic sources of information. Teachers provide mutual support by filtering the vast amount of available information, reposting what is exceptionally valuable, and offering advice about how to find resources with immediate classroom applicability.

Teaching on the Electronic Frontier

Using telecommunications in the classroom requires the development of some new teaching strategies that facilitate collaboration and encourage all students to participate. Dennis Newman (1993) observed that using a networked environment to teach earth science in an elementary school promoted "substantial movement from whole-class teaching toward more collaborative work in small groups....Instead of giving the teacher greater centralized control of individualized instruction....the network allows control to be distributed to the students." The most effective telecommunications projects feature active moderators who are familiar with the subject matter, sensitive to the needs (and anxieties) of new users, and adept at steering conversation in an educationally appropriate environment.

Telecommunications can be instrumental in promoting educational reform "because use of the Internet shifts focus away from a teacher-as-expert model and toward one of shared responsibility for learning....Much of school reform attempts to move away from teacher isolation and toward teacher collaboration, away from learning in a school-only context and toward learning in a life context, away from an emphasis on knowing and toward an emphasis on learning, away from a focus on content and toward a focus on concepts" (Sellers, 1994).

Educational practitioners who participated in the CoSN/FARNET Project on K–12 Networking agreed that "educational reform is necessary to support the needs of an Information-Age economy and reflect the values of an information-age society. We envision the Information-Age school as locus and catalyst for active, collaborative lifelong learning" (Rutkowski, 1994).

Effective telecommunications projects promote collaborative learning by engaging students' energy and enthusiasm in designing cooperative experiences and placing the responsibility for the success of those experiences squarely on the students' shoulders. The instructor's role becomes that of a mentor, a "guide on the side instead of the sage on the stage." Students explicitly recognize the value of this shift in the way they learn. As one student noted, "Sometimes I find out about things and places my teacher doesn't know about. Then I get to be the teacher and it makes me feel important."

Two excellent videotapes produced in late 1993 can help interested teachers, administrators, and school board members visualize the instructional advantages of teleconnectivity. *Experience the Power: Network Technology for Education* is a 17-minute production released by the National Center for Education Statistics, U.S. Department of Education. *NASA's Global Quest: The Internet in the Classroom* is an 11-minute video describing to schools the benefits of using the Internet.

Dave Kinnaman concludes that the Internet may provide "the last, best opportunity this century to really accomplish a major step forward for broad public education. If the National Information Infrastructure fulfills its promise during our lifetimes, every literate person can have lifelong learning and ongoing personal development as a matter of policy" (1994).

The Global Village

The capability of telecommunications to broaden students' horizons beyond their local boundaries (of home and neighborhood school) provides an environment whose ultimate impact may be immeasurable. An elementary school computer coordinator noted, "My students have learned to think more about the world as classroom—we are able to visualize the children of other nations as students just like ourselves." Another teacher commented, "I soon realized what a wonderful resource it would be for my students to learn about other cultures and to acquire English at the same time" (Honey).

Lorna Kropp reports that "students and teachers at Discovery School [Spokane, WA] have made some good friends far away. Our students have been amazed that people from New Zealand, Texas, Massachusetts, and Australia have written comments to them. They marveled at the descriptions of life in the outback of Australia and the daring feats of teens in New Brunswick. The reports have brought home similarities as well as differences in students' lives in ways that no textbook can."

An especially touching example of student awareness across time and culture was widely broadcast in the summer of 1993. Although the experience did not originate in a telecommunications forum, its impact on one individual was amplified many times over because he chose to share it with his electronic colleagues. Tacked to the wall of the Anne Frank house in Amsterdam, Raymond Harder found the following hand-printed letter:

> *Our teacher learn us about love, concord and righteous. He told to us about Anne Frank and her hiding and life. After this story we took Anne's Diary from school's library. We read her diary and acknowledge that our youth is very similar. After fifty years history repetition again in Bosnia— war, hate, killing, hiding, displacement. We are twelve years old and we can't influence on politic and war. We wait spring, we wait peace like Anne Frank fifty years before. She didn't live to see peace, but we? Many greetings for all children and all good people on the world from Bosnia.*

> ——*CoSNDISC, August 23, 1993*

K-12 Telecomputing Projects

Telecommunications projects that link students and teachers range from proprietary, commercial ventures to grassroots initiatives funded and staffed by volunteers. Regardless of their method of delivery, educators share an enthusiastic belief in the potential of teleconnectivity to enrich their students' learning experiences. Contact information for each of the following projects is provided in "K–12 Telecommunications Contacts," at the end of this chapter.

Academy One

Academy One is a grassroots network supported by volunteers and distributed by the Free-Nets of the National Public Telecomputing Network (NPTN). Students are actively involved in online interactive projects such as space shuttle simulations and the virtual Olympics, for which they must have access to an Internet account or a local Free-Net system. Other projects enable participation through newsgroups and electronic mail. Young students who send letters to Santa receive replies from older students acting in that role. Reports on international events such as the Iditarod and Whitbread Round-the-World Yachting Race are posted daily. Holidays are a traditional time for multicultural exchanges; Academy One expanded this concept to emphasize intergenerational sharing in its December 1993 request for information on how families celebrate national, cultural, and religious holidays such as Boxing Day, Chanukah, Christmas, Kwanza, the Lunar New Year, and Nirvana Day.

NPTN is significant for its emphasis on community access to telecommunications networks. Dr. Tom Grundner, founder of the Cleveland Free-Net and NPTN, compares the current state of computer technology to the development of the public library a century ago. "We reached the point in this country where literacy levels got high enough (and the cost of producing books cheap enough) that the public library became feasible. In this century, computer literacy levels have gotten high enough (and the cost of computer equipment cheap enough) that it is time for a similar movement to form around the development of free public-access computerized community information systems."

Big Sky Telegraph

Big Sky Telegraph in Montana is an exemplary model of a community information network that has integrated Internet technology with bulletin board systems (METNET) in a cooperative state-wide educational network. Its approach to training users is also significant. As part of its initial development, "Circuit Riders" were equipped with a laptop computer and a modem to use in their local communities as they explored network resources and trained their neighbors to do the same.

FrEdMail

FrEdMail originated as a grassroots network dedicated to K–12 education running Apple II computers with software developed by Al Rogers. The FrEdMail projects are now available as a distributed conferencing system on Internet as SCHLNET using the Usenet message interchange format. Forums on both FrEdMail and SCHLNET are available primarily to teachers, who then share the projects with their students. FrEdMail monitors and actively moderates many curricular, special interest groups, and project forums. The Global SchoolNet (FrEdMail) Foundation charges a subscription fee to forums. Students and teachers with access to e-mail on some other network can subscribe to the mailing lists offered by SCHLNET. Selected schools have taken advantage of live video conferencing over the Internet as members of the Global Schoolhouse Project. The Foundation also publishes a quarterly newsletter and curriculum guides to help teachers implement telecomputing.

K12Net

K12Net originated as a grassroots "network with training wheels" on FidoNet-compatible bulletin board systems. More than 35 forums distributed on six continents are devoted to specific areas of the curriculum, correspondence with native speakers in five languages other than English, and classroom-to-classroom projects designed by teachers. Projects in science and mathematics have elicited participation from the broadest geographic area because they are highly structured with well-defined goals and expectations.

Brown Bag Science promotes experiments students can perform with commonly available household materials. Each lesson features educational objectives and clear instructions for young scientists encouraged to test their hypotheses by experimenting. MathMagic is designed to capture student interest and imagination by featuring problems that have no obvious solution, can be solved using more than one strategy, and may yield more than one solution. Participating classes are required to post both their solutions and their strategies. A "River Link Project," launched in early 1995, required students to design the questions they would research about local rivers.

K12Net forums also are available as Usenet newsgroups in the k12.* hierarchy. K12Net is distinctive among K–12 initiatives in telecommunications because it is freely available to anyone who can access a K12Net BBS with a local phone call. K12Net is an all-volunteer effort with more than 50 percent of its participating BBSes located outside the United States.

KIDLINK

KIDLINK involves students between the ages of 10 and 15 in correspondence regarding the future of the world following their initial response to four questions:

1. Who am I?
2. What do I want to be when I grow up?
3. How do I want the world to be better when I grow up?
4. What can I do now to make this happen?

KIDFORUM provides a place for classroom projects devoted to the KIDLINK themes. In the fall of 1993, KIDFORUM sponsored virtual vacations to other parts of the world, attracting participants from Europe, Russia, Slovenia, and Tasmania. Participants can subscribe to the KIDLINK forums by e-mail or by accessing the archives at the KIDLINK Gopher.

KIDCAFE is a general chat area where students can discuss any topic of interest. Some cafes conduct discussions in Japanese and Portuguese. In KIDPROJ, teachers can obtain UNICEF-developed curriculum materials related to the 1989 United Nation's Rights of the Child convention. Participants can subscribe to the KIDLINK forums by electronic mail or access the archives at the KIDLINK Gopher.

KIDSPHERE (formerly KIDSNET) is a distributed and moderated mailing list devoted to ongoing issues in networking for K–12 students and teachers. Participants discuss news and mail interfaces appropriate for children's use, and the development of network services for the K–12 audience. Children can post messages to other children in the related list, KIDS. A monthly "Internet Hunt" challenges Internet users to practice their search strategies by locating the answers to specific (usually rather esoteric) questions.

Learning Link

Learning Link is an interactive computer-based communications system for K–12 educators and members of the community. Learning Link is supplied through the public broadcasting system in cooperation with education agencies and community organizations. This system offers databases, information resources, and conferencing as well as gateways to remote sites. Although the national consortium provides the editorial content, local site operators organize each system in response to the needs of their specific community. PBS announced that Learning Link is available to all its affiliates in 1994.

National Geographic Kids Network

The National Geographic Kids Network distributes highly structured telecommunications-based science and geography curriculum units of a semester's duration for older elementary students (grades 4 through 6). Students compile local data on assigned topics and then share their results with other members of their research team in geographically distant locales. The Kids Network operates using proprietary software included with a school's subscription fee.

> **NOTE**
>
> These projects all demonstrate to K–12 students and teachers how telecommunications can broaden their horizons and expand their connectivity to international resources in the Information Age. As one teacher noted, "Several specific class activities originated from FrEdMail, K12Net, and Internet projects. But most important, I no longer feel isolated behind my closed classroom doors."
>
> The individuals involved in the creation and perpetuation of these services are dedicated professionals who want to share their own enthusiasm with the upcoming generation. No single model of teleconnectivity is appropriate for every school situation. Teachers in states with established statewide networks may have access to all the K–12 educational projects listed in this chapter, but educators in less privileged locations may depend on dial-up access to a more limited number of resources.

Rodents and Spiders and Kids, Oh My!

The development of user-friendly interfaces like Gopher and World Wide Web servers and clients has dramatically impacted the K–12 networking community. No longer intimidated by challenging and esoteric UNIX commands, primary and secondary students and teachers have recently expanded their horizons beyond e-mail projects and conferencing to global information access and electronic publishing.

Educators who participated in the CoSN/FARNET Project noted that, "Today's students need to master critical Information-Age skills: finding, evaluating, and using all kinds of rapidly changing information to solve complex problems" (Rutkowski). The Internet houses a dynamic virtual library for these students and their teachers. Useful resources specifically targeted to the K–12 community include these:

- **AskERIC** is a research service available by e-mail and Gopher that provides access to the extensive national body of education-related literature held by the Educational Resources Information Center (ERIC). Educators can direct questions about K–12 education, learning, teaching, information technology, and educational administration to the AskERIC staff members, who promise to respond within 48 working hours. The AskERIC Electronic Library provides keyword-searchable directories of educational information and resources, lesson plans, network information guides, bibliographies, and the archives of K–12 related Listservs on its Gopher server.

- **The Consortium for School Networking (CoSN)** is a community of organizations, government agencies, corporations, and individuals with an interest in K–12 education. Through CoSN's distributed Listserv, CoSNDISC, participants share information and communications resources. In October 1993, CoSN assembled a significant collection of educators to share ideas with representatives of government agencies, vendors, and service providers who were directed to "Build Consensus/Build Models for K–12 Networking." Unique to this project was the extensive online discussion that preceded the physical meeting, facilitating productive working groups on the topics of equitable access, funding, curricular resources, educational reform, and technical and user support.

- **The Eisenhower National Clearinghouse for Mathematics and Science Education** provides access to a special collection of science and mathematics education resources found on the Internet through its Digital Curriculum Laboratory. In addition to curricular materials, the DCL collects information on standards, assessment, reform, and professional development. Demonstration sites are located at ten regional education laboratories.

- **The Internet School Networking Group of the Internet Engineering Task Force** publishes RFCs (Requests for Comments) that provide valuable overviews of Internet issues for K–12 educators. Working drafts and final documents (FYIs) are available by Telnet or Gopher to `ds.internic.net`.

- **SA Spacelink** is an online electronic information system for educators that is available to dial-up users as well as through the Internet. Spacelink provides teachers with NASA press releases, spacecraft launch schedules, and historical information about space exploration as well as lesson plans and classroom activities. The system also features aerospace research and adaptations of space technology for industry and public use.

The U.S. Department of Education maintains several types of Internet servers and tries to make all its holdings accessible to the public through as many of the channels commonly used by educators as possible. Reports on major Department initiatives such as GOALS 2000, School-to-Work, and Technology can be located on the Office of Educational Research and Improvement's Gopher, Web, and FTP sites.

The World Wide Web has captured the imagination of students and teachers with full Internet connectivity. Designing a home page that reflects the uniqueness of their local school and publishes their artwork and projects enables students to be electronic publishers with an international audience. Gleason Sackman maintains a "hot list" of K–12 Internet sites that tracks the dramatic growth in the number of connected primary and secondary schools. The HotList is available on the Web at `http://toons.cc.ndsu.nodak.edu/~sackmann/k12.html`. It is also possible to retrieve the list and "view" Web sites with e-mail. Hillside Elementary School maintains a list of K–12 school Web servers that can be viewed from a clickable map interface at `http://hillside.coled.umn.edu/others.html`.

Howard Rheingold reflected on the evolution of the Internet in an article about "Digital Reiko"—the popular Japanese teen idol singer, Reiko Chiba, whose home page features pictures of her wardrobe in a hand-drawn setting, "Reiko's Room":

> *I sense a strange historical inflection emanating from the moment a savvy idol singer figured out that she could live in cyberspace. The medium invented by engineers who are now in their fifties and sixties, developed by programmers now in their thirties and forties, populated by undergraduates and technology jocks in their twenties, is about to undergo another transformation. Here comes a teenage girl from Tokyo who is going to show the world how to create a cult without leaving her room, and make jillions in the process. She'll probably reveal something unexpected about what kind of medium the global multimedia communication network wants to become.*

> *——Howard Rheingold*

Danger on the Information Highway

Educators know that there are some materials available on the Internet that may be offensive to some students, teachers, and parents. Although it is possible to create network servers that obstruct the avenues to these materials, motivated students quickly identify alternative paths. Schools typically have a "code of conduct" that establishes the rights and responsibilities of students and teachers in their institution. These expectations can be extrapolated to form "Acceptable Use Policies" specifically related to Internet resources. By treating Internet access as a "virtual field trip" that requires parental permission, schools can acknowledge the dangers while indemnifying themselves. Another common metaphor treats the Internet as a "virtual library" to which access can be guided by the American Library Association's policies and interpretations of the "Library Bill of Rights."

A valuable collection of acceptable use policies is housed on the Armadillo Gopher and Web servers at `chico.rice.edu`. These policies typically describe the purpose and goals of networks in terms of collaboration, exchange of information, and the promotion of excellence in education. They emphasize respect for the rights of others, responsible and ethical use of the Internet's resources, and proscribe illegal, obscene, and commercial activities. Revocation of privileges is the usual consequence for inappropriate behavior.

The Internet holds exceptional promise for K–12 educational learning activities. That promise can best be actualized by developing thoughtful policies governing its use, promoting broad and equitable access for homes, communities, and schools, and providing appropriate training for teachers and students. This chapter barely skims the surface of the resources, opportunities, and challenges available to educators on the Internet; the contact information and bibliography that follow provide pointers to further your exploration of a dynamic, multifaceted, evolving network.

K–12 Telecommunications Contacts

Academy One
Linda Delzeit
NPTN Director of Education
714-527-5651
E-mail: linda@nptn.org

AskERIC
4-194 Center for Science & Technology
Syracuse, NY 13244-4100
315-443-3640
Fax: 315-443-5448
E-mail: askeric@ericir.syr.edu
Gopher: ericir.syr.edu (port 70)

Big Sky Telegraph
Frank Odasz, Director
Western Montana College
710 S. Atlantic
Dillon, MT 59725
406-683-7338
Fax: 406-683-7493
E-mail: franko@bigsky.dillon.mt.us
Modem: 406-683-7680
Telnet 192.231.192.1 (type **bbs**)

Consortium for School Networking
Gwen Solomon, Chair
P.O. Box 65193
Washington, D.C. 20035-5193
202-466-6296
Gopher: cosn.org (port 70)
CoSNDISC e-mail: listproc@list.cren.net
    Subject: cosndisc *yourname*

#### Chapter 48

Eisenhower National Clearinghouse
614-292-9258
E-mail: info@enc.org
Modem: 614-292-7784
Gopher: enc.org (port 70)

FrEdMail Foundation
Global SchoolNet Foundation
Al Rogers
P.O. Box 243
Bonita, CA 91908-0243
619-475-4852
E-mail: arogers@bonita.cerf.fred.org

Global Schoolhouse Project
Yvonne Marie Andrés
Director of Curriculum
7040 Avenida
Encinas, CA 92009
619-931-5934
E-mail: andresyv@cerf.net

K12Net
Janet Murray
Wilson High School
1151 S.W. Vermont St.
Portland, OR 97219
503-280-5280 x450
E-mail: jmurray@psg.com

KIDLINK
Odd de Presno
4815 Saltrod, Norway
Fax: +47-41-27111
Modem: +47-41-31378
E-mail: opresno@extern.uio.no
Telnet: 165.190.8.35 (log in as **gopher**)
Gopher: kids.ccit.duq.edu (port 70)

KIDSPHERE
Bob Carlitz
E-mail: bob@hamlet.phyast.pitt.edu

Learning Link National Consortium
WNET/13
356 West 58th Street
New York, NY 10019
212-560-6613

NASA Spacelink
NASA Marshall Space Flight Center
Mail Code CA21
Marshall Space Flight Center, AL 35812
205-544-0038
Modem: 205-895-0028
Telnet: 192.149.89.61

National Geographic Kids Network
5455 Corp. Drive, Suite 104
Troy, MI 48007
800-342-4460

National Public Telecomputing Network
Tom Grundner, President
P.O. Box 1987
Cleveland, OH 44106
216-247-5800
Fax: 216-247-3328
E-mail: tmg@nptn.org

U.S. Department of Education
INet Project Manager
Office of Educational Research and Improvement
555 New Jersey Ave., N.W., Room 214
Washington, D.C. 20208-5725
202-219-1803
Gopher: ed.gov

Videotapes:
Experience the Power: Network Technology for Education
Jim Lukesh
Nebraska Department of Education
Box 94987
Lincoln, NE 68509-4987
$6.00

Global Quest: The Internet in the Classroom
Broadcast on NASA Select TV

—or—

NASA Central Operation of Resources for Educators
Lorain County Joint Vocational School
15181 Route 58 South
Oberlin, OH 44074
216-774-1051 x293
Fax: 216-774-2144
$18.50

REFERENCE WORKS

Ellsworth, Jill H. *Education on the Internet.* Indianapolis: Sams Publishing, 1994.

Fishman, Barry and Roy D. Pea. "The Internetworked School: A Policy for the Future." *Technos: Quarterly of Education and Technology*, 3 (1), 1994.

Gargano, Joan C. and David L. Wasley. "K–12 Internetworking Guidelines." IETF School Networking Group, *Internet FYI 26*, RFC 1709. November 1994.

Grundner, Tom. "Whose Internet is it Anyway?—A Challenge." *Online! Magazine*, July 1992.

Honey, Margaret and Andrés Henr'quez. *Telecommunications and K–12 Educators: Findings from a National Study.* New York: Center for Technology in Education, June 1993.

K–12 Computer Networking. *The ERIC Review*, Winter 1993.

Kinnaman, Dave. "Internet in the Classroom." *Tricks of the Internet Gurus.* Indianapolis: Sams Publishing, 1994.

Manning, Bill and Don Perkins. "Ways To Define User Expectations." IETF School Networking Group, *Internet RFC 1746.* December 1994.

Murray, Janet. "K–12 Network: Global Education through Telecommunications." *Communications of the ACM*, August 1993.

Newman, Dennis. "Technology as Support for School Structure and School Restructuring." *Phi Delta Kappan*, December 1992.

Rutkowski, Kathleen M. "Building Consensus/Building Models: A Networking Strategy for Change." Federation of American Research Networks (FARNET), Consortium for School Networking (CoSN). March 1994.

Sellers, Jennifer. "Answers to Commonly Asked 'Primary and Secondary School Internet User' Questions." IETF School Networking Group, *Internet FYI 22, RFC 1578*. February 1994.

Strangelove, Michael. "The Essential Internet: The Rise of Virtual Culture and the Emergence of Electric Gaia." *Online Access: The Internet Special Issue*, October 1993.

K through 12 Teachers on the Internet

by Andy Carvin

The reason to build the information highway is to provide people with the opportunity to do things that could not be done without it....New information technologies, if utilized correctly, have the capability to do more than simply receive television signals from other, better staffed schools. Computers allow real interaction, and active exploratory education instead of passive listening. This means creating computer based courses that allow students to build simulated rocket ships or to try running the country by playing the President in an interactive situation....

—Roger Schank

In 1993, the Clinton administration's Information Infrastructure Task Force published its first major report on the information highway. In that report, Agenda For Action, the authors challenged the nation to "imagine a world" where "the best schools, teachers, and courses would be available to all students, without regard to geography, distance, resources, or disability." To many readers, this challenge sounded more like a telephone company commercial rather than realistic prognostication of a curricular world to come. And yet every day, thousands of students and teachers alike are doing their part to make this vision come true by accessing the one networking tool that has been used successfully by academics and researchers all over the world for over two decades: the Internet.

To the majority of K–12 educators and to the general public, the Internet is considered a brand new technology—in fact, a recent survey suggested that less than 25 percent of American adults had even heard of the Internet. But thanks to the Internet's long-established relationship with higher education and science, networking technology has matured to a point where nearly any new user can successfully use Internet tools for educational and personal development. Long gone are the days when users were required to use baffling UNIX codes and operating system gobbledygook—thanks to the development of e-mail software, Gopher, Listservs and Web browsers, students and teachers can now navigate the Net with relative ease.

The biggest problem for new users interested in K–12 networking, however, stems from the seemingly infinite, gargantuan nature of the Internet: there is simply too much information. Besides, it's often impossible to tell what resources and tools are worthwhile for classroom use in the first place. The challenge for new users is to observe what other educators and students have accomplished with the Internet, learn from their experiences, and apply that knowledge to their own classroom setting. For starters, let's take a look at two strong examples of how teachers have successfully integrated Internet tools into distinctly different curricular environments.

Case Study #1: Using KIDLINK in a Primary School

At Rosewood Elementary School in Rock Hill, South Carolina, fifth graders are exploring science, history, and culture around the world with the help of the Internet. Over the last year, they have engaged in numerous intercurricular computer projects by accessing a free international service known as KIDLINK. One of several international services linked together by what is known as the KIDS-95 Project, KIDLINK has united more than 23,000 children between the ages of 10 and 15 from over 60 nations. Through KIDLINK, children and their teachers are united in topical Internet Relay Chats (IRCs). A chat can cover a wide variety of subjects, from current events and politics to books and music. By accessing KIDLINK, a user can join a chat at any time, day or night, with children from across the globe.

The students of Rosewood, armed with their Internet accounts and KIDLINK, have tackled a variety of tasks. One project, Around the World in 80 Poems, directed the kids to use the Internet to track down at least 80 poems from dozens of countries. The students contacted kids in other parts of the world to exchange their nation's poetry. In the end, the class compiled more than 150 poems, which were analyzed, researched within a historical context, and laid out together. Additionally, the students were asked to write poems of their own on the computer for Valentine's Day. The children electronically exchanged their drafts for "peer review" and discussion; when they were satisfied with their work, the students laid it out with a desktop publishing program and mailed the final product to nursing homes in South Carolina and Iowa.

These same students have also engaged in distance education projects by way of the Internet. When three explorers recently arrived at the North Pole to conduct research for the Arctic Drift Project, they exchanged their data and observations with the class by way of e-mail, IRC, and video conferencing. In a different project, the students followed the adventures of South Carolinian astronauts who piloted several shuttle missions this past year. Project coordinator Jamie Wilkerson went down to Cape Canaveral to electronically relay questions and data back and forth between the sites.

Rosewood's most ambitious project began with the start of the 1994–1995 school year. Students are exploring the events surrounding the sinking of a gold-laden steamship off the Carolina coast in 1857. They are studying the scientific aspects of the sinking (hurricanes and weather conditions, local marine life, and so on), its historical context (pre-Civil War America, the California gold trade) and its literary context (19th century sea stories, crew and passenger records). With the Internet, students can collect, exchange, and discuss information with each other and with volunteer experts, including those involved with the actual salvaging of the ship.

Jamie Wilkerson, the fifth-grade teacher who co-manages the projects, believes that the time students spend on the Internet engages them in ways previously impossible. "I am an avid believer in using technology to expand curriculum and the experiences of teachers and students around the world," she said. "The Internet has truly revolutionized my teaching and that of many others."

Case Study #2: WWW and the Sunrise Project

Possibly the hottest item in K–12 networking at the moment is the World Wide Web. With the development of easy-to-use browsers such as Netscape and Mosaic, literally millions of new Internet users can cybernavigate the globe and track down information ranging from the Hubble telescope to tours of the Louvre in Paris. And yet some of the most incredible breakthroughs in educational Web use are occurring in the classroom, with students as young as sixth or seventh grade fast becoming veteran Web publishers. Figure 49.1 shows the Sunrise Project Web page.

FIGURE 49.1.

The Sunrise Project home page.

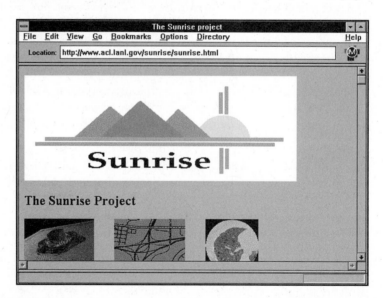

At Los Alamos High School in New Mexico, for example, students work side by side with teachers and scientists to develop Web tutorials as part of what is known as the Sunrise Project.

The Project, sponsored by Los Alamos National Laboratory (LANL), was designed as a forum to create multimedia tools for classroom use. Participating students from the local high school focus their efforts on developing educational databases on a variety of scientific subjects, including hydrodynamics, chaos theory, and the history of computing. To organize the database, students have learned how to use the HyperText Markup Language (HTML), the standardized code used by Web browsers all over the world. After spending long hours researching the ins and outs of a given subject (the history of computing, for example, contains detailed descriptions going all the way back to the 1940s), the students add the appropriate HTML codes to the text. Once the coding has been finished, the new information is placed the Web at `http://lahs.losalamos.k12.nm.us/`.

When you log on to the Sunrise Project computer, you quickly realize that what these students have accomplished is more than a mere online book report. Instead, what you find is more of a personal online tutor. Because the Web allows a publisher to write in hypertext, readers can link themselves to more and more information simply by clicking a word or a picture. And you're not required to follow a particular path, either. If a topic interests you, follow it; if not, move on to something else. The Web, in effect, lets you be your own teacher as you explore the subjects that excite you the most. And for Web users who are interested in learning more about the sciences, the students of Los Alamos High School have a lot they can teach them.

As you can see from these two brief studies, educators and students can actively integrate the Internet into class projects with widely differing methods and goals. The students of Rosewood Elementary, for example, are using the most basic Internet tools—IRC and e-mail—to collaborate with other students and gain valuable rudimentary computer skills at the same time. Gone is the notion of the insular classroom, in which students are encased by an academic wall with only the presiding teacher affecting learning and growth.

With an Internet connection, children can now reach out to other children and adults around the world in an exchange of knowledge, culture, and ideas. In contrast, the high school participants in the Sunrise Project are using the Internet to produce complex, yet highly practical, learning tools. The World Wide Web is a powerful collective of informational kiosks; through the standardization of the HTML, young people can design nonlinear multimedia environments as well as adults can. Whether schools use the WWW to create new resources or to explore pre-existing sites, the World Wide Web fosters creativity while assisting in informational discovery.

Internet and the Kids: What, Me Worry?

Because the Internet is unregulated and unmonitored, its users can be somewhat anarchic and outspoken, to put it mildly. Most Internet users take their freedom of expression quite seriously, and although you occasionally bump into folks who seem to have been educated in the Howard Stern School of Etiquette, the vast majority of cybercitizens are well behaved and desire the same respect as you do. In recent months, the media has made much of isolated cases in which con-artists and other adults have used the Internet to become "keypals" with unsuspecting kids.

As these cases began to appear before the public eye, some concerned parents proclaimed that the Internet must be a dangerous place full of people with ulterior motives. In reality, the Internet is no different than your typical public library. For example, the vast majority of it is filled with knowledge, insight, and creativity; certain scattered places contain items inappropriate for young people. The chances of a child getting sucked into a potentially upsetting or even dangerous situation is rather small—especially if parents and teachers limit or monitor student access to the Internet and lay down some token rules for kids to abide by while using the network.

In a classroom environment, this is a much easier task. Students are expected to accomplish certain goals while they are online. This isn't to say that they don't wander over to the Internet Underground Music Archive or some other cool site, but most improper Internet use can be avoided as long as a teacher is present. In addition, many schools that have access to the Internet can control the sites to which students can connect. Even if one of them knows the address to an unacceptably sexy newsgroup, for example, the school can easily lock them out of it. And some districts have gone so far as to reach out to parents in the form of a "networking contract" so that both sides agree to look out for the kids while they are online.

When children have Internet access at home, policing their access can be a more difficult task. One of the easiest deterrents for keeping kids from undesirable material is placing the computer in a public area, such as a living room. If your kids have the urge to explore the Net, they'll have to do it outside the private confines of their rooms and are less apt to go where they're not supposed to.

There are other methods a parent can use to limit access, such as not giving children the Internet password, keeping the computer locked up in a secure environment, and so on, but the best way to handle the situation is to sit down with your kids and explain to them that the Internet can be a strange place. Although most of the people they bump into will be nice and sincere, others aren't. They should never give out their full name, where they go to school, their phone number, or their address to a stranger unless the parent says it's okay. Getting to know strangers is one of the most enjoyable (and unavoidable) aspects of computer networking, but this doesn't necessarily mean your children have to tell them all their vital statistics. By teaching your children networking prudence, and using the Internet with them as often as possible, you decrease the chance of them getting into an uncomfortable scenario.

Getting Online

Once you conclude that the Internet can be a worthwhile tool for your classroom, the first thing you need to do is get an Internet account. Some schools in recent years have begun to install computer networks with direct Internet connections; if your school happens to be one of the lucky ones, check with your computer or technology coordinator. Most likely, he or she can arrange an account for you. But the vast majority of schools have yet to install or even pursue the possibilities of networking technology; if this happens to be your case, you have to go to an outside provider.

The phrase *outside provider*, however, is not cause for concern. In many states and in some major school districts, teachers and school administrators can often find low-cost or even free Internet access for educational use. Texas (TENET), Virginia (Virginia PEN), Minnesota (InforMNs/TIES), and New York (NYSERNet) are only a few of the states that offer well-established educational networks. These programs supply educators with personal e-mail accounts and offer them access to basic Internet services (often including FTP, IRC, Gopher, and sometimes the WWW by way of a text-based browser such as Lynx). In addition to these tools, state educational networks regularly coordinate Internet class projects, professional development information, and other practical services that can help you get started.

Although state and district educational networks have largely been designed with local teachers in mind, class projects and other services are often open to all educators; once you have an established Internet account, you can access programs on other state systems. For more information on state networks, contact your school's technology coordinator to find out whether your state department of education or some other local entity offers Internet access to teachers.

> **NOTE**
>
> If you can access the Internet by way of a friend, relative, or colleague, there is another easy way to find out more about state networks and department of education servers: check out Gleason Sackman's HotList of K–12 sites. Gleason has cataloged an up-to-date list of state and local Internet services on an enormous World Wide Web site. The HotList can be found at `http://toons.cc.ndsu.nodak.edu/~sackmann/k12.html`. Figure 49.2 shows the HotList page. Once you connect to the HotList, select either `state departments of education` or `state/regional networks` to get a complete listing.

FIGURE 49.2.

The K–12 HotList home page.

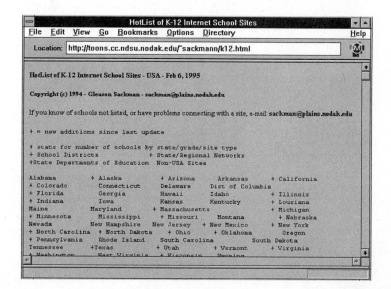

Another way to get your foot in the Internet door is to subscribe to what is known as a Free-Net. A *Free-Net* is a modem-accessible bulletin board system for community use. In general, most Free-Nets offer some form of limited Internet access, such as e-mail and Usenet newsgroups. Free-Nets often sweeten the deal by including private educational services (class projects, subject-oriented chat groups, and so on) that can be accessed only by local subscribers.

One potential problem worth noting is Free-Net traffic. Because Free-Nets are sometimes the only network game in town, logging on or getting membership approval can sometimes be an arduous task. There's also usually a request for a one-time donation. Assuming that you don't mind using the Free-Net during off-peak hours, or if you're willing to try logging on several times before giving up, Free-Nets can prove to be an invaluable resource for getting online. To learn more about Free-Nets in your community, call your local public library or contact the National Public Telecommunications Network in Cleveland at 216-247-5800.

If neither of these approaches works for you, here are some other methods that should eventually get you onto the Internet:

- **A local university.** If you're lucky enough to be in or near or town with an institution of higher learning, chances are the university has a substantial computer networking facility. If you're even luckier, the facility may offer Internet accounts to educators for a small fee. Call around, cross your fingers, and you may strike gold.

- **Commercial network services.** Many educators, as well as people who are generally interested in information technology, choose to subscribe to a commercial network service such as America Online, Prodigy, or CompuServe. Historically, these companies offer access to a variety of extremely useful educational services (such as National Geographic Network on AOL or Scholastic Network on Prodigy), but actual Internet access was rarely included. No longer is this the case. Many commercial services now offer Internet e-mail, Listserv, and newsgroups; more powerful tools such as Telnet, the WWW, and Gopher will begin to appear throughout 1995. If you skim through most major computer magazines, you can usually find special deals for free trial membership. Check your bookstore's magazine section to learn about current offerings.

- **Internet service providers.** As a final option, you can always obtain an Internet account from a local Internet service provider (ISP) such as Netcom or ClarkNet. The good news is that you get direct access to the Internet—unlike a commercial network that connects you indirectly by way of a gateway. You can also use a larger suite of Internet tools (Gopher, Telnet, and so on) than is currently available on most commercial network services. The bad news is the price tag: ISP accounts often range from $20 to $40 per month. If you're willing to spend the extra cash to have a direct gateway to the Internet, ISPs may be the best way to go.

Internet Newsletters

Once you actually establish yourself on the Internet with an account, your next (and possibly most difficult) task is to acclimate yourself to cyberspace. The Internet can be an uncomfortably odd environment for the uninitiated, so sometimes it's best to jump in with an informational safety vest of sorts—a K–12 networking newsletter. Beyond their primary function of providing readers with interesting and useful things to do on the Internet, many newsletters include monthly tips on getting started, finding basic networking information, and practicing nettiquette (the semiofficial rules of engagement for individuals who want to express themselves online).

One of the best informational periodicals, Wentworth Media's *Classroom Connect*, is only several issues old, but it has already established itself as a reliable source for what's hot in K–12 networking. In addition to highlighting the best online resources for teachers, *Classroom Connect* regularly introduces readers to unusual Internet terms and features and gives handy suggestions on how to expand your school's access to the information highway. There's also a "bulletin board" for teachers to post information about their Internet projects so that users can get into easy contact with other educators with similar interests. For subscription information, call 1-800-638-1639 or send e-mail to Amy Young at connect@wentworth.com.

My personal favorite K–12 newsletter is *NetTEACH NEWS*. Edited and published by Kathy Rutkowski, *NetTEACH* presents a detailed look at all the latest innovations in educational cyberspace. Along with her info-packed overviews of K–12 Listservs, Web sites, Gophers, and collaborative projects, Kathy always offers enlightening and articulate features on some of the most pressing issues in education technology. *NetTEACH NEWS* is available in print form as well as on the Internet by subscription only. For more information, contact Kathy Rutkowski at info@netteach.chaos.com or at this address:

> *NetTEACH NEWS*
> 13102 Weather Vane Way
> Herndon, VA 22071-2944

If free newsletters are more to your liking, you may want to get a copy of *World Link*, a K–12 guide to online curriculum resources. If you have access to Gopher, you can find *World Link* at gopher://ericir.syr.edu inside the following nest of folders: Electronic Journals, Books, and Reference Tools/Electronic Journals/World Link Newsletter. You can also contact them at the following address:

> *World Link*
> c/o Linda Joseph
> Department of Library Media Services
> Columbus Public Schools
> 737 East Hudson Street
> Columbus, OH 43211

If you choose to receive *World Link* by mail, you have to supply a self-addressed, stamped envelope for each issue.

The best way to find what you're looking for on the Internet is to do some exploring on your own. Because the vast majority of information resources are linked to like-minded sites around the world, you can usually begin with one good starting point, learn about other related resources, and move around from there. Most of the sites listed in this chapter can help you in this area. New users are often skeptical about the Internet's ability to guide them from one place to another, but whether you're on a mailing list or surfing the World Wide Web, it is next to impossible to avoid gathering an enormous collection of Internet hot spots you can use for your class, for your kids, or even for yourself.

If you want to start accumulating information quickly—and perhaps more importantly, meet other people who are trying do accomplish similar tasks—the two best places to start are with Listservs and Usenet groups. A Listserv is a computer program that automatically distributes e-mail to a group. People subscribe to a Listserv by sending it e-mail; from that point on, they receive all messages posted to the group and can send their own messages to the group (for more information on subscribing to and using Listservs, refer to Chapter 16, "Joining Discussions: Using Listservs and Mailing Lists").

Fortunately for teachers, there are scores of Listservs that focus specifically on K–12 education. Discussions range from broad topics (such as education technology or elementary schools) to extremely specific topics (such as whole language education, drug abuse counseling, and so on). Most groups have *open subscriptions*; in other words, anyone with an interest in the topic is welcome to join. A few lists, however, are members-only, so you may be asked to submit a good reason for why you should be included. In addition, discussions tend to have rather distinct character traits: some are lively and casual and others are very task oriented. And be prepared for a possible swath of e-mail cutting its way through your account.

Many groups generate as many as 50 or 60 posts a day, so try not to subscribe to too many groups without considering the consequences. Instead, find one or two that seem to be to your liking and follow the discussions for a while (this form of cyberloitering is commonly known as *lurking*); when you feel up to it, send a note introducing yourself and sharing your ideas with the group. Posting may seem a bit uncomfortable at first, but remember that each and every user had a first time. As you become a more familiar member of the discussion, you'll quickly find numerous online resources that relate to your area of interest.

One final note before listing some of the better discussions: it's a good idea to save each group's Frequently Asked Question (FAQ) archive. A FAQ often answers many of the early questions you have regarding a particular list; it also cuts down on e-mail traffic dedicated to commonly requested queries. FAQs are usually posted at least once a month (alternatively, you can write directly to the list owner for more information).

Table 49.1 lists my personal collection of high-caliber discussion groups. These groups vary quite drastically in terms of traffic and style, so choose your lists accordingly. In the end, Listservs are one of the most practical and useful aids to educational networking.

Table 49.1. Excellent K–12 Listserv groups.

Group	Address	Description
ACSOFT-L	`listserv@wuvmd.wustl.edu`	Educational software discussion
ALTLEARN	`listserv@sjuvm.stjohns.edu`	Alternative approaches to learning discussion; active
AMTEC	`mailserv@camosun.bc.ca`	Media and technology in education
APPL-L	`listserv@vm.cc.torun.edu.pl`	Computer applications in science and education
BIOPI-L	`listserv@ksuvm.ksu.edu`	Biology and education discussion
BULLY-L	`listserv@nic.surfnet.nl`	Bullying and victimization in schools list
CALIBK12	`listserv@sjsuvm1.sjsu.edu`	California K–12 librarians' discussion
CHATBACK	`listserv@sjuvm.stjohns.edu`	Special education discussion
CNEDUC-L	`listserv@tamvm1.tamu.edu`	Computer networking in education discussion
COSNDISC	`listproc@list.cren.net`	Consortium for School Networking general discussion; very active
CSHCN-L	`listserv@nervm.nerdc.ufl.edu`	Children with special health care needs list
CPI-L	`listserv@cunyvm.bitnet`	List concerning the College Preparatory Initiative
CREWRT-L	`listserv@mizzou1.missouri.edu`	Creative Writing in Education for Teachers and Students list
DISTED	`listserv@uwavm.bitnet`	Discussion on distance education

continues

Table 49.1. continued

Group	Address	Description
DRUGABUS	listserv@umab.bitnet	Drug abuse education list
ECENET-L	listserv@uiucvmd. bitnet	Early childhood education list
ECEOL-L	listserv@maine.maine. edu	Early Childhood Education Online mailing list
ECID-L	listserv@vm.cc.purdue. edu	Educational Computing and Instructional Development
EDAD-L	listserv@wvnvm.wvnet. edu	Educational Administration Discussion List
EDNET	listserv@nic.umass.edu	General discussion of education and networking; very active
EDPOLYAN	listserv@asuvm.inre. asu.edu	Educational policy analysis; active
EDRES-L	listserv@unb.ca	Discussion of online educational resources
EDSTYLE	listserv@sjuvm. stjohns.edu	Discussion of educational styles
EDTECH	listserv@msu.edu	General education and technology list; very active
EDTECPOL	listserv@umdd.bitnet	Conference on Educational Technology Policy
EDUPAGE	edupage@educom.edu	A technology news update published by EDUCOM
EFFSCHPRAC	mailserv@oregon. uoregon.edu	Effective school practices list
ELED-L	listserv@ksuvm.bitnet	Elementary Education list
ELEMUG	listserv@uicvm.uic.edu	Elementary School Users' Group
ESPAN-L	listserv@vm.tau.ac.il	Teaching Spanish literature and language list
EUITLIST	euitlist@bitnic. educom.edu	Educational uses of information technology
GEOGED	listserv@ukcc.uky.edu	Geography education list

Group	Address	Description
HSJOURN	`listserv@vm.cc.latech.edu`	High school scholastic journalism list
HYPEREDU	`listserv@itocsivm.bitnet`	Hypertext in education
IECC	`iecc-request@stolaf.edu`	International E-mail Classroom Connection Cultural exchange
INSEA-L	`listserv@unbvm1.csd.unb.ca`	International Society for Education through Art
JEI-L	`listserv@umdd.umd.edu`	Discussion of technology (especially CD-ROM) in K–12
JTE-L	`listserv@vtvm1.cc.vt.edu`	Journal of Technology in Education
KIDCAFE	`listserv@vm1.nodak.edu`	Kid's discussion group
KIDINTRO	`listserv@sjuvm.stjohns.edu`	Pen pal group for children
KIDS-ACT	`listserv@vm1.nodak.edu`	Activity projects for kids
KIDSNET	`kidsnet-request@vms.cis.pitt.edu`	Global K–12 network planning list
KIDSPHERE	`kidsphere@vms.cis.pitt.edu`	Broad KIDLINK-based discussion; very active
KIDLINK	`listserv@vm1.nodak.edu`	Information on KIDS-95
K12ADMIN	`listserv@suvm.syr.edu`	Discussions concerning educational administration
K12-EURO-TEACHERS	`majordomo@Lists.eunet.fi`	World-wide pen pal exchange
LM_NET	`LM_NET@suvm.syr.edu`	Library media specialist information exchange
LRN-ED	`listserv@suvm.syr.edu`	Support and information for K–12 teachers
MATHEDCC	`listserv@vm1.mcgill.ca`	Technology in math education discussion
MDK-12	`listserv@umdd.umd.edu`	K–12 teachers in Maryland discussion

continues

Table 49.1. continued

Group	Address	Description
MEDIA-L	listserv@bingvmb.cc.binghamton.edu	Discussion of media in education
MEMO-NET	listserv@vax1.mankato.msus.edu	Educational media discussion
MEMORIES	listserv@sjuvm.stjohns.edu	Allows kids to talk with WWII survivors
MMEDIA-L	listserv@itesmvfl.bitnet	Multimedia education discussion
MIDDLE-L	listserv@vmd.cso.uiuc.edu	Discussion of middle school-aged children; very active
MULTC-ED	listserv@umdd.umd.edu	Multicultural education discussion
MULTI-L	listserv@barilvm.bitnet	Discussion of multilingual education
MUSIC-ED	listserv@vm1.spcs.umn.edu	Music education discussion
MY-VIEW	listserv@sjuvm.stjohns.edu	A global creative writing exchange for kids
NAEATASK	listserv@arizvm1.ccit.arizona.edu	NAEA Art Teacher Education Task Force list
NAT-EDU	listserv@indycms.iupui.edu	K–12 Education and Indigenous Peoples group
NCPRSE-L	listserv@ecuvm1.bitnet	Discussion of science education reform
NCTM-L	listproc@sci-ed.fit.edu	National Council of Teachers of Mathematics discussion
NEWEDU-L	listserv@uhccvm.uhcc.hawaii.edu	New patterns in education list
NLA	majordomo@world.std.com	National Literacy Advocacy list
OUTDOOR-ED	listserv@latrobe.edu.au	Outdoor education list
PHYSHARE	listserv@psuvm.psu.edu	High school physics resources list

Group	Address	Description
SCHOOL-L	listserv@irlearn.ucd.ie	Discussion for primary and secondary schools
SHED	listserv@etsuadmn.etsu.edu	Secondary and higher education discussion
SIGTEL-L	listserv@unmvma.unm.edu	Discussion of telecommunications in education
SS435-l	listserv@ualtavm.bitnet	Elementary social studies education list
SUPERK12	listserv@suvm.syr.edu	Internet and computers in K–12 schools
SUSIG	listserv@miamiu.bitnet	Discussion of math education
T321-L	listserv@mizzou1.missouri.edu	Teaching science in elementary schools list
TAG-L	listserv@vm1.nodak.edu	Talented and gifted education discussion
TALKBACK	listserv@sjuvm.stjohns.edu	News exchange and discussion for kids
TAWL	listserv@listserv.arizona.edu	Teaching whole language discussion
TEACHEFT	listserv@wcupa.edu	Teaching effectiveness discussion
UAARTED	listserv@arizvm1.bitnet	Art education discussion
VOCNET	listserv@cmsa.berkeley.edu	Vocational Education discussion
WALDORF	listserv@sjuvm.stjohns.edu	Waldorf education discussion
WWWEDU	listserv@k12.cnidr.org	The World Wide Web in Education list; very active

A similar method of accessing and exchanging information on many subjects is by accessing Usenet newsgroups (see Chapter 17, "Reading and Posting the News: Using Usenet," for basic information on Usenet). Most Internet providers, as well as some commercial network providers, offer newsgroups as part of their services. Of the thousands of newgroups currently available, several dozen are of particular interest to the K–12 community. Nearly every one of them falls under what is known as *K12Net*. K12Net is a totally decentralized collective of educational BBSes available over the Usenet and FidoNet under the hierarchy known as K12. In other words, if you have access to Usenet groups (and depending on the type of system you use), you can get a current list of K12Net groups by implementing a newsgroup search using the letters K12. Most list titles are fairly self evident (k12.ed.music or k12.chat.teacher for example). Once you subscribe to a newsgroup, you can access that group's collection of e-mail posts.

Educational Chat Forums

Another popular scholastic use of the Internet is connecting children around the world as part of online multicultural exchanges. More than just electronic pen pal programs, chat forums allow children to enter carefully designed discussions on current events, culture, geography, personal interests, and many other topics.

One of the most popular forms of educational chats is found in what are known as Internet Relay Chats, or IRCs. IRCs are the Internet's version of a roundtable discussion, in which many people talk—live—to each other on any given subject. IRCs are simple for anyone to use: once you connect to an IRC computer, you choose the discussion you want to join by looking at the list of topics offered and typing the name of that topic. The computer automatically brings you into the discussion. When you enter an IRC, you're liable to see something like this:

```
Teacher3: Do British students learn much about American schools?
britkid1: Not really, no, but we learn a lot off of the tele.
USkid4: What's a tele?
britkid7: A television :)
USkid4: Ok.
USkid9: Like we call television a TV.
britkid1: Right.
```

As you can see, IRC chats are often very casual; anyone taking part in the discussion can jump in at any time by typing a message on the screen. When USkid9 wrote "Like we call television a TV," her words appeared on everyone's screen simultaneously. The spontaneity of real-time Internet chats can make discussions more entertaining, although some may argue that they lack the well-considered structure of other forms of discussion, such as Listservs and Usenet groups.

If you're interested in how IRCs can be used in the classroom, by far the best place to start is with KIDLINK, mentioned in the first case study at the beginning of this chapter. KIDLINK, part of a much larger program known as KIDS-95, is a global curricular conference for kids aged 10 to 15. Conducted in several languages, including English, Spanish, French, Japanese, Norwegian, and Hebrew, KIDSLINK offers free IRC access to all children within the age limit. Once a student becomes a member of KIDLINK, he or she can participate in a continuous stream of dialogs with other kids around the world on a variety of educational subjects. To learn more about KIDLINK, as well as other KIDS-95 projects, contact KIDLINK founder Odd de Presno at opresno@extern.uio.no or join one of the KIDLINK discussion groups, including KIDLINK and KIDSPHERE (see Table 49.1).

Question and Answer Services

To get kids excited about the Internet, it's often useful to give them a tool that can help them get better grades. Some of the most useful online educational services for kids are what are known as *question and answer services*. If a student has a question, needs homework help, or wants some other form of classroom advice, he or she can submit it to a service, which then forwards it to a resident "expert," often a volunteer scientist or college student. Answers are usually provided by e-mail within 48 hours. Here are some of the more useful Q&A services:

- **AskERIC.** Created by Educational Resource Information Clearinghouse (ERIC) and funded by the Education Department, AskERIC offers source materials and suggestions for the research needs of both educators and students. AskERIC receives about 300 questions per week. It's a great resource for older kids in search of annotated bibliographic information for a class project. Send all questions to askeric@ericir.syr.edu.

- **Ask Dr. Math.** Specially designed for K–12 math students, Ask Dr. Math is a service maintained by math majors and professors at Swarthmore University. Students can submit any math question they have to dr.math@forum.swarthmore.edu. If you have access to the Web, you can also look at Dr. Math's archive of past questions and answers by connecting to http://olmo.swarthmore.edu/dr-math/dr-math.html. Similar to Dr. Math is **Ask Professor Math**, coordinated by Timothy D. Kurtz at St. Bonaventure University in New York. Students should send their questions, as well as their name and grade level, to maths@sbu.edu. Figure 49.3 shows the Dr. Math page.

- **Ask A Geologist.** If you've ever wondered why Hawaii has volcanoes and Florida does not, you may want to send a message to Ask A Geologist. Sponsored by the U.S. Geological Survey, Ask A Geologist provides answers to earth science questions, thanks to the kind help of the "geologist of the day." Send your questions to geologist@octopus.wr.usgs.gov; if you have any questions about the service, contact Rex Sanders at rex@octopus.wr.usgs.gov.

- **NEWTON AskAScientist.** For burgeoning young scientists, Argonne National Laboratory offers the NEWTON AskAScientist. Students can pose questions to Argonne scientists; answers usually arrive within three days. NEWTON also archives past questions in a Frequently Asked Question (FAQ) list. To access NEWTON, you must Telnet to NEWTON.depanl.gov and register as new. Once you have registered, go to the NEWTON menu and select Teaching Topics. Next, select AskAScientist and drop your question into the appropriate box.

FIGURE 49.3.

*The Swarthmore
Dr. Math home page.*

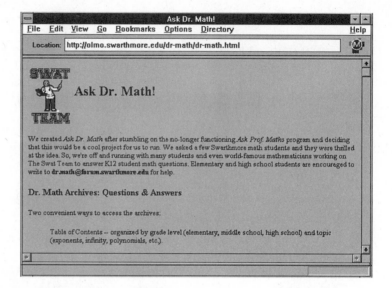

Internet Help for Teachers

One of the most common problems teachers have when they use the Internet is learning how to use the Internet in the first place. With so much information and so many ways of retrieving it, cyberspace can be a daunting place.

Following is an excellent help tool:

■ **OWL.** If it's that time of the semester and you're stuck writing a lot of book reports, you may find the Online Writing Lab to be a life saver (or at least a grade saver). Sponsored by the Purdue University Writing Lab, OWL answers questions you may have about grammar, essay styles, and anything else relevant to writing a good paper. To reach OWL by e-mail, send a message to owl@sage.cc.purdue.edu and make sure that you write owl-request in the subject line. You can also search OWL's enormous collection of documents concerning writing style and structure by way of the Web (at http://owl.trc.purdue.edu/), Gopher (at gopher://owl.trc.purdue.edu), and FTP (at ftp://owl.trc.purdue.edu).

Educational Networks

Many teachers opt to join organized educational networks that contain a wide variety of K–12 offerings. Students and teachers use these services to stay in contact with other students and teachers subscribing to the same system. The groups of learners are situated around a common goal (designed by either the service provider or the educators involved), such as surveying acid rain samples or raising fruit flies. The network is used as the medium of information exchange and review. Although most services originated as nonInternet networks, many of them now offer Internet access because of the enormous popularity of the Net. For information about some of the best educational networks, including Big Sky Telegraph, and the National Geographic Kids Network, see Chapter 48, "Schoolkids and the Net."

Gopher and the World Wide Web in Education

One of the simplest methods of accessing and publishing information over the Internet is through the use of an advanced network navigating protocol such as Gopher or the World Wide Web (often called the Web, WWW, or W3). Gopher, invented at the University of Minnesota (the Golden Gophers), is a hierarchically based text menu system that allows the user to navigate a given site's information bank, as well as connect to other information sites. Once connected to a Gopher server, you can surf around from site to site with ease, gathering information by searching menus of interest or by typing keywords of interest for which the Gopher program then searches the system. (See Chapter 25, "Using and Finding Gophers," for more information on Gopher.)

The Web, one of the most recent additions to the Internet, is an advanced navigator protocol that offers easy access to graphics and text as well as audio and video samples. Using a browsing program such as NCSA Mosaic, Netscape, or Lynx, you connect with a Web "home page," a default server connection such as the University of Illinois at Urbana-Champaign. From there, you can click highlighted text or graphics to log in to other information systems. (The WWW is discussed in detail in Chapter 28, "Navigating the World Wide Web.")

Both Gopher and the Web are excellent research tools because they let you travel the Net, following subjects of interest and guiding the computer with keywords or phrases you type. Although lacking the audio-visual capabilities of the Web, Gopher provides quick connectivity to thousands of text sources. The Web, on the other hand, includes the ability to see and hear samples and interesting bits of information (certain browsers, such as Lynx, can process only textual data).

When it comes to logging in to a Gopher or Web client, remember the basic rule: you can access a Gopher using Web software, but you usually can't access the Web with Gopher software. Because Gopher is text based, a Web program such as Netscape can handle a Gopher connection without trouble. When a Gopher program attempts to log on to a Web client, however, the attempt either fails or connects only to the textual information (and ignores any graphics or sound capabilities).

Each month, hundreds of new Web and Gopher sites pop up on the Internet; many of them are well suited for K–12 use. For examples of K–12 oriented sites, visit Web66 (at `http://web66.coled.umn.edu`), EdWeb (at `http://k12.cnidr.org:90`), and the Consortium for School Networking Gopher (at `gopher://cosn.org`) to get a sense of what types of educational servers are out there. (Figure 49.4 shows the EdWeb home page.) These sites also serve as excellent home pages for you and your classroom; because sites add links to new educational sites on a regular basis, all you have to do to find any recent network additions is check out your favorite Web or Gopher.

FIGURE 49.4.

The EdWeb home page.

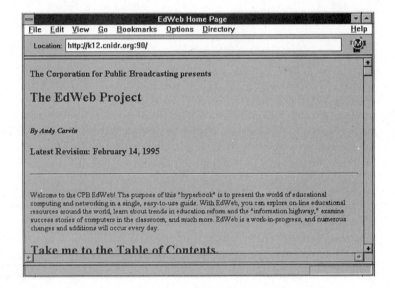

The World Wide Web also serves as an excellent tool for student publishing. If you've seen Web sites, you may be thinking, "That's silly; no middle school kid could put together something as complex as a home page." In reality, even elementary aged students are actively participating in the design of Web sites all over the globe. The example of the high school students at Los Alamos High School (cited at the beginning of this chapter) is only a sample of the quality of work young people are producing today. Because the codes for designing Web pages are standardized internationally, they are relatively easy to learn. If you or your students have access to a networked computer capable of running Web server software, you can design and publish your own Web site in short order. Later in this chapter is a Web publishing project you can do with your class.

Planning Student Internet Projects

The ultimate goal for most teachers who want to go online is to integrate the Internet into the curriculum and use it as a tool for research, dissemination, and discussion. Al Rogers, executive director of the Global SchoolNet Foundation, outlined a seven-point guide as the general steps that should be taken in designing a successful Internet project (Rogers, A., *et al.* "Telecommunications in the Classroom: Keys to Successful Telecomputing." *The Computing Teacher in 1990*, 17, No. 8, pp. 25–28). I've included some additional thoughts after each point:

1. **Clearly identify goals, tasks, and outcomes.** This step is key to any successful lesson plan. If you can connect your plan with traditional curricular goals, the more apt you are to draw in more participants.

2. **Design your project to "reward" participants.** If there's one thing people hate, it's getting involved in another person's project and getting little or nothing out of it. Share your data, thoughts, and any findings with all members of the project.

3. **Set firm beginning and ending dates and clear deadlines.** If you don't, the larger your participant pool, the more likely your project won't finish at the desired time. And as Al Rogers says, "Students often hold a teacher accountable to complete the project." You have been forewarned....

4. **Make your plans early and announce them early.** Projects take time to get ready; be prepared as many as eight weeks before the startup date.

5. **Create a formal "Call for Collaboration" and post it on a network.** The easiest way to attract other teachers to a project is to distribute it on your favorite network list or newsgroup. Make sure that it's a basic text file so that any interested reader can easily download it.

6. **Be specific in your formal description.** Tell them who you are, where you are, exactly what you want to accomplish, and with what kinds of classes. Emphasize what other teachers can gain by participating in the project.

7. **Share the results with all participants.** If possible, publish the final results on paper and distribute it to the group. In addition, post the results on any network group that may have been a medium for the project. Thank-you letters from the students are a nice touch, too.

Don't be taken aback by the seemingly large amount of work this list may require; in the end, the total time involved really isn't that bad and is well worth the effort. If you want to develop relationships with other networked teachers for future projects, you must make sure that you follow these points in some form or another. Internet educators often think of the network environment as a never-ending meeting in an online teacher's lounge—a community in which each member can contribute for the good of the whole. Those who don't put in their fair share of work may eventually be labeled selfish, so share thoughts and data whenever possible.

Sample Projects

An excellent first step to introduce students to the intricacies of Internet navigation is by way of an organized "field trip" through cyberspace. Rick Gates, a lecturer at the University of Arizona in Tucson, sponsors a series of field trips called the *Internet Hunt.* Every month, Gates poses 10 questions, all of which have answers available somewhere on the Internet. The questions are as trivial as trivia gets: In 1991, for example, the United States Postal Service issued a set of postal stamps with fishing flies on them; what five fishing flies appeared on the stamps? Players can be individual students, teams, even entire classrooms—and anyone can join at any time. To learn more about participating in the Internet Hunt, e-mail Rick Gates at rgates@locust.cic.net or call him at 602-318-3609. You can also find the Hunt archives on the CICNet Gopher at gopher://gopher.cic.net:2000/11/hunt.

Once you and your class are acclimated to traveling on the Internet, you can tackle a major lesson plan. There is actually a surprising wealth of preplanned Internet projects freely available throughout cyberspace. The following sections present a few high-caliber examples of the types of online projects you can do with your students.

The Interactive Democracy Project

One of my favorite examples of an Internet-based class project occurred this past fall in Minnesota. Interactive Democracy, sponsored by InforMNs and the League of Women Voters, taught students about the importance of public debate, voting rights, citizenship, and American government. As a launching point, the sponsors created a lesson plan made up of 15 major class activities. These activities, including "Expressing Values and Beliefs," "Exercising Rights, Accepting Responsibilities," and "Dialoging and Voting—An Empowerment Model," were largely traditional in the sense that they incorporated tried and true classroom methods, such as essay writing and class debates.

Interactive Democracy, however, departed from the mainstream with its intense use of communications technologies. On the InforMNs WWW page (shown in Figure 49.5), students and teachers could refer to databases of candidate profiles, voting polls, and state government activities. Each class activity required students to explore these topics at one point or another, so they would access the Internet as a primary source of information. In other words, students learned about the democratic process as they learned the basic methods of Internet-based research. And while they used the Internet to track down source material, they were taught how to publish on it. Teams of students conducted their own "voter surveys," canvassing their peers to gather the results. After each survey had been completed, the final product appeared as part of the online database, so all other Interactive Democracy students could access, analyze, and discuss their findings.

FIGURE 49.5.

The Interactive Democracy home page.

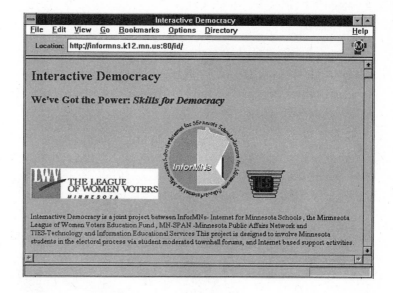

But perhaps Interactive Democracy's most innovative application of computer networking was the incorporation of an "electronic debate" into the curriculum. For the first time in Internet history, candidates from both the senate and gubernatorial races logged on to Listservs as a medium for public discourse. At appointed times in the project, candidates, teachers, and students connected to the Listserv for the "e-debate." Each candidate had been given a short list of questions that were answered and rebutted over the length of the forum. But unlike a more traditional debate, this discussion did not occur in real-time. Candidates responded to the questions over a period of days, so each answer was well considered and detailed even though candidates were maintaining a hectic engagement schedule. The students, in turn, logged on to the Internet each day to keep track of the discussion's progress. Additionally, another Listserv was set up for general use by the classes to discuss recent events in politics, to share their research, and to get a better sense of the other students involved in the project. As the candidates hammered out the issues on one Listserv, the student critiqued their responses and shared new ideas on another list.

For more information on Interactive Democracy and other projects sponsored by InforMNs, visit the InforMNs Web site at `http://informns.k12.mn.us` or Gopher to `gopher://informns.k12.mn.us`.

Live from Antarctica (And Other Worlds As Well...)

Not too long ago, some enterprising online educator came up with the grand idea of organizing *virtual field trips*. Unlike the typical class outing for which parents sign consent forms, students bring a bag lunch, and everyone gets bitten by ants, a virtual field trip allows a class to "travel" anywhere in the world (and potentially elsewhere as well) to explore the surroundings by way of a networked computer. Additionally, multiple schools can participate in a major cybertrip, which can also include expert scientists and researchers who can send e-mail to the students and discuss the nature of the visit.

One of the most successful and talked-about virtual field trips, Live from Antarctica, occurred this past winter. Figure 49.6 shows the home page of the project.

FIGURE 49.6.

The Live from Antarctica home page.

Live from Antarctica is part of a series of hi-tech field trips known as Live from Other Worlds. Using Internet tools sponsored by NASA's Ames Research Center, as well as satellite television arranged by Passport to Knowledge, Geoff Haines-Stiles Productions, and Maryland Public Television, students from around the nation teamed up with a group of explorer scientists as they traversed the frigid landscape from McMurdo Base to the South Pole. As scientists layered themselves with parkas to examine the landscape, students studied up on Antarctica with the help of a teacher's guide made available both on paper and online. The students kept meticulous journals on the progress of the explorer team, as well as on their own discoveries and questions. Over the course of the project, classrooms were connected to the team by way of interactive television, so that the students could ask about the latest findings and any other issues they wanted to bring up.

Because the satellite hookups were arranged only occasionally, kids kept track of the team by way of Internet Listserv dialogs. Using the NASA Ames network server, scientists posted regular updates on their mission and students responded online with more questions and journal entries. Additionally, teachers had their own Listserv so that they could discuss their thoughts on the project's progression and design new class plans with other participating educators.

Because all members used the Internet to exchange information, everyone kept abreast of the latest discoveries and important questions. It was the ultimate online collaborative experiment, with participants separated by over 6,000 miles.

Live from Antarctica is only one of many Live from Other Worlds projects now being considered. Future ideas include the terrestrial (Live from Mt. Vesuvius, Live from the Amazon Rain Forest), the extraterrestrial (Live from Mars, Live from the Hubble Telescope), and the chronological (Live from the Lascaux Caves, Live from the Ice Age). As each new project develops, planners will continue to find exciting ways to take advantage of Internet and other network technologies for classroom use. For more information on the Live from Other World projects, visit the NASA Ames Web page at `http://quest.arc.nasa.gov`, the Gopher site at `gopher://quest.arc.nasa.gov`, or write Geoff Haines-Stiles Productions at P.O. Box 1502, Summit, NJ, 07920-1502. For general information on virtual field trips (that is, projects other than the Live from Other Worlds program), contact Nancy Sutherland at FrEdMail (`fieldtrip@bonita.cerf.fred.org`).

Other Class Projects

What type of project do you want to try to arrange for your students? If you're pressed for time, you'll probably want to join an organized online project and pay careful attention to any Listserv or newsletter you happen to read to see what new projects are coming up. You can also use these resources as catalysts for your own plans; good projects often spark ideas for even better projects. To give you a feel for the sorts of activities you can arrange on your own, here a few basic ideas you can adapt to many different subjects.

The Music Appreciation Network

If you're a music, arts, or humanities teacher who wants to add some technological flair to your students' work, you can develop an online exchange with other classes and put together a gigantic online scrapbook of music history. After you post a request for other teachers on the Internet and have a core of maybe five or six partner classrooms, divide your goals between each class. For example, you can have a class in Saskatchewan focus on country music while a class in New Orleans works on Dixieland jazz. If you'd rather start off with a more specific topic for the whole project, tackle a genre and divide it among the participants: classical music (romantic period, avant-garde, and so on) or ethnic folk music (tribal rhythms, Japanese Kabuki theatre, and so on) can both work well. As each class studies their topic, they can put together journals and write short reports on the music and its relationship to history, culture, and other aspects of its environment. Additionally, some students in each class can act as "liaisons" for the other projects, so that the rest of the class can stay up-to-date on the inner workings of each project. As reports are put together, they are exchanged with e-mail so that classes can follow each other's progress, critique the work, and even gain some ideas on how to approach their own subject.

When the deadline approaches, participating teachers can exchange samples of each group's music by way of the Internet (by using FTP or a Web site) or, if necessary, by mail. Students submit final versions of their reports to the groups; liaisons in each class present the other work to their home room. To make the final presentations even more interesting (and if the proper technology is available), older students can put together basic Web pages for each site so that when a class is ready to present their work, other classes can connect to the Internet to read the reports, hear music, even see pictures of composers or musicians in action. Whether a music appreciation project uses e-mail only or makes use of more complex tools such as the Web or FTP, students can explore a realm of the arts in depth and at the same time work with other kids to understand the greater context of their studies.

Round Robin Creative Writing

In certain English and language arts classes, students are expected to fulfill a minimum requirement in creative writing. An interesting way to integrate writing assignments with computer use is to form partnerships with distant classes. One group of students comes up with a basic premise for a story and e-mails it to a partner group in another classroom. The receiving students must write one typed page worth of story in a certain amount of time, using the first group's premise.

Once a page is finished, it is resubmitted to the first group, or even to a third group. Whoever receives the story must add another page, without editing any of the previous writing. The teachers can determine how many iterations the story should go through before being wrapped up (so that one class can't arbitrarily kill the hero and end the story). The conclusion is written by the appropriate deadline and the story is resubmitted to each author for final editing, with comments between authors exchanged by way of e-mail. After the participants are satisfied with their story, they exchange it with other groups, who must read, discuss, and critique each work in their classroom. Any reports by the "peer review" groups are posted to the authors, who can choose to make last-minute adaptations. Finally, complete versions of all of the stories are compiled into a single document (perhaps laid out with a desktop publisher or on a Web site, depending on the age of the students) and then presented to all participants.

Online Class Resources

For teachers who have access to a World Wide Web server, one of the most rewarding online projects is to develop a Web-based class resource. Although you must first learn HTML and teach it to your students, you can get the basics in a relatively short amount of time. As the basis of your resource guide, you have to design a class home page that can have hypertext links to categories such as Class Overview, Teacher's Notes (arranged by class period or subject), Student Projects, and Frequently Asked Questions. The Class Overview can contain basic subject matters, the goals of the class, and the methods of assessment (a SyllabusWeb, if you will). All your planned discussions are placed in the Teacher's Notes section. As students ask questions that aren't already answered in your notes, you include them in the FAQ. To assist you in your development of the site, offer students extra credit for helping out with making Web documents. Limit the amount of credit they can earn so that all have a chance to help out.

For the Student Projects section, anything that the students produce—including reports, journals, and so on—should be made available online. At first, students' pages will probably not be that fancy—just a Web representation of the original document. On a regular basis, take time in class for students to look at each other's work, paying careful attention to where links could be developed from one report to another, from the teacher's notes to the reports, and so on. By taking the time to link each project, students won't feel overwhelmed early on by the hypertext aspect of their work. Eventually, as students become comfortable with HTML, they can begin to consider the role of hypertext links in their papers. Because hypertext is nonlinear, students must begin to think nonlinearly—in other words, they must consider how their work fits into a much broader environment and adapt it for that environment. As the semester runs down, students should develop an extended end-of-term project using hypertext. Once the projects have been submitted, evaluated, and returned to the students for final edits, the class again attempts to determine links between each final project and other sections of the site.

An online class resource can take a lot of effort—and you need regular access to a computer room or library so that students can do their work, in and out of class (students should never be penalized for not having computer access at home). The project also fosters teamwork, complex cognitive skills, and creativity. Perhaps most importantly, the final result can be used in future classes as a reference work or as a building block to other projects. In any case, the project remains available so that others can access it and learn from your efforts.

As you can see from these few examples, in-class Internet projects can take a variety of forms in a multitude of subjects. Don't be concerned if your projects are as simple as an intraclass e-mail exchange. The whole point of using technology in the classroom is to offer students a new medium to enhance their skills, creativity, and talents—not to create a more impressive Web site than Ms. Smith's earth science class down the hall. Take your time becoming comfortable with the technology and do the same with your students. Remember that although the Internet is an invaluable tool for online discovery in terms of learning and assessment, it is equally valuable as a way to spark new interests in your students.

Colleges and Universities on the Internet

50

by Billy Barron

Higher education (academia) has made more use of the Internet than any other group to date (although business is now taking over the lead position). Colleges and universities are largely responsible for the development of the Internet environment as it exists today. Tools such as Gopher were created in an academic setting and have been put to use by almost everyone on the Internet. Most universities these days consider their Internet connection to be a mission-critical resource. However, many smaller universities still do not have an Internet connection at all, although it is becoming less common.

Some of the traditions that make academia's use of the network unique are the access of the network by students (K–12 students are just now gaining access), the nature of free speech at colleges, the free exchange of ideas, and an attitude that is not always driven by dollars. These traditions have greatly shaped the Internet, and today the system follows these traditions even though the majority of the Internet population is now nonacademic.

Most universities have three major parts: research, instruction, and administration. This chapter divides academia's use of the Internet into these three areas. When uses and resources do not fall cleanly into one of these areas, they are included in the administration section.

History of the Internet in Academia

A few universities with strong research ties to the U.S. military have had Internet access since the beginning of the network. The number of universities connected to the Internet stayed very small for a long time. However, during the mid to late 1980s, more and more universities started connecting to the Internet.

Then the National Science Foundation Network (NSFnet) came along, funded regional networks, and gave money to universities for connecting to the Internet. This move launched the very rapid growth of the Internet in academia, which continues to this day.

In the earlier days, the Internet connection was used most by computer scientists and academic computing staffs. The hard scientists were not far behind because they needed access to the NSF supercomputing sites on the Internet. Over the years, university librarians and faculty in other departments also jumped on the bandwagon. Usually, these people start off using e-mail and then gradually discover the other functions of the Internet.

Currently, most universities in the United States have some kind of Internet connection. The state of the Internet varies greatly from campus to campus. Some sites have high-speed Internet access in all their buildings and even connections to users at home using the SLIP or PPP protocol. Additionally, these sites often have written custom Internet software for their users. Other campuses have only a single connection to a host computer system and do not provide any added functions over the basic tools (e-mail, Telnet, and File Transfer Protocol—FTP). Internet consulting at these sites tends to be minimal in many cases.

Even some of the computer-phobic people on campus are wanting Internet access because they know they are missing out on important discussions in their field. However, many people on campus still do not want anything to do with the Internet. This trend has led to an information gap between network users and network nonusers in many places. The gap may widen over time to the great disadvantage of network nonusers.

The universities on the Internet tend to exchange resources to help each other. Universities that bring up Internet resources may lose computer resources but often gain valuable goodwill and name recognition.

Research

Most universities place an important emphasis on research, especially research that brings grant money to the university. Junior professors who do not have research grants often are refused tenure and are out of a job. Therefore, finding grant opportunities is important to many researchers in academia. The Internet offers many new opportunities for faculty members to find grants and conduct research. Most research work can be broken into three major areas: finding grants, doing the actual research, and publishing the research.

Finding Grants

Quite a bit of grant information is available on the Internet, and more is appearing regularly. Many government agencies and companies that have grants to offer post announcements on relevant Internet mailing lists and Usenet newsgroups. No specific place collects all the offers, so finding them often means being on the right lists at the right time. Fortunately, a few government agencies have centralized their grant information into a single location. If you want to see how a university can use grant information on the Internet, examine the University of Texas at Dallas (UTD) Gopher server at `gopher://gopher.utdallas.edu:70/11/research/sponsor`.

The most well-known grant information source on the Internet is the NSF Science and Technology Information System (STIS). This system enables access with various methods including Gopher (`gopher://stis.nsf.gov/`), the WWW (`http://stis.nsf.gov/`), anonymous FTP, and Telnet (log in as `public`) to the node `stis.nsf.gov`. Various WAIS databases such as `nsf-awards` and `nsf-pubs` also are available. NSF even accepts the electronic submission of grant proposals over the network. Finally, the Usenet newsgroup `info.nsf.grants` contains announcements about new posts to STIS.

The National Institutes of Health (NIH) makes the *NIH Guide to Grants and Contracts* available over the network. Researchers in medical fields find this resource useful. The guide is accessible by a variety of methods including the WAIS database `NIH-Guide`; anonymous FTP to `ftp://ftp.cu.nih.gov/NIH-EGUIDE`, the WWW at `http://www.nih.gov/`, and Gopher to the server `gopher://gopher.nih.gov/11/res/nih-guide`.

Counterpoint Publishing recently added the *Federal Register* to the Internet. The *Federal Register*, potentially valuable to people in almost any academic discipline, is available on Gopher at `gopher://gopher.counterpoint.com:2002/11/`. However, only part of the information is freely available. The rest of the *Federal Register* is available on the Internet through Gopher, Telnet, or Usenet newsgroups, but at cost.

A few Internet mailing lists exist as a channel to disseminate information on grant opportunities. The `RESEARCH` list on `LISTSERV@TEMPLEVM.BITNET` provides information to people looking for outside funding sources. Another list, `APASD-L`, on `LISTSERV@VTVM1.BITNET`, is a research funding bulletin for psychologists.

Doing Research

The Internet helps researchers not only find grants but also conduct research. The Internet has an enormous amount of data, programs, and other resources to help researchers conduct their research more effectively. Even if researchers do not use the Internet to perform actual research, they often use the network for communicating with their colleagues.

More Computing Power

Many academic researchers access supercomputers around the Internet to run computer programs that are too big or take too long on their local campus. The largest and most famous of these sites are the NSF's supercomputing sites. Any professor or student in the U.S. can apply for a grant of time on one of the NSF sites. The sites typically have equipment like Crays and Connection Machines that can run most problems 3 to 100 times faster than running them locally.

For people unable to get a grant, many other supercomputer sites on the Internet sell computer time. Rates tend to range from $250 to $1,000 per Cray CPU hour. Even people who do not need supercomputing performance can find sites that sell CPU time on workstations. However, researchers often find that buying and using their own equipment is less expensive.

Another approach researchers can take to solve a problem is to break the problem in smaller pieces and ask people on the Internet to run the pieces voluntarily. On most computer systems, the CPU sits idle much of the time, especially on individual workstations. Most of these systems have a way to run programs so that they consume CPU time only when no other program is running. Therefore, running the program costs very little for most people.

The largest and most successful attempt to use this team approach took place in late 1993 and early 1994. Back in the 1970s, *Scientific American* published an article about public key encryption (a method of encrypting messages). In this article, *Scientific American* offered a $100 prize to anyone who could break a certain encrypted message. The only known method for decrypting the message is by doing a large amount of factoring. Even today, the project is not feasible to do on a supercomputer because of the sheer number of calculations to perform. A few researchers recently got together and wrote a program that individuals can run on their personal workstations. Then the workstations e-mailed their results back to a central computer at the Massachusetts Institute of Technology (MIT). The researchers then performed the final analysis work, tying together all the results from the independent workstations, and got the correct answer.

The researchers sent out e-mail messages and Usenet posts asking for volunteers. They got hundreds of volunteers who now are running the program. Hundreds of people voluntarily ran the program and the results were achieved in a matter of months instead of years. More than 1,000 MIPS of computing time was used.

Researchers thinking about using this volunteer approach must be sure that they have thought through all issues. First, the program must be designed to run on a variety of computer architectures. Second, the calculation scheme must use some redundancy in case a site on the network generates bad results. Finally, researchers must understand that people are volunteering computer time as a favor. The researcher must treat the volunteers with respect.

Software for Researchers

Some researchers do not require a computer for intense computation. Instead, they use their computers for data analysis or just running productivity software, such as word processing and spreadsheets. Researchers who need software find that the Internet offers a cornucopia of free software. The software includes editors, compilers, spreadsheets, databases, and analysis tools. Unfortunately, this software varies quite a bit in quality. Some software is superior to the commercial products available, but much of it is inferior. Always remember that a free package of poor quality can easily cost you more in time than a commercial package costs to buy. Therefore, the researcher must be careful in the selection of free software packages.

> **NOTE**
>
> Researchers who download software off the Internet should run virus protection software on their computer. Fortunately, acquiring a virus from software on the Internet is quite rare. However, taking chances is foolish.

Two of the most important software libraries for academic researchers are NetLib and StatLib. NetLib is a set of well-tested FORTRAN subroutines such as Linpack, Eispack, and Lapack that are in the public domain. All combined, NetLib totals more than 50M of source code. StatLib is similar to NetLib but focuses on statistical applications. Please note that when using StatLib with FTP, you must use the user ID `statlib` rather than the usual `anonymous`.

The free package most commonly used by academia is the GNU software, which many businesses also use heavily. You probably can find GNU software in use on almost every college campus. The GNU software generally offers good quality. GNU packages include compilers, operating systems, utilities, editors, databases, and postscript viewers. Table 50.1 lists a variety of research software.

Table 50.1. FTP sites for research software.

Software	*URL*
Anesthesiology	`ftp://gasnet.med.nyu.edu/`
Atmospheric Research	`ftp://ncardata.ucar.edu/`
Geology-NewPet/QuikPlot	`ftp://sparky2.esd.mun.ca/pub/geoprogs`
GNU Software	`ftp://ftp.gnu.ai.mit.edu/pub/gnu`
Mathematics	`ftp://archives.math.utk.edu/`
Microcomputer (Various)	`ftp://oak.oakland.edu/`
	`ftp://wuarchive.wustl.edu/mirrors`
NetLib	`ftp://netlib2.cs.utk.edu/netlib`
	`ftp://netlib.att.com/netlib`
	`ftp://unix.hensa.ac.uk/pub/netlib`
Nonlinear Dynamics	`ftp://lyapunov.ucsd.edu/pub`
Oceanography	`ftp://biome.bio.dfo.ca/bod`
Simulated Annealing	`ftp://ftp.caltech.edu/pub/ingber`
StatLib	`ftp://lib.stat.cmu.edu/`
Various	`ftp://sunsite.unc.edu/`

Surveys

The classic research method of surveying found its way into the Internet years ago. Internet users commonly are on an Internet mailing list or Usenet newsgroup and receive questionnaires. What can frustrate Internet users is that researchers do not always check the archives of the mailing list or newsgroup to see that another researcher posted a similar survey a few months earlier. This is especially true of surveys asking users why they use the Internet.

Also, poorly conducted surveys on the Internet make some network users angry at the surveyor. Researchers must make sure that the survey is clear and reasonably concise. Most importantly, the surveyor must think carefully about which mailing lists and newsgroups should receive the survey. Sending the survey to the whole world is a bad idea and a waste of network resources, especially users' time—the most valuable resource of all.

The statistical validity of these Internet surveys may be marginal at best unless the researcher understands the audience. Until fairly recently, the sample Internet population was skewed to academic people who liked computers. This tendency is becoming less true by the day, but years may pass before Internet surveys become a good technique for surveying the general population.

Library Searches

Many researchers find that their local university library does not contain all the materials they need to do their research. Using the Internet, users can search the holdings of hundreds of other academic libraries. With the results of their searches, researchers can issue interlibrary loan requests to obtain needed materials or make a research trip to the other library.

Currently, the primary way to access the libraries is by using Telnet and TN3270. Because libraries employ a variety of user interfaces, the user must understand several interfaces when dealing with library catalogs over the Internet. A text guide I wrote with Marie-Christine Mahe of Yale University is available at `ftp://ftp.utdallas.edu/pub/staff/billy/libguide` and `gopher://squirrel.utdallas.edu:70/11/Libraries`. A better way to use the libraries is with Hytelnet (refer to Chapter 28, "Opening Doors with Hytelnet,") or the Gopher library list at `gopher://libgopher.cis.yale.edu:7000/11/Libraries` or `gopher://info.anu.edu.au:70/11/other`.

Over the last few years, a new protocol called Z39.50 has been developed that enables library catalogs to communicate with each other by exchanging bibliographic records. Currently, most Z39.50 software is still being developed. One of the big gains of Z39.50 will be that the user can run a Z39.50 client program and have to use only one user interface. This client program will query the library catalogs requested and be able to search more than one catalog at a time. According to plans, the future of the WAIS software is to use the latest version of the Z39.50 protocol, which should lead to more compatibility among Internet resources. For more information, look at `http://ds.internic.net/z3950/z3950.html`.

In addition to catalogs, researchers can find many useful bibliographies or abstracts on the Internet. The bibliographies are in a variety of formats; some are on FTP sites, others in Gopher, and many in WAIS (see Table 50.2).

Table 50.2. Bibliographies in WAIS databases.

Topic	Database Name
Academic Technology (UNC)	IAT-Documents
Asian Religion	ANU-Asian-Religions
Academic Freedom	comp-acad-freedom
Biology	Cell_Lines
Cold Fusion	cold-fusion
Genomes	Arabidopsis_thaliana_Genome
Humanities in French	ANU-French-Databanks
INRIA in French	bibs-zenon-inria-fr
Journalism	journalism.periodicals
Molecular Biology	biology-journal-contents
Neuronetworks	neuroprose
Pacific Languages	ANU-Pacific-Linguistics
University of Oslo	UiO-Publications

Libraries also perform Inter Library Loans (ILLs) over the Internet. The product they use is Ariel for Windows and is sold by the Research Libraries Group (RLG). Instead of delivering a journal article by courier, mail, or fax (all of which have costs), the material is scanned, sent across the Internet, and finally printed on a laser printer. Ariel can queue documents that cannot be sent immediately and periodically retry to send them.

Research Feedback

The Internet offers a wonderful opportunity for researchers to work together on collaborative research. Although there are numerous ways for people to collaborate, I will focus on a particular example in which I was involved.

A doctoral student at my university is doing her dissertation on finding every literary and critical reference to the character Penelope in the *Odyssey*. At one point, she thought she was finished. Then she discovered the Internet and its various library catalogs. She found a large number of references she previously did not know about.

From there, she realized that the Internet community could potentially help her. With my aid, she constructed a Web page containing known references. The page was announced to appropriate Internet users who came, filled in some missing information, and added new references (the Web page can be found at http://wwwpub.utdallas.edu/~aca102/).

In addition, the student hosted some meetings regarding her work on MIT's MediaMoo. These meetings allowed researchers in this area to exchange ideas. Many humanities professors use MUDs and MOOs in similar ways.

Publishing Results

For centuries, academia has used publication as a method of writing and archiving research results. Most academic journals impose a strict peer-review system to ensure that articles are accurate. The peer-review process, although terribly slow, has generally worked. The Internet offers a convenient way to speed up the peer-review process. In addition, the Internet offers more publishing formats, such as databases and hypertext, than are possible with conventional paper-based publishing.

Academic publication can be divided into two parts. The first part is writing and publishing articles and books. The second part is reading the published articles. You actually do the reading when performing or preparing for follow-up research. This chapter has already covered some Internet uses related to the reading of materials, but the following sections discuss more.

Cowritten Papers

Historically, coauthors of a paper have had difficulty exchanging their documents over the Internet. The Internet e-mail system was originally designed to support only the transmission of text files. Most word processors, such as WordPerfect or Microsoft Word, use some type of binary file. Therefore, e-mailing a document to your coauthor was impossible.

Many savvy users have come up with ways to encode binary documents into text files (usually using the uuencode and uudecode programs). Still other users have come up with ways of using FTP, which usually involve allowing a colleague to know your password. Most universities strongly frown on password sharing, if they do not outright forbid it, so this method is not a good solution. The vast majority of coauthors have ended up sending each other floppy disks through the postal system rather than using the Internet—until now.

Fortunately, work over the last couple of years has led to a standard for e-mailing binary files (including word processing documents and graphics) across the Internet. This standard is called MIME (Multipurpose Internet Mail Extensions) and is being added to an increasing number of e-mail packages. A few packages that currently support MIME are PINE and ECS Mail. Many major commercial vendors have promised support for MIME, although most vendors have been slow in their delivery of this support. The development of MIME means that researchers can e-mail binary files to each other—if not today, then in the near future.

Mailing Lists and Newsgroups

Academic researchers can exchange and discuss ideas electronically in two primary ways over the Internet. The first way is through private e-mail messages. The other way is to conduct public discussions in mailing lists and Usenet newsgroups. Researchers find two major gains from using the Internet for this kind of exchange. First, e-mail is faster than paper mail. The other advantage is that e-mail is asynchronous, unlike the telephone.

Both individuals and workgroups can use private e-mail. This method enables researchers who are geographically distant to discuss their ideas, progress, and results quickly. E-mail also affords privacy to the discussion just like a telephone conversation, but multiuser participation is easy to establish if you want.

Mailing lists and newsgroups enable the researcher to address a wider audience than private e-mail. Many dangers accompany these methods, however. Often, the lists attract a few people who really do not know much about a subject but feel they do. These people can be very vocal, give wrong answers to questions, and state their opinions as fact. Researchers must be aware of this problem and verify any information they receive on a list or newsgroup (unless the researcher knows the author is a reliable source). Researchers who post their research ideas on the Internet take a risk that someone else on the Internet will steal their ideas and publish them as their own.

Diane Kovacs of Kent State University and others have put together a list of mailing lists organized by subject. Valuable to academia, this list is known as the *Directory of Scholarly Electronic Conferences.* You can download the list from `LISTSERV@KENTVM.KENT.EDU` or `ftp://ksuvxa.kent.edu/LIBRARY`. The first file is called `ACADLIST.README`, which explains the rest of the files that make up the directory.

> **NOTE**
>
> To read more about Listservs, see Chapter 16, "Joining Discussions: Using Listservs and Mailing Lists."

Of all the noncomputing disciplines, biologists seem to take best advantage of Usenet newsgroups. They even have formed their own newsgroup hierarchy called Bionet (see Table 50.3). Not all academic sites take the Bionet newsgroups, but many do.

Table 50.3. Some biology research newsgroups in Bionet.

Topic	Newsgroup
Neural Networking	bionet.neuroscience
Population Biology	bionet.population-bio
Botany	bionet.plants
Immunizations	bionet.immunology

The biologists are not alone in the use of the Usenet newsgroups for publishing research results and participating in discussions. Not surprisingly, computer science and other disciplines have several research-oriented newsgroups (see Table 50.4). Over time, expect to see more and more research-related newsgroups forming.

Table 50.4. A sample of other research-related newsgroups.

Topic	Newsgroup
Operating Systems	comp.os.research
File Compression	comp.compression.research
Computing Research in Japan	comp.research.japan
Computer Graphics	comp.graphics.research
Physics	sci.physics.research
Anthropology	sci.anthropology
Archaeology	sci.archaeology
Chemistry	sci.chem
Civil Engineering	sci.engr.civil
History	soc.history
Mathematics	sci.math.research
PostDoctorate Research	sci.research.postdoc
Research Methods and Grants	sci.research
Education	alt.education.research
Economics	sci.econ.research

Databases

Many research results in academia are now going into databases rather than books or journals. Some of these databases are appearing on the Internet. The available databases vary widely: from numeric databases to document databases to GIS (Geographic Information Systems) data.

One of the most successful Internet database resources is the GenBank database. GenBank lists all published sequences of nucleic acids. The database is available in a variety of formats, and you can search the database using many different keys. The newsgroup `bionet.molbio.genbank` holds discussions about GenBank. New sequences are posted to `bionet.molbio.genbank.updates`. You can find the database itself on Gopher in the IUBio Biology Archive Gopher (`gopher://ftp.bio.indiana.edu:70/11/`) and in the WAIS database `IUBio-genbank`. You can find some related files in the anonymous FTP directory `/molbio/other/genbank` and in the WAIS database `bionic-genbank-software`. The IUBio Gopher and WAIS databases contain many other Internet resources valuable to the molecular biologist.

Several astronomical databases are available over the Internet. You can access the National Space Science Data Center (NSSDC) by Telnet to `nssdca.gsfc.nasa.gov` (log in as `nodis`). NSSDC includes information on life science, microgravity, astrophysics, earth sciences, planetary sciences, and space physics. NASA's Lunar and Planetary Institute (LPI) has many resources available over the Net, including bibliographies, an Image Retrieval and Processing System (IRPS), and information on Venus and Mars. You can access all LPI resources by Telnet to `cass.jsc.nasa.gov` (use `cass` as a user ID and `online` as the password).

Geology researchers find that the United States Geological Survey's (USGS) Internet resources are a gold mine. You can find a large number of the USGS resources on the USGS's Gopher server (`gopher://oemg.er.usgs.gov/`). You also can find a few USGS resources elsewhere on the Internet. You can acquire the USGS Geological Fault Maps at `ftp://alum.wr.usgs.gov/pub/map`. Seismology information from the USGS and other sources is on the Gopher from Northwestern University's Department of Geological Sciences (`gopher://somalia.earth.nwu.edu/`).

Many universities use a collection of data called ICPSR (Interuniversity Consortium of Political and Social Research) for research. Although the data collection itself is not currently available on the Internet, the ICPSR organization has brought up its own Gopher server (`gopher://gopher.icpsr.umich.edu/`), which contains much useful related information.

The ERIC (Educational Resources Information Center) database also is available on the Internet. ERIC contains information about all types of education including academia. Even the non-academic information is of interest to education researchers in academia. You can access ERIC by a variety of methods. One way is to Telnet to `sklib.usask.ca` and use the user ID `sonia`. Then look under `Education Databases`. A part of ERIC known as AskERIC has its own Gopher server (`gopher://ericir.syr.edu/`). Finally, ERIC information is in several WAIS databases: `ERIC-archive`, `AskERIC-Helpsheets`, `AskERIC-Infoguides`, `AskERIC-Minisearches`, and `AskERIC-Questions`. For more about ERIC, see Chapter 51, "ERIC and Educational Resources."

Many other databases of interest to academic researchers exist on the Internet. Quite a few databases are available in WAIS format (see Table 50.5).

Table 50.5. Databases in WAIS.

Topic	Database Name
Climate	DOE_Climate_Data
Enzyme Restrictions	rebase-enzyme
Genetics	online-mendelian-inheritance-in-man
Hubble Telescope Exposures	hst-aec-catalog
Invertebrates	InvertPaleoDatabase
Oligonucleotides	Oligos
RIPE Network Managements	ripe-database
USDA Current Research	usda-cris
USDA Research Results	usda-rrdb

Other important databases for academia will be available on the Internet over the next few years. For example, most of the U.S. census data is now available on the Internet at this address:

```
http://www.census.gov/ and ftp://cedrd.lbl.gov/data1/merrill/docs/
LBL-census.html.
```

Electronic Journals, Preprints, and Technical Reports

Academic researchers are beginning to publish more results electronically over the Internet in addition to—or in place of—paper publications. The primary advantages of publishing electronically are faster publishing, easier distribution, and reduced cost. Articles often can be published in weeks on the Internet instead of the months or years normal publishing channels can take.

Electronic journals are scattered all across the Internet and often are hard to find. Fortunately, CICNet has a major electronic journal collection project known as the CICNet Electronic Journal Archive. Most electronic journals are in this archive, and new materials are added daily. In addition to journals, the project contains many electronic magazines and newspapers of interest to academia. To access the archive, use the CICNet Gopher server (gopher://gopher.cic.net:2000/11/e-serials/) or FTP to ftp://ftp.cic.net/pub/e-serials/. A list of journals available on the Web can be found at http://info.cern.ch/hypertext/DataSources/bySubject/Electronic_Journals.html.

In addition to journals being published in electronic form, a large number of paper publications are being scanned into electronic format and made accessible over the Internet. The Colorado Association of Research Libraries (CARL) has put hundreds of these journals into a database known as UnCover, which is a commercial database. Universities pay for connections to UnCover over the Internet. The searching of the database and its bibliographic records are free, but if you want to retrieve an article, you must pay for it. You can receive the article by fax or electronically across the Internet. The URL of CARL is `telnet://pac.carl.org/`.

Another common trend in publishing is that a researcher spends a great deal of time looking for a paper publication to print his or her article and waiting for the publication to accept the article. Many researchers in the meantime want the information to get to their colleagues as fast as possible. This situation has led to the creation of preprint collections on the Internet. The preprint may be different from the final paper and probably has not been through the peer-review process, but it still is useful to many people. One common complaint, however, is that after the paper is published in its final form, the preprint version often continues to exist on the Internet even though the preprint may be of lesser quality.

The majority of the preprint collections on the Internet are from the sciences. Several preprint collections are on the University of Virginia Gopher (`gopher://orion.lib.virginia.edu:70/11/alpha`) under `Alphabetic Organization`. These collections include philosophical preprints, scientific preprints from the American Mathematical Society, and the University of Virginia physics preprints. The University of Texas has a Gopher (`henri.ma.utexas.edu`) that contains many preprint databases including algebraic geometry preprints and physics preprints. You also can find many preprints in WAIS Databases (see Table 50.6).

Table 50.6. Preprints in WAIS databases.

Topic	Database Name
Algorithm Geometry	`Preprints-alg-geom`
Condensed Matter	`Preprints-cond-mat`
High Energy Phenomology	`Preprints-hep-ph`
National Radio Observatory	`nrao-raps`
Space Telescope (Hubble)	`stsci-preprint-db`
Theoretical Physics	`Preprints-hep-th`

Many computer science departments as well as other academic departments publish their own technical reports. You can find many of these technical reports on the Internet. Computer science technical reports are available on various Gophers, FTP sites, the Usenet newsgroup `comp.doc.techreports`, and on the following WAIS databases: `comp.doc.techreports`, `cs-techreport-abstracts`, and `cs-techreport-archives`. Purdue University has tried to tie

together all known FTP sites with technical reports into their Gopher (gopher://
arthur.cs.purdue.edu:70/11/Non_purdue/ftp/trs). This same list is in the Web with the URL
http://www.vifp.monash.edu.au/techreports/siteslist.html.

Tenure

One of the most important things in the life of a faculty member is getting tenure. Without
tenure, faculty members can lose their jobs; with tenure, it is nearly impossible for them to lose
their jobs. Getting tenure is usually based on published research in peer-reviewed journals, grant
funding, and sometimes the quality of instruction.

When peer-reviewed electronic journals first came along, they were often ignored for purposes
of tenure. Even today, electronic peer reviews are ignored at many universities. Other universities have reached the conclusion that publishing in peer-reviewed electronic journals is as valid
as publishing in paper-based peer-reviewed journals. I think we will continue to see this trend.
However, do not expect non-peer-reviewed journals (whether paper or electronic) to weigh
much in decisions of whether a faculty member gets tenure.

Instruction

This section discusses student-related activities as well as classroom instruction. An increasing
number of student activities are taking place over the Internet. College students seem to love
Internet games (such as MUDs) and chat utilities (such as IRC), but this section focuses on the
more academic instructional pursuits of the network rather than recreational pursuits.

Although a few universities restrict the use of the Internet to faculty and staff, most campuses
allow students to access the Internet. The Internet gives students a unique chance to make
national and international contacts that may help in their research and possibly in their later
careers. Therefore, the Internet is important to many students. If usage-based Internet charges
rather than flat-rate charges are ever implemented, many universities may limit their students'
access to the Internet, hurting the academic environment considerably.

Scholarships

With college costs soaring and many people out of work, going to college is more difficult than
ever. Therefore, finding scholarships is important for most students. You can find much information about student loans, grants, scholarships, and work-study programs on the Internet.

Two famous systems are FEDIX (Federal Information eXchange) and MOLIS (Minority
OnLine Information Service). FEDIX is the more general system that contains information
from at least 10 different federal agencies; MOLIS focuses on primarily black and Hispanic
education. Both systems have other academic information besides scholarships and can be

accessed by Telnet to `fedix.fie.com` (log in as `fedix` or `molis`). FEDIX and MOLIS are accessible by a Gopher server at `gopher://fedix.fie.com/` or the Web at `http://fedix.fie.com/`.

You can find even more scholarship information on the Department of Education's Office of Educational Research and Improvement Gopher (`gopher://gopher.ed.gov/`). Students should also check the systems listed in "Finding Grants," earlier in this chapter; grants and scholarship information often appear together.

Class Schedules and Catalogs

Many universities have their class schedules and catalogs available over the Internet. Although the main reason these items are available is to enable local students to access them electronically, potential students also can check out the college and see whether it has the programs and courses they are interested in. The schedules and catalogs usually are on the CWIS of the university in question. To see an example, look at `gopher://gopher.utdallas.edu:70/11/student`.

E-Mail and Usenet News in Instruction

A growing number of courses are using e-mail and Usenet news as a part of the course. E-mail is used for student-to-teacher contacts in place of an office visit. E-mail and Usenet news are both used for group discussions in classes. The majority of this usage stays local to one campus; however, in some cases, the communication is distant. For example, the University of North Texas, north of Dallas, has an adjunct faculty member who works for NASA in Houston. The faculty member teaches a graduate seminar that meets infrequently on a Saturday, when he flies there to teach. Needless to say, the students and teacher have difficulty meeting at any other time. They use e-mail on the Internet to help make up for the distance.

Some universities, such as UTD, require that students learn e-mail in their freshman rhetoric classes because they feel e-mail is a basic skill. If all universities adopted this approach, in a few years all college students and recent graduates would know how to use e-mail.

Other projects use the Internet to enable entire classes to have e-mail partners from distant locations. The usual purpose is to give students exposure to students from other countries and cultures. One such project involving academia, as well as K–12 education, is the International E-mail Classroom Connections project, which you can reach by sending e-mail to `iecc@stolaf.edu`.

Distance Learning

Many universities now are involved in remote learning projects in which university teachers are miles, if not thousands of miles, away from the students. Most projects do not involve the Internet, but a few do. The Internet now can transmit both audio and video; however, both forms require considerable bandwidth and are used only on rare occasions.

Other distance learning projects are purely e-mail and Usenet news based. Three courses on navigating the Internet have been available through mailing lists and Usenet news. One of these courses was about Gopher. The class attracted an incredible 17,769 students from across the world, which probably qualifies it as one of the largest courses ever taught. (Chapter 53, "Distance Education," discusses distance learning in more detail.)

The Internet as a Course

The University of Michigan has started an interesting course on the Internet in its School of Information and Library Studies. The students in the course not only learn to use the Internet but also are required to produce an Internet resource list for a particular topic area, such as community service or journalism. This course is part of the university's Internet Resource Discovery Project.

As another part of the project, the university has formed the Clearinghouse for Subject-Oriented Internet Resource Guides. The clearinghouse is available at `gopher://una.hh.lib.umich.edu:70/11/inetdirs` or `http://www.sils.umich.edu/Catalog/Clearinghouse.html`. The developers are trying to collect all the freely available topical resource guides on the Internet, including guides written by University of Michigan students, and are making them available from a single place. The clearinghouse is an excellent resource for students and faculty looking for information on a particular topic. For more information, contact Louis Rosenfeld at `i-guides@umich.edu`.

Starting in the Spring 1995 semester, Glenn Vanderburg and I will help teach a Computer Science class at UTD called Internet Programming. In this course, each student will have a real Internet project that would otherwise be done by the computing staff. The students may be designing Web pages for departments, solving Internet research questions, or bringing up an experimental service such as Hyper-G. A list of potential projects is maintained at `http://www.utdallas.edu/acc/projects/`. The students' goal for the semester is to produce something that can be used by the university and the Internet. The students gain valuable experience and the university gains a usable product.

Tutoring

Some students use the Internet to get assistance with their homework and studying. This process often takes place on IRC between complete strangers. Also, many friends help each other over e-mail. Although often inappropriate, students sometimes make posts on mailing lists and newsgroups begging for help.

As with all other forms of tutoring, the chance exists that the student may try to get the other person to do the work for him or her. Therefore, other Internet users must know when to draw the line between helping and actually doing the work.

Instructional Software

Many universities write CAI (computer-aided instruction) software to supplement their class-room instruction. In many cases, universities make this software available free of charge to other universities. One such example is mathematical instructional software, which can be found at `ftp://wuarchive.wustl.edu/mirrors/msdos/math`.

Student Organizations

Many national and international student organizations use the Internet for communication (see Table 50.7). They use e-mail to communicate among the various chapters and individual members. Many student organizations are relatively poor and they appreciate avoiding long-distance phone calls whenever possible. The Internet offers organizations a unique chance for inexpensive or free communication over long distances.

Table 50.7. Mailing lists of some student organizations.

Organization	List Address
Association of Japanese Business Studies	`AJBS-L@NCSUVM.CC.NCSU.EDU`
European Law Students Association	`ALL-OF-ELSA@JUS.UIO.NO`
Institute of Electrical and Electronics	`IEEE-L@BINGVMB.CC.BINGHAMTON.EDU`
Student Government Association	`SGANET@VTVM1.BITNET`
Phi Mu Alpha Sinfonia	`SINFONIA@ASUVM.INRE.ASU.EDU`
Theta Xi	`THETAXI@GITVM1.GATECH.EDU`

Some student organizations, especially individual chapters, use Gopher (see Table 50.8). Many student chapters keep their by-laws, minutes, calendar of events, and newsletters in a Gopher server for the whole world. Usually, the student chapters are buried a couple levels down in the university's CWIS, so you may have to do a little searching.

Table 50.8. Information servers of some student organization chapters.

Organization	URL
Amer. Soc. of Civil Engineers (Lehigh University)	`gopher://nss1.cc.lehigh.edu:70/1ASCE`
Amnesty International Group 124 (University of Illinois)	`gopher://gopher.uiuc.edu:70/11/UI/stuorg/amnesty`
Ballroom Dance (CMU)	`http://www.contrib.andrew.cmu.edu/org/ballroom/home`

Organization	URL
IEEE (University of Saskatchewan)	`http://www.engr.usask.ca/~ieee/`
Lesbian, Gay, Bi Alliance (Princeton)	`gopher://gopher.princeton.edu:70/` `11/.students/.organizations/.lgba`
Muslim Student Assoc. (USC)	`gopher://cwis.usc.edu:70/11/` `Campus_Life/Student_Orgs/MSA`

Tau Beta Pi (George Washington)	`gopher://gwis.circ.gwu.edu:70/11/`
	`students/Student%20Organizations/`
	`Honorary/Tau%20Beta%20Pi`

Placement

When students are near graduation, universities typically help them find jobs. Many job services are appearing on the Internet. Some list resumes, others list jobs, and some even try to make matches between the two. The Clearinghouse for Subject-Oriented Internet Resource Guides has a couple of example starting places for placement information:

```
http://asa.ugl.lib.umich.edu/chdocs/employment/job-guide.toc.html
gopher://una.hh.lib.umich.edu:70/00/inetdirsstacks/jobs%3ariley.
```

Administration

The administrative part of a university is similar to a business except that the goal is to balance a budget rather than make a profit. The administration has been the slowest area of academia to adopt the Internet. However, university administrators may find that the Internet is as useful to them as it is to faculty and students. In addition to addressing the administration's use of the Internet, the following sections discuss resources that do not fall clearly into the Research, Instruction, or Administration categories.

Vendors

A few vendors have brought up Internet services to serve their higher education customers. During 1994, almost all the vendors converted their systems to the Web and redesigned them to be of general use to all their customers (they remain important to higher education). Currently, the vendors tend to be computer vendors such as Sun Microsystems (`http://www.sun.com/`), although many other types of businesses are considering providing some business services over the Internet. When this happens, academia definitely will take advantage of it.

Nonresearch Publications

In addition to electronic journals, academia generates quite a few other publications. Almost every university has a student newspaper, personnel bulletin, and departmental newsletters. These publications are becoming increasingly common in electronic format over the Internet. In most cases, the publications are originally placed on the Internet for local use only, but they still may be useful to people at other locations. Seeing what other academic institutions are doing helps you evaluate your own institution and make needed improvements.

The majority of publications are in a CWIS such as a Gopher. To see an example, look at the University of Illinois Urbana-Champaign Gopher (`gopher://gopher.uiuc.edu:70/11/News`) which has at least 20 local publications. You can find many of these local publications in the CICNet Electronic Journal Project, mentioned earlier in this chapter.

A major publication in higher education is *The Chronicle of Higher Education*. Recently, *The Chronicle* started publishing part of its materials on the Internet in an electronic publication called *Academe This Week*, which is freely available. The *Academe* contains a guide to news in thecurrent week, a higher-education calendar of events, deadlines of grants and fellowships, and higher education job opportunities. It can be found at `gopher://chronicle.merit.edu:70/1` or `http://chronicle.merit.edu/`.

Professional Organizations

Many professional organizations that have strong ties to academia have made Internet resources available to their members as well as to other network users. The organizations find that the Internet provides an easy and efficient means to communicate with their membership.

For starters, some professional faculty organizations are available on the Internet. The Manitoba Organization of Faculty Associations (MOFA) and the Canadian Association of University Teachers (CAUT) share a Gopher server on `gopher://gopher.mofa.mb.ca/`. This Gopher contains information such as collective bargaining agreements and health plans, which are useful to faculty members.

The American Mathematical Society (AMS), which has a large number of academic members, is well established on the Internet through its E-Math (Electronic Mathematics) system. E-Math is available at `gopher://e-math.ams.com/`. E-Math contains professional information for mathematicians, such as math-related meetings, conferences, and publications.

The American Philosophical Association (APA) also has a Gopher on the Internet (`gopher://gate.oxy.edu/`). The APA lists a wide range of materials: from e-mail addresses to grants to preprints to bibliographies. Their Gopher is an excellent resource for faculty and students alike.

The American Physiological Society (APS) is another organization that uses the network to the advantage of its members, including those in academia. APS is devoted to fostering scientific research, and its Gopher server (`gopher://gopher.uth.tmc.edu:3000/`) is no exception.

Many other professional associations important to academia are on the Internet. The vast majority of these organizations have Gopher servers (see Table 50.9).

Table 50.9. Information servers of some professional associations.

Organization	URL
American Chemical Society	`gopher://acsinfo.acs.org/`
American Educational Research Association	`http://www.asu.edu/aff/aera/home.html`
Association of Computing Machinery	`http://www.acm.org/`
Coalition for Networked Information	`gopher://gopher.cni.org/`
IEEE Computer Society	`gopher://info.computer.org/`
Society of Architectural Historians	`http://akebono.stanford.edu/yahoo/Economy/Organizations/Professional/Society_of_Architectural_Historians`
Society of Women Engineers	`http://www.thesphere.com/SWE/SWE.html`
Society for the Advancement of Scandinavian Studies	`gopher://sass.byu.edu/`
Society for Industrial and Applied Math	`gopher://gopher.siam.org/`
Universities Space Research Association	`gopher://renzo.usra.edu/`

Other professional organizations have Internet mailing lists. These lists usually contain announcements as well as discussions about the organization. All the lists in Table 50.10 are on Listserv at the same nodename as the address.

Table 50.10. Mailing lists of some professional associations.

Organization	List Address
American Association of State Colleges	`AASCU-L@UBVM.CC.BUFFALO.EDU`
American Association of Universities	`AAUA-L@UBVM.CC.BUFFALO.EDU`
Association for Study of Higher Education	`ASHE-L@UMCVMB.BITNET`
Canadian Associations of Colleges & Universities	`CACUSS-L@UBVM.CC.BUFFALO.EDU`
Music Library Association	`MLA-L@VM1.NODAK.EDU`

Academic Jobs

Many services are available on the Internet for finding employment in academia. The publication *Academe This Week* was mentioned earlier, but many other services exist.

The Academic Position Network (APN) enables academic institutions to place online job advertisements for a one-time fee. People looking for employment do not have to pay a fee for searching through the list of position announcements. The APN Gopher server is at gopher://wcni.cis.umn.edu:11111/.

Some universities post their own jobs on newsgroups such as utcs.jobs for the computer science department of the University of Texas at Austin. Many universities also list available jobs in a Gopher server (see Table 50.11).

Table 50.11. Job listings in university Gophers.

University	URL
Florida State University	gopher://mailer.fsu.edu:70/11/Employees/Jobs
MIT	gopher://gopher.mit.edu:3714/ 1M%20tiserve.mit.edu%209000%2025751%20admin
Ohio State University	gopher://gopher.acs.ohio-state.edu:70/11/ Opportunities/Job%20Listings
Syracuse University	gopher://cwis.syr.edu:70/11/employment
University of California Berkeley	gopher://infocal.berkeley.edu:70/11/.p/jvl/GD
University of Minnesota	gopher://mailbox.mail.umn.edu/
University of North Texas	gopher://gopher.unt.edu:70/11/employment
University of Texas at Dallas	gopher://gopher.utdallas.edu:70/11/business/ hr/utdjobs

Many biologist positions are posted in the Usenet newsgroup bionet.jobs. Other job announcements show up in misc.jobs.offered. Resumes also are posted frequently to the newsgroup misc.jobs.resumes. Finally, many regional newsgroups exist for posting job opportunities and resumes. One example is tx.jobs, which is for jobs in the state of Texas.

You can find academic job postings on many mailing lists. A few mailing lists are dedicated to job postings, and other lists are primarily for other purposes but contain job announcements also (see Table 50.12).

Table 50.12. Some mailing lists that have academic job announcements.

Type of Position	List Address
Archaeology	ARCH-L@DGOGWDG1.BITNET
Community Colleges	COMMCOLL@UKCC.UKY.EDU
History and Philosophy of Science	HOPOS-L@UKCC.UKY.EDU
Foreign Language Education	SCOLT@CATFISH.VALDOSTA.PEACHNET.EDU
Japanese Teachers	JTIT-L@PSUVM.PSU.EDU
Libraries (especially automation)	PACS-L@UHUPVM1.UH.EDU
Library Science	SILS-L@UBVM.CC.BUFFALO.EDU
Philosophy	PHILOSOP@YORKVM1.BITNET
Political Science	PSRT-L@UMCVMB.BITNET
Quantitative Morphology	QMLIST@TBONE.BIOL.SCAROLINA.EDU
Special Libraries	SLAJOB@IUBVM.UCS.INDIANA.EDU
Urban Historians	H-URBAN@UICVM.UIC.EDU
Various in Europe (EARN members only)	JOB-LIST@FRORS12
Victorian Studies	VICTORIA@IUBVM.UCS.INDIANA.EDU
Women's Studies	WMST-L@UMDD.UMD.EDU

Academic Conferences

The Internet has become a common way to announce academic conferences. Many conferences are announced on Internet mailing lists and Usenet newsgroups that are related to the topic of the conference. Usenet also offers a group for the announcement of any conference called news.announce.conferences.

In fact, a few conferences now are announced only over the Internet. One example was GopherCon, where the announcements, session planning, and distribution of the conference schedule were handled over the Internet. This trend probably will increase over time.

Another new development is the actual broadcast of conferences over the Internet. The last few IETF (Internet Engineering Task Force) conferences have been broadcast over the Internet in real time. Unfortunately, these kinds of broadcasts use quite a bit of bandwidth on the Internet, so broadcasting several conferences at one time is not yet feasible. On the positive side, as network bandwidth increases, these kinds of broadcasts will become increasingly feasible. Over the next few years, some academic conferences will be broadcast over the Internet.

Administrative Mailing Lists

Mailing lists are not just for students and faculty anymore. Many lists now focus on the issues of upper-level administration in an academic setting (see Table 50.13).

Table 50.13. Some mailing lists for university administrators.

Topic	List Address
Academic Advising	ACADV@VM1.NODAK.EDU
Budgeting and Planning	BDGTPLAN@UVMVM.BITNET
Campus Parking Systems	CPARK-L@PSUVM.PSU.EDU
Chairpersons	CHAIRS-L@ACC.FAU.EDU
North American College and University Business Officers	NACUBO@BITNIC.BITNET
Staff Governance	STAFFGOV@VM1.NODAK.EDU

Student Recruitment

Universities now use the Internet and especially the Web to do their recruiting of students and marketing. It is becoming increasingly common to find electronic copies of paper brochures. If you want to see some examples, look at http://www.utdallas.edu/dept/ and http://www.utdallas.edu/student/.

Some universities are in the process of making their application forms available online. The goal is to have the entire application process electronic over the Internet. The potential student can look at literature electronically, e-mail questions, fill out an application form using a secure Web server (so that a credit card number can be given for the application fee), and finally get an acceptance letter back.

The Library versus the Computing Center

Many campuses are facing serious battles between the library and the computing center over who manages the Internet. The library is used to being in charge of the publications on campus. On the other hand, the computing center is used to being in charge of the computing resources. In many places, both departments are vying for control of the Internet.

Part of this conflict comes from the traditions of both organizations. The library typically wants to plan for a long time and design perfect solutions. On the other hand, the computing organization wants to react quickly to problems and user needs. The computing center knows that planning too long for any computing solution means that the solution is obsolete before it is implemented.

Another source of the conflict comes from the organizations responsible for certain types of consulting. A computing center may feel it must consult on all aspects of computing. The academic library may feel that Internet is just another research tool and should be handled only at the reference desk.

Universities can avoid this conflict easily if the computing center and library cooperate and do not draw strict borders. Librarians usually understand information organization better and computing personnel usually understand the electronic-access issues better. If the library and computing center work in cooperation, the Internet is more useful to the academic users.

At UTD, the computing center is responsible for the physical Internet connection and installation of the Internet tools. The computing staff also offers training and consulting to the librarians on request. At the same time, the librarians make suggestions to the computing center about how to make the Internet services better. The reference desk in the library helps patrons find materials on the Internet when it is the best reference. This is one possible model for other universities to follow although there are many others that work.

Internet Issues

A university has to deal with many Internet issues that do not plague businesses. By law, universities must be more accepting of free speech than businesses, especially if they are government funded. The hard part comes in determining what is free speech and what is abuse and harassment.

Many people on university campuses may not understand that a university's computing resources are limited. Limited network bandwidth, limited CPU power, and limited disk space all exist. System managers often need to decide what Internet resources they can afford to support.

Many academic system administrators cannot take a full Usenet newsfeed because of inadequate disk space. When administrators take a look at how much space Usenet is using, they often find that `alt.binaries.pictures.erotica` uses the most space by a sizable margin. Removing that one group can solve disk space problem for many sites. Most of the time, the university removes a group purely on the basis of size and not for censorship reasons. Unfortunately, academic-freedom fanatics immediately claim censorship and ignore any other interpretation of events. When this situation happens, an ugly scene often ensues on college campuses.

Some academic administrators do censor Usenet news and other electronic materials, but they are in the minority. A showdown in court will probably happen soon in one of these cases. Regardless of the outcome, the event will be bad for the academic environment. If the free-speech people win, the interpretation of the ruling will be that universities must provide unlimited computing resources. This consequence may cause some sites to remove their Usenet access totally to avoid these issues. If the case goes the other way, system administrators with authoritarian tendencies may tend to excess until more court decisions flesh out the exact boundaries.

Similar censorship issues apply to people posting Usenet news and sending e-mail. When can universities pull someone's account to stop harassment? Again, any decision by the courts could lead to a negative effect in the short term and possibly the long term. However, I am aware of one suit by a student against a university that was thrown out of court before it ever went to trial.

One issue that seems to come up regularly at public institutions is access to the Internet by people who are unrelated to the university. Some citizens have the idea that because they pay taxes, and taxes support the universities, the universities should provide them with computing access, including access to the Internet. An important note is that this position has no basis in law or in the way government allocates funds to the universities. In fact, according to the laws of many states, allowing non-university people to use the Internet may even be illegal.

The Future of the Internet in Academia

Academia has played an important role in the development of the Internet. However, many academics are still not using the Internet even though it has penetrated academia more widely than any other area. The number of people not using the network should shrink over time, but reducing the number to zero is unlikely.

Universities that have no connection or poor Internet support more and more are providing Internet support. It usually take a few years for the Internet to catch fire at these universities.

Many people may disagree about the potential growth of the Internet in universities. The Internet has been commercialized and privatized, a circumstance many academics fear. However, access costs did not go up and the quality remained about the same. Another reason commercialization is good for academia is that universities can select their level of service. For example, some of the current regional sites do not provide much more than a connection while others provide expertise on using the network. Some regionals even coordinate regional projects. For some schools, the effective coordination of the regional service provider will save money.

The Internet will see more growth in resources available from academia. Academia will continue to be an important part of the future of the Internet and of its development.

ERIC and Educational Resources

51

by Steve Bang,
Andy Carvin, and
Jill H. Ellsworth

Are you are a parent striving to help improve the quality of schools in your neighborhood? A researcher trying to keep abreast of the latest in educational technology? A teacher developing innovative lessons for your class? A company wanting to develop continuing education programs? A software developer looking for education software ideas? A member of a nonprofit organization developing adult literacy programs? Whatever your interests in education, you are certain to find information somewhere on the Internet that can help you learn more about education and achieve your goals. Internet resources relevant to education include Usenet newsgroups and mailing lists concerning education-related topics, World Wide Web sites, Gophers connected to computers at schools and libraries, file archives accessible by anonymous FTP, and online databases you can search.

The amount of educational information available on the Internet is amazing. The richest sources of references and information are found on Gopher and World Wide Web sites.

Gophers and World Wide Web Servers

For most educators, parents, and students, Gopher and the WWW represent easy-to-use protocols. Gopher provides easy-to-use text menus, and Veronica can be used to search Gopherspace for information. (Chapter 25, "Using and Finding Gophers," and Chapter 26, "Searching Gopherspace with Veronica," provide more information.)

The World Wide Web is another place where educational information abounds. You can access the WWW with GUI browsers such as Mosaic and Netscape or with the text-based browser Lynx. Several search tools are available for the Web, including Harvest, Lycos, and WebCrawler. (Part VI of this book, "Sharing Information," gives more information on the Web and its search tools.)

Following are some very good sources of information. In some cases, the sources are databases; others provide both information and access to other sites.

CICNet

```
gopher://gopher.cic.net
```

CICNet, run by the Big 10's Committee on Institution Cooperation, acts as a backbone server for Midwest education. CICNet includes Midwest servers and educational information, resource guides, and numerous educational e-texts, conferences, and serials.

The Community Learning Network

```
gopher//cln.etc.bc.ca
http://cln.etc.bc.ca
```

Although CLN is run by the Ministry of Education in British Columbia, it provides a wealth of information pertinent to U.S. education as well. CLN includes long-distance learning resource information, connections to other educational and Canadian government Gophers, and CLN software.

The C-Span Gopher

```
gopher://c-span.org
```

The C-Span Gopher offers a variety of educational resources. It includes network information and press releases, government resources, and a vast collection of historic speeches.

CoSN—The Consortium for School Networking

```
gopher://digital.cosn.org
http://digital.cosn.org
```

CoSN, a collection of leaders in educational networking, offers a Gopher that focuses on CoSN's network reform efforts, as well as general K–12 information. CoSN includes educational policy and legislation, state and local projects, educational resources, and conference information.

Claremont High School Web

```
http://www.cusd.claremont.edu
```

One of the best high school Web sites on the Net, the Claremont High School server offers a variety of teaching resources. It also offers connectivity to other school sites and detailed information on the Internet itself.

The Complete Works of William Shakespeare

```
http://the-tech.mit.edu/Shakespeare/works.html
```

Every poem and play written by the Bard himself are now available online and in hypertext. This site includes links to word definitions and cross-references to other Shakespeare works. A great place to explore. Once more unto the breach, dear friends, once more....

Dewey Web

```
http://ics.soe.umich.edu
```

The Dewey Web is the University of Michigan School of Education's interactive exploration and adventure education home page. It contains information for educators about how to get involved in online exploration and The Journey North, an arctic adventure project.

Educational Technology

```
http://tecfa.unige.ch
```

This list is maintained by the University of Geneva as a virtual library of educational resources. The list has a large collection of educational Web sites, journals, classroom materials, and software.

EdWeb

```
http://k12.cnidr.org:90
```

EdWeb is a site created by Andy Carvin, sponsored by the Corporation for Public Broadcasting and CNIDR. EdWeb explores the role of educational technology and telecommunications in education reform. EdWeb includes a discussion of the information highway debate, success stories and statistics on technology in the classroom, an online resource guide, examples of recent education reform, and the home page for WWWEdu, the Listserv for the World Wide Web in Education.

EE-Link

```
gopher://nceet.snre.umich.edu
http://www.nceet.snre.umich.edu
```

Home of the National Consortium for Environmental Education and Training, EE-Link provides a variety of materials relating to K–12 environmental education. EE-Link includes contact information, school projects, environmental literature, and connectivity to other educational and environmental sites.

EINet

```
http://galaxy.einet.net
```

In its Social Science collection, the Enterprise Integration Network's Web page offers one of the Web's most comprehensive collection of educational resources. EINet contains journals, Listservs, Internet sites, and dozens of other educational resources.

The Exploratorium ExploraNet

```
http://www.exploratorium.edu
```

San Francisco's Exploratorium maintains this virtual museum, which includes numerous audiovisual exhibits, museum journals, and numerous educational resources.

The Global SchoolHouse Gopher

```
gopher://gsh.cnidr.org
```

GSH, a leader in technology-assisted education, is constructing a Gopher to compliment its class project activities in over a dozen states and eight countries. The Gopher includes curriculum and policy information, Internet training, and access to Veronica.

HotList of K-12 Internet Sites

```
http://toons.cc.ndsu.nodak.edu/~sackmann/k12.html
```

Gleason Sackman, one of the leading archivers in educational networking, operates a site that can direct you to all known Internet sites run by schools. The HotList also includes links to departments of education and online school districts.

The Hub

```
gopher://hub.terc.edu
http://hub.terc.edu
```

Maintained by the Technology and Education Research Center (TERC) and The Regional Alliance for Mathematics and Science Education Reform, the Hub is an excellent resource for classroom projects and writings on curricular reform. The Hub also includes research information, organizational and management tools, and general teacher-assistance offerings.

InforMNs

```
gopher//informns.k12.mn.us
http://informns.k12.mn.us
```

The home server of Minnesota's teacher network, InforMNs includes teacher discussions, lesson plans, and one of the largest collections of Gopher lists available.

KIDLINK

```
gopher://kids.ccit.duq.edu
```

KIDLINK contains a variety of information concerning KIDLINK's KIDS-95 project, as well as past KIDs programs. KIDLINK also includes project information for teachers and students.

Kid's Internet Delight

```
http://www.clark.net
```

Kid's Internet Delight (KID) is designed specifically for children to provide young people with a large collection of interesting and educational Web sites.

NASA Education Sites

```
gopher://quest.arc.nasa.gov
gopher://k12mac.larc.nasa.gov
http://www.lerc.nasa.gov
http://www.nas.nasa.gov/HPCC/K12/edures.html
```

NASA and the High-Performance Computing and Communications Program offers a collection of servers specifically geared for teachers, students, and administrators. The servers offer a selection of math and science education resources, connectivity to numerous education servers, journals, and grant and project participation information. In particular, `http://www.nas.nasa.gov/HPCC/K12/edures.html` is an excellent starting point for discovering online resources.

NCSA Education Program

```
http://www.ncsa.uiuc.edu/Edu/EduHome.html
```

This site is the home base of the University of Illinois teacher networking program. It contains networking and education information for administrators and educators, K–12 subject resources, and information on the SuperQuest summer program for teachers.

NYSERNet

```
gopher//nysernet.org
http://nysernet.org
```

One of the largest state-run servers, NYSERNet offers a wide variety of K–12 tools. It includes class projects, teaching tools, discussion groups, career guidance, reference information, and school reform plans.

The Ralph Bunche School

```
gopher://ralphbunche.rbs.edu
```

The Ralph Bunche Gopher is of interest as one of the first educational servers managed and edited entirely by elementary school students. It contains writings and projects developed by Ralph Bunche students, as well as class project resources and information on the BBN testbed.

The Television News Archive

```
gopher://tvnews.Vanderbilt.Edu
http://tvnews.Vanderbilt.Edu
```

Vanderbilt University offers this archive that specializes in tracking and retrieving news clips and transcripts. It includes program abstracts, video purchasing and loan information, and specialized subject archives.

TENET

```
gopher://gopher.tenet.edu
```

The Texas Educational Network operates a Gopher for state educators and general use. TENET includes state educational news, policy and reform information, as well as college planning, field trip plans, and connectivity to educational Gophers around the world.

TIESnet

```
gopher://tiesnet.ties.k12.mn.us
http://tiesnet.ties.k12.mn.us
```

TIESnet is the online Gopher for Technology and Information Educational Services of Minnesota. The older sister of InforMNs, TIESnet is an excellent demonstration of the successes of networking educators. TIESnet includes access to numerous ongoing school projects as well as lesson plans, research information, and connectivity to InforMNs.

The U.S. Education Department/OERI

```
gopher://gopher.ed.gov
```

The ED and its Office of Educational Research and Instruction offer an information server that acts as a reference desk for all things educational. It includes educational software, Goals 2000 information, as well as primary, secondary, and vocational information.

Web66

```
http://web66.coled.umn.edu/
```

Stephen Collins at the University of Minnesota has put together this amazing site for teachers. Web66 is essentially a Web cookbook for education. It includes Web authoring information, online resources, and many other forms of guidance for Web design and Web use. Web66 is also home of the Hillside Elementary School K–12 School List, the oldest and most comprehensive collection of online schools on the Internet.

Educational Resources Information Center (ERIC)

ERIC is one of the most important resources for educators on the Internet. This section covers the wealth of education information that ERIC is developing. First, you learn how to access, search, and retrieve information from the ERIC database at the University of Saskatchewan. This chapter then offers a quick peek at the AskERIC Electronic Library at Syracuse University.

The Educational Resources Information Center (ERIC), a federally funded network of education information that collectors and providers established in 1966, consists of 16 clearinghouses specializing in information gathering and dissemination. You can find information in the following subject areas: adult, career, and vocational education; assessments and evaluation; counseling and personnel services; educational management; elementary and early childhood education; handicapped and gifted children; higher education; information and technology; junior colleges; languages and linguistics; reading and comprehension skills; rural education and small schools; science, mathematics, and environmental education; social studies/social science education; teacher education; and urban education. Along with these clearinghouses that filter education information, the ERIC system also has one facility that coordinates the editorial processes and document control, and another facility that creates microfiche copies of ERIC documents and makes printed copies available.

The ERIC clearinghouses collect, index, and abstract a wide range of education materials, including articles in magazines and scholarly journals, books, unpublished papers, conference proceedings, literature reviews, and curriculum materials. This information is then handled by the ERIC Processing and Reference Facility that coordinates the development and maintenance of the ERIC database. The resulting ERIC database is made available by both in-house services and commercial information providers in a variety of formats, including printed volumes, CD-ROMs, and online databases. The journal and magazine articles indexed in the ERIC database or mentioned in ERIC publications can be obtained in many public, school, or university libraries throughout the world. Other ERIC documents are available directly from the document delivery facility of ERIC, the ERIC Document Reproduction Service (EDRS), or through several other sources: on microfiche at over 900 locations (mostly libraries at major universities), in the original publication sources found in libraries, or even on the Internet.

> **NOTE**
>
> Be patient when exploring these resources and be prepared to wander off on your own if things have changed from the following descriptions. Frequently, the changes are the result of efforts to simplify and better organize access to information based on user feedback. At other times, the changes can be caused by the introduction of new information, either local to your system or as a result of links to other systems.

ERIC—The Database

ERIC offers the world's largest and most widely used database for access to education literature. The ERIC database is used by teachers, administrators, policy makers, parents, students, and researchers in over 3,000 locations around the world and through online access from commercial database services. In the past few years, the ERIC database has become available on the Internet in several locations. As the Internet continues to develop, even more organizations will make the ERIC database available.

The complete ERIC database currently contains around a million bibliographic references to education documents and articles dating as far back as 1966. These bibliographic records are created from documents abstracted and indexed from a variety of sources, including conference proceedings, books, theses and dissertations, literature reviews, lesson plans, handbooks, brochures, unpublished papers, and over 800 education-related journals and magazines. Each month, almost 2,600 new entries are added to the database. The size of the ERIC database you actually search on the Internet can vary considerably, depending on the number of years covered. (For example, Syracuse University offers only the last five years of ERIC records, but Auburn University offers the complete database going back to 1966.) The ERIC database is divided into two parts:

- Resources in Education (RIE), which includes references to current research findings, unpublished manuscripts, books, and technical reports

- Current Index to Journals in Education (CIJE), including references to articles from educational journals and magazines

You can search these two parts individually or combined, depending on the search capabilities of the ERIC database you use.

Many hosts on the Internet offer access to the ERIC database, but they vary in the range of years of ERIC files covered and in the quality of the search and retrieval methods they use. Three universities (Syracuse University, Auburn University, and the University of Saskatchewan) offer unrestricted, free access to the ERIC database over the Internet. Also, at least two commercial organizations offer Internet access to the ERIC database. CARL Systems, the for-profit company owned by the Colorado Alliance for Research Libraries (CARL), offers its subscribers (individuals or organizations) access to a recent selection from the ERIC database. The Dialog service also offers the complete ERIC database to its subscribers. Dialog currently offers the most powerful search capabilities for ERIC; it also offers similar search methods across all the databases the company offers. The search and retrieval methods offered by the nonprofit institutions on the Internet are subject to the availability of funding.

The following example shows how to use the ERIC database at the University of Saskatchewan, which offers a short tutorial and some advanced search capabilities.

1. Telnet from your Internet connection to `sklib.usask.ca`. (If you have access to this database from a Gopher menu, select the Telnet session from it.)

2. At the USERNAME prompt, enter **SONIA** and press Enter. The first screen you see should inform you that you are visiting the University of Saskatchewan Libraries' InfoAccess system.

3. On the first InfoAccess menu, you should see a menu item for education databases. Choose this option by typing **4** at the prompt and pressing Enter. Along with a few other education databases you may be interested in exploring later, you should see the option: ERIC (CIJE and RIE), 1983-. This option gives you access to bibliographic records in the ERIC database from 1983 to the present (CIJE and RIE are the two subsets of ERIC mentioned earlier).

   On this same screen are some tips on how to begin using InfoAccess and its search commands. Type **help** at the prompt and press Enter to display a summary of available commands.

> **NOTE**
>
> Although the on-screen note says that items listed with an ED (ERIC Document) number are available in the University of Saskatchewan library, over 900 other locations around the world also carry these microfiche documents. You may find some of these items in printed copies of conference proceedings and books—if your library owns them. You also can order ERIC documents from the ERIC Document Reproduction Service (EDRS). To find out the nearest location with ERIC microfiche collections or to get more information on ordering ERIC documents or journal articles, call ACCESS ERIC at 1-800-USE-ERIC.
>
> Item numbers with the prefix EJ are journal citations you can obtain from major university libraries or University Microform Incorporated (UMI). ACCESS ERIC can give you information about availability of journal articles from UMI. You may want to use the Internet to check the UnCover database (explained in Chapter 47, "The Virtual Library") to see whether UnCover can fax a copy of an article to you.

  4. To see the tutorial screen, enter **BEGINNER** at the prompt.

Now let's try a sample search to see what a basic search session looks like.

As mentioned on the tutorial screen, the default for searching means that if you don't specify a particular field to search, the search looks for the word string you entered in four different fields, including the author, title, descriptors, and identifiers. Try looking up some articles about science fairs.

Enter **f science fairs** at the prompt and press Enter.

ERIC found 111 titles! Because looking through all the titles would take a while, you can limit the search further by redoing the search and adding terms that might produce a list of fewer articles more closely related to your interests.

Assume that you are a parent and want information about science fairs that can help you assist your child in developing a science fair project. You can add the word *parent* to the search by reentering your search as **f science fairs & parent** (using and rather than the & does not work). This command retrieves any articles that have both the phrase *science fairs* and the word *parent* in any of the four default search fields (author, title, descriptors, and identifiers). This time you get 10 titles, which is more reasonable.

To view the results quickly, type **scan** (or **s**) and press Enter. The scan format displays a brief record including the ERIC accession number, author(s), title, and journal source information. (For more information on the scan display, enter **help scan** at any prompt.)

This search turns up an item called *Science Fairs: A Primer for Parents*, you can take a look at the longer display format by entering **list** and the number of the item. (To learn more about the list display, enter the **help list** command at any prompt.) You now see an abstract that briefly summarizes the article, giving you a better idea about whether you want to obtain this article.

If you're interested in other articles, you can scan through the rest of the titles and list (long display) any titles for which you want to read the abstracts. Or you can begin a new search at any prompt. To quit, just enter **quit** (or **q**) a couple of times at the command prompt to back up through the menus until your Telnet session closes.

As you probably realize, searching the ERIC database over the Internet helps you find answers to education-related topics from anywhere in the world and at any time of day (or night). Using the ERIC database from your home or office allows you to develop a list of references even before you enter a library. Sometimes, when I have a question about an education-related topic, I pop into ERIC, conduct a few searches, and spend some time reading the abstracts. Depending on my curiosity level, the summaries alone may answer a question. On other occasions, if I need more information, I can go to my local university library to find most of the journal articles and any of the ERIC documents.

Although this example used the University of Saskatchewan's ERIC database, two other sites offer the ERIC database: Syracuse University and Auburn University.

To connect to the ERIC database at Auburn University, your computer must support TN3270. If your site supports TN3270, enter **TN3270 auducacd.duc.auburn.edu** at your prompt. At the first screen, tab to **APPLICATION** and enter **01**. At the main menu, type **ERIC** and press Enter. Instructions on how to search appear on the screen. To end the TN3270 session, enter **STOP**. If you have access to Auburn's ERIC database, you can search all the ERIC files dating back to 1966.

AskERIC and the AskERIC Electronic Library

Two interesting ERIC services available to people involved in K–12 education are projects of the ERIC Clearinghouse on Information and Technology, located at Syracuse University in Syracuse, New York. AskERIC offers an Internet-based question-answering service for K–12 educators; the AskERIC Electronic Library offers a complementary Gopher/FTP-based electronic library of resources with answers to frequently asked questions, other education-related material, and access to ERIC information available at other ERIC clearinghouses and universities.

AskERIC, an E-Mail Question-Answering Service

AskERIC is a question-answering service available to K–12 educators, including teachers, library media specialists, and administrators. The AskERIC staff is experienced in using ERIC and other Internet-based resources relevant to K–12 education and can start you looking in the right places. The staff may even give you the precise information you need about K–12 education, learning, teaching, information technology, or education administration. You should receive replies to your questions within 48 hours (not counting holidays and weekends).

To use this service, all you need to do is e-mail your specific questions to AskERIC at askeric@ericir.syr.edu. Make sure that you include your personal e-mail address within the body of your message. If you are already experienced with Gophers, anonymous FTP, and using the ERIC database, you may want to look in the database first, reserving the tough questions for the AskERIC staff. Of course, if all this material is new to you, send the AskERIC staff your questions and they can help you get started.

The AskERIC Electronic Library

The AskERIC Electronic Library is a fairly recent addition to Internet-based resources. As a result, the service is still under development and subject to change. Because you probably are familiar with Gophers already, this section keeps the instructions to a minimum and focuses on what you can find in the AskERIC Electronic Library.

The AskERIC Electronic Library contains selected education-related information, including lesson plans, ERIC digests, AskERIC help sheets, AskERIC InfoGuides, archives for some education-related Listservs, access to other Gophers, access to online library catalogs, reference tools, and government information. The organization of these resources may change from time to time, but most of the changes will be because of the addition of new services and information.

If your UNIX host supports a Gopher client, you can connect directly to the AskERIC Electronic Library by entering **gopher ericir.syr.edu** at a UNIX prompt. Otherwise, you can Telnet directly to ericir.syr.edu (log in as gopher). You are not actually connected directly to the Gopher at this point, but after you enter your name at the next prompt, you can choose the Gopher (option 1); the AskERIC Electronic Library Gopher menu appears.

After you are connected to the AskERIC Electronic Library Gopher, you can begin exploring the various subdirectories, files, and links at this site. The following sections describe some of the most interesting items in this Gopher. You can also reach AskERIC through the WWW at http://eryx.syr.edu/.

News and Announcements About AskERIC and the Library

Check the News and Announcements About AskERIC and the Library directory to see the latest information about the electronic library. The directory includes a brief description of ERIC and AskERIC projects.

Library of Education Resources

Within the Library of Education Resources directory is access to full-text education information and pointers to other educational information. Within the Full Text Education Information directory are AskERIC help sheets, AskERIC InfoGuides, AskERIC lesson plans, and the *ERIC Directory of Information Centers*, which lists information about 400 national and international organizations providing information relevant to education. The *ERIC Directory of Information Centers* also includes information about locations offering access to ERIC microfiche, CD-ROMs, and the ERIC database in printed volumes and online. Also included are the *ERIC Review of K–12 Networking*, archives of messages from education-related Listservs (including EDNET-L, EDPOLYAN-L, EDTECH, K12ADMIN-L, KIDSPHERE-L, and LM_NET); access to a full-text, searchable database of the ERIC digests; and a recent survey on telecommunications and K–12 schools. You must explore this extensive library to see what information gems are hidden here for you.

Information on Vocational Education

The Information on Vocational Education directory contains information on policies, practices, and programs related to vocational education. The directory can help you introduce the world of work into the world of school.

ERIC Clearinghouse on Assessment and Evaluation

The ERIC Clearinghouse on Assessment and Evaluation directory links you to the Gopher at the Catholic University of America. This Gopher offers access to information about educational and psychological testing, including searchable databases with descriptions of available tests. These tests are listed in the Educational Testing Services Test File, the Buros and Pro-Ed Test Review Locators database (which offers references to reviews of specific tests), and the Measurement and Evaluation News.

ERIC on the Web

Many of ERICs clearinghouses are on the Web, and more are coming online soon. Here are the addresses of several:

- ERIC Clearinghouse on Assessment and Evaluation

  ```
  http://www.cua.edu/www/eric_ae/
  ```

- ERIC Clearinghouse on Elementary and Early Childhood

  ```
  http://ericps.ed.uiuc.edu/ericeece.html
  ```

- ERIC Clearinghouse on Reading and English

  ```
  http://www.indiana.edu/~eric_rec
  ```

- ERIC Clearinghouse on Rural Education and Small Schools

  ```
  http://aelvis.ael.org/~eric/eric.html
  ```

- ERIC Clearinghouse on Science and Mathematics

  ```
  http://gopher.ericse.ohio-state.edu/
  ```

- ERIC Clearinghouse on Urban Education

  ```
  http://eric-web.tc.columbia.edu/
  ```

- Central ERIC Gopher (OERI)

  ```
  gopher://gopher.ed.gov/11/programs/ERIC
  ```

Educational Resources and the Internet

More and more education-related information is coming online to add to the already existing flood of information. To keep up with the latest developments in educational resources, use the Web search tools, Veronica, and Gopher to search. Don't hesitate to ask your school or public librarians for assistance—keeping up with the latest information in education and educational technology is their job.

Campus-Wide Information Systems

52

by Judy Hallman

Suppose that you need a babysitter for the college basketball game next Friday, but you don't know what time the game starts; or that you are writing a paper and want to include descriptive information about your university. Where can you look for this information? Your campus-wide information system (CWIS) may be your best bet.

This chapter describes the contents of typical CWISes and addresses design and maintenance issues, topics that may be of interest to people who use CWISes, as well as those who provide these services. The chapter also suggests ways people can explore CWISes and participate in electronic discussions of CWIS-related issues.

Understanding a CWIS

A CWIS provides a wide range of campus information online, including sport schedules, campus facts and reports, job openings, and course catalogs. The information is accessible from virtually every workstation on the campus communications network. Many CWISes also are available on the Internet.

The following examples show the opening screen from the home page of the University of North Carolina at Chapel Hill (UNC-CH), which is typical of the variety of information a CWIS can provide. Figure 52.1 shows the home page as seen using a graphical World Wide Web (WWW) browser; the listing that starts at the bottom of this page shows the same page viewed using Lynx, a text-only browser.

> **NOTE**
>
> To try the UNC-CH information service, point your World Wide Web (WWW) browser to `http://www.unc.edu` or Telnet to `info.unc.edu` and log in as **info** (lowercase only).

This listing shows the UNC-CH home page seen through the text-only Lynx browser:

```
                  University of North Carolina
    [1]
    [2]Welcome to the University of North Carolina at Chapel Hill
    [3]Directories, News and Publications
    [4]Departments and Organizations
    [5]Libraries
    [6]Student Information
    [7]Faculty Information
    [8]Staff Information
    [9]Alumni Information
    [10]SunSITE and the Internet
```

```
[11]About the UNC-CH Home Page
[12]Help

[13]Mail to Webmaster

Last modified: 1995 Jan 5


Commands: Use arrow keys to move, '?' for help, 'q' to quit, '<-' to go back
 Arrow keys: Up and Down to move. Right to follow a link; Left to go back.
 H)elp O)ptions P)rint G)o M)ain screen Q)uit /=search [delete]=history list
```

FIGURE 52.1.

The home page of the UNC-CH WAIS, seen through a WWW graphical browser.

Exploring CWISes

Probably the easiest way to explore CWISes is to point your World Wide Web browser to the College and University Home Pages section (maintained by Christina DeMello, Massachusetts Institute of Technology) at the URL http://www.mit.edu:8001/people/cdemello/univ.html or the American Universities section (maintained by Mike Conlon, University of Florida) at the URL http://www.clas.ufl.edu/CLAS/american-universities.html. Or you can Telnet to info.unc.edu, log in as **info**, and select SunSITE and the Internet; a few collections are links in the Just Browsing section.

These lists provide only Web-based connections. To browse Gophers and Telnet-based services: from the UNC-Chapel Hill home page, select the Student, Faculty, or Staff section, select Global Resources, and then select Campus-Wide Information Systems. The first item (About the Campus-Wide Information Systems section) is a list of CWISes you can explore. You can also pick up a copy of this list by anonymous FTP to the URL ftp://sunsite.unc.edu/pub/docs/about-the-net/cwis/cwis-l (letter *l* is on the end). This list has been useful for people who are designing new services or contemplating major changes and who want to explore someone else's design. In addition to offering access information, the list gives the name of a contact person and describes the hardware and software the service uses. Not all CWISes are in the list—only those that have given permission for outsiders to access their services. I maintain the list using information from the electronic discussion group CWIS-L.

CWIS-L was established in January 1990 for discussing the creation and implementation of campus-wide information systems. The discussions on this list can be particularly informative for people who are interested in CWISes. To subscribe, send to listserv@msu.edu the following message:

```
subscribe cwis-l yourfirstname yourlastname
```

Messages sent to cwis-l@msu.edu go to the more than 1,200 people who are signed up for the list.

Reviewing CWIS Software

A variety of software was developed for the first CWISes. Cornell University's CUINFO, developed under the guidance of Steve Worona in 1982, was written in IBM system 370 assembler language to run on an IBM mainframe computer. Howard Strausss Princeton News Network (PNN) runs under a variety of operating systems and became quite popular in the late 1980s. Several campuses with DEC VAX computers developed CWISes using DEC's VTX product; some campuses with IBM mainframes used MUSIC/SP.

Around 1990, Massachusetts Institute of Technology developed TechInfo to run on a MacPlus with the goal of distributing responsibility for content to the information providers; for this reason, TechInfo drew a lot of attention.

Enter the Internet Gopher! The Internet Gopher, developed in 1991 at the University of Minnesota by Mark McCahill and his colleagues, revolutionized the CWIS world. The software is easy to install and runs on a variety of platforms. Using Gopher, you can develop a nice-looking system quickly and easily. Gopher also gives a CWIS user access to the world of Internet resources, as well as local campus information. Furthermore, some tools exist (such as WAIS, Veronica, and Jughead) to help Gopher users find information in a Gopher somewhere on the Internet.

Another particularly useful aspect of Gopher is that it uses client-server architecture to present information. Users can navigate through the information using the tools they have on their workstations. A server presents each database, and client software running on the user's workstation controls the user's interface to the databases. Thus, the user interface is different for each type of client and is natural to the user.

Gopher software has so many advantages that some of the earlier CWISes were reimplemented using Gopher. But Gopher isn't the end of the line in CWIS software.

The World Wide Web (WWW), a hypertext document delivery system, provides more function than Gopher. Most campuses today are initiating their CWISes with this system. The Netscape, Mosaic, and Cello graphical browsers (or clients) make WWW even more appealing. And the Lynx browser, developed at the University of Kansas, provides the textual information in a Web without the graphics. Thus, it is possible to develop high-quality CWISes that can be accessed in VT-100 mode by users who have older computers and network using modems. At the same time, users with high-end products (like UNIX workstations running Mosaic on the Internet) get a better view of the CWIS and more function. We can expect WWW clients for more platforms and continuing improvements in presentation and function. For more information on the WWW and its clients, see Chapter 28, "Navigating the World Wide Web."

One important aspect of CWIS software is the ease with which users can capture the information they see. With Web and Gopher software, you can capture files of interest very easily; you can save the files on the client computer, e-mail files to yourself or someone else, or download the files to a personal computer using a mainframe client. When someone asked me by e-mail about scholarships at UNC-CH, I was delighted to be able to e-mail back the section of the university publication about undergraduate scholarships from our CWIS.

It is clear that most CWISes are now being converted to the WWW. For example, Cornell discontinued use of its original CUINFO software in favor of a Gopher service, but quickly converted that to the WWW; UNC-Chapel Hill dropped its VTX service in July 1994 to provide only Gopher service, and converted the entry point for the CWIS from Gopher to the WWW in December 1994 (some of the underlying information is still in Gopher). In February 1995, MIT's College and University Home Pages section provided links to over 1,000 Webs, and that number is growing at a rapid rate.

Reviewing CWIS Resources

CWISes typically include a wide range of resources. Some of the different types of information that can be found in a CWIS are described in the following sections.

Popular Items

The most popular items in a CWIS tend to be job openings, directories, events, crime reports, bulletin boards, and items for sale. The following sample screen shows the Announcements, Buy/Sell, Rent, Lost/Found menu from the Appalachian State University CWIS.

```
Internet Gopher Information Client v2.0.14

                Announcements, Buy/Sell, Rent, Lost/Found

  --> 1.  Posting information to the Bulletin Board
      2.  Announcements of General Interest/
      3.  Buy/Sell, Trade, Give Away/
      4.  For Rent - Wanted To Rent/
      5.  Lost and Found Items/




Press ? for Help, q to Quit, u to go up a menu            Page: 1/1
```

Reference Information

Information used for reference is ideal for a CWIS and has the potential for reducing printing costs. Directories, class schedules, and course evaluations are items that may in the future appear only in CWISes, not on paper (currently, however, they are appearing in both forms). Reports, brochures, handbooks and guides, and policy and procedure manuals probably will continue to be published on paper but also be made available electronically for broader distribution and quick reference.

Newsletters and Journals

CWISes provide both wider distribution and archives for campus publications like newsletters and journals. In the past, printing costs have restricted distribution of scholarly works, but electronic publication enables world-wide distribution. In addition, searchable archives help users find and retrieve articles of interest.

Institution Promotion

The business of a campus is academics, and the CWIS provides a way to promote the campus's academic programs. Degree requirements, descriptions of courses, faculty bios, costs, scholarships, and alumni news is information of interest to people off-campus and on-campus. This feature is likely to become one of the most important areas of CWISes of the future as high school students explore CWISes to select colleges. It will be exciting to see how CWISes developed in the WWW use hypertext links (for example, linking courses to class schedules, course evaluations, and faculty biographies), and how CWISes use photos, sound recordings, and videos.

Counseling

Counseling services can be a particularly valuable and interesting enhancement to a CWIS. Cornell started a computer consulting service called *Dear Uncle Ezra* in 1986 in their CUINFO service. The online description of *Dear Uncle Ezra* includes the information shown here:

```
------------------------------------

D e a r     U n c l e     E z r a . . .

Do you want advice or information or help in finding something?  If so,
then ASK.  Uncle Ezra will try to provide the answer to any reasonable
question. Questions of general interest - altered for confidentiality -
will be posted for others to READ.  (You may send e-mail to Ezra at
unc@cornellc.cit.cornell.edu.)

------------------------------------
```

Dear Uncle Ezra is provided by the Office of the Vice President of Academic Programs, Campus Affairs, and Cornell Information Technologies (CIT). The service has been particularly popular; two books of the best of Uncle Ezra have been published.

Students feel more comfortable asking personal questions of a computer, avoiding direct, personal contact. To be effective, questions must be answered quickly, concisely, with sensitivity, and when appropriate, with a touch of humor. The postings to *Uncle Ezra* have been archived since 1986 and are searchable. The following screen sample shows a posting from February 1992 (the 18th of 64 postings in that month):

```
----------------------------------

--------------- Page 18 of 64 ----------------
Dear Uncle Ezra
Thanks.  Sometimes it helps so much just to know that someone's there to
listen in a caring way.
Someone you've helped
Dear Cared For,
You're welcome!  Your kind words show the beautiful caring in you, too.
Though beset by difficulties, the world still feels like a hopeful place when
we bend our energies toward helping each other - and our environment - in
whatever ways our skills and passions allow.
Uncle Ezra

----------------------------------
```

The investment of time and the commitment required to provide this type of service have hindered many campuses that would like to provide similar services. However, on the bright side, consulting services are showing up in community information systems—with a slightly different slant. Rather than allowing questions on any topic and directing all questions to one central source (like Uncle Ezra), the community systems are providing ask-an-expert services for questions in specific subject areas, like medicine, law, or auto mechanics. The questions are directed to experts who volunteer their time to find answers. The answer to a question is posted by the expert along with the original question, maintaining the confidentiality of the questioner.

Bulletin Boards

The WWW makes it easy to use bulletin boards (newsgroups) in a CWIS. The following two examples use the Lynx browser; the first example shows the unc. newsgroups and the second example shows a particular posting from the unc.support newsgroup.

```
unc.support newsgroups from the UNC-CH Web

                    BULLETIN BOARDS (NEWS GROUPS)

     * [1]unc.announce
     * [2]unc.chat
     * [3]unc.envr
     * [4]unc.facss
     * [5]unc.forum
     * [6]unc.help
     * [7]unc.ils
     * [8]unc.jomc
     * [9]unc.physics
     * [10]unc.support
     * [11]unc.test
     * [12]unc.sas-users
```

The following is a sample posting to the unc.support newsgroup at UNC-CH:

```
                    unc.studentjobs newsgroup???

    [1]Reply to: Judy Hallman

                 UNC.STUDENTJOBS NEWSGROUP???

    16 Feb 1995 16:56:48 -0000
    Supporting Guru
    Newsgroups:
          [2]unc.support
    [3]Reply to newsgroup(s)
To support list:

I see quite a few postings on this list about student jobs. It seems to me
it would be a good idea to have a newsgroup called something like
unc.studentjobs. I could then plug it into the Student Web page. What do
you think?

Judy Hallman (judy_hallman@unc.edu)
Office of Information Technology


Commands: Use arrow keys to move, '?' for help, 'q' to quit, '<-' to go back
  Arrow keys: Up and Down to move. Right to follow a link; Left to go back.
  H)elp O)ptions P)rint G)o M)ain screen Q)uit /=search [delete]=history list
```

Internet Resources

Some CWISes provide Internet resources—a feature that creates additional challenges to CWIS designers. How do users distinguish between information provided by the local service and information coming from somewhere else in the world? Is the distinction important? Does the presence of world-wide information obscure local information?

When determining how best to provide access to the world-wide resources of the Internet, consider the purpose of the CWIS. For example, the purpose of the UNC-CH information service is to provide local campus information. Off-campus information is clearly identified as such.

On the other hand, the developers of a new community information service for the Research Triangle area in North Carolina, called Triangle Free-Net, have taken a slightly different approach. Although the emphasis is on local information, the developers recognize a need to provide information at the state and global levels as well. At a subject level, the menu provides choices of local information, followed by a choice for state-wide information, and then a choice for global information, as shown in Figure 52.2.

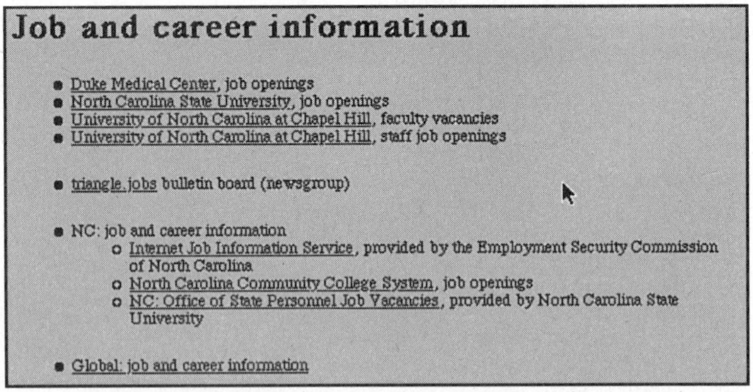

FIGURE 52.2.

The Triangle Free-Net has local as well as state and global levels.

Job and career information

- Duke Medical Center, job openings
- North Carolina State University, job openings
- University of North Carolina at Chapel Hill, faculty vacancies
- University of North Carolina at Chapel Hill, staff job openings

- triangle.jobs bulletin board (newsgroup)

- NC: job and career information
  - o Internet Job Information Service, provided by the Employment Security Commission of North Carolina
  - o North Carolina Community College System, job openings
  - o NC: Office of State Personnel Job Vacancies, provided by North Carolina State University

- Global: job and career information

NOTE

To try Triangle Free-Net, set your WWW browser to `http://tfnet.ils.unc.edu` or Telnet to `tfnet.ils.unc.edu` and log in as **lynx**.

Roadmaps and Statistics

A useful addition to a CWIS is a roadmap that provides an overview of available resources in the CWIS and their locations. The roadmap often is displayed as an outline. Some systems show usage statistics in the roadmap. Some systems use the roadmap to point out shortcuts to the information (like a "go to" or "jump to" phrase).

For a sample roadmap containing usage statistics, see North Carolina State University's (NCSU) WWW service, located at `http://www.ncsu.edu/info`. The following listing shows some selected items from a weekly report of usage statistics for a primary server, updated 19 February 1995. The sample screen shows the total transfers from each `Archive` section that has more than 10 accesses:

```
%Reqs %Byte  Bytes Sent   Requests   Archive Section
----- -----  -----------  --------   --------------------------------
 0.01  0.00       11638         23 | /../images/blueball.gif
 0.01  0.00        7992         10 | /../phonebook/
 0.67  0.34     1961693       1273 | /./
 0.06  0.24     1420668        110 | /acad/calendar.html
 0.01  0.02      123768         26 | /acad/exam_fa94.html
 0.02  0.01       46552         41 | /admin/policies/
 0.01  0.01       43875         16 | /admin/policies/software.html
 0.35  0.19     1113540        663 | /admissions_etc.html
 0.02  0.01       50738         35 | /author.html
```

```
0.14  0.07      386179      268 | /author/author.html
0.11  0.01       79366      206 | /author/greek-flag2.gif
0.01  0.00        2457       10 | /buildings/DAN.html
0.01  0.00       27596       12 | /cc/hware_svcs/
0.05  0.02       99547       95 | /cc/talks/mosaic/
0.03  0.02       95992       63 | /cc/talks/mosaic/definitions.html
0.01  0.00       14820       16 | /cc/talks/mosaic/from_home.html
0.02  0.01       53633       38 | /cc/talks/mosaic/mosaic.html
0.01  0.01       31621       20 | /cc/talks/mosaic/mosaic_start.html
0.02  0.01       32776       41 | /cc/talks/mosaic/spanning.html
0.02  0.01       72537       39 | /cc/talks/mosaic/travel.html
0.02  0.01       31504       33 | /cc/talks/mosaic/what-is-web.html
0.02  0.00       25235       39 | /cc/talks/mosaic/what_web.html
0.26  0.23     1320598      484 | /centers.html
0.01  0.00        2737       11 | /cgi-bin/mailto.pl/ccpuboff
4.31  4.32    25222686     8169 | /cgi-bin/phone/
0.08  0.01       71200      147 | /class/
0.01  0.01       82758       19 | /class/fall/PE/
0.12  0.02      144686      225 | /class/grades/
0.01  0.00       21044       17 | /class/grades/fall94/CE/
0.02  0.01       53756       38 | /class/grades/fall94/CH/
0.01  0.01       38826       20 | /class/grades/fall94/CH/CH.101.html
0.01  0.00       16368       13 | /class/grades/fall94/CH/CH.107.html
0.01  0.00        8622       10 | /class/grades/fall94/CH/CH.223.html
```

Maintaining a CWIS

Maintaining a CWIS is not as easy as most people think it should be. Converting information to a format that can be displayed clearly on the screen of the average person's computer (often called a *dumb terminal* or a workstation in *VT-100 mode*) presents some real challenges to CWIS service providers. Furthermore, as maintenance of information becomes more distributed over remote computers and a large number of information providers, it becomes more difficult for the service provider to ensure that the information in the CWIS is accurate and up to date.

Data Maintenance

The burden of maintaining the information in a CWIS database is shifting from the service provider to the information provider. In most early CWISes, essentially all the data resided on one machine and the service providers often did a lot of the maintenance work, copying files into the central database. MIT's TechInfo was one of the first CWISes designed to use a distributed database. WWW technology makes database distribution easy: just link the CWIS Web to the data on the information provider's machine. For this method to work, however, the information provider's machine must be on the Internet, up and running all the time, and running its own Web (or Gopher) server or some software the CWIS can handle.

Recent software (like the WWW) enables a service provider to give an information provider responsibility for maintaining data on a central server. The service provider simply gives the information provider permission to write into the appropriate directories or files, or creates a UNIX soft link from the user's directory to the WWW database.

Some campuses are beginning to allow the user of a CWIS to change information directly in the CWIS database. For example, at UNC-Chapel Hill, faculty, staff, and students can update their e-mail addresses in the campus directory.

Quality

As information providers assume more responsibility for the content of the database, the service provider has more difficulty ensuring the quality of the database. Written policies are becoming more important. Policies are needed to ensure that outdated information is replaced or removed. Similarly, policies are needed to ensure that the name of the person or organization to contact with questions about the information is provided, along with the date the information was last updated.

The University of Southern California has some policy and procedure documents, including a maintainer's agreement, online in its CWIS at the URL http://cwis.usc.edu in the Help section.

Before service providers link to other parts of the world for information, they must consider additional issues about quality. What if the information becomes inaccessible? What do you tell your users: "tough luck, that's not in our database?" You may want to tell users when the information they want to view is provided by a different computer. Doing so also gives you an opportunity to give credit to the source of the information. For example, in the UNC-CH service, under SunSITE and the Internet, in the Just Browsing section, the following item can be found:

```
The World Lecture Hall is a page at UT Austin Web Central that contains
links to pages created world-wide by faculty who are using the web to deliver
class materials.

In case you'd like to look at this one, it's at the URL http://www.utexas.edu
world/lecture/
```

Feedback

The quality of a service can be enhanced by providing a way for users either to tell information providers about difficulties they've had using information or to pass on compliments. Older systems typically enabled users to give feedback to information providers by showing the e-mail address of the information provider. Users could then give feedback by e-mail. But the Web makes the process more direct: the user can select an item on the page (usually a linkable e-mail address) that allows direct composition and submission of an e-mail message.

Tools and Standards

Information providers need more and better tools to help them convert files from the word processor or desktop publishing software they use to ASCII text or the HyperText Markup Language (HTML) used in WWW systems.

UNC-Chapel Hill is in the process of developing a toolbox for its users; it's at the URL `http://www.unc.edu/about/provider/provider.html`. You're welcome to use what we have.

Designing Pages and Menus

Page design is one of the more challenging aspects of providing a CWIS. Short, clear pages and consistency between pages are goals that are not always easy to achieve. Some suggestions for helping the user find the information he or she is looking for are given in the following sections.

Flowing Text versus Lists

Although one of the features of the WWW that sets it apart from the Gopher is hypertext links, presentation of a hierarchical database is often clearer in menus than in flowing text. Short simple lists, in alphabetic order, are easy to scan for information. If you are designing a Web page, remember that many people will be using the Lynx browser, so try to keep pages tight, without a lot of "white space" between lines.

Breadth versus Depth

Do you put a lot of items on a page so that you can have only a few layers, or do you keep the pages short and require the user to search through many pages to reach information? Neither method is satisfactory, but compromises are possible. Usually, 12 to 14 items are adequate to cover the categories on the home page (or main menu). If the titles are short and clear (such as *Student Information* and *Libraries*), the screen is not too heavy and users can get off to a good start. At lower levels, long pages actually can be better than short pages. For example, if a page requires the user to select a department, some users prefer to see all the departments listed in alphabetic order over a few screens rather than the arbitrary choices of *A–E, F–J*, and so on. A compromise: if the list is really long, is something like *Art to English* and *Folklore to Journalism*.

Titles and Hot Links

Short, clear titles generally are more effective than clever titles. Remember that not all users of CWISes have English as their native language and may not understand clever titles.

Using the title of a publication as the title of a list choice may seem appropriate, but titles—particularly of newsletters—are often not very descriptive. The UNC-CH CWIS uses the publisher's title but adds descriptive text when necessary; for example, *CAIS Studies (Computing and Information Services, Public Health)*. Similarly, some newsletters have columns that always have the same title, like *Helpful Hints*. These titles as list choices don't give the user useful information about the subject matter.

Titles can also give the user information about the location of the data itself, if the data is not part of the local database. In addition, the date the data was last updated can be provided in the item's title when that information cannot easily be included in the file itself.

With Web servers, be sure to make the text in the hypertext hot link meaningful; avoid phrases like *click here* because not everyone can point and click (Lynx users); in addition, such phrases break the readable flow of text.

Order of List Items

The order in which items appear in lists and the consistency of ordering from list to list are important. Some designers try to put the most important item first on the list and the least important item last. However, such lists may be harder to absorb—and people often disagree about what is the most important item. Alphabetic order shows no favoritism and provides consistency.

Use chronological order for periodicals, with the most recent as the first choice.

> **TIP**
>
> As the first item in a list, or as text preceding a list, an About... file can give an overview of available items, where the items come from, who is responsible for the items, and when they were last updated. A Web home page, for example, should contain the name of the service and the e-mail address of a contact person (although the latter is often the last item on the page).

Cross-Posting

Cross-posting is easy to do in both Gophers and the Web. For example, if the university catalog has a section on the mission of the university, you can put a link to that section in the section that talks about the university in general. Putting an item in more than one place can help people find what they need more easily.

Finding Information in a CWIS

One of the outstanding features of both the Gopher and the Web is the integration of Wide Area Information Servers (WAIS) into the system. Stand-alone WAIS databases are impressive, but the ease with which WAIS can be incorporated into Gophers and the Web is amazing. The information provider (or the service provider) identifies a block of information to make searchable (the block can include multiple files from different points in the database hierarchy).

Then the provider runs a fairly simple procedure to produce the index and adds the index choice to the appropriate menu.

Although the procedure that produces the index is simple to use, indexing is not always easy. How do you determine how big a block of information to index together? Does it make sense to index the entire CWIS database, mixing information about people (from the directory) with information about events and information (from publications)? Does it make sense to index all the campus publications together, mixing information from the course catalogs with information from the employee handbook? Does it even make sense to index all the job openings together, mixing faculty jobs with student jobs, and staff full-time jobs with staff part-time jobs?

You should consider two things when selecting items to include in a WAIS index: the headline or title that will appear in the hit list and the size of the information block the user will receive if he or she selects an item. In most cases, when you index (using the `waisindex` command), you use the `first_line` option to specify that the headline should be the first line of the file. But the first line of a file doesn't always provide enough information. At UNC-CH, job postings have the job title in the first line, but neither the job title nor the descriptive text indicates whether the job is full-time, part-time, faculty, or staff. If a program inserted that type of information into the first line, some descriptive information in a long title may be lost. The choice of UNC-CH was to index jobs separately by type.

Similarly, consider what happens when you perform a search, get back a list of items that match your request, and then select an item from that list. How big a file do you get: the information for one course, the entire section for an academic department, or an entire book? Clearly, a small file that hones in on the area of interest benefits the searcher, but that advantage requires the information provider to divide the text into the small files. Similarly, when you find the information you want, you may want to download the whole book at one time instead of downloading one section at a time. One solution is for the provider to offer large sections of text both ways.

Using Existing Resources Effectively

The World Wide Web and Gopher make it so easy to include all the information resources of the world in a CWIS that some campuses are providing rather complicated and muddled services. Information from the far corners of the world may mix with campus information. In their haste to provide links to anything interesting, some service providers create pages containing items that aren't relevant to the subject of the page.

Some of the most appealing information services have a clear statement of purpose and are well designed to fulfill that purpose; they are not cluttered with other information. For example, the purpose of the CWIS at UNC-CH is to provide campus information. The menu choice SunSITE and the Internet provides access to a variety of off-campus services (see Figure 52.3).

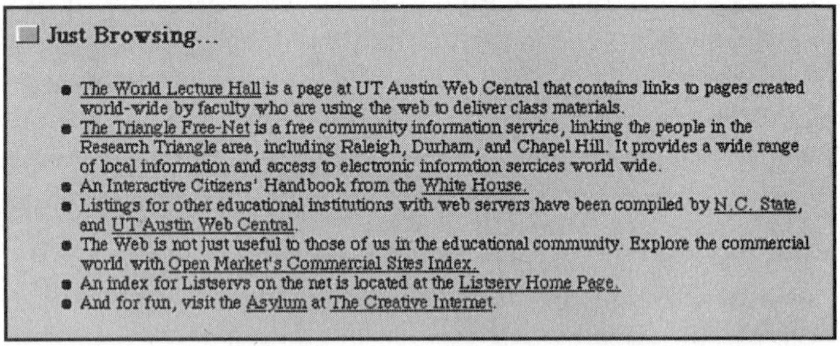

FIGURE 52.3.

With this service, you know what's what: all sites are clearly identified.

☐ **Just Browsing...**

- The World Lecture Hall is a page at UT Austin Web Central that contains links to pages created world-wide by faculty who are using the web to deliver class materials.
- The Triangle Free-Net is a free community information service, linking the people in the Research Triangle area, including Raleigh, Durham, and Chapel Hill. It provides a wide range of local information and access to electronic information services world wide.
- An Interactive Citizens' Handbook from the White House.
- Listings for other educational institutions with web servers have been compiled by N.C. State, and UT Austin Web Central.
- The Web is not just useful to those of us in the educational community. Explore the commercial world with Open Market's Commercial Sites Index.
- An index for Listservs on the net is located at the Listserv Home Page.
- And for fun, visit the Asylum at The Creative Internet.

On the other hand, the purpose of the Triangle Free-Net service (accessible from the SunSITE and the Internet page) is to provide local community information and access to information world wide. As discussed earlier in this chapter, the subject menus in Triangle Free-Net clearly identify local, state, and global information. Figure 52.4 shows the information available in Triangle Free-Net.

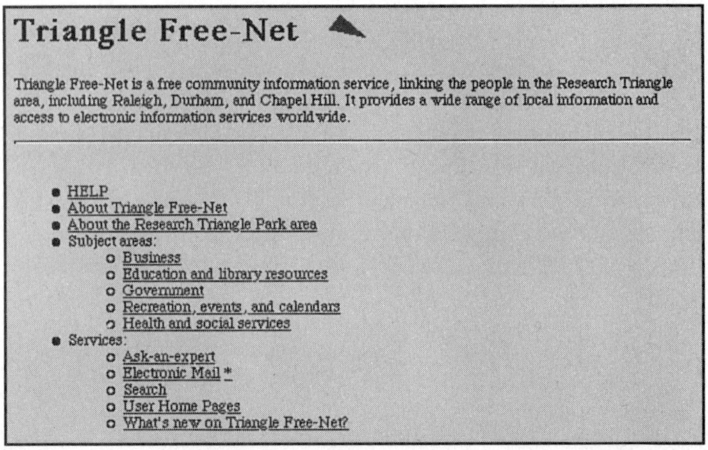

FIGURE 52.4.

The easy-to-use Triangle Free-Net page.

Triangle Free-Net

Triangle Free-Net is a free community information service, linking the people in the Research Triangle area, including Raleigh, Durham, and Chapel Hill. It provides a wide range of local information and access to electronic information services worldwide.

- HELP
- About Triangle Free-Net
- About the Research Triangle Park area
- Subject areas:
  - Business
  - Education and library resources
  - Government
  - Recreation, events, and calendars
  - Health and social services
- Services:
  - Ask-an-expert
  - Electronic Mail *
  - Search
  - User Home Pages
  - What's new on Triangle Free-Net?

Librarians are doing a good job of developing collections of useful electronic information: libraries without walls. The NCSU Libraries Webbed Information System, shown in Figure 52.5, is a good example. It has a clear statement of purpose and effective organization.

FIGURE 52.5.

A combination of graphics and clear organization makes the NCSU Libraries Webbed Information System easy to use.

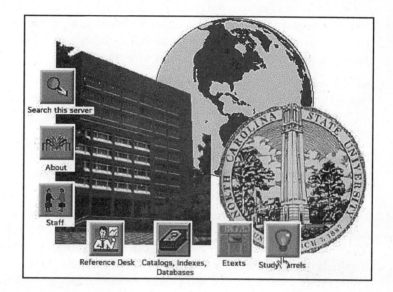

Managing a CWIS

Who decides what information a service should provide, how the information should be structured, how the pages should look, what graphics to use, and the policies and procedures for maintaining the service?

Typically, a CWIS has one central point of responsibility: a small group in the campus library or the campus computing center. The service providers usually depend on the campus community for advice and feedback. Often, this process is accomplished through a formal advisory committee that meets regularly. An alternative is a volunteer advisory committee that is solicited for advice by electronic mail whenever the need arises. The latter method works well when the service providers are considering major changes or alternative menu designs. Meetings can be particularly helpful when working out options, like choosing an initial design for the home page or main menu.

UNC-Chapel Hill has an informal group, called the Web-Walkers, that meets once a month. The Web-Walkers work together to review and revise the look and feel of the UNC-CH home page and its underlying presentations. The group has drafted a set of guidelines for developing pages for the UNC-CH Web and is working on a toolbox for the campus. More information about the Web-Walkers is available at the URL http://www.unc.edu/about/walkers/walkers.html.

Looking to the Future

CWISes are changing from "nice to have" services to essential public relations tools, providing outreach for the campuses and establishing their corporate images. The CWIS promotes the campus's programs, research, and faculty; it also showcases the campus's services to attract graduate students, grants, and partnerships, as well as undergraduate students. The CWIS also provides a means of sustaining relationships with alumni.

As community information services (such as Free-Nets) become available to the public, more high school students and alumni will use the community resources to explore campus information. Information about admission requirements, degrees, courses, faculty, expenses, and research projects will be available and searchable.

University outreach programs (such as correspondence courses) will become even more valuable as more people view the offerings, eligibility requirements, and procedures for enrolling from their homes.

Distance learning is becoming a reality. In North Carolina, classroom instruction has already moved off-campus. Using the North Carolina Research and Education Network (NC-REN) Video Network, students in Asheville can participate in classes taught in Wilmington, hundreds of miles away. TV cameras in the classrooms on both ends and voice-activated microphones allow full audio and visual communication among teachers and students at all participating sites. Several of the campuses of the University of North Carolina, private schools and colleges, and some high schools are on the NC-REN. North Carolina has made a commitment to provide services of this type throughout the state; the North Carolina Information Highway currently is being implemented.

Like libraries without walls, the national information highway will make universities into classrooms without walls. Campus-wide information systems are laying the groundwork for campuses' participation in the information highway of the future and establishing their corporate images world wide.

Distance Education

53

by Jill H. Ellsworth

Distance education entails conducting educational activities across geographical space—where the teacher or professor is not in the same classroom (or perhaps even in the same country) as the students. Distance education can involve a variety of activities, including courses, seminars, and workshops. It can also involve all levels of education, from kindergarten through postgraduate, both as formal degree-oriented activity or as informal activities outside a coordinated curriculum.

The growing popularity and availability of the Internet has vastly expanded the potential of distance education. Before the Internet became so popular, distance education was usually delivered using television, correspondence, or even radio. Now the Internet enhances these activities and serves as a delivery vehicle in its own right.

Distance education involves both alpha and beta learning activities. *Alpha learning* is usually characterized by the delivery of factual information, analogous in a regular classroom to a lecture or demonstration. Alpha activities involve the presentation of new material, concepts, facts, and information. *Beta learning* is analogous to laboratory exercises, discussions, or activities designed to support or reinforce alpha leaning. Beta activities involve working with information already covered, but in new ways or with new techniques.

Many children in Australia attend school by way of distance education, often using two-way radio systems. High school students in Alaska, Saskatchewan, and Finland have simultaneous online classes and meet face-to-face only at graduation. University students all over the world have taken courses and received degrees using distance education, primarily through broadcast television and correspondence. Recently, denizens of the Internet have been taking courses using e-mail, the World Wide Web, Gopher, FTP, and computer conferencing, all without leaving home or the office.

Characteristics of Distance Education

Using the Internet for educational activities has several advantages:

- High speed
- Not time reliant
- Not place reliant
- Can be synchronous or asynchronous
- Access to information structured by learner

The Internet has significantly increased the speed of distance education activities. Long-distance Internet messages can be sent and received in just seconds or minutes, as opposed to paper-based correspondence that can take days or weeks.

Students and teachers can exchange messages on the Internet in quick cycles. The communication tends to be more interactive and less didactic (that is, flowing one way from teacher to learner).

Distance education, supported by the Internet, helps both teacher and student by allowing each to have access at convenient times. Teacher and student don't have to be online simultaneously. For example, a student can "hand in" an assignment using the Internet at 3:00 A.M. The teacher can look at the work and respond at a convenient time in his or her own schedule. Time-shifting allows for individual schedules and eliminates concerns about time zone differences.

Distance education isn't place reliant. Student access to the Internet can be from home, from work, or from a classroom a continent away. This location can change several times during a course with no loss of continuity. There is no need for all parties to be in the same place at the same time.

Distance education can by synchronous or asynchronous. Communication can take place over time, in series, or it can take place simultaneously online. For example, in one course, the teacher came online in North America at 9:00 A.M., with students online in Finland at the same time (for them, 4:00 P.M.). They were all online together, discussing the reading assignment. The assignment, a long document, had been made available by FTP so that the students could read it before the online interactive discussion.

In a traditional learning situation, the teacher controls access to information, and often there is little encouragement to explore. The Internet enhances student learning by allowing for learning style differences. This is particularly true for documents written in HTML, which provides for both linear and nonlinear access to and use of information.

Many courses make information available over the WWW, Gopher, and FTP. This allows students to explore the material at their own pace, in the order that makes the most sense to them. Increasingly, sounds, pictures, and movies in the form of `.au`, `.wav`, `.jpg`, `.mpeg`, `.pcx`, or `.gif` files are available, and instructors are using FTP, the WWW, and portable document exchange for these files.

One of the most difficult logistical issues in traditional distance education has been access to books, materials, and libraries. For example, when delivery involved only television broadcasts, written materials were sent out, but libraries were sometimes difficult to access. However, using the Internet, students can use ERIC or the Colorado Alliance of Research Libraries system (CARL), which provides bibliographic access to thousands of magazines and journals through the UnCover service. It also provides full-text articles online and through a fax service. It is possible to use libraries world wide for catalog and index searches, as well as for some full-text retrieval. The thousands of databases and archives discussed throughout this book are available as teaching and learning resources.

Computer-Mediated Communication

When we communicate through the medium of the computer, we are using computer-mediated communication (CMC). With this type of communication, it's often difficult to convey inflection, emotion, and irony using the written word. Using CMC in Internet distance education creates the need for some special considerations. When we make a joke face to face, we can see whether the person is smiling or looking amused. On the Internet, we don't see these visual cues, so users have invented ways of communicating emotions, gestures, and expressions. The most common *communicons* are smiley faces, or smileys—this is a smiling face :). Tip your head to the left to see it. This is winking smiley ;). Gestural communications are often placed in brackets like this: [shaking my head in amazement].

Elements of the Internet Virtual Classroom

Internet distance education is increasingly being called the *virtual classroom*. The following sections look at some of the elements of a virtual classroom using the Internet.

E-Mail

E-mail is used in distance education in either one-on-one or group mailings. E-mail is personal messaging in which students and teachers can work one on one. The teacher and student can exchange messages about assignments, academic advice, or even degree planning. E-mail can supplement regular educational activities. For example, middle-school students can have e-mail pen-pals in Bosnia and get a very personal view of the unrest there.

E-mail can also support distributed messaging using Listserv or other software. This broadcast messaging allows everyone to benefit from the views, questions, and answers of others. This can be analogous to in-class discussion and presentations.

Computer Conferencing

Computer conferencing on the Internet is similar to dial-up bulletin board systems. It's characterized by public postings under various subjects, forming virtual conversations on numerous topics. These can be course related or related to logistical issues (such as times and assignments) and can allow for some educational activities not directly related to courses (such as discussions of current events).

Computer conferencing can support collaborative learning projects between students who may never meet face to face. The conferencing system, in combination with other elements, can allow students to write papers, carry out problem-solving activities, and even prepare presentations.

Gopher

Gopher supports a large number of distance learning activities. It provides menu access to texts and images, as well as connections to other Gopher links. Gopher provides access to many of the Internet databases, archives, and libraries that form the great Internet storehouse of information. By giving students information on relevant Gophers, teachers can provide massive amounts of up-to-date learning materials.

FTP

Many distance education undertakings use FTP sites to maintain ASCII and binary materials. This allows students to place and retrieve formatted word processing files, spreadsheet and database files, executable files, photographic images, graphics, and other binary and ASCII files.

FTP greatly enhances the ability to make images, programs, software, demonstrations, and texts available. Programs including uuencode, bit FTP, and Gophermail make it possible to e-mail binary files and to retrieve information from FTP and Gopher sites. As technology advances, full-motion video files also will be more readily available.

World Wide Web

World Wide Web sites or pages are becoming the most popular adjunct to distance learning with the Internet. Web pages allow for nonlinear access to materials through materials written in the HyperText Markup Language (HTML).

Web pages can contain text, images, movies, sounds, and more, making them ideally suited for the transmission of distance learning materials and information. (More information about the Web and HTML can be found in Chapter 28, "Navigating the World Wide Web.")

Resources for Distance Education

There are plenty of Internet resources available for users with an interest in distance education. Many of these listings are taken from Dr. E's Eclectic Compendium of Electronic Resources for Adult/Distance Education (http://www.oak-ridge.com/ierdrep1.html). These are the primary Listserv-based resources for distance educators:

- **AEDnet:** The Adult Education Network is an international electronic network that includes approximately 980 individuals, from 415 sites, located in 21 countries. Users may subscribe to listserv@alpha.acast.nova.edu.
- **DEOS-L:** The International Discussion Forum for Distance Learning currently has in excess of 1,400 subscribers in 47 countries. The American Center for Study of

Distance Education sponsors this large, diverse distance education list. Subscribe by way of `listserv@psuvm.psu.edu`.

■ **DEOSNEWS:** The Distance Education Online Symposium from `listserv@psuvm.psu.edu`. This electronic publication is from The American Center for the Study of Distance Education at Pennsylvania State University. It organizes DEOS and publishes *The American Journal of Distance Education*.

■ **DISTED:** The *Journal of Distance Education and Communication* from `listserv@uwavm.u.washington.edu`. The online *Journal of Distance Education and Communication* broadly covers distance education, from formal to informal education. Geographically disadvantaged learners, K–12, and postsecondary learners are covered.

Here are some additional lists and electronic journals of interest:

■ **ADLTED-L:** The Canadian Adult Education Network

```
listserv@max.cc.uregina.edu
```

■ **ALTLEARN:** Alternative Approaches to Learning Discussion

```
listserv@sjuvm.bitnet
listserv@sjuvm.stjohns.edu
```

■ **ASAT-EVA:** Distance Education Evaluation Group

```
listserv@unlvm.unl.edu
listserv@unlvm.bitnet
```

■ **AUDIOGRAPHICS-L:** Audiographics in Distance Education

```
listserv@cln.etc.bc.ca
```

■ **COLICDE:** Distance Education Research Bulletin

```
colicde-request@unixg.ubc.ca
```

■ **DERR-L:** Distance Education Research Roundtable

```
listserv@cmuvm.csv.cmich.edu
```

■ **EDISTA:** Educacion a Distancia

```
listserv@usachvm1.bitnet
```

■ **JTE-L:** Journal of Technology Education

```
listserv@vtvm1.cc.vt.edu
```

■ **NLA:** National Literacy Advocacy List

```
majordomo@world.std.com
```

■ **RESODLAA:** Research special interest group of the Open & Distance Learning Association of Australia

```
listserv@usq.edu.au
```

■ **TESLIT-L:** Adult Education & Literacy Test Literature

```
listserv@cunyvm.bitnet
listserv@cunyvm.cuny.edu
```

Here is a short list of Usenet groups of interest:

- ■ `alt.adult.literacy`: Adult literacy learners, tutors, and instructors
- ■ `alt.education.distance`: Learning over networks
- ■ `alt.education.research`: Educational research
- ■ `alt.education.university.vision2020`: The future of university education
- ■ `misc.education.adult`: Adult education discussion
- ■ `misc.education.multimedia`: Multimedia's role in education

Following are some World Wide Web pages of interest to distance educators:

■ AEDNET list archives:

```
http://alpha.acast.nova.edu/education/aednet.html
```

■ Association for Experiential Education Web Pages:

```
http://www.princeton.edu/~rcurtis/aeedown.html
```

■ Commonwealth of Learning's (COL) WWW server:

```
http://www.col.org
```

■ Distance Education Instructional Technology Group at the University of Hawaii:

```
http://www.deit.hawaii.edu/deit.html
```

■ Distance Education Related Web Links Form the Nuance Group:

```
http://www.access.digex.net/~nuance/index.html
```

■ Dr. E's Eclectic Compendium of Electronic Resources for Adult/Distance Education:

```
http://www.oak-ridge.com/ierdrep1.html
```

■ Globewide Network Academy:

```
http://uu-gna.mit.edu:8001/uu-gna/index.html
```

■ National Institute for Literacy:

```
http://novel.nifl.gov
```

■ National Resource Centre for Adult Education and Community Learning (New Zealand):

```
http://actrix.gen.nz/users/nrc/index.html
```

■ Nova Southeastern University Distance Education items:

```
http://alpha.acast.nova.edu/education/distance.html
```

■ Open University:

```
http://hcrl.open.ac.uk/ou/ouhome.html
```

■ TeleEducation, NB Distance Education Resources:

```
http://ollc.mta.ca/disted.html
```

■ Virtual Online University:

```
http://core.symnet.net/~VOU
```

■ World Lecture Hall:

```
http://wwwhost.cc.utexas.edu/world/instruction/index.html
```

■ Yahoo:

```
http://www.yahoo.com/Education/On_line_Teaching_and_Learning/
```

The National Distance Learning Center offers information on distance learning programs and resources for K–12, higher and continuing education, and teleconferences. Telnet to ndlc.occ.uky.edu and log in as ndlc.

Here is a short list of some Gopher resources you may find useful:

- **St. John's University:** learning styles and educational information:

```
gopher://sjumusic.stjohns.edu/1-GOP/%40lsi%3alsi.menu
```

- **OTAN:** The Outreach and Technical Assistance Network:

```
gopher://gopher.scoe.otan.dni.us/1D-1%3a2598%3aOTAN%20Resource%20Centers
```

- **Distance Education Resources from OISE:**

```
gopher://porpoise.oise.on.ca/11/resources/IRes4Ed/resources/distance
```

- **University of Wisconsin:** Extension database of distance education information and resources:

```
gopher://gopher.uwex.edu/11/distanceed
```

Following are some books of interest:

Burgess, William. *Oryx Guide to Distance Learning.* Oryx Press, Phoenix AZ, 1994.

The Electronic University: A Guide to Distance Learning Programs. Princeton, NJ: Peterson's Guides, 1993.

Sullivan, Eugene. *Adult Learner's Guide to Alternative and External Degree Programs.* Oryx Press, 1993.

The Future of Distance Education

Distance education is moving toward virtual reality, where the teacher and students all "meet" in a virtual classroom, using applications that include Multiple User Dungeons (MUDs), Multiuser Object-Oriented environments (MOOs), various teleconferencing programs, and virtual WWW places created using Virtual Reality Transfer Protocol (VRTP). Other technologies used include SLATE, which is a collaborative multimedia mail/white board, Internet Relay Chat (IRC), CU-SeeMe, and Internet Radio. These technologies currently exist, but require considerable bandwidth and, in some cases, special hardware.

MUDs are programs that allow users to interact in real time in a text-based virtual environment, similar to those used in text-based adventure games. Users can talk with one another, move around, use objects, and take on different personas. Unlike MUDs, MOOs use both text and graphics.

Distance education is on the verge of entering a new era of both quality and quantity caused by the environment the Internet has provided.

PART

X

Using the Internet: Community and Government

Virtual Communities: ECHO and the WELL

*by James Barnett
and Cliff Figallo*

According to one of the many wildly varying Internet statistics, there are about 20 million people online. Many of them are online through a connection at work or school, but I'll wager the majority aren't there for stock quotes, encyclopedias, or newsfeed: they're there for the people—for the human interaction so easily made possible with the crudest terminal, computer, and modem components. Why do people end up hanging around online for hours, days, and even years? The Internet's biggest resource is not its information sources, shareware, or recipes; it's the people online and the things they have to say. As people spend less and less time in public spaces, other than the bare minimum (such as at work, in the mall, and at the supermarket), they want more and more to talk, converse, joke, and flirt with other people; *computer-mediated communication (CMC)* is remarkably effective at this.

What's the worst punishment in prison? Solitary—no human contact. Humans are social by nature, and as progress rolls on in the form of more strip malls and outlet centers—and less actual "downtowns"—there are fewer public spaces for people to just hang out.

People are longing for interaction, sexual and otherwise (party lines make a lot of money). People are desperate to communicate. Even if they're not desperate, who wouldn't like the chance to participate in a good conversation, one that reaches much further than everyday chitchat? What if this conversation were available 24 hours a day? ECHO (East Coast Hang Out) offers just that.

ECHO

ECHO, which takes its tone from its location, is a conference system based in New York City's Greenwich Village. ECHO came into existence in March 1990 at the hands of founder and "cybermama," Stacy Horn. A professor at NYU's Interactive Telecommunications Program, Horn started ECHO after working for 10 years as a telecommunications analyst. Inspired by the WELL (a popular California-based conferencing system that Cliff Figallo talks a bit about later in this chapter), she started ECHO so that she "could stay home and write books and in between, pop online and have all these interesting people to talk to." She looks at ECHO as "an electronic cultural salon, like Gertrude Stein's living room in Paris." Although conversation in ECHO's Whitney or Culture conferences may live up to such ambitions, I'm not so sure about, say, the stream-of-consciousness rants in the brilliantly puerile Plain Wrapper conference (see the section entitled, "Conferences on ECHO.")

I stumbled across ECHO in the summer of 1991, reading an article in a local free weekly. I bought my first modem literally the next day and immediately signed up; I was enthralled, sometimes racking up monthly tallies of 60 hours. I never left; I now can count my hours offline. I've seen ECHO go from 7 modems and no Internet connectivity to 55 modems and a T-1 link to the Internet. At least nowadays, thanks to the fact that I'm co-host of several conferences, I don't have to imagine my ECHO bill growing bigger and bigger as the hours pile up.

As in any virtual community, ECHO's strength is in the quality of its users' postings. I haven't found any other place online that has the same high level of sharp, edgy, playful wit. ECHO also has a high percentage of female participants—about 40 percent; the percentage for hosts is about 50 percent. This mix of the sexes (compared to the usual boy's club ratios) makes the tone of conversation different than anywhere else I've been online. Male Answer Syndrome still rears its ugly head, but information isn't the only thing swapped; stories, ideas, and conversations are. I can't tell you exactly how it's different, but there's a dialog on ECHO that flows, ebbs, and has a life.

Out of humble hardware (four PCs, an Internet feed, many phone lines, and modems) comes a system that people of all persuasions log in to—not only from New York, but from Massachusetts, California, Montana, Saudi Arabia, Paris, and South Africa. However, ECHO is definitely a product of New York; users send real-time messages that pop up on the recipient's terminal with three beeps and a *"YO!!! This message comes from…."* As Echoid (what the people on ECHO call themselves) Lena Dixon puts it, "That ECHO is a superior and eccentric piece of BBS should be expected. There is, after all, only one New York. Life here plays out hard and fast. Isn't it appropriate that ECHO would reflect that?"

Echoids are students, office managers, journalists, authors, artists, TV producers, choreographers, doctors, musicians, entrepreneurs, general contractors, clerks, lawyers, teachers, playwrights, programmers, marketers, and forensic pathologists. A busy night on ECHO shows 50 or 60 users online at a time. Hundreds, sometimes thousands, of responses are posted daily. ECHO, like a lot of online services, is busiest after 11 P.M. The city doesn't sleep.

ECHO's 4,000 users frequent more than 50 conferences, such as the Elsewhere conference, for Echoids interested in travel or who live somewhere other than New York City and its environs. Inside conferences are items, which are discussion topics (such as, "England, and London, Especially"). Items contain responses; each response is a user's turn in the conversation (such as my story about the last time I was in London).

People from ECHO see each other in person a lot, too: an average week sees at least one f2f (face-to-face) group get-together. There's been an all-ECHO f2f every two weeks since 1991, housed at various downtown New York taverns. There are also regular East Village, Brooklyn, and Under 30 f2fs, as well as ECHO-wide special events such as dances, picnics, bowling, and the well-publicized welcome home party celebrating convicted hacker Phiber Optik's return to civilian life.

The first two months on ECHO cost the usual price of one ($19.95). The $19.95 includes the first 30 hours of usage ($13.75 for students and seniors). After 30 hours, ECHO is then $1.00 per hour, with a maximum fee of $48.95, for which usage is unlimited ($42.95 for students and seniors). Full Internet access costs a one-time access fee of $25 and an additional $5 a month above ECHO usage fees. SLIP/PPP accounts also are available ($25.00 setup fee and $25.00 a month for unlimited use). The phone numbers are given here:

2,400 baud 212-989-8411
9,600 baud 212-989-3124
14,400 baud 212-989-3142
28,800 baud 212-989-8239
For more information: 212-255-3839 (voice)

The Form of Communication

Personally, I have never hung out at a place like the bar in "Cheers," a place where I knew there would always be someone I could talk to—until I got on ECHO, that is. The Internet is not just a place where people blaze from FTP site to WWW server; there are plenty of places along the way to "sit and rest a while." My own particular hangout is ECHO, New York City's answer to the WELL. My observations here are based on the years I've spent there.

> **NOTE**
>
> Throughout this chapter are several real-life messages that actually appeared on ECHO. To protect the identities of the authors, their usernames have been changed.

The following is something ECHO Powerwoman wrote back when her online handle was still `msjad`:

```
7:33) msjad                                       14-AUG-91   16:47
I just figured out my persistent deja vu on Echo.

Echo is like being back in the college dorm!!!!

People awake 24 hours a day, willing to bullshit about Life, Art,
and where you can get a picture transferred to iron-on paper when
you want to Redecorate Your Room.

In my "real life", people aren't like that anymore. My friends talk
about "practical things" - where to send their kids to school, coops
and mutual funds.

I am not in that place yet in my life (and maybe never will be).

This can be called "perpetual hip" or "developmental arrest,"
depending on one's point of view.

My friends have no time to write strange, free associational verse.
They have car pool arrangements to make.

So, here I am. Where else is there a conversation going on about
The FUGS???

What a strange place!  But hits the spot.
```

In college, a group of my friends and I would hang out at our pal Andy's house almost nightly for several hours. We discussed whatever, usually in front of the TV and with a few beers. Brilliant, hysterical things came out of those conversations, or at least we thought so; there was a level of interaction that only comes from a group discussion with a room full of great people. After graduation, as we split geographically, I lost that interaction. I was without the precious resource of great conversation, and I realized how rare it was. With ECHO, I gained it back, but on a much larger scale. Now there are 4,000 of us, and it's a much bigger living room, albeit one linked by phone lines. The following is another example:

```
- - - - - 57:65) Sandy                              26-DEC-93  22:48
There are 3 special characteristics of Echo for me:    1) the
opportunity to express silly to serious thoughts in writing
whenever there's something I want to say (often) with the
belief that  someone, somewhere will read it with some degree
of interest or resonance.

2) the fact that I'm communicating with many people with one
post. that  people may have an interest in what I say without
having to have a  relationship of some kind with me. I like that
and like to be part of  others' audience in return.

3) conversely, getting to know people's thoughts and feelings
without  (or before) knowing them. Developing an interest in
people based on more  than the standard categorizations of age,
occupation, looks and gender.

Footnote to 1. the writing means you get to think before (or
after) you  write (for some of us) and the oppt'y. to think about
what others have  written - even scroll back and reread. This
is so different from  conversation. And often more satisfying. I
think this is what makes our non-Echoid  friends or intimates
puzzled and perhaps resentful.
- - - - -
```

This form of communication, the hybrid of speaking and writing that has no name yet, is more appealing than either of its progenitors in a lot of ways. You don't have to regret not thinking of a perfect response that instantly crystallizes your thoughts; you can reason, think over a question, try several times until you get it right, and write a response. At the same time, the immediacy of CMC means you don't have to wait for your written words to make their way to others by mail or for their responses to reach you. If the person you're responding to happens to be online at the same time you are, he or she can respond quickly. This "written conversation" can progress quite rapidly.

Conference software also can add levels to conversation you don't have in real life. In an online discussion, not only can participants collect their thoughts into a written response, but they can also send each other real-time, private messages (a *yo* in ECHO parlance), seen by only the recipient. In a real-life conversation, you might have to make do with a quick glance at your fellow conspirator.

This "writing" form lends itself to people opening up about themselves. I've learned more about my fellow Echoids through our years of postings than I would have in any other circumstance of knowing anyone the same amount of time. I know more about some Echoids whom I don't even like than I do about some of my closest offline friends.

Some people like to socialize at a distance. You don't have to get close until you want to; you can trade ideas with online acquaintances you wouldn't necessarily want to have coffee with, but whose opinions you still value.

Given a safe distance, people unload their psyches. Some people regret this when they meet in person and find that their anonymity is far less than they thought; others let the deep confessions stand. One Echoid refers to that early time—before people know others that they're posting to, before people recognize other names online—as "the electronic confessional."

When I was new to ECHO, my father had died a year before, and the memory was fairly fresh in my mind. Opening up in the conference Panscan about his death seemed to me a momentous event; and without ECHO, I might not have prodded my thoughts to coalesce into a cohesive statement that summed up how I felt. I've reread my posting recently, and it's not that revelatory. At the time, though, it may have been the first time I'd really thought over and communicated how I'd felt.

Not only does CMC allow you to participate in conversations you might never have encountered in person, but it is also a great leveler. I've corresponded comfortably with people I would be intimidated to meet in person. Without the physical cues, you meet mind-to-mind and also agewise. Before ECHO, my friends were just a few years older or younger than I. Now that age span has grown to several decades.

You get to recognize people, to know people from their words and their thoughts, not their appearances. Your first impression is of someone's brain, not of their face. This strips communication to its bare minimum; but you lose all the nuances of conversation, the way a point can be elucidated by a little nonverbal gesture.

All you have to communicate with online is words. If you're sloppy with your words, you may not be able to successfully express yourself; the people who communicate most successfully online are good writers. Okay writing skills are part of the cost of admission to fully participate; the form is not democratic in this way.

Membership in a virtual community such as ECHO also presupposes a certain level of financial wealth—you have to be able to afford a computer, modem, phone line, monthly fee, and so on. As the Internet reaches further into society with the availability of publicly accessible Internet-connected machines (say, in public libraries) for those who can't afford their own, some of the entry barriers may change and allow more people to successfully participate.

How This Form Builds Relationships

Sometimes, I come across little tidbits while Net surfing that I think my pals would want to read, and I forward them, the same as I clip and mail items from the newspaper. This sharing of information is like lending a cup of sugar to a neighbor. In fact, ECHO *is* a community.

ECHO provides an efficient way of finding people who share similar interests. In the real world, you have to join a club and go to meetings to meet others who are enthusiasts like you. Now you can just walk over to the computer and turn on the modem.

You can get to know people before meeting them in person. Companies are moving to virtual offices; why shouldn't there be virtual water coolers? As more and more people work from their home offices, they get less and less human interaction. A modem might help satisfy that need to talk to others. If I'm working alone at home, for example, there aren't any brief conversations in the kitchen—no chats about the news or last night's game. So I pop up a telecom window and log on.

Virtual and real relationships bleed into each other. Knowing people online and offline tends to make you act more real. People really get to know you because your words aren't as "inhibited."

Dating online happens, too. You converse much more frequently over e-mail, which tends to accelerate your relationship. The same kind of late-night, lengthy conversations happen, but you get a chance to know someone before actually meeting him or her.

As with any community or network of relationships, there are house rules (known as *netiquette*). Get used to that. Most communities are run by people (similar to hosts on a network). However, remember that you are your own words, meaning that you are responsible for what you write. This is a new frontier, and everything's still up in the air. Various groups, such as the Electronic Frontier Foundation (EFF) and the Society for Electronic Access (SEA), have formed to keep the speech as free as possible.

The Net community can become the evening's entertainment; that is, conversation occurs instead of the television talking at you. The online atmosphere is like a pub—like conversation with a stenographer present (so that you can go back and read the transcript). Invariably, the first thing I do when I get online is to see who's on. It's like seeing who's in the bar.

NOTE

ECHO's history goes back to 1990, and so do some of its posts. Although posts aren't archived, they stay on record until deleted.

How Is ECHO a Community?

People have spent a good deal of time and money to get the ECHO community. They're curious. They're also motivated and will pitch in to benefit the community. For example, no one (or almost no one) ever got paid to write a FAQ (Frequently Asked Question). ECHO, like a small town, also has gossip. After f2fs, we're all a bunch of teens, ripping each other apart, commenting on what each other wears. Lisa J. Cooley says, "Some of us have created that small town on ECHO—gossip, maliciousness, and supportiveness. And we have all the characters of a typical small town." However, people look out for and care about each other. For example, I'll recommend a record I think other members of a music conference might like. A post about a life difficulty brings many sympathetic responses.

The difference between ECHO and a real community is that ECHO is self selecting; people want to be there, or they wouldn't pay the money. So they might work harder toward a better community than people whose geographical living place is determined by a lot of things other than a simple desire to live there. Geographical proximity doesn't mean you'll become pals with those near you. I've lived in my current apartment for several months and haven't said more than *hiya* to any of my neighbors. You can carry the ECHO community with you; if you move away, you're only a local Internet provider away from your pals. Echoids have moved to California from New York, and the common thread of ECHO stays with them.

Similar to a small town, if you step out of line, someone will tell you about it. You don't have to expect the police to take care of everyone because the citizens do. For example, if you don't follow the "house rules," a host can change your password so that you can't log on again. People band together against threats to their community—for example, to oust a particularly disruptive member who's decided to use ECHO as a social testing ground for his scatological rantings.

People look for something different from their virtual-community relationships. Some want to talk shop or hobbies; some want to enter into lengthy, deep conversations about grand topics; some want to gleefully spout stream-of-consciousness rants; some want to get to know others offline; and some want conversation to be anything but serious. A well-rounded virtual community can offer all these things.

ECHO's frequent in-person get-togethers round out one's knowledge of the people behind the postings. This enhances the online experience and strengthens the feelings of community between the people there, perhaps in turn drawing people to additional f2fs and more insightful posts.

As ECHO gets larger, it gets more diffuse. The core users of ECHO have been there through the Internet/media boom. More members mean more posts, which means there will be more to read. However, ECHO's size (not too big or too small) means that there are more people there to post from their diverse viewpoints—but so many that more posts are made than the user has time to read. That is, unless you try to keep up with every single post on all of ECHO. Judicious conference-joining is encouraged.

Community comes from familiarity. Reading people's posts day in and day out lets you get to know them better (unlike Usenet, where you skim volumes of messages, making it harder to get to know people). Friendships can come out of such familiarity.

How Can a Virtual Community Be Important?

The effect of words typed on a screen (see the following example) is more powerful than one might think. I've screamed at the screen, I've chortled, and I've had my evening ruined by things I've read on ECHO. They're just words on a screen, sure—but there are feelings behind those words.

```
57:28) Aimee (And Co.)                       06-DEC-93  22:40
Earlier this year, when I was pregnant, I was hospitalized to
help fight a  virus that really had me down for the count. It was
a really scary time  - even though my doctor told us that the
baby was fine, I had my doubts. I hated being in the hospital,
and felt very lonely. My family was not  terrifically
supportive.

I was just ready to work myself up into a real pity party when
the phone  rang. It was Rwanga, who had called my house,
gotten the news from Bill,  and called because 'the WIT women
were wondering where I was, and if I was  okay'.

That was the first time, but certainly not the last time, that I
really  felt part of a community that went beyond words on a
screen. A community  that rejoiced with us at our wedding, and
at the birth of our son. A place  that saved me from going
cuckoo when I was in the house with a newborn,  and thought I'd
never be able to carry on an adult conversation again.

I know that I'll be able to show Jeff a record of his entry into
the world  - and all the people who were there to help
welcome him. And we joke  that he'll laugh at the 'primitive
ascii interface'. But I also hope that  he'll be touched, and
encouraged by the people, many of whom he'll never  'meet',
who were so thrilled to hear that he'd joined this planet.

I was so very glad that you were there to share our joy then.
And  grateful - no, honored - I can't quite find the words
here. All I know  is that I'm crying here just remembering the
outpouring of good wishes and  emotions. It meant - and means
- so much to me.
```

```
57:29) Aimee (And Co.)                                   07-DEC-93
10:09
Oh, please - someone else post in here!

I've stopped crying....I promise.
```

Since I've been on ECHO, I've seen people band together to offer support for a stabbing victim and to cheer the arrival of new births. I've also heard from a companion of an Echoid who had passed away and wanted to archive her beloved's collected ECHO writings.

The process of writing helps one think through problems and find solutions; it's easier to get motivated to write something out in response to a question, item, or posting than to write for yourself or to a friend. Sometimes the act of writing out thoughts can make you understand much better how you feel.

You get amusing conversation—and more. The more people you talk to in the world, the more you learn about the world. Something someone mentions offhandedly can change your entire life. By exposing yourself to more conversation, you expose yourself to more chances to learn, more chances to stumble on a nugget of information that could change your life—and learning about others' lives can give you insight on your own. But then, I could just be rationalizing. Spending many, many hours a month of your free time typing furiously and staring at a screen full of words teaches you to rationalize pretty quickly.

Personally, my life would be completely different had I not come across ECHO. I've met my current girlfriend there, formed a band, and made a circle of friends. Right after college, ECHO softened the blow of leaving the secure college community and of relieving the lost feeling I had after coming to New York.

As Echoid Janet Tingey says, "I've made friends here that I want to have for the rest of my life. Now, if lifelong friends aren't a serious effect on your life…. I can't imagine any other way, in this town, that I could have met so many people whom I like so much. I wonder if Stacy [Horn] really, really understands what she's accomplished here."

The Future of Virtual Communities

As more and more people come online, I think we'll see more and more conference-based virtual communities. The existing ones like ECHO will grow larger; within them, more and more subcommunities will pop up—like ECHO's Under 30 conference. When I started on ECHO in 1991, such a conference wouldn't have even been possible.

The tremendous growth of the World Wide Web (WWW) opens up all sorts of possibilities: there are larval Web-MOOs (WOOs) and Web-based conferencing systems in place as I write this, and thanks to the open-endedness of the WWW, they'll only become more sophisticated. The possibilities for adding multimedia content to text-based conferencing are exciting; an item response can be side by side with a picture of the writer or linked to a QuickTime movie of a party.

But no matter what kind of bells and whistles are on the cutting edge, text-only virtual communities won't die out. As fast as the fastest modems or ISDN lines are, there'll always be users with old equipment and a relatively slow connection to the Internet.

Cheap local Internet access providers are popping up everywhere (which is a very, very good thing), but for the ECHO or other conferencing systems, Internet access is only the icing on the cake. Their purpose isn't to solely provide an Internet connection, but to create a place for people to get to know each other and converse in depth. Especially as the number of Internet users swells, the worth of a comfortable space to call home can only increase.

Conferences on ECHO

The following conferences are currently on ECHO; conferences tend to come and go and hosts change, so *caveat emptor*. Note that the descriptions (in quotation marks) of the conferences are the hosts' descriptions.

> **NOTE**
>
> Not all conferences are listed, but this list should give you an idea of ECHO's variety. ECHO hosts' handles are used if they have them.

2600

"A place to talk about 2600 magazine and the growing hacker community."
Host:	Emmanuel Goldstein
Item 2	Off The Hook radio program, Wednesdays 10 to 11 P.M., WBAI (99.5 FM)
Item 4	The Hacker Forum
Item 5	COCOTS—Plague or what ?!

Ads

This conference lists special offers for Echoids only.
Host:	Stacy Horn
Item 3	American Symphony Orchestra
Item 5	The Children's Museum of Manhattan
Item 7	The New Museum of Contemporary Art

Books

Hosts:	M.G. Lord and Berg Man of Alcatraz
Item 2	Thomas Pynchon
Item 63	What I'm Reading Right Now…
Item 77	Book Design

Central

This is the conference you see when you log in to ECHO. It has discussions of importance to all users, as well as general "what's happening in your life?" items.

Host:	Stacy Horn
Item 138	Pointers to Items in Other Conferences
Item 139	Through the Peephole
Item 140	New Users! INTRODUCE Yourselves!

Classifieds

Host:	SuZin
Item 1	Cheap and Free
Item 63	Where do I buy a…?
Item 111	Jobs AVAILABLE

Computers

"Where people go to gripe, recommend, ask advice, and play guru."

Host:	Kevin Krooss
Item 91	You're so NeXT
Item 115	Driveway hardware rebuilding at R&Y's place
Item 177	Good Marks! (For Products/Vendors/Service People Who Deliver!)

Culture

"It's about the little and big things you stay up late talking about in somebody's kitchen at a big party…and you think you're going to leave but you just want to say one more thing…"

Hosts:	The Strange Apparatus and Topper
Item 387	Reasons To Be Depressed Again and Again
Item 380	Connoisseurship of Everyday Objects
Item 449	Life's Little Rituals

Don't Panic

"The goofy conference where fun-lovin' Echoids go to gently mock the other conferences and to make puns on the word *goat*."

Host:	Kilgore Trout
Item 44	Items that Are Too Stupid, even for Plain

Item 52   The HATE conference
Item 53   LAMBADA

Elsewhere

"The conference for those of you not in NY and those of you who wish they weren't."

Hosts: camel, cham, and Mal
Item 157   It's 4:00 AM. Do You Know Where Your Bagels Are?
Item 170   Those Elsewhere Things You just _can't_ find in NYC...
Item 184   Wanderlust and the Armchair Traveler

Feedback

This is the conference where Echoids discuss what they love and hate about ECHO, as well as where ECHO's policies are discussed.
Hosts: Abby Bowen and Sue Grady
Item 63   (52) Lurkers of the World, Unite!
Item 3   What I Don't Like About ECHO
Item 42   Private Conferences on ECHO

Food

"Hungry? This conference is for you!"
Host: Blu
Item 32   STUPID COOKING QUESTIONS
Item 29   The Best in Cooking Equipment
Item 10   What a Friend We Have in Cheeses <tm jimb>

Group

Group is a private group therapy conference; e-mail yvette for information.
Host: Yvette Colon, M.S.W. (yvette)

Health

Host: B.J. Mora, M.D. (beej)
Item 3   Diets
Item 13   Vision Quests (Eye Care)
Item 37   Vitamins'R'Us: Too Much Is Never Enough?

Humor

Host: Danny Lieberman
Item 2   Tell me a Funny Story
Item 52   The Bush Vomit Haikus. The Compleat Set
Item 7   That's not Funny, That's SICK!

Internet

"This conference is where you can find all kinds of questions and answers about the wild, wacky, wonderful, information-rich world of the Internet!"

Hosts: MoNo and Gabriel
Item 2   Internet? What's That?
Item 22   OTIS: Net Accessible Art—{Not Just SuZin's Cat}
Item 24   News Readers: What's Available?

Into the Mystic

This is ECHO's spirituality conference.

Hosts: Yankee Rose and Dorje
Item 2   What Does Spirituality Mean to You?
Item 26   Tarot Cards (ported from Culture)
Item 48   Number One Profound Experiences

Jewish

This conference is intended for people interested in Jewish religion and culture.

Host: David S. Green
Item 9   Women and Judaism
Item 16   Intermarriage
Item 46   Passover!

Lambda

"It's the Gay '90s where queer issues are everyone's issues. Bring an open mind and an honest opinion. (Sense of humor optional but highly recommended.)"

Hosts: Jane Doe and Stephen Kopp
Item 7   Domestic Partnership
Item 40   Homo-Happenings in NYC
Item 44   Queer Families—Found or Turkey Basted?

Love

"The thinking person's guide to the most enigmatic emotion."

Hosts: Neandergal and Janet Tingey
Item 29   When Did You Know it Was Over?
Item 30   Ask Dr. Lovelady : {+
Item 108   First Kisses

Matrix

"An Opinionated Review and Catalog of Other Online Places, Virtual Communities, and Other Virtual Entities."

Hosts: Steve B. and Spaceman Spiff
Item 51   Virtual Organizations

Item 56   Prodigy: Plodigy no Longer?
Item 57   ECHO as a Virtual Community

Media

Host: Xixax
Item 44   NY Radio: Yesterday, Today, and Tomorrow
Item 6   The Thin Line Between News and Entertainment
Item 56   Pixelvision: Kid Vid Tech and Other Low-Tech Media

Moe (Men on ECHO)

Moe is a private conference for men only. E-mail The Lonesome Drifter for entry.
Host: The Lonesome Drifter

Movies & TV (M/TV)

"For fans, buffs, industry types, and hoi polloi."
Hosts: Jonathan Hayes and Erin, a.k.a. EB
Item 6   Bad Movies To Rent <at your own risk>
Item 12   LINK (a new kind of Movie Ping Pong)
Item 25   The 90210 Item: Walsh with Some Strangers

Music

Hosts: Jneil and Joey X
Item 2   What's New? Hype Your Latest Musical Discovery
Item 178   What I'm Listening to Right Now
Item 184   Music For The Hypno-Tiki Bachelor Pad.

New York

This conference is all about the best and worst NYC has to offer.
Host: Twang and James Sanders
Item 94   Park Slope—Theme Park For Yuppies?
Item 127   Celebrity Watch Continued
Item 161   RESTAURANT REVIEWS II

Off Central

This conference is for public announcements that aren't quite as important as the ones in Central, such as f2f organizing.
Host: Lisa J. Cooley
Item 3   What should you *REALLY* be doing right now?
Item 7   The ECHO Addicts Online Support Network
Item 139   So, Are We Gonna Go Bowling this Year, Or What????

Panscan

Panscan is ECHO's combination of art, philosophy, and mail art conferences. Or something.

Host:	Panman
Item 4	Postal Art History
Item 25	The E-Mail Poem—An Online Experiment
Item 253	The Sociology of ECHO

Parents

This conference is "for sharing thoughts and experiences about being a parent or having parents."

Hosts:	Sarah/M and Dan Swerdlow
Item 2	Why Have Children (or Not)?
Item 8	Teenagers—Threat or Menace?
Item 35	PARENTING OUR PARENTS

Performance

"This conference is a free-for-all exchange of opinions and ideas about performance."

Hosts:	Mark Russell and flying fish
Item 7	American Splendor: Trash Culture and Wrestlemania
Item 27	Back-Stage Slap Fights: The Dish Item

Plain Wrapper

"The F*** You! Anti-Conference."

Hosts:	Scottso and JoRo
Item 828	C'mon! Admit it! You STILL HATE YOURSELF!
Item 906	The Second Most Boring Item On ECHO
Item 969	RAGING BLOWHOLE DEBATES
Item 773	Son of Revenge of the Angst Item
Item 781	The Stickboy Mocking Club
Item 571	THE BERT CONVY FAN CLUB
Item 599	That Really Really Fat Guy with the Braids Died

Politics

This conference is about global, local, and personal politics.

Host:	Margaret
Item 98	The Politics of Education
Item 113	The Rodney King Verdict
Item 153	Clinton In Transition: How's He Doing <tm ed koch>

Psych

This conference covers everything you want to know (but are afraid to ask) about psychology, psychiatry, psychotherapy, psychoanalysis, and the psyche.

Hosts: Neandergal (Liz Margoshes, Ph.D.) and Dr. Willie (Willie Kai Yee, M.D.)
Item 3   Finding the Right Therapist
Item 13   Lucid Dreams
Item 123 Did Your Parents Destroy Your Life?

Science

"Where Echoids express and satisfy their curiosity about the physical universe and the everyday manifestations of science."

Host: Gabriel
Item 20   Getting It Up—Space Technology
Item 83   Calling All Urban Zoologists!
Item 53   Sociobiology—The Beast Within

Sex

Sex is a private conference. E-mail KZ for entry.

Host: KZ

SF

"Exploring the imaginary universe."

Hosts: Danny Lieberman and Barbara Krasnoff
Item 20   Philip K Dick: Not Just Yer Average Dead SF Writer
Item 42   Why Do You Still Read SF? (That stuff'll rot yer brain kid!)
Item 57   Samurai in Orbit: The Misuse of Japanese Culture in Science Fiction

Sonic Cynic

"What's overrated, who's a joke, where not to go, and how do you make a Martini?"

Host: Amy McCutchin
Item 14   Pimple, Corns, Dandruff? You May Be Entitled to Cash Rewards
Item 17   Sonic Cynic MARTINI—only f2f
Item 22   Cat-fight!

Sports

"There's room for everyone to play."

Hosts: Don King and The Strange Apparatus
Item 8   Sports and the New York Media Experience
Item 30   NFL
Item 39   YANKEES MOVING WHERE?

Under 30

"The is the place where 20somethings, slackers, gen xers, and other members of our godforsaken generation talk about life, sex, families, careers, dope, and other fun stuff."

Under 30 is private, and restricted to, yes, those under 30.

Host: SuZin
Item 1   Can I See Some ID, Please? (The Introductions Item)
Item 17   CALLING ALL PARTY PEOPLE THE TIME HAS COME!
Item 43   PRANKS!!!!

Unix 'N' Caucus

ASCII a stupid question, get a stupid ANSI.
(Caucus is ECHO's conferencing program).

Host: Jim Baumbach
Item 11   Caucus BUGS <well, it bugs me, anyway!>
Item 14   Problems Sending Mail Outside ECHO?
Item 19   StUPiD UNiX TrICkS

Welcome!

"A place to introduce yourself and get basic technical help."

Host: Eric Hochman
Item 6   Frequently Asked Questions: The 20 Most Common ECHO Questions
Item 23   New Users! *I N T R O D U C E* Yourselves!
Item 31   ECHO Staff: Who To Call/Email For What

Wishcraft

"Team up with us to reach your personal dreams: a conference for brainstorming and barnraising."

Hosts: Arsinoe and Barbara Lynn
Item 2   Notes on "Wishcraft" Method and Philosophy
Item 11   Hard Times: What To Do When the Going Is Rough?
Item 13   Neandergal's Wish

WIT (Women in Technology)

"WIT's candid, informative, and supportive discussions on a broad range of topics are both enlightening and compelling. What makes this conference unique is that it is for women only."

WIT is a private conference. E-mail the hosts for entry.

Hosts: Faith Florer and Lynn Varsell

Working

A conference about "the world of making, doing, fetching, carrying, buying, selling, earning, and spending that we call work."
Host: David S. Green
Item 5   Freelancers Lounge
Item 7   The Recession
Item 21   When and Why To Change Jobs?

Writing

"Where established professionals can network and exchange information and newer writers can gain support and help."
Host: Lisa J. Cooley
Item 2   "Unblocking" and Other Agonies
Item 76   How Did You Get Started (And What's Your Workday Really Like?)
Item 88   Scriptwriters forum

Zines

"Where to go to talk about DIY print media and the like. Yeah! and stuff like dat!"
Hosts: Spingo and Xixax
Item 9   Non-Print 'Zines—ezines and hyperzines, etc.
Item 11   The Office Supply and Copier Machine Fetish
Item 14   The Zine Community

Zulu

"A less restful alternative to sleep," Zulu is an invitation-only, late-night hangout that's only open from 11:00 P.M. to 7:30 A.M.
Hosts: Jim Baumbach and Topper
Item 2   Best Fun
Item 10   What I shoulda posted in that OTHER item
Item 17   Situations Seen, Conversations Overheard

Whole Earth 'Lectronic Link (the WELL)

The WELL (Whole Earth 'Lectronic Link) was founded in 1985 and grew out of concepts practiced and promoted by Whole Earth publications of Sausalito, California. These print publications, which included several Whole Earth catalogs and the *Whole Earth Review* magazine, had long recognized their readers not only as customers, but as valuable contributors to their innovative and leading-edge information databases and articles. From the beginning, the WELL was envisioned by its founders, Stewart Brand and Larry Brilliant, as an "online community," regionally based in the San Francisco area, but with global access. Rather than provide prepackaged online products and "features" to sell to its customers, Whole Earth's idea was to attract interesting people to the WELL and sell them mutual access to each other.

Today, the WELL is known worldwide as an example of how community interaction—the exchange of knowledge and ideas through an electronic network—can be an end in itself in online systems, stimulating the development of new concepts and viewpoints. The WELL's product is its community and its digital conversations. It is a recognized major cultural center on the global Internet and has been referred to, in the metaphor of the times, as "the Route 66 of the Information Highway."

From its early days, the WELL's management has focused on encouraging user involvement in all aspects of the WELL's development, from policy to software. It has hired most of its staff from the ranks of former users. It also has bartered free time on the WELL for expertise and cooperation in the creation of user-friendly tools and entertaining online participation. WELL staff members maintain a conspicuous and participatory presence online, blurring the line between staff and user community.

There are many overlapping subcommunities on the WELL. Of note are the Deadheads—a community that arrived largely intact on the WELL in its early years—as well as the very knowledgeable, well-connected population of networking policy experts and consultants who frequent such conferences as Telecommunications, Information Technology, and Electronic Frontier Foundation (EFF). The creation of the EFF—the influential nonprofit advocate of fair play in the use and development of electronic communications law and policy—was inspired largely by ongoing discussions on the WELL of free speech and privacy issues in the online environment.

As of this writing, the WELL claims close to 10,000 paying subscribers and supports several hundred fully or partially subsidized accounts for users who "host" conferences and provide technical services. Compared to the CompuServes and GEnies of the online world, the WELL has been a small, slow-growing system. Slow growth allowed its community aspects to develop. However, the days of undercapitalization appear to be over, and its complex, but very flexible, interface may get a face-lift soon. At the beginning of 1994, it was announced that the WELL had been purchased in full by its former half-owner, the Rosewood Stone group—a well-endowed company that promises to invest in technical upgrades to ensure good system reliability and performance, and to provide an alternative, easy-to-use graphical front end. The obstacles that have deterred many users from joining or staying on the WELL and have kept the WELL's growth to a minimum for 10 years may soon disappear, positioning the system for very accelerated growth.

Technically, the WELL offers text-based conferences and e-mail running on a UNIX system, and uses a software interface called Picospan to support its conference/topic structure. It has more than 200 public conferences, as well as many private conferences. It categorizes its conferences as follows:

- Conferences on Social Responsibility and Politics
- Media and Communications
- Magazines, Publications, and 'Zines
- Business and Livelihood
- Body, Mind, and Health
- Cultures and Languages
- Of Place and Places
- Interactions
- Arts and Letters
- Recreation
- Entertainment
- Education, Science, and Planning
- Grateful Dead
- Computers
- Conferences About the WELL Itself
- Private Conferences

Each conference covers a general subject area and has a "host" who helps moderate or stimulate discussion and keeps the conference's "topics" up to date. Some busy conferences can have as many as several hundred topics, and topics can run into the hundreds of responses. Conferences also can feature databases of relevant files and articles that can be displayed in read-only formats or downloaded.

Users of the WELL have the option of directly logging in to Picospan or UNIX shells. UNIX software tools are available for use by WELL users, but knowledge in their use is not necessary to participate in conferences or e-mail.

WELL users also have full Internet access, including the capability to Telnet to other sites, FTP files, and use network search tools such as the WELL's Gopher client, Veronica, and the WWW.

WELL Charges and Billing

The WELL is accessible through direct dial modems, through the CompuServe X.25 packet network, and through Telnet over the Internet. Its current fee structure is as follows:

- $15/month service charge
- $2/hour WELL use
- $4/hour CompuServe Packet Network (CPN) surcharge for use within the 48 contiguous United States (300, 1,200, 2,400, or 9,600 baud access) (plus miscellaneous CPN surcharges for Alaskan, Hawaiian, or international use)

■ $1/hour connect surcharge for 9,600 bps access

■ Storage exceeding the initial allotment of 512K is billed at $20/month for each meg (1,024K)

The WELL prefers billing to MasterCard or Visa and charges a $25.00 registration fee for invoiced accounts.

New accounts are credited their initial five hours of WELL use at $2 an hour.

The WELLGopher

The WELL also supports its own Gopher site, the WELLGopher, accessible through the Internet. Its contents come largely from articles and material published in Whole Earth publications and from submissions by WELL members; so it is mostly original material, not linked in from other Gopher servers. WELLGopher's current top-level menu looks like this:

```
 1.    About this gopherspace (including a quick "How To" guide)/
 2.    See the latest additions to this gopherspace/
 3.    Search all menus on the WELLgopher <?>
 4.    Internet Outbound (*New!*)/
 5.    Art/
 6.    Business in Cyberspace: Commercial Ventures on the Matrix/
 7.    Communications/
 8.    Community/
 9.    Cyberpunk and Postmodern Culture/
10.    Environmental Issues and Ideas/
11.    Grateful Dead/
12.    Hacking/
13.    The Matrix (under construction!)/
14.    The Military, its People, Policies, and Practices/
15.    Politics/
16.    Publications (includes 'zines like FactSheet 5)/
17.    Science/
18.    The WELL itself/
19.    Whole Earth Review, the Maga'zine/
20.    Whole Systems/
```

This is an example of a second-tier menu:

```
Community
 1.    About this area of the WELLgopher.
 2.    Civic Nets, Community Nets, Free-Nets, and ToasterNets/
 3.    Advice about Privacy and Security for People New to Cyberspace.
 4.    An (almost) complete Privacy Toolkit, by Robert Luhn.
 5.    Innkeeping in Cyberspace, by John Coate.
 6.    Stephen Gaskin's The Farm as reported by Al Gore.
 7.    Protection and the Internet, by Steve Cisler.
```

```
8.    The WELL: Small Town on the Internet Highway System, by Cliff Figallo
9.    Virtual Communities, an essay by Howard Rheingold.
10.   Book List of Communities, Co-ops, Collectives 2/93.
11.   The Presidio-converting a Military Base to a Public Park/
12.   A Biased Timeline of the Counter-Culture, by Judith Goldsmith/
13.   About EFF-Austin (Grassroots Organizing in the Virtual Community)/
```

Contacting the WELL

Voice: 415-332-4335

Direct dial modem—2,400 bps max: 415-332-6106
                        —9,600 bps   415-332-8410

CompuServe Packet System: call 1-800-848-8980 to find your local CompuServe access number. Have your modem dial that number and enter **well** at the Host> prompt.

From the Internet, Telnet to well.sf.ca.us.

Mail address: The WELL
                        1750 Bridgeway #200
                        Sausalito, CA 94965.

Community Computing and Free-Nets

55

by Terrence J. Miller

Computers now supply us with a considerable number of ways to extend methods of communicating door-to-door, city-to-city, state-to-state, and especially country-to-country. Online international computer communications are making English everyone's second language—even, as the joke goes, for the English. Computing by modem, according to one cybermaster of the race, follows newspapers, radio, and television as the fourth medium. Unlike the others, he points out, this medium is truly interactive.

That cybermaster is National Public Telecomputing Network (NPTN) president and Free-Net founder Thomas M. Grundner, Ed.D., who calls community computing the niche between the SysOp owned-and-operated local electronic bulletin board and commercial online services, such as CompuServe, Delphi, Prodigy, America Online, and GEnie. (Free-Net is a registered service mark of the National Public Telecomputing Network.)

And What a Niche It Is

Internet expert Michael Strangelove, author, columnist, and publisher, calls Free-Nets "a growing phenomenon in North America that many expect will promote and strengthen democracy, enhance literacy, facilitate free access to publicly funded information and research, increase the frequency and ease of communication between voters and their elected officials, and decrease the isolation and loneliness that many experience in the midst of sprawling urban areas."

Strangelove could have added that Free-Nets are fun. Besides plates loaded with meat and potatoes, all Free-Nets offer a wide selection of desserts, ranging from forums that are as healthy as sugar- and fat-free muffins to others as addictive as chocolate bars with almonds.

Local bulletin board systems (BBSes) offer forums on dozens and even hundreds of topics. The truly local boards can be reached without paying long-distance rates. These BBSes often are free, but the better ones tend to be fee-based, just as clubs charge dues to users. Charges range from flat monthly and annual fees to time charges, or any variation thereof. The total easily can exceed that of commercial services.

The general manager at one commercial service told me that local boards are in serious competition because of their range of forums, some of which enable you to leave messages that are flashed around the world. They also offer up to several gigabytes of files, ranging from the Bible to graphic sexology. Many of these independent boards specialize in topics like genealogy, amateur radio, UNIX, guns, antiques, collecting, science fiction, and games.

In Washington, D.C., alone, according to Mike Focke, who updates an area list monthly, there are more than 1,000 boards, half of which are private. Half of the private ones are government boards, just as many of the public boards are government owned and operated.

Boardwatch Magazine editor and publisher Jack Rickard estimates the number of BBSes in the entire U.S. at more than 40,000. That's an incredible variety, as well as tough competition for commercial services. Some of the boards even offer Internet access, although the vast majority of those charge for it.

Launched in 1986 in the United States, National Public Telecomputing Network's Free-Net tentacles extend heavily into Canada and other countries. True to Dr. Grundner's doctorate, NPTN has a strong educational orientation in supporting schools and being supported by them. If Internet is an international campus, NPTN's founder is the ultimate dean—with tenure.

Dr. Grundner compares a community computer system to National Public Radio in terms of user support—but with several advantages over that medium, especially interactivity. A citizen can be active as well as passive. Although anyone can log on and read messages, a user who goes to the minimal trouble of registering on the board (often accomplished during the first session) will be given the ability to respond to topics and leave electronic mail for other users of the Free-Net. With radio and TV, the listener/viewer endures commercial interruptions during a talk show.

Everyone with access to a full-fledged community computer system gets more than Andy Warhol's promised 15 minutes of fame, and a wide selection of topics on which to expound. If you don't like the topic others select, start your own. Expound to your heart's content. If others are not interested, the subject dies. But if there is interest, the topic may rocket around the world on Internet's cyberspaceship.

Although NPTN is working on a program that will allow inexpensive, instant Free-Nets, most of them require months and even years before seeing the light of day. The new NPTN program is aimed at schools and rural areas, however, rather than metropolitan areas with a large potential of users.

Anyone can begin organizing a Free-Net. The first requirement for starting a large or small Free-Net is to gather a few people around a table. In Washington, D.C., interest began with representatives of agencies serving the homeless. They were seeking a quick and easy way to count bed availability for the homeless on a nightly basis. Free-Net offered a potential solution because of its capability to offer private, as well as public, forums. After several meetings, and as additional governmental and other organizations got involved, they decided they were getting well beyond their mission. Fortunately, Sharon Rogers stepped in and took over. Dr. Rogers was then Director of Libraries for George Washington University in Washington, D.C. Her organizational abilities helped to get the project moving.

Just as Thomas Alva Edison is inextricably linked to his inventions (and vice versa), so the story of Free-Net has to begin with Thomas Grundner, his thirsty and fertile mind, and his refusal to accept the status quo.

"The Father of the Free-Nets," who founded the concept of volunteer-driven community computing in Cleveland, is a man of many careers and whose off-career path led him to both coasts and Vietnam, and to jobs ranging from keeping cars on the road to providing security for Hollywood stars and insecurity for the Viet Cong.

As a communicator, he has used speeches, articles, books, newspaper columns, and his own radio program to reach audiences. As a means of communicating, a Free-Net has a potential for reaching more people than any other present media.

Grundner was born in 1945 and raised just across Lake Erie from Cleveland, in Detroit, Michigan. Playing virtually all sports in high school, the six-foot-four wide receiver attended college on a football scholarship, set pass receiving records, played pro ball in a minor league, joined the Navy at 21, and volunteered to work aboard high-speed small craft searching Vietnam's many little rivers.

From the Navy, Grundner joined an innovative residential treatment center for the emotionally disturbed in New Hampshire, and then earned his master's degree in just one year at a free-standing research institute outside Washington, D.C., known for its intensive experimental programs involving such internationally hailed psychologists as B. F. Skinner. He was enrolled at the University of Southern California for its very first graduate program in the nation's capital, then moved to USC's California campus, where he obtained a doctorate with a double major in educational psychology and philosophy. Income from his G. I. Bill was supplemented by paychecks from pumping gas and serving as a security guard at movie studios. His doctorate led him to a small two-year college in 1978 as its one-person philosophy department.

One of his major articles landed in the *New England Journal of Medicine* and was responsible for getting him noticed by, in particular, Case Western Reserve University's Department of Family Medicine in Cleveland.

The Creation of St. Silicon

In 1984, the Department of Family Medicine had a major problem: Its medical residents and students were scattered at sites around the city, making it difficult for them to reach staff in a timely manner, and vice versa. Grundner's solution was a simple Apple II Plus-based bulletin board system providing electronic mail and file transferring, as well as posting of meeting notices and other information.

The BBS achieved its mission as a valuable communications aid, but then came an unforeseen, and possibly unforeseeable, situation.

Within two weeks of St. Silicon's creation, lay persons discovered the board's telephone number and began posting questions about their ailments in hopes physicians would reply.

Grundner's first clue that something was amiss came from reports that the board was crashing. He quickly discovered it was overload caused by computer-knowledgeable hypochondriacs and others who preferred calling the BBS to taking two aspirins and phoning their doctor's office in the morning.

A person with less imagination would have maintained the status quo by merely closing the board to unauthorized access. Not the hero of the fields of play and war. "What would happen," Grundner wondered, "if the BBS encouraged people to get answers to their questions?" In Grundner's mind, the "what would happen" would be an opportunity for Case Western Reserve University to enhance its position as a civic-oriented and involved community organization with a strong and capable medical training program.

A One-Line Online Research Project

Grundner's software response was a BBS known as "St. Silicon's Hospital and Information Dispensary," allowing anyone with a computer, a communications program, modem, and phone line to call for information. The board's most important forum was its online medical clinic or, as it came to be labeled, "Doc in the Box." A caller could leave a question and call back a day later for the answer from a physician.

St. Silicon's single telephone line was in use continuously from 7:00 A.M. to 1:00 A.M. each day and slackened little during the other hours—a milestone in communications, as well as a tribute to the popularity of free medical advice.

Grundner's research project showed clearly, to him at least, that as often happened to Edison, hard work and creativity resulted in stumbling on a product with immense potential to medical educators: a new medium for delivering community health information.

When the *New England Journal of Medicine* published a report on Doc in the Box, Grundner received compliments and wide interest in the concept. He also received something tangible. AT&T gave him a 3B2/400 UNIX multiuser computer with multitasking. "Expand the concept and report back," AT&T told him.

Electronic Hospital to Electronic City: Cleveland Free-Net

The AT&T gift enabled Grundner to think in broader terms, and he did. The question now was, "What would happen if St. Silicon's electronic hospital concept was expanded and converted into an electronic city?"

Other questions followed. How about a post office to provide all "residents" (users) with electronic mail? An electronic school that would allow public and private schools to teach computing? A government building incorporating methods for bringing people closer to the democratic process?

To these were added a fine arts building to encompass the arts, libraries providing direct access to those of the city of Cleveland and Case Western Reserve University, and even a café with bytes rather than bites for chatting on general topics. Supply your own coffee and sandwiches, and keep up your end of the conversation. Or just eavesdrop.

In July 1986, the Cleveland Free-Net was born—a true Cyber City. Unlike electronic bulletin boards with limited topics or access, this was the first community board open to everyone with the proper equipment, regardless of their location, and at no charge to its "citizens." Just as a citizen has to register to vote, however, the Cleveland Free-Net requires registration, at no charge, before a person is allowed to participate by leaving messages. Others who sign on are given read-only status.

A city needs residents and people to run it. Grundner built the board's popularity by tramping from one organization to another, including computer groups, and spreading the word.

A key to the Cleveland Free-Net's growth and popularity was his clever method for increasing participation by enhancing its value to more users. People were invited to launch special interest groups online. When they became Free-Net moderators, Grundner says, "they brought their own constituencies." Somewhat to its founder's surprise, the biggest and most active constituency turned out to be science fiction buffs.

The Cleveland Free-Net demonstrated to hundreds, and then thousands, of people in the Cleveland area that community computing can be fun as well as valuable and educational.

Word got around and leaked outside Cleveland. But unlike Peter's dike, there was no stopping it. Grundner formed National Public Telecomputing Network (NPTN) to serve this fourth communications medium in a manner not unlike National Public Radio, but with the advantage of having interactivity between station/computer and listener/user. It's not simply "I'll talk, and you listen." To Show & Tell was added Show & Talk Back.

What Makes a Free-Net?

What is the difference between a Free-Net and other community computing systems? Grundner will tell you that it is the stamp of quality and consistency as a product is made to fit an efficient, tested, popular, and workable pattern. A constantly updated "cookbook," the National Public Telecomputing Network's organizing manual helps to ensure that local Free-Net founders from around the world will start with the same basic ingredients.

Much more sharing of talent, experience, and knowledge goes on among Free-Nets, with NPTN serving as the hub by ingesting, evaluating, and digesting the information over the Internet, and even using the old-fashioned methods of hard copy, meetings, and telephone conversations.

The stamp of quality is shown by the name "Free-Net." Only those civic computer operations organized under NPTN principles and standards are allowed to use that name as their own. While not required, incorporating the name "Free-Net" shows the world that it meets minimum standards and has the benefits provided by the network. If a company bottles "Coca-Cola" to the beverage corporation's standards, it doesn't call it "No-Name Soda."

Some community computer operations say taking the Free-Net name would make it difficult to remove themselves from the network should they ever choose to do so. With so much to be gained by being part of an accepted, major, internationally respected organization, that seems unlikely.

Picture a member of the National Public Radio network trying to go it alone. It would make listeners addicted to NPR programming very unhappy.

Organizing Committee

Helping to steer the growing organization, Free-Net representatives meet annually to provide input and exchange information, only one of the many advantages to the network.

Each Free-Net is a unique experience of individuals and organizations. At its start, the flagship, Cleveland Free-Net, was very much a one-man operation.

The Naples, Florida, Free-Net organizing committee began with two people who had been involved in other Free-Nets. They were introduced to each other by a mutual acquaintance. The Tallahassee Free-Net, the first in Florida, was the offspring of a professor of computer science at a major university.

As the Internet continues to grow in size, the Free-Nets are growing in number. They offer additional proof that one person can make a difference.

Internet Connection

Actually, a Free-Net does not need an Internet connection, just as a community does not necessarily have to be connected to another one to survive. But it helps. Without the Internet to link them, Grundner points out, Free-Nets are lonely outposts.

No community computer should be an electronic Gilligan's Island. A Free-Net's government building should be able to link a cybernaut to state and national governments, other universities, a vast array of local, state, and federal services, and even other countries.

Performing these links can be as simple as a number on the menu, such as the method the Tallahassee Free-Net uses to switch you to the Finland Free-Net.

The Free-Nets of the future will be as graphically friendly as they are now: menu-driven and user friendly.

The best superhighways, of course, are of little value to those who are unable to access them. Most Free-Nets have their connections at university sites; at least one Free-Net buys its connection from an Internet reseller.

Finding a host is a priority for establishing a Free-Net. For some, such as Cleveland Free-Net's Case Western Reserve host and Florida State University-based Tallahassee Free-Net, the host was a given. For others, such as the Florida Gulf Coast community of Naples and many other areas, getting Internet access was a major problem.

Free-Nets are not go-it-alone operations. They begin with a few people who find a few more people and then a few more people, until they have a checking account, active committees, a nonprofit corporation, and eventually and ideally, perhaps even a paid staff to obtain continuous funding and provide administration, technical services, and training.

The people who join the organizing committee have to be activists rather than talkers. Based on observation, they should represent a cross-section of the community. In some instances, librarians have been active instigators. Social services and schools can provide key components that generate the drive to provide the most worthwhile ongoing services. Connections to city hall and county government, even if the information is unofficial, are essentials, as is participation by schools and social service organizations.

Good fund-raisers and marketers are necessary, too. Nothing keeps a Free-Net free like money. Just as public broadcast stations have been forced to raise funds for decades, a Free-Net needs activities to obtain financing for hardware, software, and operating expenses.

Organizers have to remember that fund-raising is not a one-time goal. Expenses are ongoing. Money will be needed again next year and the year after that.

One major source for support are in-kind contributions. Typically, the site for the Free-Net is furnished. Computers, modems, scanners, printers, hard drives, floppy disks, and cables can be expensive, even when heavily discounted. Free-Net software, which used to be virtually free, has greatly improved but now has a cost. Technical assistance may or may not be without cost; be prepared to pay for at least some of the help the board will need. Postage, printing, and paper clips are increasingly expensive.

Volunteers to moderate the various forums are necessary and furnish the Free-Net with generally expert advice and information designed to motivate comments, questions, and general activities. Each forum or topic area should be aimed at attracting attention to the Free-Net. By keeping their part of the board active, interesting, and constantly changing, moderators assure a growing, thriving board. NPTN provides services to help attract users and maintain interest. However, there are costs for some of these services, and local sponsors are a way to finance them.

Short of running out of money, there is nothing worse for a board than inactivity. If a user pops onto a Free-Net a couple times and finds no changes, he or she may drop it. The volunteer moderators are crucial to the board's success by bringing in the users and by keeping them coming back.

Volunteer Moderators

For a vivid description of what it's like to be a moderator, let's go to the tape. Grundner's National Public Telecomputing Network has a videotape (about 14 minutes long) available. "Community Computing: If It Plays In Peoria," based on the Heartland Free-Net's own video, uses that system to demonstrate what to expect from a popular Free-Net while showing how one operates.

The tape has interviews with several people involved with or affected by the Free-Net. One of them is Terry Beachler, who owns a service station with a major repair and maintenance operation. Beachler fields automotive questions on Heartland.

"The questions go all over the place," Beachler says during the taped interview. "Some [questions] are rather complicated and defy answers; some are crackpot questions; some of the answers aren't satisfactory, so I go over and over them again and answer them with a different slant, and none of them seem to be too terribly technical.

"We keep a fair amount of reference material [at the automotive service center] with respect to automotive repairs. We have a piece of equipment with about a quarter million pages of automotive technical bulletins on compact discs, so I can go to that. I can go to one of the mechanics. And rely on my own personal experience.

"I probably have a secret desire to be a teacher somewhere down the road," the entrepreneur concludes.

Although missionary zeal counts, the effect on one's business of being a volunteer has to be a motivating force for some moderators. There are doctors, dentists, lawyers, veterinarians, florists, travel agents, and automotive technicians. As such, it is a potential source of revenue for the board if the space can be rented out or sponsored by a company. The income potential is being studied now by NPTN for possible implementation by its members.

For other moderators, a Free-Net offers opportunities to extend the reach of its social, health, education, library, and other programs and services. Tallahassee Free-Net's recent menus—which change as volunteers are added and services are increased—provides an idea as to what to expect from a Free-Net.

Here is the opening menu:

```
TALLAHASSEE FREE-NET MAIN MENU

1.   All About Free-Net (Help, Overview & News)
2.   Mail Service for Registered Users
3.   Social Services and Organizations
```

```
4.  Business & Professional Services
5.  Medical & Health Services
6.  Agriculture Center
7.  Government Complex
8.  Education Complex
9.  Religion Center
10. Science and Technology Center
11. Home and Garden Center
12. Library Complex
13. Community Center
14. Disabilities Information
15. Additional Internet & Local Services
```

Pressing 2. `Mail Service for Registered Users` takes you to the following menu:

```
MAILBOXES AND MAIL SERVICES

1.  About Tallahassee Free-Net Mail
2.  Reading and Writing Mail
3.  List all Free-Net users & addresses
4.  Search for Internet Addresses
5.  What is my Internet mail address?
6.  Are You Using Too Much Disk for Mail?
7.  Edit Your Signature File
8.  Edit the File to Redirect Your Mail
9.  Electronic Mail to Clinton & Gore
10. E-Mail Congress About the Internet
11. PINE, an Alternative Mail Program
12. UUencode/Uudecode
13. Home Directory File Services
```

Note the surprising number of Internet-related activities offered by the Tallahassee Free-Net, including the important programs (12. `UUencode/UUdecode`) that give users the ability to compress and decompress files they send and receive.

But as difficult as the Internet may be, Tallahassee enables you to jump to another member of the Free-Net family by just typing a number. Looking again at the main menu, you will see:

```
15. Additional Internet & Local Services
```

This takes you to another menu that leads to yet another menu:

```
ACCESS TO OTHER FREE-NETS

1.   About Free-Nets in General
2.   Connect to Peoria Free-Net
3.   Connect to Youngstown Free-Net
4.   Connect to Cleveland Free-Net
5.   Connect to Cincinnati Free-Net
6.   Connect to Lorain, Ohio Free-Net
7.   Connect to Denver Free-Net
8.   Connect to Victoria Free-Net
9.   Connect to Ottawa Free-Net
10.  Connect to Buffalo Free-Net
11.  Books About the Internet
(m) main menu        (p) previous menu    (x) Exit
Your Choice:
```

The Tallahassee Free-Net has a young Social Services area that it combines with Organizations. With Education, the most essential justification for a Free-Net, this section undoubtedly will grow. Here is what the Tallahassee menu showed late last year:

```
SOCIAL SERVICES AND ORGANIZATIONS

1.   About Social Services and Organizations
2.   Calder Medical Library, U. Miami  (AIDS INFO)
3.   Center For Independent Living
4.   DISC Village
5.   TCRS - Telephone Counseling & Referral Service, Inc.
6.   TCRS - The Florida HIV/AIDS Hotline
7.   TCRS - The Florida Healthy Baby Hotline
8.   TCRS - 224-NEED Crisis Helpline
9.   TCRS - Phone Friend (For Kids Home Alone After School)
10.  TCRS - The Connection (Pre-recorded Info Regarding Teen Issues)
11.  Veterans Network
12.  Tallahassee Organizations
13.  Local Civic Clubs
```

As with the Mail menu, this one is the second level of a pyramid. Moving to Peoria, with the NPTN videotape as our source, you find this listing:

```
<<< Social Services and Organizations >>>
1  Tri-County Help Resources
2  American Red Cross
3  Cub Scouts, Boy Scouts, and Explorer Scouts et cetera
```

Pressing 2 for American Red Cross moves you to the next level and presents you with yet another menu:

```
<<< American Red Cross >>>
1  About the American Red Cross
2  Blood Information
3  Disaster Relief
4  Health and Safety Services
5  Hemophilia
6  Service to Military Families
7  Volunteer Opportunities
8  Tissue Services
9  American Red Cross Questions and Answers
```

One of the older Free-Nets, the Heartland Free-Net, also has a strong educational composition, including sites on the menu for Bradley University, Illinois Central College, Peoria High School, and other secondary schools. Another feature is access to government officials.

However, board users would be bored users if not for the areas that add zest to their lives. There are many places to chat with others of like interest and argue with those holding opposing views. Let's look at a vintage Cleveland Free-Net listing for the Community Center:

```
1. About the Community Center
2. The Recreation Center
   1. Sports
      1. The Runners SIG
      2. Outdoors SIG
      3. Skier's SIG
      4. Bicycling SIG
      5. Sports SIG
   2. Games
      1. The Cleveland Chess SIG
      2. Gaming SIG
      3. Video Game SIG
      4. The Go SIG
   3. Miscellaneous
      1. Science Fiction/Fantasy SIG
      2. Culinary Arts SIG
      3. The Skeptics SIG
      4. The Travel SIG
      5. UFOlogy SIG
      6. Toastmaster's SIG
      7. Movies SIG
      8. Photographic SIG
      9. Genealogy SIG
      10. Radio Scanner SIG
      11. Amateur Radio SIG
      12. IRC SIG
      13. Internet SIG
      14. Horror SIG
3. Wanted & For Sale Board
4. Jobs Wanted/Jobs Available
```

```
5. The Religious Corner
   1. The Baha'i Faith Forum
   2. Electronic Scriptures
      1. The Bible
      2. The Book of Mormon
      3. The Koran
6. Beliefs Center
7. The Handicap Center
8. Lesbian/Gay Comm. Svc. Ctr.
9. Ohio's Finest Singles Network
```

Information Resources on Virtually Any Topic

A Free-Net also provides a tremendous amount of information on specific types of computers and provides information resources on virtually every known topic. The limitations are funding, staff, and volunteers. The Cleveland Free-Net requires hundreds of volunteers as moderators and assistants, as well as back-up for the Administration Building, Public Square, Courthouse/ Government Center, Schoolhouse, Medical Arts Building, Library, Business & Industrial Park, University Circle, Communications Center, Arts Building, Post Office, Science & Tech Center, Library, Community Center, News Center, Teleport (to libraries around the state, country, and world), and more.

Anyone can start a specific interest area if it can be shown that there are, or can reasonably be assumed to be, others who share that interest—and that there is someone reliable to serve as moderator.

When your Free-Net organizing committee is well under way, it will be time to review the services NPTN can provide to attract users from opening day. True to Tom Grundner's background and his mission for NPTN, Free-Nets are heavily weighted toward preparing future cybernauts for their place in an electronic universe. NPTN also offers additional funding possibilities for the Free-Net by attracting sponsors.

National Educational Simulations Project Using Telecommunications (NESPUT) offerings include launches, space exploration studies, and track events. For a launch, students link up with schools around the world assuming various roles in a simulated space shuttle mission. A school can be a shuttle, a docking station, or a support unit such as a weather station.

Salute to Space Exploration entertainingly teaches the history of various U.S. and other space programs. Various forms include providing hourly reports to Academy One (more on that organization later) in a supporting role or as a research project.

Teleolympics has students from around the world competing in track events without leaving their schoolyards, posting winning scores in each category to a computer network. The international winners receive recognition. The opening and closing ceremonies are conducted online.

Besides promoting physical education, the program integrates geography, writing, math, and computer science.

NPTN education director Linda Delzeit coordinates the National Education Supercomputing Program, which uses remote access to the Lawrence Livermore Laboratory's supercomputing facilities so that students can explore such areas as climate modeling, ray tracing, molecular configuration, and plant modeling. NPTN provides teacher training, software distribution, and curriculum integration.

Other science-oriented projects include educating and training youngsters in research methods using Mandeville (LA) Middle School's National Student Research Center; School-Owned Experiments and Databases (an exchange of programs among participants); Forest Day (study aids for forests and forestry); Save the Beaches (similar to Forest Day); Project Ecology Art Exchange (using e-mail and art to exchange student drawings on specific themes); and Trisphere (working with Trisphere Institute of Sports Medicine to provide information on physical training).

Foreign language studies now offer French; Spanish and German are coming online.

NPTN provides "real life" adventures, which have included frequent reports on the exciting Iditarod Dog Sled Race across Alaska and the Whitbread Round the World Sailing Race. Educational materials accompany the reports.

Writing and language arts projects have NPTN Student News Network (electronic digests of school newspapers); Spotlight on People/Spotlight on Authors (enables students to communicate with leaders, inventors, authors, and others who are successful in various aspects of their lives); Sonnet-Writing Contest (with judging by a panel of impartial literary teachers); Student Author (a creative writing exchange and progressive writing program); and Kid Trek (for young science-fiction writers).

Training in civic involvement is offered by the following:

- Project Common Ground in Ohio, a model for improving the environment and fostering student participation in civic affairs.
- Take 2, an Academy One electronic networking component to the Take 2 participatory and interactive television show by and for youngsters using videotape, performing art, creative writing, and problem-solving skills to work on youth-related problems ranging from gangs and drop-outs, drugs and smoking, to teen pregnancy.
- The Institute for Democracy in Education, founded by a group of teachers eager to provide a forum for educators, students, and teachers to discuss how to develop responsible citizens.

Education Support and Training is a curriculum exchange, starting with more than 500 lesson plans on social studies, math, language arts, and science; Teacher Education Center (for asking about Academy One and issues related to improving education); Middle School Network (with programs aimed at adolescent physical, intellectual, and social-emotional development); and Parents Are Teachers (concerning home schooling).

A particularly large NPTN project area is Social, Artistic, and Cultural Awareness. A Day in the Life of a Student has students sharing their chronological accounts: International e.Club (electronic addresses so that individual students and teachers can communicate directly with their peers); International Holiday Exchange (with students around the world comparing their holiday customs); Inter-Generational Exchange (discussions with senior citizens and others about changes in traditions, sports, music, and family roles over the years); Student Artist (exchanging pictures created with word-processing programs while training in non-alphanumeric keyboard characters); Jewish Education (for Jewish educators and students to discuss special events and share resources—open to all); and Letters to Santa (for children in grades K–2).

Academy One, which allows any K–12 school in the country to access NPTN affiliates without charge no matter where they are situated, is an umbrella educational area containing the fourth media network's educational programs. The only requirements for classroom participation are a computer/modem tie to a cooperating local college or university with an Internet connection. This will enable the school to access a Free-Net and participate in Academy One projects.

Under NPTN director of education Linda Delzeit, Academy One has delivered programs that have been used around the world by hundreds of schools and tens of thousands of students, using computers and modems as tools for expanding education into previously unknown areas.

Because of NPTN, schools have converted the world into virtual classrooms. Students from several countries have been classmates, joining in activities just as though they were in the next classroom and even the next seat, sharing curricula, materials, projects, and even the same teachers.

To enroll in Academy One, a teacher should contact Ms. Delzeit at `linda@nptn.org`.

NPTN's Online Resources

Besides projects and programs, the National Public Telecomputing Network has a host of online information resources, including the following:

- The Big Sky Curriculum Database: more than 500 curricula for grades K–12 divided into five general areas: language arts, math, social studies, science, and miscellaneous.
- College Row: electronic information about colleges and universities.
- Campaign '92: the full text of the Democratic, Republican, and Libertarian parties' campaign documents.

- Congressional Memory Project: a weekly summary of three bills each from the House and the Senate.

- Congressional Connection: a database of names, addresses, phone and fax numbers, committee assignments, and other information on federal, state, and local elected representatives.

- Daily Report Card: a weekday, eight-page electronic newsletter summarizing national, state, and local educational news from news reports, columns, and editorials.

- The Freedom Shrine: a collection of 30 full-text documents ranging from the Magna Carta to Martin Luther King's "I Have A Dream" speech, and even hard-to-find speeches such as "The Constitution of the Iroquois Nations."

- Government Accounting Office Reports: a variety of studies from the GOA in Washington, D.C.

- HIV/AIDS Information Center: a comprehensive database of AIDS crisis files.

- Pediatric Illness Database: more than 65 files with information on common childhood diseases.

- Presidential Memory Project: a full-text collection of every position paper, major press release, speech, and fact sheet produced by President Clinton during his 1992 campaign.

- Project Gutenberg: a major ongoing Internet project computerizing the full text of books and documents ranging from the Bible and the Koran to William Shakespeare's complete works and the CIA's *World FactBook*—even Lewis Carroll's *Alice in Wonderland.*

- Project Hermes: the full text of U.S. Supreme Court decisions available within minutes of being announced in Washington, D.C. Each opinion normally consists of a synopsis of the case, followed by the opinion(s) and any dissents. When Project Hermes was launched, NPTN was one of only 12 information providers selected— along with major news-gathering organizations—to provide the service.

- Youth Policy Institute Issue Overviews: policy overviews prepared by the institute, containing a summary of pros, cons, and alternatives on each issue.

Medical Information Services

NPTN offers several medical information services. Besides the HIV/AIDS Information Center and the Pediatric Illness Database mentioned in the preceding list, there are the Eye Clinic and the Pediatrics Center. The first is operated by Richard E. Gans, M.D., Diplomat, American Board of Opthalmology, and his associates to discuss ophthalmology and eye care in general. The Pediatrics Center is moderated by Dr. Norman Lavin, a Tarzana, California, physician and Diplomat in both pediatrics and endocrinology.

News

NPTN also offers information from more than 30 daily, weekly, biweekly, monthly, and quarterly news sources—most charge a fee.

In addition, there is a free news service: White House Online, daily full-text releases of major press releases, speeches, executive orders, press briefings, and other documents shipped electronically by the White House Office of Media Affairs.

The commercial news services and magazines are distributed by the American Cybercasting Corporation, of which Dr. Grundner is part owner, and are provided deeply discounted to NPTN affiliates. These are potential revenue sources because Free-Nets can seek out contributors to sponsor selected online publications.

Currently, these products include *Africa News Online*; *Animals*; *Beijing Review*; *Brookings Review*; *California Management Review*; *China Today*; *Discover Magazine*; *Educacian al Dma*; *Education Today*; *Forbes*; *France Today*; *India Abroad*; *Investors Business Daily*; *Insight Magazine*; *International Wildlife*; *The Jerusalem Post*; *Journal Français D'Amirique*; *London Daily Telegraph*; *London Financial Times*; *London Times*; *Los Angeles Times: Times Online*; *Mechanical Engineering*; *Moscow News*; *National Review*; *National Wildlife*; *New Republic*; *Ranger Rick*; *Sea Frontiers*; *USA Today Decisionline*; *U.S. News & World Report*; *Washington Post*; *Washington Times*; and *World Press Review*.

Free-Net Pioneers

The Free-Net framework has been established over several years by Tom Grundner and his Free-Net crew. Useful new experience is being accumulated daily in an area that, despite its age in computer terms, is in the early stages of an international boom.

Free-Net organizers feel as though they are pioneering, and perhaps they are. In Florida, there already is talk of a state-wide organization of Free-Nets and a "dean," Hilbert Levitz, professor of computer science at Florida State University, founder and committee chair of the Tallahassee Free-Net, and dubbed "The Father of the Florida Free-Nets."

The number of Free-Nets is growing so rapidly that there may be a Free-Net organizing committee in your vicinity now. Get active. No Free-Net has too many volunteers. No matter how much information or how many forums a Free-Net may offer, its users always want more data, more variety, and more choices.

If there isn't a Free-Net where you are, start talking one up. Meet with public, private, and special librarians, social service managers, bureaucrats, teachers and professors, technicians, computer group members, clubs, organizations, professional groups, trade associations, politicos, and media publishers and reporters.

Not all the people you need to approach are necessarily computer knowledgeable. For example, the *Naples Daily News'* expert heads the composing room. One of the Naples city government's experts is the assistant city manager who also, in this age of merging multimedia, oversees the city's cable franchising.

Here is a recent list of Free-Nets. All are organizing committees, affiliates, or K–12 affiliates holding charters from the National Public Telecomputing Network. The organizing committees are working to get online (affiliates are online as shown by the modem and Internet numbers and visitor logins, if available); K–12 educational affiliates are already online. These last are limited to students, teachers, and school officials and are not open to the general public.

This list is supplied by the National Public Telecomputing Network. (Our gratitude and thanks to Elizabeth Reid, also known as exr@nptn.org.). The following list is copyrighted 1995 by the National Public Telecomputing Network and published with permission:

> **Alabama:** Tennessee Valley Free-Net, Huntsville; Mobile Area Free-Net (modem 334-405-4636, Telnet: ns1.maf.mobile.al.us, and visitor login: visitor); Tuscaloosa Free-Net

> **Alaska:** AnchorNet, Anchorage; FairNet, Fairbanks

> **Arizona:** AzTeC, Tempe (modem 602-965-5985, Telnet: 129.219.13.60, and visitor login: guest, password: visitor)

> **California:** Northern California Regional Computing Network, Chico; Davis Free-Net; Los Angeles Free-Net (modem 818-776-5000, Telnet: lafn.org, and visitor login: Select #2 at first menu); Orange County Free-Net; Sacramento Free-Net; San Diego County Free-Net; Silicon Valley Public Access Link, San Jose; SLONET, San Luis Obispo (modem 805-781-3666, Telnet: 199.74.141.2, and visitor login: visitor); Santa Barbara RAIN; California Online Resources for Education, Seal Beach; Redwood Free-Net, Ukiah

> **Colorado:** Denver Free-Net (modem 303-270-4865, Telnet: freenet.hsc.colorado.edu, and visitor login: guest)

> **Connecticut:** Danbury Area Free-Net; CPBTI Free-Net, Hartford

> **Florida:** SEFLIN Free-Net, Broward County (modem: 305-765-4332, Telnet: befreenet.seflin.lib.fl.us, and visitor login: visitor); Alachua Free-Net, Gainesville (modem 904-334-0200, Telnet: freenet.ufl.edu, and visitor login: visitor); Miami Free-Net; Naples Free-Net; Palm Beach Free-Net; Sarasota-Manatee Area Free-Net MCNet, Stuart; Tallahassee Free-Net (modem 904-488-5056, Telnet: freenet.fsu.edu, and visitor login: visitor); Suncoast Free-Net, Tampa Bay (will be online by publication date)

> **Georgia:** 404 Free-Net, Atlanta; Worth County-Sylvester, GA Free-Net (modem 912-776-1255, Telnet and visitor login not available on this rural affiliate)

Hawaii: Aloha Free-Net Project, Honolulu; Maui Free-Net

Idaho: Sandpoint Free-Net

Illinois: Shawnee Free-Net, Carbondale; Prairienet, Champaign-Urbana (modem 217-255-9000, Telnet: `prairienet.org <192.17.3.3.>`, and visitor login: `visitor`); SWIF-NET, Edgemont

Indiana: Michiana Free-Net Society, Granger

Iowa: CedarNet, Cedar Falls; Iowa Knowledge Exchange, Des Moines; Fairfield Free-Net, Fairfield

Kentucky: Pennyrile Area Free-Net, Hopkinsville; Owensboro Free-Net, Owensboro

Louisiana: Baton Rouge Area Interactive Network; Acadiana Free-Net, Lafayette; Greater New Orleans Free-Net

Maine: Maine Community Access Network, Freeport

Maryland: Free State Free-Net, Baltimore; Community Service Network, Easton; Garrett Communiversity Central, McHenry

Massachusetts: UMassK12, Amherst (modem: 413-572-5583 or 413-572-5268, Telnet: `k12.oit.umass.edu`, and visitor login: `guest`

Michigan: Almont Expression (modem 810-798-8290, Telnet: not available, and visitor login: `visitor`, password: `visitor`); Huron Valley Free-Net, Washtenaw County; Great Lakes Free-Net, Battle Creek (modem 616-969-4536, Telnet: not available, and visitor login: `visitor`); Greater Detroit Free-Net, Detroit (modem not available, Telnet: `detroit.freenet.org`, and visitor login: `visitor`); Genesee Free-Net (modem: 810-232-9905, Telnet: `detroit.freenet.org`, and visitor login: `visitor`); Grand Rapids Free-Net; Macatawa Area Free-Net, Holland; Capitol City Free-Net, Lansing; Education Central, Mount Pleasant (modem: 517-774-3790, Telnet: `edcen.chhs.cmich.edu`, and visitor login: `visitor`)

Minnesota: Twin Cities Free-Net, Minneapolis; Northfield Free-Net

Mississippi: Magnolia Free-Net, Jackson; Meridian Area Free-Net

Missouri: Show-Me Free-Net, Cape Girardeau; Columbia Online Information Network/COIN (modem: 314-884-7000, Telnet: `bigcat.missouri.edu`, and visitor login: `guest`); KC Free-Net, Kansas City; Ozarks Regional Information On-Line Network, Springfield (modem: 417-864-6100, Telnet: `ozarks.sgcl.lib.mo.us`, and visitor login: `guest`)

Montana: Big Sky Telegraph, Dillon (modem: 406-683-7680, Telnet: `192.231.192.1`, and visitor login: `bbs`)

Nebraska: Omaha Free-Net

Nevada: Las Vegas International Free-Net

New Hampshire: Granite State Oracle, Manchester

New Mexico: New Mexico Free-Net, Albuquerque; Santa Fe Metaverse

New York: Capital Region Information Service, Albany; Buffalo Free-Net (modem: 716-645-3085, Telnet: `freenet.buffalo.edu`, and visitor login: `freeport`); CASSYnet, Corning; Southern Tier Free-Net, Endicott; East Side House Free-Net, the Bronx; Rochester Free-Net

North Carolina: Mountain Area Information Network, Asheville; Triangle Free-Net, Chapel Hill; Charlotte's Web; Forsyth County Free-Net, Winston-Salem

North Dakota: SENDIT, Fargo (modem: 701-237-3283, Telnet: `sendit.nodak.edu`, and visitor login: `bbs`, password: `sendit2me`)

Ohio: Akron Regional Free-Net; SEORF, Athens (modem: direct connect not available, Telnet: `seorf.ohiou.edu`, and visitor login: `guest`); Stark County Free-Net, Canton; Tristate Online, Cincinnati (modem: 513-579-1990, Telnet: `tso.uc.edu`, and visitor login: `visitor`); Cleveland Free-Net (modem: 216-368-3888, Telnet: `freenet-in-a.cwru.edu`, and visitor login: Select #2 at first menu); Learning Village Cleveland (modem: 216-498-4070, Telnet: `nptn.org`, and visitor login: `visitor`); Greater Columbus Free-Net (modem: 614-292-4132, Telnet: `freenet.columbus.oh.us`, and visitor login: `guest`); Dayton Free-Net (modem: 513-873-4035, Telnet: `130.108.128.174`, and visitor login: `visitor`); Lorain County Free-Net, Elyria (modem: 216-366-9721, Telnet: `freenet.lorain.oberlin.edu`, and visitor login: `guest`); Lima Free-Net; Richland Free-Net, Mansfield; Medina County Free-Net, Medina (modem: 216-723-6732, Telnet: not available, and visitor login: `visitor`); Youngstown Free-Net (modem: 216-742-3072, Telnet: `yfn2.ysu.edu`, and visitor login: `visitor`)

Oklahoma: Ponca City/Pioneer Free-Net

Pennsylvania: Lehigh Valley Free-Net, Bethlehem; Erie County Free-Net, Erie; Pittsburgh Free-Net; Mercer County Free-Net, Sharon; Chester County Interlink, West Chester

Rhode Island: Ocean State Free-Net, Providence (modem: 901-427-4435, Telnet: `192.207.24.10`, and visitor login not available)

South Carolina: MidNet, Columbia; Greenet, Greenville; GreenCo-NET, Greenwood

Tennessee: Jackson Area Free-Net (modem: 901-427-4435, Telnet: `198.146.108.99`, and visitor login: `guest`); Greater Knoxville Community Network

Texas: Big Country Free-Net, Abilene; Austin Free-Net; North Texas Free-Net, Dallas; Rio Grande Free-Net, El Paso (modem: 915-775-5600, Telnet: `rgfn.epcc.edu`, and visitor login: `visitor`); Tarrant County Free-Net, Ft. Worth; Houston Civnet; West Texas Free-Net, San Angelo; San Antonio Free-Net

Vermont: Lamoille Net, Morrisville

Virginia: SEVANET, Newport News; Central Virginia's Free-Net, Richmond (modem: phone connect not available, Telnet: `freenet.vcu.edu`, and visitor login: `visitor`); Virginia Public Electronic Network, Richmond (modem: phone connect not available, Telnet: `vdoc386.vak12ed.edu`, and visitor login: `visitor`); Blue Ridge Free-Net, Roanoke

Washington: Kitsap Free-Net, Bremerton (modem: 206-386-4140, Telnet: `198.187.135.22`, and visitor login: `visitor`); Olympic Public Electronic Network, Port Angeles; Seattle Community Network (modem: 206-386-4140, Telnet: `scn.org`, and visitor login: `visitor`); TINCAN, Spokane; Tri-Cities Free-Net (modem: 509-375-1111, Telnet: not available, and visitor login: `visitor`); Clark County Free-Net, Vancouver

Following is a list of foreign active or in-process Free-Nets:

AUSTRALIA

Melbourne Free-Net

CANADA

Alberta: Calgary Free-Net; Edmonton Free-Net; Praxis Free-Net in Medicine Hat

British Columbia: Campbell River Free-Net; Prince George Free-Net; CIAO! in Trail (modem: 604-368-5764, Telnet: `142.231.5.1`, and visitor login: `guest`); Vancouver Free-Net; Victoria Free-Net; (modem: 604-595-2300, Telnet: `freenet.victoria.bc.ca`, and visitor login: `guest`)

Manitoba: Eastmanet in Pinawa; SEARDEN Free-Net in Sprague; Blue Sky Free-Net of Manitoba in Winnipeg

New Brunswick: York Sunbury Community Server in Fredericton

Newfoundland: St. John's Free-Net

Nova Scotia: Cape Breton Free-Net; Chebucto Free-Net in Halifax

Ontario: North Shore Free-Net in Elliot Lake; Durham Free-Net in Oshawa, National Capital Free-Net in Ottawa (modem: 613-564-3600, Telnet: `freenet.carleton.ca`, and visitor login: `guest`); Niagara Free-Net in St. Catharines; Thunder Bay Free-Net; Toronto Free-Net

Quebec: Free-Net du Montreal Metropolitain

Saskatchewan: Moose Jaw Free-Net; Great Plains Free-Net in Regina; Saskatoon Free-Net

FINLAND

Finland Free-Net in Helsinki (modem: 358-929292, Telnet: `130.233.208.40`, and visitor login: `visitor`)

GERMANY

Bayreuth Free-Net (modem: direct phone not available, Telnet: `freenet.uni-bayreuth.de`, and visitor login: `gast`); Free-Net Erlangen-Nuernburg-Erlangen (modem: +49-9131-85-8111, Telnet: `131.188.192.11`, and visitor login: `gast`)

IRELAND

Connect-Ireland in Dublin

ITALY

Venice Free-Net

NEW ZEALAND

Wellington Citynet (modem: +64-4-801-3060, Telnet: `kosmos.wcc.govt.nz`, and visitor login not available)

PHILIPPINES

Philippine Public Telecomputing Network in Quezon City

SWEDEN

Medborgarnas Datanat in Norrkoping

For more information on National Public Telecomputing Network, contact NPTN, P.O. Box 1987, Cleveland, OH 44106-0187; voice 216-498-4050; fax 216-498-4051; e-mail `info@nptn.org`.

Free-Nets Without Limits

With as many as 200 Free-Nets expected to be in place by the turn of the century and the possibility of cable pushing this forecast into the stratosphere, the future for civic networks and, in particular, Free-Nets seems limited only by the interest of people around the world in connecting with each other and to information resources. In short, Free-Nets are virtually without limits.

The man who has been spearheading the project ever since he discovered that his one-line, Apple-hosted BBS was crashing because it had become a public utility, is working harder than ever at keeping Free-Nets online to destiny.

If Tom Grundner has his way, millions of children around the world will grow up trained on something more helpful to their futures than Nintendo. National and international recognition obviously are overdue. However, it is only a matter of months, rather than years, before his appreciative audience grows from hundreds of thousands to tens of millions.

Net Activism

by David H. Rothman

Dave Hughes is a retired Army colonel whom some call the Cursor Cowboy. He is to electronic activism what Louis L'Amour was to westerns; in fact, he outdoes L'Amour—he invented his own genre. Back when many home computers could not even show capital letters, Hughes used his bulletin-board system to quash a zoning bill that would have imperiled thousands of home businesses.

Around Colorado Springs, in the foothills of the Rockies, Hughes blends in well. He has a penchant for cowboy hats, western boots, and Roger's Frontier Bar, where the locals play country western music on the jukebox, watch the Broncos on television, and guzzle their Coors beer—while he logs on the Net with his laptop computer from booth number one.

Nowadays, his online activism is no longer so novel. Using the Internet, a midwestern woman fights for abortion rights and helps warn clinics when violent demonstrators are on the way. Meanwhile, a Rush Limbaugh fan goes on the Internet to post summaries of his hero's shows. And a single mother in California, a female lawyer, fights for the rights of divorced fathers.

You'll also find me on the Internet—pushing TeleRead, my plan for electronic libraries for both the rich and poor. I don't want America to replicate, online, "the savage inequalities" of today's schools and public libraries. Someday, children in Watts should be able to dial up the same electronic books as children across town in Beverly Hills.

For activists like us, which strategies and tactics work best? Just what are the pitfalls to avoid? What could the future hold for activists and others in the forthcoming era of the electronic citizen? Perhaps some inklings may be found in the experiences and teachings of Dave Hughes. Despite his Stetson hat and folksy talk, he can be as modern in some ways as the trendiest software people in Silicon Valley. Consider how he lobbied Capitol Hill electronically in 1991.

The issue touched on federal support of computer networks for children in elementary and high schools. Hughes had long been a believer in the educational benefits of the personal computer. His son, Edward, though bright, suffered from mild dyslexia and once struggled to read well. Then Dave bought a Radio Shack TRS-80 Model 1 for word processing and accounting. Soon Edward was working some spreadsheet-like calculations on the TRS-80, which was hooked up to the mainframe at his school. He was also word processing his schoolwork. By the time Edward left high school, he had sharpened his reading skills and was testing in the top sixth percentile in math. He graduated from college with a double major in computers and math. McDonnell Douglas snapped up Edward to do FORTRAN programming.

Many years later, when then-Senator Al Gore was pushing for the creation of super highways for data, Dave Hughes could understand the warm, fuzzy images that the senator invoked. Gore waxed on about a little girl using a computer to dial up the Library of Congress and learn about dinosaurs. In a town where many politicians barely knew the difference between potato chips and the silicon variety, Gore was clearly the leading friend of computer nets.

However, Hughes became incensed after reading a message on the Internet by reporter Joe Abernathy. The message alluded to Gore's bill to create a National Research and Education Network.

Unlike the House incarnation of the High Performance Computing Act, the Senate version did not involve the Department of Education. And this was taking place on Gore's watch as chair of the science subcommittee within the Commerce Committee. Despite the senator's speeches, his bill was devoid of ways to foster computer networking among schoolchildren. Only the same old crowd (academics and other researchers) would come out ahead. Even the House version of the act authorized only a measly $9 million or so—out of billions—for networking in public schools. But at least the Department of Education would enjoy a place at the table during policy decisions on the High Performance Computing Act.

Energized, Hughes posted messages on the Internet, CompuServe, the WELL system in California, ECHO in New York, Metanet in Washington, D.C., and his own Old Colorado City network. "OK, Echoids," read his alarm to ECHO members, "if you believe in the networked future, and not in the elitist present, or the robber baron past, get off your cursors."

For good measure, Hughes faxed Gore's office using CompuServe. He spoke of the need for students to enjoy networking at ages when lifelong attitudes toward technology, math, science, and work are being formed, and when talent needs to reach for the stars. College is too late. The line between education and R&D can be thin in areas such as science and math, where genius may flower most brilliantly among the young.

Hughes went to bed sometime before midnight. The next day, 13 hours after his first posting, he received a phone call from Mike Nelson, Senator Gore's specialist on data highways. Nelson told him Gore's office was receiving calls and faxes from all over. Nelson said there was quite a bit of difficulty getting the Republicans to agree to the bill. Within 24 hours of that conversation, however, reporter Abernathy told Hughes that, yes, the bill would now include the Department of Education.

Today, Mike Nelson remains at odds with Hughes over what happened. "Dave's efforts had no impact on Gore's position," he said, "and quite frankly, the dozens of phone calls his messages spurred simply wasted a lot of people's time on both ends of the phone." Nelson told me that Gore's committee lacked jurisdiction over the Department of Education, and that anyway, schools had little to do with high-level R&D. "The Labor Committee had and has its own ideas about DoEd's role in educational computing and networking, and it is not the role of the Commerce Committee to define what that role is."

But whatever the jurisdictional and political challenges, they failed to prevent the final version of the Senate bill from passing on November 22, 1991, with the Department of Education included. Hughes had won. At the least, he had shown that he could rally distant strangers around the issue of school networking.

If phone calls can pour into the Hill on an arcane issue like this, word will spread among powerful insiders. Yes, Al Gore was "for" networking at levels below college, K–12 in ed-speak, but Hughes put new pressure on Gore and other politicians to match their PR with at least token specifics.

Across the Potomac River—I live in nearby Alexandria, VA, just inside the infamous Beltway—populists like Dave Hughes do not triumph as often as they should. Instead, political action committees tend to set the tone. Working for special interest groups, everyone from phone company magnates to life insurance reps, PACs dole out millions of dollars in political gifts to members of Congress. Groups rule Washington through other means as well. Some old Congressional staffers and bureaucrats don't just fade away; they eventually end up as lobbyists.

At the symbolic level, however, and maybe at others, the white hats won the K–12 Net issue. Fittingly, they excelled when they used electronic medium itself.

"This may be the first time anyone's actually formed a *de facto* PAC to shape legislation moment-by-moment in Washington," Abernathy told Hughes over the Internet. In the end, even Mike Nelson could not ignore Hughes. Presumably with Nelson's help, Al Gore later championed legislation that advanced K–12 networking. And the next year, when Nelson was an influential member of the Clinton Administration's transition team, he solicited Dave Hughes' thoughts on low-cost networks for schools. Boosters of school networking were no longer crazies. They were part of the mainstream now, and Hughes, regardless of his disagreements with Nelson, had been key.

The question emerges: Just how can other activists—of all political beliefs—replicate Hughes' success? This chapter discusses the Rules for Electronic Citizens.

I'm blending my own thoughts with those of veteran activists and SysOps such as Hughes (dave@oldcolo.com); Frank Odasz (franko@bigsky.dillon.mt.us), a Hughes ally and a leading advocate of school networking; Cliff Figallo (fig@well.sf.ca.us), formerly a SysOp on the WELL in San Francisco, and until recently an activist for the Electronic Frontier Foundation; and Lisa Kimball (lisa@tmn.com), who helps run Metanet, a rather civil system that includes some White House staffers among its members.

Please note that the other people's opinions often clash with mine or with each other's.

What's more, as with any rules, the ones in this chapter are made to be broken. The only exception is the one about telling the truth: life is stressful enough without pushing a cause based on falsehoods.

Rule One: Decide What Issues Are Worthy of Your Time

Like any other activists, the electronic kind will enjoy more power if they don't speak up on everything. Rather than mechanically championing all good causes, the best crusaders act with both passion and knowledge. Dave Hughes is the perfect example here. School networks weren't an abstraction to him; he had seen how BBSes could help rescue his son academically. What's more, having taught at West Point and elsewhere, Hughes himself was hardly a stranger to the field of education.

My own cause right now is TeleRead, my plan to drive down the cost of knowledge. I propose a government-industry effort to slash the cost of sharp-screened, book-friendly computers through a focused procurement program; a universally affordable national library online with fair rewards for publishers and writers of books and educational software; and a way to cost-justify TeleRead through the mass use of electronic forms for federal, state, and local paper-work, as well as consumer transactions.

How could I not fight for TeleRead? I covered a poverty beat in a midwestern factory town and saw what happened when children grew up in bookless homes. Also, I'm an expert in portable computer technology, having written a laptop guide. In addition, I receive just a frac-tion of the cover prices of my books, and wish that more money would go to creators and less to printers. Imagine how much a national library online would help my bargaining power, and it would let me publish myself if publishers didn't treat me decently.

What's more, I'm a consumer as well as a producer of information: I spend thousands of dol-lars each year on information services. At the same time, like many other writers, I'm a small business person who hates government paperwork.

Going online for TeleRead, then, is a "must," not a little detail of my life. Ideally, your own cause should be heartfelt.

Rule Two: Don't Automatically Assume You Must Work Within a Traditional Group

Yes, you may well find a group whose causes you can make your own. Plenty of good organi-zations need you. What's more, when the hoods are trying to ram special-interest laws through Congress, you'll appreciate the activist groups that patrol the Hill in person. Often, however, nothing can beat the effectiveness of individuals and *ad hoc* groups online. Dave Hughes notes the tendency for politicians at all levels to think, "Oh, that's just the ACLU," or "What else do you expect of the AARP?" But if you're on your own, it is harder to pigeon-hole you or your *ad hoc* allies.

In general, although organizations still set the tone for political discourse, we need them *somewhat* less than before. Consider the major elements of a traditional political group—and the alternatives you can use on the Internet and other networks:

- **Staff.** Groups of one kind or another—mostly trade organizations, but also political ones—are a major industry in the city where I live. On some streets, you see row after row of association buildings, filled with thousands of staffers.

  Alternative: A lone activist online, or a small, *ad hoc* group organized around a particular cause, can often stand up surprisingly well against established groups. Remember, *ad hoc* groups online lack the overhead of traditional organizations. No one has to plan a Christmas party or map out a retirement plan. Besides, who's going to hang around for a gold watch? If your *ad hoc* group achieves its original goal and has no other, why the devil should it continue to exist?

  Meanwhile, for the purpose of your cause, you can build up a treasure trove of resources. People can swap files and you can even assemble an archive of each other's messages and files.

  Who needs a big publications department when each of your supporters can be a publisher online? Unlike many traditional groups, you won't see publications as a profit center so much as a way to spread the word. And without a dollars-and-cents fixation, you find you can reach more people.

- **Membership lists.** Conventional groups devote hour after hour to building up their membership rolls. They send out "mass snailings," as I'll call the mailings. People online refer to paper mail as *snail mail* because of its slowness compared with computer nets. "Snailings," alas, is all too apt—especially because many organizations do not use first-class mail.

  Alternative: You start a mailing list or newsgroup on the Internet. People come to you. The power of your cause grows apparent through the increasing number of messages posted to your list or your newsgroup.

  True, your *ad hoc* group lives only in cyberspace and lacks an imposing building on Pennsylvania Avenue. But nowadays, fewer and fewer politicians care about physical trappings. More and more groups have a token post office address in Washington and conduct their real business elsewhere. You don't think politicians are catching on?

  No, it isn't the buildings about which the politicians care. It's whether you can energize people into taking action, and whether you can build credibility within the news media and at the relevant government agencies.

- **Newsletters, magazines, and other publications.** They are among the most tangible ways for conventional groups to build bonds with members.

  Alternative: Here again, you use mailing lists and newsgroups to establish a presence in the allies' minds. You can also put out electronic publications. But electronic discussion groups really serve you best because your allies can interact with you.

Note the term *ally*. They needn't be formal members. You can very nicely run a mailing list and engage in other activities as an individual. A prime example of this is the Choice-Mail mailing list for people who work for abortion rights. Tori (vnasman@desire.wright.edu) is a scientist who, for security reasons, doesn't want her last name used; she runs Choice-Mail. She helps pro-choice people coordinate their activities and learn of new resources and warns them about threats to abortion clinics. And she does it herself: no staff. Meanwhile, she enjoys a symbiotic relationship with existing groups; they help her and she helps them.

■ **Conventions.** Traditional groups hold conventions to bond their staffers and members together.

Alternatives: Yes, so far, computer nets lack Star Trek-style wizardry of the kind that beamed up Scotty's colleagues. But if you're not together with your allies face to face, you're at least exchanging ideas more often than through conventions. You and the others are doing this at your own convenience—whenever you pick up your e-mail or download files. As Dave Hughes likes to say, "time stands still in cyberspace."

What's more, you and your allies can piggyback on the gatherings of traditional groups. Online foes of gun control, for example, can still see each other at the usual NRA gatherings.

■ **Elections.** Traditional groups vote at conventions or through the mail.

Alternatives: If you're a one-person show, people vote for you in the ultimate way; they either read your messages or ignore them. And if you're running an *ad hoc* group, you can poll each other electronically.

Indeed, the Internet itself is a form of electronic democracy, complete with votes on whether to allow the formation of new newsgroups on Usenet.

Rule Three: Be Realistic about the Possibility of Payback

If only the world were like my IBM clone. When I hit the Return key, I know I'm ready for a new paragraph. And when I press the save button, I can hear my hard drive clicking away.

Washington and City Hall, however, are not like computers: no algorithms exist to overturn stupid laws or pass good ones. The payback for your efforts may be nonexistent or far off—perhaps beyond your lifetime. To forge ahead, you may have to feel a communion with people who aren't even born yet.

Luckily, however, not all issues are this way. There are different degrees of personal influence and rewards.

In most cases, you'll enjoy the maximum influence at the local level. One example is Dave Hughes' fight against that moronic ordinance that placed home businesses in peril. Hughes tested his thinking on at least several people before he leapt into action. Very obviously, he wanted to make sure that the effort would be worth his while. Although Hughes used a BBS system, in certain cases you can also avail yourself of the Internet, which has areas devoted to happenings in various geographical regions. Some places, such as the Raleigh-Durham-Chapel Hill area of North Carolina, even have newsgroups devoted to local and state politics.

Less personal influence may come when you're working on a national or international cause that existing groups already have on the agenda. You're fighting for or against gay rights or a Constitutional amendment calling for a balanced budget. You haven't any guarantee that you'll get your way, and you're one of many, so your role is diluted; but at least your goal is on the horizon. It isn't as if you're out championing an idea on your own; you enjoy plenty of company.

And then there is the kind of cause where your personal payback may be far off and even non-existent. You're a cyber-Quixote. I plead guilty here; in TeleRead, I'm calling for major changes in the publishing, education, the international copyright system, and the computer industry. Do I think that TeleRead will happen next week? Well, the White House isn't exactly on the verge of crusading for a comprehensive national database full of affordable books and educational software. Even as politicians try to overcome the health care crisis, they may be setting us up for a knowledge crisis someday. Schoolchildren in the slums can retrieve many fewer books by modem than can those in rich suburbs; and school systems do not give written word its full due.

Should I abandon hope, then, because my goals are not as close as Dave Hughes' were back when he was fighting the ordinance? Definitely not. TeleRead is at the point where William F. Buckley, Jr., has written two columns endorsing the idea. I've testified before a hearing on the National Information Infrastructure. A letter on TeleRead has come from Gore ("I'm impressed with this detailed and very professional presentation"); although probably boilerplate, the letter is an indication that the Establishment at least knows of the idea now. And Newt Gingrich, Speaker of the House, keeps talking about the need to close the technological gap between rich and poor—not to mention his interest in fighting government-created paperwork, which TeleRead would do through its electronic forms feature.

Besides, major political and social changes are often incremental. Even if TeleRead became the law, my plan would happen over a number of years. And if it isn't law during the Clinton Administration? Future historians will hold the White House accountable for ignoring better alternatives to present policies. A TeleRead-style approach is inevitable. If the United States does not undertake one, other countries will. Meanwhile, civil rights groups will come to understand the perils of not establishing a national library online for rich and poor alike.

You may disagree with my reasoning. But keep in mind the lesson here: Don't rule out fighting for your favorite cause even if the payback is far off.

Another example is my plan for an Electronic Peace Corps, my proposal to upgrade telecommunications in the Third World and use computer networks to exchange technical knowledge. I came up with the idea in the 1980s; the government did not act. Now, lo and behold, the magazine of the influential Internet Society has published a proposal for an Internet Peace Corps that in many ways overlaps with mine. Am I charging plagiarism? Not at all. I'm delighted that the Society can see similar visions now, whether or not the writer read my EPC articles in the *Washington Post* and elsewhere. Meanwhile, a discussion of the idea has already found its way into an official report from the Office of Technology Assessment.

With a tough skin and the right genes, you may yet live to see your idea become a law. No guarantees, but remember that many members of the establishment were not always so favored in the press and society at large. How many of Bill Clinton's present supporters were on his side when it looked as if his chances of reaching the White House were zilch? The point is, most people in power have overcome major setbacks in fighting for their jobs and their ideas. If you go by your own vision, the most powerful policy makers will often respect you more, not less.

Meanwhile, take solace in an old quote from Jonathan Swift: "When a true genius appears in this world, you may know him by this sign: that the dunces are all in confederacy against him."

Rule Four: Know How To Scout the Internet Effectively and Where To Post Your Own Messages

You cannot convince people unless you know what's on their minds. When I push TeleRead, for example, I'm on the lookout for postings that discuss the shortcomings of the present copyright system. I try to keep up with those areas of the Internet that relate to what I'm doing.

I have scores of newsgroups in the file that determine what my news-reading program will call up. At the same time, I make no attempt to read all newsgroups, even those in areas of interest. My days simply aren't long enough. Instead, I keep up with mailing lists to which people often forward and crosspost messages that appear elsewhere. Many people on these lists share my concerns. In effect, they are acting as my research assistants.

Needless to say, I also use search tools on the World Wide Web, Gopher, and other information-finders to see where files and other resources exist. But as an ongoing pointer, nothing beats a good list or newsgroup whose members share your interests and keep you up to date.

If nothing else, you'll want to use lists and newsgroups to find like-minded souls. The *like-minded* part is important. Yes, you want to test your thoughts on a variety of people, some foes, some potential allies; but in the end, it's the allies and the uncommitted who count, not those who are forever destined to oppose your thinking. You want your allies to write to policy makers, and your foes to resist the urge.

In pushing my TeleRead idea, for example, I presently do not spend that much time on the general discussion areas for activists. I know who my main targets are: public librarians who share my passion for affordable knowledge; people who run community networks and have a definite populist orientation; Net-oriented educators; and academics interested in electronic publications.

Compared to the usual Internet newsgroups, fewer people read my postings on these specialized mailing lists. However, the readers who do encounter me care more about my topic than Internet users at large—what's more, it wouldn't hurt someday to have the American Library Association on my side.

At any rate, given the fact that the Net teems with at least 10,000 newsgroups, I must set priorities for reading and posting.

Rule Five: Don't Be Intrusive or Otherwise Boorish

Don't barge into a conversation on an existing topic and inflict your pet topic on others unless your subject fits in. Cliff Figallo rightly compares this to boorish behavior at a party. Still, there is a difference between a rude interruption and an explanation about how your thoughts fit in with the concerns of others.

Just try to segue gracefully; if others want your topic to be separate, please oblige them in a hurry. Good, sound, selfish reasons exist for respecting people's wishes. Some Net software, for example, offers bozo filters that can screen out messages by topic or sender. Most readers have only a limited amount of money, or time, for the Internet.

Also, in determining whether to post a message, don't forget the difference between newsgroups and mail lists. Most people—not all—have the software to wander through newsgroups by topic rather than having to suffer through every message. It's taken for granted that folks skip messages. You needn't be *quite* so choosy about the topics you post.

Mailing lists, however, often aren't set up with a high volume in mind, so be especially sure that your concerns fit within the lists of which you're a member. Granted, it's hard to generalize. Some lists bill themselves as "high volume" and others as "low volume." But normally, prudence is best.

Whether you're posting to a list or newsgroup, be very careful about messages of excessive length. Offer to e-mail—to the interested—your electronic manifesto. Or provide a way of downloading it as a file. I myself favored e-mail early on so that I could use cover letters to establish rapport with people reading `teleread.txt`. Then I started pointing people in the direction of a file posted on a Gopher.

If you go the e-mail routine, don't forget to warn requesters to write you at your regular address rather than through the list itself. Members of the list should not have their screens cluttered with messages from people requesting your file. Having learned the hard way, I sometimes use the following message in the signature that appears at the bottom of my postings on lists:

```
Please direct your responses only to me (rothman@clark.net) rather than to the
entire list. Be careful that your software does not automatically send your note
to everyone else, too.
```

Rule Six: Write for the Medium

A *National Enquirer* writer would feel at home on the Internet. As writers and readers, many Internauts favor short sentences and short paragraphs. Computer screens are harder to read than paper and can show only so much text at once. The typical posting on a newsgroup or list shouldn't be more than 400 to 500 words at most and, ideally, much shorter. That's the wisdom, and I'd agree with it most of the time.

Still, on occasion, I let my paragraphs go on. A good paragraph, after all, usually builds around a central idea. And if that idea is complex enough, the paragraph itself may end up that way.

Furthermore, the posting itself may exceed the standard length if the subject warrants it. The important thing is not to go on for thousands of words without sufficient reason.

Again, remember that you can hold down the lengths of most postings and offer to use electronic mail to send your full document. Yes, I know that 28,000 words of `teleread.txt` scares off many people. But it isn't as if I'm writing a quick little reaction to a new war or some other headline of the day. Instead, I'm proposing major changes in the copyright system. I'd rather that fewer people read my file than many people breeze through material full of gaps.

Whether I post a quick message or put out a long proposal, I try to do the following:

- Favor subject lines that stand out from the swarms of other messages but aren't obnoxious or misleading. My task is the same as that of a headline writer for a newspaper. Short of writing *Headless Corpse Found in Topless Bar*, I'll do my best to be noticed. I try to be honest, of course: If my headline doesn't jibe with my actual message, I lose credibility.

NOTE

Another caveat is to make sure that people won't mind seeing the subject line repeated when others respond to your message. Once, I was publicly debating the National Information Infrastructure with a former intelligence official who, in a private reply, used some military-strength language that I felt told everything about his attitude toward the democracy and the NII. I made two bad mistakes.

First, even though I'd warned him that I wanted public answers to some extremely legitimate questions, I shouldn't have quoted from his private message. Second, I used a subject line with the first letter of one of his colorful words, followed by three blanks. This was the Internet, I figured. People would understand what I was doing. Not so. Friends of the man successfully diverted the dialog from the real issues to the question of netiquette. Just as frustrating, I saw my original subject line—the one alluding to his salty language—assault people's eyes again and again.

- Make the beginnings as catchy as you can—with one major exception: Often I let messages lead off with a shortened quote from others' postings.

- Tell stories as much as possible. In the main part of TeleRead, for example, I write of the Kid Next Door who helped confirm the Big Bang Theory. Then I suggest that we'd have more Edward Wrights if children in the ghettos enjoyed the same access to knowledge that Ned did. I'm following an old rule for popular-level writing; that is, I explain issues in terms of people. If anything, Dave Hughes uses stories more than I do.

- Relate your message to the medium. When a *Washington Post* reporter got online to complain that people were illegally pirating an article he'd written, I came back with the suggestion that this showed the need for TeleRead. My plan would reduce the financial incentive for piracy.

- On long files, use summaries and tables of contents so that people can know in a hurry what follows. TeleRead starts off with the gist of the proposal and its benefits. Then I have a point-by-point summary of what I propose (in a way that a bureaucrat would approve). Next comes a table of contents. And only then do I have the main proposal and the shorter articles that follow.

  Not everyone approves of this format. Some say, "Just get into the main show immediately. No repetition please!" As much as anyone, however, I'm aware of the shortcomings of the present technology. Screens are much harder to read than paper. And some repetition helps my points get through.

- Favor dialogue when posting messages. I'm very liberal with quotes from people to whom I'm replying. Readers love context, as long as you don't overdo it. With popular mail-reading programs such as PINE or Eudora, it's a snap to quote other people and use symbols to set their words apart from yours.

> >I agree. But don't clutter up the nets with insipid me-too messages. See
> if you can explain why you agree.
>
> >This is turning into a dialog!
>
> Exactly! For maintaining people's interest, a dialog often beats a monolog
> any old time. In fact, one of the most popular literary forms on the Inter-
> net is a form of dialog: the FAQ.
>
> Q.   What's a FAQ?
>
> A.   Frequently Asked Questions. The same person is writing both
>   questions and answers alike.
>
> Q.   Almost Socratic.
>
> A.   Absolutely.
>
> Q.   Should look great on a computer screen.
>
> A.   Lots of white space.
>
> Q.   Where do people use FAQs?
>
> A.   You'll find them for newsgroups or on lists—one good way to get
>   the lay of the land before you start contributing. What's more,
>   you can write your own FAQs. Why not invite readers to e-mail
>   you for a FAQ about your favorite cause or group? If you're com-
>   fortable with this writing style, go for it. The disadvantage
>   is that FAQs take up more space than regular prose and can be
>   lethal if you overdose on such material. And some things just
>   flow better without FAQs.

■ Use smileys and other symbols to establish that you're joking. :-) The person at the other end may not even be a natural speaker—well, reader—of English. Even when communicating with Americans, be aware that your messages are seen by people of diverse backgrounds.

If you're a man, be aware that just as in speech, male humor on the Net can diverge considerably from female humor. Sometimes the results aren't pretty. Even with a smiley used, a woman may consider a joking remark to be mean spirited. And, as Lisa Kimball notes, the remark indeed may come across as more than a harmless joke, smiley or not.

If you're a woman and want civil discussion without the roughness of the Internet newsgroups, consider membership in a service such as Metanet, the one Kimball helps run. You can still get on the Net for information, but build your virtual community— your circle of regulars—around the smaller system. As much as I love the anarchy of the Internet, I want people to be aware of alternatives such as Metanet.

Rule Seven: Tell the Truth

Don't lie. Check your facts. Here are three good reasons:

1. Although the Constitution protects freedom of speech, it doesn't give you the right to libel anyone on the Internet—either your enemy in a flame war or a third party.

2. The Net provides enough resources for people to verify everything from the population of Australia to a quote from the U.S. Constitution.

3. If you're caught in a lie, thousands of readers just might find out about this through newsgroup postings or otherwise.

People online who are representing groups should be especially careful lest they tarnish the reputation of the whole organization. When they're wrong, they should admit it quickly. The other day, I heard from a man who had responded to an international group's human rights campaign. He said the campaign falsely accused a Latin American country of violations. A correction eventually came, but not until the man had persistently followed up on the matter. I don't know who's right or wrong here—only that individuals and groups alike should be careful about their facts.

Luckily, with the Net, you can replace the wrong information with the right information. If you're wrong about something, don't give up on your electronic manifesto. Just issue a new version with the new facts in place. When you distribute your manifesto, date your work and let people know how they can get a more recent version.

Rule Eight: Turn Flaming to Your Advantage

Don't expect to convert the person who's insulting you with obnoxious messages and doing his or her best to destroy your arguments. Unless you enjoy debate for debate's sake, don't hang around if you can spend your time in a more sympathetic newsgroup or on a more promising list.

On the other hand, there are times when flaming can actually help you. Suppose that you feel that plenty of readers do indeed sympathize with you; then argue on! The more unreasonable the other side is and the cheaper the shots against you, the more sensible you and your arguments seem to onlookers.

The Net jargon for onlookers, of course, is *lurkers*—people who read but don't post. It's been said that for every one person posting on computer nets, at least 10 others are lurking. So engage the foe, but play to the lurkers.

ETERNAL FLAMES: A CAVEAT

Eternal wars online help neither you nor your opponents. Be open to the possibility of a cease-fire even if you can never reach an agreement. Your foe on a particular issue may become a friend on another issue. After all, you both cared enough about a subject to exchange hard words over it. That shows common interest in the topic, if nothing else. Both the ex-intelligence official and I, for example, have complained again and again about the lack of a good national information strategy and the need for better databases; when we finally met each other face to face, we shook hands. I suspect he recognized the same truth that I did: The more specialized your interest, the more small-townish the Net can seem and the more likely you are to run across the same people again. Sustained feuds sap too much energy from these Net communities.

Rule Nine: Provide a Way for People To Take Action

Whether you're an individual or a group, encourage your readers to act in one way or another— and provide them guidance for that action.

Consider the example of a group called Not a Penny More, which used the Internet "as a springboard for a Federal spending-sanity campaign." Organizer G. Thomas Rush (`thomasr@cpqhou.compaq.com`) collected "individuals' pledges to pay down the Federal debt, if a Federal spending freeze is enacted and executed." Yes, he also asked readers to contact Washington, but you can bet that his pledge campaign was much catchier than a mere letter-writing campaign.

Of course, there's nothing wrong with a well-orchestrated campaign for letters. Amnesty International (reachable through `hnaylor@igc.apc.org`) doesn't just show the flag online and recruit members. It also puts out a letter-writing guide with wonderfully detailed instructions. Readers learn, for example, not to "discuss ideology or politics. Your message must be for the benefit of the victim and not a vehicle for your political opinions." The guide comes complete with sample letters and tips on how to address a King or Admiral.

From Palo Alto, California, Anne P. Mitchell (`shedevil@vix.com`), a family law attorney dealing in the rights of divorced fathers, uses the Internet to distribute a concise recruitment form with just the right questions. It asks, for example: "Which states' information interests you?" You fill out the form online, e-mail it back to her, and she adds you to her list.

Joining a mailing list can itself be a form of action. In many cases, you don't need special software to put together a small list—just check with your system administrator to make sure that you're using the system within bounds. Tori, the abortion rights crusader in the Midwest, says her operation involves "just me, via my private account," from which she reaches some 75 people in 25 states.

Rule Ten: Don't Forget To Communicate with the Media and the Policy Makers

Are you actually trying to change public policy or are you out for recreational debating? Each day, the Internet and the commercial networks carry thousands of messages from people who are more interested in arguing than in acting. Their wisdom stays within cyberspace. If it reaches the real world, it's only through indirect means.

If you really want to influence policy, however, you'd better take time off from the debate online and work up strategies for dealing with newspapers and real live politicians and other officials.

Significantly, in the United States, freedom of the press exists more for newspapers and magazines than for private individuals. No law says the *New York Times* or your local newspaper must print your letter. Such interference would be blatantly unconstitutional. And that's how it should be, even if it means that many newspapers publish a range of opinions from A to Z.

Just the same, if you can get publicity in newspapers, that can help you on the Net. When I post items about TeleRead, I'm sometimes asked for the exact dates of print citations. A reverence for paper exists even in cyberspace.

When dealing with newspapers and magazines, keep in mind that some editors see any electronic media as a rival. Many journalists cling to their old roles as gatekeepers. When I wrote about TeleRead for the *Washington Post*, an editor refused to print my electronic address for readers to contact me for further information. But your own local paper may be more sensible about this. See whether you can't get an opinion article or letter to the editor published with your Internet address included.

Should you simultaneously post the same material to the Net? Maybe. It may be harder for a newspaper to ignore you if the editors know you have other avenues. I'll add a warning. Some editors may come back and say, "Well, if it's already on the Internet, why should we give you another forum?" If a problem arises, you can counter it this way: "Okay, I'll write another letter with another angle just for you. Besides, how many of your readers scan `alt.activism` regularly?" Should the editor still not go along, he or she may just be looking for an excuse to censor you—in which case, you can post your complaint on the Net.

Luckily, newspapers are growing more comfortable with the new technology. When the *San Jose Mercury* publishes an article, the newspaper may include a code that readers can key in to the Mercury Center area of American Online and receive further information. That way, for example, readers can get documents referenced in a news article. Sooner or later, such arrangements are bound to happen on the Internet itself.

Publicity, of course, is just a means to an end—the actual actions by policy makers. Here are some tips for lobbying civil servants and politicians at all levels of government:

- ■ Mail them copies of your Net postings, and say what you're doing so that they'll know you'll have an audience.

- ■ Include in the postings the names, addresses, and phone numbers of the relevant people for readers to contact. If officials in your town lack Internet addresses to mention, let's hope that situation changes.

- ■ When you write public officials but you worry they'll ignore you, post a copy of your letter on the Net. Please note that some officials may take your actions the wrong way—there are risks here. Go by the situation.

- ■ Don't antagonize officials *needlessly*, and if you're unhappy, remember to attack ideas rather than personalities. You can never tell who may be a friend later on, or at least be a little more cooperative in another context. Dave Hughes notes he wasn't at odds with Mike Nelson personally, just his reasons for not including the Department of Education in the NREN bill.

  Nelson himself was professional enough to solicit Hughes' K–12 BBS ideas even if the two had disagreed on the NREN legislation. Today, Nelson is a power within the Office of Science and Technology Policy, and an extended public feud between him and Hughes would serve neither them nor the public.

  Of course, this does not mean you should wimp out when the public official refuses to play by the rules. I'm waging a war on the Net right now against a benighted appointee of the Clinton Administration who has succumbed to the wishes of special-interest groups opposed to the needs of schoolchildren and library users. Like Hughes and Nelson and the former intelligence man, I'll be open to friendly encounters later on. But right now, it's war. The Clintonian has made it clear that for the moment, he won't listen to reason. Under such circumstances, I'll be delighted to antagonize him, especially because I can try to bypass him on the Hill.

- ■ Most of all, in e-mail messages and public postings, show some empathy for officials who deserve it. Don't beat up on them for events and policies over which they have no control.

  How would you feel if you worked for the California Employment Development Department and someone called you to task for Irangate? This actually happened to a member of one mailing list when he was discussing his life as a state government official.

  "Of course, as a citizen," he told me, "I was as repulsed as anyone else. If I were to speak for my agency, I'd say, 'Hey, we pay unemployment, find people jobs, collect taxes, and manage a few federal programs. What's that got to do with us?' It's sort of like saying, 'Let's punish a local HMO because a German blood bank distributed tainted blood.' We don't do arms. We don't do secret international intrigue."

Also show empathy by not expecting instant agreement from officials whom you encounter online. Regardless of disclaimers that may appear at the bottom of their messages, public officials know that some people may regard them as speaking for their agencies. So, typically, they are most circumspect in any reactions they offer to your ideas. They never know when the boss may be online. What's more, is it really fair to expect public officials to make instant decisions based on your e-mail or postings?

If nothing else, remember what an acquaintance of mine has observed: There is a difference between being able to communicate with public officials and having them agree with you.

■ If the issues are local, you may want to show up at a meeting of a city council or a zoning commission. That's what David Hughes did—with plenty of supporters recruited through his BBS. Hughes posted a copy of an ordinance that could have shut down many home businesses. The ordinance was supposed to prevent home businesses from disturbing neighbors by way of traffic from customers and delivery people. But along the way, it would have shut down modem and phone-based businesses for which little came in and out but electrons. Thanks to Hughes' BBS and newspaper publicity, however, the threat went away. You yourself may spread word to allies using BBSes and a locally oriented newsgroup on the Internet. Local newsgroups exist for more cities than you expect.

Suppose that the issues are national and Washington is nearby, or you have money for a trip? Then by all means, show up in person if you can and try to testify at relevant hearings if you have enough expertise in the area under discussion. You won't just have a chance to express yourself; you can meet others with like views and forge alliances with people who are not online. What's more, you can benefit from arguments that the like-minded are making, or at least those with which you agree.

To find out about hearings, of course, you can do the obvious and subscribe to the relevant lists and track newsgroups. Using the electronic newsletter of the American Library Association, for example, I learned of an all-important hearing on electronic copyrights and related issues. I didn't pay a cent for the newsletter. I simply asked to be placed on the list for it.

Hearings are announced in the *Federal Register*, but as of this writing, it's too expensive for individual activists. We'll hope that changes. Sooner or later, if Washington wants to be truly Jeffersonian, the *Register* will be online for free or at an affordable price. And when that happens, you can search it regularly for topics of interest.

■ Try to follow up on issues and remind politicians and civil servants that your interest continues. Don't just try to testify. Write or phone your contacts to find out how the matter is progressing.

Whatever action you take, keep in mind the value of the Internet for both educating yourself for intelligent debate and, above all, for helping society arrive at a consensus.

"A few subjects are hot, such as abortion or gay rights," Dave Hughes says, "and sometimes things are so bitter and polarized that even online, a consensus doesn't emerge. But on most subjects, my finding is that by sustaining the discussion, people who are not passionate about it one way or another tend to listen. It takes three to politic. Two can bargain and argue, but the third person is the one they are actually talking to."

If you want to reach the third person—and also strengthen your efforts offline—you owe it to yourself to try the Internet.

DON'T RISK YOUR JOB OR NET PRIVILEGES

Many people are on the Net through academic or corporate accounts. Before crusading online for causes, they should check with their system administrators to find out whether there are any obstacles. Many corporations, for example, may flat out prevent people from using company Nets this way. Even some schools may do the same, saying that such activities are a waste of tax-supported computer facilities.

How to reduce such problems? Some possibilities:

■ Beyond checking with the system administrator, consult with him or her about an online disclaimer that can appear in your signature at the bottom of messages.

For example: "Do not blame MegaCorps for my opinions. I just work there."

■ Be thrifty with disk space and other system resources you're using for your cause. If in doubt, check with the administrator.

■ Don't steal time away from your company. Save the world on your own time.

■ Consider getting an account from a private Internet provider that you can use at home.

■ Also think about Telnetting into a special service such as one from Digital Express (call 1-800-969-9090 or 1-301-847-5000). For $8.95 per month, Digex gives you a private, boss-proof account with your own Net address—and no corporate identifier other than the standard `access.digex.net`.

SUMMING UP RUSH

Although I'm unabashedly liberal, that's hardly true of many on the Internet. Libertarians are very conspicuous; and so are many other non-PC folks (and I don't mean the Mac crowd).

John Switzer (jrs@netcom.com) posts summaries of the Rush Limbaugh radio show to alt.fan.rush-limbaugh and alt.rush-limbaugh. He says, "I've gotten hundreds of letters from people across the world who appreciate it as a way they can 'listen' to Rush when they're out of the country. I'm fascinated by the entire electronic publishing idea, and it seems that what I'm doing is just a small part of what's going on in the Internet. I would like to think I'm helping the conservative cause by doing the summaries, and thereby provide a record of the issues which Rush and his callers talk about. Whether it's really helpful, though, I have no idea."

It is, John. Political ideas are just as important as scientific and technical ideas. And if networks can speed up progress in medicine and supercomputers by making it easier to share facts and opinions, the same should hold true here.

A TRUE CITIZEN'S WEB: DON'T LET SOCKS MEOW FOR YOU

The White House is on the World Wide Web with *An Interactive Citizens' Handbook* (http://www.whitehouse.gov). You can see President Clinton shaking JFK's hand, call up Socks the cybercat and hear him meow, or fill out a form and fire off a letter to Bill or Al.

Unfortunately, however, if you want to meow back about taxes or gun control or your other pet cause, you will probably get only the most prosaic of replies. Chances are, you'll be just part of a public opinion sample. You are far better off focusing your efforts elsewhere—on correspondence with other, less exalted, officials; on your usual search for information; and perhaps, on a Web page of your own to which your Net postings can call attention.

Granted, the White House handbook and official congressional resources on the Web can be godsends if you understand their limitations (a good start for Capitol Hill is the legislative guide at http://thomas.loc.gov/). They're handy for, say, tracking down Bill Clinton's speeches and policy papers so that you can praise or attack them intelligently. Ditto for material from Newt Gingrich (e-mail address: georgia6@hr.house.gov) and his friends on the Hill. And of course, the WWW and Gopher areas of Congress can help you navigate the tangle of Hill committees when you're figuring out the right targets for your letters.

In many cases, however, any relationship between the official areas and "electronic democracy" is strictly coincidental. I'm glad that the texts of bills are on the Web, but what good do they do if the lobbyists get the momentum going behind closed doors? It may well be too late to stop them by the time the information is on the Web.

This isn't just talk. Recently, the Taxpayers' Assets Project (try the Web address `gopher://gopher.essential.org`—an address that also brings up the names of like-minded groups) ran across a sleazy loophole in a Paperwork Reduction Act. This stealth would have reduced public access to government information while favoring a well-connected Minnesota company. As part of the Republicans' Contract with America, this assault on citizen-taxpayers was on the fast track. And the white hats would have been up the creek if they'd lazed back and depended on official WWW or Gopher areas. The lesson is that if we citizens pay too much heed to official offerings on the World Wide Web and not enough to real life, the Web can actually harm democracy.

How do you use the Web or Gopher on your own terms? Here are some tips you can use to go beyond the official areas on the Web:

■ Latch on to WWW offerings from like-minded people—whether they're NRA activists or environmentalists. They can steer you to official links. The best activist areas put White House and Hill propaganda in context through information of their own. You may learn, for example, about the voting records of Congressmen on key issues. Liberals may be interested in such areas as the Institute for Global Communications (`http://www.igc.apc.org/igc/igcinfo.html`). Conservatives can try The Right Side of the Web (`http://www.clark.net/pub/jeffd/index.html`). People of all ideologies can try Political Participation on the Internet (`http://www.ai.mit.edu/projects/ppp/summary.html`)—even if most of the listings seem liberal, in keeping with the general nature of the groups on the Net.

■ Learn how to navigate the Web through search engines such as Lycos (`http://lycos.cs.cmu.edu/`). That way, you don't just dig up information from bureaucrats and activists, you also run across facts from noncombatants such as scientists. Think what an environmentalist can do for studies of the Amazon.

Please note that you don't need the fanciest of software to use Lycos. Lycos should work fine with the Lynx browser available to many cheap, dial-up accounts.

■ Start your own home page to develop angles that may not already be on the Web. Maybe, for example, you're a space activist but don't think enough is online about the benefits of going to Mars in particular. You can post your own opinions and links to Web areas—whether from NASA or fellow spaceniks—who support your opinions. Take a look at `http://muon.qrc.com/space/start.html`. Whatever your area of interest, try to remember the strengths and weaknesses of the Web: don't use just text—use photos that enliven your presentation, just make sure that they do not bog people down too much as they wander around your area. For the most part, make the jazzy stuff optional—many people dialing up your home page may not even be able to see the images because of the limitations of their Net connections or hardware or software. Also consider using sound clips of famous speeches relating to your cause—but check out the legal situation before posting the material. Too, try to make your WWW page interactive by using forms people can fill out to e-mail to politicians. Investigate the possibility of e-mail-to-fax bridges if that doesn't sound beyond you. Remember, most politicians still aren't on the Net.

■ Do not neglect real life. Don't get so wrapped up in prettying up your Web page that you neglect the cause itself, the page's *raison d'etre*.

■ Do not neglect other areas of the Net beyond the World Wide Web. Flaunt that Web address so that people know it exists. Add the Web URL to the signature file with which you conclude postings to newsgroups and mailing lists. Be sure to format the reference to your home page so that it serves as a true link when people use Netscape (and similar browsers) to call up newsgroups.

THE FUTURE FOR ELECTRONIC CITIZENS: FOUR PREDICTIONS

■ More public officials will go online. One of the most networked places is Santa Monica, California, where even the homeless can stand up for themselves online by using computers in public places. In Washington, at least several dozen members of Congress are available to constituents through the Internet. And these numbers should grow. More important, the big bureaucracies such as the IRS and the Social Security Administration will eventually be geared up to handle correspondence and paperwork electronically—not just in a limited way but on a truly mass basis. That's one of the goals of Vice President Gore's National Performance Review.

■ Officials will need to use software that can help them cope with the electronic onslaught of letters from citizens with praise or an attitude. Such software ideally could analyze the issues that citizens bring up, as well as tabulate their positions.

At the same time, we must remember that years and years will pass before electronic mail is representative, if ever. E-mail mustn't replace voting or scientific opinion polls.

Yes, e-mail can reduce the cost of communications between government officials and people with modems; and many intelligent people may be encouraged to share their wisdom with the Hill. But we're a long way from being able to shut down the snail operations on Capitol Hill.

- We'll be in trouble if politicians cannot resist the movement to let people vote on individual issues electronically. Unless Americans can gain a lot more leisure, they just don't have time to do their homework. That's why we elect politicians to attend to our business. If we don't like the way they are doing their jobs, we toss them out of office. I'm skeptical of people who think the whole country could be run like the Internet. Voting on the creations of a new newsgroup isn't quite the same as voting on the death penalty or abortion laws. The effects are a little more permanent.

- Video will change the balance of power on the networks, and not necessarily for the better. Right now, the Internet belongs to articulate people who can express their beliefs well in writing. But when video finally arrives, the written word will count less. Thoughts won't be as well developed. As in TV, the superficial—bodies, hair, faces, voices—will count more than they should. I'm not suggesting that we ban video for the masses, merely that we work to preserve the written word. Perhaps, as the cost of technology drops, we should figure out a way to make written e-mail free to all.

Federal Information on the Internet

57

*by Maggie
Parhamovich*

Increasingly, the United States Government is distributing information in electronic formats, including distribution on the Internet. Federal agencies are discovering the benefits of using the Internet to communicate with federal employees scattered across the nation, in addition to accessing remote files for local needs. Federal agencies are also using the Internet to distribute information to the public. In some cases, electronic information is replacing traditional print formats—such as press releases from the Bureau of the Census—which are no longer distributed in paper format to Federal Depository Libraries but are available on Cendata on DIALOG. The trend of federal information being released on the Internet is generally positive, but improvements in access and locators are necessary to integrate electronic federal information with traditional print resources.

Although there are no statistics measuring the amount of federal information available on the Internet, growth has been substantial. Federal Gophers and Web sites have increased significantly since 1993. In addition, a variety of commercial, local government, and university databases include federal information such as the University of Michigan's Gopher, which includes 1990 census data and statistics from the Economic Bulletin Board of the Department of Commerce. Better electronic technology and accessibility, combined with increased usage of personal computers in homes and offices, has contributed to the growth of federal information on the Internet.

Distributing federal information through the Internet has several advantages. Physical location of information is no longer an issue because information may be retrieved from any location in the nation. When the National Performance Review was released in Washington, D.C., in September 1993, libraries in the western part of the nation were able to download the report within 24 hours of its release, thereby eliminating a waiting period of one to three months before the report would have been distributed in paper format. The Internet plays an important role in expediting the information process by providing low-cost and expedient delivery of information.

The Internet provides the opportunity for increased citizen participation in the government process. In 1992 and 1993, the Office of Management and Budget (OMB) revised Circular A-130 and announced the process in the *Federal Register*. Citizens were able to send comments to OMB by mail or e-mail, which increased the opportunity for comments from those citizens with e-mail capabilities. E-mail communication is available to the President, Vice President, and some members of Congress. Many congressional staff members and federal employees now have e-mail and Internet capabilities. More legislative information is available on the Internet, including federal legislation on LOCIS and THOMAS at the Library of Congress, and GPO Access by the Government Printing Office. Previously, electronic delivery of federal information was limited to costly, private databases. The Internet provides a low-cost alternative for citizens who have the capability to connect to the Internet or through libraries that provide electronic connections or information.

During an era of declining budgets, the Internet is cost effective for the federal government. Electronic transmission of information eliminates the cost for typesetting, printing, and postage for distribution of information. In addition, an electronic format facilitates revisions and updates to manuals, regulations, and laws that are constantly changing. As more manuals and regulations are maintained on the Internet, citizens can be assured that they have access to current federal regulations as they are issued in Washington, D.C.

The Internet also facilitates access to federal information because it is user friendly for most databases. With the development of Gophers that provide easy menus and standardized access tools, many citizens are finding federal information easier to locate, read, and electronically mail in full text. The Internet is available 24 hours a day, and citizens are not limited to contacting a federal agency during business hours. Many federal Gophers also provide gateways to other federal Gophers, which eliminates the need to search the Internet space for new sources of federal information.

The advances in electronic information by the federal government have not been completely positive, and many changes need to be instituted before the Internet can replace traditional paper and micro formats. Information on the Internet is limited, and most information is geared toward researchers and information specialists instead of toward the average citizen. This is especially evident with the proliferation of Internet databases from the National Aeronautics and Space Administration (NASA), the National Institutes of Health (NIH), and the National Science Foundation (NSF). More information, such as the *Code of Federal Regulations, Commerce Business Daily*, and agency documents need to be uploaded and freely accessible by the public. Although commercial databases provide full-text access to many of these publications, it is imperative to expand access for citizens in support of an informed citizenry and democratization of federal information.

Federal agencies are independently developing Internet databases without interagency coordination. As a result, information is duplicated among agency databases. Multiple paths and Gophers provide the text of the Health Security Act of 1993 but, without experience, it is difficult to determine the most expedient access to text of the Act. Using the USDA Gopher (`zeus.esusda.gov`), it takes five steps to reach the full text of the Act; using the Americans Communicating Electronically (ACE) Gopher (`ace.esusda.gov`), it takes only four steps. However, both Gophers are maintained by the Department of Agriculture. Although this may appear to be only an inconvenience, during peak periods of activity on the Internet, the elimination of a couple of menus can be a real time saver. The lack of consistency in indexing and terms for federal information on the Internet also causes confusion because the same text may be given different titles—such as the Health Security Act of 1993—which is also called the Health Security Legislation of October 1993. Without locators to determine the most expedient path to information and without bibliographic control over titles and contents, librarians and individuals must search the Internet space to become fully familiar with the location of specific information.

Internet support of federal information is directly linked to federal funding. Thus, databases may cease to exist when federal funds or contracts are eliminated. Just as with paper information, if resources decline, electronic information sources may also decline. Federal agencies are being pushed more and more to recover the cost of operations. Charging fees to access federal information appears to be a viable option. Privatization of federal publications or agencies such as National Technical Information Service (NTIS) has also threatened access to government information. Although electronic information offers new opportunities for the private sector to deliver information, the public should not have to pay for both the creation and delivery of government information.

The concerns and problems with federal information can be corrected. As technology improves for electronic delivery of information, federal information on the Internet will also improve. The most significant problem confronting federal information on the Internet is the issue of who has access to the Internet and who lacks access. The situation of "haves versus have-nots" is critical for the issue of federal information. The United States has a tradition of open government; it believes the success of a democracy depends on an informed citizenry who can fully participate in the democratic process. Currently, access to the Internet is limited to those individuals who can afford the equipment and have the expertise to use electronic information, or to individuals who have access through their employer or educational institutions.

The federal Depository Library Program (DLP) was developed in an era of print formats with the primary goal of providing a "safety net" for citizens to freely access federal information. DLP is administered by the Superintendent of Documents within the Government Printing Office (GPO) and provides free documents to depository libraries that, in return, house federal documents and provide librarians and staff to process, preserve, and service federal information. Currently, over a thousand federal depository libraries exist to serve the information needs of American citizens, yet there are no guidelines for the electronic distribution of federal information to depository libraries. Only recently has Congress authorized GPO to provide electronic public access to the *Congressional Record* and *Federal Register*. This mandate is important because it supports federal agencies in their development of electronic information in addition to traditional paper formats. Federal agencies need to vigorously pursue electronic options in the delivery of federal information and make the paradigm shift from paper formats to electronic formats.

Even among depository libraries, there are disparities of access because most university and large public depository libraries have Internet access underwritten as institutional overhead, such as telephone service. Many small public libraries and specialized libraries lack Internet access and expertise, which causes a disparity of service to citizens who are depending on depository libraries as their source of information from the federal government. Depository libraries and librarians must be proactive in securing equipment and training to fully participate in today's information reality and to continue their mission of serving the public in providing access to federal information.

Electronic information presents an opportunity for Congress to develop new information policies. Congress needs to update existing statutes on privacy, copyright, dissemination, and access to electronic information. Congress must develop a distribution system that continues the tradition of depository libraries in providing access for citizens who lack the equipment or knowledge to obtain electronic information.

Locating Federal Information on the Internet

It is often said that the federal government is the largest publisher in the world; the Internet is no exception to that statement. Being the biggest does not necessarily mean the best, however, and locating federal government information on the Internet can be frustrating. Recent improvements and the development of Internet tools such as Archie, Veronica, and the World Wide Web facilitate the search for specific information. The increase in Gophers has improved access to federal information with easy-to-follow menus and keyword-searching capabilities. Gophers also provide mailing functions, which eliminate complex FTP commands and directories. Many Gophers and Web sites provide gateways to other Internet sites, leading the adventurous Internet hunters to a variety of databases. Internet guides are being developed by individuals to assist in locating specific information, as well as discussion lists that announce new Internet sites and that function as a resource for Internet expertise.

The key to accessing federal information on the Internet, however, is practice. By becoming familiar with available resources on the Internet, librarians and information professionals can easily obtain federal information. Following are several government, university, and commercial databases that illustrate the types of federal information available on the Internet.

Selected Federal Internet Sites

The best source of federal information is, not surprisingly, the federal government itself. Here is just a sampling of the many federal sources of information on the Internet.

Department of Agriculture Gopher

WWW address: `http://www.esusda.gov`

Gopher address: `esusda.gov` or `zeus.esusda.gov`

The United States Department of Agriculture Gopher includes information from the USDA Extension Service, National Agriculture Library, and a variety of federal documents including NAFTA, Clinton's Health Plan, U.S. Federal Budget, and the National Information Infrastructure report. This Gopher is easy to use and is seldom busy.

A sample session on USDA Gopher (accurate as of this writing) would begin with pointing your Gopher client to Gopher esusda.gov, which would pull up the main menu. Selected federal documents are located under menu item #12, White House and Congress. To locate publications relating to health care, select menu item #4, which lists a number of publications on the topic. Health Care publications are pulled together under one menu, and the Health Security Plan is menu #2. To read the Preliminary Health Plan Summary, select menu #5; the full text of the summary is available to read online or to mail to your e-mail account.

This is a typical session on a federal Gopher. As with other Gophers, there are layers of menus, which can be confusing. Typing = provides the address of the Gopher and path for future reference.

Air Force Gopher

Gopher address: wpdis02.wpafb.af.mil

This site contains more than Air Force information and is a good source for military information. Also included are databases on NATO, NASA, U.S. Army, international military, and general government information.

Americans Communicating Electronically (ACE)

Gopher address: ace.esusda.gov

ACE is an *ad hoc* group of federal employees gathering information with the goal of increasing access to government information for the general public without barriers. This is a good source to use for locating "hot" or new federal publications.

CancerNet

Gopher address: gopher.nih.gov/clin/cancernet

This site contains information about cancer from the National Cancer Institute's Physician Data Query (PDQ). Information is available in English or Spanish. Send an e-mail message to cancernet@icicb.nci.nih.gov. Enter **help** in the body of the message for a content list.

Central Intelligence Agency

WWW address: http://www.ic.gov

Not much information is available on the CIA site, but this is a new site with the promise of being developed into an interesting collection of materials.

Department of Commerce—STAT-USA

FTP address: `ftp.stat-usa.gov`

This is a new database and will be a central site for information on business and trade. View the `README.TXT` file for additional information on the contents of the database. The Department of Commerce will be providing access through the WWW for a fee; however, federal depository libraries will be given free access to this database. Contact your local library or the Department of Commerce for information regarding WWW access. The FTP site is free of charge.

Department of Commerce—Bureau of Census

WWW address: `http://www.census.gov`

Gopher address: `gopher.census.gov`

FTP address: `ftp.census.gov/pub/Govt-Stats`

The Census Bureau maintains a good site for current census information including press releases and basic statistics. However, some of the best sites for 1990 census files are maintained on educational sites that should be used to supplement these databases.

Consumer Information Center

WWW address: `http://www.gsa.gov`

Gopher address: `www.gsa.gov`

FTP address: `www.gsa.gov/gopher/staff/pa/cic`

In addition to the *Consumer Information Catalog*, CIC provides full text access to its publications, which can be viewed online or downloaded.

Department of Defense—DefenseLink

WWW address: `http://www.dtic.dla.mil`

The Department of Defense (DOD) site lists news releases, available DOD contracts, and general military information.

U.S. Military Academy, West Point

Gopher address: `gopher.usma.edu`

The U.S. Military Academy (USMA) Gopher contains a variety of data including math information and USMA news, plus access to the USMA library system and the U.S. Army Personnel Information Systems Command BBS.

EDGAR (Electronic Data Gathering, Analysis, and Retrieval)

WWW address: `http://townhall.org/edgar/edgar.html`

FTP address: `town.hall.org/edgar`

E-mail address: `mail@town.hall.org`

EDGAR is the database of Securities and Exchange Commission filings including 8-K, 10-K, and N-SAR. If WWW and FTP capabilities are not available, you may e-mail your request to the address listed and request an index of available company reports.

Department of Education/OERI Institutional Communications Network (INET)

Gopher address: `gopher.ed.gov`

The Department of Education maintains a number of databases on its Gopher, including National Center for Education Statistics, a listing of educational software, press releases, and information on distance learning.

National Education BBS

Telnet address: `nebbs.nersc.gov` (`128.55.128.90`) log in as `nebbs`

This bulletin board is "intended to support education by providing access to advanced computational and network resources for students in grades K through 12." Primarily a communication network for educators, this bulletin board contains information on mathematics, computer programming, network information, and political issues of the day. This is an excellent resource for educators across the United States.

Department of Education—AskERIC

WWW address: http://ericir.syr.edu

Gopher address: ericir.syr.edu

Telnet address: ericir.syr.edu

Login: gopher

A collection of recent Education Resources Information Clearinghouse (ERIC) documents. Most ERIC documents are not formally published but are excellent resources for studies in education.

Department of Energy

WWW address: http://www.doe.gov

A variety of energy information that includes full text of selected resources.

Department of Energy—Energy Efficiency and Renewable Energy Network (EREN)

WWW address: www.eren.doe.gov

This database is more technical than the main Department of Energy Web site, and it includes full text of some energy journals and reports.

Environmental Protection Agency (EPA)

Telnet address: epaibm.rtpnc.epa.gov (134.67.180.1)

This site includes EPA publications, including the full text of EPA Access and a directory of EPA resources and libraries.

Environmental Protection Agency (EPA) Future Studies Gopher

Gopher address: futures.wic.epa.gov

This collection of databases is more technical than the primary EPA Gopher and focuses on the future of the environment and related studies.

Federal Information eXchange Inc., (FEDIX) and Minority Online Information Service (MOLIS)

Telnet address: `fedix.fie.com (192.111.228.33)`

FEDIX links higher education to the federal government to facilitate research, education, and services, including information on fellowships, grants, research programs, minority programs, and relevant information from the *Commerce Business Daily* and the *Federal Register*. Several agencies support FEDIX, including NASA, Department of Commerce, U.S. Agency for International Development (AID), Department of Housing and Urban Development (HUD), and Federal Aviation Administration (FAA). Files are also available through anonymous FTP at the same address. Users are allowed 180 minutes per day, and the series of menus guides users through the various programs.

Fedworld (NTIS)

Telnet address: `fedworld.gov (192.239.93.3)` log in as `new`

This site provides connections to many government bulletin boards and online systems, as well as full text for some government publications including the *National Information Infrastructure: Agenda Action*.

Federal Deposit Insurance Corporation (FDIC)

Gopher address: `gopher.sura.net`

This database contains historical statistics since 1934 in addition to real-estate trends and consumer information.

FinanceNet

WWW address: `www.financenet.gov`

Gopher address: `gopher.financenet.gov`

FTP address: `ftp.financenet.gov`

E-mail address: `info@financenet.gov`

FinanceNet was established by Vice President Gore's National Performance Review as a clearinghouse for financial management.

FDA Bulletin Board

Telnet address: `fdabbs.fda.gov` (`150.148.8.48`) log in as `bbs`

Contains news releases, AIDS information, and consumer information.

Government Printing Office—FTP Site

FTP address: `eids04.eids.gpo.gov`

A variety of files are available for downloading from the Government Printing Office (GPO), including information on the GPO Access databases.

Government Printing Office—GPO Access

SWAIS address: `swais.access.gpo.gov`

Public Gateways:

> Columbia Online Information Network (COIN)
> Telnet address: `128.206.1.3`
> Dial in: 314-884-7000

> Seattle Public Library—Quest System
> Telnet address: `198.137.188.2`
> Dial in: 206-386-4140

> Georgia Southern University
> Telnet address: `gsvms2.cc.gasou.edu`
> Dial in: 912-681-0005

GPO Access is a fee-based database; however, free public access is available through one of the gateway systems. Federal depository libraries also have connections to this Internet site; inquire at your local library for information. GPO Access has a number of databases, including the *Federal Register, United States Code*, enrolled bills, history of bills, and the *Congressional Record*. The databases are updated daily, and most of the databases begin with the year 1994.

National Institutes of Health Server

Gopher address: `gopher.nih.gov`

FTP address: `cu.nih.gov` (`128.231.64.111`)

This includes reports from GAO, the President, the Department of Labor, and the National Institute of Health. The NIH server is also adding full text of government documents, including the *National Performance Review*.

National Institute of Allergy and Infectious Disease

Gopher address: `odie.niaid.nih.gov`

This site contains a variety of health statistics, including statistics on AIDS and the Morbidity and Mortality Weekly Reports.

Department of the Interior—Fish and Wildlife Service

WWW address: `http://www.fws.gov`

An interesting site that includes excellent information on endangered species.

Department of Interior—USGS Gopher

WWW address: `http://info.er.usgs.gov/doi/doi.html`

Gopher address: `info.er.usgs.gov` or `oemg.er.usgs.gov`

Library of Congress—Marvel

Gopher address: `marvel.loc.gov`

The Library of Congress (LOC) maintains access to their computerized catalogs in addition to copyright information and specialized collections. The LOC Gopher also includes information from other federal agencies, such as the National Archives and Records Administration (NARA). The LOC Gopher connects you to LOCIS, which contains the current status of federal legislation from 1973 until the present. (LOCIS is also available directly: Telnet to `locis.loc.gov`. Hours are limited.)

Library of Congress—LOCIS

Telnet address: `locis.loc.gov`

This site contains the current status of federal legislation from 1973 to present, as well as copyright information and the LOC *Catalog*.

Library of Congress—THOMAS

WWW address: `http://thomas.loc.gov`

Telnet address: `thomas.loc.gov`

Login: `thomas`

THOMAS is a new database of Congressional information primarily about legislation. THOMAS also has general Congressional information in addition to pointers to other Congressional Internet sites.

Library of Congress—WWW Home Page

WWW address: `http://lcweb.loc.gov/homepage/1chp.html/global electronic library`

This is a wonderful home page to browse through to get a taste of the wonders of the Library of Congress collections. Especially interesting are the historical photographs of the Civil War.

NASA Goddard Space Flight Center

Gopher address: `gopher.gsfc.nasa.gov`

NASA provides interesting and fun databases with information on shuttle launches, weather, astronomy, and the environment. NASA has many Internet sites, including Gophers, Telnet, and FTP sites; however, this primary Gopher has a variety of information and also facilitates access to other NASA Internet sites.

NASA K-12 Internet Initiative

Gopher address: `quast.arc.nasa.gov`

This is good place for teachers to explore and, as with other NASA sites, is an interesting and fun spot to check out.

NASA Lunar Planet Institute

WWW address: `http://cass.jsc.nasa.gov/lpi.html`

This site includes information on geology, solar systems, and astronomy, including NASA photos.

NASA Spacelink

WWW address: `http://spacelink.msfc.nasa.gov`

Gopher address: `spacelink.msfc.nasa.gov`

FTP address: `spacelink.msfc.nasa.gov`

Telnet address: `spacelink.msfc.nasa.gov (192.149.89.61)`

Login: `guest`

This site provides the latest NASA news, including shuttle launches and satellite updates.

NASA Technical Reports

FTP address: `techreports.larc.nasa.gov`

This site contains reports produced at NASA Langley Research Center, including technical papers and reference publications. Electronic reports may omit illustrations.

National Institute of Standards and Technology (NIST)

Gopher address: `gopher-server.nist.gov`

The best feature of this Gopher is a section on the "Malcolm Baldrige National Quality Awards." The database also contains reports and information from NIST.

National Oceanic and Atmosphere Administration (NOAA)

WWW address: `http://www.nos.noaa.gov`

NOAA's home page is a good Internet site for information on weather and reports from NOAA.

National Oceanic and Atmosphere Administration (NOAA) Earth System Data Dictionary

Gopher address: `esdim1.nodc.noaa.gov (140.90.265.168)`

National Science Foundation (NSF)

Gopher address: `stis.nsf.gov`

The NSF Gopher contains research publications on a variety of topics plus serials such as the *Antarctic Journal* and the *NSF Bulletin*. Award and program announcements are included as well. In addition to providing a wide variety of government information, the NSF Gopher provides connections to other federal Internet sites. The National Science Foundation provides a wide variety of government information, including easy access to many U.S. government Gophers.

Small Business Administration

WWW address: `http://www.sbaonline.sba.gov`

Telnet address: `sbaonline.sba.gov`

In addition to directories, the SBA site maintains information for small business, including state business profiles and business practices.

Office of Technology Assessment (OTA)

WWW address: `http://www.ota.gov`

FTP address: `otabbs.ota.gov/pub`

Telnet address: `otabbs.ota.gov`

Login: `public`

Password: `public`

OTA prepares a number of reports regarding technology and the government. This site is a collection of recent reports and information developed by the agency.

U.S. House of Representatives

WWW address: `http://www.house.gov`

Gopher address: `gopher.house.gov`

The House Internet site contains information on the legislative process and guides to Congress. Also included are directories and schedules for the House of Representatives.

U.S. Senate

Gopher address: `gopher.senate.gov`

Similar to the House of Representatives site, but the focus is on Senate information.

The White House

WWW address: `http://www.whitehouse.gov`

E-mail address: `president@whitehouse.gov` or `vice.president@whitehouse.gov`

When the WWW site was announced, it received national coverage, especially noting Sock's *meow* as a welcome. Virtual tours of the White House and photos are available in addition to press releases and information about the President.

Selected Commercial and Public Internet Sites

In addition to federal Internet sites, many commercial and university Gophers include federal information, such as full text documents, statistics, and economic data. Veronica is the best method to locate specific information, but here are a few Gophers that contain an impressive amount of data.

CapWeb

WWW address: `http://policy.net`

This is one of the key sites in locating Congressional information, including committee assignments, political party information, and directories of Congress. The WWW site also has pointers to other Internet sites of government information.

Case Western Reserve University

FTP address: `cwru.edu/hermes/word-perfect`

This is the repository for U.S. Supreme Court decisions. Be sure to download the index first, which will assist you in locating the decision you need.

Counterpoint Publishing

Gopher address: `gopher.internet.com`

Telnet address: `gopher.internet.com`

Login: `gopher`

This fee-based database contains the *Federal Register* and the *Code of Federal Regulations*. The database is updated daily with most files beginning in 1994. The Gopher software makes this a user-friendly database, which is an advantage over some other commercial providers.

Cornell Legal Information Institute (LLI)

WWW address: `http://www.law.cornell.edu/lli.table.html`

Telnet address: `www.law.cornell.edu`

Login: `www`

This is an excellent collection of law materials, including access to the U.S. Supreme Court decisions.

Internet Wiretap

Gopher address: `wiretap.spies.com`

This is a commercial database, but the public may access the database free of charge. This is a fun database with many interesting files—including federal documents.

Legi-Slate

Gopher address: `gopher.legislate.com`

A commercial site that is good for keeping up with the activities of Congress. Some of this information is available for free in other databases, but Legi-Slate supplements government information with commercial information, making it a comprehensive source.

University of Michigan Gopher

Gopher address: `una.hh.lib.umich.edu`

Telnet address: `hermes.merit.edu`

Select: `um-ulibrary`

Login: `gopher`

One of the best university Gophers, the University of Michigan uploads many federal documents, including the 1990 Census and the Economic Bulletin Board. Also check out the Political Science Law section, which contains election data, Congressional directories, and government information.

University of Missouri—St. Louis

Gopher address: `umslvma.umsl.edu/library/govdocs`

UMSL has many of the same features as other university sites, but it is known for its collection of DOD Area Handbooks and hot documents, such as the GATT agreement. This site is well maintained and easily accessible.

Integrating Federal Information with Traditional Print Resources

Electronic information is successful only after it is integrated with traditional print formats. Knowledge of existing Internet resources is developed through training and practice. The Internet requires librarians and information professionals to explore as electronic information develops and improves. In this electronic age, computer hardware and training is just as important to libraries as books and journals. It is impossible to fully integrate federal Internet information if individuals and libraries lack the appropriate equipment and expertise.

Electronic sources need to be incorporated with bibliographic instruction, guides, and reference. Libraries and computer centers should provide gateways on local systems such as online catalogs and local Gophers. Librarians and information professionals need to personally accept Internet information as no different than other formats of information. Only when we begin to incorporate electronic federal information into our existing resources will we be successful in making the technology shift toward an electronic information society.

REFERENCE WORKS

Goeffe, Bill. "Resources for Economists on the Internet," v. 7.11, August 23, 1994. (Available from the Clearinghouse for Subject-Oriented Internet Resource Guides. Gopher or FTP `una.hh.lib.umich.edu directory /inetdirs`.)

GovDoc-L (Government Documents Discussion List). Subscribe by sending message to `listserv@psuvm.psu.edu` with message `subscribe govdoc-l firstname lastname`. In addition to general discussion on the Depository Library Program, there are announcements and discussions of Internet sources. This is also a resource for questions and problems in accessing government information.

Gumprecht, Blake. "Internet Sources of Government Information," v.2, February 26, 1994. (Available from the Clearinghouse for Subject-Oriented Internet Resource Guides. Gopher or FTP `una.hh.lib.umich.edu directory /inetdirs`.)

Hancock, Lee. "Internet/Bitnet Health Sciences Resources," March 26, 1994. (Available from `gopher.ukanaix.cc.ukans.edu`. Login: `kufacts, directory /internet toolbox`.)

Net-Happenings. Subscribe by sending message to `majordomo@is.internic.net` with message `subscribe net-happenings firstname lastname`. Announcements of new Internet resources, publications, and network tools.

Network Services Announcements. Subscribe by sending message to `listserv@cerf.net` with message `subscribe nis firstname lastname`.

Parhamovich, Maggie. "Internet Resource: Federal Government Information." Release 0.8, August 1994. (Available from the Clearinghouse for Subject-Oriented Internet Resource Guides. Gopher or FTP `una.hh.lib.umich.edu, directory /inetdirs`.)

PART

XI

Internet Issues and Controversies

Crackers and Viruses

58

by Billy Barron

Computer viruses and crackers have both gotten quite a bit of press over the past few years. Both exist on the Internet, but by far, crackers are the more active and the much larger problem on the network. Even so, Internet users must be aware of both and take preventive measures—you'll be glad you did.

Long ago, the word *hacker* was a positive term that meant someone who was very good at working with computers at a low level. At some point, this word started being used by some people as a negative term. Many flame wars on the Internet have started over the use of this word. To avoid that problem, this chapter uses the clearly defined term *cracker*; I suggest you do the same.

> **NOTE**
>
> A *cracker* is a person who breaks into computer systems for good or bad (although many people say there is no such thing as a good break-in). A related term is *phreak*. A *phreak* is a person who attacks the phone system.

Every year, crackers break into literally thousands of accounts and computer systems. They sometimes delete files or crash the system. They always use CPU time and often use disk space. The scariest type of cracker, however, is the one who changes data and files for personal gain. Probably the most expensive cost is the amount of time the system administrators spend recovering from these incidents. Damages from crackers on the Internet probably run into millions of dollars per year.

Viruses seem to be more of a problem in the BBS community than on the Internet. The major reason is that most of the software available on the Internet has been screened at one point or another by responsible people before it is entered into an archive. However, do not be lulled into a false sense of security. Viruses *do* exist; downloading software without scanning it for viruses is foolish.

A Brief History

To understand the Internet's current state of security, you need to start with a history of viruses and crackers on the Internet and Bitnet. The Internet started out as the ARPAnet. ARPAnet members were originally from universities and nonclassified parts of the U.S. military involved in cooperative research. The network was also very small. The people on the network generally trusted each other. Chapter 2, "Introducing the Internet," provides additional information about the history of the Internet.

The result of this trust was that when TCP/IP was being developed, the designers did not worry enough about some security issues. Because of this oversight, many blatant security holes exist. For example, just about anyone can forge electronic mail—and has been able to for at least the past 10 years. Some fixes for this problem (such as PGP) are beginning to appear.

On Bitnet in 1987, in what was probably the first worm on a WAN, the Christmas Tree Worm struck. Many people confuse the terms *worm* and *virus*. The technical difference is that a worm is a stand-alone complete program; a virus is a piece of code that attaches itself to other files. The Christmas Tree Worm was not automated and therefore spread very slowly. It was a REXX program that ran only on VM/CMS systems. The program came into the user's spool area and the user had to run it by hand. It would print a pretty Christmas tree on the screen. While the worm was doing that, it was also reading the person's NAMES file (that is, e-mail address book) and sending a copy of itself to all the e-mail addresses. Although the worm did not do any file or system damage, it did fill up the spool space of many machines and consume a large amount of bandwidth, which was very limited on Bitnet in those days. It consumed enough bandwidth that Bitnet slowed down, and VNET, IBM's internal network, was brought to its knees.

In the late 1980s, the most famous cracker case of all time started. At Lawrence Berkeley Laboratories, astronomer Clifford Stoll was trying to track down a 75-cent accounting error. After months of investigation, he discovered that the cause was actually a West German cracker who was selling secrets to the KGB. This cracker had broken into hundreds of computers, including many unclassified U.S. military systems, looking for data the KGB was interested in.

The most famous worm, known as the Internet Worm, was released on November 2, 1988, by Robert Morris, Jr. It was supposedly an experiment to see how many machines it could run on, and it was not supposed to cause problems with the machines in question. This worm exploited problems with the sendmail and finger programs on Sun and VAX machines running UNIX. In addition, it looked for weak passwords. Because of a bug, the worm ran out of control. It brought many machines to a halt and spread at a much greater rate than Morris ever dreamed. The worm infected thousands of UNIX computer systems before the situation was brought under control.

In response to the Internet Worm, many sites, including the one I was managing at the time, cut themselves off of the network. Purdue and Berkeley quickly released fixes for the security problems the worm exploited, but it was months before the network returned to normal. Eventually, Robert Morris was sentenced to three years probation, a fine of $10,000, and 400 hours of community service.

The Internet Worm was a major turning point in the Internet security arena. Most people started taking network security much more seriously. Computer security organizations, such as Computer Emergency Response Team (CERT), were formed.

In October 1989, the last major worm struck a WAN. The WANK (Worms Against Nuclear Killers) worm attacked SPAN, NASA's network, and invaded VAX/VMS systems. The WANK worm added an antinuclear weapons message to the log-in screen of the infected computers. Although this worm did not cause any damage, it left security holes behind that crackers could later take advantage of.

Uncountable minor security incidents have happened since then. However, in late 1994, another major incident happened with regard to PANIX, an access provider in New York. Someone broke into PANIX and began capturing any data that went in and out of PANIX. The cracker was able to gain access to hundreds of sites. Eventually, the problem was solved, but the scariest part had not yet occurred.

The people at PANIX discovered a very serious security hole with the `sendmail` program that affected about 95 percent of all UNIX systems in the world. At first, they tried to work through the normal security organizations. Some of the security organizations put out a warning and a solution. The solution was not complete, however, and even sites that followed it were still at risk. The people at PANIX were upset and decided to post not only how to fix the security hole, but how to exploit it. At that point, any cracker wanna-be had enough knowledge to break into almost any UNIX system on the network. System administrators patched the hole quickly because of the risks—as PANIX had hoped—but unpatched and vulnerable systems still reside on the Internet.

This brief history should give you a sense of the security problems that exist on the Internet, including the fact that they continue to this day. If anything, they are more common today than ever.

Crackers

Historically, crackers have not been interested in damaging computers. They just like to see how many computers they can get into. However, this situation is changing. Many crackers now have motives, such as revenge or a way to profit from their cracking endeavors. Also, many of them now cause damage just for the fun of it. The future may be even grimmer.

Fortunately, the vast majority of people who attempt to crack do not really know that much about computer security. Often they try because they think it is cool or because they have recently stumbled across a file explaining how to crack into systems. These people vastly underestimate the skills of most system administrators in detecting their attacks. They additionally underestimate the power of the tools available to the system administrator in detecting their attacks. They are frequently caught almost immediately.

Cracker Communication on the Internet

Some people feel we should try to restrict the flow of information between crackers; others feel we should bring it more out into the open so that system administrators and users have better awareness of security problems. This chapter follows the second philosophy: I will discuss the methods crackers use to communicate over the Internet in the hope that you can use the information to protect yourself.

Crackers have historically had their own private BBSes in their homes. This continues to be true for many crackers. However, more and more of them are using the Internet for their communications. These communications take place in many different ways and places on the Internet.

Some crackers hang out on the #hack channel of IRC. The crackers who use this channel, which is a public arena, are very stupid. In some investigations, the authorities have gathered much useful evidence just by monitoring this channel.

Usenet newsgroups, such as alt.crackers and alt.hackers, exist to discuss cracking issues, among other things. It is possible for crackers to post anonymously to these groups; if they are careful, they do not fear detection.

Other crackers put out their own magazines. Some of them, such as *Phrack* and the *Legion of Doom Technical Journal,* are very famous and very informative. Others tend to be poorly written and even highly inaccurate. Many of the journals are available for anonymous FTP and Gopher. For Gopher, try the FTP addresses listed here (some work with Gopher, but others do not). Most of the sites listed have the same contents, so checking one of the sites should be sufficient.

```
ftp://etext.archive.umich.edu/pub/CuD/
ftp://aql.gatech.edu/pub/eff/Publications/cud
ftp://ftp.eff.org/pub/Publications/cud
ftp://ftp.warwick.ac.uk/pub/cud
ftp://ftp.funet.fi/pub/doc/cud
ftp://cair.kaist.ac.kr/doc/EFF/cud
ftp://ftp.cic.net/pub/e-serials/alphabetic
```

Cracker Attack Methods

Crackers use various methods to break into computer systems on the Internet. The first is that they try to figure out the password on an account. Some crackers try to use brute-force attacks against the front door of a system. They repeatedly try to log in as a user with different passwords until they find one that works. These kinds of attacks are the easiest to detect, and the crackers who use this method usually do not know what they are doing.

Other crackers look for security holes in the system. Most of them attempt to use the security holes that have been known for years. Fortunately, on the vast majority of systems, these holes have been fixed. Another thing these crackers look for is a misconfigured system that allows too much access, and they slip in through there. In reality, a surprising number of systems are misconfigured.

Other crackers depend on social engineering tactics. They call or e-mail a user and ask the user to either change or say their password. The cracker pretends to be the system administrator. Users should never do anything of this nature unless they are talking to the system administrator in person.

All these tactics are designed to get the crackers into the system. After they are in, their attack methods change quite a bit. The first thing most crackers look for is whether the encrypted passwords are available to all users. If so, they grab the password file and run some type of program on it that breaks passwords.

Some crackers leave behind a few Trojan horse programs. When other users run them, they cause some damage or leave a security hole in the other user's account. The major difference between a Trojan horse and a virus is that the Trojan horse does not make copies of itself (a virus does).

The cracker also looks for security holes on the system that enable them to become the system administrator. This is the eventual goal of most crackers. When crackers are successful in becoming the administrator, they often attempt to remove their tracks from the computer system so that nobody will know they have been there.

Crackers also look for other computer systems that trust the computer they are on. If they find such a computer, it is usually not too hard for the crackers to compromise the second computer also.

Some malicious crackers do not even try to break into a computer. They just attempt to make it unusable. This kind of attack is known as a *denial of service* attack. Methods include filling up the disks, slowing down response time, disconnecting network connections, and crashing the computers. Most people on the Internet take a very dim view of crackers who use this method because it threatens the existence of the network.

Crackers use many other methods. The less knowledgeable crackers use cookbook methods and are predictable. Really knowledgeable crackers do not use such methods; they adjust to the individual computer system and figure out the most effective way to compromise it.

Cracker Philosophy

The cracker community is very diverse. Although people tend to stereotype crackers, it is a mistake to do so. They have very different principles and reasons for cracking. The only generalization that can safely be made is that most crackers are young males.

Here is a list of some reasons why crackers try to crack. For any given cracker, one or more of the following reasons apply:

- **Free information.** Many older crackers believe that all information should be freely available and not hidden from people.

■ **Revenge.** Some crackers are ex-employees who want revenge against a company or a person and try to crack their systems.

■ **Competition.** Many crackers compete against one another to see who is the best cracker.

■ **Money.** Some crackers get paid to do cracking work. Spy agencies often employ such people.

■ **Software.** Many people crack because they want to have more software without paying for it.

■ **Intellectual challenge.** Many crackers think of cracking as a game between themselves and the system administrators.

■ **Practical jokes.** Some crackers crack into systems to play practical jokes on people or companies.

■ **Access to resources.** Many crackers want access to the Internet and break into your system with a modem to get that access. Others want to try out new operating systems or supercomputers. They consider it a learning experience.

■ **Report security holes.** Other crackers break in just to show the security hole to the system administrator so that the system administrator will close up the security hole as soon as possible. Typically, this kind of cracker is not destructive and can be an ally of a system administrator.

■ **Use idle resources.** Many crackers think computers are going to waste if they are not being constantly used. Therefore, they break in to use the computer's idle resources.

Cracker Relationships

As just described, crackers crack for very different reasons. Combine this with the paranoia of getting busted by the authorities and the challenge of crackers proving to each other that they are cool and you have a very chaotic community.

Crackers can be divided into advanced and novice crackers. Almost always, the novices are trying to be recognized as advanced crackers. Many novices do what they have read in some cracking magazine and repeat what has been done before. This can be dangerous because some cracking magazines print inaccurate information that is misleading and can get a cracker busted. Also, many system administrators read the same publications and know the tricks. Most advanced crackers look at what many novices are doing and sigh. The novice is usually trying to find a place in the cracking community and will do just about anything to be accepted. Such novices are frequently caught by system administrators. At times, the class difference between crackers can turn nasty: Sometimes, a novice irritates an advanced cracker; in return, the advanced cracker may do some cracking and leave evidence pointing to the novice.

Another way to look at crackers is to divide them into malicious and nonmalicious crackers. Traditionally, crackers fell into the second category (they were mainly cracking to increase their knowledge). Old-fashioned crackers lived by the hacker ethic: information and computer resources should be free to everyone, but you should never cause damage by destroying parts of a computer system. Even today, many crackers are not malicious.

However, malicious crackers do not care about what damage they may cause. Some even *want* to cause damage. These crackers are dangerous and are the type who try to get other people in trouble. Nonmalicious crackers usually despise malicious crackers. Although crackers usually do not turn each other in, nonmalicious crackers have helped authorities stop malicious crackers in a few cases.

Cracking Laws

Because computing is a fairly new field and cracking is even newer, the laws governing cracking are fairly primitive and have not been tested in court. In fact, some governments do not have laws governing computer crime at all.

In the United States, the legal situation regarding crackers is complex. On the national level, there are a variety of laws: the Computer Fraud and Abuse Statute, the Computer Security Act (EPCA) of 1987, and the Electronic Communications Privacy Act of 1986. Each of these laws cover certain classes of computer crime. The Computer Fraud and Abuse Statute, for example, makes it illegal to crack computers owned by the U.S. Government. The EPCA ruling protects private e-mail from being read by third parties.

Most states have laws that apply to cracking. In Texas, it is illegal to log in to any computer where you have not been granted permission to do so. Other states have similar laws. Usually, the state law applies when the cracker and the computer system are in the same state. If they are in different states, federal laws apply.

The most complex cracking cases are international ones. On the Internet, it is common for the cracker to be in one country but the victims in another. Whose laws apply? Often, the laws of the victim country say it is an offense but the laws of the cracker country say it is not. Obviously, we need more international cooperation and standardization of computer crime laws.

The Future of Cracking

Some authors—especially cyberpunk authors—like to paint a dismal picture of the future and the role crackers will play in it. Although these books make good fiction, I do not think they are very realistic and should be ignored as barometers of the future of cracking.

On the positive side, many developments will help track down and stop crackers. The next generation of the IP protocol, which will be implemented over the next few years, will offer some additional security features to limit the ability of crackers to forge IP addresses. Along the same lines, e-mail encryption and digital signatures will become the norm. Both features will keep crackers from reading and forging people's e-mail. More and more sites are hiding behind firewalls (see Chapter 11, "Managing Internet Security," for more information), making it much harder for external crackers to get in. Unfortunately, many companies have a strong firewall but no internal protection in case the firewall does not stop the cracker. In addition, the tools for finding crackers are becoming more widespread and more powerful. Some newer tools sit on the network, undetectable and uncrackable, but can catch many crackers in the act. These developments should make some crackers realize that they are not safe trying to crack a knowledgeable Internet site.

On the negative side, several indications suggest that things are going to get worse. Historically, crackers have been more of an annoyance than a serious problem. However, the new generation of crackers seems to be nastier and determined to cause damage. And computers are getting faster, which makes brute-force password cracking easier. Cracker techniques and tools are also becoming more powerful and advanced.

Probably, the end result will be that crackers will be no more and no less of a problem than they are today. Both sides are becoming increasingly powerful and will balance each other out.

Viruses

Viruses are common these days. Over 3,000 different viruses are known to exist. Although this number is huge, only a few viruses have caused most of the damage to date. Viruses affect microcomputers to a much greater extent than they affect minicomputer and mainframe systems. This is because microcomputers tend to have weaker security (no security in many cases), especially when compared to advanced operating systems such as UNIX and VMS. In comparison, I am unaware of any UNIX or VMS viruses, although it would not be surprising to find that a UNIX virus exists that is so good it is undetectable. That is the way of the virus world.

You should not shy away from the Internet because of your worry about viruses. Viruses are rare on the Internet. During my years on the Internet, I have downloaded literally several thousand programs and have never once seen a virus. However, I do know they are out there, and I protect my systems from them. You should do the same.

Sources of Viruses

Most viruses are written by individuals or small groups of people in secret. The intent of a virus varies quite a bit. Some are experiments just to prove it can be done. Many involve people trying to show off their programming skills and outshine other virus writers. A few viruses have tried to distribute political messages (the Macedonia virus, which infects MS-DOS systems, displays the message Macedonia to the Macedonians). The scariest viruses are the ones written by malicious people trying to cause damage.

A constant rumor on the Internet is that anti-virus authors write their own viruses and release them so that they can sell their product and the updates to their product. This rumor is unproven to date, but who knows?

Virus-Prevention Strategy

For starters, if you are downloading files from the Internet, you absolutely ***must*** consider the risk of viruses. A few people may not care whether their computer is trashed by a virus, but most of us do care.

The first part of an effective virus-prevention strategy is to get some good backup software. Equally important is that the software be used regularly. It may be necessary to keep multiple copies of backups. Often, your backups are also infected, so the more backups you have, the better the chance of finding a set that is not infected.

The second part of the strategy is to get some good anti-virus software (some recommendations are given in the following section). Even more important is to regularly update the anti-virus software. New viruses are always being written, and older software does not always detect them.

The third part is to consider the risks of every piece of software you download and try to minimize those risks. If an unknown person on the Internet offers you a piece of software that you can also acquire from a well-known anonymous FTP site, use the FTP site. Many major FTP sites check software for viruses before making it available for download. Even if they do not take this precaution, the odds are good that someone else will detect the virus before you and request that the file be removed. If the file is not removed, the person who discovered the problem will often complain about it on mailing lists or newsgroups, so you may see mention of it and learn that a particular site is not to be trusted.

The final part is to stay informed about viruses. A good way to start is to read the comp.virus newsgroup; an informative FAQ file is available there. The newsgroup also sees the announcements of new viruses that have been found and new virus software that is available to prevent them.

Anti-Virus Software

Anti-virus software is an interesting type of software; the features differ greatly between products. None of the products are capable of stopping all current viruses (more viruses are being written daily), much less of stopping all future viruses. Therefore, you should conduct some research before you select an anti-viral product. Here are some types of products:

- **Scanners.** Scanners look at files on the hard disk and find ones that are already infected. Some scanners can find viruses in compressed files; others cannot. Some programs look for the virus; others keep a database of checksums for all files on the computer and can detect when the files have changed.

- **Disinfectors.** These programs are similar to scanners except that disinfectors also attempt to remove the virus. Many disinfectors disinfect only some of the viruses they can detect.

- **Detectors.** These programs detect and prevent a virus that is just about to strike. On PCs, this kind of program runs as a TSR and uses some of your precious store of 640K RAM.

- **Write Protectors.** A few programs enable you to prevent all writes to the hard disk. This feature is effective against viruses, but also makes working difficult.

Ideally, you probably will want several layers of virus protection. Many of the packages now combine several of the types just listed.

PC

MS-DOS 6.0 includes a virus-checking program called Microsoft Anti-Virus, which is a version of Central Point Anti-Virus (see CPAV in Table 58.1). Many people have criticized Microsoft's choice in products for the product quality and the fact that many people can get a false sense of security from the software and not keep it updated.

TESTING ANTI-VIRUS SOFTWARE: A PERSONAL STORY

Several years ago, I tested many virus products. At that time, many were terribly wimpy. Later, at my place of employment at the time, we did a more thorough evaluation. Two products at that time stood out: F-Prot and McAfee. Both were frequently updated and of high quality. We went with F-Prot because of its low site license price, because our users could run it free at home, and because PCs running the McAfee software (VSHIELD in particular) seemed to take a noticeable performance hit. I continue to run F-Prot to this day and am satisfied with it. However, the state of the market—including these two products—has changed quite a bit so you should do your own evaluation and reach your own conclusions.

I compiled Table 58.1 based on personal knowledge and reviews I found with anonymous FTP on cert.org in the /pub/virus-l/docs/reviews/pc directory. I eliminated some products that had poor reviews or that I had some bad experiences with. However, other products are missing from the chart because I did not know of their existence. It is worth reading some reviews and talking to some PC experts before you select the best virus-protection software for yourself.

Table 58.1. PC anti-virus software.

Product	Commercial Status	FTP Site
AllSafe	Commercial	
Antivirus Plus	Commercial	
AvSearch	Free	ftp://oak.oakland.edu/SimTel/ msdos/virus
CPAV	Commercial	ftp://oak.oakland.edu/SimTel/ msdos/virus
DiskSecure	Commercial	
Dr. Solomon	Commercial	
Eliminator	Commercial	
F-Prot	Commercial/Free	ftp://oak.oakland.edu/SimTel/ msdos/virus
IBM Antivirus	Commercial	
Integrity Master	Commercial	
McAfee	Commercial	ftp://oak.oakland.edu/SimTel/ msdos/virus
Norton Antivirus	Commercial	ftp://oak.oakland.edu/SimTel/ msdos/virus
TBScan	Commercial	
VDS Pro	Commercial	ftp://oak.oakland.edu/SimTel/ msdos/virus
Virucide Plus	Commercial	
Virus Buster	Commercial	ftp://oak.oakland.edu/SimTel/ msdos/virus
Virus Prevention	Commercial	
ViruSafe	Commercial	
VirusCure Plus	Commercial	

Macintosh

Although I have some experience with the Macintosh, I do not work on one regularly. My only experience with Macintosh anti-virus software is with Disinfectant, which I recommend. Therefore, my comments here are minimal; instead, I offer some references on the Internet for reviews on Macintosh anti-virus software. Table 58.2 lists a few of the common Macintosh anti-virus products. Reviews of these and other products can be retrieved with anonymous FTP to `cert.org` in the `/pub/virus-l/doc/reviews/mac` directory.

Table 58.2. Macintosh anti-virus software.

Product	Commercial Status	FTP Site
Citadel	Commercial	
Disinfectant	Free	ftp://ftp.pht.com/pub/mac/umich/ util/virus/ disinfectant3.5.sea.hqx
Gatekeeper	Free	ftp://ftp.pht.com/pub/mac/umich/ util/virus/gatekeeper1.3.sit.hqx
MacTools	Commercial	
Rival	Commercial	
SAM	Commercial	
Vaccine	Commercial	ftp://ftp.pht.com/pub/mac/umich/ util/virus
Virex	Commercial	
VirusBlockade	Commercial	
VirusDetective	Commercial	ftp://ftp.pht.com/pub/mac/umich/ util/virus

UNIX

It would be difficult, but not impossible, to write a virus that attacks UNIX systems. Fortunately, to date, we have not seen any such virus. However, this security has not stopped a few vendors from trying to sell UNIX anti-virus software. Personally, I think those vendors are trying to play on people's fears. Proper use of packages mentioned in Chapter 11, "Managing Internet Security," should allow the detection of any virus that is written in the future. If you are worried about viruses on UNIX, just acquire and install COPS.

Virus Publications

A few electronic publications on viruses exist on the Internet. Although the cracker journals are easy to acquire, the virus publications are more difficult to acquire. These publications often contain virus source code, which people do not want to get into the hands of unknowledgeable but malicious programmers who can use it to make new strains of viruses not immediately detected by anti-virus software. Others agree that the source code is needed so that more people can write anti-virus software. Both sides have their points. In addition, some people are afraid that the distribution of the virus source code may lead to someone suing them for damages at some point.

What the Future Holds

Crackers and viruses both exist on the Internet just as they do in any networked computing environment. Although some of us a few years back had hoped that viruses were a passing fad, this apparently is not the case; viruses are here to stay. In addition, it is possible that another worm can be released on the Internet at some point. Although many people remember the curious, but not harmful, crackers of the past, they should not think that all crackers are this way. Many crackers are interested in causing real harm, which is sad.

Improvements in Internet security are constantly being made, but many places on the network remain very insecure. Both users and system administrators are paying more attention than ever to security, so it should be harder for crackers to succeed. One of the real sources of security problems is the computer operating system vendors. If we're fortunate, they will wake up and make their computer systems more secure with more secure default configurations and more security tools built in.

Another facet of reducing the problem is better international cooperation. Often, the hardest part in tracking down a cracker or a virus author is that you must deal with multiple nations to catch the person. Related to this problem, laws covering viruses and crackers must be enacted or strengthened by all countries.

> **NOTE**
>
> When you use the Internet, play it safe and watch for viruses and crackers. To the crackers and virus writers who are reading this: please stop and make the Internet a better place for us all.

Information Overload

59

by Andrew Kantor

In America, we like choice. When we buy a car, we want 20 colors to choose from. When we buy a computer, we like having 12 speeds of the Pentium chip to pick from. When we dine out, we want to hear, "Would you like soup or salad? What kind of dressing with that? Baked potato or French fries?" Choice is good. So it would seem the Internet is a dream come true: all those files and all those newsgroups and all those Web pages to choose from—where should we start? Need information on German exports in the 1960s? Ask in Usenet news, or check out a Gopher or World Wide Web server. (Three services to choose from. Super!) The latest tax law got you stumped? Newsgroups and their participants abound—ask a question, and you can choose from two dozen answers. It couldn't be better.

That's what many books and seminars on the Internet would have you believe—that this ragtag collection of computers is somehow the answer to all your information woes. They focus on the fact that so much information is available. What they *don't* tell you is how hard it can be to search and how difficult it can be to sort through the information to find what you want. They never mention how easily the Internet can become too much of a good thing.

Unfortunately, that's often the case—especially if you need a particular bit of data, and you need it now. Ask anyone who's ever shopped in a five-and-dime or gone to a junkyard—the more there is of something, the harder it is to find what you want.

It's called *information overload.* It's the feeling you get when you want something small but have to look through something big to find it. Imagine a six-year-old going to the grocery store to buy coffee for his mother. Which brand? What grind? What size? The Internet is no different; instead of coffee, we go there looking for information. Which computer has it? Which file is the most recent? How do I know it's correct? Where do I start?

Let your fingers do the walking through the Internet, and you're almost immediately confronted with the good and the bad of it. Millions of files to use…but millions of files to wade through. Millions of people to help you…but millions of wrong answers, too. Dozens of tools to help you find your way…but which is the right one?

Choice means responsibility, and responsibility means work. The Internet has plenty of all three.

Can We Talk?

Maybe the only thing you use the Internet for is electronic mail; you could be a CompuServe or Prodigy subscriber, for example. Or maybe that's all you really want out of it—instant messages to people around the world. You figure you're safe from being overwhelmed by the vastness of the global computer network, hidden behind your Inbox. After all, you only use it to write to friends, colleagues, or kids at college. There may be millions of people out there and terabytes of data scattered over millions of computers, but that has nothing to do with you. No overload here.

And then someone tells you about mailing lists. They've got hundreds (maybe thousands) of subscribers, all sharing the same interest—Ray Bradbury or folk music or the stock market. All you have to do is get a List of Lists (posted every once in a while to news.lists), choose a list or two, send a brief "sign me up" message, and *presto!*—you've just taken your first step toward *really* joining the Internet community.

But that first step is a doozy.

When you send a message to a mailing list, a copy is sent to everyone who has subscribed. Thus, with one note you potentially reach thousands of people. If you like to talk, it's a dream come true.

What you may not think about at first, even with the warnings that come with most of these Internet books, is that the thousands of people who read your messages will also be writing back. Imagine sending a letter to the editor of *Newsweek* and having your street address printed with it. The floodgates are open.

The first day after signing up will be relatively quiet. It takes a little time for your request to be processed, and there probably won't be too many letters in your mailbox by the end of the day. The next morning you'll have a few, and by that evening—depending on what list you chose—there might be a dozen new messages.

At first, it's no problem. You're interested in the subject, either for the moment or in general, and you like the idea of exchanging thoughts with other people who have volunteered to participate in a long-distance, possibly long-term electronic conference. So you answer your mail, and you *get* answers. Your mailbox now has a couple of dozen new messages in it every day. Figure 59.1 gives you an idea of what can happen. (Oh, and if you're doing this through CompuServe or Prodigy, you're paying for each one of those incoming messages. Beware.) Sure, you're writing a lot, but you can keep up.

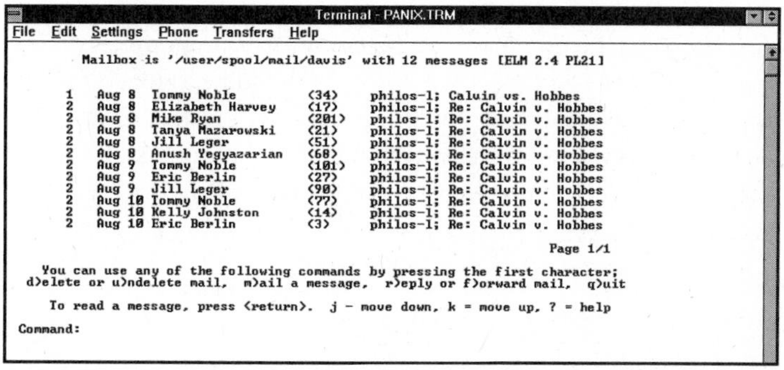

FIGURE 59.1.

After a week or so, your mailbox is filling, but it's nothing you can't handle.

```
                              Terminal - PANIX.TRM
File  Edit  Settings  Phone  Transfers  Help

        Mailbox is '/user/spool/mail/davis' with 12 messages [ELM 2.4 PL21]

     1    Aug 8   Tommy Noble          (34)     philos-l; Calvin vs. Hobbes
     2    Aug 8   Elizabeth Harvey     (17)     philos-l; Re: Calvin v. Hobbes
     2    Aug 8   Mike Ryan            (201)    philos-l; Re: Calvin v. Hobbes
     2    Aug 8   Tanya Mazarowski     (21)     philos-l; Re: Calvin v. Hobbes
     2    Aug 8   Jill Leger           (51)     philos-l; Re: Calvin v. Hobbes
     2    Aug 8   Anush Vegyazarian    (68)     philos-l; Re: Calvin v. Hobbes
     2    Aug 9   Tommy Noble          (101)    philos-l; Re: Calvin v. Hobbes
     2    Aug 9   Eric Berlin          (27)     philos-l; Re: Calvin v. Hobbes
     2    Aug 9   Jill Leger           (98)     philos-l; Re: Calvin v. Hobbes
     2    Aug 10  Tommy Noble          (77)     philos-l; Re: Calvin v. Hobbes
     2    Aug 10  Kelly Johnston       (14)     philos-l; Re: Calvin v. Hobbes
     2    Aug 10  Eric Berlin          (3)      philos-l; Re: Calvin v. Hobbes

                                                              Page 1/1

     You can use any of the following commands by pressing the first character;
   d)elete or u)ndelete mail, m)ail a message, r)eply or f)orward mail, q)uit

     To read a message, press <return>.  j - move down, k - move up, ? = help

 Command:
```

Then you go away for a weekend and don't have access to your e-mail. You come home, unpack the suitcase, water the plants, and check your messages. Surprise (and welcome to the Internet); you have 237 new mail messages, providing you with something like Figure 59.2.

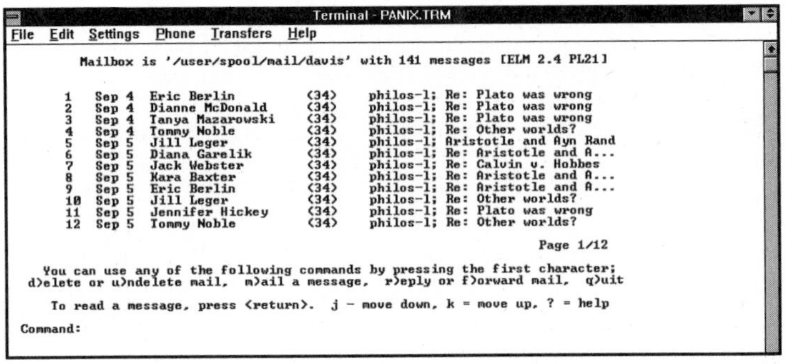

FIGURE 59.2.

Being away even for a short period of time can mean a few hundred messages have piled up.

```
┌─────────────────────── Terminal - PANIX.TRM ──────────────────────── ▾│▴│
│ File  Edit  Settings  Phone  Transfers  Help                          ▴│
├───────────────────────────────────────────────────────────────────────┤
│          Mailbox is '/user/spool/mail/davis' with 141 messages [ELM 2.4 PL21]│
│                                                                         │
│         1   Sep 4  Eric Berlin        (34)   philos-1; Re: Plato was wrong│
│         2   Sep 4  Dianne McDonald    (34)   philos-1; Re: Plato was wrong│
│         3   Sep 4  Tanya Mazarowski   (34)   philos-1; Re: Plato was wrong│
│         4   Sep 4  Tommy Noble        (34)   philos-1; Re: Other worlds? │
│         5   Sep 5  Jill Leger         (34)   philos-1; Aristotle and Ayn Rand│
│         6   Sep 5  Diana Garelik      (34)   philos-1; Re: Aristotle and A...│
│         7   Sep 5  Jack Webster       (34)   philos-1; Re: Calvin v. Hobbes│
│         8   Sep 5  Kara Baxter        (34)   philos-1; Re: Aristotle and A...│
│         9   Sep 5  Eric Berlin        (34)   philos-1; Re: Aristotle and A...│
│        10   Sep 5  Jill Leger         (34)   philos-1; Re: Other worlds? │
│        11   Sep 5  Jennifer Hickey    (34)   philos-1; Re: Plato was wrong│
│        12   Sep 5  Tommy Noble        (34)   philos-1; Re: Other worlds? │
│                                                              Page 1/12   │
│       You can use any of the following commands by pressing the first character;│
│     d)elete or u)ndelete mail,  m)ail a message,  r)eply or f)orward mail,  q)uit│
│                                                                         │
│        To read a message, press <return>.  j - move down, k = move up, ? = help│
│ Command:                                                                │
└─────────────────────────────────────────────────────────────────────────┘
```

You try reading them all, paging through slowly but steadily. Then you experience the first sign of information overload: You start deleting unread mail. Half an hour later, you've finished—having read some and discarded others—and you don't have quite the feeling of satisfaction you did when you read everything, even if you didn't answer it all. But your Inbox is empty when you go to sleep. You made it through, and your next weekend away from home isn't for another month.

Those 200 (or more) messages are from a single mailing list. What if you subscribed to more? You'd come back from every trip with a feeling of impending doom. What's waiting behind the "You have new mail" message? 10 letters? 50? 500? You could buy a notebook computer with a portable modem to check your mail from your hotel room or from a friend's house, but that makes you feel like a junkie who needs a fix—although perhaps that's not necessarily far from the truth.

You may have heard of so-called *smart* e-mail programs with "rules" you can define. Certain messages—those with a specific word in the subject line, for instance—are automatically acted on. They may be marked "urgent," or simply deleted, depending on how you define the rule. But "rules" software doesn't work well with mailing lists. Sure, you could screen messages from annoying people, but unless they write a lot of the mail you receive, it won't help you with overload.

You could simply unsubscribe to the lists, keeping up one-on-one conversations with some of the members. That way, although you might feel that you're missing out on a lot of what's happening (this is known as *withdrawal* in some circles), you're still in touch with the subject matter and the people who care about it—and you can always resubscribe.

You also can follow a newsgroup instead. If mailing lists are like magazines (you have to actively subscribe to them), newsgroups are like television stations. They're always there, and you can easily flip through the ones you're interested in to see if a message thread catches your eye (see Figure 59.3). News readers, especially those who support *threading* (the listing of "threads" of ongoing conversation), such as nn and trn, make that easy—just as they make it easy to mark entire newsgroups as read.

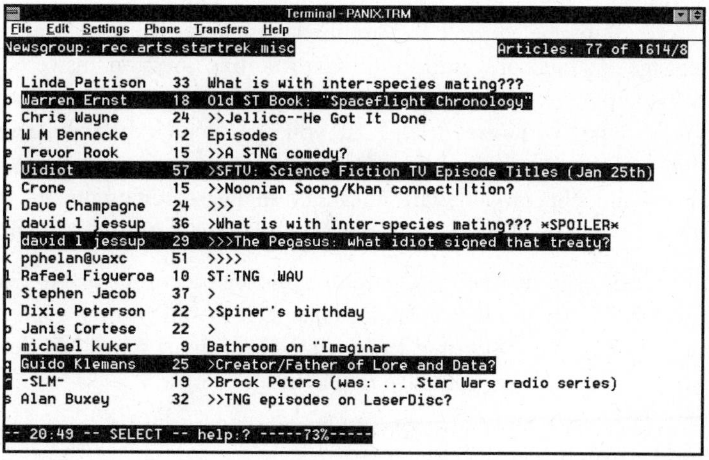

FIGURE 59.3.

When you browse through a newsgroup, you can pick and choose the messages and threads you want to read.

```
                          Terminal - PANIX.TRM
 File  Edit  Settings  Phone  Transfers  Help
Newsgroup: rec.arts.startrek.misc                 Articles: 77 of 1614/8

 a  Linda_Pattison     33   What is with inter-species mating???
 b  Warren Ernst       18   Old ST Book: "Spaceflight Chronology"
 c  Chris Wayne        24   >>Jellico--He Got It Done
 d  W M Bennecke       12   Episodes
 e  Trevor Rook        15   >>A STNG comedy?
 f  Uidiot             57   >SFTU: Science Fiction TV Episode Titles (Jan 25th)
 g  Crone              15   >>Noonian Soong/Khan connectl|tion?
 h  Dave Champagne     24   >>>
 i  david 1 jessup     36   >What is with inter-species mating??? *SPOILER*
 j  david 1 jessup     29   >>>The Pegasus: what idiot signed that treaty?
 k  pphelan@uaxc       51   >>>>
 l  Rafael Figueroa    10   ST:TNG .WAU
 m  Stephen Jacob      37   >
 n  Dixie Peterson     22   >Spiner's birthday
 o  Janis Cortese      22   >
 p  michael kuker       9   Bathroom on "Imaginar
 q  Guido Klemans      25   >Creator/Father of Lore and Data?
 r  -SLM-              19   >Brock Peters (was: ... Star Wars radio series)
 s  Alan Buxey         32   >>TNG episodes on LaserDisc?

-- 20:49 -- SELECT -- help:? -----73%-----
```

Although newsgroups may be easier to keep up with—you only deal with what you want to, rather than the whole ball of cyberwax—they present their own set of problems.

All the News that Fits...and More

Usenet news is many an Internetter's choice for conversation, explanation, suggestion, and direction. It's where you can go for a bit of information or just to banter ideas and philosophies. For newcomers and old-timers alike, it can be a bit overwhelming.

Newsgroups circulate among the millions of networks that make up the Internet. Any user on any computer connected to one of those networks can read and write to any newsgroup carried by his or her host computer. (Although many professional sites won't spend the time or disk space to carry the alt or soc hierarchies.) So, just like a mailing list, posting to a newsgroup means that potentially millions of people will see your message. Chapter 17, "Reading and Posting the News: Using Usenet," provides additional information about the alt and soc hierarchies, as well as an overall view of Usenet.

The difference is that those reading your postings don't have to subscribe to a group; they only have to *want* to read it. The postings are there for the asking whenever someone wants to browse through them—and newsgroup messages remain on the system for at least a few days, further increasing the number of people who can read them.

All this is good if you have a message you want to get out to a few million people…as long as you're prepared for the response. And that response won't only be on the newsgroup; Usenet news readers often send mail directly to your mailbox. Of course, you can probably find a service that will let you post anonymously, but that's a good deal of trouble and seems too cloak-and-daggerish for most people.

So you'll just be yourself and not use a false identity. There's no reason to if you only want to engage in some conversations or have a simple question answered. Let's say you're wondering what happened to Eve Plumb, who played Jan on *The Brady Bunch*. (Maybe you had a crush on her when you were little.) First, you have to pick the right newsgroup. You start by searching your .newsrc file for the word *Brady*. No luck. You try *1960s* and *1970s*, and several variations, and still come up with nothing. Finally, searching on *tv* gives you several responses, one of which is rec.arts.tv. It's pretty general, but it should suit your purpose.

That's newsgroup overload, part one: finding the right place to post. *The Brady Bunch* is pretty easy. But what about rockets, for instance? Would you try a space-related newsgroup, such as sci.space, or one devoted to physics? How about science fiction? There's no guide to what questions go where; you have to play it hit or miss.

Part two of newsgroup overload happens before you even write a message—when you search for a FAQ (Frequently Asked Question) file. After all, you don't want to ask about Eve Plumb if everyone has already asked. So you check the newsgroup you think is appropriate and maybe another one that might apply, including news.answers, to see if one's been posted. Then you use FTP to search the FAQ archives at rtfm.mit.edu (in the /pub/usenet/news.answers directory). There are a lot of them there. If none apply, then you can post your question.

You've read Usenet news before, so you know how to phrase your question:

```
To: rec.arts.tv
Subj: What ever happened to Eve "Jan Brady" Plumb?
I was a big fan of the Brady Bunch way back when, and I've always had a special
place in my heart for Jan. Does anyone know what happened to Eve Plumb, the
actress who played her?
```

Now you sit back and wait for an answer. (Just because there are 10 million people out there doesn't mean any of them are rushing to reply to your question.) But in a day or so, the answers start coming in to your mailbox, as well as to the newsgroup:

```
Isn't she on "One Life to Live?"
She was in the August '88 Playboy.
She works with disadvantaged kids in Oakland.
She committed suicide in 1982.
No she didn't. She was killed in a car accident.
```

```
You're both wrong. She was shot by her boyfriend.
She's married to the guy who draws "Calvin and Hobbes."
She sells clothing in a mall on Long Island.
```

Which is right? How can you tell? Chances are that correct answers are backed up with some facts—a reliable source, as opposed to rumor. But that's not always the case. (Check out the `alt.folklore.urban` newsgroup for cases of things reported to be true that simply aren't.) People tend to believe two things: computers and printed words. The Internet happily supplies both.

You've just discovered newsgroup overload, part three: A lot of information doesn't equal a lot of accurate information. With any pile of wheat, there's a lot of chaff mixed in.

Mail, mailing lists, newsgroups: They're popular, but these great communications tools aren't the real draw of the Internet. Heck, if you want to send e-mail and join mailing lists, you can sign up for Prodigy or America Online. The real attraction is the sheer volume of information available. The data—thousands of gigabytes spread around the world—is the greatest strength and potentially the greatest weakness of the Internet.

Data, Data Everywhere

There is more information available on the Internet than through any other public or private system, organization, library, or resource. More people contribute to the gathering, processing, and posting of those data than work for any news bureau, research organization, or think tank. Simply put, the Internet has it all.

That's the good news. The information is there. Here's the bad news:

It's not all there, and you can never count on something existing. Unlike a commercial service like CompuServe, no one *has* to make information available on the Internet. What's there is there by someone's good graces. For no reason other than the satisfaction of doing it, someone took the time to put it there. If you want something, you can assume it's there, somewhere among the 1s and 0s. But you have to hope that—*if* it indeed exists—you can find it, and it's accurate.

There are no guaranteed checks on what's available. Granted, users themselves provide this function, and word-of-mouth often does a better job of keeping people honest than any official organization. The information is not organized or referenced in any consistent way, either. There is no Internet card catalog. Certainly, tools such as Archie, Veronica, and WAIS make finding the information you want easier, but not easy.

Burrowing with Gopher and Veronica

Gopher is arguably the easiest of the standard Internet tools (what could be simpler than choosing a number from a list?). But using Gopher means browsing through data organized by location first, not category. It's easy to get to a server in Israel, France, or Japan (see Figure 59.4), but if you haven't been told about a specific file in a specific location, you end up browsing through virtual haystacks looking for silicon needles. On anything larger than a gigabyte or so, Gopher's usefulness begins and ends with browsing. There's simply too much to wade through.

FIGURE 59.4.

Finding a Gopher server anywhere in the world is easy. But finding a specific file isn't always.

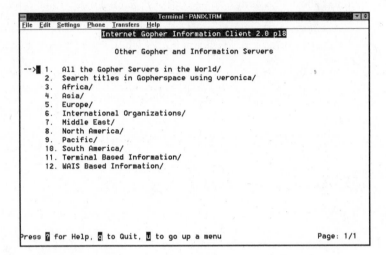

Veronica helps. Veronica lets you search Gopherspace for words in file or directory titles. If you're looking for information on *Hanover*, for example, searching with Veronica gives you a Gopher menu based on that subject (see Figure 59.5).

Searching for *Hanover* is easy because there are only a couple of dozen applicable Gopher directories. But try searching on a broader, more popular term like *business*. You'll find a lot more than a dozen entries (see Figure 59.6). There's too much there.

Indexing with Archie

Archie is the closest thing to any kind of overall index of the Internet. Archie servers keep a running record of all the publicly accessible files on all the Net's computers—a daunting (and impressive) task, to be sure—but an essential one for anyone searching for a particular file, which is what Archie lets you do. This is where the power of Archie is no match for the quantity of information on the Internet.

#### Chapter 59

FIGURE 59.5.

Searching on Hanover *with Veronica gives you a Gopher menu with entries that contain that name.*

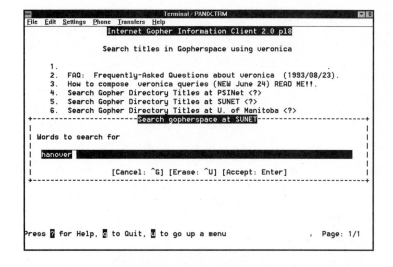

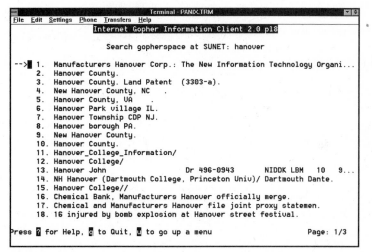

Archie is terrific for finding specific files. If you know the filename, searching finds a few servers that have it. The same applies to broad, general searches. Because Archie responds with a list of files and directories, searching on a word such as *games* or *windows* generates a list of public directories named games or windows. But you see the problem: Few people know the specific filename they want; more often they know the name of the product. But if you're looking for a program such as Apogee's Major Stryker game, what do you search on? What's the file's name?

FIGURE 59.6.

Veronica happily shows you more than 200 Gopher entries for business. Unfortunately, that's too many to be useful.

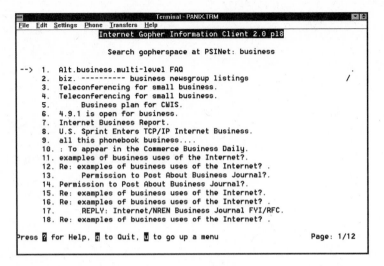

Similarly, searching on a broad topic such as *games* generates a list of directories, some of which are likely to contain the game you want. You're left to manually search each directory for the specific file, which you must identify by a possibly cryptic filename. Hopefully—but not necessarily—there's an index file you can read. For all its power, Archie is still hit-or-miss.

Scouring the Web

The fastest-growing part of the Internet—and the one thing even non-Net-savvy people seem to have heard of—is the World Wide Web. Consisting of millions of "pages" of information on thousands of computers, the Web has hit it big-time because it's got pictures.

Unlike Gopher with its text-based menu, a page on the Web can combine pictures with text of different sizes. A company's presence is no longer limited to numbered menus or an e-mail reply. Logos, pictures, catalogs—no wonder the Web is big. Anyone with a decent Internet connection can become a publisher. It's easy to get your information on the Web, too, so everyone from high school students to *Fortune 500* companies is creating a Web page. So the Web is growing and growing. There are tons of people, organizations, and—you guessed it—information.

So once again you run into the same problem: The more popular a service is, the more information there is. But the more information that's there, the harder it is to find what you want. Looking to buy a new car? Several car companies have pages on the Web. Can you find them? Maybe. There are search tools to be sure, but even they can't keep up with the explosive growth of the Web. A search on "automobile" comes up with over 200 separate pages. Some are actually the home pages of GM or Saab, but many are hobby pages, or the pages of small automobile dealers. (Yes, the Web is that vast—Rood Nissan/Volvo in Lynnwood, Washington, has a page.)

There is so much out there on the Web, and only a finite time to search through it. If you need the information *now*, there's a good chance you won't be able to get it. And even if you get close, it can take hours just to sort through all the information on a single Web page and the pages it links to.

Proof in the Virtual Pudding

Two pieces of information give testament to the incredible amount of data on the Internet. First is the monthly Internet Hunt.

Every month, teams of Internet users get together to participate in the Hunt, run by Rick Gates at the University of California's library. They have one week to answer 12 questions using Internet resources (one is a bonus question that may or may not be solvable). The first team to answer all 12 questions correctly wins.

> **NOTE**
>
> Following are two sample questions from previous Internet Hunts:
>
> 1. For 6 points: I've heard of an interesting plant, a sort of very large shrub-like tree called the Sticky Wattle. What is the genus and species for this plant?
> 2. For 3 points: What is the fax number for the Escola Tecnica Superior d'Enginyers de Telecomunicacio de Barcelona, at the Universitat Politecnica de Catalunya in Spain?

The very fact that *teams* of players have an entire *week* to answer these questions tells you something.

The second bit of information that bears witness to the overload of information on the Internet is the prices charged by Internet researchers—people who will, for a price, search its resources to find the answers to your company's questions. Looking through some of the business-related forums will tell you that the going rate is between $60 and $150 per hour. And basic capitalism tells you that the researchers wouldn't charge those rates if there weren't people willing to pay them.

The Light at the End of the Tunnel

There's hope. In fact, there's almost as much hope as there is information. Electronic mailing lists are becoming moderated for one, meaning that someone is making sure that the information posted is relevant. They're also becoming more specific—what was once a car mailing list has separated into lists for every make and model, plus collecting, repair, selling, and other specialties. The same holds true for Usenet newsgroups. There are more than ever, but they're getting more specific, and more and more are moderated to eliminate some of the chaff.

Ironically, the success of the World Wide Web has taken Gopher out of the limelight. There's a little less information there, making it a little easier to sort through. It's also more stable than the Web; you won't find a dozen new Gopher servers popping up every day.

The Web itself is starting to get sorted out. Search tools like the World Wide Web Wanderer, Wandex, and the World Wide Web Worm let you enter a keyword or phrase and will return a limited list of what's available. Lists like Yahoo (`http://www.yahoo.com/`) categorize the Web to make it easier to find what you need.

In the future you'll see *intelligent agents* abound. These pieces of software will take a request such as "What is the population of Fiji?" and scour the Net for you to find the answer. A precursor of sorts already exists: news search services that will periodically send you anything printed about a particular topic. If you tell these "knowbots" to show you everything having to do with Bruce Springsteen, each day (or hour, or week) you'll be notified of anything having to do with the Boss. Forget letting your fingers do the walking—let your computer do it for you.

If the Internet didn't have as much volume as it does—in people and in information—it wouldn't be in the news. We've always equated bigger with better, never considering the problems that enormous size can cause. Big cars make us feel safer, but we forget that they can't stop or maneuver as quickly as smaller models. (They use more gas and are tougher to park, too.) That big piece of cake sure looks appealing…until after it's finished.

People join the Internet, thinking somehow that its size and scope make it a nirvana of data and conversation. "With all that information," they think, "surely I can find what I want. With all those people, someone will tell me what I need to know."

This isn't necessarily true. We don't consider the problems that come with the Internet's bulk. All that data is hard to search, even as Internet tools and navigators get more sophisticated. Working at it, though, is likely to turn up several needles in the info-haystack. That brings up the question of accuracy: Which of the answers is correct? Which is most current? Which is most complete?

Considering the vast number of people on the Internet, we can safely assume that some of them will be able to answer our questions. But we're used to believing what we read, so it comes as a shock when we come across conflicting answers. Who's to believe? How can you be sure? Overloaded by information, sometimes it's hard to tell.

Copyright on the Networks

60

by Lance Rose

(elrose@path.net)

Early in network culture, people rarely worried about property ownership. Property claims were greeted with skepticism and subordinated to the "ethics" of using others' materials. Those who tried to protect their property often were vilified and ridiculed by other denizens of the electronic frontier. The network was primarily about connecting with other people. Who even dreamed he or she owned one end of a conversation? As the nets become more commercial, however, new users are arriving with an overriding mission to secure their property rights online. They boldly lay claim to copyrights in online conversations and in many other kinds of information found on the networks.

What Is Copyrighted?

Copyright law applies to many products of human creation. All "original works of authorship fixed in a tangible medium of expression" created in the U.S. after January 1, 1978, are copyrighted automatically under federal law the moment they are created. Works created before that time are also often copyrighted, although sometimes they accidentally fall into the public domain.

Before the widespread use of computers, it seemed intuitively clear that the *works* covered by copyright law were things experienced by the naked eye and ear, like books, plays, paintings, and music. *Authors* were the people or companies that created them. Once products of authorship started appearing on computers and networks, some asked whether the underpinnings of copyright law were crumbling. The basic requirement that a copyrightable work be an "original work of authorship fixed in a tangible medium of expression" was teased apart and subjected to withering scrutiny:

- Is it a "work of authorship" if the human creator was assisted by a computer?
- Is the work "fixed" when it is stored on a rewritable disk or in volatile RAM, as opposed to the pages of a traditional book in which the text is frozen until the distant day the page crumbles to dust?
- Is the work in a "tangible medium of expression" when it is only a pattern in the orientation of magnetic particles on a disk, or in the stream of electrons or photons streaming down a cable?

Yes—works in digitized, computerized form are copyrighted, as established in a series of court cases involving copyrights in software. In fact, computers add little to the existing copyright equation. Music and videos recorded on magnetic tape, the forerunner of magnetic floppy disks, were copyrighted for years. For decades before that, films recorded on celluloid, which must be run through a projector to achieve the illusion of motion, were fully recognized as copyrighted.

Many kinds of copyrightable works are now available on computers and the networks, including the following:

- Messages posted to Usenet, mailing lists, and bulletin boards. This includes both individual messages and message collections, or threads
- Electronic mail
- Computer software, including entire applications, patches, add-ons, and utilities
- Files of all kinds, such as the following:

    - Texts, hypertexts, and formatted documents
    - Multimedia and hypermedia works
    - Databases
    - Visual images, clip files, textures, and other image files
    - Sound and music samples, MIDI files
    - Animation loops

What Is the Purpose of Copyright?

Copyright law in the United States is based on the Constitution, Article I, Section 8, Clause 8:

> *The Congress shall have Power...To promote the Progress of Science and useful Arts, by securing for limited Times to Authors and Inventors the exclusive Right to their respective Writings and Discoveries*

When this clause was drafted, *Science* really referred to arts and letters. Ironically, 200 years later, copyright is now becoming intimate with *science* in the modern sense. Software copyrights are pivotally important to the mainstream computer industry. Even newer high-tech kinds of copyrightable works like multimedia and virtual reality (and investments in those works) promise that copyright questions will continue to arise among the latest developments in electronic science and technology.

Congress enacted the Copyright Act under its Constitutional empowerment. It encourages authors to invest their time and effort to create valuable works, by promising they will be able to charge others for copies (or, in the case of performed or displayed works, for attending the performance or viewing the work). The tradeoff is that authors can exclusively exploit their creations for a time, but their works do not remain forever in the family estate; copyrighted works eventually fall into the public domain for general use. The public gains immediate access to many new and valuable works at a market-determined price, and later obtains those works for free when the author's exclusive rights end. Underlying this scheme is the Constitutional premise that without some form of financial encouragement, many of our citizens most capable of creating great works and masterpieces will forego such efforts to seek their fortunes in other pursuits.

The exclusive rights mechanism of the copyright law is not the only way to encourage creation of valuable works. The government also pays some artists and writers to create new works and could expand on this approach if it wanted. But the exclusive rights method is shrewd and cleverly balanced: it sets up a relatively small government administration program instead of a far more expensive spending program; it promotes the creation of those works for which the public is willing to pay (one way of indicating the public value of the work); and it creates entire markets and industries for copyrighted works, such as the music, film, and software industries that contribute substantially to the U.S. economy.

In any case, the existing federal copyright system is a highly developed response to the perceived need to stimulate a steady flow of new and valuable works to the public. Some would argue that many works of little value are produced as well, but it is probably a good thing that the copyright system does not legislate matters of taste.

Computers and networks do not portend fundamental changes to the premises or reasoning underlying the copyright laws. The motivation of people to create valuable works does not change just because they start using computer networks. The main effects of the networks on the copyright system are these:

- Adding new channels for delivery of copyrighted works to customers and the public
- Enabling the development of new kinds of copyrightable works
- Creating new possibilities for joint development of copyrightable works by geographically separated authors
- Making it easier to infringe copyright, and harder to enforce certain infringements, than in the past

These are the opportunities and challenges for copyright law on the networks today and in the near future.

Basic Rights of Copyright Owners on the Networks

Copyright law, as its name indicates, regulates the copying of certain works. In fact, it goes a fair bit further than that. The exclusive rights of every copyright owner are spelled out in Section 106 of the Copyright Act:

> to *reproduce the copyrighted work...*
>
> to *prepare derivative works based on the copyrighted work*
>
> to *distribute copies...of the copyrighted work to the public...*

to *perform the copyrighted work publicly*

to *display the copyrighted work publicly*

[portions of text omitted]

The copyright owner legally can prevent others from acting under any of these exclusive rights without the owner's permission. If I write a book, other people must secure my permission before they can legally copy or distribute it, under my rights of reproduction and distribution. My permission is needed before others can write screenplay adaptations of the book, under my exclusive right to derivative works. And if I release my own authorized screenplay, others need my permission before they can publicly perform or transmit a production based on the screenplay or release any stills from the production under my rights of performance and display.

What about works on the networks? If I post my own message or file to a Usenet newsgroup, it is distributed automatically to other Usenet sites, whether I like it or not. If I place my own file in an anonymous FTP directory, everyone in the networked world can download it. In these situations, do I have any exclusive rights left?

Yes, the copyright owner retains exclusive rights when placing his or her own work on the networks, although those rights are less than if the work was not made so widely available to others. Every work is copyrighted when it is created, and remains copyrighted unless the owner expressly dedicates it to the public domain. Merely posting a message or file is not a clear dedication. In addition, the copyright owner need not publish a copyright notice with the work to retain his or her copyright—if the work was created in the U.S. after March 1989 (when the U.S. signed the Berne Convention, an international copyright agreement). As a result, all messages and files on the networks created after March 1989 should be presumed copyrighted, whether or not they have a copyright notice (except where expressly dedicated to the public domain).

But if the work is freely accessible on the network, what good is the owner's copyright? In fact, the owner does not give up that much under his or her copyright by placing the work on the network. The owner still has the exclusive right to copy and distribute the work, subject only to an implied license to network users to use the work in ways customarily accepted on the network.

What counts as "customarily accepted" use of a work depends on the local online environment. For example, in some parts of Usenet as carried on a given system, it may be customary to distribute messages only in certain geographic locales, like the Bay Area. When a copyrighted message is posted in such an area, distribution to other Bay Area Usenet sites is within the implied license granted by the author of the message. But distribution of the message outside that locale may exceed the scope of the implied license.

The copyright owner also keeps all exclusive rights not related to the normal process of transmitting or downloading the work, such as his or her right to make derivative works and to perform or display the work in public. So although a MIDI file on Usenet may be downloaded freely by other Net users, those users do not get the right to modify that file or the music it contains, nor the right to perform it. This sounds rather strange—why would someone obtain the file if not to play it for himself or herself or to provide it for someone else to play? This capability simply places emphasis on the idea that it is the *playing*, not the *copying*, that is important.

Where is the line drawn defining when the copyright owner's permission is needed to distribute a work? There is no general agreement on the exact bounds of the implied network license. This phenomenon is so new we may not see court decisions on the subject for years. In the meantime, we can point to situations in which the result is clear and say that the gray area lies somewhere in between. For example, if a copyright owner places his or her own file in a publicly accessible directory in an anonymous FTP site with the permissions set to general access by all users, we should expect an implied license to all members of the public to download the file into their own computers using anonymous FTP. On the other hand, if I engage in a spirited discussion on a mailing list, that does not mean I have granted an implied license that others can reproduce my postings in a printed book; this is not a customarily accepted use of bulletin board postings.

When there is no implied license, it is still sometimes possible to use others' work under an exception to copyright called "fair use." Some claim that any copying on the networks is fair use, but this is not true. Fair use is a recognized and valuable exception to copyright protection, but it is not *carte blanche* permission to use the works of others freely. For example, although entire magazine or newspaper articles are frequently posted verbatim online without permission under claims of fair use, such postings do not, in fact, qualify for fair use.

Fair use occurs when you use another's copyrighted work in a way that technically violates the owner's rights, but you have good reason and you do no real harm to the value of the copyright. Classic examples of fair use include making a limited number of photocopies of a magazine article to hand out to a single class in school and using excerpts from books in written book reviews. One must be careful not to generalize from such situations, however. The copyright statute requires courts to look at each claim of fair use individually on its facts, and make sure that the fair use clause is not abused in a way that damages the value of the copyright.

Section 107 of the copyright law requires considering at least four factors in each fair use decision:

> *(i) the purpose and character of the use, including whether such use is of a commercial nature or for nonprofit educational purposes; (ii) the nature of the copyrighted work; (iii) the amount and substantiality of the portion used in relation to the copyrighted work as a whole; and (iv) the effect of the use upon the potential market for or value of the copyrighted work.*

If you are uncertain whether your intended use of another's copyrighted work qualifies as fair use, it is best to seek out the advice of someone knowledgeable in this specialized subject rather than rely on the random opinions of others on the networks.

Many people use the computer networks to distribute and collect visual and audio samples, such as clip art, pieces of songs, film dialogs, and audiovisual excerpts from films. When these samples are pieces of larger copyrighted works, they are also themselves copyrighted. This was established with certainty in lawsuits involving the use of sampled pop songs in hip-hop recordings. In addition, the bulk of the samples on the networks today are not licensed by the copyright owners nor are they eligible for fair use. Thus, one should not infer merely from the availability of samples that they can be used in one's own works without infringing on copyrights. There are trends in the politics and commerce of art that may one day lead to a relaxation of copyright laws to permit free use of small samples of others' works, but that is not the case today.

A case with great importance for computer network copyrights was *Feist v. Rural Telephone*, decided by the U.S. Supreme Court in 1991. The Supreme Court held that the information in a white pages telephone directory has no copyright protection. Each entry in a phone directory consists of a name, address, and phone number, making it an objective "fact" that was not created by the compiler of the directory and that cannot be owned under copyright. Further, the entire directory is no more than a collection of such facts arranged alphabetically, and similarly is not capable of being owned under copyright. In general, there is no copyright in a fact compilation unless the compiler made some original "selection, coordination, or arrangement" of those facts. Merely gathering together some facts into an unoriginal arrangement, regardless of how much work is involved, does not confer a copyright on the gatherer.

The *Feist* case has a huge impact on the development of online database services. Existing electronic databases are often little more than collections of factual data, so many large database providers saw much of their copyright protection suddenly disappear when Feist was decided. It is not very likely that Congress will override the decision, because database owners benefit from *Feist* as well—they may lose some legal protection, but now they can plunder the data of others. For smaller network users, the *Feist* case means they can use factual data from others' databases in their own works and projects without violating any copyrights. As with the other limits on copyright protection, it is wise to consult with someone knowledgeable in copyright where the applicability of the *Feist* exception is uncertain.

Licensing and Public Domain

The main way copyright owners permit others to use their works is through licensing. We already looked at one kind of license—the implied license—that is granted automatically by the owner when he or she places his or her own work on a computer network. There are many other kinds of licenses on the networks, expressly (rather than implicitly) granted by the copyright owner. It is often useful to think of a copyright as a bundle of different rights to use the copyrighted work. When the copyright owner grants a license, he or she peels a few rights off the bundle and gives them to the licensee, either temporarily or permanently.

The most highly developed express licenses on the networks are found in connection with software. One popular approach is *shareware*, a software marketing method that exploits the rapid, broad distribution capabilities of the computer networks. The shareware license is an essential part of each shareware package. It typically grants the general public two different kinds of free licenses: an electronic distribution license and a trial-use license. The electronic distribution license usually permits unrestricted distribution of the shareware package on computer networks, as long as the online provider does not charge a fee specifically for distributing the package. The trial-use license permits individuals who download the shareware package to try the software for free during a specified test period, after which they are expected to pay a registration fee to continue using the software. Beyond such free licenses generally granted to the public, shareware copyright owners often require certain kinds of distributors, such as floppy disk vendors, to contact the owner directly for permission to distribute the software.

Other software licensing methods include *copyleft*, which uses copyright laws against themselves to prohibit those using copyleft-covered software from charging others for it; and *freeware*, which is like shareware except that no payment from the user is required to register the software copy.

A number of organizations are working on systems to make it easier to find out how to license copyrighted works and to obtain such licenses and the works themselves. Groups and systems include the Copyright Clearance Center, the Xanadu project, the Corporation for National Research Initiatives, and the VENDINFO licensing system. The different systems being explored vary in such matters as whether the licensing information is stored with the work or in centralized information sites; how the process of obtaining licenses is automated; how to obtain the works in question; and so forth. These systems are in the exploration stages, and we can only wait for the results. But as these systems become fully implemented, it will be an opportunity to see whether the power of the networks can be leveraged to create effective, new means for licensing and distributing copyrighted works.

Finally, there are works in the public domain for which there are no owners and for which no permission is necessary. As described above, a copyrighted work does not go into the public domain unless the owner expressly dedicates it to the public domain. Many works are already in the public domain. These include older works, such as classics by Shakespeare and da Vinci that preceded our copyright system, and works once copyrighted whose exclusive rights period has run out. The public domain also includes factual materials, such as the telephone directories described earlier, as well as historical facts, scientific facts, and the news.

Before using any materials from the public domain, you should always check that they do not include any copyrighted material (which can be mixed together with public domain materials in countless ways). Examples include new additions, annotations, or translations of unprotected public domain works like the Bible; expressive accounts of the facts in a text by a historian or scientist; and a novel arrangement of factual data, such as an industry-specific phone directory that adds various kinds of company data to each telephone listing. One last thing: despite claims to the contrary, a public domain text does not become copyrighted merely by putting the text into a file that can be read by computer and transmitted through the network. The mere act of literal transcription does not add any original, copyrightable authorship to the public domain text.

Enforcement of Copyrights on the Networks

The basic legal remedy for copyright owners is a court order making the infringer stop his or her infringing activity. It is often very easy for the infringer to stop infringing, so many do just that when they are threatened with a lawsuit, and the copyright owner does not proceed any further. In most cases that go to court, there is either a lot of money at stake or it is not clear whether an infringement occurred. Owners who seek money from the infringer are entitled to an award of the infringer's profits, if any, and the owner's losses caused by the infringement.

Additional remedies are available to the owner if the copyrighted work is federally registered before the infringement occurred:

- The victorious copyright owner can be awarded his or her attorneys' fees
- If the owner cannot prove any profits or losses on the infringement, there is also a provision for "statutory damages," in which the judge is permitted to make up and award an amount believed to fairly compensate the owner for the infringement

There are also criminal copyright penalties, under which infringers can pay large fines and go to jail, as we are reminded at the beginning of every commercial videocassette. The possibility of criminal penalties is often of little value to copyright owners. Only the federal government can bring criminal copyright actions, and the government acts only when it suits its own purposes.

Copyrights are easier to infringe and more difficult to enforce on computer networks than in the past. Infringing an older nonnetwork item like a book or a CD requires a large investment in copying equipment that is hard to move and easy to find—and usually results in substantial revenues to the infringer. Such infringements are hard to perform, easy to trace, and attractive to enforce, because copyright owners can take the infringer to court and obtain the illicit revenues for themselves. In contrast, anyone with Internet access can easily perform a mass infringement of any data or file available in digital form. The infringer can easily hide his or her identity. And such infringements often do not result in any revenues to the infringer, who can be a person of little means. This greatly reduces the incentive to copyright owners to pursue the infringement, because they cannot hope to recoup their costs of the lawsuit.

The infringement possibilities on the networks are not new kinds of problems. The U.S. copyright system never depended on perfect enforcement. For example, for many years bootleg copies of records, tapes, and CDs have been widely available and people have been making home tapes of music and videos. That did not stop the development of powerful music and video industries that thrive to this day. Companies, schools, and other organizations regularly make unauthorized photocopies of magazines and newspapers, but the publishing industry did not die either. The copyright system does not work perfectly, just well enough to permit copyright-based projects, businesses, and industries to flourish.

Recent and increasing copyright enforcement activity indicates that copyrights are quite effectively enforceable on the networks. Examples include the following:

- A lawsuit by Playboy Enterprises against the Event Horizons bulletin board for carrying and distributing unauthorized digital copies of *Playboy* photographs, which was settled with a $500,000 payment to *Playboy*.

- The frequent shutdown of various "pirate bulletin boards" by the Software Publishers Association, the Business Software Alliance, and large software companies like Novell, for carrying large quantities of unauthorized commercial software.

- The raid on Rusty and Edie's bulletin board system by the FBI, with assistance from the SPA, for carrying unauthorized commercial software. This is different from pirate BBS cases because Rusty and Edie's is a mainstream operation, and also because it was seized under the recently enhanced criminal provisions of the Copyright Act, which make it a felony punishable by a jail term and fine to make or distribute 10 or more unauthorized copies worth $2,500 or more.

The computer networks present new opportunities for creating, distributing, and using copyrighted works, and new opportunities for infringement. As the networks develop, you should expect to encounter many interesting and vexing questions about how copyright law applies to network activities. But the law itself, and the reasons behind it, are not fundamentally changed by the networks.

> **Lance Rose** is an attorney and writer who works with high-tech and information companies. He is the author of SysLaw, the online legal guide, and writes for *Boardwatch Magazine* and *Wired.*

Freedom of
Online Speech

61

by Lance Rose

(elrose@path.net)

In the United States, freedom of speech and of the press are guaranteed by law. The First Amendment to the Constitution states, "Congress shall make no law...abridging freedom of speech, or of the press." As long as this principle holds, the people of the United States can question their existing leadership and discuss alternatives without fear of being silenced.

The First Amendment has been upheld most purely in the realm of print publishing, especially newspapers as the traditional forum of public opinion. Radio and television fared far less well, being regulated from the very beginning by the Federal Communications Commission. The rationale for regulation was that, in the early days of radio, neighboring broadcasters competing for the same frequencies caused such interference it was difficult for any of them to be heard by the audience. The FCC was created to prevent such interference and promote an orderly allocation of broadcast frequencies. Many feel that over the decades, FCC regulation descended a slippery slope leading away from speech freedom. For example, the FCC first regulated the content of broadcasts to ensure proper use of the airwaves, then extended its reach to cable and other transmission technologies where its limited-bandwidth basis for regulation does not even apply.

As the publishing and broadcasting industries begin delivering their products on the computer networks, a major question is which will prevail: the great respect traditionally accorded freedom of speech for the print media, or the regulated environment of the broadcast media? It is too early to tell amid the current intense jockeying between multinational corporations for control of the networks. In a few years, after the dust settles, it will be clear whether regulation is needed or desirable, and if so, whether government has the will or power to impose it.

Perhaps a whole new meaning for freedom of speech under the First Amendment will develop, unique to the network environment. The computer networks provide new opportunities for speech. Millions of individuals already interact easily with others across the nation and the world, both individually and in group settings. Anyone can start his or her own electronic newsletter, Usenet newsgroup, mailing list, Internet node, or computer bulletin board, and thus become an electronic publisher in his or her own right. In addition, one can participate without revealing one's gender, race, or age, and permit ideas to flow with less hindrance by pointless prejudice. The level of connectedness within and among communities, states, and nations is at a far higher level than ever before in history, and may lead to higher and better levels of democracy. If the First Amendment can apply to the networks to protect and promote such developments, it will serve a most valuable purpose.

Unfortunately, the First Amendment online is not entirely healthy today. In the past few years, there has been a rash of government raids on computer bulletin boards for various real or imagined illegalities. A common theme of these raids is the authorities' disregard for legal safeguards against unreasonable governmental activities—seize first, figure out whether it was justified later. If a bunch of printing presses were closed down around the country by our local and federal governments, there would be an enormous outcry. But when it happens to online services—which are not yet well understood by the public—barely an eyebrow is raised. Public education on the nature of computer networks may be necessary before freedom of speech for online services will receive the general respect it deserves. With luck, such education may not even require force-feeding or the passing on of a net-illiterate generation. Within five or ten years, a significant proportion of the U.S. population may be interacting regularly on the Internet, and recognize implicitly and personally the value of their own freedom of speech.

The other source of freedom of speech is competition among network providers. If the user has multiple choices for getting into the Internet, and many different places to go once there, there will be freedom of speech. Those who cannot say their piece in one mailing list or Usenet discussion can simply go to another and state their views there. This is a practical form of speech freedom—not one based on laws—and it has international effect (unlike the First Amendment). This was displayed most stirringly in two major world events of recent years: the government-student clash at Tiananmen Square in China and the failed Russian coup attempt. In each case, forces seeking to control information flow from those under attack were unsuccessful in preventing them from spreading news of their plight throughout the world over the Internet. Being a market effect, this form of speech freedom is subject to potential control by monopoly network providers in the future. If and when that ever happens, the introduction of protective laws, perhaps in the form of antitrust-type regulation, may be necessary to keep alive our choice of services and our resulting freedom to speak.

The rest of this chapter discusses freedom of online speech as guaranteed by the First Amendment.

Three Kinds of Speech Freedom

In the short history of computer communications, the First Amendment has already been recognized to protect freedom of speech in three distinctly different ways:

1. It sharply limits the kinds of speech that can be considered illegal.
2. It assures that the overall legal burdens on distributors of speech will be kept light enough to enable them to operate effectively.
3. It limits the government's ability to search or seize online services when doing so would limit the service's ability to publish and distribute speech.

The Kinds of Illegal Speech

The first way the First Amendment protects online speech is by greatly reducing the exposure of online publishers and speakers to lawsuits based on the contents of their statements. For example, in an earlier day, disparaging statements about major public figures routinely led to potentially ruinous lawsuits. Now, such statements can be made almost with impunity. This is the result of a line of legal decisions starting with the famous case of *New York Times v. Sullivan*, in which the Supreme Court held that the *New York Times* newspaper was not liable for making false statements about a police official. The Court reasoned that newspapers must be able to report on the actions of public officials in the course of doing their job of informing the public. If officials could sue newspapers every time they made a mistake, soon the newspapers would either be out of business or avoid printing unfavorable stories about anyone to avoid expensive lawsuits. This would amount to an impermissible "chilling effect" imposed on newspapers and discussion of public affairs through use of the court system, and would violate the Constitutional right of freedom of the press.

To avoid the chilling effect, mere reporting of false facts about public officials does not subject a publisher to legal action. In subsequent decisions, the Sullivan rule was extended and refined to its current form: disparaging statements about public figures do not subject the speaker or publisher to liability unless they can be proven false, and unless it can further be proven that the speaker spoke falsely either out of malice or reckless disregard for the truth or falsity of the statement. Although the opportunity has not arisen for this principle to be applied in a reported court case to online statements, it is widely expected that the rule of *Times v. Sullivan* and its progeny will apply fully in the online context.

A related form of reduced liability for online speech under the First Amendment was recognized in the New York case *Daniel v. Dow Jones*, decided in 1987. Daniel, a subscriber to the Dow Jones News Retrieval service, invested in an oil company based on the service's report of certain dollar figures relating to the company. When the investment turned bad, he sued Dow Jones, claiming it misreported the amounts as being in U.S. dollars when they were actually measured in Canadian dollars. The investor lost under First Amendment principles because the court refused to hold Dow Jones liable merely for carrying negligently untruthful news. Again, the "chilling effect" of liability for merely making a mistake in a news report would so hobble Dow Jones and similar services that it could not effectively perform its reporting functions, so the court refused to recognize such liability.

Legal Burdens on Distributors of Free Speech

The second form of First Amendment protection limits the duty of online information distributors to monitor the materials moving through their system for illegal contents. This protection is for those who distribute the speech of others, in contrast to protecting the publisher's own statements. It has been accorded to operations like book stores and magazine distributors, who have been held not responsible for checking all the books and magazines flowing through their operations for illegal materials.

Online distributors were expressly accorded the same protection as print distributors in the case of *Cubby v. CompuServe*, decided in a New York federal court in 1991. Cubby published a small electronic newsletter that disparaged a competing newsletter. When the second newsletter sued for libel, it added CompuServe as a defendant because the Cubby newsletter was available on the CompuServe Information Service. The judge dismissed the case against CompuServe on the basis that it merely distributed Cubby's newsletter and had no actual knowledge of the alleged libel. If CompuServe had been held responsible in this situation, then to avoid further lawsuits, it would either have to monitor all materials passing through its massive information service or sharply cut down on the flow of such materials. This would result in the prohibited "chilling effect," not only on CompuServe's own business, but on the speech of hundreds of thousands of people and businesses using CompuServe at the time. Fortunately, the First Amendment was served in this case by letting CompuServe off the hook.

The Government's Ability To Search and Seize

The third way the First Amendment protects online speech is by limiting the government's ability to interfere with press and speech activities through physical searches and seizures. Students of the Constitution know that the primary protection against unreasonable searches and seizures comes from the Fourth and Fifth Amendments, and applies to all persons and businesses, not just publishers and speakers. But where the search or seizure could result in shutting down speech or press protected by the First Amendment, the Supreme Court has held that the government must be especially careful to follow all procedural requirements.

There is also a law, the Privacy Protection Act, enacted by Congress under the First, Fourth, and Fifth Amendments, to make it crystal clear that the press has special protection from government searches and seizures. The PPA requires that materials collected in preparation for publishing, and the working materials created as part of such preparation, cannot be searched or seized unless the government has good reason to suspect that the person or publisher who possesses those materials is also involved in a crime relating to the materials. Although this law does not fully protect the press from all undue searches and seizures, it helps to prevent publishers from being harassed in many situations. To explain the importance of the PPA as a restraint on the government: it is one of the few federal statutes for which federal agents can be held personally liable for damages if they violate its provisions.

The PPA was found to apply to materials on a computer bulletin board in *Steve Jackson Games v. the United States*, decided in a Texas federal court in 1992. Steve Jackson Games publishes role playing and strategy games, and ran a bulletin board for customer support and other activities. One of its employees acted as a system operator for the company BBS, and was also suspected by the Secret Service to be a phone-system hacker (based on activities he conducted at home in his spare time). Wrongly inferring that the Steve Jackson Games BBS was also being used for suspicious activities, the Secret Service raided the company and removed the BBS and most of its other computer equipment. They ended up holding the equipment for months before returning it, resulting in great injury to the business.

Steve Jackson Games sued the government under a number of laws, including the PPA. The court held that the government indeed violated the PPA when it unduly withheld materials and equipment from Steve Jackson Games after being informed that the company was involved in publishing. It awarded damages to the company for injuries to its business from the government's wrongful search and seizure. Although the result in Steve Jackson Games leaves certain things unclear—in particular, whether the court would have felt the PPA was violated if the online service was not operated by a company also involved in print publishing—it helped lay the groundwork for future protection of online services from government indiscretions.

The Online Metaphor Toy Box

The current mass movement to join the Internet is not just a bunch of computers connecting together, but a social project of exploring and defining a virtual world sometimes referred to as *cyberspace*. It is a world consisting of people's shared ideas of a computer-mediated space they occupy together, jam-packed full of metaphors based on the physical world and established social orders. It so happens that the law also operates by metaphor and analogy, so the choice of metaphor applied to an online service can be decisive in determining its treatment under the First Amendment.

We have already seen two metaphors: publisher, and magazine distributor or book store. There are certainly online analogs for each of these. The creator of a newsletter distributed through mailing lists looks like a "publisher," as does a company that sells access to a large proprietary database. Internet nodes carrying widespread Usenet discussions and FTP sites whose system administrators do not closely inspect the files made available for download look more like "distributors" or "book stores." As described in the preceding sections, these differences in metaphor can result in somewhat different First Amendment treatment. The distributor-type operations are entitled to broad relief from burdensome obligations to monitor the materials moving through their systems. Because the publisher-type operations adopt the statements and reports they carry as their own, the relief from monitoring may not apply to them, but they are still entitled to the same First Amendment limits on liability for message content enjoyed by print publishers.

Many other metaphors may apply to any given online service: innkeeper or conference hall administrator, for services that maintain online social discussion areas; common carrier, for services that merely forward messages and files between other systems; supermarket or shopping mall, for services featuring online stores; telephone chat line, for services featuring real-time chat; radio or television broadcasting, for the recently begun practice of distributing entire radio shows and audiovisual clips through the networks; news wire service, for stock quote systems and the like; postal system, for transmission of e-mail, and so on. All these metaphors have some value in determining First Amendment applicability and online rights generally. Just as importantly, none of these metaphors is the "right" one for all situations.

In fact, there are many different kinds of online services, each with unique features not entirely captured by any one metaphor. Online services ultimately will be understood on their own terms and not merely as electronic versions of older types of operations. Until that time, legal analysis necessarily stumbles along on awkward analogical legs. Fortunately, the major metaphors of "publisher" and "distributor" identified earlier in this discussion—which are already being applied by courts to online matters—are highly protective of speech in the computer networks.

The Question of Censorship

Censorship is among the most popular and controversial subjects on the networks. Any time a system administrator, SysOp, or conference moderator tampers with user messages, they run the risk of being reviled as a "censor" and threatened with lawsuits for violating the free speech rights of the user whose messages were affected.

Anti-censorship flamers often miss a critical point: the First Amendment only guarantees that federal and state governments do not interfere with freedom of speech. If a private provider of online or network services wants to interfere with a user's public message, there is no anti-censorship law preventing it from doing so. Here is where the old saw "freedom of the press means freedom of the owner of the press" is demonstrated online. If I set up my own online service, I can allow or deny any kind of messaging behavior I choose. I can even choose who I will permit to use the service and who cannot use it, without needing a good reason. Users who don't like this treatment can complain, if I let them, but they cannot legally force me to let them say their piece on my system. If they want more freedom for their speech, they can try the system down the line, or open their own.

Online services and network environments are already full of examples of private speech regulation. Prodigy, for example, has developed a reputation for monitoring almost every message that passes through the system, readily removing from its family service areas all messages that do not comport with the gentility it likes to promote. Bulletin board ECHO networks like RIME and ILINK are filled with conference moderators that routinely castigate callers who dare stray from the topic defined by the moderator, readily casting them out of the conferences altogether for repeated violations. Moderated Usenet conferences or mailing lists take moderator control a step further. The user must send his or her proposed message to the moderator, who then decides at his or her whim whether it is posted for wider viewing.

If any system administrators or moderators reading this want to run out and become message tyrants in their own domains because there is no law preventing it, they should keep a couple of things in mind. First, many users cherish the ability to speak freely online and will choose their online haunts accordingly. For example, the WELL in San Francisco takes a strongly free-speech approach, refusing to tamper with any but the most extreme or dangerous postings. Consequently, it is popular and much loved by those who like their expression of views uncut. Second, moderators or system administrators who often tamper with online messages put themselves at greater risk of being legally saddled with responsibility for all messages passing through the system. Hands-off moderators are in the best position to claim they only distribute the speech of others and are not liable for illegal materials that may be contained in such speech.

It is sometimes claimed that the most popular online services, like CompuServe and Prodigy, are so central to online communications that they are quasi-governmental, giving rise to freedom of speech rights even though they are privately owned and operated. This argument has some theoretical merit, but in fact, there is no service even close to such primacy today. The networks are growing at a frightening pace, and new major and minor providers of online services are arriving all the time. At last count, there are over 49,000 networks (and millions of individual computers) connected to the Internet on the provider side. If it ever turns out that a single monstrous online service megaprovider becomes the only place online where others can hear what you have to say, it may then be time to reexamine this question.

Lance Rose is an attorney and writer who works with high-tech and information companies. He is the author of SysLaw, the online legal guide, and writes for *Boardwatch Magazine* and *Wired*.

How the Web Is Changing the Internet

62

by John December

When I first saw the Mosaic Web browser in the spring of 1993, I knew neither I nor the networked world would ever be the same. Having toiled on the Internet using line-mode clients for FTP, Gopher, and the Web, I found in Mosaic a single graphical browser that could serve as my window into several Internet information spaces. Although the Web and graphical interfaces to network information had been around before Mosaic, Mosaic's fresh look and clean design released a flurry of new interest in the Web. The increasing number of Web servers that followed Mosaic's release created a critical mass of communication that drew still more resources and people to the Web. Major institutions and corporations joined the Web, as well as hundreds of thousands of individuals, creating thousands-fold increases in Web traffic over the year 1993.

By 1994, the prevalence of graphical browsers and the popularity of the Web as a means to disseminate information had changed forever the way the Internet would be used, taught, and explained.

But the graphical interfaces like Mosaic, Netscape, and others mark just the first steps in the Web's transformation of the Internet. Although the graphical Web browsers offer enticing views through easy-to-use point-and-click interfaces, the subtle point behind this ease of use is that the Internet user's attention can shift from the mechanics of information retrieval to the meaning of what is retrieved.

No longer focused on just the rudiments of information lookup—such as an Archie search to locate a needed file—people have begun to take part in a larger "global conversation" in hypermedia on the Web.

The Web's system of associative linking creates new relationships among people and information. Through the expressiveness of global hypermedia, the Web transforms a network of networks, the Internet, into a system for people to share meaning in ways never possible before.

The Web Integrates Information

The development of the Web at CERN in Switzerland in the early 1990s sparked interest in global hypertext as a way to organize information. Since then, the Web's chief contribution to the transformation of the Internet stems from the Web's role as an information integrator.

Web browsers serve as clients for access to many different servers. This single-client, multiple-server system transforms the line-mode retrieval of information through separate clients (shown in Figure 62.1) into a system for point-and-click to access information from a single Web browser (see Figure 62.2).

#### Chapter 62

FIGURE 62.1.

Multiple-client, line-mode access to Internet information.

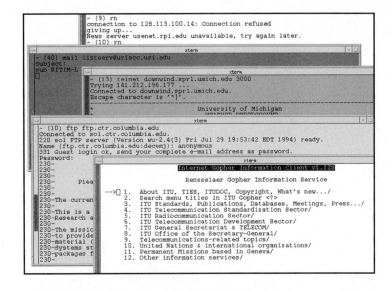

FIGURE 62.2.

A Web browser unifies Internet information access.

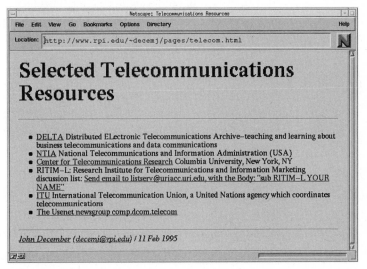

The Web's "native" language—HyperText Markup Language (HTML)—serves as the "glue" that integrates Internet resources.

Rather than requiring an Internet user to access FTP, Telnet, Gopher, and other information servers using separate procedures, users of the Web can follow hyperlinks within HTML documents to access information in several information spaces. The native protocol of the Web—HTTP—thus creates a new information space—called the *Webspace*, the set of all hypertext available on Web servers world wide—that unifies Internet information.

This elegant, seamless integration of Internet information spaces in a well-designed browser is just the visual change the Web brings to the Internet. Other changes the Web brings are perhaps more significant. These changes include new ways to train users, integral techniques for searching and indexing Internet information, and innovative practices for presenting Internet information online as well as offline.

The Web Changes Internet User Training and Literacy

A new user who first experiences the Internet through a Web browser may not know the difference between a Gopher hole and an FTP site, nor the technical details of transferring hypertext with the HTTP protocol. Instead, the user with a Web browser has a tool that graphically presents information, offers a view into content and meaning on the Internet, and hides most details of information transfer.

Therefore, an Internet trainer using the Web as a basis for teaching must still teach concepts—indeed, the Web demands a whole range of concepts for new users to grasp—but the stress of training can shift from details about information retrieval to practices of information literacy. Instead of a sometimes laborious and (highly technical) exploration of each information protocol and its inner workings, the Web-based Internet trainer can focus on a set of skills for users to discover, retrieve, analyze, understand, and use information content:

- **Information discovery.** In its role as an Internet information integrator, as well as because of the expressiveness of its hypertext language, the Web serves as a "common ground" for information on the Internet itself. Through hypertext Web pages, information providers can create structures to expressively present Internet information, allowing the users to focus on the meaning and relationships of these information pieces.

  Because the hypertext language of the Web stresses the semantic markup of documents, Webspace itself is highly amenable to indexing. In contrast, indexing Gopherspace and FTPspace is more difficult; the semantic content in these spaces is not marked but is presented in ASCII files, with only filenames, directory names, or menu entry names available to convey meaning. As a result of the Web's semantic markings, the tools that automatically traverse the Web to index its information—these tools are called *Web spiders*—are powerful searching tools (see http:// lycos.cs.cmu.edu/ for an example of a Web spider, as shown in Figure 62.3). A Web user, with a basic understanding of the limitations and use of Web spiders, can search Webspace for keywords and string patterns.

FIGURE 62.3.

The Lycos Web spider. Copyright © 1995 by Carnegie Mellon University. All Rights Reserved. Printed by Permission. Courtesy of Dr. Michael L. Mauldin.

The nature of hypertext also gives rise to information structures on the Web that serve as vast "switching stations," or "trees," that users can access to discover information.

Although the structure of these information systems on the Web is commonly tree like (not unlike Gopher's menu systems), the Web's organizational structures are not limited to hierarchical design.

A Web tree like Yahoo (`http://www.yahoo.com/`, shown in Figure 62.4) is very much list oriented. However, Web trees like the WWW Virtual Library (`http://www.w3.org/`) include individual pages that carry more narrative content and more explanations (often written by experts in the particular subject area). The extended narrative possible in Web pages adds to the significance and meaning of the resources presented.

FIGURE 62.4.

The Yahoo Web tree.
Copyright © 1994, 1995
David Filo and Jerry Yang.
Printed by permission.

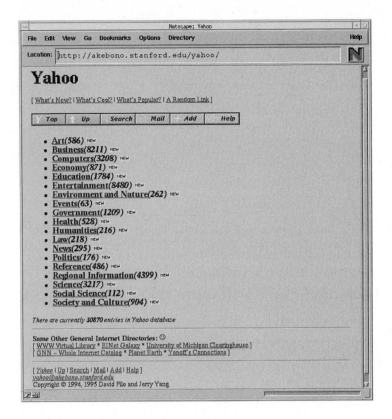

- **Information retrieval.** Because the basis for Web references is the Uniform Resource Locator (URL), and access to information referred to by URLs is the central function of Web browsers, information retrieval on the Web is consistent for many protocols. Instead of a student learning separate procedures for FTP, Gopher, Telnet, Usenet, and HTTP access, a Web browser streamlines information retrieval. The student can learn the central concepts of the client-server relationships, network relationships, and specialized techniques for navigating information spaces. Newer Web browsers like Netscape offer superior interfaces to Usenet and transform the training task for Usenet from the often-confusing and cryptic commands of a newsreader like rn into an exploration of the functions and concepts of human communication within newsgroups on Usenet.

- **Information analysis.** Networked-based information varies widely in quality, accuracy, completeness, and stability. The growing participation in Internet communication brings a great deal of information to the user. This diversity and vast quantity of Internet information requires the Internet trainer to help users make careful judgments about the value of Internet information. This process of information analysis—evaluating and placing information within a broad field of knowledge—is central to information literacy. A user who can retrieve information well but who has no skills in evaluating its quality is not well prepared. Questions users should ask about Internet information include these:

1. Can you trust the source? Is the provider of the information an expert in the field?

2. Are there others who point to the same information or resource as a reliable source?

3. What do you know about the information's accuracy? For example, is the Frequently Asked Questions (FAQ) list for the Usenet newsgroup `alt.war.civil.usa` accurate? Does someone you know who is knowledgeable in the field consider it an accurate (although not necessarily complete) source of information?

4. What is the original source of the information? For example, the Weather Underground gets its information from U.S. National Weather Service data and forecasts. This attests to a reliable, "official" source. In other cases, the source of the information may be a laboratory or a professionally run server. Remember, however, that you can't always expect "official" sources for Web-based information.

■ **Information understanding.** Closely tied to the preceding questions about information analysis is the process for information understanding. Mere data does not bring understanding, only information. Information itself is neutral in value, taking on significance only when the user has the knowledge to place that information within a larger system of specialized knowledge. Trainers using the Web as a basis for information sharing can focus on disciplinary systems of knowledge to help users achieve understanding. This disciplinary knowledge is still largely based on offline paper works such as books and journals. Transforming the Internet's vast information storehouse to actual knowledge, therefore, requires integrating the information discovery, retrieval, and analysis processes into a system of disciplinary conventions and knowledge of a particular field of study. Web trainers should focus on disciplinary knowledge as part of the information understanding component of information literacy.

■ **Information use.** Just as information has no value without understanding, understood information has little impact without use. FTP, Gopher, and other information spaces often encouraged people to use information through a process of mere duplication: copying files from one FTP site to another or including a Gopher submenu within another Gopher. In contrast, the Web's hypertext encourages annotation, explication, and contextualization of information in addition to reference. Use of information on the Web encourages an accretion of knowledge through annotation, not merely a replication of information through a file or a menu.

These transformations that the Web brings to Internet training and literacy may change as the Web gives rise to new traditions for information sharing, much in the way earlier communications media fostered traditions for sharing knowledge (some examples: in printing, the scholarly journal; in telecommunications, teleconference and distance learning).

Web trees and spiders are some of the transdisciplinary Web information systems now apparent. In the future, online Web communities may give rise to still newer systems and traditions.

The Web Alters Internet Resource Organization and Indexing

Where single protocol clients for information retrieval "ghettoized" the Internet into separate information spaces, the Web melds these spaces within a global "cloud" of hypertext.

Figure 62.5 shows how the single client-server models carve up the layout of online cyberspace into strict "zones" of information, which are each perceptible only through the specialized browsers for that space. In contrast, cyberspace viewed through a Web browser includes views into a variety of information spaces (see Figure 62.6).

FIGURE 62.5.

Specialized clients create separate information-space "zones" based on protocol.

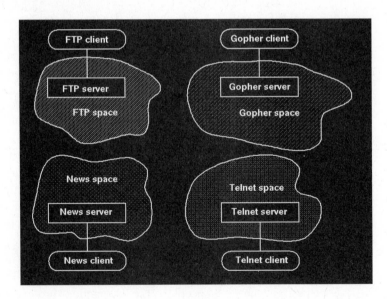

FIGURE 62.6.

The Web integrates information spaces.

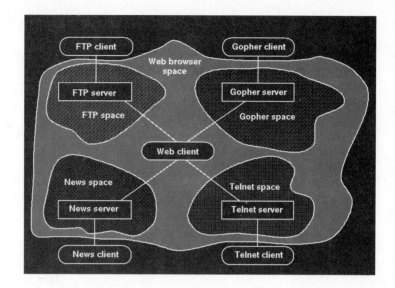

This "cloud model" of the Internet that Web browsers create fosters multiple entry points into the same information. Although information within FTPspace couldn't be even self referential (that is, it could not include a link from one file to another within an ASCII text), the Web allows multiprotocol organization of information and self reference (that is, a Web document can point to itself or another document in other information spaces, including Webspace).

The Web's cloud model for the Internet also alters information indexing. Archie and Veronica have exclusive domain over their information spaces (FTPspace and Gopherspace), but they do not index information in other information spaces.

However, some Web spiders, such as Lycos, can index not only hypertext documents in Webspace, but documents in the other information spaces referred to in Web document hyperlinks. For example, the Lycos Web spider can index an HTML document and follow the hyperlinks in that document to new documents and index those—even if these hyperlinks point into Gopherspace or FTPspace.

Of course, the spider cannot read the unstructured documents in Gopherspace or FTPspace and crawl still further into these spaces. But the ability of Web spiders to touch the Web's edges make the Web an important "common ground" for information indexing. Potentially, Web spiders communicating with Archie and Veronica could create a total indexing of online cyberspace.

The Web Alters Internet Information Presentation

The URL as the basis for referencing information on the Web creates standard, compact ways to refer to Internet resources. Instead of relying on *ad hoc* ways to refer to information retrieval activities (consider these varying references: "Telnet to `downwind.sprl.umich.edu`, port 3000" and "FTP to `ftp.rpi.edu`, the directory `pub/`, the subdirectory `communications/`, the file `internet-cmc.readme`"), the URLs `telnet://downwind.sprl.umich.edu:3000` and `ftp://ftp.rpi.edu/pub/communications/internet-cmc.readme` compactly convey the essentials for an information retrieval task in a standard format.

This standardization transforms how Internet information is presented. Online, the URL references to Internet resources are part of the hypertext "live link" to that resource. Offline, references made by URL are more uniform and compact, both typographically as well as conceptually.

Instead of a protocol-dependent way of presenting information, a protocol-unifying single "address" can be used for referring to Internet information.

And because the URL serves as a standard "catalog number" for Internet resources, the URL can serve in explanations of Internet resources in other media.

On the surface, the system of URLs may seem an incidental side effect of using the Web for information retrieval and dissemination. However, the URL profoundly transforms Internet information presentation:

- **Conceptually:** Users and information providers refer to Internet resources based on the address concept rather than using protocol-dependent retrieval procedures.
- **Operationally:** Access to Internet resources through a Web browser involves simply "opening" the URL in a browser.
- **Semantically:** A URL is the basis for constructing hot spots in Web hypertext. This associative linking is the basis for the unique meaning possible on the Web.

By integrating information, the Web transforms how people use and perceive Internet information. Instead of emphasis on how a user must manage a variety of client-server procedures, Internet training and literacy on the Web can focus on how a user finds meaning in information content.

Instead of the multiprotocol, multiserver model of information organization that carves online cyberspace into nonoverlapping zones, Web-based hypertext can meld references to multiple information spaces. And because the Web melds these protocols within hypertext, the Web's indexing mechanisms—the spiders—can serve as powerful searching tools for users to locate Web information and, with some spiders, documents in other information spaces referred to in HTML documents.

Finally, by integrating references to Internet information in the URL notation, the Web alters key conceptual, operational, and semantic aspects of presenting Internet information.

The Web Is a Powerful Tool that Can Create Meaning

The Web's system of hypertext documents containing associative links uniquely merges powerful human communication abilities. The first of these communication abilities is the textual representation of meaning in hypertext—the "surface" part of hypertext.

On top of this "surface" text are *hyperlinks*, the second communication dimension of hypertext. This melding of the "prose" and the "links" in hypertext is a powerful combination. Creating associative links taps into the associative, metaphorical realm of human language use (closely tied with poetry). Associative linking can powerfully extend or expand the meaning of a hypertext document by association with other documents or resources.

Because humans have developed techniques to shape prose and create poetry for thousands of years, it is no surprise that the Web so powerfully transforms the Internet into a system for creating meaning.

The Web's Hypertext Supports Human Expressiveness in Language

An FTP site can present the user with a list of files and directories (refer to Figure 62.7), limited by the file-naming constraints on the host computer. A Gopher hole, like the one shown in Figure 62.8, can contain menu entries that include multiple-word phrases to refer to submenus, documents, or searching mechanisms.

A Web page, like the one shown in Figure 62.9, offers a greater range of expressiveness. A Web weaver can employ narrative text, lists, graphics, or other HTML features to shape and convey meaning.

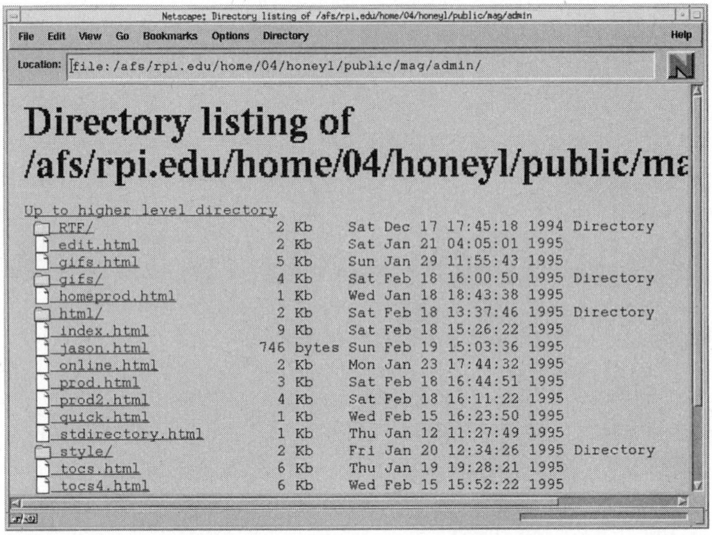

FIGURE 62.7.

An FTP site.

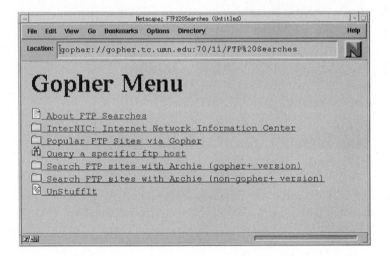

FIGURE 62.8.

A Gopher hole.

Instead of being constrained to file and directory names (as in an FTP site) or phrases and hierarchical menus (as in a Gopher site), the Web author can expressively shape prose into a web of links and associated information. Instead of working within the scaffolding of a uniform structure of menus and directories, the Web author can use language strategies, page layout, and page design to shape meaning. Instead of the linear "before" and "next" relationship of documents in file systems, and the hierarchical tree of relationships possible in Gopher, the Web author can link in nonlinear ways.

Unleashing the power of human language like this has no small consequences—the power of the written word has fostered social and cultural change throughout history. By combining human language prose expressivity with associative linking not possible in paper texts, the Web offers the potential for rich human expressiveness. This expressivity combined with the Web's ability for instant, global publishing opens up new avenues for human communication.

FIGURE 62.9.

A Web page.
Text by Nancy Kaplan.
Copyright © 1995 by
Nancy Kaplan. All Rights
Reserved. Printed by
permission.

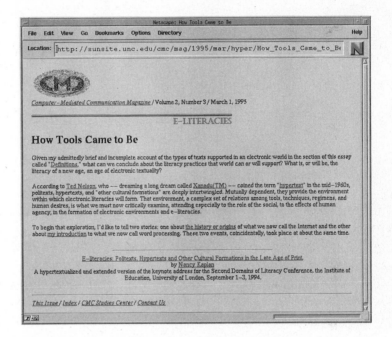

The Web's Media Characteristics Extend Meaning

The Web, like most mediated forms of communication, enables meaning to be transmitted over space and time. Unlike written works in the world of paper, however, physical distance in cyberspace doesn't matter. The (nearly) instant, round-the-clock, global access possible for Web documents allows people to choose the time for perceiving information and communication. Although most forms of Internet tools share these same characteristics for time and space transcendence, the Web has a special set of media characteristics that transform what is possible on the Internet:

■ **Associative linking:** The links possible within Web hypertext bring unique possibilities to online communication. Through associative linking, the meaning of a text on the Web is not constrained to the user's perception of a single work. Instead, text on the Web branches into Webspace, potentially linking to all documents on the Internet. This interconnection is not possible in other information spaces on the Internet, nor is this "unconstrained" nature of Web-based hypertext entirely possible within non-networked systems of hypertext.

- **Analogical thinking:** Just as hyperlinks potentially extend and relate meaning within the entire universe of Web documents, so, too, do hyperlinks create new meanings through association. *Analogical thinking* involves associating related ideas for comparison. Hyperlinks among Web documents are explicit markers of such comparisons. As a result, the Web intrinsically conveys the "relatedness" of information.

- **Empire building:** Harold Innis, in *Empire & Communications* (Press Porcepic, 1986), explains how the invention of writing was essential for creating empires (and bureaucracy). Similarly, the Web can foster "permanent" written discourse, available on demand from Web servers, that is unlike other forms of Internet communication. Unlike FTP and Gopher texts, Web communication has different media characteristics (as outlined earlier in this chapter). More dramatically, the Web differs from the ephemeral communication on Internet forums such as IRC, Usenet, MUDs, MUSHes, and so on. These discussion forums foster communication similar to preliterate communication focusing on the immediate and transitory. In contrast, Web servers offer information publishers "broadcast" stations that provide permanent repositories for global distribution. This permanence, the power of wide dissemination, and the ability of the information provider to carefully craft a message can lend a unique perception of authority to Web communication. Whether the Web will foster a new kind of empire is not known, but the opportunity to create rich texts that can be accessed on demand globally has a great potential to transform meaning and power online.

The Web transforms the "data transfer" nature of Internet communication into expressive possibilities for meaning. The free-form nature of HTML allows people to use language strategies to shape information. The Web's unique media characteristics, largely stemming from the power of associative linking, give birth to new ways for people to create meaning and, perhaps, to shift power online.

The Web Transforms Relationships Among People and Information

As explored in the preceding section, associative linking is the basis for creating meaning in hypertext. Another aspect of associative linking is in the way hyperlinks on the Web can reveal, create, or reinforce relationships among people and information.

The Web Connects Information to People

Although books in a library refer to each other in the "great conversation" of literature, these references are purely textual. That is, one author says, "Author X said this" and can refer the reader to the written volume or article written by author X. On the Web, references among works and information need not be just textual, but can be "live links" to the actual work.

Systems for organizing information on the Web (Web trees, for example) include traditions for authors to "sign" Web pages with links to their home page. This information-to-person link then serves as the basis for people to get to know others who share their same interests. When more authors link their pages of information to an existing Web, electronic interest groups grow. The resulting collection of author links reveals a community fostered by interest in information. Instead of linking just information, the Web can link people.

The Web Fosters Development of Virtual Communities

Through links from one home page to another, Web users can create "electronic tribes" that reveal the online relationships of their lives. As Usenet communities focused on discourse, MUD, MUSH, or MOO communities focused on interaction, and electronic mail lists focused on communication, the Web fosters special forms of virtual communities.

A Web-based place called *WebWorld* (which operated during 1994 but is no longer operational) demonstrated the potential for unique virtual communities on the Web. WebWorld gave people a way to "settle and live" in a world made of hypertext and inline images. Through the interactive features of forms, WebWorld's creator, Ron Britvich, provided a way for users to construct "buildings" and "containers" and to attach hyperlinks from these objects to any URL on the Internet.

The streets of WebWorld were quiet (because no direct person-to-person communication was possible), but WebWorld's implications for possible Web-based virtual communities were profound: through associative linking, people created a world mapped onto the metaphor of a city. The "city" had streets and lakes implying movement and leisure, containers and buildings symbolizing ownership and territory, and a spatial arrangement not unlike the clusters of settlements and suburbs around an actual city. WebWorld created relationships among people through proximity, common interest, and neighborhoods specialized in particular human pursuits, ranging from the serious to the scatological.

WebWorld revealed a human community, a world of hypertext in which people shared meaning through a common set of symbols. Although WebWorld had no explicit purpose other than to exist and grow, it demonstrated how people can associate with each other on the Web.

The Web as a New World

In the history of human communication, the Web is a small, recent blip. Shared only by a tiny minority of the earth's population, the Web remains far from the confluence of all human knowledge. But the Web has already transformed the Internet. By integrating the Internet's information spaces through its browsers, the Web can seamlessly connect resources and information.

From its basis for meaning in associative linking and text, the Web allows human expression both in "flat" prose as well as hypertext techniques.

By revealing relationships among people and information, the Web fosters the development of electronic tribes and virtual communities. By integrating information, fostering new ways to create meaning, and linking people to information and each other, the Web has transformed the Internet from a conduit for data exchange to a tool for expressive human communication.

Spamming and Cancelbots

63

by Kevin M. Savetz

Spam is very much on the minds of Usenet denizens.

Spam refers, of course, not to a processed meat product, but to the practice of posting a message to far too many Usenet newsgroups. Spamming is darkly frowned on by almost everyone who reads Usenet, yet spamming has become an all-too-common occurrence. Perhaps two dozen people each month misinterpret the rules of netiquette—or disregard them entirely—by sending their message to dozens—sometimes hundreds, even thousands—of newsgroups. It's hard to spend an hour cruising Usenet without finding at least one of these epistles.

Want some magic thigh-reducing cream? You may read about it in `rec.pets.cats`. Need a green card? You can find an ad for immigration lawyers on `sci.aquaria`. Coming across one of these misplaced missives in an inappropriate newsgroup can be mildly annoying or downright irritating. But finding the same message posted dozens or hundreds of times brings exasperation to new heights.

Reasons that people spam Usenet vary from simple cluelessness to the desire to announce one's product to as many people as possible. As often as the media announces that there are 20-million-plus eager customers on Internet with no rules or regulations (both statements are half truths) it's no wonder people spam.

No matter the motive, the act of spamming the Net is hard to forgive. Besides being annoying, it's also expensive. Moving even the smallest message across Usenet can cost hundreds of dollars in network connection time. Wholesale spamming can cost the Internet at large tens of thousands of dollars in network time, plus the time and attention of the system administrators, users, and others who have to deal with the problems spamming causes.

Posting messages to a hundred or more newsgroups is hard work, so these scofflaws often use simple programs, dubbed *spambots*, to do their dirty work.

> **NOTE**
>
> Spamming, by the way, is different than crossposting. When you crosspost, one copy of your message is submitted to multiple newsgroups, and each reader sees it only once. When you spam, many copies of your message are distributed, wasting bandwidth and disk space.

Several individuals, frustrated with the increased popularity of spamming on Usenet, have taken matters into their own hands. Their tack: wipe the offending messages from the face of the Net. These individuals use their own programs, dubbed *cancelbots*, to remove the offending posts. Their actions, although controversial, seem to have the general approval of Netizens aware of the battle. Indeed, casual Usenet participants may not even know what's going on—but a quick peek in `news.admin.policy` or `alt.current-events.net-abuse` reveals a constant influx of complaints and chatter about Usenet spamming. Several times a week, a spam attack is deemed wasteful enough to warrant a wholesale cancellation. When that happens, a message like this one appears in news.admin.policy (the actual spam message was removed for your safety and convenience):

```
From: jik@cam.ov.com (Jonathan I. Kamens)
Newsgroups: news.admin.misc
Subject: Spam cancelled (sfiresto@interserv.com, SAVE TAX DOLLARS!!!)
Date: 16 Feb 1995 08:00:33 -0500
I have cancelled 71 copies of a spam with the return address
and subject indicated in the subject of this message. A
single copy of the cancelled spam is included at the end of
this message.
...
These messages were cancelled only because the same article
was posted many times.  The content of the spam, or whether
it was "on-topic" in the newsgroups in which it was posted,
is irrelevant.

Note that at least a couple copies of this spam have already
been cancelled by someone else.
In addition to being posted in news.admin.misc, this message is being mailed to
the postmaster at the site from which the spam originated. If you wish to
complain, please do so (politely!) to the address(es) in the X-Complain-To header
line of this message.
The "cancel." and "cyberspam" conventions were followed in my cancel messages.
---- cut here for sample copy of spam ----
```

With that, the cancelbot slowly but surely wipes every copy of the offending message from Usenet. The cancelbot does this by masquerading as the original poster and fooling the news software into believing a legitimate request to kill each article.

The people who control the cancelbots see themselves as steadfast protectors of their terrain. Some others, including the *Wall Street Journal,* have called them "vigilantes." Some of the cancelers let their identities be known; others hide behind a cloak of anonymity. One of the most vocal cancelers, an anonymous Netizen who goes only by the unlikely name of *Cancelmoose,* has squashed dozens of Usenet spam attacks.

Cancelmoose and his ilk insist that they are not censors—they do not cancel anything because of the content of message. Inappropriate and offensive postings are left in the name of free speech. But if a message—whether it's selling thigh cream or a mandate from the Pope himself—is posted to too many newsgroups, the cancelbots jump on it. How many is too many? That is open to interpretation.

The most famous spammers (so far) are Canter and Siegel, a pair of "greencard lawyers" who became enemies of the Internet by hawking their services (their message was distributed to more than 7,000 newsgroups). In another well-publicized case in December 1994, an author was squelched after posting an announcement of his book to some 150 newsgroups. Cancelmoose did the thing he does best: nuke the cacophony of messages.

Imminent Death of the Net Predicted?

Even if Netizens see cancelbots as saviors of Usenet, the fact that they even exist raises important issues. Most notably, who has control of Usenet? A grassroots networking experiment gone right, Usenet wasn't designed to be a high-security network. The fact is, anyone with a little technical savvy can delete anything posted to Usenet.

So I asked the Cancelmoose: "Who died and made you God (or Moose, or whatever)? That's an awful lot of power for a single (if well-meaning) person to have over the Internet."

"No one made me a net.god—I am acting on my own to enforce a rule that was decided on the Net. Every action I take is explained at length, with a full copy of the posts I took action against, so that people can judge for themselves," Mr. Moose says. "I am doing this because of the danger that spamming represents, and the high net approval of such actions."

In addition, Moose points out that any site that wants to opt out can easily do so with the "cyberspam convention"—a special code is inserted in all the Moose's cancel requests that allows system administrators to ignore the Moose's spam cancels.

Almost all the noise on `news.admin.policy` and `alt.current-events.net-abuse` (perhaps surprisingly) supports the action of the cancelbots. The Moose does not act alone; there is substantial agreement among Usenet administrators who have contributed to this debate that these actions are necessary. "I think I'm doing the right thing, but of course what we're worried about here is a check on my judgment so that I can't abuse my power. All I can suggest is that you post your concerns to `news.admin.misc`. The feedback I've gotten makes me think that opinion there is highly in my favor. If that's incorrect, I'm happy to stop—Lord knows I could use the extra time," Mr. Moose says.

What will happen when others write their own cancelbots and use that software to, say, delete all messages posted by their enemies? "I am far from the first person to invent a cancelbot. Censorship is a old issue on the Net and it is frowned upon….People who cancel the articles of their enemies will be tracked and, hopefully, denied access to news [by their service providers]."

Members of the Church of Scientology last year canceled messages posted by outspoken detractors of the religion. The group said that the posts contained copyrighted material, but many on the Internet called the attempt nothing more than a foul act of censorship.

Should Usenet messages be automatically censored in software? Is Cancelmoose a hero or villain? You decide.

Kevin Fox (`kfox@ocf.berkeley.edu`) is a student at the University of California at Berkeley who takes a less drastic tactic to squelch spammers. He sends them a polite e-mail message. His eloquent message echoes the consensus of 99 percent of Usenet's populous:

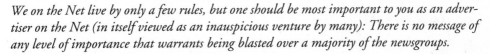

We on the Net live by only a few rules, but one should be most important to you as an adver-tiser on the Net (in itself viewed as an inauspicious venture by many): There is no message of any level of importance that warrants being blasted over a majority of the newsgroups.

While it is an appealing concept to reach the broadest possible audience, imagine if you will, the bliss you would be in if you could speak into the mind of every person on the planet. Pretty snazzy, eh? Now imagine that everyone has this ability and uses it to sell you insurance, lip gloss, and shoe spray. Would you ever be able to sleep again? How long before you go insane?

We have television channels so we can choose what to watch. We have newsgroups so we can choose what to read. Please don't force your words on us, or in the future, the voices may never let you sleep again.

Spamming from America Online

America Online, one of the nation's largest online services, offers access to Usenet. Because of its simple interface and relative ease of use, America Online has a reputation for attracting us-ers with less regard for—or perhaps knowledge of—netiquette. On `news.admin.policy`, the merest mention of AOL causes some to grumble.

"Most of the spammers from AOL are simply users who are excited at the prospect of using this great tool but who aren't aware of the 'rules of the road' when it comes to posting," David O'Donnell, AOL's system administrator says. "We go to great lengths to educate our members on what the Internet and Usenet are, their conventions and historical guidelines."

"Because AOL is the largest site on the Internet, we have a proportionally greater exposure in terms of users and notoriety," O'Donnell says. "Abusers can be characterized into three groups: the ignorant and usually accidental abuser, the commercial abuser, and the deliberate abuser. The majority of abuse by our members falls into the first two categories. Our current educa-tional efforts are helping address the issues of ignorance and inappropriate commercial activ-ity. Improved education will help further limit these kinds of abuse, and constant diligence will help stop the latter."

In addition to education as a part of policy, America Online's software makes it time consum-ing—although not impossible—to spam hundreds of newsgroups. "I think spamming from America Online is an issue, but the magnitude of the problem is usually overstated," he says. "In the roughly one year since AOL opened its Usenet system to its members, I believe the quantity of abuse has actually gone down. There have been periods of time when the trend has reversed, like during the Christmas season. It hasn't dropped as much as I would like, but we're working on some ways to help acclimate our members to being on the Usenet, which I think will help the trend continue downward."

Cacophony

Will spambots and cancelbots become the norm on Usenet? Hopefully not; in time, more sophisticated news distribution and newsreading software should stop the problem at its source. Until then, education of new Internet users will have to suffice. Unfortunately, some of us do not want to be educated and would rather exploit the Internet's resources—like the clear-cutting of virgin forest.

The voices may never let you sleep again.

PART

Internet Diversion and Fun

Interactive Multiuser Realities: MUDs, MOOs, MUCKs, and MUSHes

by Joseph R. Poirier

Many online services have "live chat" areas in which people use their keyboards to type messages that are received instantly by others.

Cyberspace has become a hot nightly gathering spot. New Year's Eve is no different. Some online services plan special events or have designated places to meet—sort of electronic ballrooms.

Delphi will open an international chat room where members can exchange greetings via the Internet with people from around the world.

— USA Today, *December 30, 1993*

The Information Superhighway was pretty much of a dud. Remember that? By the mid-90s, just about everybody was hooked up to the vast international computer network, exchanging vast quantities of information at high speeds via modems and fiber-optic cable with everybody else. The problem, of course, was that even though the information was coming a lot faster, the vast majority of it, having originated with human beings, was still wrong. Eventually people realized that the Information Superhighway was essentially CB radio, but with more typing.

—Dave Barry, *predicting the future,* Newsweek, *January 3, 1994*

Traffic volume on just the U.S. National Science Foundation's NSFnet backbone portion of the Internet exceeded 10 terabytes per month at the end of 1993…. A recent study of traffic on the NSFnet backbone…turned up the astonishing fact that just over 10 percent of the bits running back and forth belonged to MUDs.

—A. Lyman Chapin, *"The State of the Internet,"*Telecommunications, *January 1994*

The Internet isn't just electronic mail and gargantuan databases. It's also a medium for people to meet. And more and more Internet users find themselves meeting on interactive multiuser realities, more commonly known as multiuser dungeons, or MUDs.

These meeting places are similar to multiuser adventure games. Players can connect to a MUD, talk among themselves, send messages to one another, fight monsters or one another, and possibly create new objects. Friendships can begin on a MUD and extend into real life. Some MUDs have their own multiuser games, such as card games. On other MUDs, the goal is to *role play,* or pretend to be a certain type of character and go off on adventures, solve puzzles, and gather treasure to gain enough points to become a *wizard,* a MUD super-user.

Nowadays, the acronym *MUD* has become generalized to lowercase *mud.* A *mud* is an interactive multiuser virtual reality. Most muds are currently text-based; a few systems are experimenting with graphical clients. Some muds are simple chatlines. Others emphasize social aspects. Still others have combat systems and promote adventuring and puzzle solving.

Muds are similar to computer adventure games. The mud consists of a number of rooms, each having a particular description and possibly containing other objects. You wander around the mud, read the messages it displays to you, and interact with the objects in the mud. Perhaps there are puzzles to solve or monsters to kill. Or perhaps the mud enables you to build your own rooms and objects so that they, in turn, can be explored by other players.

Most importantly, however, there are other players. You aren't the only player on the mud. Other players may be exploring the mud right alongside of you. You can strike up conversations with them, play games, band together for combat, or perhaps even kill them. On popular muds, you may find more than 100 other players playing the mud at the same time you are.

Some muds have an overall theme, such as a medieval setting, a cyberspace feel, or an idyllic elfin fantasy. Other muds are based on worlds described in popular science-fiction and fantasy novels, such as Tolkien's Middle Earth, McCaffrey's Pern, *Star Trek*, Herbert's *Dune*, or Lewis's Narnia. On these types of specific muds, you may be expected to role play in a certain manner; deviating from the theme of the mud—such as playing a *Star Trek* officer in a Middle Earth setting—is frowned on by other players.

A few muds have a potpourri theme, with different sections of the mud exhibiting different themes. You get a feel for the personality of the mud as you explore it, read the room descriptions, and talk to the other players on the mud.

Some muds are not much more than multiuser talk programs, and in that sense, Dave Barry (refer to the quote at the beginning of this chapter) may be correct in saying that current multiuser Information Superhighway services are not much more than "CB radio, but with more typing." In fact, on CompuServe, the chatline is actually called "CB Simulator." From that characterization, you may get the idea that this is all a passing fad.

Comparing CBs to muds, however, is not entirely correct. Not all muds are just chatlines. Muds have CB-like qualities, such as multiuser interaction, but they offer more than that. They have a virtual reality associated with them. Currently, most muds are text-based virtual realities. However, as computers become more powerful, graphics become better, and telecommunications become faster, muds and mud-like services will turn into true graphical virtual realities. Right now, some muds can transmit GIFs to a player's screen and provide a rudimentary graphical interface. These client interfaces and the servers they talk to will get more powerful in the future.

Are all muds games, then? No. Muds are multiuser, programmable environments. Because they are programmable, they can be set up to be useful in a variety of ways. Researchers in such fields as education, writing, media, and even psychology are using muds as underlying research environments. If muds enable gamers from all over the world to meet and communicate, they can just as easily let researchers from all over the world do the same thing. Not all muds are games. Some are research or educational environments.

Players of muds—called *mudders*—can find themselves spending a lot of time connected to a mud. It can be addictive. Some students neglect their studies. Furthermore, the communications requirements can be quite large. Some universities have restricted mud use because relatively small groups of mudders are connecting to muds outside the university and using up a lot of the outgoing telecommunications bandwidth.

History

It is generally acknowledged that the first mud was created and written between 1979 and 1980 in England by Roy Trubshaw and Richard Bartle. In the spring of 1979, Trubshaw wrote a game using MACRO-10 on DECsystem-10s at Essex University. The initial game was a set of interconnected rooms in which you could wander. It was multiuser, so players could chat with each other. It was called MultiUser Dungeon, or MUD for short. It contained a language that could be used to specify how objects were defined in the game (MUD Definition Language, MUDDL). This program was later rewritten in early 1980 in BCPL. Bartle began helping out with game design and soon moved to programming with Trubshaw. When Trubshaw left Essex, Bartle took control of the game, adding such things as the point system for wizard status and improving the game design. Bartle stayed on at Essex as a postgraduate, maintaining MUD. Other students created their own games from MUD's core code.

In 1984, Bartle and Trubshaw formed MUSE Ltd., and rewrote the game as MUD2. It runs on a VAX owned by the Network Information Services Division of British Telecom. It is a commercial product. Users dial up to the game using their modems, paying the communications charges in much the same way as a user of CompuServe or America Online does today. Versions of the MUD2 interpreter have been written in C and Pascal.

MUD2 is quite advanced. It handles fluids, heat, audio-visual effects, and smells. It has a large variety of bots, some of which fly, swim, regenerate, and cast spells. The bots have expert systems that enable them to plan attacks and decide when to flee, negotiate, steal, as well as how to get past obstacles, such as locked doors. It has a safe room for chatting, many-on-many fights, and a wide range of sophisticated spells.

There are several other muds in England, such as Gods, Shades, and Avalon. Most of them descended from MUD. Many of them, in fact, were written by arch-wizzes of former muds.

In 1987, Alan Cox wrote AberMUD while he was a student at the University of Wales, Aberystwyth. It was originally written in B for a Honeywell L66 mainframe and then ported to UNIX and rewritten in C. It became the first widely available mud on the Internet when its code was made publicly available in 1988.

Soon thereafter, Lars Pensjo of Gothenburg in Sweden came across AberMUD and decided to write his own mud. This became known as Lars Pensjo MUD, or LPMUD for short. It is a combat mud, with rolling resets, quests, and bots. Wizards can create new rooms, objects, bots, and commands using LPMUD's programming language, LP-C. LPMUD is generally regarded as the most popular combat-style mud.

DikuMUD, another combat-style mud, is similar to LPMUD but can be expanded by wizards; it has no programming language as LPMUD does.

In 1989, TinyMUD, originally written by Jim Aspnes, emerged. It was inspired by MUD and the VMS game Monster, written by Rich Skrenta. TinyMUD was small and did not consume as much CPU power as its predecessors. As a result, it became popular on the Internet. In contrast to the original MUD and other games like LPMUD, with TinyMUD, anyone can create rooms and objects as long as they obtain a link with an existing exit in a room. Specific installations of TinyMUD, such as Islandia, grew to be huge databases with large mudder populations. In October 1990, Islandia had more than 3,000 players and 14,000 rooms. The idea of TinyMUD centers on conversation and room building to promote creativity and not around adventuring and combat to reach wizard level.

TinyMUCK, written initially by Stephen White, descended from TinyMUD. It restricted the building commands to designated muckers who could muck around with the environment. TinyMUCK improves on TinyMUD with its interpreted programming language, called TinyMUF (MultiUser Forth).

TinyMUSH, another TinyMUD descendent, was written by Larry Foard of Berkeley. Its claim to fame is the notion of triggered events. When a particular event occurs on an object, the corresponding code snippet is executed. In addition, it has *puppets* (objects that relay information to players) such as a crystal ball. (MUSH stands for *MultiUser Shared Hallucination.*)

TinyMOO, also written by Stephen White of Berkeley, is similar to TinyMUCK, except that normal players can create objects. It was expanded by Pavel Curtis (who wrote LambdaMOO, now running at Xerox PARC). The *OO* in *MOO* denotes *object-oriented.*

TinyMUSE extended TinyMUSH and has a class structure similar to other combat muds.

UberMUD, written by Marcus J. Ranum, moved all the rules for the universe, including commands, to its own internal programming language, U. Because of this, UberMUD is flexible but difficult to write in. It is disk-based.

UnterMUD, also written by Ranum, took a different approach to networking. The idea was that each user developed his or her own UnterMUD. Then, through the use of a portal-like property, they could connect to other people's UnterMUDs—and players on other UnterMUDs could connect to theirs. Players can wander from UnterMUD to UnterMUD by using the portal mechanism. Players can carry objects between UnterMUDs. This mud contains some of the U language from UberMUD.

Finally, several types of Internet Relay Chats (IRCs) provide very primitive multiuser communications services. Some of these chatlines are called *havens.* IRCs provide talking, acting, whispering, and paging commands, as well as "channels" in which users can gather. However, IRCs do not have actual rooms or other objects. IRCs do not support combat.

More recently, discussions of graphical muds have occurred on Internet newsgroups. It may be several years before anything truly graphical is forthcoming, although some muds now interact with GIFs to send images to players' clients. Three-dimensional graphical mudding is quite another matter. Large corporations and game companies may soon make the subject irrelevant.

Major Mud Genres

Muds can be divided into three major categories (the acronyms, such as MUD and MUSH, are explained in "History," earlier in this chapter):

- Combat-oriented muds: LPMUD, AberMUD, DikuMUD
- Social-oriented muds: TinyMUD, TinyMUSH, TinyMUCK, TinyMOO
- Chatlines: Internet Relay Chat (IRC), havens

In combat muds, you fight monsters and gain points to become a wizard. You can talk to other players, but the emphasis is on fighting. On social muds, you tend to talk to other players, get involved in group discussions, play multiuser games, create objects, and perhaps have virtual sex with someone—or at least enjoy virtual hugs and kisses. Chatlines are social muds without rooms and objects. They are similar to CB radio channels: you can talk and have group discussions on a chatline, but you can't create objects or rooms.

Each category has its own promoters and detractors, and most mudders eventually get around to trying all of the types. Some combat afficionados can't understand the attraction of social muds; they think mudding isn't really fun unless you are fighting monsters. On the other hand, some people who like social muds do it for the friendships it creates; they don't care to fight all day long or want to invest the time involved to make wizard level on a combat mud.

Try them all! See what you like. There's room for everyone!

To get a feel for the atmosphere of a mud and to learn the basic commands, run through the following sample session on an imaginary mud.

Sample Session

First, you have to choose a mud. There are mud newsgroups (described later in this chapter) that list many of the currently available muds. Or perhaps you hear of them by word of mouth, by e-mail, or by talking to mudders on other muds.

The mud actually resides on some machine at an Internet protocol port. You need the machine name (or its network address) and the port number of the mud to connect to it.

Once you have selected a mud, you must create the character you will use on it. On some muds, you can create a character immediately. On others, you must send mail to the mud administrator, who creates the character for you and provides you with an initial password. Some muds have a "guest" character you can use to explore the mud to see whether you like the mud in the first place.

Connecting to a Mud

Time for an example! Suppose that you have chosen a mud called WayCool: it is on the machine waycool.academia.edu, port 6502. You have e-mailed WayCool's administrator; a character, Speedy, with the password 4example, has been created for you. To connect to the mud, you can type this command at your machine:

```
telnet://waycool.academia.edu:6502
```

A connection between your machine and the waycool.academia.edu machine is set up. You are now connected to the mud, and you should see some kind of introductory message.

Rather than using Telnet, this example uses a mud client program. The *mud client* is a program that interprets the messages from a mud and displays them nicely for you, making sure that words wrap around lines correctly. Mud clients are discussed in "Mud Clients," later in this chapter.

For the purposes of this example, the mud client provides you with a > prompt for the time you are on the mud. This prompt helps distinguish between the commands you type and the messages the mud sends in response to those commands.

You are now connected to waycool.academia.edu at port 6502. You see something like the following:

```
Connected to waycool.academia.edu.
Escape character is '^]'.

******* WELCOME TO WAYCOOL MUD *******
To connect to your existing character, type: connect <name> <password>
To create a character, mail to admin@waycool.academia.edu.

To quit, use the 'quit' command. To see a list of players, use the 'who' command.
>
```

In this example, you have already sent e-mail to admin@waycool.academia.edu, so you are ready to connect to your actual mud character, Speedy. Type the following:

```
> connect Speedy 4example
```

Note that the > is your prompt, provided by the mud client program. You don't actually type the > character.

Once you type the preceding command, you are connected to your character; you see the following:

```
Last login:   Sat Jan 1 00:00:00 1995
You have no mail waiting.
For help, please type 'help'.

Dark Room
You find yourself in a dark room. The air is musty and stagnant. You sense you
should get out of here quickly.
```

Most muds have a starting room similar to this. By default, this is the *home room*. Your home is the place you are sent to when you are not on the mud. Later, if the mud enables you to build your own rooms, you may want to construct a room to your liking and reset your home to the new room. For now, however, this room can be your home.

Some muds have their own e-mail system. This mud informed you that you don't have any e-mail waiting.

The text also suggests typing **help** for more information on how to use the mud. If you are new to mudding or to a particular type of mud (different muds have somewhat different commands), you should definitely read the help information. Frequently, it describes an example similar to the one explained here. It also explains any idiosyncrasies of the mud and the people who keep the mud running. Some mud administrators frown on certain user activities such as swearing in public areas, amorously hitting on other users in the hopes of getting dates, or practicing extreme violence. These restrictions are usually mentioned in the help information and sometimes in the initial message displayed to the user at login. Users who behave against the policies of the mud may find their characters *toaded*, or deleted, from the mud.

Looking

One of the first things you may want to do is to look at other objects in the room. Every object in the mud has a description. When you want to see an object's description, use the look command:

```
> look object
```

The command can usually be abbreviated to simply the letter l. If you leave off the *object* portion, the mud assumes you want to look at the current room. In this example room, typing **look** by itself redisplays the room information:

```
Dark Room
You find yourself in a dark room. The air is musty and stagnant. You sense you
should get out of here quickly.
```

You also can look at particular objects or other players, including yourself. In this example, because this is your first time on the mud, when you type **look me**, you will probably see this response:

```
This object has not set its description.
```

You should take a time out and set Speedy's description.

Descriptions

Each object in the mud has a description. Your character, Speedy, has a description, but it starts with a dull default description. To set it to something else, use the describe command.

However, the actual form of the describe command varies from mud to mud. On muds of the so-called TinyMUD genre, it is the @desc command (usually pronounced *at-desk*). The @ symbol denotes commands that actually modify the database objects. The form of the command is as follows:

```
@desc object = value
```

To set your description to something else, you can type something like this:

```
> @desc me = Speedy is a happy, whizzing, blurry blue ball of fur and bare feet!
```

Now, when you type **look me**, you see this description:

```
Speedy is a happy, whizzing, blurry blue ball of fur and bare feet!
```

Someone else who types **look Speedy** sees the same thing.

Remember that the describe command varies. Consult the help information to determine the equivalent command on your mud.

Later, you can reset your description to something else. It's your character, and it's your choice! There's typically no limit to what your character can be.

Moving Around

The description of the dark room suggests that you should get out of here. Some muds make it easy to determine which commands should be used to move around. On other muds, you have to read the room descriptions and make educated guesses.

Most muds understand the basic adventure-game movement commands such as the directional commands `north`, `south`, `east`, `west`, `up`, `down`, `in`, and `out`. You also can use the `go` command to move toward a particular object:

```
> go object
```

Mud parsers vary, so some muds may not understand more complex movement commands like this one:

```
> go through the green door
```

You must experiment on the mud you are playing.

Consider the room description again:

```
Dark Room
You find yourself in a dark room. The air is musty and stagnant. You sense you
should get out of here quickly.
```

It suggests you should get out, so type **out**, which moves you out of this room. You are now in another room in the example mud:

```
Main Room
This is the main meeting room of WayCool. Everyone seems to be here! There is a
huge throng of people around you, crammed in like sardines. The level of
conversation drifts from a low roar to a loud, confusing, cacophony of sound, but
you soon get used to it. There is a set of large oaken doors leading out of the
room, to the north.
You see:
Snag
Tweedle
Zowie
Jupiter
```

```
Clarisse
Maddog
Archimedes
Shira
Napoleon
Terminator
SIGN: Please keep cussing to a minimum, dammit.
a rutabaga
a closed metal box
a rose
```

You have found the main room of the mud. Muds have different names for this room, but a central room usually can be found on most muds. Players who stay only in the main room tend to be the type that use muds for social reasons, as opposed to adventuring, exploring, and creating.

The main room has several other players, such as Snag, Napoleon, and Terminator. It also has several objects, such as the sign, the rutabaga, the box, and the rose.

Because this is all real time, the other players are typing on their computers, performing commands that let them talk, act, move around, and so forth. When the players in your room do something, you see some type of on-screen message informing you of this. When you do something, the other players see a message. In fact, when you entered the room, a message was displayed to all the other players in the room informing them that you entered:

```
Speedy has arrived.
```

You did not see this on your screen, but all the other players saw it on their screens.

Because the other players are talking and acting at the same time, you get messages at the same time you are typing some command. At first, this may be a bit confusing, but in time, you will be able to read through the barrage of messages you are getting and sort out the relevant information:

```
Snag says, "Hi there Speedy!"
Napoleon waves to Speedy.
Tweedle says, "No, no, Archimedes, you don't understand."
Terminator grunts, "Yo, Speedy."
Clarisse hugs Speedy.
Zowie waves.
Shira waves to Speedy.
Archimedes looks puzzled.
Maddog puts some tacos in the microwave... brb.
Tweedle says, "He said I shouldn't call him again."
Archimedes ohs.
```

```
Tweedle sighs.
Archimedes hugs Tweedle.
Zowie goes north.
```

Because everything is happening in real time, you probably entered right in the middle of various conversations. Sometimes, everyone in a room is talking about the same topic. Chances are, however, that different people are talking to each other about different things. You have to read the incoming messages and figure things out.

As the preceding example shows, some players saw your arrival message and decided to say hello or to wave to you. It seems that Tweedle and Archimedes are in the middle of some conversation. Maddog has left his computer to go make some tacos in real life (*brb* means *be right back*). Zowie has just left the main room for parts unknown.

Talking

At this point, you may want to say something to the other players. You use the say command:

```
> say Hello there everybody! Great to be here!
```

On your screen, you see this message:

```
You say, "Hello there everybody! Great to be here!"
```

Everyone else sees this message:

```
Speedy says, "Hello there everybody! Great to be here!"
```

The mud substitutes your name appropriately, so that everyone knows who is saying what.

After a while, however, typing **say** gets tedious, so it can be abbreviated to one double-quote (") character. There is no need to type another double-quote at the end. The mud puts that in for you. This command sends out the same messages to you and everyone else as the say command did:

```
> "Hello there everybody! Great to be here!
```

Now you can talk to your friends!

```
> "How is everyone?
You say, "How is everyone?"
Clarisse says, "I'm listening to this new CD! You gotta get it, Speedy!"
FrankNFurter has arrived.
Snag waves to FrankNFurter.
Napoleon says, "Doin' OK, Speedy."
> "What band, Clarisse?
You say, "What band, Clarisse?"
Shira waves to FrankNFurter.
FrankNFurter waves.
Napoleon waves.
Archimedes laughs.
Clarisse says, "It's the Kooky Kookaburras! You'd like them."
Napoleon has heard of them.
Tweedle goes north.
Archimedes goes north.
> "I'll hafta check it out.
You say, "I'll hafta check it out."
```

You can carry on quite a conversation simply by talking, but muds have another feature that allows for more expression. Notice that some of the players can *wave* to you. Or notice how Napoleon *mentioned* that he had heard of the Krazy Kookaburras. They didn't *say* that to you—if they had, it would have been in quotation marks. How did they do what they did? They *acted* it.

Acting

Acting adds another level to mudding. It enables you to express actions. If you want to wave to everyone, use the act command:

```
> act waves to everyone.
```

The act command takes everything after the word *act*, appends it onto your name, and sends out that whole message to everyone in the room. So, after typing this command, everyone—including you—sees the message:

```
Speedy waves to everyone.
```

The act command is also known as the pose command or the emote command. Because it is performed by players as much as talking, it also has been abbreviated to one character, the colon (:). If you type the command **:thinks this is wonderful!**, everyone sees this message:

```
Speedy thinks this is wonderful!
```

Acting adds a narrative element to the mud, as if it were a book. Here are some more examples of acting and the messages they produce:

```
> :cries.
> :understands everything now!
> :'s big toe hurts!
> :calls for a vote.
> :
> :ate the whole thing!
```

In order, the preceding commands give the following messages:

```
Speedy cries.
Speedy understands everything now!
Speedy's big toe hurts!
Speedy calls for a vote.
Speedy
Speedy ate the whole thing!
```

By talking and acting, you can interact with the other players on the mud. You can talk to them, they can talk to you, and everyone can act in literally limitless ways. Conversations can ebb and flow. Player's actions may make them seem intelligent, young, old, stupid, witty, charismatic, shy—a huge variety of personality impressions created by the messages they are sending out to the other players on the mud. It's a very public manner of communication. The commands you send to talk or act are sent to everyone in the room.

There comes a time, however, when you want to talk to someone on the mud in a more personal manner. You don't want everyone in the room to see what you are saying to that person. How do you do this? There are two ways: whispering and paging.

Whispering

You can use the whisper command to send a message to a specific player in the same room. The command has the following form:

```
whisper player-name = message
```

Suppose that you want to tell the player Snag that you just got a big raise at work. For personal reasons, you don't want everyone in the room to see this information. Type this command:

```
> whisper Snag=Guess what! I just got a big raise at work!
```

You see this message:

```
You whisper, "Guess what! I just got a big raise at work!" to Snag.
```

Snag (and only Snag) sees this message:

```
Speedy whispers, "Guess what! I just got a big raise at work!" to you.
```

In this way, you can have private conversations with people in the same room as you. You can talk to someone using whispers all day long, and only you and that person see the messages.

Some muds even offer an advanced form of whispering—a combination of whispering and acting:

```
whisper player-name = : action
```

For example, you can type this command:

```
> whisper Snag=: feels like celebrating!
```

You see this message:

```
You pose to Snag, Speedy feels like celebrating!
```

Snag sees this message:

```
In a pose to you, Speedy feels like celebrating!
```

Please be aware that not all muds offer this advanced form of whispering and acting.

Paging

What if the player you want to send a specific message to is not in the same room as you are? You could wander around the mud, find the room the player is in, and send that player a whisper. But an easier way is to *page* the player. Paging a player is similar to whispering to a player. The only difference is that the player you are paging does not have to be in the same room as you.

The page command has this form:

```
page player-name = message
```

For example, you can type this command:

```
> page Snag=Hey! Where are you?
```

You see this message:

```
You page, "Hey! Where are you?" to Snag.
```

Snag (and only Snag) sees this message:

```
Speedy pages, "Hey! Where are you?"
```

Again, note that you and Snag do not have to be in the same room for paging to work. You and Snag can be in totally different areas of the mud. Of course, you also can page someone who is in the same room.

Some muds support a paging/acting command similar to the whispering/acting command mentioned in the preceding section. Not surprisingly, it has the following form:

```
page player-name = : action
```

The command sends messages to you and the player you are paging/acting similar to the ones sent when whispering/acting. As with whispering/acting, not all muds support paging/acting commands.

By whispering or paging messages to various players, you can carry on entire private conversations that only those players can see. In fact, it is very common on muds for players to seem like they aren't doing anything—because they aren't publicly talking or acting—when they are actually paging messages back and forth with other players. Sometimes, it is quite obvious that someone is only half-listening to you because they are also trying to carry on a private page conversation with someone else at the same time, alternating between talking to you publicly and paging someone else privately.

Who Else Is Playing?

With a variety of communication commands at your disposal, you may want to know who is on the mud so that you can find them or talk to them using the page command. The who command tells you who else is playing on the mud.

Similar to the describe command, the who command varies from mud to mud. On some muds, it is simply who. On others, it is WHO (in uppercase). In our example, it is who and it displays something like this:

```
Player            On For   Idle
Speedy            0:10     0s
Snag              0:15     15s
Zowie             0:20     1m
Maddog            0:22     25s
Archimedes        0:43     54s
Shira             1:32     2m
Clarisse          1:54     43s
FrankNFurter      2:12     4m
Napoleon          2:22     2m
Jupiter           2:47     12s
Terminator        2:50     2m
Tweedle           4:29     10m
```

The first number is the amount of time that the character has been logged in to the mud; the second number is the character's idle time. You have been logged in for 10 minutes. Some muds also display the machine from which the character is connecting.

Getting and Dropping Objects

As with computer adventure games, you can pick up and put down objects. Most muds understand the basic commands:

```
> get object
> drop object
```

Other synonyms, such as take, grab, fetch, put, place, and set are also understood. Again, all mud parsers are not created equal. Some muds understand complex commands such as this one, but most do not:

```
> put the blue rose into the metal box on the table
```

Inventory

Once you have picked up an object, it is in your inventory. Your *inventory* is the list of objects you are carrying. Most muds have some type of inventory command, such as inv, which may display something like this:

```
You are carrying :
a rose
a jug of water
some cookies
a box containing:
a letter
an hourglass
```

Quitting

To quit playing, type the quit command, which is usually either quit or QUIT. On TinyMUD-genre muds, you also can go home before you quit. Typing **home** transports you back to your home room. Frequently, if you disconnect from a mud while you are still out in the public rooms, other players perform sweep commands that transport your character back home.

These commands should help get you started on a mud. For more detailed commands, such as the commands you use to build new objects on a mud, consult your specific mud's help information. Some muds have a lot of commands; others offer just the basics.

Try one out!

Combat

In addition to the basic commands described in the first part of this chapter, combat-oriented muds have additional commands related to fighting monsters and other players. Combat muds are the most common. There are hundreds of them in various states of being up or down, experimentally being added to, and being improved.

On most combat muds, you have a score that is akin to your experience. The higher score you have, the more powerful you are and the more abilities you have. To gain experience, you kill monsters, solve puzzles, and sell treasures. On some muds, you can gain experience by inter-acting with other players.

Initially, you can choose a gender, race, and class for your character, such as *female, human fighter* or *female, elfin magician.* Common classes for your character include fighters, magicians, priests, and thieves. *Fighters* can use all sorts of weaponry. *Magicians* cast spells. *Priests* can heal themselves and other players. *Thieves* are adept at stealing, searching, and other covert activities.

Most muds implement some sort of trait system to provide a way for you to get better at some-thing. Initially, you may be given a certain number of points, which you can allocate to your various traits. Fighters need strength and dexterity. Magicians need intelligence. As you gain experience, you gain more points to increase your traits and make your character better at his or her profession. Trait systems vary from mud to mud. Some muds have special rooms that are training centers; these areas also can be used to increase your traits.

Next, you can buy weapons and armor. You may have to search around to find a room where these items are sold. Perhaps you can get items from other players or from monsters you have killed. Once you have a weapon, you have to wield it. There is usually a command to do this:

```
> wield sword on right hand
```

To use armor, you have to wear it:

```
> wear shield on left arm
```

Some muds keep track of various body parts, for more realism. Others enable you to use only a certain number of items at one time.

With your traits allocated as you desire, weapon in hand, clothed in armor, you set out for the great unknown areas of the mud. You meet up with monsters. Some monsters are good—you can gain information from them. Other monsters try to defeat you. To battle them, you might type this command:

```
> kill monster
```

You replace `monster` with the type of monster you are fighting, such as `kill goblin`. A battle will occur. You may win, in which case you gain a higher score and perhaps some treasure you can use or sell. You may lose and be sent back to a central area to regenerate. Getting killed lowers your score. Perhaps you run away, or maybe someone else happens along and helps you out. Or maybe someone else helps the monsters defeat you! When players kill other players, it is known as *player killing*.

Player Killing

On most combat muds, you can be killed by other players, but only in areas where player killing is allowed. You decide for yourself when it's appropriate to venture into these areas.

In the early days of combat muds—when no area was safe—a powerful player could wait around for a new player to appear and then immediately kill off that player to gain experience. This led to muds being dominated by a few powerful players, and no one else could get a foothold. So the idea of safe areas, or *havens*, was created. Most muds now have a safe central town or castle. No player can kill another player in that area. New players can ready themselves for combat safely. They can fight in areas that have monsters but are still safe from player killing. Then, when they feel they are ready, they can go to the really nasty areas.

Resets

On combat muds, you must frequently solve puzzles to gain a higher score. You may have to answer riddles. More likely, you may have to pick up objects and place them in a certain manner. For example, you may find a key and use it to open a locked door, or you may have to place a special jewel in a certain spot to activate something.

With many people playing, objects are moved from their original locations to other places within the mud. Other players won't be able to solve the puzzles. Hence the idea of the *reset*. Every so often, objects are placed back in their original positions. Unlocked doors are closed and relocked. Dead guardian monsters are revived. Some games eject the players before doing this, but others use *rolling resets*, in which objects are replaced without the game being interrupted.

On some combat muds, the player has to perform quests, such as finding a magic sword. When the player completes the quest, the special object may be sold, offered as a gift, or perhaps thrown into a pit—and thus replaced behind-the-scenes, ready for another adventurer to find it.

When you try out a new combat mud, make sure that you read the help information. It provides details about the combat system, traits, weapons, armor, and safe areas.

Happy adventuring!

Bots

In addition to the other players on a mud, you may encounter robots, or *bots*, that seem like other players but are actually little programs that send out responses based on your interactions with it. Bots are programmed to use the same commands that players use; with clever programming, they can fool players into thinking that the bots actually *are* other real players.

Bots can automatically explore the mud, retaining mapping information, so that players can ask a bot how to get from one place to another; the bot can inform the player of the shortest distance to use. Bots can log all information they receive to a file on a disk.

Bots can have trigger phrases, so that they say a particular thing—or perhaps perform a random action—when a player does something or says something. For example, a bartender bot may greet everyone who enters the room with an encouragement to order a drink.

Bots can be programmed to favor or disfavor certain players.

Some muds enable players to connect themselves, or *attach*, to a bot and use it like a character. This can really make it tough to determine whether a character is a player or a computerized bot—because it could be both!

One of the most famous bots, written by Michael Mauldin, was named Julia. She was similar to the famous AI Eliza program. Legend has it that she fooled many players into thinking she was an actual real-life player; she had clever responses to players' speech and actions.

Mud-Related Internet Resources

In addition to the muds themselves, there are several mud-related resources that the inquiring mudder may find useful.

Newsgroups

Several Usenet newsgroups are devoted to the discussion of muds:

`rec.games.mud.admin`	Administrative issues of muds
`rec.games.mud.announce`	Informational articles on muds
`rec.games.mud.lp`	Discussion about LPMUDs (combat-oriented)
`rec.games.mud.misc`	Various aspects of muds
`rec.games.mud.tiny`	Discussion about TinyMUDs (social-oriented)

Several articles of interest are regularly posted to these newsgroups, such as the list of Frequently Asked Questions (FAQs).

The Frequently Asked Questions (FAQs) List

The FAQ is actually a series of three articles posted regularly to `rec.games.mud.announce`. It contains valuable information similar to the information contained in this chapter. It also gives more detailed information about mud clients and mud servers and where source code for these are located.

Part 1 contains information similar to this chapter. Part 2 details mud clients and servers extensively, including where source code for various programs can be found. Part 3 describes the mechanism you use to find out who is on a particular mud without having to connect to it.

The FAQ is written and maintained by Jennifer Smith (jds@math.okstate.edu). It can also be FTPed from ftp://ftp.math.okstate.edu:/pub/muds/misc/mud-faq.

Mud Clients

A *mud client* is a program you can use to connect to a mud. Although you can use the Telnet program as a client, there are better programs available. A mud client is a communications program written specially for a mud (or a type of mud). You can think of it as a mud front-end.

Mud clients make mudding easier. They break output up for you so that lines wrap at word boundaries rather than in the middle of words. They separate your input line from the mud output messages being sent to you. They provide better line-editing features than Telnet. They usually have an output buffer area so that you can scroll back and reread output that has scrolled off the top of your screen. Some clients allow you to load a file and transmit it to the mud as if you had typed the whole thing yourself.

Here are some of the other features that mud clients provide:

Feature	Description
autologin	Enables you to log in to a mud automatically, without having to type your character name and password. You specify your character name and password once, and the mud client remembers this; it uses this information the next time you log in to that mud.
gag	Enables you to suppress, or gag, output from a player. If an obnoxious player is swearing and sending out a lot of spam (see the definition of *spam* in "Mud Terms," later in this chapter), you can gag that player and never have to read it.
highlight	Enables you to highlight certain players or print lines containing their names in reverse video. Alternatively, you can highlight all whispers and pages directed towards you, so that you don't miss them.

Feature	Description
log	Enables you to record all the output from a mud session to a file.
macros	Macros are short commands that expand to longer commands. If there are certain sequences you type frequently, you can make them into macros.
trigger	Enables you to send commands when a certain event happens, such as automatically saying *hello* whenever someone enters a room.

Finally, some mud clients are programmable; you can add functionality to them if you desire.

Popular Mud Clients

There are many mud clients. A few of the more popular ones are listed here:

TinyFugue	Commonly known as tf, it works best with TinyMUD-style muds and runs on BSD or System V.
TinyTalk	Works best with TinyMUD-style muds and runs on BSD or System V.
VT	Works best with TinyMUD-style muds. It's programmable and runs on BSD or System V.
LPTalk	Used for LPMUD-style muds and runs on BSD or System V.
mud.el	Usable for TinyMUD-style muds. It's programmable and runs on GNU emacs.
lpmud.el	Usable for LPMUD-style muds. It's programmable and runs on GNU emacs.
BSXMUD	Enables certain muds (BSXMUDs) to transmit graphics to them. It runs on a variety of platforms.

Where To Find More Information About Mud Clients

For information about mud clients, your best bet is to consult the Frequently Asked Questions series, Part 2, which is all about mud servers (the muds themselves) and mud clients (the front-end programs). The FAQ document describes over two dozen mud clients, what they run on, and what capabilities they have. It also lists machines and FTP directories from which you can get source code for a mud client (in case one is not on your machine and you want to compile it yourself).

Mud Terms

As you play a mud, you may come across some terms you are not familiar with:

Term	Definition
newbie	A mudder who has just started mudding. An inexperienced player.
dino	An experienced mudder. Someone who has been mudding for several years or someone who has been a player on a particularly famous mud.
mav	A mudder who accidentally leaves a colon or quote in front of a whisper or a page, thus sending private messages to everyone in the whole room. This can be very embarrassing, especially if the message contains sensitive information that the player does not want everyone to know. The term comes from a famous TinyMUD player who had a tendency to do this often.
lag	The delay time you experience when the network is overloaded. Lag can also occur if the computer running the mud becomes overloaded. Eventually, the bottleneck dissipates, and response time returns to normal. Network lags that last several minutes are not uncommon.
spam	Flooding a mud with useless messages, such as very long say commands or quoting ASCII pictures line by line and sending them to the mud. Spam has a tendency to occur a lot on chatlines. Mud administratiors get upset with players who intentionally spam a mud. If a mud enables player killing, spamming a mud is a good way to get killed by other annoyed players. The term comes from the Monty Python sketch about spam.
spoof	Sending out messages that look like messages the game itself would send out, such as a message informing everyone that another player has been killed (when, in fact, he or she has not) or running a say command on someone else, thus "putting words in his or her mouth." On some muds, this is a wizard ability. On others, it is a result of security breaches.
TinySex	Sending commands, usually act commands, to imitate having sex with someone else. The phrase "mudding with one hand on the keyboard" is related to this. TinySex is similar to so-called "phone sex."

Term	Definition
bonk/oif	It is somewhat traditional in muds to "bonk" someone who says something silly or acts in a dumb or goofy manner. Bonk someone by typing something like this: `> :bonks Bob!` In turn, it is traditional to acknowledge being bonked by saying "`Oif!`" Some muds have actual commands that implement these two things. This practice is less common than it used to be.

Social Issues

Like other forms of role playing, muds can become terribly addictive in both their combat-oriented and social-oriented manifestations. Most mudders are teenagers who have managed to obtain connections to a local university or undergraduate college students tapping into the Internet world for the first time. The experience can be exhilarating. A mud player's immediate previous experience may have been interacting with the local neighborhood crowd or fellow students at high school. Now, a community that encompasses the whole country—or even the whole world—beckons. Mudders from San Francisco, Chicago, New York, Toronto, and a city in Sweden can all talk to each other and play games with each other at the same time. The world becomes smaller on a popular mud. Players tend to be more tolerant of cultural diversity and intolerant of players who express prejudice.

Most muds tend towards liberalism. Staunch conservatives are usually shunned and argued against. Freedom of speech on muds is taken seriously. Rousing debates are not uncommon, but because muds are detached from real life, long-standing grudges are infrequent—although, when they do occur, they can be quite fierce. Most conversations revolve around computers, sex, music, politics, boredom, and loneliness. On combat-oriented muds, players can go off in groups to kill monsters. They can gang up and kill someone they don't like.

Muds—and virtual interactive forums in general—are less socially inhibitive than real-life encounters. Because the body language cues that dictate acceptable behavior do not exist on muds—except in a very rudimentary form through acting—people feel less constrained in their actions. Shy, introverted people find the medium inviting because they feel they can act the way they really are, to be how they really want to be. Extroverted people tend to find their personalities amplified on muds.

There is also a sense of technological superiority on muds—the feeling that you are playing in a cutting-edge environment. Mom and Dad never did anything like this when they were young. Non-mudders aren't connected like you are. They don't get it. The world is going global and you are part of it. Why, you are talking to someone from some other country right now. Suddenly, a conversation switches languages, and everyone starts talking in French or German.

Non-mudders see news on television, but you have talked to someone who has actually been there. Perhaps someone who saw the Berlin Wall being removed. Or someone was in the crowd around the Russian White House when Yeltsin brought in the tanks. They are here, on a mud, talking to you in real time. You want to know about such people, and they want to find out about you.

All these factors add up to a powerful environment, in which you are much more likely to be accepted than rejected and you can find other people who think and act like you do. The large variety of muds enables people to find their niche. With more than 200 muds available, you can find an environment suitable to your tastes simply by connecting and interacting for a while with the players there. If a particular mud is harsh or otherwise displeasing, simply try another! Social flow is reversed. Rather than society choosing you, you have the opportunity, not just to choose you own friends and your own types of conversations and interactions, but to choose your own reality. That's the real attraction behind mud playing: it's fun, it's high-tech, you get to be whoever you want to be, and you are interacting with people who, for the most part, are just like you.

Addiction

Such freedom can lead to addiction. Players have been known to spend huge amounts of time on muds; 16 hours a day playing a mud is not uncommon. Perhaps the time is spent trying to attain wizard level. It may be spent talking with all the other players on the mud or playing interactive games with them. Or perhaps it is spent adding to a mud and using one's creativity as one pleases. It may even lead to real romance. Time can indeed pass quickly.

This can lead to neglecting other areas of one's life, such as one's studies. Cases of mudders dropping out of college because they spent too much time playing muds and not enough time studying are still fairly common. If the player was gaining access to the mud through a fee-based service, the end may occur when the bill for connection time arrives. Sometimes, this sudden removal from the mud environment can be a shock.

Gender Issues

In the late 1980s, when Internet muds first appeared, they were populated mainly by undergraduate students in computer science or engineering. This was not surprising because muds initially were based on computer programming and computer game playing. Most of the players were male. Gradually, however, more and more female players found out about muds and started playing. Some of this came about by real-life word of mouth and also because of changing demographics (as the Internet grew out of engineering departments and began reaching students in other subjects such as liberal arts, management, and the arts). This, in turn, led to bigger chances of male-female interaction over muds. Some of that interaction is playful interpersonal communication, and some of it is harassment. The harassment issue has forced some mud administrators to enforce policies in which players that talk or act in a harassing manner are removed from the mud.

Mudders are generally uncomfortable with censorship of speech that comes from administration, although the trend is changing as more people find out about the medium and the events that occur there. Most mudders prefer to sort the problem out for themselves through *social conditioning*. A particularly obnoxious or bad-mouthed player is ignored or told to shape up by other mudders; this social conditioning usually suffices in maintaining balance in all but the most glaring cases. However, as more women use muds, both in total number and percentages on a given mud, issues such as nondiscriminatory hitting on women for sexual reasons are becoming more widely discussed—following trends in real life. Muds vary, but most have an implied contract of male-female interaction that includes such events as getting to know one another, or even having virtual sex, but frowns on pick-up lines, wanton advances, and lewd remarks in public. Some muds state this as explicit policy and quickly deal with players who refuse to adhere to the stated social agreements. Other muds eschew censorship and suggest that certain players may find the mud harassing and perhaps should look elsewhere.

You can play any type of character or personality you want on a mud; this implies that you can even play a different gender. Gender-switching is common in muds. Males play female characters, and females play males. Some players do it simply to see what it is like; others do it as a role-playing challenge. Some mudders do it to avoid being treated a certain way. Female players may switch to male characters to avoid being hit upon. Other females may simply quit mudding because the mud has become too sleazy or perhaps because they feel that they should not have to switch genders to be left alone. A mud with strong administration and stated guidelines has a better chance of attracting and maintaining strong male and female user populations than one in which any behavior—no matter how rude or offensive—is permitted.

It's good to keep gender switching in mind when playing a mud. That coy, playful girl you come across may actually be being played by a man! Or a suave, handsome man may actually be being played by a woman!

Violence

In addition to gender issues, violence is also an issue. In combat-oriented muds, violence is the whole point of the game! In social-oriented muds, combat tends to be frowned on, unless a player is being obnoxious.

In combat muds, you can kill the monsters on the mud, which has a satisfaction similar to destroying the bad guys on a video game. Some people love this kind of stuff; others don't.

Perhaps more interesting is when you yourself get killed— especially if you were killed by another player rather than by some programmed monster. This can be quite shocking and depressing, especially if you have spent a lot of time developing your character's abilities. Some players spend weeks and months playing a mud, striving for wizard level. This leads to a close association between the player and the mud character. Some players have said that they themselves experienced a feeling of death and total nothingness when their characters were killed. These feelings can lead to depression. For these types of players—typically young males in their teens and early college years—it is important to remember that muds are games. The games aren't real life. They reflect real life, but are not a replacement for it.

However, it's worthwhile to point out that the social aspects of mudding may be quite real. Friendships that are just as close as real-life friendships can develop over a mud. Relationships can blossom. Some people have met over a mud, gotten to know each other well, and eventually have married. From a social point of view, muds may not be that different from real life at all.

Education

Muds are coming into use as educational tools too. Some are simply gathering points in which people talk about certain topics. In this way, information can be disseminated and discussed. Better yet, muds can be used as creativity enhancers.

Consider MariMUSE. MariMUSE was based on MicroMUSE, one of the first educational muds. MariMUSE was developed as a constructive learning environment for college students; local primary school students were also able to connect to it. Some of these students were low performers. Some of them had a history of missing a lot of school. When they started using the MUSE, a curious thing happened. They became involved. They developed friendships. They started coming to school early so that they could spend a bit of time before school on the mud. Their grades improved. They created new areas on the mud, writing the descriptions for these areas and creating new objects. They learned how to program the mud, and some wanted to know more about computer programming and mathematics. MariMUSE helped them become better students.

MediaMOO, developed about a year after MariMUSE, is a mud devoted to media research and populated by media researchers. It is an environment professionals use to get in contact with other people with similar research interests and to socialize and communicate with each other.

These types of educational environments will appear more and more. It's easy to think of a mud that can teach a player about a certain topic, with the rooms being informational snippets and the objects relating to the topic at hand. On EON, the successor to MariMUSE, learners can explore a Gopher exhibit that contains pointers to information about the Internet Gopher service. They can actually use Gopher itself through the mud. Users of the mud learn about Internet resources in a hands-on manner. Electronic communication replaces classroom buildings. More detailed information can be added by other players, with the mud expanding, perhaps having links to other muds on other related topics—somewhat like hypertext. Graphical muds will even improve on this.

The Future

The future looks bright for muds. Although it remains to be seen how text-only muds will fare in the coming years, it's clear that multiuser virtual realities will begin to go mainstream. Just think of all the millions of video game players out there, and how a graphical multiuser virtual reality would affect them. Some online services and game companies are already providing such environments. There's a lot of money to be made.

The question is will muds be only a pastime for computer enthusiasts or will everyone find the new medium exciting? Yorg the PowerMudder may think that widely available graphical muds are the wave of the future, but what about other people? Will there come a day when Joe Sixpack finds himself clicking off the weekend sports game on television and connecting up to a game where he himself can play alongside other players and perhaps computer-generated sports legends? Will muds let armchair quarterbacks become "real" quarterbacks? After all, muds are just a small step away from the much ballyhooed cyberspace of the future.

Time To Try It Out!

Now that you've read about the mud basics, it's time for you to go try one out! See what all the fuss is! Pick a mud and log in as a guest. Create a character. Play for a while and see how you like it. Try the different varieties of muds; you may like one type of mud more than another. For a challenge, try role-playing a character who is very different from your real-life personality. Solve the puzzles, join the card games, toast the monsters, offer your own opinion in conversations, and above all, feel free to talk and interact with the other players on the mud. You might meet someone you like!

Soon, you, too, may be a mudder!

And if you happen to bump into a character named Snag, feel free to page me and say hello!

Virtual Reality on the Internet

by David H. Mitchell

- ■ "What is all this I hear about virtual reality?"
- ■ "What is virtual reality?"
- ■ "Why would I want it?"
- ■ "What does the Internet have to do with it?"
- ■ "How will the Internet and virtual reality work together?"
- ■ "How do virtual reality, tele-presence, and the Internet fit together?"
- ■ "What's beyond the global Internet and virtual reality?"
- ■ "How can I use the Internet to learn more?"
- ■ "What's the bottom line?"

A few years ago, *virtual reality* was a phrase and a concept known only to a few people. Today, virtual reality (VR) is still more virtual than real. By the turn of the century (that's only five years away—where has this century gone?!), people may well be spending more time each day in virtual reality than watching television.

What Is All This I Hear About Virtual Reality?

Perhaps the first book to deal with virtual reality was Arthur C. Clarke's *The City and the Stars*, written almost half a century ago. In this book, the citizens of a future city could hold meetings in which each person's presence was electronically projected and mingled with the others. This created the illusion of everyone being at a meeting without the need for being physically assembled. And even more to the point, the city dwellers could participate in "sagas" in which one or more people would enter an artificial adventure created by an artist. In this adventure, the player could explore things, alter the events, and be a part of what was going on—not just be a passive observer.

Clarke is also considered by many to be the father of the communications satellite. So not only did Clarke show how the world could be wired together with communications satellites placed in orbit, but he might as well have also pointed out how we can be "wired" together socially.

In these days when terms such as *global village, wired world, electronic town meetings*, and *virtual communities* are being bantered about with great fanfare, it is important to remember that the concepts have been around a long time. So what we're hearing today are the whispers from the past overlaid with new technology and new excitement. Such is the route science fiction travels in becoming science fact! Those who seek a crystal ball to see the future need only read science fiction!

What Is Virtual Reality?

This question often leads to a philosophical discussion of "What is reality?" After all, how can we define virtual reality if we don't know what reality is? Happily, we can avoid that problem by looking at early atomic theory! `<grin>` Don't panic—I mean *really* early atomic theory, back in Greek times. Back then, the term *atom* was coined to mean "indivisible." So by defining the basic unit, the Greeks started building useful information—knowing when to stop trying to figure out what was unknowable at the time. Only in the past 200 years have new tools and technologies come about that enable us to explore things smaller than atoms. And only in the past 30 years have tools come about to enable us to define and explore virtual reality. We can safely leave studying reality to the scientists and philosophers for now.

Virtual reality, in a nutshell, is fake reality. Have you ever gotten so heavily involved in a book that you didn't notice someone asking you a question? Ever had a lucid dream? Ever been so wrapped up in a television show that you didn't notice someone walk in front of the TV screen? The human mind, these days cheerfully referred to as our *personal neural net* or *private wetware*, is a truly wonderful thing. We even occasionally use it—although there are plenty of skeptics who say the vote is not in on that issue! But the point is that reality is what the mind perceives.

We each have our own subjective universe, based on what our senses tell us, what we think it is, and how we manipulate it. The goal of a system using virtual-reality techniques is to give us some sense of being "somewhere else" rather than "here." This "here/there" concept opens up all kinds of possibilities—leaving someone trying to get started with a huge feeling of "Gee, how am I supposed to figure it out?" This is the same way many of us felt a few years ago about personal computers and this year about the Internet. Well, the good news is that you don't have to worry because by the time you are done reading this chapter, you will have some feel of what virtual reality is all about, and you will know how to find out more, without fear of embarrassment.

So what does fake reality mean? The goal of a good movie is to get your senses and then your emotions involved to the point where you become part of the adventure. Of course, good luck trying to change the corny ending or be part of the action. To be part of the action, you have to become a movie star, and most people with such ambitions end up in Little Theater. In theater, one of the golden rules is not to "break the fourth wall"—the wall between the actors onstage and the audience. For many, virtual reality can be seen as the tool not just to break the fourth wall, but to put everyone on stage.

In the real world, the plot is often boring, sometimes not to your liking, but you have some control. You can take that freeway off-ramp and get out of the gridlock if you choose, you can decide to go vegetarian or have a steak, and you can decide who to vote for as President. But in the real world, you still may not have much influence in the plot or be able to change the corny ending. Now imagine, just imagine, if you could have the best of both worlds—the movie *and* reality! Imagine choosing a place to be and what you do there—and having an influence on where you end up and how you end up. This is the promise of virtual reality that is first seen by most people. The promise goes much deeper and is more far-reaching than simple escapism. But everyone needs some time and place to escape every now and then. It's called a vacation.

To create a fake reality, two important factors are your immersion in this synthetic reality and your ability to interact with it. If you feel you are really there (immersed) but can't manipulate anything, you end up with the same thrill as you get with a roller coaster ride and about the same amount of control. If you can move about in this fake reality, move objects around, and control what you do, but it doesn't look real, you have a good time but don't accept it as much more than a game or diversion. The battle that virtual reality has faced for many years is meeting people's expectations for both immersion and interactivity. You want it to be real! This desire has led to a lot of hype and a lot of disappointment as expectations exceed the capability of software and hardware. This limitation is changing slowly.

The tools of virtual reality are varied. To many, seeing someone put on a modified motorcycle helmet and gloves exuding wires is the first clue that something is afoot. To others, seeing things float on a computer screen in three-dimensional perspective and being able to move them around is the clue. The simple fact is that virtual-reality-in-a-box is not yet here. You can't point at one thing and say, "That's virtual reality!" This may change in a year, two at most. The essence of virtual reality is to be able to project yourself somewhere else, involving as many senses as possible—and having as much control over what you do there as possible. The big word at the moment is *immersive*, followed by *interactive*. Throw in things such as Head-Mounted Display (putting the TVs in your face), gloves (we can't use joysticks, not cool), and Worlds (the software that puts us "there" rather than "here"), and for good measure, say *rendering* (the act of drawing the images you see), and you may pass as an expert on VR if you aren't careful. <grin>

But pretty soon, everyday virtual reality will mean putting on some device to give you visual images (I hope it won't be too long before the device will be a replacement for a pair of glasses), and it will be wired (or wireless) to a box that does the work. Sound and touch sensations will be handled by your clothing ("What! Clothes used to just sit there?"), and you won't think about this technology much more than you think about your television, car, or phone—it will be just another tool. Although this may sound silly to you now, the thought of 20 million-plus people all sitting down pushing little rows of buttons very fast while staring at a box for hours on end seems quite hilarious! And they all wonder why their backs hurt. The idea of having the images projected in front of you in full perspective regardless of position sounds mighty appealing. We'll need to lose the keyboard as soon as possible, too. Who came up with our current interface? Some sadist, no doubt. Why would anyone want to move a wired box around in their hand to aim an arrow at a little box with a picture in it? So maybe the question is not "What is virtual reality?" but "What the heck do we have now?"

Why Would I Want It?

Why not? You read books, have a computer (or are considering getting one), and you probably even own a television. (See how much I can deduce from the fact that you are reading this?) Because you are reading about the Internet, you are surely interested in exploring new stuff. Well, if the Internet is going to open the world to you, do you really want to explore the world by keyboard and monitor screen? Heck no! Text is great, but there is more out there than just text. So depending on your desires, virtual reality can be an escape/vacation, or now maybe an interface.

But wait! There's more. With virtual reality, you can slice and dice yourself into new modes of learning. Before you are done with this chapter, you will learn how you can use virtual reality and the Internet to drive a model of a lunar rover vehicle on a mockup of a moon colony! You will see the learning methods of the future and how people will be able to explore space from their chairs at home. In the next few years, you can actually become a tele-naut, operating real spacecraft from home. And a lot of this capability is available now. With your computer, a modem, and access to the Internet, you can get a taste of virtual reality and home *tele-operations* (operating remote robots, androids, and vehicles)—not at some hopeful future date, or next year, but now. There are exciting islands you can reach by the global information highway!

What Does the Internet Have To Do with It?

"OK, you have my interest—now what?" If you gave 20 million people the capability to communicate with each other and said, "Do whatever you want!" guess what you would get? The Internet! So trying to describe the Internet is like trying to explain what 20 million people are doing—and throw in a growth rate of 15 percent a month to that figure. My task here is much easier because maybe 60,000 people are all that have intimate interest in virtual reality at the moment. (It's much easier to get intimate with 60,000 people than 20 million.) What the Internet has done is provide places to share information about virtual reality research (the newsgroups), ways to communicate with individuals (e-mail), and ways to get to groups and systems doing virtual reality experiments (Telnet). And when you get comfortable with moving files of information around, there are places to get information (FTP). By reading other chapters in this book, you will learn exactly how to read and contribute to newsgroups, how to receive and send e-mail, and how to connect to various computers on the Internet by *Telnetting*. Telnetting is much like teleporting or "beaming" yourself to another computer and is a form of virtual reality in itself. When you Telnet, you connect your computer to a remote computer.

You shift your "here" to a "there" for the purpose of checking out an Information Island. When you Telnet, you use the Internet like a highway. The place you Telnet to is the place at the end of the off ramp. When you're there, it is its own community; you have to check it out and learn the customs.

Here is where you can take a look at your "shyness index" and decide whether you are the bold one who at a party says, "Hi! I'm here!" or whether you are the one who walks in quietly and meets people as they come—or the one who avoids the party completely. I have worked my way over the years from avoidance to acceptance to annoyance (the stages of losing shyness), but shyness, like virginity, is probably best not discussed at length. The key here is that we are all virtual reality virgins now (except for a very few), and most of us are also Internet virgins.

The easy and safe way to start learning about virtual reality using the Internet, without risk of embarrassment, is to read the newsgroups about virtual reality. Then, when you have your virtual Internet legs, you can fire off a short e-mail or two to people with whom you have shared information you find interesting, asking a quick question and thanking them for sharing their information. Most people who do share information in the newsgroups like to hear that what they are doing is read about and appreciated. Then, the day will actually come when you have something to share, and you will make a post to a newsgroup. But if you really want more than words, you will have to Telnet to some of the Information Islands to get some hands-on virtual reality. The Internet does not have any inherent virtual reality capabilities (yet), but that limitation is being worked on by a lot of people.

Even the largest commercial online computer networks have subscriber bases only a tenth as large as the number of Internet users. And none of the commercial networks can boast a growth rate anywhere near the Internet's. Some say this is caused by the flexibility of the Internet. Others say that the Internet, in being a loose organization, has actually been a model example of individual intellectual capitalism at its best (freed from government regulations that control and limit competition in other areas of communication). And some say it is so successful simply because it costs less. Whatever the reason, the Internet is going to be a major source of information about virtual reality, and the tools of virtual reality will begin to make the Internet easier to use and explore. In the years to come, we can expect to be able to find things faster by using virtual-reality-based Gophers (the Internet equivalent of a phone book) rather than text-based Gophers.

So the Internet will probably be the experimental playground for new methods of using virtual reality to bring people together. After all, while software is being developed to enable you to escape into a fake reality, why not bring a few friends with you? As long as you are in a fake reality, it doesn't much matter where your friends live—as long as they can plug in to the Internet. For better and worse, we can expect to see communities of first hundreds and then thousands linking in artificial realities to conduct business, learn, play, and socialize. Anyone for tea on the summit of the Matterhorn today?

How Will the Internet and Virtual Reality Work Together?

To really see all the ways in which the Internet and virtual reality can work together, one must step back and look at the characteristics of each, as well as the needs, goals, and dreams of the user. That means you. What are you hoping to get out of the Internet? What do you want from virtual reality?

The Internet offers you access to e-mail, newsgroups, computers, and archives of information. Virtual reality offers you new methods of connecting to your computer and new ways of sharing information. The Internet is a collection of places, or "there," and virtual reality is a method of making "there" be like "here." Virtual reality offers a way to get at all the good stuff without the keyboard and monitor screen being filled with text.

What a delight that now that the Internet global village has formed, we are about to have some decent virtual reality clothes to wear. Having the proper attire for a global village meeting is only logical, and keyboards and monitor screens are the loincloths of the Information Society—fine for primitive meetings but hardly suave and debonair.

Following are some explicit examples of how the Internet and virtual reality can work together:

- **Example 1:** You like Rodin. You do not live near the Rodin Museum in Paris. Indeed, you do not live in France. So you take a "cyber-tour" of the museum. You put on your head-mounted display, Telnet to the Rodin Museum computer, and request to take a Virtual Tour. You are shown images just as if you were standing at the door of the museum. As you press keys on your keyboard or gesture with your glove, you move about the gallery as if by magic. You are seeing the sculptures as they are created (rendered) based on the information stored in the museum's computer. It is almost as good as being there. You can float above the sculptures to see them from other angles. If you are wearing sensory gloves, you can reach out and touch the sculptures— something not always allowed in the real world. (I have always been of the opinion that sculptures should be felt, and that only seeing a sculpture is like going to an opera with no sound.) This capability is not available yet, but it will be. The question is when, not if. My guess is from 1998 to 2001.

- **Example 2:** You like real things—no computer simulations for you. You want to take a drive. As a matter of fact, you want to get the hang of driving something while sitting at home. Say, a model of a lunar rover vehicle. So you put on a head-mounted display (or use your conventional computer monitor screen) and Telnet to the Lunar Tele-Operations Model 1. You can now take a turn at driving a rover vehicle model on a miniature lunar colony model. You receive live television images from the vehicle from the driver's point of view. Why not? You're the driver! You can remote control something that is half a world away from you. The whole field of tele-operations and virtual reality are intertwined because virtual reality can put you into a "fake there," and tele-operations can put you into a "real there"—and the tools and techniques are very similar. But about this example—you can do it now! The Lunar Tele-Operations Model 1 exists and is operational.

■ **Example 3:** You like people and want to relax. You want to try your hand at virtual reality and actually get into a Virtual World with someone. You want to move a few objects around and play hide-and-seek and not have to buy any special hardware to do it. So you Telnet to a system and download a program called POLY (Polygon Playground). You have a friend do the same. Then, you both Telnet to the system that runs POLY. On-screen, you and your friend see each other represented as a cat's face. You can use your mouse to move a hand on the screen to pick up and move various objects. You can change your point-of-view and move yourself so that your friend can't see you. You spend time building things from the objects, moving about, and looking at the place from many perspectives. You play tag and hide-and-seek with your friend. Again, this is something you can do now! POLY does exist and there is a system that runs it.

■ **Example 4:** You are studying the Constitution at school. Your entire class puts on head-mounted displays and Telnets to a computer in Washington, DC. You are now all members of the Constitutional Convention as it occurred more than 200 years ago. You have been randomly assigned to be one of the participants. Information about you (as a member of the Convention) is displayed floating in mid-air in front of you. Other members are identified. You are prompted for your "lines," but you can also try your own ideas. The group is a mix of your classmates and computer-generated members. You have the ability to see history, to alter it, and to learn deeply not just what happened, but why it happened. You also gain insight on how each member of the Convention influenced the outcome that we call the Great American Experiment. My guess on availability for this remote learning tool is 2001 to 2010.

■ **Example 5:** You are doing a survey for a Mars colony location. You put on your "glasses" (head-mounted display) and Telnet to a planetary database computer. You enter a Virtual World that is an accurate landscape of Mars based on the data from planetary probes. You drive a simulated rover vehicle up and over mountains, through valleys and plains. Occasionally, you request to move a few kilometers at a time or switch to "fly mode" and zoom along the terrain at high speed. In the comfort of your own home, you explore thousands of square kilometers in a few hours. My estimate for this simulated Mars tour is two years or less.

These are just a few of the ways the Internet and virtual reality will work together. The Internet is the information highway, and virtual reality is the information automobile. Now you can go anywhere in style, and the speed limit is a safe 186,232 miles per second!

How Do Virtual Reality, Tele-Presence, and the Internet Fit Together?

With virtual reality, you use hardware and software to end up in an artificial or synthetic (fake) reality. With tele-presence, you use a lot of the same hardware and software to get, not to a fake reality, but to another real place. This means there has to be something at the other end—a robot with TV cameras mounted on it, a mechanical hand, or maybe a rover vehicle. The goal is to make you think you are somewhere else—the "there" being a place that really exists. Being able to be somewhere else through tele-presence is the next best thing to teleportation and "beaming."

For several years, I have been exploring the role of "Android Agents" and have coined Mitchell's Law: *Everyone should have at least one Android Agent.*

We have been living with telephones and televisions for a long time now, but a lot of new "teles" are about to be thrust on us. Tele-presence, tele-operations, tele-tourism, tele-creation, tele-EduTainment, tele-toys, and tele-creation, to name a few.

Don't worry too much about remembering all the tele-flavors; you can always refer to this menu later if you need to.

Tele-presence is like virtual reality in that you are put in a "there" that is different from your "here." But when you are in a fake reality, it is just that. In the case of tele-presence, all the effort electronically is to make you feel as though you are in the remote location. If it were perfect, you would have all your senses fooled and be convinced you had just been moved to a new locale. So your head-mounted display shows you a real view of another location, and your gloves can do real work at the other end. Kind of a video phone with hands and feet coming out of each end. Of course, tele-presence is just taking its first tele-steps, but the next five to ten years will have us walking around in New York while standing in Los Angeles. Considering earthquakes, maybe it's better the other way around, and we can just settle for watching the holodeck on *Star Trek: The Next Generation.*

Tele-operations is getting into full swing now. With tele-operations, you are remotely controlling something, but you can sure tell that you aren't there. Usually, you get video images to see from a driver's point of view, and you can control the robot or rover vehicle using keys, a mouse, or a joystick. Tele-operations can enable firemen to send androids into places too hot to handle, undersea divers to work at great depths without leaving the house, and security guards to never leave the safety of the control room. Tele-operations holds keys to almost being in two places at once—and it gives us hands to help with work that can be far from where our body happens to be. With tele-operations, you are concentrating on getting work done, not creating the illusion that you are where the work is being done.

Tele-tourism will be something between riding a roller coaster from home and exploring native Hawaii from your desktop. Combining aspects of tele-presence, tele-operations, and a bit of theatrics, groups and individuals will be able to conduct expeditions and explorations from the safety of home. Companies such as Digital Expeditions have just been formed, working in association with groups such as The Planetary Society. Tele-tourism can gradually evolve into an entire service industry, taking you on serious expeditions as well as simple tours. Hang on to your head-mounted display—dinosaur parks may be tame by comparison!

Tele-EduTainment will be remote learning in many forms. This education can include seminars in which lecturers give presentations to an audience spread all over the world. So-called town meetings plus virtual reality and the Internet open the door to all kinds of group gatherings. Language education will reach new levels of quality as people practice by taking a walk in another country. Of course, because you are really at home, you will not have to learn "where is the restroom?" as your first sentence. And as people get used to meeting in global groups, it's only a matter of time before international rock concerts become common.

Tele-toys will plug into your home computer, enabling children of all ages to play with your trains and race cars from anywhere in the world. Dancing android dolls may well provide choreographers new dimensions in dance. A chorus line may stretch across a continent!

Tele-creation may see the end of manufacturing as we know it today. As the capability to use nano-technology to build small machines and objects improves, we will see the advent of home assembly units and then home manufacturing units. You will be able to receive "recipes" for everything from a diamond to a computer. The Internet can send you text to read on your screen just as easily as it can send assembly instructions to build something atom by atom in your home.

For bigger tasks, you can rent an assembly android to provide the manpower (androidpower?) to assemble a desk. For those heavy tasks, you may well expect that android to be tele-operated by an experienced tradesperson working from her home. Instead of packing up tools and driving off in a pickup, the craftsperson will step into a set of coveralls rigged with sensors so that the android 50 or 500 miles away mimes every move, with the Internet information highway transporting skills, not people and pickups.

We can expect the rise of a new industry—the tele-op services industry. We will see everything from housecleaning using robots operated by "crews" in another city to security patrol androids to renting time on lunar dune buggies for armchair exploration. Home diagnostics and tele-medicine may offer lifesaving treatments faster, and doctors may start making house calls of a sort. Solar sailing clubs will be formed, with people using sunsails to pilot space yacht models in orbit. At the conference "Making Orbit 93" in Berkeley, I stated my long-term goal of renting tele-operated rides on the moon. In many cases, the highway linking all these diverse activities will be the Internet and SolNet.

What's Beyond the Global Internet and Virtual Reality?

SolNet. We seem to have wired the world ahead of the predictions of science fiction. The next step will be SolNet—the solar system Internet. The star we are attached to, Sol, will soon have a net extending outward. In the years to come, we will be using the Internet and SolNet not just to move information around, but to project our presence to remote corners of the globe and to the far reaches of the solar system. Remote-controlled robots, rovers, hands, spaceships, and androids will be extensions of ourselves.

What is so amazing is that this is not the far future. We will see a lot of this technology in the next decade. I have already driven the NASA Ames rover vehicle from my home, assisted with communications links allowing the Russian Mars rover in Moscow to be driven from Washington, D.C., and built a model lunar rover vehicle that has been driven by people thousands of miles away.

I have watched the launch and landing of a tele-operated spaceship at White Sands Missile Range in 1993. This revolutionary spaceship (called the DC-X) is a one-third-size experimental spaceship that takes off and then lands on its own tail of fire. The DC-X was tele-operated by astronaut Pete Conrad from a mobile trailer, and was built in less than two years for less than $60 million—a tiny amount for space hardware. As of this writing, testing has stopped because the Advanced Research Projects Agency refuses to spend the $5 million allocated for continued testing by Congress. Only in America could the Democrats and Republicans agree to lower the cost of getting into space and have the decision blocked by an "Advanced Projects" agency. This is the same ARPA that got the Internet started many years ago as the ARPAnet, so I was rather surprised to see major innovation bottlenecked by such a normally forward-thinking group.

NASA, space societies, and private industry are all rushing to mix virtual reality, tele-operations, the Internet, and space capabilities into a new revolution in space exploration and development. New kinds of planetary probes are being designed to give the ground control stations more capability—including allowing the use of Internet links to enable universities and others to access data directly from the probes.

Access to space by the ordinary person will become a reality in the next 20 years. Not only will you take simulated rides and explorations, but you will operate real space hardware and remote data-collection colonies using SolNet. Our first presence in space may well be robotic, but as time progresses, the robots and androids will make it affordable and desirable to develop and colonize space. The improved standard of living from low-cost access to energy and raw materials in space, coupled with the desire to reduce pollution on earth, will provide an economic imperative far beyond any gold rush to extend mankind into the solar system.

SolNet will be the information highway beyond the sky!

How Can I Use the Internet To Learn More?

The Internet is rich with information about virtual reality and the Information Islands where you can explore virtual reality and the "teles." The following information is given on the assumption that you have learned how to read newsgroups, send and receive e-mail, and use the Telnet and FTP commands on the Internet. Be sure to take the time to learn the basics of navigating the Internet so that when you are ready to explore virtual reality on the Internet, you won't get stuck.

Many newsgroups are devoted to related subjects, but an excellent place to start is with the newsgroup sci.virtual-worlds. As you read the messages posted there, you will begin to see who is doing what and where the state of the art is. This moderated newsgroup is hosted by the Human Interface Technology Laboratory (HIT Lab) at the University of Washington. Lists of Frequently Asked Questions (FAQs) are posted regularly in the newsgroup. You can get more information by e-mailing scivw@hitl.washington.edu.

Here are other newsgroups that have information about various aspects of virtual reality:

```
alt.3d
alt.cyberpunk
alt.cyberspace
alt.education.distance
alt.toys.high-tech
alt.uu.virtual-worlds.misc
alt.wired
comp.multimedia
comp.robotics
sci.virtual-worlds.apps
```

New newsgroups are forming at a fast rate, so be sure to read the newsgroups for more information.

Because the field of virtual reality is evolving very quickly, it is best to refer to the newsgroups for current software and files and the location of FTP sites where you can get these files. Popular virtual reality rendering programs such as REND386 (written by Bernie Roehl and Dave Stampe) are available at many archive sites, but the primary site is the University of Waterloo. Dave Stampe's new VR-386 is at a site at the University of Toronto. Refer to the newsgroup sci.virtual-worlds for the latest version and FTP site information.

Several commercial online services have solid virtual reality forums and conferences that you can access using the TELNET command on the Internet. Not only do the "big guy" services offer information, but services such as the WELL (Telnet to well.sf.ca.us) and the Diaspar Virtual Reality Network (Telnet to diaspar.com) have forums and conferences with quality information.

Diaspar stands apart from the other commercial online systems because of the operational shared worlds, online video, and tele-operations capabilities. Because Diaspar uses a revenue-sharing system with virtual reality world developers, Dan Duncan (whom many refer to as the "Poet Laureate" of virtual reality) has said, "Diaspar is an experiment in Open Capitalism." Diaspar is also the online home of other companies and societies involved with virtual reality, media, publishing, tele-operations, and space exploration.

The Diaspar Virtual Reality Network is experimenting with shared virtual worlds created by individual "world artists." The first such release is a two-person shared world called POLY, which stands for Polygon Playground. Two people anywhere in the world can move about, move objects, and perform other simple tasks in this world. POLY was developed by *PCVR Magazine* editor Joe Gradecki, based on REND386.

The nonprofit Lunar Tele-Operations Model 1—a miniature moon-colony model with vehicles that can be operated through the Internet from anywhere in the world—is sponsored by Diaspar.

What's the Bottom Line?

We are at the beginning of two Golden Ages: the Golden Age of Information and the Golden Age of Space Development. The Internet may well be the glue that not only holds this planet's civilization together but also binds the solar system into a community of people and machines. This community has the potential of great progress in a renaissance for the human condition and spirit. We are on the verge of taking our first steps toward being a cohesive global village and into new eras of education, exploration, and development. We are about to become a space-faring people.

There are unlimited intellectual resources available on the Internet now. There will be unlimited tangible and intellectual resources on SolNet as it forms in the next 50 years.

Virtual reality is the interface between man and machine and man again. We are about to wear the cosmic attire. We can look up, out, and now reach to the stars and touch them. With virtual hat and glove in hand, the future is in our grasp!

Games Online

by Kevin M. Savetz

66

It should come as no surprise that the Internet is home to a huge population of people who play games—and have found in the Internet a way to find and interact with fellow players.

We're not just talking intrinsically computer-based games here, like MUDs (Multi-User Dungeons) and Bolo, although the Internet does have a substantial population of those. We're also talking about classic board and card games that can, but don't have to, involve computers—for example, backgammon, Reversi, chess, and Go.

Games on the Internet may not be as flashy as those on your Nintendo and Sega, but the Internet can offer the ability to play against other folks—not just computerized opponents. As with other Internet tools, the people you're playing with may be right down the hall or across the globe. Besides, it's certainly more satisfying to play (and beat) a human opponent than a digital one.

Actually, if you have a graphical Web browser, some of today's games can approach the graphical snazziness of your Nintendo—but they tend to be much (*much!*) slower. If you don't have graphical access to the Internet, you're stuck (in most cases) with text-based games.

The Internet is home to two styles of games: interactive and play by mail. *Interactive games* let you play and converse in real time with your opponents; *play-by-mail games* take longer and are more involved. Unlike interactive games, play-by mail games let people who have only e-mail access join the fun. As you may expect, play-by-mail games on the Internet aren't far removed from play-by-mail games that have taken place by snail mail for decades.

Is gaming allowed on the Internet? Sure; it's okay to use your system and the Internet to play games as long as it's not against the policies of your site. Some institutions have strict rules against that sort of thing. If you use the Internet from a school or business computer, ask the system administrators about your site's policy. Then again, "it is easier to get forgiveness than permission." (Don't tell your system administrator I said that.)

Interactive Games

For instant gratification, try playing an interactive game. Pick your poison: there are classics like chess, Go, and Reversi as well as modern diversions like Bolo.

Some games are available using Telnet, but increasingly, the World Wide Web is the interface of choice for Internet gamers. The Web, fast becoming a convenience of modern life, provides color graphics, a friendly interface, and is simply a whole lot more gamer-friendly than that dusty old Telnet program.

Once connected to a server, you can play, watch, or kibitz with other users. Depending on the game, a server may have just one or several games running simultaneously.

Board Games

The game Go (a two-player strategy board game) is available by Telnetting to one of several Go servers. The Internet Go server has been home to international tournaments as well as a haven for more casual players. Telnet to `telnet://telnet igs.nuri.net:6969` to give it a— uhm—*go*. For more information about Go and online Go games, read the Go Frequently Asked Questions (FAQ) list. It is available through FTP at `ftp://rtfm.mit.edu:/pub/usenet/news.answers/games/go-faq`.

Backgammon, another classic board game, is also available online. You can reach the First Internet Backgammon Server (FIBS) by Telnetting to `telnet://fraggel65.md-stud./chalmers.se:4321`.

Fans of Reversi (also known by the commercial name Othello) can play with players or computerized opponents by Telnetting to `telnet://faust.uni-paderborn.de:5000`. Even better, if you have a graphical Web browser, point it to `http://www.cis.ohio-state.edu/htbin/othello`. This program supports a blissfully simple, intuitive interface (see Figure 66.1). And it's fast— even at 9,600 bps. There's another Web-based Reversi game at `http://www.pt.hk-r.se:80/~roos/othello1/`—there's a Telnetable one at `telnet://faust.uni-paderborn.de:5000`.

FIGURE 66.1.

The classic board game Reversi is available on the World Wide Web.

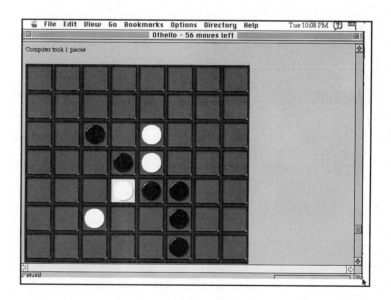

The strategy game Ataxx is available at `http://www.sun.com/events/sid/sid.html`. This game is strictly you against the computer, but it's a lot of fun anyway (see Figure 66.2).

FIGURE 66.2.

Test your skill against that of the computer in Ataxx.

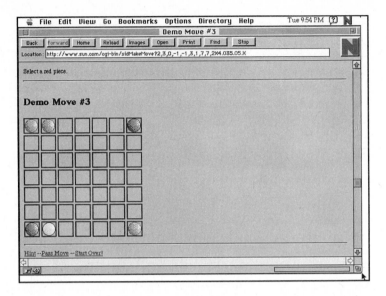

There's a mighty fine chess server at `http://www.willamette.edu/wdbin/starter.pl`. Figure 66.3 shows this version of the chess game. If you can't do the Web, don't fret—there are Telnetable chess servers at `telnet://iris4.metiu.ucsb.edu port:5000` and `telnet://coot.lcs.mit.edu:5000`. While we're on the subject, a Chinese chess server is available for anyone with access to Telnet. Just Telnet to `telnet://coolidge.harvard.edu:5555`.

FIGURE 66.3.

You can play chess with a real person instead of against a computer when you use the World Wide Web.

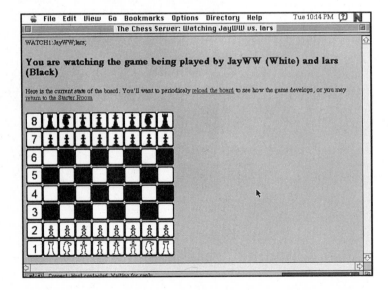

Although I promised Joseph I wouldn't talk about MUDs and MOOs in this chapter because that's his bailiwick (refer to Chapter 64, "Interactive Multiuser Realities: MUDs, MOOs, MUCKs, and MUSHes"), I will point you to WisDOOM at `telnet://next7.cas.muohio.edu:8888`. This is a MOO with plenty of games, especially word games in the style of Scrabble.

Bolo

Bolo is a real-time, graphical, networked tank battle game. Bolo has attracted a loyal following (especially among the college crowd) because it is challenging and fast paced; and (perhaps best of all) you can play against 15 of your friends (see Figure 66.4). Bolo has elements of arcade-style shoot-em-up action, but serious players have been known to engage in strategic 12-hour games, with all 16 players forming alliances, taking over land, blowing each other up, and generally having a good time.

FIGURE 66.4.

Round up 15 other players on the network and you can battle out your frustrations with tanks.

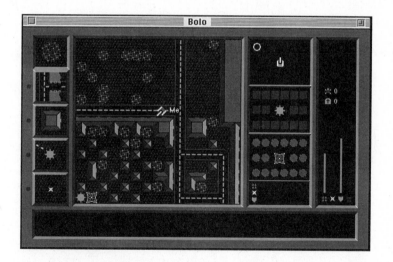

The bad news is that Bolo is only for the Macintosh (although some folks are attempting to write DOS and Windows versions). The good news is that you can play over the Internet. Bolo works best over a dedicated Internet connection. Although it will work over a SLIP or PPP connection, doing so isn't recommended because it can slow down the gameplay for everyone.

For more information, check out the Bolo FAQ (posted to `rec.games.bolo`) and the Bolo Web site `http://student_97ffa.williams.edu/bolo.html`. For real-time tank talk, there's also the IRC channel `#bolo`.

You can get Bolo from `aim.stanfrd.edu` and `mac.archive.umich.edu`. There's also a nice "Bolo Starter Kit" available (it's an archive of a variety of Bolo-related tools and resources); you can get it through FTP from `ftp://noproblem.uchicago.edu/pub/Bolo/Start_Kits/MegaWatts_Bolo_Start_Kit.hqx`.

Lite Brite and Maze

Some games are decidedly wacky. As people explore the possibilities of presenting information on the World Wide Web, the creative juices flow. Among the myriad of diversions on the Web are a maze program (in which you are given a rat's-eye view and asked to find your way out) and Lite Brite, a Webified version of the classic diversion. With it, you can create your own masterpieces and view others' works of pixelized art. Although Lite Bright requires a graphical Web browser, it is especially suited to users with slow Internet connections because of the simplistic and elegant way it sends pictures (see Figure 66.5). The maze is at `http://metnet.geog.pdx.edu/~mcnalley/game/index.html` and the game of light is at `http://www.galcit.caltech.edu/~ta/lb/lb.html`. No batteries required.

FIGURE 66.5.

Play Lite Brite on your computer and you won't have to worry about vacuuming up all the little pegs when you're done.

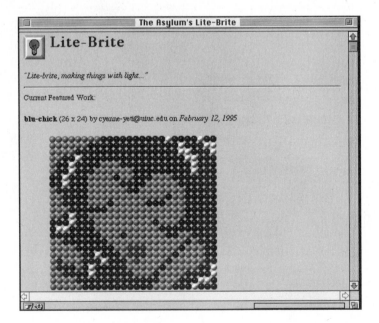

Outland

If you use a Mac and enjoy interactive gaming, forget about the hodgepodge of board games, MUDs, and other diversions on the Net: Outland is the one place to go for your gaming fix (see Figure 66.6). This service gives Mac gamers a central place to meet and play, offering a variety of parlor and card games (including classics like Chess, Reversi, and Go) as well as Galley (a naval battle simulation), and the ever-popular time-sucker, Spaceward Ho! Outland lets you play against human opponents rather than canned computerized foes. You can kibitz as you play using on-screen chat boxes.

FIGURE 66.6.

Use your Mac to take a trip to Outland for the best assortment of interactive games at a single site.

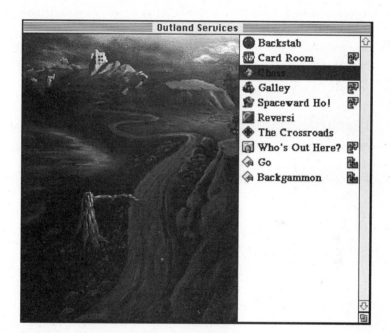

My favorite part about Outland is this: it costs $9.95 a month for unlimited use (on top of whatever you're already paying for Internet access.) It works with SLIP and PPP, but you don't even need 'em; amazingly, Outland allows anyone with access to Telnet to use its graphical games.

My only criticism of Outland is that there aren't always a whole lot of other players online. You may tire of seeing the same old faces, especially after you've beaten someone at Hearts (or have been beaten) 300 times. Outland is small but growing, so this problem should resolve itself soon enough,

For more information, Web on over to http://www.outland.com/ or send e-mail to info@outland.com.

Play-by-Mail Games

If your Net connection leaves something to be desired, don't fret—there are plenty of games to play using electronic mail.

Crossword Puzzles

If you're a crossword fanatic whose subscription to the daily paper just doesn't provide enough crosswording to fill your day, rejoice! Send e-mail to xword@acy.digex.net with the subject of send puzzle for a crossword puzzle. There's a new one daily that will arrive in your e-mailbox within moments. The crosswords are actually an elegant marketing tool; they're created by a program called Crossword Express, which (of course) the company would like you to buy. Finger xword@acy.digex.net for more information about this service, this program, and this company.

The following is a sample crossword puzzle:

```
===================================================================
       _____  _                 _____   _    _   _____   _____   _       _____
      |_   _|| |_   ___        |  __ \ | |  | | |___  /  |___  /  | |     |  ___|
        | |  | '_ \ / _ \       | |__) || |  | |    / /      / /   | |     | |__
        | |  | | | |  __/       |  ___/ | |  | |   / /      / /    | |     |  __|
        |_|  |_| |_|\___|       |_|      \__,_|  /____|   /____|   |_____| |_____|

===================================================================

                    Wednesday, 03/01/95

===================================================================
+ — + — + — + — + — + — + — + — + — + — + — + — + — + — + — +
|1   |2   |3   |4   |####|5   |6   |7   |8   |9   |####|10  |11  |12  |13  |
|    |    |    |    |####|    |    |    |    |    |####|    |    |    |    |
+ — + — + — + — + — + — + — + — + — + — + — + — + — + — + — +
|14  |    |    |    |####|15  |    |    |    |    |####|16  |    |    |    |
|    |    |    |    |####|    |    |    |    |    |####|    |    |    |    |
+ — + — + — + — + — + — + — + — + — + — + — + — + — + — + — +
|17  |    |    |    |####|18  |    |    |    |    |####|19  |    |    |    |
|    |    |    |    |####|    |    |    |    |    |####|    |    |    |    |
+ — + — + — + — + — + — + — + — + — + — + — + — + — + — + — +
|20  |    |    |    |    |    |    |####|21  |    |    |    |    |    |    |
|    |    |    |    |    |    |    |####|    |    |    |    |    |    |    |
+ — + — + — + — + — + — + — + — + — + — + — + — + — + — + — +
|####|####|####|    |####|22  |    |    |23  |    |    |####|    |####|####|####|
|####|####|####|    |####|    |    |    |    |    |    |####|    |####|####|####|
+ — + — + — + — + — + — + — + — + — + — + — + — + — + — + — +
|24  |25  |26  |    |27  |####|28  |    |    |####|29  |    |    |30  |31  |32  |
|    |    |    |    |    |####|    |    |    |####|    |    |    |    |    |    |
+ — + — + — + — + — + — + — + — + — + — + — + — + — + — + — +
|33  |    |    |    |    |34  |####|    |####|35  |    |    |    |    |    |    |
|    |    |    |    |    |    |####|    |####|    |    |    |    |    |    |    |
+ — + — + — + — + — + — + — + — + — + — + — + — + — + — + — +
```

```
+---+---+---+---+---+---+---+---+---+---+---+---+---+---+---+
|36 |   |   |####|37 |   |   |   |   |   |####|38 |   |   |   |
|   |   |   |####|   |   |   |   |   |   |####|   |   |   |   |
+---+---+---+---+---+---+---+---+---+---+---+---+---+---+---+
|39 |   |   |40 |   |   |####|   |####|41 |   |42 |   |   |   |
|   |   |   |   |   |   |####|   |####|   |   |   |   |   |   |
+---+---+---+---+---+---+---+---+---+---+---+---+---+---+---+
|43 |   |   |   |####|44 |   |45 |####|46 |   |   |   |   |   |
|   |   |   |   |####|   |   |   |####|   |   |   |   |   |   |
+---+---+---+---+---+---+---+---+---+---+---+---+---+---+---+
|####|####|####|####|47 |   |   |   |48 |####|   |####|####|####|
|####|####|####|####|   |   |   |   |   |####|   |####|####|####|
+---+---+---+---+---+---+---+---+---+---+---+---+---+---+---+
|49 |50 |51 |   |   |   |####|52 |   |   |   |53 |54 |55 |
|   |   |   |   |   |   |####|   |   |   |   |   |   |   |
+---+---+---+---+---+---+---+---+---+---+---+---+---+---+---+
|56 |   |   |####|57 |   |58 |   |   |####|59 |   |   |   |
|   |   |   |####|   |   |   |   |   |####|   |   |   |   |
+---+---+---+---+---+---+---+---+---+---+---+---+---+---+---+
|60 |   |   |####|61 |   |   |   |   |####|62 |   |   |   |
|   |   |   |####|   |   |   |   |   |####|   |   |   |   |
+---+---+---+---+---+---+---+---+---+---+---+---+---+---+---+
|63 |   |   |####|64 |   |   |   |   |####|65 |   |   |   |
|   |   |   |####|   |   |   |   |   |####|   |   |   |   |
+---+---+---+---+---+---+---+---+---+---+---+---+---+---+---+
```

Wednesday, 03/01/95

ACROSS	DOWN
1 Ship's small boat	1 Tibetan oxen
5 Genre	2 Continuous dull pain
10 Large almost tailless rodent	3 Enclose in paper
14 Land measure	4 Freckle
15 Mosquito bite	5 Quickly
16 Roman Numeral for 53	6 Filament
17 Asian prince	7 Affirmative reply
18 Angry	8 Hidden
19 Among	9 Choose
20 Divided by a septum	10 Short play
21 Molting	11 Intentions
22 Contraction of has not	12 Roman Numeral for 103
24 Wild dog of Australia	13 Helps
28 Speck	23 Gliding

29	Cults	24	Threnody
33	Mental deficiency	25	Standard of perfection
35	Slice of meat	26	Lustrous
36	Soak	27	Red earth pigment
37	Become hoarse	29	Traditional portion of Muslim law
38	Lever for rowing	30	Cuff
39	Having a specified gait	31	Crews
41	Soul	32	Wander
43	Senior	34	10th letter of the Hebrew alphabet
44	Besides	35	Brown-capped boletus mushroom
46	Restless	40	Instructor
47	Automatic pistol	42	Betrothed
49	Broken	44	Aural
52	Stronghold	45	Pour from one container to another
56	Apiece	47	Flat shelf
57	Sofa	48	Wash lightly
59	Fool	49	King mackerel
60	Hoar	50	Sudden assault
61	Profits	51	Peak
62	Greek god of love	53	Venture
63	River in central Europe	54	Ebony
64	Overjoy	55	Undergo lysis
65	Sandy tract	58	By way of

Core War

Core War is a game in which players compete to write the most vicious computer program. The programs, written in an assembly language called RedCode, run in a simulated computer; the object of the game is to cause opposing programs to terminate, leaving your program in sole possession of the machine. This is pure hacker fun...sort of like writing your own virus without the chance of going to jail.

Core War has been around for many years and is available for dozens of computer systems. Not surprisingly, you can also play Core War on the Internet against other hackers. The Internet's ongoing Core War tourney is called *King of the Hill.* Once you've written a nasty RedCode program, you can e-mail it to the King of the Hill server, which pits your program against 20 others on "the hill." E-mail replies indicate how your program fares.

Core War is only for true hackers. If the following example program doesn't frighten you, find out more about Core War and King of the Hill by getting the Core War FAQ through FTP at `rtfm.mit.edu:/pub/usenet/news.answers/games/corewar-faq`:

```
;redcode
;name Dwarf
;author A. K. Dewdney
;strategy Throw DAT bombs around memory, hitting every 4th memory cell.
```

```
bomb    DAT  #0
dwarf   ADD  #4,    bomb
        MOV  bomb, @bomb
        JMP  dwarf
        END  dwarf ; Programs start at the first line unless
                   ; an "END start" pseudo-op appears to indicate
                   ; the first logical instruction.
```

Diplomacy and Other Play-by-Mail Games

A variety of other play-by-mail games are available. Most play-by-mail games are strategy and war games, including Diplomacy.

For information on Diplomacy, send mail to judge@shrike.und.ac.za or judge@u.washington.edu with **help** in the body of the message.

For complete information on play-by-mail games (both traditional ones and Internet-based games) read the play-by-mail FAQ, available through FTP at ftp://rtfm.mit.edu:/pub/usenet/news.answers/games/play-by-mail.

What Else Is There?

But wait, there's more! Other games are available on the Internet for your pleasure. Internet services come and go daily—it's probable that several new games have popped up somewhere or that one mentioned here has disappeared.

Start by pointing your Web browser to the following address:

```
http://www.cs.cmu.edu:8001/afs/cs.cmu.edu/user/zarf/www/games.html
```

This is *Zarf's List of Interactive Games on the Web*, a magnificent catalog of hundreds of goofy things to do, from classics like Mastermind and crossword puzzle games to toys available only in cyberspace, like the Rome Lab Snowball Camera (http://www.rl.af.mil:8001/Odds-n-Ends/sbcam/rlsbcam.html) and Cindy Crawford Concentration—classic Concentration updated with pictures of Cindy Crawford, as shown in Figure 66.7 (http://cad.ucla.edu:8001/concentration). In the words of the page's creator: who better to make you lose your concentration than Cindy Crawford?

And while you've got your Web browser loaded, point it to the Games Domain at http://wcl-rs.bham.ac.uk/GamesDomain. This is a one-stop shop for gamers, including sundries such as a central collection of game FAQs, cheats and walkthroughs for your favorite adventure games, game-related FTP links, and online gaming magazines (see Figure 66.8).

FIGURE 66.7.

*Let Cindy help you lose
your Concentration.*

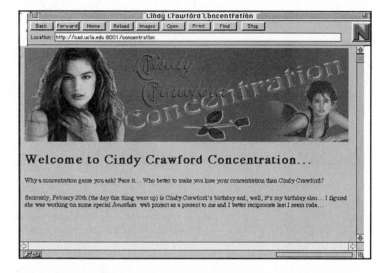

FIGURE 66.8.

*Take a trip to the Games
Domain for one-stop
gaming accessories.*

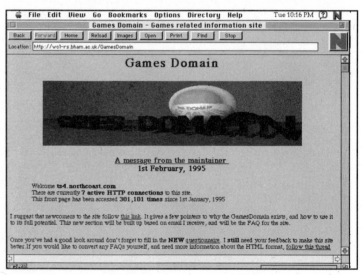

Remember, someone once said that all work and no play is a bad thing. So have fun.

Cool Web Worlds

67

by Angela Gunn

The Web stretches out on all sides of your browser, unmapped for the most part. All around you are whispers of fabulous treasures and venues: "Check out that music site with the..." and "You know the one that..." and "these incredible movies at the..." and "a whole list of..." and "you can spend hours playing the..." and "it's got the most amazing...." And here you sit, with a map that stretches exactly as far as the next screen and a compass that can't seem to find magnetic north.

There isn't one on the Web—a magnetic north, that is. (After all, magnetism isn't good for computers.) Your map of the Web's high points and landmarks won't match anyone else's. But a few friendly pointers can start you on the right path; a few great sites can take you on a trip no one has made before you.

What's your pleasure? There are two ways to set out on Web adventures. You can take the whirlwind tour and collect a bunch of great souvenir URLs to ponder later, or you can settle in and really root around a single site with a bit of style and a lot of substance. Or, as far as that goes, you can do both.

Web Tour #1: Scooping Up Goodies Left and Right

Pump up that list of bookmarks! Get out and see the (Web) world! Give yourself an excuse to log in every 24 hours! The sites on our first tour have something fresh for you nearly every day. We have frivolous sites and fabulous sites; sites that may substitute for your morning paper and sites that fill needs you never dreamed existed.

Some people can't start the day without reading the paper, and don't start reading the paper without a look at the funny pages. Take a look at the Web-only comic strip in Figure 67.1 by pointing your browser to `http://sunsite.unc.edu/Dave/drfun.html`.

David Farley designs *Dr. Fun* as a strictly-Web page; he's based in Chicago, but we just dropped by North Carolina to check the daily strip. There are other comic strips distributed over the Net; one of the most popular is *NetBoy*, a weekly Internet-only strip (`http://www.intelli.com/netboy/`).

You'd like us—reading over your shoulder—to believe that you flip to the news next, wouldn't you? If you must persist in this charade, skip the next few paragraphs. But we caught you looking at the astrology page, updated weekly at `http://bazaar.com/Megadeth/horrorscopes.com` and shown in Figure 67.2.

This electronic version of Rob Breszny's slightly surreal *Real Astrology* column runs in a number of papers nationwide. On this site, you find the current week's forecast; those using slower browsers see a duplicate all-text listing at the bottom of the page shown.

FIGURE 67.1.

The art is straightforward but the humor is twisted at Dr. Fun's page.

FIGURE 67.2.

So, what IS your sign?

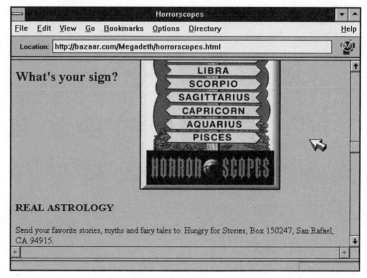

Oh, *now* you want to check the news. Let's check the daily edition of *Time*—yes, that's *Time* magazine, the well-known weekly. Everything moves faster on the World Wide Web, as we see in Figure 67.3. Point your browser to http://www.timeinc.com/pathfinder/Welcome.html.

Click any of the headlines to go directly to that story. Of course, any community of a decent size has several daily papers from which to pick (or at least they used to); the Web can take us back to those more civilized and well-informed days. For a different view, try the *San Jose Mercury News*, seen in Figure 67.4 and found at http://www.sjmercury.com/.

FIGURE 67.3.

The front page of your daily Web paper—one of them.

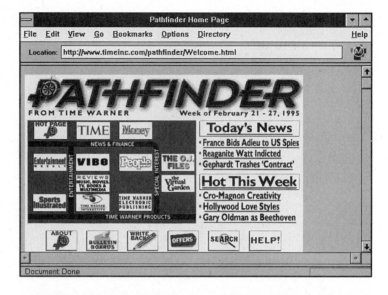

FIGURE 67.4.

The San Jose Mercury News can be your local paper anywhere in the world.

Notice that both *Pathfinder* and the *San Jose* paper have links on their screen today about the magnificent cave paintings discovered recently in southern France. However, the *Pathfinder* link goes to a story from *Time*'s art critic Robert Hughes, while the *San Jose* link connects you to a profusely illustrated essay sponsored by the French government (and available in French and English at http://www.culture.fr/gvpda-en.html). Lions and panthers and bears and ibexes and megaloceroses, oh my!

Because I'm reading over your shoulder and tend to get impatient easily, you flip to the Internet daily news to keep me happy. Let's drop by Mecklerweb for my daily dose of geekspeak (see Figure 67.5), available at `http://www.mecklerweb.com/mags/iw/news/newsmenu.html`.

FIGURE 67.5.

All the news that's fit to IP.

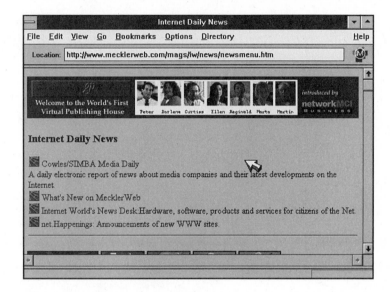

Note the ad for MCI's Gramercy Press Publishing house at the top. Web advertising is becoming more common on the larger sites. Resist (if you can) the urge to point the Web browser to `http://www.mci.com/gramercy/`—how will we get anything done if you're sidetracked by the continuing saga of the world's first virtual publishing house?

Really, we must move along. If you want to add a new wrinkle to your brain in one quick click, the Cool Word/Phrase of the Day is the site most likely to do that painlessly and efficiently, bringing a smile to your face and fear to the heart of the next person you talk to. See it in Figure 67.6 and give it a whirl at `http://www.dsu.edu/projects/word_of_day/word.html`.

A lot of people keep a quote-of-the-day calendar on their desks. If one quote isn't enough for you, the Quotes of the Day site will pop out several for your amusement. Point your browser to `http://www.xmission.com:80/~mgm/quotes/qotd.html`. As you see in Figure 67.7, it's not much to look at, but it serves up several fresh quotes at a time.

FIGURE 67.6.

*Here it is! It means
"descended from a common
ancestor"—what most of us
would refer to as "related."*

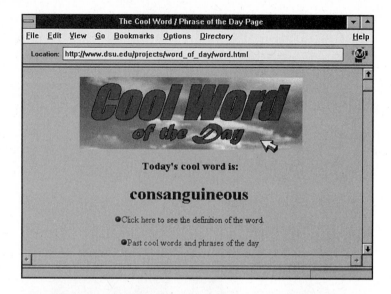

FIGURE 67.7.

*Woody Allen ponders the
ineffable on today's quote
page.*

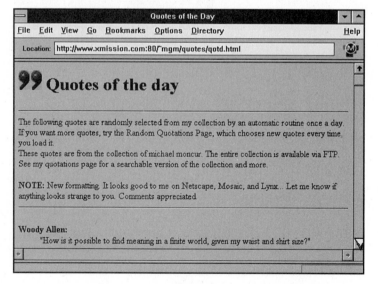

You're only stalling if you go up to web-weaver Michael Moncur's home page and over to his
Virtual Keyboard at `http://www.xmission.com:80/~mgm/misc/keyboard.html`. Sure, if you click
a key it plays a little `.au`-format sound file of the proper note, but don't you have better things
to do? This page actually made Paul Phillips' *Useless WWW Pages* list at `http://www.primus.com/
staff/paulp/useless.html`, a fact of which Michael is quite proud.

We'll conclude this whirlwind tour by heading off on an entirely new tangent. Scattered about the Web are several sites designed to set you on such a tangent, catapulting you to someplace new every day. There are a number of good random-URL dispensers: one click on the proper button at the Yahoo Web searcher (`www.yahoo.com`) or the URouLette Wheel (`http://kuhttp.cc.ukans.edu/cwis/organizations/kucia/uroulette/uroulette.html`) and you're hurtling off heaven knows where. But for a cooler experience, it's time to point your Web browser to the page shown in Figure 67.8, at `http://www.infi.net/cool.html`.

FIGURE 67.8.

Feel the refreshment at the Cool Site of the Day.

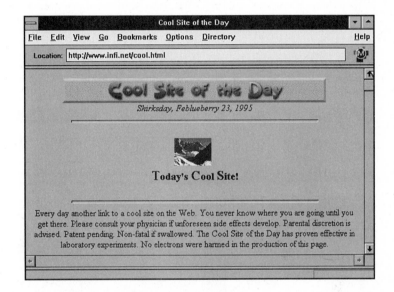

Every day, the kind folks at the Cool Site page sift through their notes and find a brand-new URL to hide behind that innocuous-looking link in the middle of the screen. Click, and *boom!* You're sailing away to parts unknown. It's a mighty Web that can generate at least one cool site each day; aren't you glad you're checking in regularly?

Web Tour #2: If You Liked It Any Better Here, You'd Move In

Some sites, on the other hand, ought to be savored, mulled over, returned to as a regular pilgrimage. Some sites are so good that they exist as more than a collection of URLs; they are *places*, existing perhaps only as a shared hallucination (but plenty real even that way). Such sites on the Web are as rare as such places off the Web.

A really good Web site—a *really* good Web site—has something akin to a personality, which is, of course, the sensibility of the Web designer shining through. This is not an accident. A great Web site may contain entire sections of bizarre information and its links may span the globe, but the designer bringing those topics and links together uses discretion and care when presenting them to you. A *great* Web site reads well. A great Web site pleases the eye. And a great Web site *works*; if it's not well taken care of and its links and pages are not maintained, it may be a great ruin of a site but it is not a great site. (And unlike archaeological ruins in the everyday world, there's nothing interesting or mysterious about an abandoned, decaying Web site.)

That said, shall we look at a great Web site? Point your Web browser to `http://www.glasswings.com.au/GlassWings/welcome.html`—and the Glass Wings home page shown in Figure 67.9.

FIGURE 67.9.

The opening screen at Glass Wings.

This Australian site is possessed of what can only be called —sorry—a sparkling personality. It uses a unifying metaphor of a journey through a semi-mystical land full of friendly inhabitants: you'll travel by teleporter, horse-drawn carriage, subway, flying armchair, and other curious conveyances courtesy of the fertile minds of Katherine Phelps and Andrew Pam.

The main page continues as shown in Figures 67.10 and 67.11. Figure 67.10 shows a continuation of the main-page list; Figure 67.11 shows the colorful image map also available for navigation. Unlike some sites, Glass Wings is thoughtful about using smallish image maps and placing them on the page so that those using text browsers can still make sense of what's offered.

FIGURE 67.10.

Sections in Glass Wings are listed and described briefly.

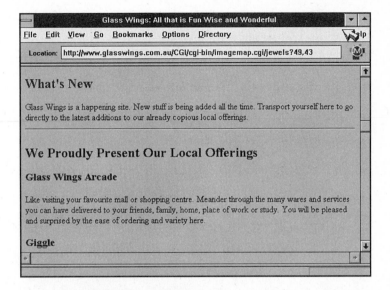

FIGURE 67.11.

A colorful image map (check it out if you don't believe me) guides users to the most popular areas of the service.

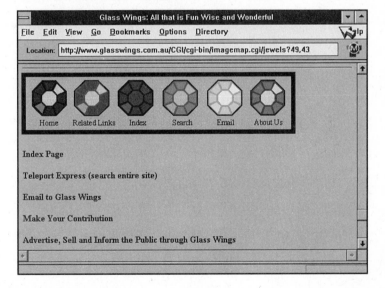

Let's glance briefly through the sections offered for our amusement. In your own explorations, you'll find that Glass Wings has marvelous depth; unexpected surprises are waiting around almost every corner. All areas of the site are well kempt, and very few items are included without explanation. This is a nice feature, geared toward providing Net surfers with a bit of information about what's behind each link before they go spinning into odd corners of the Web.

Glass Wings is a commercial site; the Arcade section lists businesses with advertisements on the Glass Wings system. The page text nicely presents the sites as part of a narrative (a walk though a bustling street bazaar); click a link to see an individual ad (which doesn't necessarily fit the theme of the page). See Figure 67.12; the narrative gives the ad a prominent spot on the site without calling undue attention to its "ad-ness."

FIGURE 67.12.

An ad from the Arcade *section.*

The site has several mini-publications of its own. Its humor 'zine, *Giggle*, takes reader submissions (over e-mail, of course). By and large, the humor and stories are gentle and suitable for all ages. Less so are the entries in *Sensual Celebrations*, another 'zine for the adult Glass Wings reader. The first screen is shown in Figure 67.13.

Presentation of explicit material is an ongoing issue on the Web. Until recently, it was understood that most Internet users were of an age to view whatever materials were allowed by the laws of their country; however, it's now understood that the population of the Web (not to mention the laws affecting it) are in rapid flux. Glass Wings offers a good compromise between providing mature materials for mature readers and not making them the focus of the site.

Further down is a computer-gaming 'zine and *Modern Adventure*, both exclusive to Glass Wings; *Utopia Now*, which has links and information on various progressive causes; the *Armchair Travel Service*, which contains everything from a beautiful lighthouse tour to instructions on how to refold a map (!!!); a recipe page with many sugar-fest concoctions; and the full electronic version of Bruce Sterling's classic *The Hacker Crackdown: Law and Disorder on the Electronic Frontier*. (Although Mr. Sterling retains rights to the book, published in 1992, he makes it freely available electronically.)

FIGURE 67.13.

There's nothing to wince at on the first screen—more sexually direct offerings are a level further down.

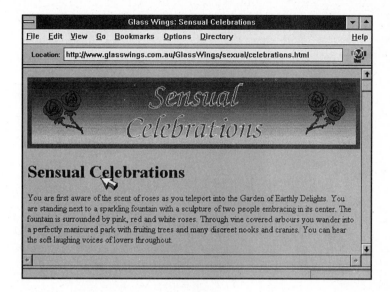

Each of the topic areas offers a page of selected *teleports* (links reaching off-site and around the world). See Figure 67.14. Because the main page is arranged by topic areas, this means that links to (for example) pages concerned with the environment and spirituality are always found on the third level of the site—under the link to the local pages on the environment and spirituality. (Glass Wings has a pronounced "New Age" feel in certain areas.) Local links are on the second level; the main page is, of course, on the first. The structure of Glass Wings is never pointed out explicitly, but because it's consistently organized, it's easy to surf the site, feeling reassured that you'll never wander too far astray (accidentally at least).

Links to the outside are collected in the `Teleports of Call` section, seen in Figure 67.14. All the off-site links are relisted here under their respective headings; also, links to news, health information, entertainment, and a wonderful page of museums and exhibits (`Wings to Discovery`) are here. The items in the `Wings to Discovery` section are particularly well chosen; there's a good mix of well-known sites (such as the Expo Ticket Site at `http://sunsite.unc.edu/expo/ticket_office.html`, with links to the Vatican, the Dead Sea Scrolls, and other cultural wonders) and things you might otherwise have missed (such as the Smithsonian Gem and Mineral Collection, on the Web at `http://galaxy.einet.net/images/gems/gems-icons.html` and shown in Figure 67.15).

Glass Wings fine-tunes itself by including fewer outside links than other Web sites of its ilk. The links that *are* included are well-matched to the editorial content of the site (and they are well documented when they do occur). The areas that accept reader input—*Modern Adventure, Sensual Celebrations, Utopia Now*—have definite guidelines for submissions. Glass Wings differs from a "traditional" commercial site by offering a great amount of information that's not at all related to the site's business; on the other hand, it's more structured than many of the "personal" Web pages that exist mainly for the amusement of the creators and whoever drops by.

FIGURE 67.14.

The Glass Wings teleport can send you anywhere in the world.

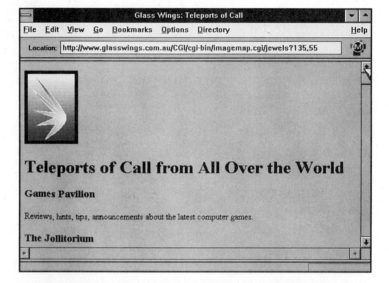

FIGURE 67.15.

Better than the windows at Tiffany's: pretty sparkly things made by humankind and nature.

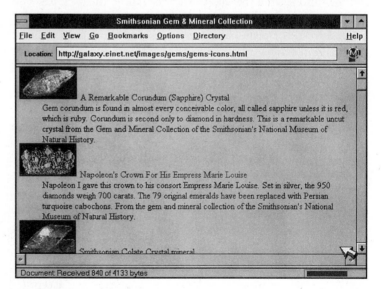

Be Your Own Tour Guide

It's good to check out other sites of this caliber to see how various wizards of Web design have envisioned the browsing experience. The following selected sites are equally worthy of your time; each has its own unique sensibility and each, large or small, can give you hours of contented Web cruising.

Site	Address
Addicted to Noise	`http://www.addict.com/ATN/`
bianca's Smut Shack	`http://www.bianca.com/`
Internet Underground Music Archives (IUMA)	`http://www.iuma.com/`
The SUNsite at the University of North Carolina	`http://sunsite.unc.edu/`
TeleCircus	`http://www.well.com/www/` `tcircus/index.html`
UC-Berkeley Museum of Paleontology	`http://ucmp1.berkeley.edu/` `server.html`

Online Art Galleries

68

by Angela Gunn

Art and technology historically go 'round and 'round—for every scientifically curious Renaissance, there is a Romantic era in which science and new technology are considered "anti-art." Current artistic interest in the Internet may not signal a new Renaissance, but it does mean that artists are building new ways of bringing their work to the masses and to each other—and they are, increasingly, creating entirely new varieties of art.

The arts information you find online is of roughly four types:

- Exhibits, in which several works are presented for viewing or downloading (often with commentary or other text)
- Web pages and other information about museums and other non-Internet exhibits that make the pages exhibits *about* exhibits
- Internet-specific and Internet-based pieces of art, which treat the Net as the medium for both creation and dissemination
- A great deal of commentary and discussion in arts-oriented mailing lists, newsgroups, and e-zines

The types of art available include every variety of visual arts (the focus of this chapter) as well as architecture, music, dance, theater, and creative writing.

Arts exhibits on the Internet are the online equivalent of walking through a museum, a sculpture garden, or an artist's workshop. It's no surprise that many of the most popular exhibits are presented on Web pages; the ability to easily show images and video has been perhaps the most important aspect of bringing arts to the Internet and vice versa. An *online exhibit* is generally a collection of images of art that exists in the "real world" (that is, that exist somewhere other than on a computer). The exhibits are often (although not always) accompanied by commentary and pointers to other online resources.

ArtAIDS and Fluxus

ArtAIDS (`http://artaids.dcs.qmw.ac.uk:8001/` or `ftp://artaids.dcs.qmw.ac.uk`) and Fluxus (`http://www.panix.com/fluxus/`) are two collections currently online. The former is sponsored by the Arts Council of England and the University of London and presented as an artistic response to the modern-day plague; the latter is an exhibit and exploration of the work of the Fluxists, a mid-century art movement.

The ArtAIDS site, the top of which is shown in Figure 68.1, includes an element of participation by the Net at large. If you have artwork you want to contribute, you can do so through the Internet or through more traditional means. The gallery began with original works from twenty digital artists; by choosing one of the thumbnail images, you can get more information and download the image itself. Additional images are added to the various galleries, which are curated by guest artists. So far, the exhibited images are marvelous—a compelling response to what one arts critic has called "the story of our time."

FIGURE 68.1.

The top of the remarkable ArtAIDS site.

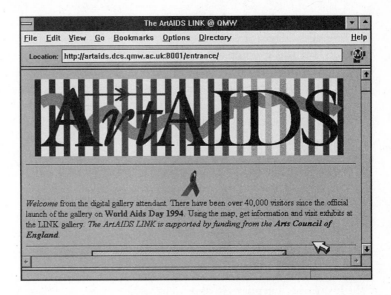

The Fluxus site covers a movement that has already created most of its art; the large (and ever so brightly colored) imagemap shown in Figure 68.2 is based on an artwork by George Marciunas. The Fluxus site includes works by a number of artists prominent in the Flux movement, with an absolute minimum of commentary; navigation is through this semi-inscrutable imagemap or through an only slightly less inscrutable text menu. Definitely in accord with the post-Dada spirit of the movement itself, this exhibit as presented couldn't exist in our real-life, space-time dimension, let alone in your average museum.

FIGURE 68.2.

The Fluxus imagemap will take you places; it just won't tell you where first.

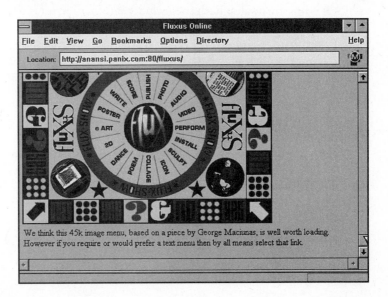

Both these exhibits present works that have an existence outside the Internet, but they rely on the Internet to display the collection of works that make them up. The Enlightenment exhibit created by the French Ministry of Culture (`http://dmf.culture.fr/files/imaginary_exhibition.html`) is another good example of this. The URL sums it up: this exhibition, although it consists entirely of art that has existed for centuries, doesn't actually exist anywhere in the world. The hundred paintings included hang in eighteen museums scattered across France. You can't stroll from work to work; you can only click.

Real-World Museums in Cyberspace

Museums and other non-Internet institutions, on the other hand, already exist quite comfortably without the Internet. Museums have made uneven progress in bringing themselves online—certain world-class organizations such as the Louvre have been remarkably benighted when approached by people interested in making their works available over the Internet (they are, however, coming around).

The Institute of Egyptian Art and Archaeology (`http://www.memst.edu/egypt/main.html`) and the UIUC Krannert Art Museum (`http://www.ncsa.uiuc.edu/General/UIUC/KrannertArtMuseum/KrannertArtHome.html`) are two prominent museums currently available on the Web. The former is part of the University of Memphis in Tennessee; the other is located at the University of Illinois at Urbana-Champaign.

Both sites focus on the museums themselves, including just a portion of the works you'd see if you made the trip to Tennessee or Illinois. In this way, they differ from the exhibits—when you view a museum site, you're aware that you're looking at not only art but the institution in which it currently resides. Each site includes information on reaching the actual museum, on other exhibits that are planned or showing, and on the collection as a whole. (Some museum sites try very hard to replicate the physical experience of museum-going; the Krannert site isn't the only museum that includes a loving description of its cafeteria.) Additionally, most museum sites include the kinds of background material and auxiliary information you find in a regular museum or in a Web exhibition like those just described.

The Memphis pages have a short tour of various sites in Egypt, the beginning of which is shown in Figure 68.3. The GIF images can be expanded separately (a kind gesture to modem users!); the commentary briefly describes what you're seeing and puts it in the context of the art in the exhibit. It's very much like the sort of photo exhibit you find in a standard museum as you approach a display of artifacts from an unfamiliar culture.

FIGURE 68.3.

See the pyramids along the Nile at the University of Memphis's tour of Egypt.

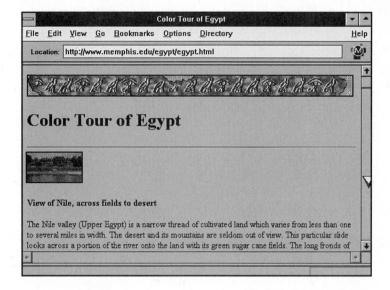

The exhibit itself, the beginning of which is shown in Figure 68.4, is fairly short. You see just five of the central objects in the museum's exhibition (out of over 150 pieces). Still, the commentary is good, and the page includes several views of the larger works. The pieces selected give a nice overview of what's in the museum's exhibit and provide a bit of context for the collection—the story of how Nedjem's artifacts came to be in America is itself a nifty historical tale. Overall, it's a small site but nicely executed and attractively presented.

FIGURE 68.4.

The exhibit gives multiple views of statuary, in lieu of being able to walk around it in person.

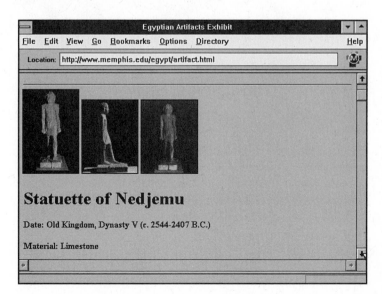

The Krannert museum, existing as it does in the cradle of Mosaic, is much more extensive. It really does include sample menus from the cafe (although, inexplicably, nothing at all from the bookstore). More seriously, it has a sampler of the museum's permanent collection, information on upcoming exhibits and special events, and a guide to the resources available for teachers and students in the area. There's even access to maps of the museum and the campus.

Again, the Krannert site is an adjunct to the physical museum. The various collections are each represented by a main Web page (as shown in Figure 68.5), which has a few sub-pages with information on individual artworks. Buttons at the bottom of each page let you move between the collections quickly. The commentary on these pages isn't as expansive as that in the Memphis site; there's a greater emphasis on art history and less on the art's other contexts. Like the Memphis page, the Krannert pages are modem friendly by providing thumbnail views that can be expanded into detailed photos as desired. (The Memphis site's multiple views of large pieces of sculpture is a lovely idea that the Krannert might consider adopting.)

FIGURE 68.5.

Glance over the list of gallery contents and then click a word or an image to delve further.

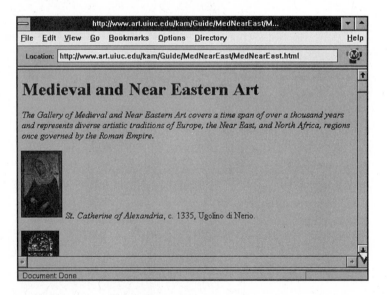

The portion of the museum devoted to outreach has links to the Education Resource Center and to a joint project between UIUC and the Cicognara Library at the Vatican. The Krannert site also has information on a major exhibit planned for 1997, in which the Krannert is working with a guest curator and several American and Japanese outfits to incorporate print, CD-ROM, and the Internet in the presentation of an exhibit of posters.

Art Exclusively for the Internet

A growing number of artists are already experimenting with the structures and advantages of the Internet: working with faraway collaborators, replicating and manipulating a piece over time while keeping it available in its original form, using hyperlinks and the multimedia abilities of the Web. The art they're creating is related to the Web in the same way that the Mona Lisa is related to canvas and paints: made within the format and strictures of the medium, the best works express something that glorifies the tools used.

Two of the more interesting Internet-specific works are Joseph Squier's *the place* (`http://gertrude.art.uiuc.edu/ludgate/the/place.html`) and the various projects that make up OTIS (`http://sunsite.unc.edu/otis/`). *the place* is a mainly visual exhibit with lots of use of the graphical and hypertext capabilities of the Web; OTIS encompasses a number of arts projects, most of which take great advantage of the abilities of the Net to bring together artists around the world.

the place incorporates several of Squier's works. *Urban Diary*, a portion of which is shown in Figure 68.6, is a dense and complex web of fragments of thought, image, and language. *Urban Diary* is composed primarily of images and pieces of art (mainly found art), doodles, and various pages that could have come from the diary or notebook of some anonymous citydweller. The images are extensively linked to other images, phrases, and reiterations of portions of the main pages. You find yourself clicking relentlessly, trying to discover more about the person whose journal you have apparently run across. Without the Web, this work couldn't exist in this form. *Urban Diary* plays on our curiosity about strangers and our fascination with artifacts and random debris from the lives of others; its themes are desire, power, and art.

FIGURE 68.6.

Part of the first page of the Urban Diary work.

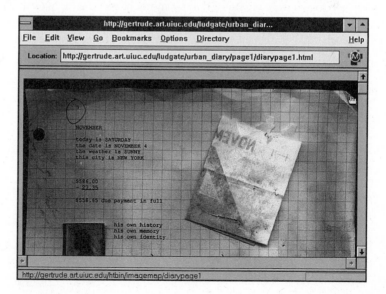

The projects of OTIS, on the other hand, vary widely in theme and intent. The hallmark of many of OTIS's projects (particularly those in the Synergy section) is their basis in collaboration and group creation. As the banner in Figure 68.7 says, the operative term here is *stimulate*. There's even a "what is art?" graffiti page for the philosophically minded.

FIGURE 68.7.

The OTIS main page is a simple beginning to a large and sprawling site.

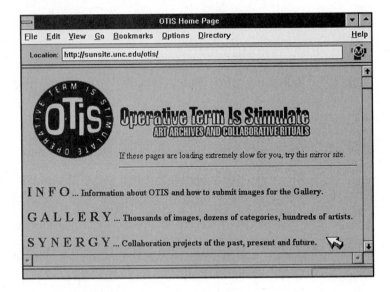

The Grid Gallery contains the results of several of the OTISts' collaborations. The idea behind the grids is that an artist with even a basic understanding of how to get around on the Net can download an image file submitted by another artist, manipulate and change it at will, and then upload it for the next creative soul. The rules for creating the various grid forms were loosely set forth to all comers; evolution of the technique is permitted and discussion of the whole shebang is encouraged.

Artistic Discussion Online

Commentary and discussion are important as Internet artists work to build communities while the Internet balloons around them. Let's finish by looking at one of the Internet's most important clearinghouses for arts information.

FineArt Forum (`http://www.msstate.edu/Fineart_Online/home.html`) is an Internet-based news service covering art and technology. It's available to both simple and sophisticated Internet connections as a monthly e-mail digest, a set of files available through FTP, a Gopher-based database, and a large Web site.

Figure 68.8 shows the main Web page for *FineArt Forum*. (It's ironic that a major nexus for the arts is itself a relatively plain page, isn't it?) The journal, which provides news, views, and announcements of current arts events online, is in the process of converting to HTML (hypermedia). The Gallery is actually a listing of links to several interesting current shows.

FIGURE 68.8.

The top of the FineArt Forum.

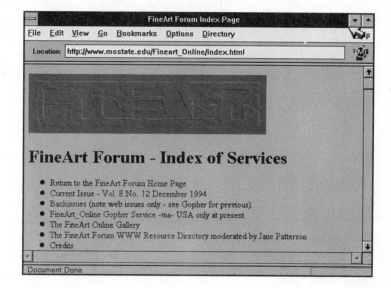

The *FineArt Forum* WWW Resource Directory, maintained by Jane Elizabeth Patterson, is an important resource for further explorations in the arts online. Patterson accumulates and sorts arts-related links of all kinds into various categories. Additionally, the list acts as a clearing-house for information on current projects, conferences, festivals, and other items of interest for the working artist.

For Further Internautting

Other excellent online exhibits include the following:

- Through Lover's Eyes (http://www.potsdam.edu/art_expo/titlpage.html), by Linda Strauss

- The strange and lovely MKZDK collection (http://www.mkzdk.org/)

- ArtHole (http://www.mcs.net/~wallach/arthole.html), which has a collaborative Net project in addition to Harlan Wallach's wonderful exhibition of his pinhole-camera photos, a portion of which is shown in Figure 68.9

- The well selected Frida Kahlo home page (http://www.cascade.net/kahlo.html; art available through FTP at ftp.cascade.net)

FIGURE 68.9.

Photos and narrative from ArtHole.

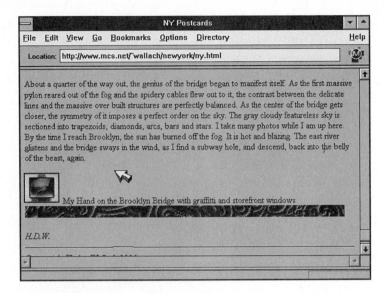

- The knockout Art Crimes (`http://www.gatech.edu/desoto/graf/Index.Art_Crimes.html`), which presents images of graffiti art (most of which has, of course, been obliterated by the time you see it online) from around the world

A few of the many museums worth touring on the Internet are listed here:

- Pixel Pushers (`http://www.wimsey.bc.ca/Pixel_Pushers/`), shown in Figure 68.10, which is designed explicitly as an Internet-aware space

FIGURE 68.10.

Pixel Pushers' main page is whimsical.

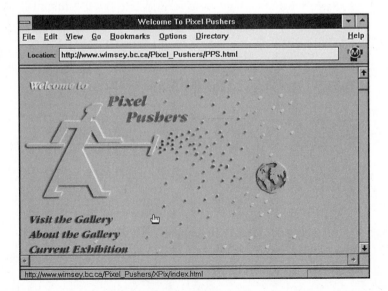

- ArtMetal (`http://wuarchive.wustl.edu/edu/arts/metal/ArtMetal.html` or through FTP at `wuarchive.wustl.edu` in the directory `edu/arts/metal`), which brings metalsmiths and sculptors to the Net

- The Academy of Media Arts in Cologne (`http://www.khm.uni-koeln.de/`), which shows both traditional and Net-based works

- The Anecdote (`http://anecdote.com`), which proves that the underground is alive and well in Ann Arbor, MI

Following are several Internet-specific works:

- HypArt (`http://rzsun01.rrz.uni-hamburg.de/cgi-bin/HypArt.sh`), a collaborative area

- Beauty For Ashes (`http://neuromancer.ucr.edu/beauty/`), a hypertext piece (a portion of which is shown in Figure 68.11)

FIGURE 68.11.

The Beauty for Ashes main page; the image is also a map for navigation.

- The not entirely serious but still interesting Lite Brite Gallery (`http://www.galcit.caltech.edu/~ta/lb/lb.html`), modeled after that famous toy

- Core (`http://arts.ucsc.edu/Core/core.html`), a better-than-average collection of computer-generated art

- The multimedia WAXWeb (`http://bug.village.virginia.edu`)

To receive *FineArt Forum* through e-mail, send a message to `fast@garnet.berkeley.edu`, omitting the subject line and putting the following in the body of the message:

```
SUBSCRIBE FineArt yourname yourstreetaddress yourtelephone yourfax your e-mail
```

The FTP archive is accessible with anonymous FTP at `ra.msstate.edu` in the directory `/pub/archives/fineart_online`. If you prefer the Gopher site, that's at `gopher.msstate.edu/11/Online_services/fineart_online/` (that has a number of good links to other important places).

Other significant sources for arts (and discussion thereof) on the Net include the list of links at OTIS (`http://sunsite.unc.edu/otis/art-links.html`); Canada's ANIMA (`http://www.wimsey.bc.ca/anima/ANIMAhome.html`); the Public Domain site (`http://noel.pd.org/`), which includes the multimedia journal *Perforations*; and ArtNetWeb, an NYC-based spot for discussing, showing, and promoting art online (`http://www.awa.com/artnet/artnetweb/`).

PART

Appendixes

Internet
Access Providers

A

This appendix lists companies and organizations that provide dial-up Internet accounts for individuals and organizations. The list includes providers in the United States, Canada, and other countries.

If you already are connected to the Internet but are searching for alternatives, check online at `ftp://nis.nsf.net/internet/providers/` or `http://www.internic.net/internic/provider.html`. The National Science Foundataion (NSF) and InterNIC maintain lists of providers and update them frequently. Note, however, that Web addresses are subject to change, so it's possible that either or both of these addresses may have changed by the time you read this. If you're not already connected, other good sources are your local newspaper and yellow pages.

For more information on different types of Internet access and what to look for in a provider, see Chapter 7, "Finding Access as a User," and Chapter 8, "Finding Access as an Organization."

Geographical and Area-Code Summary of Providers in the United States and Canada

This section presents North American Internet provider names grouped by the state or province serviced by the provider, by area code, and then alphabetically by provider name. Details and contact information for each provider follow in the next section. The first (and largest) portion of this list presents providers that supply standard access. At the end of this list are the providers that supply packet/network or toll-free access.

Standard Access

Alabama—205
InterQuest Inc.
Nuance Network Service
Planet Access Networks

Alaska—907
Internet Alaska

Alberta—403
Alberta SuperNet Inc.
CCI Networks

Arizona—602
ACES Research
CRL Network Services
Evergreen Internet
Internet Direct, Inc.
Internet Express
Network 99, Inc.
New Mexico Technet, Inc.
Primenet

Arkansas—501
Sibylline, Inc.

British Columbia—604

Cyberstore Systems Inc.
DataFlux Systems Limited
Wimsey Information Services

California—209

Sacremento Network Access
West Coast Online

California—213

CRL Network Services
CSUnet (California State University)
DHM Information Management, Inc.
DigiLink Network Services
Earthlink Network, Inc.
KAIWAN Corporation
Primenet

California—310

CERFnet
CRL Network Services
CSUnet (California State University)
DHM Information Management, Inc.
DigiLink Network Services
Earthlink Network, Inc.
KAIWAN Corporation
Lightside, Inc.
Netcom On-Line Communication Services

California—408

Aimnet Information Services
Best Internet Communications, Inc.
 (BEST)
CSUnet (California State University)
ElectriCiti Incorporated
Internet Connection
InterNex Information Services, Inc.
Netcom On-Line Communication Services
Portal Communications Company
Scruz-Net

South Valley Internet
West Coast Online
zNET

California—415

Aimnet Information Services
APlatform
Best Internet Communications, Inc.
 (BEST)
CERFnet
CRL Network Services
CSUnet (California State University)
ElectriCiti Incorporated
Institute for Global Communications
 (IGC)
InterNex Information Services, Inc.
LineX Communcations
Netcom On-Line Communication Services
QuakeNet
Scruz-Net
The WELL
West Coast Online

California—510

Access InfoSystems
Aimnet Information Services
Best Internet Communications, Inc.
 (BEST)
CCnet Communications
CERFnet
Community ConneXion
CRL Network Services
CSUnet (California State University)
ElectriCiti Incorporated
HoloNet
InterNex Information Services, Inc.
Netcom On-Line Communication Services
Sacramento Network Access, Inc.
West Coast Online

California—619

CERFnet
CSUnet (California State University)
CTS Network Services (CTSNet)
ElectriCiti Incorporated
ESNET Communications
Netcom On-Line Communication Services
Network Link, Inc.

California—707

Access InfoSystems
CRL Network Services
CSUnet (California State University)
Northcoast Internet
Pacific Internet
West Coast Online

California—714

CERFnet
CSUnet (California State University)
DHM Information Management, Inc.
DigiLink Network Services
Digital Express Group (Digex)
KAIWAN Corporation
Lightside, Inc.
Netcom On-Line Communication Services
Network Intensive

California—805

Dataware Network Services
KAIWAN Corporation

California—818

CERFnet
CSUnet (California State University)
DHM Information Management, Inc.
DigiLink Network Services
Earthlink Network, Inc.
KAIWAN Corporation
Lightside, Inc.

Netcom On-Line Communication Services
Primenet

California—909

CSUnet (California State University)
Digital Express Group (Digex)
KAIWAN Corporation
Lightside, Inc.

California—916

CSUnet (California State University)
Netcom On-Line Communication Services
Sacramento Network Access, Inc.
Sierra-Net
West Coast Online

Colorado—303

CNS
Colorado Internet Cooperative Association
Colorado SuperNet
DASH—Denver Area Super Highway
Internet Express
Netcom On-Line Communication Services
New Mexico Technet, Inc.
Nyx
Rocky Mountain Internet, Inc.

Colorado—719

CNS
Colorado SuperNet
Internet Express
Old Colorado City Communications
Rocky Mountain Internet, Inc.

Connecticut—203

Connix: The Connecticut Internet
 Exchange
I-2000
New York Net
PCNet
The Dorsai Embassy

Delaware—302
SSNet, Inc.

District of Columbia—202
CAPCON LibrARY Network
Capitol Area Internet Service (CAIS)
ClarkNet (Clark Internet Services, Inc.)
NovaNet, Inc.
US Net, Inc.

Florida—305
Acquired Knowledge Systems, Inc.
CyberGate
Florida Online
Gateway to the World, Inc.
IDS World Network
SatelNET Communications

Florida—407
Florida Online
IDS World Network

Florida—813
CENTURION Technology, Inc.
Florida Online
PacketWorks, Inc.

Florida—904
Florida Online
SymNet

Georgia—404
CRL Network Services
Internet Atlanta
MindSpring Enterprises, Inc.
Netcom On-Line Communication Services
Ping

Georgia—706
Mind Spring Enterprises, Inc.

Hawaii—808
Hawaii OnLine

Idaho—208
WLN

Illinois—217
FGInet, Inc.

Illinois—312
American Information Systems, Inc. (AIS)
InterAccess Co.
MCSNet
Netcom On-Line Communication Services
Ripco Communcations, Inc.
Tezcatlipoca, Inc.
WorldWide Access

Illinois—708
American Information Systems, Inc. (AIS)
CICNet
InterAccess Co.
MCSNet
Ripco Communcations, Inc.
Tezcatlipoca, Inc.
WorldWide Access
XNet Information Systems

Illinois—815
American Information Systems, Inc. (AIS)
InterAccess Co.
MCSNet
WorldWide Access

Indiana—317
IQuest Network Services
Network Link, Inc.

Indiana—812
IgLou Internet Services

Michigan—616

ICNet/Innovative Concepts
MichNet
Msen, Inc.

Michigan—810

ICNet/Innovative Concepts
Innovative Data (ID-Net)
MichNet
Msen, Inc.
Rabbit Network, Inc.

Michigan—906

ICNet/Innovative Concepts
MichNet
Msen, Inc.

Minnesota—218

Minnesota Regional Network (MRNET)
Red River Net

Minnesota—507

Millenium Communications
Minnesota Regional Network (MRNet)

Minnesota—612

Cloudnet
Millenium Communications
Minnesota MicroNet
Minnesota Regional Network (MRNet)
StarNet Communications, Inc. (Winternet)

Missouri—314

Neosoft, Inc.

Missouri—816

SkyNET Corp.
Tyrell Corp.

Montana—406

WLN

Nebraska—402

INS Info Services
Internet Nebraska Corp.

Nevada—702

Evergreen Internet
Great Basin Internet Services
Network 99, Inc.
Sacramento Network Access, Inc.
Sierra-Net

New Hampshire—603

MV Communications, Inc.

New Jersey—201

Internet Online Services
Neighborhood Internet Connection
New York Net
Planet Access Networks
The Dorsai Embassy
Zone One Network Exchange (ZONE)

New Jersey—609

Digital Express Group (Digex)
New Jersey Computer Connection
New York Net

New Jersey—908

Digital Express Group (Digex)
I-2000
New York Net
Planet Access Networks
Zone One Network Exchange (ZONE)

New Mexico—505

Internet Express
New Mexico Technet, Inc.

New York—212

Blythe Systems
Creative Data Consultants
CRL Network Services
ECHO
Escape (Kazan Corp)
Ingress Communications, Inc.
Internet Online Services
Interport Communications Corp
Maestro Technologies, Inc.
Netcom On-Line Communication Services
Network 23, Inc.
New York Net
NYSERNet
Panix
Phantom Access Technologies, Inc.
Pipeline Network
The Dorsai Embassy
Zone One Network Exchange (ZONE)

New York—315

NYSERNet

New York—516

Creative Data Consultants
I-2000
LI Net, Inc.
Long Island Information, Inc.
Maestro Technologies, Inc.
Network Internet Services
New York Net
NYSERNet
Panix
Phantom Access Technologies, Inc.
The Dorsai Embassy
Zone One Network Exchange (ZONE)

New York—518

Internet Online Services
NYSERNet
Wizvax Communications

New York—607

NYSERNet

New York—716

NYSERNet

New York—718

Blythe Systems
Creative Data Consultants
ECHO
Escape (Kazan Corp)
I-2000
Ingress Communications, Inc.
Interport Communications Corp.
Maestro Technologies, Inc.
New York Net
NYSERNet
Phantom Access Technologies, Inc.
The Dorsai Embassy
Zone One Network Exchange (ZONE)

New York—914

Cloud 9 Internet
I-2000
New York Net
NYSERNet
Phantom Access Technologies, Inc.
The Dorsai Embassy
TZ-Link
WestNet
Zone One Network Exchange (ZONE)

New York—917

Network 23, Inc.
New York Net
Zone One Network Exchange (ZONE)

North Carolina—704

FXnet
Interpath
Northcoast Internet
VNet Internet Access, Inc.

North Carolina—910

Interpath

North Carolina—919

Interpath

North Dakota—701

Red River Net

Ohio—216

APK Public Access UNI*
Exchange Network Services, Inc.

Ohio—513

EriNet Online Communications
Freelance Systems Programming
IgLou Internet Services

Ohio—614

OARNet

Oklahoma—405

GSS Internet

Oklahoma—918

GSS Internet
South Coast Computing Services, Inc.

Ontario—416

UUNorth Incorporated

Ontario—519

Hookup Communication Corporation

Oregon—503

Agora
Hevanet Communications
Internetworks
Netcom On-Line Communication Services

Teleport
Teleport, Inc.
WLN

Pennsylvania—215

FishNet (Prometheus Information Corp.)
VoiceNet/DCS
You Tools Corporation (FAST.NET)

Pennsylvania—412

Telerama

Pennsylvania—610

FishNet (Prometheus Information Corp.)
SSNet, Inc.
You Tools Corporation (FAST.NET)

Pennsylvania—717

You Tools Corporation (FAST.NET)

Rhode Island—401

IDS World Network

Quebec—514

Communications Accessibles
 Montreal, Inc.

South Carolina—803

A World of Difference, Inc.
FXnet
Global Vision, Inc.
SIMS, Inc.
South Carolina SuperNet, Inc.

Tennessee—615

Edge

Texas—210

Freeside Communications

Texas—214

DFW Internet Services, Inc.
Metronet, Inc.
Neosoft, Inc.
Netcom On-Line Communication Services
Texas Metronet

Texas—409

Info-Highway International, Inc.
Internet Connect Services, Inc.
Neosoft, Inc.

Texas—512

Eden Matrix
Freeside Communications
Illuminati Online
Internet Connect Services, Inc.
Netcom On-Line Communication Services
Onramp Access, Inc.
Real/Time Communications
Zilker Internet Park

Texas—713

Black Box
Info-Highway International, Inc.
Internet Connect Services, Inc.
Neosoft, Inc.
South Coast Computing Services, Inc.

Texas—817

ACM Network Services
DFW Internet Services, Inc.
Metronet, Inc.
Texas Metronet

Texas—915

New Mexico Technet, Inc.

Utah—801

Evergreen Internet
Internet Direct of Utah
XMission

Virginia—703

CAPCON LibrARY Network
Capitol Area Internet Service (CAIS)
ClarkNet (Clark Internet Services, Inc.)
Digital Express Group (Digex)
Netcom On-Line Communication Services
NovaNet, Inc.
PSI
US Net, Inc.

Virginia—804

Global Connect Inc.
Widowmaker Communications

Washington—206

Cyberlink Communications
Eskimo North
Netcom On-Line Communication Services
NorthWest CommLink
Northwest Nexus, Inc.
Pacific Rim Network, Inc.
Pacifier Computers
Skagit On-Line Services
Teleport
Teleport, Inc.
Townsend Communcations, Inc.
WLN

Washington—509

Internet On-Ramp, Inc.
WLN

Wisconsin—414
BINCnet
Exec-PC BBS
FullFeed Communications
Internet Connect, Inc.
MIX Communications
WorldWide Access

Wisconsin—608
BINCnet
FullFeed Communications

Wisconsin—715
BINCnet
FullFeed Communications

Packet Network/Toll-Free Access

CompuServe Packet Network
IDS World Network

PSINet
HoloNet

SprintNet
Neosoft, Inc.
Portal Communications Company

Toll-free/800 Access
AlterNet (UUNET Technologies)
American Information Systems, Inc. (AIS)
BIX (Delphi Internet Services)
CENTURION Technology, Inc.
CERFnet
CICNet
CNS
CRL
DASH—Denver Area Super Highway
Digital Express Group (Digex)
Exec-PC BBS
Freeside Communications
FXnet
Hookup Communication Corporation
IgLou Internet Services
Info-Highway International, Inc.
INS Info Services
InterAccess Co.
Internet Express

Internet Online Services
Interpath
IQuest Network Services
Msen, Inc.
Neosoft, Inc.
Netcom On-Line Communications
 Services
Network Intensive
New Mexico Technet, Inc.
OARNet
Pacific Rim Network, Inc.
PCNet
Ping
Primenet
Rabbit Network, Inc.
Rocky Mountain Internet, Inc.
Sacramento Network Access, Inc.
Scruz-Net
South Coast Computing Services, Inc.
Traveller Information Services
Tyrell Corp.
UltraNet Communications, Inc.
VNet Internet Access, Inc.
VoiceNet/DCS
West Coast Online
WLN
Zone One Network Exchange (ZONE)

Tymnet
Holonet

Alphabetical List of Providers

This section presents an alphabetical list of providers grouped by country and then by provider name. Countries included are the United States, Canada, Australia, Germany, Netherlands, New Zealand, Switzerland, and the United Kingdom.

United States and Canada

The following is a list of North American Internet provider names in alphabetical order by provider name.

A World of Difference, Inc.

Area code(s):	803
Voice phone:	803-769-4488
E-mail address:	info@awod.com
Services provided:	Shell, PPP

Access InfoSystems

Area code(s):	707, 510
Voice phone:	707-422-1034
E-mail address:	info@community.net
Services provided:	Shell, SLIP, PPP

ACES Research

Area code(s):	602
Voice phone:	602-322-6500
E-mail address:	sales@aces.com
Services provided:	SLIP, 56 to T1

ACM Network Services

Area code(s):	National/International
Voice phone:	817-776-6876
E-mail address:	account-info@acm.org
Services provided:	Shell, SLIP, PPP, T1

Acquired Knowledge Systems, Inc.

Area code(s):	305
Voice phone:	305-525-2574
E-mail address:	samek@aksi.net
Services provided:	Shell, SLIP, PPP

Agora

Area code(s):	503
E-mail address:	info@agora.rain.com
Dialup number:	503-293-1772
Services provided:	Shell, Usenet, FTP, Telnet, Gopher, Lynx, IRC, mail; SLIP/PPP coming

Aimnet Information Services

Area code(s):	408, 415, 510
Voice phone:	408-257-0900
E-mail address:	info@aimnet.com
Services provided:	Shell, SLIP, PPP, DNS

Alberta SuperNet Inc.

Area code(s):	403
Voice phone:	403-441-3663
E-mail address:	info@supernet.ab.ca
Services provided:	Shell, e-mail, Usenet, FTP, Telnet, Gopher, SLIP/PPP

AlterNet (UUNET Technologies)

Area code(s):	All
Voice phone:	800-4UUNET4
E-mail address:	info@uunet.uu.net
Services provided:	Telnet only, SLIP, PPP, 56, 128 T1, 10Mps

American Information Systems, Inc. (AIS)

Area code(s):	312, 708, 800, 815
Voice phone:	708-413-8400
E-mail address:	schneid@ais.net
Services provided:	Shell, SLIP, PPP, leased lines

APK Public Access UNI*

Area code(s):	216
Voice phone:	216-481-9428
E-mail address:	support@wariat.org
Services provided:	Shell, SLIP, PPP

APlatform

Area code(s):	415
Voice phone:	415-941-2641
E-mail address:	support@aplatform.com
Services provided:	Shell, SLIP, PPP

Best Internet Communications, Inc. (BEST)

Area code(s):	408, 415, 510
Voice phone:	415-964-2378
E-mail address:	info@best.com
Services provided:	Shell, SLIP, PPP, leased lines

BINCnet

Area code(s):	608, 414, 715
Voice phone:	608-233-5222
E-mail address:	ward@binc.net
Services provided:	SLIP, PPP, 56 to T1

BIX (Delphi Internet Services)

Area code(s):	National/International
Voice phone:	800-695-4775, 617-354-4137
E-mail address:	info@bix.com
Services provided:	Shell

Black Box

Area code(s):	713
Voice phone:	713-480-2684
E-mail address:	info@blkbox.com
Services provided:	Shell, SLIP, PPP, ISDN

Blythe Systems

Area code(s):	212, 718
Voice phone:	212-348-2875
E-mail address:	accounts@blythe.org
Services provided:	Shell

CAPCON LibrARY Network

Area code(s):	202, 301, 410, 703
Voice phone:	202-331-5771
E-mail address:	info@capcon.net
Services provided:	Shell, SLIP, PPP

Capitol Area Internet Service (CAIS)

Area code(s):	202, 301, 410, 703
Voice phone:	703-448-4470
E-mail address:	dalston@cais.com
Services provided:	Shell, SLIP, PPP, ISDN, 56 to T1

CCI Networks

Area code(s):	403
Voice phone:	403-450-6787
E-mail address:	info@ccinet.ab.ca
Services provided:	Shell, e-mail, Usenet, FTP, Telnet, Gopher, WAIS, WWW, IRC, Hytelnet, SLIP/PPP

CCnet Communications

Area code(s):	510
Voice phone:	510-988-0680
E-mail address:	info@ccnet.com
Dialup number:	510-988-7140, log in as guest
Services provided:	Shell, SLIP/PPP, Telnet, e-mail, FTP, Usenet, IRC, WWW

CENTURION Technology, Inc.

Area code(s):	800, 813
Voice phone:	813-572-5556
E-mail address:	jablow@cent.com
Services provided:	Shell, PPP, 56, 128, T1

CERFnet

Area code(s):	619, 510, 415, 818, 714, 310, 800
Voice phone:	800-876-2373
E-mail address:	sales@cerf.net
Services provided:	Full range of Internet services

CICNet

Area code(s):	313, 708, 800
Voice phone:	800-947-4754, 313-998-6703
E-mail address:	info@cic.net
Services provided:	SLIP, FTP, Telnet, Gopher, e-mail, Usenet

ClarkNet (Clark Internet Services, Inc.)

Area code(s):	410, 301, 202, 703
Voice phone:	800-735-2258, 410-730-9764
E-mail address:	info@clark.net
Dialup number:	301-596-1626, log in as guest, no password
Services provided:	Shell/optional menu, FTP, Gopher, Telnet, IRC, news, Mosaic, Lynx, MUD, SLIP/PPP/CSLIP, and much more

Cloud 9 Internet

Area code(s):	914
Voice phone:	914-682-0626
E-mail address:	scottd@cloud9.net
Services provided:	Shell, SLIP, PPP, ISDN, 56 and up

Cloudnet

Area code(s):	612
Voice phone:	612-240-8243
E-mail address:	info@cloudnet.com
Services provided:	Shell

CNS

Area code(s):	303, 719, 800
Voice phone:	800-748-1200
E-mail address:	service@cscns.com
Dialup number:	719-520-1700, 303-758-2656
Services provided:	Shell/menu, e-mail, FTP, Telnet, all newsgroups, IRC, 4m, Gopher, WAIS, SLIP, and more

Colorado Internet Cooperative Association

Area code(s):   303
Voice phone: 303-443-3786
E-mail address: contact@coop.net
Services provided: SLIP, PPP, 56, T1, ISDN

Colorado SuperNet

Area code(s):   303, 719
Voice phone: 303-273-3471
E-mail address: info@csn.org or help@csn.org
Services provided: Shell, e-mail, Usenet news, Telnet, FTP, SLIP/PPP, and other
                       Internet tools

Communications Accessibles Montreal, Inc.

Area code(s):   514
Voice phone: 514-931-0749
E-mail address: info@cam.org
Dialup number: 514-596-2255
Services provided: Shell, FTP, Telnet, Gopher, WAIS, WWW, IRC, Hytelnet,
                       SLIP/CSLIP/PPP, news

Community ConneXion

Area code(s):   510
Voice phone: 510-841-2014
E-mail address: info@c2.org
Services provided: Shell, SLIP/PPP

Connix: The Connecticut Internet Exchange

Area code(s):   203
Voice phone: 203-349-7059
E-mail address: office@connix.com
Services provided: Shell, SLIP, PPP, leased lines

Creative Data Consultants

Area code(s):   718, 212, 516
Voice phone: 718-229-0489 x23
E-mail address: info@silly.com
Services provided: Shell

CRL

Area code(s):	213, 310, 404, 415, 510, 602, 707, 800
Voice phone:	415-837-5300
E-mail address:	support@crl.com
Dialup number:	415-705-6060, log in as newuser, no password
Services provided:	Shell, e-mail, Usenet, UUCP, FTP, Telnet, SLIP/PPP, and more

CSUnet (California State Unversity)

Area code(s):	All in California
Voice phone:	310-985-9445
E-mail address:	maryjane@csu.net
Services provided:	56, 128, 384, T1

CTS Network Services (CTSNet)

Area code(s):	619
Voice phone:	619-637-3737
E-mail address:	support@cts.com
Dialup number:	619-637-3660
Services provided:	Shell, e-mail, Usenet, FTP, Telnet, Gopher, IRC, MUD, SLIP/PPP, and more

CyberGate

Area code(s):	305
Voice phone:	305-428-4283
E-mail address:	sales@gate.net
Services provided:	Shell, e-mail, Usenet, FTP, Telnet, Gopher, Lynx, IRC, SLIP/PPP

Cyberlink Communications

Area code(s):	206
Voice phone:	206-281-5397, 515-945-7000
E-mail address:	sales@cyberspace.com
Services provided:	Shell, SLIP, PPP

Cyberstore Systems, Inc.

Area code(s):	604
Voice phone:	604-526-3373
E-mail address:	info@cyberstore.ca
Dialup number:	604-526-3676, log in as guest
Services provided:	E-mail, Usenet, FTP, Telnet, Gopher, WAIS, WWW, IRC, SLIP/PPP

DASH—Denver Area Super Highway

Area code(s):	303
Voice phone:	800-624-8597, 303-674-9784
E-mail address:	info@dash.com, custserv@dash.com
Services provided:	Shell, SLIP, PPP, leased lines

DataFlux Systems Limited

Area code(s):	604
Voice phone:	604-744-4553
E-mail address:	info@dataflux.bc.ca
Services provided:	Shell, e-mail, Usenet, FTP, Telnet, Gopher, WAIS, WWW, IRC, SLIP/PPP

Datawave Network Services

Area code(s):	805
Voice phone:	805-730-7775
E-mail address:	sales@datawave.net
Services provided:	56

DFW Internet Services, Inc.

Area code(s):	214, 817
Voice phone:	817-332-5116
E-mail address:	sales@dfw.net
Services provided:	Shell, SLIP, PPP, 56 to T1

DHM Information Management, Inc.

Area code(s):	213, 310, 714, 818
Voice phone:	310-214-3349
E-mail address:	dharms@dhm.com
Services provided:	LAN, PPP, SLIP, T1-56, Shell

DigiLink Network Services

Area code(s):	213, 310, 714, 818
Voice phone:	310-542-7421
E-mail address:	info@digilink.net, bob@digilink.net
Services provided:	ISDN, PPP

Digital Express Group (Digex)

Area code(s):	301, 410, 609, 703, 714, 908, 909
Voice phone:	800-969-9090
E-mail address:	info@digex.net
Dialup number:	301-220-0258, 410-605-2700, 609-348-6203, 703-281-7997, 714-261-5201, 908-937-9481, 909-222-2204, log in as new
Services provided:	Shell, SLIP/PPP, e-mail, newsgroups, Telnet, FTP, IRC, Gopher, WAIS, and more

Earthlink Network, Inc.

Area code(s):	213, 310, 818
Voice phone:	213-644-9500
E-mail address:	info@earthlink.net
Services provided:	Shell, SLIP, PPP, ISDN, 56, T1, DNS

ECHO

Area code(s):	212, 718
Voice phone:	212-255-3839
E-mail address:	info@echonyc.com
Dialup number:	212-989-3382
Services provided:	Conferencing, e-mail, Shell, complete Internet access including Telnet, FTP, SLIP/PPP

Eden Matrix

Area code(s):	512
Voice phone:	512-478-9900
E-mail address:	jch@eden.com
Services provided:	Shell, SLIP, PPP, T1

Edge

Area code(s):	615
Voice phone:	615-455-9915 (Tullahoma), 615-726-8700 (Nashville)
E-mail address:	info@edge.net
Services provided:	Shell, SLIP, PPP, ISDN, 56

ElectriCiti Incorporated

Area code(s):	619, 408, 415, 510
Voice phone:	619-338-9000
E-mail address:	info@electriciti.com
Services provided:	SLIP, CSLIP, PPP

EriNet Online Communications

Area code(s):	513
Voice phone:	513-436-1700
E-mail address:	info@erinet.com
Services provided:	Shell, SLIP, PPP

Escape (Kazan Corp)

Area code(s):	212, 718
Voice phone:	212-888-8780
E-mail address:	info@escape.com
Services provided:	Shell, SLIP, PPP, 56

Eskimo North

Area code(s):	206
Voice phone:	206-367-7457
E-mail address:	nanook@eskimo.com
Services provided:	Shell

ESNET Communications

Area code(s):	619
Voice phone:	619-287-5943
E-mail address:	steve@cg57.esnet.com
Services provided:	Shell

Evergreen Internet

Area code(s):	602, 702, 801
Voice phone:	602-230-9339
E-mail address:	evergreen@libre.com
Services provided:	Shell, FTP, Telnet, SLIP, PPP, others

Exchange Network Services, Inc.

Area code(s):	216
Voice phone:	216-261-4593
E-mail address:	info@en.com
Services provided:	Shell

Exec-PC BBS

Area code(s):	414
Voice phone:	800-EXECPC-1, 414-789-4200
E-mail address:	info@earth.execpc.com
Services provided:	Shell

FGInet, Inc.

Area code(s):	217
Voice phone:	217-544-2775
E-mail address:	newuser@mail.fgi.net
Services provided:	Shell, SLIP, PPP

FishNet (Prometheus Information Corp)

Area code(s):	215, 610
Voice phone:	610-337-9994
E-mail address:	info@pond.com
Services provided:	Shell, SLIP, PPP

Florida Online

Area code(s):	407, 305, 904, 813
Voice phone:	407-635-8888
E-mail address:	jerry@digital.net
Services provided:	Shell, SLIP, PPP, ISDN, 56 to T1

FredNet

Area code(s):	301
Voice phone:	301-698-2386
E-mail address:	info@fred.net
Services provided:	Shell, SLIP

Freelance Systems Programming

Area code(s):	513
Voice phone:	513-254-7246
E-mail address:	fsp@dayton.fsp.com
Services provided:	Shell, SLIP

Freeside Communications

Area code(s):	210, 512
Voice phone:	800-968-8750
E-mail address:	`sales@fc.net`
Services provided:	Shell, SLIP, PPP, ISDN, 56 to T1

FullFeed Communications

Area code(s):	608, 414, 715
Voice phone:	608-246-4239
E-mail address:	`info@fullfeed.com`
Services provided:	Shell, PPP, 28.8, 56, 384, T1

FXnet

Area code(s):	800, 704, 803
Voice phone:	704-338-4670
E-mail address:	`info@fx.net`
Services provided:	Shell, SLIP, PPP, ISDN, 56, T1

Gateway to the World, Inc.

Area code(s):	National/International
Voice phone:	305-670-2930
E-mail address:	`mjansen@gate.com`
Services provided:	Shell

Global Connect, Inc.

Area code(s):	National/International
Voice phone:	804-229-4484
E-mail address:	`info@gc.net`
Services provided:	SLIP, CSLIP, PPP, DNS

Global Vision, Inc.

Area code(s):	803
Voice phone:	803-241-0901
E-mail address:	`derdziak@globalvision.net`
Services provided:	Shell, SLIP, PPP, ISDN, 56 to T1

Great Basin Internet Services

Area code(s):   702
Voice phone: 702-829-2244
E-mail address: info@greatbasin.com
Services provided: UUCP, SLIP, PPP

GSS Internet

Area code(s):   405, 918
Voice phone: 918-835-3655
E-mail address: info@galstar.com
Services provided: Shell, SLIP, PPP

Hawaii OnLine

Area code(s):   808
Voice phone: 808-246-1880, 808-533-6981
E-mail address: info@aloha.net
Services provided: Shell, SLIP, PPP, 56 to T1, DNS, ISDN

Hevanet Communications

Area code(s):   503
Voice phone: 503-228-3520
E-mail address: info@hevanet.com
Services provided: Shell, SLIP, PPP, Telnet

HoloNet

Area code(s):   510, PSINet, Tymnet
Voice phone: 510-704-0160
E-mail address: support@holonet.net
Dialup number: 510-704-1058
Services provided: Complete Internet access

Hookup Communication Corporation

Area code(s):   519, Canada-wide
Voice phone: 800-363-0400
E-mail address: info@hookup.net
Services provided: Shell, e-mail, Usenet, FTP, Telnet, Gopher, WAIS, WWW, IRC,
                    Hytelnet, Archie, SLIP/PPP

I-2000

Area code(s):	203, 516, 718, 908, 914
Voice phone:	516-867-6379
E-mail address:	mikef@i-2000.com
Services provided:	SLIP, PPP

ICNet/Innovative Concepts

Area code(s):	313, 810, 616, 517, 906
Voice phone:	313-998-0090
E-mail address:	info@ic.net
Services provided:	Shell, SLIP, PPP, DNS, ISDN, 56K, T1

IDS World Network

Area code(s):	401, 305, 407, CompuServe Network
Voice phone:	401-885-6855
E-mail address:	info@ids.net
Dialup number:	401-884-9002
Services provided:	Shell, FTP, Gopher, Telnet, Talk, Usenet news, SLIP

IgLou Internet Services

Area code(s):	502, 812, 606, 513
Voice phone:	800-436-IGLOU
E-mail address:	info@iglou.com
Services provided:	Shell, SLIP, PPP, ISDN

Illuminati Online

Area code(s):	512
Voice phone:	512-462-0999, 512-447-7866
E-mail address:	admin@io.com
Services provided:	Shell, SLIP, PPP, ISDN

Info-Highway International, Inc.

Area code(s):	409, 713
Voice phone:	713-447-7025, 800-256-1370
E-mail address:	smcneely@infohwy.com
Services provided:	Shell, SLIP, PPP

Ingress Communications, Inc.

Area code(s):	212, 718
Voice phone:	212-679-8592
E-mail address:	info@ingress.com
Services provided:	Shell, SLIP, PPP, 56 to T1

Innovative Data (ID-Net)

Area code(s):	313, 810
Voice phone:	810-478-3554
E-mail address:	info@id.net
Services provided:	Shell, [C]SLIP, PPP, 56 to T1

INS Info Services

Area code(s):	800, 319, 402, 515, 712
Voice phone:	800-546-6587
E-mail address:	service@ins.infonet.net
Services provided:	Shell, SLIP, 56 to T1

Institute for Global Communications (IGC)

Area code(s):	415
Voice phone:	415-442-0220
E-mail address:	support@igc.apc.org
Dialup number:	415-322-0284
Services provided:	E-mail, Telnet, FTP, Gopher, Archie, Veronica, WAIS, SLIP/PPP

InterAccess Co.

Area code(s):	312, 708, 815
Voice phone:	800-967-1580
E-mail address:	info@interaccess.com
Dialup number:	708-671-0237
Services provided:	Shell, FTP, Telnet, SLIP, PPP, and so on

Internet Access Company

Area code(s):	617, 508
Voice phone:	617-276-7200
E-mail address:	info@tiac.net
Services provided:	Shell, SLIP, PPP, ISDN, 56

Internet Alaska

Area code(s):   907
Voice phone: 907-562-4638
E-mail address: `info@alaska.net`
Services provided: Shell, 56 to T1

Internet Atlanta

Area code(s):   National/International
Voice phone: 404-410-9000
E-mail address: `info@atlanta.com`
Services provided: UUCP, SLIP, PPP, ISDN, 56, T1

Internet Connect Services, Inc.

Area code(s):   409, 512, 713
Voice phone: 512-572-9987, 713-439-0949
E-mail address: `staff@icsi.net`
Services provided: Shell, SLIP, PPP, ISDN, 56 to T1

Internet Connect, Inc.

Area code(s):   414
Voice phone: 414-476-ICON (4266)
E-mail address: `info@inc.net`
Services provided: Shell, SLIP, PPP, ISDN, 56 to T1

Internet Connection

Area code(s):   408
Voice phone: 408-461-INET
E-mail address: `sales@ico.net`
Services provided: SLIP, PPP, ISDN, 56 to T1

Internet Direct of Utah

Area code(s):   801
Voice phone: 801-578-0300
E-mail address: `johnh@indirect.com`
Services provided: Shell, SLIP, PPP, 56 to T1

Internet Direct, Inc.

Area code(s):   602
Voice phone: 602-274-0100, 602-324-0100
E-mail address: `sales@indirect.com`
Services provided: Shell, SLIP, PPP

Internet Express

Area code(s):   719, 303, 505, 602, 800
Voice phone: 800-592-1240
E-mail address: `service@usa.net`
Services provided: Shell, SLIP, PPP, dedicated lines

Internet Nebraska Corp.

Area code(s):   402
Voice phone: 402-434-8680
E-mail address: `info@inetnebr.com`
Services provided: Shell, SLIP, PPP

Internet On-Ramp, Inc.

Area code(s):   509
Voice phone: 509-927-RAMP (7267), 509-927-7267
E-mail address: `info@on-ramp.ior.com`
Services provided: Shell, SLIP, CSLIP, PPP, leased lines

Internet Online Services

Area code(s):   201, 212, 518, 800
Voice phone: 800-221-3756
E-mail address: `accounts@ios.com`
Services provided: Shell, SLIP, PPP, leased lines, DNS

Internetworks

Area code(s):   National/International
Voice phone: 503-233-4774
E-mail address: `info@i.net`
Services provided: SLIP, PPP, ISDN, leased lines

InterNex Information Services, Inc.

Area code(s):   415, 408, 510
Voice phone: 415-473-3060
E-mail address: sales@internex.net
Services provided: ISDN

Interpath

Area code(s):   919, 910, 704
Voice phone: 800-849-6305
E-mail address: info@infopath.net
Services provided: Full shell for UNIX, SLIP, PPP

Interport Communications Corp.

Area code(s):   212, 718
Voice phone: 212-989-1128
E-mail address: sales@interport.net, info@interport.net (autoreply)
Services provided: Shell, SLIP, PPP, dedicated lines

interQuest inc.

Area code(s):   205
Voice phone: 205-464-8280
E-mail address: paul@iquest.com
Services provided: Shell, SLIP, PPP

intuitive information, inc.

Area code(s):   508
Voice phone: 508-342-1100
E-mail address: info@iii.net
Services provided: Shell, [C]SLIP, PPP, 56

IQuest Network Services

Area code(s):   317
Voice phone: 317-259-5050, 800-844-UNIX
E-mail address: info@iquest.net
Services provided: Shell, SLIP, PPP, ISDN, 56, T1

KAIWAN Corporation

Area code(s):	714, 213, 310, 818, 909, 805
Voice phone:	714-638-2139
E-mail address:	sales@kaiwan.com
Services provided:	Shell, SLIP, PPP, 56, 256, 512, 768, T1

LI Net, Inc.

Area code(s):	516
Voice phone:	516-476-1168
E-mail address:	questions@li.net
Services provided:	Shell, SLIP, 56, T1

Lightside, Inc.

Area code(s):	818, 310, 714, 909
Voice phone:	818-858-9261
E-mail address:	lightside@lightside.com
Services provided:	Shell, SLIP, PPP, 56 to T1

LineX Communcations

Area code(s):	415
Voice phone:	415-455-1650
E-mail address:	info@linex.com
Services provided:	Shell

Long Island Information, Inc.

Area code(s):	516
Voice phone:	516-248-5381
E-mail address:	info@liii.com
Services provided:	Shell, SLIP

Maestro Technologies, Inc.

Area code(s):	212, 718, 516
Voice phone:	212-240-9600
E-mail address:	staff@maestro.com, rlekhi@maestro.com
Services provided:	Shell, SLIP, PPP

maine.net, Inc.

Area code(s):	207
Voice phone:	207-780-6381
E-mail address:	atr@maine.net
Services provided:	SLIP, PPP, 56, T1

MBnet

Area code(s):	204
Voice phone:	204-474-9590
E-mail address:	info@mbnet.mb.ca
Dialup number:	204-275-6132, log in as mbnet with password guest
Services provided:	Shell, e-mail, Usenet, FTP, Telnet, Gopher, WAIS, WWW, IRC, Archie, Hytelnet, SLIP/PPP

MCSNet

Area code(s):	312, 708, 815
Voice phone:	312-248-8649
E-mail address:	info@mcs.net
Services provided:	Shell, SLIP, PPP, dedicated lines, ISDN

Metronet, Inc.

Area code(s):	214, 817
Voice phone:	214-705-2900, 817-543-8756
E-mail address:	info@metronet.com
Services provided:	Shell, SLIP, PPP

MichNet

Area code(s):	313, 616, 517, 810, 906
Voice phone:	313-764-9430
E-mail address:	recruiting@merit.edu
Services provided:	SLIP, PPP, host services, 56, T1

Millennium Communications

Area code(s):	507, 612
Voice phone:	507-282-8943, 612-338-5509
E-mail address:	info@millcom.com
Services provided:	Shell, SLIP, PPP

MindSpring Enterprises, Inc.

Area code(s):   404, 706
Voice phone: 404-888-0725
E-mail address: sales@mindspring.com
Services provided: Shell, SLIP, PPP

Minnesota MicroNet

Area code(s):   612
Voice phone: 612-681-8018
E-mail address: info@mm.com
Services provided: SLIP, SLIP, PPP

Minnesota Regional Network (MRNet)

Area code(s):   612, 507, 218
Voice phone: 612-342-2570
E-mail address: sales@mr.net
Services provided: SLIP, 56, T1

MIX Communications

Area code(s):   414
Voice phone: 414-228-0739
E-mail address: sales@mixcom.com
Services provided: BBS, SLIP, PPP

Msen, Inc.

Area code(s):   800, 313, 517, 616, 906
Voice phone: 313-998-4562
E-mail address: info@msen.com
Services provided: Shell, SLIP, PPP, ISDN, 56 to T1

MV Communications

Area code(s):   603
Voice phone: 603-429-2223
E-mail address: info@mv.mv.com
Services provided: Shell, SLIP, PPP, 56

Neighborhood Internet Connection

Area code(s):	201
Voice phone:	201-934-1445
E-mail address:	info@nic.com, combes@nic.com
Services provided:	Shell

NeoSoft, Inc.

Area code(s):	800, 713, 409, 214, 504, 314
Voice phone:	713-684-5969
E-mail address:	jmw3@neosoft.com
Services provided:	Shell, SLIP, PPP, ISDN, 56, T1

Netcom On-Line Communications Services

Area code(s):	206, 212, 214, 303, 310, 312, 404, 408, 415, 503, 510, 512, 617, 619, 703, 714, 818, 916
Voice phone:	800-501-8649
E-mail address:	info@netcom.com
Dialup number:	206-547-5992, 212-354-3870, 214-753-0045, 303-758-0101, 310-842-8835, 312-380-0340, 404-303-9765, 408-261-4700, 408-459-9851, 415-328-9940, 415-985-5650, 503-626-6833, 510-274-2900, 510-426-6610, 510-865-9004, 512-206-4950, 617-237-8600, 619-234-0524, 703-255-5951, 714-708-3800, 818-585-3400, 916-965-1371; log in as guest
Services provided:	Shell, e-mail, Usenet, FTP, Telnet, Gopher, IRC, WAIS, SLIP/PPP

Network 23, Inc.

Area code(s):	212, 917
Voice phone:	212-786-4810
E-mail address:	info@net23.com
Services provided:	Shell

Network 99, Inc.

Area code(s):	National/International
Voice phone:	702-442-7353, 602-780-7533, 800-NET-99IP
E-mail address:	net99@cluster.mcs.net
Services provided:	56 to T3

Network Intensive

Area code(s):	714
Voice phone:	800-273-5600
E-mail address:	info@ni.net
Services provided:	Shell, SLIP, PPP, 56, ISDN, T1

Network Internet Services

Area code(s):	516
Voice phone:	516-543-0234
E-mail address:	info@netusa.net
Services provided:	Shell, SLIP, PPP

Network Link, Inc.

Area code(s):	619, 317
Voice phone:	619-278-5943
E-mail address:	stevef@tnl1.tnwl.com
Services provided:	Shell, NNTP, IDSN, 56, T1

New Jersey Computer Connection

Area code(s):	609
Voice phone:	609-896-2799
E-mail address:	info@pluto.njcc.com
Services provided:	Shell, SLIP, PPP

New Mexico Technet, Inc.

Area code(s):	505, 602, 303, 915, 800
Voice phone:	505-345-6555
E-mail address:	granoff@technet.nm.org
Services provided:	Shell, SLIP, PPP, leased lines

New York Net

Area code(s):	201, 203, 212, 516, 609, 718, 908, 914, 917
Voice phone:	718-776-6811
E-mail address:	sales@new-york.net
Services provided:	SLIP, PPP, 56, 64, 128 to T1

North Shore Access

Area code(s):	617
Voice phone:	617-593-3110
E-mail address:	info@shore.net
Dialup number:	617-593-4557, log in as new
Services provided:	Shell, FTP, Telnet, Gopher, Archie, SLIP/PPP

Northcoast Internet

Area code(s):	707
Voice phone:	707-444-1913
Services provided:	Shell, FTP, Telnet, Gopher, SLIP/PPP

NorthWest CommLink

Area code(s):	206
Voice phone:	206-336-0103
E-mail address:	gtyacke@nwcl.net
Services provided:	Shell, SLIP, PPP, 56 to T1

Northwest Nexus, Inc.

Area code(s):	206
Voice phone:	206-455-3505
E-mail address:	info@nwnexus.wa.com
Services provided:	Shell, SLIP, PPP, 56, T1

NovaNet, Inc.

Area code(s):	703, 202, 301
Voice phone:	703-524-4800
E-mail address:	sales@novanet.com
Services provided:	Shell, SLIP, PPP, 56 to T1

Nuance Network Services

Area code(s):	205
Voice phone:	205-533-4296
E-mail address:	info@nuance.com
Services provided:	Shell, Usenet, FTP, Telnet, Gopher, SLIP/PPP

NYSERNet

Area code(s):	212, 315, 516, 518, 607, 716, 718, 914
Voice phone:	315-453-2912
E-mail address:	info@nysernet.org
Services provided:	Shell, 56 to T3

Nyx

Area code(s):	303
Voice phone:	303-871-3308
E-mail address:	info@nyx.cs.du.edu
Services provided:	Shell, semi-anonymous accounts

OARNet

Area code(s):	614
Voice phone:	800-627-8101
E-mail address:	info@oar.net
Services provided:	Shell, SLIP/PPP

Old Colorado City Communications

Area code(s):	719
Voice phone:	719-528-5849
E-mail address:	thefox@oldcolo.com
Services provided:	Shell, 56

Onramp Access, Inc.

Area code(s):	512
Voice phone:	512-322-9200
E-mail address:	info@onr.com
Services provided:	SLIP, PPP

Pacific Internet

Area code(s):	707
Voice phone:	707-468-1005
E-mail address:	info@pacific.net
Services provided:	Shell, SLIP, PPP, 56 to T1

Pacific Rim Network, Inc.

Area code(s):	800, 206
Voice phone:	206-650-0442
E-mail address:	sales@pacificrim.com
Services provided:	Shell, SLIP, PPP, ISDN, 56 to T1

Pacifier Computers

Area code(s):	206
Voice phone:	206-693-2116
E-mail address:	sales@pacifier.com
Services provided:	Shell, SLIP, PPP

PacketWorks, Inc.

Area code(s):	813
Voice phone:	813-446-8826
E-mail address:	info@packet.net
Services provided:	PPP, ISDN

Panix Public Access UNIX and Internet

Area code(s):	212, 516
Voice phone:	212-787-6160
E-mail address:	info@panix.com
Dialup number:	212-787-3100, 516-626-7863, log in as newuser
Services provided:	Shell, Usenet, FTP, Telnet, Gopher, Archie, WWW, WAIS, SLIP/PPP

PCNet

Area code(s):	203
Voice phone:	800-66-4INET
E-mail address:	sales@pcnet.com
Services provided:	Shell, SLIP, PPP, ISDN, 56, T1

Phantom Access Technologies, Inc.

Area code(s):	212, 718, 516, 914
Voice phone:	212-989-2418
E-mail address:	info@phantom.com
Services provided:	Shell, SLIP, PPP, 56 to T1

Ping

Area code(s):   404, 800 (includes Hawaii and Alaska)
Voice phone: 800-746-4835, 404-399-1670
E-mail address: bdk@ping.com
Services provided: Shell, SLIP, PPP, 56

Pioneer Global

Area code(s):   617
Voice phone: 617-375-0200
E-mail address: sales@pn.com
Services provided: Shell, 28.8, 56, T1

Pipeline Network

Area code(s):   National/International
Voice phone: 212-267-3636
E-mail address: staff@pipeline.com
Services provided: Shell

Planet Access Networks

Area code(s):   201, 908, 319, 205
Voice phone: 201-691-4704
E-mail address: fred@planet.net
Services provided: Shell, SLIP, PPP, dedicated lines

Portal Communications Company

Area code(s):   408, SprintNet
Voice phone: 408-973-9111
E-mail address: info@portal.com
Services provided: Shell, e-mail, Usenet, FTP, Telnet, Gopher, IRC, SLIP/PPP

Primenet

Area code(s):   602, 213, 818
Voice phone: 602-870-1010, 800-4 NET FUN
E-mail address: info@primenet.com
Services provided: Shell, SLIP, PPP, 56, 128, T1

PSI

Area code(s):	North America, Europe and Pacific Basin; send e-mail to `numbers-info@psi.com` for list
Voice phone:	703-709-0300
E-mail address:	`all-info@psi.com`
Services provided:	Complete Internet services

QuakeNet

Area code(s):	415
Voice phone:	415-655-6607
E-mail address:	`info@quake.net` (autoreply), `admin@quake.net` (human)
Services provided:	SLIP, PPP, DNS, 56 to T1

Rabbit Network, Inc.

Area code(s):	810, 800 (entire U.S. and Canada)
Voice phone:	800-456-0094
E-mail address:	`info@rabbit.net`
Services provided:	Shell, SLIP, PPP, leased lines

Real/Time Communications

Area code(s):	512
Voice phone:	512-451-0046
E-mail address:	`info@realtime.net`
Services provided:	Shell, SLIP, PPP, IDSN, custom services

Red River Net

Area code(s):	701, 218
Voice phone:	701-232-2227
E-mail address:	`lien@rrnet.com`
Services provided:	Shell, SLIP, 56, T1

Ripco Communcations, Inc.

Area code(s):	312, 708
Voice phone:	312-665-0065
E-mail address:	`info@ripco.com`
Services provided:	Shell

Rocky Mountain Internet, Inc.

Area code(s):	303, 719
Voice phone:	800-900-RMII
E-mail address:	`mountr@rmii.com, jimw@rmii.com`
Services provided:	Shell, SLIP, PPP, 56, T1

Sacramento Network Access, Inc.

Area code(s):	800, 916, 209, 510, 702
Voice phone:	916-565-4500
E-mail address:	`sales@sna.com`
Services provided:	Shell, SLIP, PPP

SatelNET Communications

Area code(s):	305
Voice phone:	305-434-8738
E-mail address:	`martinson@satelnet.org`
Services provided:	Shell, SLIP, PPP

Schunix

Area code(s):	508
Voice phone:	508-853-0258
E-mail address:	`info@schunix.com`
Services provided:	Shell, SLIP, PPP, ISDN, 56, 128, T1

Scruz-Net

Area code(s):	408, 415
Voice phone:	800-319-5555, 408-457-5050
E-mail address:	`info@scruz.net`
Services provided:	SLIP, PPP, ISDN, 56, T1

Sibylline, Inc.

Area code(s):	501
Voice phone:	501-521-4660
E-mail address:	`info@sibylline.com`
Services provided:	Shell, SLIP, PPP, 56, 128, T1, DNS, advertising

Sierra-Net

Area code(s):	702, 916
Voice phone:	702-832-6911
E-mail address:	info@sierra.net
Services provided:	Shell, SLIP, PPP, 56 to T1

SIMS, Inc.

Area code(s):	803
Voice phone:	803-762-4956
E-mail address:	info@sims.net
Services provided:	Shell, SLIP, PPP, ISDN, 56, 128, 256

Skagit On-Line Services

Area code(s):	206
Voice phone:	206-755-0190
E-mail address:	info@sos.net
Services provided:	Shell, SLIP, PPP

SkyNET Corp.

Area code(s):	816, 913
Voice phone:	816-483-0002
E-mail address:	info@sky.net
Services provided:	Shell, SLIP, PPP, 56 to T1

South Carolina SuperNet, Inc.

Area code(s):	803
Voice phone:	803-748-1207
E-mail address:	info@scsn.net
Services provided:	SLIP, PPP, 56, T1

South Coast Computing Services, Inc.

Area code(s):	800, 713, 918
Voice phone:	800-221-6478
E-mail address:	sales@sccsi.com
Services provided:	Shell, SLIP, PPP, 56, T1

South Valley Internet

Area code(s):   408
Voice phone: 408-683-4533
E-mail address: info@garlic.com
Services provided: Shell, SLIP, PPP, dedicated and leased lines

SouthWind Internet Access, Inc.

Area code(s):   316
Voice phone: 316-263-7963
E-mail address: staff@southwind.net
Services provided: Shell, TIA-SLIP

SSNet, Inc.

Area code(s):   610, 302
Voice phone: 302-378-1386
E-mail address: info@ssnet.com, sharris@ssnet.com
Services provided: Shell, SLIP, PPP, UUCP

StarNet Communications, Inc. (Winternet)

Area code(s):   612
Voice phone: 612-941-9177
E-mail address: info@winternet.com
Services provided: Shell, SLIP, PPP

SymNet

Area code(s):   904
Voice phone: 904-385-1061
E-mail address: info@symnet.net
Services provided: Shell, SLIP, PPP

Teleport

Area code(s):   503, 206
Voice phone: 503-223-4245
E-mail address: info@teleport.com
Dialup number: 503-220-1016
Services provided: Shell, e-mail, Usenet, FTP, Telnet, Gopher, SLIP/PPP

Teleport, Inc.

Area code(s):	503, 206
Voice phone:	503-223-0076
E-mail address:	sales@teleport.com
Services provided:	Shell, SLIP, PPP, ISDN

Telerama

Area code(s):	412
Voice phone:	412-481-3505
E-mail address:	sysop@telerama.lm.com
Dialup number:	412-481-4644
Services provided:	Shell, e-mail, Telnet, Usenet, FTP, Telnet, Gopher, IRC, SLIP/PPP

Texas Metronet

Area code(s):	214, 817
Voice phone:	214-705-2900
E-mail address:	info@metronet.com
Dialup number:	214-705-2901, 817-261-1127; log in as info, with password info
Services provided:	Shell, e-mail, Usenet, FTP, Telnet, Gopher, IRC, SLIP/PPP

Tezcatlipoca, Inc.

Area code(s):	312, 708
Voice phone:	312-850-0181
E-mail address:	ilixi@tezcat.com
Services provided:	Shell, TIA

The Dorsai Embassy

Area code(s):	718, 212, 201, 203, 914, 516
Voice phone:	718-392-3667
E-mail address:	system@dorsai.dorsai.org
Services provided:	Shell, SLIP, PPP

The WELL

Area code(s):	415
Voice phone:	415-332-4335
E-mail address:	info@well.com
Services provided:	Shell

The World

Area code(s):	617, 508
Voice phone:	617-739-0202
E-mail address:	staff@world.std.com
Services provided:	Shell, DNS

Townsend Communcations, Inc.

Area code(s):	206
Voice phone:	206-385-0464
E-mail address:	inquiries@olympus.net
Services provided:	PPP, 56

Traveller Information Services

Area code(s):	204
Voice phone:	800-840-TNET, 204-883-2686
E-mail address:	info@traveller.com
Services provided:	Shell, CSLIP, PPP, ISDN

Tyrell Corp.

Area code(s):	816, 913, 504, 316
Voice phone:	800-TYRELL-1
E-mail address:	support@tyrell.net
Services provided:	Shell, [C]SLIP, PPP

TZ-Link

Area code(s):	914
Voice phone:	914-353-5443
E-mail address:	drew@j51.com
Services provided:	Shell

UltraNet Communications, Inc.

Area code(s):	508
Voice phone:	508-229-8400, 800-763-8111
E-mail address:	info@ultranet.com
Services provided:	SLIP, PPP, ISDN, 56, 128, 384

US Net, Inc.

Area code(s):	301, 202, 703
Voice phone:	301-572-5926
E-mail address:	info@us.net
Services provided:	Shell, SLIP, PPP, DNS, 56 to T1

UUNorth Incorporated

Area code(s):	416
Voice phone:	416-225-8649
E-mail address:	uunorth@north.net
Dialup number:	416-221-0200, log in as new
Services provided:	E-mail, Usenet, FTP, Telnet, Gopher, WAIS, WWW, IRC, Archie, SLIP/PPP

VNet Internet Access, Inc.

Area code(s):	704, public data network
Voice phone:	800-377-3282
E-mail address:	info@vnet.net
Dialup number:	704-347-8839, log in as new
Services provided:	Shell, e-mail, Usenet, FTP, Telnet, Gopher, IRC, SLIP/PPP, UUCP

VoiceNet/DCS

Area code(s):	800, 215
Voice phone:	215-674-9290
E-mail address:	info@voicenet.com
Services provided:	Shell, SLIP, PPP, ISDN

West Coast Online

Area code(s):	415, 510, 707, 408, 916, 209
Voice phone:	800-WCO INTERNET
E-mail address:	info@calon.com
Services provided:	Shell, SLIP, PPP, ISDN, 56 to T1

WestNet

Area code(s):	914
Voice phone:	914-967-7816
E-mail address:	staff@westnet.com
Services provided:	Shell

Widomaker Communications

Area code(s):	804
Voice phone:	804-253-7621
E-mail address:	bloyall@widomaker.com
Services provided:	Shell, SLIP, PPP

Wilder Systems, Inc.

Area code(s):	617
Voice phone:	617-933-8810
E-mail address:	info@id.wing.net
Services provided:	Shell, pipeline, PPP, SLIP, ISDN, 56 to T1

Wimsey Information Services

Area code(s):	604
Voice phone:	604-936-8649
E-mail address:	admin@wimsey.com
Services provided:	Shell, e-mail, Usenet, FTP, Telnet, Gopher, WAIS, WWW, IRC, Archie, SLIP/PPP

Wizvax Communications

Area code(s):	518
Voice phone:	518-271-6005
E-mail address:	root@wizvax.com
Services provided:	Shell, SLIP, CSLIP, PPP

WLN

Area code(s):	800, 206, 509, 503, 208, 406, 360
Voice phone:	800-DIAL-WLN, 800-342-5956, 206-923-4000
E-mail address:	info@wln.com
Services provided:	Shell, SLIP, PPP, 56 to T1

WorldWide Access

Area code(s):	312, 708, 815, 414
Voice phone:	708-367-1870
E-mail address:	support@wwa.com
Services provided:	Shell, SLIP, PPP, ISDN, leased lines

Xensei Corporation

Area code(s):   617
Voice phone: 617-773-4785
E-mail address: sales@xensei.com, terri@xensei.com
Services provided: SLIP, PPP, ISDN, 56K

XMission

Area code(s):   801
Voice phone: 801-539-0852
E-mail address: support@xmission.com
Services provided: Shell, SLIP, PPP, leased lines

XNet Information Systems

Area code(s):   708
Voice phone: 708-983-6064
E-mail address: info@xnet.com
Dialup number: 708-983-6435, 708-882-1101
Services provided: Shell, e-mail, Usenet, FTP, Telnet, Gopher, Archie, IRC,
                        SLIP/PPP, UUCP

You Tools Corporation (FAST.NET)

Area code(s):   610, 215, 717
Voice phone: 610-954-5910
E-mail address: internet@youtools.com
Services provided: SLIP, PPP, ISDN, 56 to T1

Zilker Internet Park

Area code(s):   512
Voice phone: 512-206-3850
E-mail address: info@zilker.net
Services provided: Shell, SLIP, PPP, ISDN

zNET

Area code(s):   408
Voice phone: 408-477-9638
E-mail address: info@znet.com
Services provided: SLIP, PPP, ISDN, DNS

Zone One Network Exchange (ZONE)

Area code(s):	800, 718, 212, 914, 516, 917, 201, 908
Voice phone:	718-549-8078
E-mail address:	info@zone.net
Services provided:	UUCP, SLIP, PPP, 56 to T1

Australia

Aarnet

Voice phone:	+61 6-249-3385
E-mail address:	aarnet@aarnet.edu.au

Connect.com.au P/L

Areas serviced:	Major Australian capital cities (2, 3, 6, 7, 8, 9)
Voice phone:	1-800-818-262 or +61 3-528-2239
E-mail address:	connect@connect.com.au
Services provided:	Shell, SLIP/PPP, UUCP

Germany

Contributed Software

Voice phone:	+49 30-694-69-07
E-mail address:	info@contrib.de
Dialup number:	+49 30-694-60-55, log in as guest or gast

Individual Network e.V.

Area serviced:	All of Germany
Voice phone:	+49 0441 9808556
E-mail address:	in-info@individual.net
Dialup number:	02238 15071, log in as info
Services provided:	UUCP throughout Germany; FTP, SLIP, Telnet and other services in some major cities

Inter Networking System (INS)

Voice phone:	+49 2305 356505
E-mail address:	info@ins.net

Netherlands

Knoware
E-mail address: info@knoware.nl
Dialup number: 030 896775

NetLand
Voice phone: 020 6943664
E-mail address: Info@netland.nl
Dialup number: 020 6940350, log in as new or info

Simplex
E-mail address: simplex@simplex.nl
Dialup number: 020 6653388, log in as new or info

New Zealand

Actrix
Voice phone: 04-389-6316
E-mail address: john@actrix.gen.nz

Switzerland

SWITCH - Swiss Academic and Research Network
Voice phone: +41 1 268 1515
E-mail address: postmaster@switch.ch

United Kingdom

Almac
Voice phone: +44 0324-665371
E-mail address: alastair.mcintyre@almac.co.uk

Cix
Voice phone: +44 49 2641 961
E-mail address: cixadmin@cix.compulink.co.uk

Demon Internet Limited

Voice phone:	081-349-0063 (London)
	031-552-0344 (Edinburgh)
E-mail address:	internet@demon.net
Services provided:	SLIP/PPP accounts

The Direct Connection (UK)

Voice phone:	+44 (0)81 317 0100
E-mail address:	helpdesk@dircon.cu.uk
Dialup number:	+44 (0)81 317 2222

NOTE TO PROVIDERS

If you would like to be included in future versions of this list, for use in subsequent editions of this book as well as other Sams Internet books, send an e-mail message to Mark Taber at mtaber@netcom.com.

Tools Every Internetter Should Have

by Ron Dippold

B

So you're surfing the Internet, riding waves of data. Hang ten, Moon Doggie! *Uh-oh*—here comes a megawave, and your board is, shall we say, not in pristine condition. *Wipeout!* Bummer. Good tools are important. Find the guy with the killer board and just make a copy.

The analogy was pushing it to begin with, but here's where it really breaks down: on the Internet, your tools are just computer data, and the only cost involved is in finding and keeping a copy.

The Internet is a very hackerish community. That's in the good sense of the term *hacker*: a solitary programmer churning out fantastic code, not the popular media picture of the slobbering pre-teen breaking into top-secret computer databases. Most Internet tools are either free or *shareware* (try now, pay later if you want to continue using it), and most of them are available on the Internet. This makes wonderful sense—leave the tools where you want to use them and where others who might want to use them can find them.

Free Tools Can Be Good Tools

"Free?" you cry (go ahead, try it)! "How good can it be? Who'd give away their software if it were any good?" Plenty of people. Free and shareware programs are often as good as or better than their commercial counterparts. You won't get a sense of it from the software racks or browsing most magazines, but there is a very large community of people who write software and give it away (at least initially). I'm one of them. Why?

First, there may not be enough of a market. My tool may be indispensable to a group of Internet users, but that's a far cry from convincing a software firm to carry the tool. Is it going to sell enough to be worth their while? Hard to say—the Internet craze is just taking off: two years ago, you couldn't find a book publisher willing to touch an Internet book, much less convince a software publisher that your Internet software will be as marketable as King's Quest LXVIII. And the burdens of self-publishing require a whole separate level of effort.

Second, your software may be "too small" for sale by traditional means. A full-featured uudecode for DOS may be a great program and a joy to use, but it still doesn't do all that much. It may do it well, but it still decodes only uuencoded files. You'd have to sell it as part of a suite of utilities. Ah, just give it away.

Third, making your software freely available is great advertising if you're trying to sell it as shareware—let the users try it first.

Fourth, some of us are egotists—we put in the effort to write the damned thing (as we affectionately refer to our creations at times), so we'd like to know that as many people as possible are using it. The best way to do that is to make it as widely available as possible and make it free.

Fifth, some people (such as the Free Software Foundation) believe that all software should be free. They are dedicated to producing commercial-quality software and giving it away. After seeing the GNU line of programs, who am I to tell them not to?

Sixth, the Internet has a long history of voluntary personal contribution to the Internet community. You "pay" for all the nifty free software you used in the past by contributing your own software.

Seventh, with a huge team effort involving widely spread members of the Net, like FractInt (fractal generator) or POV (a raytracer), dividing up the loot may be a problem of Gordian complexity.

Eighth, upgrades are easy with freely distributed software. Just release a new version and it'll find its way to all the FTP sites and BBSes.

Ninth, many people enjoy the image of corporate purchasing persons' heads exploding as they try to do accounting for free or shareware packages.

Last, does it matter? The free software is good. It's just a matter of finding it, which is where Archie comes in (see Chapter 24, "Archie: An Archive of Archives").

Commercial Software Is Pretty Good, Too

All this great stuff about free software doesn't mean that commercial software is bad. It's just more expensive (meaning that it had better be *really* good), and it's harder to find. The latter is changing as interest in the Internet increases.

You should ask yourself, however, whether you really want to use a package that doesn't let you try it out first. Generally, the "if you can't find it on the Internet, you don't use it" rule works fairly well. Because of the complexity of networking, a product you can't try (even in crippled form) is a product that may have hidden problems.

Currently, most commercial Internet software tends to be either TCP/IP "suites," or dedicated programs such as e-mail, Gopher, or newsreader clients.

Software Preliminaries

The following few pages lay the ground rules about Internet software: where to get it, how it's described in this appendix, and what kinds of file formats you can expect to encounter.

Where To Get the Software

The software I'm going to discuss is available through FTP. If you don't have FTP access, you'll have to use a mail server (discussed elsewhere in the book) to grab the programs—I'm not going to cover that again.

> **NOTE**
>
> For your convenience, most files mentioned in this appendix are available on the *Sams Internet Software Library* at the Macmillan Computer Publishing Internet site, which is accessible through the World Wide Web or by FTP:
>
> ```
> http://www.mcp.com/sams/software/internet
> ftp://ftp.mcp.com/pub/sams/internet
> ```
>
> Retrieving the files from our site is faster and easier than searching across dozens of sites. Some sites are also very difficult to reach, and transfer speeds can sometimes be very slow.
>
> When you retrieve a file from other sites, you may discover that a filename has changed. This usually happens because the software has been updated and the version of the software is a part of the filename. You won't have to worry about this if you retrieve files through our Web pages.
>
> If you're retrieving files by FTP, read the INDEX.TXT file in the /pub/sams/internet directory for updated information on these files. There are subdirectories for UNIX, Windows, Macintosh, DOS, and OS/2 programs.
>
> A few files could not be included on our site—you'll have to retrieve them from the home site in the listing. This is noted in the listing for each of the files that aren't on our site.
>
> And remember, this list of software is growing because new software is being introduced all the time. Look on our Web or FTP site for new and exciting software as it becomes available.

Software List Format

The software list in this appendix has the following format:

Tool Name

```
Platforms:          Supported platforms (UNIX, DOS, OS/2, Mac, etc.)
Description:         Short description
Location:            Where to get it
Author:              Who wrote it
Cost:                The price, if anything
```

And then I'll blab on and on here with a description of the product, which will no doubt be absolutely fascinating reading and should hold your rapt attention.

The location of the software is in the following format: `oak.oakland.edu:` `/pub/misc/unix/` `wowsah.Z`—the `oak.oakland.edu` is the FTP site and the `/pub/misc/unix/wowsah.Z` is the directory and filename. In this case, the `.Z` tells you that the file is a UNIX compressed file.

Note that the author of the software isn't always willing to talk to people about a program, especially if it's an old one. Contact information is usually given inside the program. The author's name is listed to give credit where it's due. Because of the volatile nature of the Internet, however, addresses may go out of date at any time.

Cost given is for personal use only. If you want to include the program in something you're selling, it may cost you some money—contact the author.

Finally, remember that the only thing more volatile than information on the Internet is a politician's promises. Some of this information is *guaranteed* to be out of date within a month.

File Formats

Files on FTP sites come in many formats. They are indicated by a suffix, such as `foobar.uue`, `foobar.c`, `foobar.gz`, `foobar.exe`, `foobar.lzh`, and so on. As a quick refresher, the most common formats you encounter are listed here:

Format	Description
`.abe`	This is the ABE (ASCII-Binary Encoding) format. It never really caught on, but it performs the task of sending data over a text connection (such as mail) well.
`.arc`	The old SEA ARC format; it's pretty much obsolete, but some old archives are still stored in this format. You need PKXARC, PKUNPAK, DEARC, or almost anything with ARC in the format to unpack this.
`.arj`	Almost exclusively used for PC software, this format was produced by the ARJ packer. Use ARJ to unpack it, or find UnARJ to unpack it if you're not using a PC.
`.bin`	MacBinary—this is basically a header wrapped around a file to preserve some of what the Mac considers vital statistics (and all other systems consider junk). Macs can use one of the standard decompression programs such as StuffIt Expander. Others can use `mcvert` or Mac utilities for OS/2 to get rid of it.

continues

Format	Description
.c	This is a C program; it usually indicates a simple program you just compile (use this command on many UNIX systems: cc `filename`.c -o `filename`).
.cpt	Macintosh CompactPro archive.
.exe	An executable program. Usually, this format is under a directory for a specific operating or computer system; you can just download it (in binary mode) and run it. Often, this format is actually an executable archive that unpacks into the actual program files.
.gz	Packed with GNU Zip (gzip); use GNU Zip (gzip or gunzip) to unpack it.
.hqx	Macintosh BinHex file, used for sending binary data over text links. There are actually two incompatible formats (4.0 and 5.0), but every one ignores 5.0—look at the first line in the file to see whether it mentions BinHex 4.0.
.lha or .lzh	These are generally known as LHarc files and are fairly common for intersystem exchange. Very popular on the Amiga. There are several versions floating around—for example, LHa format is a popular variation which surpasses LHarc in compression capabilities. You may find some incompatibilities, however.
.sea	Macintosh self-extracting archive. Just run it to unpack it.
.shar	A program in executable shell format. You must have the UNIX Bourne shell available to unpack this (use this command to unpack: sh `filename`.shar).
.sit	Macintosh StuffIt 1.5, 2.0, or 3.0. Use StuffIt Expander to unpack it.
.tar	UNIX tar format turns several files into one large file for purposes of tape backup. Use tar (or detar) to unpack the file into its components. Because tar doesn't compress at all, you usually find the software tarred and then compressed.
.tar.gz or .tgz	A file that has been tarred and then gzipped. Use gzip to unpack it (you may have to rename `filename`.tgz to `filename`.tar.gz first if you have an old gzip) and then detar it.
.tar.Z or .tZ or .tarZ	A file that has been tarred and then compressed. Use uncompress and then detar it. You may have to rename `filename`.tZ or `filename`.tarZ to `filename`.tar.Z first.
.txt	A text file. Just read it.

.uue	A uuencoded file, used to send binary data over text links. Use uudecode to decode it.
.z	Created by the UNIX pack program. Do unpack *filename.z* to unpack it.
.zip	The near ubiquitous (under DOS) PKZIP format. You can use PKUNZIP to unpack these files or use the Info-ZIP program. Info-ZIP is slower, but more portable, and it's free. There are two major versions of .zip files: those from PKZIP 1.10 and those from PKZIP 2.04g.
.zoo	The zoo format is popular for inter-platform exchange. Use Booz 2.0 or Zoo 2.10 to unpack.
.Z	UNIX compress format—very common. You can use uncompress or gzip to decompress it.

The Software

Finally! Keep in mind that I'm not listing all possible software, or even major TCP/IP suites— I could fill a whole book with just product information if I wanted to, which could distress my editor.

This is a list of "critical" programs for those who make a habit of hanging around the Internet. You may not need the xxdecode program right this moment, but you should know where to find it when you do. More specific stuff can be found with Archie and in the rest of this book, where our authors have hustled their butts and given you plenty of listings of things like mail programs and Web browsers. I've made a specific effort to reference files on oak.oakland.edu if it is available there because this is a large and reliable FTP site.

NOTE

In fact, because this note won't take up much space, keep these great sites in mind when you're hunting software:

Mac:	sumex-aim.stanford.edu, mac.archive.umich.edu
OS/2:	ftp.cdrom.com
General:	oak.oakland.edu, sunsite.unc.edu, ftp.demon.co.uk, wuarchive.wustl.edu
Windows:	ftp.cica.indiana.edu

Because of their popularity, some of these sites can be very difficult to access during peak hours. You can either try again at a later time or go instead to one of the mirror sites. America Online, for example, maintains reliable mirrors (at mirrors.aol.com) of the Macintosh archives at Michigan and Stanford, and of the Indiana University CICA Windows archive.

Archivers

Data on the Internet comes packed in dozens of formats, each with its own advantages and disadvantages. You don't want to be able to pack all the different formats, just the most popular ones. But it would be nice to be able to unpack them. For that reason, the Internet Scout (motto: "Be Prepared") makes sure that he or she has access to all the necessary unpackers, and I've emphasized the Archivers section here. I suggest you grab the entire contents of `oak.oakland.edu:` `/pub/misc/unix` and have an unpack and compile party.

ABE

```
Platforms:      Any
Description:    Sends/receives binary programs over text links
Location:       oak.oakland.edu: /pub/misc/unix/abe.tar.Z
Author:         Brad Templeton
                <brad@clarinet.com>
Cost:           Free
```

ABE never really caught on, but it is a very nice way to send binary (8-bit) data over a text link, such as mail, where only a certain printable subset of characters is allowed. ABE the file on one side, mail it, then deABE it on the other side. It's written in portable C, and all the source code is included, so you can use it on just about any system with a C compiler. It has many more features than most of the other programs in this genre, including a good file error check.

ARC

```
Platforms:      UNIX, other
Description:    Archive program that handles .arc files
Location:       oak.oakland.edu: /pub/misc/unix/arc521e.tar.Z
Author:         Howard Chu
                <hyc@hanauma.jpl.nasa.gov>
Cost:           Free
```

ARC is the old PC SEA `.arc` format. This UNIX version also handles the more efficient "squashed" format introduced in the PKARC `.arc` packer. You'll only need this to unpack `.arc` files (you don't want to actually use it to pack something because other formats offer much greater compression). The source code is included so, theoretically, you can make this work on any system for which you have a C compiler.

ARCA and ARCE

```
Platforms:      DOS
Description:    .arc file packer and unpacker
Location:       oak.oakland.edu: /SimTel/msdos/archiver/arca129.zip
                oak.oakland.edu: /pub/SimTel/archiver/arce41a.zip
Authors:        Wayne Chin and Vernon D. Buerg
Cost:           Free
```

These are no-cost tools for adding to and extracting from any `.arc` files you happen to run across. No frills, but they work.

ARJ

```
Platforms:      DOS
Description:    .arj file packer/unpacker
Location:       oak.oakland.edu: /SimTel/msdos/archiver/arj241a.exe
Author:         Robert K. Jung
Cost:           Free for noncommercial, $40 other, volume discounts
```

ARJ is the "other" packer for DOS systems. It's superior to ZIP in many ways, but PKZIP has the momentum (and speed in most cases). ARJ is worth taking a look at anyhow, and certainly worth getting so that you can unpack any `.arj` files you find. It includes the `rearj` program, which converts archives from one format to another. There's no required registration for individual users, but you are strongly encouraged to send in your $40 if you use it regularly.

BinHex

```
Platforms:      DOS
Description:    Mac BinHex 4.0 encoder/decoder
Location:       oak.oakland.edu: /SimTel/msdos/mac/binhex13.zip
Author:         University of Minnesota
Cost:           Free
```

This program lets PC users work with BinHex files (basically the Mac version of uuencode/ uudecode) to send binary files over text links. It uses a full-screen interface. See `xbin`, later in this appendix, for an alternative.

boo

```
Platforms:      Many
Description:    Sends/receives binary program over text links
Location:       oak.oakland.edu: /pub/misc/unix/makeboo.c.Z
                oak.oakland.edu: /pub/misc/unix/unboo.c.Z
Author:         Robert Weiner
                <rweiner@watsun.cc.columbia.edu>
Cost:           Free
```

The boo program is yet another format looking to unseat uuencode as the format for sending a binary (8-bit) file over a link that can handle only ASCII characters (such as most mail systems). Use makeboo to encode the file (.boo) and unboo to decode it. Both are fairly portable C programs and come with specific support for Microsoft C 5.1 for DOS, GCC++ 1.05 for DOS, VMS, SunOS 4.1, UNIXPC 3.51, OS-9, MANX C for Amiga, and MWC for Atari ST. In the absence of a "real" transfer protocol like ZModem or Kermit, boo also offers a way to move files from system to system.

Booz

```
Platforms:      UNIX, other
Description:    Bare-bones ZOO file lister and extractor
Location:       oak.oakland.edu: /pub/misc/unix/booz20.tar.Z
Author:         Rahul Dhesi
                <dhesi@bsu-cs.bsu.edu>
Cost:           Free
```

This is a small and simple program that lists the contents of ZOO files and allows their extraction. The *ooz* comes from undoing zoo, and the *b* is for *bare-bones*. This is prime UNIX humor. It doesn't have all the fancy options of the full fledged ZOO, but that's not its purpose. It comes with source code and is fairly simple, so it should be usable on any system for which you have a C compiler. Booz 2.0 unpacks files created by ZOO 2.10 (the latest), which is somewhat strange naming.

Brik

```
Platforms:      UNIX, DOS, other
Description:    Makes 32-bit checksum files
Location:       oak.oakland.edu: /pub/misc/unix/brik2src.tar.Z
                oak.oakland.edu: /SimTel/msdos/fileutil/brik2exe.zip
Author:         Rahul Dhesi
                <dhesi@bsu-cs.bsu.edu>
Cost:           Free
```

Brik isn't, strictly speaking, an archive program, but it belongs with them. It allows you to generate 32-bit checksums for a file or series of files (ASCII or binary), save them, and then check them later. This is an excellent way to make sure that your file came through the mail (or whatever perils it traversed) intact. Brik isn't quite as useful as it used to be, now that most new archive programs use 32-bit checksums. The brik2exe.zip file contains the executables for DOS.

DeArj

```
Platforms:      Mac
Description:    .arj unpacker for Macs
Location:       sumex-aim.stanford.edu: /info-mac/cmp/de-arj.hqx
Author:         <ArgOn>buccolm@CSOS.ORST.EDU
Cost:           Unknown
```

DeArj claims to be the fastest .arj decompressor on the Mac and has a real Mac interface ("no command lines, thank you"). If you have to decompress .arj files on a Mac, this one is worth a look.

dosmap

```
Platforms:      UNIX
Description:    Translates UNIX file trees to DOS filenames
Location:       oak.oakland.edu: /pub/misc/unix/dosmap.prl
Author:         Afzal Ballim
                <afzal@divsun.unige.ch>
Cost:           Free
```

This perl script (most versions of UNIX have perl) takes a UNIX hierarchy and turns it into one that is DOS compatible. This can be desirable because DOS is so incredibly limiting with names. Not only are the filenames changed (simple), but any references to them in uncompressed files such as makefiles or documentation are changed as well.

gzip (GNU Zip)

Platforms:	UNIX, PC, OS/2, other
Description:	Handles .Z and .gz compressed files
Location:	prep.ai.mit.edu: /pub/gnu/
	ftp.cdrom.com: /.1/os2/unix/gz124-32.zip
Authors:	Many, but primary Jean-loup Gailly
	<jloup@chorus.fr>
Cost:	Free

gzip (GNU Zip) is the Free Software Foundation's answer to the ubiquitous ZIP format in the PC world and is a replacement for UNIX compress. It's not compatible with PC .zip files, so the name is slightly misleading, but its intent is to be as common in UNIX as .zip is for DOS—and it seems to be succeeding. gzip's .gz files are everywhere on the Internet. It fixes two serious problems with UNIX compress: First, compress is covered by two patents—gzip is guaranteed patent free, which means no legal or money hassles. And compress is seriously out of date—its compression ratios are pathetic by today's standards. gzip uses modern compression algorithms to get very respectable compression.

gzip offers nine levels of compression (from fast and inefficient to slower and much compression); it can unpack compress's .Z files and pack's .z files as well. It's a complete compress, decompress, pack, and unpack replacement.

gzip also includes gzexe—this phenomenal little program allows you to pack your UNIX executable files so that they take up less space on disk. Whenever you run a program, it is quickly unpacked (in /tmp) and run. Because UNIX executables often compress very well, this program can save you a lot of space.

Because the filenames change with every release, and there are multiple file options, the following locations may have changed. The current version of gzip is 1.2.4, so I'll use that:

gzip-1.2.4.msdos.exe	gzip in executable DOS format
gzip-1.2.4.shar	gzip source code in shar format
gzip-1.2.4.tar	gzip source code in tar format
gzip-1.2.4.tar.gz	gzip source code tarred and compressed

If you use DOS, you'll want to grab the gzip-1.2.4.msdos.exe version. If you already have gzip for your UNIX system, you should grab gzp-1.2.4.tar.gz. If you don't have gzip yet, grab gzip-1.2.4.tar if you have tar; grab gzip-1.2.4.shar if you have the Bourne shell available. The .tar and .shar files are four times larger, which is why you don't always want to grab them. For OS/2, the gz124.-32.zip file on ftp.cdrom.com contains executables.

The source code includes makefiles for Amiga, Atari ST, DOS, Windows NT, OS/2, PRIMOS, generic UNIX, and VMS.

```
Platforms:      Mac
Description:    gzip for Macs (see gzip, just described)
Location:       sumex-aim.stanford.edu: /info-mac/cmp/mac-gzip-022.hqx
Author:         Jose A. Gutierrez
                <MacSPD@ivo.cps.unizar.es>
Cost:           Free
```

This is gzip for Macs; it's separate because it's a work in progress (it is in version 0.2 at press time). Perhaps soon after you purchase this wonderful book, the full 1.0 version will come out. Call me and we'll throw a party.

HQXer

```
Platforms:      Mac
Description:    BinHex encoder/decoder for Macs
Location:       sumex-aim.stanford.edu: /info-mac/cmp/hqxer-11.hqx
Author:         John Stiles
                <LTAYLOR@academic.csubak.edu>
Cost:           $10
```

This is a fast, System 7-aware program that creates and decodes BinHex files. Requires System 6.0.7 or later.

LHA for UNIX

```
Platforms:      UNIX
Description:    .lha/.lzh file packer/unpacker
Location:       oak.oakland.edu: /pub/misc/unix/lha101u.tar.Z
Authors:        Several
Cost:           Free
```

LHarc format is popular for intersystem transfer, mostly because the format is well known and source code is freely available. This is the LHA program, which supersedes the LHarc format— it can unpack LHarc files, but LHarc programs (such as LHarc 1.02 for UNIX) can't unpack LHA files. LHA is competitive with the other major archive programs (PKZIP 2.04g, ARJ 2.41, ZOO 2.10) in terms of packed files sizes. It includes source code, so it can be compiled on most systems.

Unfortunately for uneducated Westerners, the original authors are Japanese, and so is the included documentation. But LHA works like almost any other archiver, and the built-in short instructions are in English, so you should be able to cope.

Mac Archive Utilities for OS/2

```
Platforms:      OS/2, UNIX, other
Description:    Unpacks Mac .hqx, .sit, and .cpt files
Location:       ftp.cdrom.com: /.1/os2/archiver/macutils.zip
Authors:        Compiled by John Paul Morrison
                <jmorriso@ee.ubc.ca>
                Most source code by Dik Winter
                <dik@cwi.nl>
                Unpost code by I. Lee Hetherington
                <ilh@lcs.mit.edu>
                Many others
Cost:           Free
```

Impressive! With this little set of utilities, you can unpack those pesky Macintosh archive files. It will handle the following formats and archivers: BinHex 5.0, MacBinary, UIMCP, Compress II, ShrinkToFit, MacCompress, AutoDoubler, PackIt, StuffIt, Diamond, Compactor/Compact Pro, Zoom, LHArc/MacLHa, most StuffIt Classic/StuffIt Deluxe, and later versions of DiskDoubler.

This file comes with OS/2 executable versions, but includes all source code and should compile under UNIX as well (or on other platforms with a little massaging).

mcvert 2.15

```
Platforms:      All
Description:    Converts Mac file interchange formats
Location:       sumex-aim.stanford.edu: /info-mac/cmp/mcvert-216.shar
Authors:        Many, including Joseph Skudlarek
                <jskud@wv.MENTORG.COM>
Cost:           Free
```

This one converts between Macintosh file interchange formats, such as BinHex and MacBinary, on a UNIX machine or just about any system that can compile the C programs.

PKPAK 3.61

```
Platforms:      DOS
Description:    .arc file packer/depacker
Location:       oak.oakland.edu: /SimTel/msdos/archiver/pk361.exe
Author:         Phil Katz
Cost:           $45 (volume discounts)
```

After SEA created their ARC package and the first "standard" archive file format for DOS, Phil Katz came along with PKARC, which was far faster and included a new compression type for better compression. SEA eventually took legal action to stop Katz from doing anything with ARC. He came back with the now famous PKZIP program and .arc files haven't been heard from since. However, the last PKARC file massagers are still available for your use if you come across .arc files and don't want to use the public domain .arc file extractors. For free utilities, see ARCA and ARCE, earlier in this appendix.

PKZIP

```
Platforms:      DOS
Description:    .zip file packer/unpacker
Location:       oak.oakland.edu: /SimTel/msdos/zip/pkz204g.exe
Author:         PKWare
Cost:           $47 (volume discounts)
```

.zip is the premiere file format for the PC, and PKZIP is the program that sets the standard. It can't be beat for speed in .zip file manipulation, but if you want free versions, see UnZip and Zip, later in this appendix. They don't have multiple floppy disk archive support (PKZIP does). Make sure that you have version 2.04g, and not anything earlier—earlier 2.xx versions were extremely buggy and tended to explode in your face.

Post/Unpost

```
Platforms:      All
Description:    Highly featured uuencode/uudecode programs
Location:       oak.oakland.edu: /SimTel/msdos/decode/post110.zip
                oak.oakland.edu: /SimTel/msdos/decode/unpos234.zip
Author:         John W. M. Stevens
                <jstevens@csn.org>
Cost:           Free
```

See uuencode, uudecode, and uucat, later in this appendix for more information—and then realize that Post and Unpost are the premiere programs for dealing with the headaches you encounter with the other three programs. Both Post and Unpost are in the msdos directories but should work with almost any system that has a C compiler.

Post handles all the problems involved in uuencoding a file and posting it in multiple parts. It even handles generating the different headers and subject lines. It comes with a utility that lets you automatically post the results to Usenet using NNTP.

Unpost handles all the travails involved in uudecoding files, including multiple files in one source file, one file in multiple source files, and combinations thereof. It sorts pieces that are out of order. It can discard or save "garbage" messages, such as all text commentary messages. It comes with a utility that lets you automatically grab new articles from Usenet using NNTP and then decodes them.

The programs are full featured and highly configurable. I like them. If they're a bit intimidating for you, see uuencode/uudecode for PC, later in this appendix.

StuffIt Expander 3.7

```
Platforms:      Mac
Description:    Great unpacker of most Mac packed formats
Location:       sumex-aim.stanford.edu: /info-mac/cmp/stuffit-expander-352.hqx
                sumex-aim.stanford.edu: /info-mac/cmp/stuff-expander-352.bin
Author:         Aladdin Systems, Inc.
                Leonard Rosenthol
                <leonardr@netcom.com>
Cost:           Free
```

If you get no other unpacker for your Mac, get this one. It handles AppleLink packages, BinHex files, and CompactPro and StuffIt archives. Nice user interface. They're trying to sell you their StuffIt Deluxe or StuffIt Lite packages—more power to them—and you get your free software.

suntar

```
Platforms:      Mac
Description:    .tar creator/unpacker for Macintosh
Location:       sumex-aim.stanford.edu: /info-mac/cmp/suntar-204.hqx
Author:         Sauro Speranza
                <speranza@cirfid.unibo.it>
Cost:           Free
```

This is a beta release, so by the time you decide to make that difference in your life and buy this book, a full version should be out there. Suntar is the most powerful .tar file manager for the Mac. It is mostly useful for unpacking UNIX .tar files, but it can be used as a backup program if you can't stand to part with the money for a commercial tape backup program.

UnARJ

```
Platforms:      Any
Description:    Unpacker for ARJ files
Location:       oak.oakland.edu: /pub/misc/unix/unarj241.tar.Z
                oak.oakland.edu: /SimTel/msdos/archiver/unarj241.zip
                ftp.cdrom.com: /.1/os2/archiver/unarj241.zip
Author:         Robert K. Jung
                <robjung@world.std.com>
Cost:           Free
```

ARJ is a fairly popular DOS compressor, initially because it compressed much better than PKZIP 1.10 and currently because it has more features (such as decent multidisk archives, which PKZIP 2.04g still doesn't have). Unfortunately, it's not available for any platform other than DOS. Fortunately, however, the author has made decompression source code freely available, so you can make the UnARJ de-archive on any system. It's fairly no-frills, but it works. unarj241.zip at oak is the DOS compiled version, unarj241.zip at cdrom is the OS/2 compiled version.

Unsea

```
Platforms:      UNIX, other
Description:    Handles Mac self-expanding (.sea) files
Location:       sumex-aim.stanford.edu: /info-mac/cmp/unsea-10-unix.shar
Author:         David W. Rankin
                <rankin@ms.uky.edu>
Cost:           Free
```

Unsea removes the self-expanding code from self-expanding archive (.sea) Mac binary files created by StuffIt or CompactPro. It's ANSI C code, so it should work if you have an ANSI-compliant C compiler.

Unshar

```
Platforms:      DOS, other
Description:    Extracts files from .shar archives
Location:       oak.oakland.edu: /SimTel/msdos/fileutil/unshar.zip
Authors:        Fred Smith
                <uunet!samsung!wizvax!fcshome!fredex>
                Warren Toomey
                <wtoomey@csadfa.oz.au@munnari.oz>
Cost:           Free
```

If you have access to the UNIX Bourne shell, .shar files are very nice because they are self extracting. You just run them through the shell and unbundle the files within. If you don't have access to sh, you're in trouble. You can panic, or you can grab this program. It does a quick and dirty job of looking through the .shar file and grabbing the individual files for extraction. It should run on almost any platform with a C compiler. It comes with a DOS executable.

unsit for UNIX

```
Platforms:      UNIX, other
Description:    Unpacks Macintosh .sit files
Location:       sumex-aim.stanford.edu: /info-mac/cmp/unsit-15-unix.shar
Author:         Jeff Wasilko
                <jjw7384@ultb.isc.rit.edu>
Cost:           Free
```

This is a small set of C programs that unpack Mac StuffIt 1.5 (not the latest 3.0) files.

UNSIT

```
Platforms:      DOS
Description:    Unpacker for Mac .sit files
Location:       oak.oakland.edu: /SimTel/msdos/mac/unsit30.zip
Author:         Brian K. Uechi
                <brian_u@verifone.com>
Cost:           Free
```

If you have to unpack Mac .sit files, this will do it for you. No source code.

UnStuff/PC

```
Platforms:      DOS
Description:    Unpacker for Mac .sit files
Location:       sumex-aim.stanford.edu: /info-mac/cmp/unstuff-msdos.hqx
Author:         Aladdin Systems, Inc.
                Leonard Rosenthol
                <leonardr@netcom.com>
Cost:           Free
```

This is a Mac .sit file unpacker from the makers of StuffIt, who should know what they're doing.

UnZip 5.01

```
Platforms:      UNIX, DOS, OS/2, Mac, other
Description:    Info-ZIP unpacker for .zip files
Location:       oak.oakland.edu: /pub/misc/unix/unzip512.tar.Z
                oak.oakland.edu: /SimTel/msdos/zip/unz512x.exe
                ftp.cdrom.com: /.1/os2/archiver/unz512x1.exe
Author:         Info-ZIP project
                <info-zip@wkuvx1.bitnet>
Cost:           Free
```

See the information on Zip 2.0.1, later in this appendix, for more explanation. This comes with source code and compile support for Amiga (partial), Macintosh, Minix, DOS, OS/2, UNIX, VMS, Windows, and Windows NT. Version 5.1 will have full Amiga, Atari ST, and TOPS-20 support. unz50p1.exe is the DOS executable. unz50x32.exe is the OS/2 32-bit package.

uucat

```
Platforms:      All
Description:    Recombines split uuencoded files
Location:       oak.oakland.edu: /pub/misc/unix/uucat.c
                oak.oakland.edu: /pub/misc/unix/uucat.msg
Author:         Stefan Parmark
                <d84sp@efd.lth.se>
Cost:           Free
```

This small utility recombines split uuencoded files. Because many links limit the size of messages (64K is common), you may have to split a uuencoded file into several pieces and send the pieces individually. The person receiving the pieces has to recombine the files, edit out all the extraneous mail crud, and then uudecode it. The uucat utility does the first two steps for you.

uuencode/uudecode

```
Platforms:       All
Description:     Sends/receives binary files over a text link
Location:        oak.oakland.edu: /pub/misc/unix/uuencode.c
                 oak.oakland.edu: /pub/misc/unix/uudecode.c
Authors:         Many
Cost:            Free
```

This is the mother of all methods for sending binary (8-bit) data over a link that can accept only ASCII characters (such as most e-mail transfers). You uuencode the file, which turns it into a gibberish of printable characters, and send the file to the other person; they uudecode it and, supposedly, they then have the file.

These program files are very portable C and should be usable on almost any system. Your only worry may be truncating file names if your system allows limited filenames (like DOS, but it already comes with DOS support). See uucat (the preceding description) for another useful utility.

For a more fully featured set of programs that do more of the grunt work for you, see Post/Unpost, earlier in this appendix, and uuencode/uudecode for PC, in the following section.

uuencode/uudecode for PC

```
Platforms:       DOS
Description:     Full featured uuencode/uudecode for DOS
Location:        oak.oakland.edu: /SimTel/msdos/decode/uuexe532.zip
Author:          Richard Marks
Cost:            Free
```

uuencode/uudecode and xxencode/xxdecode can be a pain in the rear. Because many links limit the size of messages (64K is common), you may have to split a uuencoded file into several pieces and send the pieces individually. This causes many headaches, much unnecessary manual labor, and conniptions when things arrive in the wrong order. uuencode/uudecode 5.25 for PC takes care of most of this for you. It automatically handles splitting and de-splitting, even when the split pieces are out of order. Very convenient and easy to use, especially for decoding. This software also handles the xxencode/xxdecode format (in case anyone uses that).

For a more fully featured set of programs, see Post/Unpost, earlier in this appendix.

UULite

```
Platforms:      Macintosh
Description:    Decodes uuencoded files on the Mac
Location:       sumex-aim.stanford.edu: /info-mac/cmp/uu-lite-17.hqx
Author:         Jeff Strobel
                <jstrobel@world.std.com>
```

UULite does only one thing: decode split uuencoded files. And it does a good job of it. Includes completely automatic encoding and splitting, special decoding for "problem files," automatic and manual type/creator setup, and more. It's completely disk based, so it's limited only by the space available.

uuprep 1.0

```
Platforms:      OS/2, UNIX, other
Description:    Split uuencode file unpacker
Location:       ftp.cdrom.com: /.1/os2/2_x/archiver/uuprep10.zip
Author:         Johannes Martin
                <JMARTIN@VZDMZX.ZDV.UNI-MAINZ.DE>
Cost:           Free
```

This program is specifically written to process the contents of a Usenet newsgroup in preparation for uudecoding. Just dump all the pieces into the big stewpot file and run uuprep on it to produce a sorted and cleaned file. It then sends that through uudecode (included in the package). Source code is included, so it can fairly easily be recompiled on other systems. Its simplicity of operation makes it worth a look.

xbin

```
Platforms:      DOS, other
Description:    Mac BinHex 4.0 decoder
Location:       oak.oakland.edu: /SimTel/msdos/mac/xbin23.zip
Author:         Jochen Roderburg
                <Ro@RRZ.Uni-Koeln.DE>
Cost:           Free
```

This program lets PC users decode BinHex files (basically the Mac version of uuencode/uudecode) and allows you to send binary files over text links. It comes with simple C source for DOS and UNIX, so it should work on other systems as well. If you want to make BinHex files, see BinHex 1.3, earlier in this appendix.

xxencode and xxdecode

```
Platforms:      All
Description:    Sends/receives binary files over a text link
Location:       oak.oakland.edu: /pub/misc/unix/xxencode.c
                oak.oakland.edu: /pub/misc/unix/xxdecode.c
                oak.oakland.edu: /pub/misc/unix/xxencode.man
Authors:        Phil Howard and David J. Camp
                <david@wubios.wustl.edu>
Cost:           Free
```

Yet another program trying to replace uuencode/uudecode. This is mostly a bust, but it's worth mentioning in case you find an .xxe file and because xxdecode includes the equivalent of uucat for uudecode. It's also worth mentioning because xxencoded and uuencoded files look a lot alike (and produce the same size files!), but their files are incompatible. xxdecode will happily chew on a uuencoded file and spit out an incorrect file, with no errors. For your information, lines in uuencode files start with M and lines in xxencode files start with h.

Wincode

```
Platforms:      Microsoft Windows
Description:    Sends/receives binary files over a text link
Location:       oak.oakland.edu: /SimTel/win3/encode/wncode261.zip
Author:         George H. Silva
                <George.Silva@wadsworth.org>
Cost:           Free
```

A multipurpose encoder/decoder for Windows; supports uuencode. A help file and e-mail support is available for a $5 payment to the author.

WinZip

```
Platforms:      Microsoft Windows
Description:    Zip packer/unpacker for Windows
Location:       oak.oakland.edu: /SimTel/win3/archiver/winzip56.exe
Author:         Niko Mak
                <info@winzip.com>
Cost:           Shareware: $29 registration
```

Windows tool that allows the use of ZIP files without requiring PKZIP and PKUNZIP. ARJ, LZH, and ARC files are supported with external programs. Version 5.6 includes built-in support for popular Internet file formats, including `tar`, `gzip`, and UNIX `compress`. Both Windows and Win32 (Windows/NT and Windows 95) versions are available.

Zip

```
Platforms:      UNIX, DOS, OS/2, Mac, other
Description:    Info-ZIP .zip file packer
Location:       oak.oakland.edu: /pub/misc/unix/zip201.zip
                oak.oakland.edu: /SimTel/msdos/zip/zip20x.zip
                ftp.cdrom.com: /.1/os2/archiver/zip201x2.zip
Author:         Info-ZIP project
                <info-zip@wkuvx1.bitnet>
Cost:           Free
```

The `.zip` format is the archiving format of choice in the DOS world. These programs are manipulated by PKZIP, from PKWare. Unfortunately, the latest PKZIP is available only for DOS, and although PKWare has made noises about porting it to other platforms, that could take forever (PKZIP 2.0 was a year late). Enter the Info-ZIP team with Zip 2.0.1 (sometimes known as portable Zip 2.0.1). This program is compatible with the files created by the latest PKZIP (2.04g) and reproduces most of its features (and adds a few). Even better, it comes with source code and is portable between platforms. You can have Zip (and companion UnZip, described earlier in this appendix) for free and use it on almost any computer. It's not as fast as PKZIP, which is the price you pay for portablility, and it doesn't do PKZIP's multivolume archive support.

Zip 2.0.1 goes with UnZip 5.0p1—they use a different numbering scheme on each to make your life more difficult. Support includes Amiga, Atari ST, Mac, DOS (Borland and Microsoft C), Human68k, OS/2, TOPS-20, UNIX, VMS, and Windows NT. The `zip20x.zip` is the DOS executable. `zip201x2.zip` is the 32-bit OS/2 version.

ZipIt

```
Platforms:      Mac
Description:    .zip packer/unpacker for Macs
Location:       sumex-aim.stanford.edu: /info-mac/cmp/zip-it-131.hqx
Author:         Tommy Brown
Cost:           $10
```

ZipIt seems to be the ultimate `.zip` file utility for the Mac. It understands the latest PKZIP 2.0 format and retains special Mac file information within the packed file. It is a full Mac interface, which is a change (usually, `.zip` utilities for the Mac are quick ports). It's even System 7-aware. If you deal with lots of `.zip` files, $10 is a bargain.

ZiPMe

```
Platforms:      OS/2
Description:    Graphical interface for Info-ZIP's Zip and UnZip
Location:       ftp.cdrom.com: /.1/os2/archiver/zipme121.zip
Author:         Peter Eggert
                <eggert@uni-paderborn.de>
Cost:           Free
```

This is a slick little Presentation Manager shell that manipulates ZIP files using Zip and UnZip (described earlier in this appendix).

Zoo

```
Platforms:      UNIX, DOS, other
Description:    ZOO file packer/unpacker
Location:       oak.oakland.edu: /pub/misc/unix/zoo210.tar.Z
                oak.oakland.edu: /SimTel/msdos/zoo/zoo210.exe
                ftp.cdrom.com: /.1/os2/archiver/zoo210e.zip
Author:         Rahul Dhesi
                <dhesi@bsu-cs.bsu.edu>
Cost:           Free
```

ZOO is a popular compressor file inter-platform file exchange and a favorite of UNIX hacker types. It comes with source code, has a very Free Software Foundation-like license, has a seemingly infinite number of options, and behaves like a UNIX tool "should" behave. It's lost its favored position to GNU Zip and Info-ZIP's Zip, which share many of the same attractions. It comes with fiz 2.0, a damaged-ZOO-file repair utility. zoo210.exe is the DOS executable. zoo21_2.zip is the 32-bit HPFS aware OS/2 version.

File Transfer (FTP)

Most of your problems involve what to do with the files once you have them, but if you want something else to worry about, moving files around is a good candidate.

AutoFtp

```
Platforms:      UNIX
Description:    Automatic FTP without user babysitting
Location:       oak.oakland.edu: /pub/misc/unix/autoftp30.tar.Z
Author:         Mingqi Deng
                <deng@shire.cs.psu.edu>
Cost:           Free
```

This program consists of three C files and a Bourne shell script that allow you to set up automatic FTP of a group of files from a remote server without any user intervention. This arrangement is desirable for several reasons. First, many sites allow only a limited number of users, so you have to keep trying to get on. Second, because it can take a while to fetch files, with AutoFtp, you don't have to wait, enter a new file name, wait, and so forth.

You have to change the default FTP server (SIMTEL-20 no longer exists), and you need in advance a list of files you want to get from your FTP server. FTP to it normally, download the index, make a list of files to grab, and then use AutoFtp. This comes with source code.

BatchFtp

```
Platforms:      UNIX
Description:    Automatic FTP without user babysitting
Location:       oak.oakland.edu: /pub/misc/unix/batchftp102.tar.Z
Author:         Shawn Cooper
                <cooper@rex.cs.tulane.edu>
Cost:           Free
```

If AutoFtp is too underpowered for you, BatchFtp is its descendant. It has a much more powerful set of options and commands (such as FTP upload). For basic operation principles, however, see the AutoFtp description in the preceding section. BatchFtp comes with source code and should work on any Berkeley-style UNIX system.

Fetch

```
Platforms:      Macintosh
Description:    MacTCP-based FTP client
Location:       sumex-aim.stanford.edu: /info-mac/comm/tcp/fetch-212.hqx
Cost:           Shareware: $25 registration
```

rz and sz

```
Platforms:      UNIX
Description:    Zmodem, Ymodem, Xmodem file transfers
Location:       oak.oakland.edu: /pub/misc/unix/rzsz3_36.sh.Z
                oak.oakland.edu: /pub/misc/unix/rzsz-pd.zip
Author:         Chuck Forsberg
                <...!tektronix!reed!omen!caf>
Cost:           Free/$20 per port (see description); volume discounts
```

There's a good chance your UNIX box already has Kermit or Xmodem, but they're both incredibly slow (newer versions of Kermit are much faster, but your term program probably doesn't support it). Use rz and sz on UNIX, and your modern term program on your personal computer, and get full Zmodem speed and functionality. rz and sz can also do Ymodem and Xmodem.

There is a bit of a "gotcha"—the latest versions of rz and sz are not public domain. They are free for educational use or if you use them to talk to other Omen Technology (Chuck Forsberg's company) products. Otherwise, you must pay $20 per port to register them. The rz and sz programs in rzsz-pd.zip are completely free, but they're not as recent and don't have all the features of the latest versions.

Xmodem

```
Platforms:      UNIX
Description:    Xmodem and Ymodem file transfers
Location:       oak.oakland.edu: /pub/misc/unix/xmodem3-10.tar.Z
Author:         Steve Grandi
                <grandi@noau.edu>
Cost:           Free
```

This is an implementation of Xmodem and Ymodem for UNIX. It supports batch, 1K mode, CRC, and MODEM7. It has special text and Macintosh text modes as well for automatic CR/CRLF/LF translation. Unlike rz/sz, this is absolutely free. If you don't need Zmodem, this should fit your needs.

WS_FTP

```
Platforms:      Windows
Description:    FTP file transfers
Location:       oak.oakland.edu: /SimTel/win3/winsock/ws_ftp.zip
Author:         John A. Junod
                <72321.366@compuserve.com>
Cost:           Free for individual noncommercial use and by any U.S.
                government organization.
```

Excellent WinSock FTP client. Retains site profiles.

VX FTP

```
Platforms:      OS/2
Description:    Multithreaded PM FTP client
Location:       ftp.cdrom.com
```

Mail

There's more information about Internet mail in Chapter 12, "Internet E-Mail: An Overview," but here is a short selection of some mail programs you can try out.

Elm for OS/2

```
Platforms:      OS/2
Description:    Elm e-mail front-end for OS/2
Location:       ftp.cdrom.com: /pub/os2/unix/elm23exe.zip
```

Eudora

```
Platforms:      Windows, Macintosh
Description:    E-mail program
Location:       ftp.qualcomm.com
Cost:           Freeware for noncommercial use. Upgraded commercial version 2.0
                available for $65.
```

Easy-to-use e-mail program that features mailboxes, MIME and BinHex support, automatic checking for new mail, and address books.

Pegasus Mail

```
Platforms:      Windows
Description:    E-mail program
Location:       risc.ua.edu: /pub/network/pegasus
Author:         David Harris
Cost:           Free; manuals available from author for a fee
```

A Windows e-mail program that has more features than many commercial programs. Supports MIME, uuencode, BinHex, message filtering, and automatic mail checking; includes a spell checker and address book.

POP3d

```
Platforms:      UNIX
Description:    POP3 Mail Server
Location:       oak.oakland.edu: /pub/misc/unix/pop3d.tar.Z
Author:         Katie Stevens
                <dkstevens@ucdavis.edu>
Cost:           Free
```

This is a simple POP3 mail server for UNIX. For more information about POP3, see Chapter 13, "Internet E-Mail: UNIX." It should run under generic UNIX and SunOS. It's small, it's portable, it's easily changed, and it's free. Elegant.

UnDigest

```
Platforms:      UNIX
Description:    Turns mail digests into individual messages
Location:       oak.oakland.edu: /pub/misc/unix/undigest.c
Author:         (Maintainer) Keith B. Petersen
                <w8sdz@TACOM-EMH1.Army.Mil>
Cost:           Free
```

Many mailing lists "digestify" their messages by combining them into a single message and sending it out. This greatly reduces the strain on routers and mailers. If you prefer to read these digested messages as individual messages, however, you need a mail reader that automatically "undigestifies"—or you can use this program. It turns the digest message into a mailbox files with lots of individual messages. It's very portable C, so it should work on almost any system for which you have a C compiler.

Newsreaders

Your Usenet newsreader is a highly personal thing, capable of sparking wars nearly as heated as the "My UNIX editor is better than yours" wars (just for the record, emacs is better than vi). If you bought one of the TCP/IP suites, you may already have a newsreader. But the UNIX newsreaders have had longer to evolve—I've got more newsreaders than I can shake a stick at (although the rationale for doing that is fuzzy) and I still Telnet to a UNIX box to run nn. I'd probably do the same for trn if nn wasn't available.

In the beginning, the UNIX newsreader was rn and rn was the UNIX newsreader. This was back in the days when an individual could still read every message posted to news every day. Now Usenet traffic is huge, and it can be almost impossible to keep up with the few groups that interest you—and people are still using rn, which was written for a low-traffic, low-noise situation. If you can move up to something else, you will be astounded at the time you can save.

News XPress

```
Platforms:      Windows
Description:    Usenet news reader
Location:       boris.infomagic.com: /pub/mirrors/cica/winsock/nx10b3.zip
Author:         W.L. Ken Ng
                <kenng@hk.super.net>
Cost:           Freeware
```

One of the top WinSock newsreaders, commercial or free. Supports threads, signatures, built-in uuencode/uudecode, kill and autoselect, and local folders for filing articles.

Newswatcher

```
Platforms:      Macintosh
Description:    MacTCP-based FTP client
Location:       sumex-aim.stanford.edu: /info-mac/comm/tcp/news-watcher-
                20b24.hqx
Cost:           Free
```

The most popular Mac newsreader. Drag-and-drop subscribing. Articles display Reply and Followup buttons. Automatic uudecoding.

nn (No News Is Good News)

```
Platforms:      UNIX
Description:    Best Usenet group reader on the planet
Location:       dkuug.dk: /pub/nn6.4.tar.Z
Author:         Kim Fabricius Storm
                <storm@texas.dk>
Cost:           Free
```

You may have your own custom Usenet newsreader for your platform. But if you're stuck with rn, you owe yourself a look at nn—it may already be on your system: just try typing **nn**. The nn program's features are far too many to go into here, but its basic philosophy is doable: although rn makes you work to *not* read articles, nn reads nothing unless you want it to. Everything is presented in overview format, and you can choose which articles/authors look interesting. A little practice and you'll be zipping through groups—it can literally take less than a tenth of the time to read the same articles and extract the same information. As you have no doubt guessed, I'm biased. I've tried all the major newsreaders, and this is what I use.

trn

```
Platforms:      UNIX
Description:    Usenet newsgroup reader, better than rn
Location:       vixen.cso.uiuc.edu: /usenet/trn-3.4/
Author:         Wayne Davison
                <davison@borland.com>
                (based on rn by Larry Wall and Stan Barber)
Cost:           Free
```

The other major newsreader. This takes rn and makes it more like nn...or not, depending on your whims. It can behave just like rn if you want, or you can use the new trn features as needed or wanted. If you're attached or addicted to rn, this is a great way to move up: it's like a familiar friend but with a lot of new qualifications. As with nn, you'll find that you can search the same mass of data in a fraction of the time it takes with rn.

TRN for OS/2

```
Platforms:      OS/2
Description:    trn newsreader for OS/2
Location:       hobbes.nmsu.edu: /network/tcpip/trn_197b.zip
```

OS/2 version of the popular UNIX newsreader.

Trumpet Newsreader

```
Platforms:      Windows
Description:    Usenet newsreader
Location:       ftp.trumpet.com.au: /ftp/pub/beta/wintrump/wt_wsk.zip
Cost:           Shareware: $4 registration
```

An easy-to-use Windows newsreader. Shows new groups since you have last subscribed and can save articles to disk or in folders.

WinVN

```
Platforms:      Windows
Description:    Usenet newsreader
Location:       ftp.ksc.nasa.gov: /pub/winvn.win3
Cost:           Free
```

Popular WinSock newsreader that supports threading and built-in uudecoding.

YARN/2

```
Platforms:      OS/2
Description:    A text-mode offline news and mail handler
Location:       hobbes.nmsu.edu: /comm/yrn2_083.zip
```

The NewsReader/2 application included with OS/2 Warp can read only newsgroup articles when you are logged on to the Internet. This OS/2 version of YARN allows you to do offline reading of groups.

Search Tools

Here's a collection of some of the best UNIX, Windows, OS/2, and Macintosh Archie and Gopher clients.

Anarchie

```
Platforms:      Macintosh
Description:    Archie client
Location:       sumex-aim.stanford.edu: /info-mac/comm/tcp/anarchie-14.hqx
Cost:           Shareware: $10 registration
```

A nifty program that combines Archie searching and FTP.

Archie

```
Platforms:      UNIX, DOS, NeXT
Description:    Clients for Archie
Location:       nic.sura.net: /pub/archie/clients/
Authors:        Brendan Kehoe and others
Cost:           Free
```

There are several files of interest in this directory. I suggest you look through the directory and read the README file to see which client is best suited for you. If you don't know, try the c-Archie client.

Archie for OS/2

```
Platforms:      OS/2
Description:    Text-mode Archie client
Location:       hobbes.nmsu.edu: /network/tcpip/archie.zip
```

Archie for OS/2 is a command-line Archie client. It allows you to store the results of a search in a file if you think the results won't fit onto a single screen of data (which often is the case).

Gopher for OS/2

```
Platforms:      OS/2
Description:    Gopher client
Location:       hobbes.nmsu.edu: /network/tcpip/gopher.zip
```

TurboGopher

```
Platforms:      Macintosh
Description:    MacTCP-based Gopher client
Location:       sumex-aim.stanford.edu: /info-mac/Communication/MacTCP/turbo-
                gopher-20.hqx
Cost:           Free
```

WSArchie

```
Platforms:      Windows
Description:    WinSock Archie client
Location:       oak.oakland.edu: /SimTel/win3/winsock/wsarch07.zip
Author:         David Woakes
Cost:           Free for noncommercial use
```

Well-designed Archie program that can work with WS_FTP to retrieve files.

Other Tools

The programs described in the following sections don't quite fit into any of the preceding categories, but still come in handy at times.

CRLF

```
Platforms:      Macintosh
Description:    Converts text file formats
Location:       sumex-aim.stanford.edu: /info-mac/cmp/crlf-120.hqx
Author:         Natsu Sakimura
                <SAKIMURA@vaxr.sscl.uwo.ca>
Cost:           Free
```

DOS uses a CR/LF (Carriage Return/Line Feed) combination to mark the end of a line. UNIX uses just an LF. Macs use just a CR. *Sheesh.* CRLF lets you easily convert between these formats. It also supports Japanese text.

flip 1.0

```
Platforms:      UNIX, DOS, other
Description:    Converts text files between LF and CR/LF format
Location:       oak.oakland.edu: /pub/misc/unix/flip1src.tar.Z
Author:         Rahul Dhesi
                <dhesi@bsu-cs.bsu.edu>
Cost:           Free
```

DOS likes a Carriage Return/Line Feed (CR/LF) at the end of every line of text. UNIX likes just a simple Line Feed (LF). This can cause problems when manipulating text on one system that was created for another system. The flip program does conversion of text files from one format to the other; as an added bonus, it detects binary files and avoids changing those (because that would be disaster). It's simple C source and should work on any system for which you have a C compiler. It comes with project files for Turbo C 2.0 for DOS.

GNUish Tools for DOS

```
Platforms:      DOS
Description:    DOS versions of GNU UNIX tools
Location:       oak.oakland.edu: /SimTel/msdos/gnuish/
Authors:        Various
Cost:           Free
```

If you become a UNIX addict and can't stand the thought of using nonUNIX-like DOS programs, you can find many DOS equivalents in this directory. Especially look at the file futil4ax.zip, which contains a host of miscellaneous UNIX-like file utilities, including cat, chmod, cmp, cp, dir, head, ls, mkdir, mv, paste, rm, rmdir, tac, tail, touch, and vdir.

GNUish Tools for OS/2

```
Platforms:      OS/2
Description:    OS/2 versions of UNIX tools
Location:       ftp.cdrom.com: /.1/os2/unix/
Authors:        Various (Kai Uwe Rommel deserves an extra pat on the back,
                however)
Cost:           Most are free
```

Again, if the sinister urge for UNIX gets the better of you and you decide that your OS/2 should behave like UNIX, you can get a full set of standard UNIX utilities here. You can even find some UNIX shells if you want to make OS/2 command shells look more like UNIX.

host

```
Platforms:      UNIX, possibly other
Description:    Returns host information
Location:       oak.oakland.edu: /pub/misc/unix/host.c.Z
Author:         Berkeley
Cost:           Free
```

The host program is an interesting little network information tool that returns information about a host given its domain name or IP address. This is sometimes useful, sometimes useless, but at the very least, it allows you to get some host information if you have its address or name. It's in very simple C, but your system must support the networking calls it uses, such as gethostbyname() and gethostbyaddr().

VT-100 Test

```
Platforms:      UNIX
Description:    Tests VT-52/VT-100/VT-102 terminals
Location:       oak.oakland.edu: /pub/misc/unix/vttest9207.tar.Z
Author:         Per Lindberg
                <(mcvax,seismo)!enea!suadb!lindberg>
Cost:           Free
```

The old VT-100 terminal is probably the most popular ever. Most terminal programs or terminal emulators offer some form of VT-100 compatibility. Or so they claim—some of them don't do the right thing in all situations, which can lead to garbage on your screen. This program lets you put your terminal emulator through a VT-stress test. It also comes with a few sample VT-100 escape sequence "movies" for your enjoyment.

By the way, my terminal program failed a few tests, but I haven't noticed any problems—most software just doesn't use the fancy commands.

UNIX Basics and Tips

by Steve Bang

On the Internet, UNIX is pervasive. In fact, it is virtually impossible to roam the Internet without encountering computer hosts that operate on the UNIX operating system. Also, your own connection to the Internet is likely to be from a host that is running UNIX.

> **NOTE**
>
> UNIX is a multitasking, multiuser operating system originally developed in the 1960s at AT&T's Bell Labs. Largely because of its power and flexibility, UNIX is an ideal operating system for running computers that offer simultaneous access to many users; it is also capable of performing many different tasks at the same time. Currently, the majority of computer hosts on the Internet are Sun workstations that use the power and flexibility of UNIX and the connectivity of TCP/IP to offer resources and services to local and remote users.

Throughout the Internet, the development of UNIX *shells* (front-ends, or interfaces, that attempt to eliminate direct contact between you and the UNIX operating system) have reduced the need to learn UNIX commands. You will probably find yourself learning some UNIX, however, whether you intend to or not.

Because many computer sites offering connections to the Internet run the UNIX operating system, you may encounter UNIX even sooner than you expected. When you log in to an anonymous FTP site, it is frequently a UNIX system. The more you understand about UNIX, the more quickly you can do what you want to do.

This appendix is designed to acquaint you with UNIX; it teaches you some basic UNIX features and commands that will make your use of the Internet more productive and enjoyable. If you find yourself wanting to learn more about UNIX than is presented here, or need a more complete explanation of some feature, take a look at the "Further Assistance" section at the end of this appendix.

Getting Started

Without initially describing anything about the UNIX file system or the details of some of the UNIX commands, the next few sections help you get your feet wet by helping you make some useful changes within your UNIX account. These are changes you may want to make before using e-mail or posting messages to Usenet newsgroups.

Your UNIX Account

Before you can use UNIX, you must have a login name and a password. Usually, you get your UNIX account from the organization from which you gain access to the Internet. Some users obtain their account through their employer, if their access is work related. Either the system administrator or an account manager can assist you in establishing an account.

When you first get an account on a UNIX system, your *login name* (or account) may be assigned to you by the system administrator or an account administrator. If your login name is an account number, or a name you do not particularly like, see whether you can get a *system alias* for your account that is easier to remember.

For example, the procedure for establishing login accounts used at one of my UNIX sites gave me the login name 2034bang. I was lucky to have a short last name that fit in the four-character space available after the assigned number. If my last name had been *Johnson*, my account would have been 2034john. Not only would that be confusing to others trying to send me e-mail, but I wouldn't like it either. In my case, however, I convinced the system administrator to give me a system alias, skbang, so that I can tell others to contact me at skbang instead of 2034bang.

If, for whatever reason, you don't like your login name and cannot get it changed, check to see whether the system administrator can give you a system alias. If you can't think of a good login alias or need time to think about it, you can always send the system administrator e-mail later requesting one. A warning: if you are printing business cards or will be telling lots of people your account address soon after your account is established, it is best to take care of this issue as soon as possible. One point to remember is that although e-mail can be sent to you at your system alias address, you must enter the real login name when you log in to your UNIX account.

When your UNIX account is set up, the system administrator usually specifies one of two *shells* (interfaces between the UNIX operating system and you): the Bourne shell (sh), which uses the dollar sign ($) as the system prompt, or the C shell (csh), which uses a percent sign (%) as the prompt. Depending on the shell to which you are initially assigned, you see one of these two prompts. For this introduction to UNIX, I assume that you are offered the C shell and have the % prompt. Most of the basic UNIX commands work the same in both shells, although some more sophisticated features may work differently on the different shells. Ask another user or the system administrator if you encounter any problems. Now, assuming you have an account, you can log in.

Logging In

When logging in to a UNIX account by dial-up access or from a networked terminal, have your login name and password handy. The initial messages that appear as you connect to a UNIX computer may vary among systems, but after these messages appear, you enter your login name in lowercase letters. For example, if your login name is rsmith, at the login prompt, type this:

```
log in: rsmith
```

Then press the Enter or Return key. The system should prompt you to enter your password. Enter your password carefully (it is not displayed on the screen as you type it):

```
password:
```

Again, press Return. After the system verifies your login name and password, you will probably see some more system messages, news, or warnings, followed by your system prompt. On some systems, a menu may be displayed, in an attempt to simplify your access to UNIX or Internet resources and services.

Depending on how helpful the menuing system is, you may be able to avoid the UNIX system prompt for some time. Most menuing systems have an option that gets you to the system prompt, but even if you don't choose it, you will probably stumble across a system prompt when choosing one of the available services or resources. Many system administrators offer a menu system to new users, but if you feel confident and don't like menuing systems, talk to (or e-mail) your system administrator about having your account open up at a system prompt. If you are logging in for the first time, or if you haven't done so in a while, you may want to *change* your password, but first you should learn how to *choose* a good password.

Choosing a Password

Your password is the key to your account and your primary defense against unauthorized access. Without the password, it is much more difficult for someone to break into your account. If your password is too easy to guess, someone can log in to your account, snoop in your files and e-mail, and post messages before you notice the damage.

So what makes a good password? Although a password should be easy enough for you to remember, it should be difficult enough that someone (or a password cracker program) would find it extremely difficult to figure out. The simplest rule is to make your password at least six characters long and contain at least two alphabetic characters and one numeric digit or special character. To help you find an even better password, here are some guidelines to follow:

- Use six to eight characters (anything beyond the eighth character is ignored).
- Use both uppercase and lowercase alphabetic characters, numeric digits, and one or more of the following special characters:

    ~ ! $ % ^ & * ( ) - = [ ] { } \ ¦ / , . / < > ; :

- Don't use words that can be found in either English or foreign language dictionaries. Cracker programs frequently use any available dictionary words to guess passwords.
- Don't use slang or commonly used phrases.
- Don't use the proper names of people, places, or companies. This includes your favorite fictional characters from science fiction books or movies.

■ Don't use personal information that others may have access to, including your birthdate, social security number, license plate, driver's license number, or any personal information about your family, relatives, friends, or pets.

Once you have a password that is easy to remember, yet difficult for others to guess, avoid writing it down. At least not in a place accessible to others (and especially not on or near your computer or desk). Also, don't allow others to watch you enter your password. Even if you take all these precautions, it's a good idea to change your password regularly (every few months or so).

If you forget your password, the system administrator can give you a new one you can use until you get a chance to change it to a better one.

Once you have chosen a password, you need to know how to change it.

Changing Your Password

To change your password, type **passwd** at the system prompt and press Return. You are prompted to enter your old password (the current one, the one you want to change). While you are entering your old and new passwords, the display of your keystrokes is suppressed.

```
% passwd
Changing password for bang on coyote.
Old password:
```

After entering your old password, you are prompted to type a new password, then asked to retype it (to verify that what you thought you entered is what you did enter):

```
New password:
Retype new password:
%
```

If you retype your new password correctly, you return to the system prompt, as shown in the preceding example. Otherwise, you see a message that the password has not been changed. If you get this message, just retry the passwd command—you probably hit a wrong key accidentally.

After you change your password, you may want to change your *finger name*, which is the name others see if they finger your account.

Changing Your Finger Name

The finger command is frequently used to find out information about a user, either on the local system or at a distant location. For example, assume that you fingered your own login name; the system might return the following log in information about yourself:

```
% finger rsmith
Log in name: rsmith       In real life: Raymond J. Smith III
```

Although your formal name is Raymond J. Smith III, you may prefer to be known as Ray Smith, but because you put your formal name on the application for a UNIX account, you ended up with a formal name showing in the line where your finger name appears.

If you have an unusual name, you may want to check your finger name to make sure that the spelling is correct. I went crazy once looking for someone's login name. I couldn't find it because the name had been entered incorrectly by the system administrator. Luckily, you can change this finger name yourself by using the chfn (change finger) command.

To change your finger name, enter **chfn** at the system prompt and press Enter. You should see the following:

```
Changing NIS finger information for rsmith on coyote.
Default values are printed inside of '[]'.
To accept the default, type <return>.
To have a blank entry, type the word 'none'.
Name [Raymond J. Smith III]: Ray Smith
```

Just in case someone is screwing around with your account while you are away from the terminal, you are prompted for your account password to verify that it's really you making the changes.

```
Password:
NIS entry changed on coyote
%
```

After entering your password, the change in your finger name is noted by the system, and you are returned to the system prompt. You have successfully changed your finger name.

One important point to consider is that whatever you put in the finger name is searchable by others using the finger command. Depending on your inclination, you may want to make it easier for people to find you if they know your computer host address but can't seem to remember your account name.

Now that you've tidied up some things in your account, you may want to begin sending e-mail and posting messages to Usenet newsgroups. You may have already noticed many e-mail messages and Usenet postings with information at the end of the messages about the person who sent it.

Unless the person is foolish, they are not manually entering this information each time. How do they do it? I'm glad you asked. Because you may not have sent any messages yet (or are embarrassed to admit that you have been manually appending personal information at the end of every message), now is a good time to learn how to set up your own automated signature file.

Signature Files and How To Create Them

A *signature file* (or *signature*) is a short text file containing personal information that, depending on your mail program and its settings, can be automatically appended to any e-mail message you send. If your mail program doesn't automatically append your signature file, it is still much easier to add a pretyped message yourself than to retype it for each message you send. Also, signatures are usually appended automatically to Usenet newsgroup postings if the signature file exists within your home directory.

Signatures offer a chance for you to be clever, to insert a disclaimer that your employer should not be held responsible for what you're saying or doing, or to include personal information that you typically include in a letter.

You can consider signatures as substitutes for letterheads and return addresses on paper letters. Signatures can also include quotations or comments that help assert your personality or beliefs. Many people deem long signatures to be wasted bandwidth (a waste of download time and storage space) when they exceed the conventional four-line length, so be careful what you include when you create one. Some newsgroups or mailing lists even refuse or truncate messages with signatures that are longer than four lines. Take a look at a few Usenet postings or e-mail messages if you need some ideas for what to include in your signature.

To create your own signature file, you create a file named `.signature` in your home directory. If you don't know how to use a UNIX text editor (such as vi or pico), you can either learn how to use one before creating your file or you can try the following shortcut. This shortcut can be done easily on your Windows PC or Macintosh, assuming that you use your personal computer as a terminal. First, open a new file using a word processing program you are familiar with. Set the font to 12-point Courier and the line length no greater than 80 characters. Also, make sure that you press Return at the end of each line rather than allowing the words to wrap.

Now get creative. A simple, but effective signature file can include your full name, current job title, snail mail address, e-mail addresses, and phone numbers. When you have finished creating the text you want to become your signature, save the file, put your word processing program in the background, open your UNIX account, and type the following at the system prompt in your home directory:

```
% cat > .signature
```

When you have done this, switch back to your word processing program, highlight (or select) your text, copy it to memory, switch back to your UNIX screen, and paste the text. At this point, your screen should look something like this:

```
---------------------------------
John Gear - Manager, Manufacturing - Widgets & Gadgets, Inc.
jgear@widget.com                              (202) 555-1234
-Thoughts expressed here belong to me and not my employer-
```

If you break the four-line rule slightly and create something a little bit more imaginative, your pasted text may look something like this:

```
---------------------------------
John Gear               | Furious activity is no
Mgr., Manufacturing     | substitute for understanding.
Widgets & Gadgets, Inc. |
jgear@widget.com        |    - H. H. Williams
---------------------------------
```

After the text has been pasted, enter Ctrl+D (the end-of-file key) to complete the file. To check that everything went well, enter the following command to see the new signature file:

```
% cat .signature
```

If everything looks fine, you now have a signature file that should automatically be appended to your e-mail and Usenet postings. If you want to change the signature file, delete the file using the rm command and repeat the preceding steps. Remember, because there is a dot (.) as the first character in the filename, you cannot see this file when you use the ls command unless you use the *all files* option (ls -a). Try it out by mailing yourself a message and seeing whether the signature is appended. Later, you can learn a UNIX text editor and use it to modify your signature file, but here I have at least shown you a quick, painless way to put together a signature.

Along with all of the other changes you have made, you may be wondering about all that other information (or nonsense) you may have seen in other people's finger information. How did it get there? Here's how to find out.

Don't You Have a Project and a Plan?

When someone fingers your account address, not only does this person see your finger name, but other information about you that appears automatically. This includes the last time you logged on, whether or not you're currently online, and how long it's been since you've read your mail.

This finger information also displays the names of two fields, `Project` and `Plan`, as well as any information placed in their respective hidden files, `.project` and `.plan`, if they exist in your home directory. Usually, these two fields of information remain blank until you figure out how to put some information in them.

Like your signature file, the information that goes in these two fields should give useful information to someone about who you are or where they can get hold of you. You may also choose to include something that makes your finger information reflect your personality or style. These fields sometimes display creative ASCII artwork, animated displays, or just about anything you can imagine. The four-line rule doesn't apply here, but people who finger your account aren't expecting to see pages of information scroll by. So now that you know about them, how do you go about creating your own `.project` and `.plan` files?

Simply create these files using either a UNIX text editor or the trick I described in the preceding section on creating your own signature file. The same directions apply here, but make sure to name your two files `.project` and `.plan`. Realize that only the first line of the `.project` file appears under the `Project` field, so any extra lines you create are a waste of time.

Now that you have created several useful, and possibly interesting files, and have whetted your appetite for knowing more about UNIX, it's a good time to explain how the UNIX file system works.

An Introduction to the UNIX File System

The UNIX file system consists of a set of three different types of files:

1. Ordinary files, which contain data such as text, binary programs, or any information stored in eight-bit bytes.
2. Special files, such as the device files, which provide access to terminals and printers.
3. Directories, which are files containing pointers with links to other files, including other directories.

The directories are organized hierarchically in what looks like an upside-down family tree. At the top level of this inverted tree is the root directory, denoted by a slash (/). Beneath the root are several standard UNIX subdirectories, usually called `bin`, `etc`, `usr`, `tmp`, and `lib`. Each of these standard root subdirectories are important, and contain specific types of files. Your home directory is usually, but not always, located within the `usr` directory.

Files are represented in the UNIX file system with *filenames*. The specific location of files and directories are represented with *pathnames*. Pathnames can be *absolute*, telling you the exact path of the directories required to go from the root to where you want to go, or *relative*, pointing to a file relative to your current working directory. When you log in to UNIX, you are automatically placed within your home directory. Knowing how to move about within the UNIX file system is important because it makes your Internet forays more productive and less tedious.

Creating and Naming Files

Files can be created in your home directory in many ways. You can import them from a remote host, save them from e-mail messages sent to you, upload them from your PC or Macintosh, or create them using UNIX text editors.

As you become more familiar with the Internet, you'll find that your home directory can swell rapidly with files. These include text, image, and binary files saved from your mail, or downloaded from anonymous FTP sites and Gophers. When files are created, they must be given filenames. Unlike DOS—in which filenames can use only 8 characters before the dot and 3 characters after it, for a total of 11 characters—UNIX is a bit more generous. UNIX filenames can have 14 characters, and most newer versions of UNIX support much longer filenames.

The rules for creating and naming files on UNIX are very liberal, but here are some general guidelines that are good to follow:

- Although files and directories can be named using both uppercase and lowercase letters or digits from 0 to 9, you may find it helpful to name regular files using lowercase letters and directories with either the first letter or the entire filename in uppercase letters. This helps differentiate directories and files that are otherwise not distinguishable when you use the `ls` command to display their names.

- Avoid beginning filenames with periods. Files that begin with periods become hidden files and are treated as initialization files if located in your home directory. Even worse, you may forget that they exist because they don't display with the standard `ls` command (use the `ls -a` command to see these *dot files*).

- Use the period, hyphen, and underline characters to separate words within a filename. This increases the readability of the names.

- Avoid using spaces in filenames, even though UNIX allows it. Files created with spaces in them are not only more difficult to remove, they also may appear as several different files when displayed using the `ls` command. To remove a file created with spaces, use the `rm` command, but remember to put quotation marks around the whole filename.

- Try to remember to use the conventional suffixes, when appropriate, to differentiate files in unique formats. For example, `.zip` should be reserved for files compressed using PKWare's ZIP compression program, `.ps` for PostScript files, `.bin` for binary files, and `.z` for compressed files. These file suffixes help users determine what type of files they have and which software tools to use to work with them.

Creating and Naming Directories

A directory is really a file, but unlike ordinary files, a directory includes pointers linking it to other files and directories. To create a directory, you use the `mkdir` command followed by the new directory's name. For example, type the following command to create a new directory named `Files.to.get` (where you may want to store information on Internet files you want to remember to get later):

```
% mkdir Files.to.get
```

Other than using the `mkdir` command, all the file-naming guidelines given in the preceding section apply to directories as well. Now that you know some basics about how to make and name both files and directories, it is a good time to learn how to use absolute and relative pathnames to get to files.

Paths and Directories

When you log in to a UNIX account, you are automatically placed within your home directory. When you move to different directories, the directory you are currently in is called the *working directory.*

If you want to know what the current working directory is, use the `pwd` command to display the path of the working directory. If you become lost or just want to get back to your home directory quickly, enter the `cd` command by itself to jump back home. When you enter the `pwd` command, notice that the pathname displayed starts with a slash (/) representing the root directory. Depending on where you are, the path displayed varies—the one constant is that the pathname starts at the root directory of your UNIX system and lists all directories in between, separated by slashes. For example, when I enter the `pwd` command as soon as I log in, this pathname is displayed:

```
% pwd
/user/users2/bang
```

According to the pathname displayed, I am currently in a directory named `bang` (the last name in the list is the current working directory); the rest of the pathname gives the path between the root directory and my current working directory (which, in this case, happens to also be my home directory). This long pathname is called the *absolute pathname* because it always uses the root directory as its starting point and terminates in your current working directory. The absolute pathname can be used with the `cd` (change directory) command to move to other directories within your UNIX system. To move to the directory one level up (known as the *parent directory*), I enter the following command:

```
% cd /user/users2
```

My current working directory becomes /user/users2. Using absolute pathnames, you can move anywhere within the UNIX system that you have permission to enter, but there is another way to move between directories that can be much easier. For example, if you log in to an anonymous FTP site called sumex-aim.stanford.edu, you enter the UNIX system there at the root FTP directory. Assume that you read in a Usenet newsgroup posting somewhere that there is a listing of recently added files there and were given the absolute pathname /info-mac/help/ recent-files.txt. You can now easily get to the recent-files.txt file by moving to the help directory. At the FTP prompt, enter the cd command followed by the pathname that gets you to the help directory:

```
FTP> cd /info-mac/help
250 CWD command successful.
FTP>
```

If you entered the pathname correctly, you are told that you have succeeded and are presented with the FTP prompt. To get the file, enter the FTP get command (this command copies the file to your home directory) followed by the filename you want to copy (in this case, recent-files.txt):

```
FTP> get recent-files.txt
200 PORT command successful.
150 Opening ASCII mode data connection for recent-files.txt (14590 bytes).
226 Transfer complete.
local: recent-files.txt remote: recent-files.txt
14874 bytes received in 4.9 seconds (2.9 Kbytes/s)
FTP>
```

According to the response from the FTP site, you have transferred a copy of recent-files.txt to your local working directory (shown here as remote, because your computer is remote from this computer at Stanford University). This is great—using absolute pathnames lets you jump right to the directory where the file is and grab a copy of it. Perhaps you also wrote down the name of a new version of a game you wanted to get, slime-invaders-201.hqx, which you know is in the arc (arcade) subdirectory of the game directory. You can enter the following command at the FTP prompt to go to that directory:

```
FTP> cd /info-mac/game/arc
```

However, there is another, easier way. Instead, you could enter the following command:

```
FTP> cd ../game/arc
```

You still get to where you want to go, but with fewer keystrokes. Interested?

This example used the other type of pathname, the *relative pathname*. This pathname treats your working directory as the starting point for changing to another directory (rather than using the root directory as the starting point). Because the working directory varies depending on where you currently are, it's known as *relative*.

The UNIX convention is that entering cd .. moves you up one level in the path to the parent directory—on this site, the info-mac directory. To move down into a subdirectory (or child directory), you can change directories by entering the cd command followed by the pathname for the path from where you are to where you want to go. So, when you enter cd ../game/arc, you move back to the parent directory and over to a different directory two levels deep. Learning to use both absolute and relative pathnames can greatly assist your movement on your local UNIX computer and any others you might venture to with the Internet. If you want to read a longer explanation of absolute and relative pathnames, take a look at a basic UNIX book.

Listing Files and Directories

An important thing to know is how to display files within any UNIX directory. To see a list of the files and directories without any additional information, just enter the **ls** command by itself at the UNIX prompt within the directory whose files you want to see.

When listing files using the ls command, the names of directories and files appear the same—unless you have followed a naming convention that differentiates between them. Also, the hidden files (or dot files) do not appear in the display.

If you use a variation of the ls command, the ls -l (list using long format) command, the listing includes additional information that indicates whether the name listed is a file or a directory. If the first letter in the long listing of a filename is a d, it is a directory. The first character is a hyphen if the filename is an ordinary file. The information in the first section of the display listing also shows the access permissions established for each file. Although this can be important to know, you are less likely to need this and can always check a UNIX book if you do need it.

Viewing Files

To view the contents of a file, you have several options in UNIX. The cat command, followed by the filename, displays the file's contents continuously on the screen.

Press Ctrl+S to temporarily stop the scrolling of the screen display; press Ctrl+Q to resume the scrolling. An easier method is to use the more command. Enter **more** followed by the filename to display the contents of a file, one screenful at a time. When you use the more command, the word *more* appears in the bottom left side of the screen. Also displayed is the percentage of the file left to be viewed. To move to the next screen in the file, press the spacebar. To quit during the display of the file, type **q** to make the system prompt quickly reappear. More information on more's capabilities can be found by referring to the online manual pages.

Renaming or Moving Files

If you decide you want to rename a file, or want to correct a spelling error in the filename, use the mv command. To rename a file, enter **mv** followed by the current filename, then a space, and then the new filename. When this command is used within a directory, it removes the old filename and replaces it with the new one. You can also use this command to move a file into a directory. To do this, enter **mv** followed by the filename, then a space, and finally the pathname of the directory the file should be moved into.

Removing Files and Directories

Removing files and directories generally requires the use of two commands: rm and rmdir. To remove files from a directory, enter **rm** followed by the file or filenames (separated by spaces). Be careful: UNIX does not provide any utilities to undelete a file once it has been deleted.

To remove directories, enter the **rmdir** command followed by the name of the directory. This command does not work unless the directory is empty (that is, unless the directory contains no files). Another command, rm -rf, followed by the directory name, deletes any files within a directory as well as the directory itself. Although it isn't important to understand how some of these commands work, you can check the online UNIX help or refer to a UNIX book for details.

Tips and Tricks

The following sections provide helpful information on piping and filtering commands and using wildcards.

Piping and Filtering

Learning how to pipe commands expands the functionality of UNIX beyond some apparent limitations. Most UNIX commands are simple, yet when they are combined using pipes, you can create more complex operations on files. Following are a few of the more commonly used forms for piping commands:

command1 ¦ *command2*	Redirect the output of *command1* to the input of *command2*.
command1 ¦ *command2* > *file*	Redirect the output of *command1* to the input of *command2*, then redirect the output of *command2* to *file*.

```
command1 ¦ command2 < file
```
Redirect the output of *command1* to the input of *command2*, then redirect the input from *file*.

Wildcards

Wildcards are special characters that represent one or more other characters. They are useful for quickly specifying many files at once or to help find files about which you can't remember all the details. One wildcard, the asterisk (*), can represent any string of characters, including no characters. Depending on where it is placed in a string, the meaning varies. If you place a wildcard at the beginning of the character string .pcx, for example, all files that end with the string .pcx are listed:

```
ls *.pcx
```

When you place a wildcard at the end of a character string, the string refers to all strings beginning with the defined string. The following example moves all files beginning with the string chapter into a predefined directory called Book:

```
mv chapter* Book
```

When you place the wildcard within a defined character string, all strings having both the defined beginning and ending characters are specified. This example initiates a zmodem download of all files beginning with the letter a and ending with .zip:

```
sz a*.zip
```

Finally, when used by itself, the asterisk represents any character string. For example, if you want to delete all the files in your home directory, enter the following command:

```
rm *
```

This command causes all files (except for directories and hidden files) to be deleted. This particular command can be useful for cleaning up your home directory, or emptying a directory so that it can then be deleted using the rmdir command.

Two other wildcards can also be used. The question mark (?) can be used to indicate any single character, and brackets ([ ]) can be used to surround a string of characters you want to match. Although used less frequently than the asterisk, they can be useful for specific needs.

UNIX Overview

The following sections provide a brief overview of special keys and characters used in UNIX; following that is a brief introduction to some useful UNIX commands.

Special Keys and Characters

When you use UNIX, you use special keys and characters; the following sections will help you make sense of these elements.

|

A *pipe* is represented on UNIX by a vertical bar (¦) between two commands on the command line. The output of the first command becomes the input for the second command.

>

Directs output to a file.

>>

Appends to a file.

<

Redirects input from a file.

Ctrl+C

Interrupts the current process.

Ctrl+D

The end-of-file character.

Ctrl+H

Erases the previously typed character. This is also known as the *backspace key*. The backspace key on your PC keyboard should be mapped to this key. If your physical backspace key doesn't work, you can use Ctrl+H, but you may want to learn how to change the keyboard mapping or ask the system administrator to do it for you.

Ctrl+J

Resets the terminal. Some systems support this command. Even if your system does, there is no guarantee that this command will work.

If this command doesn't work, you should abort the session any way you can and attempt to log in again.

Ctrl+S

Temporarily stops the screen display from scrolling. You use this keystroke in conjunction with the Ctrl+Q key to control the scrolling of the screen display when you use the cat command to view a text file.

Ctrl+Q

Starts the screen display scrolling again. You use this keystroke in conjunction with the Ctrl+S key to control the scrolling of the screen display when you use the cat command to view a text file.

Some UNIX Commands Worth Knowing About

The following sections provide a brief introduction to some of the most-used UNIX commands.

apropos *keywords*

This prints the manual pages of the system's online reference manual that contain at least one of the keywords in the title. It's identical to the man -k command.

cat *file*

Concatenates and prints files continuously. Following are some options and variants you can use with the cat command:

```
cat file
```

Displays *file* continuously. Use the more command to display *file* one screenful at a time.

Takes input from the keyboard and redirects it to *file*.

```
cat > file
```

```
cat >> file
```

Appends input from the keyboard to *file*.

```
cat file2 >> file1
```

Appends the contents of *file2* to *file1*.

> **TIP**
>
> Entering **cat** *file* can be handy for capturing ASCII text to your personal computer. However, if there is any line noise, the text may contain errors. It is safer to download the text file using error correction protocols.

cd directory

Changes the directory. Following are some options and variants you can use with the cd command:

```
cd
```

Used by itself, this command moves the current directory back to your home directory.

> **TIP**
>
> The cd command can be handy in case you lose track of where you are or if you accidentally end up somewhere else in your UNIX system's file structure.

```
cd ..
```

Moves you from the current directory up a level to its parent directory. If you enter this command when you are in your home directory, you may find yourself wandering around in the parent directories of your UNIX system's file structure. If you are adventuresome and find yourself lost in the file structure, or if you just want to quickly return to your home directory, use the cd command by itself.

```
cd directory1/directory2
```

Moves you down two levels from the current directory into *directory2*, a subdirectory of *directory1*.

> **TIP**
>
> This command is useful for quickly getting into a deep subdirectory of an anonymous FTP site.

chmod [*options*] file (or directory)

Changes access modes (permissions). For information on how to use this command to change the access permissions of files, consult a basic UNIX book.

cp file/directory

Copies a file to a new file, or into a directory. Following are some variants for the cp command:

```
cp file1 file2
```

Copies a file to a new file.

```
cp file directory
```

Copies *file* into *directory*.

date

Displays the current date and time.

grep "pattern" files

Searches files for lines that match a pattern. If the pattern is a single character string, the quotation marks are unnecessary. Following are some options and variants for using the grep command:

```
grep -l "pattern" files
```

Finds files that contain lines that match the *pattern*.

```
grep -i "pattern" files
```

Finds files that contain lines matching the *pattern*, ignoring whether the characters are uppercase or lowercase.

```
grep -n "pattern" files
```

Finds files that contain lines that match the *pattern* and displays line numbers for each occurrence.

head *files*

Prints the first few lines of *files*.

> **TIP**
>
> The head command is a quick way to look at the first few (usually 10) lines of a file.

help *command/error*

Gives a brief explanation of a command or error message.

kill [*pid*]

Terminates the current processes. Following are some options and variants you can use with the kill command:

```
-9
```

This option, a signal number, terminates stubborn processes.

> **TIP**
>
> The `kill` command is handy when you attempt to log off your account and UNIX informs you that there are active processes. Using the `ps` command, you can find out the pid (process ID) number for those processes and then use `kill` to terminate those processes.

ls

Lists the contents, of a directory. Following are some options you can use with the `ls` command:

```
ls
```

By itself, `ls` lists all files, excluding hidden files (dot files), in the current directory.

```
ls -l
```

Lists all non-hidden files or directories within the current directory, including file sizes, access permissions, and other useful information.

```
ls -a
```

Lists all files and directories, including hidden files (dot files).

```
ls ¦ more
```

Lists all files, and filters the list through the `more` command.

> **TIP**
>
> The `ls ¦ more` command is handy to use if you have so many files in a directory that they scroll by too fast to read.

man *command*

Displays continuously the manual pages for *command* from your system's online reference manual. Some systems may have this command pipe display through the more command. If not, you can do it yourself. Following are some of the options and variants you can use with the man command:

```
man command ¦ more
```

Displays the manual pages one screen at a time using the more command.

```
man -k keyword
```

Lists relevant commands covered in the online reference manual that contain *keyword*. Also supported is the apropos command, which performs the identical function.

mesg [y/n]

Prints the current state of write permission on your account. Following are some options and variants you can use with the mesg command:

    mesg n denies write messages
    mesg y allows write messages (default)

mkdir *directory*

Makes a new directory.

more *file*

Prints *file* one screenful at a time. Here are some of the keystrokes you can use with the more command:

Key	*Purpose*
Spacebar	Moves the display forward one screenful
b	Moves the display backward one screenful
q	Quits displaying the file

mv *file1* [*file2/directory*]

Moves or renames a file. Here are some of the variants for the mv command:

```
mv file1 file2
```

Renames a file with a new name.

```
mv file directory
```

Moves a file to a directory.

passwd

Changes the current password. When this command is entered, the system prompts you for a new password. See "Changing Your Password," earlier in this appendix, for further explanation.

ps

Reports a list of the current processes that are running. Use this command in conjunction with the kill command to end a session if you seem to be stuck trying to log out and get a response like current active processes. See the kill command, earlier in this chapter, for more information on how to get past this message.

pwd

Prints the working directory (the full pathname of the current directory).

rm [*options*] *files*

Removes files or directories. Here are some options and variants that apply to the rm command:

```
-i
```

Requests confirmation before removing.

```
-r
```

Recursively removes directories.

> **TIP**
>
> Use the wildcard (*) to cut down on the keystrokes necessary to type filenames. If you
> saved a file with a long filename, you may find it easier (and lazier) to type just enough
> of the filename to uniquely identify it for deletion. Be careful so that you don't
> accidentally remove other files you intended to keep.

rmdir *directory*

Removes empty directories. To remove directories that are not empty, use the `rm -rf`
command.

tail *file*

Displays the last 10 lines of *file*.

> **TIP**
>
> The `tail` command is handy for looking at the tail end of an e-mail message to see the
> signature of the sender.

users

Lists the currently logged in users.

vi *file*

Opens *file* with the `vi` editor. If the file doesn't exist, `vi` creates a new file with the name *file*.
To learn more about the `vi` editor, consult a basic UNIX text.

w

Displays who is on the system and what they are doing. The `w` command takes a moment longer
to get results than the `who` or `users` commands. If you're curious about what other users on
your system are doing, try it.

who

Lists who is currently on your system.

whoami

Displays the account name you are currently logged in under.

write *user*

Initiates a `write` session in which you can initiate or respond to another user who is logged in on your system or a remote site. The user sees your message as you type it—including all the errors and corrections. When you are finished typing a message, terminate the session by pressing Ctrl+D.

TIP

Use the `write` command respectfully; the user to whom you are sending a message may not appreciate being interrupted. Also, it's a good idea to make sure that the user to whom you want to talk is logged on before you use the `write` command. To check whether the user is logged on, use one of the following commands: `user`, `who`, or `w`. If you use the `w` command, you may even get an idea what the user is doing before you interrupt his or her session.

Further Assistance

If you get stuck, there is help available. Following are some of the resources available to you.

Local Online Help

To learn more about UNIX commands supported on your system without having to find a book, use the online reference manual supported by the `man` command.

Usenet Newsgroups

You can learn more than you ever wanted to know about UNIX by hanging out in some of the following Usenet newsgroups: `comp.unix.questions`, `comp.unix.wizards`, and `comp.unix.user-friendly`.

FAQs

Consult the UNIX Frequently Asked Question files (FAQs) that appear regularly in the Usenet newsgroup `news.answers`. In particular, look for the multipart UNIX FAQ file, `unix-faq`. There is also a UNIX FAQ for information on UNIX books called *The Guide to UNIX Books* at `unix-books-faq`.

Books

Abrahams, Paul W. and Bruce A. Larson. 1992. *UNIX for the Impatient.* Reading, Massachusetts: Addison-Wesley.

Anderson, Bart, Barry Costales, and Harry Henderson. 1991. *The Waite Group's UNIX Communications.* Indianapolis, Indiana: Sams Publishing.

Hahn, Harley. 1993. *The Student's Guide to UNIX.* Berkeley, California: Osborne McGraw-Hill.

O'Reilly & Associates. 1989. *UNIX in a Nutshell* [various editions]. Sebastopol, California: O'Reilly & Associates.

Internet Domain Names

D

Organization Domains

com	Commercial organizations
edu	Educational institutions
gov	Governmental entities
int	International organizations
mil	Miltary (U.S.)
net	Network operations and service centers
org	Other organizations

Geographic Domains

ad	Andorra
ae	United Arab Emirates
af	Afghanistan
ag	Antigua and Barbuda
ai	Anguilla
al	Albania
am	Armenia
an	Dutch Antilles
ao	Angola
aq	Antarctica
ar	Argentina
as	American Samoa
at	Austria
au	Australia
aw	Aruba
az	Azerbaijan
ba	Bosnia Hercegovina
bb	Barbados
bd	Bangladesh
be	Belgium
bf	Burkina Faso
bg	Bulgaria
bh	Bahrain
bi	Burundi
bj	Benin
bm	Bermuda
bn	Brunei Darussalam
bo	Bolivia
br	Brazil
bs	Bahamas
bt	Bhutan
bv	Bouvet Island
bw	Botswana
by	Belarus
bz	Belize
ca	Canada
cc	Cocos Islands
cf	Central African Republic
cg	Congo
ch	Switzerland
ci	Ivory Coast
ck	Cook Islands
cl	Chile
cm	Cameroon
cn	China
co	Colombia
cq	Equatorial Guinea
cr	Costa Rica
cu	Cuba
cv	Cape Verde
cx	Christmas Island
cy	Cyprus

cz	Czech Republic	hr	Croatia
de	Germany	ht	Haiti
dj	Djibouti	hu	Hungary
dk	Denmark	id	Indonesia
dm	Dominica	ie	Ireland
do	Dominican	il	Israel
	Republic	in	India
dz	Algeria	io	British Indian
ec	Ecuador		Ocean Territory
ee	Estonia	iq	Iraq
eg	Egypt	ir	Iran
eh	Western Sahara	is	Iceland
es	Spain	it	Italy
et	Ethiopia	jm	Jamaica
ev	El Salvador	jo	Jordan
fi	Finland	jp	Japan
fj	Fiji	ke	Kenya
fk	Falkland Islands	kg	Kyrgyzstan
fm	Micronesia	kh	Cambodia
fo	Faroe Islands	ki	Kiribati
fr	France	km	Comoros
ga	Gabon	kn	St. Kitts & Nevis
gb	Great Britain (UK)	kp	Korea, North
gd	Grenada	kr	Korea, South
ge	Georgia	kw	Kuwait
gf	French Guiana	ky	Cayman Islands
gh	Ghana	kz	Kazakhstan
gi	Gibraltar	la	Lao People's
gl	Greenland		Republic
gm	Gambia	lb	Lebanon
gn	Guinea	lc	St. Lucia
gp	Guadeloupe	li	Liechtenstein
gr	Greece	lk	Sri Lanka
gt	Guatemala	lr	Liberia
gu	Guam	ls	Lesotho
gw	Guinea-Bissau	lt	Lithuania
gy	Guyana	lu	Luxembourg
hk	Hong Kong	lv	Latvia
hm	Heard &	ly	Libya
	McDonald Islands	ma	Morocco
hn	Honduras	mc	Monaco

md	Moldova	pn	Pitcairn Island
mg	Madagascar	pr	Puerto Rico
mh	Marshall Islands	pt	Portugal
ml	Mali	pw	Palau
mm	Myanmar	py	Paraguay
mn	Mongolia	qa	Qatar
mo	Macau	re	Reunion Island
mp	Northern Mariana	ro	Romania
	Islands	ru	Russian Federation
mq	Martinique	rw	Rwanda
mr	Mauritania	sa	Saudi Arabia
ms	Montserrat	sb	Solomon Islands
mt	Malta	sc	Seychelles
mv	Maldives	sd	Sudan
mw	Malawi	se	Sweden
mx	Mexico	sg	Singapore
my	Malaysia	sh	St. Helena
mz	Mozambique	si	Slovenia
na	Namibia	sj	Svalbard & Jan
nc	New Caledonia		Mayen
ne	Niger	sk	Slovakia
nf	Norfolk Island	sl	Sierra Leone
ng	Nigeria	sm	San Marino
ni	Nicaragua	sn	Senegal
nl	Netherlands	so	Somalia
no	Norway	sr	Suriname
np	Nepal	st	Sao Tome &
nr	Nauru		Principe
nt	Neutral Zone	su	USSR
nu	Niue	sy	Syrian Arab
nz	New Zealand		Republic
om	Oman	sz	Swaziland
pa	Panama	tc	Turks & Caicos
pe	Peru		Islands
pf	French Polynesia	td	Chad
pg	Papua New Guinea	tf	French Southern
ph	Philippines		Territories
pk	Pakistan	tg	Togo
pl	Poland	th	Thailand
pm	St. Pierre &	tj	Tajikistan
	Mequielon	tk	Tokelau

tm	Turkmenistan	vc	St. Vincent & the Grenadines
tn	Tunisia		Grenadines
to	Tonga	ve	Venezuela
tp	East Timor	vg	Virgin Islands
tr	Turkey	vn	Vietnam
tt	Trinidad & Tobago	vu	Vanuatu
	Tobago	wf	Wallis & Fortuna Islands
tv	Tuvalu		Islands
tw	Taiwan	ws	Samoa
tz	Tanzania	ye	Yemen
ua	Ukrainian SSR	yu	Yugoslavia
ug	Uganda	za	South Africa
us	United States	zm	Zambia
uy	Uruguay	zr	Zaire
va	Vatican City State	zw	Zimbabwe

Favorite Internet Books

by Kevin M. Savetz

E

There are hundreds of books available about every facet of the Internet—the culture, the programs, the computers, the history, the future. Reading them can be a full-time job. Because most of us don't have that kind of time, this appendix provides a list of some of our very favorite Internet-related books.

The Unofficial Internet Booklist

The list in this appendix is culled from the *Unofficial Internet Booklist*, a massive bibliography of books about the Internet. The *Booklist* is posted twice monthly (on the 5th and 19th of each month) to the Usenet newsgroups `alt.internet.services`, `misc.books.technical`, and `news.answers`.

You can receive the *Booklist* through anonymous FTP at `ftp://rtfm.mit.edu/pub/usenet/news.answers/internet-services/book-list`. Or with electronic mail:

```
To: booklist-request@northcoast.com
Subject: archive
Body: send booklist
```

Introductions to the Internet

Title: *The Complete Idiot's Guide to the Internet*
Author: Peter Kent
Publisher: Alpha Books
ISBN: 1-56761-414-0
Price: $19.95
Pages: 386
Goodies: DOS disk
For more information: `http://www.mcp.com/cgi-bin/bag?isbn=1-56761-535-X&last=/bookstore`
Notes: This best-selling book provides an easy-to-understand introduction to the Internet. It covers virtually all important Internet services in a light-hearted, straightforward way. It includes coupons for Internet-service discounts and a disk containing files that list thousands of Internet resources.

Title: *Connecting to the Internet*
Author: Susan Estrada
Publisher: O'Reilly & Associates
ISBN: 1-56592-061-9

Price: $15.95
Pages: 170
For more information: `http://gnn.com/gnn/bus/ora/item/connect.html`
Notes: This small book focuses on choosing the best type of network connection for your personal, school, or business needs; it also explains how to get the best price for the type of access you require. The book explains the differences between SLIP, PPP, ISDN, X.25 and other options; it also includes an extensive list of Internet service providers. This is a single-purpose book: it explains how to choose a connection and get online. It doesn't try to teach you how to use the Net once you're there. That is graceful in its simplicity.

Title: *How the Internet Works*
Author: Joshua Eddings
Publisher: Ziff-Davis Press
ISBN: 1-56276-192-7
Price: $24.95
Pages: 218

and

Title: *How To Use the Internet*
Author: Mark Butler
Publisher: Ziff-Davis Press
ISBN: 1-56276-222-2
Price: $17.95
Pages: 144
For more information: 800-688-0448

Notes: These graphically engaging books are certainly the prettiest of the slew of Internet books out there. They both feature copious, nicely drawn images to explain the basics of how the Internet works (including topics such as who pays for the Internet and how video conferencing works) and how to use the Internet (logging in to UNIX, using FTP, searching text, and so on). Although they're not very detailed, they do explain in simple terms the concepts and issues of the Internet. Heavy on art, they use graphics to quickly explain what the Internet is all about. They're readable, informative, and downright pretty.

Title: *Internet: The Complete Reference*
Authors: Harley Hahn and Rick Stout
Publisher: Osborne McGraw-Hill
ISBN: 0-07-881980-6
Price: $29.95

Pages: 818

Notes: A grassroots guide to learning about the Internet. It takes clueless newbies and leads them from the fundamentals—like understanding what the Internet is, how to connect, and how addressing works—through the Internet's most important tools. This book delivers the information in a lively, always interesting manner. No topics are glossed over and the authors never get mired in the dirty technical details. This book is intended for folks who will be accessing the Internet using a UNIX command-line prompt. If you are just trying to get started on the Internet, but don't know which of 100 step-by-step hold-your-hand books in your bookstore you should buy, *Internet: The Complete Reference* won't disappoint you.

Title: *The Internet for Dummies*
Authors: John Levine and Carol Baroudi
Publisher: IDG Books
ISBN: 1-56884-222-8
Price: $19.95
Pages: 427

and

Title: *More Internet for Dummies*
Authors: John Levine and Carol Baroudi
Publisher: IDG Books
ISBN: 1-56884-164-7
Price: $19.95
Pages: 430
For more information: 415-312-0650 or `dummies@iecc.com`
Notes: If the Internet frightens you—if they laugh when you sit down at the computer—then perhaps these are the books you need. These light-hearted tomes are intended to set novices at ease as they explore the Net. These books walk the fine line between thoroughness and readability—they are both.

Title: *The Internet Navigator*
Author: Paul Gilster
Publisher: John Wiley & Sons, Inc.
ISBN: 0-471-05260-4
Price: $24.95
Pages: 590
For more information: 800-263-1590 or `gilster@interpath.net`
Notes: The Internet Navigator is for readers accessing the Internet through a UNIX command-line account. Is it very thorough, providing the basics of UNIX, e-mail, Usenet, and resource discovery. It's not flashy like many other beginners' books; it is somewhat academic in tone. If you prefer a text-bookish manual for accessing the Internet from UNIX, *The Internet Naviga-*

tor will suit you.

Title: *The Internet Passport: NorthWestNet's Guide to Our World Online*
Author: Jonathan Kochmer
Publisher: NorthWestNet and the Northwest Academic Computing Consortium
ISBN: 0-9635281-0-6
Price: $29.95
Pages: 667
For more information: 800-223-2336 or e-mail `passport@nwnet.net`
Notes: An introductory guide to the Internet, with emphasis on databases, e-texts, libraries, mailing lists, K–12 newsgroups, health care resources, and becoming an information provider. This book presents a lot of densely-packed information and can be overwhelming. But the *Passport* has heft and breadth—it covers a lot of ground and can be useful to everyone, although it is skewed toward UNIX users.

Title: *Internet Starter Kit for Macintosh*
Author: Adam Engst
Publisher: Hayden Books
ISBN: 1-56830-111-1
Price: $29.95
Pages: 640
Goodies: Mac floppy disk filled with great software and free connect time
For more information: `http://www.mcp.com/cgi-bin/bag?isbn=1-56830-111-1&last=/bookstore`
Notes: If you use a Macintosh and only have $30 to spend, buy this book. This is simply the best Internet book for Macintosh users that was ever—or could ever be—written. This book claims to be "everything you need to get on the Internet" and it delivers: everything from the software you need to get connected to more than 600 pages of knowledge. This is a fun, enlightening, excellent book. If you own a Mac and are on the Internet (or want to connect), this is the one to get.

Title: *Internet Starter Kit for Windows*
Authors: Adam Engst, Corwin Low, and Michael Simon
Publisher: Hayden Books
ISBN: 1-56830-094-8
Price: $29.95
Pages: 600
Goodies: Disk containing a limited version of Chameleon, WinVN news reader, Eudora, WSGopher, and free connect time
For more information: `iskw@tidbits.com` or `http://www.mcp.com/cgi-bin/bag?isbn=1-`

`56830-094-8&last=/bookstore`

Notes: This book is an excellent resource dedicated to Microsoft Windows users. It isn't quite as strong as The *Internet Starter Kit* for Macintosh but is nonetheless a wonderful guide for teaching Windows users about the Internet and getting them online. It contains all the software you need to get online and explains how to use it.

Title: *The Internet Yellow Pages*
Authors: Harley Hahn and Rick Stout
Publisher: Osborne Publishing (McGraw Hill)
ISBN: 0-07-882098-7
Price: $27.95
Pages: 800
Notes: *The Internet Yellow Pages* strives to be an unmatched subject-oriented index to the Internet's resources, a lofty goal given the number of competing indexes available. Hahn and Stout do it right—this book is a resource that long-time Internet addicts and new users will enjoy equally. Organization is intuitive and consistent. The online resources it points to are high-quality and truly interesting sites to visit. Well researched and well indexed.

Title: *Netiquette*
Author: Virginia Shea
Publisher: Albion Books
ISBN: 0-9637025-1-3
Price: $19.95
Pages: 154
For more information: info@albion.com
Notes: This slim book does an excellent job of helping those new to cyberspace learn the basic tenants of network etiquette, or "netiquette." It's easy to read and loaded with interesting real-life examples. This book should be required reading for anyone collecting their Internet Learner's Permit. (You can retrieve a brief excerpt from *Netiquette*—"The Core Rules of Netiquette"—by sending e-mail to netiquette-request@albion.com with the words archive send core in the subject line.)

Title: *The Whole Internet User's Guide and Catalog*
Author: Ed Krol
Publisher: O'Reilly & Associates
ISBN: 1-56592-063-5
Price: $24.95
Pages: 572
For more information: http://gnn.com/gnn/bus/ora/item/twi2.html or info@ora.com
Notes: This book covers the basic utilities used to access the network and then guides users through the Internet's "databases of databases" to access the millions of files and thousands of

archives available. It includes a resource index that covers a broad selection of approximately 300 important resources available on the Internet. The second edition has been completely updated to reflect the development of new Internet tools, including Mosaic, MIME, tin, PINE, xarchie, and a greatly expanded resource catalog. Highly recommended.

Title: *Your Internet Consultant: The FAQs of Life Online*
Author: Kevin M. Savetz
Publisher: Sams Publishing
ISBN: 0-672-30520-8
Price: $25 US $34.95 CAN
Pages: 550
For more information: `http://www.northcoast.com/savetz/yic/yic.html` or `http://www.mcp.com/cgi-bin/bag?isbn=0-672-30520-8&last=/bookstore`
Notes: *Your Internet Consultant: The FAQs of List Online* (written by the author of this appendix) provides simple, enlightening answers to hundreds (361, to be exact) of frequently asked questions about the Internet (as well as answers to a few questions that aren't frequently asked, but should be.) The book is arranged in a question-and-answer format, making it blissfully simple to find just the information you need. I think you'll find the book unique, useful, and a little silly.

Title: *Zen & the Art of Internet*
Author: Brendan Kehoe
Publisher: Prentice Hall
ISBN: 0-13-121492-6
Price: $23.95
Notes: I've never actually read this book, but everyone tells me it's a classic not to be missed. So I'll steal a review from J. Matisse Enzer, who says: "This guide should give you a reference to consult if you're curious about what can be done with the Internet. It also presents the fundamental topics that are all too often assumed and considered trivial by many network users. It covers the basic utilities and information reaching other networks."

Intermediate/Advanced User Books

Title: *Finding It on the Internet*
Author: Paul Gilster
Publisher: John Wiley & Sons, Inc.
ISBN: 0-471-0387-1
Price: $19.95
Pages: 300
For more information: 800-263-1590 or `gilster@interpath.net`
Notes: Everyone knows the Internet has an incredible amount of information…the problem is locating the information you need. In *Finding It on the Internet*, Internet denizen Paul Glis-

ter shows how to use the Internet's vast (but sometimes daunting) search tools—Archie, Veronica, WAIS, the WWW, and others—to find information on the Internet. It leaves no stone unturned, covering with grace some of the applications—like WAIS and Hytelnet—that baffle even some experts.

Title: *Internet CD*
Author: Vivian Neou
Publisher: Prentice Hall
ISBN: 0-13-123852-3
Price: $49.95
Pages: 260
Goodies: CD-ROM
Notes: As the title suggests, the core of this book is a CD-ROM laden with Internet software for DOS, Windows, and UNIX computers. The disc contains a variety of Internet client software for doing e-mail, Telnet, Gopher, FTP, UUCP, and so on. It even includes a full implementation of Linux, a popular UNIX variant. The book itself is a no-frills guide to using the software. You should be familiar with the Internet and using your computer before picking up this package because it doesn't dwell on the basics.

Title: *Internet Slick Tricks*
Authors: Alfred and Emily Glossbrenner
Publisher: Random House
ISBN: 0-679-75611-6
Price: $16.00
Pages: 262
For more information: Send blank e-mail message to books@infomat.com or call 800-345-8112.
Notes: If you've been on the Internet forever (or at least for a couple months) and you think you know it all, pick up *Internet Slick Tricks*. I bet you'll learn something new. This slim guide will show you hundreds of tips and tricks on using the Internet. It's readable and honest and full of fascinating facts on decoding graphic images, using Archie, finding information online, and much more. One of my favorites.

Title: *Teach Yourself the Internet: Around the World in 21 Days*
Author: Neil Randall
Publisher: Sams Publishing
ISBN: 0-672-30519-4
Price: $27.00
Pages: 700
For more information: http://www.mcp.com:80/cgi-bin/bag?isbn=0-672-30519-4&last=/

sams

Notes: A well-organized tutorial that shows, in a topic-oriented (rather than tool-oriented) fashion, how to find information online. If you're interested in reading (or publishing) an online magazine, it shows you where to go for the goods on Usenet, in mailing lists, and on the WWW. If you're looking for a job, the authors show you not only how to find job listings online, but how to use the Net to research prospective employers and find international job sources. It also covers lots of ground in education, art, entertainment, and business. Even if you've been on the Net for years, this book can show you corners of the Net you've never imagined.

Title: *Tricks of the Internet Gurus*
Authors: 21 of 'em
Publisher: Sams Publishing
ISBN: 0-672-30599-2
Price: $35.00 US $47.95 CAN
Pages: 809
For more information: `http://www.mcp.com/cgi-bin/bag?isbn=0-672-30599-2&last=/bookstore`
Notes: A collection of chapters written by 21 well-known Internet user/authors, each of whom is an Internet "expert" in his or her own field. This book is not for the newbie or novice Internaut, but is filled with Internet tricks and secrets that will help turn a moderately experienced person into a seasoned veteran. These are not mere tutorials, but detailed high-level essays written by visible, online personalities. Chapters cover how to send a fax from the Internet, discussion forums, educational uses of the Internet, research, business, and commerce. Well written and well presented.

The World Wide Web

Title: *Plug-n-Play Mosaic for Windows*
Author: Angela Gunn
Publisher: Sams Publishing
ISBN: 0-672-30627-1
Price: $29.99
Pages: 300
Goodies: Disks with Enhanced NCSA Mosaic and TCP/IP software
For more information: `http://www.mcp.com:80/sams/books/mos/initial.html`
Notes: An exceptional introduction to the World Wide Web. Very readable, includes sections on getting online, sight-seeing, basic HTML. Of the many WWW introduction books out there, this is a favorite. (Keep an eye out for the Macintosh edition, available in mid-1995, co-

authored by yours truly.)

Title: *The World Wide Web Unleashed*
Authors: John December and Neil Randall
Publisher: Sams Publishing
ISBN: 0-672-30617-4
Price: $25.00
Pages: 1,058
For more information: `http://www.rpi.edu/~decemj/works/wwwu.html`
Notes: Not only the largest book on the Web, but also the most complete. Covers fundamental concepts and individual Web browsers for different platforms; describes navigation and searching techniques; lists Web sites by subject. Written by a team of WWW experts, the best part is the inclusion of details on technical information. Loads of information on designing and creating a Web site, working with HTML editors and filters, creating forms, and image mapping.

Guides for Specific People

Title: *Canadian Internet Handbook, 1995 Edition*
Authors: Jim Carroll and Rick Broadhead
Publisher: Prentice Hall Canada
ISBN: 0-13-329350-5
Price: $21.95
Pages: 800
For more information: `info@handbook.com` or `http://www.csi.nb.ca/handbook/handbook.html`.
Notes: If you live in Canada, get this book. It's an excellent general introduction to the Internet, slanted for Canadian users. It also contains detailed lists of Canadian service providers, Gopher sites, Web servers, newsgroups, and IRC servers. There are also listings of Canadian community networking organizations, Internet service bureaus, and Canadian companies on the Net. The authors have done an excellent job of teaching the basics and keeping an eye on their audience.

Title: *The Internet for Scientists and Engineers*
Author: Brian J. Thomas
Publisher: Optical Engineering Press
ISBN: 0-8194-1806-4
Price: $30.00
Pages: 485
For more information: `suep@spie.org` or `http://www.spie.org/book.html`
Notes: The first half of this book covers the oft-repeated basics of getting online and using the

basic Internet tools. However, the book shines in its second half, in which it includes excellent, thorough indexes of online resources in many scientific fields (like aerospace, agriculture, anthropology, archaeology, biology, chemistry, electronics and electrical engineering, energy, engineering, geology, mathematics, medicine, meteorology, oceanography, physics, and statistics). Engineers and scientists looking for information on the Net will not be disappointed.

Title: *51 Reasons: How We Use the Internet and What It Says About the Information Superhighway*
Authors: Martha Stone-Martin and Laura Breeden
Publisher: FARNET
ISBN: None
Price: $19.95
Pages: 124
For more information: 617-860-9445 or `stories@farnet.org`
Notes: This is a unique book exploring how people and organizations in all 50 United States (plus the capitol) are using the Internet as the first stepping stone toward the Clinton Administration's "information superhighway." Written as an oral narrative from the mouths of the people making these projects work, the book covers uses of the Internet in libraries, K–12 education, agriculture, economic development, government, health care, and higher education. Although brief, *51 Reasons* gives novel ideas for the use of the Internet and provides contact information for each of the individuals and projects mentioned. You can get the text of the book online from Gopher (`gopher://gopher.cni.org:70/11/cniftp/miscdocs/farnet`) and FTP (`ftp://ftp.cni.org:/CNI/documents/farnet/stories-index`).

Doing Business on the Internet

Title: *How To Advertise on the Internet*
Authors: Michael Strangelove and Aneurin Bosley
Publisher: *The Internet Business Journal*
ISSN: 1201-0758
Price: $49.50
Pages: 221
For more information: `mstrange@fonorola.net`
Notes: From the editor and publisher of the *Internet Business Journal*, this book takes a nononsense approach for those who want to market their products and services on the Internet. After a brief look at demographics of the Internet, *How To Advertise* examines marketing through online conferences, selling through classified ads, and reaching the right target audience. It also talks about the dangers of ads on the Net, the challenge of demonstrating products online, and

explains all the fuss about the World Wide Web.

Title: *The Internet Business Book*
Author: Jill Ellsworth
Publisher: John Wiley & Sons, Inc.
ISBN: 0-471-05809-2
Price: $22.95
Pages: 376
For more information: `je@world.std.com` or 800-879-4539
Notes: Unlike the other business-related books mentioned here, *The Internet Business Book* looks at the Internet from two angles: first, it's a substantive guide that offers practical business advice about marketing on the Internet and creating a corporate presence. Second, it serves as a general introduction for how to use the Internet. The business advice is first rate, but the book's chapter-long tangents about how to use Telnet, e-mail, and FTP can be distracting.

Title: *The Internet Business Guide: Riding the Information Superhighway to Profit*
Authors: Rosalind Resnick and Dave Taylor
Publisher: Sams Publishing
ISBN: 0-672-30530-5
Price: $25.00 US, $34.95 CAN
Pages: 418
For more information: `http://www.mcp.com/cgi-bin/bag?isbn=0-672-30530-5&last=/bookstore`
Notes: Of the various books on doing business on the Internet, this is my personal favorite. By reading this book, you'll find out how to use the Internet to build market share, track down business leads, communicate with colleagues, and search online databases—all through extensive examples and detailed case studies. The authors also explain how you can offer cost-effective customer support and access critical information using the Net.

Having Fun on the Net

Title: *net.sex*
Authors: Candi Rose and Dirk Thomas
Publisher: Sams Publishing
ISBN: 0-672-30702-2
Price: $19.99
Pages: 250
For more information: `http://www.mcp.com/sams/books/net.sex/`
Notes: Subtitled *The Complete Guide to the Adult Side of the Internet*, it gives practical advice on how to access the back alleys of the information superhighway. Indeed, it does. It's a sur-

prisingly well-written, thoughtful, and detailed guide to finding adult-oriented stuff on the Net. Lots of insightful text and not one sleazy picture. Includes information on discussion lists, anonymity, finding dirty pictures, and so on.

Title: *Planet Internet*
Author: Steve Rimmer
Publisher: McGraw-Hill
ISBN: 0-07-053015-7
Price: $24.95
Pages: 315
For more information: `http://uunorth.north.net:8000/alchemy/html/alchemy.html` or `70007.1531@compuserve.com` or 800-352-3566
Notes: Colorful and engaging, *Planet Internet* explores the oddball side of the Internet culture. From devilbunnies to purity tests to a collective obsession with *Star Trek*, Internauts are a wacky bunch—and *Planet Internet* picks up on the craziness. It's basically just a bunch of pointers to funky newsgroups and FTPable files, but Rimmer offers plenty of enlightening information and notes—for example, he explains what Esperanto is and tells why the TV show The *Prisoner* has such a devoted following. Reading it is sort of like surfing the Internet: you never quite know what you're going to get.

Jargon and Dictionaries

Title: *Internet in Plain English*
Author: Bryan Pfaffenberger
Publisher: MIS Press
ISBN: 1-55828-385-4
Price: $19.95
Pages: 463
Notes: Of the various glossaries and dictionaries of Internet jargon, *Internet in Plain English* is among the most complete. Arranged like a dictionary, it defines just about every term you're likely to hear on and about the Internet and UNIX, from *abbrev* to *'zine*. It contains a lot of technical terms that tech-heads bandy about relentlessly (like *CSO name server*, *ISDN*, and *OSI protocol suite*) and can give beginners and intermediate users a leg up in understanding what everyone's talking about.

Title: *net.speak—The Internet Dictionary*
Authors: Tom Fahey
Publisher: Hayden Books
ISBN: 1-56830-095-6
Price: $12.95

Pages: 250

Notes: If you've ever wondered just what the *InterNIC* is or what *MIME* stands for or the difference between a *bridge* and a *router*, pick up *net.speak—The Internet Dictionary*. This is a dictionary of all things Internet, listing some 2,000 Internet-related phrases, acronyms, and jargon. Although the definitions are brief, this book contains a useful mix of tech-speak (like *High-Level Data Link Control*), common Internet slang (like *spam*), and those hard-to-decrypt acronyms (like *RTFM*, *KIS*, and *NIC*). To keep things from getting dull, the book is peppered with cartoons, interesting stories about the Net, and netiquette tips.

Title: *The New Hacker's Dictionary*
Authors: Edited by Eric Raymond and Guy L. Steele
Publisher: MIT press
ISBN: 0-262-68079-3
Price: $14.95
Pages: 453
For more information: 800-356-0343 or 617-625-8481

Notes: *The New Hacker's Dictionary* is a great book for learning about the various slang, jargon, customs, and folklore of the Net (as well as other lairs of the hacker). Doesn't take itself seriously at all. Very silly and highly recommended. You can get it for free online (The Jargon File) at `http://www.ccil.org/jargon/jargon.html`, but the bound book makes great bathroom reading and contains silly cartoons and stuff.

Hackers and Internet Lore

Title: *The Cuckoo's Egg: Tracking a Spy Through the Maze of Computer Espionage*
Author: Clifford Stoll
Publisher: Doubleday
ISBN: 0-385-24946-2
Price: $5.95
Pages: 332

Notes: A spy novel, except it's true: a first-person account by a down-on-his-luck Berkeley astronomer who, with others, tracked down a KGB network spy. Contains a very good recipe for chocolate chip cookies, too.

Title: *The Hacker Crackdown: Law and Disorder on the Electronic Frontier*
Author: Bruce Sterling
Publisher: Bantam
ISBN: 0-553-08058-X
Price: $23.00

Pages: 352

Notes: An in-depth examination of the forces of law who try to deal with computer crime, and of the issues involved. Written by one of the science fiction writers who invented cyberpunk. The real story behind Operation Sundevil and the Legion of Doom. Readable, informative, and amusing. You can also get it online: `ftp://ftp.eff.org/pub/Publications/Bruce_Sterling/ Hacker_Crackdown/` or `http://www.eff.org/pub/Publications/Bruce_Sterling/ Hacker_Crackdown/`.

Technical Stuff

Title: *Firewalls and Internet Security*
Authors: Cheswick/Bellovin
Publisher: Addison-Wesley
ISBN: 0-201-63357-4
Price: $26.95
Pages: 306
For more information: `firewall-book@research.att.com`
Notes: If you're in charge of keeping your company's computer on the Internet, and that computer has information you need to keep safe, *Firewalls and Internet Security* is a must read. It offers practical suggestions for firewall construction and other aspects of Internet security. It's surprisingly easy to read, considering its technical slant.

Title: *Managing Internet Information Services*
Authors: Liu, Peek, and Jones
Publisher: O'Reilly and Associates
ISBN: 1-56592-062-7
Price: $29.95
Pages: 400
For more information: `http://gnn.com/gnn/bus/ora/item/miis.html` or `info@ora.com`
Notes: Written for database maintainers and system administrators, this UNIX-based technical guide covers installing, setting up, and running Internet applications such as Gopher sites, FTP servers, mailing lists, WAIS, and World Wide Web pages. It delves into areas shunned by many other books, including the elusive concepts of clickable images and forms in the WWW,

creating WAIS sources, and keeping your server site secure.

Title: *TCP/IP Illustrated, Volume 1: The Protocols*
Author: W. Richard Stevens
Publisher: Addison-Wesley
ISBN: 0-201-63346-9
Price: $47.50
Pages: 576

and

Title: *TCP/IP Illustrated, Volume 2: The Implementation*
Authors: Gary Wright and W. Richard Stevens
Publisher: Addison-Wesley
ISBN: 0-201-63354-X
Price: $52.75
Pages: 1,200
Notes: These textbooks explain the real nuts and bolts behind how the Internet works. These guys understand concepts like TCP bulk data flow, Internet group management protocol, and multicast input processing. Frankly, I don't understand a word of it, but these books give a thorough examination of how the TCP/IP protocols are implemented, and are known for being the best books in their field.

INDEX

SYMBOLS

, (commas), Usenet newsgroups, 294
- (hyphen), FTP operator, 405
! (bang), 60
   Usenet newsgroups, 294, 298
(pound sign), undeleting e-mail, 200
#hack channel (IRC), 1033
$ (dollar sign), Archie regular expressions, 440
% (percent sign), 60
&& (double ampersands), rn newsreader macros, 319
( ) parentheses, Gopher searches, 450
* (asterisk)
   Archie regular expressions, 440
   Usenet newsgroup conventions, 285
+ command (readnews program), 297
- (hyphens), Usenet newsgroups, 294, 297
. (period), Archie regular expressions, 440
</DL> (HTML), 652
</TYPE> (HTML), 652
<ADDRESS> (HTML), 651
<BASE HREF="URL"> (HTML), 647
<BLOCKQUOTE> (HTML), 651

Add to Your Sams Library Today with the Best Books for Programming, Operating Systems, and New Technologies

The easiest way to order is to pick up the phone and call

1-800-428-5331

between 9:00 a.m. and 5:00 p.m. EST.
For faster service please have your credit card available.

ISBN	Quantity	Description of Item	Unit Cost	Total Cost
0-672-30617-4		The World Wide Web Unleashed	$35.00	
0-672-30667-0		Teach Yourself HTML Web Publishing in a Week	$25.00	
0-672-30627-1		Plug-N-Play Mosaic for Windows (book/disks)	$29.99	
0-672-30669-7		Plug-N-Play Internet for Windows (book/disks)	$35.00	
0-672-30702-2		net.sex	$19.99	
0-672-30599-2		Tricks of the Internet Gurus	$35.00	
0-672-30530-5		The Internet Business Guide: Riding the Information Superhighway to Profit	$25.00	
0-672-30595-X		Education on the Internet	$25.00	
0-672-30519-4		Teach Yourself the Internet: Around the World in 21 Days	$25.00	
0-672-30520-8		Your Internet Consultant: The FAQs of Life Online	$24.99	
0-672-30299-3		The Waite Group's UNIX Communications and the Internet, Third Edition	$35.00	
❏ 3 ½" Disk		Shipping and Handling: See information below.		
❏ 5 ¼" Disk		TOTAL		

Shipping and Handling: $4.00 for the first book, and $1.75 for each additional book. Floppy disk: add $1.75 for shipping and handling. If you need to have it NOW, we can ship product to you in 24 hours for an additional charge of approximately $18.00, and you will receive your item overnight or in two days. Overseas shipping and handling adds $2.00 per book and $8.00 for up to three disks. Prices subject to change. Call for availability and pricing information on latest editions.

201 W. 103rd Street, Indianapolis, Indiana 46290

1-800-428-5331 — Orders   1-800-835-3202 — FAX   1-800-858-7674 — Customer Service

Book ISBN 0-672-30714-6

GET CONNECTED
to the ultimate source of computer information!

The MCP Forum on CompuServe

Go online with the world's leading computer book publisher!
Macmillan Computer Publishing offers everything
you need for computer success!

Find the books that are right for you!

A complete online catalog,
plus sample chapters and tables of contents
give you an in-depth look at all our books.
The best way to shop or browse!

➤ Get fast answers and technical support for
MCP books and software

➤ Join discussion groups on major computer
subjects

➤ Interact with our expert authors via e-mail
and conferences

➤ Download software from our immense
library:

  ▷ Source code from books
  ▷ Demos of hot software
  ▷ The best shareware and freeware
  ▷ Graphics files

Join now and get a free CompuServe Starter Kit!

To receive your free CompuServe Introductory Membership, call **1-800-848-8199** and ask for representative #597.

The Starter Kit includes:
➤ Personal ID number and password
➤ $15 credit on the system
➤ Subscription to *CompuServe Magazine*

Once on the CompuServe System, type:

GO MACMILLAN

for the most computer information anywhere!

MACMILLAN
COMPUTER
PUBLISHING

 CompuServe

PLUG YOURSELF INTO...

THE MACMILLAN INFORMATION SUPERLIBRARY™

Free information and vast computer resources from the world's leading computer book publisher—online!

FIND THE BOOKS THAT ARE RIGHT FOR YOU!

A complete online catalog, plus sample chapters and tables of contents give you an in-depth look at *all* of our books, including hard-to-find titles. It's the best way to find the books you need!

● STAY INFORMED with the latest computer industry news through our online newsletter, press releases, and customized Information SuperLibrary Reports.

● GET FAST ANSWERS to your questions about MCP books and software.

● VISIT our online bookstore for the latest information and editions!

● COMMUNICATE with our expert authors through e-mail and conferences.

● DOWNLOAD SOFTWARE from the immense MCP library:
  - Source code and files from MCP books
  - The best shareware, freeware, and demos

● DISCOVER HOT SPOTS on other parts of the Internet.

● WIN BOOKS in ongoing contests and giveaways!

TO PLUG INTO MCP: ➤   WORLD WIDE WEB: **http://www.mcp.com**

GOPHER: gopher.mcp.com

FTP: ftp.mcp.com